OUT
of the
ASHES

OUT
of the
ASHES

LIFE, DEATH AND TRANSFIGURATION
OF DEMOCRACY IN CHILE,
1833-1988

James R. Whelan

Regnery Gateway
Washington, D.C.

Library of Congress Cataloging-in-Publication Data

Whalen, James R. (James Robert). 1933–
    Out of the ashes : Life, Death and Transfiguration of
Democracy in Chile, 1833–1988 / James R. Whalen.
    p.   cm.
    Bibliography: p.
    Includes index.
    ISBN 0-89526-553-2 : $49.95
    1. Chile—Politics and government.   I. Title.
    F3081.W43   1988   88-18533
    983—dc19   CIP

Published by Regnery Gateway,
1130 17th Street, NW, Washington, DC 20036

Distributed to the trade by Kampmann & Company, Inc.,
226 W. 26th Street, New York, NY 10001

Manufactured in the United States of America

Designed by Irving Perkins Associates

10 9 8 7 6 5 4 3 2 1

ACKNOWLEDGMENTS

I began work on this book just a little over fourteen years ago. Inevitably, that translates as a very large measure of indebtedness—and the risk of overlooking or slighting those who deserve better. They have my thanks, as well as my apologies.

There are those one could never forget. That list must, for me, begin with the Clan Martínez—Manolo and Morita, and their wonderful brood, a family of incomparable warmth and affection and geniality. Inexplicably, some years ago, they opened their home and their hearts to me and made me one of them. With the passage of the years, the ties which bind me to them have grown only stronger, richer. I suppose I might have done this book without them, but I know that it would have been a lesser book, just as I would have been a lesser person had I not been privileged to call myself a Martínez-by-adoption. In the measure that I have failed of their expectations, it is because I fell short, not their love, caring, or counsel.

So many, many others in Chile helped. There is the wise and witty Tomás MacHale, offering friendship as well as the benefits of his awesome experience and network of sources, both those he agrees with and those with whom he does not.

In these later stages, Luís Valentín Ferrada put at my disposal not only his own office, but also his wonderful secretary, Anita, who stitched together appointments for me with a diligence and perseverance bordering on relentlessness.

There were the Washington Chileans, too. None, through the years, would contribute more than Mario Correa, a perspicacious critic, a patient helpmate; unraveling with unflagging good humor everything from obscure episodes to inscrutable translations (*zapato chino*, for example, means "Chinese shoe," but what does a Chilean really mean when he speaks of a *zapato chino*? Mario knows). María Pincus worked an unconscionable number of hours transcribing often scratchy, and sometimes barely audible tapes to give me an indispensable record of innumerable interviews. For arranging so many of those interviews, I am indebted in earlier years to (then) Air Force Col. Eduardo (Caco) Sepúlveda; in more recent years, to Chile's extraordinarily able young ambassador in Washington, Hernán Felipe Errázuriz.

Yet another ambassador helped: my friend of so many years, Jim Theberge, whose death earlier this year left a large gap in the lives of so many of us. James D. Theberge had served as U.S. ambassador to Chile from 1982–1985, his second post as ambassador, and he shared many insights with me even as he worked on a book of his own.

But authors do not live by friends and sources alone, and so I am deeply grateful to those who provided financial support: the Earhart Foundation, for a most generous grant, and L. Francis Bouchey and his Council for Inter-American Security, for his and their important support at especially critical times.

Because of such support, I was able to enlist the assistance of fine researchers: in Chile, Oscar Burgos Acuña, here in Washington, Sarah Dye and, most especially, Anne McKinney, who so painstakingly constructed the "road map" leading me out of the wilderness and into the final completion of the book. J. Paul Wyatt strengthened and refined the appendices. Patricia (Trish) Bozell, a fine editor, moved in at the end to attempt the impossible: to bring polish and precision to the work. Neither she—nor any of the others who contributed—ought be in any fashion held accountable for the failings and shortcomings; those, alas, belong to me.

There are those who contribute in other, subtler ways, giving nothing less than of themselves, giving love and caring. My son, Bobby, has through all these years, not a few of them years of privation, material and emotional. So, too, has my daughter, Heather, home from school in the afternoon in time to make sure that her very distracted father had his tea-and-niblets, on what otherwise were often foodless days. Two more wonderful children, no father ever had.

When I wrote my first book—on Chile, as it happens—I said I might have never turned to writing had it not been for the encouragement and guidance of a lady who really had no time to give either—but did, ceaselessly. That woman was my mother, Margaret Mary Southard Whelan. It was true then. It still is, yet I know that thanking her again is not the same as thanking her enough. Few of us ever could, I suppose, thank a loving mother sufficiently, and I am no exception.

James R. Whelan
Arlington, Virginia
October 1988

CONTENTS

TABLES

PREFACE

To write a truthful history, Hilaire Belloc has observed, one must know the towns, the country houses, the landscape, the whole physical setting of the country of one's studies; one must talk with old men and women, besides reading other people's books; one must peer imaginatively behind the veil of yesteryear. Or, as Russell Kirk reminds us of the message of Edmund Burke, to master grand policies, "I must see the things, I must see the men."

These, then, are the principles I have brought to the daunting task of writing a truthful political history of Chile. The task has been made the more daunting because Chile is a country which, because of the prevailing intellectual conceits of the modern world, because of its own apostasies vis-á-vis those conceits, is, I am quite persuaded, a country which lives far more in caricature beyond its remote borders than it does in realistic portraiture. Still, such queasiness as I feel springs not from the expectable disapprobation of those professional political scientists and others who have created the caricature, so much as it does from the reverence I feel for two who so honored those principles I have cited at the outset of this essay in their monumental and imperishable works, Alexis de Tocqueville and the Marquis de Custine.*

Those, then, who demand only detached and arid abstraction will not find it in these pages. To the degree possible, I have, for thirty years, explored the towns and the landscape of Chile, and talked to men and women young and old, including the country's last four presidents. But the quest for original sources has taken me to the weak and the scorned as well, including men and women who have risked their lives and fortunes fighting against one or another of those self-same presidents. I have spoken to others who have stood at or near the pinnacle of power, and I have spoken to those who knew the degradation of exile or prison, or both. I have spoken, also, to those who looked on as outsiders, and I have read the books of others, many, many books.

The sum of it all is a book which strives to be truthful while not denying an explicit point of view, and even passion at times. Such a book may not satisfy those who pretend that neither point of view nor passion are appropriate to such works. I will leave it to others to protest that neither history nor political science lend themselves to analysis devoid of point of view, however dissembled, however disguised. This is particularly true of political or historical studies of the region of the world I

---

* I refer, of course, to De Tocqueville's *Democracy in America*, and Custine's *Journey For Our Time: The Russian Journals of the Marquis de Custine*, translated from the original, *Russie en 1839*.

know best, Latin America. It is certainly true of the country which is the subject of this book, Chile. It was, indeed, the discovery, so many years ago, of a suffocatingly prevailing "point of view" in scholarship on Latin America which impelled me to embark on my own long and arduous journey of research, investigation, study, and reflection: a search not to find facts to fit yet another theory, this one mine, nor to prove a preconceived point; rather, to submit the evidence of my own senses to serious scrutiny, to examine "objective" phenomena as thoroughly as I could, so as to decode a persistent riddle. That riddle revolved around the distance I have, for many years, observed, again and again, between reality as I lived and perceived it in the region, and the images dominating the literature of political science and history of the region.

To take the example which first gave me pause: Uruguay. Uruguay was, for many years, extolled in scholarship and the mass media as "The Switzerland of the Americas." Scholars and specialists continued to so refer to the country into the late-1960s, long past the point where it was true, if it was ever true at all. By "Switzerland of the Americas," it was meant that Uruguay enjoyed a political and economic system, created and driven by a European-style population, which combined to make it an enviable and exemplary island of enlightened political and economic prosperity in Latin America. This is not a book about Uruguay, nor even about cant in political science, and so I will limit myself to a single comment: Uruguay was, in fact, the first full-scale welfare state in Latin America, a circumstance which no doubt accounted for much of the scholarly acclamation, just as it accounted for the decline and ultimate collapse of both the political and economic systems of that country. By the mid-1960s, I recall quite vividly, a majority of Uruguayans were telling Gallup and other pollsters that they believed the problems of their country were beyond solution. That was the view from inside America's "Switzerland."

Chile "enjoyed" similar adulation. In 1967, two American political scientists presented a paper on Chile at the annual meeting of the American Political Science Association, meeting that year in Chicago, which apotheosized the point. In it, they argued that, using a variety of indices, Chile continued then to enjoy the same rank among the world's democracies, as they had found it to occupy in 1965: fifth. Fifth, in the entire world. The researchers based their finding on a comparative analysis of the development of democratic institutions around the world to that point in the twentieth century.* Yet another political

---

* William Flanigin and Edwin Fogleman, "Patterns of Development and Democratization: A Quantitative Analysis." In his book, *The Chilean Senate*, Weston H. Agor says the index updated to 1968 would not alter the ranking of Chile as number five. He goes on to explain why he believes that in Chile, political democracy equates with political development (Austin: University of Texas Press, 1971, p. 5).

scientist, viewing their work, observed that, in the case of Chile, there was no reason to suppose that the practice of democracy had not achieved the same level of development as the facilitating institutions themselves, and that there was no reason, either, to suppose that in 1968, Chile did not still rank number five. Those analysts were far, far from alone; indeed, if there were important voices in the political science or modern history academies of Latin America, North America, or Europe expressing contrary views, they were small voices indeed.

Knowing this helps to understand the subsequent furor following the collapse of Chilean democracy just five years later, in 1973. Indeed, in 1968 Chile was enjoying a ranking as a functioning democracy which located it ahead of such other states as Austria, Belgium, France, the Netherlands, Italy, and Australia (all of which could be disqualified for one reason or another—remember, the year of the measurements was 1967, and the period measured 1900–1967, updated, as noted, to 1968). Still, however precise or however narrow the grounds for the ranking, it remains that there stood Chile, in the orthodoxy of academia, trumpeted inevitably by the echoing mass media as a shining example of an extraordinarily successful democracy.

The truth, as in the case of Uruguay, was otherwise. In 1968, Chile was only two years away from becoming the first country of any consequence in the world freely to elect a Marxist-Leninist government. That event, by itself, would be unimportant only if one were willing to believe that Marxist-Leninist governments, once in power, deny their own philosophical essence, which is to exercise power in perpetuity and monopolistically. There is a good deal more on this subject in the text; for the moment, suffice to remark that history awaits the example of the first Marxist-Leninist regime to relinquish power—or even share it, for that matter—voluntarily.

But even putting aside the Marxist-Leninist construct, it remains that the practice of democracy in Chile had deteriorated into a series of dogmatic and unyielding political factionalisms. Expressed differently, as one eminent Chilean historian has, by 1973, "not even a vestige" remained of political consensus; in its stead, there was "the imperative necessity of liquidating political and ideological adversaries."[*]

The present point is this: the Chile of reality, in 1968, in 1970, in 1973, bore very little resemblance to the images so fashionable in Western scholarship and mass media reporting.

More than a few reputations had, in fact, been invested in the confabulation of those images. Many others merely parroted the confabulators.

[*] Gonzalo Vial Correa, "Decadencia, Consensos y Unidad Nacional en 1973," in *Política y Geoestrategia*, #36 (Santiago: Academia Nacional de Estudios Políticos y Estratégicos, 1985), p. 29. A former education minister, Vial Correa was an early member of the Chilean Academy of History.

And a great number more believed because they wanted to believe: the Chile of orthodoxy was an exquisite paradigm not only of "progressive" thought, but also of progressive prescriptions for other countries. To admit that it was the prescription that had failed would have demanded repudiation of the theories themselves, an exercise highly menacing to one's reputation as an analyst. There was, of course, an alternative: to adduce that what really had happened was that some few Chileans—the generals, mainly, and those hapless Chileans who agreed with the revolution-making generals—had failed to measure up to the splendor of the paradigm. (So obstinate were many among the theoreticians that they reserved their most venomous abuse for the very man who had, until then, been the very paragon of the paradigm, President Eduardo Frei Montalva. Frei, you see, defended the revolution of 1973 as necessary, just as he would declare that democracy in Chile had died not at the hands of the generals, but at the hand of the Marxist-Leninist government of Salvador Allende. And yes, Frei did describe Allende's regime not with the empty euphemism, "Marxist," but as "Marxist-Leninist," as did Allende's Popular Unity itself. For his pains, Frei found himself summarily excommunicated from the priesthood of the world's progressives.)*

There was yet a second reason why Chile would find itself immediately condemned, from Stockholm to Hyannis Port, from Mexico City to Moscow: The generals who took power in 1973 quickly made it plain that they were discarding the old order, the one so warmly endorsed by the likes of France's François Mitterrand and Sweden's Olaf Palme, as well, of course, as by Allende's soul mates, Cuba's Fidel Castro and the USSR's Leonid Brezhnev. They made it equally plain that they intended to build a new one, rigorously traditional in its social framework, corporatist in its political structure, exuberantly free market in its economic one.

As Paul Johnson would remark in his epochal work, *Modern Times*, the regime of Augusto Pinochet Ugarte had not only deposed an incompetent Marxist-Leninist, but had opted to "reverse the growth of the public sector . . . and open the economy to market forces, on the lines of other Pacific economies." As a result, Chile suffered the kind of vilification directed at Thailand, South Korea, Singapore and Taiwan.† (Vil-

---

* Stanford Professor Richard R. Fagen, who would become one of the shrillest voices in the pro-Allende chorus, described Frei as "one of the shrillest voices in the anti-Allende chorus," in "The United States and Chile: Roots and Branches," *Foreign Affairs*, January 1975.

† Paul Johnson, *Modern Times: The World from the Twenties to the Eighties* (New York: Harper & Row, 1983), p. 725.

ification and severe ostracism notwithstanding, Chile would come to share another distinction with those countries: its economy actually grew and prospered.)

Yet another author, of yet another remarkable work, the aforementioned Marquis de Custine, wrote that "nothing colossal is obtained without pain." The test needs be that the end sought is worthy of the pain, of the exertion (a proposition not to be confused with the-ends-justifies-the-means, since we are talking about nation-building strategies, not moral choices). Although at the very beginning, Chile's new rulers only dimly glimpsed the task before them—if, indeed, they understood it at all—the goals they would eventually set were colossal. Yet it needs be remembered that the condemnation of them began the moment their goals, and the ends they intended to pursue to achieve them, became visible. This was long before "human rights" violations could become the club with which to bludgeon them. They continued to be bludgeoned even when, years later, the success of their endeavors in building a Chile far sounder and saner and healthier for *most* Chileans could any longer be seriously doubted.

Human rights abuses there were, and some would continue for too many years. That these abuses were far fewer than those committed in the name of "progressive" revolutions in no way excuses them; yet it need also be remarked that those least willing to forgive Chile tend to be those most willing to exculpate the wrongs committed in the name of such "progressive" revolutions as those of the Soviet Union, Cuba, Nicaragua, and the China of Mao.

I have, in the preceding paragraph, insinuated a theorem: a government, and most certainly a revolutionary government, must be judged ultimately by the question: do those who have ruled leave their country better off than when they found it? In the case of the revolutions cited above, the ones which find so many apologists among Western literati and intelligentsia, the answer is clearly and resoundingly no. In the case of Chile, I believe that a jury of honest judges, unshackled by preconceptions, would find that the answer is yes.

I hear already what Russell Kirk has called "the howl of the fanatic," causing the modern mob to bow down before "the stony idols of Unreason and Devastation," demanding, for example, that "South Africa be reduced to the happy condition of Uganda or Chad." Or Chile to the "happy condition" of Cuba or Nicaragua.

I said, a few lines ago, that this revolution without recognition has created a better Chile for *most* Chileans. Perfection is not part of the human condition, though we properly aspire to approach it. In the case of Chile, the striving is made more vexatious by the reality that Chile is truly a house divided against itself; there dwell in that land a hard core of Marxist-Leninist revolutionaries—perhaps as much as 10 percent of the populace—who will settle for nothing less than absolute power for themselves and their prescriptions. It is conceivable, in the fullness of time, that these violence-prone fanatics might learn to coexist within the system; more probably, they will mainly fade away. The more crucial question is whether the ostensibly "legalistic" Communist and Socialist parties—both now outlawed—would also agree to accommodate to the system, renouncing the violent path they, too, chose a decade ago. And if they were to do so, would they accept genuine accommodation, as do Communist parties in France and Italy, or would they view the system, as they did in Chile's past, as merely a malleable means for achieving their own ends: total and permanent power? True accommodation will be possible only when Chile achieves a level of true political maturity, when the Marxist-Leninists in Chile reconcile themselves to the proposition that they have lost, irrevocably, the ability to impose their will. There are, of course, those who would argue that they *did* coexist within the system prior to 1970, and in a narrowly formal sense that is true. But it is true only to the degree that "they" referred to the Communist party and the relatively sane wing of the Socialist party, both of which patiently probed and exploited the weaknesses and opportunities of the system. Coexistence within the system was never true of the radicals within the coalition which put Allende in power, and it is even less true of them today. It is, then, an idle flummery to suppose that those who believe that power grows out of the barrel of a gun either can or will lay down their arms and/or accept peacefully the new country which has been raised up around them. The end result of this constellation of factors is a continuing state of internal strife and violence—a circumstance easily exploited by those who use images of violence to indict not the violent, but those attempting to control the violence.

There is yet another small minority—very vocal and very visible—for whom the new Chile is anathema: the political professionals of yesteryear and a few (not many) ordinary citizens who yearn yet for a past that is mainly illusion. The difficulty of incorporating this group into a consensual democracy is obvious. But, because of their network of international political and ideological alliances, they are powerful far out of proportion to their own numbers, or to the loyalties they actually command.

There is yet another factor likely to assure that Chile continues to be subject to outside hectoring: the indictment of those who demand levels of purity and perfection in the forms and practices of democracy which exist mainly in theory and which are utterly unheard of among the struggling nations of the Third World. The democracy now emerging in Chile is neither pure nor perfect. It is, however, better than what is available in most of the rest of the civilized world. And, to return to the point of departure: the great majority of Chile's citizens are, in the meantime, clearly better off than they were in 1970, their country a sounder and saner place, better able to provide for the future of its citizens. In 1988, at least, there can be little serious dispute that most (that word again) citizens of Chile are demonstrably better off than the inhabitants of the tottering democracies of surrounding countries: Peru, Argentina, Brazil, and Uruguay. Yet those countries continue to bask in the uncritical admiration of the world's "progressives" simply because they are nominally democratic; few examine the texture of those democracies too closely, and fewer yet bother to observe that those governments are impoverishing their populations. The latter seems not to matter to those who live in ease and luxury elsewhere, so long as the impoverishing is done within a "democratic" framework.

But this is not a book about those countries either. Nor even about Salvador Allende. But, in the measure that the Allende years would become the chasm between past and present, much of the book is devoted to chronicling those years. A few words about them are in order here.

He called it *la vía chilena al socialismo*, the Chilean path to socialism, but what Salvador Allende Gossens gave Chile was a nightmarish journey without maps. There was but a single objective at the end of that road, and that objective was power, including the power to destroy, forever, the power of those who would oppose him or his heirs in Marxism.

He never had any real chance of reaching that objective, because he—and those who accompanied him—were a minority, not only in the land, but even within the coalition that put him into the presidency. And so he plunged the country into a thousand days of strife and lawlessness, ending in economic ruin and civil war, the fabric of Chilean society torn to tatters. But as the damage had begun long before, so it would take long years to repair it.

That is the reality of Chile, of Allende, of the years since, a reality so radically at odds with the image incomprehensibly fashionable, even now, fifteen years after Allende's fall. To this observer at least, those images often appear as though in a time warp, judgments formed then, not to be reviewed since: on the one side, the images of Allende as a humanitarian crusader fighting for a better life for the country's underdogs; on the other, those of the men who struck him down—mad barons of privilege, domestic and foreign.

Salvador Allende, as we have already remarked, was not some freak phenomenon suddenly exploding onto Chilean life, a guided missile bringing to Chile the clash between capitalism and communism. If he had been, his example would be little more than a curiosity of the Cold War. He was, on the contrary, the culmination of a political process already fifty years old when he lurched into the presidency, and of social forces as old as the enlightened republic he would lead to its ruin. Even his programs—for such limited time as he could lay serious claim to having conscious programs—were hardly distinguishable from those of his principal rivals, the Christian Democrats, nor had they been for a number of years. There was, indeed, very little "revolutionary" about him in the Chilean context of his era, which made the more beguiling yet the siren song that disguised its totalitarian trap.

In that light, Allende stands as a lesson for those Third World countries entranced by what Jean François-Revel has called the "totalitarian temptation." The temptation is reinforced by the illusion that Allende marched in the tradition of an authentic democratic system so widely admired, particularly in Latin America, that its solvency is simply asserted as a matter of faith. The lie will perish only after the bramble of cant is cleared away, and Chile's political processes are seen for what they really were by 1973: not the flowering of a civilization, but the deflowering of a society.

There is a lesson in all of this that goes beyond, that transcends Allende, that transcends the generals and the free market technocrats who followed him, and it is a lesson of much larger and more lasting value. It is fashionable for those of us of the self-assured ("developed") nations to imagine that we cannot learn from the misadventures of the "lesser" states. Indeed, we view the developing world—and certainly this is the case with Latin America—with a special kind of contempt: through the prism of *our* issues, of the ones that matter to *us*. As if those "lesser" states had no history, no past, no traditions, no will, no force, no destiny of their own.

In the case of Allende, international cross-currents, such as the conflict between capitalism and communism, surely were part of the turbulence. But they were also diluted into the very real and very powerful mainstream of Chilean reality, a reality with intellectual headwaters as old and as vital and as autochthonous as the competing outside ideologies themselves. The ideas that coalesced in collision under Allende were not imperatives imposed from without, grafted onto an inert body politic, as if Chile were a kind of convenient guinea pig. Rather, these ideas represented forces that had been evolving within the country for many years, adapted to the personality of the country and its leaders.

In the case of Pinochet, volumes have been written force-fitting the regime into elaborate political science constructs. Others have attempted to assess the regime in terms of political developments, leaders, or movements elsewhere, from Franco's Spain to Chun Hoo

Hwan's Korea. Almost all coincide: the general's most egregious error has been his refusal to return to the political system in place before Allende. Except for a passing phrase or two, none I have seen locates the behavior of the Pinochet regime within the one philosophical and ideological framework which *does* underpin it: the very Chilean antecedent of the Portalian Republic, the nineteenth-century creation of Diego Portales that laid the foundations for the subsequent growth and development of the Chilean nation, of Chilean democracy.

Unless these propositions are understood, then the true message of Chile will be lost, and it is a message as real as the daily agonies of the rich countries now coping with the unfamiliar and frightening spectres of debt, social fragmentation, and chronic economic malaise.

Chile went through this, over fifty beguiling years of it, until the wrong that had been done could no longer be evaded. To the point: Chile lived through the experience of sliding into political and economic bankruptcy while the outside world marveled at the system's capacity to extend the frontiers of social and political opportunity. What really happened? As to social opportunity, the economic vitality of the country was being sapped and drained until it finally could promote the general welfare of no one; the rich had been leveled, but so too had the poor. As to political expansion, instead of securing the blessings of liberty, long years of demagoguery had created a legacy of a society torn asunder, irreconcilably polarized. It happened because Chile's political leaders repeatedly opted for policies that bought quick political advantage at the expense of weakening the economic foundations of the nation. It happened because they practiced the politics of Polyanna, a promise of plenty for all at the expense of responsibility, promises paid for by deficit spending, by browbeating business, by spreading state control, and finally, having divided classes, by pitting them against one another, the better to conquer them.

The men who took command of Chile's destinies in 1973 understood this, or came to understand this, and they understood it in terms indigenous to their own experience, to their own country. The political model they sought was not, then, imported, but one rooted in what they perceived to be the true strength of their own historic past. And so they saw their task in the same terms as did Portales, 140 years before: not as mere arbiters between competing bands, but as the builders of a new and sturdier country. The evidence, in this crucial year of transition, seems to suggest that they have succeeded, despite the hostility and despite the harassment of both superpowers, and of virtually every major nation on the planet. The final verdict must, of course, await time and history.

In ways that will surprise and even annoy North Americans and Europeans, Chile is and has been a valid laboratory—in microcosm, to be sure, but valid all the same—for testing many of the same sets of choices we have faced and must yet face in the developed world. Details vary, as they always do, in time and space; but the fundamental choices for ordering societies that men and their leaders must make, do not.

This book represents an honest effort to chronicle what Chile's men and leaders did, the choices they made, the consequences they had to cope with. I confessed at the beginning to a point of view. But then, how to come away from a cataclysm and not suppose that something had gone wrong?

OUT
of the
ASHES

1

The Crucible

THE PLACE

It is by now a cliché to point out that each of the twenty traditional republics[1] south of the Río Grande is an entity unto itself, each with its own eccentricities. There is really no need to prove that one is more eccentric than the next, and yet Chile represents an irresistible temptation.

To begin with, there is the matter of geography. Chile is so unusual that once spied on the map, one knows, to paraphrase an old jingle, there is nowhere else in the world quite like it. For example: "Chile stretches 2,625 miles along the South Pacific coast and averages only 120 miles in width. At its very widest, far south at the Strait of Magellan, the width reaches 312 miles, and at its narrowest spot, Illapel, it is but 56 miles wide."[2] One imagines this lump of geographical ludicrousness in the deft hands of Rostand, immortalizing its ungainly shape much as he did Cyrano's nose. Lesser writers struggling to describe Chile have envisioned the land as an eel (of the knobby and nibbled variety, presumably), a snake (uncoiled, of course), and a twig (but stripped of its branches, forsooth), or my own favorite, "a bell rope full of knots and kinks . . . hanging down the west coast of South America."[3]

I prefer that because it conveys a sense of physical detachment, which is one of the four or five basic keys to understanding Chile. A Chilean political scientist, Claudio Véliz, wrote some years ago that "for the last century and a half, Latin America has been a faithful echoing chamber for every political noise uttered in the more civilized regions of the Northern Hemisphere."[4] Chile was no exception. But unlike other Latin nations, Chile ingested ideas in lonely seclusion, in an isolation perhaps without parallel anywhere else in the industrial world.[5]

Consider: Chile's nearest western neighbor of any consequence is New Zealand, across 5,500 miles of the South Pacific. Chile's eastern

3

borders are formed by a solid wall of Andean mountains, including no fewer than twenty-five peaks towering six thousand meters (19,200 feet) or higher and literally dozens of active volcanoes. To the north is the Atacama Desert, six hundred miles of some of the world's most barren desolation, including spots were rain has not fallen in four hundred years, followed by a strip four hundred miles wide of semidesert. At Chile's southern tip is frigid Tierra del Fuego, and beyond, the emptiness of Antarctica. In all, desert to the north, mountains to the east, ice to the south, and ocean to the west.[6]

As a result, Chile looked to the sea and developed early as a maritime power. By 1851 Chile's naval reach extended all the way to San Francisco; it possessed enough maritime muscle even to jostle Uncle Sam.[7] Trade also gave Chile the means—and the need—to organize a federal bureaucracy, an important factor in the development of a broadly based state apparatus. It was in sharp contrast to most other Latin nations, where small cliques operated shoebox governments—so small, the affairs of state could have been filed in just about that space. In Chile, government began early to assume an active and expanding role in the lives of the citizenry, a phenomenon engendering stability and dependence.

THE PEOPLE

> ... *la gente que produce es tan granada,*
> *tan soberbia, gallarda y belicosa, que*
> *no ha sido por rey jamás regida ni a*
> *extranjero dominio sometida.*[8]

Isolation fostered another, profounder phenomenon: the formation of a Chilean character, distinct as it is elusive. So elusive that a distinguished Chilean writer would writhe and grope and finally confess that Chile is "a country that is characterized by its intellectual and artistic preoccupations [but it] has not succeeded in creating a style of its own in which the national soul can recognize itself . . . these seemingly insignificant facts are the symptoms of something deep and transcendental: something has not yet been detected in our typical man, and this prevents him from externalizing his real personality."[9]

This is a country that has nurtured two Nobel laureates in poetry, for this "something deep and transcendental" is as much a part of Chile's reality as the high Andes that cradle the country. Its character bespeaks spontaneity and independence and naturalness, unaffected good nature masking carefully concealed toughness, and a quality of kindness and generosity—of *amabilidad*, the evocative Spanish word every visitor soon learns must have been coined to describe Chileans. The great Colombian novelist Gabriel García Márquez has expanded provocatively on this theme:

> Chileans are very much like their country in a certain way. They are the most pleasant people on the continent, they like being alive, and they know how to live in the best way possible and even a little more. But they have a dangerous tendency toward skepticism and intellectual speculation. A Chilean once told me on a Monday that "no Chilean believes tomorrow is Tuesday," and he didn't believe it, either. Still, even with that deep-seated incredulity, or thanks to it, perhaps, the Chileans have attained a degree of natural civilization, a political maturity, and a level of culture that set them apart from the rest of the region.[10]

The British writer Robert Moss sees them set apart in still another important way: "It is in some ways easier to understand the pattern of Chilean politics if one tries to imagine it (Chile) as a kind of lost island of Europe than as an integral part of Latin America." Half a century earlier, a German philosopher and man of letters, Count Hermann Keyserling, synthesized those two strands of thought: "Of all the peoples of South America, Chileans possess the greatest character. They are also a plain people, inasmuch as they are less liars, less presumptuous, less boastful and less given to promise what they cannot deliver. They are upright and open to the degree that the spirit of the continent allows. . . ."[11]

To greater or lesser degree, every people is an echo of its past. In the case of Chile, it is a past with a pioneering flavor rarely rivaled in the world.

Of the eleven major tribes[12] originally inhabiting the land now known as Chile, none other left a more indelible stamp than the Araucanian Indians.[13] It cost the conquistadors more men trying to subdue these warriors than they were to lose in all their other campaigns combined throughout South America—and they never did prevail.[14] The Spaniards were not the first to fail. The Incas managed to extend their domain as far south as the River Maule in Chile, about 180 miles south of present-day Santiago. In approximately 1485 the Inca Huayna Cápac attempted to lead an army even farther south. He got as far as Araucanian country, at the Itata River, about eighty miles from the Maule. There, the Incas were repulsed in a bloody two-day battle. They never again ventured south of the Maule. Successive invaders suffered the same fate for the next four hundred years, a record of resistance that has few parallels in history, and one that probably changed the course of Chile's history.[15]

The Araucanians ruled an area of exquisite beauty and natural abundance, stretching roughly 180 miles between the present-day city of Chillán and the Toltén River, just north of Valdivia.[16] Tawny-skinned, round-faced with wide foreheads and high cheekbones, the Araucanians were as adept at fishing and farming as at hunting. Nearly 200,000 of their descendants are clustered today in the province of Cautín in that same area, and they make up about forty-five percent of the population of the province. The Cautín concentration also accounts for about one-third of Chile's total Indian-descended population.[17]

Recently, archeologists in Monte Verde, Chile, claim to have found evidence that people lived in South America 33,000 years ago, twenty thousand years earlier than the accepted findings at the Clovis site in New Mexico.[18]

One is tempted to tarry over the fascinating episodes of Chile's early history, a saga resembling the winning of the American West more than the tales of looting and plunder usually associated with the conquistadors. A few broad strokes will suffice to suggest the main outlines of the country's infancy and adolescence.

The first known white man in Chile was an earless wonder named Gonzalo Calvo de Barrientos. He was a former soldier of Pizarro, and his ears had been lopped off as punishment for small crimes. In anger and humiliation, he had fled alone to the southern wilderness. One sketch shows him bearded and fittingly bald (calvo means bald), wearing a tunic, clutching a spear, and surrounded by Indians who, believing he had come down from heaven, obeyed him slavishly. Much later Calvo helped ease the way for Diego de Almagro, a Spanish conquistador. Almagro, then in his fifties, shared with Pizarro sovereignty over most of the west coast of South America. Pizarro got the northern part, which embraces most of what is now Peru, and Almagro the southern part, including present-day Chile. A later border dispute would lead to Almagro's death.

Like Pizarro, Almagro was illiterate. And like Pizarro, he was a man of extraordinary shrewdness and courage; yet where Pizarro was crafty and cold-blooded, Almagro was generous and warm-hearted. On July 3, 1535, Almagro set out from Cuzco to explore his new domain at the head of a force of about fifty Spaniards. Eventually his forces would include 300 infantrymen, 200 cavalrymen, and a "multitude" of Indian slaves—their number was estimated at 10,000 to 15,000. Guiding him were Paullo Túpac, brother of the Inca Manco, and Villal Umu, high priest of all the Incas.

They made their way through Bolivia, traversing the three-mile-high

Puna (Plateau) of Atacama, descending into the Copiapó valley in April 1536. The journey across that one hundred-mile defile was an agony for the Spaniards. For the Indian bearers, it was a death march—it was said that as many as ten thousand perished along the route. An expedition retracing their footsteps a few months later used the frozen corpses of the Indians to build parapets for shelter.

Once in central Chile, Almagro found fertile lands and an agreeable climate. (Santiago's weather is very much like San Francisco's, except drier.) But he also found that the gold which had lured them was a mirage—or, more probably, a trap set for them by the Incas, who, anxious for the Spaniards to divert a large part of their forces from Peru, sent them on a fool's errand. Such gold mines as they did find were, in the phrase of one explorer, "as well worked as if Spaniards had been engaged in them, and so worked out that the best pan produced a bare twelve grains."

Almagro also met an unbudgeable barrier. On a July day in 1536, at the junction of the Itata and Ñuble rivers, the Spaniards clashed for the first time with a foe that would defy white men for the next 350 years: the Araucanians. For these bold warriors, it was their first combat ever against cavalry. Their losses were high, but the Indians fought so stubbornly that the Spaniards were forced to withdraw. Thoroughly discouraged, Almagro headed back to Peru. The march back—this time across the four hundred-mile desolation of the Atacama Desert—was stigmatized by the unusual cruelty of the Spaniards toward their Indian slaves. As for Almagro, captivity and death at the hands of Pizarro's sons were the rewards awaiting him.

The next, and decisive, expedition was led by Captain Pedro de Valdivia, a career military man who had already distinguished himself in battle in Italy, Flanders, Spain, Venezuela, and Peru.[19] For his latter services, Valdivia was rewarded by Pizarro with an estate and silver mine which made him the rival in wealth of Pizarro himself. Yet, responding to an apparently unassuaged sense of adventure and fulfillment, he left his quiet life of opulence and set out in January 1540 with seven other Spaniards and a thousand Indians. (His force was later bolstered to number about 150 Spaniards.) On December 13, 1540, he reached the site of what is now Santiago, and on February 12, 1541, he formally founded the city, which he named for the patron saint of Spain.

Santiaguinos are fond of pointing out that Valdivia chose to halt and found the first city at a point just halfway between the two Pacific Coast extremes of the country. Although those measurements check close enough to be convincing, Chile had to fight a war and annex northern territory three and-a-half centuries later to validate Valdivia's prescience.

The tiny settlement was barely seven months old when it underwent the first Indian siege: 50 Spaniards against an attacking force of 8,000 to 10,000 Indians. Anticipating the attack, Valdivia had set out with a main force in hopes of intercepting and surprising the Indians. He missed. The Indian chief Michimalongo put to the torch every building in the settlement, and probably would have finished off the defenders but for the dramatic intervention of Inés de Suárez. The only white woman in the expedition and the consort of Valdivia, Inés proposed that seven Indian chieftains the Spaniards were holding hostage be decapitated and their heads thrown among the attacking hordes. When others hesitated, she took a sword, one version has it, and did part of the job herself. Brandishing a sword, she then led a counterattack that repulsed the Indians.[20] It was the first instance of a woman playing a decisive role in Chilean history, but it would establish a tradition reverberating down to and including the time of Allende.[21] The date of that first dramatic event: September 11, 1541.

Valdivia was captured in 1553 in a battle in which a twenty-year-old Indian chieftain named Lautaro displayed brilliant strategy. Legend has it that the Indians put Valdivia to death by forcing molten gold down his throat. A more prosaic—and probable—version is that he was struck down by a single blow from a mace wielded by an enraged chieftain named Leocotón while Lautaro and the great leader Caupolicán debated Valdivia's fate.[22]

As noted, the Indian wars were to continue[23] for over three more centuries, but the colony prospered slowly as the burgeoning number of inhabitants gave up dreams of easy riches—the curse of other colonies— and dedicated themselves to farming and livestock. But Chile was not entirely free of the pernicious forces at work in other Spanish colonies. One was a government system that fostered excessive dependence on the central administration. Another, the practice whereby officers were given huge tracts of land, creating landholding patterns that were to become a political plague.

Frequent cohabitation between the Spaniards and the native Indians produced a distinctive mestizo strain, which, according to a Pan American Union handbook, helped form a homogeneous population with few, if any, rivals in Latin America.[24]

Most of the earlier settlers were from Spain's Basque and Castilian regions. But Spaniards were not the only Europeans drawn to Chile. As the name of the great liberator Bernardo O'Higgins attests,[25] the Spanish influence was later diluted by emigrations from other European countries, including Ireland, England, and Scotland, so that names like Cochrane, Edwards, Walker, and MacKenna loom large in Chilean history. The arrival of 225 German colonists in 1850 ushered in a ninety-year era of German immigration, which eventually saw the German-descended population reach an estimated sixty thousand, mostly scattered on the small farms to the south. Late in the last century, there was also another major surge of Spanish immigration. Since then, with the exception of a handful of displaced persons admitted after World War II, Chile's population growth has been ingrown, accentuating the formation of a distinct Chilean prototype.[26]

Chile's population was 9,340,200 in the 1970 census, 11,329,726 in the 1982 census, and was estimated, at mid-1986, at 12,271,173. A 1967 study revealed that 45 percent of the population was clustered in the three main urban centers (Santiago, Valparaíso, and Concepción) and that these three centers, with less than 4 percent of the national area, absorbed 75 percent of Chile's public health expenditures and 95 percent of investments in manufacturing and processing industries. This concentration of people and power in the cities helps to account for the strength of the country's middle class—and to understand the woes of agriculture. The magnet of urban jobs also explains accelerating migration to the cities; by 1985, those three metropolitan centers were bulging with 63 percent of the country's total population; Santiago, alone, had increased from 32 percent of the total population in 1960, to 40 percent in 1985 (with a metropolitan area total of 4,772.9 million population).[27]

Stale statistics and a quick excursion into the country's musty past fail to illuminate two other essential human characteristics.

One is the phlegmatic style of Chileans, a stubborn regard for the niceties of form and convention, qualities that have moved many observers to view Chileans as the British of South America.[28] Some have become so infatuated with the theory, that they have virtually equated the Chilean Congress with the British Parliament. This comparison bred the belief that Allende's socialist revolution would be carried out within the framework of democratic institutions. Or that the end could not but come peaceably. Interesting, but the theory overlooked the fact that the Chileans—unlike the British—have had few qualms about resorting to extrainstitutional means (that is, force) when political tensions became badly taxed. Expressed differently, beneath his austere surface, in every Chilean lurks the soul of a Latino.

The other quality—commented upon by countless other writers—I offer into evidence without a demurrer. And that is, the extraordinary beauty of Chilean women. I am not sure how this relates to the soundness of this narrative, but undaunted, I am prepared to propose a theory. My own theory—endearing to few women's libbers, I am sure—is that their special charm is their ability to make each man seem important to them as a man. What is relevant to our tale is the catalytic role they played in mobilizing men in the Allende drama, faithful to a tradition reaching back to the days of Inés de Suárez and kept alive by women playing conspicuous roles at crucial times ever since. In the rest of Latin America, until very recently, women have been for the most part seen but not heard and rarely heeded.

Even such a perfunctory glimpse of Chile's people is incomplete without a word on similarities and dissimilarities between Chileans and their Latin confreres. Faithful to the Hispanic tradition, Chileans were, until recently, more comfortable in the world of law, the social sciences, and letters than in the world of science, technology, and the practical applications of man's energies. One is tempted to add "even more so." In law, for example, the Chilean civil code, drafted in 1855, became the model for most of Latin America.[29] The notion of organized labor first took root in Chile, with the formation in 1847 of the first workers' social organizations. Chile also was a pacesetter in putting into effect labor legislation (the day of Sunday rest, in 1807, for example). Chile's social-security system, adopted in 1925, ten full years ahead of the United States, also became a model for Latin America. The short-lived regime of Marmaduke Grove in 1932 was the hemisphere's first Socialist Republic, and the Popular Front in 1933 the first in the Americas (and with France and Spain, among the first three in the world). In letters, this small and improbable republic has produced two Nobel laureates: Gabriela Mistral (real name: Lucila Godoy Alcayaga) and Pablo Neruda (real name: Neftalí Ricardo Reyes Basoalto), both poets—a distinction Chile shares with no other country on earth.

Chileans are also much more emancipated, more "modern," than other Latins in matters of morality: machismo and the double standard are far more passé in Chile than elsewhere in Latin America. Chile also shared, during the Allende years, another distinction "endemic to developed countries only": alone among Latin countries, pornography ("soft-core," but pornography not found elsewhere in Latin America) and bawdy shows abounded (later abolished under the military junta).

But the quality that marks Chileans above all, is their admirable ability to laugh easily, spontaneously and—most loudly—at themselves. And that sets them apart from just about any peoples anywhere.

THE LAND

Nobel laureate Gabriela Mistral once described her native land as "a desire to exist." For the most part, it is a scowling land, harsh and unyielding, a bilious and brutal land. Beauty, yes, rawboned and bountiful and breathtaking, and along a narrow vein, subtle and soft. But for the most part it is a land perverse and impudent, and impervious to man and his purposes. In the north, a thousand miles of parched barrenness— and the clearest, cleanest skies in the Western world, and below, unexpected geysers and eerie earthly remains and awesome unearthly remains.[30] In the south, a thousand miles of fjords and gulfs and bays and inlets and canyons and capes and glaciers and islands and towering trees and howling winds—an irredeemable paradise. Along the coast, an ocean that runs cold and swift and deep and often at savage odds with the restraining shore. Along the country's back, the restive Andes, young, assertive peaks, higher than any others on earth save for the remote Himalayas, a barrier so formidable that less than a third of the world's weather can make it across their scraggy, gnarled, and fuming battlements. Wedged in the middle is that thin and verdant vein of loveliness, the Central Valley.

It is the youth of the Andes that accounts for the violence of the land— the volcanoes, the earthquakes. There are 2,085 volcanoes, fifty-five of which are active,[31] including the exquisite Osorno,[32] a worthy trans-Pacific companion piece to Fujiyama. But earthquakes are Chile's special purgatory, and in their ubiquity, they traumatize Chileans in a confraternity of terror.[33] When one totters interminably on the edge of a hideous abyss, the experience is bound at the least to affect one's view of abysses. I am not suggesting that Chileans live in permanent fear of earthquakes. I am suggesting that earthquakes happen in Chile with such regularity over an area encompassing 90 percent of the country's population as to be routine, an experience shared by virtually all Chileans.

The effect on Chileans, I believe, is to imbue them with a mysticism that goes beyond fatalism. For them, it is not so much that Victoria's messenger *must* come riding to save Mac the Knife from the gallows, as that the bloomin' blackguard has always made it in time before. So it was that in the final days of the Allende regime, when each day brought word of some terrible new crisis, even the most sober of men were heard to say that "we'll work it out somehow; always have before, you know," or "we've been to the brink before without going over; we won't this time either, you'll see." Victoria's messenger did not, of course, reward mystical faith in September 1973.[34]

In Chile now, cherries are dancing
the dark mysterious girls are singing
and in guitars, water is shining
The sun is touching every door
and making wonder of the wheat

I have no wish to change my planet.[35]

A harsh and defiant land, true, allotting man less than one acre in twelve as suitable for growing the food he needs to survive—and even that pittance he mistreats.[36] But it is also a benign, generous land. The county's greatest mineral riches—copper, nitrate, iron, and oil—are found in areas otherwise inimical to man. The country's agricultural riches are found in an area superbly beckoning to man, and it is there—between Copiapó to the north and Puerto Montt to the south, about a quarter of the country's area—that 76.9 percent of the population live.

This is the home of the great cities: Santiago, a deceptive city, a dreary place to the casual eye, but to the patiently perceptive, a cornucopia of subtle delights; Valparaíso, the mountain-muscular port city publicists call the "Pearl of the Pacific," and the poet Neruda called a "filthy rose"; Valparaíso's fair sister Viña del Mar, queen of Chile's resorts (but surpassed, in my judgment, for sheer charm and seductive simplicity, by Algarrobo, El Quisco, Santo Domingo, and Neruda's own favorite, Isla Negra—all down the coast from Viña); Concepción, a stubborn city which has risen from the ashes of six devastating earthquakes and rules as the most important city in southern Chile; Temuco, marketplace for the country's corn and grains; Valdivia, a prim microcosm of the Germany so many of its inhabitants left behind.

Valdivia is also an area of incomparable bucolic beauty, as the explorer Valdivia noted nearly four and–a–half centuries ago.[37] It was late summer when I first drove the 420 miles from Santiago to Temuco, a journey that sealed my great romance with Chile. Agronomists say Chile's Central Valley, cupped by the Andes and the Costal Range, rivals in fertility and lushness California's Imperial Valley. I remember it as a magic-carpet escape into a fantasy world of gentle folk and simple pleasures and a serenity so delicate as to tinge my contentment with melancholy. I remember watermelon at roadside stands and barefoot children and the smell of hay in a passing wagon and mud walls and poplar trees and apple orchards and rushing rivers and crisp air and the perfume of pine groves, of tangy *empanadas* (meat pies) shared with wizened men and giggling children and washed down with a twenty-five-cent jug of lusty red wine; of somnolent towns and snow-preened peaks and eucalyptus trees and dusty roads leading past stables, granaries, barns, and sheds to the remnants of another world of unpretentious manor houses where the welcome is warm and spontaneous and there is no such word as stranger. I remember too the first gusts of the whirlwind of ugly class war that would soon blight those quiet green valleys: small knots of people in huts and tents, a Chilean flag hooked on a scraggy stick, and the strapping young buck coming forward saying that these lands had been seized in the name of the socialist revolution. While the others, certain only that they were poor and always had been, cringed about, awaiting the hand of Authority to be laid upon them, in blessing or violent rebuke.

Throughout most of its history, Chile produced enough food on its relatively meager farmlands for its own people, as well as for the tables of Peru and Europe.[38] But, by 1942, net food exporter Chile became net importer Chile, a situation that worsened progressively and reached catastrophic dimensions under Allende.[39] It would take the military government of Pinochet to restore vigor to the farm economy. We leave for later chapters a closer look at what happened to collapse farm production, and why, as well as a discussion of the comeback of Chilean agriculture in the post-Allende years. Here we offer in Table 1 a few preliminary highlights:

TABLE 1
AGRICULTURAL OVERVIEW, 1948–1983

FARM DEFICIT IN INTERNATIONAL TRADE (NET, IN MILLIONS OF DOLLARS)					FOOD IMPORTS, ALLENDE YEARS (GROSS, IN MILLIONS OF US$)			
1948	1955	1956	1959	1961	1970	1971	1972	1973
−6	−79	−55.4	−67	−83	171.3	310.9	447.5	594.9

	OUTPUT, KEY CROPS, ALLENDE YEARS (THOUSANDS OF METRIC QUINTALS)				FOUR PINOCHET YEARS			
	1970	1971	1972	1973	1980	1981	1982	1983
Wheat	13,069	13,679	11,951	7,466	9,660	6,859	6,504	5,858
Rice	762	670	862	549	954	997	1,311	1,155
Corn	2,390	2,583	2,829	2,940	4,051	5,181	4,840	5,115
Beans	655	721	829	649	842	1,382	1,624	843
Potatoes	6,838	8,358	7,330	6,235	9,031	10,072	8,414	6,836

(It should be noted that two of the Pinochet years, 1982 and 1983, span a deep recession, induced largely by a constellation of international factors. Output of all five crops increased in the 1984 and 1985 harvest years, in some cases dramatically.)

Sources: Alain Labrousse, El Experimento Chileno (Barcelona and Mexico: Ediciones Grijalbo, S.A., 1973), p. 109; For food imports: "Situation, Principal Problems and Prospects of the Chilean Economy," Ad-hoc Country Review Group of the Inter-American Economic and Social Council, Permanent Executive Committee, Washington, D.C., March 6, 1975, p. 129; for Output figures, "Indicadores Económicos Y Sociales, 1960–1985," op. cit., p. 63.

The Central Valley is cattle country, farmland, and fruit country, producing wheat, corn, potatoes, sugar, and onions. In the "north central" region—the provinces immediately to the south of Santiago—were the big estates. Farther south, where the valley bulges to a width of sixty miles, smaller farms predominated. Vineyards in the Central Valley also make Chile Latin America's second-largest wine producer (after Argentina).

Chileans prefer consuming their wines at home to selling them abroad. For many years they ranked sixth in the world in per capita wine consumption.[40] Until the 1980s, Chileans exported only one-half to 1 percent of what they produced: in 1966, for example, they produced 473 million liters and exported 4.7 million; in 1971, production was 525 million liters, exports 3.5 million. By the mid-1980s, production was not only dramatically higher; so too were exports.[41] Most connoisseurs, including the French, who import Chilean wine, agree that it ranks second only to the world's very best in quality.

To the south of Concepción and extending to Puerto Montt, is Forest Chile. Here are the great timberlands that have made Chile a major producer of pulp and paper products. This is also the area of the biggest cattle herds and most bountiful wheatfields. The southern third of Chile, below Puerto Montt—archipelagic Chile—is also blanketed with dense forests. But it is one of the rainiest and stormiest areas on earth, and the land is of little use to humans.[42]

By 1983, agriculture (including fishing, forestry, and hunting) provided jobs for only 13 percent of the economically active population, and contributed 5.7 percent to the gross domestic product.[43] Though recent statistics on farm income are hard to come by, a study done during the Allende years showed that annual income per farm worker in 1972 was no more than seven thousand escudos—less than half the then legal *minimum* wage of 15,876 escudos per year; and a sample of farmers on *minifundios* ("minifarms") in three provinces (Aconcagua, O'Higgins, and Osorno, all prime farm areas) showed them subsisting in 1972 on four thousand escudos per year.[44] Low wages are, of course, a key reason why in Chile, as elsewhere in Latin America, it is all but impossible to keep people down on the farms and away from swelling city slums. The shift in population from rural areas to the city (Table 2) has been much more pronounced in Chile than almost anywhere else in the hemisphere.[45]

The seas off Chile were, until recently, less important as a source of jobs than as a staple of Chilean diets, above all in times of acute meat shortages. Successive Chilean governments have tried to stimulate an even healthier appetite for fish, but given their druthers, Chileans persistently pass up their delicious crayfish, abalones, swordfish, and shrimp in favor of old-fashioned steak. (In recent times, they *must* pass up their abalones, or "locos," as they are known in Chile; overharvesting

TABLE 2
POPULATION DISTRIBUTION 1875–1985

CENSUS	URBAN POPULATION	% OF TOTAL	RURAL POPULATION	% OF TOTAL
1875	599,181	27.0	1,620,000	73.0
1885	762,517	30.6	1,729,369	69.4
1895	1,065,634	38.0	1,738,666	62.0
1907	1,394,737	43.2	1,833,821	56.8
1920	1,732,567	46.4	1,999,006	53.6
1930	2,119,221	49.4	2,168,224	50.6
1940	2,564,634	52.5	2,320,384	47.5
1952	3,464,869	58.4	2,469,126	41.6
1960	5,144,143	68.2	2,332,966	31.2
1970	7,023,800	75.2	2,316,400	24.8
1982	9,316,100	82.2	2,013,600	17.8
1985 (Est.)	10,084,700	83.5	1,989,800	16.5

Sources: For period 1875–1960: *Atlas de la República de Chile*, 2d ed. (Santiago: Instituto Geográfico Militar, 1982), p. 193; For 1970, 1982 and 1985: *Indicadores Económicos Y Sociales, 1960–1985*, op. cit., p. 363.

of that shellfish threatened to wipe it out, leading to a government-imposed, four-year ban on its sale within Chile.) With world demand for fish rising steeply, commercial fishing in Chilean waters has taken on much greater importance, and beyond the two hundred-mile limit, huge fleets of Japanese, Russian, American and other commercial vessels are fishing the Humboldt Current as never before.

But, above all, copper was the traditional king in Chile, a reign that dates back to World War I, when saltpeter fell casualty to synthetics. Copper has been produced commercially in Chile since the birth of the republic, and by 1860 Chile's production of 50,000 tons was accounting for 40 percent of the world market. Until 1875, when displaced by booming U.S. production, Chile was the world's principal source of copper, a leadership Chile has recaptured in recent years.

By 1891 Chilean output was down to 20,000 tons, and at the turn of the century Chile accounted for a scant 5 percent of world output. The Chilean owners of the ninety-year-old El Teniente mine tried unsuccessfully to raise capital from Chilean and European sources to underwrite modern operating methods. Finally, in 1904, William Braden, an American mining engineer, persuaded Guggenheim associates to buy the property. In August 1904 the newly acquired property was named the Braden Copper Company, later (in 1915) to be melded with five U.S. mines into the Kennecott Copper Corporation.

It was the first U.S. beachhead in the industry, and marked the beginning of the resurgence of Chilean copper in the world context. It also marked the onset of a mood that would become a movement—the mood of resentment against *dependencia*. The word began as the expression of a carefully conceived rebellion against excessive control over internal affairs by outsiders and ended, as it became increasingly debased in the politics of demagoguery, as a snarl in a vendetta aimed mostly at the United States.[46]

Nine years after the emergence of Kennecott as a single force, Anaconda Copper won the concession to exploit the Chuquicamata mine. It was the beginning of sixty years of American ascendancy over Chile's basic industry. Eventually, Anaconda and Kennecott came to account for 20 percent of Chile's gross domestic product, 40 percent of all government tax revenues, and 80 percent of hard currency earnings. In the words of one acute analyst of the industry, "All of *Fortune*'s 500 largest corporations combined do not play nearly the role in the economy of the United States or pay more than a fraction of the percentage of U.S. taxes that Anaconda and Kennecott alone supplied in Chile."[47] Increasingly, in the context of Chilean politics, it was a kingdom without glory.

Chile's copper deposits speckle a one thousand-mile strip, extending from Chuquicamata in the Atacama Desert in the north to El Teniente, hard against the Andes seventy miles south of Santiago. Chile is number one in the world in known copper reserves: 100 million tons, or 25 percent of the world's known reserves. Even though Chile increased its share of the world market from the 13.2 percent it averaged from 1801 to 1974 to 20 percent by 1981, Chile's reserves were sufficient to continue production at 1986 levels for about 112 years, while the rest of the western world would exhaust its reserves in about 67 years.

Chuquicamata—Chuqui, as it is called in Chile—and El Teniente are the giants of the five mines that make up the *gran minería*, the large mines. Chuqui is the world's largest open-pit copper mine, and El Teniente the world's largest underground copper mine. In recent years these two mines have accounted for 80 percent of Chile's total copper output. Tables 3 and 4 profile the big mines, and put Chile's production in a world perspective.

TABLE 3
RESERVES, OUTPUT, WORKFORCE AND PRODUCTION, CHILE'S
MAJOR COPPER MINES, 1973–1974

MINES	RESERVES[a]	WORK FORCE	PRODUCTION[b]	
			1973	1974[c]
Chuquicamata	30.0	10,421	265,252	318,000
Exótica	3.0	418	31,837	49,000
El Salvador	5.5	5,929	84,028	79,000
Andina	2.5	2,020	56,064	61,000
El Teniente	40.0	12,656	178,129	233,000
ALL OTHERS	19.0	TOTALS:	615,310	740,000

Sources: Work force and production, El Mercurio, April 14, 1974. Volume of reserves, El Mercurio, October 12, 1974.

[a] In millions of metric tons.
[b] In metric tons.
[c] Figures are provisional.

Total production from all mines for 1973—Salvador Allende's last year in power—was 746,800 metric tons. It has continued to climb virtually ever year since, standing at an estimated 1.357 million tons for 1986—pushing Chile ahead of the United States into first place among the world's producers.[48] Chile sells copper to more than forty countries, mainly in Europe, although Japan came up rapidly in the seventies to rank as Chile's second customer. The United States has not led the list since 1952, when Chile passed a law in retaliation for U.S. actions during World War II and the Korean War, actions that unilaterally fixed ceiling prices for copper, without consulting the Chileans.[49]

Of the big five, until Allende nationalized the mines, Anaconda controlled Chuqui, El Salvador, and Exótica; Kennecott had El Teniente; and Cerro Corporation, the Andina mine. Kennecott and Anaconda had for decades ranked one and two among the world's copper-producing companies.

Chuquicamata is an ever-deepening elliptical amphitheater two miles long, one mile wide, and situated 10,000-feet high in a barren desert. About 1.2 billion tons of material have been gouged from the earth since the Guggenheim interests began serious operations there six decades ago, using steam shovels that had helped dig the Panama Canal. In 1923 the Guggenheims sold a 51 percent interest to Anaconda for $77 million, the biggest deal recorded to that point on Wall Street. Anaconda created in those inhospitable surroundings a pleasant company town of 30,000, with American-style amenities that included a country club. The company was handsomely rewarded for its risks and efforts, but not

TABLE 4

CHILEAN COPPER IN A WORLD CONTEXT, 1800–1974

PERIOD	WORLD PRODUCTION (IN METRIC TONS)	CHILEAN PRODUCTION (IN METRIC TONS)	CHILE AS % OF WORLD
1801–1810	163,000	15,000	9.2
1811–1820	168,000	15,000	8.9
1821–1830	244,000	65,000	8.5
1831–1840	325,000		
1841–1850	441,000	100,000	22.7
1851–1860	678,000	220,000	32.4
1861–1870	1,000,000	401,000	40.1
1871–1880	1,250,000	457,000	36.6
1881–1890	2,254,000	367,000	16.3
1891–1900	3,750,000	236,000	6.3
1801–1900	10,273,000	1,876,000	18.3
1901–1910	6,940,000	352,000	5.1
1911–1920	10,928,000	676,000	6.2
1921–1930	13,407,000	2,027,000	15.1
1931–1940	16,276,000	2,702,000	16.6
1941–1950	23,387,000	4,347,000	18.6
1951–1960	33,671,000	4,451,000	13.2
1961–1970	51,683,000	6,391,000	12.4
1971–1974	28,914,000	3,070,000	10.6
1901–1974	185,206,000	24,016,000	13.0
1801–1974	195,479,000	25,892,000	13.2

Source: El Mercurio, October 12, 1974.

COPPER OUTPUT IN A WORLD CONTEXT, 1983–1985

	WORLD (MILLION METRIC TONS)	CHILE (MILLION METRIC TONS)	CHILE AS % OF WORLD
1983 (A)	7.9	1.25	15.8
1984 (B)	8.1	1.290	15.9
1985 (C)	7.8	1.360	17.4

A—1985 Year Book, p. 330.
B—1986 Year Book, pp. 331–332.
C—1987 Year Book, p. 300.

nearly so handsomely as Allende and a legion of latter-day propagandists, abetted by an uncritical press, would have had the world believe.[50]

Nitrate—once a source of gunpowder, still important as a source of fertilizer—is next in the country's traditional mining picture, but it took a war to put nitrate on Chile's map. It happens that most of the nitrate deposits are situated in an elongated stretch of territory roughly fifteen miles across and five hundred miles long in the northern desert region, lands that formerly belonged to Bolivia and Peru. Chile wrested these lands from her two neighbors in the War of the Pacific (1879–83).[51]

For fifty years, nitrate dominated the Chilean economy, eventually accounting for 52 percent of Chile's income.[52] At the beginning of this century, Chile was producing 70 percent of the world's nitrate, a total of 1.5 million tons, and by 1917, had doubled that output figure.[53] But when the country's biggest nitrate customer, Germany, was blockaded during World War I, the Germans hurried the development of synthetics.[54] Stimulated by the creation in 1968 of a new, U.S.–controlled sulphate complex, nitrate production came out of a long slump. From 1970 to 1971, the increase was 49.4 percent, and nitrate exports in 1971 rose to $36.6 million, or 3.2 percent of total exports (only to collapse under Allende the following year to $24.5 million).[55] Chile remains the only sizable producer of natural nitrates in the world, and, in the 1980s, the industry enjoyed a new resurgence of importance.

In importance, iron ore displaced nitrate as a moneymaker for the country in 1961 ($44.7 million versus $34.4 million for nitrate), reaching an absolute peak in terms of its export value in 1981 ($161.9 million, beginning a slide that year which has continued since.) Nitrate—Chile is the world's only producer of pure nitrate—has, interestingly, staged a comeback in recent years. Though production levels are nowhere near the "golden era" peaks, improved mining techniques coupled with rising prices have combined to push the value (and profitability) of Chile's nitrate sales to unprecedented levels.[57]

But Chile is rich in many other minerals, as well: second in the world (behind the U.S.) in molybdenum reserves (as well as in production); second only to Japan in iodine, and to Russia in lithium; third to the U.S. and USSR in rhenium—accounting for 17 to 22 percent of the world's production of these minerals. Chile also has significant reserves of coal (and growing output) of gold, silver, boron, and less-sizable reserves of manganese (26,000 tons output in 1986), cobalt, lead, zinc and mercury. Chile's first oil well began producing on December 29, 1945 in Magallanes, in the far south; In 1973, domestic production from 366 wells in Tierra del Fuego covered about one-third of the country's domestic needs; by 1985, it was about half the total.[58]

Mining and quarrying were long the traditional kingpins of the Chilean economy—first nitrate, then copper. That, of course, meant the country was at the permanent mercy of price fluctuations and demand factors in world markets Chile could not control. The Pinochet administration set out purposefully to change that—and succeeded. In 1972, mining and quarrying represented 9.9 percent of gross domestic product, and copper a shade over 80 percent of all exports. Employment was only 3.2 percent of the labor force at the time. As elsewhere in Latin America where a single crop or product dominated the economy, workers in that industry were the industrial wage elite. In Chile, wages in the copper industry traditionally averaged anywhere from 50 to 100 percent higher than those for other industrial workers, and copper workers held a trump card in national economic affairs which could not be underestimated—as Salvador Allende ruefully discovered.[59] By 1987, copper had dropped to 41 percent of the total value of exports, thanks mainly to a systematic development of the country's farm, fishing and forestry riches—a subject to be explored in a later section.[60]

Before leaving the matter of mining, it is useful to examine in closer detail the "catastrophe of 1929," when the bottom fell out of Chile's metal riches. More than any other event, before or since, it focused the country's attention on the issue of dependence, inasmuch as the two main sources of wealth were then in foreign hands, where they were to remain for many more years to come. That meant the country had little maneuverability in the midst of worldwide economic storms.[61] The wounds opened then remained a festering sore in the country's body politic, culminating in the "final solutions" of the Allende regime.

But there were other, more subtle consequences rooted in habits formed during the palmy days of prosperity and never really rectified to meet new realities. André Siegfried, a widely admired French political and social scientist, visited South America in the early 1930s and published, in 1933, a book called *Impressions of South America*. In it he broke important intellectual ground on the topic of dependence and also discussed the subtle ramifications of economic collapse hinted at above. Paul Kramer and Robert McNicoll included a chapter of Siegfried's book in an anthology thirty-five years later.[62]

They remarked that the importance of Siegfried's observations lay much more in the fact that they were *thought* to be authoritative than in his "depth of penetration into the details of Chile's economic predicament." Later generations of brisk technocrats echoed Siegfied's ideas, often unwittingly.

"What the Frenchman Siegfried said about the Chilean economy in 1931," Kramer and McNicoll assert, "was eventually adopted by the Chileans as political doctrine, implemented by an elected government thirty-five years later, and accepted as a solution for overcoming difficult problems in U.S.–Latin American relations by a leading U.S. newspaper."[63] The government they cite is that of Eduardo Frei and his now highly suspect "Revolution in Freedom" (1964–70), and the newspaper, the *New York Times*, and its October 12, 1966, editorial cheering Frei's plan for "Chileanization" (that is, buyout) of U.S. copper interests. A scheme, by the way, excoriated by Marxists (see, for example, pages 131–37 of the Alain Labrousse book), scrapped by Allende, and, in retrospect, defensible largely as a self-fulfilling prophecy of doom. A later chapter will dwell in more detail on this theme. For the moment, it is important to clarify, emphatically, what is *not* meant, and that is, that a country, large or small, developing or developed, should not fail to control its basic riches. But "control" became equated—fallaciously, uncritically—with ownership, and many a poor country has pursued this mirage with ruinous results.[64]

Siegfried, in his work, isolated five factors as underlying the Chilean predicament, the first two purely empirical, the third a political judgment, the fourth the (then) bombshell, and the last, social critique.

The first two: the fall in world prices of raw materials, and nitrate's decline in the face of synthetics. Number three is what he calls the "foolhardy" borrowing of the populist dictator, Carlos Ibáñez, and his borrowing heavily from a single source, the U.S.[65]

Siegfried's fourth factor would later become a preferred weapon in the war on private foreign investment, a weapon which, in careless hands, resembled a blunderbuss, scattering shot indiscriminately. "Thus," Siegfried wrote, "the profits from this [mining] wealth, when there are any, leave the country in the form of dividends. It is easy to realize how foreign payments under such conditions can only be compared to a hemorrhage." He also chided Chileans for brashness in bringing in outsiders. "The country naturally could not be developed without foreign capital, but it was tempted to go ahead too quickly and borrow too heavily, beyond the limits of prudence."[66]

Siegfried named the Chilean temperament as the fifth—and, in his estimate, vilest—villain of his piece. Chileans, he said, squander their money, taking it out of the country and dissipating capital on showy buildings. (He pinpointed several, presumably those surrounding the Plaza Constitución in downtown Santiago; a less austere observer might describe them not as showy, but as serviceably dreary, and certainly after three decades of wear and tear.) He also said Chileans live excessively on borrowed money, private indviduals as well as the state, a weakness that would grow markedly worse with the passing of time.

"It is difficult," Siegfried wrote, "to build up a sound public economy on a private economy which is unsound. Individually, the Chilians [*sic*] are charming, cultivated, generous and kind, but in this country, as in many others on this continent, one feels that they do not take economic matters seriously enough."

Were Siegfried to have viewed the wreckage of Chile's economy forty-two years later, one cannot help feeling that he could have been excused a harumph or two of self-satisfaction. And perhaps a sign of remorse, that so many of his ideas later would become bludgeons in accursed causes.[67]

Notes

CHAPTER 1

1. An arbitrary division, admittedly, which includes the Spanish-speaking republics as well as Brazil and Haiti, but excludes Cuba, the English-speaking countries of the Caribbean, and the three Guianas.
2. I resort to direct quotation in such seemingly innocent circumstances to illustrate a peril all Latinists soon discover: statistics on Latin America must be approached with caution and care. One would imagine that statistics on geography ought to be harmless. They aren't. These, for example, come from *Fodor's South America* (New York: David McKay Company, 1974), p. 260. On the very next line of that volume, Chile's area is given as 463,600 square miles. The actual figure is 292,000 give or take a few square miles, or at least the World Bank, the Inter-American Development Bank, *The Encyclopaedia Britannica*, the *South American Handbook*, and the *New York Times Almanac* agree on the lower figure in their publications. (Evidently the Fodor people had in mind Chile's Antarctic claim, which isn't 463,600 square miles, but 482,625 square miles.) To add injury to this hodgepodge of confusion, another reference work, *The Latin American Scene of the Seventies: A Basic Fact Book* (Miami: Center for Advanced International Studies, University of Miami, 1972), gives Chile's area as 286,396 square miles, "still greater than Texas, and larger by one-third than any European country save for Russia." Practically all of the aforementioned publications quibble among themselves over the proper length and width figures for Chile. I labor the point to condition the reader to deal gingerly with statistics on Latin America, in this volume and elsewhere.
3. John Gunther, *Inside South America* (New York: Harper & Row, 1966), p. 280. Gunther adds: "The land is a kind of narrow shelf between the Andes and the Pacific, a balcony." As somebody said to me in Santiago, "You have to be thin to be a Chileno. Otherwise you fall off."
4. Claudio Véliz, "Centralism and Nationalism," *Foreign Affairs* 47, no. 1 (October 1968): 68.
5. K. H. Silvert, among others, disputes this interpretation, pointing to Chilean fondness for foreign travel, his cosmopolitan quality (he cites the old saw, "whenever a good Chilean dies, he goes to Paris"), and the Geneva-like quality of Santiago as a seat of international agencies (which, I remark in passing, are actually few in number and significant chiefly in that they contain a high percentage of technocrats whose own leftist biases reinforced the ascendancy of leftist thought in Chile)—Silvert, "The Prospects of Chilean Democracy," in *Latin American Politics*, ed. Robert D. Tomasek (Garden City, N.Y.: Doubleday, Anchor Books, 1966). Silvert's article was reprinted from "Some Propositions on Chile," American Universities Field Staff Report, January 1964.

   The point I make is that there is a great difference between an elite that travels abroad to dip into the well of world ideas, and a nation that digests

23

ideas in the solitude of isolation, itself off the beaten track of international ideas. And that, I believe, *is* the point. For details of my claim about the international agencies in Santiago nurturing leftist thinkers, see Robert Moss, *Chile's Marxist Experiment* (New York: John Wiley & Sons, Halstead Press, 1973), p. 53; and Marcos Chamudes, *Chile: Una Advertencia Americana* (Santiago: Ediciones P.E.C., 1972), pp. 112–16.

6. It is beyond the scope of this work, but no mention of Chile's geography would be complete without alluding to two of the country's most interesting possessions: Easter Island (Rapa Nui), 2,350 miles out in the Pacific, famed for its huge carved-stone monuments; and the three Juan Fernández Islands, 520 miles west of Valparaiso. One of them is called Marino Alejandro Selkirk, for the Scottish sailor Alexander Selkirk, marooned there in 1704, whose escapades later inspired Daniel Defoe's book *Robinson Crusoe*.

7. In 1851, the minister of war and navy announced that a warship would regularly patrol between Valparaíso and San Francisco "so that our merchant fleet will be encouraged and our consuls will have nearby a force with which to make their decisions respected. . . ." Years later the fleet did, in fact, make "their decisions respected." In 1885, the cruiser *Esmeralda* took a force of Chilean marines to Panama with orders to oust an American force which was there scouting a canal route. The Chilean marines landed and ousted the gringos.

8.   *. . . those the land produces are so haughty,*
              so proud, so indomitable and fierce,
              that mastered by kind they never were
              nor to foreign rule submitted.

From the epic poem "La Araucana," by Alonso de Ercilla y Zúñiga, translated by María de la Concepción González. Ercilla came to Chile at twenty-one, fought in seven battles against the Araucanians. His poem is the most cherished literary landmark of the Conquest and Araucanian heroism.

9. Enrique Campos Menéndez, "Chile Today: Concern and Hope," in *Chile: A Critical Survey* (Santiago: Institute of General Studies, 1972), pp. 16–17.

10. Gabriel García Márquez, "The Death of Salvador Allende," *Harper's*, March 1974.

11. Moss, op. cit., p. 11. Keyserling is quoted by Chilean historian Francisco Antonio Encina in an essay on the Chilean race in *Nueva Enciclopedia de Chile* (Argentina: Ediciones Copihue, Fotomecánica Futura SRL, Ediciones Libra, 1974), 1:170. (Hereafter *Nueva Enciclopedia*.)

12. Walterio Millar lists eleven tribes in his serviceable primer, *Historia de Chile*, 29th ed. (Santiago: Editorial Zig-Zag, 1973), p. 47. H. R. S. Pocock speaks of five major Indian groups in his book, *The Conquest of Chile* (New York: Stein & Day, 1967), p. 229. Unless otherwise noted, references to Chile's Indian past were taken from these two works.

13. There are two theories about the origin of Chile's name. One holds that it is derived from the Quechua Indian word *tchili*, meaning "cold" or "snow"; the first conquistadors experienced plenty of both as they made their way down through the Andes from Peru with Quechua-speaking guides and porters. The other is that the name resembles the sound *chee-lee, chee-lee*, made by a bird then common to the area, Triles. In both cases, the Spaniards made the *ee* sound at the end of the word an *ay*, as in *day*. As Pocock notes (op. cit., pp. 232–33), the word *Araucano* was invented by Ercilla to describe

the fighting Indians who belonged to one of three tribes (the Picunches, Mapuches, and Huilliches) speaking the same language and inhabiting the area from the Itata River to the Gulf of Reloncaví. The Mapuches were the fighters.

14. The claim about Spanish losses to the Araucanians appears in Gunther, op. cit., p. 293. Pocock makes no such claim, although he makes numerous references to the ferocity of Araucanian resistance, including tribute paid them by no less a soldier than Pedro de Valdivia: "I have warred with men of many nations," Valdivia wrote his sovereign, Charles V, "but never have I seen such fighting tenacity as is displayed by these Indians" (Pocock, op. cit., p. 238).

"For more than 300 years," Pocock wrote (p. 9), "the members of this primitive race, probably never numbering as many as 400,000 individuals, stubbornly maintained their independence in the face of all that could be brought against them by their European aggressors. While the Picunches, their northern neighbors, and the Huilliches to the south of them, succumbed almost at the first contact, the Araucanians successfully defended a solid strip of territory running right across the middle of Chile from mountain to ocean, dividing it into two separate halves. Only when their numbers had been pitifully thinned, their blood ruthlessly drained by combined ravages of disease and ten generations of warfare, was it possible to impose permanent terms of settlement upon them."

The *Encyclopaedia Britannica* (15th ed. [1975], Micropaedia, 1:479) refers to the Araucanians as "the fiercest warriors whom any Europeans had yet encountered in the Americas"—but makes no mention of the toll they exacted on the conquistadors.

15. The Indian wars ended, for all practical purposes, in 1861, after two and-a-half years of renewed fighting, but it was not until 1877 that the Araucanian allowed immigrants to settle their lands unmolested. Early in the 1860s there was a bizarre flare-up, kindled by an eccentric Frenchman named Aurelio Antonio de Tounens. Shortly after he began trading with the Indians, Tounens persuaded them to proclaim him their king—"Orélie-Antoine I, King of Araucania and Patagonia." Col. Cornelio Saavedra, who only shortly before had managed to bring peace to the frontier, had "King" Orélie-Antoine arrested, tried, and deported, ending the one-week reign. Orélie lost little time in returning, however, and led another uprising. This time a price was put on his head, but he vanished mysteriously and was not heard from again. Millar, op. cit., p. 265; Luis Galdames, *Historia de Chile,* 14th ed. (Santiago: Productos RAVAL, 1974), pp. 359–88; and Andrew Marshall, ed., *The South American Handbook* (London: Trade & Travel Publications, 1971), p. 265.

Pocock notes (op. cit., p. 190) that when the Araucanian lands finally were opened, "enthusiasm for this part of the country knew no bounds. . . . We may conclude with Encina that had the Araucanians been merely of the same caliber as Picunches and Huilliches, then it is likely that the center of gravity of Chile would have shifted from Santiago to the area which the Spaniards settled in the early 1550s. It was the Araucanians' stubborn resistance which gave Santiago some three hundred years' start, too large a handicap for the south ever to overcome."

16. *Atlas de la República de Chile,* 2d ed. (Santiago: Instituto Geográfico Militar, 1972), ethnographic map, p. 192.

17. Until a very few years ago, many Chileans denied the Indian presence in

their midst. Professor Lipschutz of the University of Chile, in an article a few years ago, showed that Chile's Araucanian population probably exceeded 600,000, and remarked that "many in Santiago take umbrage with that figure." He reported that at one meeting of educators he attended, the number of Araucanians was put at 10,000, a figure accepted without comment by the other educators present. Alejandro Lipschutz, "Cuántos Araucanos Hay en Chile?" *El Mercurio* (Santiago), March 4, 1971, p. 3.

In quoting Professor Lipschutz's work since, I have collided repeatedly with the same resentment-tinged incredulity. It should be noted that Professor Lipschutz undoubtedly was using the term *Araucano* in the generic sense, in which it is often (and misleadingly) applied in modern Chile to the descendants of all the southern Indian tribes. Similarly, the term *Mapuche*—"people of the land"—is often applied to all Indians of tribes from the Choapa River south to the Gulf of Reloncaví. Cautín figures from *Atlas Regionalizado de Chile* (Santiago: Instituto Geográfico Militar, 1981), p. 56.

18. Science Notebook, *Washington Post*, March 14, 1988, p. A-7.

19. Chileans are also fond of pointing out that Valdivia was a man of "superior polish and character" (which he was) in contrast to the "rude adventurers" and greedy plunderers who stayed behind in Peru. See, for example, Galdames, op. cit., p. 64.

20. Galdames (ibid., p. 68) reports that the attackers killed four Spaniards and slaughtered about twenty of their horses, destroyed stores and equipment, and most of the domestic animals the Spaniards had brought, leaving them with only three pigs and two chickens, plus a handful of wheat seeds. "It was," he wrote, "a complete disaster." Strangely, he makes no mention whatever of Inés de Suárez, much less of her role in repulsing the Indian attack. Pocock (op. cit., pp. 92–93) notes that Inés was "believed to have assisted in the executions, on the authority of evidence submitted at Valdivia's trial in Peru by Valdivia himself." (Pocock gives two as the number of Spaniards killed, but adds that all the defenders were "more or less severely wounded.")

21. Still another example of a different kind of feminine fury was provided by Fresia, wife of Caupolicán, first great Araucanian field general. Betrayed and taken by surprise in 1558, Caupolicán was about to be put to death (by being forced to sit on a spiked stake) when Fresia dumped their infant son at his feet and shouted: "Weren't you the one who vowed to conquer Spain itself? Don't you know that death in battle is glory and honor for a warrior? Take your son, raise him yourself, you've turned into a woman. As for myself, I would not be known as the mother of a child of an infamous father" (Millar, op. cit., p. 88). There is not a woman in Chile who cannot recite that story, and during the Allende years, women increasingly taunted their men in ways reminiscent of Fresia.

22. Ibid., p. 81. Pocock says (op. cit., p. 223) that "the most probable version" is the one that had Valdivia killed by a single blow of a club, and his heart cut into small pieces and eaten by the principal chieftains—the prevailing Araucanian custom at the time. He says the fact that there are so many conflicting versions of Valdivia's death "is itself the best proof that nothing was in fact known at all." Galdames (op. cit., p. 74) says simply that details of Valdivia's death are not known.

23. After a bloody battle in 1770, the peace was, however, disrupted over the

next century by ever-diminishing clashes, and pacification all but finally achieved in 1861.

24. *Chile*, American Nation series of Organization of American States (Washington, D.C., 1969), p. 7. Only Uruguay, where fully 90 percent of the population is of European extraction, has a more homogeneous population. The *New York Times Encyclopedic Almanac*, p. 745, puts Chile's population at 68 percent "Spanish-Mestizo," 30 percent European, and 2 percent Indian. As we have seen earlier, the last figure is almost certainly too low.

25. O'Higgins' father, Ambrosio, was born in Ballinary, Ireland. He arrived in Lima at the age of forty and worked for a year as a street peddler before moving to Chile, where his background in construction and engineering enabled him to move up in the administration. He was mayor of Concepción, then governor of Chile, and eventually viceroy of Peru.

26. My appointment book for a not untypical week in Chile included the following names, each and every one belonging to a distinguished Chilean: Cox, Ewing, Willoughby, Beckett, and Brady. A further example: three of the four combat battalions of the Chilean Marine Corps are named for the following military heroes: Lynch, Miller, and Cochrane. (The fourth: Aldea.) Francisco Antonio Encina offers a scholarly discussion of the formation of the Chilean "race" in *Nueva Enciclopedia*, 1:162–70.

27. In 1650 Chile's population was estimated at half a million. By 1831 it had reached a million. In 1875, it stood at 2,075,000, in 1935 at 4.7 million, and in 1960, 7.6 million [Alain Labrousse, *El Experimento Chileno* (Barcelona and Mexico: Ediciones Grijalbo, S.A., 1973), p. 101]. The 1970 figures are from *Indicadores Económicos Y Sociales 1960–1985; Dirección de Estudios, Banco Central de Chile* (Santiago, 1986) p. 357. (Hereafter *Indicadores Económicos Y Sociales 1960–1985.*) The 1982 figures and 1986 estimates are from *Compendio Estadístico 1986;* Instituto Nacional de Estadísticas; Ministerio de Economía, Fomento y Reconstrucción (Santiago, 1986), p. XLV. (Hereafter *Compendio Estadístico 1986.*) The 1967 data are taken from a speech delivered by Radomiro Tomic, then Chilean ambassador to the United States, at the University of Notre Dame, March 8, 1967, at a "Colloquium on Overall Development of Chile," p. 5 of a mimeograph copy distributed by the Embassy of Chile in Washington, D.C. The 1985 percentage figure for the three largest metropolitan areas was extrapolated from data appearing in *"Statistical Synthesis of Chile, 1981–1985; Dirección de Estudios, Banco Central de Chile,"* (Santiago, 1986), p. 10 (hereafter *Statistical Synthesis of Chile, 1981–1985*); and for Santiago's share of the national population and 1985 population from *Indicadores Económicos Y Sociales 1960–1985*, op. cit., p. 357.

28. In his dashingly witty, anecdotally entertaining, and occasionally scholarly travelogue on several South American countries he confessed to having discovered recently, the British historian Alistair Horne titled a chapter "The England of South America"—Horne, *Small Earthquake in Chile* (New York: Viking Press, 1972).

29. Significantly, it was drafted by Andrés Bello, a Venezuelan who became a transplanted Chilean. Still another grace of Chileans is their unaffected hospitality to foreigners, a quality which, until Allende, stood them in good stead.

30. The earthly remains are a collection of ossified mummies discovered in the area around San Pedro de Atacama in northeastern Chile, about 210 miles

28 OUT OF THE ASHES

northeast of Antofagasta, near the Bolivian border. The unearthly remains
are formed by the crater of a meteor measuring 470 meters (1,500 feet) in
diameter, one of the biggest in the world. From *Chile, Guía Turística '71*
(Santiago: Sección Publicaciones, Ferrocarriles del Estado, 1971), pp. 24, 25.
As to matchlessly clean, clear skies: astronomers from around the world
rushed to the three major observatories clustered around La Serena, Chile,
in 1987 following the sighting, on February 23, of a phenomenom with
few—if any—parallels in the history of astronomy. From one of those international observatories, scientists spotted an exploding star 170,000 light
years away, the closest supernova discovered since 1604, just before Galileo
invented the reflecting telescope. That event, viewed from a region freer of
air pollution than any other in the Western Hemisphere, was said to revolutionize the study of such supernovas and "spawned at least one field of
science." ("Star Explosion in Nearby Galaxy is Revolutionizing Astronomy," *Washington Post*, March 22, 1987, P. A-3.)

31. "Las Forjas de Vulcano," *Qué Pasa*, September 27, 1974.

32. Though one of the smaller peaks (8,700 feet), Osorno has few rivals for
beauty in the world. Situated in the ruggedly picturesque southern lakes
region, Osorno is a visual masterpiece of symmetry, color, and setting.
Imagine a conical shape of sculpted perfection, a crown of eternal snow,
green-forested flanks, all mirrored in the deep blue of Lake Todos los Santos,
and you have an impoverished word picture of glorious Osorno.

33. Anyone who has ever experienced a severe tremor knows their heart-
stopping terror, and Chile experiences a tremor on the average of every other
day. The country has also been wracked by some of the most violent quakes
on record. In May 1960, for instance, Chile's midsection was convulsed
repeatedly by a series of gargantuan earthquakes, registering between 7.25
and 8.5 on the Richter scale. For comparative purposes, the San Francisco
earthquake registered 8.3, and the worst on record anywhere, at Assam,
India, in 1950, 8.7. A shock wave raced from Chile across the Pacific at 520
miles an hour, creating an arc of terror extending through Los Angeles to
Alaska and New Zealand to Japan. *Time* magazine reported at the time:
"Farther south, quakes heaved up a 24-foot wave of lava-heated water and
smashed it against the village of Lebu, washing away 100 people. Six old
volcanoes and three new ones came to angry life as channels cracked open
to lava beds. Just north of the town of Rupanco, a flood of boiling lava poured
into Lake Ranco and swept over the town. Short moments before, an avalanche had thundered down a nearby mountain burying 113. In the raging
seas off Puerto Corral, two Chilean freighters went down without a survivor. Two small mountains sank out of sight, a 25-mile stretch of high
ground dropped 1,000 feet and new lakes were formed. Thick slices of the
island of Chiloé slipped into the Pacific. Volcanic ash rose 23,000 feet into
the sky. Seismic waves washed away 630 of the 800 citizens of the fishing
village of Queilén. In the inferno of lava, smoke, fire, water, avalanche, and
death, the helpless victims first scurried around in panic, then subsided into
resigned silence. The death toll in Chile was 5,000, damage nearly half a
billion dollars. The provisional count then showed 56 dead in Hawaii, 107 in
Japan, 20 in the Philippines" (*Time*, June 6, 1960, pp. 17, 18).

34. A reference to the final scene of *The Threepenny Opera*. Macheath (Mac the
Knife) is mounting the steps to the gallows when Victoria's messenger rides
up and announces that Her Majesty, in view of her coronation that day, had

granted him a reprieve. In the epilogue, we are reminded that in real life, Victoria's messenger does not come riding to save us from the consequences of our follies. The final act of Chile's drama was real life, not theater. From *The Threepenny Opera* (*Die Dreigroschenoper*), by Kurt Weill and Bertolt Brecht, adapted to English by Marc Blitzstein; original cast record by MGM Records (E3121).

35. Pablo Neruda, "El Perezoso," *Estravagario* (1958), in *Pablo Neruda, Selected Poems*, ed. Nathaniel Tarn (New York: Delacorte Press, 1972). Translation of "El Perezoso" by Alastair Reid. I am indebted to Alistair Horne (op. cit., p. 166) for reminding me of this evocative passage.

36. *La Nueva República*, a booklet published by the National party, outlining the party's program for the 1970 elections. The booklet gives (pp. 47–49) the total of arable lands as 6 million hectares (of the total land mass of 74 million hectares), and notes that a very high percentage of even that land is lost to erosion. The report also quoted an Italian scientist on the faculty of the University of Chile, Francesco di Castri, as estimating that Chilean soil had lost more than 80 percent of its biological potential through abuses, including burning off lands to clear them, intensive or irrational use of land (which the conservative National party attributed largely to fragmentation of the land into small plots), and bad use of fertilizers. The booklet quotes the illustrious nineteenth-century figure Benjamín Vicuña Mackenna as saying Chileans should give the vote to trees because they might then learn to take care of them and the land they are on.

37. In his first letter to the king of Spain—which it took him five years to get around to writing—Valdivia rhapsodized about the Mapocho Valley around Santiago: "There is no better land than this in the world whence to live and put down roots. . . . [I]t is flat and extremely healthy, a contented land, lush pastures and cropland, right for all kinds of cattle and plants; abundant and fine wood for building houses, and water, firewood, and feed for cattle; so much so that it would seem that God made it thus so as to have everything at hand" (Enrique Bunster, "Valdivia Entre las Ruinas de Santiago," *El Mercurio*, March 10, 1974).

38. In 1850, Chile exported 300,000 hundredweight to Peru and Europe (Labrousse, op. cit, p. 43).

39. Even as Chilean agriculture under Allende was collapsing, there were those who insisted that Chile could feed itself. For example, in 1972, Pablo Baraona Urzúa wrote: "There is a general consensus that under fair conditions, Chilean agriculture would be able to cover all the country's needs for food and agricultural raw material" (Baraona Urzúa, "The Reality of Chilean Agriculture," in *Chile: A Critical Survey* [Santiago: Institute of General Studies, 1972], p. 167). Those "fair conditions" were created by junta policies, proving Baraona Urzúa right.

40. By the mid-eighties, Chile had been overtaken by Luxembourg, Switzerland, Greece, and Austria because Chileans were drinking dramatically less wine, and inhabitants of those countries more. For example, in 1968, the ranking of countries in terms of per capita wine consumption was: Italy, France, Portugal, Argentina, Spain, and Chile. Souce: *1971 Encyclopaedia Britannica Book of the Year*, p. 91, Table 3. The 1988 *Year Book*, p. 216, showed lower rates of consumption in all the leading countries (except Argentina), and Greece and Austria slipping behind Chile. The 1986 ranking: France, Italy, Portugal, Argentina, Luxembourg, Switzerland, Spain,

Chile. In the case of Chile wine consumption (48.9 liters per person in 1968, 40 liters in 1986) may have been partially affected by widespread availability (and competitive prices) of long-banished imported spirits of all kinds. Interestingly, the U.S. has yet to make the "Top 25" list.

41. Sources for 1966 and 1971 figures: *Nueva Enciclopédia de Chile,* op. cit, Vol. 2, p. 241. Long a blip so small as not to appear on the trade statistics screen, wine had, by 1986, generated $11 million in export earnings, up 30 percent over the previous year. Thanks to a sharp increase in productivity, Chile in 1986 produced nearly as much wine (450 million liters) on 75,000 hectares as it had in earlier years in half again as much land. Sources: *Chile Today,* August 1987, #56, pp. 10–11, monthly publication of the Ministry of Foreign Affairs, Santiago (exports), and *Statistical Synthesis of Chile* (Santiago: Banco Central, 1986), p. 20 (output).

42. According to *The South American Handbook,* 200 inches of rain fall on some of it; seven days of the year are classified as tempestuous, twenty-five as stormy, ninety-three as squally—and the sun shines through a blanket of mist and cloud only fifty-one days per year. Marshall, op. cit., p. 315.

43. *Statistical Synthesis of Chile, 1981–1985,* op. cit., pp 17, 43 and 44.

44. Baraona Urzúa, op. cit., p. 176. Though more recent statistics are strangely absent amid the welter of statistical reports churned out by official and unofficial sources, there are a few clues, and perhaps none more revealing than published statistics on extreme poverty—a relatively new and decidedly trendy topic in Chile's political and economic debates. The studies use 1970 and 1982 census data. The first one was published in 1974, and was a joint undertaking of the Catholic University of Chile's Institute of Economics and the government's National Planning Office (ODEPLAN). ODEPLAN did the second. According to those studies, 21 percent of all Chileans were living in extreme poverty in 1972: 14.2 percent of them in the cities, 6.8 percent in rural areas. In 1982, the figures were: 14.2 percent, total; 10.6 percent, urban, and 3.6 percent, rural. In other words, while urban population was increasing by 32 percent, urban extreme poverty was dropping by 25 percent. In rural areas, the population declined by 13 percent; extreme poverty, meantime, plummeted by 47 percent. To complete the picture, it should, however, be noted that in the four prime agricultural regions—Maule, Bío-Bío, Auracanía and De Los Lagos—though there was progress, the rate of drop in the extreme poverty index was below the overall averages for the total rural population, and in De Los Lagos, the extreme poverty index (21.1) was the highest in the country. More on this in the chapter on the Pinochet years. Source for extreme poverty discussion: *Indicadores Económicos y Sociales, 1960–1985,* op. cit., p. 370, and *Statistical Synthesis of Chile, 1981–1985,* op. cit, pp. 4 and 48.

45. Indeed, in 1983, farming-fishing-forestry provided fewer jobs in Chile than in only three Latin American countries. Source: *1986 Britannica Book of the Year* (Encyclopaedia Britannica, Inc., Chicago, 1986), pp. 856–860.

46. Theodore H. Moran (*Multinational Corporations and the Politics of Dependence: Copper in Chile* [Princeton, N.J.: Princeton University Press, 1974], p. 3) observes that Encina wrote "with despair" in 1912 as he looked back over the history of nitrates and forward toward the future of copper. The Chilean historian's despair centered on what he termed the "denationalization" of those industries, a term which eventually would become "dependence." Moran notes (p. 4) that what the idea of dependence gained in

popularity after World War II, it lost in precision—in academic as well as political discussion. His book is an excellent survey of what dependence really meant in the case of copper in Chile.

47. Ibid., pp. 6–7. Moran does not exaggerate. In fiscal year 1974, for example, *all* corporate taxes in the U.S. represented only slightly over 14 percent of U.S. government revenues, and about 30 percent of taxes paid by individual taxpayers. Yet for all of their very real weight in the Chilean economy, the U.S. copper corporations were powerless to stave off even their own final executions: Allende's confiscation-without-compensation in 1971. This runs directly counter to the popular myth about the vaunted "power" of big corporations. As Moran notes (p. 10): "Despite widely advanced hypotheses to the contrary, as the foreign copper companies expanded operations in Chile, they did not gain power, or influence, or allies on the domestic scene. Rather, their power became attenuated, their position became more precarious, their alliances proved most fragile."

48. The total production figure for 1973 is from a presentation made before the Inter-American Economic and Social Committee of the Alliance for Progress by Raúl Sáez, principal economic adviser at that time to the Chilean military junta, in January 1974, and quoted in *Programa de Desarrollo de Chile a Corto y Mediano Plazo* (Santiago: Editora Nacional Gabriela Mistral, 1974), p. 20; and the 1986 figure and future projections from *Chilean Cultural Panorama: Agriculture, Flora and Mining*, vol. 2 (Washington: Embassy of Chile, 1987), Mario Correa, ed., p. 25.

49. Discussed in further detail in chap. 3. Under law 10.255, copper was sold through the Central Bank, which paid the companies the U.S. price while selling at the "world" price, the difference remaining in the Chilean treasury. The state sales monopoly thus set up—"with two local functionaries, two secretaries, and a man who worked half days . . . trying to price and sell 13 percent of the world's copper output to customers on four continents"—was, Moran notes, "the first major attempt to end the condition of 'dependencia' " (Moran, op. cit., p. 88). The law was repealed in 1954. During the time it was in effect, production slipped, the country's copper earnings dropped, and the companies put a lid on new investment—understandably, since the artificial exchange rate applied to their production costs pushed their taxes up sharply. In the 1951–54 period, Moran observes (p. 93), the level of effective taxation on Anaconda and Kennecott ranged from 65 percent to 92 percent.

50. In his melodramatic speech before the United Nations General Assembly on December 4, 1972, President Allende told a sympatic Third-World audience that for the period 1955 to 1970, Anaconda's annual profits averaged 21.5 percent of its book value. He failed to tell his audience that 21.5 percent was *before* payment of taxes to the Chilean Treasury. In the same speech, Allende asserted that Kennecott's profits over the same period averaged 52.8 percent, "even reaching such incredible rates as 106 percent in 1967, 113 percent in 1968, and over 205 percent in 1969. Kennecott's average profits in other countries during that period amounted to less than 10 percent per annum."

The fact is that Kennecott's earnings for that fifteen-year period were 32 percent higher than that for the company's U.S. mines . . . but again, *before* taxes. After the high Chilean taxes, which deposited in the Chilean Treasury around 85 cents of every copper dollar, Kennecott's earnings were 45 percent *below* the company's U.S. earnings. Kennecott says its actual earnings during the fifty-five years it operated in Chile averaged $9.3 million per year, and that from 1904 to 1927 the Chilean operations yielded no dividends at all. Source for Allende data: publication of the Embassy of Chile in Washington, containing the text of Allende's United Nations speech of December 4, 1972. Source for Kennecott rebuttal: publication of Kennecott Copper Corporation, *Expropriation of El Teniente* (1971).

It is interesting that in press reports, the inflated Chilean figures were used repeatedly, those of the five-volume Kennecott rebuttal rarely, demonstrating anew the efficacy of the big-lie technique. Other figures used repeatedly were taken from paid advertisements published in major newspapers around the world at the height of the nationalization dispute, which included at least half a dozen deliberately mixed comparisons to produce a wholly distorted image. See, for example, "The Recovery of Basic Resources Is a Sovereign Decision Reflecting the Feelings of All Chilean People," *New York Times*, January 25, 1971, p. 72-C.

51. Acquisition of these lands and the rich nitrate fields ushered in an era of opulence in Chile. Federal treasury receipts quadrupled (from 16 to 60 million pesos) in the ten years following the war. Exports soared from 27 million pesos in 1870 to 68 million in 1890. But it must be noted that the big expansion in nitrate production happened after Chile took over; output in 1880 was worth 25 million pesos; by 1890 the Chileans, with heavy British investment, had pushed it to nearly 80 million. Galdames, op. cit., pp. 448–49.

52. On the eve of the War of the Pacific, 54 percent of the nitrate industry was in the hands of Peruvians, 18 percent belonged to Chileans, and 15 percent to English interests. Interpretations vary, but all agree that nitrate detonated the war. What is also clear is that by 1887, British interests, led by crafty John Thomas North and Robert Harvey, had captured 70 percent of the industry. They were eventually to yield to American interests under Harry Guggenheim. Labrousse, whose book is an unabashedly Marxist interpretation of Chilean history and Marxist apologia for the Allende regime, attempts to show how British interests preyed on the differences between Peru, Bolivia, and Chile to maneuver the industry into their own hands and then milk it for exorbitant profits. He maintains the same exercise was repeated later, sans warfare, by the U.S. copper companies. For an unabashedly partisan Chilean version of the causes of the conflict, see Galdames, ibid., pp. 399–404. In this scenario, war came only after repeated Peruvian-Bolivian abuse of Chilean nationals and companies working the nitrate fields, and despite official Chilean restraint over a period extending from 1866 to the outbreak of hostilities in 1879.

53. Labrousse, op. cit., p. 45.

54. The bottom fell out altogether during the Great Depression. In 1929 Chile's copper production was 482,700 tons and nitrate output 972,000. The following year they plummeted to 277,000 and 479,300 tons, respectively. It was the end of an era of economic opulence for Chile, a collapse which impacted in profound ways. From ibid., p. 148.

55. In 1894, in the early heyday of the industry, natural fertilizers obtained from nitrates accounted for 73 percent of the world's production. By 1926 it was already down to 26 percent and has been shrinking ever since. André Siegfried, "Chile: The Economic Crisis," in *Latin American Panorama*, ed.

Paul Kramer and Robert McNicoll (New York: G. P. Putnam's Sons, 1968), p. 240. The 1972 figure is from *Comentarios Sobre la Situación Económica* (Santiago: University of Chile, Facultad de Ciencias Económicas y Administrativas, 1973), pub. 8, p. 112.

56. Despite massive American investment in Chilean industry, the country's character is little affected by American influences, and certainly far less so than other countries with comparable American investments, such as Venezuela. Quite apart from the sturdiness of Chilean character, there is another possible explanation: Chile teems with small industries and shopkeepers. The American stake, while large in a strictly investment sense, was insignificant in that those industries employed a small fraction of the labor force, and only a fistful of Americans, and were all export-oriented.

57. Iron ore production was 3.8 million pure tons in 1961, 6.8 million in 1971, 5.1 million in 1981, and by 1985 was down to 3.9 million. But the value of iron ore exports had risen from 1961's $44.7 million to $69.1 million in 1971 and $161.9 million in 1981, dropping to $90.3 million in 1985. Iron ore production was in American hands (Bethlehem Steel) almost from the time Chile began exporting high-grade ore in the late 1920s. Until 1946, when a national steel company was founded, Chile exported almost its entire production; that steel company was also, until Allende, under U.S. ownership. By 1969, steel production stood at 601,000 metric tons; in 1986, pig iron production (the bulk of the output) was 590,000 metric tons. Nitrate production, which declined steadily from 1.1-million ton levels until 1966, dropped to a low of 529 million tons in 1978, then began a climb which saw it reach 900,000 tons in 1985. The value of nitrate and iodine exports (the two are lumped together in export statistics) remained constant in the $30–35 million range until 1967, slumped sharply for a few years, and began its steep climb in 1977 (from $44.2) that year to an estimated $85 million in 1985. Profits in 1986 were estimated at an unprecedented $30 million. Communist China was a principal importer of Chilean nitrate, all of which was produced by the formerly state-owned Chemical and Mining Society of Chile (SOQUIMICH) which, under the Pinochet government's aggressive privatization program, was already 65 percent in private hands by mid-1987. Sources: *1971* and *1988* editions of the *Encyclopaedia Britannica Book of the Year* (Chicago: Encyclopaedia Britannica), pp. 188 and 223, respectively (for 1969 and 1986 figures); *Indicadores Económicos y Sociales*, op. cit., pp. 81–82 (nitrate production) and pp. 327–328 (value of exports); "Habrá Inversionistas Interesados en el Salitre?," *El Mercurio*, Feb. 15, 1987, p. B-1 (1985 figures, including profits); Shirley Christian, "Chile's Privatization Pleases Investors," Santiago-datelined dispatch in *The New York Times*, July 20, 1987, p. D-6.

58. Gordon Young, "Chile, Republic on a Shoestring," *National Geographic*, October 1973, p. 468 (for 1973 petroleum data); "Mining: Chile's Resources," in *Chilean Review*, Vol. 1, #13, March 1988, p. 5 (a monthly publication of the Chilean Embassy in Washington); *Chilean Cultural Panorama: Agriculture, Flora and Mining*, op. cit., p. 26 (for first well). Chile's crude oil output hit the two million cubic meter level in 1963, and hit an all-time peak of 2.4 million in 1982; for 1985, it had dipped to 2.074 million again. In common with other struggling oil-importing nations, Chile was hard hit by the oil price shocks of the mid-1970s and again in the early 1980s: the country's oil import bill went from $79 million in 1973 to $418

million in 1977, peaking at $983 million in 1981. For 1986, it was estimated at $322 million. Sources for 1963–1985 figures, *Indicadores Económicos y Sociales*, op. cit., pp. 135–136; for import bill, *Economic and Social Progress in Latin America* (1987), op. cit., Table 72, p. 482.

59. 1972 figures from *Economic and Social Progress* (1973) (Washington: Inter-American Development Bank, 1974), pp. 162–163; Jonathan Kandell, "Confronting the Copper Strikers," *The New York Times*, June 24, 1973. Kandell gave wage discrepancies as anywhere from three to six times higher in copper than other industries. *Indicadores Económicos y Sociales*, op. cit., p. 194, shows average real wages for Chilean mining workers, expressed in 1978 Chilean pesos adjusted for inflation, as follows: 1960, 3,340; 1970, 7,820 (rising sharply the next year to 9,670); and for 1982, last year for which I have found reliable figures, 10,568. For those same years, laborer (*obrero*) wage levels in manufacturing were 2,386; 4,385 (and 4,975); and 6,097. The true wage "elites," in all of those years were found, however, in public utility services.

60. The transformation of Chile from an import-substitution economy to an export economy, now fully diversified and no longer dependent on a single commodity, is at the heart of the Chilean economic miracle, which has made the country more akin to the miracle economies of the Pacific Rim than to the floundering economies of virtually all of Latin America. Exports shot up from $1.2 billion in 1973 to more than $5 billion in 1987, an increase in percentage of GDP from 12 percent to 28 percent. The number of products exported has risen from 412 to 1,343, the number of countries receiving Chilean goods from 60 to 117. Fruit exports have shot up from $14 million in 1973 to $550 million in 1987; forest products from $36 million to $550 million; fisheries from $22 million to $640 million. Chile now sells abroad even military hardware (an industry whose growth was in large measure fostered by the U.S. embargo on arms sales to the anti-communist Pinochet regime) to computer software (reflecting Chile's emergence as the most thoroughly-computerized and computer-literate society in Latin America.) Source: José Piñera, "A New Chile," in *Economía y Sociedad*, April 1988. Piñera served as both Mining and Labor minister in Pinochet's Cabinet.

61. Gil cites a League of Nations study of thirty-nine nations, representing 90 percent of world commerce, as showing that Chile was the Latin American country most seriously hurt by the 1929 world depression. Federico G. Gil, *El Sistema Político de Chile* (Santiago: Editorial Andrés Bello, 1969), p. 78.

62. Siegfried, op. cit., pp. 237–42.

63. Ibid., p. 238.

64. Moran, research associate at Harvard's Center for International Affairs, wrote illuminatingly on the subject in 1971 after a year as visiting professor at the University of Chile. "Even if economic nationalism can manage to surmount the problem of maintaining efficiency at the production stage, they (the so-called 'nationalists') may still find that they have not gained their independence; rather, they are more dependent than ever." This, he said, would happen as a result of the defensive moves of multinational firms responding to the new pressures, above all in "vertical" industries (production through marketing) such as copper. Moran, "New Deal or Raw Deal in Raw Materials," *Foreign Policy* 5 (Winter 1971–72).

In an article generally sympathetic to Allende's nationalization of the copper mines, Normal Galt ratifies the Moran prophecy. After cataloguing the misadventures and blunders of Marxist management of the mines, Galt concludes: "These difficulties, unfortunately, have undermined the potential advantages of socialism which in a country like Chile is not state ownership as an end in itself, but the rationalization of production and distribution of limited resources." Far from achieving such "rationalization," he adds, the result of headlong nationalization of farms, factories, and big copper, accompanied by political intrigues and rivalries, was that "Chile today is experiencing its worst economic crisis since the Great Depression"—Normal Galt, "Chile: The Struggle in the Copper Mines," *Dissent* (Winter 1973).

65. John Gunther puts the amount at $208 million, and adds: "The Ibáñez loans were among the most famous 'sucker loans' that drained money out of small investors in the United States in the Twenties; most have long since been defaulted" (Gunther, op. cit., p. 266).

66. Siegfried, op. cit., p. 240. There is no doubt that the copper companies profited handsomely in Chile over the years, but it should also be remembered that the investment climate of the 1920s was not the same as that of today, nor were the rules of business the same, internationally or within national borders. It is also wise to examine closely claims about exorbitant profits, since this is an area in which the unscrupulous and the innocent tend to frolic heedless of restraints.

67. Ibid., pp. 237–42.

2

Birth of a Nation

THE BAD SEED

Throughout the colonial period, Chile was a colony of a colony: a satellite of the viceroyalty headquartered in Lima. In Chile, as in Venezuela at the other end of the continent, being twice removed from the metropolis and its influences engendered a sturdy sense of independence wedded to a hearty disdain for the remote sovereign. One of the suffocating conditions of Chile's lowly colonial status was that it was allowed to trade only with Peru.[1] But such confinement also breeds stealth, with the result that Chileans learned early how to go it alone in the international arena. By 1715 there were forty French ships trading illegally along the coast.[2] Smugglers attracted pirates, which through the years included Sir Francis Drake, Bart Sharp, Thomas Cavendish, and Henry Brouwer.

Slavery was phased out during the eighteenth century under constant pressure from clerics,[3] but its death rattle raised another evil, which continued to vex Chile down to modern times: the *inquilino* system of agriculture. Basically, it was designed to provide a cheap and reliable manpower substitute for slavery, since estate owners still needed field hands and helpers.

The *inquilino* was a contract farm laborer, a tenant farmer, who worked the land of the *patrón* in exchange for a small plot of his own (usually from one-fourth to one-half of an acre), the right to graze his livestock on the owner's land, and housing for himself and family. As late as 1953 the law required that he be paid only 25 percent of his wages in money, the rest either in kind (farm produce) or in the use of a small parcel of land. In 1963 that percentage was hiked to 35 percent, and as of 1965, *inquilinos* had to be paid a minimum of 75 percent in cash. The Inter-American Committee for Agricultural Development (ICAD) re-

36

ported in a landmark 1966 study of Chilean agriculture that *"inquilinos* constitute a miserable lot, with a high percentage of illiteracy, housed in rudimentary conditions, underfed and tied to the land for generations."[4]

Even more miserable was the lot of those below the *inquilino* on the labor scale—the migrant laborers (*afuerinos*, "outsiders," and *voluntarios*, "volunteers"). The *voluntario* usually lives with the *inquilino*, but since he has no contract, he is paid only for days worked. The *afuerino* is a true migrant laborer.

The *afuerinos* were indeed *les misérables* of rural life, particularly those unlucky enough—as the overwhelming majority were—to work on the tiny scraps of land known as the *minifundios*, economically unworkable minifarms, the counterpoint of the sprawling estates known as *latifundios*. Contrary to the usual image of the big plantation owners as the vilest of the villains, the worst abuses tended to happen on the smaller farms. Salvador Allende's own agriculture minister, Jacques Chonchol, the Robespierre of Chile's agrarian revolution, pinpointed this in 1972: "Exploitation of the peasantry . . . frequently is greater in the medium- and small-scale farms than in the large estates," he wrote. "Although the medium- and small-scale farms function in the same way as the large estates, the economic conditions are more difficult and the enterprise is therefore frequently financed by exploiting the peasantry to a greater extent. . . ."[5]

Above the *inquilino* on the social scale came the *medieros*, fifty-fifty sharecroppers. Next came the owners of small farms—a huge majority—and so on up to the relative handful owning the giant estates.

In few other ways, if any other, has the dead hand of the colonial past lain more heavily on Latin America's present than in relation to the land. In Chile the problem was more acute than in most countries.[6] The 1966 ICAD study of land tenure and development in Latin America (see table 5) showed that Chile—at least then—was better off than most countries regarding its "middle class" in farming, but worse off than all but one country (Peru) in the percentage of land controlled by the big operators.

Latifundios, the sprawling estates, are good in that they create an aristocracy which can play a benign, civilizing role in the formation of new countries. Such was the case in Chile, at least for the most part.[8] Provided they are worked wisely and conscientiously—more often the case in Chile than almost anywhere else in Latin America—big farms can also be the most efficient farms.[9] *Latifundios* are bad in that they limit to a few the fruits of the land. Table 6, also from the ICAD study, shows how badly skewed farm income was in Chile as late as 1960.

TABLE 5[7]

RELATIVE NUMBER AND AREAS OF FARM UNITS BY SIZE GROUPS IN ICAD STUDY COUNTRIES (Percentage of country total in each size class)

COUNTRIES	SUB-FAMILY[a]	FAMILY[b]	MULTI-FAMILY MEDIUM[c]	MULTI-FAMILY LARGE[d]	TOTAL
Argentina					
Number of farm units	43.2	48.7	7.3	0.8	100.0
Area in farms	3.4	44.7	15.0	36.9	100.0
Brazil					
Number of farm units	22.5	39.1	33.7	4.7	100.0
Area in farms	0.5	6.0	34.0	59.5	100.0
Chile					
Number of farm units	36.9	40.0	16.2	6.9	100.0
Area in farms	0.2	7.1	11.4	81.3	100.0
Colombia					
Number of farm units	64.0	30.2	4.5	1.3	100.0
Area in farms	4.9	22.3	23.3	49.5	100.0
Ecuador					
Number of farm units	89.0	8.9	1.7	0.4	100.0
Area in farms	16.6	19.0	19.3	45.1	100.0
Guatemala					
Number of farm units	88.4	9.5	2.0	0.1	100.0
Area in farms	14.3	13.4	31.5	40.8	100.0
Peru					
Number of farm units	88.0	8.5	2.4	1.1	100.0
Area in farms	7.4	4.5	5.7	82.4	100.0

[a] Subfamily: Farms large enough to provide employment for fewer than two persons with the typical incomes, markets, and levels of technology and capital prevailing in each region.

[b] Family: Farms large enough to provide employment for 2.0 to 3.9 persons on the assumption that most of the farmwork is being carried out by members of the farm family.

[c] Multifamily medium: Farms large enough to provide employment for four to twelve persons.

[d] Multifamily large: Farms large enough to provide employment for over twelve persons.

TABLE 6[10]
DISTRIBUTION OF AGRICULTURAL INCOME IN CHILE, 1960

| | FARM FAMILIES | | INCOME | | |
	THOU-SANDS	PER-CENTAGE	MILLIONS OF ESCUDOS	PER-CENTAGE	AVERAGE FAMILY INCOME (E°)
Workers and small-scale owners	243.9[a]	70.7	155.2[b]	33.4	636
Family-scale producers[c]	61.1	17.7	59.0	12.7	966
Supervisory personnel	7.3	2.1	8.6	1.8	1,178
Medium-scale producers	22.3	6.5	71.4	15.4	3,202
Large-scale producers	10.3	3.0	170.8	36.7	16,582
	344.9	100.0	465.0	100.0	1,348

[a] Includes families of producers with subfamily-scale units and sharecroppers.
[b] Includes salaries, payment in kind, social-security contribution, and incomes on sub-family units from shares and from the land ceded as part payment for labor to *inquilinos*.
[c] Includes for the most part producers with from five to twenty hectares in irrigated zones, and greater area in the middle and extreme south. Barraclough and Domike add that some such units had incomes close to those of sub-family producers.
Source: Solon L. Barraclough and Arthur L. Domike, "Agrarian Structure in Seven Latin American Countries" in *Agrarian Problems and Peasant Movements in Latin America,* Rodolfo Stavenhagen, ed. (New York: Anchor Books, 1970), p. 65. They cite the third agricultural census, the national accounts of CORFO, and case-study data in the ICAD study for their estimates.

Minifundios are bad because they are universally inefficient. When the land is atomized under a system of serfdom such as in the *inquilino-mediero* pattern, efficiency is no longer the issue. The raw, flagrant injustice of it is.[11] Unfortunately, flagrant injustice in Latin America has invited as often demagoguery and disastrous tinkering as enlightened leadership and real solutions. Such has been the sorry record of Chile, a record ignominiously highlighted by the nearly volcanic eruption of class warfare in the countryside during the Allende regime.

Agrarian reform got started in Chile in 1962, was rapidly accelerated during the Frei years (1964–70), and became a whirling dervish during the Allende years (1970–73). Yet for all of that, the main visible effect was sharply to reduce the number of big farms, including some of the most productive, while greatly increasing the number of hopelessly inefficient small plots. The 1974 *Nueva Enciclopedia de Chile* shows that of Chile's 151,082 farm units (including forestry operations), 75,627 (or 50 percent) were 10 hectares or less (compared with 36.9 percent classified as subfamily in the 1966 study; see table 5); 53,766 (36 percent) were 10 to 99 hectares (compared with 40 percent classified as family-size in the 1966 study); 18,316 (or 12 percent) were 100 to 999 hectares (compared with 16.2 percent multifamily medium in the earlier study); and 3,373 (or 2 percent) were 1,000 hectares or more (compared with 6.9 percent) classified as multifamily large.[12] Furthermore, as to work force, a "rough breakdown" in 1972 estimated that about 1 percent of the farm work force were *latifundistas* (about 6,000 owners); 4 percent were on medium-size farms (20–80 hectares); 9 percent worked small family plots (5–20 hectares), consuming most of their own produce and seldom employing outsiders; 35 percent were *minifundistas* (with less than 5 basic hectares); 7 percent belonged to the new "reformed" area (that is, expropriated farms) and they worked 30 percent of the country's farmland; 18 percent were *inquilinos*; and 22 percent migrant laborers (or semirooted *voluntarios*). The percentage of supervisors/administrators remained unchanged at 2 percent.[13]

Thus the proportion of people at the bottom of the scale actually increased (from 70 percent in 1960—see table 6—to 75 percent in the early 1970s). In part, this was a function of the constant growth in absolute numbers of the agricultural work force: from roughly 560,000 in 1930 to somewhere around 750,000 in the early seventies. The real problem was the same at the end as at the beginning: farms in Chile were carrying a work force much larger than they could support. In the 1966 study it was estimated that 30 percent of the agricultural work force was redundant; in 1972 it was estimated that the number of surplus farmworkers had actually increased.[14] Even Chonchol, the man more than any other responsible for Chile's headlong rush into rapid agrarian reform, acknowledged in 1972 that the small peasant population (7 percent) on the big chunk of lands expropriated into the "reform" sector (30 percent) had "become very egoistic. They do not wish to incorporate into the *asentamiento* [state-run farm settlement] more people than those originally working on the farm, because they argue that when the time comes for the distribution of land they will each get less. So, when extra labor is taken on, it is only as wage earners [that is, migrants], and not as full *asentados* [peasants destined to share ownership of the settlement]."[15]

Agrarian reform, it seems, not only failed to solve the ancient people problem; it created new aggravants to it.

To make matters worse, productivity went into a tailspin. Per capita production of food in 1960 was indexed at 101; by 1973, it was down to 83. Furthermore, as shown by table 1 (chapter 1), the country's food import bill went from $83 million in 1961 to $594.9 million during Allende's last year.

The limitation of rural opportunities hastened the growth of the cities.[16] This in turn hastened the decline of rural political power. By the mid-1930s urban areas had begun to bleed the farm sector, mostly through price ceilings, which favored consumers while ruining farmers. Inevitably, farm production suffered. Agriculture was now a wounded bull, easy prey for later *picadores* of politics: first, the Christian Democrats, who saw the countryside as a problem in distributive justice, but who were never really in command of their own fashionable but fuzzy ideas on agrarian reform. Next came Allende's Unidad Popular, which viewed the peasantry as a vehicle for political power.

THREE CRISES

As noted earlier, one of the more persistent homilies of the Allende era held that traditional institutions lorded it over men and their political passions. It was a homily preached by friend and foe alike of the Marxist regime. Foes used it in the beginning to reassure themselves that things weren't so bad after all, much as children cope with the formless terrors of the night by shouting or singing or stomping their feet. This was especially true of the Hamlets of Chilean politics, the Christian Democrats. Later on, they brandished institutions much as schoolmasters of an earlier time would a hickory stick—to intimidate the unruly. And so they lectured and scolded and even threatened to bring the full force of the law down upon Allende's head. But Allende by then had become a truant, skipping out on the law, out of reach of the institutional hickory stick.

Friends of the Marxist regime in the early days invoked institutions as a siren song to lure the waverers and allay the fears of the more suspicious, pointing out that no real harm could come from an adventure in Marxism because the country rested on a bedrock of democratic institutions. Disgruntled revolutionaries inside Chile and elsewhere protested that Allende's *Vía Chilena* was little more than a Southern Hemisphere version of British socialism. In the exhilaration of witnessing the birth of the hemisphere's first freely elected Marxist government, many observers—conspicuously foreigners and foreign newsmen—overlooked the obvious: the dominant partners of the Allende alliance made it explicitly and repeatedly plain that they at no time thought of democractic institutions as more than springboards to power, to be discarded once they had served their purposes.[17] As Allende's end neared, friends of the regime invoked institutions as amulets to ward off the evil spirits of revolution. Not respected, mind you, just invoked, as if intoning enough verses from the Good Book of Democracy would cancel Judgment Day.

Alas, friend and foe alike credited democratic institutions with a force and finality in Chilean life which they simply did not have.[18] A more serious appraisal of the country's past would show a pragmatic pattern of behavior that said: respect institutions while they work; get rid of them when they don't. This does not put Chile into the category of those precarious states that have rarely, if ever, been able to develop workable institutions of any kind, and that go through life careening from one caudillo to another. It does, however, clearly separate Chile from the company of such representative governments and parliamentary systems as the United States and Great Britain, where faith in democratic institutions and their ability to cope with any problem, no matter how conflictive, has been demonstrated time and again.[19]

A brief look at three crises in the country's past suffices to make the point—but at the peril of omitting huge and significant chunks of the country's history. One such hunk deliberately left out is the War of the Pacific (1879–83), in which German-trained Chilean forces prevailed over the disarray of combined Peruvian and Bolivian forces. For our purposes, it is enough to note that such a triumph should have guaranteed the country's armed forces a permanent place of honor, respect, and devotion in the country's affections. It didn't, as Christian Democrats were to demonstrate three-quarters of a century later— much to their eventual chagrin.

THE FALLEN IDOL

Independence came to Chile—as it did to most other American nations—for reasons that at the beginning were quite beyond the colony's control. In 1808 Napoleon Bonaparte invaded Spain and installed his brother Joseph on the Spanish throne. In common with other Spanish colonies in the New World, Chile made ready a provisional junta, ostensibly to protect the authority of the deposed king, Ferdinand VII. But when the junta met on September 8, 1810, it instead decreed the country's independence, responding to revolutionary ferment dating back to 1780. It would take eight more years of intermittent war, internecine rivalries, and counterrevolution before independence could be truly consolidated.[20]

More than any other, the man who did it was Bernardo O'Higgins. O'Higgins was born in Chillán, in the heart of the lush Central Valley, on August 20, 1778, the illegitimate son of the Irishman Ambrosio O'Higgins (see note 25, chapter 1) and a Chilean mother, Isabel Riquelme. At the age of ten he was sent to school in Lima, and from there to London for further studies. He returned to Chile at the age of twenty-three to take charge of the hacienda left him by his father, and shortly became caught up in the politics of independence.

In 1811 he was elected to the first Congress. He distinguished himself in a number of battles in 1813, receiving the first of several wounds in bold combat, and eventually displaced his former commander and political mentor, José Miguel Carrera, as commander in chief. But on October 1 and 2, 1814, forces under him were routed at the city of Rancagua, enabling the Spaniards to regain control of the country. O'Higgins made his way with the remnants of his army across the Andes to Mendoza, Argentina, where he joined the forces of Gen. José de San Martín, the great Argentine patriot.

After more than two years of training and organizing, San Martín led his Army of the Andes back across the mountains and on February 12, 1817, defeated the Spaniards in the decisive battle of the war for Chilean independence at Chacabuco. O'Higgins led the daring cavalry attack on the forces of the Spaniard Gen. Rafael Maroto that opened the battle— and sealed the outcome. More battles were fought the following year in the south to finish off the remaining Spanish forces, but they were anticlimactic.

Grateful Chileans offered San Martín the leadership of their liberated country. But he declined, and instead O'Higgins was named supreme director. O'Higgins ordered that two books be opened in each city and town, one for the signatures of those in favor of independence, one for those favoring continued ties with the defeated mother country. The pages of the second remained blank. With that, O'Higgins, on February 12, 1818—one year to the day after the decisive battle—declared Chile's formal independence.

O'Higgins' rule degenerated into heavy-handed dictatorship. He refused, for instance, to create a legislative Senate and to draft a constitution which the public demanded. Finally, in 1822, he promulgated a constitution without submitting it to popular referendum of any kind. Parallel with his refusal to submit to outside control were his attempts at breaking up some of the big estates and distributing the land to those willing to work it. These and proposed fiscal reforms put him on a collision course with the country's landed gentry. The mayor of Concepción led an armed uprising, and on January 23, 1823, Santiago's ruling elite called a council meeting and asked O'Higgins to resign.

At first he refused to acknowledge the authority of the meeting, touching off a shouting match. "I am not frightened by seditious shouts nor by threats," O'Higgins cried over the tumult. "I hold death in contempt today, just as I did on the battlefield."

Anxious to avoid civil war, he proposed that a provisional junta be named, and once done, wrote out in their presence his resignation. Then, turning to the multitude, he said: "Now I am a simple private citizen. I am willing to answer any and all accusations you make. And if these failings of mine have caused damage which can only be purged with my blood, then take the vengeance you wish."

Then, with a dramatic gesture, he tore open his tunic, and said: "Here is my breast."

"No, no. We have nothing against O'Higgins. Viva the Father of our Country," the crowd shouted. O'Higgins left the forum amid applause, and sailed a few days later for Peru. There, for the next twenty years, he lived as a gentleman farmer, awaiting the summons from Santiago that never came. He died in Lima, October 24, 1842.

A TIME TO REMEMBER

O'Higgins' ouster was followed by eight years of dictatorship and anarchy. In 1831 Joaquín Prieto began a ten-year term, ushering in sixty years of (mostly) political tranquility. A new constitution went into effect, and would remain so for over ninety years, until 1925.

The power behind this first stable throne was a man whose image was destined to reappear on Chile's stage 140 years later: Diego Portales. A merchant who wielded one of the most satiric pens of his day, Portales served as a minister under two presidents and was the iron fist crushing incipient revolutions in the early, faltering years of the Prieto government. Elected vice president with Prieto, he resigned, preferring his shadowy role of gray eminence. He is credited with the organization of that first government. He was also the man who engineered the defeat of the liberal forces contesting control of government, and molding the ideological shape of the republic, a shape which had as its essence a strong, central government. The formation of such a government spared Chile the endless cycle of caudillo pocket revolutions which ravaged other Latin countries. In 1973 the figure of Portales emerged powerfully from history's shadows, as the ideological inspiration for the military that sacked Allende.

From 1831 to 1871, Chile was virtually a monarchy,[21] in which two elitist strains—old monarchists and new aristocrats—contended for power.[22] For the first thirty years, three conservative presidents firmly wedded to the autocratic ideas of Diego Portales governed with near absolute power. A transition presidency was followed by twenty years marking the rise of partisan politics and a corresponding decline in stability. Those early years witnessed two bloody but abortive uprisings,[23] and the later years the increasing cacophony of politicking dominated by so-called theological questions: a liberal-led movement to break the power of the church in civil affairs. In the main, it was a period of prosperity and progress, during which Chile was an example and a force admired and envied throughout the Americas. The Indians were subdued, South America's first telegraph inaugurated and first railroad built,[24] Chile's longest-lived political party founded (the Radical party, in 1861), pioneering civil and commercial codes drafted, and bold social innovations introduced.[25] As noted earlier, Chile also fought and won a profitable war that added one-third to its size and immeasurably to its wealth.

But it was also a period that saw the appearance of the first of a trinity of fiscal nightmares that would haunt the republic relentlessly to this day: chronic inflation.[26] And it came at a time of unprecedented prosperity, when prudent policies would have spared the country that plague. It was also a time when the first major foreign investments appeared in the country.

The end of that era came with a man with a thick handlebar mustache, a towering ego, a silvery tongue—and a reformist's zeal. The leader of a liberal, anticlerical group (though in his youth he had considered the priesthood), José Manuel Balmaceda first won fame in 1878 when he persuaded Argentina to stay out of the War of the Pacific.

Elected in 1886 over the bitter opposition of a coalition of conservatives and a splinter group of traditionalist liberals, Balmaceda presided over an interlude of splendor with few equals in Chilean history.

Bankrolled by a swollen public treasury (receipts rose from 37 million pesos in 1886 to nearly 60 million in 1890, thanks to nitrate coming on stream), Balmaceda gave an important push to public education. He built three hundred schools (among them the first public high school for girls) and two teachers' colleges, and hired German educators to staff the system. He also created a Public Works Ministry to execute an unprecedented building program: more than one thousand kilometers of railroad, government buildings, waterworks, hospitals, docks, and bridges, including a three hundred-foot-high railroad bridge that served Eiffel as an important reference for building his famous tower.[27]

Repeated efforts to placate his political foes were rebuffed, however, and in 1890 he lost control of Congress to what resembled a concatenation of squabbling factions more than a coherent opposition. The fact is that he did not have the votes to effect his programs, which included banking and tax reforms, an overhaul of the bureaucracy, and electoral reforms. He also proposed to "Chileanize" the nitrate industry and use the profits to build a state-owned industrial infrastructure.

Both ideas were revolutionary at the time, and Balmaceda is often portrayed as a prophet of socialism and the precursor of Uruguay's José Battle y Ordóñez, pioneer of social reform in Latin America. But this is largely a superficial view of a nationalist whose real reformist ideas were harnessed to implacable political ambition.[28] His political tactics included packing the courts, bypassing the Congress, and unleashing in the government-controlled press a campaign of vituperation and vilification against his enemies without parallel until then.[29]

When Congress refused to approve the budget for 1891, Balmaceda began ruling by decree, a de facto dictatorship. He was opposed by a powerful front composed of bankers, landowners, and—foreign nitrate interests.[30] The gunpowder of revolution was provided by the navy—despite Balmaceda's largess in outfitting it with two new cruisers and two destroyers (torpedo boats).

In January 1891 a squadron commanded by Jorge Montt sailed from Valparaíso for the northern port of Iquique. Aboard were Waldo Silva, vice president of the Senate, and Ramón Barros Luco, president of the Chamber of Deputies.[31] Charging Balmaceda with mocking the constitution, the Congress declared him outside the law and deposed him, naming a junta headed by Montt, Silva, and Barros Luco. Iquique was made the provisional seat of government.

The army remained loyal to Balmaceda, as did fragments of the fleet (and the two new torpedo boats, one of which would later sink the battleship *Blanco Encalada*, pride and flagship of the fleet). The rebels controlled the four northern provinces, including the two nitrate-rich provinces of Antofagasta and Tarapacá. With money and the support of friendly populations in that region, the revolutionaries were able to raise a ten thousand-man army that finally defeated government forces four times that number.

Besides battles between regular naval and ground forces during the seven months the revolution lasted, there also were increasingly bloody sabotage, repression, and countermeasures in and around Santiago, culminating in the ruthless sacking of both Valparaíso and Santiago and the murderous persecution of Balmaceda loyalists.[32] It was a civil war that cost ten thousand lives, an appalling cost to a country with only 2.5 million inhabitants.[33]

The end came in bloody battles at Concón and Placilla, August 21 and 28, 1891—just a few weeks before Balmaceda's presidential term was to have ended. Balmaceda took refuge in the Argentine embassy, and there waited out the end of his term. On the day it ended, September 19, 1891, he ended his life with a bullet in his right temple. (When the end would come for Allende, he would still be only midway through his six-year term. And the bullets did not pierce his head. They blew off the top of it.)

With Balmaceda dead, Montt took over the presidency, but under new rules. Growing fretfulness with the strong presidential system had boiled over because of Balmaceda, and in the new scheme of things, Congress was made supreme. In the years ahead, the number of contenders for power multiplied, and beneath the apparently placid surface of organized democratic life, political power became an end in itself and the chances for consensus on national goals more and more remote.[34] Francisco Orrego Vicuña, a respected professor of international law in

Chile, wrote in 1972 that the switch to a parliamentary system led to "a deterioration of institutions and civic values that has been carried on to this day in the form of a destructive political struggle and of a standing crisis of public authority."[35]

As with the fall of O'Higgins seventy years before, an entire system collapsed with the man and a dramatically new one was erected in its place. It was a pattern destined to repeat itself again—and again.

LEFT FACE

One of the most persistent fictions in newspaper and magazine accounts of events in Chile is that until Allende, the Right ruled the country. The fact of the matter is that the Right in Chile went to its political grave in 1924. Ghosts of a conservative past would waft into view from time to time in the form of "rightist" regimes, notably those of the Alessandris, father Arturo Alessandri Palma (rightist in his second administration, 1932–38), and son Jorge Alessandri Rodríguez (1958–64). Table 7 traces the steady march into oblivion of the parties of the Right—the Conservative and Liberal, which in 1969 teamed to form the National party.

TABLE 7
VOTING IN CHAMBER OF DEPUTIES ELECTIONS, 1925–1969

YEARS	TOTAL VOTES CAST	CONSERVATIVE PARTY		LIBERAL PARTY	
		ACTUAL VOTES	PERCENTAGE OF TOTAL	ACTUAL VOTES	PERCENTAGE OF TOTAL
1925	261,779	51,902	19.83%	84,895	32.43%
1932	327,162	55,260	16.89	51,530	15.75
1937	412,230	87,845	21.31	85,515	20.74
1941	450,248	77,243	17.07	63,118	13.95
1945	449,930	106,264	23.62	80,597	17.91
1949	464,872	106,603	22.72	83,582	17.98
1953	779,174	78,383	10.06	84,924	10.90
1957	878,229	121,223	13.80	134,741	15.34
1961	1,339,896	198,260	14.80	222,485	16.60
1965	2,282,443	121,882	5.30	171,979	7.50

		NATIONAL PARTY			
1969	2,307,512	480,523	20.82		

Source: Estadísticas Electorales, 1925–1969 (Oficina de Informaciones, Chilean Senate, Boletín de Información General, no. 66, June 25, 1970).

In the same period, the parties of the far Left achieved and held the commanding electoral heights for most of the years after the mid-1930s, the exception being the eight-year (1949–57) hiatus when the Communist party was outlawed. I include in the far-Left category the Radical party, for it consistently lent itself to the purposes of the more militant Socialist and Communist parties. Table 9 traces the fortunes of far-Left parties in those same elections:

TABLE 8

VOTES FOR PARTIES OF THE LEFT, 1925–1969

	RADICAL PARTY		SOCIALIST PARTY		COMMUNIST PARTY	
		PER-		PER-		PER-
	ACTUAL	CENTAGE	ACTUAL	CENTAGE	ACTUAL	CENTAGE
YEAR	VOTE	OF TOTAL	VOTE	OF TOTAL	VOTE	OF TOTAL
1925	56,001	21.39	—	—	—	—
1932	59,413	18.16	18,642	5.70	—	—
1937	76,941	18.66	46,050	11.17	17,162	4.16
1941	98,296	21.72	75,500	16.69	53,144	11.80
1945	89,922	19.99	57,418	12.76	46,133	10.25
1949	100,869	21.70	43,432	9.34	—	—
1953	103,650	13.30	109,897	14.10	—	—
1957	188,526	21.47	93,787	10.68	—	—
1961	296,828	22.15	149,122	11.13	157,572	11.76
1965	312,912	13.71	241,593	10.58	290,635	12.73
1969	313,559	13.59	294,448	12.76	383,049	16.60

Source: Estadísticas Electorales, 1925–1969 (Oficina de Informaciones, Chilean Senate, Boletín de Información General, no. 66, June 25, 1970).

The Christian Democrats made their appearance on the electoral stage in 1941, and in 1964 emerged as the largest single party. At the beginning, they were left-center, but by 1969 their programs were barely distinguishable from those of Allende's coalition, and the leftist faction of the party eventually would prove to be left even of Allende himself.

TABLE 9

CHRISTIAN DEMOCRAT VOTE IN CHAMBER ELECTIONS, 1941–1969

	1941	1945	1949	1953	1957	1961	1965	1969
Votes	15,553	11,565	18,221	22,353	82,710	213,468	995,187	716,574
% of Total	3.44	2.57	3.92	2.87	9.42	15.93	43.60	31.05

Source: Estadísticas Electorales, 1925–1969 (Oficina de Informaciones, Chilean Senate, Boletín de Información General, no. 66, June 25, 1970).

The trouble grew out of the turbulent twenties, when the rules of Chile's political game were decisively changed: new power relationships were established, and an entirely different set of political values were enthroned.[36] The most important change was the irrevocable shift of economic power away from the old oligarchies—once the landowners, later the entrepreneurs—to the state. Cox refers to what he describes as the "excessive growth" during this period of a "welfare state, bureaucratism, and demagogy." They created, he says, "a rigid and static national structure and a strong parasitic habit regarding the state."[37]

Those rightist relapses were "rightist" within the confining limits of a new sociopolitical context. Furthermore, if Jorge Alessandri's administration was intolerably "rightist," the country's Communist party did not think so. For most of the Alessandri years (1958–64), it treated Alessandri with unusual deference and circumspection, and reports persisted of a nonaggression pact between Alessandri and the Communists.[38] Communist party political fortunes prospered as never before during Alessandri's government, provoking warnings that Alessandri was sowing a whirlwind.[39]

Friendly relations between supposedly antithetical forces are not, of course, the same as an alliance between them, and insofar as is known, no such alliance existed between Alessandri and the Communists. But the fact of such friendly relations ought to silence much of the gibberish about the existence of a rigid and reactionary Right in Chile, implacably opposed to reform and the agents of most extreme reform, the Communists.[40]

It was none less than the elder Alessandri who presided over the atomization of the Right. Known as the Lion of Tarapacá—for the northern province he represented in Congress—Alessandri was a man with a powerful voice and a physique to match. John Gunther relates that once Alessandri single-handedly dragged a wounded policeman out of a mob, and another time used a stick on an opposition deputy before heaving him over a fence. He also was a remarkable orator, fond of haranguing crowds from the balcony of La Moneda.

As indicated earlier, Chile went into an economic tailspin during World War I because of the loss of its major nitrate customer, Germany. Labor strife had beset the country for years. Violent clashes between workers and the police—and frequently the army—began in the nitrate camps in the 1880s and were climaxed by a massacre during a 1907 strike that cost two thousand lives.[41] Between 1911 and 1920 there were 293 strikes in an only incipiently industrialized nation of just over 3 million inhabitants. On July 4, 1912, a self-taught typographer named Emilio Recabarren founded a workers' party, which in 1922 became the Communist party.

In the midst of this ferment, Alessandri emerged as the presidential candidate of the Liberal Alliance, a conglomerate of groups dedicated to breaking conservative power. His platform was a frankly populist appeal for the votes of labor, peasants, and the poor.[42]

Once in power, Alessandri attempted to make good his campaign promises. He had a majority in the Chamber of Deputies, but the conservative-controlled Senate rejected one after another of his reform proposals: a labor code, which formed the basis of Chile's advanced social legislation; the right to organize in unions; the eight-hour workday; an income tax. The Senate also impeached one after another of his ministers—many lasted only weeks in their jobs, creating administrative anarchy. It was a problem which had plagued presidents ever since the enthronement of the parliamentary system thirty years before, but now it reached dangerously destructive extremes. (It was also a problem Allende would later face, albeit for different reasons.)

Alessandri's Alianza Liberal (Liberal Alliance), a coalition of (for then) leftist parties, won control of both houses of Congress in the March 1924 elections, amid charges of widespread fraud and rigged elections. To make matters worse, personal and party rivalries were rife within the coalition. When Congress convened in June, it frittered away three months in sterile political debates. In September, bypassing a number of pending, urgent matters (including the budget for that very year), the lawmakers turned their attention to a matter dearer to their own hearts: a two thousand-peso monthly salary for themselves, a handsome sum in the best of times, and the country was then in an economic crisis.

Out of the black hole of national frustration, there suddenly emerged a new force in Chilean political life: a group of young army officers allied to leftist causes (as well as one of their own: Congress had also failed to act on pay raises for inflation-squeezed soldiers). Outraged that Congress should put itself first, a group of these young turks appeared in uniform in the visitor's gallery of Congress on September 5, 1924, to heckle the lawmakers, sending shock waves through Congress and the government. They later formed a military committee to back their claims, and enlisted the support of Gen. Luis Altamirano, inspector general of the army.

Congress caved in, and in rapid succession approved the labor code, the social-security act, and sixteen other long-stalled reform measures (including military pay raises).[43] But by then, the young officers were demanding more: the dissolution of Congress.

To this point Alessandri had welcomed them as allies. But this was more than he had bargained for. He presented his resignation on September 8 and took refuge in the U.S. embassy. Congress refused his resignation, but authorized a six-month "leave of absence," and Alessandri headed over the Andes bound for Europe. A junta of government, headed by General Altamirano, was formed, accepted Alessandri's resignation, and dissolved Congress.[44] Alessandri was accompanied into exile by his principal political lieutenant, Pedro Aguirre Cerda, a sagacious Radical party leader who would be heard from again.

A few months later, on January 23, 1925, the young officers ousted the old-guard generals, accusing them of disregarding the purposes of the September 5 movement and of abetting the presidential aspirations of Ladislao Errázuriz, leader of the conservative Unión Nacional. The young officers organized their own junta and recalled Alessandri. While he was making his way back from Europe, the young officers prepared a fusillade of decree-laws embodying important social and economic reforms, especially strong in the areas of labor and health. Although little noted in conventional annals of the role of military men in Latin affairs, this was probably the first time regular military forces had intervened in Latin America on the side of social revolution.

Alessandri finally made it back on March 20, returning to an apotheosis of public enthusiasm as yet without precedent. He lasted only six months and ten days, but it was long enough for him to draft and submit for public approval a new constitution, promulgated on September 18, 1925.

This constitution partly restored presidential power, provided for direct election of the president, and established the separation of church and state, a goal of liberals in Chile since the middle of the nineteenth century.[45] The new constitution also contained a specific threat to private property, a threat because it was a gratuitous hedge on the right to hold private property, reflecting the onset of socialist thought in Chilean politics.[46] It also contained a provision that, had it been honored, would have changed the course of the country's history: the provision calling for the creation of provincial legislatures and a redistribution of federal power (and revenues) among the provinces. Such decentralization would have acted as a brake on the country's rollercoaster ride into Marxism over political tracks greased by the demagoguery of frenzied competition for popular favor. But the provision was never honored, despite the promises of candidate after candidate, down to Salvador Allende.

The new constitution survived until the fall of Allende. By then, it was tattered, treasured more for what it might have been than for what it was.

The man behind the scenes during this period of tumult—and the man who provoked Alessandri's second resignation—was Col. Carlos Ibáñez, of the later "sucker loans."[47] Ibáñez emerged as a strong man while minister of war under Alessandri, and then as minister of the interior in the regime of Emiliano Figueroa Larraín (1925–27), when he maneuvered to muscle Figueroa out.[48] A nationalist who espoused a mixed bag of unassorted leftist and fascist ideas, Ibáñez embarked on a borrow-and-spend program never before seen in Chile. The spending binge (highways, railroads, port facilities, etc.) created a climate of artificial prosperity and enabled Ibáñez to impose his will on a complacent Congress without protest from a self-indulgent public.[49]

Ibáñez purged the army of officers identifed with the old civilian elites. He also created a paramilitary national police organization, the Corps of Carabineros, as a middle-class counterweight to unrestricted army power (while taking care to pamper his former comrades-in-arms, providing the army and navy with new weaponry and elevating the air force to full parity as a separate service).

On the one hand he outlawed the Communist party, and on the other declared May 1 a holiday and promulgated a new and more liberal labor code.

When the bottom fell out of Chile's mineral exports as a result of the worldwide depression of 1929, Ibáñez instituted a series of emergency measures, including suspending payment on the country's debt. But the dike had already burst, and following a "general strike of intellectuals"—including doctors, lawyers, and engineers, groups that would also figure in the fall of Allende—Ibáñez was deposed on July 26, 1931.[50]

The next government was barely in office when a group of navy noncommissioned officers claiming to represent the Chilean Worker Federation and the Communist party staged a lightning revolt. They arrested their officers, seized the ships, and announced they were forming a government. It was the first noncom revolt in Chilean history; forty-one years later another group of navy noncoms, also with leftist allegiances, would attempt another, one of the crucial events sealing the fate of Salvador Allende.

But the noncoms were suppressed in a single week by the army and the air force. A short time later, on June 4, 1932, one of the most colorful characters in Chilean history, Col. Marmaduke Grove, exploded onto the scene. His slogan was Bread, a Roof, and Shelter, and he preached a 150-point socialist program he called Grovismo, which included a sharp attack on foreign control of Chile's basic industries. He lasted only twelve days himself, but the socialist republic he proclaimed survived 103 days—and a move was afoot to convert Chile into a permanent socialist state.[51]

There is a temptation to see comic opera in this, were it not for the far-reaching implications.[52] Much of the legislation Allende would later resurrect to his advantage was promulgated during that wacky era. None was more controversial than a device called *resquicios*, a legal instrument enabling the president to seize industries or businesses in certain circumstances.

The picturesque career of a man who was an officer in both the army and the navy concurrently, then joined the air force and rose to become chief of staff, and then headed a political revolution called Grovismo, invites attention.[53] But he was blipped off history's screen as suddenly as he had appeared (temporarily, as it would turn out). Four other presidents followed Grove and his associates in that year of 1932, bringing the twelve-month total to six.

The fourth was Alessandri, back this time in earnest, for a full term (1932–38), at the head of a center-right coalition and backed by an overwhelming popular mandate.[54] Two crises competed for top priority, the crisis of authority and the economic crisis. On the latter, unemployment was still at 160,000 (it had peaked at 200,000, perhaps one-fifth of the nonagricultural work force), the treasury was empty, foreign creditors clamored for payment (the foreign debt stood at a staggering 4 billion pesos), and spiraling inflation strangled wage earners. Furthermore, by 1933, an outbreak of a particularly scurvy form of typhus (exanthematic typhus) had reached alarming dimensions.

The crisis of authority was reflected in strikes and lawlessness, legacies of demagoguery and economic collapse. Violence begat more violence, much as it would forty years later. Well-to-do youths organized the Republican Militia, armed vigilantes whose number reached fifty thousand before they decided to disband in 1935. A small but virulent Nazi movement, complete with a Black Shirts brigade, was forming under the leadership of Jorge González von Marées. The new (1933) Socialist party and the increasingly influential Communist party[55] harassed Alessandri implacably.

Hardly an auspicious rebirth for Chile's Right, and the flickering hope was soon forfeited in a maelstrom of crisis, its own political opacity, a new and demolishing challenge from the Left, and freak circumstance.

To tackle the economic problems, Alessandri turned to Gustavo Ross Santa María, a man who would earn a reputation as an economic wizard—and a highhanded autocrat. He restored Chile to economic health, but his brusque tactics made him an easy target for leftist propaganda.[56]

Alessandri's efforts to press forward with his social reforms were blocked by the conservative coalition that controlled Congress, a political blunder it would repeat twenty years later with another Alessandri in the presidency. Alessandri did, however, manage to put through two important pieces of legislation: one, at the end of his term, providing minimum wages for industrial and commercial workers, the other establishing a program of free preventive medicine for workers. The minimum-wage program was, however, a case of too little too late—and not even enough of too little: Congress refused to pass Alessandri's companion proposal establishing minimum wages for farmworkers. The previous year, in 1936, the country had been torn by a new wave of violent strikes, mainly in the nitrate fields and railroads. Alessandri responded with increasing repression, further weakening popular support for his government.

In the midst of this ferment, the Communist party, displaying "the patience of ants and the political flight of eagles,"[57] persuaded its old antagonists of the Left, the Radical party, and its permanent rivals of the even more extreme Left, the fledgling Socialist party, to forge an electoral coalition. It was the world's second Popular Front—following by a few months the French version, preceding by a few the Spanish—and it came just one year after the Comintern in 1935 had decreed Communist party alliances with democratic forces. It was destined to last longer than either of the other fronts, surviving in one form or another until April 16, 1947. The man commissioned by Moscow to implant the Popular Front in Chile credits the front with finishing off the "softening up" of the intellectual and political climate.

"After the collective experience with the Popular Front in the thirties and forties," he wrote, "Communism ceased to appear to the eyes of Chileans so nefarious as they had regarded it up to 1934. Theory and practice implanted in Chile the idea that communism was not the grave risk nor mortal danger portrayed by the cold war. . . . Chileans were clearly massaged to accept, with a minimum of resistance, the communist assault of 1970."[58]

That man was a flamboyant Peruvian named Eudocio Ravines, whose real role was later lost in the mix-master of Communist party infighting and "revisionism."[59] What is known is that Ravines, then secretary-general of the Peruvian Communist party, arrived in Chile in 1935 from Moscow with orders to patch together the electoral alliance. The main object of the party's affection was the Radical party, biggest of the leftist parties, and Ravines skillfully played to the Radicals' impatience for the spoils of power after so many years in destiny's shadows.[60]

The coalition rallied behind the candidacy of Pedro Aguirre Cerda, a moderate Radical. To head the front, the bedmates-of-convenience selected the irrepressible Colonel Grove, head then of the Socialist party. The Communists would later subject Grove to withering abuse, but he served their purposes in the campaign. The Conservatives and Liberals backed the candidacy of the controversial Gustavo Ross.

The new leftist coalition—Radicals, Socialists, Communists, the tiny Democratic party, and the (renamed) Confederation of Workers of Chile—created its own first opportunity. On May 21, 1938, Alessandri went before a traditional joint session of Congress to deliver his last State of the Union message. As Alessandri himself would later tell it,[61] Popular Front congressmen turned a reception in Congress's Salon of Honor for diplomats and lawmakers into a shouting brawl, before storming out of the building. Later, as Alessandri rose to deliver his message, a shot rang out from the adjoining Salon of Honor, followed by the explosion of a petard. Next, two front deputies attempted to push their way through police lines back into the building. In the ensuing melee, which Alessandri ascribes to the "excitement, agitation, and nervousness" of the moment, several lawmakers were clubbed by Carabineros.

The next incident happened on September 5, 1938, just seven weeks before the elections. A group of Nazis occupied the social-security building, across the street from La Moneda, in a slapstick attempt at revolution. A Carabinero was shot in the back and killed just outside the president's office. Several other persons fell wounded from shots fired from inside the University of Chile, a block and-a-half from the palace on Alameda. Rumors circulated of an army uprising, and several radio stations were seized and power pylons felled, causing some power outages. For four hours, the rebels fired on La Moneda from the twelfth floor of the social-security building, also tossing handmade bombs. In those circumstances, Alessandri ordered the Carabineros to oust the rebels without mercy.

Of sixty-two Nazis inside, only one came out alive. Ibáñez, their candidate, switched his support to the front, and Aguirre Cerda edged Ross by four-thousand of the 441,441 votes cast.[62]

The political power of the Left, sputtering to life in the twenties and thirties, was now an irreversible and entrenched reality.[63]

The 1920 and 1938 elections were significant for yet another reason: in both, military commanders played decisive (albeit, secret, behind-the-scene) roles in tipping the balance to the men who would then—but only then—occupy the presidency. As Chilean historian Gonzalo Vial Correa wrote years later, the two instances of military leaders giving the constitution a "nudge" shared these characteristics: (1) they were unconstitutional; (2) they were provoked by a grave civil crisis; (3) the willingness of civilians to go along with these "nudges" averted what might have been more ominous military moves.[64]

Salvador Allende made his political debut during this period, in a 1931 Communist-front student organization called Avance. Some of his more enthusiastic biographers would later portray Allende as a key man in the fight to oust Ibáñez. But, according to implacable foe Marcos Chamudes, who was himself in the thick of the affair, Allende arrived on the scene after the dust had settled, and arrived "pedantically," at that.[65] Allende went on to become president of the student medical center and later vice chairman of the student federation and a delegate to the university council.

His radical student activities caused him to be arrested twice and expelled once from the university. In 1933, a year after his delayed graduation from medical school, Allende joined more prominent public figures in founding the Socialist party. He was elected to the Chamber of Deputies in 1937, and the following year, he managed the successful presidential campaign of Aguirre Cerda. In return, the young doctor, whose medical career was largely limited to a job in the city morgue, was named Aguirre Cerda's health minister.[66] He was then (1938) thirty years old.

Allende was one of three Socialists in the cabinet, and dropped out with the others in 1941 when Aguirre Cerda took a turn to the right. The Communists, on orders from Moscow, never did join in the government they had really created. The Communists used their influence, however, to keep Chile friendly to Hitler's Germany, at least until the Nazi-Russian Nonaggression Pact of 1939 blew up in Germany's lightning attack on Russia in 1941. (This obeisance of the Chilean Communist party was the beginning of a long record of truckling subservience to Moscow with few parallels in the world.) The Socialists attacked the fascists from the beginning, but neither of the leftist parties ever prevailed on that issue: Chile waited until the spring of 1945 to declare war on Japan, and was the only South American country never to declare war on Germany.

Out of this period came a set of legal and constitutional instruments for the care and preservation of democracy believed to have few equals elsewhere in the world. Yet those instruments—for all the euphoria of those inside and outside Chile who hosannaed them, be they of the Right or the Left—obviously were flawed.

If democracy is supposed to be the goal of political development, then those instruments were fatally flawed in that they allowed a minority to inflict its policies on a reluctant majority; in other words, they failed to provide "a political marketplace for the ordering of the periodic intervention of the electorate in the policy affairs of government."[67] The reference is, of course, to Salvador Allende, a man who came to the presidency with only 36.2 percent of the voters behind him, and who was to lose the next two national elections, the second of them an unmistakable plebiscite on his policies. And yet, he could, and did, refuse to modify those policies, with the result that democracy in Chile came crashing down.

In reality, democracy died a slow death in Chile. The death penalty was asked in 1920, and sentence passed in 1925. In 1938 the scaffold was erected. Allende was merely the executioner.

Notes

CHAPTER 2

1. Andrew Marshall, ed., *The South American Handbook* (London: Trade & Travel Publications, 1971), p. 263.
2. Ibid.
3. A law in 1811 freed children of slaves born after that date; complete emancipation came under a second law in 1823, making Chile the first American nation to free slaves. The United States was the second, forty years later. Walterio Millar, *Historia de Chile*, 29th ed. (Santiago: Editorial Zig-Zag, 1973), p. 222.
4. Inter-American Committee on Agricultural Development, quoted by Alain Labrousse, in *El Experimento Chileno* (Barcelona and Mexico: Ediciones Grijalbo, S.A., 1973), p. 103. Labrousse's Marxist biases have already been mentioned. This report reflected fancies fashionable among international technocrats—then, as now, mostly of leftist persuasion—about the right remedies to the very real problems afflicting Latin America's rural areas. For the most part, the palliatives they prescribed exacerbated the ills of the countryside: inefficient production and inhuman living conditions. The point here is that this study tilts left in agrarian matters, and references to it should be understood in that light.
5. Jacques Chonchol, "The Agrarian Policy of Popular Government," in *The Chilean Road to Socialism*, ed. J. Ann Zammit, with cooperation of Gabriel Palma (Austin and England: University of Texas Press and Institute of Development Studies [IDS]; University of Sussex, 1973), pp. 108–9. The book was based on the proceedings of Round Table in Santiago in March 1972, sponsored by the Chilean National Planning Office (ODEPLAN) and IDS. Chonchol cites the incidence of greater abuses among smaller farmers more to justify the government's breakneck policy at that point in seizing small farms as well as the big ones, than to mourn the fate of the peasantry.
6. The purely statistical problem of poor land distribution in Chile has been aggravated by the emergence of a broad-based middle class with only one or two rivals for size in Latin America. Nirvana for Chile's rural poor was thus not some unattainable never-never land, but the bountiful life in plain view all around them.
7. From "Land Economics," vol. 42, no. 4 (November 1966) (copyright 1966 by Regents of University of Wisconsin), pp. 391–424; reproduced in Solon L. Barraclough and Arthur L. Domike, "Agrarian Structure in Seven Latin American Countries," in *Agrarian Problems and Peasant Movements in Latin America*, ed. Rodolfo Stavenhagen (New York: Doubleday, Anchor Books, 1970), p. 48.
8. Ricardo Cox, Chilean author, politician, and university professor, has pointed out that the men who owned the highly productive irrigated lands between Aconcagua, in the north, and Talca, in the south, became compara-

57

tively prosperous and settled down in Santiago long before independence, a "caste" of rich landlords that grew as agriculture further developed. He said the group was influential but not privileged, "because aristocracy held talent and merits in high esteem. Our statesmen of old times were industrious men who excelled in agriculture, industry, and liberal professions. Aristocracy assimilated worthy men and helped them to the highest positions regardless of their origin. Its sense of genuine values is also manifest in its rich and flexible political judgment, which created advanced juridical institutions and strove constantly, often amidst violent controversies, to adapt them to the necessities of changing times." This interpretation enamors few Marxists, and Cox is a commentator who finds little favor among them. But the fact is, Chile's history shines with examples of social advances engineered by the country's patricians, the automatic hobgoblins of leftist lore. Ricardo Cox, "The Collapse of Democracy," in *Chile: A Critical Survey* (Santiago: Institute of General Studies, 1972) pp. 30–35.

9. Commenting on the ICAD study, Barraclough and Domike (op. cit., p. 49) attack the notion that land ownership in large-size holdings is as prevalent in developed countries as in Latin America: "This is false. An examination of United States census data, for example, reveals that, using the ICAD criteria of farms big enough to employ permanently more than twelve laborers, only about 1 percent of the country's cultivated lands are in large multi-family sized holdings as contrasted with 65 percent in Chile or 20 percent in Argentina, the lowest percentage encountered in the ICAD survey." It is an outrageous commonplace, yet it must be noted that the fundamental differences in land-tenure patterns between the United States and Latin America are that the United States was settled mainly by men claiming the land for themselves, and that the opportunities to possess land were later reinforced by the Homestead Act. In Latin America, men came to claim land in the name of a distant sovereign, who then, through an *encomienda* system of land distribution, created permanent patterns of conflict between the land-endowed and the land-denied. Besides, in the U.S.—as in many other developed countries—the trend in recent years has been toward ever-larger farms. By 1982, 71.6 percent of all U.S. farms were 50 acres or larger, and just under 40 percent were 185 acres or larger. (Source for 1982 figures: *1986 Britannica Book of the Year*, op. cit., p. 866.) op. cit., p. 65.

10. Stavenhagen, op. cit., p. 65.

11. For a more benign, but not uncritical, view on life on Chilean farms in the late nineteenth century, see Luis Galdames, *Historia de Chile*, 14th ed. (Santiago: Productos RAVAL, 1974), pp. 445–48.

12. *Nueva Enciclopedia de Chile* (Argentina: Ediciones Copihue, Fotomecánica Futura SRL, Ediciones Libra, 1974), 2:194–95. (Hereafter *Nueva Enciclopedia*.) The encyclopedia, in a distressingly common failing, neither dates the information in question nor provides clear sourcing for it, but it is clear that these data refer to the early 1970s. Unfortunately, the comparison with the data in the 1966 study must be approximate, but it seems to be an acceptably close comparison.

13. Solon L. Barraclough, "The Structure and Problems of the Chilean Agrarian Sector," in Zammit, op. cit., pp. 119–20. Barraclough was at that time international director of the Institute for Training and Research in Agrarian Reform in Santiago, an agency sponsored by the UN Food and Agriculture Organization.

14. Ibid., p. 120.

15. Chonchol, op. cit., p. 111.
16. Pablo Baraona Urzúa, who earned his master's degree in economics at the University of Chicago, and who taught at the Catholic University of Chile, estimates an annual immigration of thirty thousand peasants to the cities over a thirty-year period ending in the early 1970s. Indeed: the decline in Chile's rural population, 1960–1980, was the greatest in percentage terms (44.5 percent) in all of Latin America, by a wide margin. That is a generally positive development given that in Latin America (as in much of the rest of the world), the incidence of extreme poverty tends to be highest in rural areas. Baraona Urzúa echoes that in taking note of the pitifully low level of farm income; in 1972, he reported, the 800,000 persons then earning their living in farming had to divide a total income pie that would have given them less than half the legal minimum wage in force, and that did not take into account the lopsided distribution of income within the farming sector itself. But, as a World Bank study would point out fifteen years later, the Pinochet government's decision to focus government social spending on the poorest segments of the population—a "performance unequaled in the region"—eased the plight of that shrunken rural sector of the population. Sources: Baraona Urzúa, "The Reality of Chilean Agriculture," in *Chile: A Critical Survey* (Santiago: Institute of General Studies, 1972), pp. 169, 176. For 1960–1980, "Rural Development and Social Growth," in *Economic and Social Progress in Latin America: 1986 Report* (Washington: Inter-American Development Bank, 1986), p. 125. For social spending under Pinochet: *"Poverty in Latin America: The Impact of Depression"* (Washington: The World Bank, 1986), p. 20. Baraona went on to become one of the original "Chicago Boys" blueprinting—and guiding—Pinochet's free-market revolution.
17. I chose almost at random from among countless examples. Oscar Waiss, a Socialist, then editor of the official newspaper *La Nación*, and therefore a principal interpreter of official ideology, wrote revealingly less than a year after Allende came to power, when legality was still moot. He chided those who would slow the pace of the revolution just because they lacked the votes. "We Chilean Socialists," he wrote, "in this period of transition and transformation, are not willing to limit ourselves to counting how many deputies the National party has, how many the Christian Democrats have, how many we have in our own trenches. We see in the elections a mere approximate index of overall trends, but in no case do we regard them as a mathematical expression of the correlation of the social forces in conflict. Bourgeoise democracy is, necessarily, limited, arbitrary, deformed, and unjust" (*Ercilla* magazine [Santiago], August 18–24, 1971, p. 14).

Even more revealingly, the Socialist party pronunciamiento at its Twenty-second Congress in Chillán in November 1967, stated: "Revolutionary violence is inevitable and legitimate. It is an inevitable result of the regressive and armed character of the class state. [Violence] represents the only means leading to taking political and economic power and to its later defense and strengthening. Only by destroying the bureaucratic and military apparatus of the bourgeois state can the socialist revolution be consolidated. The peaceful and legal forms of struggle (labor, ideological, electoral, etc.) do not, by themselves, lead to power. The Socialist party considers them as limited instruments of action, built into the political process which leads us to armed struggle" (quoted by Labrousse, op. cit., p. 199).

It is useful to note that the hard-liners in the Socialist party, Allende's own party and the one regarded by many (Labrousse included; see p. 213) as the most influential in the coalition, never backed away from this position (Labrousse, p. 210). Herein lie the most toxic seeds of Allende's eventual destruction.

18. Indeed, Weston H. Agor notes that two American political scientists, William Flanigan and Edwin Fogleman, had developed an index to measure "democratization" around the world. They concluded that for the period 1900–50, Chile ranked fifth in the world, behind Canada, England, the United States, and Switzerland, but ahead of France, Italy, and Germany. Agor quickly adds that political democracy does not necessarily mean the same thing as political development. But he then goes on to say that in the case of Chile the two do mean the same thing. Agor, *The Chilean Senate* (Austin and London: University of Texas Press, 1971), p. 5.

I am not familiar with the Flanigan-Fogleman study, presented at the 1967 annual meeting of the American Political Science Association, and so I cannot comment on it. But I do criticize the conclusion, and speculate that they failed to reckon sufficiently with the fragility of Chile's institutions in time of crisis, a fragility notably demonstrated over a period of nearly a decade (1924–33), smack in the middle of the time the country was supposedly consolidating its democratic personality. It is interesting to note that Chile finally solved that institutional crisis by scrapping one system (parliamentary) for another (presidential).

It is also curious to observe the contrast between the enthusiasm of foreign academics for Chilean democracy and their failure to see how deeply flawed the process had become. Commenting on foreign regard for the country's republican forms under the parliamentary system (1891–1924), historian Galdames observes: although true that no other Hispanic nation had achieved such institutional development, it was also true that if foreigners had understood better "the workings of the electoral system which served as the basis of that political regime, perhaps their observations would have contained important reservations. In fact, the parliamentary regime not only exercised powerful influence on the conduct of public affairs, but modified also the electoral habits in a way that can only be regretted." He refers to the proliferation of widespread fraud, vote buying, and other noxious practices that weakened civic spirit. Galdames, op. cit., pp. 459–66. The evidence is overwhelming, in my view, that Chile's republican processes were even more corroded under the later presidential system, certainly to a degree that should have but usually did not restrain the writings of foreign commentators on that period.

19. Even Chileans believed in recent years in the *principle* of rule of law— institutions commanding men. Agor quotes a public opinion survey taken in January 1965, at a time when President Eduardo Frei's popularity was presumed to be at a peak. The question was: "Returning to the subject of the actual government, let us suppose that Frei cannot govern, because Congress obstructs his work. Would you be in favor of dissolving Congress so that the government could complete its program, or would you be in favor of waiting until the parliamentary elections of 1969 in order to obtain a favorable Congress?" Agor reports that although 67.1 percent of the sample recognized that a conflict existed between the president and the Congress, and 73 percent felt the president was correct (versus 12 percent for Con-

gress), only 36.8 percent favored dissolving Congress as the solution, 44.9 percent preferred to wait until the 1969 congressional elections, and only 1.3 percent favored a plebiscite. Agor, op. cit., pp. 22–23.

Yet a scant eight years later, an unmistakably overwhelming majority of Chileans clamored for the ouster of the president by whatever means, legal or other, and there were very few signs of mourning over the closing of the Congress. As remarked earlier, this is the difference between a survey of Chilean attitudes in relatively normal times, when institutions operate more or less according to specifications, and their view in times of severe crisis because they are incapable of protecting themselves from their own destruction.

20. Chile's first formal government was headed by José Miguel Carrera (1812), who gave the country its first constitution, created the flag and coat of arms, ordered free schools opened in convents in villages of fifty or more inhabitants, established diplomatic relations with the U.S., and bought from a naturalized American, Matthew Arnold Hoevel, the press for the country's first newspaper, *Aurora de Chile*, founded February 13, 1812. Millar op. cit., pp. 140, 146.

21. Ricardo Cox (op. cit., p. 39) notes that the president not only ruled in his own administration, but appointed his successor, intervened in the nomination of candidates for Congress, and eventually manipulated parliamentary elections.

22. Chilean historian Alberto Edwards discusses this rivalry in his *La Fronda Aristocrática* (Santiago: Editorial del Pacífico, 1952).

23. The calm was punctured violently twice—by armed uprisings in 1851 and again in 1859. Both were sizable revolutions, involving major battles. Ibid., pp. 257, 261. Chile also fought another foreign war, joining Peru in beating back a halfhearted Spanish attempt to recover Peru. The six months of hostilities peaked on March 21, 1866, when a Spanish squadron mercilessly bombarded Valparaíso.

24. By a U.S. citizen, William Wheelwright, though Peru disputes the claim that Chile's railroad was first. Anyway, Wheelwright inaugurated his, which ran from the northern port of Caldera to the iron mines at Copiapó, on July 4, 1851. Millar, op. cit., p. 248.

25. Even before the Indians were subdued, the brilliant Amunátegui brothers were demanding a place of equality for Chile's Indians. In a book published in 1859, they argued that it was economically counterproductive to exclude anyone from the benefits of education, so as to enable all to "escape from the misery of the soul, ignorance, and the misery of the body, poverty. That will be achieved," they wrote, "the day in which general and complete education is cemented throughout the country" (Miguel Luis and Gregorio Víctor Amunátegui, *De la Instrucción Primaria en Chile: Lo Que Es y Lo Que Debería Ser* [Santiago: Imprenta del Ferrocarril, 1859], p. 9).

26. Following the War of the Pacific, the government used its new riches, as Galdames points out, for everything except to keep its solemn obligation to redeem paper money issued to finance the war and ameliorate an earlier recession. The result: paper money fell to half its face value. Foreign creditors refused to honor it, while pressing for payment. This produced an outflow of gold and hard currencies, and forced an inevitable sharp rise in the prices of indispensable imported goods, a chain of events ending in runaway inflation. The two other fiscal evils—heavy borrowing abroad and resorting to the printing presses to provide (debased) money to finance

failures—date from a later era, the administrations of Ibáñez and Alessandri, respectively.

27. Government investment in plant and equipment went from 12,036,796 pesos in 1886, when Balmaceda took office, to 26,196,417 in 1890, his last full year in office. Labrousse, op. cit., p. 37.

28. Uruguay's president from 1903 to 1907 and 1911 to 1915, Battle y Ordóñez, the first great reformer to reach power in Latin America. The welfare-state innovations he introduced in Uruguay were widely admired and copied throughout the hemisphere. Long admired (superficially) as the Switzerland of the Americas, Uruguay would, in later years, become an economic basket case and a political shambles, only recently returning to a shaky democracy astride a tattered economy.

29. During the Allende administration, the press in Chile—pro and con the president—was the most rabid and ribald in the hemisphere. But raucousness was an old tradition in Chilean political reportage. A few samples from the earlier, Balmaceda era—from an editorial in *La Nación*, June 12, 1891: "The likes of Matte, Edwards, and Ross [bankers and opposition leaders] should be tried in accord with the law and their ugly and repulsive beings strung up in the middle of Huérfanos Street [in downtown Santiago] as a permanent warning for those who would traffic in the peace and honor of the country." From *El Correo* of July 16, 1891: "The gallows is a terrible thing. So be it. If it existed for the people then it now exists as well for the aristocracy, who wept only for their own kind but never gave a thought to the common man, whom they tricked, sacrificed, and exploited." The same newspaper characterized Augusto Matte as a "prototype of a vampire"; Augusto Edwards as a "slavedriver" (the Spanish word used in the text is *cangallero*—now archaic—taken from *canga*, describing a type of yoke used by Chinese for convicts); and Isidoro Errázuriz as a "caricature of every kind of immorality."

El Recluta, edited for loyalist conscripts, reacted to rumors of a revolt in Santiago with a sinister warning for "aristocratic millionaires": If you dare try it, the paper said, "tremble for your palaces, reduced to ashes by just popular rage, and tremble for your wives and daughters, fair game for the lust of our soldiers." The article ended with a call to arms strikingly similar to a front-page appeal in the Communist party newspaper, *El Siglo*, of September 11, 1973. *El Recluta* wrote: "People: Come to the aid of your brothers left hungry by the proud aristocracy. Citizens: To your duty stations, at the side of your friends of the army of order, to avenge the swindles and abuses of three quarters of a century! Death to the Aristocratic Millionaires!"

From "Balmaceda y la Crisis del '91," *Qué Pasa*, February 22, 1973, pp. 30–31.

30. A Marxist interpretation offered by Labrousse is that Balmaceda's ouster was sponsored, in large measure, by British nitrate interests headed by John Thomas North, who had acquired a dominant position in Chilean industry. He refers to a U.S. diplomat (but does not name him) as saying that North had contributed £100,000 to the revolt, and even provided British ships to transport volunteers. Labrousse, op. cit., p. 39.

31. One version has it that the parliamentary leaders traveled to Valparaíso only for a last-ditch try at persuading Montt and the other naval leaders to prevail on Balmaceda to install a new cabinet. Instead, they were persuaded to join

the rebellion and sail with the fleet. Silva was so unprepared for such a dramatic turn of events that he arrived at the port with no other luggage than a woolen wrap for his feet. J. Rogers Sotomayor, "La Revolución del '91 y la del '73," *La Tercera de la Hora* (Santiago), April 10, 1974, p. 4.

32. The point-of-no-return on violence was reached with the execution of Ricardo Cumming Durme on July 12, 1891. Cumming was caught in a conspiracy to blow up navy ships. Civic leaders, foreign diplomats, and the Catholic archbishop all pleaded with Balmaceda for clemency. His answer: "What would you have me do? Give myself up with my hands tied to the opposition? I well know that my head is on the block in this game, but by sending Cumming to the firing squad, I put the opposition on notice that their heads are at stake, too." Bloodletting reached a frenzy following a series of guerrilla attacks around the capital. At 4 A.M., on August 19, an army unit surprised a group of youthful conspirators at an estate in the foothills of the Andes outside Santiago. Several were shot out of hand. Balmaceda was inflexible in demanding death for the rest, and they were shot the next day. Estimates of the number executed run from thirty to forty. "Balmaceda y la Crisis del '91," *Qué Pasa*, February 23, 1973, p. 33. This episode is instructive too in spiking still another oft-told tale of recent years, namely, that violence has been a stranger to Chilean life. To the contrary; it has been a persistent marauder.

33. Hermógenes Pérez de Arce, "Between Socialism and Freedom," in *Chile: A Critical Survey* (Santiago: Institute of General Studies, 1972), p. 118. The 1851 revolution also was bloody: more than two thousand dead in a country with only 1.5 million inhabitants. Galdames, op. cit. pp. 360–61.

34. Peter G. Snow points out that Chilean politics have been characterized since early in the century by the multiplicity of political parties. Fifty different parties gained seats in Congress in the three decades up to the midsixties (and two or three more since), and as many as twenty parties were represented in Congress at one time—Snow, "The Chilean Multiparty System," in *Latin American Politics* ed. Robert D. Tomasek (Garden City, N.Y.: Doubleday, Anchor Books, 1966), p. 399.

35. Francisco Orrego Vicuña, "The System of Chilean Foreign Policy: Rise or Fall," in *Chile: A Critical Survey* (Santiago: Institute of General Studies, 1972), p. 95. Gil cites a study done by Julio González Heise which reveals another dimension of the crisis: between 1831 and 1886, Chile had thirty-one cabinets; during fewer years of the parliamentary system, 1891–1922, Chile had 212 cabinets and a total of 530 ministers. Federico G. Gil, *El Sistema Político de Chile* (Santiago: Editorial Andrés Bello, 1969), p. 67.

36. Ricardo Cox points out that the emergence of the popular socialist parties at this time produced a "deep change in the political structure . . . concern for social problems became predominant . . . [but] remained at the level of ideologies and of hostilities among groups and social levels which concealed a mentality that was incompatible with democratic life." He argues that the "old" parties were run by men who were basically men of action, and that Chile owes to them the landmarks of social legislation. The new ones—the Communist, Socialist, and later Christian Democrat parties—belong, he says, to doctrinaire men who force-fit objective reality to their subjective theories. "The whole organization of society is rejected because it does not harmonize with (their) particular doctrine," he writes; ". . . every intellectualist movement aims at undivided power . . . this clamor of protest and

revolution. . . . This wild struggle has a very serious consequence: those who seek total and undivided power and those who aim at transitory power are now on the same level in the eyes of the public." He specifically includes the Christian Democrats with the Communists and Socialists as espousing doctrinaire ideas of this type. Cox, op. cit., pp. 41–42, 51–54.

37. Ibid., p. 54. Cox's views may appear too conservative for some tastes. Witness Claudio Véliz, a man of impeccably leftist intellectual credentials, who took up his pen in spirited defense of the Allende experiment early in the life of the regime. He noted that even before Allende, in 1968, the state already accounted for 60 percent of total investment. As to the growth of bureaucracy in the wake of the 1925 constitution, Véliz agrees, except that he calls it "enlightened bureaucratic centralism"—Véliz, "The Chilean Experiment," *Foreign Affairs*: 444, 446.

The modern record of the Right in economic affairs in Chile has been one of resiliency and ruse—and strategic retreat. Crafty evasion of officialdom where they could get away with it, connivance in the form of tradeoffs where they couldn't (protective tariffs, immunity from tax scrutiny in return for contributions and public support). Mario Arnello observed: "Enough that we remember that it was the Popular Front, with its policies of price fixing, protective tariffs, and shocking favoritism of foreign exchange, which went about creating monopolies and magnates who came to control vast economic sectors of the country and who, in combination with professional politicians, have put together a powerful oligarchical empire" (Arnello, *Proceso a una Democracia: Pensamiento Político de Jorge Prat* [Santiago: Talleres Gráficos "El Imparcial," n.d.], p. 41).

Chile teems, in fact, with "parlor pinks," whose radical politics—and impressive fortunes—date from that "populist" era. Those who remained on the Right found themselves in constant retreat, whereas those on the Left jealously protected private nests, with the overall result that statism proliferated while capitalism disintegrated.

The web of state controls in Chile over production, distribution, imports, banking currency, etc., is dizzying. The *Wall Street Journal's* former (and outstanding) Latin America correspondent, Everett G. Martin, summarized the situation in a similar vein: "Since the 1930s, experimenting by government has left a massive network of state ownership of business and interference in private operations. . . . State funds were even used to support private business ventures so that a Chilean industrialist became a complacent soul sitting comfortably inside high-tariff walls, never challenged to cut his costs, improve his product nor expand to go after broader markets" (Martin, "Chile's Reconstruction Formula," *Wall Street Journal*, June 3, 1974).

38. Marcos Chamudes cites reports he wrote for the magazine *Visión* in 1961–62, and again in his own, Santiago-based magazine *P.E.C.*, in 1963, and similar claims made in a radio broadcast at that time. Chamudes, *Chile: Una Advertercia Americana* (Santiago: Ediciones P.E.C., 1972), pp. 149–50. Chamudes was a Communist in the 1930s and was expelled from the party in 1940. He later became a resolute, unflinching—and frequently solitary—fighter against communism in Chile.

This book often lapses into personal vendettas, but it is an invaluable source of factual data. More important, it provides insights into the personalities of Chilean personages from one angle not usually available: the relationship between these figures and their decisions and the inevitable rise to power thereafter of a Marxist regime. In discussing the decline and fall of Chile's aristocracy—"more than any other in Latin America, comparatively exemplary"—Chamudes says that in its period of decadence, the aristocracy not only lost its creative spark, but was too inept to defend what it had created. The middle class, which succeeded the old aristocracy, never coalesced, he said, into a homogeneous, coherent force capable of shoring up democracy against the erosive ideologies of the far Left. Ibid., p. 31.

39. Julio Durán, presidential candidate of the Radical party in 1964 and confidant of Alessandri in 1980, said in a campaign radio speech July 8, 1964: "I affirm that Alessandri, together with several of his ministers, have served communism in Chile . . . he has given all kinds of facilities to the Communists . . . it's a question of accommodating. Leave me in peace during my government, go about your business, and after me, the deluge. An easy way to live peaceably. But will the conscience of a government leader who took that position later let him live in peace?" Durán cited the fact that Chile's doors were then wide open to Communists and all the meetings, conferences, and the like they wanted to stage in the country, and that in foreign policy, Chile was cozying up to the then very much quarantined Fidel Castro. Ibid., pp. 154–55. It should be remembered that at this time, Castro was financing and supporting, materially and morally, guerrilla forces in Africa, Guatemala, and elsewhere in Latin America; that he had just been defeated in a three-year virtual war on Venezuela; and that Che Guevara would later attempt to bring down by force of arms the government of Chile's northeastern neighbor, Bolivia.

40. It was under the aegis of the Right that most important reforms were achieved in Chile. Furthermore, the very existence of Chile's liberal democracy of this century is a monument to the patricians of the past century—aristocrats, all, as Edwards and other writers have pointed out. Few "rightists" in recent times gave the lie to this myth better by their own lives and example than Jorge Prat Echaurren, independent candidate for the presidency in 1964. He was a novice to politics, and completely independent—not a single congressman campaigned with him. And he was also a reformer, campaigning, above all, against political bosses and political hacks, those who were systematically sacrificing national interest to ambition and party. Although he withdrew five months before the 1964 elections, his ideas took powerful root and have found significant echo among those who succeeded Allende in power. For a detailed account of Prat's thought, and his eleven-month presidential campaign, see Arnello, op. cit.

41. According to the Labrousse version, troops opened fire on the families of striking workers who had seized a school in Iquique. Labrousse, op. cit., p. 57. Moss also uses the two thousand figure in his *Chile's Marxist Experiment* (New York: John Wiley & Sons, Halstead Press, 1973), p. 43. The French journalist Régis Debray, who fought with Che Guevara in Bolivia, lists five separate labor battles with a toll of dead and wounded for the period 1903–34, the bloodiest being the Coruña massacre of 1925, costing three thousand lives. Debray, *The Chilean Revolution: Conversations with Allende* (New York: Random House, Vintage Books, 1971), p. 31.

42. But not too poor. The 1888 legislation granting universal suffrage excluded illiterates. On the subject of the vote: women weren't enfranchised to vote in national elections until 1949.

43. Even Marxist Debray describes the labor code as "remarkable for its time" (Debray, op. cit., p. 37).

44. There is some confusion about just who was in charge of what at this point. According to Galdames (op. cit., p. 469), Alessandri first resigned, a junta took over and dissolved Congress, and then the president left, carrying an authorization to leave the country given by Congress before it was dissolved.

45. In return, the state agreed to compensate the church 2.5 million pesos per year for five years so as to enable the church to assume financial responsibility for activities (schools, for example) previously subsidized by the state. The new constitution is interesting also in that it called for governmental decentralization, through the creation of provincial assemblies with power of taxation. This was never done, because Congress never enacted the enabling legislation, legislation that obviously would have weakened the authority of Congress and the political parties dominated by congressmen. The modern history of Chile undoubtedly would have been completely distinct had power been so dispersed. The new constitution, approved by decree of the military junta on October 21, 1980, after nearly six years of study and debate by a constitutional commission, reorganizes Chile into regions, provinces, and "comunes" (cities, towns, or clusters of small cities/ towns/villages). More on this in chapter 6. Dispositions governing regions/ provinces/ "comunes" are contained in Chapter XIII, Articles 99–115, of the 1980 constitution.

46. The right to own private property was specifically subordinated to "the limitations and rules needed for the maintenance and progress of the social order." As Galdames notes (op. cit., pp. 471–73), the new constitution was designed to facilitate "such reforms as may be warranted for the readjustment of the economic structure of society to the greater benefit of the working classes [clases asalariadas]. The constitution contained, at the same time, the concept that property is not an inalienable individual right for the exclusive benefit of those who possess it, but rather a social function which is exercised by these same persons, a function susceptible of being subordinated to the public interest or the demands of the common weal [progreso común]." While referring also to the "social function" as to the uses, enjoyment, and disposition of private property, the 1980 constitution (Chapter III, Article 24) is much more liberal in safeguarding property against seizure or expropriation, as well as providing for indemnization.

47. For details of the "sucker loans," see n. 65, chapter 1.

48. Ibáñez represented the progressive officer corps, and from his position as war minister, pressured a reluctant Figueroa to push ahead with reform measures. By early 1927, Ibáñez was all but dictating to the president, so Figueroa quit on May 4. Eighteen days later, Ibáñez was elected in new elections in which there was no opposition candidate.

49. In 1930 Ibáñez created—with the eager connivance of political leaders—a Hot Springs Congress, so called because its members were hand-picked (and installed without benefit of elections in an elaborate legal farce) at the Hot Springs of Chillán. Public impatience with his freewheeling style erupted when the economic crunch began. Galdames, op. cit., p. 480.

50. Allende, who was just cutting his political teeth at the time, later remembered the Ibáñez dictatorship as "a benign dictatorship, the outcome of a

chaotic government and a chaotic economic situation . . . not typical of dictatorships in Latin America" (Debray, op. cit., pp. 62–63).

51. A military coup ended the Socialist interlude September 13, 1932, just one month before elections were to be held to elect a new Congress, which was to rewrite the constitution to implant a socialist state. As we have seen, the 1925 constitution not only simplified the amendment and revision procedure, but even anticipated the possibility of a socialist economic structure. Galdames, op. cit., p. 491.

52. In its one hundred days in power, the socialist government promulgated a phenomenal 590 decree laws, one of which would later become a major economic bludgeon in Allende's hands. It gave the executive authority to expropriate any company, provided one of three conditions existed: (1) acute shortages of the product produced by that company; (2) deliberate attempts by that company to sabotage market mechanisms; (3) the company was paralyzed by an irreconcilable dispute with its workers. (Allende usually invoked that decree law with or without the conditions.) From the vantage point of his presidency, forty years later, Allende would describe the 1932 revolution as having had "a profound influence on vanguard thought" (Debray, op. cit., p. 7).

53. For a brief but tangy account of Marmaduke Grove, see John Gunther, *Inside South America* (New York: Harper & Row, 1966), pp. 266–67.

54. Alessandri outpolled four opponents, winning handily with 187,914 of the 342,990 votes cast in the 1932 election. Interestingly, the runner-up—with 60,856 votes—was Colonel Grove, who dashed back from exile on Easter Island to make his bid. The Communist party candidate, Elías Lafertte, ran dead last with 4,128 votes, an experience the Communists would turn to advantage in the next elections. Election figures from *Estadísticas Electorales, 1925–1969* (Oficina de Informaciones, Chilean Senate, Boletín de Información General, no. 66, June 25, 1970), p. 7.

Interestingly, too, Alessandri had tried a comeback in the elections of October 4, 1931, as the candidate of a far-left coalition. He was beaten, nearly two to one, by Juan Esteban Montero, representing a center-right coalition. The results indicated that the Chilean electorate was not in step with the avant-garde leftist wave promoted by the political leadership, a lesson the electorate also attempted to transmit in several other elections up to and including September 1970.

55. As early as the midtwenties, the Communists controlled the 200,000-member Chilean Worker Federation. Six party members were among the 122 framers of the 1925 constitution, though the Communist thesis was defeated in the plebiscite held to ratify the constitution. For an account of the haste in drafting the constitution and the cockeyed technique used for ratifying it, see Gil, op. cit., pp. 105–6.

56. Demonstrating a certain cynicism, if not outright hypocrisy, because Ross's economics should have been to the ideological liking of the Left: economic nationalism, taxes on commerce and industry, a doubling of the federal budget (from 1 billion pesos in 1934 to 2 billion in 1938), and rapid expansion of the money supply (from 550 million pesos in 1932 to 1 billion in 1937)—third in the trinity of fiscal evils that plague the country down to the present. "Printing-press prosperity" was a device Allende would use to unimagined extremes, creating a momentary illusion of bonanza, followed by a whirlpool of ruin. In the 1930s the economic structure had not yet been

so thoroughly weakened and the immediate impact was less: a worsening of the inflationary cycle, but a cure for unemployment. But the acid of recklessness had begun its corrosive work.

57. The quote is from former communist Chamudes op. cit., p. 26.

58. Eudocio Ravines, *El Rescate de Chile* (Santiago: Empresa Editora e Impresora Edimpres, 1974), p. 16.

59. Ravines' own version is contained in his book, *La Gran Estafa* (no pub date). Gil, in his widely admired book, fails even to mention Ravines' name, or at least not in the Spanish edition that I have (*El Sistema Político de Chile*, pp. 84–86). Moss (op. cit., p. 35) reproduces the official Communist party version—solemnized by party elder Lafertte in his 1957 book, *Vida de un Comunista*—that Ravines was really a Nazi agent in disguise, and that he later gorged himself on funds from the German embassy in wartime Santiago. Chamudes, himself a member of the Communist party and in the thick of events at that time, disputes Lafertte's timetable, says Lafertte wanted to smear Ravines to hog credit for the front himself, and says he doubts that Lafertte could have known about secret payoffs from the German embassy anyway—if in fact there were any. Chamudes, op. cit., pp. 40–50. There is, of course, nothing unusual in Communist smear campaigns to discredit defectors.

60. Ravines writes that the first overtures were made to Grove, but the Socialists—and particularly Oscar Schnake and Salvador Allende, two men whose fates would remain bracketed to the very end of their days—rejected any talk of alliance. The Communists then began wooing the Radicals; two Radical leaders, Justiniano Sotomayor and Santiago Labarca, swayed the others to join the front. Ravines, *El Rescate*, pp. 23–24.

61. In his *Rectificaciones al Tomo IX de la Historia de América*, of Ricardo Levene, a rebuttal of a section of that book authored by Ricardo Donoso and dealing with the history of Chile, 1833–1938. Galdames, op. cit., pp. 500–502, cites the Alessandri rebuttal.

62. This was actually the second electoral appearance for the Popular Front. In the parliamentary elections of 1937, the three main front parties polled 34 percent of the vote, 7 percentage points fewer than the Liberals and Conservatives. Despite his withdrawal, incidentally, Ibáñez was far from finished; he would reappear as democratically elected president for the period 1952–58.

63. Allende, in his conversations with Debray, called the victory of the Popular Front "a great advance, because it marked the point at which the petty bourgeoisie took a share in the exercise of power. . . ." But he said it did not bring about "political liberation or complete sovereignty" because the "obstacle of economic dependence stood in the way" (Debray, op. cit., p. 70).

64. Gonzalo Vial Correa, "Decadencia, Consensos y Unidad Nacional en 1973," in *Política y Geostrategia* 36 (Santiago: Académia Nacional de Estudios Políticos y Estratégicos, 1985), pp. 9–10. Vial Correa reports that with the election deadlocked in 1920, Alessandri's people sponsored a "Tribunal of Honor" to choose between Alessandri and Luis Barros. Barros' people rejected the proposal on the grounds that the election should be decided by the Congress, where Barros had majority backing. Parallel with this developing civil crisis, there was a military one: a general mobilization to meet new threats from old enemies Peru and Bolivia, which meant that virtually the entire army was clustered in the north—Alessandri country. According

to Vial Correa, among the many elements in the still-shrouded drama, it appears the crucial one was a coded message from the Army of the North, saying it would not be responsible for maintaining public order if the Tribunal idea were not accepted. Suddenly, Barros caved in, and Alessandri was chosen.

In 1938, Aguirre Cerda nosed out Gustavo Ross by 1 percent. Ross charged irregularities caused by Popular Front (FP) storm-trooper tactics and said the electoral Tribunal (created by the 1925 constitution) should decide the election. The FP rejected that proposal out-of-hand, saying Aguirre Cerda had won. On November 12, Ross received two letters, one from army commander-in-chief Gen. Oscar Novoa, the other from Carabinero commandant Humberto Arriagada. Both warned of serious disorders in the inflamed opinion climate of the moment if Ross didn't concede—the army chief invoking "patriotism," the Carabinero chief saying failure to concede would "trample the popular will." Ross got the message, saying the country was in "a revolutionary state." He said the two letters made it impossible for him to continue contesting the election.

65. Chamudes, op. cit., p. 67.
66. Allende also worked as a dental-school assistant, a physician in a mental hospital, and an official reporter at medical conventions, and practiced among public-welfare patients in and around Valparaíso. Despite his limited professional experience, he would later become president of the Chilean Medical Association, chairman of the College of Physicians, president of the Pan-American Medical Confederation, and editor of the *Chilean Medical Bulletin*. See *Current Biography* (New York: H. W. Wilson, September 1971), p. 6. Allende blamed his political activity for his inability to get a firm foothold on a medical career. As for his relations with the man who rescued him from disrepute, the Radical president Aguirre Cerda, Allende described him as "a man of great human qualities, a very kind man . . . to begin with, he was the bourgeois radical political 'par excellence,' and in response to the loyalty and affection of the people, he was gradually transformed into a man of deeper conviction, much closer to the aspirations of the people . . ." (Debray, op. cit., p. 67).
67. The definition is courtesy of K. H. Silvert, "The Prospects of Chilean Democracy," in *Latin American Politics*, ed. Robert D. Tomasek (Garden City, N.Y.: Doubleday, Anchor Books, 1966), p. 387. Professor Silvert, a political scientist and prolific writer on Latin affairs (and much admired by Professor Gil for his work on Chile), detected the danger signals ("persistent and stable strength can flow only from an electorate able to put aside small group and class loyalties in favor of the national community"—p. 398). I believe he erred in his optimism in failing to see that fragmentation and sectarianism were part and poisonous parcel of Chilean political institutions. I also believe he erred in accepting the reformist economic strategies of the Christian Democrats and others as the right ones for achieving the objectives of development—the creation, in his words, of "a strong and free national community" (p. 398). Instead, the Christian Democrats polarized Chilean politics as never before and legitimized the politics of class warfare.

3

The Beguiling Intermezzo

THE MIRAGE

For many within Chile—and even more beyond those spindly borders—the forties, fifties, and sixties were a time of political apotheosis. In the aftermath of the Allende holocaust, it was plain that it was really the protasis of democracy's death.

The omens were everywhere visible, even then, amid the carnival of democratic sights and sounds that excited the enthusiastic admiration of political scientists celebrating the Chilean model as an example for all Latin America. On a purely formal level, democracy did, for the most part, flourish. On a more substantial level, it was cannibalistic democracy, consuming itself. Most commentators seem to have suffered its imperfections and overlooked the miasma enveloping it—out of loyalty to two latter-day truths: any democracy is better than anything else, and any regime of the Left is better than any regime of the Right.

The appearances were there all right. In 1927 only 7.3 percent of the population was registered to vote. In 1949 the figure was 9.1 percent. With full suffrage for women (January 8, 1949) that number had jumped to 17.6 percent by 1952, 20.5 percent by 1958. Then a strong drive to bring eligible voters into active participation in the country's decision-making process produced an even more spectacular leap, from 23.6 percent in 1959 to 34.8 percent in 1964 and 38.1 percent in 1971—a year in which, as provided for in the constitutional reforms of 1970, still another amendment of the electoral laws took effect (lowering the voting age from twenty-one to eighteen and giving illiterates the vote). Thus, while Chile's population was increasing by 54 percent from 1950 to 1970 (from 6.062 million to 9.276 million), the number of registered voters was increasing by 325 percent (from 833,000 to 3,539,000).[1]

Political transitions were carried out in an orderly way throughout this period, and the Congress operated continuously. The Communist party was twice outlawed, but other than that, there was little interference with political parties, and they, indeed, multiplied and divided.[2] Except for the Communists during their two exiles, basic freedoms were respected: assembly, press, worship.

On a socioeconomic level, industrial workers and peasants banded together in increasing numbers in unions. The number of workers enrolled in unions jumped from 270,542 in 1964—equivalent to 10.3 percent of the nonagricultural work force—to 551,086 in 1970, or 19.4 percent. In the countryside the picture was the same: in 1964, peasant organizations, technically illegal, numbered 1,658 members. By 1970 that number had climbed to 114,122,[3] or about one-sixth of the farm labor force.

Interestingly, it was the Right that had authorized peasant unions in the first place, and the Left, the verbal "champions" of the peasants, that had struck them down. Interestingly also, it was the Right that gave Chilean workers a comprehensive minimum-wage law (in 1937, a year before a limited minimum-wage law went on the books in the U.S.), so that by the mid-1960s, a United Nations study would show that Chilean blue-collar workers were ranked fourth in wage scales among twelve leading industrial countries in the entire world. (By then Chile also was first in Latin America in per capita industrial output, first in per capita consumption of energy, and third in literacy.)[4]

Under the Christian Democrats, popular participation in government was also extended: in the cities, through the creation of legally recognized Neighborhood Committees and Centers of Mothers; in rural areas, Committees of Cooperatives (organized—and dominated—by the party, however, and really operating as branches of it).

The *patrones* already had their organizations, of course; landowners had their once powerful National Agricultural Society, founded May 18, 1838, and industrialists and merchants their chambers and associations, foremost among them the Society for Industrial Development* (SOFOFA—Sociedad de Fomento Fabril), founded in 1883. But still another type of organization, highly developed, marked Chile apart: the organizations of professionals and small businessmen, both of which included virtually all of their groups in the country.

Superficially, then, Chile was a country in which consensus was forged in the controlled fires of orderly, ordered debate, a country in which the clash of ideas and the crossfire of conflicting interests never got beyond the shouting stage at worst. True, there were already a few hotheads committed to imposing their views by force: by 1971, no fewer than twenty-nine groups of extremists, all but one of the extreme Left, had been identified in Chile.[5] But they were thought to be little more than an ugly blemish on democracy's fair, Chilean face.

---

* Sometimes loosely translated as National Manufacturers Association, so as to equate it with the similarly-named U.S. organization.

The truth was another.

The politics of solutions had long since given way to the politics of power, power as an end in itself. Reasonableness, rationality, and responsibility vanished in the charnel house of demagoguery, as political parties and politicians competed with each other in a frenzy of promises and pandering that emptied the country's treasury, sapped its self-reliance, and locked the country inside an ideological ballistic missile with a nation-wrecking warhead.

The Right had lost its historic stamina and self-confidence and wallowed in the irrelevance of intransigence and incompetence.

The Left, increasingly self-confident, never wavered in the relentless pursuit of its objective, the conquest of total power, first by manipulating the mechanisms of the despised bourgeois democracy, then dismantling and discarding it.

The center—first the Radicals and then, in startlingly similar circumstances and style, the Christian Democrats—confident that it could outsmart and outmaneuver both Left and Right, fidgeted, fumbled, and hesitated until it was too late and the center found itself ground to smithereens in the inevitable collision between Left and Right.

To make matters worse, political parties themselves became a cancer consuming the larger body politic. The malignancy grew out of the 1925 constitution. Although the document made a single passing reference (in Article 25) to political parties, the effect was to give them a virtual stranglehold on the political process. Nor were their activities restricted, either constitutionally or legally. The first consequence was ruinously divisive, an all-spoils-to-the-victor mindset which required that presidents submit to the dictates of their own parties rather than rule as chief executives for the entire nation. (Relations between those who first backed Pedro Aguirre Cerda and his party, the Radicals, became so bad that when he died, his widow, Juanita Aguirre, refused to accept the condolences of the party's Central Board.) Party councils increasingly became the battlegrounds of Young Turks and demagogues practicing the politics of what historian Vial Correa calls "demolition": undermining leaders, stirring up and fanning the flames of factionalism, carping, criticizing, destroying consensus. The second consequence of unrestrained party power was guerrilla warfare waged by party vigilantes against presidential policies and appointments they disapproved.

Next, party fund-raising degenerated, from questionable sources and practices at home to, beginning in the late 1950s, increasing willingness to accept funds from abroad. The sources ranged from the Vatican to the Kremlin, the CIA to Fidel Castro, Argentine Dictator Juan Perón to European Social and Christian Democrats.

The frenzied search for voters, for funds, made parties easy prey for ambitious special interests. Finally, their own ambition fueled messianic visions which first fostered atomization, splitting parties into factions and new parties (by 1970 there were fifteen), and then drove the parties, both Left and Right, to politicize every sector and segment of the society, from the churches to factories, from classrooms to labor unions, business, and professional organizations and even, in the end, the armed forces.

It was, Vial Correa remarks, fatal for the survival of a truly democratic society.[6]

First there were the Radicals.

THE "MOLDERING PILLAR"

Marcos Chamudes, the ex-Communist turned Radical,[7] has called it the "moldering pillar."

"That the century-old Radical party constituted one of the most solid pillars of Chilean democracy," he wrote, "was one of the hackneyed commonplaces of the political oratory and literature of the country."

In the beginning, the Radical party did not, of course, represent the center, but was part of a "leftist" movement already a quarter of a century old and with two cardinal aims: religious freedom, through the separation of church and state (the constitution of 1833 established the Roman Catholic church as the exclusive state religion), and a more representative democracy. (The 1833 constitution limited the vote to males twenty-five or older who could read and write and had a certain income level, and stipulated election of senators through an indirect vote and the president through special electors.)

Nowhere else in Latin America, with the possible exception of Brazil, did the seeds of positivism—that man should seek happiness within the finite boundaries of the knowable world—find more fertile soil than in Chile. Elsewhere in Latin America the philosophy of Auguste Comte was bent to serve local purposes: as an ideological weapon in the war against frankly oppressive regimes; later, as a palliative for the emerging middle classes to justify their taste for material comforts; throughout, as a rationalization for ruling classes, who saw anarchy as the only alternative to their rule.[8]

At the beginning, in the so-called intellectual movement of 1842, there was much of the sword about positivism in Chile, particularly as the new ideology was brandished by a young (twenty-one-year-old) law school student, Francisco Bilbao, in the pages of a periodical called *El Crepúsculo* (*The Twilight*). But what distinguished the growth of positivism's influence in Chile was that it would soon become the instrument of the elite wielded in behalf of the less privileged—foreshadowing by a full century the New Deal and Democratic Left regimes of other countries.

The elite in Chile was not merely the intellectual vanguard, sniping at the establishment from behind the barricades of exile or within the musty irrelevance of cafes, academia, or artists' garrets. By 1860 a new artistocracy had arisen in Chile, an aristocracy of miners, merchants, and traders to challenge the hegemony of the landed gentry. And these new aristocrats, in turn, legitimized a new meritocracy, which became part and parcel of the accepted establishment, and brought with them the baggage of their liberal thought and reformist ideals.[9]

Decades would pass, of course, before the aristocrats would become dominant—the power of the oligarchy was not finally broken until 1920.[10] But what set Chile apart from all but its sister countries of the Southern Cone (Chile, Argentina, and Uruguay) was that liberal thought occupied a permanent place at the banquet table of power.

It was in this setting that the Radical party was founded, by the Matta brothers, Manuel Antonio and Guillermo, in 1861.[11] In the early years it was the party of the cutting edges of society: the new class of small shopkeepers and nouveau riche miners and later the frontiersmen of the seventies and eighties. Still later it was the party of the expanding industrial proletariat and the ever-multiplying legions of civil servants. The latter group—the inevitable outcropping of an economy based on metal riches, riches which sent profits abroad and taxes into government coffers, but which precluded the growth of a home-grown entrepreneurial class—was a force for stability and governmental paternalism, both consequences of its own vested interest in the system. Inevitably, too, the burgeoning bureaucracy identified with Radicalism.

The Radicals early in their career became the champions of the movement to separate church and state and to reduce the church's power. They won their first important political triumph precisely on that battlefield in 1874 when they spearheaded an alliance with other liberal forces to pass a law that permitted clerics to be tried in regular courts for certain crimes, followed a year later by another law that abolished altogether the existence of special courts for clerics. Henceforth, priests and other religious were subject to the jurisdiction of regular criminal and civil courts, and henceforth, the Radicals became known as an anticlerical party.

They won their first taste of power with the formation of the Popular Front and the election of Aguirre Cerda in 1938. The Radicals rolled up the largest single vote in only four of the eight parliamentary elections during the thirty years they played a decisive role on the country's political stage: 1932, 1941, 1957, and 1961. It was their lot throughout this period to be the balance of power between the declining, but still checkmating, combination of rightist parties (the Liberal and the Conservative) and the emerging leftist parties (the Socialist and the Communist).

In the beginning the Radicals were a party of idealists, crusaders in the fight to lead the unwashed out of the wilderness of political privation and economic misery. "The workers," wrote Enrique MacIver, one of the party's early ideologues, "lack the necessary culture and preparation for understanding the problems of government, let alone constituting part of it."[12] So the intellectual elite battled for reform in behalf of the untutored masses, while giving them schools and coaching them in the ways of strikes, political action, and revolutionary zeal.

By the time the party reached maturity and political power, it was torn between the allures of the new religion, Marxism-Leninism, and the old ways of utopian socialism. For the most part, it was a party of dilettantes, the "parlor pinks" of a later era, men of elaborate social consciences and lofty principles resting on a bedrock of comfortable fortunes and "sensible" revolutionary ideals, still imbued with a vanguard vision of themselves. Such decent men of principle were, of course, easy prey for the single-minded cynics for whom the only scruple was the conquest of power.[13] And so it was that the Radicals, so long frustrated in their quest for power, put aside their own qualms and entered into successive alliances with the Left that put three of their men in La Moneda.

For all outward appearances, the Radicals ruled Chile from 1938 to 1952, the arbiters between the contending forces of Right and Left, tilting first one way, then another, but always blunting the extremist edges of both, a force of moderation in Chilean life.

Indeed, as more than one Chilean scholar has noted, the Radicals, for a time, managed to offer hope of a new national consensus in a country long lacking in one. The problem, as Gonzalo Vial Correa has noted, is that the experiment in consensus-building soon gave way to *caudillismo*, the cult of the personality, which was the cult of less advanced Latin American states.[14]

Ultimately, the Radicals became the handmaidens of extremism, doing their bidding in order to retain their indispensable support, until finally becoming the skulking satraps of the relentless Left.

Their policies during this delusion of power constructed the scaffolding on which they would finally go to a despised execution.

THE RADICAL YEARS

Two earthquakes early in the Radical years overshadowed the subtler shift in the country's political topography.

The first of them was physical. On January 24, 1939, a cataclysmic earthquake took an estimated forty thousand lives and wreaked widespread destruction in the southern provinces of Linares, Maule, Ñuble, and Concepción.

The second one was external, with deep ramifications. On September 3, 1939, World War II broke out. The Socialist party demanded an immediate break with the Nazis. The Communist party, responding to the German-Russian Nonaggression Pact, urged neutrality and tilted toward the Nazis. It was the major factor in the Socialist decision to pull out of the coalition early in 1940. There was another: although the Socialists were in the government (with three Cabinet posts) and the Communists were not, the latter gained ground in winning control of the unions, the battleground the bourgeois-based Radicals had long since forfeited to the Communists and the Socialists. Within the Socialists a faction led by César Godoy Urrutia,[15] charged that sharing power with the disappointingly moderate Radicals was costing them labor support; he bolted the party and formed the Socialist Workers party. The remnants, led by Marmaduke Grove, quit the coalition shortly afterward.

The war brought another consequence: unable to sell copper to traditional buyers of the Axis bloc, Chile found most of its booming production[16] diverted to the United States, where by unilateral decision, a price of 11.75 cents per pound had been fixed. As a result of this action, Chile protested that it had been "cheated" out of anywhere from $100 million to $500 million during the war.[17]

The man who presided over the country's destinies at this time was a prototype of the traditional Radical leader of that era. Teacher, lawyer, congressman, presidential confidant, and finally president, Pedro Aguirre Cerda was a man admired for his long climb from humble beginnings to the pinnacle of political power. Along the way he also amassed a fortune—part of it his private enterprise, a larger part of it by marriage—and collected a piquant nickname of the sort Chileans are fond of pinning on their public figures. They called him Don Tinto, a name which reflected in part his position as the husband of Juanita Luco, a member of the wealthy clan that owned the Conchalí winery near Santiago, and in even larger part his enthusiasm for the beverage (tinto is the Spanish term for red wine).

Don Tinto was, in a word, a burgher whose profession happened to be politics and whose views were avant-garde—but not too much so, because, like so many of his confreres of the Radical movement, the "what I am" about him frequently overruled the "what I say" about him. He was, in fact, one of an increasingly conspicuous brand of Radical with close ties to the establishment it excoriated—a group of revolutionary fat cats doomed to political extinction.[18]

The fifty-nine-year-old Aguirre Cerda was, in fact, chosen as the party's candidate to calm the anxieties of moderates inside and outside the party alarmed by the electoral pact with the Communists and the Socialists. As was the familiar case with Radicals, Don Tinto's oratorical bark was worse than his executive bite, unless one remembers that oratory itself has a deep, special, and lasting sting of its own.

In his very first message to Congress, Aguirre Cerda leveled a broadside at foreign control of Chile's mineral riches. That gripe henceforth would be blared by the Left until it became an irrepressible battle hymn of the republic.

"There can be no real progress, nor meaningful social stability, nor the kind of civilization that ennobles the country," Aguirre Cerda said, "until such time as our own people, in their entirety, share fairly in the fruits of our raw materials along with the indispensable representatives of more advanced civilizations."[19]

Aguirre Cerda did nothing to modify foreign control of the copper mines—nearly thirty years would elapse before that would come to pass—but the gauntlet had been thrown. Meanwhile, the Radicals did move in other directions to extend state control over the economy.

No move in that regard was more significant than the creation, in April 1939, of the Development Corporation (CORFO, from Corporación de Fomento de la Producción), a much copied pacesetter for all of Latin America. Interestingly, it was legislated into existence by a Congress controlled by the supposedly hidebound Right. Until very recently, few Chileans—or non-Chileans—had anything but undiluted praise for CORFO.[20] In the longer perspective of time and the evidence, there is a growing tendency to view CORFO as the disguised but decisive Trojan horse behind the systematic dismantling of the capitalist economy in Chile.

Governmental support for industry in Chile dates back to 1847, when import duties were eased for a sugar-beet factory, and to 1854, when the government loaned money to a struggling chinaware factory. On October 7, 1883, leading industrialists, responding to government prodding, formed the Society for Industrial Development (SOFOFA). Over the years, the Society organized vocational training for workers, studied and imported advanced technologies from foreign countries, staged expositions, and lobbied for protection for home industries.

CORFO marked a shift away from private to state economic initiative. From the very beginning CORFO was less an agency for stimulating production than one for expanding state control of the economy. In the long run the two—increased production and state control—were only occasionally synonymous. CORFO's first major achievement was to implement, in 1944, a plan developed eight years earlier by private sources (the Institute of Engineers) for coherent electrification of the country. To do this, CORFO created a state electric company (Empresa Nacional de Electricidad—ENDESA) to compete with a U.S.-owned electric utility. ENDESA was widely, and wrongly, credited with unprecedented expansion of electric energy output; what ENDESA did do was extend power grids to the remotest corners of the country, providing service where none had previously existed.[21]

CORFO was the catalyst in the creation of a number of other enterprises, the two most notable being the National Petroleum Company (ENAP—Empresa Nacional de Petróleo), in 1939; and, seven years later, the Pacific Steel Company (CAP—Compañía de Aceros del Pacífico). Steel is, however, another case in point where CORFO is routinely given greater credit than is its due. The bulk of the funds for the plant came from the U.S. Export-Import Bank, which agreed in 1942 to finance that project and Brazil's Volta Redonda steel mill in order to prod those two countries into breaking with the Axis.[22] The two plants were the first integrated steel mills in Latin America; and for many years after they went into operation, ranked one and two (Volta Redonda first, Chile's Huachipato second) in size in Latin America.

ENAP remained entirely in state hands. CAP was held originally 25 percent by the Chilean government (CORFO), 18 percent by foreign investors (mostly U.S.), and the rest by seven thousand small shareholders, two thousand of them employees of the company.[23] Under Allende, the state took over total control.

Before Allende's administration, the usual CORFO pattern was: establishing new, joint ventures, or helping develop struggling, established ones—with special emphasis on industries producing goods formerly imported from abroad. Under Allende those traditional roles would be perverted altogether: CORFO would become the agent for illegal acquisition of everything from banks to the only brewery, most of them thriving when the state muscled in.

The policy of import substitution promoted by the Radical governments made them especially popular with industrialists, who immensely prospered behind comfortable barriers of high protective tariffs.[24] More local production also meant more wages for more local industrial workers, and with it a consumer boom.[25] But it was a bonanza built on quicksand: high-tariff walls almost always protect inefficient industries, and this inefficiency translates into ever higher prices, the base ingredient of inflation (and the Radical years marked the onset of an ever accelerating spiral of the world's most gluttonous inflation).

Pioneering Chile also discovered—as other emulating underdeveloped countries would later—that far from easing the drain on foreign exchange, substituting homemade products for imported ones created a number of artificial industries with an insatiable appetite for raw materials or semifinished goods from abroad. Once established, industries that provide jobs are difficult to dismantle no matter how inefficient they may be, and so in addition to breeding a new vicious cycle of imports, these industries require increasing state support to stay alive. Thus the bonanza was also accompanied by pervasive expansion of state intervention, direct and indirect, in the productive life of the country, intervention with the usual favoritism and chronic corruption.

The Popular Front concentrated on three other targets: education, health, and labor. In his campaign, Aguirre Cerda had trumpeted the slogan To Govern Is to Teach, the continuation of the notion of an elitist vanguard leading the way for the unenlightened masses. Apart from attempting to instill in Chileans the socioeconomic ideology of the Left, Aguirre Cerda also set out to revitalize, and reshape, the country's educational system. In public instruction the emphasis was shifted from classical to vocational education, and room was cleared on teaching staffs for previously proscribed Communist party members and other Marxists. Construction of new schools was pushed, along with sizable pay raises for teachers. Poor pupils were given uniforms and school lunches. From 1938 to 1941, enrollment in primary schools jumped from 110,000 to 615,983.[26]

Public health facilities were greatly expanded, the beginning of what would soon become the virtual socialization of medicine in Chile. A determined effort was launched to reduce Chile's shocking infant mortality rate.[27] Under the leadership of his young health minister, Salvador Allende, Aguirre Cerda's government also pushed ahead with reforms in the social-security program and industrial safety laws. During his term as minister (1939–41), Allende wrote a book published by the ministry called *La Realidad Médico-Social Chilena* (*The Medical-Social Reality of Chile*), in which he blamed capitalism for much of the poverty and sickness in the country. In the book he outlined an elaborate program for reforms in public health, housing, nutrition, and social security.[28]

In the labor field the government encouraged unionization, recognizing nearly two thousand unions in 1941 with more than 200,000 members. Labor trouble, sporadic in the past, would, in the years ahead, become a plague. It was a plague fomented, in large part, by the combination of government policies which trapped labor and the middle class in a perpetual wage-price vise, and by political parties of the Left fueling labor's expectations as part of its own strategy of class warfare.

Taken sick in 1941, Aguirre Cerda had to step aside, and designated his interior minister, Jerónimo Méndez, to succeed him. On November 25, 1941, Aguirre Cerda died. The Popular Front, which had already disintegrated because of the endless squabbling between Socialists and Communists, re-formed in a loose alliance that this time included the Falange Nacional, a splinter group from the Right destined to become the Christian Democrat party a few years later.

An external circumstance facilitated the formation of the new alliance between Socialists and Communists: the Nazi invasion of Russia in 1941. With Russia now antifascist, the Chilean Communist party dutifully became antifascist and joined forces with the Socialists in opposing Germany.[29] The Communists, in the 1941 congressional elections, made the best showing they had to that time, winning 11.80 percent of the total vote.[30] The Socialists did even better, winning the largest share of the vote they ever had (16.69 percent), or would have until Allende. The year 1941 also saw the forces of the Right lose control of Congress for the first time in history; in 1945 they regained control, by a narrow margin, and for the last time.

The Radicals have been described, by one of their own leaders, as a "party with a bad memory," a reference to the fact that in the (then) free atmosphere of the party's councils, prodigal sons were always welcomed back. The Radicals rallied round just such a prodigal as their candidate to succeed Aguirre Cerda: Juan Antonio Ríos, a man who had once been expelled from the party. Backed by the loose leftist coalition known as the Democratic Alliance, Ríos defeated Carlos Ibáñez in the special elections of February 1, 1942, by 55,000 of the 464,669 votes cast. More moderate than his predecessor, Ríos also was resolutely anti-Communist, a circumstance which kept Communist party members out of his government but which did not slow the party's impressive gains in organized labor and in forging a nationwide electoral apparatus.

In part, the Communists were favored by continuing fratricide within the Socialist party, a party torn by factional dissension from the day of its birth to the day of its death. The left wing of the party which had bolted with Godoy teamed with the Communists and Radicals in the 1941 parliamentary elections, while the original cadres loyal to Marmaduke Grove and Oscar Schnake presented their own candidates. New infighting erupted after the election over the question of whether to continue to support Ríos. This time, in mid-1944, Grove led a split, forming the Authentic Socialist party, and control of what was left of the party fell to Salvador Allende.

The Allende forces controlled the Socialist-dominated unions and forced new and more bitter battles with the Communists for control of organized labor. The Radicals and Christian Democrats (still called the Falange Nacional) backed the Communists, who retained control of the Federation of Labor. Allende's Socialists formed a rump organization of their own.

The endless bickering and backbiting within his own ranks led Ríos to turn increasingly to independents for his cabinet ministers. Thus, the Left forfeited the first genuine opportunity ever given it to govern. For the first time the Left controlled both the executive and legislative branches of government. But in practice, because it was unable to overcome its rivalries and jealousies, it actually controlled neither.

Ríos's major concern was in the foreign field: to break or not to break with the Axis. Two strategic considerations inclined Chile to the side of maintaining relations: first, the futility of such a militarily weak nation attempting to defend a three thousand-mile coastline; and second, the fact that Chile's shipments of vital metals crossed the oceans unmolested so long as it remained neutral.

Sentiment within the country grew, however, for making the break. Sentiment impelled in large measure by the Communists and Socialists and massaged by the offer from the U.S. Export-Import Bank to finance the steel mill. On January 1, 1943, Ríos asked the Senate for an advisory opinion. The vote was overwhelming in favor of breaking with Germany, Italy, and Japan. On January 20, 1943, Ríos took the step.[31]

Although several years would elapse before production would actually begin—it did a few minutes past midnight, June 2, 1950—work began almost immediately on the steel plant. It was situated on San Vicente Bay, near Concepción, the nucleus for an eventual industrial complex in that area to compete with the traditional Santiago-Valparaíso industrial corridor.

There was an economic development of parallel importance which took place during Ríos's term. After years of trying, and 60 million pesos worth of looking, oil was discovered on December 29, 1945, at Springhill (now named Manantiales) on Tierra del Fuego. By 1974 the country was producing 2.2 million cubic meters of oil, 30 percent of total consumption; by 1983, crude oil output covered 48 percent of the country's needs and 64 percent by 1986.[32]

Public education also commanded high priority, but this time at the secondary level. Ríos commissioned a study by a task force of teachers to "convert this branch of teaching into an efficient instrument for social and economic progress." From this study emerged a number of experimental institutes.

On September 28, 1945, Ríos set out on a tour of several hemispheric nations, including the U.S.—the first Chilean president to visit the U.S. while in office. Like Aguirre Cerda before him, Ríos did not survive the rigors of the presidency. On June 27, 1946, at the age of fifty-eight and following a six-month illness, he died, and with him, a brief era with reverberations that not even a profound revolution could control.

Still another Radical administration was waiting in history's wings, and it would veer off on a tangent all its own. But the forces already set in motion were so powerful that they would engulf mere men as well as their administrations.

THE INFAMOUS YEARS

It was a time for rejoicing. Pablo Neruda, later a Nobel laureate in poetry, dedicated a poem to him: "The People Call Him Gabriel" ("El Pueblo Lo Llama Gabriel").

Actually, the people preferred to call Gabriel González Videla by the name Gaby, but militant Communist Neruda may be forgiven a déclassé touch.[33]

Gaby González Videla had just given the Communist party the gift it had received from only one other ruler in the Western Hemisphere: posts in the presidential Cabinet. (The earlier precedent: Cuba, where dictator Fulgencio Batista in 1940 rewarded the Communists with three Cabinet posts in return for their electoral support. He kept them in the Cabinet for four years. The Communists in Cuba would again support Batista years later, when he returned as dictator, siding with Fidel Castro only at the very end.)

González Videla—the most radical, the toughest, the brawlingest of the three Radical presidents—reached power thanks to the decisive support of the Communists, and at a high price which they extracted from him. In return for their support, the Communists demanded that their candidate be nominated at a convention of all three coalition partners (Radicals, Communists, and the small Democratic party), and that the candidate swear to uphold the platform that would be hammered out at that convention. González Videla agreed, but attempted to renege early on the agreement (as he would ruthlessly renege on it once in power).

In his acceptance speech at the convention, González Videla failed to swear to support the program, to thank the Communists for their support, and to pledge to govern with the full participation of all of his partners. Ricardo Fonseca, a tough former primary school teacher who would soon seize control of the Communist party, was seated behind the speaker, and slipped a note to González Videla reminding him of his "oversight." When that failed to produce the desired results, Fonseca—to the astonishment of those present—ostentatiously rose from his chair and sidled up to González Videla, reminding him in a very loud stage whisper of the missing pledge. Only then did the candidate remember to give the stipulated pledges.[34]

The Right in that election was a victim of its own overconfidence, a mistake it would not repeat, but Chile's other non-Marxist parties would. In the 1945 parliamentary elections, both parties of the Right—the Conservatives and the Liberals—had scored impressive gains, increasing their share of the vote from 1941's 31 percent to 41 percent. At the same time the three parties of the Left—Radicals, Communists, and Socialists—were sliding from 50 percent to 43 percent.

As a result, the Conservatives ran a highly respected physician and former public health minister, Eduardo Cruz Coke, a man whose politics were liberal enough to earn him also the support of the Falange and Marmaduke Grove's Authentic Socialist party. The Liberals went their own way with Fernando Alessandri, son of the former president. Allende's Socialists nominated Bernardo Ibáñez (no kin of the former president), while the Radicals offered González Videla, the scrappy political heir of Aguirre Cerda.

The two candidates of the Right divided a whopping 57 percent of the total vote to 20.23 percent for González Videla. (Allende's man scrounged 2.5 percent of the vote and faded into political oblivion.) The election was thrown into Congress, where the Liberals negotiated a pact that gave the Radical candidate the presidency. It was the first time in Chilean history the Congress had decided an election under the constitutional provision for a circumstance in which no candidate polled a majority of the votes. It was a device that would be used in all but one election thereafter, and established the "tradition" that Congress give the election to the candidate who had polled the highest number of votes (although the constitution made no such stipulation). The Liberals actually threw their votes to González Videla for other reasons: a share of power.

The new Cabinet contained three Liberal ministers, three Radicals—and the three Communists. Until then, in no other country in the Western world had the Communists achieved so much power and influence—all within the letter of the law. Furthermore, they were still climbing the heights of power. In the municipal elections of 1947 they won control of every major city in the country,[35] polling 91,204 of the 552,034 votes cast, or 16.52 percent of the total, nearly double the total of the Socialists, and enough to make them the third largest party in the country (after the Conservatives and Radicals). In Congress, they had 5 senators and 15 deputies, of a total of 45 senators and 147 deputies.

The Communists, and the Radical era, would shortly come tumbling down together. For the Communists, it was not a wreckage that they left behind but a lode of political capital they would later exploit to a level of advantage also without parallel in the Western world. In Chile—and in the rest of Latin America, as well as in Europe, particularly France and Italy—the ascent to power of the Communist party had been watched with a mixture of fear and fascination. That the Communists abided by the rules of bourgeois democracy befuddled their foes and lulled their lukewarm friends. "Softly, gradually," ex-Communist Ravines wrote, the Popular Front "softened national resistance toward communism, eased the tensions surrounding the danger of Marxism, caused even the most wide awake to lower their guard and anesthetized the vigilance of even the most alert."[36]

Little noticed was the fact that the Communists did not need to resort to violence to achieve their purposes: both the intellectual climate and the political rules supported them. And so it was that they could pose as loyal servants of democratic processes, while laying the groundwork for their destruction. It was a groundwork that included raking up the embers of class hatred, so that politics in Chile deteriorated increasingly from a competition between political ideologies to a competition between economic classes; the search for solutions to the very real problems of poverty and political imperfection gave way to frenzied pandering to popular favor. Among parties of the Left, partisan loyalty took decisive precedence over private conscience. A detailed study of the Chilean Senate showed that among congressmen of the Right—a steadily vanishing breed in Chilean politics—party discipline on voting matters mattered "little," whereas for Socialists it was "strong" and for Communists "absolute."[37] And there is, of course, no record anywhere in all of Chilean politics of the Communists sacrificing party advantage to the national interest.

There was still another reason why the Communists could view their temporary eclipse with equanimity: the country had taken an irrevocable turn to the left. The political and economic debate in Chile might occasionally favor them and might occasionally go against them, but it was being conducted ever more inexorably on their intellectual terrain. Silvia Pinto, one of Chile's most combative women journalists during the Allende years, summed it up in her book, *Los Días del Arco Iris:* "To be of the Left in Chile was, until a very short time ago, synonymous with progressive, elegant, and fashionable."[38]

The man who temporarily derailed the Communist train was true in doing so to his mercurial temperament, if not to his political prejudices. In his career in Congress, González Videla was known for the "vehemence of his character"[39] as well as the radicalism of his ideas. Following the April 1947 municipal elections, the Liberals—alarmed by the fact that the Communists alone among the coalition partners had scored gains—maneuvered to oust the Communists from the Cabinet. They were not alone. The Radical leadership also panicked at the exodus of the faithful from their ranks into the Communist camp. From outside the coalition, pressure also came from the Socialists, a group with which the Radicals felt ideologically more comfortable.

The Socialists had reason to be angry; the Communists were using their newfound power to weaken their old rivals, and settle an old score. The vendetta dated from 1940, when the Socialists turned on their Communist allies and backed a Conservative initiative in Congress to have the Communists outlawed, a maneuver that failed only because the Radical president, Aguirre Cerda, vetoed the bill. One of the ministers in González Videla's Cabinet was Carlos Contreras Labarca, secretary-general of the Communist party. He ordered a wholesale purge of the Socialists employed in his Ministry of Transport, Development, and Public Works. One casualty was Raúl Ampuero Díaz, who had succeeded Allende as secretary-general of the Socialist party. The Communists also used their leverage to dislodge Socialists from many of the outposts of power remaining to them in the labor movement, touching off a series of violent confrontations among Communists, Socialists, and anarchists.[40]

At Liberal prodding, González Videla dissolved the Cabinet. It was the end of five months of Communist ascendancy, and the beginning of a Cabinet adagio that would see the president experiment first with an all-Radical Cabinet, and next with a Cabinet of "national concentration," which included Radicals, Liberals, Socialists, Conservatives—and military men. It was the first time a civilian government would press military men into service as political counterweights in a power-balancing act—a precedent Salvador Allende would later copy.

But fifteen months would pass before the executioner's ax finally fell on the Communists. On October 3, 1947, Communist-led coal miners at Lota (the Communists had concentrated their earliest and most effective organizing efforts on coal, nitrate, and copper miners) went on strike. The vengeance-prone Socialists sided with the government in ousting the Communists from leadership of the union and breaking the strike. Next, González Videla announced that he had uncovered evidence that the strike had been financed and directed from Moscow through the Yugoslav and Czech embassies in Santiago, and broke relations with those two countries. When the Russian ambassador announced that his embassy would assume responsibility for Czech and Yugoslav affairs, it was interpreted as a deliberate slap at Chilean national dignity. Furthermore, González Videla announced discovery of still more secret documents, this time showing that the Chilean Communists "were instruments of a worldwide plan to deprive the United States of primary materials in event of war." Chile broke diplomatic relations with Russia—only four years after becoming one of the first Latin American nations to have them.

There were widespread claims, amplified afterward, that the entire episode had been stage-managed by the Right in Chile, with U.S. encouragement, as a ploy to win economic aid from the United States, and to further its own political fortunes at the expense of the aggressive and growing Left. What is clear is that the Communist party had fomented labor strife in a two-level pattern of tactics it would repeat in Chile and elsewhere: the pursuit of power by means legal and illegal. What is equally clear is that the Right reneged on one of its major pledges: concessions to the U.S. copper companies in return for new investments.[41]

The climax of the skirmishing came on September 3, 1948, with the promulgation of law 8967, "The Law for the Permanent Defense of Democracy." Communists called it the "Accursed Law," or the "Infamous Law." Under it, the party was outlawed and barred from presenting candidates for public office or in the trade unions. Communist party publications, including the Santiago daily, El Siglo, were closed. The 26,000 registered Communist voters were stricken from the electoral rolls. More than one thousand party leaders were jailed or deported. Among them the secretary-general, the fiery Ricardo Fonseca, the man who had forced González Videla to his knees in public as the price for Communist party support in the 1946 elections; Luis Corvalán Lepe, who would eventually take over as party boss; and Volodia Teitelboim, an urbane and velvet-tongued man with a razor-sharp wit, destined to become the party's chief ideologue.[42]

How effective the law was—or how zealously it was applied—depends on who does the analyzing.[43] But most agree that enforcement was lax. What is clear is that law 8967 secured González Videla a place in the Communists party annals of infamy—Debray, for example, not only heaps abuse on this "frivolous and commonplace" man, but also subjects him to the ultimate scorn: he misspells his name.[44] It is equally clear that the law failed to stem the tide of Marxism in Chile, the custody of which now shifted irrevocably to the erratic and irascible Socialists.

An immediate consequence of the law was to produce a new split in the Socialist party. Three Socialist deputies who had voted for the law were expelled from the party.

Allende and Ampuero teamed to form a new anti-Videla party, the Popular Socialist party (PSP). In the congressional elections the following year, the PSP rolled up a vote total greater than the combined vote for the two other Socialist parties, and managed to get six deputies and one senator elected. The senator: Salvador Allende. Though he had attracted little notice outside Chile, and still not much even within the country, there were those who already detected in this tireless manipulator the earmarks of a man on the move. One such observer was González Videla himself, who at a dinner party in 1947 prophesied that Allende would soon be president of Chile.[45]

It was, in fact, a time of accelerating fragmentation of Chilean political life: in the 1945 congressional elections twelve parties competed; in 1949, eighteen; by 1953 there would be thirty-six.

Despite the fragmentation, the 1949 elections contained a message that somehow failed to register with the political bosses: the electorate plainly was disenchanted with the far Left. For the now tame-talking Radicals, it was their last big hurrah, the last time they would ever roll up the largest single vote total in an election in Chile. (And even that outcome was clouded, inasmuch as the votes of the Conservative and Traditional Conservative parties, close ideological kin, were lumped together and added up to 105,603—4,800 more than the Radicals got.) The Radicals elected thirty-four deputies and five senators. The Conservatives elected thirty-one deputies and three senators. The Liberals finished third in votes (83,000) but first in seats—thirty-three deputies and six senators. The reason for that was Chile's complicated electoral formula (a proportional representation system devised during the nineteenth century by the Belgian Victor D'Hondt). Together, the combined Conservative and Liberals, the parties of the Right, ran up 41.53 percent of the vote. There was one man on whom the lesson of disenchantment with the Left was not lost: perennial candidate Carlos Ibáñez. He formed a new right-wing party called the Agrarian-Labor party and led it to a fourth-place finish, electing fourteen deputies and five senators.

All in all, González Videla's hodgepodge coalition, the National Concentration, controlled two-thirds of both houses of Congress following the 1949 landslide, an opportunity that would soon vanish in interparty feuding and politics-fomented labor strife.

Three other developments during that administration bear mentioning. In 1940 Pedro Aguirre Cerda signed a decree laying formal claim on behalf of Chile to 482,625 square miles of Antarctic territory shaped like a piece of pie, which nearly touches the southern tip of Chile. Aguirre Cerda had done nothing about protecting the claim. Under González Videla one naval base was established there in February 1947, and a second one inaugurated by him personally one year later. (Traveler González Videla also would visit Brazil, Argentina, and the U.S. while in office.)

The second event was a time bomb with international repercussions that wouldn't be felt until the 1960s. In 1947, Chile proclaimed that its territorial sovereignty extended over two hundred miles of Pacific waters, far more than the traditional three or twelve miles of other countries. By August 18, 1952, Chile had persuaded Pacific neighbors Ecuador and Peru to sign a document in which they joined in laying claim to a similar slice of continental shelf. Little attention would be paid this eccentric claim until the "tuna wars" of the late 1960s in which both Ecuador and Peru began to seize vessels of the United States and other countries fishing within the two hundred-mile limit. By the time the 1974 Conference on the Law of the Sea rolled around, what was once a lonely Chilean initiative had become a clamor supported by a majority of the world's coastal nations.

The third development was the law, on January 8, 1949, giving women full voting rights; previously they had been able to vote only in municipal elections. Chilean women, far more liberated than the women of most Latin American nations, would emerge as an independent and powerful electoral force to be reckoned with on their own highly practical terms.

As table 10 indicates, women consistently supported the most conservative candidate in each race, a reality the parties just as consistently chose to ignore as they continued their leftward march.

TABLE 10
WOMEN'S VOTE IN PRESIDENTIAL ELECTIONS, 1952–1970

CANDIDATE	TOTAL VOTE	PERCENTAGE OF TOTAL	HOW MEN VOTED (PERCENTAGE)	WOMEN'S VOTE (PERCENTAGE)
1952				
Carlos Ibáñez	446,439	46.8%	48.4	43.0
Arturo Matte	265,357	27.8	26.0	32.0
Pedro Alfonso	190,360	19.9	19.9	20.2
Salvador Allende	51,975	5.5	5.8	4.6
1958				
Jorge Alessandri	389,909	31.6	30.2	34.1
Salvador Allende	356,493	28.9	32.4	22.3
Eduardo Frei	255,769	20.7	19.0	23.9
Luis Bossay	192,077	15.6	15.2	16.1
Antonio Zamorano	41,304	3.3	3.2	3.6

			ACTUAL VOTE	
			MEN	WOMEN
1964*				
Eduardo Frei	1,409,012	56.09	644,589	744,423
Salvador Allende	977,902	38.93	602,136	375,766

	VOTES RECEIVED	PER-CENT-AGE OF TOTAL	MEN NUMBER	%	WOMEN NUMBER	%
1970						
Radomiro Tomic	821,801	27.8	392,719	25.9	429,082	29.9
Jorge Alessandri	1,031,159	34.9	478,902	31.5	552,257	38.4
Salvador Allende	1,070,334	36.2	631,488	41.6	438,846	30.5
Void/Blank	31,505	1.1	14,882	1.0	16,623	1.1

Sources: 1952 and 1958: *Chile: Election Factbook, September 4, 1964* (Washington, D.C.: Institute for the Comparative Study of Political Systems), p. 33. 1964: Teresa Donoso, *La Epopeya de las Ollas Vacías* (Santiago: Editora Nacional Gabriela Mistral, 1974), p. 110. 1970: Dirección del Registro Electoral, "Elección Ordinaria de Presidente de la República," Viernes 4 de Septiembre de 1970 (a mimeographed report).

By the time the presidential elections of 1952 approached, it was plain to all but the professional politicians that the Chilean public was fed up with political parties. Historian Galdames notes that the end of the Radical era coincided with a "marked loss of prestige of the political parties which, in the majority opinion of the country, had demonstrated the incapacity to orient and guide national aspirations."[46]

Conservative commentator Mario Arnello concurred: "The decomposition of the political parties is a national drama, because it is not only destroying the parties themselves, but the Chilean juridical system, democratic life, the system, freedom, the self-sufficiency which great Chileans, and especially Don Diego Portales, had given us."[47]

Into this breach marched seventy-five-year-old Carlos Ibáñez, the military man turned public figure who touted himself as a man above politics—although his name had not only appeared twice on the presidential ballot since leaving La Moneda, he was also then serving as a senator under the auspices of a party he had created, the Agrarian-Labor party. To a country shell shocked by the long siege of increasingly strident partisan politics, Ibáñez held out the nostalgic hope of a return to the order and stability of a quarter of a century earlier, when he had ruled the country with a firm and strong autocratic hand. He campaigned with a broom and he promised a clean sweep.

Deprived of the counsel of the crafty allies they had banished into illegality, the Radicals had to content themselves with heading a coalition that included a pair of political apprentices: the Falange (Christian Democrats) and the Democratic Conservatives (Social Christians). The Liberals and the Traditionalist Conservatives supported a businessman-politician, Arturo Matte Larraín. The Socialists ran their own man, who made his debut on the national electoral stage: Salvador Allende Gossens.[48]

Ibáñez won by the biggest margin accorded any candidate since the voters had swept Arturo Alessandri to power in 1932 with a resounding mandate to end the disorder and disarray in public affairs. Ibáñez polled 446,439 votes, 46.79 percent of the total. Conservative candidate Arturo Matte trailed at a distance: 265,357 votes, or 27.81 percent of the total. The Radical coalition candidate was Pedro Enrique Alfonso Barrios, a moderate who had served in the Cabinets of three Radical presidents. He had to settle for 190,360 votes, a poor 19.95 percent of the total. The only authentic "leftist" in the race was Allende, who managed to attract only 51,975 votes, a paltry 5.45 percent.

Ibáñez had promised a clean sweep. What he actually gave the country was a regime of unprecedented corruption reaching to the very pinnacle of power. The economic mess deepened, and when an attempt was made to cure the politically created economic ills, that attempt would die in the morass of even more politics. On the political front there was disintegration instead of consolidation: as noted, 1953, a year after Ibáñez came to power on the crest of a tidal wave repudiating incessant politicking, an unprecedented thirty-six parties appeared to woo the electorate. The results were predictable: the voters once again backed the apolitical mavericks rallying around Ibáñez.[49] But far from achieving stability, the Ibáñez administration was a period of administrative roulette: Ibáñez reshuffled his Cabinet a dizzying forty-one times in the first thirty-three months of office, and finally resorted to "apolitical" figures to see him through to a harrowing end.[50]

Out of the disarray of this period would emerge the two forces destined to compete for power in a political minuet that would be often eerie and would have been endlessly fascinating, had it not become so deadly. The two were the Popular Action Front (FRAP—Frente de Acción Popular) and the Christian Democrats.[51] FRAP,[52] a fatally flawed alliance of the parties of the far Left, would succeed, despite itself, in eventually electing Allende president, on his fourth try, and then in incinerating itself once power had been achieved. The Christian Democrats represented themselves as the one best hope of thwarting the far Left.

The longer the Christian Democrats remained on the political scene, however, the more they looked and sounded and talked like FRAP, and many—perhaps most—of their prominent leaders never were able to shake off their deep infatuation with it.

The result was a love-hate relationship between the two that was sometimes a dance and sometimes a duel, suspending them in a trance-like state of mutual hypnosis. At the end they destroyed each other, reluctantly, ruefully, and with it, the synthesis of social thought and action each side believed possible on its own terms. The synthesis was never more than an illusion, though, because one side believed the forms and terms of democracy could be twisted and bent indefinitely and still survive to serve its utopian aims, and the other twisted and bent them because it knew that those forms and terms had to be destroyed if ever they were to achieve their aims.

Salvador Allende surfaced on the national electoral stage at that time, but only after he had again (the third time in eight years) crossed party lines in a byzantine maneuver of a sort that already was becoming his political trademark.[53] The Popular Socialist party, which Allende, together with Raúl Ampuero, had formed a few years earlier, resisted Allende's efforts to have himself nominated and decided, instead, to support Ibáñez's candidacy. Ampuero, a moderate on the Socialist spectrum—and unlike Allende, anti-Communist—also maneuvered Allende out of his job as party secretary-general.

Allende bolted the party and returned to the Socialist party of Chile. Next he persuaded this party—until then, the socialist faction most bitterly opposed to the Communists—not only to present him as its presidential candidate, but to accept Communist party support as well.

In that, he had competition: Ibáñez also wooed Communist support by promising, if elected, to work to repeal the hated Permanent Law for the Defense of Democracy, a pledge he dawdled in keeping until the very end of his term. Even then, he kept it as only part of a scheme to block the powerful candidacy of Jorge Alessandri,[54] the reluctant Abraham of the Right. But then the Communists, still underground, concentrated most of their efforts on Allende's candidacy, with an eye less to 1952 than to building a base for the future, as befitted a party that had already demonstrated the "patience of ants and political flight of eagles."

Allende left behind in the faction he cofounded and then deserted several of the men who would later play vital roles in his own presidency: Carlos Altamirano Orrego, the well-born radical of the Socialist movement; Clodomiro Almeyda Medina, later a self-styled Maoist, who served Allende as foreign minister; Felipe Herrera Lane,[55] who went on to become president of the Washington-based Inter-American Development Bank, an agency which owes its existence in large measure to Chilean initiatives.[56]

Altamirano and Almeyda both would later merge to the left of Allende; that they would then be willing to support the candidacy of an ex-dictator and military man is a measure of the ideological aimlessness of the Chilean Socialist movement. Unlike the Communists, superb and patient strategists who demonstrated repeatedly their willingness to sacrifice immediate tactical aims to long-range strategic advantage, the Socialists were the party of the manipulators and the hotheads, of impromptu decisions and a dangerous admixture of recklessness and rigidity. Altamirano, a petulant martinet who started his career as a lawyer for an American-owned power company, was en route to consolidating his career on the party's extreme left, where recklessness and rigidity ruled. Almeyda applied a cooler style to comparably incandescent ideas, and Allende was, as indicated, the high prince of manipulation.

Faced with rampant inflation and a foreign credit squeeze, Ibáñez, midway through his term, hired a U.S. management consulting firm to advise him on the economy. The Klein-Saks Mission, as it was called, began its two-year work in September 1955 and achieved relatively impressive results in a short time through a severe austerity program. It included loose wage controls and looser price controls, a sharp reduction of government spending, a crackdown on tax evaders, and a number of fiscal measures including the lifting of foreign exchange controls. In 1955, living costs had risen 83.8 percent; in 1956, the increase was 37.7 percent, and in 1957, it was down to 17.3 percent.

Such stringent measures, however, could not long survive in the volatile political climate that had been created in Chile. Until January 1956, workers had been given an automatic pay raise equivalent to 100 percent of the cost of living the previous year. In accord with a Klein-Saks recommendation, those automatic increases were cut in half. In 1956, salaries rose 30 percent and prices 37 percent,[57] a modest wage-price spread compared with what Chileans had experienced already, and a trifling compared with what would come, but it was enough to aggravate a problem complicated by the convergence of competing international currents.

The International Monetary Fund (IMF)—then the hobgoblin of the Left in Latin America for the austerity of the fiscal policies it imposed on countries as the price for its financial support, and indispensable credit worthiness certifications—joined United States institutions in extending $75 million in credits to Chile. Arrayed against the "monetarists" of the IMF were the "structuralist" economists then on the ascendancy in other international agencies, many of them later associated with the Alliance for Progress, many more based in UN and OAS agencies in Santiago.

Despite the evident progress, labor turmoil escalated in 1955 and 1956, much of it fomented by the Communist-dominated Confederation of Labor (CUT—Central Única de Trabajadores), which in 1953 claimed 300,000 members in 35 national federations and associations, and 913 unions.[58] Amid such powerful crosscurrents, the precarious coalition that put Ibáñez in power disintegrated, and he turned increasingly to the Right and to independents for support. They would prove

themselves—first with Ibáñez, then, more disastrously for their ultimate cause, with Alessandri in the next administration—unequal to the
burden of persevering with austerity. Controls were gradually relaxed,
and in 1958 inflation went up to 32.5 percent.

In spite of the economic crunch and labor unrest, the electorate
remained indifferent to politics. The 1956 municipal elections attracted
the lowest turnout of any national elections in modern times. Table 11
traces voter turnout for the years 1950–70.

TABLE 11
VOTER TURNOUT, 1950–1970

YEAR	TYPE OF ELECTION	TOTAL[a] POPULATION	ELIGIBLE[b] VOTERS	REGISTERED VOTERS	VOTES CAST	PER- CENTAGE[c]
1970	Presidential	9,276,561	na	3,539,747	2,954,799	83.47%
1969	Congressional	8,999,588	na	3,244,892	2,406,129	74.15
1967	Municipal	8,565,657	3,649,009	3,073,992	2,321,184	75.51
1965	Congressional	8,152,916	3,543,970	2,948,461	2,353,123	79.81
1964	Presidential	7,954,066	3,501,943	2,915,121	2,530,697	86.81
1963	Municipal	7,735,990	3,459,919	2,570,291	2,070,188	80.54
1961	Congressional	7,394,187	3,777,378	1,858,980	1,385,676	74.54
1960	Municipal	7,374,712	3,333,472	1,769,681	1,229,503	69.48
1958	Presidential	6,984,507	3,244,064	1,497,902	1,250,350	83.47
1957	Congressional	6,739,699	3,201,891	1,284,154	878,229	68.39
1956	Municipal	6,488,483	3,152,486	1,184,882	731,449	61.73
1953	Municipal	6,083,211	2,906,233	1,106,709	759,379	68.82
1953	Congressional	"	"	1,100,027	786,811	71.53
1952	Presidential	6,162,000[d]	2,871,358	1,105,029	957,102	86.61
1950	Municipal	6,062,000[d]	2,802,565	833,460	619,724	74.36

Sources: Chile: Election Factbook, September 4, 1964 (Washington, D.C.: Institute for the Compar-
ative Study of Political Systems), p. 15; Garrido Rojas, in *Chile: A Critical Survey* (Santiago:
Institute of General Studies, 1972), p. 198; *CORFO: Geografía Económica de Chile* (Santiago:
Editorial Nascimento, 1965), pp. 369–70; *Estudio Social de América Latina* (Washington, D.C.:
Unión Panamericana, 1964), pp. 11–17. Garrido Rojas uses figures taken from the Santiago-based
Latin American Center for Demographic Studies (CELADE). In cases of conflict for the period before
1967 between the *Factbook* figures and those contained in *Estadísticas Electorales, 1925–1969*
(Oficina de Informaciones, Chilean Senate, Boletín de Información General, no. 66, June 25, 1970), I
have opted for the latter.

[a] The 1970 and 1960 population figures are based on census data as given in *Nueva Enciclopedia de
Chile* (Argentina: Ediciones Copihue, Fotomecánica Futura SRL, Ediciones Libra, 1974), 1:337–38.
The figures for noncensus years represent an extrapolation based on demographic growth.
[b] Estimated.
[c] Percentage of registered voters actually voting.
[d] Approximations given by Garrido Rojas in *Chile: A Critical Survey* (Santiago: Institute of General
Studies, 1972), p. 198. The corresponding percentage figures for voter turnout are also approximations.

The winners in 1956 were the Right, but because they remained divided, they were also the losers. The two traditional parties of the Right polled 27.98 percent of the total vote; the Radicals took 23.81 percent; the fledgling Christian Democrats 6.37 percent. The Socialists were still divided: Allende's Socialist Party of Chile was the smaller, by far, of the two, collecting only 10,563 votes to 72,359 for the Popular Socialist party; taken together, the two accounted for 11.98 percent of the total. The two factions finally patched up their differences the following year, joining forces on July 7, 1957, after suffering a shellacking in the parliamentary elections that April. The two Socialist parties saw their share of the vote drop that April to 10.68 percent (from 1953's 14.10 percent), and the leftist coalition—the still clandestine Communists, the two Socialist parties, and the tiny People's Democratic party—lost sixteen of the thirty-seven seats they had held in the Chamber of Deputies.

Ibáñez's own Agrarian-Labor party began its tailspin into political oblivion, dropping from twenty-three to eleven Chamber seats. The Radicals bounced back in the 1957 election, capturing 21.47 percent of the vote (up from 13.30 percent in 1953), and regained their position as the top party in the Chamber (with thirty-six seats).

But the election was especially significant for another reason: it marked the emergence of two men who would tower over the political landscape for years to come. One was Eduardo Frei, who paced the explosive growth of the Falange party (which went from five to sixteen Chamber seats in that election); Frei himself rolled up the highest vote total of any senatorial candidate in Santiago (sixty thousand). The other emerging figure was Jorge Alessandri, the businessman son of the former president who now found himself reluctantly drawn deeper into politics. Alessandri, making his debut as a senatorial candidate, led a resurgence of the Liberal party, which placed a solid second behind the Radicals among the seventeen parties vying in the 1957 elections. The Liberals did half again as well as they had in 1953, pushing their share of the vote from 10.90 percent in 1953 to 15.34 percent in 1957.

In both cases—Falange and Liberals—the voters seemed to be leaning more to the man than to the party, catapulting both into a confrontation neither could escape.

RESURRECTION OF THE RIGHT

The Chilean bourgeoisie, one of the least stupid in the world, defends itself by opening its arms to its rival. . . .

Régis Debray[59]

Jorge Alessandri Rodríguez had little taste for public life and even less for occupying the presidency. He was, in fact, the antithesis not only of

his gregarious and garrulous father but also of anyone else of any prominence in Chilean political life. His own public life to this point—
finance minister for two years (1947–49) in González Videla's government, deputy for four years (1926–30), and now a freshman senator—
was a reluctant concession to noblesse oblige.

A civil engineer by training, Alessandri was a businessman by preference, and an eminently good one. Under his guidance, the Compañía
Manufacturera de Papeles y Cartones (Paper and Cardboard Manufacturing Company) became one of the most modern and efficient pulp
manufacturers in Latin America, the largest exporter of newsprint and
other paper products in the region, and Latin America's largest cellulose
plant. Alessandri also was active in banking, insurance, and other businesses.

Tall, stately, taciturn, Jorge Alessandri had a reputation as an irascible
man who not only disliked politics but also detested speechmaking and
large crowds. There were those who remarked that he even disliked
small crowds: he never married. Austere and unimpeachably honest, he
lived in stark simplicity in a small bachelor apartment on the Plaza de
Armas in downtown Santiago, and walked to and from most of his
appointments. He continued both traditions—the small apartment and
walking to and from the "office"—even after he was elected president of
the republic.

Chile was ripe for such a man. But fate needed to intervene for the
man to accept his destiny.

Following the 1957 parliamentary elections, the buoyant and purpose-
ful young men of the Christian Democrats swashbuckled into prominence as the wave of the future, and the gangling, earnest, and eloquent
Eduardo Frei was their best hope of making the future happen now. The
Liberals, themselves resurgent, tilted strongly for supporting Frei's candidacy. Even the Traditional Conservatives wanted him, and asked, as a
sole condition, that he give them a letter asking for their support—a
written assurance, of sorts, that they would not then be forgotten in the
later councils of government. Frei declined, confident that they would
have to back him anyway to head off the victory of a leftist coalition.

Within Liberal ranks, there was one group with a different idea. They
were headed by a senator, Raúl Marín Balmaceda, and they wanted
Alessandri. Marín launched a movement to draft Alessandri, and Alessandri insisted stubbornly that he was not interested. Finally, on the eve
of the Liberal convention, Marín went to Alessandri's quarters to plead
with him personally. Alessandri persisted in his refusal. Undaunted,
Marín said he would offer Alessandri's name in nomination anyway,
and, as he was leaving, added, "Remember El Cid—he won his best
battles after death."

At the convention, Marín made a brilliant speech in support of Alessandri's candidacy—then collapsed to the floor and died. The event stunned and electrified the convention, which went on to acclaim Alessandri's candidacy. The event also deeply affected Alessandri.[60] He accepted—the third Alessandri to become a presidential candidate, and of the three, the only one who did it with deep, melancholy misgivings.[61]

The 1957 congressional elections should have portended the advent of the most powerful leftist coalition yet, or at the very minimum, the inevitability of such a coalition. The Radicals had rallied in 1957 to recapture their place as the country's largest single party; the Socialists, though now reunited, had fizzled the last time at the polls; the Communists were just beginning to regroup after their long political exile, although in the relaxed environment of the previous six years, the Communists had been anything but idle or actually exiled. Besides, the Left faced the threat of a triple alliance that would decimate it: the newly emerging Christian Democrats with the two traditional parties of the Right, behind the candidacy of Eduardo Frei. In such circumstances, a coalition of the Left, organized by the preeminent Radicals, on their terms, was a natural.

Only this time, the Communists and Socialists wanted it on their own terms, and the coalition never happened. The Socialists and Communists decided to go all out behind Salvador Allende, a decision facilitated when they saw the opposition divide into two irreconcilable camps, one supporting Frei, the other Alessandri. But the Communists first flirted with the endlessly ambitious Radicals, extracting from them the votes they needed in Congress to repeal the anti-Communist Law for the Permanent Defense of Democracy, a law enacted ten years earlier by many of the same Radical senators and deputies. That accomplished—in the dying days of the Ibáñez regime—they closed ranks with the Socialists.

That left the Radicals to go it alone for the first time in twenty years, with a man who was, in so many ways, as much a messenger of their death as a symbol of it: Luis Bossay Leiva. Senator Bossay was an apt target for Communist blandishments then, and he would remain so down to the final funeral days of Radicalism in the Allende delirium.[62]

Both the Conservatives and the Liberals finally backed Alessandri, while Frei had the support of his Christian Democrats plus a smattering of miniparties.

There was a fifth contender, notable chiefly for the confusion he would contribute to later analysis of the outcome. His name was Antonio Zamorano, a former priest who had won election to the Chamber of Deputies the year before under the banner of FRAP, the far-left coalition.

In such circumstances, the campaign of 1958 was the wildest free-for-all in the history of Chilean presidential elections, a classic of divide-and-conquer that flushed the Communist party with optimism. The outcome very nearly rewarded its hopes (see table 12). Alessandri nosed out Allende thanks largely to the women's vote (table 10).

TABLE 12
RESULTS OF THE PRESIDENTIAL ELECTION SEPTEMBER 4, 1958

CANDIDATE	TOTAL VALID VOTES	PERCENTAGE OF TOTAL VOTE (VALID + THOSE VOIDED)
Alessandri	389,909	31.2
Allende	356,493	28.5
Frei	255,769	20.5
Bossay	192,077	15.4
Zamorano	41,304	3.3
Void/blank votes	14,798	1.1
TOTAL VOTES	1,250,350	100.0
Not voting	247,552	16.5
Total registered	1,497,902	

Source: Estadísticas Electorales, 1925–1969 (Oficina de Informaciones, Chilean Senate, Boletín de Información General, no. 66, June 25, 1970), p. 64.

To come so close, and yet be so far, filled Marxists then—and for years to come—with something resembling apoplexy at the mere mention of Zamorano's name. Labrousse said flat out that Zamorano was "bought";[63] even non-Marxists accepted the notion that the Cura of Catapilco (Priest of Catapilco, the small town in Aconcagua Province about seventy-five miles northwest of Santiago where he came from) had cost Allende the election. Gil, for example, also says flat out that "if Zamorano had not run, Allende would have won," and adds that it is "logical" to assume that Allende would have picked up Zamorano's votes. Finally, he adds that Zamorano's votes came from "small farmers and slumdwellers, the ones who had elected him deputy in 1957 under the FRAP banner."[64]

The episode bears examining because it is one of the two mythologies created by those elections with repercussions in the future.

To begin with, Zamorano ran a poor fifth in his own home province of Aconcagua, polling a scant 1,530 of the 29,293 votes cast in that province, so the people who supported him in 1957 deserted him in 1958. Next, the Cura of Catapilco got 17,000 of his votes in heavily urbanized Santiago and Valparaíso provinces. Next, Zamorano fared best in rightist strongholds, poorest in leftist bastions.[65] And finally, Zamorano rolled up his highest total (7,206 votes, or 19.8 percent of the provincial total) in Talca, and his lowest two totals in two of the three provinces (Arauco and Concepción, 0.4 and 0.7 percent, respectively) where Allende was compiling his best results (47.6 and 40.6 percent, respectively; Zamorano didn't do very well, either, in Magallanes, where Allende scored highest of all; the former priest got a paltry 1.1 percent of the votes; Allende, in that Socialist stronghold at the icy tip of Chile, a thumping 47.8 percent). It is interesting that Talca was the *only* province in 1958 where none of the three front runners managed to come up to his own national share of the vote, strongly suggesting that Zamorano was, in fact, pulling votes away from *all* of them.

The second myth was based on the shaky premise that the 1957 and 1958 elections had signaled the rebirth of voter confidence in the party system—and that the Christian Democrats were the party of the future.[66] The latter was a conceit the Christian Democrats not only fostered but came to believe themselves, leading them into the politics of arrogance and exclusivity, a game they played with growing ferocity and diminishing returns. In point of fact, the Christian Democrats succeeded in 1958 in the only way—with a single exception—that they ever would: by compounding the fracture between Right and Left, and usually with an eye to finishing off the wounded Right.

The 1958 elections did not mark the return to a party system; they marked the irrevocable division of the country along ideological lines, Right and Left. In that ambiance, the political parties became the mere spear carriers of contending forces in an ideological war. In Chile, as elsewhere in the world, the Right failed to devise an effective message, a set of positive principles to explain its cause, and fell back, increasingly, on the politics of skirmishing and retreat. At the end the rightists leaned on an aging and unwilling general to save the political and economic institutions they had themselves crafted.

The Left had the message of Marxism, of salvation from the imperfections of a "capitalist" economy and its bourgeois political trappings, imperfections to which they devoted their best efforts to deepening beyond repair. They disagreed on tactics but not on goals, and so it was relatively easy for them to agree on a candidate, since he was merely an agent they would manipulate in the service of a prefabricated revolution.

The Christian Democrats, ostensibly, occupied a position between the two natural enemies. In reality, they would demonstrate repeatedly, beginning in the Alessandri administration, when they moved to the left of the Radicals to oppose him, that they thought of the Right as their real enemies. They advertised themselves as a "democratic alternative" to the Left, but embraced so many of the same ideals—and frequently, so many of the same political tactics—that what they finally did was join in obliterating the real alternative. Along the way, they disintegrated into a cacophonous chimera.

The elections of 1958 should have destroyed another myth, but they didn't; namely, that the Right still controlled the political destinies of the countryside. This power was supposedly based on the sway of *patrones*, the landed gentry, over the peons in their employ. There were three things wrong with that fashionable legend, a favorite of American political scientists and journalists—and, of course, of the Chilean Left—down to Allende's day.[67]

The first is a function of pre-Pinochet Chilean electoral law. Voters could only vote in the district where they were registered, and that excluded, almost automatically, the *voluntarios* or *afuerinos*, the migrant laborers who, as noted in chapter 2, accounted for 35 percent of all field hands in the Central Valley as late as 1961. Add to that the fact that illiterates did not become eligible to vote until 1971, and the size of this supposed horde of human cattle, being driven to the polls to do their masters' bidding (even in secret balloting), diminishes even further. The 1952 census pegged overall illiteracy at close to 20 percent, but at 40 percent in the rural sector, the one under consideration.[68] Thus relatively few farm hands were even theoretically eligible to vote in the first place, still another consideration overlooked in the facile description of rural "fiefdoms."

Next, there is the matter of sheer numbers. As tables 2 and 6 show, the bulk of the land was in relatively few hands, but there were, according to an exhaustive 1960 study, 340,000 families with farms of their own, or fully 53 percent of the agricultural labor force. Even the small holders, as Marx pointed out over a century ago, are not easily mobilized for "class warfare." In the specific case of Chile, as the authors of the report containing these observations point out: "Those independent proprietors who are, in reality, 'family farmers,' entrepreneurs selling most of their production regularly on the market and calculating their incomes in terms of profits and losses, tend to consider themselves part of the propertied classes; they identify their interests with the landowning class in particular, and private property rights in general."[69] This would then leave somewhere around 300,000 landless laborers, including the patron-tied sharecroppers. Illiteracy among these was, of course, much higher than for other social groups—at the 40 percent level indicated earlier. The conclusion, then, is that the landed gentry controlled far fewer votes than it was routinely claimed.

Third, there is the record itself. As noted, Ibáñez won the countryside in 1952. In 1958 Allende finished first in only two of the sixteen provinces from Aconcagua in the north to Chiloé in the south, where agriculture provided most jobs—but he finished second in ten more of them. James Petras and Maurice Zeitlin, authors of the aforementioned report, show that Allende consistently harvested more than 40 percent of the male vote in agricultural municipalities where landless peasants predominated; Robert R. Kaufman, in his invaluable study of the politics of Chilean agriculture, notes that "by 1956, much of the peasant vote had shifted to the FRAP, and in 1958, it nearly provided the margin of victory for the FRAP presidential candidate, Salvador Allende."[70] Furthermore, if one assumes that Frei, Bossay, and Allende were all candidates of the Left—at the indisputable minimum, all three stood for programs unpalatable to large landowners—then it is even more revealing that these three outpolled Alessandri, the "oligarch's" choice, in all sixteen of these provinces, and in almost all of them by margins of two to one or more. If the big landowners were so "adept in the exercise of their influence in rural districts so as to assure the election of liberal or conservative candidates"—as Gil, for example, asserted (p. 94)—this sort of thing obviously would not happen.

Even the notion of oligarchy was two parts myth and one part misrepresentation to one part grain of truth. Because *oligarchy*, as political scientist James L. Payne showed in an innovative study a few years ago,[71] is a term honored in the breach in writing on Latin America. Chile, where the term was less applicable than perhaps anywhere else in Latin America, did not escape this form of ideological tar and feathering, even from those who acknowledged that it was, at best, wrong to use the term uncautiously if the term is to have any meaning at all.[72] In Chile, the "oligarchy" forfeited decisive political power with the appearance of the so-called liberal Republic in 1861; by 1920 they were permanently on the defensive, fighting a rear-guard action. Big landowners had, of course, survived, but, as noted earlier, these men were closer to the traditions of the patricians than the caudillos and despots marauding the rest of Latin America. They were the architects of liberal democracy, and later its ideologues of change, rational and orderly change, but change in the deepest sense. Furthermore, the balance of power was shifting against them even within their own political ranks, and so too were the patterns of landowning.[73] *Latifundistas*, big landowners, there were, but a special breed uncommon elsewhere in Latin America; oligarchs there were not.

The independent voting patterns of the countryside were, then, the product not of crass manipulation of defenseless voters, but of the same spirit of conservatism that characterizes men who work the soil everywhere. The change in Chile came with the disruption of the old life-cycle patterns of land occupancy, and their replacement by peasant settlements and collective farms—and the raucous politics that preceded those changes. The man who lived and died on a parcel of land was soon outnumbered, when not displaced altogether, by others for whom that parcel of land was no more than circumstance: an immediate opportunity, or a new and sorrowful deception.

As so often happened in Chile, it was the Right, and not the Left, which would deliver the final coup de grâce to the landed gentry, for it was the Right, and not the Left, which would initiate agrarian reform.

The countryside was not, however, the first priority that awaited the new president. Jorge Alessandri found a country in a state of near collapse, and approached the job he did not want with the energy and resolve he had always brought to his private enterprises. At sixty-two Alessandri was at the peak of his intellectual powers and perception of the country's problems. Among these problems:

- The inflationary spiral was gaining momentum again, increasing the pressure on wage earners caught in the wage-price squeeze.
- Unemployment had climbed to 150,000, the consequence of stagnating industrial production (down 10 percent in three years).
- The 1959 budget of $465 million, which he inherited, was unbalanced by an awesome $242.5 million.
- Food production failed to keep pace with a rapidly expanding population, pushing the country's bill for food imports steadily upward[74] (see table 1, tracing the growing farm deficit).

Alessandri marshaled a decisive majority in Congress by recruiting Radical support and he moved vigorously, asking for—and getting—virtual dictatorial powers over the economy. Less than six months after he had taken office, Congress empowered him to undertake drastic measures which included streamlining government-owned or -financed agencies, and tax and monetary reform (in 1960, the peso was abandoned and the escudo, worth one thousand pesos, erected in its place, on a par with the dollar). The cuts were counterbalanced by a spurt of spending on public works (paving the Pan American Highway, for example, was finished—3,128 kilometers, roughly two thousand miles, from Arica in the north to Puerto Montt in the south) and housing (the biggest housing program ever yet which would see 150,000 units constructed during his six-year term). He also got an important boost from the international situation: copper prices by mid-March of 1959 stood at 31.5 cents per pound, 6.5 cents above the 1958 low, at a time when each one-cent difference represented $10 million in income for Chile. But copper would provide a brief bonanza.[75]

The economy responded quickly: industrial production in 1959 increased 14 percent. Labor unrest subsided, unemployment dropped, the budget was balanced, and foreign credit began flowing in. On August 10, 1959, *Time* wrote:

> No ordinary business notice was the letter posted by the Finance Ministry in Santiago last week, urging government contractors to stop in and pick up their monthly checks—cashable immediately. In Chile, where contractors are resigned to waiting years for the government to pay, it was a sign of real progress. In the nine months since paper tycoon Jorge Alessandri, 63, moved in as president, on a free-enterprise platform, the long-time degeneration of the national economy has been halted, even reversed in spots.[76]

Nor did he stick labor with the bill for recovery. Wages were hiked an average of 32.5 percent before he initiated the austerity program, with the result that prices jumped 22.2 percent in Alessandri's first six months in office—a premeditated rise, he said.

"It was a social and political impossibility," he said, "to permit rising living costs to be thrown totally on the shoulders of the working classes." But by June 1959, costs had risen only 2.1 percent, compared with 4.7 percent in January, following the massive pay adjustments.[77]

A balanced budget was a phenomenon not seen in spendthrift Chile since 1949, and the author of the earlier accomplishment was the self-same Jorge Alessandri, then finance minister. In fact, from the time the Left ascended to power in Chile in 1938 until the Pinochet years, the country would live within its national means only five times: the two years when Alessandri was finance minister (1947–49), and again during the first three years of his presidency.

The voters got their chance to react in April 1960, eighteen months after he took office. They gave him a resounding vote of confidence: parties supporting him collected 607,000 of the 1,173,000 votes cast in municipal elections. Of the seventeen parties contesting the election, the Radicals, basking in the reflected glory of their shift to the right behind Alessandri, increased their share of the vote from 1958's 15.5 percent to 20.93 percent, to recapture their political primacy. The Christian Democrats, who had opposed Alessandri from the start, saw their share of the vote drop from 1958's 20.70 percent to 15.55 percent, a debacle those presumably committed to the invincibility of the Christian Democrats would manage to represent as a triumph.[78] To make the message of repudiation of the Left crystal-clear, the voters also dumped the far Left, chopping the Socialist-Communist share of the vote from 28.85 percent in 1958 to 19.82 in 1960. The left had but a single consolation: 1960 marked the return to the ballot of the Communists and the resumption of their long and patient march to power.

Nature dealt Alessandri's efforts the first blow, with a series of violent earthquakes in May 1960 (see note 33, chapter 1, for details). As noted, that catastrophe cost an already staggering country half a billion dollars, nearly an eighth of the country's entire gross national product.

Man did the rest. To boost the economy, Alessandri had picked Roberto Vergara Herrera, a civil engineer who had been chief of finances in CORFO and headed the development corporation's New York office in 1940. Taking his cue from Alessandri, Vergara cracked down hard on the causes of inflation, zeroing in along the way on waste in government-run businesses. The Left, diametrically opposed to such austere measures, unleashed an unmerciful attack on Vergara, dubbing him Ruca (slang meaning worn-out or has-been). Labor problems, spearheaded by the Communist-dominated Confederation of Labor (CUT), finally forced Vergara to quit in 1960.

The labor strife came although Alessandri—and Vergara—had succeeded in holding prices stable from the middle of 1959 through most of 1960 for the first time in twenty years, that is, since the Left had first come to full power. In 1958, strikes had cost 196,000 man-days. In 1959, Alessandri's first full year in office, the number slipped slightly below that. The dam burst in 1960, despite the spectacular vote of confidence in the April elections, and despite the success to that point of phase one (stabilization) of his two-phase economic program (stabilization, then development). An epidemic of strikes swept the country. In 1960, strikes cost the economy 3.3 million man-days, and in 1961, matters got worse.[79]

Inevitably, such pressures buckled economic as well as political resistance. Rising wages were followed by rising prices. In 1960, Alessandri's second year in office, prices had increased a meager 7.5 percent. But in 1961 the inflationary spiral started another steep climb. It was the beginning of a climb from which Chile would not recover for a quarter of a century, a phenomenon with "incalculable effects on Chilean society and the body politic,"[80] and it was a spiral which would lead to endless tinkering and tampering with the economy in an atmosphere of increasing demagoguery. Even the century-old Conservative party, the bastion of principles and Portalian rectitude, would join in the prostitution of politics to immediate advantage.[81]

"The Right was blind because it wasn't politically smart," the Chilean intellectual and later Alessandri collaborator Jaime Guzmán Errázuriz commented. "It joined in the cacophony of demagoguery, competing in promises with the parties of the Left, because it thought that was the one best way of holding power. At the end, it even repudiated Alessandri himself."[82]

In both judgments, the Right was wrong, as its later slide into oblivion would demonstrate.

Three other aspects of the Alessandri administration require comment, because all three also give the lie to what might be termed "reflexive wisdom" regarding regimes of the Right. The first is that, despite labor unrest, much of it politically inspired, Alessandri's government was the freest and least autocratic of any in the twentieth century. During his six years in office, Alessandri only once resorted to the power to suspend civil liberties, and that was following the 1960 earthquakes. He declared, briefly, a state of emergency, the least drastic of the measures available to Chilean presidents.

The others were, in large measure, in response to the reformist euphoria of the times generated by the proclamation, in August 1961 at Punta del Este, Uruguay, of the Alliance for Progress. The fact is that rightist-ruled Chile was, with the possible exceptions of Venezuela and Colombia, the Latin nation which moved most energetically to effect Alliance-blessed reforms.

The first of these was to introduce in Chile long-range economic planning as an instrument of state policy. The ten-year plan (1961–70) anticipated investment over the decade of $10 billion—55 percent from the public sector, both the Chilean government and international lenders—to boost the country's gross national product by 55 percent by the end of 1970.[83] The plan was unveiled in January 1961, and approved subsequently by the so-called Committee of Wise Men created by the Alliance.

Next, the Alessandri administration enacted the most sweeping, and effective, package of tax reforms the country had ever seen, including improved collection procedures. The government's program, first submitted to Congress in 1961, included higher taxes on land—the rightist-sheltered sacred cow of reflexive wisdom—inheritance, gifts, sales, business volume, and others. The result was that fiscal revenues increased by 15 percent between 1961 and 1962, and Chile already had the third-highest ratio of tax income to gross national product in Latin America.[84]

Finally, Alessandri introduced agrarian reform in Chile. In 1960 the Caja de Colonización (Colonization Fund), first established in 1928, was reorganized and revitalized. In 1961 it distributed 300,000 hectares. On November 15, 1962, law 15020, the Agrarian Reform Law, became final. Cynics would protest that it was a sop offered by oligarchs to stave off a massive mutiny of land-hungry peasants (presumably the same ones meekly obeying the electoral whims of the land barons); the fact remains that legislation admired as a model throughout Latin America was proposed by a rightist president to a Congress controlled by forces loyal to him.[85]

Actually, the Right was collaborating in a self-destructive myth in accepting the then fashionable notion that agrarian reform was the answer to the growing food crisis. As table 5 (chapter 2) shows, Chile did suffer an acute problem of land distribution. But this was a social problem and not, essentially, one of efficiency.

Not even the social issues were clear, [86] a point repeatedly missed by Alliance planners and most commentators when they dutifully trotted out statistics and landholding patterns. It was, however, a point well understood by the radicals of land reform, such as Jacques Chonchol, who would supervise agrarian reform for an unsuspecting Frei and later a grateful Allende. "In the last analysis," Chonchol wrote, in one of his little-noticed treatises on the subject, "agrarian reform is not a techni-cal process, but basically a political process."[87] The well meaning, in a word, viewed agrarian reform as the answer to a social and economic problem; the cynics capitalized on their innocence as a road to power.

In Chile, the fundamental, and fundamentally overlooked, cause of sagging food output was price policies penalizing farmers to favor city dwellers. The supposedly powerful landowners watched helplessly while artificially low ceilings were kept on farm prices as a means of courting the favor of burgeoning urban populations, a practice perfected by the Radicals and accelerated in later years. Systematically robbed of incentives, farmers produced less. Agrarian reform caused output to sag even further, as experience would show and as power-conscious manip-ulators such as Chonchol already knew it would.

Alessandri knew he was gambling when he chose to put stability ahead of development in his economic strategies: banking inflation's fires almost inevitably puts a crimp in production. Yet production did increase and the gross national product, which had slowed to a snail's pace of growth barely keeping pace with population, increased by an impressive 7 percent in 1961. However, strikes and tax reform were taking a heavy toll by 1962, triggering a huge flight of capital and a slowdown of production.[88]

The government stepped up foreign borrowing to offset a drain on its international reserves and to finance a sharp rise in imports to buy raw materials and foreign capital goods for home industry.[89] The 1963 bud-get leaned on foreign loans for the financing of nearly half of greatly enlarged public investments, but was able to pay for the rest from a large (107 million escudos, slightly over $100 million) budget surplus, a van-ishing species in Chilean life.

In the congressional elections of April 1961 the voters rendered a confusing verdict. With fewer parties competing than in 1961 (ten instead of seventeen), all six major parties gained—the three backing Alessandri (Radicals, Liberals, and Conservatives); the solo Christian Democrats; and the two on the far left, Communists and Socialists. All of them picked up a percentage point and-a-half or less over 1961, except for the Communists, who gained 2.2 points. But the Communists were the big winners in still another way: they went from zero to sixteen seats in the Chamber of Deputies and zero to four seats in the Senate. Altogether, the far-left Popular Front wound up with forty (of 147) Chamber seats and thirteen (of forty-five) Senate seats. Still, Alessandri's forces held comfortable control of both houses: eighty-four Chamber seats and twenty-six Senate seats. The Christian Democrats had twenty-three deputies and six senators in the new Congress.

The 1963 municipal elections produced an entirely different result. A phenomenal 80.5 percent of registered voters—the highest percentage ever to vote in a municipal election—thronged to the polls. Table 13 shows the shifting fortunes of Right and Left in the off-year elections of the Alessandri era.

TABLE 13

VOTE FOR MAJOR PARTIES, CONGRESSIONAL AND MUNICIPAL ELECTIONS, 1957–1963

| | 1957 | | 1960 | | 1961 | | 1963 | |
| | CONGRESSIONAL | | MUNICIPAL | | CONGRESSIONAL | | MUNICIPAL | |
PARTIES	VOTES	%	VOTES	%	VOTES	%	VOTES	%
Communist			112,251	9.2	157,572	11.4	225,776	12.4
Conservative	154,887	17.6	173,875	14.1	198,260	14.3	226,717	11.0
C. Democrat	82,710[a]	9.4	171,503	13.9	213,468	15.4	455,522	22.0
Liberal	134,741	15.4	188,314	15.4	222,485	16.1	260,197	12.6
Radical	188,526	21.5	245,911	20.0	296,828	21.4	431,470	20.8
Socialist	93,787[b]	10.7	128,724	10.4[c]	149,122	10.7	229,229	11.1

Source: *Estadísticas Electorales, 1925–1969* (Oficina de Informaciones, Chilean Senate, Boletín de Información General, no. 66, June 25, 1970), p. 63

[a] In 1957 it was still the Falange Nacional; the Christian Democrat party was formally founded July 28, 1957, four months after those elections.
[b] The 1957 totals combine the votes of the Socialist and Popular Socialist parties.
[c] The 1960 totals combine the votes of the Socialist and Socialist Democrat parties.

As table 13 indicates, the Christian Democrats were the biggest single winners. The three parties supporting Alessandri in the Democratic Front saw their share of the vote drop from 1961's 51.5 percent to 44.4 percent. For the Radicals, who had formally joined the front only in October 1963, it was the last time they would ever achieve 20 percent of the vote. Immediately after the elections, they pulled out of the government and began their descent into oblivion.

The outcome was a stinging rebuke for the parties of the Right, but not for Alessandri personally, as even such an acerb critic as Gil would acknowledge.[90] In fact, Allessandri would, in the phrase of the *Nueva Enciclopedia de Chile,* "conserve intact his popularity until the end of his term, truly extraordinary in the political history of Chile."[91]

That popularity did not, however, extend to the political parties, busily jockeying for advantage as the 1964 presidential elections neared.

So great, in fact, was Alessandri's popularity that a move was made to reform the constitution to permit him to run again. But his Conservative and Liberal allies, who had already scuttled his programs in Congress,[92] had pledged to support a Radical candidate in exchange for Radical support in Congress. Alessandri himself vetoed the stillborn initiative.

The Radical candidate was drawn from its moderate ranks, Julio Durán Newman, a self-made man whose nimble mind and engaging style had enabled him to climb to the peak through the democratically organized ranks of the Radical party. The crusty elements of the Radicals' partners of the Right never did feel comfortable with the candidacy of a man they regarded as a *roto*—Chilean slang for trash, white or mestizo. Nor was he palatable to the left wing of the party, headed by Luis Bossay Leiva, the man the Communists had puffed up six years earlier with a hint of their backing for his presidential ambitions.

Durán was staunchly anti-Communist. Senator Bossay was not. At a public rally organized by the left wing of the party to honor him in mid-February 1964, Bossay said: "Those politicians among us who insist—in a selfish way—in forcing the issue as a fight between Marxism and democracy, those politicians are just plain ridiculous."[93] With the presidential elections only seven months away, it was a signal for internecine war that would obliterate Durán's hopes, and with them, the Radicals and the future of the Right in Chile.

Because, by campaign time 1964, the squabbling, foundering, confused coalition that called itself the Democratic Front was the fragile and fragmented remnant of a politically visible right in Chile.

The Christian Democrats, at their 1961 convention, had debated three possibilities: a loose alliance with the Right; an alliance with the "moderate" Left; a decided shift to the left themselves, with their own candidate. They opted for the last choice, but the decision really did no more than confirm a course they had long since charted for themselves. Their program, in the phrase of one Marxist observer, had in fact "come to resemble that of Allende."[94]

The Socialists and the Communists (and two junior partners, the National Democrats and National Vanguard of People) banded together in the Popular Front and decided to go with Salvador Allende for a third time.

For all practical purposes, Chile did not have to wait for the presidential elections in September to glimpse the future. The Waterloo of the Chilean Right came on March 15, 1964, in an inconspicuous and forgotten corner of the country called Curicó. Curicó is lush farm country 125 miles south of Santiago, hard by a rugged rib of Andes peaks and volcanoes, a province which is home to Chile's three native species of fauna: the mountain lion, the condor, and deer. In size, it is the third-smallest province; in population, the fifth smallest; in history, a nullity, until then.

In the erroneous arithmetic of the reflexive wisdom, Curicó—because it was agricultural, presumably—was "normally conservative."[95] It was not, and it had not been for years. In 1958, for example, Curicó was the farm province that gave Allende the second-highest share of the vote in the country (the first, Arauco, is an interesting case where the Radicals, who had formerly dominated, earning 45.8 percent in 1957, for example, were displaced by the far Left the very next year when the Radicals switched their allegiance from left to right). It is also notable that in only one other predominantly farm province (O'Higgins, immediately south of the politically effervescent capital) did Allende receive a percentage of the vote even close to the 32 percent he harvested in Curicó in 1958.

The March contest was a by-election to fill a vacant Chamber of Deputies seat. Durán made the mistake of advertising the election as a sort of "national plebiscite," because he too misread arithmetic. Durán made the mistake of adding the combined vote of Radicals, Liberals, and Conservatives in 1963 in the province, 47.5 percent, and assuming that the three parties of this threadbare coalition of the Right were bigger than the monolithic forces of the two far-left parties.

The calculation was wrong for three reasons. First, as pointed out, the Radicals were themselves badly divided, and the coalition far from cohesive. Next, that arithmetic overlooked the superior overall strength of the Left in the province. Finally, the experience of recent years in Chile had shown repeatedly that political parties, with the exception of those of the far Left, could not "deliver" votes willy-nilly to the candidates or combinations of their choice; the voters reacted increasingly to men and programs, and less and less to parties.

Personalities, in fact, very much clouded the issue in Curicó. The Communist-Socialist coalition ran as its candidate a young doctor, Oscar Naranjo Arias, son of the deceased deputy who had held the seat. Naranjo was born and raised in Curicó, a man who radiated the warmth, humor, and special wryness of the land. He would have been a formidable candidate under any banner.

Naranjo won with 9,566 votes, followed by Rodolfo Ramírez Valenzuela, candidate of the Right, with 7,950. Third was Christian Democrat Mario Fuenzalida Madriaza with 6,621 votes. In the aftermath, the Right, in panic, caved in. For these tremulous men, Curicó presaged a Communist victory in September. Foxy Salvador Allende and other FRAP leaders fueled the fears of the Right. Allende said Curicó was a "veritable political earthquake," and he was right, but only in that decisions were made in the fumes and confusion of unnerving events.

In reality, for the reasons described above, Curicó should not have been that alarming, and probably would not have been had it not been for the stance of the Christian Democrats. During the rollicking campaign in Curicó, the Christian Democrats left no doubt that they were out to get the Right, whatever the cost. At one point, for instance, they joined FRAP agitators in laying siege to a local bank after discovering that employees had worked overtime there to sort and package 250,000 worth of escudos in E^0 5 and E^0 10 notes—planting suspicions in the process of a government plot to buy votes. But even more decisive was the arrogance of the Christian Democrats: they would join in a pact with no one, an attitude they would persist in until it was too late to rescue Chile's decimated democracy. Inflexibility in 1964 meant that the votes in the presidential elections would be divided a dangerous three ways.

It also gave Durán little room to maneuver, especially in light of dissension within his own Radical ranks, and the carping and whining emanating from his circumstantial allies of the Right. Shortly after Curicó, Durán withdrew as the front's candidate.[96] The Liberals and Conservatives then merged their electoral fortunes with those of the Christian Democrats, a party which viewed them as the real enemies of Chile.

"The FRAP's analyses of the structural causes of Chile's under-development," wrote Marxist Labrousse, "were not fundamentally different from those of the Christian Democrats."[97] Christian Democrats would later express their contempt of the Right and what it stood for in even blunter terms.

"The Right," ex-Communist Ravines wrote, "capitulated without a fight. Nothing did greater damage to the mentality of the Chilean people than being deprived of that face-to-face encounter, one that should have been the one great focusing of the ideological issues."[98]

"What the politicians did not understand," Guzmán said, "is that what the public wanted was another Alessandri. First they were offered Durán, a man cut from the same old style of politicking. Next they were given Frei, who was obviously even more demagogic and even more subordinated to party than Durán. So there never was a real choice."[99]

A measure of Alessandri's popularity was the outpouring of hundreds of thousands of Chileans who walked with him in a procession without precedent to the National Congress on November 3, 1964, for the ceremonies in which he turned over the sash of office to Eduardo Frei, and then followed him out and back to his modest apartment on the Plaza de Armas, a few blocks away. Observers have described the event as an apotheosis.

In a sense, it was really a wake.

THE TRANSITION YEARS—AN INVENTORY

In all of Latin America, there was no country more admired than Chile during these years of change. Its political institutions were held in reverent awe; its social innovations and forward-looking legislation commented on and copied. Its people were the envy of all, for their stability, for the egalitarian society they were forging, for their relative prosperity.

Furthermore, Chileans wore success gracefully, and this reinforced their position as perhaps the most universally popular of all Latin American peoples.

The truth, as noted at the outset of this chapter, was another. In reality, it was not that the Chileans were doing so well, but that the others were doing so poorly. When Argentina fell under the jackboot of Col. Juan Perón in 1945 and began its long economic and political decline, only Uruguay and Chile remained as paradigms of long-established democratic virtue in Latin America. Both would experience the thralldom of the boundless, and uncritical, admiration of academics and others while both were, in fact, sinking into a suffocating morass of political chicanery and economic ruin.

Chile's constitution of 1925 was born in indecent haste[100] and rotting under the weight of what even admirer Gil would describe as a "confusing, imperfect, and inefficient political system."[101] It was a political system in which as many as thirty-six parties disputed the spoils of power, and a political system in which the Congress, one of the most frequently cited pillars of Chile's democracy, had become, in the words of a justice minister, a "regime of clienteles."[102] Arnello, in a 1964 essay, showed how: of all laws approved by the Chilean Congress over the previous thirty-eight years, 7.36 percent were for the general public, 40.43 percent for particular groups or places, and 51.4 percent for private individuals. Furthermore, Arnello notes that the Senate, over the course of a year, was putting in a total of about two hundred hours of work in session. Arnello also noted that because of quorum rules designed to make attendance nonessential, a law could be passed in the Chamber by as few as sixteen (of 147 deputies) and in the Senate by as few as six (of forty-five senators).[103]

Increasingly, the Congress was at the service not only of individuals, but of political parties: by 1968, the president of every political party (except the right-wing Nationals) was a senator. As Weston Agor shows in his study of the Chilean Senate, there was a high degree of interlocking relationship not only between key Senate assignments and positions of party leadership, but also between party discipline and votes on issues.[104]

The economic picture was also a mirage, and by the mid-1960s it was evident that Chile was stagnating, if not actually "skidding backward," as Gil concluded.[105] Yet, the cure prescribed by the Christian Democrats was an even more massive dose of statism and paternalism, policies that made them the paladins of the Americas.

The first eight years of Radical rule left a debt of better than a billion pesos.[106] Inflation from 1940 to 1955 amounted to a sickening 2,887 percent, and once released, the demon of inflation would grow ever faster, except for brief periods under Ibáñez and Alessandri when conservative economics were applied. Between 1950 and 1958, money in circulation increased seventeen times, as the government turned increasingly to the printing presses to finance its largess. The gross national product for the five-year period 1955–59 was down to an annual growth rate of 0.9 percent, which, taking into account population increase, actually represented a 1.6 percent backslide. The balance-of-payments deficit from 1950 to 1955 was $71 million, and for 1955–60 it reached $244 million. A country that had long exported food was after 1942 an importer, as the increase in output from 1948 to 1961, for example, was only 1.8 percent while the population was increasing 2.5 percent.[107]

The government payroll was swollen by 60 percent from 1940 to 1955, as the parties scrambled to pad payrolls with political loyalists and at the same time expanded the apparatus of the welfare state they were creating.

Runaway inflation took its toll too on the already wobbly savings habits of the country: it destroyed them, at the public as well as the private level. In 1960 Chile had the lowest coefficient of savings and investment to gross domestic product in the hemisphere.[108]

An American academic, writing from the scene in 1957, echoed the sentiments that were to become fashionable. "Chilean politicians," Prof. K. H. Silvert wrote, "can debate which side of the economic street they ought to occupy, but they can no longer debate whether the route is the right one."[109]

A British historian, viewing the same period from the vantage point of a later perspective, entered a different verdict. "From 1942," wrote Alistair Horne, "the Radicals, cut loose from the Popular Front, ruled for ten years; ten years of inefficiency, galloping inflation, and vast expansion of the bureaucracy."[110]

Hardly a promising route. But it was only the beginning.

Notes

CHAPTER 3

1. José Garrido Rojas, "The Increasing Social Participation in Chile," in *Chile: A Critical Survey* (Santiago: Institute of General Studies, 1972), pp. 197–99. Garrido Rojas was himself one of the reformist-minded young turks of the Liberal party in the early 1960s, and one of the leaders of the movement for the country's ground-breaking agrarian reform law. He later became head of the government agricultural-planning agency under Alessandri. I have adjusted Garrido's figures for the 1970 population—and, therefore, the percentage increase from 1950 to 1970—to conform to the actual population figures as given in the 1970 census in *Nueva Enciclopedia de Chile* (Argentina: Ediciones Copihue, Fotomecánica SRL, Ediciones Libra, 1974), 1:338. (Hereafter *Nueva Enciclopedia.*) As the encyclopedia notes, Chile's 1970 population fell short of the 9.7 million forecast, the estimated figure used by Garrido and others.
2. In 1953 twenty-four new parties joined the twelve represented in Congress to vie in the municipal elections. In 1957 sixteen parties, plus a number of independent candidates, contested seats in Congress. In 1965 there were still twelve parties slugging it out. Even in 1969, with the polarization of forces in Chile approaching the flash point, there were still eight parties contesting congressional seats. *Chile: Election Factbook, September 4, 1964* (Washington, D.C.: Institute for the Comparative Study of Political Systems) and *Estadísticas Electorales, 1925–1969* (Oficina de Informaciones, Chilean Senate, Boletín de Información General, no. 66, June 25, 1970). Unless otherwise indicated, election statistics in this book are taken from the latter, Chilean government report. Old political habits apparently die hard. As the military government eased up—but even before political parties were formally legalized—at least fifteen "parties" were already jockeying for position in early 1987. That was a full fourteen years after all parties were banned, and a year before elections, the 1988 presidential plebiscite.
3. Genaro Arriagada Herrera, *De la "Vía Chilena" a la "Vía Insurreccional"* (Santiago: Editorial del Pacífico, S.A., 1974), p. 54. Like practically every other statistic, these must be taken with a grain of salt. Labrousse, for example, claims that as early as 1953, the Communist-dominated CUT had 300,000 members, almost certainly an inflated figure. Alain Labrousse, *El Experimento Chileno* (Barcelona and Mexico: Ediciones Grijalbo, S.A., 1973).
4. Arturo Alessandri's labor minister recognized the legality of peasant unions in 1933. Marxist author Labrousse notes that, "paradoxically enough, it would be the Popular Front which would outlaw by decree the formation of peasant unions, a ban which would not be repealed officialy until 1967." Labrousse ascribes this to a tactical move of the Communists and Social-

112

ists, anxious to share power alongside the middle class and industrial bourgeoisie, without "breaking the dominant structure of society." The Peasant League way back then—March 38, 1939, the date it was outlawed—had twenty thousand members. Labrousse, op. cit., p. 107. It was during Alessandri's administration too that the minimum-wage law was enacted. The United Nations study is quoted in *New Deal in Chile: Will "Revolution in Liberty" Succeed?* Great Decisions, no. 6 (New York: Foreign Policy Association, 1967), p. 4.

5. Quoted by Garrido Rojas, op. cit., p. 183, from an interview published in *El Mercurio*, December 5, 1971, by Silvia Pinto, with Sen. Victor García G.

6. Gonzalo Vial Correa, "Decadencia, Consenso y Unidad Nacional en 1973," in *Política y Geoestrategia*, #36 (Santiago: Academia Nacional de Estudios Políticos y Estratégicos, 1985), pp. 23–26. Article 25 of the 1925 constitution is the second in Chapter 6 covering the Congress. It says: "In elections for Deputies and Senators, a procedure will be employed which will have as its practical outcome an effective proportionality of representation of opinions and political parties." Obviously, those who framed the constitution in such haste never imagined that they were creating a Frankenstein, yet later generations declined to rein in the parties, although the weaknesses of the system had become obvious. Ultimately, Frankenstein was too strong to be tamed.

7. Chamudes was expelled from that party too in 1967. But again, expulsion was a badge of honor for him, because the once proud party had by then become a cloying mendicant of Communist party favors. In 1969 the party finished off its self-immolation as an independent force, expelling Julio Durán, its 1964 presidential candidate, along with eight others, the last remnants of moderation in the party. Chamudes's vindication came two years later, in the Hall of Honor of the National Congress, when he, together with two former presidential candidates, was unanimously elected a member of the national executive board of the newly formed Democratic Radical party. Chamudes describes that as one of the two greatest moments of his public life—Marcos Chamudes, *Chile: Una Advertencia Americana* (Santiago: Ediciones P.E.C., 1972), pp. 142–43; quotation "hackneyed commonplaces" from p. 120.

8. Francisco Miró Quesada, "El Impacto de la Metafísica en la Ideología Latinoamericana," in *Antología de la Filosofía Americana Contemporánea*, ed. Leopoldo Zea (Mexico, D.F.: B. Costa-Amic, 1968), pp. 182–83.

9. Galdames remarks that men such as José Victorino Lastarría and Miguel Luis Amunátegui, bereft of a financial future, achieved social and political eminence "thanks exclusively to their qualities of intelligence and character" (Luis Galdames, *Historia de Chile*, 14th ed. [Santiago: Products RAVAL, 1974], p. 375). Amunátegui's equally bereft brother, Gregorio, who collaborated with him on many literary works, went on to become chief justice of the Supreme Court. Artists had been allowed to adorn high society ever since the Medicis, but not participate in it, and certainly not in Latin America. That is what distinguished the Chilean experience.

10. Even Gil, an observer of undisguised sympathies for the Christian Democrats, a professedly leftist movement, concedes that "oligarchic dominion came tumbling down in 1920" (Federico G. Gil, *El Sistema Político de Chile* [Santiago: Editorial Andrés Bello, 1969], p. 74). I say "concedes" because, again, the fashion among Western liberals has been to describe Chile as a

country ruled by the Right until the advent of Allende, a misleading and inaccurate judgment.

11. The authoritative *Diccionario Político de Chile*, ed. Jordi Fuentes and Lía Cortés (Santiago: Editorial Orbe, 1967)—hereafter *Diccionario*—dates the founding of the party from 1857, but notes (p. 403) that it remained an ideological movement until 1888 when the first convention was held, on November 19, to organize it as a political party. The *Diccionario* identifies Manuel Antonio Matta Goyenechea and Pedro León Gallo Goyenechea as the first "directors" of the movement. In 1858 Gallo led a breakaway from the Liberal party, and the following year he, a rich miner, bankrolled the formation of a one thousand-man rebel army which defeated government troops in the battle of Los Loros, occupying the city of La Serena. Gallo's forces were defeated in April 1859 at Cerro Grande, and the revolution ended. According to the *Nueva Enciclopedia* (1:208), Gallo founded the Radical Assembly at Copiapó in 1863. The party routinely referred to itself as the oldest in Latin America, and indicated a birthdate at the close of the 1850s.

12. Quoted by Régis Debray, *The Chilean Revolution: Conversations with Allende* (New York: Random House, Vintage Books, 1971), p. 137.

13. According to Hugh Thomas in his epic, *The Spanish Civil War*, rev. ed. (Middlesex, Eng.: Penguin Books, 1965), p. 130, the minutes of the Seventh Congress of the Comintern, held in Moscow in 1935—the meeting that sponsored the popular-front concept—included the following statement by the secretary-general, the Bulgarian firebrand Georgi Dimitrov: "The formation of a joint People's Front providing for joint action with Social Democratic parties is a necessity. Cannot we endeavor to unite the Communists, Social Democratic, Catholic, and other workers? Comrades, you will remember the ancient tale of the capture of Troy. The attacking army was unable to achieve victory until, with the aid of the Trojan Horse, it penetrated to the very heart of the enemy camp. We revolutionary workers should not be shy of using the same tactics." Former Communist Eudocio Ravines quoted the Hungarian Communist Eugene Varga as preaching at that time, "We can reach communism not only via the armed insurrection of coup d'etat of our Comrade Lenin, but also by means of a succession of 'New Deals'; that is, a progressive statization of private enterprise" (Ravines, *El Rescate de Chile* [Santiago: Empresa Editora e Impresora Edimpres, 1974], p. 21. And, of course, there is the byzantine record of Lenin's own life, a record of alliances of convenience, made and betrayed—a leitmotif summarized in his dictim: "In politics, there is only one principle and one truth: what profits my opponent hurts me and vice versa" (Adam B. Ulam, *The Bolsheviks* [New York: Macmillan Co., 1965], p. 226).

14. Gonzalo Vial Correa, op. cit., p. 22. Vial Correa argues that, beginning around 1910, Chileans lost not only a common perception of the world beyond their borders, but also "faith in their political system [and] the social class leading them." The *caudillo* who undermined Radical institution-building was Gen. Carlos Ibáñez.

15. Urrutia had been defeated in 1935 by Grove in the contest to choose a successor to Eugenio Matte as secretary-general.

16. In 1943 and 1944, production peaked at 540,000 tons, a level which would not be reached again until 1962. Part of the bloom was taken off the copper boom, in any case, by official efforts to stimulate production of alumi-

num—lighter, cheaper, and subject to fewer supply and price fluctuations—for copper (which is, however, less bulky and more efficient than aluminum for conducting electricity and heat). From 1939 to 1943, production of aluminum in the Allied countries more than tripled, while copper output increased by about 25 percent. Theodore H. Moran, *Multinational Corporations and the Politics of Dependence: Copper in Chile* (Princeton, N.J.: Princeton University Press, 1974) p. 46.

17. Copper prices had averaged from 10 cents to 13.167 cents per pound from 1937 to 1940, peaking at 16.775 cents. Copper companies, faced with what they rightly described as a "systematic campaign" by U.S. government officials to promote the substitution of aluminum for copper, agreed to moderate their price ambitions when ceilings were negotiated in Washington for the duration of World War II. The average price paid Chile during the war was about 11 cents per pound. On this basis, Chileans claimed they "lost" between $107 million and $500 million; the low figure represented the difference between their price and the price of 17.35 cents allowed for subsidized mines in the United States. The higher figure represented the difference between the Chilean price and an estimate (24.5 cents) of what open-market prices would have been. (During World War I and the Vietnam War, no price ceilings were fixed, and open-market prices rose 200–300 percent.)

Whatever the merits of the argument, Moran points out (op. cit., p. 63) that "Chile was being denied full enjoyment of the boom side of the business cycle in the developed countries while having the recession side of the cycle exported with exaggeration into the Chilean economy" (such as the 1949 recession in the United States when copper prices fell by 40 percent). Data in this footnote taken from Moran (ibid., pp. 47, 63, 66, 68).

In the competition for political advantage and headlines in the years ahead, the half-billion-dollar figure came to be accepted as an article of faith in Chile, by persons on the Right as well as on the political Left. Yet, as Moran points out, the so-called open market for copper—the London Metals Exchange and the New York Commodity Exchange—represented "thin markets," buying marginal amounts for new or sporadic users. On that basis, those markets routinely paid 10 percent to 15 percent above corporate quotations for big lots of contract copper sales. This fine distinction, he adds, "was not clearly understood in Chile nor carefully explored," and led Chile's politicians into a familiar kind of Third-World arithmetic used in adding up what the industrialized nations "owe" them. Ibid., p. 78.

18. As Radical governments extended state control over the country's economic life, businessmen inevitably cozied up to Radical politicians. The result: more and more Radical politicians drifted into business, until an entire class of businessman-Radicals had sprung up. Aguirre Cerda, as noted, was a wealthy landowner. Radical congressmen often doubled as lawyers for big companies, and several even represented those foreign hobgoblins, the copper companies. Gabriel González Videla, who started out as one of the most Radical radicals of all, went into banking after leaving the presidency. At the grass-roots level, the Radicals became the party of the bureaucracy, precisely because they were the ones responsible for its gargantuan growth. So, in its old age, the party of revolution became the party of privilege and patronage.

19. Galdames, op. cit., p. 504.

20. Gil (op. cit., p. 180), for example, says: "The splendid role of CORFO in the development of domestic industries in Chile is cited frequently as the most successful example in Latin America." In *Nueva Enciclopedia* (2:140) CORFO is referred to as the "push-rod [*palanca*] of development in Chile since Pedro Aguirre Cerda founded it."

21. In relative terms, the most spectacular increase occurred entirely under private auspices, in the period 1930–45, when output tripled (from 965 million kilowatt hours to 2.6 million kwh). From 1945 to 1960 the increase was from 2.6 billion to 4.5 billion kwh; by 1969 the total was 7.1 billion kwh; of installed capacity in 1969 (1.9 billion kilowatts), 64.6 percent was in public hands, the rest private; and ENDESA, in turn, accounted for 69 percent of the state-held sector. *Nueva Enciclopedia* 2:176–77.

22. The role of the Export-Import Bank, or any other outside agency, rarely is even mentioned. It was by Jerome Levinson and Juan de Onís, *The Alliance That Lost Its Way,* (Chicago: Quadrangle Books, Twentieth Century Fund Study, 1970), p. 36.

23. The division of shares in CAP was given by John Gunther, *Inside South America* (New York: Harper & Row, 1966), p. 291. By contrast, Marxist Labrousse (op. cit., p. 82) said 63 percent of CAP's shares were in private hands, "particularly" in those of a consortium that included copper giants Anaconda and Kennecott. He does not tell us how much "particularly" represents, but presumably it was Gunther's 18 percent. Nor does Labrousse mention the small shareholders.

    Nitrate was another example of CORFO's investment technique—and the eventual fate of private partners. In 1968 CORFO joined the Anglo-Lautaro Nitrate Co., to create a new entity, the Chemical and Mining Enterprise of Chile (SOQUIMICH—Sociedad Química y Minera de Chile). Anglo-Lautaro (a U.S.–British consortium founded in 1926 and controlled by the Guggenheim group of New York) not only had dominated the industry in modern times (accounting for 70 percent of output), but had revolutionized it (through the introduction of the so-called Guggenheim system for processing crude sodium nitrate). In the words of the *Nueva Enciclopedia* (2:135): "The modernization of the Chilean nitrate industry has been due, in large measure, to the spirit of enterprise and financial efforts of the Guggenheim group which has invested in the industry more than $115 million over the past thirty-five years." Such exemplary behavior would not, however, save the company when the winds of nationalization began howling in the sixties, and so Anglo-Lautaro not only put into the new mixed company its installations and know-how, but also led the way in arranging the financing for a $25 million expansion program. Anglo-Lautaro completed its retreat by agreeing to sell out to the government early in the Allende regime, in May 1971.

    Not so "lucky," however, was Dow Chemical. Dow held a 70 percent controlling interest in a SOQUIMICH offspring, called Petroquímica Chilena. Dow's holdings were "intervened" in by Allende, a lightly disguised form of theft. It was June 1974 before Dow would receive the first return of any kind on its $35 million investment: a $13,900 royalty payment from the military government, which had just then returned the operation to the company.

24. Manufacturing's share of the gross national product increased 42 percent from 1940 to 1955. For the period 1946 to 1955, industrial output increased 50 percent. The textiles industry was one of the genuine success stories.

Before the Popular Front, Chile imported 90 percent of all the cotton fiber used in the country. By 1960 only 11 percent was imported. In 1929, 85 percent of iron and steel supplies were imported; by 1952 only 9 percent. That rosy picture is incomplete, however, without pointing out that as late as 1970, machinery, the backbone of industry, was by far the largest single item in Chile's $930 million import bill, costing $185 million. Next came chemicals ($98 million), then automobiles ($97 million), to feed an incredibly inefficient local assembly industry. As of January 1972 the cheapest of the eight models then assembled in Chile, the tiny Fiat 600, was priced at E⁰ 58,102, or $3,052, at the then-prevailing exchange rate for those transactions (E⁰ 19 to the dollar). The most expensive car then available—a Dodge Dart—cost $5,390. Production increase figures, Gil, op. cit., pp. 179–80. Local production figures, *Nueva Enciclopedia,* 2:193; import figures, Banco Central de Chile, "Estadísticas de Comercio Exterior al 30 de Abril de 1974," mimeographed, July 5, 1974; automobile prices, *Qué Pasa,* May 4, 1972, p. 37; and exchange rates, *La Economía de Chile Durante el Período de Gobierno de la Unidad Popular* (Escuela de Negocios de Valparaíso, March 1974), p. 76. As we shall see in chapter 6, the trade situation improved considerably in the post-Allende years.

25. Consumption of iron and steel products increased 75 percent from the period 1925–29 to 1956–60; electrical energy consumption in the same period 540 percent; petroleum 213 percent; shoes 128.6 percent (from one pair of shoes, on the average, every fifteen months, to a pair every seven months). *Nueva Enciclopedia,* 2:187.

26. Balmaceda had given education the first big push sixty years earlier, when about one-fourth of all school-age children were enrolled. By 1970 the number in grade schools, plus the first two years of high school, had reached 2,123,400. Galdames, op. cit., pp. 438, 505, 556.

27. During the early 1930s Chile had one of the most shocking rates of infant mortality in the world: 250 per one thousand. By 1960 the rate was down to 127.9 per one thousand live births, a level still so bad that it was exceeded in the Western Hemisphere only by chronically backward Haiti. Chile achieved the greatest reduction of any Latin American country in its infant mortality rate during 1960–66, when the rate dropped from 127.9 to 101.9 per one thousand. But even more impressive progress was made under the military government, so that by 1985, infant mortality had been cut to 17.8 percent. That, coupled with a concerted attack on malnutrition, gave Chile one of the best performance rates in the entire developing world. Sources, for 1930s: Labrousse, op. cit., p. 49; for 1960: *Institutional Reforms and Social Development Trends in Latin America* (Washington, D.C.: Inter-American Development Bank, March 1963), p. 101 (hereafter *Institutional Reforms*); for 1960–1966, *Economic and Social Progress in Latin America,* annual report (Washington, D.C., Inter-American Development Bank, 1972), p. 153 (hereafter *Economic and Social Progress 1972*); for 1985, *Statistical Synthesis,* op. cit., p. 47; for malnutrition, *Poverty in Latin America: the Impact of Depression,* op. cit., p. 21.

28. The *Diccionario* presumably erred in the biographical sketch of Allende by indicating (p. 36) that he began his second term as minister on December 14, 1941. The same reference work, in its sketch of the history of the Socialist party, notes (p. 472) that the Socialists pulled out of the government in 1941, a few months after joining right-wing parties in attempting to get the

Communist party outlawed (a bill vetoed by the Radical president Aguirre Cerda). Socialist ministers again formed part of the cabinet announced on April 1, 1942. The reference to Allende's book is from *Current Biography* (New York: H. W. Wilson, September 1971), p. 4.

29. The honeymoon lasted on the labor front until 1943, when Communists and Socialists presented for the first (and last) time a joint slate of candidates at the Third Congress of the Chilean Labor Federation. In politics, acrimonious competition remained the rule.

30. They did much better on the local level in the 1947 municipal elections.

31. As pointed out earlier, however, Chile was the only South American country that never did declare war on the Axis.

32. *Programa de Desarrollo de Chile a Corto y Mediano Plazo* (presentation by Raúl Sáez, government economic coordinator, before Inter-American Economic and Social Committee of Alliance for Progress, 1974, reproduced in a booklet (Santiago: Editora Nacional Gabriela Mistral, 1974), p. 7. Crude oil production in 1983 totaled 13.3 million barrels, consumption 27.4 million barrels. In the area of petroleum products, domestic production by then covered 86 percent of the country's needs, including virtually all of the gasoline needs. Source for 1983 figures: *1986 Britannica Book of the Year*, op. cit., p. 652. Source for 1986: *Economic and Social Progress in Latin America*, 1987 Report, pp. 479–480. For gasoline production/consumption: *Indicadores Económicos y Sociales, 1960–1985*, op. cit., p. 136.

33. Neruda was a Communist sympathizer in the thirties, and joined the party publicly in the early forties. Ex-Communist Chamudes relates that the party's Central Committee debated several times Neruda's offer to serve the party as it best saw fit: as an open, declared member, lending the prestige of his name; or as an underground member, so that his propagandizing in their behalf would have the ring of "independence." Chamudes says the party finally asked Neruda to decide, and he opted for open membership, saying his entire life had been a record of openness. Chamudes, op. cit., pp. 116–17.

34. As recounted in "Cincuenta Años del Partido Comunista: de Recabarren a Corvalán," *Qué Pasa*, December 30, 1971, p. 10. This Chilean version, if correct, would leave Professor Gil (a Cuban with long experience in Chile) out on an ingenious limb: he describes the Radicals as "again heading a coalition of the center and left" (Gil, op. cit., p. 89). But then, Gil repeatedly underestimates the astuteness of the Communists. Through the long years of their existence in Chile, the Communists displayed that astuteness constantly, never succumbing to the allure of the trappings of power if that would imperil their grip on the substance of power. In 1938 it was to their advantage to maneuver in the shadows, building their own organization, radicalizing the terms and tone of politics and the policies of government— but without polarizing the opposition by surfacing in positions of visible power. So they declined ministerial posts, giving the Right a chance to get used to living in a leftist world. Similarly, they knew in 1970 that they could not win with a candidate of their own, but knew that their cause would win if they supported a candidate they could manipulate. Salvador Allende went to his doom largely because he would not, or could not, allow himself to be manipulated by the Communists.

35. Lautaro Silva, *Allende: El Fin de una Aventura* (Santiago: Ediciones Patria Nueva, 1974), p. 13. I have seen the same claim made nowhere else, and suspect a trace of characteristic enthusiasm for polemic.

36. Ravines, op. cit., p. 16.

37. Agor includes the following table to demonstrate the degree of individual autonomy vs. party disipline in the voting behavior of Senate committee members:

DISCIPLINE AND INFLUENCE OF SENATORS BY PARTY

PARTY	DEGREE OF DISCIPLINE	INFLUENCE OF SENATORS ON PARTY POLICY
Communists	Absolute	One factor
Socialist	Strong	Less important
Christian Democrat	More than Radical but similar	Important
Radical	Tends to be individualistic	Decisive
National	Little	Absolute

Source: Agor, *The Chilean Senate* (Austin and London: University of Texas Press, 1971), p. 53.

In other words, senators of the Right (the National party) could tell the party what to do, but the party had little sway over them; the farther one moved to the Left, the less influence senators had on party policy—but the greater party control over them. Agor also noted (p. 43) that the National party was the "least disciplined" (that is, their senators were the most independent in evaluating and voting on issues); several times (pp. 37–60) he demonstrates how Communist party discipline ties not only the votes, but the tongues of Communist senators in committee, which is "where you see the real man . . . where you talk about the interests of Chile, and less about the party" (p. 54).

38. Silvia Pinto, *Los Días del Arco Iris* (Santiago: Editorial del Pacífico, 1972), p. 36. With Allende in power they discovered, too late, how little, in reality, there was of the "progressive, elegant, and fashionable" in the Left.

39. Galdames, op. cit., p. 54.

40. Robert J. Alexander, *Communism in Latin America* (New Brunswick, N.J.: Rutgers University Press, 1957), pp. 200–202, cited by Gil, op. cit., p. 90.

41. The account of the Russian offer to represent the Czechs and Yugoslavs appears in Silva, op. cit., p. 14. He adds that the Kremlin retaliated by "kidnaping" the Chilean ambassador in Moscow, preventing him or his family from leaving the country. There is a detailed discussion of the interplay between U.S. and Chilean interests, official and unofficial, in Moran, op. cit., pp. 174–80. The main thrust of Moran's narrative is that it was the Chilean Right, and particularly the Liberals, that clamored for the outlawing of the Communists as a condition for U.S. official aid. Once they were outlawed, there was indeed a flood of new U.S. private investment, including $130 million by Anaconda, the largest single investment in Chilean history. It is also true that new official loans were granted in 1949. But nothing so complex is uncomplicated, except to political propagandists. The copper companies were responding, for the most part, to pledges of substantial tax breaks in return for new investments. And those reviewing official loans to Chile must have taken into account the fact that the country's financial affairs were then in the no-nonsense hands of Jorge

Alessandri Rodríguez who, as finance minister, gave the country the last balanced budget it would see until he himself was president, a decade later (and would not see again until the Pinochet years). Or at least it would seem reasonable to assume that bankers and businessmen might *also* be influenced by signs of solvency and fiscal austerity in lieu of earlier inflationary recklessness. As to copper companies, far from their getting a tax break, the effective tax rate on them was hiked from 50 percent at the end of World War II to over 70 percent in 1950.

42. Teitelboim's extraction—a Jewish family that had fled the Ukraine—did not prevent him from returning to the land of the persecutors of his ancestors and to serve as a Radio Moscow propagandist following the fall of Allende.

43. Marxist Labrousse says the campaign of persecution "provoked a movement of solidarity which, together with the stepped-up labor struggles, would, little by little, clear the way for leftist unity" (op. cit., p. 63). For anti-Communist Chamudes, the Chilean experience contradicts the belief that persecution favors the persecuted. He notes (op. cit., p. 123) that in their last election before the law—the municipal elections of 1947—the Communists captured 16.52 percent of the vote. In their first postrepeal appearance, the municipal elections of 1960, they won only 9.55 percent (the actual figure was 9.2 percent). Ravines, also an ex-Communist, says (op. cit., p. 31) the repeal of the law saw the Communists "not only cleanly resurrected and strengthened but adorned by the halo of martyrdom unjustly inflicted." Ravines blames González Videla and the Radical leadership for failing to convince Chileans that he acted because of rampant subversive activity of the Communists. The result of that failure was that most Chileans, jealous of their tradition of civil liberties, frowned on the move and wrote it off as back-alley politics.

As to the harshness of the law, leftist writers wax choleric on the subject. Debray refers to the "bloody persecution" of Communists, and Labrousse refers to the Pisagua "concentration camp." Chamudes (op. cit., p. 123) describes Pisagua as a place of "deserted beaches in the extreme north of Chile, with a magnificent climate." He says that, far from a concentration camp, there were neither walls nor barbed-wire fences, and inmates moved about freely within a restricted zone. Nor were all "persecuted." Chamudes relates (ibid., pp. 123–24) that the Communist leader and writer Elías Lafertte interceded with ex-President Arturo Alessandri, then president of the Senate, on behalf of poet Pablo Neruda, whose Senate-granted immunity was about to expire. Alessandri, on his own authority as Senate president, extended Neruda's permit after a lengthy chat with Lafertte, a tale that contrasts with widespread reports that Neruda was among those "persecuted." Britisher Robert Moss avers that, in fact, "the law was never applied very firmly" (Moss, *Chile's Marxist Experiment* [New York: John Wiley & Sons, Halstead Press, 1973], p. 58).

44. Debray, op. cit., pp. 156–57.

45. This episode was related to me by Tobías Barros, former career diplomat and member of one of the country's most distinguished families, during an interview in Santiago, April 11, 1974. Barros said he arrived for dinner with the president in company of his mother (who was from González Videla's hometown of La Serena), father, and grandmother. They were introduced there to a couple Barros had not met before: Salvador and Tencha Allende. Said the president in introducing the strangers: "This man is going to be

president of Chile one of these days." González Videla lived to see his prophecy (ruefully) realized twenty-three years later.

46. Galdames, op. cit., p. 515.

47. Mario Arnello, *Proceso a una Democracia: Pensamiento Político de Jorge Prat* (Santiago: Talleres Gráficos "El Imparcial," n.d.), p. 39.

48. Ibáñez, at the head of a mishmash of ad hoc parties and groups, a movement so ideologically amorphous it merited no better name than Ibañismo, polled 446,439 of the 954,131 votes cast in the four-way race. The candidate of the right, Matte Larraín, was the runner-up, with 265,357. Next came Radical candidate Pedro Enrique Alfonso, with 190,360. Fourth was newcomer Allende, who cornered a piddling 5.45 percent of the vote, 51,975. The elections were held September 4, 1952, starting a tradition that they be held on that date.

49. Ibáñez's forces won decisive control of both houses of Congress. Galdames describes the outcome as a "personal triumph" for Ibáñez (op. cit., p. 516). Gil interprets 1953 as "the high-water mark of voter sentiment against the traditional parties" (op. cit., p. 97). Interestingly—perhaps for what it reveals of the author's biases—Gil interprets the Ibáñez phenomenon as "the voters [trying] to elude their responsibility by electing a paternalistic figure who would assume their responsibilities" (ibid., p. 96). The same author had noted (ibid., p. 95) that the "failure of the Left was in not knowing what to do with what they had helped to construct"—which, according to him at this point in his prose, was a country "economically robust and with its democratic institutions intact." On the level of appearances, true. However, Gil himself remarks (ibid., p. 96, fn) how cleverly the Radicals used state-of-emergency decrees (suspending civil rights) and the very undemocratic Law for the Permanent Defense of Democracy (of their own invention) and the Internal Security Law (dating from Alessandri's second term) to exile opponents, particularly Communists; on p. 225 he characterizes the country's political system as "confusing, imperfect, and inefficient"; on p. 216 he notes that popular discontent over politicking led in April 1957 to another, and uglier, kind of protest: rioting in Santiago and Valparaíso (which, according to Labrousse, op. cit., p. 76, left seventy dead and saw angry mobs for a time attempting to seize the presidential palace). Democratic institutions may have survived "intact" (more or less) under the Radicals, but democracy was sick, and in such circumstances, perhaps the citizens were not "eluding their responsibilities" in rejecting still more politicking in favor of a man who offered the hope of responsible government.

50. Gil describes Ibáñez's last two years—with a touch of hyperbole—as "the period of the most dangerous instability in the history of the country" and says Ibáñez survived thanks to the loyalty of his former comrades-in-arms, the military, and because his lack of partisanship enabled him to recruit improbable, but effective, independents for his administration. (Gil, op. cit., pp. 217–18). One thinks of the twenties and thirties, not to mention the turbulence on at least three occasions during the nineteenth century, as offering comparable instability.

51. The Christian Democrat party was founded July 28, 1957, the fusion of the Falange and Conservative Social Christian parties, the latter a small splinter of a liberal faction of the parent Conservative party.

52. Née Frente del Pueblo, November 25, 1951, transformed into the Frente de

Acción Popular on February 29, 1956, died September 11, 1973, as Unidad Popular.

53. The verb most frequently applied to Allende's penchant for dark maneuvering was the Chilean slang term *muñequear* ("puppeteer"). Allende believed himself a master at manipulating others, and was still *muñequeando* as rockets rained into La Moneda. The term is from the Spanish word muñeca, meaning "wrist," hence an agile wrist.

54. *Qué Pasa*, December 30, 1971, p. 12.

55. Hermógenes Pérez de Arce, "Between Socialism and Freedom," in *Chile: A Critical Survey* (Santiago: Institute of General Studies, 1972), p. 108, cites these three as among the Socialists backing Ibáñez.

56. Herrera was the first president of the bank. The bank was an outgrowth of the ideas and proposals of many men in many countries, chief among them, Frei in Chile; Carlos Lleras Restrepo, later president of Colombia; the Argentine economist Raúl Prebicsh; former President Juscelino Kubitschek of Brazil; and the brilliant Brazilian economist Roberto de Oliveira Campos. But basically, it was Chile that, in 1958 during the Ibáñez presidency, quarterbacked the creation of the bank, and a largely unsung Chilean economist who brainstormed the blueprint of the bank.

57. Figures on living costs are from *Situation, Principal Problems and Prospects of the Chilean Economy*, report of the Ad-Hoc Country Review Group of the Inter-American Economic and Social Council of the OAS, February 20, 1975, p. 126, table AE-3: "Chile: Rate of Inflation According to General Consumer Price Indez (1969 = 100), 1941–74." Figures on wages are from Gil, op. cit., pp. 209–10.

58. Labrousse, op. cit., pp. 63–54. As noted earlier, in n. 3 of this chapter, the figure 300,000 for CUT members is almost certainly inflated.

59. Debray, op. cit., p. 34.

60. This account was related to me by Jaime Guzmán Errázuriz during an interview in Santiago, October 13, 1974. Guzmán was close to Alessandri from the time of his days as a law student at the Catholic University (he graduated in 1967), becoming leader of the Youth Movement supporting Alessandri in the 1970 campaign, and the candidate's confidential secretary.

61. The two others were, of course, his father, Arturo, and older brother, Fernando, who ran against González Videla in 1946 and later became Senate president (as did his father). Jorge was the second of five sons, all of whom distinguished themselves in professional careers. Jorge Alessandri's brilliance surfaced in his student days: he graduated as a civil engineer with 870 out of a possible one thousand points, the highest score recorded at the University of Chile for the period 1917–19.

62. Chamudes (op. cit., p. 130) notes that the Communists played to Bossay's ambitions in the days before the repeal of the "Accursed Law," thereby implying that he would have their backing in the presidential elections. Bossay would later protagonize two splits in the disintegrating Radical ranks, the first of which left the party forever prostrate.

63. Labrousse, op. cit., p. 64.

64. Gil, op. cit., pp. 98–99.

65. Zamorano failed to match his own national share of the vote (3.3 percent) in *any* of the nine voting jurisdictions won by Allende, with the single exception of Santiago's second district. By contrast, he equaled or exceeded his average in eight jurisdictions won by Alessandri (all but the one mentioned).

66. Gil, for example, remarks: "It was plain that there had been another of those great shifts in Chilean politics and that, after the Ibáñez fiasco, the voters were decided to put their trust again in the well-established political organization" (op. cit., p. 97). Balderdash. He himself records that the Falange—barely twenty years old and hardly well established—achieved "imposing progress" (p. 252). Furthermore, he singles out for special mention two men making their debut at the level of senatorial politics: Frei and Alessandri, and notes that the two of them attracted the greatest individual outpouring of votes. He also cites the split in the Socialist camp, which doubtless contributed to their pratfall (a fact that further undermines the Gil analysis).

Another—and, I believe, more probable interpretation—is that the voters were transferring their hopes from one strong man (Ibáñez), who had disappointed their expectations, to two others (Frei and Alessandri). Chilean historian Galdames supports this interpretation: "The outcome signified that the concept of the person mattering more than the party continued in full force, as it had in the election of President Ibáñez. The voters backed Alessandri because of his personal qualities, without taking into account the fact that he was backed by parties of the Right" (op. cit., p. 518). As for the Radicals, what they lacked in program or personal charisma, they more than made up for in organization, still the country's most widespread. But the Radicals would later prove themselves capable of frittering away even that advantage in their frenzied pursuit of power at any price.

As to the PDC "wave of the future," Gil again sacrifices scholarship to partisanship, this time attempting to disparage Alessandri's victory, and gild Frei's showing. For example (op. cit., p. 252): "By scant margin, Alessandri obtained a plurality in 1958: 31.6 percent of the vote, and the presidency. Alessandri did well in many provinces but could not win a clear majority in any." That he should fail to win a "clear majority" in any province in a five-way race, in which four of the five contenders had national organizations behind them, should surprise no one. One limited to the Gil account would not discover, on the other hand, that Alessandri captured the highest percentage in a province of any candidate (47.9 percent in Maule; Frei's high-water mark, 27.1 percent, was in the so-called oligarch-dominated cattle and timber province of Llanquihué). It is also notable that Alessandri won in nineteen of the twenty-eight jurisdictions; Allende won the remaining nine. Frei won none.

Gil dismissed Alessandri as "another member of the famous family" and described Frei as "a figure of great attraction for intellectuals, technocrats and non-Marxist leftists, as well as Catholics" (p. 98). Gil later reports (p. 252) that "the Christian Democrat Frei received throughout the country the solid backing of approximately 20 percent of the electorate. His percentages fell below 15 percent in only three small jurisdictions of 29 [sic] and exceeded 25 percent in three others, including Valparaíso." Another way of describing the "solid support" for Frei would be to point out that he managed to equal (or come within 1 percentage point of) his nationwide average (20.5 percent) in only fourteen of twenty-eight (correct) jurisdictions and failed to do so in some mighty big ones (Linares, Valdivia, Talca, Antofagasta, O'Higgins) as well as "small ones." Next, I am puzzled at the significance of 15.5 percent, except as a great divide Frei managed to cross on his way to nowhere. Finally, it was true that Frei exceeded 25 percent in Valparaíso: he got 25.7 percent. It is not clear, though, why

Valparaíso should have been singled out, inasmuch as it was only the fourth largest jurisdiction in the country. One possibility: the line about 15 percent and Valparaíso is copied almost word for word from *Chile: Election Factbook*, p. 36. In all of Chile, Frei finished second in only eight jurisdictions, three of them small (fewer than thirty thousand voters), and had to settle for third in all four Santiago districts, which means in the first and second largest in the country.

67. Gil, in his 1969 work (op. cit.)—an oft-cited classic, quoted by scholars Chilean and non-Chilean—says the "most significant feature of the 1958 elections was the confirmation of the trend started in 1952, when rural districts, dominated by conservatives, supported Ibáñez." Father figure Ibáñez was, of course, more rightist than the candidate of the already vacillating Right. This consideration should not be allowed to confuse the issue. And that issue is that he wrested votes away from the supposedly invincible barons of the feudal estates. Gil acknowledges as much in discussing the 1952 election ("for the first time, the majority of migrant workers and tenant farmers defied the landowners and voted for Ibáñez"— p. 95).

Such facts should not, however, disturb theory. "A key to the power of the parties of the Right," Gil writes on the very preceding page, p. 94, "resided in the fact that the bulk of Chile's rural areas were practically unchanged" during the years of leftist rule. Obviously, in political terms—and that is what we are talking about—they *were* changing, as the 1952 vote demonstrated, and as the Allende-Frei successes in the countryside would again demonstrate in 1958. It is true that the Left did nothing to improve the plight of the peasantry or alter the pattern of landholding: it would remain for the Right to do that.

The error of these analyses lies in equating the landed gentry of Chile with the brutal caudillos of the other countries. As pointed out earlier, the Chilean plutocracy of the nineteenth century was heavily influenced by the classical liberalism of the nineteenth-century Enlightenment: Comte's positivism and Bentham's philosophical radicals. As disciples of those liberating movements, they became the instruments of change and progressivism, which made Chile the showcase of the continent. Landholding patterns remained unaltered, but the politics of the countryside evolved, and evolved from within.

68. Institutional Reforms, p. 104. The new electoral law governing registration, promulgated September 11, 1986, established (Article 34) that voters could register only where legally domiciled.

69. James Petras and Maurice Zeitlin, "Agrarian Radicalism in Chile," reprinted from *British Journal of Sociology* 19, No. 3 (September 1968), in *Agrarian Problems and Peasant Movements in Latin America*, ed. Rodolfo Stavenhagen (New York: Doubleday, Anchor Books, 1970). The 1960 study they cite was done by Solon Barraclough et al., *Chile: Tenencia de la Tierra y Desarrollo Socioeconómico del Sector Agrícola* (Santiago: Comité Interamericano de Desarrollo Agrícola), pp. 291 ff. (tables B-12, B-13, B-14), 507–8, 523–24.

70. Petras and Zeitlin, op. cit., p. 525. Not unexpectedly, the converse was also true: the higher the proportion of proprietors of farms, the lower the Allende vote. They note that what appeared as a "tendency" in 1958 had by 1964 solidified as a "far stronger [and] direct" relationship. Pp. 518–519. Kaufman

is the author of the monograph *The Chilean Political Right and Agrarian Reform: Resistance and Moderation* (Washington, D.C.: Institute for Comparative Study of Political Systems, 1967). Although Kaufman makes plain his belief in agrarian reform as an imperative of Chilean political life—a premise I do not share—his is the least hectoring and most scholarly study of the problem I have been able to find. The quote is from p. 10 of the study.

71. James L. Payne, *The Oligarchy Muddle*, a monograph prepared for delivery at the 1967 annual meeting of the American Political Science Association in Chicago, September 5–9, 1967; copyright 1967, American Political Science Association.

72. Gil writes: "In reality, the term 'oligarchy' could no longer be applied indiscriminately to the Right and in particular to the landowning class, since the latter had lost their monopoly on political power in 1925" (op. cit., p. 94). He then goes ahead (p. 253) and does it anyway; in describing leftist inroads into the rural vote in 1958, Gil refers to the "agricultural zones of the Central Valley, traditional oligarchical bulwarks." Even the cautious Kaufman demonstrates by the thrust and sense of his paper how Chilean landowners would fail to fit into a workable definition of *oligarch*, yet he proceeds to use it several times.

I like Payne's definition; an oligarchy ought to have two components: (a) be a "group," and (b) have considerable "power." The groups might be families, individuals of great prestige or wealthy employers, landowners, the armed forces, Roman Catholic church, or high public officeholders. Their power might flow from "occupying top political positions over a long period of time," prevailing against other members of society on selected issues, or controlling opinion so that other members of society do not protest against the group's position, or one which, he says, embodies a fallacy. Payne writes about power which enables them to "benefit from the state of affairs, and therefore cause a state of affairs" (op. cit., pp. 3–5). Even assuming a cohesive landowner group in Chile—and there were, in fact, at least three distinct groups (the German-dominated farmers of the south, those of the central region, and the family and small holders)—it is clear that they had not possessed significant power in any of those four ways for forty years.

73. The Liberal party had long since directed its appeals to professionals and middle-class bureaucrats and tradesmen, and even within the ranks of the Conservative party, industrialists steadily displaced landowners in power and influence. Though there were links among these groups, Kaufman (op. cit., pp. 12–19, 30–41) shows how divided they really had become when the moment of truth finally came: the debates in the 1960s over the two agrarian reform laws.

As to landowning patterns, not only was the breakup of the big estates accelerating by the fifties, but agribusinesses already were appearing. Petras and Zeitlin wrote: "Agricultural corporations have gained in importance relative to the large individual landowner, and these corporations now own a significant (though unknown) proportion of the arable land, especially that held by the large *fundos.*" They refer to a then still incomplete study done by Zeitlin of the twenty largest *fundos* (in hectares of first-class land) in the ten major agricultural provinces from Aconcagua to Ñuble. Six, with 29 percent of the land, belonged to corporations; two, with 9 percent of the land, belonged to limited partnerships by inheritance; two more, with 10 percent of the land, belonged to government institutions; one, with 4 percent of the land, belonged to the Roman Catholic church. Nine individuals owned the rest, 49 percent of the land. Petras and Zeitlin, op. cit., p. 511. A sharply different picture this, from the usual one of crusty land barons lording it over a peasant serfdom. (Percentages total 101 because they were rounded to nearest whole numbers.)

74. "Chile: Down to Business," *Time*, March 23, 1968, p. 22.

75. World copper prices soared to 60 cents-plus during the Korean War, in the early 1950s, but then slid continuously, year after year, except for 1960, when the price bounced back, averaging 30.77 cents as opposed to 1959's 29.7 cents. In 1961, prices started another slide, which continued until a dramatic jump in 1964 (from 29.30 cents to 43.99 cents). Statistics from "Cobre: El Mejor Precio y Su Realidad para Chile," *El Mercurio* April 14, 1974, p. 2. Thus, copper was more problem than palliative for Alessandri.

76. "Chile: Balance Sheet," *Time*, August 10, 1959, pp. 26–27.

77. Ibid.

78. *Time*, for instance, enthused that the Christian Democrats had "soared to 171,000 last week" ("Chile: Vote of Approval," April 18, 1960, p. 21). *Time* gave its readers not so much as a hint that the "soaring" Christian Democrats had actually suffered a shellacking. It is true that they had "soared" in comparison with their performance in 1956, but *Time* was nowhere else in that article comparing 1960 to 1956. In comparison with 1958, the benchmark used by *Time* for everyone else, the Christian Democrats actually *lost* 85,000 votes. But then, the Christian Democrats were born with a silver media spoon in their mouths, coddled and cooed over by the international press almost from the time they first appeared on the political scene.

79. As of the end of September 1961, the tally was 4.5 million man-days lost that year. Figure from, "Chile: Stable but Striking," *Time*, October 6, 1961, p. 27.

80. Gil, op. cit., p. 211.

81. Arnello remarks that the Conservatives had gone the way of "making bedfellows of politics and wheeling-dealing" (op. cit., p. 36).

82. Interview in Santiago, October 13, 1974.

83. The gross domestic product stood at $8.4 billion in 1971, a 90 percent improvement over 1961. But the 1971 figure is expressed in 1970 dollars. The acutal rate of annual growth in the gross domestic product, 1960–71, was 4.7 percent, while the plan called for 5.5 percent per annum. *Economic and Social Progress*, p. 152.

84. 12.6 percent of the GNP in 1961, which put Chile behind Ecuador and the Dominican Republic. *Institutional Reforms* p. 102.

85. Kaufman notes that the Right "began to make concessions during a period in which it still retained considerable influence within the political system." In other words, it didn't have to. He gives three basic reasons for the change in position. First, agrarian reform was a *quid pro quo* Alessandri offered the Radicals, eager for an issue that would placate their own left wing, in return for their support in Congress. By August 1961, negotiations had ended, and the Radicals joined his government. Second, changes within Chilean society and political groups: the shift in the position of the Roman Catholic church, "the steady erosion of the social and economic power of the landed elite, relative to new industrial and commercial groups that have moved into the upper class" (op. cit., p. 5), pressure from the urban middle class and the "non-Marxist intellectual community," and finally a liberal

revolt within the Conservative party itself in the spring of 1961 which put "reformist" Héctor Correa in command of the party. Third, external pressures, which included the boisterousness of the Castro revolution, the fact that "through the Alliance for Progress, the United States officially endorsed the idea of land-tenure changes and held out the incentive of massive economic aid if such changes were effected," and the fact that "the economists of the [UN] Food and Agriculture Organization and [UN] Economic Commission for Latin America lent respectability to the idea of agrarian reform and provided technical economic arguments to support their position" (ibid., p. 10). Evidently it did not occur to anyone that most of those technicians were lending "respectability" to their own Marxist biases.

Kaufman also notes that criticisms of the alleged weaknesses of the Alessandri law "may be somewhat overdrawn." He adds that if the Alessandri goal of the careful creation of five thousand to seven thousand new farm owners per year were carried out, "in ten years such a program could make a considerable change in rural property" (ibid., p. 20). Kaufman remarks that the law was most significant both for the profound change it represented in the thinking of the Right and because it created the legal machinery for later large-scale agrarian "reform" (in quotation marks because neither Frei nor Allende conducted programs for transforming the countryside on grounds that could be described as rational Frei gave a handful of peasants to land; Allende gave none.

86. Kaufman operates in his study on the fundamental premise that unless there were agrarian reform, there would be revolution. If demagogic political leaders are permitted to fan class hatreds for their own ends, that is, of course, a possibility, but one which does not derive necessarily from the realities of rural life. Revolutionaries from Marx forward have noted repeatedly the need to galvanize a listless peasantry into action, and when they fail to act, to act "for" them.

As to the social "justice" of agrarian reform, Kaufman has the floor: ". . . the making of adjustments to prevent revolution should not be confused with the larger issue of whether these adjustments are steps to a more just social order in the countryside. 'Social justice' may be necessary to maintain stability, but there is no *a priori* reason to assume that this must be the case" (ibid., p. ii). One would need to be utterly dogmatic to claim that what emerged from nine years of Frei-Allende "reforms" yielded greater social justice in the countryside. There can be no dispute whatever that those nine years seriously weakened the capacity of Chilean agriculture to feed the nation's people, and it would seem that there ought to be a consideration of "social justice" in that reality too.

87. Jacques Chonchol, *El Desarrollo de América Latina y la Reforma Agraria* (Santiago: Editorial del Pacífico, S.A., 1964), reproduced in *Agrarian Problems and Peasant Movements in Latin America*, ed. Rodolfo Stavenhagen (New York: Doubleday, Anchor Books, 1970), p. 162. A World Bank study trips all over itself in making, with the utmost reluctance, the same point on the economic weakness of agrarian reform: "Where the program has been vigorously prosecuted, the results have sometimes been adverse, in that agricultural output has fallen and the condition of those whom it is intended to benefit has not been improved, or has even deteriorated" (*World Bank Operations: Sectoral Programs and Policies* [Baltimore and London: Johns Hopkins University Press, 1972], p. 35). (Hereafter *World Bank Opera-*

tions.) Although the report gingerly slips in the qualifier "sometimes," the fact is that it shows no instances where the opposite has occurred: where output has not been affected adversely. In the following line, a further apology is offered: "The record is, in a sense, unfair to land reform in that it has often been implemented in times of great social tension, and against strong opposition, by radical governments."

88. *Institutional Reforms*, p. 102.

89. Ibid., p. 102. Labrousse (op. cit., p. 72) put borrowing 1961–62 at $410 million, as compared with $540 million for the entire 1950–60 decade. It should, however, be pointed out that heavy borrowing by Latin governments was encouraged in the early years of the Alliance for Progress, a device supposedly designed to give a sharp push to floundering economies.

90. Gil, op. cit., p. 256.

91. *Nueva Enciclopedia*, 1:135.

92. Although the Radicals joined formally in an electoral front only in October 1963, they had supported Alessandri from the very beginning, and in April 1961 had joined Liberals and Conservatives in parceling out committee chairmanships and assignments in the new Congress.

93. A few weeks later, following the Curicó debacle, Bossay would turn up in Moscow, as a guest of the Supreme Soviet. On April 3, 1964, *El Siglo*, the Communist party daily in Santiago, trumpeted a statement made by Bossay in Moscow. Chamudes says the statement "was a vulgar repetition of Khrushchev's propaganda about Communist triumphs which would mean the 'burial' of world capitalism by 1970" (op. cit., p. 131).

94. Labrousse, op. cit., p. 93.

95. Gil, for example, uses these words, on p. 99. Later (p. 261) he goes even further, describing the province as having been "always regarded as a conservative bulwark." Curicó was a "conservative bulwark" in no sense at all. If you were to add the votes of the Liberal and Conservative parties in the 1957, 1960, 1961, and 1963 off-elections, it is true that they were the biggest single "bloc," except they weren't a bloc. Furthermore, the analysis overlooks the strength of the Left, which *was* a bloc. In 1963 the Socialists and Communists jointly polled 27.2 percent (vs. 29.5 percent for the Conservatives and Liberals). But the Christian Democrats, self-proclaimed leftists themselves, collected the biggest single vote in the province, 21.4 percent, which means the *total* vote for the Left in that "conservative bulwark" was 48.6 percent, nearly 20 percentage points more than that of the combined Right. The flip-flopping Radicals got most of the rest.

96. Durán later reappeared as the candidate of the Radicals to siphon votes away from Allende, particularly those of anticlerical Radicals, who could not swallow a Christian Democrat candidate.

97. Labrousse, op. cit., p. 94.

98. Ravines, op. cit., p. 80.

99. Interview in Santiago, October 13, 1974.

100. Gil (op. cit., pp. 105–6) notes that the 1925 constitution was drafted in less than five months. It was approved at a plebiscite in which fewer than half the eligible voters reacted to one of three drafts. The result was that 127,483 people, or less than 3 percent of the population, agreed to accept a blueprint for the future charted by fifteen persons in the midst of great political turmoil.

101. Gil, ibid., p. 225.

102. President Ríos's justice minister, in a July 6, 1943, speech to Congress, cited by Gustavo Lagos in the Christian Democrat–produced *Reforma Constitucional 1970* (Santiago: Editorial Juridico de Chile, 1970), p. 63.

103. Arnello, op. cit., pp. 42–43.

104. Weston Agor, *The Chilean Senate* (Austin and London: University of Texas Press, 1971), pp. 52–60.

105. Gil, op. cit., p. 219. Except that Gil saw the recent Right as the essential villain of the piece, ignoring his own impressive evidence to the contrary (pp. 202–9, for example).

106. Galdames, op. cit., p. 513.

107. A World Bank study of nineteen countries showed that in 1960, Chile had the lowest agricultural output per hectare of arable land of any of them: $59. By contrast Israel had $557, Egypt $643, Japan $961; even among the poorest, India had $91, Yugoslavia $141, and Brazil $104. *World Bank Operations,* p. 67. Source for the GNP, balance of payments, and output figures herein cited: Labrousse, op. cit., pp. 72–73, 109.

108. In 1961 that coefficient was 4.7 percent; Alessandri managed to boost it considerably—to 8.1 percent in 1962, 7.2 percent in 1963, and 8.3 percent in 1964—but even the higher figures kept Chile at the bottom of the list. Richard S. Thorn, "The Alliance for Progress: The Flickering Flame," in *Constructive Change in Latin America,* ed. Cole Blasier (Pittsburgh: University of Pittsburgh Press, 1968), p. 139. Thorn gives the Agency for International Development, Statistics and Reports Division as his source.

109. Quoted by Gil, op. cit., p. 214; from K. H. Silvert, *A Political Economic Sketch of Chilean History from 1879* (Santiago: American University Field Staff Letter, January 29, 1957), p. 2.

110. Alistair Horne, *Small Earthquake in Chile* (New York: Viking Press, 1972), p. 104.

4

The Precipice

FALSE LIGHTS AND UNDISGUISED CALAMITIES[1]

The early sixties was a time of great expectations, a time for believing even in fairy tales, like Camelot. It was a time of superpowers and supersolutions. America was making plans to put a man on the moon, and Russia was making plans to bury America. Lesser rivals had fallen away: China into the abyss of its Great Leap; France and Britain into the quagmire of Suez. An entire generation of international technocrats proclaimed that they had taken the measure of man's oldest and vilest maladies—poverty and violence—and relief was just a master plan or two away. Reason sulked in rhetoric's shadow.

In the Americas, John F. Kennedy and a supporting cast of soothsayers who ranged from the sublime to the ridiculous stumbled over Fidel Castro at the Bay of Pigs and landed on Latin America at Punta del Este. They decided to kill Castro—or at least the threat of Castroism in the hemisphere—with kindness, and fashioned, for the purpose, the Alliance for Progress. It was to become an international Tower of Babel from the day Kennedy first announced it at the White House on March 13, 1961. True, it was immensely valuable in mobilizing resources and energies for an ambitious onslaught on the very real problems of poverty and inequality. But it was also immensely destructive of realistic dialogue, launched as it was amid "excessive rhetoric, exaggerated urgency, and unwarranted optimism," and characterized by "slogans without much substance and programs without clear purpose."[2] Kennedy sold Americans on the notion that the Alliance constituted a set of political and economic canons for conferring the better life on the peoples of Latin America, and that these principles were shared by men of the two Americas, in the rich and increasingly paternalistic one in the North and the struggling but proud one in the South. "It was assumed," one scholar wrote in a post-mortem, "that economic growth, social equity,

130

political stability, and constitutional democracy all went hand in hand and could therefore be advanced simultaneously in Latin America."[3]

The trouble is that Latins never had the slightest intention of accepting U.S. tutelage, economic or political, as the price of access to U.S. treasure. Many among them understood that achieving each of those goals individually was a long and arduous process, and that achieving all simultaneously might be not only impossible but undesirable, because those four goals could be mutually exclusive. The Alliance that Latins wanted was one in which the United States and other developed countries would help them build their own better worlds, but according to their own lights.

The ink was barely dry on the Alliance's lofty charter and the lyrical "Declaration to the Peoples of America"—gossamered during two weeks in August 1961 at Punta del Este, Uruguay—when the governments of two of the three largest Latin nations (Brazil and Argentina) were toppled. When Peru joined them a few months later, Kennedy expressed his dismay and reminded his Alliance associates of their commitment to democratic institutions. Admonition notwithstanding, it was the beginning of the end of an illusion,[4] the illusion that we had witnessed in the Americas the Twilight of the Tyrants, the euphoric title of a book then in vogue.[5]

Illusions die hard, however, especially those reflecting the American penchant for devising gimmicks to Cinderella away the drudgeries of the real world. So the United States continued to divide up those who walked in darkness from those who walked in the Alliance's light. No other country "benefited" more from this largess than Chile,[6] because Chile was one of the "showcases" of the Alliance.

Ironically—or perhaps not so ironically if one views the overall record of U.S. aid programs in winning influence with the benefiting countries—it was Chile that would lead the movement to coalesce Latin America into an effective force for engaging the U.S. through the politics of collective confrontation.

Chile also illustrated one of the hidden traps of the Alliance: the decisive shift in the terms and control of the debates over development strategies, a shift fostered by Alliance rhetoric and the inter-American bureaucracies feeding off it. The new technocrats, overwhelmingly, were legionnaires of the Left. In their designs they gave priority to the state over private or personal initiative, and deflected attention from the bitter truth that "the reasons for Latin America's problems are mostly in Latin America."[7] The effect of this was to deny legitimacy to the arguments of the Right.

In Chile, the Right was already in its death rattle, cowed into submission by its own fear, like a wounded soldier wandering a battleground without his glasses. The Alliance obliterated the safe ground the wounded soldier sought.

The far Left already had the blood of revolution in its eyes—and more while its arguments acquired a new legitimacy—by focusing on the now common enemy, but it still lacked the strength to convert truculent defiance into the fact of power. Only the Christian Democrats—young, arrogant, doctrinaire—were ready to be swept along by the new parade, because only they marched to the beat of the new drummers, cocky and confident that they could beat the Communists at their own society-engineering game.

As the election of 1964 neared, two melancholy and deeply important changes seeped into Chile's institutional life. Note was taken of them, but, in the heat of battle and euphoria so characteristic of those stampeding times, they were not really noted at all.

The first was that politics, at the national level, emerged from its protective cocoon of parochialism, and Chile became an Ouija board of international politics. To a truly alarming degree, the electoral battle that year was waged less on the terrain of local issues than in the context of the collision of international systems. Much of the money for the campaign came from outside the country. Lyndon Johnson, upon the advice of Robert F. Kennedy and the secret undercover intelligence panel later to become infamous, decided that the best bet for spreading the benefits of the Great Society to Chile was via the Christian Democrats.

Accordingly, the U.S. provided, sub rosa, $3 million for Frei's campaign chest, and "all but drowned Chile in AID dollars" ($127.4 million in 1964 alone). One U.S. intelligence official reportedly characterized U.S. intervention in Chile that year as "blatant and almost obscene." Unable to buy all the Chilean escudos it needed through New York banks, the CIA embarked on a mad scramble to obtain Chilean currency through operatives in Lima, Rio de Janeiro, and Montevideo.[8]

The United States government was far from alone in trying to influence the outcome of an election that, in the end, was beyond the power of outsiders to influence. Funds poured into the Christian Democrats from sister parties, particularly in Europe, and from Roman Catholic church sources, particularly in the U.S. The far Left was, of course, handsomely provided for by its allies, particularly in Cuba and Russia.

The second development was the polarization of politics, the division of the country into classes at war with each other. Some of the old forms and habits would linger on a few more years, but for all practical purposes, 1964 marked the end of noblesse oblige and civility in Chilean public life.

It was ironic, really. At the level of the superpowers, the spirit of détente, which began at Camp David and which survived the traumas of the U-2 and the October missile crisis, was still alive. Vietnam was on the horizon, but it never would directly affect the U.S.–Soviet thaw.

Yet, "Chile, in 1964, had become," in the words of two authors, "a cold-war battlefield."[9]

Late in 1963 Eduardo Frei fished for and received an invitation to visit the Soviet Union. Ostensibly, he was a pilgrim of understanding. Cynics said he went to woo the votes of the far (but not hard-core) Left, and noted that he measured his remarks well enough to win the plaudits of *El Siglo,* the Communist party daily in Santiago.[10]

The United States, meanwhile, fearing a recession that would favor Allende, rushed a loan of $40 million to the Alessandri government late in 1963 for "general commodity imports." In the first years of massive U.S. giving, Chile had already become far and away the favored Latin recipient of U.S. largess.

The Curicó debacle had paralyzed the Right, and it found itself believing the Soviet premier Nikita Khrushchev's boast about communism as the wave of the future.

But the rightists were also victims of home-grown propaganda, which had begun years before, when one of their own eminences bolted Conservative ranks to join in founding the Falange (forerunner of the Christian Democrats). Said the maverick, "The Christian Democrats are the only political entity with efficient force to halt the advance of communism."[11]

But they were more than just scared; they also were spent after a century of political life,[12] yet not so dazed or driven as to bring an entire order down with them,[13] and so they rallied behind the Christian Democrats in what was to become one of the most faintly praised swan songs on record.[14]

Not everyone shared even in those giddy times the notion that the best way to combat communism was by competing with the Communists on their own ideological terrain. Nowhere in the Western world had the experiment failed more conspicuously than in Italy, where the reaction to fascism obliterated altogether the Right as a political alternative. In that ambiance, in which the ideas of the Left are canonized as the only legitimate ones, the Italian Communist party became the biggest and strongest in the Western world and kept the country in a state of permanent labor and political crisis. In the 1963 elections the Communists scored huge gains, at the expense of the Italian Christian Democrats led by Amintore Fanfani.

Eduardo Frei, returning from his European tour, pooh-poohed the significance of the elections. But the great Milan newspaper *Il Corriere della Sera* thought otherwise. "The most disturbing and alarming and negative fact in the center-left policy of Fanfanian stripe," the newspaper wrote, "is the increase of more than a million votes for the Communist party. A sign that where political, moral, and religious barriers are erased or blurred in order to compete with the Communist party with its own methods, the result is to improve their chances. . . ."[15]

Nor were all Americans sold on the Christian Democrats. Ambassador Charles Cole, an early Kennedy appointee, made plain his support for Durán up until the time of the Curicó by-election. Back in Washington, Ralph Dungan, part of the New Frontier inner circle, carped to the president about Cole's position, and urged support for Frei. Furthermore, John Robinson, the Agency for International Development (AID) mission director in Chile, "maintained open lines to the Christian Democratic leadership despite Cole's policy"—in clear violation of an edict of the man who had appointed both Cole and Dungan, John F. Kennedy.[16] As noted earlier, the Frei faction carried the day, and the U.S.-backed Frei's campaign materially as well as morally. (Frei was not the only winner; Dungan went on to become the U.S. ambassador in Chile, one of the most dismal ones ever.)

Even on the domestic front, there were dissenters. Former Communist Marcos Chamudes wrote on March 1, 1964:

"He who sows the winds reaps whirlwinds. And he who sows illusions reaps desperation.

"The Christian Democrats have gone about that kind of sowing. The communist reaper will later collect the fruits of their harvest."[17]

But an Italian newspaper, an American ambassador, and a Chilean journalist all were voices in the wilderness. It was, after all, a time for charisma, not caution.

HOW LEFT IS LEFT?

REBELS AND THEIR CAUSE

John Gunther reports that he once asked one of Eduardo Frei's best friends, "How leftist is Frei?"

"So much so," the friend responded, "that he would be a Marxist except for his allegiance to the church."[18]

Like the phenomenon of anamorphosis in optics, that answer must be viewed from just the right angle to be seen clearly. That angle is economics, because in common with most Christian Democrat leaders, Eduardo Frei applied Marxist criteria to the analysis of economic problems, including the idea that private property was at the root of most of man's collective ills.[19]

"Those who founded Christian Democracy in Chile," Frei wrote, "rejected capitalism as a system; they believed and believe that it was, in its origins, materialist and inhumane. . . ."[20]

In common with other Christian Democrat thinkers, he also believed in the inevitability of "at least a restricted kind of class struggle."[21] Gabriel García Márquez, the great Colombian novelist and long-time Communist, said Frei "was the one who took the best advantage of the class struggle, the one who stimulated it and brought it to a head"[22] during the Allende years. García Márquez might have added that the same pattern was part and parcel of the Christian Democrat program while that party was in power itself.

In politics it was also true that the Marxist parties, and particularly the Communists, always held for Christian Democrats what Chamudes has described as "the fascination of the forbidden fruit." Frei himself did not share that fascination, which is why it would be wrong to describe him as a Marxist, but he did yield repeatedly to the party's Marxist-accommodating purposes. In part because Frei, in common with other Christian Democrat thinkers, accepted Kerensky's dictum: "For the cause of democracy, there are no enemies on the Left."[23] Indeed, in 1966, a book by the Brazilian writer Fabio Vidigal Xavier de Silveira entitled, *Frei, el Kerensky chileno*, went so far as to argue that Frei and his policies were preparing the way for a Communist takeover in Chile. The book was banned in Chile—but the thesis it espoused would reverberate through Chile for years to come.[24]

But in these, as in other issues, Frei's views were more moderate than those of the party's other high commanders, Bernardo Leighton Guzmán and Radomiro Tomic Romero. His views were more moderate too than those of a Roman Catholic clique, composed mainly of Jesuits headed by the Belgian priest Roger Vekemans, that was enormously influential in radicalizing Christian Democrat thought.

Not unexpectedly for a public figure trying to appeal to the greatest possible range of voters, Frei's views tended to be more mottled as well as more moderate.

For example, he repeatedly portrayed himself as anti-Communist, and yet one of the most famous phrases in Chilean political lore is from a speech he made June 27, 1947: "There is something worse than communism: anticommunism."

On May 30, 1961, responding to a letter sent him a month earlier by Luis Corvalán Lepe, secretary-general of the Communist party, Frei said: "The time has come for a great effort to achieve harmony among those who aspire to give Chile a new regime of institutions to bring about necessary and inevitable social changes! Naturally, such agreement is easier and certainly deeper among those who share a common scale of moral and ideological values, but we do not exclude other human groups who also form part of this country and its destiny. In this regard I must tell you that it is not true that Christian Democracy conceives of its task in Chile, nor interprets its past and present, in terms of antagonism between Christian Democracy and communism."[25]

Two years later he made his one-week pilgrimage to Moscow, ostensibly to see for himself what the people and leaders thought and felt. But the conciliatory tone of the public remarks of "anticommunist" Frei about what he found behind the Iron Curtain was widely interpreted in Chile as a bold bid for Communist party support.

Later, his revived disdain for communism overcame again his disdain for anticommunism, so that he sanctioned a "Campaign of Terror," as part of his crisply and professionally organized 1964 campaign. The Campaign of Terror was designed to frighten Chileans with horror stories of what awaited them if the Communist party came to power.[26] So much for the non-anti-Communist anticommunism of un-Communist Frei.

In point of fact, Frei was profoundly anti-Communist, a devoutly religious man, devoutly dedicated also to representative democracy. His greatest weakness was deferring repeatedly to those who put power and party above principle, and in the Christian Democrat constellation, those were overwhelmingly the party's radical leftists. Not until 1972 would Frei finally assert his authority decisively in the party's councils and seek a desperation alliance with the Right, but by then it was too little, too late.

Eduardo Frei Montalva was born in Santiago on January 16, 1911, son of a Swiss immigrant who worked as an accountant on the national railways. He grew up in a middle-class neighborhood, and studied law at the Catholic University in Santiago. His classmates included three men who would join him in founding the party: Leighton, Tomic, and Manuel Garretón. All four were political activists, leaders of a group called the National Catholic Association; and all were caught up in the effervescence of reform and social experimentation then so rife in Chile. Under the tutelage of a senator and a reform-minded patriarch of the Conservative party, Rafael Luis Gumucio, they became the young turks of that party.

Following his graduation in 1933, Frei went briefly to Iquique in the north to edit the newspaper *El Tarapacá*. Next, he and Garretón traveled to Europe, where they met the brilliant French philosopher Jacques Maritain. Maritain's neo-Thomist thought was to have a profound influence on Frei as well as on the Christian Democrat party ideologue, Jamie Castillo, who wrote often on his work. Maritain's thought emerged as the leitmotif of the early era of the entire worldwide Christian Democrat movement.

Of the commonly accepted five dominant themes of Maritain, the one which evidently impacted most directly on Frei's thought was the last: "the pluralistic cooperation among men of different beliefs in the pursuit of the common good of political life."[26] But, as in so many other facets of his public career, Frei preached a better line than he practiced, excluding all but Christian Democrats from his government, and excluding the Right even from the political debate.

To a degree far greater than was the case in most other Latin American countries, the Roman Catholic church in Chile was agitated by the 1891 encyclical of Pope Leo XIII, "Rerum Novarum," a remarkably bold statement for its day. In it, the pope defended the inviolability of private property, but also decried the excesses of capitalism. Young Catholic radicals in 1909 founded the Chilean Worker Federation, later to fall under Communist control; and in 1920 two European Jesuits, Fathers Fernando Vivas Soler and Jorge Fernández Pradel, founded the Social League, which advocated collective land ownership.

Christian Democrat social and economic thought was also deeply influenced in its formative years by Catholic social doctrine, particularly as expressed in "Rerum Novarum" and Pius XI's 1931 encyecical "Quadregisimo Anno," both of which were critical of the excesses of liberal capitalism and collectivist socialism. As the assiduous American scholar Paul Sigmund points out, these encyclicals called for the establishment of a new form of society responding to both the individual and social aspects of man's nature. That doctrine, he adds, could be given an authoritarian or corporatist character, as in Portugal, Austria of the 1930s, and Franco's Spain. But, as mentioned, Jacques Maritain exerted his own prestige. "Chilean Christian Democrats," Sigmund writes, "like their European counterparts, saw democracy as the form of government most in keeping with the Gospel message. . . . Catholic in terms of the sources of its ideology and of the educational background of most (but not all) of its leaders, it [the PDC] was not a confessional party."[27]

Frei and his contemporaries challenged the stance of the Conservative leadership, which held that the church condemned the excesses of the capitalist system but not the system itself. The rebels insisted on the validity of a third position between socialism and capitalism, a position they described as "communitarianism."

The distance between the young radicals—Frei, Leighton, Tomic, Garretón, Ignacio Palma, Jorge Rogers Sotomayor—and the elder statesmen of the Conservative party widened steadily. The final break came in 1938, when the youth group refused to support the candidacy of

Gustavo Ross, the party-backed candidate narrowly nosed out by the leftist coalition. Their defection was a key factor in the Left's ascendancy to power.

The dissidents first called themselves Conservative Falange, and later National Falange. Garretón emerged as the party's first ideologue, constructing a twenty-six-point program closely paralleling that of the fascist Spanish Falange.[28] The resemblance was understandable. During the European trip with Frei, the two had met Benito Mussolini, the Italian dictator, and Garretón described him as a "giant." Although rejecting fascism as "contrary to the dignity of the human being," Garretón found much to admire in the system, which he described as "the greatest attempt to remedy the evils of the liberal-democratic regime."[29] He proposed for Chile a "national state, hierarchically organized above parties, groups, or classes." In the distressing tenor of the times, the Falange also organized uniformed paramilitary groups.

Leighton succeeded Garretón as the party's mentor. Two years older than Frei, Leighton was as unlike Frei ideologically as he was in appearance, and yet the two men were, in the phrase of a gushing admirer of both, "as close as fingers for thirty years or more."[30] Leighton looked for most of his life like a boy, and his critics asserted that he had never grown up politically either. Eduardo Frei was tall and gaunt in the way of Lincoln, except that he tended to plumpness below the waist. A great beaky nose split a rugged face from north to south, and he looked at the visitor out of deep-set, brow-shrouded eyes that reflected the grave and studious person that he was. John Gunther said he thought "he looked like an El Greco saint, but not so tortured."[32] Like Leighton, Frei suffered for most of his career from a certain ingenuousness in public affairs, but there any political resemblance between the two men ended.

At age twenty-seven Leighton joined the ranks of Chile's boy wonders; he became Arturo Alessandri's labor minister, reputedly in defiance of his fellow Falangists, who would shortly torpedo Alessandri's man, Gustavo Ross.[33] According to Chamudes, one of Leighton's first acts was to fall hook, line, and sinker for a Communist trick.[34] Leighton would later become education minister in the González Videla government and first president of the Christian Democrat party.

Leighton presided over the drift away from the ideas of Maritain, when the party embraced the "progressivism" of French, German, Dutch, and Belgian clergy, a moral relativism which rejected absolute qualities of Catholic dogma. Leighton and company rejected also Maritain's vision of a close link between church and public life. The Chilean church shortly would become a haven for a number of these European clerics, destined to become the spinal cord of the Christian Democrat Left, and by 1973 some of Salvador Allende's most articulate defenders.

What distinguished Leighton throughout this period—as it would throughout his career—was his affinity with the men and ideas of the far Left. He was followed as the party's top chieftain by Tomic, but the Tomic era introduced no change in the party's commitment to the Left; it simply hastened and deepened it.

Frei occupied himself during these years building political fortunes— the party's and his own. In 1945, after failing to win election as a deputy, he was named public works minister; in 1949 he was elected a senator— first of his party to reach the Senate. He made such a good showing in the 1953 parliamentary elections that Ibáñez invited him to join his polyglot government, even though the Falange had opposed Ibáñez the year before. The party that year did dismally, making the second-lowest showing (2.87 percent) of the four congressional elections in which it had participated, still another example of what by then was becoming a phenomenon as familiar as it was ignored among the democratic parties in Chilean politics: the appeal of the man rather than of the party. But it was Frei's showing in the 1957 elections (the highest vote total of any senatorial candidate in Santiago) which established his indisputable leadership of the Christian Democrat party. Austere, scholarly, and implacably ambitious, Eduardo Frei had done his job well: he had built for the Christian Democrats a platform to power.

Garretón, Leighton, Tomic, and others who shaped the party's program had done the rest: they had constructed the ideological quicksand in which both the proud past and the promise of a better future would perish.

"REVOLUTION IN LIBERTY"

> *Will [Latin America] waste its efforts on a collectivism or statism that will absorb and subjugate man?*
>
> Eduardo Frei[35]

One of the paradoxes of Eduardo Frei is that he so often enunciated so well, in affairs both domestic and foreign, the pitfalls into which he had just led his own followers, national and international. One admiring American journalist put aside his adulation long enough to write: "Sometimes, it seems, President Frei relishes more his picture of himself as Latin America's voice and conscience than he does the irritating business of simply being the leader of a single country constantly in a state of hypertension."[36]

In his campaign for the presidency in 1964, for example, Frei promised the electorate a "Revolution with Liberty." The twin pillars of the revolution were collectivism (on the farms, in government-sponsored urban organization, in labor affairs) and statism (the rapid expansion of state control—direct control—over the country's economic affairs). The revolution, as far as it went, did not "absorb and subjugate" Chilean man. But it did make inevitable a later regime that brought the country to the brink of that abyss and then, because of the bullheadedness of both its promoters and its detractors, pushed the country over.

One of Frei's heroes was Konrad Adenauer. German Christian Democrats rewarded Frei's admiration of their leader richly during the electoral campaign: one American journalist estimated that European Christian Democrats in West Germany, Italy, and Belgium pumped from $18 million to $20 million into Frei's campaign,[37] and most sources agree that the West Germans were the most openhanded of all. The reputed conduit for the European funds: the Jesuit Roger Vekemans.[38] The U.S. journalist also asserted that U.S. sources contributed $1 million a month "for many months" to Frei's campaign. Presumably that would not include $3 million appropriated clandestinely under the auspices of Robert Kennedy for use by the CIA.[39] One former CIA man (turned exposé author) even repeats a newspaper report that up to $20 million in American money was funneled into the country clandestinely.[40]

Allende's campaign was lavishly bankrolled too, and much of the money also came from abroad, principally from Russia and Cuba. But not only the Left supported him. Leading banks—those bastions of capitalism—loaned candidate Allende money, a variation on the old Leninist prophecy that the last two capitalists on earth would bid against each other to sell the executioner the rope with which to hang them. One bank loaned Allende 230 million pesos ($85,000) on his signature alone, a handsome sum for a man whose only income was his Senate salary.[41]

The only campaign that was not well funded, in fact, was the brief but vigorous one of independent Jorge Prat Echaurren, the only authentically "right-wing" candidate in the race. He quit on April 26, 1964, blaming lack of finances after an intense ten-month campaign, but he left behind an ideological legacy that would be retrieved a few years later. In quitting and throwing his support reluctantly to Frei, Prat said: "If they [Allende's Popular Action Front, FRAP] win, it cannot be written in Chilean history that I was the one who facilitated a Communist victory." His remark paralleled the one of Radical Julio Durán: "Many people are trying to determine which group, the FRAP or the Christian Democrats, is the lesser evil"—except that Durán believed the best way of blocking FRAP was for him to remain in the race and siphon off leftist votes from Allende.[42]

Allende went into the race oozing confidence. Nearly a year and-a-half before the elections, he sent a message to Fidel Castro saying that

Chile would soon stand shoulder to shoulder with Cuba as the second socialist state in the hemisphere,[43] a sentiment frequently reflected in foreign press comment on the 1964 elections. During the early months of his campaign, Allende was outspoken in his praise of Castro's revolution.

So confident was Allende that he did not even use his influence to prevent the staging in Santiago, less than one week before the crucial Curicó by-election, of the Havana-organized Second Latin American Youth Congress. On opening day the conference theme was unveiled: For the Liberation of Latin America, the slogan then identified with Castroite guerrilla movements. The conference collapsed in a spasm of denunciations that many of the delegates belonged not to youth organizations but to underground terrorist groups. Allende and his cohorts were aware that the mere staging of such an incendiary conference would heighten tension, but evidently felt they were invincible.

Another incident revealed their impudence. A Communist senator, Jaime Barros, made a savage attack on Catholic priests in a June 23 speech in Congress, calling them "vampires." But this one backfired immediately, galvanizing the church into action, including dusting off and widely publicizing a two-year pastoral message of the country's bishops. The pastoral was mostly a church blessing for Christian Democrat–style reformist programs, but also included a dramatic warning:

"Communism has never imposed itself by conviction, by the value of its doctrine, but always due to the feebleness of states and parties which call themselves democratic, and has risen to power only to become the implacable foe of all who do not think alike, including those who made its ascension possible. From the triumph of communism in Chile, the church and all of its children can expect only persecution, tears, and blood."[44]

The collapse of the Democratic Front after Curicó meant that it would no longer be a triangular race but, for all practical purposes, a head-on between Allende and Frei. This, plus church hostility, caused Allende to tone down his praise of Castro, and he even invented a group called "Catholics for Allende." Allende emphasized in his speeches his commitment to Chile's democratic institutions, insisting that he would carry out his revolution legally and constitutionally.

But then, so did Frei; and as countless observers, friends, and critics alike have observed, the differences in their program were a matter more of emphasis than of substance.[45] The U.S. government and press, both enthusiastic supporters of Frei, were significant exceptions to this rule. But the fact remains that there was little difference between the two. In fact, two months before the elections, the managing editor of

Santiago's Socialist daily summed up the view of the Left. "Electorally," he said, "the Marxists may suffer a defeat, but politically they have already scored a victory." He explained that the Right was dead and the differences between Christian Democrats and the Popular Front were slight. In that, the Socialist was not far from the youth wing of the Christian Democrats.

In a statement on March 24, 1964, commenting on the Curicó election, the National Council for the Christian Democrat Youth praised both Frei and FRAP for eliminating the Right. "By means of their support for the Chrisitan Democratic party and for the Popular Action Front," the statement said, "the people of Curicó expressed their repudiation of the existing system of government and their irrevocable desire for social change. . . . The Democratic Front [the coalition of the Radicals and the Right] suffered a historic defeat."[46]

On September 4, 1964, after the costliest and most bombastic campaign in Chilean political history, the voters returned their verdict in an election in which the specter of explicit totalitarianism towered over all else. The result was a decisive win for Frei, though not nearly the "smashing triumph" portrayed by the international press.[47] The result:

Frei	1,409,012	56.09%
Allende	977,902	38.93
Durán	125,233	4.98

As noted earlier, Allende did almost as well as Frei among men: 602,136 men voted for him, 664,589 for Frei. It was the women who gave Frei his decisive margin: 744,423 women voted for him, only 375,766 for Allende.

Immediately after the election, Lyndon Johnson said Frei's victory was "an omen for a very bright future in South America," adding that U.S. aid to Chile under the Alliance for Progress deserved "some credit."[48]

Fidel Castro "angrily denounced" the defeat of Allende and said it again demonstrated that the "armed revolutionary fight is unavoidable." He ascribed Allende's defeat to "lies, fear, and money."[49]

While Frei's followers celebrated on Santiago's streets, mobs of angry Allende followers shouted "revolution, revolution," charging that Johnson and Pope Paul VI had sabotaged their man with money. Speaking from a balcony, Allende urged them to avoid violence. "We must remain calm," he said. "I am not broken nor defeated. I have strength to continue fighting and remain side by side with those who supported me." Few believed Allende would rise again from the ashes of his third defeat, however.[50]

Following his inauguration on November 3, 1964, Frei told Adlai E. Stevenson, head of the U.S. delegation: "I am responsible now." Later, he told José Mayobre, the Venezuelan who then headed the UN Economic Commission for Latin America—an agency Frei greatly admired: "No one can ask me to do more than I promised, but neither can anybody ask me to do less."[51]

Even in defeat, Fidel Castro glimpsed victory. The influence of the Cuban revolution, he said, had forced "reactionaries out of the election and limited the contest to revolutionaries and reformers."[52]

Following his election, Frei retreated to a country estate outside Santiago. A coterie of close advisers shuttled back and forth, helping him to hammer out his immediate program. Among them: Leighton, Tomic, Gabriel Valdés Subercaseaux, Jacques Chonchol Chait, Alvaro Marfán, and, especially, the economist Jorge Ahumada. Two independents joined them: Sergio Molina Silva and William Thayer. From this group would come four members (Leighton, Valdés, Molina, and Thayer) of his Cabinet, a slick elite of mostly young men (seven of the twelve ministers were under fifty, and one, Molina, was only thirty-five; only two ministers, of education and health, were over sixty).[53] Gunther said that together "these comprise what has been called the most 'brilliant' Cabinet in the world. All its members are intellectuals, most were professors, who have known one another for years, and form an integrated team; they still do their homework, and are not unconscious of their own merit. One of them said to me with engaging audacity: 'We make a strong group. We have spent our lives preparing for this role, and we will be the government for thirty years.' "[54] The composition and snobbishness of the group—reminiscent of Franklin D. Roosevelt's Brain Trust and the Ivy League clubbishness of the New Frontier—may help to explain why Frei's government began with what British historian Horne described as the "liberal adoration of Frei in the U.S."[55]

The group also included two other key men: Tomic, who would become sort of a surrogate foreign minister from his post as ambassador to Washington, and later go on to lead the party to its final ruin in the 1970 presidential elections; and Chonchol, who had warmed up for his job as architect of Frei's agrarian reform program by spending two years as a United Nations adviser to Fidel Castro. The group was also notable in that, of the Christian Democrats, all were recruited from the Left to far-Left ranks of the party.[56] Molina, an independent destined to become finance minister, was the only authentic moderate among them.

Out of these meetings came Frei's action plan. First on that agenda, sweeping constitutional reforms, unveiled in the first weeks of his government. Among the proposed amendments were measures to strip Congress of much of its power, while greatly expanding presidential power (including "exclusive" authority to initiate economic and social legislation); another to create a Constitutional Tribunal to hear all constitutional disputes; yet another to create an Economic and Social Counsel, a superagency with vast powers over the entire economy. (It would take Frei five years to get most of those constitutional reforms—with ominous consequences in the final death duel of democracy in Chile. He did, however, ram through Congress in 1967 a constitutional amendment peeling away private property rights from farmers in order to facilitate his agrarian reform schemes, yet another legal Frankenstein in the hands of Allende and his agrarian "reformers," chief among them that selfsame Jacques Chonchol).

Next: a Cabinet made up entirely of Christian Democrats and sympathetic independents, leaving in the cold the parties of the Right which were crucial to his election. Third: a decision not to try to work with the existing Congress, where the Radicals and parties of the Right still held control, but rather to mobilize massively for the congressional elections the following March (where they would come within a whisker of achieving absolute control). Finally: Frei began to blitz the Congress with his proposals, forcing them to gag on so many radical programs as to give the Christian Democrats the electoral ammunition they needed for those 1965 elections.

Such acrimony followed Frei's election that when the day came for Congress to meet and formally accept the results of the election, so many senators and deputies stayed away that there was no quorum. Frei had to wait until the next day, when, under the constitution, no quorum was needed to invest him as president.[57]

On November 24, 1964, twenty days after Frei's inauguration, Molina laid before Congress the new government's program, a program which began by identifying five major national problems:

(1) The endemic inflation and need for higher levels of production;
(2) Social injustice;
(3) The lack of educational opportunities;
(4) The lack of participation of the people in the nation's political life;
(5) The imperfections of national sovereignty.

To meet these problems, the government proposed a six-point program:

(1) ... the eradication of punitive inflation within a period of four years. The government's goals are a lowering of the rate of inflation to 25 percent by the end of 1965, to 15 percent in 1966, to 10 percent in 1967, and to zero in 1968;

(2) ... increase of exports by 100 percent within six years. The government believes that the increase would help to give Chile the means to reduce the heavy external debt which has compromised her national sovereignty;

(3) ... the solution of the problem of the fundo [large estate] system within six years. The government aims at both the increase of agriculture production through the encouragement of commercial agriculture, the increase in the amount of land under cultivation, and the improvement of irrigation systems, improvement of the system of agricultural credits, and the creation of 100,000 new agricultural properties;

(4) The reduction of the housing deficit within six years by the construction of 360,000 new houses;

(5) The offering of educational opportunities to all children of school age. The government plans to accomplish this within one year;

(6) The providing of minimum public services to the poor neighborhoods within four years.

To finance these objectives, Molina proposed:

(1) Forcing both businesses and individuals to fulfill strictly their tax obligations;

(2) Raising the taxes of those most able to pay;

(3) Encouraging voluntary savings directly through the perfecting of the savings institutions, and indirectly through monetary stabilization and voluntary cooperation of the most patriotic Chileans.

(4) Renegotiating the external debt [Chilean foreign debt in 1964 was about $1.127 billion, or about $140 for each Chilean] and acquiring new credits.[58]

Frei was in office less than one month when he sacrificed the first of his goals to politics: the government ordered pay raises equal to the increase in the cost of living, opening inflation's floodgates anew; through price controls, the increase the next year was contained to the targeted level, but the horse of inflation had departed the barn of restraint.

Writing a few years later, Olympian Frei, as opposed to politician Frei, would remark: "One of the main features of democratic cycles is a 'something for nothing' attitude, where everyone demands concessions but not at the expense of hard, sustained effort; and this is perhaps the gravest danger that faces Latin American societies in search of full equality after generations of constraint."[59]

There was, of course, no hint of austerity or "hard, sustained effort" in Frei's blueprint of bonanza. The money, basically, would come from the rich, those at home, and the creditors abroad.

Tax evasion in Chile, it is true, was about as endemic as elsewhere in Latin America; basically, only the despised foreign firms paid their taxes according to the letter of the law. But in zeroing in on business, for example—a politically safe thing to do—Frei was pandering to the myth of fat business profits. A 1965 study showed that "holders of corporate equities received only about 2 percent per annum in real terms on their investment over the 1929–1959 period," and that "profits by the large corporations were reduced by the rapid rise in wage costs and that wages were higher for large enterprises than in the case of small firms."[60] As for the American-owned mining giants, the source of 70 percent of government revenues, they already were paying the highest mining taxes in the world, from sixty-seven to eighty-three cents on every taxable dollar. (Less than two years later, one of the two American giants, Kennecott [Braden] was paying eighty-one to eighty-seven cents on every dollar.)

How well did Frei do?

If he were to be measured against the rhetoric of the Alliance for Progress, then the answer is very well, indeed. Levinson and de Onís, in their book *The Alliance That Lost Its Way*, include a table (see table 14) that is based on what they describe as Alliance criteria, and that measures the performance of the three major aid recipients during the first decade of the Alliance.[61]

The authors concede that columns B and C are highly subjective, but that column A can be pinpointed with a fairly high degree of precision.[62] Is progress in agriculture, for example, carving up big estates to create state farms, or is it increasing the food supply? Is progress in politics a

TABLE 14

PROGRESS ON ECONOMIC, SOCIAL, AND POLITICAL FRONTS

	A MACROECONOMIC MANAGEMENT (FISCAL, MONETARY, EXCHANGE POLICY)	B SOCIAL REFORM (EDUCATION, HOUS- ING, AGRICULTURE)	C REPRESENTATIVE POLITICAL INSTITUTIONS	TOTAL
Brazil	4.5	2.5	1.0	8.0
Chile	2.0	4.0	5.0	11.0
Colombia	4.0	3.5	4.0	11.5

(On a scale of 1 to 5)

Source: Jerome Levinson and Juan de Onís, *The Alliance That Lost Its Way* (Chicago: Quandrangle Books, Twentieth Century Fund Study, 1970), p. 207.

single man or group of men claiming to represent the broadest possible interests (as the authors seem to indicate it can be in their approval of Mexico's one-party system), or is it a multiplicity of parties? And is Left better than Right, or Right better than Left?

And how good were Alliance criteria anyway? Levinson and de Onís quote an official of one international financial institution as saying: "Look at Chile. They have done all the things called for under the Charter of Punta del Este [creating the Alliance]. And what a mess!" The authors go on to say that what a "look at Chile also suggests is that fundamentally transforming social, economic, and political relationships within the framework of genuinely representative political institutions may have to be expensive and messy." Apart from the fact that "expensive and messy" is not what the American framers of the Alliance promised, the Levinson–de Onís premises were superficial even in 1970, when they wrote those lines, and were soon to become not an accolade to progress but a prescription for doom.

How well did Frei do, as measured against his own six goals?

1. *Inflation In Chile, 1965–1970*

TABLE 15
INFLATION IN CHILE, 1956–1970: GOALS vs. PERFORMANCE

	1965	1966	1967	1968	1969	1970
Frei's goals	25%	15%	10%	0	0	0
Actual	26	17	22	27	29	35

Source: For actual figures, International Monetary Fund Statistics, November 1971, December data, p. 35. Percentages are extrapolated from the year-to-year increase in the consumer price index.

Note: Frei's six-year term ended November 4, 1970.

A two-year drought in 1967 and 1968, the worst of the century, is frequently cited by Frei apologists as one of two principal causes for his losing the war on inflation; but as table 16 indicates, the impact was felt only in 1969, and was limited in scope.

The other frequently invoked defense is that the government was "unable" to cope with the demands of labor unions. The Frei years were a time when the "inhumanity" of capitalism was being replaced by the "humanitarianism" of communitarianism in the early years, socialism in the later ones. The Frei years were also a time of the worst labor turmoil yet on record in Chile.

Plainly, Frei failed dismally to achieve his first goal.

TABLE 16
AGRICULTURAL OUTPUT IN CHILE, 1965–1970

	1965	1966	1967	1968	1969	1970
Index of per capita						
Food production	102	101	102	104	95	101
Milk production[a]	835	855	875	875	900	1,100
Production of principal crops[b]						
Corn	221	246	362	321	154	250
Potatoes	737	717	717	725	603	618
Rapeseed	60	77	61	48	64	65
Sugar beet	710	768	1,048	1,194	1,238	1,635
Wheat	1,276	1,167	1,203	1,220	1,214	1,300
Meat production[c]	232	237	244	262	274	280

Source: Summary of Economic and Social Indicators, 18 Latin American Countries: 1960–1970 (Washington, D.C.: Office of Development Programs, Bureau for Latin America, Agency for International Development, April 1971), pp. 51, 52, 53, 55.

[a] In thousands of metric tons.
[b] In thousands of metric tons.
[c] In thousands of metric tons; includes chicken.

2. *Increase exports 100 percent in six years, to reduce heavy external debt*

Thanks largely to a sustained high level of prices for copper, which gave Frei a $1.7 billion windfall over six years, Frei did boost the value of exports by 79 percent (from $624 million at the end of 1964 to $1.1 billion at the end of 1970).[63] But no Chilean government has yet managed to claim credit for the world price of copper, and copper was the principal reason for the increase. It is also interesting that during the same period, imports rose at a similar rate (from 1964's $607 million to 1970's $1.096 billion).[64]

Manufacturing—where most of the badly needed new jobs would come from—grew from 1965 to 1970 at the paltry rate of 3.3 percent (the third-lowest level in all of Latin America) and in 1970 actually showed the only decline (–0.3 percent) in Latin America. For the region as a whole, the growth rate for those years was 7.3 percent.[65] In 1964 manufacturing represented 26.3 percent of the gross national product; by 1968 it was down to 25.6 percent and still sliding. A 1969 study reported: "Between 1960 and 1966 industrial production rose by 6.4 percent a year, due, among other factors, to a vigorous industrial development policy. . . ." There was a brief spurt in 1964 when Frei indulged in wage-price policies, which Allende would use six years later to create the illusion of prosperity. Then, "in 1967 and 1968, the rate of growth of industrial output declined to about 2.5 percent a year because of labor disputes, credit restrictions, the reduction of general economic activity, and the stagnation of manufactured exports caused by more difficult competitive conditions."[66]

The report does not say so, but there was another villain. By 1969 the state controlled half the country's banking and 50 percent of total investment. The net result was that unemployment, which had been 5 percent in 1963, stood at 6.2 percent in 1970.[67]

Thus the ranks of the jobless increased. How about those who were working? As table 15 shows, inflation started accelerating upward under Frei: the consumer price index, according to those same International Monetary Fund figures, and using 1963 as a base year of 100, went from 174 in 1965 to 555 at the end of 1970, an increase of 218.9 percent, a sickening performance matched by only one or two countries in the world.

In the same period the index of industrial earnings also advanced, from 113 to 168,[68] but that modest increase (48 percent) fell far short of keeping pace with rocketing costs. The result was that the wage earner in 1970 was able to buy far less with his fatter paycheck than when the revolution to free man from capitalism's "inhumane materialism" started in 1965.

As to his plans for reducing the "heavy external debt which has compromised [our] sovereignty," Frei did not fare too well either. His finance minister pegged the foreign debt at the time Frei took office at $1.127 billion, the equivalent of $140 for each Chilean. At the end of 1970 it stood at $2.566 billion,[69] meaning he had more than doubled it. The 1970 census figures for the total population was 9,276,561 and that meant the government had run up the amount owed by each Chilean to $276.

Plainly, Frei flopped on point two also.

3. Agriculture

In his first State of the Union speech, Frei said: "It is an undebatable fact that the most critical issue in our economic development resides fundamentally in the backwardness of our agrarian sector."[70] Frei accepted the fashionable premise that bigness was bad in Chilean agriculture, and so forged a constitutional amendment, enacted in 1967, to suspend usual property rights in rural areas. That amendment enabled the state to seize farmlands through court orders, paying 10 percent of the adjudicated value of the land, the rest in equal installments spread over 15 years. The amendment was ostensibly aimed at stripping rural property owners of their rights only when their lands were inefficiently worked.

But the executors of his policies would soon demonstrate their willingness to sacrifice even "efficiency" in order to attack the "evil" of bigness. Frei also promised to increase production by encouraging commercial agriculture, to increase the land under cultivation, and to give land to 100,000 peasants by breaking up the big estates.

In the beginning the altruists of the Alliance—and that included most of the brisk young men around Kennedy—reacted to the farm problem with the same messianic impetuosity they brought to most other issues. Their operating syllogism for the farm "crusade" was: big farms hog most of the rural land in Latin America; Latin America is both hungry and seething with menacing hordes of landless peasants; therefore, big farms are bad and must be broken up. The minor premise does not, of course, follow from the major, and the conclusion rests on nothing.

The "logic" of the arguments in favor of land reform was reinforced by fear of Castro: "The Kennedy administration," de Onís and Levinson wrote, "regarded peasant unrest in Latin America as a warning signal of incipient Castro-style revolution. Kennedy and his liberal advisers looked upon agrarian reform as a historical imperative for Latin America."[71] As Kaufman pointed out, those notions were reinforced and made "respectable" by the technocrats of the Marxist-dominated UN agencies in the field, with the inevitable result that the Kennedy zealots backed their fervor with cash. "Through the Alliance for Progress," Kaufman wrote, "the United States officially endorsed the idea of land-tenure changes and held out the incentive of massive economic aid if such changes were effected."[72]

In the process, far from pacifying the peasantry, the technocrats stoked artificial fires of unrest, artificial because, as Marx recognized a century earlier, peasant unrest does not just happen, it must be fomented—as it shortly would be by government agitators under Jacques Chonchol in Chile. And once the peasant appetite for land reform is stimulated, it becomes—in the phrase of Mexican writer Edmundo Flores, one of the radicalizing elements of agrarian-reform movements—"a supremely effective device to gain and to retain the support of the peasants, and a deadly weapon against the landed oligarchy." He quotes John H. Kautsky:

> Intellectuals echo and support that demand [for land reform], for one thing, because it is in accord with their new ideas of justice and equality. These ideas also make it desirable for them to become the leaders of a mass movement, of "the people. . . .
>
> "Finally, they press for land reform not because of anything it will do *for* the peasants, but because of what it will do *to* the aristocracy.

The latter is the intellectuals' only powerful domestic enemy, and land reform strikes at the very root of its economic and social position."[73]

Reform enthusiasts Petras and Zeitlin found that in Chile, the land-reform siren song of the far Left had little appeal for the 53 percent of the agricultural labor force who were landowners. Accordingly, the far Left concentrated on the rootless rural laborers—the *voluntarios* (contract laborers who live on the estate and do occasional work) and the *afuerinos* (the outsiders, the migrant laborers). "It is necessary," Luis Corvalán, secretary-general of the Communist party, said in 1960, "to know whom to support to the greatest extent. Of all the rural sectors, the agricultural laborers are, naturally, the most determined, especially the *afuerinos*, who receive their payment in cash, have no other ties to the *fundo* [estate], and only work irregularly."[74]

So, while the altruists viewed the countryside as a caldron of discontent, seething with angry masses clamoring for a better life, the far Left saw it as a vehicle to power, and the inhabitants as impassive targets who could be riled up to smite their ancient masters. This was particularly so of those on society's lowest rung, the migrants, those with the smallest stake in society, reachable via the oldest deceit of all—the chance to get something for nothing.

Chile was as true to Marx's vision of the dynamics of conflict as it was untrue to that of Kennedy's New Frontiersmen. The pressure for reform came from "the urban middle class and non-Marxist intellectual community, and to a lesser extent, *even* the peasants themselves. . . ."[75] There were those in the ranks of the Right who understood that what was at stake was nothing less than their survival as a viable force in Chilean society.[76] But in the main, they were shouted down, and when the chips were down, abandoned even by their own natural "allies," big businessmen.[77] For contrary to facile journalistic accounts of "an extraordinarily powerful and deeply entrenched landowner class which blocks reform," the Right, once its collective mind was made up, went along with agrarian reform, limiting its opposition to rear-guard skirmishing on a few vital issues.[78]

Warnings went unheeded that the Right was merely playing into the hands of those who would be content not merely to defeat it politically, but to destroy it altogether.

"The superficiality with which this subject was been approached," said one such Cassandra in a radio speech, "is due to one cause: agrarian reform has been made a political problem and what interests its proponents is the effect it can have on the electorate."[79]

Carlos Bulnes Correa had an answer for those who argued that by consenting to agrarian reform, the Right would win new followers. "The people have an instinct," he said. "It is not easy to fool them. They will think, and correctly so, that what can be conviction in the Left is simple, occasional demagogy in the Conservatives and Liberals. They [the people] will continue following their leaders, and with much more good reason, after seeing them triumph [by] destroying the bastion of private property."[80]

Eduardo Frei, for his part, all but guaranteed that his agrarian reform would travel a political road by his choice of his top agricultural adviser: Jacques Chonchol. Because of the two years he spent in Cuba, Chonchol was too "hot" to be given the top job as director of the Agrarian Reform Corporation (CORA, for its Spanish initials).[81] So he was given a job that, in many ways, was even more dangerous: head of the newly created Farm and Fisheries Development Bureau (INDAP), charged with working with small farmers and organizing rural labor unions. From the very outset, to the applause of even the Communists,[82] he made clear that his notion of agrarian reform was the molding of *afuerinos* and *voluntarios* into a potent political force.

Eventually, Chonchol became even too hot for eternally temporizing Frei to handle[83]—but not before he had unleashed a veritable tumult in the countryside. Petras and Zeitlin reported that "the number of peasants involved in strikes (protected somewhat by the umbrella of the reform-oriented government) trebled from 1964 to 1965."

The same authors quote Corvalán, the Communist party secretary-general, as pointing out that strikes, even the fear of strikes at harvest time, are a weapon that "makes the large landowner tremble."[84] Under Chonchol's prodding, the supposedly omnipotent land barons would tremble again and again in the years ahead, as table 17 demonstrates.

Sowing the wind with such volatile explosives might have been justified had it accomplished the two goals Frei had set for the program at the beginning: increasing food production and giving land to 100,000 peasant families, as part of providing them with a better life.

TABLE 17
FARM STRIKES, 1960–1969

	1960	1961–64	1965	1966	1967–68	1969
Claims presented	6	74	305	506	3,026	—
Strikes	3	97	141	586	1,341	—
Land seizures	—	5	13	18	21	80

Source: Alain Labrousse, *El Experimento Chileno* (Barcelona and Mexico: Edicions Grijalbo, S.A., p. 101), p. 124, from a study done by A. Alfonso, "Sindicato Campesino: Agente del Cambio,"*CEREN*, no. 5, September 1970, Santiago.

Using 1961–65 as a base period, food output per capita in Chile was 103 on a scale of 100 in 1964, the year Frei took office. As table 16 indicates, only once over the next six years was that level equaled (in 1968). Expressed still a different way, agriculture represented 10.2 percent of gross domestic product in 1965, but dropped to 9.6 percent in 1970.[85]

From 1950 to 1962, pre-Frei years, production of foodstuffs (aside from milk and beef) increased at a rate of nearly 5 percent per year, well ahead of the population growth of 3 percent per year.[86] For the period 1965–70 the increase in overall agricultural output was down to 2.5 percent; what's worse, farm output for 1966–70 slipped 2.2 percent behind population growth.[87] When Frei took over, Chile was spending $130 million on food imports; by 1966 that figure was up to $170 million; in 1967 it dropped to $155 million, only to bounce back the next year to $161 million, before soaring to $186 million in 1969 (the year the effects of the drought hit hardest). He closed out his term with a food deficit of $168 million,[86] a hike of nearly 30 percent over the situation he inherited.

Furthermore, by 1968 "U.S. food gifts to Chile were providing school lunches for 800,000 children a day," and "an estimated 1.9 million persons—one-quarter of Chile's population—were receiving U.S. food aid through voluntary agencies, particularly Caritas. The food grants," authors Levinson and de Onís add, "are a measure of the inadequacies of Chilean production."[89] This little-noted program, which would continue under Allende but with even less recognition, was part of the $534 million in U.S. aid "in direct support of the broad program of economic and social reform undertaken by the Christian Democratic government" of Frei.[90]

Frei's agrarian "reform" benefited directly from a $23 million U.S. loan in 1967, and three Inter-American Development Bank loans: $10 million to Chonchol's INDAP for a supervised credit program to small farmers, $8 million to CORA to help finance peasant settlements, and $10 million in drought relief. In addition, Frei's government was able to divert resources from his budget for agrarian reform thanks to the $80 million annual U.S. program loan, which generated local currency for the regular budget.[91]

Yet, despite such massive outside assistance, Frei also failed to achieve one of his two basic goals for Chilean agriculture: increased output.

The second was to give land to 100,000 peasants. He failed in that one too. Badly, in ways obvious and not so obvious.

As of November 1970, when he left office, 28,700 families had "benefited,"[92] but precious few even of this number received title to the land.

Instead, they were clustered on *asentamientos,* cooperative settlements similar to Mexico's *ejidos.* They were put there at a fantastically high cost: one estimate was $6,000 to $10,000 per family, and that would have made the total cost well over $2 billion, nearly a quarter of all the moneys spent by the Chilean government during Frei's six years in office. The same source said administrative overhead gobbled up a fifth of those costs.[93]

Furthermore, far from solving the problem of the landless laborers, the program tended to create a new ruling rural class. Labrousse, for example, reports that on one *asentamiento,* "Peralillo de Lampa," members of the cooperative hired laborers to help them till their two thousand-acre spread; soon laborers constituted one-third the work force—low-paid laborers, at that. He also notes that following the 1968 drought, laborers were fired in droves, despite the new collective-bargaining contracts, because the government was reluctant to move against its own "reform" creature, the *asentamientos.*[94]

These observations reflect a hidden reality of Chilean rural life, namely, that Chilean agriculture was employing perhaps double the number of field hands it actually needed. Getting rid of the excess might have improved "efficiency," one of the alleged goals of agrarian reform, but it also would have aggravated the problem of unemployment in the cities. This is, in fact, one of the bitterest internal contradictions of agricultural reality in Chile and many other parts of Latin America. It is one so deeply rooted in the structure of the economy as to make lasting solutions virtually impossible.

But in the fifties and early sixties, land reform was an intellectual stampede, and so the Right acquiesced, and thereby preserved the stability of Chilean political institutions, because it was plain that the Left would not relent.[95]

Chile's adventure in agrarian reform under the Christian Democrats was legitimized by one of the most radical land-reform laws on the books anywhere in Latin America, a set of proposals so bold as to surprise even the Chilean Left.[96] The vindictiveness of Chonchol and others within the dominant left wing of the Christian Democrat party made resistance inevitable.

"The Chilean agrarian reform," Levinson and de Onís wrote, "ran into political complications it might have avoided or reduced if its primary objective had been to promote efficient farm production, regardless of the size of the farm....

"Some officials of the Ministry of Agriculture and CORA favored this approach. However, the left wing of the Christian Democratic party was committed to breaking the political power base of the traditional commercial agrarian sector, which it blamed for much of Chile's inequitable social structure."[95]

Landowners could not, of course, acquiesce indefinitely in such a clear threat to their very survival, and so by 1966 there already were press reports of farmers in the south arming to resist.

There was still another reason for alarm. The *asentamiento* system was integrated into the same "wide network of bureaucratic and political relationships" as the *ejidos,* a situation which led even an ardent admirer of *ejidos* to point out the "vulnerability of the *ejido*'s independence and its capacity for autonomous decision and action as a social unit," since it was exposed to "official authoritarianism and paternalism, bureaucratization and, particularly, corruption."[98] This was, of course, precisely the Orwellian scenario forecast and feared by unheeded critics years earlier.

Political gains there were—for the Christian Democrats, for Chonchol. A 1968 study showed something over 73 percent of the newly organized peasants in organizations loyal to the Christian Democrats, and 24 percent in a federation controlled by Chonchol himself.[99]

What price such "progress"!

"We are moving into an institutional crisis," one prominent leader of the Right said, in 1969, "in which eventually the military may have to step in and take over."[100]

In 1966 such a prophecy would have been written off as bordering on hysteria. Didn't Chile, after all, have the sturdiest democratic institutions in all of Latin America? And weren't Chile's military leaders strictly letter-of-the-law boys?

Even before Frei's social engineers began dismantling the old order, the answer should have been a guarded maybe. By the late 1960s, only a hammer and a sickle were needed to complete the demolition.

4. Housing

Frei promised to build 360,000 new publicly financed houses; Alessandri had built 150,000.[101]

In 1966 Frei established Latin America's first Ministry of Housing and Urbanization. Even before it got started, 1965 was already the biggest single year of public-housing building to that point in the country's history, thanks in no small measure to the biggest outpouring of Alliance financing then available to any country.

But Frei missed his housing target too. From 1965 through 1970, 132,926 new units were added by the public sector. The private sector did somewhat better: 150,367,[102] mostly under the aegis of a home mortgage program—one of the best in the Americas—set up earlier under Alliance guidance.

More dismaying, the housing shortage was worse, much worse. Organization of American States and Inter-American Development Bank Studies put Chile's housing deficit around 1960 at 375,000 units.

Around 1965, at the outset of Frei's term, it was 400,000. In 1969, as he was leaving the presidency, it was 630,000.[103]

5. Education

The offering of educational opportunities to all children of school age, to be accomplished within one year, was another goal of Frei's program. This was one genuine success story of the Frei years, though accomplishment was not quite so total or fast as promised.

Enrollment in primary schools jumped from 1,355,000 in 1964 to 1,681,000 two years later, and by 1970, had leaped to 2,100,000, a 55 percent increase. Even more impressive was the percentage of school-age children (five to fourteen years of age) enrolled in schools: 68.5 percent in 1964 (which ranked Chile third in that respect in Latin America) to 93.8 percent in 1970 (putting Chile far out in front of every other country, a full 10 percentage points better than runner-up Argentina). The number of teachers employed in primary schools went from 36,227 in 1964 to 56,000 in 1970, so that even with the huge enrollment bulge, the teacher-pupil ratio remained virtually unchanged. In 1965 alone, 6,595 classrooms were constructed, more than during the previous five years combined; the pace would slacken, but for the six years, 13,231 primary school classrooms were added. Similar successes were registered in enrollment figures in secondary and higher schools. A constantly expanding share of the gross national product went for education, so that by 1970 Chile—traditionally third or fourth among Latin countries in the proportion of total national income dedicated to education—had taken over as a solid number one.[104]

Spending by the Chilean central government on education went up dramatically under Frei, from $145.6 million in 1964 to $245.6 million in 1969; allowing for inflation, that is a jump of more than 75 percent in five years.[105] Not to be overlooked, however, is the fact that Chile received during this time a sizable amount of aid for education, including $20 million from the United States,[106] and $17.25 million from the Inter-American Development Bank and the World Bank.[107]

By 1970 Chile, along with Venezuela, was said to have made the most far-reaching educational reforms in Latin America outside Cuba. Frei had made the realization of educational reforms one of his top priorities. To carry out the task, he assembled an aggressive young team of administrators, including thirty-one-year-old Patricio Rojas, who was appointed undersecretary of education.[108]

Frei and his team initially emphasized the goal of a quantitative increase in enrollment. They formulated a five-year plan to overhaul the entire system of education, involving, on the primary level, a large campaign to reduce the dropout rate by means of a modernized curriculum, the introduction of guidance and testing systems, and an automatic promotion system designed to move students expeditiously through their primary schooling. On the secondary level, the plan called for the establishment of a dual-track system: a college preparatory track and a vocational track teaching middle-level technical skills. The plan also called for a decentralized administrative structure and the creation of eight to ten regional educational districts.

However, no accounting of educational institutions under Frei would be complete without recognizing that student agitation, including violence, was remarkable during the Frei presidency.[109]

Student agitation in Chile began in the early 1960s at the Concepción campus of the University of Chile, the birthplace and main bastion of the Maoist-tinted Movement of the Revolutionary Left (MIR). That agitation boiled over in 1967,[110] first as a move to oust the president of a small Catholic college who was then off on a pilgrimage to Moscow, later as a protest against the gift of a cyclotron by the University of California at Berkeley, still later as a series of high school riots, and finally as a battle royal involving the cardinal and, ultimately, the Vatican. From the Catholic campuses it spread to the state-run University of Chile in Santiago, and before ending, it would see the far leftists win by violence, coercion, and deceit—and the ingenuousness of its opponents—what they could not win with votes: a new set of rules that would permit them to control the universities as redoubts in their war to revolutionize society, with or without the consent of the governed.

A radical wing of the Christian Democrats, which called itself *terceristas* (roughly, "advocates of a third way"),[111] controlled the student federations of both the University of Chile and the Catholic University. As part of the "Revolution with Liberty," the *terceristas* had been agitating for university reform from the time Frei came to power. The twin objectives: (1) make the university a more efficient instrument for the creation of the new society in which state planning and direction would supplant individual initiative; (2) make the university more "democratic." That meant giving students an enlarged vote and voice in the conduct of university affairs, including seats on the policymaking university council, as well as in the selection of the president and deans. The Communists, next largest and next best organized group of students, demanded even more: voice and vote as well for university employees, everyone from dishwashers and janitors to campus police, groups they, of course, held considerable sway over, as later events would demonstrate.[112]

Both Christian Democrats and Communists denied any ideological intent in their "reforms," claiming they wanted only the "modernization" and "democratization" of the university. Smaller groups, led by the violence-prone MIR, wanted to "revolutionize" the university, "put it at the service of the missing masses—workers and peasants."[113]

The first important crisis occurred at the Catholic University in Santiago. There students on August 11, 1967, broke off reform talks and occupied the main building in downtown Santiago. Under the slogan New Men for a New University, they demanded the ouster of the moderate president, Monsignor Alfredo Silva Santiago, who opposed their demands for student "cogovernment" of the university. Eventually, the Vatican backed Cardinal Raúl Silva Henríquez, who yielded to student demands. Monsignor Silva Santiago resigned and was replaced by Fernando Castillo Velasco, then the mayor of a Santiago suburb, a man of brimless belief in the honorable intentions of the Left.[114] He appointed to prominent positions in the university a number of the young "idealists" who had substituted violence for dialogue, the beginning of leftist ascendancy at the university under his leadership, a trend arrested finally by students themselves and a handful of faculty. The leader of the Catholic University revolt of 1967 was Miguel Angel Solar, a young medical student who would eventually be expelled by the Christian Democrats, but only after he had implanted Marxist rule in the university.

The following May, the University of Chile was the target. Lengthy negotiations on reform proposals between the Christian Democrats and the Communists failed to produce agreement. The issue was submitted to a referendum, a device the Communists persistently tried to block because they persistently lost it. They lost that one too, but not the war, because their more radical rivals, the MIR, refused to accept the verdict.

In the big School of Philosophy and Teacher's College—commonly called *El Pedagógico* in Chile—leftist students had forced the resignation of the dean and his replacement by Communist historian Hernán Ramírez Necochea. Under his direction students and faculty went ahead and promulgated the very reforms just rejected in the referendum. They were promptly overruled by the University Council. On May 3, 1968, a small group of students led by MIR agitators occupied buildings and barred entry to professors opposed to their views. Three weeks later others seized the university television station, fighting a pitched battle with the police, which tried to oust them.

Christian Democrats, not to be upstaged, then seized the main building of the university in downtown Santiago; Communists seized other buildings; and a forty-one-day general university strike was on. Eventually it would force the resignation of the president, deans, and University Council; the acceptance of the selfsame proposals the Communists had made and been unable to advance through elections; and the beginning of a prolonged period of negotiations and reorganization, which would not finally end until Allende signed into law a new university code on June 4, 1971.

With the two major institutions vanquished, the six other private and state universities then operating in Chile were easy prey. The road had been cleared for converting the universities into bastions of revolution.

Statistically, Frei's report card on education was impressive. In a large sense it was not, because educational plants and the educational system, at the high school and college levels, had been converted into ideological battlefields, once again on terrain chosen by Communists and Maoists masquerading as reformers. Inevitably, it was terrain they ruled. In the aftermath, one Chilean writer observed: "Only when they seized power did the reformers begin to modify their strategy and their real purposes became apparent."[115]

That judgment would appear touchingly naive, were it not so similar to most made about the Frei years—and were the error not so universal.

6. *Minimum public service for neighborhoods*

To overlord the efforts to incorporate the disadvantaged into the mainstream of society, and particularly the growing number of slumdwellers, Frei proposed the creation of a new ministry of popular promotion. He was not able to get that—opponents feared the Big Brother qualities of such an organization—but he did create organizations that brought the power of participation to many who had never before experienced it. Among them: Neighborhood Councils (*Juntas de Vecinos*) and Centers for Mothers in the cities, the Co-Op Committees on the farm settlements. The councils developed self-help projects for their neighborhoods administered through town-meeting organizations, a rare initiation into democratic procedures for many, and enabled council members to deal with the formal government agencies and entities on an organized, collective basis. The Centers for Mothers provided home-economics training for women, day-care centers, and an outlet for cottage industry handicraft. Four-H-type training and services were provided by the rural cooperatives.

The Frei government made rapid strides on still another social front: cooperatives. In 1964 Chile had 160 consumer cooperatives; by 1970 that number had grown to an estimated 230. In rural areas the growth was even more dramatic: 266 in 1964, approximately 473 in 1970.[116]

Under Alessandri—and with the heavy backing of the Alliance for Progress, Inter-American Development Bank, and World Bank—Chile embarked on a program to extend water and sewerage service. Rough 1960 estimates showed that only 66 percent of the urban population had potable water and only 40 percent had sewerage service. Estimates were not available for the rural population, but even as late as 1969 only 5.7 percent had drinking water piped into their homes. Even with the rapid growth of the cities, much of it involving the creation of new shanty-towns called *poblaciones,* the program, accelerated under Frei, paid dividends. By 1971, 69 percent of the urban population had a home water connection, 28 percent had "easy access to water" (mostly pumps provided for the shantytowns). Only Uruguay and Venezuela (100 percent) and Panama (99 percent) in all of Latin America had higher levels of potable water service for their urban inhabitants. By mid-1969 it was estimated that 2.1 million urban dwellers, 32.2 percent of the total, were served by existing sewerage networks. In the countryside, works were already under way in 1969 to bring piped drinking water to a total of 33.1 percent of the then rural population.[117]

Illiteracy in Chile in 1960 was pegged at 16.4 percent, although in the rural areas that percentage climbed to an estimated 40 percent. During the Frei years a significant dent was made in that already good record, both through putting more children into classrooms and through an adult-education program supervised by a special bureau established in 1965.[118]

More universal health care was also a major goal. Infant mortality, an old nemesis in Chile, was reduced from 127.9 per one thousand live births in 1960 to 79.3 in 1970; the overall mortality rate dropped from 12.2 per one thousand in 1960 to 8.6 in 1970.[119]

Finally, of the housing units built during the Frei years, an estimated 57,000 went to low-income families,[120] a low figure considering the swollen size of the city slums.

In general, the Frei record in the area of incorporating the huge masses of disadvantaged into the mainstream of society was a good one in making available to them the instruments of participatory democracy, a less good one in providing the material comforts. Frei would later boast that during his presidency, no fewer than 19,901 such neighborhood, mothers, youth, sports, fathers/guardians centers had been created in Chile. He would also point to a doubling in union membership: up from 270,502 at the end of 1964 (or 10.3 percent of the work force) to 533,713 when he left office, and that the number of farm workers organized in unions had gone from 1,658 to 104,666 in the same period. These organizations inevitably drew participants not only into political life, but into Christian Democrat cadres as well—though not necessarily as an electoral bloc loyal to the party.[121]

Indeed, in light of the electoral successes of the far Left among slum dwellers, it would appear that Christian Democrat oratory stimulated a taste for the rhetoric of exaggerated expectations, an appetite with disastrous consequences for the survival of that *sine qua non* of democracy, rational, reasonable dialogue and debate.

Frei himself saw this process of mass agitation and involvement as vital to his vision of a new Chilean society, and felt that what had started out under his administration to be a purely technical process (which it most decidedly was not) had been perverted by Allende into a political process. "If this effort had not been made," Frei would write after nearly three years of Allende, "Chile would today be defenseless in the face of the totalitarian and statist onslaught."

One other major area of Frei's domestic policies must be explored, for what it reveals about the distance between political promises and economic facts during the Christian Democrat years, and for what it reveals as a case study of frequently self-destruct attitudes of developing countries toward foreign investment. That area is copper.

As noted earlier, copper had dominated Chilean economic life since World War I. In 1970 it accounted for 70 percent of all exports and 9.8 percent of the entire gross domestic product. Better than 80 percent of the industry was in the hands of three American companies: Anaconda, Kennecott (in Chile, called the Braden Copper Co.), and Cerro Corporation (in Chile, Compañía Minera Andina). The bulk of the industry was held by oldtimers Anaconda and Kennecott, which together had, at various times, accounted all by themselves for anywhere from 7 percent to 20 percent of Chilean gross domestic product. Together, they paid more into government coffers, in direct and indirect taxes and royalties, than all other sources put together—a fact almost never mentioned.

For years, the Left in Chile had drummed away on the claim that the copper giants were plundering the country's riches. Contorted statistics were repeated so often that they became gospel, and a public frame of mind was created that no politician dared dispute. The Christian Democrats, congenitally hostile to capitalism anyway, contributed to the cacophony. But they were far from alone. At the time Eduardo Frei reached the presidency, few doubted the essential villainy of the copper companies.

As so often is the case, the serious woes of the U.S. copper companies began at home (in the United States). A 1947 study of the copper industry, done by the U.S. Federal Trade Commission and containing highly questionable premises, was quoted—and mostly misquoted—by Chilean politicians of all persuasions for years thereafter to "prove" that the American companies were a monopolistic octopus strangling the economic life out of Chile. Fallout from that study weakened the support the companies got from their only domestic allies, the Right, which to that point continued to champion free enterprise, foreign and domestic, as the best bulwark against communist encroachment.[122] That such a flawed study should be accepted so uncritically even by the Right was a reflection of Chilean innocence at that time about the realities of their major industry and breadwinner, an innocence that would lead the country's comptroller general to testify, five years later, that "except for the foreign management of the companies nobody, including himself, had any idea of what was going on in the industry or had ever had the basis for making a judgment!"[123]

Two other forces eroded the intellectual ground from beneath the Right. The first was the fashionableness of Raúl Prebisch's *dependencia* theories, reinforced by economists at the Santiago-based United Nations Economic Commission for Latin America (ECLA [frequently referred to as CEPAL, from the Spanish initials for Comisión Económica para América Latina]).[124] The second was the growing "respectability" of Communists, enhanced in 1946 when President González Videla brought them into his government as full-fledged partners.

But it was an external event which would put the companies permanently on the defensive. Following the outbreak of the Korean War in June 1950, the U.S. Office of Economic Mobilization announced a price of 24.5 cents per pound for copper for the duration of the war—without so much as inviting the Chileans to participate in the discussions. Chilean indignation was so great and immediate that the U.S. relented to the extent of calling in May 1951 a conference in Washington at which the Chileans won two concessions: a three-cent-a-pound increase, and the right to sell up to 20 percent of the output of the American companies in Chile at "free"-market prices. The bonanza flowing from the second concession—"free" prices reached 55 cents per pound—served simply to deepen the conviction that Chile was a dependent stepchild at the mercy of international monopolies.

The solution, it was argued, was to control not 20 percent of the output, but 100 percent of what was, after all, the country's basic riches. In May 1952 González Videla notified President Truman that Chile was voiding the Washington agreement and would henceforth market all of its copper through a state monopoly. As noted earlier, the experiment was a dismal flop and was ended in 1954.[125]

Out of the ashes of this ruin came the *Nuevo Trato*, the New Deal of 1955, built on the notion that replacing a "bad investment climate" with a "good investment climate" would stimulate the companies to invest and expand their Chilean operations. The formula, as finally translated into legislation, proved far too simplistic for the circumstances. It was the Right's last significant chance to manage copper in accord with the beatitudes of a "free-enterprise" system. In a sense, it was the Right's last significant chance of any kind to prove the superiority of a capitalist approach to economics in Chile. It was a chance it bungled badly. *Nuevo*

Trato failed to reward the Right's expectations (though it was, by no means, an unmitigated failure). In anger and frustration, the Right turned on the copper companies with a vengeance.

Once again, external events interceded decisively. Those events were the evangelistic sermons of the Alliance for Progress. Disillusioned already, the Right was thus ripe for offering the copper companies as sacrificial lambs to the missionaries of reform. "Nationalize the copper companies" became a clamor of the Right—as well as a mere slogan of the Left—so as to spare the Right an onslaught on what were its most vital interests: control of the land.[126]

Bereft of allies, and caught between the Scylla and Charybdis of Frei vs. Allende in the 1964 elections, the companies groped for the right strategy to save as much skin as they could. In 1960 Kennecott had offered the Conservative government of Jorge Alessandri a plan to finance a 55 percent increase in the output of its El Teniente mine—a $200 million investment. Because of the adverse political climate that had been created toward the copper companies, the government failed to go through with the deal.[127]

On the assumption that its days in Chile were numbered, Kennecott startled the president-elect, Eduardo Frei, by offering to sell 51 percent of its holdings in El Teniente. The offer, exceeding even Frei's own ambitions for "Chileanization" of the industry at that point, also infuriated the high command of Anaconda, which had stoutly resisted the overtures of Frei's emissaries that they surrender substantial ownership of their Chilean holdings. According to one account, the Anaconda people continued to believe that they "could keep manipulating the politics of Chile behind the scenes...."[128]

On December 21, 1965, an exultant Frei went on nationwide television to announce a major new deal in copper as the result of extended negotiations with the U.S. companies. He did not mention that a major element of that deal—the 55 percent increase in output at Kennecott's mine—actually was an initiative of the company, the same one made four years earlier, except that then, Kennecott offered to finance the entire deal.

Main points of the agreement announced by Frei were:

1. The government acquired 51 percent of Kennecott's interest in the El Teniente mine, a 25 percent interest in a new Anaconda mine, Exótica, and 30 percent of Cerro's brand new Río Blanco mine. Kennecott got $80 million, payable over fifteen years at 4.5 percent interest, plus a sharply higher reassessment of the assets it kept.[129]

2. In return, the companies were given tax, import, and dividend repatriation concessions. The most controversial one permitted the companies to retain their share of exchange earnings from foreign

sales in the United States. Since the government set the selling price, and skimmed off everything above that,[130] this was actually a marginal advantage.

3. The companies agreed to a $600 million expansion program aimed at doubling production by 1972, and tripling the volume of copper refined in the country. Anaconda covered its own financing arrangements; Kennecott and Cerro entered into elaborate "fail-safe" arrangements.[131]

Christian Democrats, from Frei down, had made no secret that they shared the ambition of the far Left for a complete takeover of the industry, an extreme step they hesitated to take only because it wasn't practical; for one thing, they still hadn't had time to hone enough "new men" with the "right" outlook on society.[132] And so they assigned to the negotiations Raúl Sáez, a civil engineer who headed the first Committee of Wise Men of the Alliance for Progress, the nine-man panel directing Alliance strategies and policies. Because he was one of the few authentic moderates around Frei,[133] Sáez was able to drive a bargain with which the copper companies could live.

But no sooner had Frei announced the agreement and, on January 4, 1965, sent the enabling legislation to Congress for action, than the Left pounced on the agreements as a sellout. Debate over copper in Chile already had been so badly polluted by the politics of demagoguery as to make the issues almost unrecognizable. Over the next eight years, reason and reality would vanish altogether in a quagmire of untruths, half-truths, and distortions, solemnly made in forums ranging from streetcorner rallies to chambers of the United Nations, and most were just as solemnly—and uncritically—parroted by the world's press.

The major charges, as they coalesced over the years, were summarized in a full-page advertisement in the *New York Times*, January 25, 1971, paid for by the Chilean Copper Corporation, CODELCO—an ad heralding the final expropriation of the companies. Interestingly, CODELCO was a full-scale partner in the deals it was then denouncing. Also interestingly, CODELCO people were a party to every single important decision taken by the companies during this period, and most of those decisions could be made only with the *approval* of the Chilean government. Yet these points were glossed over as if the companies had been operating on the planet Mars. So too were the later rebuttals of the companies. One such was an extensive white paper (actually five separate booklets) prepared by Kennecott Copper Corporation; its side of the story remained astonishingly invisible.[134]

The charges were:

1. *The companies had made no "fresh, new" investment in Chile, but had financed expansion programs by loading the country with*

debts. Rebuttal: Kennecott put up the largest single amount—$92 million—from its own money. The U.S. government Export-Import Bank, interested (as always) in stimulating the sale of U.S.–made machinery needed for the $26 million expansion program at El Teniente, had originally been down for the largest share, $110 million. But that was later trimmed to $83 million by the availability of more Chilean-made products. CODELCO kicked in a total of $37 million, which Kennecott said was at Chilean government insistence. The rest ($46 million) came from the Banca Commerciale Italiana and Mitsui & Co., Ltd. So, actually there was "fresh, new capital" aplenty. That Kennecott's came not from corporate headquarters in New York does not change by one iota the fact that the $92 million was, after all, the company's own money.

Still another gripe of critics in this issue is that Kennecott insured its new investments through the U.S. government's Agency for International Development program designed to encourage American investors to put their money where it was needed most: in high-risk countries and situations. That meant that the U.S. government had a financial as well as a policy stake in Chile's later scuttling of the agreements.

2. *Huge profits.* During the period 1965 through 1970, Kennecott supposedly earned $446 million from El Teniente. That sum was indeed earned—but not by Kennecott, a subtle distinction somehow overlooked. Kennecott received $126 million in earnings or dividends, or 28.3 percent of total earnings during a period when it either owned 100 percent of the mine (1965–67) or was a 49 percent partner. The rest went to partner CODELCO, or to the government, in taxes.

3. *Excessive return on investment.* Allende and his minions, chief among them his long-time ambassador to the United States, Orlando Letelier, made much of the fact that the companies made far fatter profits from their Chilean operations than they did from their U.S. domestic operations. Before taxes, true. After taxes, Kennecott points out that its net earnings were 45 percent *below* domestic earnings, and that in no year since 1955 had El Teniente earned more after taxes or on investment than on Kennecott's U.S. operations.

4. *The overall earnings record.* Frequently and loudly trumpeted was the claim that U.S. copper companies had made "fabulous, almost incredible profits with minimum investment in Chile." In the *New York Times* ad, and elsewhere, the case was made even more lurid: "The four [*sic*] big U.S. companies that have been working these natural resources in Chile collected earnings of $10.9 billion in the course of the past 60 years. This figure is of tremendous significance for Chile if one compares it with the fact that the gnp achieved through the entire existence of the country, that is, approximately 400 years, amounts to $10.5

billion. The conclusion is clear: in a little over half a century, these U.S. companies took out from our country an amount greater than that created by Chileans in terms of industries, highways, ports, schools, hospitals, trade, etc., during our country's entire history."

Appalling, positively appalling. Except that it happens to be a brazen lie, made the more brazen by the fact that before the court of world opinion, the lie was allowed to go mostly unchallenged.

Kennecott points out that in its own case, its gross income was $3.4 billion during the fifty-five years it operated El Teniente (1916–70). But that was the total realized on the operations: from that total, the company paid $2.491 billion for salaries, materials and supplies, services, taxes, etc. An additional $430 million was spent outside Chile to buy needed machinery, materials, and services. So what was left was $509 million, an average profit of $9.3 million per year.

As to "minimum investment," the advertisement made no mention of the fact that from 1904 to 1927, Kennecott operations in Chile paid no dividends at all. It would make little sense to put dollars invested fifty years ago on the scale of today, the dollar having been through so many wringers of devaluation and inflation. Kennecott does make the claim, however, that at 1972 costs, it would take $700 million to finance even a 180,000-ton-per-year operation, the level at which Kennecott was operating before going into the $267 million expansion program.

Since the Christian Democrats had already conceded to their leftist foes the major premise—that foreign ownership of the mines was essentially evil—they were less than enthusiastic defenders of the factual record. Rather, they concentrated during the long public and congressional debates on the supposed advantages of the deal for Chile, a process which, inevitably, led them into exaggerated claims.

The biggest one, of course, was that by greatly increasing output, and pocketing those huge profits that formerly went abroad, Chile would make far more money from copper: an average of $47 million per year in tax revenues alone. Neither happened.

One of the recurring fictions about those events in Chile is that the Right thwarted Frei on copper. The Left did—unrelentingly. The Right used copper for a time to extract certain concessions from him on agrarian reform—and modest concessions they were[135]—in return for its votes on copper. In April 1966, the concessions made, the Right threw its support to Frei, and he got his copper law.

Labor also had a hand in thwarting Frei. On January 1, 1966, workers at El Teniente went on strike for higher wages. That legal strike led to other, wildcat strikes at Chuquicamata, Potrerillos, and El Salvador. At the last, on March 11, 1966, there was a clash between workers and troops commanded by Col. Manuel Pinochet—no kin of the later president, though he has often been confused with him in press reports. Eight workers were killed and sixty wounded in the fracas.

In copper, as in other issues, far from standing as "a bulwark against the extreme Left,"[136] Frei's government loosed a chain of events that could not be contained. On June 27, 1969, responding to stepped-up political pressures, and with an eye to the elections just a little over a year away, Frei announced phase two of the Chileanization of the industry. The pressure came from the left wing of his own party. Phase two consisted of a forced sellout by Anaconda of 41 percent of its holdings in the three mines it was working (Potrerillos, El Salvador, and Chuquicamata), with the rest to be acquired starting in 1973 (provided that Chile had paid at least 60 percent of the first purchase price by the end of 1972). Frei, who had described copper in 1964 as the mainspring (*viga maestra*) of his social and economic programs, called the new deal "Chile's second independence." But it was really only a dress rehearsal for the final execution of the companies. Allende was in power only a few months when the companies lost everything they had in Chile.

"In return for their cooperation," British historian Horne wrote of the copper deals of the 1960s, "the U.S. companies were to be guaranteed against expropriation." He adds that the "guarantees" later proved to be "a scrap of paper." Henry Kissinger, later National Security Adviser and then Secretary of State under President Richard Nixon, described it as a surrender of principle to pressure despite "generous U.S. aid."[137]

How well did the deals work out for Chile? As to production, the goals were missed by a mile—and Allende was not the only villain of that piece, as is so often wrongly asserted. As to the value of copper to the Chilean state, the picture is rosier, but it must be remembered that world market prices were abnormally high throughout this period, so the government's share would have increased sharply anyway. Indeed, much of the big jump from 1968 to 1969 is attributable to the government's skimming off the top the "cream" of unexpected high prices—a deal the government rammed down the companies' throats in 1969 *after* they had kept their end of the bargain regarding heavy investment in expanding production. The results are summarized in table 18.

So, under Frei, copper failed in his final year to meet the target by 128,000 tons, a whopping 17 percent off target. (Under Allende, of course, the record was worse.) Relative stagnation of production— 582,000 tons in 1964, 595,000 tons in 1970—also occurred, although two new and rich mines, Anaconda's Exótica and Cerro's Río Blanco, had come on stream.

TABLE 18
COPPER, 1964–1971

	1964	1965	1966	1967	1968	1969	1970	1971[a]
Actual	582	528	592	591	573	603	595	628
PRODUCTION								
Frei's target	—	—	—	—	—	634	723	964
Taxes paid	105	126	197	194	167	217	137	32
GOVERNMENT SHARE								
CODELCO dividends	—	—	—	36	42	124	162	66
TOTAL	105	126	197	230	209	341	299	98

Source: Adapted from *Portada* magazine (Santiago) August 1972, p. 8.

Note: Production figures in thousands of tons; government share figures in millions of dollars.

[a] An Allende year, of course; it is included for comparative purposes, since it was the first year of total state control of the industry.

"A DYNAMIC NEW HOPE"[138]

> *If . . . Latin America believes that it can build its economic develop-*
> *ment in an atmosphere of strategically nurtured antagonism to the*
> *United States, it will only succeed in imposing on its people extreme*
> *and unnecessary hardships and compromising its future in a sense-*
> *less policy.*
>
> Eduardo Frei[139]

It is hard to know whether Chile's foreign policy toward the United States under Frei was the product of a "strategically nurtured antagonism" or a viscerally nurtured antagonism. Or perhaps it was simply the fact that in the house of Frei, everybody made foreign policy but Frei, and those who did nurtured strategic, visceral, and opportunistic antagonisms toward the United States. Because what is clear is that during the Frei years, no other nation in all of South America pursued a foreign policy more consistently and persistently inimical to the United States than Chile.

And yet Chile managed to bask in the admiration, if not actual adulation, of American leaders from John F. Kennedy and Lyndon B. Johnson on down, and enjoyed the almost unanimous acclaim of American commentators, media and academic—part of what Horne describes as the "liberal adoration of Frei in the United States."[140]

Similarly, no other country in all of Latin America benefited more during those years from Alliance for Progress aid than Chile, and yet Frei carped constantly about the Alliance. Apologists justified such ingratitude as a necessary expedient in the context of domestic politics,[141] a context of leftist-permeated sloganeering which the Christian Democrats did much to create.

Not that anti-Americanism was confined to the Left in Chile. The case of copper demonstrated how easily the Right could jettison "natural" alliances with international capitalism, for reasons of conviction, or for reasons of selfish political or economic advantage. But on an even deeper level, some of the most articulate and conspicuous figures of the Right were philosophically and pungently anti-American. Some, because they saw the United States as a society so materialistic and socialized itself (witness the Alliance, they argued) that it would destroy ethical and political values they cherished,[142] a view which would grow with the years. Others were hostile to the United States for grubby, commercial reasons: they simply wanted to exclude foreign business which, until the late sixties, meant almost entirely U.S. business, for the simple reason that it was more comfortable not to have to compete.

The antipathy of many among the Right for the United States contradicted the popular cliché about Uncle Sam cozying up to the oligarchs and vice versa. The cliché outlasted reality until, finally, the circumstance of sheer survival in the face of a real threat from communism forced many on the Right to seek shelter in the embrace of the U.S., a shelter more often than not denied them. Chile should have served to bury another cliché, and that was the refusal of the U.S. to side with "reformist" regimes; as noted, no other nation in Latin America benefited more during this period than Chile, few nations during this period could claim to be more "reformist," and few undermined American influence in the area more significantly than the Chile of Frei.

Under Alessandri, Chile joined perennial fence sitter Mexico in opposing sanctions against Fidel Castro, after an Organization of American States investigating team, acting on charges brought by Venezuela, found that Castro had aided guerrillas and terrorists trying to topple the democratically elected government of Rómulo Betancourt.[143] Frei went one step further, taking up the cudgels in behalf of the doctrine of nonintervention, a doctrine then being promoted chiefly by those attempting to spare Castro any effective countermeasures against his revolutionary adventures.

Those around Frei would take an even more protective attitude toward Castro, a circumstance that would not spare Frei Castro's special brand of vitriol.

"He promised revolution without blood," Castro said of Frei, following a clash between police and miners which left several dead, "and has given blood without revolution."[144]

Yet even before his election, Frei was reported to be toying with the idea of making a "fresh attempt to draw Cuba back into the hemispheric community." The same newspaper report quoted Frei as attacking the OAS because it "no longer has any vitality" (it had just voted the embargo against Cuba).

The Venezuelan foreign minister, Ignacio Iribarren, a quiet and scholarly man representing a country that had felt the lash of Castro's attacks in its own flesh, suggested that Frei was out of touch with the realities of Castro's threat.[145] Three years later, Frei and his Christian Democrats would again draw the wrath of Venezuela, this time when the party issued a statement saying the Havana-based Latin American Solidarity Organization (OLAS) was not responsible for escalating guerrilla activity in Latin America. The enemies, the Christian Democrats said, were "misery and underdevelopment"—as if OLAS, which in fact claimed credit for guerrilla insurgency and actively fomented it, was the antidote to those real ills.

When Frei's government permitted OLAS to set up shop in Chile (Allende was by then president of the organization), President Rafael Caldera of Venezuela, himself the leader of a Christian Democrat party, said he was "shocked by the news that the Christian Democrats of Chile will permit the installation of the OLAS." The party replied that allowing an avowedly subversive organization to operate there did not mean approval.[146]

Before Frei, Chile had maintained diplomatic relations with a single communist country: Yugoslavia. Frei was in office less than three weeks when, on November 24, he established diplomatic relations with the Soviet Union. Not long thereafter he added Poland (January 7, 1965), Czechoslovakia (January 15), Hungary (January 17), Bulgaria (January 25), and Rumania (March 31). With Czechoslovakia, Frei's government would become especially chummy, even to turning over to it Alliance for Progress plans for Chile's development.[147] In that, he was taking a cue from Christian Democrat Youth leaders, who, a few months before the election, had issued in Santiago a joint statement with the Czechoslovak Youth Union expressing the "need for consolidation of peaceful coexistence among all countries with different social systems."[148]

Relations with Russia were resumed not only in accord with the party's avowed policy of diplomatic détente, but also for the ostensible reason of increasing trade with the Soviet bloc. Yet not a year and-a-half earlier, Alessandri had sent a mission to Moscow headed by an eminent law professor named Julio Philippi to explore trade possibilities. Shortly after he returned, Alessandri, in his typically dry style, said: "They tell us there will be more resources if we increase our trade with all countries in the world. Fantasies. The possibilities for trade with the Soviet bloc countries are very limited." Specifically, the Philippi mission estimated trade opportunities at $5 million per year, tops. In point of fact, trade with Russia never rose above half a million dollars per year during Frei's administration.[149] Overall, the Philippi mission's estimates held up: for 1966 through 1970, trade between Chile and Czechoslovakia and Poland—the only Soviet-bloc countries with which any measurable trade was developed—did hover close to the $5 million mark. But it was far from the bonanza Frei's people advertised. In fact, it cost Chile $8.6 million for the privilege of trading with those countries (exports, $7.212 million; imports, $15.813 million).[150]

Frei named Máximo Pacheco as the first ambassador to Moscow. Pacheco, a young University of Chile professor, later became Frei's education minister. His work in Moscow won him accolades from *El Siglo,* the Communist party daily in Santiago. "During his assignment in Moscow," the newspaper wrote, "he distinguished himself by developing a positive action which created for him a favorable image in Chilean public opinion...." The newspaper referred to Pacheco's "atmosphere of respectability and seriousness"; according to Chamudes, Pacheco earned good marks from the Communists in particular for his unqualified praise of Patrice Lumumba University, the institution Moscow set up primarily for training Third-World militants.[151]

The Russians dispatched some forty persons to staff their embassy in Santiago (the Chileans sent four or five to Moscow), and took advantage of their new travel privileges to step up contacts with the Chilean Communist party, not only the largest in Latin America but by far the most slavishly loyal to Moscow. The control point for Communist activity on the continent was the semiclandestine South American Bureau, headquartered at the big Russian embassy in Montevideo. With diplomatic relations reestablished, traffic between Montevideo and Santiago picked up, as did infusions of money into the party's coffers, to the point where even the official newspaper *La Nación,* breaking with its policy of coy flirtation with the Communists, remarked on July 26, 1966: "Some observers might find it strange that the Communist party now asks its members for less money. But then, relations with Moscow are, after all, very good...."

The embassy also operated a veritable travel bureau to arrange Iron Curtain junkets for Chilean leaders. One to make the trip was Frei's first labor minister, William Thayer, who returned with a "very fine impression" of what he saw in Moscow. Someone asked him about labor problems.

"From what was explained to me," law Professor Thayer said, "strikes are not forbidden in the Soviet Union. There are none because problems are solved before reaching that stage, and at another level. What happens—they contend—is that with the disappearance of private enterprise, the exploitation of man by man has also disappeared. Now worker and enterprise are one and the same, the business belongs to the workers themselves."[152]

Despite Frei's admonition, there were three other main areas in which his government nurtured policies that were strategically antagonistic to U.S. interests: Cuba, the Dominican Republic, and on the larger question of the proper place of the U.S. within the inter-American system.

Even under Alessandri's so-called rightist government, Chile temporized on sanctions for the Castro regime. Following the 1962 Cuban missile crisis, Castroites throughout the hemisphere promoted the line that since Cuba was no longer a nuclear menace, it should be regarded as just another country with a different form of government. Chile's Christian Democrats were among the first to embrace the idea, and Frei offered to compete with Castro to see which accomplished more for its people. The idea—ingenuous, at best—was warmly endorsed by liberal commentators in the U.S. and elsewhere, and icily ignored by Castro.

Gabriel Valdés, Chile's "Tin-Can Foreign Minister"[153] who would later distinguish himself for the virulence of his antagonisms toward the U.S., conveyed the cherubic qualities of the Christian Democrat attitude toward Cuba on the eve of Frei's inauguration:

"I believe that Cuba is one of those political regimes which, because of its extra-continental ties, represents a disquieting element within the American family. But it's up to the Cubans to show that their form of government is democratic, and that they harbor no aggressive or dangerous intentions to the American community; then Chile is disposed to use her good offices [to have Cuba return to the OAS]."[154]

Quite apart from the fact that there was nothing remotely "democratic" about Castro's form of totalitarian government, Cuba of the midsixties was far from finished with its subversive ambitions. Cuba-supported guerrillas were still operating in at least two countries: Guatemala and Bolivia. Furthermore, even after repeated repulses on the field of battle and Russian muzzling of Castro's guerrilla bite, his antidemocratic bark remained the same—as Chileans themselves would later discover when Castro joined forces enthusiastically with Allende in attempting to turn their country into an armed police state. But in the case of Cuba—as in so many others—it was the Christian Democrats, and not Allende, who would provide the initial opening. With only eight months remaining in his term, Frei, in February 1970, announced the signing of a trade agreement with Cuba. Chilean defiance of the hemisphere quarantine of Castro was now complete.

Chile's behavior in the case of Bolivia put it into collision with still another nation plagued by Castroite aggression in the form of a guerrilla band led by Ernesto (Che) Guevara. Late in February 1968 five remnants of Guevara's force made it across the high Andes into Chile. Frei spurned the appeals of Allende, who rushed to the border to assure "protection" for the fugitive guerrillas and who asked that Chile grant them asylum. But Frei also spurned the appeals of the pursuing Bolivians, who asked for the extradition of the five. Instead, Frei ordered the five promptly deported, and they began a round-the-world trip back to Cuba (via Chile's Easter Island, Tahiti, Paris, and Prague). Bolivia's ambassador to the OAS, Raúl Díaz de Medina, later protested that Chile's action not only violated the Inter-American Treaty of Mutual Assistance, but also converted Chile into a sanctuary for guerrillas.

Despite repeated evidence that Castro had turned to a new form of subversion—supporting domestic terrorist organizations such as the Tupamaros in Uruguay, the Montoneros in Argentina, urban terrorists in Brazil, not to mention the MIR in Chile itself, as well as its continuing aid to conventional guerrilla forces in Colombia, Peru, and elsewhere[155]—Frei's government continued pressuring for a relaxing of the sanctions against Castro. Valdés, for example, said in June 1969: "Cuba no longer intervenes in the internal affairs of our countries; I believe Cuba has reached the conclusion that guerrillas of this type no longer make sense in Latin America. In such circumstances, it seems to me that not to have relations with Cuba is abnormal."[156]

Given the stance of the Christian Democrats on communism in general and Castro's subversion in particular, it was, of course, no surprise that Frei would fail to sympathize with U.S. purposes in sending troops ashore in the Dominican Republic in April 1965 to forestall what President Lyndon Johnson believed was a Castro-supported takeover attempt. A number of other Latin American leaders of the democratic Left found themselves in a similar quandary, but none other reacted so spitefully as the Frei government. As Christian Democrat ideologue Genaro Arriagada wrote: "Chile was the only Latin American country which condemned in unqualified terms the North American invasion of Santo Domingo."[157]

When the United States asked for OAS support for ending the civil war, Frei said it was "disgraceful" for the OAS to implicate itself in the affair. Foreign Minister Valdés scoffed at reports that the rebel movement had been infiltrated or that the country might have been taken over by Communists had the U.S. not intervened. "It is dangerous," he said, "to put the label of Communist on every movement. The Dominican Republic is not Vietnam."[158] (Later, Christian Democrats, under the goading of their youth wing, would hammer away at the U.S. over Vietnam as well.)

No other conspicuous leader of the party was more outspoken on the Dominican Republic question than Radomiro Tomic, who managed to butt in from a most improbable perch: he was then Chilean ambassador to the White House. That did not prevent Tomic from cabling Col. Francisco Caamaño, the rebel leader, expressing his support for Caamaño's "government." Later, Tomic attacked the U.S. action in Santo Domingo before a world conference of Christian Democrat Youth in Berlin, and said the United States "deals with Latin America as though it is its own backyard."[159]

The Chilean magazine *P.E.C.*, as saucily anti–Christian Democrat as it was anti-Communist, claimed that in his private conversation with Averell Harriman, dispatched by Johnson to explain the U.S. action to Latin governments, Frei said he had to do what he did or he would have lost control of the party, and the party could not jeopardize its prestige.[160]

Chile's position on Cuba and the Dominican Republic formed part of a larger stategy of antagonism to the United States. On February 17, 1969, President Richard Nixon announced that he had named Nelson Rockefeller, governor of New York and a man with professional and personal ties to Latin American reaching back nearly thirty years, to head a special fact-finding mission to Latin America. Later, in his first major message on Latin America, a speech before the OAS on April 14, 1969, the newly inaugurated president followed up by saying he would await Rockefeller's findings before shaping a new American hemisphere policy to replace the long-languishing Alliance for Progress. Predictably, Nixon's announcement brought shrieks of protest from Kennedy loyalists, who had not yet discovered the corpse the Alliance had become.[161] Frei's reaction was to use the Nixon posture as a pretext for pursuing an old foreign policy goal: reducing U.S. power in hemispheric affairs. Frei himself, of course, had long been a critic of the Alliance, and from the very outset of his administration had lacerated the Organization of American States.

Thus the Chileans led the way in reactivating a dormant organization that had been created as an appendage of the United Nations, the Special Latin American Coordinating Committee (CECLA). CECLA had originally been created in 1964 to coordinate the positions of Latin American governments at the United Nations Conference on Trade and Development. It was significant because it was the first important hemisphere group that excluded the United States.

At the initiative of the Chileans, a CECLA meeting was convoked at Viña del Mar, the queen of Chile's beach resorts. What emerged, in May 1969, was a forty-six-point program that represented a stunning triumph for the Left in its choices of political and economic strategies; the preamble, furthermore, was a ringing Bill of International Rights for Latin America, a sulking indictment (by indirection) of the United States for failing to achieve for Latin America the Alliance-promised millennium, and a belligerent formalization of confrontation between Latin America and the United States, the clear implication being that the proper place for the United States was in the dock. Never mind that very few Latin leaders themselves—beginning with the host Chileans—had much faith in the Alliance. As Chamudes points out, it was one thing to grouse about the quality and quantity of the aid given, quite another for the one country that had most benefited to head the prosecution.

What emerged was, finally, what Roberto Campos, the brilliant Brazilian economist who masterminded that country's economic miracle, called a "tear-gas theory of economic development."[162] (Campos then, and later, was a perennial target of the high priests of righteousness in international affairs because, contrary to the fashionable "structuralist" school of economics, he was a "monetarist," and called for savings, sacrifice, and solvency as the indispensable prerequisites of economic growth and development.)

Host Valdés was given the assignment of communicating the Consensus of Viña del Mar formally to Nixon, which he did at a White House dinner attended by the entire Latin American diplomatic corps in Washington. Valdés reportedly had been puffed up by the Communists to believe he could be their choice as a compromise presidential candidate in the 1970 elections, a ruse they had used a few years earlier with a Radical senator. Putting such a rare publicity opportunity to full advantage, Valdés used the occasion to read a riot act to Nixon. Even the Communist daily in Santiago, *El Siglo*, commented that his speech had "gone beyond even the agreements reached by CECLA."

Drew Pearson, in his widely syndicated column, commented afterward: "Informed diplomatic sources explained that Minister Valdés is not really anti-American, but is seeking the presidency of Chile and the easiest way to get elected in some countries is by running against the United States." Valdés may not have been anti-American, but he was far from anathema to the Soviets; the Russians did not object to his being named to head the UN aid program for Latin America, even though he was a member of the major opposition party to their man Allende, then in power.[163]

Through the Frei years, the atmosphere of hostility to the United States flourished in inverse proportion, in fact, to the aid given Frei's government. In 1965 Senator Robert F. Kennedy and his entire retinue were ousted from the University of Concepción by rioting students led by a young man named Luciano Cruz (later to become famous). The same year, Christian Democrats joined the far Left in a near hysterical attack on a U.S. army–sponsored research study of counterinsurgency techniques in Latin America, even though Chile was not, in fact, one of the main countries covered by the study. (But the revelations originating in Chile led eventually to cancellation of the entire research project.) Edward M. Korry, who succeeded Dungan as ambassador, recalls that when he arrived in Santiago, on October 12, 1967, "there were machine guns set up by the Carabineros of Chile all around my house, and every day, without exception, for the entire four years until I departed, October 12, 1971, my wife, my children, and I received threats. . . ."[164]

Renán Fuentealba Moena, several times president of the Christian Democrat party, and a man with an uncanny instinct for the wrong causes, introduced a baroque element in December 1969, when he joined the silver-tongued Communist senator Volodia Teitelboim in denouncing an alleged CIA plot to overthrow Frei. Even a Communist columnist, Eduardo Labarca, writing in the party newspaper December 13, 1969, alluded to Fuentealba's "glaring weakness" before the TV cameras; the party publicly repudiated the "revelations," and Fuentealba himself later admitted on the floor of the Senate that he lacked proof to support his charges.[165] The irony of ironies of this slapstick episode is that it was later discovered that at this precise time, the CIA was slipping half a million dollars under the table to the Christian Democrats to shore them up for the forthcoming electoral clash with Allende.[166]

Yet through the Johnson administration, at least, Frei continued to enjoy the good opinion of official Washington. Johnson even invited Frei to make a state visit to the United States on February 1 and 2, 1967. Two weeks before he was to leave, the Chilean Senate did to Frei what it had never done to any other president: it exercised its prerogative to refuse him permission to leave the country. It was a stinging rebuke in which Left and Right vented their wrath for widely different reasons over the arrogance of power displayed by the Christian Democrats.

There was one other area in which Frei's government took a tack contrary to U.S. interests in Latin America: his government, as Arriagada points out,[167] fired salvo after salvo at the Inter-American Defense Board. The board, founded in 1942, had long been a target of leftists in the hemisphere; not because it coordinates military strategy throughout the hemisphere (which it does), nor because that strategy through most of the fifties and sixties was aimed principally at containing Communist insurgency (it was), nor even because the board arranges for advanced training for Latin American military men (it does), but because, above all, the board over the years had become a club of sorts at which senior Latin military men could become chummy with their U.S. counterparts, and vice versa. Such chumminess inevitably consolidated U.S. influence in the minds and affections of men who, when they did not rule themselves, played pivotal roles in their Latin homelands. Such a relationship was, of course, galling to the far Left, and so it attacked military programs of all kinds, setting up a spurious cause-effect relationship between professionalism in military affairs and the abuses of military power (which, of course, existed long before there were military aid programs, and would exist without them). To a flabbergasting degree, the far Left managed to get away with the sophistry.

Chile also was the catalyst in the creation in 1967 of an organization of principal copper-exporting nations (Zambia, the Congo, and Peru were the others), a legitimate and laudable effort to protect the price stability of the country's principal export commodity.

Defense of copper was, of course, the expression of a sovereign and independent foreign policy, and that is the way Frei liked to describe his. It just happened that his "sovereignty and independence" routinely translated as opposition to American purposes, a "strategically nurtured antagonism," or, as Lenin put it: "In politics there is only one principle and one truth: what profits my opponent hurts me and vice versa."[168]

In more recent times, Soviet analysts overcame their traditional reticence about Latin America as an impenetrable sphere of American influence and refined Lenin's maxim. "The focus of Soviet interests and the main thrust of its purposes," two Sovietologists wrote, ". . . is not so much an extension of Soviet control or the attainment of outright communist regimes, as the buildup of opposition and hostility toward the U.S. and toward those elements in Latin American societies which have ties with the U.S.. . . . 'To sap and undermine U.S. positions' there [in Latin America] is said to inflict significant damage to the U.S. positions not only in that region but in the world at large, and thereby help shift the 'correlation of world forces' in favor of the Soviet Union."[169]

In Chile of the Frei years, opposition to U.S. positions bordered at times on insolence. Tomic, for example, while ambassador to the United States, made a number of speeches in the United States harshly critical of the country's involvement in Vietnam, flagrant interference in the internal affairs of the host country. On one such occasion, he was even formally seconded by an announcement from Santiago. Later, Tomic was quoted as bragging that despite his sharp criticism of the U.S. intervention in the Dominican Republic, he obtained "U.S. aid for Chile which was eight times higher per capita than any other Latin American country could obtain. . . ."[170]

Gil observed that the Christian Democrats attracted to their ranks many "romantic leftists."[171] Their behavior, once in power, particularly their handling of the Communists and the even more dangerous Socialists, is perhaps most kindly described as "romantic leftism." But it was a romantic leftism that not only affected the U.S. position in the country and hemisphere—a matter that ought to be of no small concern to nations devoted to the survival of democracy—but also affected the course and content of Chilean political life itself.

"We know how to handle the Communists," the Christian Democrats boasted, and the world believed them. The formula they offered was to outpromise and outreform them by using programs and principles and premises expropriated from the Communists, and through all of it, maintaining an abiding faith in the commitment of their far-left rivals to the very rules of democracy they themselves cherished.

"The world in general recognizes the effort that is being made in Chile," Frei said, "and the most outstanding figures in the world come here to express their warm interest and respect, and even their enthusiasm, for what is happening here."[172]

One who did not make the pilgrimage but certainly must have felt enthusiasm for what was happening there was Nikita Khrushchev, then the boisterous ruler of Russia. Khrushchev told the Twentieth Communist Party Congress in 1965 that the world no longer was divided into capitalist and socialist camps but included other states, many new but all underdeveloped, which were "seeking to break away from alignments with the imperialist camp to form a 'zone of peace.' " These new states were characterized by "anti-imperialism," an emphasis on the state rather than on the private sector in domestic affairs, a willingness to accept compromises in principle as far as the role of local Communist parties was concerned, "even to the point of ignoring suppressive activities against them." Signs that the full-scale conversion into a socialist state were not far off would include "expansion of the state economic sector and restriction of the private sector, nationalization of foreign trade, banks and utilities, land reform, increased participation of the 'masses' in the political process. . . ."[173]

The Frei government had not yet nationalized foreign trade, banks, and utilities, although it was moving swiftly in that direction, but it tightly controlled all of them. But it had a high degree of tolerance of, bordering frequently on connivance with, the Communists, and it had greatly expanded the state sector, accelerated land reform, and mobilized the "masses." So it was that, "from the Soviet point of view, Frei had adopted a number of positions which fitted into Soviet ideas on proper directions for policy in Latin America. . . ." He did not adopt these strategies to please Moscow, yet the end result was that "his regime [was] in the category of those which Moscow looked on with some favor."[174]

But there were others who were not so pleased about events in Chile. They were troubled, for example, that although Frei was unstinting in his criticism of U.S. transgressions, when he visited the Berlin Wall and was asked for his reaction, he declined comment.[175] The irreverent even began to pin on Frei a name that would haunt him: the "Kerensky of Chile," reviving memories of what happened in Russia during the four fateful months when Aleksandr Feodorovich Kerensky ruled the country as provisional premier. His failure to deal with urgent economic problems, and his moderation, cleared the way for the destiny-riding Bolsheviks to seize power in November 1917, a minority (even the word *Bolshevik* means minority) displacing a fragmented and immobilized majority—much as would soon happen in Chile.

"We will win out over the Communists," Gabriel Valdés said.

The Communists thought better.

"Push them! Push them!" Luis Corvalán, secretary-general of the Chilean Communist party told a party congress, "until their measures are our measures." He was referring to the measures of the Christian Democrats.

"In truth," the Christian Democrat Arriagada would write later, "it would be difficult to find in the foreign policy of Allende a break with respect to that of his predecessor. For all practical purposes, all he did was develop the policies formulated during the previous government."[176]

The government was, of course, the Christian Democrat one of Eduardo Frei.

THE LAST YEARS: TRIUMPH TO TUMULT

Eduardo Frei came to power at the head of a great crusade. He led his country to its political grave. Although the outside world would little notice or remark it, the crusade disintegrated after its first great triumph.

That triumph came in the congressional elections of March 7, 1965. Going into the elections, the Christian Democrats held little more than a toehold in Congress. After 1965, they held an absolute majority in the Chamber of Deputies, the first party to accomplish that in forty years. In the Senate they went from run-of-the-mill to number one, though they were still two agonizing votes shy of veto power in the Senate.[177] Tables 19 and 20 tell the story.

TABLE 19
COMPOSITION OF CHAMBER OF DEPUTIES AFTER 1961 AND 1965 ELECTIONS

	NO. OF DEPUTIES	
PARTY	1961	1965
Conservative party (PCU)	17	3
Christian Democrats (PDC)	23	82
Liberal party (PL)	28	6
Radical party (PR)	39	20
Communist party (PCCh)	16	18
Socialist party (PS)	12	15
National Democratic party (PADENA)[a]	12	3
TOTAL	147	147

Source: "The Chilean Congressional Election of March 7, 1965: An Analysis" (Washington, D.C.: Institute for the Comparative Study of Political Systems, 1966), p. 24.

[a] PADENA was the largest of the minor parties, remnants ot the non-Marxist leftist groups that had supported Ibáñez. In the 1961 elections the party lost all six Senate seats, but managed to elect twelve deputies. It supported Allende in 1964.

TABLE 20
COMPOSITION OF SENATE AFTER 1961 AND 1965 ELECTIONS

	NO. OF SENATORS	
PARTY	1961	1965
PCU	4	2
PDC	4	13
PL	9	5
PR	13	9
PCCh	4	5
PS	7	7
PADENA	0	1
National Vanguard of the People (VNP)	1	1
Independents	3	2
TOTAL	45	45

Source: "The Chilean Congressional Election of March 7, 1965: An Analysis" (Washington, D.C.: Institute for the Comparative Study of Political Systems, 1966), p. 24.

The Radicals, for so many years the courtesans of Chilean politics, were already evidencing the ravages of dissoluteness, the ineluctable fate of aging among excessively promiscuous courtesans, even political ones. The Right, having forfeited its identity and, with it, a valid claim to voter allegiance by running scared behind Frei in the 1964 elections, was all but wiped out. Some of its major leaders were buried in the very avalanche the Right had helped to create, and there were those who would prophesy that even Jorge Alessandri himself was finished. (Others would perpetuate the myth of a powerful and stubborn Right standing foursquare in the way of progress.)[178] Out of the ashes of total defeat would rise, however, a new and more virile Right, sobered by the experience of frittering away 150 years of proud past. In the aftermath of the debacle, all ten nonpolitical farm leaders interviewed by Kaufman in connection with the agrarian-reform debate agreed that it would have been better if FRAP had won in 1964. As one said: "If Allende had won in 1964, the only way we could have moved into a Marxist society was through civil war. Frei may do it peacefully. In that sense, it might very well have been better if FRAP had won. The issues would have been clearer and the lines would have been drawn more firmly."[179]

These ten were representative of a new breed of men of the Right who worked to form the National party, fused from the frankly conservative remnants of the Conservative and Liberal parties. It was a process that caused some old-guard political pros to stomp out in a huff, but they represented precisely the dead hand of an ideological and opportunistic past the new leaders were trying to amputate. It was also a process that brought jeers of derision and doomsaying, especially from those who found a frankly conservative party not to their own taste.[180]

As for the far Left, it was the real winner. Not only did the Communists and their even more leftist ally-rivals, the Socialists, increase their number of seats in Congress from thirty-nine to forty-five, but they also witnessed the destruction of their primary enemy, the Right. They could now turn their skills and energies to extracting from the Christian Democrats the maximum advantage for reshaping the country to their own ideological image. Having done that, they would then concentrate on displacing the Christian Democrats in power, and finishing the job themselves. That job would include finishing off political rivals, including the Christian Democrats.

But for the moment victory belonged to the Christian Democrats, and that was the message the world got. "In the eyes of most observers, particularly foreigners, the Christian Democrat victory obliterated major stumbling blocks in the path of democratic development in Chile. Here was an able leader, backed by a vigorous party, who had dedicated himself to a sweeping reform of his country. Now he had power; what was left for him was to use it," was the way it looked to some. Tomic saw in the outcome of those elections the birth of a dynasty; Christian Democrats, he said, would rule for thirty years. More cautious observers settled for twenty.[181]

In a way, they could be forgiven their euphoria, because the Christian Democrats did far better than they had dared imagine, or that anyone else had, for that matter. *Ercilla* magazine polled political leaders before the 1965 election, asking them for their forecasts of how many seats their parties would win. Table 21 shows how far off the mark they were—far even allowing for a little electoral razzle-dazzle and the eternal optimism of candidates.

TABLE 21

PREDICTIONS VS. ACTUAL OUTCOME—1965 CONGRESSIONAL ELECTIONS

| | PREDICTIONS | | ACTUAL OUTCOME | |
PARTY	SENATE	CHAMBER	SENATE	CHAMBER
Conservative	4	24	0	3
Liberal	3	25	0	6
Radical	6	42	3	20
Christian Democrat	9	65	12	82
Socialist	4	20	3	15
Communist	2	24	2	18
PADENA	2	12	1	3

Source: Ercilla, February 10, 1965, pp. 6–7, as cited in "The Chilean Congressional Election of March 7, 1965: An Analysis" (Washington, D.C.: Institute for the Comparative Study of Political Systems, 1966), pp. 18, 21.

The landslide was such that two Christian Democrats who had run for Senate seats strictly on a pro forma basis, so as to round out the party's ticket, suddenly found themselves elected. In Santiago the party discovered that if it had run four candidates instead of three, the fourth man would have bested Socialist Carlos Altamirano Orrego.[182] Altamirano was on his way to becoming the leader of the radical wing of the Socialist party; later he would be the single most powerful force in preventing an Allende rapprochement with more moderate elements. At the very end, his provocations facilitated the overthrow of Allende. In that light, it is interesting to speculate what Chilean history might have been had Altamirano's political career been ended in 1965.

Impressive as the victory was, it was not the apocalypse that Christian Democrat believers and boosters made it out to be. For one thing, the numbers were misleading. Chile's complicated electoral formula (the D'Hondt system of proportional representation) was tilted to favor the larger parties at the expense of smaller ones. The Christian Democrats, for example, elected one deputy for about every 12,100 votes, whereas it took the Liberals about 28,700 votes to elect one deputy. Thus, although the Liberals and Conservatives between them got 12.8 percent of the votes cast for deputies, they won only 6 percent of the seats; conversely, the Christian Democrats, with 43.6 percent of the vote, won 56 percent of the seats in the Chamber of Deputies.[183]

Furthermore, elections for the Chamber of Deputies were based on the 1930 census, when Chile was still an overwhelmingly rural country. (Indeed: the 1930 census would *remain* the basis for Chamber seats down to the final apocalypse of 1973.[184])

Next, although the Christian Democrats held commanding control of the lower house, they were stymied in the Senate.

Most important, they weren't able to convert votes into action. Although few saw it then, their day had really come and gone.

One reason for this was the inability of the Christian Democrats to work effectively with other parties, to muster coalitions. In common with most reformist parties, the Christian Democrats exercised their power with the arrogance of those confident that they walk in the ways of moral certitude. Even the *New York Times,* a newspaper consistently devoted to Frei before, during, and after his term of office, felt constrained to point this out in a 1967 editorial: "Chileans, whom many consider the most democratic of all Latin Americans, are accustomed to the adjustments and give-and-take of party politics. In the Frei regime they faced a stiffness that many considered to be arrogance."[185] During the six years the Christian Democrats reigned, no other party was invited to share their banquet table of power.

They were hobbled too by the fact that, as Gil observed,[186] they were a party more of men than of ideas; thus it was that Tomic from Washington functioned pretty much as his own foreign minister, and Chonchol back home ran his agrarian-reform program, and Leighton, from his powerful perch as interior minister, repeatedly muzzled the Carabineros and allowed the MIR to mount its terrorist-guerrilla organization.[187]

And they were frustrated by an even larger and inescapable internal contradiction: political reality was against them. It was against them because they were zealots playing with the fires of revolution. Analysts Parrish, von Lazar, and Tapia Videla wrote at the time:

> The essence of pluralistic democracy is that it cannot be quickly moved in one direction or another, except, of course, in a crisis. . . . It may be that the problems of Chile are serious enough to be classed as a crisis, but the tone and manner of life in the country at the present time do not suggest such an analogy.

President Frei promised a "Revolution with Liberty" to the Chilean voters, and it may be that the next few years will show these terms ill-suited to one another in Chile . . . .

The essence of a revolution is that basic social and economic relationships are greatly changed. This means that, necessarily, political power relationships must be drastically altered. In contrast, the term "liberty" means, basically, that people will be left alone, and that there will be a minimum of interference with the daily activities of citizens . . . .[188]

That same dilemma would be the undoing of Allende a few years later, except that Allende and his cohorts did not submit to the same scruples about democratic processes and institutional forms. But the fact that Frei had sowed the wild whirlwind of revolution enabled Allende to try to bring it to its conclusion: in his case, a logical one, because it was unabashedly Marxist.

Frei had bequeathed Allende weapons of incalculable value in pursuing his revolutionary goals, in the form of the Constitutional Reforms of 1970, reforms which Frei described as the "culmination of his government." Those reforms, which Frei could only wheedle from Congress by making them effective the day after he would leave office (but when, all the betting was, he would be succeeded by a succession of other Christian Democrat presidents in any case), would not only confer upon Allende wide-ranging powers, but also enable him to maintain the masquerade of legitimacy long after he had, in reality, torn it asunder.

Frei first proposed his package of revolutionary reforms in his first month in office. The Christian Democrat-controlled House approved the package, the Senate buried the proposals after long and bitter debate. In 1969, Frei tried again, and after arduous lobbying and compromise, finally won approval for seven of his nine points on December 29, 1969, signing them into law on January 21, 1970 (and hence the 1970 designation). Congress balked at creating the Economic and Social Council and at delegating to the president exclusive legislative control over the private sector. But—in addition to granting the vote to illiterates and eighteen to twenty-one year olds—the reforms greatly strengthened the powers of the presidency at the expense of the Congress. For example: all legislation dealing with social and economic matters could originate only with the president; empowering the president to force Congress to act on his initiatives within thirty days; barring Congress from straying from the sense of Executive legislation during the amendment process.

Frei would fight hard for this shift in power, arguing that the country, during its 150 years as a republic, had been governed best during the first forty years, under a strong executive system; disastrously (and corruptly) during the period of so-called "parliamentary" democracy

(1891–1925); and with increasing inefficiency during the deterioration of strong executive control after 1925. While ending the era of parliamentary democracy, the 1925 constitution, he would argue, did not go far enough in restoring presidential authority. (That judgment—that Chile is governed best under a strong presidential system—has been widely accepted by politically aware Chileans of all political colorations for many years, down to the present day). Of all the developments since adoption of the 1925 constitution, Frei would cite the emergence and importance of centralized economic planning as the most important justification for a more streamlined constitution, quoting—at one point—a former justice minister as saying that if government economic policy is to be rational in a democracy, there could be only one hand on the throttle. In the fast-moving modern world, he argued, Congress should confine itself to legislating broad policy outlines, leaving management and administration of fiscal affairs to the Executive. (Interestingly, he defended yet another of the reforms, the creation of the Constitutional Tribunal, by citing only two countries specifically where such courts had been created: France, until the autocratic rule of Charles DeGaulle, and Yugoslavia, in the sixties even less democratic than it is today.)

Under Frei, the tension between "revolution" and "liberty" was usually resolved on the side of revolution. Interference in daily lives even extended to the abolishing in 1966 of a cherished Latin institution, the siesta (which he ended—temporarily—by ordering government offices to work a straight seven-and-one-half-hour day; Allende, the proletarian's guardian angel, restored the three-hour siesta, in no small measure because he was exceedingly fond of taking one himself).

Frei made another bold move in the area of personal behavior: in nominally Catholic Chile, he instituted family-planning programs throughout the country. Birth control was justified in Chile not because of runaway population growth (Chile had one of the lower population growth rates in the world) but to counter illegal abortions (rampant and highly dangerous).

On the economic front, the government moved rapidly to extend state control over the economy, and the economic lives of its citizens, not only on the farms, and in the banks, but in industry in general. The lopsided nature of the Chilean economy—copper dwarfing everything else—facilitated the task, the need for new capital to expand complicated it. On the first score, a 1969 study showed that 288 companies controlled the entire interlocking network of Chilean economic activity; 144 companies controlled the entire sphere of industrial activity.

By 1969 the state had increased its investment in the 850 corporations that made up the industrial sector from 1967's 7.4 percent to 16.7 percent.

But in the same period foreign investment, principally American, also increased its stake, from 16.5 percent in 1967 to 20.3 percent in 1969.[189] The sixties were a time of explosive growth of U.S. private investment in Latin America—from $8.3 billion in 1960 to $14.2 billion at the start of the next decade—and Chile was not excluded from the dance of the dollars. The fact that Frei's government permitted that investment, particularly in new areas such as the revitalized nitrate industry, drew the unrelenting fire of the far Left. Though no friend of private capital, Frei justified this as a temporary expedient: the country was short of investment capital.

Frei's problems multiplied after the municipal elections of April 2, 1967. Confident of their strength, the Christian Democrats characterized the elections as a national plebiscite on Frei's policies and they expected to pull at least the 43.6 percent share they had won in the 1965 congressional elections. When the votes were counted, Frei had been dealt an unmistakable rebuke, and what appeared in 1966 as only a freakish relapse now was an unmistakable trend: the Christian Democrats were on the skids, and would continue to skid. It was a message it would take commentators, especially foreign commentators, years to digest, mesmerized as so many were by the supposed invincibility of the party. In the immediate aftermath, one noted foreign analyst indulged in the sort of apologetic harumphing reminiscent of U.S. radio commentator H. V. Kaltenborn's celebrated report on the outcome of the U.S. presidential elections in 1948.[190]

The Christian Democrats got 36.43 percent of the vote. The Communists went from 12.73 percent in 1965 to 15.09 percent, the Socialists from 10.58 percent to 14.20 percent. The Radicals wobbled up from 13.71 percent to 16.46 percent, and the new National party, picking up the pieces of the two decimated parties of the Right, picked up 14.61 percent, just under two percentage points better than the two parties did in 1965. Inevitably, Frei found himself on the defensive within his own party.

Student demonstrations at the Catholic universities in Santiago and Valparaíso in mid-1967 brought into the open the tension between those forces in the party demanding a more radical program and the moderates led by Frei. At the party's National Assembly, July 15, 1967, a political-technical committee headed by Jacques Chonchol presented a report entitled "Proposals for Political Action for a Noncapitalistic Road to Development During the Period 1967–1970." Rejecting the "developmentalist" approach, the report called for war on the Right, rapprochement with the Left: ". . . active confrontation with the Right, especially its ultrareactionary elements . . ." and "active and constructive dialogue with . . . political forces . . . from whom we can gain support for the execution of this program." Though not named, it was clear the authors had in mind the left-wing Popular Action Front (FRAP). In the economic arena, the report called for: increased control of copper; nationalization of the nitrate industry and largest coal company; nationalization of the Bethlehem Steel 58 percent share in the national steel company; takeover of ITT's telephone company; and total government control of the Central Bank.

Though the entire program was an implied attack on Frei and his policies, the five hundred-member assembly approved the program and referred it to the party council for application. Frei suffered further humiliation when the *rebeldes* and *terceristas* decisively defeated the *oficialista* slate in voting to choose party officers for the coming year. The *rebeldes* elected three officers, the *terceristas* two, Frei's *oficialistas* none. Sen. Rafael Gumucio, leader of the *rebelde* faction, ousted Jaime Castillo as chairman.

The now-dominant left wing of the party kept unrelenting pressure on Frei through the year. When, on November 11, 1968, Chonchol quit as head of the agrarian reform institute (INDAP), fifty-three of the eighty-one Christian Democrats in the Chamber of Deputies supported Frei and his embattled interior minister, Edmundo Pérez Zújovic, the principal target of left-wing fire. But three thousand party members turned out for a banquet honoring Chonchol two weeks later. Among them: Radomiro Tomic, who had just returned from the United States to prepare for his presidential campaign, and the new party president, Renán Fuentealba, leader of the *tercerista* wing.

The long-smoldering tensions erupted with the presidential campaign already in full swing. On May 1, 1970, the party's Assembly met to vote on policy in the elections. One proposal, supported by *terceristas* and *rebeldes*, and presented by Fuentealba, called for "rejection of any possible understanding, whether direct or indirect, with the Right, rejection of a position of isolation for Christian Democrats. . . ." The other, the *oficialista* resolution, ruled out "any possibility of agreement with the [conservative] National party," but called for "the replacement of capitalist structures by a way to development which is neither capitalist nor collectivist." As Sigmund observed: "The choice was thus between a proposal for negotiations with the Left for a common candidate, preferably but not necessarily a Christian Democrat, and the nomination of a candidate first, followed by possible negotiations for support later."

It took all of Frei's waning prestige to prevail—his close friend and party ideologue Jaime Castillo was elected chairman—but by a cliffhanging 233–215 margin. In the wake of that meeting, Sens. Gumucio and Alberto Jerez, Deputy Julio Silva Solar—and Chonchol—all bolted the party to form the Movement for Unitary Popular Action (MAPU), with Chonchol at its head.[191]

The vote followed months of rough infighting. In November 1967 a group of young rebels attacked Freismo as the "iron hand of revolution in liberty." Their wrath was directed principally at the Grupo Móvil, a specially trained and equipped strike force within the Carabineros created by General Huerta for dealing with mounting disorders in the countryside and in the cities. Huerta was vilified constantly because he was a graduate of the International Police Academy, established in Washington under the auspices of AID, and the Grupo Móvil was characterized almost reflexively as "murderous." Despite restraints Leighton managed to impose on it, the force was hated for its efficiency in keeping the MIR at bay and for checkmating attempts by farm and factory workers, goaded by political agitators, to take the law into their own hands and seize farms and factories.

Interestingly, Frei owed a portion of his problems with the Left—inside and outside his party—to a man named Pinochet—though, as noted earlier, not the later president of that name.

In March 1966, the Left-dominated copper unions declared sympathy strikes in support of miners at El Teniente who had been on strike since January. The government declared the strikes illegal. Eighty-five soldiers under the command of Colonel Manuel Pinochet found themselves opposed by a thousand miners and their families when they attempted to occupy the El Salvador mine. The troops opened fire, killing six workers and two housewives. Wrote Sigmund: "The Left called the incident a 'massacre' and cited it for years to prove that Frei was opposed to the workers."[192]

In the politically excited atmosphere of "revolution" then abroad in Chile, such confrontations worsened, as did labor trouble. Table 22 illustrates the growth of the labor crisis.

The year 1963 was, of course the final one in power for Alessandri's conservative government, and the years 1965–69 cover the administration of a government supposedly representing the coalescence of workers and peasants.

Nor was strife limited to farms, factories, and schools. On August 11, 1968, a group of young priests, nuns, and laymen occupied the Roman Catholic cathedral in downtown Santiago. Calling itself the Movement of the Young Church, the group issued a manifesto demanding that the church "renounce its dependency" on international finance. "The church," said the manifesto, "should not serve the scandalous division of classes. Its schools, which shelter Chilean aristocracy, are institutions contrary to the gospel." Leader of the movement was a thirty-three-year-old priest named Diego Palma, who said he believed the MIR

TABLE 22
STRIKES, 1963–1969

YEARS	STRIKES	NO. OF STRIKERS	MAN-DAYS LOST
1963	642	115,331	585,514
1965	772	212,397	1,952,494
1966	712	195,435	2,015,253
1967	2,177	386,801	2,252,478
1969	977	275,405	972,382

Sources: For 1963, 1965, 1967, Manuel Becerra, "Perspectiva Histórica de la Huelga Obrera en Chile," Centro de Estudios de la Realidad Nacional, Catholic University of Chile, September 9, 1971, p. 146, cited by Alain Labrousse, *El Experimento Chileno* (Barcelona and Mexico: Ediciones Grijalbo, S.A., 1973), p. 168. For 1966, 1969, "Mensaje del Presidente," May 21, 1970, pp. 366, 368–69, cited by Henry A. Landsberger and Tim McDaniel in "Mobilization as a Double-Edged Sword: The Allende Government's Uneasy Relationship with Labor, 1970–1973," in *United States and Chile During the Allende Years, 1970–1973*, report of Hearings of the Subcommittee on Inter-American Affairs of the Committee on Foreign Affairs, U.S. House of Representatives (Washington, D.C.: Government Printing Office, 1975), p. 623.

was the only group capable of bringing about the "changes" Chile needed, because "they have clean hands."[193]

It was in this climate that Ambrosio won the presidency of the Christian Democratic Youth organization that year, deepening the split between leftists and moderates in the party.

Still another and even more electrifying protest was yet to come. One of the trademarks of the Frei years was an attitude of studied contempt toward the country's armed forces, and it reflected the unrelenting campaign throughout the hemisphere against the military. In Latin America it was, in part, a reaction against the penchant of the military in so many countries for seizing power for itself, and when not doing that, allowing itself to be maneuvered into the position of protecting the power of "oligarchs." Yet in Chile, neither charge was valid; with the exception of the civil war of 1891 and the tumultuous events of the twenties and early thirties, the Chilean military had studiously avoided politics. This won it the almost ritualistic accolades of those who relished baiting the military elsewhere—but did not spare them the same penalties. The attack was usually mounted on the grounds that the military gobbled up too large a share of the meager resources, although throughout the sixties, defense spending in Latin America was lower than that of any other region of the world, Africa included.

In Chile the result was constant erosion of force levels, obsolescence of equipment, and deteriorating pay and living conditions for the military. Roberto Viaux Marambio, a general whose name would soon reverberate through Chilean history, complained that noncommissioned officers in his First Army Division, based at Antofagasta, were living in shanties with no roofs, and that new "housing" being built for them by the government consisted of tiny apartments lacking hot water, or doors for the two closetless bedrooms, so small they barely held two cots. Fifty First Division officers had to crowd into bachelor officer quarters built to house twenty-five. The pay was so bad that a lieutenant colonel, with twenty-five years of service, earned no more than the starting pay for the lowest-graded laborer at the Chuquicamata copper mine. A foreign diplomat observed that in their 1967 regular maneuvers, the Chilean armed forces performed poorly, in large measure because they had not been able to call up the conscripts due to be called that year "because they didn't even have enough shoes to shod them."[194]

By 1967 "vamos a tomar una pilsener en el Club Militar" ("let's have a beer at the officers' club") had become the catchword among young officers in the Santiago garrison, a signal to the high command that they were about to walk out unless relief were given quickly. It wasn't, and in 1968, four hundred (of around two thousand army officers) resigned en masse. A new defense minister, Gen. Tulio Marambio Marchant, and new army commandant, Gen. Sergio Castillo Aránguiz (a man with family ties to top Christian Democrats) were named. They promised action within nine months. They failed to deliver.

Amid this growing military restiveness, the tough-minded artillery officer, Roberto Viaux Marambio, was promoted to general. From his new and higher perch, Viaux waged his own private war on the high command. Late in September 1969, nine months after his promotion and assignment as commandant of the First Division, he was summoned to Santiago and he began immediately to seek a meeting with Frei—through regular channels, and outside them. Instead, a few days after his arrival, Gen. Sergio Castillo Aránguiz called Viaux to his office and told him he was being retired and would be relieved the following day of his command.

Making his way back to his headquarters, nine hundred miles away, Viaux was given a hero's welcome by his men, who urged him not to resign. Finally, after some confusion, he was summoned back to Santiago. As Viaux told the story,[195] officers began arriving at his house in Santiago that night, telling him they were fed up and wanted to act. At 2:30 A.M. October 21, 1969, he agreed to take over command of the Tacna armored regiment, and declared himself in "professional rebellion" against the government.

Within hours, he said, numerous other units had pledged support and a stream of visitors began arriving at the regiment headquarters, situated a short distance from downtown Santiago. Among them were Juan de Dios Carmona, former defense minister and a prominent member of the moderate wing of the Christian Democrats; Sen. Renán Fuentealba; representatives of the Radical and Socialist parties; and the commandant of the Santiago garrison.

Viaux tried to telephone Frei to assure him that the uprising was aimed not at toppling the government, but only at enforcing the military's demands for decent pay, housing, and career conditions. Significantly, no move was made to oust him by force, though garbage trucks were drawn up around La Moneda to defend it in case of attack. At one point a mob of about one hundred persons gathered outside the rebellious regiment, and when the latter dispersed them, one man was shot in the thigh and several hurt in the stampede to flee.

Late in the afternoon, Patricio Silva Garín, undersecretary of health, arrived as a personal emissary of Frei. The sides finally hammered out a five-point agreement, under which Viaux ended the revolt in return for the resignation of the defense minister and Frei's pledge to "resolve in urgent form the economic problem of the armed forces." At 3:30 A.M., October 22, twenty-five hours after the "revolt" had begun, Viaux went home to bed. He would later reappear in another and more shocking drama.

For the Christian Democrats, communism always held the fascination of the forbidden fruit. It was an impulse stronger than anything so commonplace as evidence of its distance from the objective world, and so they courted the Communist party almost despite themselves—the pathetic suitor in the starched suit pursuing the painted lady he knows isn't right for him, and his family would never accept anyway, and yet, how to stay away?

At one point, early in the regime, they joined in an alliance with the Communists to elect one of their men president of the College of Journalists, the powerful professional organization of the country's newspapermen. As the July 1965 annual convention of the Chilean Labor Federation (CUTCH) neared, the Christian Democrats approached the Communists on the possibility of sharing power in the federation. The Communists, who already ran things themselves, would have none of it.

The Christian Democrats continued tilting to the left, even though it was clear that it was the far Left that was blocking them in Congress, and the even farther Left that was making violence a way of life in the country. They continued their wooing even after another electoral reverse, the 1969 congressional elections, a prelude to the presidential elections the following year. And the dynasty-minded Christian Democrats, unweary and unwary, would court the Left once more—one disastrous time more.

But then, how could they do otherwise? As one of their young ideologues put it in 1967: "Christian Democracy, being Christian and democratic, is closer to communism in its ends than any other Chilean party." Besides, he said, "to be Communist in Chile is perfectly respectable and that does not automatically amount to subversion or submission to the Kremlin."[196]

Notes

CHAPTER 4

1. Nearly two centuries earlier, a great liberal thinker warned of the perils of despising the past and those who had forged it—much as the Christian Democrats were doing in Chile in 1964. Edmund Burke, in a letter written to a friend in France in 1790 commenting on the excesses of the French Revolution, said: "Compute your gains: see what is got by those extravagant and presumptuous speculations which have taught your leaders to despise themselves, until the moment in which they became truly despicable. By following those false lights, France has bought undisguised calamities at a higher price than any nation has purchased the most unequivocal blessings. France has bought poverty by crime. France has not sacrificed her virtue to her interest, but she has abandoned her interest, that she might prostitute her virtue.... All other people have laid the foundations of civil freedom in severer manners, and a system of more austere and masculine morality. France, when she let loose the reins of regal authority, doubled the license of a ferocious dissoluteness in manners, and of an insolent irreligion in opinions and practices; and has extended through all ranks of life, as if she were communicating some privilege, or laying open some secluded benefit, all the unhappy corruptions that usually were the disease of wealth and power" (Burke, "Reflections on the Revolution in France: In a Letter Intended to Have Been Sent to a Gentleman in Paris, 1790," *Edmund Burke* [New York: P. F. Collier & Son, Harvard Classics, 1968], p. 166).

2. Abraham F. Lowenthal, "Alliance Rhetoric Versus Latin American Reality," *Foreign Affairs* 48, no. 3 (April 1970): 494, 501. I must add, in fairness to Professor Lowenthal—and myself—that I agree with many of his analyses of the Alliance's roots, but with few of his recommended remedies as expressed in that article. In still another essay on the Alliance, Lowenthal returns this verdict: "That so many North Americans (including officials as well as the authors of liberal accounts) apparently took the Alliance's early rhetoric seriously can only be attributed to self-delusion or hypocrisy" (Lowenthal, " 'Liberal,' 'Radical,' and 'Bureaucratic' Perspectives on U.S. Latin American Policy: The Alliance for Progress in Retrospect," in *Latin America and the United States; The Changing Political Realities*, ed. Julio Cutler and Richard R. Fagen [Stanford: Stanford University Press, 1974], p. 277).

3. Lowenthal, in *Foreign Policy*, p. 496.

4. And a lollapalooza it was. By the time the tenth anniversary of the by then moribund Alliance rolled around, seven of the ten Latin states on the South American continent were dictatorships, as were two of the three in the Caribbean and two of the five Central American states. Mexico, nominally a "guided democracy," was then marking its forty-third year of rule by the Institutional Revolutionary party, and therefore was and is in a class by itself.

When the Alliance got started, democratic governments were in power in all but one of seven South American countries, and all but one of the five Central American States. In the Caribbean, all three traditional OAS countries (Cuba, Haiti, and the Dominican Republic) were dictatorships, but the Trujillo dynasty was already disintegrating in Santo Domingo.

5. Tad Szulc, *Twilight of the Tyrants* (New York: Henry Holt, 1959).

6. Chile was the largest per capita recipient of Alliance assistance in Latin America, and only one or two countries on earth had, until 1973, received more U.S. aid, per capita, than Chile. I put "benefited" in quotes because while it is clear that Alliance aid was of crucial importance to Eduardo Frei and his Christian Democrats, it is far less clear whether helping them was the same as helping Chile—or merely complicating and postponing the day of realistic reckoning.

7. Covey T. Oliver, "Foreign and Human Relations with Latin America," *Foreign Affairs* 47, no. 3 (April 1969): 521. Professor Oliver was assistant secretary of state for inter-American affairs in the late sixties and U.S. coordinator of the Alliance for Progress.

The "victim syndrome," one of the hoariest and most enervating legends in Latin America, was given considerable impetus by Alliance rhetoric. The cornerstone of the "victim" theory was the work of the Argentine economist Raúl Prebisch, in attempting to show that the terms of international trade worked to favor the advanced, industrialized countries at the expense of the backward, raw-materials-supplying countries. Despite flaws in the original Prebisch study, and mounting evidence over the years to contradict it, the Prebisch model long remained, for most Latin Americans, an article of faith.

Theodore H. Moran, in *Multinational Corporations and the Politics of Dependence: Copper in Chile* (Princeton, N.J.: Princeton University Press, 1974), demonstrates how in the case of Chile, the Prebisch model was a key factor in leading the country into an erroneous strategy: "trying to reverse the trend in the terms of trade through pressing for the highest commodity prices market power would allow in the short run" (p. 84). This happened, he said, because a thorough analysis of the Prebisch model was never attempted for the case of Chile as a copper exporter, but, rather, "a Prebisch 'cast of thought' was permitted to flourish . . . without any insistence that the able and sophisticated Chilean economists think through the technical aspects of their model and the implications for policy in the copper industry" (p. 79). For Moran's analysis of the impact of the Prebisch model on Chilean copper strategy, see pp. 66–84. Socialists, Communists, Radicals, the Christian Democrats, and many even on the Right, shaped their policies, and attitudes, on the strength (or, more to the point, weakness) of those theories with the predictable ultimate consequence of nationalization.

8. The secret panel was then known as the 303 Committee. First established in 1947, these top-secret groups under the direct authority of the White House achieved instant fame in September 1974 with the (largely spurious) disclosures of CIA activity in Chile. By then the five-man committee was known as the 40 Committee, after National Security Council Intelligence Decision Memorandum No. 40, which reorganized the panel in 1969. Henry Kissinger says the committee was renamed after a news leak simply *named* it. "In those faraway days of innocence," Kissinger wrote, "This was enough of a breach of security to require a change of name." (Henry Kissinger, *The White House Years* [Boston: Little, Brown, & Co., 1979], p. 660).

The "drowning" quote is from a confidential *Time* memorandum prepared in 1970 following Allende's election, and reproduced in U.S. Congress, Senate, Subcommittee on Multinational Corporations of the Committee on Foreign Relations, *Multinational Corporations and United States Foreign Policy*, pt. 2, p. 704. The "blatant" quote is from Victor Marchetti and John D. Marks, *The CIA and the Cult of Intelligence* (New York: Dell Publishing Co., 1974), p. 39, fn. The report of the CIA's scramble to buy escudos is from Philip Agee, *Inside the Company: CIA Diary* (New York: Stonehill Publishing Co., 1975), p. 382. Agee, then a CIA operative stationed in Montevideo, said the purchase in Montevideo at that time "was also worth over $100,000 and, according to the Finance Officer, is only a drop in the bucket. He says we are spending money in the Chilean election practically like we did in Brazil two years ago."

9. Jerome Levinson and Juan de Onís, *The Alliance That Lost Its Way*, (Chicago: Quadrangle Books, Twentieth Century Fund Study, 1970), p. 9. Chile was, indeed "a cold-war battlefield" in 1964, but the authors fail to remark that the decisive forces, and personalities, were purely the internal ones.

10. Said the newspaper, a slavish mouthpiece for the official party line, in its October 20, 1963 edition: "Eduardo Frei traveled to the Soviet Union and, fair man that he is, returned with a balanced account of what he found there, revising old and outdated ideas that really are more prejudice than idea. . . . Senator Frei's statements clearly gainsay those sectors of his party who still try to traffick in sterile and stubborn anti-communism" (in Marcos Chamudes, *Chile: Una Advertencia Americana* [Santiago: Ediciones P.E.C., 1972], p. 204). In today's context that may sound so innocuous as to be quaint; in the sixties, it was fraught with significance, especially since Frei was about to make his second run against their man Allende for the presidency.

11. Ibid., p. 247. The author of that remark was Sen. Rafael Agustín Gumucio, a founder of the Falange.

12. It is, of course, no accident that in the fifty years after 1920, when politics in Chile became a cacophony of sloganeering, only the Communist party suffered no splits, no serious internal decay. However much the party line might zigzag—and it did so in lockstep with Moscow—that line was law for its members. And so it reached what most observers regarded as a saturation level of about 50,000 card-carrying members by the late 1960s, and held fast at the level.

The Christian Democrats, like the Radicals before them, were doctrinaire and feisty—so long as they were in the opposition. Once in power, confronted with the responsibility of creating a new order rather than dismantling an old one, their doctrines and dogma bedeviled them in two ways: internally, as the source of endless infighting and eventual ruptures between moderates and extremists; externally, doctrine was honored in the breach as the party attempted to become all things to all men and finally clearly represented very few. The process of disintegration that began immediately after the party's greatest triumph, in 1965, was accelerating in September 1973.

The Right never had a body of doctrine to weld it together, and so for over one hundred years, Liberals and Conservatives, individualists all, shared the same strategic vision of society but failed to reconcile their tactical and attitudinal differences. The Conservatives were traditionalist Catholics, the Liberals anticlerical; the Conservatives wanted a strong parliamentary system, the Liberals felt a presidential system was better suited to the country's idiosyncrasies; Conservative leadership was drawn mainly from landowner ranks, that of the Liberals from mercantile backgrounds; the Conservatives relied internally on rules and regulations to guide them, whereas the Liberals were subdivided into personalist factions and cliques. And so the two parties that together might have constituted an alternative helped instead to annihilate each other. It would take an electoral catastrophe in 1965 to bring them together.

13. Numerous commentators have noted the traditional flexibility of the Chilean Right. For instance, Federico Gil, in *El Sistema Político de Chile* (Santiago: Editorial Andrés Bello, 1969), refers to the "long tradition of adaptability" of the Right (p. 216). Chamudes (op. cit., p. 220), who is as polemic in his boisterous way as Gil is insidiously so in his seemingly austere way, refers to the Right's "exemplary sense of civic responsibility" in putting aside what amounted to "political revulsion" for some and "fears" for others in deciding to support Frei, rather than risk a Marxist conquest.

14. Newspaper accounts at the time almost invariably referred to Frei's win as a smashing triumph for the Christian Democrats, and rarely even mentioned the role of the Right in putting him in the presidency. Some commentators went even further, and erroneously put the Right in Durán's camp to the very end. As for Frei, he ignored the Right altogether in forming his government, excluding it entirely from power.

15. Quoted by Chamudes, op. cit., p. 198.

16. Reported by Levinson and de Onís, op. cit., pp. 92–93. Cole was former president of Amherst. Dungan was Kennedy's legislative assistant.

17. In his magazine *P.E.C.* Quoted by Chamudes, op. cit., p. 198.

18. John Gunther, *Inside South America* (New York: Harper & Row, 1966), p. 270. Gunther added that the evaluation was "dubious," and then gives some highly dubious reasons for saying it was dubious.

19. Gil notes that "some important leaders of the PDC are not very distant from Marxism in their political philosophy. In their advocacy of what they call a 'communitarian society,' they share with Marx the idea that private capital is the root of most evils, and therefore are for the abolition of private property" (op. cit., p. 289).

20. Eduardo Frei, *Un Mundo Nuevo* (Santiago: Ediciones Nueva Universidad, Universidad Católica de Chile, 1973), p. 12.

21. Gil, op. cit., p. 289. Frei, in the aforementioned work (n. 20), refers to the "clash between obviously antagonistic classes" coming about as the result of the gulf between rich and poor (p. 13).

22. Gabriel García Márquez, "The Death of Salvador Allende," *Harper's*, March 1974.

23. In Eudocio Ravines, *El Rescate de Chile* (Santiago: Empresa Editora e Impresora Edimpres, 1974), p. 91.

24. Paul E. Sigmund, *The Overthrow of Allende and the Politics of Chile, 1964–1976* (Pittsburgh: University of Pittsburgh Press, 1977), p. 54.

25. In Chamudes, op. cit., p. 202.

26. Alain Labrousse describes one of the elements of the Campaign of Terror as consisting of frequent radio spots which opened with the rat-a-tat of a machine gun, followed by the scream of a woman shrieking that the Communists had killed her son. Then, the emotion-choked announcer's voice: To avoid this in Chile, elect Eduardo Frei. The spot ended with another burst of machine-gun fire and dramatic music. Labrousse quotes a U.S. doctoral candidate, George Grayson, as saying he had interviewed dozens of PDC leaders and militants who confessed they never really believed the

Communist "peril," but staged the campaign solely to win votes. Labrousse, *El Experimento Chileno* (Barcelona and Mexico: Ediciones Gribalbo, S.A., 1973), p. 94. Frei himself behaved as if he didn't know about the campaign, exhorting listeners to vote for him not because they feared communism, but because they believed in his programs.

27. Paul E. Sigmund, op. cit., pp. 31–32.

28. *Encyclopaedia Britannica* (Chicago: Encyclopaedia Britannica, 1967), 14:896.

29. Gil, op. cit., p. 288. Gil describes the similarity as "surprising," yet also describes Garretón's ideas as "contaminated by nazism."

30. Labrousse, op. cit., p. 88.

31. Gunther, op. cit., p. 271.

32. Ibid., p. 258.

33. Garretón, according to several accounts, wired Leighton: "Impossible to accept post in cabinet; for a leader of a movement, there is nothing but the leadership of the nation" (Gil, op. cit., p. 288). Most accounts make Leighton to be an even more wondrous boy, a mere twenty-five when named. On the other hand, his age is put at twenty-nine by *Nueva Enciclopedia de Chile* (Argentina: Ediciones Copihue, Fotomecánica Futura SRL, Ediciones Libra, 1974), 1:136.

34. Chamudes says he was sent to the coal fields of Lota to settle a strike by the Communist-dominated union. The party sent him because of his popularity: he was the top vote-getter in the country in the 1937 congressional elections (doubling the vote, for instance, of another upstart named Salvador Allende). Chamudes said the party feared a bloody strike there which would jeopardize the fragile electoral alliance they had stitched together with the jittery Radicals. He says that upon his return from Lota, after ending the strike, he found a note from Leighton congratulating him for his "patriotism." Chamudes, op. cit., p. 102.

35. Frei, "The Second Latin American Revolution," *Foreign Affairs* 50, no. 1 (October 1971): 93. He was referring specifically to socialism, and by implication, the socialism of Allende, but as numerous commentators—including Christian Democrats—have pointed out, the differences between Christian Democrat tactics and those of their rivals of the Left are measured in millimeters. The essential difference, according to them, is that they believe their socialism will leave democratic pluralism intact, whereas that of others would destroy it.

36. Bernard Collier, "A Revolution Without the Execution Wall," *New York Times Magazine*, January 17, 1967. Collier, a former *New York Herald-Tribune* and *New York Times* correspondent in Latin America, had a reputation among his colleagues for stylistic flamboyance not always matched by reportorial caution; this article, for example, contains several major bloopers.

37. Ibid. Gunther notes that Pope John XXIII and John F. Kennedy were two other Christian Democrat heroes, and that U.S. aid to Chile, especially during the Frei years, was lavish, as was U.S. help to get him elected. Gunther, op. cit., p. 262. Vatican secrets are, of course, safer than CIA secrets, so details of church largess are not available; there is no secret, on the other hand, that the Roman Catholic church in Chile has consistently and constantly allied itself with the Christian Democrats.

38. Labrousse, op. cit., p. 92.

39. Collier, op. cit. Although you would vainly scour the almost gleeful news-

paper and magazine accounts of alleged CIA wickedness in Chile in 1964 and again in shoring up Allende's political foes for even mention of his name, the fact is, Robert Kennedy was a member of the 303 Committee (as it was then called) which controlled the CIA's clandestine operations. The former U.S. ambassador Edward M. Korry was, however, less skittish. Appearing on the September 29, 1974, Public Broadcasting Television program "Firing Line," hosted by William F. Buckley, Jr., Korry said the late president's brother was a member of the committee, and that word of CIA activity in Chile in the 1964 elections was common gossip in Washington in September-October 1967 when he was being briefed before going to Chile. Among those who knew, he said, were members of the same Senate subcommittee (on Inter-American Affairs) headed by Sen. Frank Church (D.–Idaho), who a few years later would wax so indignant about the "revelations" of CIA activity in Chile. The indignation was confined, however, to reports of CIA efforts to undermine Allende, reports which were largely erroneous and/or misleading anyway. Korry's comments from a transcript of program, prepared by Radio TV Reports, Inc., New York, New York.

40. Marchetti and Marks, op. cit., p. 39. In contrast to the diligence displayed on other matters, the authors make a single reference to Robert Kennedy—one which neither connects him to the 303 Committee nor compromises him in any other way.

41. Chamudes, op. cit., pp. 110–11.

42. Both Prat's and Durán's remarks are from Paul D. Bethel, *The Losers* (New Rochelle, N.Y.: Arlington House, 1969), p. 515.

43. Quoted in an editorial in the *Miami Herald*, April 9, 1963. Bethel quotes university professor Enrique Paris, a member of the Communist party's Central Committee, as saying: "Those participating in our campaign are willing to give everything they have in order to make our country into the second Free Territory of the Americas." The phrase echoed one Castro invented for his Cuba. The remark touched off a backlash. Bethel, op. cit., p. 515.

44. In Jaime Guzmán E., "The Church in Chile and the Political Debate," in *Chile: A Critical Survey* (Santiago: Institute of General Studies, 1972), p. 284.

45. Gil, for example, an ardent admirer of the Christian Democrats, writes: "Senator Eduardo Frei also adopted in his campaign a strong reformist line. His differed from that of the FRAP more in tone and emphasis than in essence" (op. cit., p. 322). Marxist Labrousse writes: "The analysis of the FRAP of the structural causes of Chilean underdevelopment were not fundamentally different from those of the Christian Democrats." He says the FRAP was only more "radical" in the matter of nationalization of banks, public utilities, industry and insurance companies (op. cit., p. 94).

46. Both quotes from Bethel, op. cit., pp. 511, 514.

47. Gunther, for example, exulted that Frei "had won an amazing personal triumph—the largest plurality of any presidential candidate in Chilean history" (op. cit., p. 263). As we have seen, it was anything but a "personal triumph," and as to the pluralities, one need search no further back in Chilean "history" than 1931 (when Montero won 63 percent of the vote) or 1925 (when Figueroa got 71 percent). In 1942 Ríos got 55.96 percent, or only a sixth of a percentage point less than Frei.

An even more flagrantly distorted "analysis" was offered by Prof. Harry

Kantor in his *Patterns of Politics and Political Systems in Latin America* (Chicago: Rand McNally, 1969). He wrote (p. 549): "By 1964, the need for reform was so obvious that the Conservative and Liberal parties did not even offer a presidential candidate."

Alistair Horne points out that Frei's campaign undoubtedly gained a certain amount of "sympathy votes" because of the death of Frei's sister in an automobile accident shortly before the election, as she was returning from a speaking engagement in his behalf. For Frei, it was a severe personal loss since he was close to her and leaned on her frequently for advice. Horne, *Small Earthquake in Chile* (New York: Viking Press, 1972), p. 106, fn.

Of much greater significance for its impact on the outcome was a 1962 electoral reform sponsored by the Conservative Jorge Alessandri, which, in easing the rules for registration, extended the vote to many of the country's landless and poor. The result was that more than half of those who voted in 1964 had never before voted for a president, and those votes went overwhelmingly to Frei.

48. "Johnson Credits Alliance for Frei Victory," *Miami Herald*, September 6, 1964.

49. "Fidel Hits Defeat in Chile," *Miami Herald*, September 12, 1964.

50. An Associated Press story, "Losing Socialists Shout Revolution," *Miami Herald*, September 5, 1964. The dispatch ended with the aside that "observers doubted he [Allende] would try again."

51. Gunther, op. cit., p. 263. Of CEPAL, Frei himself wrote: The United Nations CEPAL "... played an important role in Chile and Latin America in implanting new ideas [of economic planning]. ... CEPAL played a major role in the consolidation of these new concepts and, under its influence and the renewal of economic thought which this signified, governments throughout the hemisphere, and particularly ours, began to extend the techniques of economic planning to all areas of state activity." Eduardo Frei, in *Reforma Constitucional 1970* (Santiago: Editorial Jurídica de Chile, 1970), p. 38. As we shall see later, CEPAL's ideas were mainly Marxist, and CEPAL would strongly influence Allende, as Allende would influence it.

52. From Charles J. Parrish, Arpad J. von Lazar, and Jorge Tapia Videla, *The Chilean Congressional Election of March 7, 1965: An Analysis* (Washington, D.C.: Institute for the Comparative Study of Political Systems, 1966), p. 11.

53. The ages of the ministers fit with the youthful profile of the party itself: an estimated 65 percent of the party's members were under thirty years of age, and the average age of PDC deputies was 39.8 (compared with 47.6 for Radicals, 47.5 for Communists, and 44.6 for Socialists). From a study by George W. Grayson, Jr., "Significance of the Frei Administration for Latin America," quoted by Kantor, op. cit., p. 554.

54. Gunther, op. cit., p. 271. Gunther did not say so, but the thirty-year remark probably was made by Tomic, a man of towering arrogance. Chamudes recalls how Tomic in 1969 denied ever saying such a thing, and offered a million pesos (then about $2,100) to the person proving he did. The next day, Germán Gamonal, a newsman for Radio Portales, said he could prove it because his station had taped Tomic making just that statement—and still had the tape. Gamonal collected. Chamudes, op. cit., p. 240.

55. Horne, op. cit., p. 27.

56. Ahumada was recruited by Frei from the UN's Economic Commission for Latin America (CEPAL), which served as a talent bank of leftist economists

for Frei and later Allende. Frei thought very highly of Ahumada, and Ahumada was on his way to a central role in affairs when he died, early in the first Frei administration.

57. Parrish et al., op. cit., p. 12. The summary of the proposed constitutional reforms is from *Reforma Constitucional 1970* (Santiago: Editorial Jurídica de Chile, 1970), pp. 9–11.

58. Ibid., pp. 12–13. Quoted from *El Mercurio* report, November 25, 1964, of the text of Molina's speech the day before in Congress.

59. Frei, in *Foreign Affairs*, p. 90.

60. Tom E. Davis, "Changing Conceptions of the Developmental Problem: The Chilean Example," in *Economic Development and Cultural Change* (Chicago: October 1965), pp. 21–32, as quoted in U.S., Congress, Senate, Committee on Foreign Relations, *Survey of the Alliance for Progress: Inflation in Latin America*, by Prof. Raymond F. Mikesell, 91st Cong., document 91-17, September 25, 1967 (Washington, D.C.: Government Printing Office, 1969), p. 63.

61. Levinson and de Onís, op. cit., p. 207.

62. Ibid., p. 208.

63. At the levels of production of those years, each penny fluctuation in price represents $17 million, plus or minus, for Chile, and for Frei, they were all pluses, big pluses. Copper statistics, like most others, are subject to skepticism; but these, from Chile's Central Bank, are about as authoritative as any: 1955: 44.0 cents; 1956: 40.8 cents; 1957: 27.5 cents; 1958: 24.7 cents; 1959: 29.7 cents; 1960: 30.77 cents; 1961: 28.7 cents; 1962: 29.26 cents; 1963: 29.30 cents; 1964: 43.99 cents.

The Frei years: 1965: 58.64 cents; 1966: 69.47 cents; 1967: 51.13 cents; 1968: 56.10 cents; 1969: 66.56 cents; 1970: 64.10 cents. So, even using the freakish high figure of 1964 as a base figure, copper prices alone gave Frei a whopping $1.7 billion windfall over his six years in office. Central Bank figures from "Los Precios en 20 Años," *El Mercurio*, April 14, 1974, p. 23.

64. Source for export figures 1965–69, International Monetary Fund Statistics, November 1971, p. 36; for 1970, a mimeographed bulletin of the Banco Central de Chile, Gerencia de Estudios, July 5, 1974; IMF statistics (p. 37) were used for all import figures.

65. "Evolution of the Main Sectors of Economic Activity" *Economic Survey of Latin America, 1971* (New York: Economic Commission for Latin America, United Nations: 1973), p. 41.

66. Figures for manufacturing as a share of GNP and the following quotes are from *Socio-Economic Progress in Latin America, Ninth Annual Report, 1969* (Washington, D.C.: Inter-American Development Bank, March 1970), pp. 16, 253–54. Hereafter *Socio-Economic Progress*.

67. *Economic and Social Progress in Latin America, Annual Report* (Washington, D.C.: Inter-American Development Bank, 1972), p. 8. Hereafter *Economic and Social Progress*.

68. *Summary of Economic and Social Indicators, 18 Latin American Countries: 1960–1970* (Washington, D.C.: Office of Development Programs, Bureau for Latin America, Agency for International Development, April 1971), p. 91. Hereafter *Summary of Economic and Social Indicators*.

69. *Economic and Social Progress*, p. 407.

70. In Frances M. Foland, "Agrarian Reform in Latin America," *Foreign Affairs* 48, no. 1 (October 1969): 102.

71. Levinson and de Onís, op. cit., p. 227.
72. Kaufman, *The Chilean Political Right and Agrarian Reform: Resistance and Moderation* (Washington, D.C.: Institute for Comparative Study of Political Systems, 1967), p. 10. The U.S. ambassador in Chile, Ralph Dungan, parroted the cliché. The U.S., he told a Chilean interviewer, believed in agrarian reform "as an act of humanity," and added that "the rights of private property are not unlimited." Dungan made the statement in January 1966, at the peak of congressional and national debate on the bill—a most undiplomatic intrusion into internal politics. The Dungan quotes are from Levinson and de Onís, op. cit., p. 238, from an interview in "Reforma Agraria Sin Diplomacia," *Ercilla* magazine, January 5, 1966. Dungan behaved in Chile as though he were an unpaid consultant to Frei, alternately boosting and chiding, and lobbied ostentatiously for "his" man at the White House.
73. Edmundo Flores, "The Economics of Land Reform," in *Agrarian Problems and Peasant Movements in Latin America*, ed. Rodolfo Stavenhagen (New York: Doubleday, Anchor Books, 1970), p. 146. He cites Marx's observation that "peasants do not form a class, because the limited interconnection that exists among them is strictly local, and, wrote Marx, the 'identity of their interests begets no unity, no national union, and no political organization.' " The Marx quote is from Karl Marx, *The Eighteenth Brumaire of Louis Napoleon: Selected Works* (New York: International Publishers, n.d.), p. 415. The Kautsky quote is from John H. Kautsky, *Political Change in Underdeveloped Countries: Nationalism and Communism* (New York: John Wiley & Sons, n.d.), p. 47. (Italics are Kautsky's.)
74. James Petras and Maurice Zeitlin, "Agrarian Radicalism in Chile," in *Agrarian Problems and Peasant Movements in Latin America*, ed. Rodolfo Stavenhagen (New York: Doubleday, Anchor Books, 1970), pp. 507, 520–21. They add: "much of the political radicalism of the agricultural proletariat [that is, the *voluntarios* and *afuerinos*] in Chile and elsewhere, such as France, Italy, or Cuba, may have resulted not only from 'natural' social processes that make them more likely than other peasants to respond to radical agitation addressed to them, but also because they were differentially selected as organizational and political *targets*" (p. 528).
75. Kaufman, op. cit., p. 5. (Italics are mine.)
76. Most resistance in 1961 centered on Alessandri's proposal to amend the 1925 constitution to permit deferred (rather than cash) payment for expropriated land. Opponents tended to equate that amendment with the destruction of private property and one (Carlos Bulnes Correa) wrote in *Diario Ilustrado* on November 23, 1961: "Payment that is disguised under the euphemism of deferred payments is not payment . . . the Liberal and Conservative parties thus abandon, at a stroke, one of the basic principles of their existence: respect for private property" (in Kaufman, op. cit., p. 15). Kaufman notes that for these men, "acceptance of the reform would unleash a dynamic that ultimately would be far more dangerous than a refusal to do anything at all" (ibid.).
77. Relates Kaufman: "The powerful industrial pressure group—the Society for Industrial Development (SOFOFA)—remained neutral in the battle over the constitutional reform, and in general showed a reluctance during this period to be drawn into a position on the agrarian reform issue." He adds (p. 36) that there is "some evidence" that the soft-line position advocated by the major farm lobby, the National Agriculture Society, may have backfired and helped

to isolate farmers in their battle against the carving up of their lands. Conversely, the hard-line pushed by farm groups with no political ties "might, in fact, [have served] to mobilize industrial allies." A few years later, during the debate over the much more radical Christian Democrat law, the SNA—the supposedly omnipotent bastion of feudalism—withheld funds from a militant committee formed to fight some of the more radical features of the bill, a move which destroyed that committee, and with it, effective farm resistance. Kaufman shows, revealingly, how strongly SNA was a handmaiden of political, rather than class, ambitions. Kaufman, op. cit., pp. 33, 34.

78. The quote is from Gunther, op. cit., p. 257, and is typical of constant press reports then and thereafter on events in Chile. The features of the Christian Democrat bill which farmers found most objectionable:

1. The mere size of a farm—and not how well or badly it was being farmed—would now justify expropriation; anything over eighty "basic hectares" could be grabbed, and even "exceptionally efficient" owners might keep only 320 "basic hectares." (Eighty basic hectares refer to 192 acres of irrigated prime land in the Central Valley, equivalent areas elsewhere in the country.)

2. The Agrarian Reform Corp. (CORA) could seize land immediately, without awaiting a court decision, and, in case of dispute, reformist-stacked special courts would decide, with no appeal to regular courts. Furthermore, the burden of proving "efficiency" would rest with owners.

3. The provision created government cooperatives (instead of giving peasants title to land). Theoretically, this would be a two-year transitional period; but in practice, CORA could, at its discretion, prolong cooperative status indefinitely. Furthermore, the peasants themselves could vote to continue farming on a "communitarian" basis rather than divying up the land into individual parcels. Given the "communitarian" proclivities of so many Christian Democrats, and most emphatically, of the CORA technocrats, peasants were under heavy pressure to do just that. This was the clause that drew the greatest fire, because it was a direct threat to the survival of private property and the philosophical system underpinning it, and because it opened the way to the creation of sprawling state farms, an ominous expansion of the power of the state and those who happened to be in charge. Christian Democrat assurances were based mainly on their own conceit that they would be in charge of Chile, and the program, for decades to come, and that legality would therefore triumph. Even if they had remained in power—and their power had already peaked—the point remained that they themselves were philosophically antagonistic to private property, contrary to the innocent optimism of so many of their foreign fans.

4. Such substantative issues as jurisdiction of the courts and the old constitutional safeguards on payment—carefully spelled out in keeping with the traditional Chilean strong reliance on the Roman system of minutely written legal codes—would be left to ordinary legislation, covered in the meantime by a few dashed-off and conflict-breeding generalities.

5. CORA, not the owners, would decide which land could be kept by the farmer, so that he might even find himself deprived of his house, barns, and principal improvements on the land.

6. All land divided after November 1962, date of the original Agrarian Reform law, would be subject to automatic expropriation. Ostensibly, this was designed to thwart landowners who had given children, relatives, and

even friends plots of land so as to evade seizure on the grounds of mere size, a possibility not covered by the original law, but one raised by the rhetoric of both the Christian Democrats and Allende's FRAP. Rhetoric is not law, however, and even Luis Larraín Marín, the generally liberal head of the SNA, said this would mean that "an act that was legal under existing law becomes now illegal. It is a vindictive disposition and it introduces a fact of hatred unknown until now in Chilean law." Kaufman goes on to record that SNA was more moderate in its opposition to the law than farm groups with fewer political ties, and the charge that SNA was "simply trying to stale-mate agrarian reform" is "probably false." This summary is from Kaufman, op. cit., pp. 25, 26, 31. Larraín quote from p. 31.

In the final crunch, the Christian Democrats were forced to water down some of the most objectionable features: limited appeal to regular courts was permitted, the automatic expropriation feature was made retroactive only to November 1965, when the Christian Democrat bill went to Con-gress, and owners were given the right to decide which sections of their land they would keep for themselves.

79. R. Ossa, in a radio speech; text in *El Mercurio*, January 6, 1963, p. 27, and quoted in Kaufman, op. cit., p. 15.

80. *Diario Ilustrado*, November 23, 1961.

81. Labrousse remarks as much, op. cit., p. 115.

82. Chamudes reports that even *El Siglo*, the Communist newspaper, rushed to defend Chonchol, already under heavy fire only a year from the starting gate. Reporting on a banquet in his honor, December 20, 1965, *El Siglo* the next day said, "Jacques Chonchol has earned for himself the solid respect of the popular movement in the face of the attacks on him by landowners and their servants." Frei sent word that Chonchol counted with the "full backing of the president of the Republic" (Chamudes, op. cit., p. 251). Kaufman also relates how government leaders "closed ranks" behind Chonchol to defend him against charges about his Marxism, and "a series of public assemblies were held on Chonchol's behalf." Patricio Aylwin, then president of the party, engaged in "a bitter exchange of public letters" with Pedro Enrique Alfonso, a prominent Radical leader and head of a group of northern farmers fighting the Christian Democrat bill. Kaufman, op. cit., p. 38. In the case of Chonchol, as in so many others, the Christian Democrats underestimated the wiliness of the Marxists, as they would discover too late a few years later.

83. Infighting within the party to oust Chonchol grew in bitterness until Frei in August 1968 asked for his resignation, only to be persuaded to relent by Renán Fuentealba Moena, a Christian Democrat chieftain with a perma-nent place in his affections for the wrong people. Three months later Chonchol bolted the party, formed his own, entered into an electoral alli-ance with Allende, and later wound up as Allende's ultraradical agriculture minister.

Kaufman evidently succumbed to that phobia of the fifties and sixties—part of the bilious fallout of McCarthyism—a reluctance to call a Commu-nist a Communist. Reporting attacks on Chonchol by militant farm groups in 1965, Kaufman pooh-poohs charges that Chonchol was a "Marxist," an "international agent," and one of Fidel Castro's major farm advisers: "In reality, Chonchol has long been affiliated with the more militant wing of the Christian Democrat party. He has served as an expert in many interna-tional organizations. During a period of service with the United Nations

Food and Agricultural Organization (FAO), he was stationed in Cuba as an adviser to the Cuban government on its agrarian-reform program. It was on this activity that the committee based its charges" (Kaufman, op. cit., p. 38, fn. 7). One suspects that the committee might also have had in mind Chonchol's explicit views and activities within Chile in arriving at its judgment. Of course, Kaufman wrote this nearly two years before Chonchol advertised his ideological colors as well as wore them.

McCarthyism took its toll in Chile as elsewhere in the world in inhibiting debate. Kaufman records that politicians of the Right, unlike nonpolitical farm leaders and others, were unwilling "to charge that there were 'Marxists' in government" (ibid., p. 35). There were, of course, plenty, some of whom would later serve Allende conspicuously, others who would proclaim their Marxism while remaining within PDC ranks. Chamudes (op. cit., p. 213) makes mention of the muzzling effects of the bitter aftermath of McCarthyism. As Chamudes points out, moral fervor on such issues tends to depend on whose hand is being bitten. By 1971 the Christian Democrats had lost their inhibitions. With Allende firmly entrenched in power, the official PDC newspaper, La Prensa, was describing as "a patriotic duty" the denunciation of communism and Communists. La Prensa, September 26, 1971, cited by Chamudes, op. cit., pp. 211–14.

84. Petras and Zeitlin, op. cit., pp. 505, 529. The parenthetical aside about "reform-oriented government" is theirs.

85. Economic Survey of Latin America, 1971, p. 109, table 38, "Chile: Gross Domestic Product at Factor Cost, by Sector of Economic Activity."

86. Levinson and de Onís, op. cit., p. 235.

87. Statistics for 1965–70 from Economic Survey of Latin America, 1971, p. 41, table 2, "Latin America: Evaluation of the Main Sectors of Economic Activity"; for 1966–70, from Economic and Social Progress, p. 397, table 20, "Annual Growth Rates of Agricultural Production."

88. The figures for 1966 through 1970 are from Nueva Enciclopedia, 2:208.

89. Levinson and de Onís, op. cit., p. 239.

90. Thomas M. Rees (D.–Calif.), "Latin American Economic Study," Committee on Banking and Currency of the U.S. House of Representatives, 1969, p. 19. Rees was one of the congressional clan that, even at that late date, remained mesmerized by the mirage of reform under Frei.

91. Levinson and de Onís, op. cit., p. 239.

92. Pablo Baraona Urzúa, "The Reality of Chilean Agriculture," in Chile: A Critical Survey (Santiago: Institute of General Studies, 1972), p. 172. Baraona says that under Frei 1,408 farms covering a total of 3,564,300 hectares (approximately 8.8 million acres) were expropriated. His original, announced target was approximately four thousand of the country's ten thousand large farms. Labrousse also notes that of twenty thousand families settled on asentamientos by 1969, fully 65 percent of them had lived on that same land even before it was expropriated. On asentamientos, peasants did not receive title to the land until the two-year training period was up, or until CORA decided they were ready. On the Mexican ejidos, peasants took immediate, collective title to the land and farmed it as a cooperative. Labrousse quotes Chonchol as saying that of 257 asentamientos that had completed their two-year break-in period by 1970, on only 77 were peasants given title to the land. Labrousse, op. cit., p. 287.

93. Labrousse, op. cit., p. 117. According to Alliance statistics, the Chilean government spent, for the years 1965 through 1970, $9.5 billion (Summary

of Economic and Social Indicators, p. 35). The same source puts total agriculture spending at $702.8 million (p. 47) during the same period, a figure almost certainly too low. Labrousse relies on the previously cited Barraclough study (chap. 3, n. 67) for his per family estimate. I have taken the median point ($8,000) in projecting total cost of agrarian reform alone at $2.2 billion, which, if true, would represent 23 percent of total government spending.

94. Labrousse, op. cit., p. 123. Labrousse also quotes Chonchol regarding a 1968 study which showed that of 15,621 persons then working on collective farms, 10,540 were *asentados,* and thus potential owners, and 5,121 hired field hands. In some instances, hired hands outnumbered *asentados* two to one—a classical case of the creation of a new ruling class. Ibid., p. 285.

95. Kaufman notes that the Right's accommodation "has discouraged a polarization of political forces and the grave threat to social stability that even such a development might imply" (op. cit., p. 1). He particularly lauded the willingness of the National Agriculture Society "to accept not simply legislative but 'real' sacrifices on the part of the landowning class" (p. 41). Kaufman coupled that with a warning that the key to "restraining" future conflict would lie in the retention of "some institutional channels through which the Right could defend itself at the governmental level" (p. 45). Those channels were increasingly clogged under Frei, choked off under Allende. Implicit in the Kaufman commentary, characteristic of many, was the notion that the Right had a responsibility to cave in to save Chilean democracy—the intransigence of both the Christian Democrats and of the even farther Left was seen as somehow part of a natural historical imperative. The Chilean experience is important in this regard, as in so many others, in that it demonstrates that by "caving in" the Right did not prevent polarization, but merely made a deeper and more destructive polarization inevitable.

96. Ibid., p. 25.

97. Levinson and de Onís, op. cit., p. 237.

98. Rodolfo Stavenhagen, "Social Aspects of Agrarian Structure in Mexico," in *Agrarian Problems and Peasant Movements in Latin America,* ed. Rodolfo Stavenhagen (New York: Doubleday, Anchor Books, 1970), p. 253.

99. Labrousse, op. cit., pp. 123–24. The late Adlai Stevenson, in his excursions into Latin America, discovered what he believed was a "revolution of rising expectations." It was, in reality and for the most part, a revolution of demagogically fired expectations. Labrousse notes that as the Christian Democrats raised the level of expectations with their promises, the result was that workers resorted increasingly to strikes to achieve those demands (pp. 165, 168). The result was not a better life for all, but chaos for all and the concomitant of inevitable economic collapse.

100. Quoted by Kaufman, op. cit., from an interview in Santiago, May 23, 1966. Kaufman says (p. ii) that he interviewed "27 prominent rightist leaders" during the year he spent in Chile researching his study.

101. *Nueva Enciclopedia,* 1:135.

102. *Summary of Economic and Social Indicators,* pp. 98–99. It is revealing that the 32.3 percent average increase in public housing for the period 1966–69 achieved by Chile's much admired reformist government pales alongside the increase achieved in the same period by Brazil's much mauled military government: 1,285 percent, the highest level (by far) in Latin America. The military there took over from a succession of three

"reformist" governments. Source for comparative growth statistics: *Analysis of the Economic and Social Evolution of Latin America Since the Inception of the Alliance for Progress* (Washington, D.C.: Inter-American Economic and Social Council of the Organization of American States, August 1971), p. 67, table II-14. Hereafter *Analysis*.

103. *Analysis*, p. 68, table II-15. The housing shortage was aggravated not by population growth—Chile's demographic growth for 1960–70 was a paltry 1.5 percent, one of the lowest rates in the world—but by factors such as earthquake damage and, above all, accelerating migration to the cities.

104. Education statistics are from *Summary of Economic and Social Indicators*, pp. 63–68. It is interesting to track Chile's education spending during the Alliance's first decade. The following figures represent central government educational expenditures (in millions of dollars) as a percentage of gross national product; the numbers in parentheses indicate Chile's ranking in Latin America, with respect to education spending as a percentage of GNP:

1961	1962	1963	1964	1965	1966	1967	1968	1969	1970[a]
3.3	3.6	3.2	3.2	3.7	3.9	4.7	4.6	4.9	5.7
(3)	(3)	(4)	(4)	(4)	(4)	(3)	(3)	(3)	(1)

Source: p. 63.

[a] provisional.

105. Ibid., p. 65.
106. Levinson and de Onís, op. cit., p. 303.
107. Of which $6.0 million came from the IADB and $11.25 million from the World Bank. Chile was the only country in the world during this period to have three educational loan projects approved by the then hard-nosed World Bank—a record surpassed only by Pakistan, which received four grants. Sources: for Inter-American Development Bank, *1971 Statement of Loans, Appendix to the Annual Report*, pp. 32–33, 56; World Bank, *World Bank Operations: Sectoral Programs and Policies* (Baltimore and London: Johns Hopkins University Press, 1972), pp. 286–87. Hereafter *World Bank Operations*.
108. Levinson and de Onís, op. cit., p. 301. They relate that Rojas, a medical student, had been president of the Chilean Federation of Students and the man who headed Frei's task force on education during the 1964 electoral campaign. Most of the information in the following paragraph is also from Levinson and de Onís, pp. 239, 302–03.
109. Labrousse (op. cit., pp. 173, 186–90) refers to the impact of Alliance rhetoric and the radical sloganeering of the Christian Democrats as factors impelling student revolt. Although Christian Democrats remained a majority in the Chilean Federation of University Students (FECH), their Marxist sympathies were so strong that by 1969 they would vote a Communist in as president of the federation. The impact of these events on the party in general is examined in a later section.
110. In June 1967, students at the Catholic University in Valparaíso, taking advantage of the fact that the university president was in Moscow on a junket with the presidents of other Chilean universities, occupied buildings and demanded his ouster. He eventually resigned, and student-

demanded "reforms" were granted. In Santiago, MIR-led students rioted to protest acceptance by the University of Chile of a cyclotron donated by the University of California at Berkeley. On August 2, high school students in Santiago attacked the U.S.–run Chilean–North American Institute. The big blowup followed nine days later at the Catholic University in Santiago. Basic data on these events from Tomás P. MacHale, "Ideologies in the Reform of the Universities," in *Chile: A Critical Survey,* pp. 255–63; and Labrousse, op. cit., pp. 171–77.

111. Christian Democrats, during the early years of the Frei administration, heaped vitriol on outsiders who dared to find cracks in their organizational facade. By 1966 factional infighting could no longer be hidden, however, and a number of pro-Castro university and other leaders were expelled from the party, notable among them a deputy (Patricio Hurtado) who had attacked Frei bitterly. Three factions emerged: *Oficialistas,* mainly the old guard headed by Frei; *rebeldes,* radicals who would tilt the party as far left as they could before bailing out (a group which included Chonchol; Sen. Rafael Agustín Gumucio, son of the party patriarch; and two obstreperous deputies, Julio Silva Solar and Alberto Jerez); and *terceristas,* a leftist group that would not desert at once, but would wait until Allende was in power. In the meantime, they joined in pushing the party even further left.

The *terceristas* backed Rodrigo Ambrosio in his successful 1967 bid for leadership of the Christian Democrat Youth, a process that intensified the radicalization of that group. A young socialist recently returned from Europe, Ambrosio espoused a noncapitalist road to development as a transition to socialism. Other *tercerista* leaders were Juan Bosco Parra and Luís Maira. For a time—until the very survival of the party was imperiled—they were supported by inveterate leftists Leighton, Tomic, and Renán Fuentealba. Labrousse, op. cit., pp. 186–90; Chamudes, op. cit., pp. 243–48.

112. In 1972, for instance, Claudio Véliz was ousted from his post as director of the Institute of International Studies of the University of Chile, in voting decided by the kitchen help and janitors. The fact that he had written extensively—and very tellingly, since two of his articles represented the total image of revolutionary Chile the prestigious *Foreign Affairs* magazine offered its readers during the early years of Allende—did not save Véliz from such an indecorous pratfall. I had seen Véliz in Santiago a few months before and he was already so fretful that most of our conversation had to be conducted in his car while driving up a mountainside.

113. Labrousse, op. cit., p. 174.

114. Christian Democrat Castillo Velasco had ideological problems on his own home front as well: his wife was a militant leftist, and two of his children were members of MIR. Daughter Carmen was, in fact, wounded October 5, 1974, when police stumbled onto the house where MIR overlord Miguel Enríquez Espinoza was hiding. Carmen was then estranged from her husband, Andrés Pascal Allende, nephew of the late president. (Pascal was himself a MIR chieftain.) Her brother, Christian, also a MIRista, was believed wounded during that same pitched, two-hour battle, but managed to escape. By then Castillo Velasco was living in self-imposed exile in London.

115. MacHale, op. cit., p. 260. Author-editor MacHale also was an editorial writer for *El Mercurio.*

116. *Summary of Economic and Social Indicators,* pp. 89–90.

117. Sources: the "rough 1960 estimates" from *Social Progress Trust Fund, Second Annual Report, 1962* (Washington, D.C.: Inter-American Development Bank, February 1963), p. 210. Hereafter *Social Progress Trust Fund*. For 1969, *Socio-Economic Progress*, pp. 259–60. For 1971, *Economic and Social Progress*, p. 92.

118. Literacy-illiteracy figures are a statistical grab bag too. For example: *Summary of Economic and Social Indicators*, p. 84, puts illiteracy in 1960 at 11.8 percent. The 1969 *Socio-Economic Progress* report asserts (p. 260) that it was 16.4 percent—a more probable figure, which I have used. As to 1970, take your pick: the aforementioned 1969 report says (p. 251) it was already down to 10.4 percent by 1968, and still sliding, of course. Yet the 1972 report says (p. 152) that illiteracy in 1970 stood at 14 percent. Anyway, progress was made.

119. Sources: the 127.9 figure is from the 1962 *Social Progress Trust Fund*, p. 207; 79.3 is from the 1971 report (p. 155); 12.2 is from the 1969 report (p. 259); 8.6 is from the 1971 report (p. 155). Again, there are discrepancies among these, and other, "official statistics." On these figures too I use the probable ones.

120. *Socio-Economic Progress*, p. 161.

121. Frei, *Un Mundo Nuevo*, p. 108. Figures on community centers and unionization are from an article by Frei, "La Reforma Constitucional en su Contexto Histórico-Político," in *Reforma Constitucional 1970*, op. cit., pp. 42–43.

122. In reporting on the 1947 study, Moran (op. cit., p. 26) notes that the study "boldly went on to identify *six men* who, the study claimed, 'directly or indirectly are in a position to dictate the production and price policies of about 60 percent of the world output of primary copper'!" (The italics and exclamation point are Moran's.) Moran was quoting from pp. 176 f. of the *Report of the Federal Trade Commission on the Copper Industry* (Washington, D.C.: Government Printing Office, 1947). Moran cites several studies (op. cit., p. 28, fn. 19) to show that in point of fact, the industry has met with "continually decreasing success" in this century in its efforts to control prices, and that all seven major attempts since the beginning of the twentieth century to form copper cartels "were short-lived and unsuccessful." Besides, the study in question was constructed for the benefit of consumers, who suffer the consequences of monopoly control of an industry and its prices, and *not* a producer country, a beneficiary of such arrangements.

The higher the prices, the higher tax revenues that would accrue to a producer country, and Chile was then extracting between 50 percent and 60 percent taxes from the profits of the copper companies. Such facts did not, however, stand in the way of the demagogic theories that would be "based" on the study for years to come. (Moran on p. 27 quotes a number of such reactions all the way down to 1964.) The reference to the Right's inclination to identify with the companies is from pp. 172–73. Moran identifies several leading Conservatives as joining the Left in attacking the companies as early as the late 1940s and early 1950s, on pp. 183–84, 189–90. He also points out that attitudes toward North American investors were "inseparably bound up with the attitude the country would adopt toward communism" (pp. 174–75).

123. Moran, op. cit., p. 121.

124. CEPAL (or, ECLA, in the English acronym), heavily influenced by the work of its superstar Raúl Prebisch, was the principal "think tank" for leftist

economists, not only in Chile but throughout Latin America, for many years. Allende recruited many of his top economic policymakers from among the ranks of CEPAL alumni.

125. For details of the state sales monopoly, see chap. 1, n. 48. With the end of the Korean War in 1953, the Chileans found themselves less and less able to market their output. To offset sagging sales, the artificial exchange rate tax on companies was increased, until for the period 1951–54, Anaconda was paying effective tax rates ranging from 65 percent to 92 percent. Inevitably, the companies tightened up on badly needed new investment. Moran notes that the government "had huge stocks accumulating on its hands, weak prices and a major mine (Potrerillos, belonging to Anaconda) about to give out" (op. cit., p. 93).

126. Comments Moran: "The new element that was responsible for the deterioration in support for the U.S. copper companies was the Alliance for Progress and the resentment it caused among conservative political and business groups." He adds that the conservative parties "became more Machiavellian," proposing the nationalization of Anaconda and Kennecott "in an effort to hold them as hostages to gain concessions on land reform." The rationale used by the Right "was to use the companies' failure under the *Nuevo Trato* as a scapegoat for the development problems of Chile—while denying the allegations about domestic maldistribution of income, about local monopolies, about the need for social reform" (op. cit., p. 131). For a discussion of the Right's rationale in proposing *Nuevo Trato* as a palliative for the industry's ills, see ibid., pp. 94–96.

Basically, *Nuevo Trato* gave the companies everything they wanted—a lower tax base, elimination of artificial exchange controls, etc.—without exacting from them specific new obligations. The authors of *Nuevo Trato* assumed, naively, that it was enough to provide profit incentives.

Moran comments: "Careful negotiations structured to give the foreign companies an inducement to do what the host country wanted would have had a better chance of success than a mere display of generosity" (ibid., p. 114). Moran concludes that *Nuevo Trato* was a "failure" because of the exaggerated expectations conservatives brought to it, a "success" because of what would have happened if no new legislation had been passed at all, and "left much to be desired" measured against what could have been accomplished through tougher, more realistic negotiations. Production, which had been slumping, did rebound; refining output stagnated; there was new investment, but nowhere near the avalanche expected; tax revenues increased very substantially. In one area, there was no room for argument: Kennecott and Anaconda profits on their Chilean operations doubled. For a discussion of the effects of the *Nuevo Trato* legislation, see ibid., pp. 99–118.

127. Moran says that because of "the disintegration of domestic support for the foreign copper companies," Kennecott could not get the twenty-year guarantees of inviolability it sought in return for making the investment. In a later white paper on the subject, the company itself said simply that "for reasons best known to itself, the Chilean government elected not to pursue the venture or provide the necessary guarantees." *Expropriation of El Teniente* (Kennecott Copper Corp., 1971), p. 43.

128. Moran, op. cit., p. 132, fn. 20. Moran notes that, in contrast to Anaconda, Braden (Kennecott) "had never been an aggressive copper miner in Chile" (p. 129). That, fundamentally, explained Kennecott's willingness to sell, an

offer which was "a stroke of good fortune for the newly elected [Frei] regime," and one which "startled (and irritated) Anaconda" (p. 128). According to Moran, Kennecott by 1964 understood what Anaconda did not: "Long-term guarantees for operations in Chile—risky even in the best of times—were losing their meaning" (p. 132). In the atmosphere of the Alliance, the Kennecott offer was "greeted as an act of statesmanship" (p. 129). The leftist magazine *New Republic* clucked in an article at the time: "When Chile has a stake in the ownership of those mines, the threat of expropriation may thin, even vanish" ("President Frei and the Copper Goose," *New Republic*, December 18, 1965, p. 11). Quite the opposite; as events would later demonstrate, "Chileanization" made expropriation under Allende inevitable.

129. That $80 million represented twice the book value, and the reassessment meant that Kennecott still owned 49 percent of a company "worth four times as much ($286 million) as it had been ($69 million) before. From a cash-flow perspective, Kennecott would be receiving 49 percent of the proceeds from an operation exporting almost 64 percent more output at a tax rate reduced from over 80 percent to 44 percent" (Moran, op. cit., p. 134).

130. After the agreement had been reached, the government, unilaterally, decided on an arbitrary price for copper—and kept the rest for itself. Prices had been pushed abnormally high both because of the Vietnam War and because of the worldwide boycott of white Rhodesia (now Zimbabwe), a major producer. Skimming off "overprice" income gave the government $62 million in windfall profits from Kennecott alone, an even larger amount from Anaconda.

131. Anaconda pledged to increase output by over 200,000 tons per year, investing $72.55 million itself, and guaranteeing an additional $58.7 million loan from the Export-Import Bank in Washington. The Chilean government paid $3.75 million for a 25 percent share of the new Exótica mine. In return, Anaconda got a tax break that would really not benefit it until the 1970s, and retained sole ownership of its two biggest mines.

Kennecott made a much more elaborate deal. The company agreed to loan back to the new mixed venture the $80 million paid it for its 51 percent share. (The company later had to put in an additional $12 million, generated from internal earnings.) The Chilean government put up $27.3 million, later boosted to $37.3 million. The company's investment was insured by the U.S. government. Next, the company demanded that the Chilean government unconditionally guarantee the sale amount and the $110 million loaned for the expansion program by the Export-Import Bank, and that the deal be made subject to the laws of the state of New York. Finally, Kennecott involved a consortium of Japanese and Italian firms in a $45 million cost-overrun investment. Robert Haldeman, head of Kennecott's Chilean operations, was quoted as saying: "The aim of these arrangements is to ensure that nobody expropriates Kennecott without upsetting relations to customers, creditors, and governments on three continents" (Moran, op. cit., p. 136). The Kennecott package finally totaled $267 million and a ten-year management contract. Production was to increase from 180,000 to 280,000 tons yearly.

The deal with Cerro more closely resembled the Kennecott settlement than the one the government made with Anaconda. The result was that Kennecott and Cerro were hailed as "enlightened" companies because, in the spirit of the times, they were willing to "go partners" with the host government; Anaconda, though bearing the burden of expansion itself, was on the defensive from the outset. The twenty-year guarantee of inviolability, which Anaconda won as its only "prize," would be torn from it less than four years later by that same Christian Democrat government—*after* Anaconda had put up the risk capital to expand the industry.

132. Genaro Arriagada Herrera, *De la Vía Chilena a la Vía Insurreccional* (Santiago: Editorial del Pacífico, 1974), p. 59. Arriagada is a major Christian Democrat writer, so much so that his book contains a foreword by Frei, the only one Frei consented to do in the first years after the September revolution.

133. Sáez was Frei's finance minister for a few months. He quit when he saw that the party's radicals were firmly in charge of policy. He later surfaced as economic czar (briefly) for the military junta.

134. I have pored over hundreds, perhaps thousands, of newspaper and magazine articles, from well over a hundred publications in the U.S., Latin America, and Europe, both during the time I was a correspondent myself and in researching this book. Rare is the mention of the company viewpoint, much less a detailed rebuttal of the cliché-ridden charges. The charges against Anaconda were similar to those against Kennecott (Cerro was too new to get much embroiled). I use Kennecott as a case study because the takeover of that company started earlier, and because the record is more abundant. Kennecott's case was presented in its booklet *Expropriation of El Teniente* (1971), followed by supplements dated 1972, December 1972, and May 1973, a total of just under four hundred pages. Moran (op. cit., pp. 140–43) notes that representatives of CODELCO and other government officials were closely involved with copper company officials in everything from audits to construction to sales to finance, and by 1969, Chileans were supervising operations—mining, smelting, and refining. The newspaper ad appeared in the *New York Times*, January 25, 1971, p. 72-C, under the headline: "The Recovery of Basic Resources Is a Sovereign Decision Reflecting the Feelings of All Chilean People."

135. Kaufman (op. cit., pp. 38–39) writes: "The FRAP, arguing for outright nationalization, had consistently opposed all aspects of the programs, not only in Congress, but in the mines themselves, where the leftist unions had organized a series of strikes that paralyzed operations for several months." The Radicals, beginning their slide into a suicidal embrace with the far Left, joined in opposing the program. As for the Right, Kaufman remarks: "It is interesting to note the cheapness of the 'price' which the rightist senators finally accepted [on agrarian reform] in return for their support on copper." The big one was that CORA be made subject to the courts; in other words, made to obey the law.

136. The phrase is from Levinson and de Onís, op. cit., p. 157. But they were far, far from alone. Gunther, for example, wrote: "But the companies had come to heel because, in the long run, this being the modern world, their position was untenable, and after all, Frei was better for them than Allende and the Communists" (op. cit., p. 297). He also passed along, without comment, the leftist barb that the companies were "shameless exploiters." Even the then conservative newsweekly *U.S. News & World Report* echoed the same either-or theme. The magazine quoted H. Danforth Starr, vice president and treasurer of Cerro, as saying the companies must help the Frei

government because "the alternatives were not very attractive." Added the magazine: "Major alternative: control by the Communists. . . ." ("Chile's New 'Deal' with U.S. Firms," *U.S. News & World Report*, January 4, 1965). By the time the Right realized that the chance for a real choice had passed, a choice between free enterprise and statism, Salvador Allende was in La Moneda.

137. Phase two was a synergism of leftist ideology, misplaced euphoria, and bad faith, all at the service of a misguided notion of "liberation." The cult of *dependencia* had long since ceded the ideological battle to the leftists. The euphoria was a product of a steady climb in production and prices, apparently under the aegis of Chileans themselves.

Bad faith evidenced itself when the "take" got too temptingly high, not only for the government, but for the companies. Frei's first move was to impose the arbitrary surtax, a move the companies could scarcely oppose, since they had just completed major investment outlays. Next, under the leadership of the Christian Democrat deputy Narciso Irueta (later president of the party), a move was launched to "reevaluate" the contracts signed only four years before by those same Christian Democrats. Anaconda resisted (in vain), arguing for nationalization with compensation rather than to submit to such a forced sellout. (The payment terms offered Anaconda were generous, but the company was, by then, wary of such deals. Its wariness was well placed. Allende's "nationalization" scheme, ratified by the full Congress on July 16, 1971, provided for deduction of "excess" profits all the way back to 1955, so that the companies wound up owing Chile money!)

By the simple expedient of treating guarantees as "a scrap of paper" (Horne, op. cit., p. 108), Chile had "liberated" itself from foreign "domination"—except that five years would pass before the Chilean nation would again profit so much from copper as it did while supposedly being "exploited." Kissinger wrote that supporting Frei had been, for U.S. policymakers, "a morally simple decision because it enabled us to be both anti-Communist and on the side of reformist and progressive forces. . . ."—a sophistry of seemingly incorrigible durability. He adds: "The polarization of Chilean political life was evidenced when Frei, in spite of the generous U.S. aid program, felt obliged by leftist pressures" in early 1969 to cancel a visit by special presidential envoy Nelson Rockefeller (dispatched on a tour of Latin America by Nixon to chart a new course for U.S. policy in the hemisphere), and to repudiate the copper agreement negotiated "by his own government . . . only two years before." He also observed that Anaconda, "with a lack of foresight characteristic of many multinational companies," had allowed its expropriation insurance to lapse so as to save the premium expense, confident that the 1967 agreement would be honored. Henry Kissinger, *The White House Years* (Boston: Little, Brown & Company, 1979), p. 662.

138. Thomas G. Sanders, "The Church in Latin America," *Foreign Affairs* 48, no. 2 (January 1970): 290. For Sanders, the Christian Democrats were "a dynamic new hope under the leadership of outstanding intellectuals like Eduardo Frei and Radomiro Tomic." What makes Sanders' euphoria curious is the timing: by January 1970 the ground had vanished from beneath such ecstasy. Sanders is closer to the target when he refers to the Christian Democrats' "messianic sense of being Latin America's alterna-

tive to Marxism [attracting] admiration and support from abroad" (pp. 290–91). Alas, the target was misplaced.

139. Frei, "Second Latin American Revolution," p. 96.

140. Horne, op. cit., p. 27.

141. During the 1964 campaign Frei agreed with Allende that the Alliance was "inoperable." Bethel, op. cit., p. 516. He said so even though from January 1960 to May 1965 (a few months after he had made the remark), the Alliance had lavished on Chile $734.5 million, or the equivalent of $86 for every man, woman, and child in the country. That was a full 20 percent more than was given runner-up Panama, 28 percent more than the sum for third-place Bolivia, and nearly eleven times as much as was given Haiti, the poorest country in the hemisphere. AID statistics, Richard S. Thorn, "The Alliance for Progress: The Flickering Flame," in *Constructive Change in Latin America*, ed. Cole Blasier (Pittsburgh: University of Pittsburgh Press, 1968), p. 136. (I did not use his per capita extrapolations, because they are very inaccurate.) By April 1967 Frei was writing in *Foreign Affairs* about "the Alliance that lost its way," giving admirers Levinson and de Onís the title for their book.

142. Frederick Pike, for example, has observed that since the nineteenth century, the Chilean Right has been firm in its distaste for U.S. culture and lifestyle and resolved to defend Chilean values, which it deemed superior. Pike, *Chile and the United States, 1880–1962* (South Bend, Ind.: University of Notre Dame Press, 1963), pp. 250–56, cited by Gil, op. cit., p. 268. Conservative leader Jorge Prat was also outspokenly anti–U.S.

   A Chilean Jesuit, finishing his Ph.D. at Harvard, once told me that the reason Latin Americans found nothing to emulate in the American experience was that America had never developed a philosophical base more substantial than the pragmatism of William James—and for Latins, that wasn't philosophy. The comment not only cheated James (by failing to acknowledge the two other strains of his work, voluntarism and radical empiricism) but also misinterprets the American experience, leaving out, for example, the formative and tempering influences of Christian thought—not to mention the other lesser but important religious roles—in shaping American character. But it does capsulize an important Latin prejudice about Americans, important because it is real even if not true.

143. But, unlike Mexico, legalistic Chile did accept the verdict of the OAS majority and agreed to break relations with Cuba. Betancourt, by the way, is a name that demonstrates how threadbare the actual devotion of the far Left to "democracy." Betancourt was one of the earliest effective fighters for democratic reform in Latin America, a giant by any reckoning. But he also (1) was an ex-Communist, and faced with the most vicious campaign of Castro-sponsored violence then seen in Latin America; and (2) became as unflinching in his opposition to Communist Castro as he had been in his opposition to reactionary Rafael Leonidas Trujillo of the Dominican Republic. The two sins earned him the undying hatred of the far Left. Witness, for example, Marxist Debray's description of Betancourt's "repressive, proimperialist government . . . one of the most sinister in Venezuelan history" (op. cit., pp. 141–42). This is the same Debray who clamored for Betancourt's democratic scalp, and who would a few years later fill the pages of the world's newspapers with elegies to the death of democracy in Chile—and be allowed to get away with the fraud. Although

Betancourt and his government gave me personally, as UPI country manager there, more hassling than I would care to remember, I will affirm that he was pro only one thing, pro-Venezuelan, and in the pursuit of that policy was as often on a bruising collision course with the United States as he was in harmony with it.

144. In Horne, op. cit., p. 109.

145. Bethel, op. cit., p. 519.

146. Ibid., p. 526. Bethel notes that shortly afterward, Sen. Rafael Agustín Gumucio (who would later bolt the party) went further, announcing "solidarity" with OLAS. By mid-1967, the Christian Democrats would have second thoughts about OLAS. In July the government charged Socialist Sen. Carlos Altamirano Orrego—OLAS' most active backer in Chile—with openly insulting the president and the armed forces and with openly encouraging violence. The Supreme Court upheld the charges, and Altamirano was suspended from his seat in Congress. At the same time, the government filed similar charges, for different reasons, against the conservative National party. The party's entire leadership was detained for making allegedly inflammatory statements on government defense policies, but those charges were thrown out by the Supreme Court. Source: *The 1968 Britannica Book of the Year* (Chicago: Encyclopaedia Britannica, Inc., 1968), p. 194. Altamirano's OLAS activities were the first important instance in which he would preempt the left flank of his (supposed) party elder Salvador Allende—but not the last.

147. Bethel, op. cit., p. 519.

148. Ibid., p. 514. Christian Democrat Youth also would later demand (but not get) diplomatic relations with North Vietnam and Cuba, and the "eradication" of U.S. influence in Latin America. The party's elders did, however, cooperate in advancing the last two ambitions (eradication and Cuba).

149. Chamudes, op. cit., pp. 155–56, 180–81.

150. "Estadísticas de Comercio Exterior al 30 de Abril de 1974," mimeographed, July 5, 1974, tables 2, 6.

151. Chamudes, op. cit., p. 184.

152. Ibid., p. 186.

153. Ibid., p. 165. Chamudes says Valdés's antagonists pinned the label on him because at the time he was named foreign minister, he was the obscure lawyer for a firm that manufactured tin used for processed-food cans.

154. Ibid., p. 165.

155. Examples: "Colombian Leader Speaks Out Against 'Intervention' by Cuba," in *Miami Herald*, July 22, 1972, reporting on a speech made by President Misael Pastrana Borrero to a joint session of the Colombian Congress. "Peru Guerrillas Trained by Reds," a *Miami Herald* story, August 6, 1972, reporting on the crushing of a guerrilla band led by a Communist the government said had been trained in Cuba and China. Among numerous reports on the training of Chileans in Cuba was one written in 1964 by Tom Stacey of the *London Sunday Times* and published in the *Miami Herald*, April 26, 1964, under the headline "Red Boss a Puzzling Figure." He said it was estimated that some two thousand Chileans were then undergoing training in Cuba.

156. Chamudes, op. cit., p. 170.

157. Arriagada, op. cit., p. 59.

158. Bethel, op. cit., p. 521.

159. Ibid.

160. Chamudes, op. cit., pp. 177–78. Another instance—of numerous ones—that would becloud Gunther's judgment: "His [Frei's] approach to life is uncompromisingly ethical" (op. cit., p. 258).

161. Two years later, Ben S. Stephansky, one of the original cadre of Kennedy advisers on Latin America, and one of the woolliest, was still pouting, even impugning Rockefeller's Latin America credentials. But then Stephansky's philosophy—in this article and elsewhere—scarcely recommends him as a judge; it seems to reduce to the proposition that what is good for Latin America is good foreign policy for us—provided, of course, that we are listening to the "right" Latin America (the left one, that is). In cases of conflict, Latin interests should take precedence. The article in question: "Latin America: Toward a New Nationalism," Headline Series, no. 211 (New York: Foreign Policy Association, June 1972.)

162. Chamudes, op. cit., p. 67.

163. The account of Valdés's role—plus the *El Siglo*, Drew Pearson, and UN references—is from Chamudes, op. cit., pp. 166–68. He gives the dates as June 13, 1967, for the *El Siglo* article and June 17, 1969, for the Pearson column (which I have translated from Chamudes's Spanish).

164. Edward M. Korry, in testimony March 27, 1973, before the Subcommittee on Multinational Corporations of the Foreign Relations Committee, of the U.S. Senate, pt. 1, p. 282.

165 Chamudes, op. cit., pp. 192–193.

166. Laurence Stern of the *Washington Post* quoted Rep. Michael J. Harrington (D.–Mass.)—the man behind the original CIA-Chile flap in 1974—as saying $500,000 was authorized by the Forty Committee in 1969 to "fund individuals who could be nurtured [ironic choice of words] to keep the anti-Allende forces active and intact" ("CIA Allegedly Had Anti-Allende Fund," *Washington Post* Service dispatch in the *Miami Herald*, September 8, 1974). It was later disclosed that the bulk of that money went to the Christian Democrats.

167. Arriagada, op. cit., p. 59.

168. In Adam B. Ulam, *The Bolsheviks* (New York: Macmillan Co., 1964), p. 226.

169. Leon Gouré and Morris Rothenberg, *Soviet Penetration of Latin America* (Miami: Center for Advanced International Studies, University of Miami, 1975), pp. 5–6.

170. Bethel wrote that in a speech before the Chilean–U.S. Association in New York, Tomic said U.S. involvement in Vietnam was wrong, too expensive, could provoke a nuclear war, and would, at best, lead only to a negative victory. "By comparison," he said, "Chile is showing the way positively by demonstrating to twenty Latin American countries that the democratic system can mobilize a country, overcome underdevelopment, and modernize civilization" (op. cit., p. 522; Bethel does not give date of speech). Bethel (p. 530) says the boast was "a bid for Communist support" in the forthcoming elections and was quoted by the strident Socialist paper *Clarín*, December 1, 1968.

171. Gil, op. cit., p. 292.

172. In Collier, op. cit.

173. Gouré and Rothenberg, op. cit., pp. 8–10.

174. Ibid., p. 97.

175. Reported by Bethel, op. cit., p. 522.

176. Arriagada, op. cit., p. 59.

177. A vote of two-thirds plus one—in other words, thirty-one—was needed for

overriding a presidential veto. Exactly two-thirds was necessary for enacting certain legislation; or for the originating house of the Congress to spike legislation that it had proposed and that the other house wanted to amend. After 1965 the opposition had thirty-two votes in the Senate counting the two "independents," and both very emphatically belonged to the opposition. One, Jaime Barros Pérez Cotapos, was an avowed Communist, who later moved to the left of the Communists, siding with the violence-minded Maoists of the MIR. The other, Exequiel González Madariaga, talked like a Communist, acted like a Communist, and in fact faithfully served the Communists—until dumped from his seat in 1969 in a maneuver designed to clear the way for Salvador Allende to run for reelection from a "safe" district.

178. Jorge Prat was among those defeated; he would later reappear as a founder of the National party. So too was Liberal Hugo Zepeda, the president of the Senate. The defeat of two men close to Jorge Alessandri—Hugo Rosende and Javier Echeverría Alessandri—led analysts Parrish, von Lazar, and Tapia Videla (op. cit., p. 23) to predict: "It must be added that it is improbable anyway that Alessandri will again wield much power in politics." They added that "these matters are difficult to predict," and in that, at least, they were right; three years after they wrote that line, Alessandri was candidate for the presidency, and missed winning by fewer than forty thousand votes.

    As to the myth, Horne, to take a handy example, refers to the "conservatively oriented Senate," and later speaks of Frei and his Christian Democrats "frustrated by the intransigence of the vested interests of the right wing" (op. cit., pp. 107, 113). As we have seen, the Right, after 1965, had 9 of 147 Chamber of Deputy seats, 7 of 45 Senate seats. In point of fact, the Right gave Frei the votes he needed to enact the two biggest pieces of legislation of his administration, agrarian reform and copper nationalization.

179. Kaufman, op. cit., p. 34.

180. Kaufman, for example, wrote: "But the merger seems to have marked the further decline, rather than a resurgence. . . . Many members of the new party itself are privately pessimistic about its chances for success, and others feel that the merger was a tactical mistake" (op. cit., p. 27). In fact, the National party would rack up progressively higher vote percentages: it made its debut in 1967 with 14.61 percent (surpassing the 12.8 percent swan song of its two progenitors in the 1965 election), climbed to 20.82 percent in 1969, and 34.9 percent in 1970. By contrast, the Christian Democrats declined in inverse proportion: in 1965 they cornered 43.60 percent of the vote, by 1967 that had dropped to 31.05 percent, and by 1970 to 27.8 percent.

181. Parrish, von Lazar, and Tapia Videla, op. cit., p. 25. "If anything," they wrote, "the entire scene suggested that the Christian Democratic party might be able to settle down quietly to about twenty years of uninterrupted domination of the political scene." But such euphoria was not entirely warranted, they add. After ticking off some of the major problems facing Frei, they do hedge and say that, as a result, "the future of the Christian Democrats is not at all clear" (ibid., pp. 27–31).

182. Members of the Chamber of Deputies were elected from districts, which roughly correspond to the provinces. Their term of office was four years. Senators were elected to eight-year terms from nine geographical districts called *agrupaciones,* so constituted as to defy logic. In 1969, for example, Allende was one of five senators elected from the tenth *agrupación,* a

traditional leftist bulwark sprawling over the southern-tip provinces of Chiloé, Aisén, and Magallanes. Allende was the top vote getter, with 14,472 votes, and yet his pacesetting total was well below the 17,555 polled by Jorge Molina Valdiveso in the third *agrupación* (Aconcagua and Valparaíso), and Molina Valdivieso was not elected. Furthermore, the idea of regional representation would have some sense if the congressmen actually represented the areas that elected them, but in the main they did not. Anyway, twenty-five senators were elected at one time, twenty were elected four years later, so as to ensure continuity in the Senate. All 147 deputies ran at the same time.

183. Parrish, von Lazar, and Tapia Videla, op. cit., p. 23.
184. Francisco Cumplido Cereceda, in *Una Salida Política-Constitucional Para Chile* (Santiago: Instituto Chileno de Estudios Humanísticos, 1985), p. 86. Cereceda points out that staggered elections of senators also distorted the relationship between that body and political reality (one-half the Senate stood for election every four years; senators served for eight years). That was increasingly crucial in an era of rapidly shifting correlation of political forces (the decline of the Christian Democrats beginning with the 1965 elections). It would, of course, prove *decisive* in 1970, when Congress would elect Allende president, a Congress dominated overwhelmingly by a party in decline, a party which in the presidential elections finished third, behind Allende and the candidate of the Right.
185. "Another Blow to President Frei," *New York Times*, April 17, 1967, in Weston Agor, *The Chilean Senate* (Austin and London: University of Texas Press, 1971), p. 158.
186. Gil, op. cit., p. 288.
187. Vicente Huerta Celis, the general who commanded the Carabineros throughout the Frei presidency, told me in an interview in Santiago, October 9, 1974, that he was repeatedly rebuffed when he went to his boss, Leighton, for permission to move against the MIR. "We had them heavily infiltrated," he said, "and we knew every move they were making. But when I would go to Leighton, he would say to me: 'Why do you come to me with these crazy stories?' Needless to say, I didn't get the authority I needed to act more decisively." Huerta's case demonstrates the internal anarchy during Frei's years. That Huerta continued to occupy such a sensitive post obviously meant that he continued to enjoy the confidence of Frei, who put him there in the first place. Yet he could be, and was, repeatedly checkmated by the man who came between himself and Frei— Leighton. As indicated elsewhere, Leighton was throughout his career always congenial to the leftists and their causes just as he viscerally and reflexively opposed those who opposed the Left. (Those who observed the Reagan presidency in the U.S. will understand the role of buffers between the president and those committed to his policies who are unable, because of the buffers, to connect with him.)
188. Parrish et al., op. cit., p. 29.
189. Oscar Guillermo Garretón and Jaime Cisternas Pinto, "Algunas características del proceso de toma de decisiones en la gran empresa y la dinámica de concentración," ODEPLAN (Office of Planning), March 1970, mimeographed study, p. 8; and, "La presencia de la empresa extranjera en la industria chilena," Centro de Estudios de la Planificación Nacional, University of Chile, Serie de Estudios de Planificación, no. 21, November 1972, cited by Arriagada, op. cit., pp. 47, 63.

190. Gil (op. cit., pp. 332–34) trips all over himself trying to find a message of triumph in the ruins of defeat. He duly notes the plebiscite character of the election, and the fact that Frei had laid his prestige on the line by stumping the country personally. "Despite this effort," Gil wrote, "the outcome, without being adverse for the Christian Democrats, was below their expectations...." Later: "It is logical to expect that, given the greater importance of the parliamentary and presidential elections (of 1969 and 1970, respectively), the Christian Democrats will be able to recover at least part of the vigor they had lost."

Again, reporting on a special election on June 11, 1967, to fill a vacancy created by the death of Socialist Sen. Salomón Corbalán, Gil notes that the FRAP, backed by the Radicals, retained the seat. Corbalán's widow, their candidate, got 46.15 percent of the vote. Christian Democrat candidate Jaime Castillo got 35.9 percent and Víctor García, the National party candidate, got 17.56 percent.

Gil also relates that the election was invested with the same weather-vane significance as the Curicó election of 1964. Yet, even though the Christian Democrat share of the total vote slid for the third straight time, and even though it was the second straight increase for the Right, Gil managed to stand those facts on their head and read into the outcome "stabilization" for the Christian Democrats, at between 35 percent and 40 percent of the electorate, and see also "the continued decline of the forces of the Right, indicating small chance of [their] recovery in the future." He was, of course, as wrong on every count as he was illogical.

H. V. Kaltenborn, a distinguished radio news commentator, allowed his enthusiasm for Republican candidate Thomas E. Dewey to overcome his professional prudence. In an early morning broadcast the day after the 1948 presidential election, Kaltenborn reported that President Harry S. Truman was ahead, but added that this was certain to change as the vote from the preponderantly Republican Midwest came in. It didn't.

191. Sigmund, *The Overthrow of Allende and the Politics of Chile, 1964–1976*, op. cit., pp. 62–63, 72–73 and 78–79. The three factions first surfaced at the Second National Congress of the PDC, August 26–29, 1966. The *rebeldes*, led by Gumucio and Silva Solar, were far more strident in their criticism of Frei than were the *terceristas*, headed by Fuentealba. Ibid., p. 53.

192. Sigmund, op. cit., p. 50. Sigmund mistakenly identifies the army officer as Augusto Pinochet, at that time, the later president was serving as deputy director of the war academy in Santiago.

193. The manifesto quote is from Labrousse, op. cit., p. 188. The remark about the MIR was quoted by Silva Pinto in *Los Días del Arco Iris* (Santiago: Editorial de Pacífico, 1972), p. 43.

194. Florencia Varas, *Conversaciones con Viaux* (Santiago: Talleres Impressiones Eire, 1972), pp. 62, 81–82. The quote about the shoes is from a conference record of a symposium at Georgetown University in Washington, D.C., August 15, 1974, and was made by the former ambassador Edward Korry. It appears in *United States and Chile During the Allende Years, 1970–1973*, pp. 640–41.

195. Varas, op. cit., pp. 99–106.

196. Patricio Silva Echeñique, Undersecretary of Foreign Affairs, interview with *Washington Star*, April 7, 1967, cited by Chamudes, op. cit., p. 191.

5

In Harm's Way

"We will be known by our acts, and only by our acts"
—Salvador Allende.[1]

It was, as Richard Nixon would remark, a time of revolutions. But a time, he would add, for creating a world such as the world had never known.[2]

For Nixon, for most Americans, such ringing words were a summons to do better what, essentially, we had done in the past. But for Salvador Allende, and the implacable men and women around him, the revolution they planned would bury the past in the debris of a world turned upside down.

But as 1969 drew to a close and the electioneering of 1970 intensified, Salvador Allende and his dreams of revolution might have amounted to little more than the last hurrah of a has-been, hack politician. For the dreams to become nightmare, it would take, as so often it does in revolution, the connivance of those blinded by their own ambitions, or hatreds—or stupidities.

THE CANDIDATE

The world would little note it, but the man who appeared at the head of this impending revolution was little more than a cat's paw, at the mercy of the irreconcilably squabbling forces that put him, reluctantly, in power. Consuming ambition and the craftiness of his cohorts overcame the resistance of those who, in 1969, viewed Allende as a worn-out ward healer.

Allende's relentless ambition had become as famed in Chile as the man's towering vanity. In 1964, a Chilean newsman asked Allende, then making his third run for the presidency, whether he had any special caprices.

"Yes," he said, "for thirty years, I have had the caprice of wanting to be president."

He was asked to imagine what the year 3000 would be like.

"A year," he said, "without me as a candidate." Then, laughing, "Probably."[3]

Salvador Allende was born in the seaport city of Valparaíso July 26, 1908, the first of four children of a moderately well-to-do family with deep roots on both sides in the legal and medical professions. One grandfather was a lawyer and the other a doctor who organized the medical services of the Chilean army during the War of the Pacific. (Another ancestor, on his mother's side, achieved a different kind of distinction. He was shot for his role in leading an uprising against President Balmaceda [1886–1891].) His father, Salvador Allende Castro, was a lawyer. Allende's mother, Laura Gossens, was a devout Roman Catholic, a member of the Third Order of Carmelite Nuns, an organization of lay women closely allied to that religious order. Her influence was reflected in the name he was baptized with: Salvador Isabelino del Sagrado Corazón de Jesús Allende. (*Salvador* means "savior" and *del Sagrado de Jesús* translates as "of the sacred heart of Jesus.") Once in the presidency, atheist Allende dropped the religious names, changing his birth certificate to read "Salvador Guillermo Allende."

Much has been made of Allende's bourgeois background, as if his later life were a repudiation of that "capitalistic" past. It is true that he grew up in a decidedly upper-crust neighborhood, and was educated at private schools in Talca, Valdivia, and Valparaíso. He even volunteered for military service, which he performed at the Coraceros Cavalry Regiment, at the beach resort of Viña del Mar, immediately north of his hometown (he later even achieved officer's rank in the reserve). But the fact is, Allende's ancestors had belonged to the Chilean Left for better than three-quarters of a century, and his earliest intellectual influences were profoundly leftist.

Allende's paternal grandfather, Dr. Allende Padín, a medical doctor, was a Most Serene Grand Master of the Masonic Order and a Radical senator. Allende himself would later become a member of the equally secret, equally elitist Lautarian Lodge, avant-garde from the days of its creation as the political arm of the movement for independence from Spain. In his conversations with French Marxist Régis Debray, Allende remarked that his grandfather founded the first lay school in Chile at a time when secular education was the battleground between liberals and conservatives. Radical ideas earned the elder Allende the nickname Red Allende.[4] Allende's father and all his uncles were activists in the Radical party, the party of the anticlerical Left in those days.

Allende told Debray that his family, though well off, was "not associated with the economically powerful sector of the bourgeoisie"—a circumstance that may later have stimulated Allende's own inordinate appetite for the perquisites of economic power. Allende told Debray:

> When I was a boy of about fourteen or fifteen, I used to hang around the shop of a shoemaker, an anarchist called Juan Demarchi, to hear him talk and exchange views with him.
>
> That was in Valparaíso, at the time I was in grammar school. After the school day, I used to go and converse with this anarchist, who was a great influence on my life as a boy. He was sixty or perhaps sixty-three and he was quite happy to talk with me. He taught me how to play chess, he spoke to me of the things of life, and he lent me books . . . all the essentially theoretical works, so to speak, like Bakunin, for example, but the most important thing was Demarchi's commentaries, because I didn't have the temperament for reading in depth; he explained things to me with the simplicity and clarity that one finds in self-taught workers.[5]

Disdain for reading in depth dogged Allende throughout his life; political associates remembered Allende as a man who would, at best, skim-read, or, more usually, rely on his phenomenal memory and capacity for picking the brains of others for his ideas.[6]

In 1926, Allende began his studies at the medical school of the University of Chile in Santiago, already a hotbed of political activism.

"Medical students were traditionally the most advanced," Allende would recall later. "At the time, we lived in a very humble district, we practically lived with the people; most of us were from the provinces, and those of us living in the same hostel used to meet at night for readings of *Das Kapital* and Lenin, and also Trotsky. . . ."[7]

While at the university, Allende began his own career as a political activist, a career which cost him two arrests and temporary expulsion from the university. He was president of the Student Medical Center and later became vice chairman of the Student Federation and a delegate to the University Council.

One of his arrests was for taking part in a student strike that ended in student seizure of the university.[8] Jailed with him was a brother who was, for the most part, aloof from politics, and a brother-in-law who was, in turn, the brother of Marmaduke Grove, the flamboyant Socialist leader. Allende boasted of his family ties with Grove in his conversations with Debray; those ties would not spare Grove in 1944 when Allende led an assault on the old leadership headed by Grove. Grove was driven from the ranks of the party in that battle, and into political oblivion.

Allende and his brother were released from prison to be with their father, who had had one leg amputated, and was dying of gangrene in the other.

"I was able to talk with him for a few minutes," Allende told Debray, "and he managed to tell us that all he had to leave us was a clean, honest upbringing—he had no material wealth. He died the next day, and at his funeral I made the promise that I would dedicate my life to the social struggle, and I believe that I have fulfilled that promise."[9]

With his father gone, Allende's mother took firm charge of the family. Allende's sister, Laura, remembers:

> My mother was a woman who, even for her time, behaved differently than other women. During the time my father was failing, it was she who took charge of the notary's office in Valparaíso despite the fact that she had never worked outside the house.
>
> People came to her just as they would to a professional, so that my father only had to review and sign documents. [In Chile, notaries must be lawyers, and as a rule, they enjoy considerable prestige and great earning power.]
>
> Salvador was extremely close to her and felt so proud when she, already on in years, but very erect and very cute, would hook her arm in his and go to vote. Salvador felt reassured because she was always behind him in his political fights, even though they cost her a good deal of suffering.
>
> In the 1958 presidential campaign, for example, when she was 80 years old, she was besieged with threatening or insulting telephone calls. But she never complained because she understood that Salvador was fighting for the people and against those who oppressed them.
>
> One day during that same campaign, all of us were seated at the table at dinnertime when someone said to Salvador: "You could be president of Chile if only you would break with the Communist party, so much resisted in this country."
>
> Before Salvador could answer, my mother, a deeply religious woman, answered herself: "Salvador, you should never leave the Communist party because it has been loyal to you and that would be betrayal." And that was always Salvador's stand: loyalty.[10]

Laura was herself one of several women who played decisively influential roles in Allende's life. She was herself a Socialist deputy and if for no other reason than loyalty to her own son Andrés Pascal, a firebrand of the Maoist terrorist organization, the MIR. Laura was regarded as on the Left of her famous brother. Together with her son, she remained, to the very end, a link between the MIR and the government, and a permanent gadfly in the ointment of closer alliances with the Communists, the strategists of Allende's coalition.

There was another woman who played an important role in Allende's early life, his nanny, Rosa, affectionately known to the family as Mama

Rosa. Young Salvador was her favorite, and she gave him the nickname Chicho because, Laura related,[11] he was to her as pretty as *chiche*, a slang word in Chile for a shiny trinket. Years later, when Allende reached the presidency, Mama Rosa walked on his arm to Congress for his investiture as chief executive.

Allende was barely out of the university when he joined the fledgling Socialist party, a fusion of several small groups that had backed Marmaduke Grove Vallejos in the short-lived Socialist republic of 1932. The Socialist party was founded by Eugenio Matte Hurtado, an eminent lawyer and scion of one of Chile's oldest and most moneyed families. Allende, conspicuous already as a student agitator but otherwise a minor figure, would later style himself a founding father of the party, a touch-up of history "interviewer" Debray and others would allow him to get away with.[12]

Why a Socialist party, rather than closing ranks behind the strong-willed revolutionaries of the Communist party? Allende's answer betrayed the kind of confusion and contradictions that characterized not only his career, but that of other Chilean Socialists: "We analyzed the situation in Chile, and we believed that there was a place for a party which, while holding similar views in terms of philosophy and doctrine—a Marxist approach to the interpretation of history—would be a party free of ties of an international nature. However, this did not mean that we would disavow proletarian internationalism."

Far from it, in fact. As early as 1949, at a time when most of his Socialist colleagues were still locked in mortal ideological combat with the Communists, Allende demonstrated his willingness to do their bidding. He did so by becoming a member of the Executive Committee of the Committee for World Peace, a front organization organized by the (then proscribed) Chilean Communist party in advance of a Mexico City "peace conference." Five years later, he headed a delegation invited by the Chilean-Soviet Cultural Institute to tour the USSR and Czechoslovakia. (The same year, he spent six months in Communist China.)[13]

In later years, as he courted the support of the Communists, Allende would repeatedly and heatedly defend Chilean Communists against charges they belonged to an international conspiracy, or followed orders from abroad. If, then, they believed only in a Marxist interpretation of history, and their only foreign ties were spiritual, as members of the international proletariat, how to differentiate Communists from Socialists?

The answer had precious little to do with the theoretical hairsplitting of Allende or others who would cast Chilean Socialists in the ideological mold of international socialism—a mistake Europeans, especially, would persist in down through and beyond Allende's own time in power. Allende himself told Debray that Chilean socialism did not "have anything to do with certain self-styled Socialist parties in Europe."[14] In fact, Chilean socialism never did manage to enunciate a coherent body of theoretical thought, certainly none that lasted until the ink was dry.

Rather, the answer was to be found in the practical proposition of the perceptions of Allende and others on the best means of pursuing and achieving power.

Allende's first experiences in the pursuit of power, his student politicking, put a crimp in his medical career: "In order to be able to work in the hospitals in Valparaíso, I had to take four examinations and although I was the only candidate, I was rejected because of what I had been as a student. I started to work as a pathology assistant, and that means that my first job was very hard and very dull. I had to carry out autopsies."[15]

Cadavers were not, however, Allende's main interest then, just as it is doubtful that medicine was then or ever would have been, either. No sooner back in Valparaíso, Allende became "practically" the founder of the Socialist party in the port city (the qualification "practically" was Allende's own in his talks with Debray). He spent far more time stumping the city and rural environs proselytizing for the party than he did in the laboratory.

Within a few short years, he began the visible climb to power: first, in 1937, getting himself elected to the Chamber of Deputies, then on September 28, 1939, getting a toehold on the national stage as minister of health in the Popular Front government of Pedro Aguirre Cerda, one of three Socialists named to cabinet posts in the government. (Allende, then thirty-one, had managed Aguirre Cerda's campaign.) Allende remained in the Cabinet until February 1943, pulling out with other Socialists in protest against the Radical government's refusal to declare war on Nazi Germany.

In 1945 Allende was elected to the Senate, winning reelection in 1953, 1961, and 1969. In all of those elections except 1961, he was elected from the sparsely populated and traditionally Socialist southernmost district. In 1961 he switched to the much more populous Third District—Aconcagua and Valparaíso—a move that very nearly cost him his career. Despite running in his home territory, and despite the backing of the Communists and lesser allies of the far left Popular Action Front (FRAP), Allende ran a flaccid fourth in the field. That year marked the thunderous arrival of the FRAP as a major electoral force; in the highly fragmented election lineup, the FRAP commanded the highest single vote total. That year also marked the last time the parties could pool their votes in a senatorial election under the byzantine system already outlawed (in 1958) in the elections of deputies and municipal councilmen.

In such circumstances, Allende chose discretion over valor and retreated to the safety of the south for the 1969 elections, a district which not only was a stronghold of the far Left but one in which candidates needed far fewer votes to get elected. (Concretely, the fourteen thousand votes that Allende won with in 1969 in the Tenth District—Chiloé, Aisén, and Magallanes—would have put him far out of the running, in seventh place, that year in Aconcagua-Valparaíso; in point of fact, the Socialists did so badly in those provinces that year that the total vote for all three of their candidates was only 13,289 votes—even if combined, not enough to elect one of them.)

Of the mythologies encrusting Allende's career as it has been interpreted by foreign observers, few are more pervasive than the one that portrays him as a conscientious parliamentarian, devoted to the traditions and norms of parliament and, thus, parliamentary democracy. The much neglected record demonstrates otherwise. Just as he confessed to "lacking the temperament" for in-depth reading, Allende lacked the temperament for sustained hard work, substituting his formidable powers of personal persuasion, his sense of the dramatic, and his engaging charm. Allende had his eye, unflinchingly, on the main avenue to total power, and not on winning temporary, tactical control even of important events.

So it was in his political career; as he maneuvered to win control of the party machinery. Each time he was blocked, he would force a split and emerge at the head of a faction, shunning alliances he could not control (such as with Ibáñez) but always welcoming those he could, even at the sacrifice of ideological principles (as he did in joining the Radical government and later would in actively wooing the Communists, the archenemies of orthodox Socialists).[16]

So it was too in his Senate career. A survey of attendance at Senate sessions for the sixteen-month period ending September 18, 1966—a critical time when the fate of issues such as agrarian reform and control of the copper industries was being decided—showed that of the forty-five senators, only one managed to attend fewer sessions than Senator Allende. Allende attended 66 sessions, or 27 percent of those held during that period, whereas the overall average of all senators was 154 sessions, or 63 percent. Interestingly, the one senator who was even less faithful to his Senate duties than Allende was Luis Corvalán, secretary-general of the Communist party. Weston Agor, who made these observations, commented that Corvalán "places greater emphasis on his party duties." Agor also commented that most Chilean senators since World War II "take their work seriously . . . [and] have devoted more and more time to their legislative careers."[17]

Serious-minded and almost reverential about the Senate and its role in Chilean politics, most senators attached high importance to committee work, developing along the way a clear notion of the relative importance of committees. A measure of Allende's indifference to the institution—and the low esteem in which he was held by his fellow senators—is that despite his years in the Senate, Allende never chaired a committee more important than that on public health. Ostensibly, this was a reflection of his special expertise as a doctor; in point of fact, other senators preened themselves for control of key committees. Allende's Public Health Committee was ranked by senators themselves somewhere between sixth and tenth among the fourteen Senate committees in a survey done by Agor, and was ranked twelfth by Senate staffers in the same survey.[18] Of the three Senate committees chaired by Socialists in the 1965–69 period, Allende's was, in fact, the lowest-ranking; the others were national defense, headed by frequent party rival Raúl Ampuero, a man regarded as more charismatic but less single-minded than Allende; and top-ranked finance, headed by Carlos Altamirano, the *enfant terrible* of the Socialists (and a case in point of a senator who learned the skills he needed as he climbed toward his committee goal).

But Allende got what Allende wanted—not a share of substantial power, control of a powerful committee, but the unshared limelight of ceremonial power: the presidency of the entire Senate. In theory, presidency of the Senate is "a force for nonpartisanship, conciliation, and the search for the national interest."[19] Under Allende it became a fulcrum for catapulting him to the ultimate power he had long sought, and he insinuated into the role contempt for the rules of "bourgeois democracy," as he would so often disparagingly call them—rules which would later vex his administration.

Allende served a disarming apprenticeship of sorts as Senate vice president from 1951 to 1955. Since the vice president's job is more honorary than real, he emerged from that period with an altogether respectable reputation.

Following the Christian Democrat's congressional landslide in 1965, the Right, stung by Frei's pariahlike treatment of them, refused to back a Christian Democrat for the Senate presidency, a post traditionally a plum in political deals. As for the Christian Democrats, they demonstrated then as they would again in 1970 that they would far rather deed the country over to the far Left than support a man of the Right, even though the Right had swallowed its own misgivings in 1964 to help elect Frei.

The failure of the Christian Democrats and the Right to patch together a coalition (together they would have had twenty-two votes, one shy of what they needed to prevail) undoubtedly contributed to nudging the Radicals, with their nine pivotal votes, into the FRAP camp.

The scrambling got so bad that for two days a man with an almost peerless record of mediocrity served as interim president. The regular session ended without agreement on a new president.

Out of the melee came Allende, emerging at a special session in December 1966 as Senate president, put there by the twenty-five votes of the Communists, Socialists, Radicals, and their lesser allies—and the stubbornness of the Christian Democrats. In the process, the Christian Democrats rescued Allende's political career from decline and gave him the national forum he needed to overcome the stigma of repeated defeat and run again in 1970. But even with such a forum, Allende only barely made it.

Allende began his new career with a profession of his fealty to the traditions of nonpartisanship of the Senate presidency, a speech presaging the pious one he would make four years later on winning congressional ratification of his election as president of Chile.

"Notwithstanding the political position of those who elected us," Allende assured his Senate colleagues in 1966, "we will not have a Senate habitually opposed [to the government]. . . . I can say that all of the senators will receive equal and just treatment, which has been the constant norm of the Chilean Parliament."[20]

Once in office, what he did was not, however, what he said. In the narrow sense of applying and interpreting Senate rules, Agor, a sympathetic critic, gave him good marks, but with a hedge. Agor quoted one senator as making what he described as a "typical comment" on Allende's behavior as Senate president.

"Allende," the senator told Agor, "is a combatant; he is trying to take advantage of the visibility of this position to push himself." Said another: "There is a lot more partisanship under Allende than there should be. For example, he told Bulnes [of the rightist National party] to hurry up, when he was debating the salary readjustment bill. But when [Communist] Teitelboim spoke, he didn't. Why? Because they are political friends."[21]

Such incidents would be trivia were it not for an image of Allende built far more on his words than on his deeds, a deceit he got away with to an astonishing degree.[22]

But there was one area in which not even Allende's most dogged defenders could whitewash him, because Allende himself could never make up his own mind: his bird-snake fascination with violence. In his choice of causes and heroes, at home and abroad, he tilted almost invariably to the messages and messengers of violence, even when his well-honed instincts for survival should have dictated otherwise.

It was Allende, for instance, who proposed, at the Tri-Continental Conference in Havana in January 1966, the creation of the Latin American Solidarity Organization (OLAS). Those who would celebrate his frequent protestations of "dedication" to democratic practices and institutions just as routinely overlooked his inflammatory streak. He told five hundred delegates from one hundred countries at that conference that out of it would come a realization that "action cannot be taken in isolated struggles but must come by a united fight in all countries."[23] A few years later, ensconced in power, he would tell Debray that he never thought of OLAS as more than an informational clearinghouse for revolutionary activity.[24] Yet from the very outset, OLAS advocated the armed overthrow of noncommunist governments; the manifesto at the close of the first OLAS conference in Havana in July 1967 said that "the revolutionary armed struggle constitutes the fundamental line for the Latin American revolution." A year later, with Allende still a conspicuous member of the OLAS directorate, the organization went on record as asserting that "armed revolution is the only solution for Latin America's social and economic ills." Such sword rattling was not, however, limited to foreign arenas. Allende's own Socialist party, in its twenty-third convention, called for "active resistance to the present economic and social order, then armed resistance and finally insurrection."[25]

When he rushed north in 1968 to defend and then escort out of the country the five survivors of Che Guevara's guerrillas—an act that shocked the Chilean sense of decorum and political neutrality expected in a Senate president—only the reluctance of the Christian Democrats to act saved him from impeachment proceedings. The Christian Democrats were by then hard put to keep their own radical Left under control, particularly their youth organization, which sympathized with virtually every radical cause then fashionable, including OLAS.

As to his heroes, Allende rhapsodized in his conversations with Debray over three who, for him, towered above all others: Fidel Castro (the affection was not always mutual), Ernesto (Che) Guevara, and Ho Chi Minh, whom he had met in Hanoi on an Asian junket in 1968. He expressed deep admiration for the Vietcong ("an example of breadth of vision") and China's Cultural Revolution. Said Allende: "I understand that Mao Tse-tung, as a revolutionary, has sought to destroy the elements that were paralyzing and neutralizing the Revolution. Such elements must be singled out and eliminated."[26]

El Mercurio, the grand doyen of the Chilean press, opposed Salvador Allende throughout most of his public life, and in the end nearly perished in the process. Yet for all its political coloration, *El Mercurio* only occasionally sacrificed scholarship to partisanship, above all in the years before Allende converted the country into a caldron of hatreds and tensions.

In an editorial published June 7, 1967, the newspaper posed the dilemma of Allende squarely: "Which is the real Allende? The old parliamentarian who today presides over the debates of senators in a solid and traditional regime of law, or the guerrilla who applauds and stimulates the 'struggles of the people' against the order he himself represents in his country? These are questions that are being asked by partisans of guerrillas and partisans of democracy. . . ."

Allende responded with tirades against the newspaper, but the question would not go away. Four and-a-half years later, early in his presidency, guerrilla-partisan Debray put essentially the same question to him again, with a persistence rare in Debray's reverential interview of Allende:

> DEBRAY: Comrade President, Allow me to look ahead a little. You know that Leninism has nothing against compromises, as long as they are absolutely necessary, and do not jeopardize the long-term development of the class struggle. . . . The problem now is whether these [conciliatory] conditions can continue to favor the advancement of this [revolutionary] process: in other words, how can the transition from a bourgeois system to another more democratic, more revolutionary, more proletarian system be achieved without a break? . . . One may wonder whether the proletariat and their allies are going to be hemmed in by the bourgeois institutions, and pacified with a few reforms here and there, or whether at a given moment the framework will be broken to create a proletarian democracy? Is the proletariat going to assert itself over the bourgeoisie, or will the bourgeoisie gradually remold the proletariat and reabsorb it into its world? Doubtless, I'm overgeneralizing, but basically my question would be: "Who is using whom? Who is taking whom for a ride?" That's putting it brutally and perhaps a little provocatively. . . .
>
> ALLENDE: I don't believe that a comrade can ask questions whose intention is to provoke.
>
> DEBRAY: Well, there are those who say I'm a professional *agent provocateur*, comrade President.
>
> ALLENDE: I shall not allow myself to be provoked.
>
> DEBRAY: The question is important.
>
> ALLENDE: And the answer is short: the proletariat. . . .[27]

Inevitably, the conflict between revolution and institutions grew as a minority president attempted to uproot an entire social, economic, and political system over the rising clamor of an increasingly vocal majority. Predictably, Salvador Allende allowed institutions to slip into the limbo of worthless words.

They called him El Pije ("the Dandy"), this champion of the working classes, this dapper man of drawing-room charm, tailored suits, and a lifelong taste for fine whiskeys and pretty women.

In the ripeness of his years, Allende cut a stocky rather than a swashbuckling figure. He ate and drank zestfully and yet managed to hold dissoluteness at bay by submitting himself, in the dawn of most of the days of his life, to the discipline of strenuous exercises. He slept little at night—three or four hours (to the despair of many cronies or subordinates inveigled into accompanying him). But he compensated for the lack of nighttime sleep with an almost daily ritual of a siesta in an alcove bedroom just off his presidential office. He exuded an air of vitality, yet he had kidney trouble, hepatitis twice, a heart attack, and two minor strokes, one of which left the right side of his face partially paralyzed.

He stood 5 feet 7 inches, a height that gave him a two-inch advantage over the average for his countrymen.[28] His face was full without being fat, and suggested for all the world the visage of a self-satisfied bourgeois businessman. He was not unattractive, and neither was he handsome, but there was an impish quality about his appearance and mien, much as there was about his private life. He loved humor, especially ribald humor, and he was a renowned storyteller, but he also was feared for his temper and was capable of cutting down those who crossed him with cold arrogance. With time and experience, his self-confidence grew and he bore himself with the air of a man of self-assured authority, strutting more than walking when on public display. And yet, he was fidgety and restless, and his green eyes, half-shaded behind thick horn-rimmed glasses, would as often as not evade meeting the gaze of the person to whom he was talking. Until the very end, his ruddy rectangular face was fuzzed across the middle by a trim gray mustache and crowned by a thick shock of mostly curly dark brown hair.

Salvador Allende was never a spellbinder as a speaker; he excelled in one-on-one contacts, in drawing rooms, and in close personal persuasion. Similarly, he was able to mesmerize the women who came into his life, but Chilean women at large remained forever his nemeses. Noting that women had once cost him a byelection in his hometown of Valparaíso, Allende said, with a touch of wryness, "and every day I'm more a partisan of women."[29] Allende was, of course, perfectly willing to allow his "macho" image to grow, as evidenced by his widely quoted remark, "I have been accused of everything except being a thief or a homosexual." Once in the presidency, he didn't even try to keep up pretenses of a normal married life with his still attractive wife, Hortensia (Tencha), and his escapades were common gossip in Chile.

He used his formidable powers of charm and persuasion as a surrogate for studiousness or substance. The Chilean author Lautaro Silva noted Allende's reputation as "la mejor muñeca de Chile" ("the best manipulator of Chile"), and the former president Eduardo Frei said, "Allende was a frivolous man, more frivolous politically than morally. He was, no doubt, intelligent, a facile but superficial speaker, a backslapper, a politician of the ward-heeling type. But Allende was not an ideologue, he was not a statesman, but a maneuverer. . . ."[30]

U.S. Ambassador Nathaniel Davis, who served in Santiago the last two years of Allende's life—and who professed personal admiration for Allende, as well as clear faith in his programs—noted that, for all his charm and cleverness, Allende could not be trusted. Wrote Davis: "Few of his friends have ever claimed that he [Allende] was altogether truthful in his political dealings . . . for myself, I liked the president wholeheartedly, but I did not always believe him. . . . It was in Allende's nature to make political bargains rather easily, always with the possibility of being able to wiggle out of them later. . . ."

Davis also quotes his predecessor in Santiago, Amb. Edward M. Korry, as saying Allende not only was "personally" financed by foreign Communists "for many, many years," but that he had accepted bribes from multinational corporations—as much as $500,000 from a mining company. (Davis adds that "no one should conclude, however, that Allende was 'bought' in terms of his policies or convictions. If he was 'rented,' the rent was high, and the leases were short if observed at all.")[31]

He posed, for most of his adult life, as a champion of the downtrodden, but he never relented in his pursuit of physical and sensual comforts for himself. For most of his married life, he lived with his wife and three daughters in a pink stucco and stone duplex house on Guardia Vieja Street in the tony Providencia section of Santiago. The couple employed a maid, cook, and driver. The Allendes also had a small but handsome seashore villa smack on the bay in the choicest real estate in Algarrobo, a seacoast fishing village and summer resort for select Santiago families. (The village managed to retain its charm largely because it was, rather pointedly, not served by public transportation.) The Allendes' house was almost directly across the road in Algarrobo from the yacht club, a club distinguished more for the quality of the seafaring than for the size or opulence of the boats. Around the club Allende is remembered, contrary to his image as an avid yachtsman, as an indifferent boatsman who toyed with a small boat more as an occasional escape than as a measure of his love for the sea. (Allende himself, in a snit over repeated references to his "yacht," told the Senate in 1968 that it was "a sailboat just big enough for four persons and which doesn't even have an outboard motor. Yet for some, it's an ocean liner.")

In his later years Allende gave up yachting, and, for the most part, Algarrobo, preferring during his presidency El Cañaveral, a secluded hideaway in El Arrayán, the foothills of the Andes east of Santiago. He bought that sprawling estate for his long-time mistress Miría Contreras Bell (La Payita). Once in the presidency, Allende surrounded himself with a wealth and splendor never before seen in austere Chile: cars, houses, banquets, and finery on a lavish scale. (Forty expensive suits were found in one closet alone following his death in 1973.) His reputation as a bon vivant grew to the point where it was said he could identify with a sip the brand of Scotch whisky, though for himself he preferred the very fine (and expensive) Chivas Regal. (Yet as late as March of 1972, Allende would be asserting that he drank Scotch only occasionally "because it is very expensive." In point of fact, he drank it right up to the hour of his death.)

In 1964 a British newspaperman, on Allende's campaign trail, wrote: "In peasant lands, where he campaigned recently, he chooses a plebeian windjammer. He is not a man of the people. He relishes bourgeois comforts his youth accustomed him to. He sent his daughters to English schools. . . .

"Perhaps he might be called, in the Churchillean phrase for Bevan, a Bollinger Bolshevik—if, that is, he had the personality and roundness of humor. . . . His bolshevism is obscurely qualified."[32]

But on one subject, Allende was not at all obscure: his quest for power. It was a quest that would see the manipulator become manipulated.

THE MANIPULATORS

For all the development of democratic processes in Chile, the citizens of that country, in common with those of most democracies, were basically passive about their politics. In fact, the best estimate made by the Senate Information Service in Chile pegged party membership in the early seventies at 8 percent of all voters.[33] In 1964, the last year for which the Christian Democrats released official figures, they claimed 45,792 members (while rolling up a vote that year of 1.4 million). In 1970, peak estimates put their membership at twice that number, or just about 1 percent of the country's total population, a (rarely cited) statistic in sharp contrast to the colossuslike image conjured up by the repeated ballyhooing of them as "Chile's largest party."

There was, however, one party where membership was significant: the Communist party of Chile (PCCh). By 1971 the Communists could boast of 50,000 card-carrying members, 22 deputies, 6 senators, 230 municipal councilmen, and 17 percent of the electorate, not to mention a daily newspaper, a number of weekly papers and magazines, radio stations, and a business empire that included drugstores, bus lines, and bookstores,[34] all of which made the party the best financed in Chile. Discipline, tight organization, and single-mindedness—plus a fat purse—gave the party a power far out of proportion to its numbers. The organization ranged from a National Congress, theoretically the supreme organ of the party (but actually subservient to the Central Committee), down to cells grouped in regional organizations—all managed by full-time paid staff (the Communists were the only Chilean party with the means to maintain such a professional, career staff).

The PCCh was, in fact, the largest and best-organized Communist party in Latin America, and the third largest (after France and Italy) in the entire free world. In Gunther's phrase, the PCCh was "a *real* Communist party . . . a long way from the dreamer-dilettantes in Brazil, or those who, as in Argentina, merely hope for change." Debray noted that it was the Communist party in South America that was not composed primarily of elites who claimed to speak for the working class, but actually drew its "lifeblood from the workers' movement itself," making Chile "the only country in which the ruling class has had to face a century's defiance from a proletarian resistance movement." A U.S. ambassador, with broad experience observing Communist parties on both sides of the Iron Curtain, said he rated the PCCh as "the most able of any in a nontotalitarian state" he had witnessed. He noted that the Chilean party was the prime adviser on Latin America to the Kremlin, and added that the PCCh was "the most successful Communist party that I have ever seen in operation."[35]

On the fiftieth anniversary of the party in 1972, for example, the Kremlin sent a message referring to the "revolutionary transformations in Chile as a new page in the creation of the socialist world. . . ." The message made plain that for Moscow the Communist party was the "correct" agent for leading Chile to socialism by noting "the clear classist position [of the party] with respect to the role and importance of the October Revolution, the premier country of socialism."[36]

The party's secretary-general, Luis Corvalán Lepe, once stated that workers made up 75 percent of the membership, but the figure was contradicted by the other party claims about the high percentage of youth and peasants—not to mention "intellectuals"—in their ranks. Debray was indulging in a bit of histrionics in any case when he referred to a "proletarian resistance movement." The reality, of course, was that the party's elders were long-time bureaucrats, as alien to the pick and the plow as most of the "oligarchy" they reviled.

Just as the electoral fortunes of the Christian Democrats and the Radicals declined as they (and the country) moved steadily leftward, those of the PCCh climbed steadily: from 11.76 percent of the vote in the congressional elections of 1961 to 12.73 percent in 1965 and 17.3 percent in 1969.

Through its long and mostly docile life, the PCCh had a love-hate relationship with the issue of revolutionary violence, preferring to believe it could collapse the system from within without resorting to arms. Yet the party never foreswore violence, and buried even its revered founding father, Luis Emilio Recabarren, because of his stubborn faith in the peaceful triumph of the cause.

Elías Lafertte, Recabarren's secretary and later himself the elder statesman and president of the party, carried away from his first encounter with Recabarren the memory of a man who at first blush appeared "ungainly of bearing and of hooded eyes," and who through simple, quiet, yet stimulating phrases caused nine and-a-half hours to evaporate before the entranced Lafertte regained his sense of time.

Recabarren was born in 1876 in Valparaíso, son of small shopkeepers. At eighteen he married Guadalupe del Canto and fathered a son by her, but the couple soon split up. In 1912 he met Teresa Flores, the woman he would live with for the rest of his days.

Recabarren began his studies at St. Thomas Aquinas School but at fourteen had to drop out and go to work as a printer's devil. It was that experience, amid ink and the printing press, which kindled in him an insatiable appetite for learning and reading; and it was that experience, amid the effervescence of an awakening and brawling labor movement, which shaped his political fervor. He became a missionary of reform, first within the ranks of the populist and labor-championing Democratic party, founded in 1887 by the avant-garde dissidents from the Radical party, and later (in 1912) at the head of his own Socialist Worker party. Lafertte remembers his crossing the desert in a donkey cart, burdened down by books, pamphlets, and his own zeal, hounded by authorities and his employers, carrying his message of labor unity to nitrate workers.

In 1906 he managed to get himself elected a deputy, only to have his election invalidated by the Chamber. The second time, the ostensible reason was his refusal, as an atheist, to swear by God to discharge his duties. Noting that he castigated the deputies for breaking faith with the law and constitution by excluding him in defiance of the will of those who had elected him, Debray expressed the scorn of latter-day revolutionaries when he wrote: "When Recabarren thus appealed for the application of law, he was not just engaging in a tactical maneuver ... so much as expressing his nostalgic faith in the authentic rule of law, his inner conviction that he had common sense and justice on his side."[37] Recabarren would finally return to the Chamber, remaining from 1921 to 1924, but by then the Socialist had become a Communist.

In 1907, Recabarren traveled to France and Belgium, and, presumably, on to Stuttgart for the Congress of the Second International. The Stuttgart Congress was "the best ever," in Lenin's phrase, bringing together the superstars of world socialism, and was the fountainhead of the tradition of loyalty to party above loyalty to country, the principle which decisively weakened the czarist government in Russia and paved the way for the 1917 Revolution.[38] Having temporarily smoothed over the chronic differences that divided them at a London conference of the All-Russian Social Democratic Labor party in April-May of that year, the Russians were able to field an unprecedented delegation at Stuttgart in August: sixty-three representatives of all factions and parties, including Lenin, Plekhanov, Litvinov, Lunacharsky, and Trotsky. A total of 884 delegates from twenty-five nations and every continent attended that conference, and of the non-Russians no name loomed larger than that of Rosa Luxemburg.

There is no record of Recabarren having met these luminaries of world revolution, but the thirty-one-year-old Chilean could not help carrying away a deep sense of revolutionary zeal himself.

In 1917 Recabarren won control of the foundering Chilean Workers Federation (FOCh), shaping it as a potent political force; it went from 20,000 members in 1919 to 80,000 in 1921. An important factor in the election of the reformist Alessandri government, the FOCh was able to win for itself legal status for unions in 1924. Recabarren believed in an authentic dictatorship of the proletariat, a government controlled by unions rather than by a party, and an economy based on collective rather than on private property. By 1919 he had converted the FOCh from a labor organization into a revolutionary force; and having broken the power of the U.S.–based Industrial Workers of the World (IWW), he led the federation into the Moscow-based Red International of Unions.

In January 1922, in the copper-mining city of Rancagua, fifty-five miles south of Santiago, Recabarren transformed his Socialist Worker party into the Communist party of Chile. It would be several years before Moscow would formally accept the PCCh into full membership in the Third International, but the new Chilean party immediately accepted the famous, and occasionally infamously ludicrous, "twenty-one points" laid down by Lenin as a condition for membership binding on all foreign parties. For the Chilean party, unlike many others around the world, those twenty-one points would become a combination of commandment and orientation over the years.[39]

The same year (1922) Recabarren traveled to Russia and returned so enthralled with what he had seen that he wrote a rhapsodic paean called "Peasant and Worker Russia." Chilean analysts would repeatedly describe as a "home-grown version" of communism the type he preached upon his return: repudiation of violence, burrowing from within the parliamentary system to achieve revolutionary aims. Actually, these were echoes of the Master's Voice: at the Second Congress of the Comintern in July 1920, Lenin disappointed foreign delegates when he urged them to temporize with capitalist regimes—the same Lenin who until only a few months before had preached total war against capitalists. He urged them to be "not doctrinaire but flexible." They should not spurn the opportunities that the capitalist state affords through its rotten freedoms. "Thus the Communists," Adam B. Ulam recounts of Lenin's counsels, "ought not to reject the chance to use parliaments, and to work through the trade unions; if an occasion warrants they should join in a bloc or even enter the opportunist Socialist parties."[40]

To fiery revolutionaries eager for their own October Revolution, such counsel bordered on heresy; not to Recabarren and the Chileans, already familiar with the advantages of recruiting labor to their cause and using parliament to attain their ends.

That course was derailed, temporarily, by events in the Kremlin, a familiar and recurring circumstance for the Chilean party. In December 1922 Lenin suffered a second and virtually incapacitating stroke. In April 1923 Stalin succeeded him as party secretary-general. Later that year a Communist uprising in the province of Saxony in Germany, hastily blessed by the Comintern, failed miserably. As Isaac Deutscher has observed: "These events were to have a powerful impact on the Soviet Union. They destroyed the chances of revolution in Germany and Europe for many years ahead. They imparted to Russian communism a deep and definite sense of isolation. . . . The Comintern, anxious to save face, belittled the importance of its setback, forecast a new revolutionary situation in Germany, and encouraged 'ultraleft' policies."[41]

More than nine thousand miles away, in Santiago, these events would have a powerful impact too on the aging Recabarren and the fledgling party he headed. On December 13, 1924, over his strenuous objections, six young "ultraleftists" were elected to the party's Executive Committee. On December 19, Recabarren rose early and, while Teresa prepared breakfast, went into his small study. Minutes later Teresa heard a single shot and went in to find him dead, a bullet through his forehead.

His suicide consolidated the power of the Russian-oriented leadership of the party. Forced underground by Ibáñez a few years later, the party became even more conspiratorial, and enmeshed in an international web. A final circumstance made the party almost totally dependent on the Russians: the collapse of the nitrate industry in the Great Depression. The party's greatest strength was among workers in that industry, catechized by Recabarren years before. In 1930 nitrate provided 40,465 jobs; by 1933 that number was down to 8,137.

The party's dependence on outside help was made evident at its 1933 conference; there, at the prodding of the South American Bureau of the International, even the memory of Recabarren was smeared. A resolution passed at the conference said that "his conceptions of patriotism, of revolution, of the building of the party are, at present, a serious obstacle to fulfilling our mission." The resolution added that the party had to free itself from "the ideological ballast of Recabarren, a very serious ideological, political, and organic obstacle for the infusion of Marxist-Leninism into the Communist party."[42]

From that time forward, the Chilean Communist party never wavered in its fidelity to Moscow, earning for itself a reputation as the most slavish Communist party in the world beyond the Iron Curtain. Indeed, it was a loyalty openly proclaimed. In 1962, for example, Secretary-General Luis Corvalán Lepe said that "the communist movement has been, since its origins, essentially internationalist . . . in it, there has always been a guiding center in the best sense of the word, a center as vanguard of advanced ideas. . . . For a very long time now, that center has been there, in the Soviet Union." (He added that notwithstanding its role as "guiding center," the Communist party of the Soviet Union did not rule the Communist party in Chile.)

While perhaps not ruled from Moscow, the Chilean party did march in lockstep behind Moscow. A few examples: the party swallowed without a murmur the Russian Non-Aggression Pact with the Nazis (after their earlier, dutiful tirades against Hitler); it praised Stalin lavishly until Khrushchev denounced him in 1956 at the Twentieth Party Congress; but when Khrushchev fell, he fell also in Chile, so that his death in 1971 rated a single paragraph buried inside the official party newspaper, *El Siglo*; by contrast, that year an old biography of the life of onetime party secretary-general Ricardo Fonseca, written by Luis Corvalán, the man who succeeded him, was revived in a new edition, one containing a prologue with long quotes from the resurrected Stalin. The Chilean party also supported the Russian rape of Budapest in 1956, sided with the Kremlin against Tito and, later, Mao Tse-tung, and was the first in the entire noncommunist world to leap to defend the Russian invasion of Czechoslovakia in 1968.

Events in Moscow reverberated even in the internal organization of the Chilean party: in 1931 the party split into two groups (headed by Lafertte and Manual Hidalgo, the latter Recabarren's successor) as a result of the fight in the Comintern between Stalinists and Trotskyites.

In 1945 Moscow lashed out at "Browderism," the insistence of Earl Browder, secretary-general of the Communist party in the United States, on a peaceful evolution to socialism. One of the casualties was Carlos Contreras Labarca, who was accused of practicing this heresy for his role at the San Francisco conference creating the United Nations. Contreras Labarca, a former president of the Federation of Students, also represented an intellectual faction within the party now being challenged by a resurgent "proletarian" faction headed by the brusque and bruising Ricardo Fonseca, offspring of impoverished peasants.

The triumph of hard-liner Fonseca was Pyrrhic for the party, however: President González Videla could coexist with Contreras Labarca, but could not stomach the tough-talking Fonseca, and shortly afterward decreed the "Accursed Law" outlawing the party. Fonseca died of cancer in 1949 and was succeeded by a Stalinist, Galo González. When Khrushchev denounced Stalinism, González got the ax and was replaced in 1958 by Corvalán, who guided the party's ascending fortunes for the next fifteen years with much skill.

Pint-sized (5 feet 1 inch), a prolific writer, frequent speaker, and the affectionate father of four children, Corvalán was born in 1914 in the picturesque southern city of Puerto Montt. In 1936, in his second year as a grade school teacher, Corvalán, already a Communist, was fired from his job for making political speeches to workers in Iquique (where a young Santiago lawyer by the name of Eduardo Frei was then editing the local newspaper). Although he would be given back his teaching rights two years later when the Communist-backed Popular Front government of Pedro Aguirre Cerda came to power, Corvalán preferred the world of journalism, rising through the ranks of *El Siglo* from sportswriter and politics writer until, in 1946, he became the editor.

In 1948 his prominence as editor of the Communist party newspaper cost him imprisonment along with other Communist leaders caught up in the collapse of the Radical-Communist alliance. Seven years later he would be jailed again, this time at Pisagua, the "concentration camp" that Ibáñez reopened in response to a Communist-called general strike, the first in the country's history. Pisagua symbolized for Communists an important lesson: they could afford to be successful—but not too successful. González Videla turned on them in 1948 when they became too successful at the polls and began to throw their weight around, openly and clandestinely. In 1955 they were corralled because their control of labor had become too alarming, as the general strike testified. Never again would Chilean Communists appear in conspicuously commanding roles, but instead would attempt to convert others to being their cat's-paws.

In 1961, Corvalán made his first try for public office, running for senator. He was elected from a "safe" southern district (Ñuble, Concepción, and Arauco), winning reelection eight years later.[43]

Corvalán embodied the deliberate ambivalence of the party on the question of violence, an ambivalence that began with the ouster of Recabarren, and that was complicated by two factors. The first was external: the party's meek submission to the dictates of Moscow, meaning that the PCCh zigged when the Kremlin zigged and zagged when the Kremlin zagged. The second was internal, rooted in the nature of the Chilean political system—its liberalism and its "bureaucratization." Liberalism so systematically inflated the currency of socialist thought in the Chilean debate that *conservative* finally became in the country's parlance a far "dirtier" word that *communist*. The "bureaucratization" of politics—government of and by politicians for their parties, which in turn arrogated to themselves the claim to represent the "people"— created malleable and available clients for Communist manipulation. So it was that the Communists were able to achieve their purposes by manipulating the levers of power of a progressively diseased system.

They began early. Hidalgo, who had succeeded Recabarren, was one of six Communists on the commission that drafted the 1925 constitution. They were the only ones to fight for continuation of the anarchic parliamentary system; and failing in that, they turned later to manipulating "strong" presidents. When they were unable to do that, they worked to undermine the power of the presidency by exacting high political prices in return for allowing his programs to get through Congress. They did the latter in 1938, with the Popular Front government they masterminded into being, and again in 1946, when they helped propel another Radical to the presidency, and themselves into positions of unprecedented (albeit brief) power. Eventually they destroyed the rightist forces within that party, and with them, the Radical party itself, converting it into a craven beggar at the banquet table of power. During the Radical years, new forces were set into motion to weaken their enemies by expanding the role of the state in the economy at the expense of an increasingly cowering private enterprise.

Nor was it devotion to democracy but cold self-interest that led the Communists to support General Ibáñez in 1952, Ibáñez, the very man who had persecuted them for a time a quarter of a century earlier, and would a few years later when they overplayed their hand. From Ibáñez they won the chance to rebuild their shattered forces, and finally, despite the midterm falling out, the repeal of the "Accursed Law," which had prostrated them.

Not even "hated" rightist Jorge Alessandri was immune to their blandishments. In 1963, near the end of his term, there were insistent published reports of an informal "nonaggression" pact between Alessandri and the Communists. Whether the pact existed or not, the fact is that Communist fortunes flourished during his administration, and Chile was in that same year one of two countries in the hemisphere opposing the break in diplomatic relations with Castro because of his persistent attempts to subvert the Venezuelan government of President Romulo Betancourt. The Alessandri years were not only a period of unfettered freedom for the Communists, but also a time when the first agrarian-reform law was enacted, the beginning of the end for the second of the two major pillars of conservative power.

Next, the Communists courted the Christian Democrats, a party as ripe for plucking as the Radicals before them. Where the Radicals succumbed because of their greed for power, the Christian Democrats did out of commitment to their fuzzy brand of humanist Marxism. In August 1965 Corvalán wrote an open letter offering to support the Christian Democrats provided they constituted a government of the Left. Shortly afterward the Communists followed with a tantalizing display of comradely cooperation: they gave the Christian Democrats the votes they needed to get one of their pet projects through a recalcitrant Senate (the Socialists abstained, and the Radicals and the Right openly balked). The project: funds for the Centers for Mothers and Neighborhood Councils, one of the public-involvement schemes of Frei's "Popular Promotion." The Christian Democrats tripped over themselves to hail the Communists for their patriotism. Bernardo Leighton, the man then second in command in the Christian Democrat power structure, said, "We could not remain silent in the face of this service which they [the Communists] have done for the country."

Little noted in the exulting was an analysis presented to the PCCh's Central Committee six months earlier by José González, then number two man in the party. "What's at stake here is that we must be IN the masses. We must be where the bulk of the masses are . . . not to serve the interests of the government party, but to give these organizations their true class character and instill in them fighting spirit."[44] In other words, the Communists saw in these organizations a chance to shape them into pliable mass battering rams in the class war, supplementing their control of labor, their formidable grip on the loyalties of youth, and their growing influence in the newly emerging peasant movement.

The Communists' control of labor dated back to the days of Recabarren. It was intensified following the 1936 creation, under their auspices, of the Chilean Workers Federation,* a potent factor in turn in the formation of the Popular Front coalition that year. Ironically, it was not until Marxism would be in power that a half century of Communist

---

* Central Unica de Trabajadores—CUT, sometimes given the more literal translation, Central Workers' Confederation. Both are used in this book.

hegemony over labor would be challenged. As for youth, by 1970 nearly half the party's total membership was in its youth organization, headed by a "youth" named Gladys Marín, then thirty-one-years-old, six years over the statutory age for membership in the Communist Youth (JCC). Although the Communists never could wrest control of the student federations from the Christian Democrats, they did the next best thing: they converted the federations into disciples of their causes.

Until the 1950s, the Communists ignored the rural area, but a change in the voting law in 1952 gave them grand new opportunities,[45] and they moved swiftly to capitalize on them. In 1960 Corvalán asserted that peasants made up 20 percent of the party's "fighters," and in agricultural provinces that percentage rose to 50 percent.[46] Of particular interest to the Communists were the migrant laborers or the landless contract laborers. To capture their loyalties, the Communists unleashed a new phenomenon until then unknown in Chile: *tomas*, the illegal seizure of land by force, a tactic later preempted by the extreme leftists and one that would return to haunt the Communists once in power. In 1961 the Communists organized the First Congress of Peasants and out of that came the National Peasant Federation. Communist-inspired agitation in the countryside and the reformist impulses sponsored by the Alliance for Progress, then in its period of ecstasy, were the decisive forces impelling passage of an agrarian-reform law. Although the Communists would later be upstaged by the Christian Democrats, who would command a majority in the countryside, the Communists were effective in mobilizing the most volatile and aggressive of the peasant groups: the migrants and contract laborers.

From the outset the Communists used carrot-and-stick tactics with the Christian Democrats, changing tactics but rarely retreating. "Push them! Push them!" Corvalán had told a party congress early in Frei's regime, "until their measures are our measures."[47] In 1968 an Italian Communist, Giuliano Pajetta, would write in *L'Unita*, the offical newspaper of the Italian Communist party, remarks he said were made to him by "Chilean comrades" during a trip to Chile: "For us Christian Democracy is not the principal enemy, and that is a difference of orientation between ourselves and the Socialists. . . . The principal enemy is the Right, including the Right within Christian Democracy."[48]

How well the strategy worked—marooning moderates within the ranks of the Christian Democrats, much as they had done with the Radicals years before, by cooperating with the "progressive" elements of those parties, boycotting "reactionaries"—would soon be abundantly clear.

In February 1969 Renán Fuentealba, once again president of the Christian Democrats, said that as far as he could see, "our enemy is the Right."

A year later, with Allende in La Moneda, the Spaniard who had become Allende's "gray eminence," Joan Garcés, could cluck of the Christian Democrats that they had been "moved by a sincere will to carry out social changes and showed themselves to be an anticonservative and populist political movement."[49]

Burrowing from within, the Communists, then, had little need to resort to violence, a state of affairs which elicited extravagant testimonials to their respectability. As early as 1960, two U.S. authors wrote: "In the U.S. we recognize in communism a dreadful threat to the enjoyment of privileges, the intellectual and cultural developments and freedom which our high material standard of living has made possible. Chilean advocates of reform, on the other hand, see in communism one of the possible means of achieving the physical prosperity which is the necessary point of departure for the fuller total life they ultimately envision for their country."[50]

But although it is true that they rarely resorted to violence, they never renounced it. The tone of Communist party strategy was set early, at the Eighth Party Congress in January 1927, three years after Recabarren had been sent to his grave. "The party will strengthen the process of bolshevization," a manifesto read. "Communists do not enter Parliament in order to consecrate the capitalist regime, but to destroy it. The proletariat's emancipation will be achieved, not by democratic but by revolutionary methods. Its liberation lies not in Parliament, but in the Soviets." During the abortive naval revolts of 1931, Galo González—the Stalinist Corvalán would years later replace as secretary-general— reportedly urged rebels to shoot their officers so "there would be no turning back."[51]

Stalin's denunciations of Browderism in 1945 pushed the party into a renewed hard-line posture, a posture that would soon afterward send it hurtling into a near fatal abyss of illegality. Then, in 1960, at the Twentieth Party Congress in Moscow, the Kremlin dictated a switch in tactics to "peaceful coexistence," based on Khrushchev's boast that communism would bury capitalism in peaceful competition. The following year, Corvalán published a series of articles in the Communist magazine *Principios*, later collected in a booklet called *Nuestra Vía Revolucionaria*, in which he echoed Moscow's thinking: "The triumph of the Popular Front in 1938 and of the Democratic Alliance in 1946 demonstrated, precisely, the possibility that the worker class and the people of Chile could win the government by a path which is not that of insurrection." In the same publication, Corvalán ruled out as "sectarian" and "leftist"—two epithets then in vogue in international communism—moving along parallel electoral and armed paths. "Besides," he said, "such tactics could expose the popular movement, or a part of it," to retaliation by superior armed force.

But he did not rule out altogether the resort to arms, which he said could occur "at the opportune moment through the action of the masses on a grand scale" and which would include "attracting [that is, subverting] a grand part of the army to the revolutionary side."[52] That, in fact, is precisely what did happen in the final phase of the Allende regime, with the creation of *cordones industriales* ("industrial belts") as a Maginot line of Maquis-type guerrillas encircling Santiago, and the increasingly bold attempts to drive a wedge between military enlisted men and their officers.

Despite their remarkable success in bending Chilean institutions, politics, and opinion to their purposes, the Chilean Communists were not altogether comfortable with the "peaceful-way" theme. At the 1969 Congress of Communist Parties in Moscow, the Chileans tried, unsuccessfully, to have the slogan changed to revolution "without arms." That slogan would allow for a type of violence they were already practicing: seizure of farmlands, street riots, wildcat strikes. Corvalán gave a clear indication of his "devotion to legality" in a statement on strikes: "Our party has pointed out the good sense of the presentation of simultaneous demands in different branches of industry, coordinating movements and strikes, in many cases without waiting for the expiration of contracts, ignoring the Labor Code wherever that code would tie our hands."

On the *tomas*, the illegal land seizures: "Our party has been and is also the principal organizer of the actions of the rural workers in the seizures of land."

On the *vía pacífica* (peaceful way): "*La vía pacífica* presupposes class struggle and not class cooperation; not a friendly coexistence between exploiters and the exploited; nor renouncing the resort to arms if that should be necessary."

Again, at the Twentieth General Congress of the Socialist Party, speaking on behalf of the Communists: "The struggle for the conquest of power is in full bloom, and has multiple forms of expression. It is carried out within and outside of the bounds of bourgeois legality and includes not a few acts of violence, organized and responsible, as have been the land seizures."

Again, in *Nuestra Vía Revolucionaria*: "There are those who identify *la vía pacífica* with legal or constitutional channels, a completely mistaken idea. Believers though we are in the *vía pacífica*, we want at the same time for the worker and popular movement to break with the ballast of legalism and be guided, rather than by laws and a constitution promulgated by the bourgeoisie, by their own class interests, taking into account the concrete situation at each juncture."[53]

With such a vision of "legality" or morality, it was, of course, a short jump to jettisoning earlier reluctance to move on parallel armed and electoral paths. "We must be prepared," Corvalán wrote in 1971 (in the characteristically-convoluted style of communist dialecticians), "for any change in the situation, and therefore, for moving out on the other path [that is, violence]. When we speak of preparing for any change in the situation, and therefore to move out on the other path, should that time come, the way of violence, we are referring, above all, to the necessity of having ideological and political clarity; of studying the art of revolution, in any and all of its forms, of the work of the party in relation to the armed groups and also that the party understand that, even having won its legality, not to show all of itself and its work but to continue its triple facets—legal, clandestine, and secret."

Nor did Corvalán change his tune once Allende had reached power. In May 1972 he said that "under certain conditions, if the path of the revolution is obstructed by the opposition, it may become necessary to resort to armed struggle."[54]

Indeed, the Communists began "preparing" early for the "eventuality" of violence, organizing in the late sixties armed groups called the Ramona Parra Brigades (named for a popular Communist folksinger).

By means legal, clandestine, or secret, the goal never changed, not before they would finally control the citadel of government, nor even afterward: "All power to the Popular Unity," Corvalán proclaimed six months after Allende took office. Not just control of the presidency, which they had won by a precarious margin; but control of the economy, which they would set about by means fair and foul to achieve, and control of the Congress, the courts, the armed forces, and, finally, the whole of Chilean life.

It was a style reminiscent of Lenin's over fifty years earlier, when he cried, "All power to the Soviets," the worker and soldier councils that were the cannon fodder of revolution. Like Lenin, Corvalán had curmudgeonly and highly suspicious partners to beguile, the better to manipulate them.

Unlike Lenin, Corvalán never had a chance to amend that cry to "All power to the party!"[55]

Of all the elements in Chilean society, none other managed to enjoy the fruits of democracy more while barking at it incessantly than the Chilean Socialist party. Unlike the Communists, the Socialists were never jailed or hounded or forced to cringe in hiding as legal outcasts. Unlike the Communists, they never relented in demanding the dismemberment of the bourgeois democracy that protected them.

They were for nearly forty years the companions of convenience of the Communists—a companionship contrived mostly by the Communists, who tempered their own distaste of it for the sake of necessity; and scorned by the Socialists, who profited the most and contributed the least. The companionship was of the sort that must have compelled the Communists to ask themselves, plaintively and often, with friends like these, who needs enemies? At the end their Socialists friends were in fact their deadliest enemies.

Unlike the Communists, the Socialists were neither well organized nor well disciplined, although in later years they would not only conduct party affairs in the shadows of secrecy, but be notoriously autocratic—little rank-and-file participation existed in their decision process. Nor did they ever develop a leader of sufficient stature to surrogate for the ideology they never had—unless revolutionary nihilism can be an ideology.

It was a party made for a man of ingratiating, wily, and shallow ways. It was a party made for Salvador Allende.

Allende was, indeed, one of the men who, on April 19, 1933, in the dark days following the fall of the short-lived Socialist Republic, founded the Socialist party. It was not really so much a new party as leftovers from the deeply divided Communist party, torn by the dissension between Trotskyites and Stalinists, and fragments of the Socialist parties that had supported Marmaduke Grove. In its first pronunciamiento, the founders said that "the party adheres to Marxism as the method for interpreting reality and recognizes the class struggle as the motive force of history." In the same declaration, the party criticized the Second and Third Internationals. For Marxist Debray and others, this represented one of the crucial differences between the Socialists, with their limited vision of revolutionary solidarity, and the internationalist communists. (The Chilean Socialists envisioned a Continental Federation of Socialist Republics.)

In point of fact, criticism of the Second International was beating a dead horse—Lenin, Trotsky, Rosa Luxemburg, and others had buried it years before with the outbreak of World War I. As to the Third International, it happened that Trotsky had himself broken with it only one month before the founding of the Chilean Socialist party. He did so in anger over the Comintern's position on the rise to power of Hitler in Germany; for Trotsky, that was "not a temporary reverse or a tactical setback, but a decisive strategic defeat, which would leave the working class prostrated and paralyzed for a whole epoch." For the Comintern, Hitler's "victory [was] devoid of significance" and the strategy and tactics of the German Communist party were pronounced "flawless from beginning to end, and it [the Comintern] forbade any Communist party to open any debate over the issue."[56]

A child of heresy, the Chilean Socialist party remained forever an apostate in the eyes of orthodox Marxists, at least to those who looked to the Kremlin for orthodoxy. The Socialists fought bitterly with the Communists during the period of the Russian honeymoon with Hitler. Chilean Socialists made no secret of their admiration for the later "apostates": Tito, then Mao, and even later, Castro (during the period when the Russians had not yet brought Castro to heel and he continued to export violence in defiance of "peaceful coexistence"). So the Socialists were as heretical toward Moscow as their Communist countrymen were mincing, a fact that all by itself should have kept them permanently separated.

If the Communists displayed "the patience of ants and the political flight of eagles," in the phrase of Chamudes, then the Socialists, left to their own devices, would have immolated themselves much sooner than they finally did, because they possessed neither patience nor finesse. The Communists saw to it, however, that they would rarely be left to their own devices. In their very first fusillade, the Socialists said a "dictatorship of the working class" would be unavoidable during the total transformation of society, a challenge to rattle more than just the teacups of little old ladies.

In the early years, the Socialists were more coalition than party, a loosely knit coalition of Trotskyites, anarchists, utopian socialists, and romantic Marxists. In 1933 they supported the candidacy of their nominal leader, Marmaduke Grove, but with the death of Matte in 1935, two upstart names were beginning to insinuate themselves: Oscar Schnake for his ideas, Salvador Allende for his astuteness. The two of them teamed to rebuff the first feelers of the Communists, anxious to form a Popular Front for the 1938 elections.

The Communists were not easily put off. First, they maneuvered the Socialists into joining them in supporting the senatorial candidacy of a journalist named Juan Luis Mery, who had been ordered expelled from the country by the courts. Next, the Communists softened the resistance of the Radicals by demonstrating how "disinterestedly" they would support a non-Communist candidate of the Left. Next, they worked on the vanity of Grove, joining in a street chant they helped make popular: "Quién manda el buque . . . ? Marmaduke!" ("Who captains the ship? . . . Marmaduke!" In Spanish, it forms a singsong rhyme.) When the Radicals decided to join the Popular Front, the Socialists found themselves stampeded and the five leftist parties (Communists, Socialists, Radicals, Democrats and the Radical Socialists) joined in propelling Aguirre Cerda into the presidency at the head of one of the world's first Popular Front governments.

The first split in the party occurred shortly after Allende and two other Socialists jumped aboard the bandwagon of power, taking cabinet posts in the new government. César Godoy, defeated earlier in a challenge to Grove's command of the party, led a faction out of the party, charging that the party had prostituted itself and was losing credibility among workers; Godoy and his Socialist Workers party would later join the Communists.

A similar squabble over participation in the government split the party again, in 1944, this time with Grove pulling out and Allende assuming control of the party.

Endless internecine warfare and the lack of a coherent program had cost the party not only the labor movement—assiduously cultivated by the Communists—but almost political life itself. In the 1946 elections the Socialists polled a meager 12,000 votes, 2.54 percent of the total cast; only one year earlier, in congressional elections, the Socialists had obtained 57,418 votes or 12.76 percent of the total; and five years earlier they had won 16.69 percent, a percentage they would not again see until 1971, when there was a Socialist in the presidency.

Out of the tumult of that year emerged the most charismatic rival Allende would ever face—and eventually vanquish—within the ranks of the party: Raúl Ampuero. Ampuero, backed that year by Allende, blueprinted a party program that narrowed the ideological gap between themselves and the Communists and paved the way for twenty years of enforced cohabitation between the two within the same electoral tent, culminating in Allende's triumph. There would be later splits and purges (including the ouster of Ampuero himself)[57]—with Allende the protagonist in most of them—but the basic hard line of the party was set.

As Marxist Labrousse has observed, a study of the party's behavior over the years "reveals a very considerable distance between theoretical formulation and concrete policy," in contrast to the Communists' behavior. For example, the Socialists were able to rationalize support of Ibáñez in 1952 and of the neofascist/populist/*sui generis* Argentine dictator, Juan Perón, on the grounds of affinity with "nationalism" in Latin America.

The combination of "respectability" (the Socialists were never outlawed), ideological anarchy, and elitist style may account for the party's attractiveness to Chilean "intellectuals." They were strong in the University of Chile, theoreticians' havens such as the Development Corporation, and international agencies, including the Santiago-based UN Economic Commission for Latin America (CEPAL) and the Inter-American Development Bank (the first and long-time president Felipe Herrera, was a Socialist, as was the next highest-ranking Chilean in the bank, Orlando Letelier).

"Respectability" and ideological disarray notwithstanding, the party never wavered on one theme: its resolve to destroy the system of bourgeois democracy—and to do so by violent means.

The party's Twenty-first Congress, in June 1965, for example, attributed the defeat of the Popular Action Front at the hands of the Christian Democrats the previous year to the failure to focus the social struggle on the inevitability of "a decisive confrontation of classes." The Congress called for the creation of a Revolutionary Workers Front (FTR) with the FRAP as its political expression, to lead the struggle in the name of the working class and the "exploited masses" against the "bourgeoisie [middle class] linked to the native oligarchies and imperialism."[58]

Thus it was that in 1965 the Socialists singled out the middle class as one of their three deadly enemies. Their persistence once in power in trying to suffocate that class would lead to Allende's downfall.

"What means to use?" the Congress's resolution asked. "Our strategy discards out of hand the electoral route as a method for achieving our objective, the taking of power."

The Socialists did not rule out continuing to take advantage of what Lenin described as the "rotten freedoms" of the parliamentary system, and thus of continuing to take part in elections. "A revolutionary party, one which is truly revolutionary," the resolution said, "will give a revolutionary character and a revolutionary imprint to all its steps. . . . Insurrection will have to come when the leadership of the popular movement understands that the social process, which it has itself impelled, has reached maturity and is ready to serve as the midwife of revolution."

That was far from a random expression of momentary wrath. Allende and fellow Socialists Clodomiro Almeyda and Walterio Fierro were, that same year, the main proponents in Havana of the creation of the Latin American Solidarity Organization (OLAS), the organization dedicated to the violent overthrow of "bourgeois" governments.

For Carlos Altamirano, the signal for the onset of direct action was not long in coming. Altamirano found it in the continuing decline of the Christian Democrats and resurgence of the Left, as reflected in the municipal elections in the spring of 1967. "The conditions for guerrilla warfare, though they may not be as good as in other nations, are present in Chile," Altamirano proclaimed, and the Socialist party seconded him by sponsoring the establishment of OLAS in Chile, a statement and an act which demonstrated vividly that their "respect" for the country's hullabalooed democracy was pure hokum.

His record notwithstanding, Altamirano would manage to get away with being described as, for instance, a "concerned Socialist senator," and was quoted, a few years later, as saying: "Unfortunately, as a result of the tasks a legislator must perform and the spirit of life Congress imposes, a professional congressman is created who is the antithesis and negation of what an authentic revolutionary agitator should be.

This system of gradual and subtle assimilation unconsciously transforms one into support of the status quo versus being against it."

Altamirano was singularly immune to that assimilation process, before and after expressing such "concern." As noted previously (chapter 4 note 144), Altamirano, as the principal proponent of OLAS in Chile, was suspended from his seat in Congress in July 1967 for insulting the president and the armed forces and openly encouraging violence. The charges were later upheld by the Supreme Court.

That did not, however, deter the party from its sponsorship of violent solutions, although a fairly sizable chunk of the party, led by Ampuero Díaz, Allende's chief rival for power, did split off in protest to form the Popular Socialist party. At the Twenty-second Congress in Chillán, in November 1967, the Socialists banished any lingering doubts about their faith in democratic institutions.

"Revolutionary violence," the Congress proclaimed,

> is inevitable and legitimate. It springs necessarily from the regressive and armed character of the class state. It constitutes the only means which leads to the taking of political and economic power and to its ultimate defense and strengthening. Only by destroying the bureaucratic and military apparatus of the bourgeois state can the socialist revolution be consolidated.
>
> The peaceful or legal means of struggle (strikes, ideological, electoral) do not of themselves lead to power. The Socialist party considers them as limited instruments of action, an integral part of the political process which leads us to the armed struggle.[59]

At the same Congress, the Socialists also banished any lingering doubts about their attitude toward the middle class: "The national bourgeoisie is allied to imperialism and is, in fact, its instrument, and is, therefore, irreversibly counterrevolutionary." With those words, the party ruled out any possibility of transaction with "legalistic" forces, such as the Christian Democrats, still another attitude they would cling to stubbornly until their doom was irrevocably sealed.

There was one brief—but entirely tactical—retreat from this position, and a short one it was. At the party's June 1969 Congress, the *vía electoral* ("electoral path") forces of Allende won out over the *vía revolucionaria* forces of Carlos Altamirano. But only to the extent that the Socialists agreed to enter into an electoral pact with such "organizations and persons openly committed to the anti-imperialist fight and which are for the substitution of the capitalist regime by a socialist society."

Small wonder that when Debray would remark to Allende that his Socialist party "has had nothing to do with the European Social Democrats for a long time," Allende would agree and add: "Nor does it have anything to do with certain self-styled Socialist parties in Europe."[60] A respected political scientist put it bluntly: "The Socialists were vehement anarchists—and remember, Allende was a Socialist."[61]

THOSE WHO HATE, AND THOSE WHO STAND AND WAIT

Fidel Castro's seizure of power in January 1959 ushered in an era of new and frequently destructive mythologies in Latin America. None other would bloody the hemisphere more than the notion of the invincibility of dedicated guerrilla movements.

Castro himself fed the hoax, boasting that he would turn the Andes into the Sierra Maestra of the Americas. It was a boast founded on a fiction, the fiction that he had defeated the dictator Fulgencio Batista on the field of battle rather than in the sludge of Batista's own dissoluteness. Moscow finally muzzled Castro, in the late sixties, when Russian control over the Cuban economy became completely decisive. But by then virtually every country in the hemisphere had suffered the agonies of violence executed by those determined to get their messianic way at the point of a gun and emboldened by Castro to believe they could get away with it.

In no country did they succeed. No country, no matter how "liberal," was safe from them: Castro's first target was Venezuela, a country then constructing a solid but leftist democracy. By the time Ernesto (Che) Guevara went to his death in Bolivia in 1968, Castroite and Maoist theories about elite-led peasant uprisings had been discarded in favor of urban terrorism. It seems surprising, yet probably should not be, that the country which suffered the most ruthless bloodletting of all was the one most admired for its "Swiss-like" democratic past: Uruguay. Another widely admired democracy was not spared, either, despite the fast and deep pace of its socializing revolution. That country was Chile.

Before 1964 the apostles of violence in Chile were scattered among three or four tiny and ineffectual groups. The event that gave rise to the organization of a cohesive force dedicated to armed violence was the decision of the Socialist party at its Twentieth Congress in 1964 to expel a small group of youthful hotheads. The group was headed by two brothers, Miguel and Edgardo Enríquez Espinoza, whose father, Edgardo Enríquez Froeden, would later become chancellor of the University of Concepción and still later Salvador Allende's education minister. The young militants represented a peril to the party's efforts to appear "respectable" in the presidential elections in which their man Allende was running as a Socialist-Communist candidate. (At the very next Congress, a year later, the party would proclaim its belief in the inevitability of the armed struggle.) The Espinoza brothers and Bautista Van Schouwen formed the Marxist Revolutionary Vanguard (VRM), which shortly afterward subdivided into two other warring factions, one identified with Maoist ideology, the other a pro-Castro group, but both committed to armed violence.

In August 1965 the Castroite wing joined the dissident Communists headed by Luciano Cruz Aguayo and leftist "Christians" headed by Andrés Pascal Allende (son of the later deputy Laura Allende and favorite nephew of Salvador Allende) to found the Movement of the Revolution Left (Movimiento de Izquierda Revolucionaria—MIR). Eventually they would number between three thousand and fifty thousand, an estimated 40 percent to 51 percent of them trained in urban "warfare" tactics.

Luciano Cruz was the cutting edge of the MIR during its early years. His entire brief life was, in fact, a record of violence. In 1961, at the age of sixteen, he was leading street demonstrations of high school students in support of striking workers. The following year he entered medical school and immediately became an activist in the Young Communist Movement. But Cruz was too wild for the party's tastes, and he was expelled from it in 1963, after agitating among the *sin viviendas*, the homeless ones crowding into urban area slums. In 1965 he led student-worker clashes with the Carabineros in protests over a hike in bus fares. He was arrested for the first time following demonstrations a short time later protesting joint naval maneuvers between U.S. and Chilean units.

In the same year, Cruz led student storm troopers who drove visiting Sen. Robert Kennedy from the University of Concepción. The following year Cruz was arrested again, leading students supporting a strike of sanitation workers. In 1967 Cruz was elected secretary of the Concepción Students Federation.

On September 6, 1967, Cruz was arrested following rioting that lasted five hours. In the course of it, the U.S. Information Service library and offices were destroyed and a U.S. flag burned. A news photographer covering the riot was attacked and his roll of film seized. Cruz harangued his followers about the Peace Corps before being taken prisoner. En route to the police station, Cruz broke loose from the two men guarding him and ten others nearby and escaped. Cruz returned to the university to resume command of the rioting students, still waging a pitched battle with Carabineros. That night they proposed a "prisoner exchange": students for a Carabinero they had captured, Héctor Gutiérrez Orellana. Eventually Cruz was recaptured and spent several weeks in jail.

Those riots pushed the MIR to national prominence. At the MIR's Third Congress in December 1967, Edgardo Enríquez was elected to the top post, secretary-general, and Cruz was elected a member of the Central Committee and the National Secretariat. The new leaders gave high priority to rousing peasants and slumdwellers—and training clandestine paramilitary cadres. As early as 1964 there had been reports of two thousand Chileans receiving guerrilla training in Cuba and an additional 150 undergoing instruction in "the niceties of totalitarian policing" in Hungary.[62]

In 1967 Emilio Oelckers, director-general of the nationwide police detective force, Investigaciones, revealed that his men had located a training center for terrorists on the outskirts of Concepción. Oelckers said twenty university students belonging to the MIR had been receiving training in detonating high explosives, a prelude to a planned wave of urban violence.[63] In still another raid, in Guayacán, near Santiago, Carabineros seized arms, explosives, and a number of Socialists enrolled in the MIRista guerrilla training school. Among them was Adrián Vásquez, later named by Allende to head the Farm and Fisheries Development Bureau (INDAP—Instituto de Desarrollo Agropecuario).

Such guerrilla training centers were central to the MIR's strategic approach to "solving" Chile's problems. Secret MIR documents captured in 1969 included one dating from that period which said the "armed struggle" in Chile would be, from the outset, anti-imperialist and anticapitalist, and one which would exclude alliances with so-called progressives (then still busily wooing the MIR in the belief that they could be co-opted into the progressive movement—an error the Communists never made). The document predicted a long and irregular fight and said basic to it was "the formation of the revolutionary army and power."

Well over a year would pass before the MIR, and the even more reckless and radical splinter group broken off from it known as the MR 2, would swing into armed action. But when the MIR did, it marauded for several months with seeming impunity, leading violent seizures of city lands by squatters, robbing banks and supermarkets, capturing arms, committing arson, attempting to drive a wedge between military enlisted men and their officers, kidnapping, and even hijacking an airplane.

The MIR terrorists posed, for the most part, as Robin Hoods, much as Uruguay's even more ruthless Tupamaros had in their early days. "The MIR will return all this money to the peasants and workers," the leaders said after one bank robbery on January 23, 1970, "by investing it to arm and organize the armed apparatuses necessary to return to all the workers what has been stolen from them by the owner class of Chile, in other words, by founding a worker-peasant government for constructing socialism in Chile. This is still one more proof that the MIR has nothing in common with common crime." The statement was, in fact, a flagrant lie. MIR's "common crimes" included a brutal attack, on June 6, 1969, on Hernán Osses, publisher of the newspaper *Noticias de la Tarde* of Talcahuano. Osses was lured to a rendezvous at 1:15 A.M. and seized by three individuals, one of whom he identified as Luciano Cruz. He was taken to a cabin on the outskirts of Concepción and there stripped and beaten and his hair scissored off. His crime: attacking the MIR in his newspaper. Later, the Robin Hoods of the MIR threatened a woman journalist, Silvia Pinto, with the "Osses treatment" after she had tangled with Víctor Toro, a top MIR leader, in a television program.[64]

Gen. Vicente Huerta Celis, commander of the Carabineros and creator of the highly trained (and, for subversives, highly hated) strike force (Grupo Móvil), recalled later that he had succeeded in infiltrating the MIRista high command at that time to the very top. But he said his efforts to squelch them were repeatedly frustrated by political interference from leftist-leaning elements who dominated the Christian Democrat administration.[65]

Toro was another key figure to emerge from this period of violence. Born in Coquimbo in 1943, Toro brought to the revolution background as an authentic proletariat—one of the very few in it, in fact. He had worked as a miner, fisherman, and waiter, and possessed a burning zeal to destroy bourgeois society, which was forever alien to him. Toro would later become for Salvador Allende a political hair shirt, but one Allende could not bring himself to remove. (In fact, it was a hair shirt that Allende himself had fashioned, since Allende would be in office only ten days before he would order charges dropped against Toro and seven other MIRista fugitives, including his nephew, Andrés Pascal Allende, the Enríquez brothers, Luciano Cruz, and Van Schouwen. They had been long sought for their participation in the wave of robberies and other armed actions.)

Two others in that group deserve mention. One was Humberto Sotomayor. On November 13, 1969, Sotomayor had led a group of twelve guerrillas in a daylight assault on the Banco de Crédito in the upper-crust Providencia section. A few days later police cornered Sotomayor in a raid on the home of a French psychologist sent by the French government to teach at the University of Chile. Sotomayor escaped by threatening to pull the pin on a grenade, but a confederate was captured. The professor, Benjamin Fabre, said he knew Sotomayor was a MIRista, but did not know he had taken part in the bank heist. Fabre, who would later be deported, also said that he had been manhandled by police and even subjected to the *picana eléctrica*, a device used for applying electric shocks, usually to the genitals of the victims. The episode evoked cries of protest from the University Council and others, and formed part of what was already becoming a widespread pattern of interference by foreigners in Chile's internal affairs.

The other was Max Joel Marambio. Marambio had earned a reputation as a formidable gunslinger, a reputation which would land him, a few months following the presidential pardon, the job of chief of an illegal palace guard Allende had formed called the Grupo de Amigos Personales (GAP)—Group of Personal Friends. Marambio, a squat, pudgy man with a pug nose, puffy jowls, and a thick shock of curly black hair, had been trained in Cuba and used the pseudonym Ariel Fontanarosa. Eventually Marambio and other MIRistas would leave the GAP to be replaced by Socialists, but not before he had forged it into a swashbuckling, and feared, force numbering several highly trained pistoleros.

The MIR road to violence was, for the most part, mapped in the pages of the "party" publication *Punto Final*, and seconded by a cast of Marxist newsmen headed by Augusto Olivares, destined to become Salvador Allende's closest confidant and companion in death. (Olivares was then news director of the University of Chile's television network, one of three in the country. He was called to testify in connection with one MIRista bank robbery, and made little secret of his close ties to the MIR.)

Through much of 1967 and 1968, *Punto Final* lionized the murderous deeds of Uruguay's Tupamaros, then in their apogee. Such instigation was needed less by MIR's own small cadres of activists than by those the MIR proposed to "save," especially peasants. Peasants normally are singularly unresponsive to messianic messages of violence; but, as leftist writers Petras and Zeitlin observe, "The possibility of providing the link between dispersed peasants is, of course, very important for guerrilla movements . . . guerrilla mobility and selective use of violence against hated landlords or their henchmen creates [sic] bonds between the guerrillas and the peasants. . . ."[66]

In an August 1969 manifesto, the MIR said the primordial goal must be "to destroy the bourgeois legal superstructure and install a revolutionary government of workers and peasants, so as to lay immediately the groundwork for the construction of socialism." The same document said that goal could be achieved only through simultaneous armed and political class struggle, in the cities as well as in the countryside.

"From the strategic standpoint," the document read,

> the fight will be fundamentally rural, so as to assure stability and continuity of the armed struggle and permit the formation of a revolu-

tionary power and army and, at specified stages of combat, permit the carrying out of reforms in the interior of the liberated zones.

It will be fundamentally urban from a tactical standpoint because, despite the inherent difficulties, it is in the cities where the masses of working classes are concentrated.... All other forms of struggle, legal or illegal, will be used: infiltration of the armed forces, general strikes, creation of militias, etc.[67]

The MIR was, to an astonishing degree, successful in seducing those who, intoxicated already by the messages of "reform" so much in vogue, saw it as a group of youthful idealists fighting for "right and justice." Father Diego Palma, the thirty-three-year-old priest and leader of the "New Church" group of young clerics and nuns who seized Santiago's Cathedral in August of 1968, said he believed only the MIR revolutionists could effect the changes Chile "needed" because "only they have clean hands."

The MIR never, however, managed to seduce the far wilier Communists, who saw them as rambunctious hotheads compromising the delicate job of removing by more surgical means the enemies of Marxism. Although the MIR and Communists would come to an uneasy truce during the final stages of the Allende campaign and the years he was in power, neither ever trusted the other. The Communists were quick to charge the MIR with a major share of the blame in Allende's final downfall, probably an accurate judgment.[68]

Though the MIR was by far the most effective and unrelenting of the extremist organizations, the remaining leftists could scarcely forfeit the field of violence to them, nor did they. Even the Communists had their Ramona Parra Brigade. For the most part, however, the brigade remained covert while the Communists maintained their public pose of respect for legality.

Although publicly frowning on violence, the Communists were not above practicing it. Communist journalist Eduardo Labarca boasted that Communist goon squads had sent more than sixty right-wingers to the hospital during the 1970 electoral campaign. As for the Socialists, they had their Elmo Catalán Brigade (named for a former secretary of Socialist leader Carlos Altamirano; Catalán was killed while fighting with guerrilla forces in Bolivia in 1971). But the Socialists, like the Communists, kept their storm troopers in check and out of sight for the most part, using them instead as training cadres for clandestine paramilitary forces built up during the Allende years.

Eventually, there would be half a dozen significant underground organizations, including the right-wing Patria y Libertad (Fatherland and Freedom). It was the onset of three years of hatred and violence.

Nor were "civilians" idle. On February 9, 1968, Allende's sister Laura, a Socialist deputy, led 340 families in seizing vacant lots in Santiago, lots they finally held after a three-hour pitched battle with Carabineros. Not to be upstaged, the Communists showed up with one thousand families and later the Christian Democrats themselves installed a group of "their" families on the spontaneously expropriated lands, this time aided by Carabineros. (It was the beginning of the practice of using Carabineros to connive in breaking the law, a practice that was made routine by Allende and one that would build in Carabineros pent-up resentments which made them among his deadliest enemies in the end.)

In a country with an acute housing shortage—a condition only aggravated by Christian Democrat oratory promising quick, but impossible, solutions—once such lawlessness had been uncorked, it could not be contained. A few weeks after Laura Allende led the Santiago seizure, another Socialist deputy, Luis Espinoza Villalobos, led seventy families onto a plot of land two miles from the center of the southern fishing and lumber city of Puerto Montt. The following morning, at four o'clock, a force of two hundred Carabineros moved in to dislodge the squatters. Inevitably, reports of conflict abounded as to who did what to whom first or when, but few debated the aftermath: eight dead, twenty-six wounded.

The Left immediately baptized it "the Puerto Montt Massacre," and began a campaign to pin responsibility for it on Edmundo Pérez Zújovic, who had only shortly before been tapped to replace Leighton as interior minister. At the time of the clash, Pérez Zújovic was in Santiago, nearly seven hundred miles to the north. The order to dislodge the squatters had been given by a provincial chief who had not even consulted him, and been carried out by Carabineros inexperienced in riot control. (One reason the crack Grupo Móvil had earned the wrath of the far Left was that it efficiently broke up riots without resorting to anything meaner than tear gas and nightsticks, thus depriving the extremists of "martyrs.")

But the Left was not alone in attacking Pérez Zújovic. He also came under fire from the left wing of his own Christian Democrat party, ever ready to repudiate anything or anyone with the taint of "law and order." Jaime Ravinet, president of the Federation of University Students (FECH) and a Christian Democrat, issued a statement shortly after the incident saying that "the continuance of Pérez Zújovic in the post of minister constitutes a permanent danger of the repetition of repressive measures which will occasion painful consequences for workers and students." Renán Fuentealba, then in the party's presidency, proposed to Frei that Pérez Zújovic be removed for the good of the party. And Radomiro Tomic, emerging as the visible leader of the party's left wing, said the Puerto Montt incident ruled out any possibility of Pérez Zújovic being the party's presidential nominee. The possibility had been actively discussed by those within the party who believed the only hope of stopping the Left was by putting forward a candidate the resurgent Right could support. To Tomic, such an opening to the Right was, of course, anathema.

The campaign of slander against Pérez Zújovic did not let up even after he had been bypassed as a presidential candidate. It ended finally with his murder in 1971, a crucial turning point in the construction of the historic gallows on which the Left would itself perish.

Pérez Zújovic, the victim of this vilification, was a self-made man from a family wiped out financially by the collapse of the nitrate industry. He was forced to quit school after the sixth grade to go to work as a bricklayer. The father of nine children, a mild-mannered and devout man, he was unflinchingly anti-Communist, but equally committed to Frei's version of noncapitalist economics. He once remarked to an interviewer that he was greatly pleased to read in a U.S. magazine that Chile's Corps of Carabineros was rated the best police force in Latin America and one of the four best in the world. Not surprisingly, he was—in contrast to his predecessor, Leighton—one of the few men who backed Carabineros chief General Huerta in what was now becoming a successful war against extremist violence, and that, of course, made Pérez Zújovic a marked man.

According to leftist folklore, the underground extremists, and chiefly the MIR, "patriotically" decided to call a truce to their violent activities in June 1970, just three months before the presidential elections, because they sensed the coming of the "proletariat" triumph. A more sober evaluation would note that all of the top leaders were by then in hiding, and their training camps had been smashed. On May 22, 1970, for example, a force of 1,500 Carabineros and soldiers uncovered and raided a guerrilla camp in a heavily wooded area near the port of Corral, south of Valdivia.

That raid also served to reveal the deep crack in the facade of respectability of the leftist coalition backing Allende. Aniceto Rodríguez, then secretary-general of the Socialist party, and Rafael Tarud, coordinator of the Popular Unity campaign, both repudiated the existence of the camp. The political committee of the Socialist youth wing, however, issued a statement saying, "We understand that political-military training of the worker class and of students is a legitimate means of responding to the repressive apparatus of the bourgeois state. . . ." It was a defiant statement echoing one made two months earlier by Víctor Toro, who then described the squatters, a movement actively supported by the Socialists, as "militias which, together with other revolutionary organizations, finally will take power and form a government; not one step at a time, but when a Revolutionary Army of the People destroys the military apparatus and the grip of the overlords, the bourgeois state."[69]

Such battle cries, and the actions that accompanied them, were more than mere episodes in the Chilean drama. Rather they were, as Marxist Labrousse points out, "an element which contributed to the radicalization of the popular struggle on all levels and, as such, helped to convert the campaign into something more than a mere electoral contest."[70]

As the country would soon discover, that "radicalization" was now an irrevocable sentence.

Of all the political parties and political forces, native and foreign, that played a role in the rise to power of Marxism in Chile, none other was fairer in its youth, or fouler in its senility, than the Radical party. By the time the party weaseled its way into power in 1938, it was intellectually spent, most of the goals it had set for itself having been achieved. All that remained were the instincts: the instinct to be decent, to be democratic, to be progressive, to be open. Because the party developed no new ideologies to replace the old ones, it attracted the independents and mavericks who shunned dogmatism. But without a cause to champion, it also forfeited the chance to lead. Because it was a genuinely democratic party, it attracted the men who believed most deeply in democracy. It was, in a word, the purest expression of liberalism—nineteenth-century liberalism, a brand of liberalism which may yet acquire new luster. Inevitably, such a party (and such men) fell prey to the powerbrokers, the manipulators, the schemers.

Following the debacle of 1964 (when the party's presidential candidate, Julio Durán, polled a feeble 4.98 percent of the vote), the party was ripe for opportunistic plucking. The stage was set at the 1965 convention, when Sen. Humberto Enríquez, a man as decent as he was ineffectual, was elected to lead the party. The anti-Durán forces next managed to insert in the party's National Executive Committee a chameleonic man named Alberto Baltra Cortés, while welcoming back into their ranks a number of leftists who had supported Allende in 1964 over the party's own candidate. (One of them, Alejandro Ríos Valdivia, would later be rewarded with the post of defense minister in Allende's first Cabinet.) When the party's convention rolled around in June 1967, there was no question any longer which group was in command. Several "right-wingers," including Chamudes, were expelled.

Baltra, a professor of economics who had served in González Videla's Cabinet, had won the affection of the far Left in 1958 when he moved in the Chamber of Deputies for the repeal of the "Accursed Law," outlawing the Communist party. He was also warmly remembered for his defense of the Berlin Wall, a stance of "independence" which earned him the presidency of the Chilean-Soviet Institute of Culture. He also was a board member of several mining and industrial concerns. A tribute, perhaps, to the irrepressible masochism—or ingenuousness—of capitalists. (Baltra would later repent his coziness with the Communists, and once Allende was in power, an event to which he contributed in no small way, he would become one of Allende's most fearless and effectively outspoken critics.)

Baltra's political position was strengthened enormously in December 1967. With the support of the Communists and Social Democrats, he upset Christian Democrat Jorge Lavandero in a special election for the Senate seat from the provinces of Bío-Bío, Cautín, and Malleco. This not only gave the opposition a two-thirds majority in the Senate, enough to block any Frei initiatives, but also emboldened the Radicals to believe that they once again could hold the trump card in the formation of any alliances for the 1970 presidential elections. (In the municipal elections earlier that year, the Radicals had bounced back to become the country's second-largest single party, a distinction of utterly no value and one they would never again achieve; it was valueless because no party would again matter by itself, whether first, second, or whatever. More to the point, in those elections *all* parties gained ground, all at the expense of the still lionized Christian Democrats.)

A youthful Rasputin was emerging in the party's ranks during this period: Patricio Valdés Bastías, president of the Revolutionary Radical Youth ("Revolutionary" was added at his insistence). For seven years before this, he had served as the salaried vice president of a communist-front organization called the World Federation of Democratic Youths. It was a measure of Valdés's calloused affection for communist causes that he had served his apostleship in Budapest, scene, of course, of the bloody Russian massacre of 1956.

By the time of the fourteenth national convention of the Radical party in June 1969, the stage had been so carefully set that it would become more lynch mob than political assembly. Four days before the convention opened, the Communist party newspaper *El Siglo* could safely "predict" in its June 23 edition that Baltra would be proclaimed Radical standard-bearer for the presidential elections and add that "his nomination is not intransigent. The PR [Radicals] will propose his name to the other parties of the Left, but will point out that in the last of cases, the PR would back another candidate of the Left if the UP [Popular Unity] coalesces favorably."

A few details remained, however, before the Radicals would consummate what would become their morganatic marriage with the avowed Marxists, the Socialists and the Communists. Scores of "objectionable" delegates to the convention were barred, among them the grand old man of the party, Pedro Enrique Alfonso, a lifelong Radical, several times minister, former vice president, and his party's 1952 candidate for the presidency. The grounds: "behind in his dues."

Next the convention elected as president of the party Carlos Morales Abarzúa, former president of the Chilean–North Korean Institute of Culture.[71] Senator Enríquez, who had presided over the party during the period of leftist takeover, was moved then to protest: "The Marxist fifth column has demonstrated its effectiveness. Morales has taken over the party. There is nothing left but to organize a radical movement in exile."[72]

Next the Radicals moved to purge their ranks of all remaining "retarded" (that is, rightist) elements, headed by Julio Durán, the 1964 presidential candidate. Valdés and Baltra had signed a pact a few days before the convention opened pledging to join forces in that purge, a pact denounced on June 24 in the newspaper *La Segunda*. Once the convention opened, the purge was put in motion, and according to the Communist newspaper *El Siglo*, it was Valdés who focused the issue most sharply: "You delegates," he said, "will have to choose between continuing to enjoy the support of the sound and revolutionary forces of youth or to continue with the gentlemen of the Right." It was no idle threat: Valdés's youth organization had already voted 582–34 to eliminate the "gentlemen of the Right." The convention quickly fell into line, voting 548–43 to oust Durán and a legion of his followers (who promptly formed a new party called Radical Democracy).[73]

True to *El Siglo*'s prediction, Baltra, then fifty-seven, was chosen as the party's candidate for president. For the gleeful onlookers of the far Left, he was in fact what he would become: a cat's-paw in an unholy alliance.

There was, inevitably, a cast of minor supporting actors. Chief among them was the Movement of Unitarian Popular Action (MAPU), headed by the principal strategist of Frei's agrarian reform program, Jacques Chonchol. Chonchol had returned from Cuba in 1964 to join those within the ranks of the Christian Democrats pushing the party ever leftward. Eventually, they formed a powerful coalition which included the ultraleftist "Rebels," the almost equally leftist *terceristas* (roughly, "third position"), and a galaxy of party elders including Renán Fuentealba, Bernardo Leighton, and Radomiro Tomic. Their thesis, warmly applauded by the Communists, was called "the noncapitalist path to development," a set of economic theses hardly distinguishable from those of avowed Marxists. For most of Frei's presidency, this leftist coalition held the balance of power within party councils. They even succeeded in thwarting Frei's plans to fire Chonchol for his flagrant agitation of the peasantry.

In November 1968 Chonchol turned the tables on Frei by resigning himself. The rest of the Rebels bided their time until after the March 1969 parliamentary elections. In May, making a mockery of their repeated protestations of fealty to the party that had elected them, they bolted to join Chonchol in forming MAPU. Among them were Sen. Rafael Agustín Gumucio V. and Sen. Alberto Jerez Horta, the latter elected with PDC votes only two months before; Deputies Julio Silva Solar and Vicente Sota, who had done so much to push the party leftward; and PDC Youth leader Juan Enrique Vega. On September 29, 1969, MAPU named Chonchol as its presidential candidate. But, in a move to make itself more appetizing as a vehicle of compromise to the coalition-hunting Communists, they named the better-known Gumucio as a "reserve candidate."

(The *terceristas* were somewhat more circumspect. They remained in the party long enough to use their influence to get left-winger Tomic nominated. In 1971 they bolted the party, formed another called the Christian Left [IC], and joined Allende's government. Among those who would go were three of Tomic's sons, his son-in-law, and former Christian Democrat Youth leader Luis Badilla, the man who had gained fame as a human megaphone for Tomic.)

Next, in descending order, came the Social Democratic party, which, as Régis Debray points out, "bears no relation to international Social Democracy nor to traditional social democratic concepts."[74] This party was formed in 1966 by Patricio Hurtado, the Christian Democrat deputy who was the first ranking party member in modern times expelled, in his case for his avid propaganda work in Chile in behalf of Fidel Castro, precisely at a time when Castro was busiest insulting Frei. Hurtado's service to leftist causes was recognized the following year with a medal bestowed by the Vietcong and relayed by Castro.

As the presidential derby began, Hurtado's miniparty was joined by the Democratic National party (PADENA), founded in 1960 from the remnants of leftist elements that had backed President Ibáñez. PADENA began with a bang, mustering nearly 7 percent of the vote in the 1961 parliamentary elections (in which it lost its six Senate seats but won a surprising twelve Chamber seats). The party backed Allende in 1964, but by the 1969 parliamentary elections it was all but spent, picking up a meager 1.94 percent of the vote and electing no one to Congress. Together the Social Democrats and PADENA would first plunk for the candidacy of Sen. Rafael Tarud Siwady, a runaway Socialist, and, as their second choice, Baltra.

Tarud rounds out the cast of supporting characters. The son of Syrian immigrants and economy minister in the mishmash government of Ibáñez, Tarud surfaced in April 1969 at the head of a miniglomerate called Independent Popular Action (API), made up of populists, retired military officers, and a miscellany of leftists. Tarud became API's hoped-for compromise candidate of what it expected would be an irreconcilably divided leftist movement.

API was very nearly right.

It is well to remember these minor players in the cast of characters, the ones who stood and waited. In the reports of countless newspaper, magazine, and academic commentators, the world was repeatedly assured that however sinister the Communist and Socialist Big Brothers might be, the democratic purity of the coalition was vouchsafed by these "democratic" partners. Reference was made especially and repeatedly to the "century-old" Radical party as the best guarantee of democratic purity.

And well it might have been, were it not that those wearing the finery of the party in the Allende procession were little more than the hollow mockery of a once proud name.

THE FATAL FLAW

The March 1969 elections were, by all lights, crucial for shaping the destiny of the country. In a logical and rational world, they might have been. But the Chile of 1969—in common with so many other places on the planet where politicking replaces statesmanship and dogmatism eviscerates debate—there was little room for logic or reason in the jockeying for political power. The elections were, nonetheless, crucial in the empirical sense that they shaped the Congress Allende would inherit and have to work with (see table 23) down to the last days of his regime and life.

The Christian Democrats, despite the advantages of power and the bonanza of record world copper prices, continued their decline; only the phenomenon of proportional representation allowed them to fare as well as they did in the enlarged Congress. The Radicals stagnated, while the Nationals, representing the revitalized Right, scored the most spectacular gains of all.

Both major parties of the far Left—Communists and Socialists— gained significantly. Interestingly, the six parties that would shortly join in the Popular Unity coalition polled 47.8 percent of the vote; subtract the Radical vote (13.5) and the result (34.3) comes within a few whiskers of what Allende would later get (36.2 percent) in the presidential elections. On the other hand, add that 13.5 to the National party's total, the result is 34.3, even closer to what it actually got (34.9). Such doodling powerfully suggests that the Radicals went the wrong way when they went left, and that the voters who stayed behind went right.

What those elections unmistakably demonstrated was that no one party could any longer hope to triumph alone. It was a lesson the Communists had long understood, and the Christian Democrats had not yet learned. Throughout the Frei regime, the Communists never

TABLE 23
COMPOSITION OF CONGRESS AFTER 1969 ELECTIONS
(Numbers in parentheses reflect results of 1965 elections)

PARTY	DEPUTIES		SENATORS		% OF OVERALL VOTE	
					1969	1965
Christian Democrats	55	(82)	22	(13)	31.0	43.6
National party	33	(9)[a]	5	(7)[a]	20.8	12.8[a]
Communist party	22	(18)	6	(5)	16.6	12.7
Radical party	20	(20)	8	(9)	13.5	13.7
Socialist party	15	(15)	4	(7)	12.7	10.5
Radical Democracy	3	(0)	1	(0)	na	—[b]
MAPU	1	(0)	0	(0)	na	—[b]
Social Democrats	0	(0)	1	(1)	.9	—[b]
Popular Socialist Union	0	(0)	2	(0)	2.2	—
PADENA	0	(3)	0	(1)	1.9	3.2
API	0	(0)	1	(0)	na	—[b]
Independents	1	(0)	0	(2)	0.1	0.2
TOTAL	150	(147)	50	(45)		

NOTE: Numbers in parentheses represent party totals following 1965 elections. The size of both the Chamber and the Senate was increased effective in 1969.

[a] 1969 figures represent combined totals of Conservative and Liberal parties, later fused into the new National party.
[b] These parties either were nonexistent in 1965 or did not present candidates.

Several developments affected the composition of the Congress before the 1973 elections:

—A Socialist won the seat vacated by Allende in 1970, keeping that party's Senate total constant at fifteen.
—The Christian Democrats lost eight of their Chamber seats in 1971 when the *terceristas* bolted the party to join Allende under the Christian Left banner.
—The Radicals lost another Senate seat to Durán's Radical Democracy party in 1970.
—The Christian Democrats retained a Senate seat and the Nationals gained one (at the expense of the Radicals) in special elections in January 1972.

really gave up the hope of teasing the Christian Democrats into an acceptably Marxist alliance of the Left. While the Socialists, with their characteristic intemperance, opposed Frei with all the resources at their command, the Communists used all the wiles at their disposal to seduce the Christian Democrats. In June 1966 the exasperated Socialists accused the Communists of "an unspoken understanding" with the Christian Democrats, "or, in the best of cases, a critical but officious support" of them. Their goal was ever the same: to nudge the Christian Democrats ever more onto Marxist terrain, there the better to compete with them for the loyalties of a rank and file made ever more responsive to the blandishments of Communist nostrums.

The strategy envisioned driving a wedge between the party's "progressives"—Leighton, Tomic, Fuentealba, and the youth faction—and the "reactionaries," led by Frei, Sen. Juan de Dios Carmona, and Pérez Zújovic. That strategy had worked with the Radicals, bending them to the Communists' purposes. (That strategy was also on the verge of working on September 11, 1973, too late for electoral pacts, but not too late for attempts to rescue Allende from the tomb of failure.) As late as May 1968 a Communist spokesman forecast an election alliance that would include "a good part" of the Christian Democrats, the Radicals, and the moderate Socialist parties (Ampuero's Popular Socialists and PDC outcast Patricio Hurtado's Social Democrats), as well as the bulwarks of the earlier FRAP coalitions, the Communists and Socialists.[75]

Frei's narrow victory in the 1968 PDC convention, coupled with Socialist refusal to pact with the bourgeois enemy, forced the Communists to shift their tactics—long before, as it happened, left-wingers among the Christian Democrats realized they were no longer wanted. In April 1969 the Communists tried, in vain, to persuade their rambunctious partners of the Left to put aside their pettifogging over candidates and close ranks in intensifying the "revolutionary struggle." "The first order of business," a Communist party manifesto read, "is to continue pushing the popular struggle, molding with action understanding among all advanced forces, wherever they may be [politically situated] at this time. Next, we should agree on a clear, concrete program and agree on what kind of popular government should be constituted. The matter of a candidate should come later."[76]

The manifesto was barely public when Tarud tossed his hat in the leftist ring as a candidate of transaction. Next the Radicals named Baltra. In August the Socialists settled for Allende. Next, on September 29, came MAPU's Chonchol-Gumucio parley. Finally, the following day, the Communists announced their "choice": the poet Pablo Neruda. The man who would become the 1971 Nobel laureate in literature (and who thirty-six years earlier had won the homage of the great Spanish poet and dramatist Federico García Lorca) was, for most of his life, a devoted Communist.

Neruda had been Chilean consul for seventeen years in Rangoon, Colombo, Batavia, Singapore, Buenos Aires, Barcelona, Madrid, Paris, and Mexico City. He would end his life as Allende's ambassador to France. The Spanish civil war fired his latent sympathies for communism, and he joined the Communist party in 1943. But even before formally joining, he had served the party clandestinely.[77] In 1945 Neruda was elected a senator on the Communist ticket, and in 1948, the party outlawed, he began a long series of travels that would take him to Russia, Eastern Europe, and China. In 1950 he shared the Moscow-conferred World Peace Prize with the American singer and political activist Paul Robeson and Spain's Pablo Picasso. In 1953, a year after his return to Chile, he was awarded the Stalin Prize.

Salvador Allende was a flawed candidate even before he reached the cannibalistic contest to choose a coalition contender. To begin with, his own Socialist party was badly fragmented. The upstarts of MAPU were stealing its extremist thunder among peasants, the MIR was stealing its thunder in the city slums and orchestrating a series of violent strikes.

At the party's national plenum in June 1969, the *vía electoral* wing headed by Allende and the *vía revolucionaria* wing headed by Altamirano reached an uneasy truce. Out of the convention came a compromise that would permit the inclusion within the future electoral alliance of non-Marxist parties—provided they supported Marxist strategies. "There is room in this grouping," the statement said, "for all parties, organizations, and persons openly committed to the anti-imperialist fight and who are for the substitution of the capitalist regime by socialist society." It was the final capitulation of the Socialists to the stealth-and-stalk strategies of the Communists. (A year before, at the one and only conference to ratify the warlike protocols of the Latin American Solidarity Organization in Chile, the Socialist senator Aniceto Rodríguez was chosen as president of the Chilean branch. But the Communists refused to sit at the same conference table with the MIRistas, a stance which threatened to destroy the precarious Socialist-Communist alliance once and for all, given the unanimous support for OLAS within the Socialist party.)

But the capitulation to Communist pragmatism was, as it would turn out, on paper only. As Marxist Labrousse observed, the hard-liners within the Socialist party retained an important influence, "if not the preponderant one," within party councils.[78]

One important consequence of this intramural feuding was to fuel the aspirations of Rodríguez, a man who had managed to rise through party ranks largely by remaining innocuous, a trait which would continue to characterize him afterward. For Altamirano's hard-liners, Rodríguez represented a more malleable quantity than the old fox Allende. The soft-liners saw in the younger and more moderate Rodríguez a more attractive alternative to Allende, a man they perceived to be a useless fossil, burned out in his three previous tries at the presidency.

Rodríguez, then party secretary-general, might have been proclaimed the party's candidate by acclamation in June 1969 had it not been for a Byzantine incident. Allende was then on a junket to North Korea, North Vietnam (where he was one of the last world Marxist leaders to see Ho Chi Minh alive), and Cuba, attempting (with very limited success) to enlist a reluctant Fidel Castro to his cause. Rodríguez backers planned to spring their acclamation surprise at a banquet they had organized in his honor.

A few hours before the banquet was to begin, a cable from Cuba arrived bearing Allende's name. It said: "Having learned acclamation [plans] independent groups [of the] Left and preparations reception my arrival, I declare: I am profoundly grateful [for] revolutionary loyalty of those who have remembered my name. I irrevocably decline any proclamation [my candidacy]. I believe there is no room for personalist postures in face of situation Chile and America, and much less in a militant of the Socialist party."

Rodríguez, as party chieftain, had to read the cablegram at the banquet. Hopes of proclaiming him by acclamation that night were, of course, dashed. The ploy gave Allende's men time to rally and regroup until the junketing leader could return a few days later. The irony is that this masterstroke of political tactics was, in all probability, not Allende's but that of one of his anonymous henchmen. As Marxist Labrousse points out, Allende never did deny that he was not the author of the cablegram.[79]

Two months later Allende won the support of his candidacy of Socialist regional organizations. Finally, on August 29, 1969, the party's Central Committee, the court of last resort, reluctantly agreed to name him Socialist party candidate. The vote: twelve in favor, thirteen absentions. From that moment forward, Salvador Allende was astride a suicidal bronco he never would manage to master.

On October 9, 1969, the Socialists and Communists organized a Committee of Coordination with an eye to creating the electoral alliance that would become the Popular Unity. Their first act was to form a committee to draft a program. The committee, made up of three representatives of each of the six parties in the coalition, completed its work on December 10. The result was a 4,800-word document replete with the usual pieties of electoral platforms, including several concessions to "women's liberation," evidently designed to overcome the traditional antipathy of Chilean women for Marxist candidates. The preamble promised the "most democratic political regime in the history of the country," but warned also that the UP had been formed not "for the simple substitution of one president by another, not to re-emplace one party with others in government, but to carry out the profound changes which the national situation demands." This was to be accomplished by "transforming present institutions in order to install a new system of power in which the working classes and the people are the ones who really exercise power."[80]

(To the uncritical eye, such heroic phrases have the ring of righteousness about them, until it is remembered that in the Chile of 1970, 38.1

percent of all Chilean, men, women, and children, were registered to vote, and 31.8 percent of them actually did vote, a turnout of 83.3 percent. By contrast, only 61.8 percent of the total voting population of the U.S. bothered to turn out to elect Richard Nixon in 1968, and the turnout figure for 1964, an all-time high, was 63 percent.[81] More on voter data later in this chapter.)

The constitution would be rewritten, Congress would be scrapped in favor of a unicameral "Peoples' Assembly," bureaucratic power would be decentralized, and the court system would be overhauled so that "a whole new concept of the judicial process [would] replace the existing individualistic and bourgeois one." (UP strategists, and especially the Communists, understood from the outset that the Congress and the courts represented the two insurmountable obstacles to achieving their ambition of total power. In point of fact, despite much brouhaha, they never dared change the constitution, Congress, or courts by legal means, but simply resorted to ignoring, defying, or subverting them. Apologists would complain of the difficulty of changing them when the government didn't have the votes to do so, a complaint which struck at the heart of Chile's ills under the Popular Unity government of Salvador Allende—namely, Allende's disregard for the realities of majority rule in a democracy.)

In economic affairs, the program envisioned the nationalization (expropriation) of all "basic resources" (copper, nitrate, and the like), as well as of banks and other elements of the financial system (insurance companies, loan companies), foreign trade, "large" distribution firms, and "strategic industrial monopolies." High priority also went to speeding agrarian reform.

Loose language—with sinister intent—also characterized an ominous passage on the mass media. The program said, "It is necessary to redefine [the] purpose" of the mass media, "putting emphasis on their educative role and ending their commercialization, and to adopt measures which allow social organizations the use of these communications media, eliminating the harmful effects of the monopolies." Strange language indeed, for two television networks were operated by universities and the third by the state, and every major political party had its own newspapers, radio stations, and magazines (a field in which the Communists excelled). The only "monopoly," in fact, was the glint in the UP's eye, the one it hankered to create.

In foreign policy, the program promised friendship with all nations, while leaving no doubt whatever who the enemy was: the United States. Besides genuflecting before the long and usual litany of leftist international and hemispheric shibboleths, the program specifically promised to "review, denounce, or renounce ... those treaties or agreements which involve commitments limiting our sovereignty, and, in particular, treaties of reciprocal assistance, pacts of mutual aid or other pacts which Chile signed with the U.S.A." As the framers roamed the world in search of targets for their righteous wrath, they found, coincidentally, only American villains: "Likewise, we shall condemn all forms of economic, political, and military aggression provoked by imperialist powers. Chile's foreign policy must be one of condemnation of North American aggression in Vietnam, and one of recognition of and active solidarity with the heroic struggle of the Vietnamese people." (No mention of the "heroic struggle" of the 19 million southerners then resisting the "blandishments" of the 22 million North Vietnamese.) The program said Chile would be especially sympathetic to those "colonized countries . . . fighting for their liberation and independence," yet had this to say of what, by then, had become the most conspicuous puppet state in the Americas: "In the same way, the Chilean people will demonstrate meaningful solidarity with the Cuban Revolution, which is the vanguard of revolution and construction of socialism in Latin America."

There was one other target, apart from the U.S., of Marxist wrath, though not mentioned by name in the document (only Cuba, Vietnam and the U.S. merited that distinction). That was Bolivia, governed since the previous year by a right-wing military government.

"The Popular State," the program said, "will remain alert before those threats to our territorial integrity and the country's independence, which are encouraged by the imperialists and by those groups of the oligarchy in power in neighboring countries who encourage expansionist and retaliatory pretensions as well as repressing their own people."

Tough talk coming from such peace-loving folk was aimed, of course, at discouraging the Bolivians in any ideas they might have of realizing their ninety-year-old dream of recovering their outlet to the sea, lost to Chile in the War of the Pacific. It was also aimed at the Peruvians, but to a lesser degree, because while the Peruvian military junta was still new on the job, its leftist leanings were already surfacing. And if the Peruvian generals were leftist, they couldn't be all that expanionist, retaliatory, or bad, could they?

The six parties making up the Popular Unity were the Communists, Socialists, Radicals, MAPU, API, and Social Democrats. Throughout the spring and early summer (October–late December) of 1969, skirmishing among them to agree on a candidate intensified. Allende, the best known among the contenders, was unable to muster a majority, mostly because of the deep-seated feeling that he was passé, over the hill politically. To this, he had a stock answer: "Just like Coca-Cola, I am a product already established. Everybody in the country knows Allende." A later collaborator, Carlos Briones, expressed it differently: "Allende was known from Arica to Magallanes. His rivals were just not marketable."

The Socialists backed Allende, while not ruling out the possibility of falling back on Rodríguez; they were flat out against Baltra, Tarud, or reserve-hitter Gumucio. The Communists were flexible, insisting only that the candidate who emerged must be backed by themselves, the Socialists, and Radicals. They added that they would accept any candidate supported by four of the six coalition partners. The Radicals pushed their man Baltra, and said no new names other than those already under consideration should be admitted. The tiny MAPU touted Chonchol or Gumucio, and the even tinier API and Social Democrats held out for Tarud. Only MAPU among them indicated it would accept Allende, but its acceptance was decidedly lukewarm.

On December 26, the still divided parties of the coalition published a pact of far-reaching and crucial importance, yet one that was little noted during the years Allende pranced in the presidency. The "Pact of the Popular Unity" proclaimed that the new government would be one neither of one man nor of one party, and that its decisions would be rooted not only in the parties that had constituted it, but also in the entire cluster of "popular organizations"—a concession that left room for the MIR and other terrorist organizations at that time very much underground. A few days later another document prescribed a campaign built on "ideological and practical confrontation with the government, Christian Democracy, imperialism, and the Right." A third and final document bound the candidate to adhere to the program of the Popular Unity and the aforementioned commitments, and bound him also to include in his cabinet three Communists, three Socialists, three Radicals, two from MAPU, and two from Tarud's two miniparties (which left two cabinet posts to the president's discretion). Allende would often boast of the heterogeneity of his Cabinet; he did not add that his hands were tied not only in this respect, but, and far more important, as to his independence in the presidency, even before he was selected as the UP's puppet candidate.

That selection was to be made before the end of December. But despite round-the-clock sessions the last two days of the year, the leaders of the UP parties were unable to reach agreement. The voting, during those last days:

Socialists:	Allende-Neruda
Communists:	Neruda-Allende
Radicals:	Baltra-Tarud
MAPU:	Chonchol-Neruda
Social Democrats:	Tarud-Baltra
API:	Tarud-Baltra

Thus, Tarud had two first-choice votes (his own parties) and one second-choice vote; Allende had one first (his own party), one second;

Neruda had one first and two seconds; Baltra one first, two seconds; Chonchol one first. Of the candidates in the race, only Chonchol fared more poorly than Allende. That day MAPU announced the withdrawal of its candidate. The Radicals, API, and Social Democrats all announced that they would consider themselves free to pull out of the coalition if a candidate were not chosen by midnight, December 31. The witching hour came and went and the bickering went on. On January 7, Allende announced he would withdraw as a candidate unless agreement were reached "soon." The break finally came on January 20. Baltra, under instructions from his party, withdrew as a candidate. A few hours later Neruda also pulled out. That left Allende and the upstart Tarud. Next the Social Democrats switched their support to Allende, and on Thursday, January 22, Tarud quit. Chonchol, on behalf of the Committee of Coordination of the Popular Unity, proclaimed Allende the candidate.

Two days later, Salvador Allende announced his acceptance.[82]

Carmen Puelma Accorsi, a voluptuous beauty who would become a buzzsaw of Chilean broadcast journalism, tells the story of an interview she had with Radomiro Tomic Romero during the time when Tomic was still serving (1964–68) as Frei's ambassador to the United States.

La Puelma, as colleagues called the indefatigable woman with the blue-green eyes, was an unknown quality to Tomic.

"As you will understand," Tomic therefore told her, "I would like to know whether you are really a suitable person for interviewing me, capable of understanding what I am going to tell you. Tell me, for example, what does 'fata morgana' mean?"

" 'Fata—' what?" she asked.

"Fata morgana," Tomic repeated.

"Well," she said, "the 'morgana' part suggests Captain Morgan, or pirates or some such. Perhaps it's some kind of fatalism. . . ."

"Out!" said Tomic. "How dare you request an interview with me without knowing what any university-trained person should know, how to handle the language without difficulty. And so that you don't remain in the dark, 'fata morgana' means mirage, illusion. . . ."[83]

This, then, is the unlovely side of Tomic's personality, the caustic pedant. He had been, in common with many figures in Chilean political life, a university professor—in his case, of social legislation.

There was, of course, another side: his handsome good looks, flashing smile, and silky oratorical skills that won him the nickname Golden Voice. He used that voice and those charms tirelessly in the U.S. He used them to such singularly good advantage that he was able to boast in a speech at the University of Notre Dame in 1967 that during the previous two years, Chile had managed to extract from the United States per capita aid in excess of $16 per person, "at least three times more than was promised in 1961" when the Alliance for Progress was created.[84]

Still another dimension to Tomic, the public man, was his lifelong devotion to leftist causes. He was born in 1914, was a lawyer and a journalist, and, with Frei, a founder of the Christian Democratic party and its forerunner, the Falange. Tomic was one of the first two PDC men elected to Congress, in 1941, and was reelected to the Chamber of Deputies in 1945 (the year Frei was losing his first try at a seat in Congress). In 1950 he was elected to the Senate to fill the vacancy left by Pablo Neruda, who had left the country without permission of the Senate. In 1961 he was again elected a senator, but resigned to assume the ambassadorship in Washington.

There were those who described Tomic as Frei's close friend and foil, but the record demonstrates that Tomic not only was consistently to the left of Frei but visibly chafed under his leadership as well. Following his return to Chile from the United States in 1968, Tomic connived ceaselessly to maneuver the party into an electoral alliance with the Communists. It was Tomic, in fact, who created the Popular Unity concept, a concept which forced many in the party to attempt to disassociate the party and its policies from Frei, the hobgoblin of the Communists.

On April 10, 1969, in the aftermath of the ruinous (for the PDC) parliamentary elections, Tomic addressed a letter to Frei in which he said that despite Communist-Socialist rebuffs and barbs aimed at him, "it is clear that without them, there is no Popular Unity." In another letter to Luis Maira Aguirre, a PDC deputy identified with the *tercerista* wing of the party, Tomic said: "My duty is to be honest, serious, and clear. There is no agreement in favor of the Popular Unity, and as a result, there will be no Tomic candidacy. I will not agree, under any circumstances, to be a candidate if only my party supports me."[85] It was a statement Tomic had made many times, but by putting it in writing then, it amounted to an ultimatum to the party on the eve of its crucial 1969 national convention.

It took all the support Frei could muster to defeat, at that convention in May 1969, the move to negotiate an electoral pact with the Left, the alliance so long caressed by Tomic, Leighton, Fuentealba, new party boss Benjamin Prado, and lesser luminaries of the party's left wing. Supported by the long-time party ideologue Jaime Castillo, the controversial but deeply respected Pérez Zújovic, Sen. Juan de Dios Carmona, and others, Frei won 233–215. The *terceristas* below the top leadership party promptly quit the party. It was the last time Frei could, or would, get his way in party councils until the country was plunged deeply into the maelstrom of Allende.

Three months later, in August 1969, the party leaders picked Tomic as their candidate. Tomic, of course, had not changed his leftist stripes. As Salvador Allende would later put it, responding to a Debray observation that Tomic represented the "radicalization of the petty bourgeoisie": "Exactly. Nobody can dispute this. There were many respects in which Tomic's program had very much in common with our own, and some would say that it was even more advanced than ours on some points."[86]

Tomic had simply put aside his scruples about representing a single party. And Frei had simply succeeded in destroying any chance of a united opposition front to defeat the united Marxist front, much as the one which had put himself in the presidency five years earlier.

The Right, after all, could scarcely rally behind a man whose program was "even more advanced . . . on some points" than that of the far Left.

So the Right turned to a man it regarded more as a savior than as a candidate. That man was Jorge Alessandri Rodríguez, whose presidency half a dozen years earlier was remembered with increasing nostalgia as a time of sobriety and civility,[87] because those qualities were rapidly vanishing from Chilean life, and whose father's presidency thirty years earlier was the farewell to conservative power in Chilean public life. Though he had served as president of his country, Alessandri's disdain for politics was so great that he had never been active in any political party. During the six frenzied years of the Frei presidency, he remained aloof from public affairs, making no speeches and shunning involvement in the great controversies reverberating through Chilean life. He did so not for lack of concern about his country, but, in the words of a man close to him, "because he believed that the greatest evil afflicting Chile was demagoguery, and he did not wish to add his voice to the din."[88] In 1958 Alessandri had reached the presidency as the reluctant standard-bearer of a conservative movement that was badly fragmented and already rife with demagogic tendencies of its own, and then was forced to govern with the votes of a party (the Radicals) that was ideologically antagonistic to almost everything he stood for. In 1969 those who approached him in behalf of the National party at least represented a movement that was unabashedly and cohesively conservative. Still, Alessandri rebuffed them repeatedly and finally relented only when he became the first presidential candidate in Chilean history drafted by popular petition. This is all the more remarkable when it is realized that Chilean election law was stacked against such independent candidacies; a minimum of twenty thousand registered voters had to sign the petition in the presence of two election notaries, a process that cost each signer an investment in time of several hours. And yet, from one end of Chile to the other, they did it, thirty thousand persons, far above the legal requirement. On November 2, 1969, Alessandri accepted—with characteristic independence: "If I win the election, I will govern in an absolutely independent fashion, searching constantly for contact with the workers; and I will govern for all Chileans, without exception, without establishing differences among them, being guided [in the choice of collaborators] only by the capacity, honesty, and sense of service to the country."

It was a bold and inspiring beginning. But the man called upon to lead this crusade was bereft of organization and staff, and lacked not only the stomach but even the experience for the campaign trail. And he was seventy-four years of age.

So it was almost foredoomed that the country would hear, just one year later, from another man, an agonizingly different version of what it meant to preside over the destinies of the country and its people.

Notes

CHAPTER 5

1. In Armando Uribe, *The Black Book of American Intervention in Chile* (Boston: Beacon Press, 1973), translated from the Spanish by Jonathan Casart, p. 75. Uribe, Allende's ambassador to Beijing, reproduces on pages 74–80, what he describes as the official transcript of Allende's thirty-five-minute meeting on November 4, 1970, with Assistant Secretary of State Charles Meyer, who headed the U.S. delegation to Allende's inauguration. It was Allende's first meeting as president with a foreign dignitary, and he spent most of the time lecturing Meyer on the rights of Chile and the responsibilities of the United States.
2. Ibid., p. 32. Nixon made the remarks during a tense meeting with Gabriel Valdés, then Chile's U.S.-baiting foreign minister, and later president of the Christian Democrat party. Valdés, flanked by the ambassadors of every Latin nation accredited to the White House, presented Nixon on that occasion with a document drafted at a conference orchestrated by Chile's Christian Democrats and held at the beach resort of Viña del Mar in April 1969 at which Latin nations agreed to take a united stance against the U.S. on trade and finance matters. Valdés added to the tension with a frontal assault of his own on the U.S.
3. In Emilio Filippi and Hernán Millas, *Anatomía de un Fracaso* (Santiago: Empresa Editora Zig-Zag, S.A., 1973), p. 21.
4. Régis Debray, *The Chilean Revolution: Conversations with Allende* (New York: Random House, 1971), pp. 65–66.
5. Ibid., p. 66.
6. Héctor Valenzuela Valderrama, a Christian Democrat who served an unprecedented three terms as president of the Chamber of Deputies, says Allende had a problem with his eyesight the last ten years of his life and had reports digested and read to him. For a year and-a-half, when Valenzuela's term overlapped with that of Allende as Senate president, the two men worked in particularly close proximity. Valenzuela recalls one incident when he arrived ten minutes late to his office for an appointment with Allende and found him leafing through a book that was then very much in vogue and that Valenzuela had just finished reading: Lester B. Pearson's *Partners in Development.*

"What's the gist of this book?" Allende asked him. "I've heard a good deal about it." Valenzuela said he gave Allende a detailed summary of the book's highlights, answered several of Allende's questions and then went on to the business at hand. Later Allende excused himself to leave for a scheduled news conference.

"Imagine my surprise the next day," Valenzuela said, "when I picked up a newspaper and found that one of the questions concerned the Pearson book and that Allende had acquitted himself with a 'brilliant exposition' of the book and Pearson's main ideas. What's more, he was almost 100 percent accurate!" Interview with Valenzuela in Santiago, April 25, 1974.

7. Debray, op. cit., pp. 63–66.
8. For details of Allende's involvement in that strike, or his lack of it, see Marcos Chamudes, *Chile: Una Advertencia Americana* (Santiago: Ediciones P.E.C., 1972), pp. 67–68. Allende refers to his arrest in his interview with Debray, op. cit., pp. 62–63.
9. Debray, op. cit., p. 63.
10. Quoted by Florencia Varas and José Manuel Vergara in *Operación Chile* (Santiago: Editorial Pomaire, 1973), pp. 120–21.
11. Ibid., p. 122.
12. Debray, op. cit., p. 61.

DEBRAY: How did you come to join the Socialist party?

ALLENDE: I didn't join the Socialist party, Régis—I am a founder, one of the founders of the Socialist party.

Debray manages to keep his "journalistic" talents well camouflaged through the sixty-seven pages of this book, which contains his actual interviews with Allende, and he appears rather in a role somewhere between disciple and straight man. The reader is thus left to himself to sift the abundant fiction from the occasional fact in the "conversations."

As to Allende's role in founding the party, the authoritative *Diccionario Político de Chile* (ed. Jordi Fuentes and Lía Cortes [Santiago: Editorial Orbe, 1967]; hereafter *Diccionario*) doesn't even mention his name until fully four-fifths of the way through its account of the party's history (on p. 473 of the section, which runs from p. 469 through most of p. 474). Nor does the *Diccionario* list the founding of the party as one of Allende's achievements in the biographical sketch of him (pp. 36–37). It does, however, identify Matte Hurtado as the founder in the biographic sketch of him (p. 307).

13. The analysis quote is from Debray, op. cit., p. 62. The account of Allende's activities in Communist causes is from a confidential *Time* magazine memorandum of October 26, 1970, reproduced in *Multinational Corporations and United States Foreign Policy*, a report of the hearings before the Subcommittee on Multinational Corporations of the Foreign Relations Committee of the U.S. Senate (Washington, D.C.: Government Printing Office, 1973), pt. 2, p. 703.
14. Debray, op. cit., p. 72.
15. Ibid., pp. 66–67.
16. For details of that zigzag phase of Allende's career, see chap. 5.
17. Weston Agor, *The Chilean Senate* (Austin and London: University of Texas Press, 1971), pp. 148–50.
18. Ibid., pp. 71.
19. Ibid., p. 118.
20. Ibid., p. 117, from "Diario de Sesiones del Senado, Legislatura Extraordinaria," Sesión 43A, December 27, 1966, pp. 2594–95.
21. Agor, op. cit., p. 19.
22. Agor, in a "conclusion" section written shortly after Allende's election, put caution—and his own, earlier reservations—aside and wrote: "Third, and perhaps most important, is the style of President Salvador Allende himself, which suggests that Allende does not personally favor and probably will not seek to weaken or close down Congress, despite campaign rhetoric to the contrary. This [Agor's] study clearly demonstrates that when President

Allende was president of the Senate, he normally abided by role expectations that required him to preside over the Senate in a nonpartisan manner. Allende's role behavior as a senator also suggests that he may well be more solicitous and responsive to opposition political parties' points of view in the Senate than was characteristic of the Christian Democrats' administration." Agor's optimism also included confidence that "elements within President Allende's coalition (particularly factions of the Radical party) will resist attempts to reform radically the role of Congress." Ibid., pp. 168–69.

Events, of course, quickly demolished such romantic hopes and evaluations. Once in power, Allende "followed the constitutional rules of the game" only insofar as they served his purposes, and ignored them—and the Congress and courts, above all—whenever and wherever he could get away with it, much as he had done in a more muted but no less obvious way during the time he supposedly "normally abided by role expectations."

As for the Radicals, they never did get more than a small share of the spoils of power, never any real power in the Allende "coalition." Those few Radicals who remained in the coalition to the end did so only because they sold out, lock, stock, and barrel, to Allende and his whims.

As for Allende's allegiance to Congress, one of his first proposals was to abolish it and replace it with a unicameral Congress, more malleable to his "revolutionary" purposes. Failing to find support for that scheme, he scrapped the idea and with it, even a semblance of respect for Congress, which he spoke of with increasing contempt as one of the "relics of bourgeois legality."

23. "Chilean Leftist Raps U.S.," Associated Press dispatch datelined Havana, in *Miami Herald*, January 10, 1966, p. 16-A.

24. Allende rationalized the inconsistency between his oath in Chile to uphold the constitution and his commitment to OLAS's "revolutionary armed struggle," by saying that he had "always maintained that OLAS could not be the supranational revolutionary headquarters," but rather an "information organization, a unit for coordination and demonstration of solidarity." Debray, op. cit., p. 124. Of course Allende was saying that not from the vantage point of an outsider clamoring for power but from his comforting perch as the self-styled senior statesman of "peaceful revolution."

25. David F. Belnap's *Los Angeles Times* Service dispatch, "Che Band Gets Aid in Chile," *Miami Herald*, March 5, 1968, reporting not only Allende's intercession in behalf of the Guevara guerrillas but also his role in OLAS and the public stance of that organization.

26. Debray, op. cit., p. 80.

27. Ibid., p. 122. The interview took place in January 1971, fourteen months after Allende's inauguration.

28. According to estimates reported by the archaeologist Francisco Antonio Encina, the average Chilean man measures 5 feet 5 inches, the average woman just a shade over 5 feet. *Nueva Enciclopedia de Chile* (Argentina: Ediciones Copihue, Fotomecánica Futura SRL, Ediciones Libra, 1974), 1:164.

29. Lewis H. Diuguid's Santiago-datelined dispatch: "Chilean President Develops Dynamic Style," *Washington Post*, January 31, 1972.

30. Lautaro Silva, *Allende: El fin de una aventura* (Santiago: Ediciones Patria Nueva, 1974) p. 26. The Frei quote is from the same work, same page.

31. Nathaniel Davis, *The Last Two Years of Salvador Allende* (Ithica: Cornell University Press, 1985), p. 50. As to Davis's own views, the following pas-

sages reflect one of the two biases implicit throughout Davis's book: enthusiasm for Allende and most of his ideas (the other: an equally strong aversion to the junta which ousted Allende): "was Salvador Allende a Democrat ... I believe the answer is yes!. . . . In 1948 Allende had criticized the Soviets' negation of 'rights which we deem inalienable to the human personality.' During the intervening years most of his positions with this assertion were consistent. It was only the road to socialism, however, that Allende wanted to make democratic and institutional. He did not envisage the Chilean people voting exploitative and capitalist institutions back into power. Once 'the people' took over in the complete Senate, Allende believed that they would continue to rule." Ibid., p. 51. And again: ". . . his 'flexible wrist' and propensity to renege on his commitments, his willingness to let his dirty work be done, his dissembling—all were part of Salvador Allende. But Allende was also called by some 'the First Dreamer of the Republic': and he dreamed marvelous, soaring dreams. His aspiration was for a better Chile and for happiness and fulfillment for his compatriots. Not just personally, but in the selfless political sense. He loved the women and children of Chile . . ." Ibid., p. 53. One needs to jump to the endnotes to discover the identity of "some" who saw Allende as a "dreamer": Régis Debray and Camilo Taufic. Davis does not, however, clarify that both are doctrinaire Marxists. Davis gives as the source for the Korry remarks, "Satements and Discussion," U.S. Congress, Senate Committee on Foreign Relations, *Nominations on Hon. Cyrus R. Vance to be Secretary of State*, January 1977 Hearings (Washington, D.C. 1977), pp. 57, 67.

   In sharp contrast to his successor, Korry saw Allende quite differently—as did virtually every non-Marxist I have ever read, including the three Chilean presidents who preceded Allende. Korry samples: (1) "As far as the motivation behind Allende's domestic economic policies, the evidence is overwhelming that their objective was political—to destroy the middle class . . ."; (2) "Allende did not believe in democratic socialism by anybody's definition . . ."; (3) "He [Allende] had no intention of ever negotiating seriously with the United States. . . ." From the report of a Conference on Chile, held at Georgetown University's Center for Strategic and International Studies (CSIS), August 15, 1974, and chaired by CSIS Latin Studies Director Dr. James D. Theberge as reproduced in *United States and Chile during the Allende Years, 1970–1973*, Hearings of the Subcommittee on Inter-American Affairs, U.S. House of Representatives, July 1 and Oct. 15, 1971; September 11, 1972; March 6, September 20, 25, October 11, 31, December 7, 1973; August 5, September 17–18, 1974 (Washington, D.C., 1975) pp. 644–645. (Hereafter: *United States and Chile*.)

32. "Red Boss in Chile a Puzzling Figure," by Tom Stacey of the *London Sunday Times*, in *Miami Herald*, April 26, 1964.

33. This information was given to me in response to a request I made during a visit to the Senate Information Service in April 1974. The Service had attempted to pinpoint party membership in a 1968 survey. Only two parties responded, the Christian Democrats and the Popular Socialist Union. Their replies: Christian Democrats (née Falange), 1942—3,210; 1946—3,602; 1952—5,798; 1958—13,216; 1964—45,792. Popular Socialist Union: 1952—9,800 members.

34. "Cincuenta Años del Partido Comunista," *Qué Pasa* December 30, 1971, p. 6.

35. John Gunther, *Inside South America* (New York: Harper & Row, 1966),

p. 278 (italics his). The Debray quote is from his work, op. cit., p. 32. Labrousse quotes Corvalán in 1967 in an article in the June issue of *Nuestra Epoca,* entitled "Unión de las Fuerzas Anti-Imperialistas," as saying the party membership consisted of: 66.4 percent urban and farm workers; 7.7 percent small farmer landowners; 20 percent craftsmen, small businessmen, white collar workes, intellectuals and others. Alain Labrousse, *El Experimento Chileno* (Barcelona and Mexico: Ediciones Grijalbo, S.A., 1973), p. 201. The ambassador was Edward M. Korry, who had spent seventeen years as a news correspondent on both sides of the Iron Curtain in Europe. From his testimony before the Subcommittee on Inter-American Affairs, U.S. House of Representatives, July 1, 1971, *United States and Chile during the Allende Years, 1970–1973* (Washington: U.S. Government Printing Office, 1975) p. 29. (Referred to hereafter as *United States and Chile.*)

36. Cited by Joaquín Fermandois in *Chile y el Mundo, 1970–1973; La Política Exterior del Gobierno de la Unidad Popular y el Sistema Internacional* (Santiago: Ediciones Universidad Católica de Chile, 1985), p. 368. Fermandois quoted from the Communist party daily, *El Siglo,* of January 3, 1972.

37. Debray, op. cit., p. 38.

38. Bertram D. Wolfe, *Three Who Made a Revolution* (New York: Dell Publishing Co., Delta Book, 1948), pp. 591–92, and 600–01. A resolution approved at that Congress called upon the proletariat "to exert every effort to prevent the outbreak of war by means they consider most effective. . . . Should war break out, nonetheless, it is their duty to intervene in favor of its speedy termination and to do all in their power to utilize the economic and political crisis caused by the war to hasten the abolition of capitalist class rule." In Russia, the intervention for a speedy termination became refusal to fight, forcing the czar to sue for a ruinous peace, an event which sealed his own fate. In Chile, sixty-five years later, the far Left would use another precept laid down then—"agitation among military recruits"—to weaken the power of the "counterrevolutionaries," that is, the military commanders.

39. The twenty-one points included maintaining an illegal as well as a legal apparatus, a point Corvalán would later preach and the party practice with the creation of "revolutionary brigades"; periodic purges of the party to cleanse it of "bourgeois elements"; a command making it the duty of every Communist party to lend assistance to Soviet Russia, a command born out of the insecurity of a new and hemmed-in revolutionary regime, but one the Chileans would later, and repeatedly, honor by backing Russian causes on the international stage; and a requirement that Communists who won election to Parliament "were not to be bound by any democratic or parliamentary scruples [but] be under the strictest discipline of the Central party." As we have seen, Communist congressmen in Chile followed party orders to a *t;* and as to "scruples," any they might have had evaporated in the mortal contention between Allende and Parliament once they were in power.

One point was awkward for others, but not for the Chilean Communists: the one that required working through "*worker*-revolutionaries who have their ties to the villages." This dictum was almost quaint to American or British Communists, conjuring up, in Ulam's phrase, "the vision of the Communist worker from New York or London beating on the door of a peasant's hut in Iowa or Norfolk and stirring him up against the local landlord and government official." But to the Chilean Communists, it made sense—eventually, if not immediately because the party hierarchy always was heavy on worker representation. The quote is from Adam B. Ulam, *The Bolsheviks* (New York: Macmillan Co., 1965), p. 501., as is the synopsis of the twenty-one points, pp. 501, 502, 504, and 507.

40. Ibid., p. 497. The Chilean magazine *Qué Pasa*, in its admirable survey of the first fifty years of the Chilean Communist party, refers, for instance, to Recabarren's "national communism," and describes it as "deeply different from Russian Communism." "Cincuenta Años del Partido Comunista," pp. 7–8.

41. Isaac Deutscher, *The Prophet Unarmed: Trotsky, 1921–1929* (New York: Random House, Vintage Books, 1965), 2:144, 212.

42. Except where noted, the details of the Communist party's development are from *Qué Pasa*, December 30, 1971, pp. 6–10.

43. Details of Corvalán's career from "Luis Corvalán Lepe: Un Pacifista Violento," *Sepa* magazine, March 9–15, 1981, pp. 6–7.

44. From *El Siglo*, June 28, 1965, as cited by Chamudes, op. cit., p. 217.

45. Before 1952, each political party could not only print its own ballots but distribute them, a practice that gave landowners easy access to the votes of their laborers. Thus, the ballot the peasant deposited was most often the one the "patrón" gave him. However, it must be noted that until another change in the electoral law in 1970, illiterates could not vote and a high percentage—perhaps a majority—of farm laborers were illiterate. What is significant is the Communist proselytizing of those who could vote, and efforts to capture the loyalties of those who would later vote.

46. James Petras and Maurice Zeitlin, "Agrarian Radicalism in Chile," in *Agrarian Problems and Peasant Movements in Latin America*, ed. Rodolfo Stavenhagen (New York: Doubleday, Anchor Books, 1970), p. 520.

47. Paul Bethel, *The Losers* (New Rochelle, N.Y.: Arlington House, 1969), p. 40.

48. *L'Unita*, no. 276 (October 1968), quoted by Chamudes, op. cit., p. 219.

49. Joan E. Garcés, "1970, La Pugna Política por la Presidencia de Chile," pp. 43, 47; cited by Labrousse, op. cit., p. 219.

50. Frederick Pike and Donald Bray, *A Vista of Catastrophe: The Future of U.S.-Chilean Relations*, cited in U.S. House report, *Multinational Corporations and United States Foreign Policy*, pt. 2, p. 707. Following the fall of Allende, Chileans would be justified in protesting that it was now they who recognized "in Communism a dreadful threat" and Americans who thought of it as simply "one of the possible means of achieving physical prosperity," etc.

51. The bolshevization quote is from Debray, op. cit., p. 131. The shooting quote is from Chamudes, in Robert Moss, *Chile's Marxist Experiment* (New York: John Wiley & Sons, Halstead Press, 1973), p. 44.

52. From the 1961 booklet, *Nuestra Vía Revolucionaria*, quoted by Labrousse, op. cit., pp. 193–94.

53. Except where noted, all the foregoing Corvalán quotes are from "Luis Corvalán Lepe, Un Pacifista Violento," *Sepa* magazine (Santiago), March 9–15, 1971, pp. 6–9.

54. Luis Corvalán Lepe, *Camino de Victoria* (Santiago: Sociedad Impresora Horizonte, 1971), p. 26. The 1972 quote is from I. Rybalkin, "The Chilean Experience: General Laws and Peculiarities of the Revolutionary Process," *Kommunist*, no. 8 (May 1972): 121, cited by Leon Gouré and Morris Rothenberg, *Soviet Penetration of Latin America*, (Miami: Center for Advanced International Studies, University of Miami, 1975), p. 111.

55. The Chilean Communists did, however, have a parallel slogan of sorts to the cunning All Power to the Soviets. Their platform in 1970 called for All Power to the People through the abolition of Congress and its replacement by a unicameral legislature, empowered to elect the president and cabinet ministers, as well as to name justices of the Supreme Court (who, in turn, named judges of lower courts). The Communists' strategy was obvious: once in power, they would use the power and leverage of the presidency, plus the combined voting strength of their coalition, to claim decisive control over the commanding heights of Chilean politics, as well as the economy—in a word, total power, and all gotten very "legally." Of course, they first had to persuade the existing Congress to abolish itself, which Allende, with more bravado than political sense, said he would accomplish through a plebiscite. Against such a backdrop, one can only wonder at the boundless faith in words of writer after writer who would refer to the "commitment" of the Communists—or Allende—to the Congress or parliamentary democracy. (In fact, and not surprisingly, Allende never dared even call for that or any other plebiscite.)

56. Isaac Deutscher, *The Prophet Outcast: Trotsky, 1929–1940* (New York: Random House, Vintage Books, 1965), 3:200–201.

57. Expelled in 1967, Ampuero founded the Popular Socialist Union (USOPO). Accused of "personalism and *caudillismo*," Ampuero replied: "I succumbed to a spurious coalition of guerrilla theosophists, career politicians, and local bosses" ("El Lado Oculto del P.S.," *Ercilla*, September 13, 1972; quoted by Moss, op. cit., p. 48).

58. Labrousse, op. cit., p. 198.

59. Ibid., p. 199. Notes on the 1965, 1967, and 1969 Congresses of the Socialist party are, except where noted, from ibid., pp. 197–200.

60. Debray, op. cit., pp. 71–72.

61. Gonzalo Vial Correa, "Decadencia, Consensos y Unidad Nacional en 1973," in *Política y Geoestrategia* #36 (Santiago: Academia Nacional de Estudios Políticos Estratégicos, 1985).

62. Gustavo Cuevas, director of the University of Chile's Institute of Political Science, in an interview with the author in Santiago, January 29, 1987.

63. Bethel, op. cit., p. 528.

64. Data on secret MIR documents in Silvia Pinto, *Los Días del Arco Iris* (Santiago: Editorial del Pacífico, January 1972), p. 61. The quote on returning stolen monies in Labrousse, op. cit., p. 234. Details of attack on Osses and threat to Mrs. Pinto are in ibid., pp. 62, 73–75.

65. Interview with General Huerta in Santiago, October 9, 1974. General Huerta was Frei's top lawman throughout Frei's six years in office. One of fourteen sons of a poor postal official, he took over the Carabineros at a time when the organization was suffering moral and material decomposition. He inveigled more than $5 million in U.S. aid to modernize the Carabineros from stem to stern, creating the Grupo Móvil, crack riot-control troops, and arming the group with 1,000-round-a-minute machine guns (which, to the best of my knowledge, the troops never had to fire in anger before September 11, 1973).

When he took over the Carabineros, the organization was so arms-poor that a man going off duty had to turn over his weapon to the man relieving him. But Huerta used the bulk of the aid money ($3 million, plus $3 million in Chilean funds) to connect the 1,200 Carabinero posts from one end of the country to the other with a modern communications system, a "weapon" of incalculable value in combating crime and subversion. Huerta was proud of the fact that he was an honors graduate of the FBI-run International Police Academy in Washington, D.C. The combination of his efficiency and effectiveness, plus the FBI "taint," made him, for leftists, a man thrice accursed. But the fact that he had served Frei loyally would later cost Huerta the esteem of the Right, which saw him as one of the men responsible for facilitating the later holocaust.

66. Reference to Olivares in Pinto, op. cit., p. 64. The peasant reference is in Petras and Zeitlin, op. cit., pp. 529–30.

67. In Labrousse, op. cit., pp. 156–57.

68. An example of the long-festering hostility: Luciano Cruz died under mysterious circumstances in 1971. Two years later, less than one month before Allende's overthrow, Miguel Enríquez made an impassioned speech in which he noted tribute paid Cruz by other leftist organizations, adding: "Only one group soiled itself." That group, he said, was the Communist-controlled Labor Federation (Central Única de Trabajadores), which, he said, refused the MIR request to make its headquarters available for the wake, even though Allende himself would lead the mourners at the funeral. The incident is in Ricardo Boizard, *Proceso a Una Traición* (Santiago: Ediciones Encina, 1974), pp. 124–25. The Chilean Communist party's top theoretician, Volodia Teitelboim, wrote, following Allende's overthrow, a series of analyses in *World Marxist Review,* in which he noted that the action of radical leftist groups caused "the working class [to be] isolated from its allies," a theme repeatedly echoed by Soviet commentators. See Gouré and Rothenberg, op. cit., pp. 107–210.

69. In Labrousse, op. cit., p. 235.

70. Ibid., p. 238.

71. Just nineteen months later, with Allende barely three months in power, an alarmed Morales would be warning that the Radicals might have to pull out of the government unless illegal land seizures were halted (which they were not). The Radicals were hurting because the land piracy was taking place in the southern provinces, where what remained of their electoral strength resided.

72. *El Mercurio,* June 30, 1969, quoted by Chamudes, op. cit., p. 138.

73. The Valdés and Enríquez quotes are from Chamudes, op. cit., pp. 138, 139.

74. Debray, op. cit., p. 196.

75. The June 1966 and May 1968 references to the Communists are from Labrousse, op. cit., pp. 201–2.

76. Ibid., p. 207.

77. Chamudes, op. cit., p. 116, says Neruda participated in a number of party debates before 1940 over the issue of whether it would be preferable to have Neruda declare his communism openly or serve party causes as an "independent."

78. Labrousse, op. cit., p. 200. The compromise statement is from the same page.

79. Ibid., p. 207. Text of cable, ibid. p. 206.

80. *The Chilean Road to Socialism,* ed. J. Ann Zammit, with cooperation of Gabriel Palma (Austin and England: University of Texas Press and Institute of Development Studies [IDS], University of Sussex, 1973), p. 261. Unless otherwise noted, further references to the Unidad Popular program are taken from this work, pp. 263–77.

81. *Pocket Data Book, U.S.A., 1971* (Washington, D.C.: U.S. Department of

Commerce, May 1971), p. 101. The comparison is not precise because the U.S. "voter population" figures include all those of voting age, rather than those actually registered to vote. But even those voter figures in the U.S. never approached Chile's latter-day "eligible voter" levels—much less did the percentage of registered voters approach the Chilean levels.

I am, of course, familiar with the infinite capacity of Marxists for pseudodialectical caterwauling: participation does not a democracy make, they will argue, because the "capitalists" control the levers of economic power (in Chile, resoundingly false, and it had been for many years) or because the "institutions" are corrupt (Communists would substitute their own "vanguard" institutions). Bilge, of course. As Chileans would soon discover, the Communists and their companions of the Left cared not one whit about majority rule, as they went about twisting institutions to their own purposes and flouting the wishes of the majority.

82. Details of Allende's selection as UP candidate are taken, for the most part, from Labrousse, op. cit., pp. 205–11. The Briones quote is from an interview with the author in Santiago, May 13, 1974.

83. Pinto, op. cit., p. 150. Another would-be interviewer felt the lash of Tomic's celebrated arrogance before they could even meet. William Buckley, in Chile in 1971, requested an interview with Tomic and received the curt refusal on the grounds that they "had nothing in common." To which Buckley, recalling his own somewhat quixotic candidacy for mayor of New York, replied: wrong. "After all," Buckley shot back, "we both lost an election" (Horne, op. cit., p. 136).

84. "Chile Faces Human Development," speech by Tomic at the "Colloquium on Overall Development of Chile," at Notre Dame University, March 8, 1967; from mimeographed text provided by Chilean embassy, Washington, D.C., p. 16. In that same speech, Tomic took a (characteristic) number of liberties with the facts, such as when he described the Christian Democrats as accounting for "something less than 45 percent of the electorate" (p. 15), a level they never in fact attained at any time. Tomic did manage to make influential friends at Notre Dame (and other U.S. campuses), foremost among them Notre Dame's president, Father T. M. Hesburgh, who would remain a champion of the Christian Democrats long after they had botched their mandate—and let down their country.

85. Quoted by Labrousse, op. cit., p. 216. Maira would later skip the party and join Allende's Unidad Popular.

86. Debray, op. cit., pp. 121–22.

87. Though not, alas, by the far Left. Debray, for example, says Alessandri's government "is remembered as one of the most reactionary in the last three decades" (op. cit., p. 150).

88. Interview in Santiago, October 13, 1974, with Jaime Guzmán Errázuriz.

6

Over the Brink

It was as if "the child on whom we devoted the most attention and care had decided, upon finishing graduate school, to embrace cannibalism."[1]

"OUT OF THE VALLEY OF HINNOM ..."

On Saturday, September 5, 1970, the people of Chile awoke to discover that they had done what no other people, anywhere, had ever done. They had elected a Marxist president, in elections so simon-pure clean that one newspaper would describe them as "honest, open, and unchallenged."

"Marxist" was actually a euphemism commonly used then and thereafter, obscuring the simple fact that Salvador Allende Gossens came to power at the head of a Communist-Socialist coalition. There might be some quibbling about whether any other people had ever before elected a Marxist—and others had, in free elections—but no free people had ever before elected a Marxist-Leninist government, pledged to transforming the entire state and society into a Communist-Socialist state. And it is well to remember that in Chile, the Socialist party bore no resemblance to similarly named parties in Europe and elsewhere, and was, in fact, well to the left of the Communists, in tactics, style and totalitarian taste.

The fact that the Radicals formed part of Allende's winning Popular Unity (UP—*Unidad Popular*) coalition caused some to shy away from the more forthright Communist-Socialist label. Yet the Communists and Socialists would pull the strings that made puppet Allende dance, and the Radicals, electoral cannon fodder, had nothing important to say about the conduct of affairs from the day of Allende's triumph until the day of his death.

The sense of shock at what had happened in Chile was heightened precisely because of the bloated reputation the country had come to enjoy as a model of political perfection and the virtues of reform. A few years earlier, for example, that peripatetic chronicler of the contemporary world of yesteryear, John Gunther, had described Chile as "the most important country in South America and Eduardo Frei as its most important man." Even *le grand* Charles de Gaulle, during that interlude in the midsixties when he allowed his preternatural gaze to sweep over Latin America, had described Chile as "the pilot country of Latin America."

Don Bohning, long-time Latin America editor of the *Miami Herald*, surveying the scene a week after the election, described Allende's victory as the "single most significant event in Latin America since Fidel Castro seized power more than a decade ago." He was not alone. U.S. Ambassador Edward M. Korry, in a confidential report forwarded to President Richard M. Nixon, said Allende's election "will have the most profound effect on Latin America and beyond; we have suffered a grievous defeat . . ."

Henry Kissinger, then the national security adviser, said Nixon underlined the following passages in Korry's report:

> Chile voted calmly to have a Marxist-Leninist state, the first nation in the world to make this choice freely and knowingly. *His margin is only about one percent but it is large enough in the Chilean constitutional framework to nail down his triumph as final.* There is no reason to believe that the Chilean armed forces will unleash a civil war or that any other intervening miracle will undo his victory. It is a sad fact that Chile has taken the path to communism with only a little more than a third (36 percent) of the nation approving this choice, but it is an immutable fact. *It will have the most profound effect on Latin America and beyond; we have suffered a grievous defeat; the consequences will be domestic and international;* the repercussions will have immediate impact in some lands and delayed effect in others.[2]

In Moscow the celebration was tinged with caution. The stakes for the Russians were high, exceedingly high. Allende gave powerful support to the claim, then fashionable, that communism was the inevitable wave of the future, cascading to power by peaceful means. For years the Kremlin had pushed the peaceful line in competition with the violent prescriptions of Mao (and, at that time, Moscow's unruly puppet, Fidel Castro). Allende not only vindicated the strategy of conquest by peaceful stealth, but also soothed the anxieties of those who though attracted by the intellectual allures of Marxism were repulsed by its addiction to violence.

Moscow's enthusiasm was tinged with caution because the Soviets understood that this battle they had fought so hard to win was far from over on September 5, 1970. Chile was, after all, still reeling from a full year of the most raucous political fratricide and electioneering of its history and shell-shocked by the final verdict.

Since Allende had failed to win a majority, the final decision rested with the Congress, and that meant fifty days more of nerve-racking cliffhanging. Russian commentators apparently had not expected Allende to win in the first place, and were apprehensive in any case about the durability of the Popular Unity coaliton (and would remain so to the end). So they withheld full-scale pop-corking until the Congress acted.[3]

Before the postelectoral skirmishing was over, the casualties would include not only the country's top soldier, but also, in one way or another, a legion of foreigners such as Henry Kissinger, the CIA, and ITT.

And, of course, Chile's civilized past.

As 1958 had demonstrated, the Left had a clear advantage with more than two candidates in the race. It was for that reason that the Right backed Frei in 1964. But the Christian Democrats (PDC) had repeatedly echoed the sentiments of party President Renán Fuentealba, who said in February 1969: "Our enemy is the Right."[4] The entire Frei administration was a systematic dismantling of everything the Right stood for, in social theory as well as economic practice. Even Moscow smiled on Frei's performance.[5] Furthermore, the Christian Democrats—despite their boasts that they would "govern for thirty years" and were the "wave of the future"—actually had declined steadily since 1964 (when they won with the support of the Right); whereas the Right, following its reorganization in 1967, had gone from 14.6 percent of the vote that year to 20.8 percent in 1969.

In such circumstances, there was no hope of the Right and the Christian Democrats uniting to stop Allende—before or after the elections.

Besides, Radomiro Tomic, the Christian Democrat standard-bearer in that electoral Armageddon of 1970, had no wish of stopping Allende.

Four months before the elections, in May 1970, Christian Democrat deputies backed Popular Unity candidates in elections to select the new presiding officers of the Chamber. Osvaldo Giannini Iñíguez, deputy PDC floor-leader, explained that the PDC bloc had voted thus out of deference to Tomic who had requested it as part of "closing ranks ever more with the Left, with a view to an understanding at the Joint Session (of Congress) which will have to decide between the two highest candidates."[6]

Tomic already knew, of course, that with three in the race, none had a chance of getting the absolute majority needed to win a clear-cut victory. The Chilean constitution provided that in such cases, the two

Houses of Congress should meet in joint session to choose between one of the two highest vote-getters, although not binding the Congress to pick the man with the highest total.[7]

Tomic's contempt for the Right became further evident when he entered into a secret pact with Allende to block Alessandri's chances in the Congress. The pact was revealed by a Communist, Eduardo Labarca Goddard, in his book *Chile al Rojo (Chile Going Red)*. Allende flatly denied the existence of the pact, and Tomic said it wasn't a pact, but a "clarification of intentions." Earlier, U.S. intelligence picked up a report that Allende had sufficient support in the Congress—which, inevitably, meant from Christian Democrats—to be elected even if Alessandri ran first but failed to compile a margin of victory of more than 5 percent.[8] Tomic himself, in an interview with a fellow Christian Democrat, Sen. Tomás Pablos Elorza, explained that he and Allende "agreed that if either of us won with a difference of 30,000 votes, we would recognize and support publicly the first relative majority."[9] In other words, he pledged to attempt to sway the Congress for Allende, since it was obvious from early in the campaign that Tomic had no chance of finishing first and very little even of second. And he would do so if Allende managed to nose out Alessandri by a meager 1 percent of the expected vote.

Tomic was as good as his word.

In the voting on September 4, 1970, the outcome was:

TABLE 24
RESULTS OF 1970 PRESIDENTIAL ELECTIONS

	VOTES	% OF TOTAL
Allende	1,070,334	36.2
Alessandri	1,031,159	34.9
Tomic	821,801	27.8
Void/Blank	31,505	1.1
TOTAL	2,954,799	

Source: Elección Ordinaria de Presidente de la República; Viernes 4 de Septiembre de 1970; Dirección del Registro Electoral, Santiago.

Allende edged Alessandri by 1.3 percentage points; 39,175 votes. It was up to Congress, where the Christian Democrats held the balance of power. They accounted for 77 of the 200 senators and deputies; the party of the Right, the Nationals, held 38 seats; Allende's Unidad Popular parties held 78 seats.[10] The rest were scattered among dissidents and independents. Needed to elect: 101 votes.

The very day after the elections, Tomic rushed to Allende's house on Guardia Vieja Street to congratulate him on his "victory," although, under Chile's constitution, it was up to Congress to decide who had won.

Five days after the elections, Alessandri announced his decision: if chosen by Congress, he would resign, so as to force new elections, and he would refuse, irrevocably, to take part in the new elections.

A few days later, on September 13, Salvador Allende gave his answer: "Let them [his opponents] know," he shouted at a street rally, "that the entire country will grind to a halt. There will not be a factory, nor company, nor shop, nor school, nor hospital, nor farm that works, as the first demonstration of our power. Let them know that the workers will occupy the factories and the peasants will take over the farms. Let them know that the white collar workers will be in the offices, awaiting the command and the voice of the Popular Unity."[11] In other words: elect me—or else!

He needn't have shouted. Within the Christian Democrat party, the left wing, led by Tomic, Leighton, Fuentealba, Prado, and a young rebel group, maneuvered to ease the way for Allende. (A few months later, the young rebels, having won their way, bolted the party and joined forces with Allende—much as Chonchol's group had done a year earlier.)

In keeping with his Olympian style, Eduardo Frei, leader of the party's moderate forces and the man with the greatest sway over the rank-and-file, shunned taking the public position that might have been decisive. In private, he told a number of associates he believed the election of Allende would "be a disaster for Chile."[12] The man who headed a badly bungled attempt to force a preemptive coup d'état, Gen. Roberto Viaux Marambio, claimed Frei had even given a guarded "green light" for his plan. He said the green light was conveyed by a cousin of Frei, a Catholic priest named Father Ruiz Tagle.[13] Two experienced reporters on the scene—one working for International Telephone and Telegraph Co., the other reporting confidentially to *Time* magazine—both reported, in harsh language, that Frei was in a Hamlet-like trance, one minute tilting in the direction of blocking Allende, the next saying no.[14]

There were others in Frei's inner circle pressuring him to act. Their number was said to include his defense minister, Sergio Ossa Pretot, Finance Minister Andrés Zaldívar, and Economy Minister Carlos Figueroa.[15] Other moderates, such as Sen. Juan de Dios Carmona, argued that the Christian Democrats should hold out for seats in Allende's Cabinet in return for their votes so as to be able to checkmate his actions. But they were outflanked at the top leadership levels which Tomic, as the party's candidate, had captured. Bernardo Leighton, vice president of the party, told Frei flat-out after September 4 that he would deliver his votes to Allende.

On September 24, the party published a statement: "We are convinced that many of the points defended by the candidacy of Salvador Allende aimed at the transformation and development of society, have been and remain ours today." The statement was careful to disassociate the party from many of Allende's programs, and called upon him specifically to renounce plans for creating a "popular power" as a parallel force or counterweight to the armed forces. The manifesto then timidly asked Allende whether he would be willing to swear to a list of "constitutional guarantees" in return for their votes.

On September 29, Allende reacted angrily with a seven-page statement of his own. "I have a right to expect," he said, "that my permanent democratic attitude guarantees by itself the future conduct of my government." The Christian Democrats responded that Allende's reply was "incomplete" and "unsatisfactory," and that it was "indispensable" that their demand for the guarantees be met "as soon as possible." His rough stand was backed by the Socialists—but not by the Communists, who managed to prevail. Provincial and community leaders of the Christian Democrats, known to be anti-Allende, were showing signs of rebelling against the national leadership. Without so much as a bow to candidate Allende's protest, the coalition parties, goaded by the Communists, notified the Christian Democrats that they were ready to negotiate.

On Monday, October 5, after a marathon convention that ran through the weekend, the Christian Democrats voted 271–191 to back Allende provided that the Congress passed and he accepted a Statute of Guarantees. Negotiations to draft the Statute were opened immediately with a UP team. "The intervention of . . . Bernardo Leighton at the meeting," one of Chile's leading journalists wrote, "was decisive. He displayed all his brilliant abilities to calm his party colleagues about the personality and attitudes [tendencias] of Dr. Allende and the Popular Unity."[16]

There was another "lobby" working to influence the Christian Democrats. On September 26, the country's Roman Catholic bishops—dominated by an elite group sympathetic to the left wing of the Christian Democrats—issued a statement urging their countrymen to eschew violence. But the statement was even more significant as an implied acceptance of Allende's candidacy: the bishops said they were in favor of social change to help the "millions of underprivileged in Chile. We know changes are difficult, and bring great risks for everyone." They added that Allende's supporters "harbor great hopes and show constructive willingness" to work for solutions.

Inasmuch as a substantial number of Chileans—including many Christian Democrats—feared an Allende victory as a plague on their land, the bishops' statement clearly amounted to a gratuitous defense of Allende. It was, in fact, in a perfect line of progression for the church in Chile which, starting in the mid-1960s, drifted steadily left. The intellectual fountainhead of this movement was the Centro Belarmino, a Jesuit institute dominated by a Belgian priest named Roger Vekemans.

Under the influence of other church "progressives" from Holland, France, and Belgium, the church barely disguised its affection for Tomic during the campaign—and for Allende during the cliff-hanger period. Jesuit enthusiasm for Allende veritably exploded when he was barely in office: "When Chile and the world pass judgment on Allende, he will be judged as a revolutionary. As to his work in La Moneda [the presidential palace]: will it have meant a decisive step toward the appearance of that New Man, sane, free, whole, responsible and creative? The antivalues fostered by the capitalist system: will they have fled before the collapse of structures sheltering them today? . . . As the government of Popular Unity advances towards that New Man, a Christian cannot but march by its side, since that New Man is none other than the same one which Christ came to install upon this earth."

They were, of course, talking about the New Man to be molded by Salvador Allende according to his Marxist lights and tenets. And "they" were the editors of the Jesuit magazine, *Mensaje*, in their issue #194, in November 1970, a hosanna written as Allende was barely settling in office.[17]

In all of this, the Right—whose candidate had run only 39,000 votes behind Allende—was not even consulted. This casts an interesting light on the thesis developed by Benjamín Prado, then president of the Christian Democrats, to justify their position vis-à-vis Allende: "To deny Allende the possibility of assuming the presidency would be as if to have said to 36 percent of the electorate, you have the right to take part in the elections, but you can't win."[18]

Evidently, however, it was fair to exclude altogether from negotiations of uttermost importance for the future of the country 34.9 percent of the electorate (not to mention the very considerable bloc of moderate Christian Democrats whose voices were drowned out by the party's left-wing leadership). The fact is, the PDC, in excluding the Right, was acquiescing in a stratagem devised by the Communists, who stage-managed the "guarantees" negotiations; Allende's own Socialist party opposed the negotiations, and, if it had gotten its hot-headed way, even the PDC would have been hard put to vote Allende into the presidency. The stratagem: break off and isolate the Right, both the frankly inimical National party as well as the moderates within the PDC, so as to glue the Marxist-leaning leftists of the PDC to an invincible coalition of the Left. Part of that strategy included dangling offers of Cabinet posts before top Christian Democrats. One of them, Frei's Yankee-baiting foreign minister, Gabriel Valdés Subercaseaux (of the confrontation with Nixon), did, in fact, win Allende's support for an international plum: head of the United Nation's Economic Commission for Latin America (CEPAL).

On October 19, Alessandri withdrew as a candidate, but as Arturo Fontaine Aldunate, the respected Chilean newspaper editor, observed, "Alessandri collapsed that very evening" of the elections.[19] On October 22, a small armed band directed by Viaux ambushed Gen. René Schneider, commander-in-chief of the army. They intended kidnapping him, but in their panic, wounded him mortally. Two days later, the Congress elected Allende president: the vote: 153 for Allende, thirty-five for Alessandri, seven blank. On November 3, Allende was sworn in as president.

The head of the National party, Sen. Francisco Bulnes Sanfuentes, explained on October 22 why his party would abstain on the constitutional amendments.

> We affirm that the proposal amounts to deceiving the public, giving the public to understand that this proposal definitively assures the survival in Chile of a State of Law and representative democracy. In the first place, that is not going to depend on the letter of the law . . . but rather on the respect the next government has or does not have for it . . . In the second place, the proposed reforms are, for the most part, useless, because in the majority of the cases, they do nothing more than fill in unnecessary details or needless expressions of intent which the Constitution already establishes with sufficient clarity, while the few real changes of practical importance are actually gravely prejudicial . . .[20]

But it would remain for Salvador Allende to have the last word on the seven "guarantees." Safely ensconced in the presidency, he would have this exchange with fellow Marxist Régis Debray four months later:

> DEBRAY: Was it absolutely necessary? Was it essential to negotiate that Statute on democratic guarantees?
> ALLENDE: Yes, that's why we did it. I am still convinced that it was right to introduce the guarantees Statute, but I should make it clear that the use of the word negotiation is unjustified here, because we did not give ground on a single line of our Government program. Put yourself in the period in which this Statute got on the books, and you will see it as a tactical necessity.[21]

His later actions would speak much more loudly than mere cynical words.

THE TOOTHLESS TIGER

"Red Rule in Chile?
U.S. Keeps Hands Off"

That headline appeared in the *Miami Herald*, July 5, 1970, over a Santiago-datelined story written by the *Herald*'s Latin America editor,

Don Bohning. Bohning wrote that, in keeping with the doctrine of "low profile" in hemisphere affairs, enunciated by President Richard Nixon October 31, 1969, sources in both Santiago and Washington indicated the U.S. was "ready to tolerate a second Communist State in this hemisphere." He noted the contrast to Lyndon B. Johnson's stance in justifying U.S. intervention in the Dominican Republic in 1965—that the U.S. would never accept a second Communist regime in the hemisphere. Bohning also referred to a Washington dispatch by José M. Navasal in *El Mercurio* at that time, in which Navasal quoted a "top State Department official" as saying that the U.S. considers "the preservation of democracy is a responsibility incumbent on the citizens of each free country. We have stopped thinking," the official told Navasal, "that we [the U.S.] have the duty to aid in impeding every anti-democratic threat." The same official added that the U.S. would like to see Chilean voters again demonstrate faith in representative democracy, but if Chileans were to reach a different decision, "if a candidate is elected who opposed the concept of democracy that we sustain, then we would do no less than accept the verdict of the Chilean people. It would be painful, but we would have to respect it."

The "top official"—Charles A. Meyer, assistant secretary of state for Inter-American Affairs[22]—was doing more than merely mouthing reassuring platitudes. Several weeks earlier, a top-level group in Washington—including representatives of the White House, State and Defense departments, and the CIA, gathered as the "Forty Committee" (see note 8, chapter 4)—had reached the decision "that nothing should be done . . . that might affect the election." That decision was communicated in "late May or early June" by Richard Helms, then director of the CIA, to John A. McCone, a former CIA director and then member of the board of directors of ITT. McCone had gone to Helms to "reflect to him, and through him, to the policymakers of the Government" the views of ITT specialists that Allende was going to win the September election, and that if he did, it "would have a very serious effect on this country as well as the business interests involved." Helms did say some "minimal effort" to influence the election would be made by the CIA within its existing budget. Helms also told McCone he agreed with the ITT assessment that "there were no prospects" of Alessandri defeating Allende.[23]

Nor was Meyer merely mouthing platitudes when he spoke of how "painful" an Allende victory would be for the United States.

From the end of World War II to 1970, the U.S. had poured a total of $1.281 billion in aid to Chile, $957.6 million of it in official development assistance, not counting military aid.[24] At the time Allende came to power, U.S. private companies had a book value investment in Chile of $750 million, of which $313 million was insured by the U.S. government. Of Chile's external debt of $2.9 billion, nearly half of it, $1.357 billion, was owed to U.S. official and private agencies ($864 million and $493 million, respectively).[25]

The House Appropriations Committee, in a special 1970 study, showed that of 123 nations and seven territories which had received U.S. aid after 1946—including the war-ravaged countries of Europe, and later war allies in the Far East—only twenty-one had received more aid in total dollars than Chile. Of those, only one was in the Western Hemisphere: Brazil, a country with ten times the population (but which received only twice as much aid). In that list of countries receiving more aid in absolute terms, only five (Belgium-Luxembourg, France and Greece, South Vietnam and South Korea) received more aid per capita than Chile.[26] As to foreign investment, U.S. companies in 1970 had more invested in only five Latin countries: Argentina, Brazil, Mexico, Venezuela, and Panama (the first three with much larger populations; Venezuela then the number one source of foreign oil for the U.S.; and Panama, because of the canal, a special case). In few countries in the world, was the U.S. insurance exposure greater; the risk was so great, in fact, that Chile was regarded, by October 1971, as belonging, "potentially," to the "catastrophic loss" category.[27]

Allende had campaigned on a platform calling for nationalization of the vast bulk of those U.S. investments. His economic programs also menaced the stability of the already precarious Chilean economy.

The political diagnosis was at least as "painful." One of the main objectives of the Alliance for Progress was to contain Castro—and the spread of communism—in the hemisphere. As Henry Kissinger noted, ". . . two previous administrations had concluded that Salvador Allende and the forces behind him posed a sufficient threat to our interests to warrant our opposing him . . . That an Allende government threatened our national interests was conventional wisdom when Nixon entered office . . ."[28]

An Allende victory would create a pro-Soviet Havana-Santiago axis further weakening U.S. hegemony in the hemisphere. A leftist military regime had seized power in Peru a year earlier, and at that very moment of decision in Chile, another leftist military junta had seized power in Bolivia. In Argentina, the rightist military regime was tottering, and in Uruguay, the Tupamaros, a radical-left terrorist organization, seemed invincible. The U.S. was faced with the prospect of a hostile bloc of countries covering practically the entire southern cone of South America, a prospect which led to exultant claims in the Kremlin-mouthpiece Soviet press that "a revolutionary situation of a general character" existed in Latin America.[29] Anatoly A. Gromyko, son of the Soviet foreign minister and a specialist on U.S. affairs, would write just before the fall

of Allende: "The Cuban revolution and positive anti-imperialist transformations in a number of Latin American states have shown that the
socio-economic processes on that continent can sap and even undermine U.S. positions there."[30]

The pressures on the U.S. to act were not limited to the view from
Washington—or Moscow, or Peiping (later Beijing). Edward Malcolm
Korry, a feisty and voluble man then rounding out his third year as U.S.
ambassador to Chile, was under heavy siege from all three contenders as
the presidential campaign gathered momentum. As Korry would testify
later: "All three camps, three political camps, approached me directly for
funds, as did other people, for the electoral campaign. The United States
never responded." Among those soliciting Korry: Salvador Allende's
fundraiser, who asked for $1 million in U.S. money.[31]

Henry Kissinger told the Senate Foreign Relations Committee a similar story. "The CIA was heavily involved in 1964 in the election, was in a
very minor way involved in the 1970 elections, and since then we have
absolutely stayed away from any coups."[32] Kissinger went on to characterize as "blatant and almost obscene" the U.S. intervention to defeat
Allende in 1964, when the CIA pumped an estimated $20 million into
the election campaign of Christian Democrat Frei. As noted in chapter
4, such outside meddling was unnecessary since the Right had closed
ranks behind Frei, and Allende's chances in a two-way race were next to
nil. The most probable explanation for U.S. interference: official Washington was in the grip of a paroxsym of paternalism during the New
Frontier-Great Society years, dabbling in assassination plots, manipulating elections and governments.

As Ambassador Korry would note[33], the intervention in 1964 was
cocktail circuit gossip in Washington, but the media would remain
curiously silent about it for nine years, until the post-Watergate exor-
cisms—and until the targets of indignation were all on the Right.

Korry also had a large American "family" to keep in check during that
tumultuous election campaign. The "official" family included 120 officers and staffers at the American Embassy, AID (Agency for International Development) and U.S. Information Service (of whom, a
Communist source claimed in 1968, 42 were CIA agents, a number
presumably swollen by 1970);[34] 85 Peace Corps staffers and volunteers;
13 officers and enlisted men advising the Chilean armed forces; 8 officers, 81 airmen, and 53 dependents serving at U.S. air force observation
stations (on remote Easter Island and equally remote Punta Arenas, at
the frozen tip of the continent); and an estimated 3,000 civilians, many
of them long-term residents employed by 55 American companies ranging from small sales or distribution offices to the huge copper and iron
mining companies.

Korry did not know it, but still other pressures for U.S. intervention were boiling up in an elegant, eighth-floor suite in an old world hotel, just a few blocks up 16th Street from the White House. The hotel was the Sheraton-Carlton and the suite belonged to Harold S. Geneen, chairman and chief executive officer of International Telephone and Telegraph Corporation.

International Telephone and Telegraph (ITT) was a logical—and in some ways—an inevitable catalyst for the commotion which was to follow. Long before the terms "conglomerate" or "multinational" were coined, ITT had pyramided from a small telephone company in the Virgin Islands into a corporate colossus, and had done so largely under the guidance of an iron-willed genius, Harold Sydney Geneen. In 1970, Geneen was at the peak of his intimidating power, and ITT at the dizzying heights of its intoxication with power. By 1970, it employed 450,000 persons in sixty-odd countries, and its $6.6 billion in sales that year gave it eighth ranking among U.S. industrial corporations. Until the late 1960s, ITT concentrated its growth, and assets, outside the U.S. Along the way, it collected wounds as well as wealth, and a bruising style of survival in the treacherous arena of international politics and intrigue. The company also developed a wariness of leftist regimes: when the Iron Curtain clanged down on Eastern Europe, it cut ITT off from two of its telephone companies and other assets. The Communist takeover in China cost the company loss of the Shanghai Telephone and Electric companies. Later, Fidel Castro would seize the Cuban Telephone Co., a $50.6-million prize, the seventh time ITT had lost out to a Communist regime. One of the first acts of the leftist military junta in Peru in 1969 was to squeeze ITT out of the telephone business there.

By the early 1960s, ITT, which a decade earlier had constructed the Distant Early Warning (DEW) line defense system for the U.S., was constructing a political DEW line of its own: a corps of top-notch journalists and former diplomats at posts around the world to help steer the company through the shoals of international turmoil. In Washington, the company assembled a staff with specialties going far beyond the traditional bounds of lobbying: men and women with expert knowledge of and contacts in the defense and foreign service establishments, media, the Congress, and specialized agencies. Inevitably, the Washington office became the most militant of the ITT information and influence operations.

The office was headed by William R. Merriam, a corporate vice president who reported—theoretically—to Edward J. (Ned) Gerrity, the shrewd and disarmingly affable senior vice president who headed up ITT's huge worldwide corporate relations and advertising establishment. (Gerrity was also highly skilled at corporate survival; he had, in fact, survived longer than anyone else in ITT's top hierarchy alongside the hard-driving and demanding Geneen.) In common with many Washington corporate operatives, Merriam wriggled and squirmed constantly to escape the control of an intermediary (Gerrity) at the home office. Inevitably, too, this resulted in the Washington office attempting to do more than it should, and claiming more clout than it had.

ITT won a reputation as a brawler on the international scene in 1962 when Leonel Brizola, the leftist governor of the Brazilian State of Rio Grande do Sul, expropriated the company's small ($6-million) telephone company. Since it seemed that the leftist regime of Brazilian President João Goulart would go on a rampage against all American companies in the country, Geneen prodded Sen. Bourke B. Hickenlooper (R-Iowa) to throw a protective mantle over American business. Hickenlooper introduced an amendment to the Foreign Assistance Act of 1962 which required the president to suspend all economic assistance to any country that expropriated the property of a U.S. company, repudiated a contract with a U.S. company, or made a U.S. company subject to discriminatory taxation or administration.[35] That amendment remained a point of friction between the U.S. and Latin America for years until its repeal in the early seventies, especially among those regimes which equated economic nationalism with the ouster of American (and other foreign) private investment. (Prior to its repeal, liberals in the Congress and the foreign policy establishment in the U.S. teamed up to prevent the measure from ever actually being invoked, though there were several episodes which cried out for its application.)

With only seven weeks left until the Chilean elections, a man walked into the lobby of the Sheraton-Carlton and took a seat in one of the plush leather chairs. The man was William V. Broe, then chief of the Western Hemisphere Division of the CIA's Directorate of Plans—better known as Clandestine Services, irreverently known as the "department of dirty tricks."

A few minutes later, another man entered the lobby. "He came up to me and asked me" whether I was William Broe, the CIA man said. "I was the only one, frankly, sitting in the lobby at the time."

The man was Merriam. The time was about 10:30 on the evening of July 16, 1970, and the occasion was a meeting between Broe and Geneen which McCone, at his initiative, had suggested Helms set up.[36] Geneen said he agreed to the meeting "in order to get a detailed rundown from the Government as to the prospects of an Allende victory and what might happen thereafter." As for Broe, he learned that he was to meet Geneen only that day when Helms called Broe and said that McCone "had suggested or asked that someone who was knowledgeable about the situation in Chile get in touch with Geneen, who was going to be in

Washington that day." Beyond that, Broe said, his only instructions were to "keep open this channel of communication" with ITT.[37]

Geneen had ample cause for concern. In 1927, the company had acquired an English utility, the Chilean Telephone Co., Ltd. (ChilTelco). In 1967, the company negotiated a deal with the statist-minded government of the Christian Democrats to sell a 24 percent interest to the government's development corporation (CORFO), and 6 percent to the public. The agreement also contained a mechanism for a complete buy-out of the company by the Chilean government. By 1970, ITT valued its holdings in the company at $153 million, and until then, despite constant government audits of the company's books, that valuation had not been disputed by the Chilean government.

ITT had other interests in Chile: a telecommunications equipment factory founded in 1942 (eight hundred employees and an investment of $2.2 million); two cable companies, ITT World Communications and All America Cables and Radio (160 employees); ITT World Directories (whose 150 employees published telephone directories for ChilTelco); and two hotels worth $8.4 million and employing about seven hundred, the Sheraton-Carrera and the brand-new Sheraton San Cristóbal (both acquired in 1968). But these companies were not facing an economic firing squad; ChilTelco was.

In the platform of Allende's coalition, drafted the previous December, communications was one of six areas of the economy targeted for quick nationalization. Shortly before Broe and Geneen met, the coalition released its detailed communications plan. The plan not only banished any lingering doubts as to whether Allende would nationalize the company; it also laid the groundwork for the kind of "excess profits" arithmetic that would later be used to seize American copper interests without paying any compensation whatever. The document also said that "while the necessary legal instruments are being perfected . . . the Popular Government will take the necessary steps so that immediately the workers have participation in the Boards of Directors or Advisory Boards under which the companies and organizations mentioned operate at present."[38] This, of course, was a standard ruse for throwing a monkey wrench in management's machinery, since the "workers" were represented by Communist-controlled unions bent (as events would later demonstrate) on sabotaging the operation of the company.

Merriam took Broe up to Geneen's suite, and when Geneen arrived, left the two alone. Most of the meeting, which lasted slightly less than one hour, was given over to Broe's briefing on the development of the political campaign in Chile. In the course of that conversation, Geneen told Broe that in 1964 a group of American businessmen had contacted McCone, then head of the CIA, and told him they wished to contribute to an election fund. McCone told them the CIA "would not accept such a fund."

Geneen then told Broe ITT would again be willing to "assemble an election fund . . . a substantial fund" to support conservative candidate Jorge Alessandri in the 1970 campaign, then in the home stretch.

"Well," Broe said, "I told him we could not absorb the funds and serve as a funding channel. I also told him that the U.S. Government was not supporting any candidate in the Chilean election."[39]

Had Geneen bothered to ask McCone again, this time in McCone's capacity as ITT board member, the subject might never have come up at all. McCone said Geneen never mentioned his intention to make such an offer, and "if Geneen had made any suggestion to me that ITT or other corporations offer money to CIA for use in political purposes, I would have said CIA under no circumstances would consider such an offer, and I would advise against it."[40]

In fact, the evidence indicates the fund offer was an impetuous fishing expedition undertaken by Geneen as he groped for some means to protect ITT's imperiled stake in Chile. "We did not have a plan," Geneen would later recall. ". . . We hoped the government would have a plan, and we felt that we had something that we could offer that might be helpful to such a plan." He also made the point that he would have had to take such an "unusual" matter to ITT's board, but lacking "something tangible," he never did. "I come back to my point," Geneen said. "There was no real offer other than to go with whatever a government plan was . . .[41]

Neither Geneen nor anyone else in ITT again mentioned the "fund" idea during the campaign. Geneen was leaving the next day for a ten-day European trip. As the two men were parting, he asked Broe to call him on July 27th, and in the meantime, should he need to talk to anyone in ITT, to call Ned Gerrity. He did not ask Broe to contact Merriam.[42]

On July 27, Broe called Geneen. "We talked very briefly about the progress of the candidates," Broe said. "I do not think we talked more than two or three minutes actually, because he was obviously very busy; he took the call and I talked to him very briefly, and that was all."[43] Broe said there was no mention of the fund idea.

Salvador Allende's election, when it finally happened, was a bombshell everybody knew about but few actually expected to explode. A few days before the election, the State Department predicted privately that Alessandri would win handily.[44] Ambassador Korry predicted a narrow Alessandri victory. ITT's Robert Berrellez cabled his home office from Santiago on September 1 saying the "most reliable indicators" pointed to Alessandri winning with 40 percent to 41 percent of the vote. Berrellez added that he also had information from "the uppermost Chilean intelligence sources" that left-wing radicals were ready to spring a "three-stage sabotage and violence maneuver" in Santiago and other major cities should the vote appear to be going against Allende.

In the same report, Berrellez said, "reliable sources caution us to proceed slowly, not to panic even if pressures are strong in the beginning . . . Strong outside political and economic pressures, resulting in unemployment and unrest internally, will certainly strengthen the hand of left-wing extremists and convert Allende into merely a puppet of a machine dedicated to violent anti-U.S. revolution on a hemispheric scale."[45] Berrellez did not know it, but there were more readers for his coded messages sent "urgent system confidential," than he imagined, and one of those secret kibitzers would shortly be hatching exactly the sort of disruptive scheme he was cautioning against. That man was William V. Broe.

Berrellez wasn't the only Santiago observor urging calm. A few days after the election, Ambassador Korry met with representatives of the American business community in Santiago and urged them to: "(a) eschew any activity that could be interpreted as political; (b) avoid discussions involving the internal Chile political future . . . (c) seek to maintain normal production and normal activities at their firms to the maximum extent possible; (d) prepare for the possibility of nationalization or state intervention . . ."

To his own embassy people, Korry laid down even tougher guidelines. For weeks, they had been under orders to reduce their contacts with the Chilean military to a minimum. Beyond that, one man, "his family or any of his political lieutenants," had been declared positively off-limits for a year already. That man: Gen. Roberto Viaux Marambio. Earlier, Korry had even told Frei he would take measures to reduce the flow of American military and even tourists to Chile during the preelection period, an offer Frei rejected as unnecessary. With the votes counted and Chile plunged into a state of turmoil, tension and anxiety without precedent, Korry tightened up further and ordered all official Americans to avoid contacts with known extremists of the Right or Left. Over the next eight weeks, he himself would see Frei only twice, once to exchange a quick greeting at a municipal theater function, the second time on September 12, when he served for half an hour as interpreter for a visiting assistant secretary of state for cultural affairs.

American businessmen attending Korry's postelection meeting accepted the ambassador's advice without protest—almost. "Only one of the several dozen Americans present challenged this view," Korry said, "and sought to read a prepared statement calling for opposition to Dr. Allende's election by the Congress. I cut him short and forbade him to use U.S. Government premises for such inappropriate remarks. He was supported by no one else present. No American businessman in Chile ever involved the U.S. Embassy in any effort to interrupt the constitutional process that led to the election of Dr. Allende by the Congress . . ."[46]

The shattered forces of Alessandri attempted to regroup quickly behind a dispirited leader. Two days after the election, Alessandri's campaign manager, Dr. Arturo Matte Larraín, like Alessandri, his brother-in-law, a man in his seventies, unveiled for Berrellez the last-ditch scheme for blocking Allende legally. It became known as the "Alessandri formula," and called for moderate Christian Democrats to give their votes in Congress to Alessandri so as to elect him. He would then resign, new elections would be called—in which he would refuse to run—and Frei, presumably, would be elected with the backing of the Right, as he was in 1964. Such a maneuver would bypass the constitutional prohibition against a president succeeding himself, since an interim president would have served pending the new elections. The scheme was perfectly legal, but fraught with danger.

"The Alessandri camp," Berrellez wrote, "is fully aware of the consequences of such a maneuver—a bloodbath, since the far Left extremists would not take this without reacting violently." Matte, acknowledging this, said it was necessary in order to prevent communism from taking over the country.[47]

"About this Alessandri formula," Korry would testify later in Congress, "one, it is Chilean, it was Chilean-conceived. It is constitutional; the drafters of the Chilean constitution wrote it in because they wanted this option. It is not sleazy, a surreptitious thing. It was openly debated and discussed in any and all forms of Chilean communications for many weeks."[48]

But to work, the plan needed one crucial element: the active support of Frei. And that it never got.

FROM DISARRAY TO DESPERATION

Even before policy planners in the U.S.—public or private—had a chance to ponder their next move, economic disarray was setting in in Chile.

On the Monday following the Friday election, the small Santiago stock exchange failed to open as scheduled for the first time since 1938. When it did open on Tuesday, trading on the exchange's one hundred stocks was off by 60 percent, and prices fell by as much as 73 percent, especially of companies marked by Allende for nationalization. There was also a run on banks that Monday which one American banker said saw withdrawals total $13.5 million. In the first three days of business, that total would rise to the escudo equivalent of $25 million.

Foreigners in Santiago were approached on the streets during those first anxious days by Chileans willing to give them thirty-five and forty escudos to the dollar when the official exchange was 12.21 to the dollar. (In Miami, Perera Co., Inc., a leading exchange house, suspended trading in the Chilean escudo when the price, already well padded to allow for the escudo's weakness, tumbled from twenty-five to the dollar to forty to the dollar in the week following the election.) Weak currencies, it should be noted, routinely trade for considerably less beyond their home borders, and, when the margin is great, it is an indication of how artificially overvalued the currency is at home.

On Wednesday, September 9, Treasury Minister Andrés Zaldívar Larraín said the government had printed new money to meet the wave of withdrawals. "It is also true," he said, "that the government has taken all the steps necessary to assure depositors that they will be able to make their withdrawals." The next night, Allende went on nationwide radio to denounce what he called "a campaign of fear." He said the campaign would not stop with scare tactics, but that his opponents could be expected to resort in the future to "new means of sabotage, threatening imminent layoffs, suspending payment of salaries, and breaking other commitments, with even worse to come." He appealed for calm and said his plans to nationalize banks did not mean that deposits would be confiscated.

Appeals were not enough, however, especially against the backdrop of Allende's announced plans for the economy. On September 23, Zaldívar said "financial reactions in the week following the election had provoked a credit and banking crisis." He said the Central Bank had to supply $48 million to banks—three times the average for a full month—during the first two weeks of September alone to cover runs on those banks. Sales of all goods except food had fallen by 30 percent to 80 percent, he said. He added that the inflow of capital from abroad had stopped, and that inflation and further unemployment threatened. Allende's partisans said Zaldívar's report came at a time when panic was subsiding and that it was designed to tip the balance in Congress against Allende.[49]

"It would be unwise to conclude," American correspondent William Montalbano wrote a few days after Allende's election, "that the Right, which has ruled Chile in one fashion or another for four centuries, has surrendered totally. But, for the moment at least, what is most evident among Alessandri's partisans is despair."[50] The reporter was wrong in repeating the glib sophistry about "four centuries of rightist rule"—the Right had lost its political power in Chile in 1920, and irrevocably in 1938, and its economic power, fading ever since the midtwenties, had all but vanished in the sixties. But he was right about despair. That despair would soon turn to desperation.

For some, like the women who staged what Montalbano described as "a mournful march, chanting 'Cuba no, Chile sí' " it was the beginning of a long and often bitter campaign of peaceful resistance.

For others, the solution was flight. On his postelection rounds of Santiago, Montalbano discovered lines stretching from the counters to the streets at centers issuing vaccination certificates needed for international travel. A woman asked Montalbano, half in jest, he remarked, "Do you think that the Cuban exiles could find room for all of us in Miami?" Eventually, thousands of Chileans would leave their country during Allende's three years. (How many is anybody's guess; Chileans did not have to register to emigrate. What is known is that more than twenty thousand returned to Chile from the opulent U.S. alone in the first two years after the fall of Allende, to share the bitter harvest of economic hardship, and—at least in the vision of the international press—"fascist repression.")

Within a few weeks, U.S. Consul Frederick D. Purdy would report swarms of long-time American residents of Chile turning up to get their outdated passports validated. "We issued 126 passports in September. In the past ten years," he added, "this consulate never issued more than sixty in a month." Purdy also reported a 100 percent increase in inquiries from Hungarians and Czechs who had fled to Chile following Soviet-crushed uprisings against the Communist rulers in their native lands and who now wanted to escape to the United States. Long lines of Chileans formed daily outside the American consulate in an almost hopeless wait for visas.[51]

For others, the situation called for decisive action. A few days after the votes were in, a young buzzsaw of a lawyer named Pablo Rodríguez Grez organized two hundred fellow lawyers and others in an organization called Movimiento Nacional Patria y Libertad (National Fatherland and Liberty Movement). Its purpose: to persuade whatever Christian Democrats were needed to back the "Alessandri formula." When, on September 24, it became plain that the Christian Democrats were going to back Allende, most of the members of the movement drifted away in a spell of despair. A few decided that, the law having failed them, they would resort to lawlessness.

For a few desperate days, the idea of armed struggle would grow in the minds of a handful of the vanquished, until in an instant of panic, they would immolate themselves, and the hopes of many others. Three men played pivotal roles in the plotting: retired Gen. Roberto Viaux Marambio, the hero (to many, in and out of the armed forces) of the October 21, 1969, pocket uprising against Frei; a forty-one-year-old industrial chemist named Luis Gallardo Gallardo; and José Jaime Melgoza Garay, who brought passion and a mercurial personality to his new-found political activism. Their scheming, which, at various times, involved some of the senior commanders of the armed forces, came to an explosive climax early on the morning of October 22. Four carloads of armed men surrounded the car of army commander-in-chief Gen. René Schneider Chereau, with orders to kidnap him. The idea: hold him for forty-eight hours and demand of Frei the formation of a military cabinet as a first step toward calling new elections. Instead, Schneider was slain in a hail of gunfire.* Two days later, a stunned Congress voted to confirm Allende as president.

DAYS OF WINE AND *EMPANADAS*

He called it *"la vía chilena al socialismo,"* the Chilean road to socialism, a revolution replete with *"empanadas y vino tinto"* (meat pies and red wine). It would be, Salvador Allende said, a revolution such as the world had never known, a journey without maps, yet one "anticipated by the classics of Marxism," by the oracle Friedrich Engels himself.[52]

Russia, half a century before, had pioneered one path to socialism, through the dictatorship of the proletariat. Now, Chile would show the world a second way. We are today, Allende would boldly proclaim, "the first nation on earth called to construct the second model of transition to a socialist state. The task is extraordinarily complex, because there is no precedent to inspire us. We walk a new road, we march through trackless terrain without benefit of a guide, our only compass our faithfulness to the humanism of the ages, and particularly Marxist humanism; having as our true north the outline of the society we wish to have . . . our task is to define in practice the Chilean road to socialism, a new model for the State, for the economy, for society, centered on man, his needs and aspirations . . . There are no previous experiences that we might use as a model; we must develop the theory and the practice of new forms of social, political and economic organization, both so as to break the grip of underdevelopment as well as to create socialism . . ."[53]

Salvador Allende was in the presidency over six months before, on May 21, 1971, he announced that journey without maps, one that would rapidly become a nightmarish journey without maps. There was but a single objective at the end of his road, and that objective was power, including the power to destroy, forever, those who would oppose him or his heirs in Marxism.

---

* Details of the plot are contained in the Appendix. As fascinating as they are, I have also reserved for the Appendix details of the ITT, CIA, Nixon-Kissinger, and Moscow machinations since, in the end, none of them amounted to more than a bombastic media sideshow to the larger Chilean drama.

He never had any real chance, either, of reaching that objective, because he and those who accompanied him were a minority not only in the land, but even within the coalition that put him in the presidency. And so, on November 3, 1970, he began to plunge the country into a thousand days of strife and lawlessness, ending in economic ruin and civil war, the fabric of Chilean society torn to tatters.

There were ominous signs, even in those first days, but with spring in the air, the days were, for the most part, days of wine and *empanadas*.

Delegations from sixty countries gathered at the Capitol to watch as Senate President Tomás Pablo administered the thirty-word oath of office to Salvador Allende, inaugurating him as Chile's twenty-eighth constitutional president. Among the onlookers were unofficial observors from Cuba, North Vietnam, the Peoples' Republic of China (Red China, as it was then known), the German Democratic Republic (East Germany)—and the pro-Communist (and tiny) Puerto Rican independence movement. Ten days later, defying the solemn decision six years earlier of the Organization of American States to break relations collectively with the Fidel Castro dictatorship because of its repeated subversion of other American states, Allende announced the resumption of diplomatic relations with Cuba. It was his first significant foreign policy initiative. (Within seven months, all of those "unofficial" delegations would become official; on January 5, Chile became the second country in the hemisphere [after Cuba] to establish diplomatic relations with Peiping [Beijing]; East Germany was next, three months later, and North Vietnam and North Korea followed—also, after Cuba, hemispheric "firsts"—on June 1, 1971.)

The new, fifteen-member Cabinet contained no surprises: Socialists got two key portfolios: Interior (key because it controlled the 26,300-man national police force, the paramilitary Carabineros); and the Foreign Ministry, plus two lesser ministries. The Communists and Radicals got three apiece, the Social Democrats two, one went to the miniscule API (Independent Popular Action), and the remaining one to a self-styled "independent." Of the other key posts, Castro crony Jacques Chonchol, head of a tiny splinter party (MAPU), got Agriculture, and was on the job only two days when he would announce: "from here out, the peasants are in charge." Pedro Vuskovic, a doctrinaire Marxist who presented himself as an independent, got the Economy Ministry—and promptly declared a war on inflation. The new labor minister, Communist José Oyarce, initiated his reign by announcing that the right to strike would be scrupulously respected by the Popular Unity government.[54]

There was cruel irony in all of this. Peasants never ruled; they became, instead, the pawns of an ideological fanaticism designed not to bring "justice" to the countryside, but to install a new order, a new lawlessness which would very nearly devastate Chilean agriculture. As for controlling inflation, the new economic enlightenment would not only drain Chile's treasury, but bring the country to virtual bankruptcy, unable to pay its debts—and reeling under the worst inflation in its history, and one of the worst on the face of the earth. And strikes? This government which claimed to rule in the name of the peasants and the workers would vent such violence on labor as to convert labor into an avenging angel crucial to driving Allende from power.

Thanks largely to a boom in copper prices—Chile's copper earnings had more than doubled in the five years before he came to power, rising from $428 million in 1965 to $925 million at the end of 1969—Allende inherited an economy which gave at least the illusion of prosperity. As a direct result of the copper boom, Chile's international reserves in 1970 stood at an all-time high, $393 million (a figure that would not be equalled until the Pinochet boom of 1978–1981, when reserves would reach more than ten times that level). Urban unemployment had been declining steadily, from 7.6 percent in 1966 to 3.8 percent as Allende took office (in 1972, it would fall even lower, to 3.6 percent, an all-time low, until, the economy shattered, it would soar to the teens, remaining there for over a decade). Rural unemployment was even lower, down from 4.5 percent in 1966 to 2.4 percent in 1970 (bottoming out at 1.8 percent the following year, before, it, too, would rise steeply, plateauing at 5.7 percent in 1985). Inflation, which had inched up to 30 percent in 1970, would drop by 50 percent during Allende's first full year in office—before skyrocketing to more than a crushing 500 percent at the end. There was another disquieting statistic, little noted amid the artificially stimulated economic euphoria and political paroxysms of that turbulent interlude: The growth of the economy, sluggish during most of the Christian Democrat years, had dropped to a dismal 2.1 percent in 1970. Once again, Allende's first full year in office (1971) would see it shoot up to 9 percent—before plunging to minus levels his last two years.[55]

As his cartographer of the economy, Allende turned to Pedro Vuskovic, a man steeped in the "structuralist" ideas of the UN Economic Commission for Latin America (ECLA). Dominated by the Argentine economist Raúl Prebisch, ECLA, through the sixties and early seventies, exerted great power over development strategies and spending (much of it U.S.-funded) in Latin America, preaching its gospel of economic salvation through rigorous state control and government planning for a better tomorrow. Though nominally an independent,

Vuskovic, who worked for ECLA from 1949 to 1969 before joining the Allende campaign, had close ties to Communists, helping Communist economist José Cademartori in his run for a Chamber of Deputies seat.[56] Vuskovic was only one of a number of Marxists Allende would lure back to Chile from cushy jobs in a number of international agencies. Still others were recruited locally from ECLA. One such: Max Nolff, a Communist, who became Allende's minister of mines.

What Vuskovic charted was an erratic course which contained two main features: "socialist consumerism," an ersatz version of Keynesian "pump-priming,"[57] and galloping state control of the economy, a concept pleasing to the Christian Democrats, inasmuch as they had practiced it themselves, but displeasing when they witnessed the breakneck pace of it under Allende/Vuskovic. Following the very first Cabinet meeting, on November 9, Vuskovic announced a fourteen-month battle plan to bring about "a rapid rise in the levels of economic activity, substantial headway against unemployment, a significant change in the distribution of income and containment of inflationary pressures."[58] Measures included a 50 percent cut in interest rates—a bonanza for debtors, a disaster for lenders, with the result that bank shares "came tumbling down" on the stock market. The government moved swiftly to buy control of those weakened banks, ultimately controlling virtually the entirety of the credit system (with ruinous consequences, as well, for the once solvent banking system).[59] *El Mercurio*, for a century Chile's leading newspaper—and, increasingly, an embattled beacon of opposition to Allende—editorialized dryly: It is hard to understand how "a program which raises wages by a minimum of 35 percent while at the same time claims to stabilize prices and the value of the money—including the exchange rate for the dollar—a measure which, nonetheless, would imply an increase in money in circulation of approximately 5 billion escudos, can yet promise a 10 percent increase in gross domestic product in one year." (*El Mercurio* not only did not exaggerate, it understated the suicidal means Allende would take to "finance" his journey without maps: printing-press money. Before he was finished, Allende would preside over a tenfold increase in money in circulation until, in the end, the bills were literally not worth the paper they were printed on.)[60]

The very first targets of business takeover were the small Chilean branches of two U.S. firms, Indiana Brass Co., and Ralston Purina, seized on November 20, under a 1945 labor law on the grounds they had deprived their workers of jobs. (Satisfactory payment terms were later worked out.) A month later, on December 21, Allende unveiled his promised constitutional amendment to seize the copper companies (Congress would approve that proposal 158–0 the following July; more on copper later), and on December 30, his intention to nationalize banks, moving in the meantime to buy them out. It would be almost a year before he would take aim at Chilean businesses, on October 19, 1971, announcing the nationalization of 150 firms which he said played a key role in the overall economy. He would, at that same time, pledge to retain a mixed state-private economy.[61]

There was one other "economic" measure worth remembering from those giddy first days. "Man of the people" Allende rented for himself a walled and opulent estate, called Tomás Moro, in one of the ritziest neighborhoods of Santiago, consisting of a Moorish-styled manor house, large terrace, grounds and swimming pool and outbuildings which, among other things, housed as many as seventy-five heavily armed palace guards. The new tenant was the same man who had told his countrymen, two days after his inauguration: "In this Government, we might put our foot in it—but never our hand. We will be unbending in safeguarding the morality of the regime." Now, one month later, he put an Allende-style spin on his acquisition. In a meeting with top administration officials, Allende said: "If anyone in the Popular Unity thinks we have come here to perpetuate self-serving 'advantage-taking,' they are wrong. I, for example, have rented a comfortable house because mine, the one in which I have lived since 1953, is not adequate in terms of security for a man who is going to expropriate the copper companies, the banks, the big estates and the monopolies."[62] Chile's two previous presidents lived out their entire terms in their own modest homes, and one of them—Alessandri—even walked to work at the palace. Allende would not even bother to explain his later real estate acquisitions, including a sprawling estate on the outskirts of Santiago called El Cañaveral, where, increasingly, he spent much of his time in the company of his long-time mistress, Miría Contreras Bell de Ropert, and which, like Tomás Moro, was also an armed camp.

Even before the incendiary agriculture minister, Jacques Chonchol, announced on February 15 that all farms which could be legally taken would be by the end of 1971, illegal seizures and violence had begun to disfigure the face of rural Chile. Allende's ambivalence in reacting to that violence—as well as the officially sanctioned (and often officially encouraged) violence in the factories—was one of the fatal flaws of his rule.

On the one side was Allende, the career civil servant, the lawmaker, the Man of La Mancha, riding out to fight and right injustice wherever he found it, blazing a new revolutionary trail as he went. This was the romantic Allende, the one nourished by his vanity and his yearning to make his mark on posterity.

But there was a darker side, the side molded and shaped during so many years of struggle and survival in a party that prided itself on its revolutionary flame, a party that defiantly asserted, with Salvador Allende already in the presidency: "The bourgeois state in Chile will not serve as a basis for socialism, and it is necessary to destroy it."[63]

And it was this side, fed by his own weakness and superficiality, which would persistently yield a man whose deeds mocked his noble words. It was this side, too, which was reflected in his intoxication with class warfare. Witness, for example, what he told a Valparaíso audience on February 4, 1971, in a speech: "I am not the president of the Socialist Party. I am the president of the Popular Unity. Nor am I president of all Chileans. I am not a hypocrite . . . I am not the president of all Chileans." Later, in his first State of the Union message, on May 21, he expanded on that theme: "the People's Government is inspired in its policy by a premise that is artificaly denied by some—the existence of classes and social sectors with antagonistic and opposing interests."[64]

Tolerance for "revolutionary violence" also echoed—as already indicated—the dominant thrust of his own Socialist party. The party was then largely under the sway of Carlos Altamirano, a man whose fiery impetuosity would later cost Allende dearly. To Altamirano—and to the Maoist-inspired Movement of the Revolutionary Left (MIR)—"civil war in Chile was inevitable and the role of the Left was to prepare for armed insurrection. They aimed to bring about the classical prerevolutionary situation of 'dual power' by building up militant organizations inside state-run industries, in the workers' suburbs of Santiago, and among peasant groups. The members of these 'soviets' were to be trained and organized for a violent insurrection in which Santiago's vital services would be crippled and the industrial suburbs and revolutionary campamentos would 'encircle' the capital."[65] It was a strategy Allende had brandished as a threat during the sixty days of decision before his inauguration, it was one he connived in while denouncing it down to the last days of his presidency, and it was one he would, in fact, believe was his final salvation down to the moment of his death.

It was a strategy which his Communist partners warned him against repeatedly. And it ultimately would cost him the support of the Christian Democrats, and tip the balance of power against him.

He was on the job less than a week when his government moved to quash proceedings against imprisoned or fugitive MIR leaders. On January 4, he made it official by granting a presidential pardon to forty-three guerrillas belonging to MIR and a similar organization, the Organized Vanguard of the People (VOP). One of those pardoned, Arturo Rivera Calderón, later committed a crime that, as much as any other event, incinerated Salvador Allende's chances of success in the presidency. (Among the others pardoned were men of equally violent character, including Luciano Cruz, Miguel and Edgardo Enríquez, Juan Bautista von Schowen, Sergio Zorrilla, Humberto Sotomayor, Max Joel Marambio—all of whom would confer upon Allende's presidency an aura of violence which both fascinated and enfeebled him. For further background on the MIR, and the above-named, see pages 250–258, chapter 5.)

Had words indeed been deeds, those violent men (and the violent women with them) would have remained neutralized. The words, for example, of his interior minister, José Tohá, reassuring an apprehensive Chilean Congress investigating the first clash between Carabineros and armed participants in an illegal *toma* (seizure) of a farm: "The government will never permit, anywhere in the country, under any circumstances whatever, the existence of armed groups organized outside the law." While saying that, Tohá also ordered an investigation—into the behavior of the officer in charge of the Carabinero detail which had returned the fire of an armed band seizing a farm ("Lo Prado Abajo") in a tiny village about one hundred miles southwest of Santiago. The incident, which took place November 26, was the first such in the new administration, and the administration's response was a clear slap at the forces of law-and-order—the first of many.[66]

A French writer, Suzanne Labin, vividly described a *toma:* "A band armed with clubs and rifles forces its way onto a farm, orders the whole of the owner's family to pack their bags; pushes them out onto the road; gathers together all those who work on the farm; tells them that it is their property from now on, and sets up a banner with the words: 'This property has been seized by the people.' " She also noted that despite protestations of innocence from the Allende government, by July of 1971, "police records showed that 658 farms had been illegally seized—as well as 339 industrial firms, 218 parcels of urban land, and 154 schools."[67] "Legal" expropriations of farmland would, during that first year alone, exceed the number taken by Frei during his six years of ambitious "land reform."[68]

As Allende neared the end of his first six months in office, he nevertheless found support in the objective universe for his characteristic ebullience. On April 4, voters went to the polls in 280 municipal elections, the first electoral test of Allende's strength since his election. His Popular Unity coalition scored a smashing victory, collecting 49.73 percent of the votes; an impressive 13.4 percent increase over the previous September. But there were three important caveats. The first, and most important: although the victory was impressive it still did not give Allende the clear majority he needed to rule by fiat, particularly since cracks were already appearing within his coalition. The second:

for the first time, not only were eighteen-to-twenty-one year olds voting in that election, an electorate predictably more responsive to "revolutionary" rhetoric, but also illiterates, a group easy prey for demagogues and the politics of hand-outs. The third, as pointed out by seasoned observor Alistair Horne: absenteeism in those elections reached 25 percent as compared with the usual 19 percent.[69]

There was, then, a touch of complacency in the land. And why not?—why not, that is, because, if you didn't look too closely, Chile was actually enjoying an economic boom of sorts, and unless you happened to be among the few hundreds whose properties had been wrenched from them, and if you weren't terribly fastidious about the letter of the law, then that "paper dam," the Statute of Guarantees, was still in place, and calamity had not, after all, been visited upon the anxious land.

Writing four years later, Prof. Paul E. Sigmund, a scholar with extensive experience in Chile (and generally sympathetic to the leftish views of the Christian Democrats), would say: "The period after the municipal elections now appears to have been crucial for the long-term survival of the regime. The Right was still in disarray. The Christian Democrats had elected a compromise leadership which was not committed to either of the party's wings, and the short-run economic and political indicators were favorable. Yet, instead of taking action on the economic front to stem the loss of foreign reserves and to dampen inflationary pressures—and on the political to prevent the movement of the Christian Democrats into an alliance with the right-wing opposition parties—the regime continued its previous policies, confidently assuming that in the long run, 'the people' would support it and ignoring the warnings of 'bourgeois' economists that the loss of foreign reserves, the expansion of demand, and the sharp decline in investment would produce disastrous consequences in the following year."

Yet, as Sigmund would observe in that same essay, there was a fatal flaw in Allende's reasoning: "Allende acted as if he had that [majority] support, but even at the highest point of his popularity in the April 1971 elections, he never achieved it."[70]

FIRST BLOOD

On the morning of June 8, 1971, the poison of radical rhetoric, long festering in Chile's body politic, a poison which was the very mother's milk of the regime then in power, exploded on the streets of Santiago in the cruel and cowardly rat-a-tat of machinegun fire. The immediate victim was a man, but the real casualty was Salvador Allende and his vainglorious deliriums of dynasty.

Edmondo Pérez Zújovic was driving to work when, before the horrified eyes of his daughter, three men opened fire. Nine bullets pierced his body. The man who had served his country, first as minister of public works, then as vice president and interior minister under Eduardo Frei, was dead before the first ambulance reached the scene. He was fifty-nine.

All Chile was shocked. Salvador Allende went on nationwide radio and television to denounce "the introduction into our country of practices absolutely alien to our tradition." He ordered a massive manhunt to track down the perpetrators.

There were those who found hollowness in his words, because they remembered that Arturo Rivera Calderón, the head of the hit squad, was among the forty-three violent terrorists pardoned by Allende only six weeks after he assumed the presidency.

Christian Democrat leaders from Eduardo Frei on down denounced the crime and demanded that the investigation be turned over to the military, because they didn't trust Eduardo (Coco) Paredes, the man who headed the police investigative force. Wasn't Paredes himself linked previously to the VOP (Vanguardia Organizada del Pueblo), and the larger and equally violent Movement of the Revolutionary Left (MIR), one of their leaders asserted on the floor of the Senate? When the slain leader's daughter identified the assassins from police photos, the army joined the manhunt.

There were those who found irony along with the anguish in the cries of the Christian Democrats. They remembered that in 1969, when the Left screamed for Zújovic's scalp over a "massacre" he had nothing to do with, Renán Fuentealba, then the party's president, and Radomiro Tomic, later the party's presidential candidate, were among the party leaders calling for Zújovic's ouster (see pp. 256–257, chapter 5).

But, beyond the shock, and beyond the remembrance of wrongs, there arose in the land an anxiety that could not be abated, not even when, five days later, Ronald Rivera Calderón, the triggerman, would die in a blaze of gunfire as he attempted to flee across rooftops. His brother Arturo, the mastermind, would end his own life rather than accept capture. Three days later, the third hit man, VOP leader Heriberto Salazar Bello, forced his way into a police station in Santiago and activated a bomb strapped to his waist, killing himself and two policemen, wounding a third. Arturo Fontaine, the author and journalist, would express it as follows: "The eyes of the country looked not only at the hand that pulled the trigger but also at the whole system of hatred that had produced this cold-blooded murder . . ."[71]

It was the beginning of a fateful political realignment, within the principal parties of the so-called "democratic left," and then in their relationship to the Allende government. But for that to happen, the façade of unity within those parties, masking deep divisions between Left and Right, first had to melt in the white hot debate over a question which could no longer be evaded: whether to submit—connive, even— in Salvador Allende's *vía chilena al socialismo.* By the winter of 1971, less than one year after Allende had assumed the presidency, it was clear beyond any dispute where that path would lead: the profound transformation of Chile, from a Western-style democracy into a Marxist-Leninist regime in which democracy as a meaningful term would become moot. Moot, because Allende made it clear (the behavior of his cohorts even clearer) that he intended to transform not only the economy, not only the social arrangements, but the most basic elements of the democracy itself, the court system, the legislature. And change them, not gradually, but roughly, rapidly, uprooting in a matter of mere months the century-and-a-half evolutionary processes in those societal structures and arrangements, jamming the new and jerry-built ones into place as though there were a mandate to do so. But, as noted earlier, roughly two-thirds of all Chileans had voted for no such violent revolution in their country, in their lives, and with the murder of Pérez Zújovic, now not even the leadership of the political parties could any longer support what their constitutents clearly did not.

And so, over the vehement objections of the ultraleftists who had until then controlled the party, the Christian Democrats entered into the first ever tactical alliance of their own choosing with the Right. That decision led to yet another major split within the party: eight deputies and a number of other leaders pulled out to form a pro-Allende party, the Izquierda Cristiana (Christian Left). The same anguished debate produced a similar split in the Radical party, that one member of the Popular Unity coalition so vital to the appearance of legitimacy of the Allende government because of the party's long democratic record. Five of seven Radical senators and seven of nineteen deputies quit to form the Partido de la Izquierda Radical (Party of the Radical Left-PIR). Though the PIR would continue to give lukewarm backing to Allende for a time, by mid-1972, it, too, had gone over to the ranks of the outright opposition. (On August 11, three Radical ministers and MAPU Minister Chonchol offered their resignations to Allende in the wake of the divisions within their parties; Allende refused them, and Chonchol bolted the microcosmic MAPU party he helped create in 1970 when he deserted the PDC for the equally miniscule Christian Left formed in July of 1971 by the ultraleft Christian Democrat dissidents, the so-called terceristas).[72]

The decision to break with Allende was a traumatic one for the Christian Democrats, and made possible only because Eduardo Frei, reluctantly abandoning his Olympian perch above the life-and-death struggles raging around him, once again invested his own energies and matchless following into the struggle, as he had done in 1970. The decision was traumatic because it went against the very grain of the socialist mindset of the PDC. Indeed, months later, in March 1972, their presidential standard-bearer, Radomiro Tomic, would still lament that Allende had committed a "fatal political error" in failing to forge an "institutional majority" in the Congress through a "far-reaching agreement between socialists inspired by Christianity and socialists inspired by Marxism—that is, between the Christian Democrats and the Popular Unity—in the period following the presidential election."[73] Yet those splits within the parties facilitated a new clarity of purpose; on September 26, responding to increasingly vituperative Allende attacks on Frei, the Christian Democrats announced their formal opposition to the government.

The tactical alliance between the PDC and the Right found expression a few days after another kind of earthquake—a physical one—jolted the provinces of Coquimbo, Aconcagua, and Valparaíso, on July 8, 1971. A by-election was held in Valparaíso to fill a vacancy in the Chamber of Deputies created by the death of the office-holder. Although the government poured massive relief aid into the province, and although it was on Allende's own home turf—where, indeed, he had temporarily established the seat of government—an independent backed by the united forces of the Right and the Christian Democrats defeated Hernán del Canto, secretary-general of the labor federation (and later Allende's law-defying interior minister and secretary-general of government).

This marriage of convenience between the Christian Democrats and the Right would survive down to the very end of the drama. In no small measure, this rickety, wobbly and even improbable alliance lasted because of the pig-headedness of Allende himself—and the worsening climate of violence, confrontation, and class-warfare promoted by the many around him who never really believed power came from anywhere but the barrel of a gun. Before allowing himself to be swept along in the avalanche of violence during his last year in La Moneda, Allende himself seemed to waver between a yearning to believe he could construct his "socialist" new state through peaceful means, and his own lifelong fascination with the swashbucklers of armed revolution. He professed special admiration for Fidel Castro, Ernesto (Che) Guevara, Ho Chi Minh, and Chou en Lai—all of whom he had met personally, all of them proponents and practitioners of the armed struggle. He was, after all, the man who, while serving as president of the Senate, also served as a director of the Organization of Latin American Solidarity (OLAS), dedicated to violent revolution. He was, after all, the man who would throw his own cloak of parliamentary immunity around three survivors of the rag-tag Che Guevara guerrilla band routed by Bolivian special forces, accompanying them to final safety all the way to Tahiti. And he was the man who told the French Marxist writer Régis Debray: "To begin with, we are going to contain it with their own laws. Then we shall meet reactionary violence with revolutionary violence, because we know that they are going to break the rules. For the time being, to stay within the domain of legality, I shall say this . . ."[74]

On July 3, 1971, ten members of the notorious Uruguayan terrorist organization, the Tupamaros, were released from jail and arrived in Chile. Among them: the wife of Raúl Sendic, chieftain of the Tupamaros, who broke with his Socialist party a decade earlier because of scorn for the electoral route to power, and whose "achievements" would include the kidnapping and murder of Dan Mitrione, a civilian employee of the U.S. Embassy in Montevideo. They chose Chile, they said on arrival, because "we know that in Chile, there is an almost fanatical respect for legality . . ." The Allende government welcomed them, not as political exiles, but with tourist visas.[75]

> Régis Debray: In other words, the workers are perhaps in power, but they certainly have no power in the judiciary.
> Salvador Allende: Precisely.
> Debray: Aren't you worried by these restrictions?
> Allende: Yes, very worried. But as we have said, I shall respect the limitations imposed by a system which is not of our making while the three powers exist independently . . .[76]

In his electoral platform, Allende announced his intention to abolish the bicameral legislature and replace it with a unicameral Congress. He reserved particular venom for the Supreme Court (which he said stood accused of "exercising its duties with a clear class bias," and later mocked and caricatured it as a redoubt of aged and irrelevant dinosaurs). Once in power, he made increasingly plain his intention not only to transform the court system, but to curb dramatically the power of the other two branches of government, so that they might continue to "exist independently"—but just barely. In all of this, however, there remained that fatal flaw: whether he actually would have the backing of the people to do so.

> Debray: But bourgeois democracy remains intact here. You, in fact, hold the executive power . . . but not legislative or judicial power; nor the apparatus of police power. Legality, the institutions, these were not the work of the proletariat, the bourgeoisie formulated the constitution to suit its own ends.

> ALLENDE: Of course ... we said we would take advantage of what openings there are in the present constitution to open the way to the new constitution, the people's constitution ... If we put forward a bill and Congress rejects it, we invoke the plebiscite ...[77]

Those words were uttered only two months after he had assumed office. A few months later, on May 21, 1971, he delivered his first State of the Union message. Now, flushed with the sense of power that came from his stunning victory in the municipal elections a month earlier, he gave Congress what amounted to a defiant ultimatum: "Our legal system must be modified. Hence the great responsibility of the two Houses at the present time: to help and not to hinder the changes in this system. On whether the Congress takes a realistic attitude depends to a great extent whether capitalist legality will be succeeded by socialist legality in conformity with the social and economic changes we are making and without a violent break in jurisdiction which would open the door to arbitrary acts and excesses which we, as responsible people, wish to avoid."[78]

Allende chose a curious moment to pursue his revolutionary ambitions. He signed the proposed legislation on November 10, 1971, the very day Fidel Castro would arrive in Chile on his first visit to Latin America since 1959, the year he seized power. (In the intervening years, he had been busy with other kinds of "visits" to Latin America: sending arms and revolutionaries such as Che Guevara in a futile attempt—in Castro's phrase—to convert the Andes Mountains into the equivalent of Cuba's Sierra Maestra, the spinal cord of violent revolution.) Castro's visit to Chile, like Castro's speeches, was a rambling marathon, lasting twenty-five days, memorable mainly for energizing opposition to Allende—and for a fateful souvenir he would leave behind: an AK-47 sub-machinegun, with a gold-plated inscription: "To my friend and comrade-in-arms. Fidel Castro." (Breaking fourteen years of self-imposed silence, Allende's mistress and confidante, Miría Contreras Bell de Ropert, revealed that Castro's "militant tourism" in Chile was, at first, a source of joshing for Allende, later of deep concern. "By the looks of things, Fidel won't ever leave Chile; he likes it here too much." Thus, she said, they joked among themselves as the visit, originally expected to last ten days, dragged on and on. "Kidding aside, the President realized that Castro's visit was transforming itself into a veritable political catastrophe. And the worst of it was that Allende didn't know how to tell Castro to leave ...")[79]

On November 21, the Christian Democrats announced their opposition to the constitutional changes. Six days later, the Constitutional Committee of the Congress voted them down. Allende never did call for the plebiscite, nor did he ever resubmit his proposals. Instead, he would resort, ever more boldly, to bending, twisting, and just plain ignoring the laws he had sworn to uphold and defend.

To the extent that it had ever existed at all, as more than merely a smorgasbord of overheated rhetoric, *la vía chilena al socialismo* was now dead. Indeed, Allende would not again ever seriously mention it.

EMPTY POTS, ANGRY PANS

By late 1972, a survey done by a popular chain of cooperative stores showed that of three thousand basic products normally stocked, more than five hundred were unavailable.[80] But even as the summer of 1971 approached, shortages, skyrocketing prices, and long lines had already become fixtures of Chilean life. On December 1, 1971, thousands of Chilean women—the largest outpouring of women demonstrators within memory, according to *El Mercurio*[81]—took to the streets of Santiago. Many of the women brandished—and banged on—empty pots and pans. As we have seen in chapter 1, and will see later, this was not the first time that the women of Chile had taken a decisive stand in times of crisis—nor would it be the last. As the demonstrators streamed onto the city's main artery, the Alameda, from streets edging Santa Lucía Hill, they were attacked by mobs from the Communist party's Ramona Parra and "Elmo Catalán" Brigades and the radical-left MIR. The attackers wielded clubs and hurled rocks and potatoes embedded with razor blades. Soon, Carabineros, acting under orders from the Interior Ministry, moved in with tear gas. When the dust settled, ninety-nine persons were injured—some suffering gunshot wounds—and 187 persons were under arrest. The next day, Allende declared a state-of-emergency (and later a curfew) in Santiago Province. Under that state-of-emergency, street demonstrations were banned, news censorship imposed, and persons became subject to arrest without warrant. Interior Minister José Tohá, charging that the demonstrations were part of an "orchestrated, seditious plan," also ordered the closing of two Christian Democrat-controlled radio stations which had supported the demonstrations. (Efforts to bully and muzzle the press, while bankrolling an ever-expanding official press, began in the early days of the regime and continued to the very last.)

The Christian Democrats, joined the following day by the National party, responded by voting to begin impeachment proceedings against Tohá for failing to act against illegal armed groups (the MIR, Elmo Catalán, and other brigades). (A month later, the day after the Chamber of Deputies voted to impeach Tohá, but two weeks before the Senate would take the same action, Allende countered, not by removing Tohá, but by reshuffling his Cabinet, naming Tohá to a new post, as defense minister. Allende would repeat this revolving door technique over and over again to mock congressional efforts to oust renegade Cabinet ministers, reshuffling his Cabinet twenty-eight times in his thirty-six months in power.)

Allende's reaction to food shortages was similarly obtuse. Instead of responding to a real problem, Allende resorted to yet another political maneuver. On December 8, Allende announced that the government would take full control of food distribution, obviously a powerful weapon in the hands of any government. To give that weapon an even sharper edge, in the same speech he urged the formation of "neighborhood vigilance committees," ostensibly to guard against food hoarding and black marketeers. But, inevitably, the move was seen as an ominous parallel of standard procedure in totalitarian regimes to control and crush opposition, such as the neighborhood committees set up in Communist Cuba which not only control dissidents, but also reward "apparatchiks" with jobs, scarce rations, and other plums, while punishing dissidents.

Although dramatic—and, because of the violence, significant in further hardening opposition to Allende—the March of the Pots and Pans, as that protest came to be known, was merely symptomatic of deepening cracks in the Chilean economy. During Allende's first six months in office, the binge of government spending and reality-bending wage increases and price controls produced a brief but feverish economic boom. By May of 1971, industrial output was up 13.5 percent over the previous year, unemployment had dropped to 5.2 percent (bottoming out at around 3.8 percent by year's end), and inflation, as measured by the Consumer Price Index, had slowed to a (for Chile) creeping 6 percent, the lowest in many years. Salaries and wages, meantime, increased by 27 percent in real terms.[82]

On November 9, 1971, Allende announced that Chile was suspending payment on its foreign debt.[83] It was a move that really should have surprised no one. In the Popular Unity's platform, one of the "first forty measures" called for "reneging on commitments with the International Monetary Fund." And, only two months before Allende spoke, the Communist Gonzalo Martner, Chile's delegate to the Seventh Meeting of the Inter-American Economic and Social Council, proposed a ten-year suspension of Latin American debt payments to the United States. Martner told the Panama meeting that this would be a "new strategy for the independent development of Latin American economies."[84] When Allende announced his debt decision, the country's reserves—which had been at an historic high of $394 million when he took office—had dwindled to $163 million. The consumer price index, at the same time, had already begun the steep climb which would see it top a staggering 500 percent-plus in 1973.

The following tables illustrate vividly the accelerating slide into collapse of the economy during the Allende years:

TABLE 25

MONTHLY FLUCTUATIONS IN CONSUMER PRICES AND INDUSTRIAL OUTPUT

YEAR AND MONTH	CONSUMER PRICE INDEX	INDUSTRIAL OUTPUT[1]
1970		
October	35.6	−8.0
November	35.3	4.3
December	34.9	− .3
1971		
January	28.1	−4.5
February	22.8	−7.3
March	20.1	6.3
April	20.2	1.6
May	21.0	13.5
June	21.1	10.7
July	19.1	6.7
August	17.4	10.7
September	15.6	25.5
October	16.5	22.6
November	18.8	22.1
December	22.1	19.5
1972		
January	24.8	18.5
February	32.0	11.9
March	34.0	10.2
April	38.1	12.6
May	40.0	11.4
June	40.1	2.5
July	45.9	5.0
August	77.2	3.6
September	114.3	−7.8
October	142.9	−7.7

[1] Percentage of change from the same month of the previous year.

MONTHLY FLUCTUATIONS IN CONSUMER PRICES AND INDUSTRIAL OUTPUT (continued)

YEAR AND MONTH	CONSUMER PRICE INDEX	INDUSTRIAL OUTPUT[1]
1972		
November	149.9	−8.1
December	163.4	−11.1
1973		
January	180.3	−6.8
February	174.1	−4.7
March	183.3	−2.8
April	195.5	−11.3
May	233.5	−11.0
June	283.4	−14.8
July	323.2	−10.7
August	303.6	−11.9
September	286.0	−22.9
October	528.4	18.0
November	528.9	5.1

Source: Instituto Nacional de Estadísticas, Santiago: Sociedad de Fomento Fabril (Society for the Development of Manufacturing), Santiago. As presented by Sigmund in "Allende in Retrospect," reproduced in *United States and Chile,* op. cit., p. 604.

[1] Percentage of change from the same month of the previous year.

TABLE 26

SOME INDICES OF THE CHILEAN ECONOMY, 1970–1972

	1970	1971	1972
Gross Domestic product (percentage of change)	3.7	8.3	1.4
Investment (percent change)	8.6	−24.2	−8.5
Real wages & salaries (percent change)	13.0	30.0	−9.0
Exports (millions of dollars)	1,129	1,045	853
Imports (millions of dollars)	1,020	1,124	1,287

Source: Department of Economics, University of Chile, as presented by Sigmund, ibid., p. 604.

(None of the figures in the above two tables squares exactly with those in *Indicadores Económicos y Sociales,* op. cit., but the two sets of statistics are close enough to accept the above as illustrative. As pointed out elsewhere in this volume, all such economic statistics must be taken with at least a grain of salt, although statistical discipline and seriousness is considerably greater in Chile than in most Third World countries.)

THE U.S. AND CHILE

On February 25, 1971, in his State of the World Message, President Richard Nixon said: "We are prepared to have the kind of relationship with the Chilean Government that it is prepared to have with us."

A few months later, in a postscript he penned for his "conversations" with the Marxist writer Régis Debray, Allende wrote: "We have always said that we wish to have better relations with all countries in the world, and naturally with the United States, the most powerful nation in the hemisphere . . . We have said clearly that we will not accept the tutelage of any great power . . . We know that our Government's action against the monopolies which have plundered the Chilean economy and our attempts to recover the basic natural resources of the country for the Chilean people will affect certain North American private interests. However, we are sure that these interests cannot be identified with the great historical purposes of the North American people . . ."[85]

For Allende—and for many in the United States and elsewhere—it was natural to postulate a distinction between U.S. national interests and the right, responsibility even, of any sovereign nation to look out for and protect the legitimate interests of its citizens, the private ones, the corporate ones. Allende himself, from the very beginning of his administration, in his very first meeting with a U.S. official, had insisted that "we will be known by our acts and only by our acts."[86]

His action, in hiring Soviet "experts" to assist in appraising the value of the U.S. copper companies,[87] and then seizing them without compensation, did, indeed, trigger a sharp U.S. reaction. Testifying before the U.S. Congress, a few days after the decision to pay the companies nothing, Assistant Secretary of State Charles Meyer articulated the U.S. position:

> The United States Government is deeply disappointed and disturbed at this serious departure from accepted standards of international law . . . It appears that the major factor in the Controller General's decision with respect to the largest producers [Anaconda and Kennecott] was the determination on September 28 of alleged "excess profits." The unprecedented retroactive application of the excess profits concept, which was not obligatory under the expropriation legislation adopted by the Chilean Congress, is particularly disquieting. The U.S. companies . . . earned their profits in Chile in accordance with Chilean law and under specific contractual agreements made directly with the Government of Chile. The excess profits deductions punish the companies today for acts that were legal and approved by the Government at the time. No claim is being made

that these excess profits deductions are based on violations of Chilean law. This retroactive determination has serious implications for the rule of law . . ."[88]

Meyer did not add that those same acts were carried out under the close supervision of democratic governments as widely admired at the time for their enlightenment as for the sturdiness of their democratic institutions and practices.

Meyer did not add either, that for all the bluster, all the liberal cater-wauling, defense of U.S. corporate interests was not central to the foreign policy thinking of the Nixon administration. As Nixon's national security adviser (and later secretary of state) Henry Kissinger remarked, "we inherited legislation—the so-called Hickenlooper amendment—that required a cutoff of American aid if American property was expropriated without fair compensation. But the Nixon administration did not view our foreign policy interests through the prism of the financial concerns of American companies. In 1969, we had cooperated with Chile's Christian Democratic president, Eduardo Frei Montalva, and negotiated fair terms for the nationalization of majority ownership of the Anaconda copper company. That same year, in Peru, we stretched the Hickenlooper amendment almost to the breaking point to avoid cutting off aid after Peru's seizure of the International Petroleum Company. We repeatedly sought a basis to avoid invoking the legislation and finally worked out a modus vivendi with Peru despite the fact that its government leaned toward the more radical factions of the Third World."[89] Those lessons of American flaccidness in failing to defend the interests of U.S. business obviously were not lost on Salvador Allende—as they were not on so many of the world's other "reformist" predators.

There is an Arab proverb which holds, roughly, that the height of stupidity is the inability to distinguish between friend and foe. Neither the Allende government in Santiago, nor the Nixon government in Washington—nor, for that matter, such onlookers as the Soviets or their Western Hemisphere satrap, Fidel Castro—suffered any such delusions. Salvador Allende set a course to convert his nation into a Marxist-Leninist state, and, in the process move it ever more inexorably into the Soviet camp, proclaiming the USSR as Chile's "Big Brother." Indeed, early on, Chile even explored links to Comecon, the Soviet-dominated "common market."[90] He wasn't in office one year before the Soviets would offer a staggering $300 million in military credits[91]—five times the total of all U.S. military credits to Chile in the period 1953–1975.[92] That offer was rejected because the Chilean military refused to enter into such an embrace with the Soviets.

For those who hold that the only legitimate U.S. national interest is to subordinate our wishes and needs to the wishes and needs of other countries, no matter how unfriendly their behavior, then the debate over who did what to whom and when wallows in a murky sea of minutiae. For such people, it was enough that Salvador Allende *said* he intended to construct something bold, something grand, and it was wrong for the United States to interpose its wishes in any fashion[93]—not even as Allende savaged the rights of U.S. corporate citizens, not even as Allende reneged on his bills to the U.S. treasury, to U.S. taxpayers, not even as Allende became ever closer to the U.S.'s deadliest enemies, not even as it became shatteringly clear that Allende was attempting to ride rough-shod over the wishes of an overwhelming majority of his own people.

We will wallow in no such sea. For those so compelled, this volume alone contains an ample bibliography of the most virulent and hostile essays of that tenor. In the Appendix, we have attempted to deal at great length with the most incandescent—and caricatured—episodes, the plots to prevent Allende from assuming the presidency, the ITT-CIA "conspiracies."

Distaste, disdain, antagonism, hostility even, there was—on both sides. Wishful thinking—Richard Nixon's September 1971 outbursts about stopping Allende at all costs, outbursts which came to nothing; a senior Nixon official predicting Allende wouldn't last long, nearly two years before he would, in fact, fall[94]—this, too, there was. But, in the end, the United States was largely marginal to the unfolding of the Allende drama, just as, in the end, Salvador Allende not only failed to alter the worldwide strategic balance of forces, but even set back the Soviet cause in the hemisphere.[95]

Nixon or no, the centrifugal pull in official Washington, vis-à-vis Allende, as on virtually all foreign policy issues in the postwar period, was in the direction most favored by the foreign policy establishment in Washington: to those on the Left. Contrary to the usual image-mongering, even the CIA itself was dominated by the same breed of "progressives" as those who peopled the State Department, far more comfortable with the politics and ideologies of Social Democrats than with those of any political strains on the Right. How effective they were, in the behind-the-scenes infighting, stands as a little examined case study of the ability of the unelected Washington Establishment to thwart the will of the elected government it allegedly serves. Henry Kissinger, who witnessed those events of 1970 as Nixon's National Security Adviser, documents in his memoirs State Department maneu-vers to block support for "a candidate [Alessandri] of impeccable demo-cratic antecedents whose principal liability in the eyes of our bureaucracy was that he was conservative. That this opinion could be held at all—much less prevail—in a Nixon Administration shows once again how difficult it is even for a President to impose his views on the entrenched bureaucracy." The result of that behind-the-scenes obstructionism and sabotage was that, contrary to sensationalized images fostered by Democrats in Congress and the media, "the United States acted in only the most minimal and ineffectual fashion prior to the Chilean election . . ." One who felt he had been particularly snookered: Henry Kissinger. "By the time of the election," he wrote, "I had come to the view that I had been maneuvered into a position incompatible with my convictions—and, more important, those of Nixon. Had I believed in the spring and summer of 1970 that there was a significant likelihood of an Allende victory, I would have had an obligation to the President to give him an opportunity to consider a covert program of 1964 proportions, including the backing of a single candidate. I was resentful that this option had been foreclosed without even being discussed . . ."[96]

That same Establishment, through adroit manipulation of "leaks" to cronies in the media, managed to oust Edward M. Korry as the U.S. ambassador to Chile, and replace him with Nathaniel Davis, a careerist. Korry was as hard-headed about the peril Allende represented for Chileans, for the U.S., as Davis would show himself to be starry-eyed about Allende.[97]

Though a political appointee, the tough-talking Korry was sufficiently effective to earn appointment and reappointment by three different presidents: John F. Kennedy (to Ethiopia, in 1963), Lyndon B. Johnson (to Chile, in 1967), and reconfirmed when Richard Nixon took office in 1969. During the crucial months leading up to the 1970 elections, Korry was virtually alone in warning of the consequences of an Allende victory, and in urging that the U.S. support the democratic forces in Chile capable of defeating him at the polls. His messages vanished in the maw of a bureaucracy which demonstrated again and again a conviction that the worst thing that could happen to Chile would be the election of a conservative, and that the worst thing the United States could do would be to aid and abet that outcome. Once Allende did win, Korry used his formidable powers of persuasion (and arm-twisting) to tamp down emotions and tempers in the large and volatile U.S. official and unofficial communities in Chile. He played a similar role in his dealings with official Washington—including a fateful session with President Nixon which ultimately cost him the support he would have needed to survive the left-wing onslaught against him.[98] (Korry's moderating role was borne out fully in the exhaustive—and, as Kissinger observes, "tendentious"—Senate investigation led by the late Sen. Frank Church [D-Idaho] a few years later.) The campaign to "get" Korry, spearheaded largely by *Washington Post* reporter Marilyn Berger, portrayed Korry as a truculent obstacle to "dialogue" between Allende and the United States.

(Korry would subsequently be the target of an even sorrier spectacle, one which ultimately left his career in ruins: spurious charges made by *New York Times* investigative reporter Seymour Hersh. The *Times* would later recant—but too late to save Korry's career.)[99]

That view from the Left was reflected in an article written by the American political scientist Federico G. Gil, an ardent champion of the Christian Democrats who would later find more to praise than to damn in Allende: "Removal of the United States Ambassador Edward Korry, of hawkish inclinations, and his replacement by Nathaniel Davis, a smoother and much better-qualified negotiator, was interpreted as a conciliatory gesture."[100] (During several reporting trips to Chile at that time, senior officials in the Allende administration told me Allende actually liked dealing with Korry because he spoke clearly and forthrightly.)[101] But Korry was ousted, and that he was reflects the ability of the decidedly dovish (and mainly left-wing) foreign policy establishment to "get" an ambassador perceived to be too "tough" on a "progressive" regime, no matter how intrinsically hostile that government may be to the United States. (Fifteen years later, yet another U.S. ambassador to Chile, the late James Theberge, would find himself under Establishment fire because he was perceived as not being tough enough on a right-wing government eager for closer ties to the United States, the Pinochet government.)

Davis, a career foreign service officer, was serving as U.S. ambassador to Guatemala when notified on November 20, 1970, that he was being recommended for Chile. A specialist on Communist Eastern Europe as well as Latin America, Davis said, "Had I been wiser, I might have declined the honor. At the time, I had no knowledge of U.S. covert action in Chile and little knowledge of the depth of hostility to Allende in the White House . . ."[102] By his deeds and later words, Davis would make it plain he never did understand why there should have been U.S. "hostility to Allende."

As Davis knew, U.S. "hostility" to Allende was confined mainly to fulminations. By the time the Chilean situation came under sustained scrutiny at the policy-making level in Washington, the Senior Review Group of the "Forty Committee" concluded that "we are faced only with a choice in tactics." Following review by the full National Security Council, Nixon issued a directive on November 9 that the public posture of the United States would be "correct but cool, to avoid giving the Allende government a basis on which to rally domestic and international support for consolidation of the regime." On a confidential level, the directive called for assembling pressures to prevent the consolidation of "a communist state in Chile hostile to the interests of the United States and other hemispheric nations." But, as Kissinger noted, "the directive was stern but less drastic and decisive than it sounded . . . [and] was much less so than the policy later pursued against Augusto Pinochet of Chile or Anastasio Somoza of Nicaragua."[103]

Relations between the United States and Chile during the Allende years revolved around two large, intertwined and sprawling issues: the nationalization of the U.S. copper mines (and other companies) without compensation, and whether in retaliation the U.S. did or did not attempt to crush Chile through an "invisible economic blockade."

The copper issue came to a head rapidly. On July 11, 1971, Allende cited a French and Soviet study to prove the big copper companies had been mismanaged and had extracted excess profits from their operations. Referring to their nationalization, he said, "We will pay if it is just, and we will not pay what is not just." That same day, 158 (of the total of two hundred) senators and deputies, meeting in joint session, unanimously approved a nationalization measure heavily amended since its first approval by the Senate, five months earlier. That bill provided for compensation to the companies over thirty years, the amounts to be fixed by Chile's comptroller general. On September 28, Allende announced those findings: since 1955, Kennecott and Anaconda's profits exceeded 10 percent per year, and $774 million in "excess profits" would be deducted from any payment to them. In addition, $250 million would be deducted for "technical deficiencies" and "other expenses" related to the operation of the mines. That was, of course, far above the $629 million book value of their holdings—$388 million above in all. The comptroller general said Chile would not attempt to collect that $388 million because it was not contemplated by the legislation. But it also meant the two big producers, Anaconda and Kennecott, would get nothing. Furthermore, the Allende government repudiated the $150 million debt still outstanding to Anaconda under the terms of the Chileanization buy-out of its mines. Though claiming to honor the $92.9 million debt owed Kennecott, minus $8.1 million for "deficiencies," the Allende government did not, in fact, make good its payments to Kennecott, and those issues, too, would wind up in international dispute. (The third U.S. copper company, Cerro, was not affected by excess profits considerations because its new Río Blanco mine had not yet produced a profit. But, in some ways, Cerro suffered the cruelest fate of all. Its mine was built in a remote site in the Andes where, as Ambassador Korry would testify before the U.S. House Subcommittee on Inter-American Affairs [July 1, 1971], "every copper company in the world said it was impossible to do." It was, Korry said, not only built underground, using the most advanced technology in the world, but it represented "the realization of a dream by one American with a special affection for Chile against the advice of everybody"—and at a much higher investment cost than anticipated. Cerro made its first sale of copper from the mine just five months before Allende seized it—without turning so much as a penny's profit on one man's expensive dream.) There was no mention in the announcements (1) that the government itself had been, since the Chileanization of the Frei years, a 51 percent partner in Kennecott's El Teniente mine (the country's second biggest), a one-quarter partner in Anaconda's Exotica mine, and, beginning in 1969, a 51 percent owner of both of Anaconda's biggest mines, El Salvador and giant Chuquicamata; (2) that, for the first quarter of a century, Kennecott, for example, had made no profit at all on its Chilean investments; (3) that the profit figures were pretaxes paid to the Chilean government (see pages 161–168, chapter 4, for a detailed discussion of the background of Chileanization and the debate over profits, investments, and operating conditions).

The table on the following page demonstrates the arithmetic used in the "excess profits" exercise, and the implications for the U.S. Overseas Private Investment Corporation (OPIC).

Allende gave the companies a single avenue of appeal: a specially created, five-member Copper Tribunal, composed of two government representatives and three judges, one of them from the Allende-appointed Constitutional Tribunal, which meant, in effect, that Allende named three of the five members of the court. The tribunal began operations October 28, 1971. On August 11, 1972, the court announced its decision: the "excess profits" rulings must stand because the decision of the Allende government was a political act, and thus not subject to its jurisdiction or review. (On December 5, the court awarded Cerro $19 million compensation, one half of what Cerro sought.) The chief justice of Chile's Supreme Court expressed the view that the companies should have been allowed a way out of the Catch-22 created for them: an appeal to the high court, which did have authority in judging "political acts." Confronting the retroactive formula for calculating "excess profits," one leading Chilean constitutional scholar, in a painstakingly worded analysis of the legal issues, wrote that "authority for retroactive measures cannot be found" within the statute adjusting Chilean law to international law. That same scholar, Francisco Orrego Vicuña, also argued that "the opinion of the majority of the Congress was that compensation should be paid.[104]

On September 29, 1971, the day after announcing the copper companies would receive nothing for their holdings, the Allende government picked off the next largest U.S. holding in Chile: ITT's Chilean Telephone Company, even though nine years remained on its half-century concession to operate in the country. As observed at the outset of this chapter, Allende had invented the "excess profits" stratagem

TABLE 27

COMPARISON, CHILEAN CONTROLLER GENERAL'S EVALUATION AND OPIC EXPROPRIATION COVERAGE[1], U.S.-OWNED COPPER MINES (THE VIEW IN 1971)

COMPANY AND MINE	EVALUATION	OPIC COVERAGE (MAXIMUM)
Anaconda:		
Chuquicamata Mine:		
book value (net worth)	$242,958,862.43	
Deductions:		
For mine	5,398,937.59	
Defective property	13,060,861.91	(2)
Excess profits (3)	300,000,000.00	
Result: deficit of:	76,500,937.07	
La Exótica Mine:		
book value (net worth)	14,815,052.52	
Deductions:		
For mine	250,000.00	
Defective property	4,554,607.41	
Excess profits (3)	0.00	Equity $22,500,000 (4)
Result: compensation of	10,010,445.11	
Less payment by GOC* for		
25% equity interest	3,750,000.00	
Payment to U.S. company	6,260,445.11	
El Salvador Mine:		
book value (net worth)	68,372,196.57	
Deductions:		
For mine	353,692.06	
Defective property	5,596,139.09	(5)
Excess profits (3)	64,000,000.00	
Result: deficit of	1,577,634.58	
Kennecott:		
El Teniente Mine:		
book value (net worth)	318,801,198.77	
Deductions:		
Revaluation	198,483,929.92	
For mine	223,519.00	
Defective property	20,520,167.05	Debt $84,600,000

TABLE 27 *(continued)*

COMPANY AND MINE	EVALUATION	OPIC COVERAGE (MAXIMUM)
Excess profits (3)	410,000,000.00	
Result: deficit of	310,426,417.21	
Cerro:		
Andina Mine: (Río Blanco) book value (net worth)	20,145,469.44	
Deductions:		
For mine	1,532,176.09	
Defective property	343,592.00	
Result: compensation of	18,269,701.35	
Less, payment by GOC* for 30% equity	6,300,000.00	
Payment to U.S. company	11,969,701.35	

* GOC Government of Chile.

Source: Documents provided by Marshall T. Mays, general counsel of OPIC, October 19, 1971, to Rep. Dante B. Fascell (D-Florida), chairman of the Subcommittee on Inter-American Affairs, Committee on Foreign Affairs, U.S. House of Representatives, appearing as Appendix D in *United States and Chile,* op. cit., p. 451.

[1] Prepared from information supplied by OPIC; (2) Coverage disputed. OPIC maintains that there is no coverage on these contracts. Anaconda claims equity coverage of $184,000,000; (3) As determined by President Allende in decree No. 92, Sept. 28, 1971; (4) Coverage on debt is disputed. OPIC maintains that there is no coverage for debt. Anaconda claims coverage of $11,225,000; (5) Coverage disputed. OPIC maintains that there is no coverage on these contracts. Anaconda claims equity coverage of $51,400,000.

during his electoral campaign in first taking aim at the telephone company. Within two weeks, ITT filed the biggest claim ever with the U.S. taxpayer-funded Overseas Private Investment Corporation (OPIC): $108.5 million, to cover the insured portion of what ITT said was the $153 million of its 70 percent remaining share in the company. The entire question of payment to ITT would become snarled in controversy six months later when columnist Jack Anderson on March 22 began publishing reports of ITT efforts to enlist U.S. government support for blocking Allende's accession to office in 1970, and then, failing in that, trying (also without success) to engage the U.S. in a campaign of sabotage to bring him down).[105]

The seized companies went over to a three-pronged counterattack: first, to persuade the U.S. government to support their claims; second, to seek indemnification through the Overseas Private Investment Corp., and third (in the case of the copper companies) through courts in the

U.S. and in other countries (including France, Sweden, the Netherlands and Germany, winning preliminary skirmishes to freeze Chilean assets, losing on appeal, not on the merits, but rather on questions of jurisdiction).

For OPIC, Chile represented a grave crisis. As Ambassador Davis noted, OPIC's accumulated reserves from premiums and the original congressional seed money fluctuated at around $100 million. The Anaconda, Kennecott, and ITT claims alone added up to over half a billion dollars, enough, if paid, to bankrupt OPIC several times over. The result: "OPIC's interest in Chilean developments was incandescent, and its activism in U.S. policy toward Chile was considerable."[106]

Although the embattled companies did win U.S. support, it was mainly of the lip-service category. In the wake of the reaffirmation of Chile's decision to pay the seized companies no compensation, President Nixon on January 19, 1972, issued a broad U.S. policy statement on expropriation, containing his toughest language yet:

> Under international law, the United States has a right to expect . . . that its citizens will receive prompt, adequate, and effective compensation from the expropriating country. Thus, when a country expropriates a significant U.S. interest without making reasonable provision for such compensation to U.S. citizens, we will presume that the U.S. will not extend new bilateral economic benefits to the expropriating country unless and until it is determined that the country is taking reasonable steps to provide adequate compensation or that there are major factors affecting U.S. interests which require continuance of all or part of these benefits . . . In the face of the expropriatory circumstances just described, we will presume that the United States Government will withhold its support from loans under consideration in multilateral development banks . . ."

But, as the following section will show, the well had been drying up for U.S. government and international loans to Chile even before Allende assumed office. Further, Nixon's stern words notwithstanding, U.S. officials within the international lending agencies repeatedly stated that "criteria for judging financial assistance to Chile are based principally on considerations of the Chilean Government's credit worthiness and other considerations relating to Chile's current financial state . . ."[107]

Anaconda and Kennecott fared no better at first in collecting on their insurance claims. On September 19, 1972, OPIC announced the biggest settlement in its history: $11.9 million to Anaconda, the full amount of its insurance for its Exotica mine. But OPIC that day also disallowed altogether Anaconda's $154 million claim for its Chuquicamata and El Salvador mines, claiming that those had been nationalized in 1969, before Anaconda's coverage was in effect.

On December 14, 1972, OPIC announced it would issue a guarantee to Kennecott of $66.9 million as insurance on the company's 1965 loan of $92 million to the government (see p. 163, and note 129, chapter 4, for details)—but nothing for the $319-million book value in its El Teniente mine. As for ITT, it faced the prospect of getting nothing at all.[108]

The following tables reveal the broad picture of U.S. investments in Chile during the Allende years, as well as the consequences for OPIC during the Allende years of nationalizations/expropriations:

TABLE 28

SELECTED* U.S. FIRMS WITH MAJORITY INVESTMENTS IN CHILE PRIOR TO COPPER NATIONALIZATION

FIRM	DATE OF OPERATION IN CHILE	PRINCIPAL ACTIVITY
W. R. Grace	1891	Transportation
Bethlehem Steel	1913	Iron mining
Anaconda	Circa 1916	Copper mining
1st National City Bank—N.Y.	1916	Banking & finance
Kennecott	Circa 1920s	Copper mining
Dupont	1920	Explosives
ITT	1927	Telephone
RCA	1942	Radio & television
ITT	1942	Radio & television
Kaiser (Argentina)	1946	Iron & steel products
Oscar Kohorn & Co.	1948	Textiles & fibers
Englehard Minerals & Chemicals	1955	Iron mining
American Cyanamid	1955	Pharmaceuticals
Standard Oil (N.J.)	1959	Oil distribution
Parke, Davis & Co.	Pre 1960	Pharmaceuticals
Chas. Pfizer	Pre 1960	Pharmaceuticals
Sterling Drugs	1960	Pharmaceuticals
Armco Steel	1960	Iron & steel products
Mobil Oil	1961	Oil distribution
International Basic Economy Corp.	1961	Banking & finance
W. R. Grace	1961	Food manufacturing
CPC International	1961	Food manufacturing
General Motors	Pre 1962	Auto assembly
Simpson Timber Corp.	1965	Pulp & paper
Sperry Rand Corp.	1966	Office equipment
Singer Sewing Machine	1966	Iron & steel products

Table 28 *(continued)*

FIRM	DATE OF OPERATION IN CHILE	PRINCIPAL ACTIVITY
General Mills	1967	Food manufacturing
Ralston Purina	1967	Food manufacturing
Dow Chemical	1967	Petrochemicals
Firestone Tire & Rubber	1967	Rubber tires
Northern Indiana Brass	1967	Copper fabricating
Bank of America	1967	Banking & finance
Ford Motor Co.	1968	Auto assembly
Monsanto Co.	1969	Petrochemicals
General Tire	1969	Rubber tires
IRECO Chemicals	1969	Explosives
Cerro	Late 1960s	Copper mining
General Telephone & Electronics	1970	Radio & television
Chemtex Inc.	1971	Textiles & fibers

* The above list is not all-inclusive. There was a total of around fifty-five American companies operating in Chile when Allende took office.

Source: James F. Petras and Robert LaPorte, Jr., "Can We Do Business With Radical Nationalists? Chile: No," in *Foreign Policy,* Summer 1972, as reproduced in *United States and Chile,* op. cit., pp. 490–491.

The authors cite: North American Congress on Latin America, *New Chile* (California: NACLA, 1972), pp. 150–168; *Recent Developments in Chile, October 1971,* Report of the Subcommittee on Inter-American Affairs of the Committee on Foreign Affairs, U.S. House of Representatives (Washington: Government Printing Office, Oct. 15, 1971), p. 18; and D. Lynne Kaltreider, "A Tale of Two Interventions and Other Related Actions," unpublished paper, Nov. 1971.

Table 29

IMPACT OF NATIONALIZATIONS IN CHILE ON U.S. OVERSEAS PRIVATE INVESTMENT CORPORATION (OPIC)

1. CLAIMS PENDING AS OF FEB. 28, 1973:

NAME OF COMPANY	AMOUNT OF CLAIM	TYPE OF CLAIM	STATUS
Bank of America	$ 2,913,021	Inconvertibility	Application in process (A-I-C)
Cerro Corp.	14,201,000	Expropriation	Investor negotiating with GOC (Chile)
Ensign Bickford	20,000	Inconvertibility	A-I-C
Ensign Bickford	300,000	Expropriation	OPIC awaiting documents
1st Nat'l City Bank	140,000	Expropriation	A-I-C
Int'l Chemical Fibers	29,494	Inconvertibility	A-I-C

Table 29 (*continued*)

1. CLAIMS PENDING AS OF FEB. 28, 1973:

NAME OF COMPANY	AMOUNT OF CLAIM	TYPE OF CLAIM	STATUS
ITT	92,000,000	Expropriation	A-I-C
Johns-Manville Corp.	10,000	Inconvertibility	OPIC awaiting documents
Ralston-Purina	212,000	Expropriation	A-I-C
Ford Motor Co.	276,000	Expropriation	OPIC awaiting documents
Soconet	60,000	Inconvertibility	A-I-C

2. CLAIMS RESOLVED BY OPIC CASH SETTLEMENTS TO INSURED INVESTORS:

COMPANY	COVERAGE	AMOUNT PAID	OPIC RECOVERY
Ford Motor Co.	Inconvertibility	$ 910,885	$879,698
Anaconda	Expropriation	11,890,000	—
Ralston-Purina	Expropriation	614,417	448,000
NIBCO	Expropriation	110,000	—

3. CLAIMS SETTLED BY AN OPIC GUARANTY WHICH ENABLED THE INVESTOR TO RECEIVE CASH PAYMENT:

Kennecott	Expropriation	66,900,000	—

4. CLAIMS SETTLED BY HOST GOVERNMENT COMMITMENT, BACKED BY AN OPIC GUARANTY:

Parsons & Whittemore	Expropriation	3,259,365	(1)
Bethlehem Steel	Expropriation	23,598,095	(2)

5. CLAIMS DENIED BY OPIC (CONTRACTS PROVIDE THAT ANY DISPUTES MAY BE SETTLED BY ARBITRATION):

Anaconda	Expropriation	154,000,000	(3)

(1) OPIC liability; (2) including interest; (3) amount denied.

Source: Testimony presented March 6, 1973, before the Subcommittee on Inter-American Affairs of the Committee on Foreign Affairs, U.S. House of Representatives, by John H. Crimmins, Acting Assistant Secretary of State for Inter-American Affairs, reproduced in *United States and Chile,* op. cit., p. 73.

When Crimmins testified—March 6, 1973, six months and five days before Allende's fall—only twenty-four American companies, with a book value of $70 million, remained in Chile (among them, curiously, the archdemon ITT, which continued to operate its two Sheraton hotels in Santiago through the Allende years). When Allende came to power, there were around fifty-five American companies in Chile with a book value of $750 million. Of them, three (the copper companies) had been nationalized; twelve had been subjected to varying degrees of shotgun "buy-outs" (most of which would lead to OPIC claims); and sixteen had been "intervened or requisitioned" (including ITT's 70 percent remaining interest in the telephone company)—euphemisms, usually, for seizure–without–compensation.

Prior to Allende, U.S. private investment in Chile was, in per capita terms, the third highest in all of Latin America, behind only Panama (inflated by canal-related investments) and Venezuela (where the giant oil companies had made that country then the world's largest oil exporting nation).

For many years, the United States had been the number one buyer of Chile's exports. In 1969, Frei's last full year in office, Chile exported $186 million to the U.S. In 1972, Allende's last full year, exports were down to $80.2 million, putting the U.S. in fourth place (behind Japan, West Germany, and the United Kingdom, in that order). As for sales to Chile, the United States had not only been the principal supplier for many years, but in 1969 sold more to Chile singly ($349 million) than any other region of the world (East and West Europe combined, all of Latin America, all other countries). In 1969, U.S. exports to Chile amounted to 38 percent of the total. In 1972, not only had that percentage dropped (to 17 percent), but the Europe total ($512 million) was more than double the U.S. total ($240 million). The Latin American regional total ($437 million) was also much higher, and Argentina alone ($215 million) was only slightly behind the U.S. (because, by 1972, Allende's agriculture policies had taken their awesome toll and Argentina was all but feeding neighboring Chile). In 1969, the "miscellaneous" category in All-Other Countries—a category which included the Soviet Union—was a piddling $7.1 million (in a total of $907 million); in 1972, that total had leaped to $110.8 million).[109]

THE INTERNATIONAL DIMENSION

For many "progressive" thinkers, who could see no evil in Salvador Allende, the proper role of the United States—and the rest of the world community—might be summarized: (1) if slapped, turn the other cheek, because, after all, those slaps were only administered under Chilean "law" (as "progressives" would interpret it), and besides, Allende had that electoral platform to execute, hadn't he?; (2) open your pocketbooks to help ease Allende's way into the promised land of socialist revolution; (3) whatever else, keep hands off Chile because, after all, the country does possess the political maturity to manage its own affairs, find its own way—not to mention the twin and cardinal principles of self-determination and nonintervention. Not surprisingly, many of those who most loudly—and, not infrequently, vituperatively—proclaimed those principles would later see no good in the Pinochet government which followed Allende. Instead, they would argue, with equal vigor, equal venom: (1) slap Pinochet's face, as well as his wrists; (2) close all pocketbooks to that regime; (3) use every means possible to bring the regime down, so as to save Chileans from themselves: nonintervention and self-determination are more a matter of passion and prejudice than principle.

Out of this smorgasbord of dogmatism and devotion there would bubble up a conspiracy theory which came to be known as the "invisible blockade" and which was held accountable for the economic ruin visited upon Chile during the Allende hecatomb. According to the theory, international lending agencies choked off credits to Chile, under pressure from a vindictive Washington, bent on vengeance for Chile's decision to end the era of plunder by the "imperialist" and "exploitive" foreign capitalists. (Less was said about the home-grown "exploiters" whose assets were also seized wholesale.)

Those charges were nowhere made more flamboyantly nor with greater reverberation than by Salvador Allende himself, in his only speech before the United Nations, December 4, 1972. With the economy crashing down all round him, Allende told the General Assembly:

> We are suffering from yet another manifestation of imperialism, one that is more subtle, more cunning and more terrifyingly effective in preventing us from exercising out rights as a sovereign State.
>
> From the very day of our electoral triumph ... we have felt the effects of a large-scale external pressure against us which tried to prevent the inauguration of a Government freely elected by the people, and has attempted to bring it down ever since, an action that has tried to cut us off from the world, to strangle our economy and paralyze trade in our principal export, copper, and to deprive us of access to sources of international financing ... This aggression is not overt and has not been openly declared to the world; on the contrary, it is an oblique, underhanded, indirect form of aggression, although this does not make it any less damaging to Chile ... This financial strangulation ... has led to the severe limitation of our ability to secure the equipment, spare parts, manufacturing inputs, foodstuffs and medicines which we need. Each and every Chilean is suffering from the consequences of these measures ... What I have just described to the Assembly amounts to a perversion of the fundamental nature of international agencies ... in a word ... imperialist insolence ...

To hyperbole, Allende then added factual fatuity. The man who came to power with 36.2 percent of the vote, nosing out an opponent who stood for diametrically opposite policies by 39,000 votes (of 2.954 million cast), told the UN: "Chile is a nation which has attained the political maturity to decide by majority vote to replace the capitalist economic system by the socialist."[110]

For political scientist Federico Gil—among others—Allende's UN speech "was an impassioned and eloquent denunciation of economic aggression." Professor Gil said he viewed Allende's accusations as "seemingly well-founded."

For a Chilean political leader, Sergio Onofre Jarpa, president of the National party (the one which missed by 39,000 votes defeating Allende in 1970), Allende's UN speech "constitutes a model of distortion and falsification of the history and reality of Chile. The crisis which confronts our country has not stemmed from external pressures, but from the forced application of an anachronic, unjust and inefficient Marxist system; from the incompetence, sectarianism and premeditated robbery carried out by the ruling cadres of the Popular Unity parties."[111]

Superficially, the case for the "invisible blockade" appeared persuasive. The World Bank did not approve a single new loan for Chile during the entire Allende presidency. The Board of Directors of the Inter-American Development Bank (IDB) did not act on a single new Chilean loan proposal after approving two small ones ($7 million and $4.5 million) in the first months of the Allende presidency. Furthermore, U.S. official aid to Chile all but dried up during the Allende years. (Although even Allende would allow that "the United States, in its sovereignty, may grant or withhold loans in respect to any country it chooses."[112] Not all the regime's supporters were so tolerant, however, as witness the outcry which followed the decision of the quasi-autonomous U.S. Export-Import Bank, in 1972, to deny Chile a $21 million loan to finance the purchase of three U.S.-made Boeing 727 jet airliners.) Finally, Allende raised the issue of the disappearance of private bank credits to Chile—though few would join him in that chorus, a difficult one to sustain since he had squeezed all foreign banks out of the country in the first year, and by November of 1971, had suspended payment on the official foreign debt.

Closer inspection fails to validate the "invisible blockade" theory. First, the United States does not have a majority vote in either the World Bank or the Inter-American Development Bank. Further: I have pored over hundreds—perhaps thousands—of pages of the most virulent criticism of U.S. behavior toward Chile in the Allende years and have never come across a single specific, concrete scrap of evidence of U.S. "pressure" to force those institutions to deny credit to Allende. Beyond that, tracking of the IDB has persuaded many observers—including this one—that it has, over the past quarter-century or more, behaved not only with independence of the U.S., but frequently at cross-purposes to its wishes. The argument that Chile was denied loans because it had taken a "socialist" path flies in the face of the long and large history of World Bank lending to Soviet-bloc (and other) socialist countries. The argument that the banks withheld their monies because of the dispute over compensation for the copper companies flies in the face of the fact that the World Bank had, on several occasions, made loans over the objections of one or more of the great powers to countries then embroiled in disputes over nationalizations (Bolivia, Guyana, and Iraq to that time).

A quirkish footnote to the dispute: Chile actually exercised great influence in the affairs of IDB—until Allende. Felipe Herrera resigned the presidency to return to Chile after Allende's election, and Allende recruited from the bank Orlando Letelier, one of the top loan officers, to become his ambassador to Washington. Both Herrera and Letelier were Chilean Socialists, and as we have seen in an earlier chapter, Socialist in Chilean political parlance bears no resemblance to the term as it exists in Europe. Clearly, the U.S. was less than vigilant, and conspicuously ineffectual, if enforcing ideological purity in the upper echelons of the bank had been a goal.

Chile, in 1948, was the very first country to receive a development loan granted by the World Bank. In the twenty-five ensuing years, Chile would receive a total of $234.7 million in loans from the bank, as well as a $19 million "soft loan" for earthquake recovery in 1961. '

But, by the mid-1960s, the bank was already "disenchanted" with Chile's economic performance and prospects. Indeed, in the five years before Allende took office—a fact rarely mentioned—the World Bank granted but a single loan to Chile. As with any sanely managed financial institution, the World Bank had bottom-line criteria to measure "credit-worthiness": "... the primary conditions of bank lending—a soundly managed economy with a clear potential for utilizing additional funds efficiently."[113]

A full five years before Allende discovered an "invisible blockade," international economists warned of "underlying weakness in the Chilean economy."[114] Despite windfall earnings resulting from a sharp rise in copper prices (which nearly doubled, from 36 cents a pound in 1965 to 66 cents in 1969), Chile's current accounts (the difference between international payments—debt service and profit repatriation—and international earnings) were in the red all but one of the Frei years.

The problems were two: borrowing and a steady rise in imports, both of which fueled inflation as well as mortgaging the future of the country. As to the first: the country resorted, increasingly, to borrowing from abroad to finance its ambitious social welfare programs. In 1960, debt service claimed 11 percent of export earnings; by 1971, the figure was 37 percent. In 1962, the government financed 58 percent of its debt from internal borrowing, 42 percent from external sources; by 1966, those percentages were 27 percent and 73 percent, respectively. As to imports: the share of national income devoted to imports rose from 13 percent of gross domestic product in 1964 to 17 percent in 1969.

Analyst Jonathan Sanford, writing of these developments, would remark: "Because of the World Bank's disenchantment with Chile's high rate of inflation and its lack of internal economic stability, the country received little assistance from that institution during the last three years of this period [1967–1969, inclusive, the last Frei years]."[115] Inter-American Development Bank lending did, however, continue throughout the Frei years, reaching an all-time, one-year record peak of $62.5 million in 1969, all but $13.8 million of that in "soft" loans for social development projects.

In his even-handed study, Sanford notes:

> The World Bank seems to have maintained a relatively consistent approach toward Chile during the entire 1961–1974 timespan. During the Frei government, this Bank was reluctant (as it has been in other cases) to provide loans to Chile because of the inflation and economic instability which the country experienced late in the decade; economic conditions during the Allende period were also sufficiently problematic as to justify some hesitation . . .
>
> . . . it seems proper to conclude that the Inter-American Development Bank was less consistent than was the World Bank in its approach to Chilean lending. Perhaps because of its view that development problems emanate from weaknesses in national economic structures rather than simply from poor macroeconomic policy decisions by governments, the IDB lent to Chile during periods of substantial inflation (1966–1970), and during periods of large balance of payments deficits (1961–1963). If that Bank were consistent in its treatment of Chile, one might have expected it to continue making new loans to Chile throughout the Allende period or at least until it became evident in late 1971 and early 1972 that the future economic conditions in Chile would be significantly worse than those experienced under the Frei regime . . .[116]

Sanford is correct in his analysis—as far as he goes. But, as the IDB pointed out in a white paper on its policies toward Chile during the Allende years, the bank bent its own rules to aid Allende's Chile in the aftermath of the 1971 earthquake. Bank President Antonio Ortiz Mena (a Mexican) toured the devastated areas with Allende. Back in Washington, he persuaded the Board of Directors to redirect to Chile the unused portions of nine previously approved loans, a total of $16.1 million. Those monies were for projects that, for one reason or another, could no longer be used. Under usual bank practice, the loan agreements would have been cancelled. Instead, the $16.1 million which Ortiz Mena "rescued" for Chile, taken together with other disbursements for loans submitted and approved during the Frei administration, meant that Chile would receive, during the Allende years, the largest annual disbursement of foreign exchange in the bank's history: $33.8 million in 1971, $21.7 million in 1972, and $14.5 million between January and September 1973.[117]

But the bone of contention was not monies flowing from previously approved loans, but the absence of new loans. Again, the IDB would point out that, when Allende assumed the presidency, Chile had two Frei proposals under study. But when Allende's government withdrew the priority formerly assigned to them, the bank discontinued its study of them. Then, between Allende's election and December of 1972, his government presented only one new proposal to the bank: a $31.5 million loan for a petrochemical project. But since the plan envisioned sale of two-thirds of the project's output to Argentina and Andean Pact countries (most of which were experiencing serious economic problems of their own), the bank balked. It was agreed to have a British consulting firm do a feasibility study: that study wasn't finished until one month after Allende's fall, in October 1973.

Chile would make no new proposals until December 1972, when two were presented: one, to help finance export of natural gas to various other countries (not approved); the other for the huge Antuco hydroelectric project (named for the small Andean village of the same name, about five hundred miles south of Santiago). That project—which envisioned 1.8-million kilowatt hours of annual electrical output, and irrigation of 1 million acres—was one of Allende's top priorities. By early January, the basic project studies were delivered to the bank. In May, a field mission went to Chile for close-up study; on July 26, a bank project study approved the proposal. As negotiations neared an end, the Allende government, on August 28, requested an increase in the original loan amount. That is where the matter rested when Allende fell.[118]

There were one or two other lesser transactions involving the IDB and Chile during the Allende years. Overall, it would be difficult to indict the IDB of a deliberate "blockade" on the strength of the actual record—though results (no loans), not the reasons why formed the basis for most "invisible blockade" claims. Sanford did examine the detailed record, yet seems to center most of his criticism on slow reaction time on the hydroelectric project, a debatable proposition, at best, given the $75 million magnitude of the project—not only the largest single project (by far) ever proposed by Chile, but bigger alone than the highest one-year total of all IDB loans to Chile ($62.5 million in 1969). Yet another extrapolation was made: the bank approved no new loans to Chile during most of the Allende government, but quickly approved major loans during its first year to the military government that followed.

Again, on the surface, true. However: the biggest of the loans was for the Antuco power project, which by the time it was approved on March 29, 1974, had been thoroughly studied. The other, a $22 million agricultural loan (which the "United States Government did not disapprove"),[119] was approved on March 30, 1974, on a clearly accelerated timetable. But the IDB frequently put itself on a fast-track footing when conditions in a country warranted—and in 1974 Chile's agriculture was not only showing the ruinous ravages of Allende's destructive agricultural policies, but the country had only recently emerged from a shooting-war revolution.

Since World Bank performance during the same period cannot be responsibly faulted, only two additional observations need be made. On September 11, 1971, a World Bank economic mission began a one-month, on-site evaluation visit. In its report, issued mid-October, the mission "stated clearly that Chile's economic policies would prevent the effective utilization of Bank lending even if the country were somehow deemed capable of servicing its debt ... The mission's prediction of severe problems was almost immediately upheld when in November Chile suspended all service on external debts to international organizations ..."[120]

Throughout 1972, Chilean officials from Allende on down kept up a drumfire criticism of the bank. Finally, in response to one of those attacks, Bank President Robert McNamara reiterated that the reason for a hold on bank lending to Chile had nothing to do with the expropriation/nationalization dispute, but everything to do with the creditworthiness of the country: "The Chilean economy is in severe difficulty with the cost of living having risen 96 percent in the first nine months of 1972, 20 percent in the month of September alone. The balance of payments deficit for 1972 would be, by the government's own figures, $370 million even after suspending most payments on external debt ... In this situation it is clear that internal measures to reestablish economic stability are required, and no amount of external financial assistance can substitute for them. As matters stand—in the absence of such fundamental economic stability—it is simply impossible for Bank funds to be used productively for the benefit of the Chilean people, and with the reasonable probability of repayment, which the Bank's articles of Agreement require ..." Three months later, Chile suspended service on all payments of interest and principal to the bank.[121]

Even if there had been an "invisible blockade," there was no shortage of foreign capital. Most of it came from the Soviet Union and its satellites in Eastern Europe—though far more was promised than was ever actually delivered. By one reckoning, the Soviet Union and other "socialist camp" countries offered the Allende government $620 million—$156.5 million in short-term bank credit and $463.5 million in project aid and supplier credits, of which $260.5 million came from the USSR. As of September 1973, according to another analyst, only $91 million committed by the Soviet Union, Comecon countries, and Red China had actually been disbursed. Yet another writer claimed Chile's actual indebtedness to the Soviet Union-Eastern bloc countries and Red China increased by only $31 million during the Allende years. (During the Frei years, a total of $592 million was authorized—but not all of it disbursed—by the World Bank, Inter-American Development Bank, and the U.S. Agency for International Development, a total, in other words, significantly below the amount Communist-bloc countries offered [i.e., "authorized"] Allende in only half the time Frei was in the presidency.)

Other credits were proferred Allende by Canada, Argentina, Mexico, Australia, and Western Europe ($250 million), as well as other Latin American nations ($70 million).

Nor was the Allende government denied access to the vaults of all of the Washington-based international agencies: on December 10, 1971, the International Monetary Fund granted Chile $39.5 million credit as an offset against the drop in export earnings occasioned by the fall in copper. A year later, on December 20, 1972, the IMF granted a second such credit, for $42.8 million.

Putting aside the discrepancies between amounts authorized and those actually disbursed, it remains a fact that Chile's public debt inreased by $600 million in Allende's three years in power. During Frei's six years, the increase was just over double that amount, yet no one claimed that Frei, riding the crest of a copper-fueled chimerical boom (and even more chimerical international reputation), had been the target of a credit blockade, visible or invisible.[122]

Even such an Allende booster as Professor Emanuel De Kadt, one of four members of the University of Sussex' Institute of Development Studies to take part in the March 1972 symposium in Santiago cohosted by the institute, would write after Allende's fall: "Whatever the importance of the U.S.-inspired economic quasi blockade and of the obstructiveness of Chilean private enterprise, very few observers disagree that the [Popular Unity's] management of the economy was disastrous . . ."[123]

It would remain for one of Allende's heroes—China's Chou En-lai—to put the matter of outside help in perspective. In a letter he wrote to Allende February 3, 1973, apologizing, in part, for his own country's niggardly contribution to the Chilean revolution, Chou said: "Basic for developing countries is to support themselves through their own efforts, in other words, make self-support the principal means and foreign aid a complementary measure . . ."[124]

FROM RHETORIC TO RUIN

In 1891, one of Allende's home-grown heroes, the populist president José Manuel Balmaceda, took aim at the British-owned nitrate industry, then the towering giant of the Chilean economy. Ultimately, that decision—plus a number of others aimed at the country's economic barons—would cost Balmaceda his presidency, and his life. (Ironically, Balmaceda would end his life a suicide on September 19, a date very much in Salvador Allende's mind on a mid-September day, eighty-two years later.)

Nitrate would become the very first major nationalization acquisition of the Allende regime. Though no longer the giant it once was (and by 1971, American-owned), nitrate still loomed large on Chile's emotional landscape, and so it was with great fanfare that Allende would announce on May 28, 1971, the buy-out of Anglo-Lautaro Nitrate Co. Ltd., and its subsidiary, Chilean Mining and Chemical Co., for a total of $42.2 million.

Although he would enjoy the enthusiastic initial support of the Christian Democrat-controlled Congress in nationalizing copper, that support would eventually turn sour, so nitrate was Allende's one unquestioned nationalization triumph.

Indeed, by February 19, 1972, Congress had become so chary of Allende's swashbuckling assault on the domestic private sector, that, meeting as a Committee of the Whole, it voted 100–33 to approve a series of constitutional amendments requiring specific approval of Congress for the expropriation of any enterprise. The amendments were made retroactive to October 14, 1971—back to, but not to include the copper nationalizations. On April 6, Allende vetoed the measure and threatened to dissolve Congress or call a plebiscite if Congress continued its "obstructionist attitude toward the executive." (Allende would hurl that threat again, but never dared to call the plebiscite; actually, the opposition had already challenged him, on February 21, to call one to give the people of Chile the opportunity to vote on whether they wanted a socialist economy.) Angered by his remarks, the Party of the Radical Left—which had broken away from the Radical party in the wake of the Pérez Zújovic murder (see p. 331), pulled out of the government coalition.

But the confrontation had another consequence with ominous ramifications. To replace one of the two resigned Radical ministers, Allende named an air force general, Pedro Palacios Cameron, as minister of mines—the first member of the armed forces to serve in the Cabinet in more than ten years.

On October 19, 1971, Allende submitted legislation defining three areas of the economy: state, mixed, and private. The real purpose of the bill was to facilitate the nationalization of the first ninety-one of 150 companies portrayed as pivotal to control of the entire economy. That legislation ultimately boiled up into a full-scale constitutional confrontation between Allende and the Congress; first Congress voted to void the "three areas" scheme, a measure which, on April 6 (as noted above) Allende vetoed. The following July 7, the Senate overrode his veto, and the dispute went to the newly created Constitutional Tribunal.

As more than one observer had noted, Chile was already second in the Western Hemisphere only to Communist Cuba in terms of the state's role in the economy—even before Allende was inaugurated. True to Christian Democrat doctrine that the government which governs most, governs best, the public sector (the state) already accounted for 40 percent of the gross internal product; the state payroll was one-third of the total of all wages and salaries in the economy; state investment was half the total in the economy, and the state financed 70 percent of all investment; the government's Banco del Estado (State Bank) had on deposit a sum almost equal to the total of all private banks combined; and the state already owned outright, had controlling interest or substantial investments in such industries as electricity, telecommunications, oil, steel, sugar, petrochemicals, electronics, cellulose and paper, wood, computers, agribusiness and others.[125]

Economic factors facilitated the steady expansion of the state's role: income from the biggest source of wealth, copper, flowed either abroad in profits or remained in state coffers through taxes and royalties; given the smallness and relative isolation of the market, there was no opportunity for the emergence of industrial or commercial powerhouses in other areas, which meant the private sector was relatively weak vis-à-vis the state.

But fundamentally it was ideology which propelled Chile into ersatz socialism: the ideology of the Christian Democrats, both during the six years they ruled Chile, and through the crucial support they gave Allende in reaching the presidency as well as the support extended him during the first third of his presidency. Had Allende—and those around him, those he never really could control—behaved with more restraint, there is little doubt that the Christian Democrats would have continued to support him, because he was moving along a path they had blazed themselves.

A 1969 study asserted that, as of 1966, 284 companies controlled the entire primary and secondary sectors of the Chilean economy, and that 144 companies controlled the entirety of the primary and secondary sectors of the country's industry.[126] It was that central nervous system of the economy—the "monopolies"—Allende targeted with his October 19 legislation, while piously proclaiming respect for the rightful role of the private sector in the economy. In fact, he and his minions took not ninety-one, not 150, but 450 Chilean companies, most of them without benefit of law. What would be left of that private sector could be glimpsed by the definition of "monopolies" developed by his Planning Office: all companies with capital in excess of $500,000.[127]

By the onset of his second year in the presidency, Allende's deeds finally mattered more to the Christian Democrats than Allende's words, and the deeds bespoke violence, class warfare, economic ruin—and mortal peril for democracy itself. The Christian Democrats were no longer willing to buy caricatures of their own ideas.

And so it was that, a few months later, Congress would throw down the gauntlet, and locate it at October 14, a date that included takeover of the copper companies, but blocked all others, the rebuff to his "three areas" which precipitated the aforementioned constitutional confrontation. Mere legality, meanwhile, would scarcely stay Allende's hand: more and more industries were taken over ("requisitioned," ostensibly a short-term measure) in the wake of trumped-up labor, production or financial problems, or subjected to de facto "popular" seizure (with government connivance at worst, tolerance at best). Among them: fourteen companies producing half the country's textiles, beer, coal, fishing, poultry, smoked pork or beef, and ninety other small companies. This path led, of course, not to socialism, but only to confrontation—and fiscal bankruptcy. In 1972, the deficit for public and semipublic enterprises was 21.8 billion escudos; a year later, it stood at 175 billion—a 703 percent increase.[128]

Inevitably, spiralling inflation, spiralling imports, spiralling demand for funds to finance this phantasmagoric frenzy, caused the printing presses to work overtime churning out ever more money, ever more worthless. The first time the government would face up to the reality that the value of the money had skidded was on July 26, 1971 (just fifteen days after Allende's Day of National Dignity, commemorating the announced take-over of the copper companies). The Central Bank devalued the escudo by 100 percent, dropping the open rate from 14.23 to 28 escudos to the dollar. (On the by-then flourishing black market, the rate was already much higher than that.) That slide would gain speed, until by the time Allende fell, the rate was literally in the thousands, the bills not worth the paper they were printed on, a farce that continued until the military government was firmly in place.

Perhaps in no area was the disaster—a combination of chaos in the countryside and palsied planning—more evident, more painful, than in foodstuffs. On February 1, 1972, two months after the March of the Pots and Pans, Economy Minister Pedro Vuskovic announced new measures to overcome shortages the government had heretofore denied existed. Subsidies for basic foodstuffs were ended; prices would be raised in excess of 1971's 22 percent cost-of-living increase. Faced with the failure of those policies—designed to stimulate investment and encourage farmers to market their produce—the government later began requiring that employers provide a monthly differential to their employees to offset price increases. The latter measure, of course, only fueled further the fires of inflation.

Once lawlessness had been unloosed, inflamed by the heat of revolutionary rhetoric, it could not be contained—and particularly in the countryside. As food shortages mounted, the import bills rose ever higher, the lines outside shops lengthened. And the need for stability in agriculture grew ever greater, but that is not what Chile got; what Chile got was more rural violence, more expropriations—as the following table illustrates.

TABLE 30

FARM EXPROPRIATIONS, FREI AND ALLENDE YEARS

	# OF FARMS	AREA	FAMILIES AFFECTED
From 1965 to 11/31/70	1,408	3,564,552.9	20,976
From 11/4/70 to 3/22/73	3,628	5,585,327.2	33,948

Source: Presidential Message of 1973 (extracted from *Chile: The Balanced View*, ed. Francisco Orrego Vicuña, op. cit., table 18, p. 185.) Though Allende claimed the expropriation phase officially ended in March of 1973, another source—drawing on Agrarian Reform Corporation figures—claimed that, in just three months, June–August of that year, the pace of expropriation reached record-breaking proportions: 648 farms covering 599,922 hectares. (*Source:* Genaro Arriagada Herrera, *De La Vía Chilena A La Vía Insurreccional*, op. cit., p. 310.)

Production inevitably suffered. In 1970, Chilean agriculture supplied 82 percent of the country's wheat needs; in 1973, that was down to 45 percent. Rice went from 69 percent to 46 percent, maize (corn) from 46 percent to 29 percent, potatoes 93 percent to 73 percent, beef 75 percent to 57 percent, lamb 93 percent to 57 percent, milk products 83 percent to 55 percent. The country's import bill for agricultural products shot up from $168.4 million in 1970 to $555.6 million in 1973. Economic chaos encouraged economic corruption. The magazine *Ercilla* estimated that by mid-1973, an estimated sixty thousand people were working full-time in the black market, where 35 percent of the national income was being spent or earned. Commenting on this, Sigmund noted that peasants diverted much of their produce to the far more lucrative black market, and that a new "profession" emerged: *coleros* (from the Spanish word, *cola*, or line), for persons who spent their time in lines foraging for scarce items for resale. A maid shortage developed as servants discovered that they could earn more plying this new trade than in domestic service. The emergence of such a huge underground economy also cost the government revenues, the 18 percent sales tax on legal transactions.[129]

Though rarely mentioned, the impact of the shortages was eased somewhat by U.S. Food for Peace shipments, which actually increased during the Allende years, to a total of $16.8 million (plus $250,000 in special disaster relief).

The picture was similar in industrial production. After the artificial boom of 1971, industrial output began a steady slide. The binge in printing press money reached historic proportions: on June 19, 1973, the Society for Industrial Development (Sociedad de Fomento Fabril*) reported that the expansion in the money supply already that year— 274.3 percent—was the highest in Chile's history.[130]

Inflation, as indicated previously, reached similar, sickeningly historic proportions. The following table reflects—to the extent that statistics ever can—the economic wreckage Chile would become as Allende led the country along "the Chilean road to socialism":

TABLE 31
CHILE'S ECONOMY, THE ALLENDE YEARS

	DEC. 1970	DEC. 1971	DEC. 1972	SEPT. 1973
Consumer Price Index	100.0	122.1	321.7	942.2
Issue of Money Index	100.0	267.6	700.7	2,118.2
Industrial Production Index	100.0	110.0	107.3	95.1
Agricultural Production Index	100.0	100.9	90.2	70.4 (1)
Cattle Production Index	100.0	106.8	108.1	97.6
Copper Production (2)	534.5	571.3	592.7	404.6
Exports (millions of US$)	1,254.7	1,086.0	963.7	1,194.5 (1)
Imports (millions of US$)	1,177.9	1,198.8	1,463.0	1,632.4 (1)
Balance of Payments	98.21	−309.0	−318.9	−253.2 (1)
International Reserves	343.2	34.2	−441.7	−605.6
External Debt (3)	2,632.0	2,696.6	3,124.9	3,454.7
Investment Index	100.0	76.0	71.0	80.0
Fiscal Revenues (3)	19,309.2	23,924.4	38,375.1	137,777.0
Fiscal Expenditures (3)	22,191.4	36,456.6	64,950.5	281,211.0
Money supply (percentage increase in 12-month period)	62.1	119.0	138.8	329.8

(1) as of December 1973
(2) thousands of metric tons—figures are for the four major mines, plus Andina (Río Blanco)
(3) in millions of escudos

Source: Adapted from Statistical Synthesis, Table 1, in *Chile: The Balanced View,* ed. Francisco Orrego Vicuña, op. cit., p. 168. That volume cites as the source *The Chilean Economy Under the Popular Unity Government* (Santiago: Impreso Editora Nacional Gabriela Mistral, 1974), pp. 33–80.

* Sometimes translated as National Association of Manufacturers, more closely reflecting its role in Chilean business.

As indicated previously, not all of Chile's economic hardships were of Allende's making. The dramatic drop in world copper prices—from 76 cents per pound in 1970 to 48 cents in 1972; 48 cents in 1972 (though it would bounce back strongly) to 66 cents in 1973—cost Chile dearly, inasmuch as each one-cent fluctuation in copper prices then represented the equivalent of $16 million in export earnings.[131] Nor, conversely, was the external situation entirely adverse: apart from the massive inflow of credits from Communist and other countries, the International Monetary Fund (see p. 339) did provide offset credits for copper price losses, and, on June 12, 1972, twenty-eight U.S. banks agreed to refinance, over eight years, Chile's $160 million debt to them, but only after Allende's envoy, Orlando Letelier, agreed to submit any nonperformance dispute to the jursidiction of U.S. courts. Allende had denounced similar concessions made by the Frei government as an offense to the country's dignity.[132]

On that same date, Allende's Cabinet resigned to give him a free hand in dealing with the economic crisis. Vuskovic was replaced by the more "pragmatic" Carlos Matus (a Socialist). On July 24, Allende unveiled his new economic plan. The plan called for a two-year government investment in agriculture and industry of $760 million (much of it to come from Communist countries), compulsory salary increases, compulsory insurance, tax increases for the middle and upper classes, and further price controls (to force the nationalization of the ninety-one major industries nominally left in private hands; a Chamber of Deputies study showed that, by mid-June, sixty-five of them in one fashion or another, under one pretext or another, had already been taken over by the government).[133] For good measure, Allende included in his address an attack on the U.S. for its "invisible blockade."[134] The Communist credits would never materialize at anything resembling a fraction of that figure, the government would invest less, not more, and compulsory wage increases (which did materialize) only fanned inflations's fires.

The fumbling, the tinkering went on; on September 27, Allende's new economy minister announced that, effective in October, prices would be frozen across-the-board. The stagnating productive sectors stagnated even more. (Already, going into 1972, chaos in the economy began to paralyze public transportation: Juan Vergara, president of the taxi and bus drivers' union, revealed that 30 percent of Santiago's microbuses, and 25 percent of the taxis were sidelined for lack of parts.)[135]

With shortages reaching epidemic proportions, Allende began his last year in power, by exploding his biggest bomb yet. For Chile's "suffering, humiliated middle classes"—as a former radical president would describe those people who made up the very essence of the country's political and social and economic vitality—the worst was yet to come.

Notes

CHAPTER 6

1. William Buckley's wry remark on the shock in the U.S. following the election of Allende, as quoted by Alistair Horne, *Small Earthquake in Chile* (New York: Viking Press, 1972), p. 28. The U.S. had, of course, bankrolled Chile more heavily than any other country in the hemisphere during the sixties in the belief that Chile, and, particularly, the reformist government of Frei, were the best alternatives to communism.
2. Henry Kissinger, *White House Years* (Boston: Little, Brown & Company, 1979), p. 653. Kissinger notes that "the Chilean election results came in just as Moscow and Cairo were rejecting our protests of Middle East cease-fire violations; Jordan feared an imminent move by Iraqi troops against the king; a Soviet naval force was steaming toward Cuba. By September 8, the day the Chilean developments were first discussed by an interagency committee, several airplanes had just been hijacked in the Middle East and the Soviet flotilla was nearing the port of Cienfuegos. Six days later, on September 14, when Chile was next considered, the Jordan situation had deteriorated, and Cuban MiGs intercepted a U-2 flight seeking to photograph Cienfuegos and the mission had to be aborted. In the weeks that followed, our government pondered Chilean events not in isolation but against the backdrop of the Syrian invasion of Jordan and our effort to force the Soviet Union to dismantle its installation for servicing nuclear submarines in the Caribbean. The reaction must be seen in that context." The foregoing is useful in framing Chile in a realistic perspective, inasmuch as so many commentators have focused on the U.S. reaction to Chilean events "in isolation." Kissinger also notes that, largely because of the strong leftist bias within the State Department against doing anything to help the rightist Alessandri, and a corollary belief that an Allende presidency would not be seriously harmful to U.S. interests, the Forty Committee dealt with Chile only four times in the twenty-one months before Allende's election win, and on two of those occasions, took no action. Ibid., p. 665.
3. *Miami Herald*, September 13, 1970, p. 1-F. I think the most significant event of that dysphoric decade was the Cuban missile crisis of October 1962, when the fate of all mankind hung in the balance. But in strictly hemispheric terms, the impact of the event on the hemisphere itself, I would probably side with Bohning—and the Russians. References to Russian reactions are from Leon Gouré and Morris Rothenberg, *Soviet Penetration of Latin America* (Miami: Center for Advanced International Studies, University of Miami, 1975), pp. 97–98. On the significance, V. G. Spirin, "USA Imperialism and Latin American Reality," *S.Sh.A.i. Ekonomika Politika, Ideologia,* no. 8 (August 1971): p. 33. On the peaceful tack, Radio Moscow, January 8, 1971. On Latin America as new front, V. Tkachenko, "Latin America: Problems of Liberation Struggle," *International Affairs* (Moscow), no. 5, May 5, 1972; on apprehension, Gouré and Rothenberg, op. cit., p. 98.
4. Quoted by Marcos Chamudes, *Chile: Una Advertencia Americana* (Santiago: Ediciones P.E.C., 1972), p. 216.

5. Gouré and Rothenberg, op. cit., p. 99.
6. Chamudes, op. cit., p. 216.
7. The provision was written into the 1925 constitution, but it did not need to be invoked until 1946. That year—and in the next two presidential elections (1952 and 1958)—the Congress chose the top vote-getter, establishing the "tradition" (but not the legal requirement) that the candidate finishing first be chosen (just as the U.S. Electoral College is not bound by the popular vote totals, and, in fact, ignored them in 1888 in choosing close runner-up Benjamin Harrison as president over "winner" Grover Cleveland). The Chilean Congress did not need to intervene in the 1964 elections because Frei, backed by the Right, won with 56.09 percent of the vote. Congress passed the 1970 guarantees seven weeks after Allende's election, on December 21, 1970, and he signed them into law January 9, 1971, to gather dust, thereafter. (Painfully) mindful of Chile's fractious political past, the framers of Chile's new constitution, approved in a 1980 plebiscite, provide that in presidential elections with three or more candidates, if none wins an absolute majority, a run-off election must be called pitting the top two vote-getters against each other—the French system.
8. Eduardo Labarca Goddard, *Chile al Rojo*, cited by Chamudes, op. cit., p. 236. The Tomic quote appears on the same page of Chamudes. The intelligence report is in Kissinger, op. cit., p. 666. He wrote that by June 27, "both CIA and State Department experts suddenly and unexpectedly concluded that Allende's supporters in the Chilean Congress might prevail even if Allende lost, unless Alessandri's margin of victory . . . was more than 5 percent." He adds that such a margin was still "confidently assumed," a clearly preposterous assumption in a three-way race and given the circumstances of the campaign.
9. Quoted by Arturo Fontaine A., in "Revolution on Official Stamped Paper," in *Chile: A Critical Survey*, ed. Tomás P. MacHale (Santiago: Institute of General Studies, 1972), p. 60.
10. Figures for the party break-down in Congress vary from source to source. I have taken mine from *Nueva Enciclopedia de Chile*, Francisco Javier Díaz Salazar, ed. (Buenos Aires: Ediciones Copihue, Fotomecánica Futura, S.R.L., 1974), vol. II, pp. 32–42—a listing of legislators by names, district and party.
11. Alain Labrousse, *El Experimento Chileno: ¿Reformismo o Revolución?* (Barcelona: Ediciones Grisalbo, S.A., 1973), p. 243.
12. Among them was the man who fought Frei's street battles for him for six years, Gen. Vicente Huerta Celis, director of the corps of Caribineros. He said Frei "several times," in private meetings following the elections, expressed the wish that Allende would be spurned by the Congress. Interview with the author in Santiago, October 9, 1974.
13. Viaux' statement appears in Florencia Varas, *Conversaciones con Viaux*, (Santiago: Impresiones Eire, July 1972), p. 133. Watch for that phrase— "green light"—to appear again.
14. The ITT man was Robert Berrellez, a veteran of twenty-two years with the Associated Press in Latin America, winner of many awards and, perhaps the highest of all, the respect and confidence of his professional colleagues. (As a former competitor, I knew of no Latin "regular" who did not respect Berrellez.) In 1970, he was ITT's director of Inter-American Relations, based in Buenos Aires. In a September 29 memo to his New York headquarters,

Berrellez reported from Santiago: "All past evaluations of Frei's weakness in a crisis are being confirmed. Worse, it has been established beyond any doubt that he has been double-dealing to preserve his own stature and image as the champion of Latin American democracy. For instance, he told some of his ministers he would be quite willing to be removed by a military coup that would, in turn, upset Allende. Then he turned around and told the military chief that he was totally against a coup." The *Time* memo quoted Frei as telling a departing confidant (identified as Manuel Trucco, former Chilean ambassador to the Organization of American States): "I don't know what I did wrong now that the Government is about to be delivered to the Communists." The memo adds: "Perhaps harshly, many of Frei's old friends and political contemporaries view him as a Chilean Hamlet, wringing his hands." Both memos appear in *Multinational Corporations and United States Foreign Policy*, Vol. II., pp. 737 and 707, respectively, based on hearings before the Subcommittee on Multinational Corporations of the Committee on Foreign Relations, U.S. Senate, 93rd Congress, on March 20, 21, 22, 27, 28, 29 and April 2, 1973. Hereafter, those two volumes will be referred to as *Multinational Corporations*.

15. The names were cited by Viaux in Florencia Varas and José Manuel Vergara, *Operación Chile* (Santiago: Editorial Pomaire, 1973) p. 127.

16. Fontaine, op. cit., p. 65. A lawyer and university professor, Fontaine was then deputy editor of *El Mercurio*. That put him in opposition to Allende, but I have never heard anyone seriously question his integrity as a journalist; his opinions, perhaps, but not the honesty of his reporting.

17. Jaime Guzmán E., in "The Church and the Political Debate," *Chile: A Critical Survey*, op. cit., p. 297.

18. Quoted by Emilio Filippi and Hernán Millas, in *Anatomía de un Fracaso (La Experiencia Socialista Chilena)*, (Santiago: Empresa Editora Zig-Zag, 1973), p. 31. (Hereafter: *Anatomía de un Fracaso*.) Prado added: "We lost power and will win it again, but only when we can do so cleanly"—a statement which glossed over the fact that the PDC had lost power so decisively that it wasn't even eligible to compete in the run-off it would so "nobly" give away.

19. Fontaine, op. cit., p. 60.

20. *La Lucha por la Juridicidad en Chile*, eds. Andrés Echeverría B., and Luis Frei B. (Santiago: Editorial del Pacífico, 1974), vol. I, p. 37.

21. Régis Debray, *The Chilean Revolution: Conversations with Allende* (New York: Random House, 1971) p. 60. One cannot resist the remark how little some learn—or, more to point, are *willing* to learn—about the worthlessness of scraps of paper signed by those who know no scruples other than the triumph, by whatever means, of their own fanaticism. One thinks of the "Peace Declaration" Adolf Hitler signed at Munich on September 30, 1938, in order to pacify spineless British and French leaders ("peace in our time," proclaimed British Prime Minister Neville Chamberlain, brandishing that particular scrap of paper; World War II erupted eleven months later). Or the August 24, 1939, nonaggression pact between Hitler and the equally cynical Soviet Union. That pact gave Hitler his cheap shot to march on Poland one week later, and the Soviets the two years they needed to build their own military arsenal. Or in more recent and proximate times: the statement of guarantees which the Sandinistas in Nicaragua gave a gullible Organization of American States in June 1979, a month before they seized power, in order

to achieve crucial OAS backing. The Sandinistas have honored none of those guarantees in the intervening years.

22. Navasal told me in Santiago May 7, 1974, that the "top official" was Meyer.

23. Testimony of McCone March 21, 1973, before Sen. Frank Church's Senate subcommittee, *Multinational Corporations*, op. cit., pp. 94–96.

24. These figures are from *Recent Developments In Chile, Oct. 1971*, report of the subcommittee on Inter-American Affairs of the Committee on Foreign Affairs, House of Representatives, October 15, 1971, p. 14, testimony given by Meyer, then assistant secretary of state. The larger figure includes "all other" forms of U.S. government development assistance (except military) which, in the case of Chile, involved only Export-Import Bank loans for commercial transactions with the U.S. Neither figure includes repayments by the Chileans. Interestingly, to finance his "Revolution with Liberty," Frei tripled the size of Chile's public debt during his six years in power, raising it from $700 million at the end of 1970 to $2.2 billion at the end of 1970. (Source: *Indicadores Económicos y Sociales, 1960–1985* [Santiago: Banco Central de Chile, 1986], p. 312.) A 1974 mimeograph report of the U.S. Agency for International Development, summarizing Official Development Assistance (ODA), Military Assistance, and "Other" U.S. government loans and grants to Latin America on a country-by-country basis reveals the usual discrepancies: the AID report gives the ODA total ("Loans and Grants-Obligations and Loan Authorizations") as $869.9 for 1946–1970, and the total of ODA plus "other" at $1,437.7 billion. None of these figures includes repayments. The same report gives the repayment plus interest total for 1946–1973 inclusive as $103.7 million, and for "other" $430.5 million. That would leave a net, for both, 1946–1973 inclusive, of $1.127.6 billion. Again, using the AID figures, it is interesting to note that ODA assistance to Chile during the Alliance for Progress years (1962–1970 inclusive) was $769.5 million, and "other" amounted to $295.0 million—far and away the highest per capita of any hemisphere country. For comparative purposes, it should be noted that military aid for these periods was: 1946–1969 inclusive: $150.6 million; 1962–1970: $103.7 million. Repayments, 1946–1973 inclusive: $11.1 million. Since there was relatively little new lending—and less repayment—during the Allende years, the 1973-inclusive figures are usable as comparisons.

25. Figures for U.S. private investment from *United States and Chile During The Allende Years, 1970–1973*, p. 70 (referred to hereafter as *United States and Chile*), report of the hearings before the subcommittee on Inter-American Affairs of the Committee on Foreign Affairs, U.S. House of Representatives, July 1, October 15, 1971; September 11, 1972; March 6, September 20 and 25 and October 11 and 31 and December 7, 1973; August 5, September 17–18, 1974. Figures given in the testimony, March 6, 1973, of John H. Crimmins, acting assistant secretary of state for Inter-American Affairs. Figures for the amount underwritten by U.S. Overseas Private Investment Corp. (OPIC) from *Recent Developments in Chile*, October 1971, op. cit., p. 66, testimony given by Marshall T. Mays, then general counsel of OPIC, p. 6. Debt figures were given by Crimmins, op. cit., p. 66.

26. *Foreign Assistance and Related Programs: Appropriation Bill, 1971*, Report # 91–1134, U.S. House of Representatives, submitted June 1, 1970, by the Committee on Appropriations to the Committee of the Whole House on the State of the Union, pp. 4–5.

27. The quote is from the House testimony of OPIC General Counsel Marshall Mays, op. cit., p. 22. Indeed, by 1968, the U.S. had already virtually halted issuance of insurance to private American companies in Chile, so bad had the investment climate become.

28. Kissinger, op. cit., p. 661. Kissinger notes that "the Nixon Administration was initially less active against Allende than its Democratic predecessors [John F. Kennedy and Lyndon B. Johnson] had been . . ." He ascribes that partly to more pressing crises elsewhere, but also to a wrong estimate of the likely outcome of the Chilean election. Ibid., p. 662.

29. The statement was attributed to R. Arismendi, first secretary of the Uruguayan Communist party, but—as coauthors Gouré and Rothenberg observe—"as early as the first few months of 1971, Soviet articles were quoting the Arismendi statement." Gouré and Rothenberg, op. cit., p. 99.

30. Ibid., pp. 5–6. They note (also on p. 6) that an "authoritative 1972 Soviet study pointed out growing U.S. problems of supply by Latin America of raw materials needed in missile, communications, and atomic industries, electronics, etc." (The analysis was done by K. S. Tarasov in *S.Sh.A.i. Latinskaia Amerika* [Moscow: Politizdit] p. 29.)

31. Testimony March 27, 1973, before Senate subcommittee on *Multinational Corporations*, op. cit., p. 281. Korry's testimony was corroborated by Assistant Secretary Meyer in his testimony before the same subcommittee, March 29, 1973, p. 402. "The policy of the Government, Mr. Chairman," Meyer said, "was that there would be no intervention in the political affairs of Chile. We were consistent in that we financed no candidates, no political parties, before or after Sept. 8, Sept. 4 rather." Korry's remark about Allende's bid for $1 million appears in *United States and Chile*, op. cit., p. 649. He adds that the pitch to the embassy on their behalf may have been made without the knowledge of Allende or the other candidates.

32. Kissinger gave that testimony during his confirmation hearings as secretary of state in 1973. The quote is from a *Washington Post* Service story as published in the *Miami Herald*, July 7, 1975: "Did CIA Plot Result in Chilean General's Assassination?" The Washington-datelined story referred to a "confidential Senate staff report" done in September 1974 which accused Kissinger of having "deceived" the Foreign Relations committee in saying that. The authors of the "confidential" Senate report—in common with the authors of the mostly polemic *Post* story—appear to have lumped as one the preelection campaign period and the cliff-hanging sixty-day postelection period in arriving at their conclusion.

33. In a televised exchange with William Buckley on September 29, 1974, Korry denied flatly an American role in the 1970 election campaign. Buckley then asked him to speculate about the "general ethics" of using American money in the politics of another country.

KORRY: "The principle has been well established and practiced for so many years that it was taken as a matter of course . . . When I was being briefed to go to Chile in 1967, in October, September/October 1967, I was told, not asked, by well-known reporters of our leading media outlets, by congressmen, senators and their staffs, of the very large United States role in the election of 1964 in Chile; that is, making all of these allegations [they] spoke to me gratuitously about their knowledge in private. So they knew, and presumably Senator Church, who is chairman of the subcommittee [on multinational corporations], is not being kept in the dark by his own staff . . .

In any event, it was an open secret, but for ten years to this date, nobody has written about that . . ." From Radio-TV Reports, Inc., New York, transcript of Buckley's "Firing Line" program on WNET-TV, New York, and the Public Broadcasting System, September 29, 1974. Korry errs—slightly. The *Washington Post*'s Laurence Stern had written about the 1964 intervention, in 1973. Barnard Collier, then a correspondent for the *New York Times* in Latin America, alluded to U.S. support at the rate of a million dollars a month during the 1964 campaign in a February 17, 1967, article for the *Times'* Sunday Magazine ("A Revolution Without The Execution Wall"), but Collier did not name the CIA. Despite the "open secret" quality of the episode, the news remained in a protective capsule in Washington; Don Bohning, Latin America editor of the *Miami Herald*, a studious and conscientious reporter, could muster nothing stronger in the previously cited July 5, 1970, dispatch than an observation that Korry and the U.S. were not an issue in the campaign, "in contrast to charges, apparently with some justification, that the U.S. was involved in the anti-Allende effort of 1964."

34. The figure appears in a mysterious, 605-page book titled *Who's Who In CIA*, published in East Berlin, in English, in 1968, by Julius Mader (1066 Berlin W 66, Mauerstrasse 69) and quoted by Dan Pinck, a former Office of Strategic Services agent and later senior research associate at Harvard, in an article distributed by the *New York Times'* Special Features Syndicate division, for release March 23, 1975. The article was titled: "Is Everyone In The CIA?" Pinck relates that he was unable—on a one-hour "research" mission—to find a trace of either Mader or of one Fernando Gamarro in Mexico City, listed as a Mader resource and compiler of information. But, he said, six months after his original article on the book appeared, he "received a note from Mr. Mader, in East Germany," assuring Pinck (in English) that he (Mader) "liked your article. I do exist. I am alive." *Punto Final*, official organ of the Chilean Revolutionary Leftist Movement (MIR), claimed that after the September 4 election, a total of 550 CIA agents swarmed into Chile, many of them Cubans. Like so much which appeared in *Punto Final*, the report was regarded as a wild exaggeration.

35. This account is from Jerome Levinson and Juan de Onis, *The Alliance That Lost Its Way* (New York: A Twentieth Century Fund Study, Quadrangle Books, 1970), pp. 143–144.

36. McCone told the Church subcommittee that he had discussed the Chilean presidential elections several times with Helms, whom he described as a "close, personal friend." He indicated those conversations took place following an ITT board meeting (probably in June), at which Geneen had expressed concern for the fate of the company's extensive holdings in Chile (*Multinational Corporations*, op. cit., pp. 93–94 and 96). The account of Broe's meeting with Geneen, as well as subsequent telephone and personal contacts with Merrian and Gerrity, are taken from the same report, pp. 244, ff.

37. Ibid., p. 458 (for Geneen's remarks) and p. 258 (for Broe's). Much of the questioning of Broe (and Merriam, and Geneen) centered on why a cloak-and-dagger man should be assigned to what was, essentially, a briefing function. Geneen's answer, given on April 9, 1973—long before the spate of exposé stories of the CIA would show how it was organized and operated— was: "I think the best answer I can give you, Senator—I never knew, until this hearing, that there was a distinction between a clandestine group and an intelligence group. I thought they were all the same" (p. 465). Broe, for his

part, said simply that he did not know why he had been selected to meet with the ITT executives (pp. 257–258). However naive Mr. Geneen's 1973 answer may sound to 1988 ears, it ought to be pointed out that until Senator Church, aided and abetted by a Watergate-spastic media, began his public dismemberment of the CIA, the agency was cloaked, if not in secrecy, at least in decorous camouflage. For what it is worth, despite twenty years of professional experience in journalism, including ten as a foreign correspondent and two as a Washington correspondent, in 1973 I did not know about the clandestine-intelligence dichotomy, either. So effective was Senator Church in dismembering the CIA that, by 1974, a former deputy director would report that the already meager level of covert funding (1 percent to 2 percent of the total intelligence community budget), was "falling. There are no political-action programs underway now." (From an article by Ray S. Cline in the *New York Times,* November 1, 1974: "The Value of the CIA," as reproduced in United States and Chile during the Allende Years, 1970–1973, op. cit., p. 651.

38. Ibid., vol. 2, pp. 522–527.

39. Ibid., vol. 1, p. 246.

40. Ibid., p. 96.

41. Ibid., pp. 475–476. Geneen was talking mostly at this point about the second "fund" episode, which came up after the election, but his remarks were reinforcing his earlier testimony that ITT did not have a "plan."

42. Ibid., p. 243.

43. Ibid., p. 247.

44. Kissinger hints at—but does not make explicit—another possible explanation for the inaccurate forecasts: deep antipathy in the State Department to the candidate of the Right, Alessandri. That bias, as Kissinger documents in detail, translated as a policy of allowing only a trickle of money to oppose Allende, while going to great lengths to avoid helping the only candidate able to defeat him, Alessandri. Pointing out that no agency had called the attention of the White House, or the Forty Committee, to "the gravity of the situation" in Chile until the hour for effective action had passed, Kissinger ascribed this to a "State Department predisposition against an active covert role," intimidating those who might have opted for a more activist course. Kissinger understood that "if Allende was to be stopped, it would have to be by the conservative Jorge Alessandri. Though he had impeccable democratic credentials ... the Latin American Bureau [of State] disliked him, ostensibly for being too old, in reality because he was considered insufficiently progressive. Some in the Latin American Bureau, confusing social reform with geopolitics, did not consider an Allende presidency dangerous enough to overcome their ideological prejudices against Alessandri ..." Kissinger, op. cit., p. 663.

45. Ibid., vol. 2, pp. 562–565. Berrellez would later identify those "uppermost sources" as "an acquaintance in police intelligence" he happened to meet on a Santiago street. That even such a pro of Berrellez' standing would lapse into feverish prose reflects not only the superheated political atmosphere then reigning in Santiago, but also suggests the caution readers ought generally bring to anonymous sources in news stories (or, as in this case, confidential corporate reports).

46. Ibid., pp. 278–279.

47. Ibid., vol. 2, pp. 583–584.

48. Ibid., p. 282.

49. The account of the details of economic events immediately following Allende's election was distilled mainly from two *Miami Herald* stories: "Establishment in Chile Lets Despair Show," September 11, 1970, a Santiago-datelined dispatch written by William Montalbano; and, "Chilean Government Moves to Allay Fears on Economy," September 10, a combined wire services dispatch from Santiago. Zaldívar's September 23 remarks are from *Chile Since the Election of Salvador Allende: A Chronology*, prepared by Arthur J. Rynearson, Foreign Affairs Analyst in the Foreign Affairs Division of the Library of Congress, covering the period September 4, 1970–March 22, 1973, and reproduced in the appendix of the House subcommittee report, *United States and Chile* op. cit., pp. 373–374. It should also be noted that the Perera Co., leading traders in foreign exchange in Miami (and elsewhere), suspended trading at the same time in two other then-wobbling currencies, the Peruvian sol and Ecuadorean sucre. As for the escudo, the government would maintain the fiction of the official price of 12.21 to the dollar until December 31, 1970. Thereafter it began an uninterrupted slide which saw it hit 6,000 to the dollar five years later, and virtually lose any meaning whatever as a medium of exchange. Ultimately, with the escudo hovering around an official rate of 6,400 to the dollar, the military government, on September 29, 1975, scrapped the escudo in favor of the peso (1,000 escudos to one peso).

50. Montalbano, in the above-cited *Miami Herald* article of September 11, 1970.

51. Purdy's remarks are from an Associated Press dispatch in the *Miami Herald*, October 12, 1970: "Many Leaving Chile Over Marxist Leader." There was no quota for individual countries in the Western Hemisphere, but the annual limit for the entire hemisphere—Canada and the Caribbean included—was then 120,000. One of the Chileans who fled shortly after September 4 was Agustín Edwards, publisher of *El Mercurio*, the leading newspaper in Chile and frequent target of Allende's wrath. Allende had threatened in his platform to expropriate the paper, but later relented. Edwards himself was told he was on a "liquidation" list.

52. Allende quoted Engels on the possibility of ". . . a peaceful evolution from the old society to the new in countries where the representatives of the people have all power and in accord with the constitution can do what they desire when they have the majority of the nation behind them." Cited by Prof. Paul E. Sigmund, in an article in *Problems of Communism*, May–June 1974, as reproduced in *United States and Chile*, op. cit., p. 598. But, as Professor Sigmund goes on to point out, lack of majority support was precisely Allende's "central problem" as he fumbled to do what he could only have done with "the majority of the nation behind" him.

53. Genaro Arriagada Herrera, *De La Vía Chilena A La Vía Insurreccional* (Santiago: Editorial del Pacífico, 1974), pp. 66–67.

54. *Breve Historia de la Unidad Popular: Documento de "El Mercurio"* (Santiago: Editorial Lord Cochraine, S.A., 1974), Teresa Donoso L., ed., p. 31. (Hereafter *Breve Historia*.)

55. All from *Indicadores Económicos*, op. cit.: copper earnings, p. 327; international reserves, pp. 332–333; unemployment figures, pp. 244–245; inflation, p. 148; gross national product figures, p. 16.

56. Background on Vuskovic from Robert Moss, *Chile's Marxist Experiment* (New York/Toronto: A Halsted Press Book, John Wiley & Sons, 1973), p. 53.

57. Vuskovic's ideas were a particularly ersatz brand of Keynesian thinking inasmuch as Keynes postulated his theory of stimulating aggregate demand for depressed or stagnant economies, and, where possible, stipulated private participation in stimulating demand. Chile's economy was not then stagnant, and the private sector, still preponderant in the economy, could have played such a role, but under Allende/Vuskovic, was so emasculated as to be rendered incapable of doing so. Indeed: capital investment as a percentage of gross domestic product actually declined each of the years Allende was in La Moneda, shrinking to a level in 1973 (7.8 percent) below that of modern-day Chad or Mozambique. (Investment figures from *Indicadores Económicos*, op. cit., p. 40, and Chad-Mozambique comparison from *1986 Encyclopaedia Britannica Book of the Year*, op. cit., pp. 850, 852.)

58. *Breve Historia*, op.cit., p. 31.

59. Allende used another device to squeeze the banks: on January 7, 1971, it was reported that the State Development Corporation (CORFO) had withdrawn its very sizable deposits from private banks. By July of that year, the Allende administration had captured 60 percent of Chile's private banks. Two large foreign banks—Bank of America and the Bank of London and South America, the latter, a pioneer in Chile—had also sold out to the government by late July. City Bank of New York followed suit six months later. Source for the foregoing: *United States and Chile*, op. cit., p. 375. For the drop in bank shares, ibid., p. 591. As to the "ruinous consequences": in 1970, Chile's private banks were $16 million in the black; by 1973, $235 million in the red. Source: *Indicadores Económicos*, op. cit., pp. 332–333.

60. *Breve Historia*, op. cit., pp. 33–34. When Salvador Allende took office, money in circulation totaled 3.7 billion pesos; when he left, it stood at 74 billion, zooming to an astounding 202 billion in September of 1974, before that runaway horse could be brought under control. Source: *Indicadores Económicos*, op. cit., p. 288.

61. Source for seizure of Ralston and Indiana Brass, *United States and Chile*, op. cit., p. 375. For compensation agreement, Robert Moss, *Chile's Marxist Experiment*, op. cit., p. 68. For copper and banks, *United States and Chile*, op. cit., p. 379, and for 150 Chilean firms, ibid., p. 379.

62. *Breve Historia*, op. cit., pp. 31 and 34. Details on Tomás Moro from James R. Whelan, *Allende: Death of a Marxist Dream* (Westport, Ct.: Arlington House, 1981), p. 87.

63. Moss, op. cit., p. 59.

64. "I am not president" quote from *Breve Historia*, op. cit., p. 40; State of the Union remarks from *United States and Chile*, op. cit., p. 599.

65. Moss, op. cit., p. 18.

66. *Breve Historia*, op. cit., pp. 35, 32.

67. Suzanne Labin, *Chile: The Crime of Resistance* (Richmond, Surrey, England: Foreign Affairs Publishing Co. Ltd., 1982), p. 1982. As a Scripps-Howard Newspaper Alliance correspondent reporting on Latin America, I had the opportunity to witness many similar scenes, most memorably on a driving trip south to the farm city of Temuco, around four hundred miles south of Santiago, in the spring of 1971. Jacques Chonchol was in Temuco at that time, still denying the existence of armed bands; we encountered their roadblocks just a few miles outside of Temuco.

68. According to a National Planning Office presentation made in March of
    1972, at an international round-table in Santiago organized jointly by the
    Planning Office and the British Institute of Development Studies of the
    University of Sussex, England, 1,300 large farms (*latifundia*), with a total of
    2.3 million hectares, were expropriated in 1971. Conference proceedings are
    in *The Chilean Road to Socialism*, ed. J. Ann Zammit (Austin: University of
    Texas Press, 1973), statistics p. 325. According to official government fig-
    ures, by early 1973, 3,628 farms had been taken under Allende, covering a
    total of 5.5 million hectares (Presidential Message of 1973). For comparative
    purposes, Chile, in 1976, had a total of 311,324 "farms" (including or chards,
    lumbering operations, forest preserves, pasturelands, and the like), covering
    a total of 28.7 million hectares (*Indicadores Económicos*, op. cit., p. 56).
69. Alistair Horne, *Small Earthquake in Chile*, op. cit., p. 322.
70. Sigmund, *Problems of Communism*, in *United States and Chile*, op. cit., pp.
    606–602.
71. Details of Pérez Zújovic murder from *Breve Historia*, op. cit., pp. 59–60, 62;
    Robert Moss, *Chile's Marxist Experiment*, op. cit., p. 124; Chile: Arturo
    Fontaine A., "Revolution on Official Stamped Paper," in *Chile: A Critical
    Survey*, op. cit., p. 74; Fontaine quote, ibid., p. 74. Following the June 13
    shoot-out, police found in the pockets of Ronald Rivera a note addressed to
    his mother: "Happy at having killed Pérez Zújovic." Next to the body: a sub-
    machinegun taken from Carabineros. Tomás Arnoldo Gutiérrez Urrútia,
    shot and killed May 24 during a hold-up staged by four VOP (Vanguardia
    Organizada del Pueblo) gunmen. These details from *Breve Historia*, pp.
    62, 56.
72. Data on the splits in the political parties from Professor Paul E. Sigmund,
    "Allende in Retrospect," in *Problems of Communism*, May–June 1974, as
    reproduced in *United States and Chile*, op. cit., p. 601. Sigmund provides
    much greater detail on the in-fighting in the party in his later book, *The
    Overthrow of Allende and the Politics of Chile, 1964–1976* op. cit., pp. 50–
    54, 61–64, 72–73, 78–80, 149–152.
73. Ibid., p. 603. Tomic made the remark at a March 1972 Round Table in
    Santiago jointly sponsored by the University of Sussex (England) and the
    Chilean Planning Office. That conference, ignoring the massive evidence
    already mounting in Chile, was mainly a rally of pro-Allende ideologues,
    from Britain, the United States, the Soviet Union, East and West Europe,
    Asia, Africa, and Latin America. The proceedings were later published in
    The Chilean Road to Socialism, ed. J. Ann Zammitt, op. cit.
74. Debray, *The Chilean Revolution: Conversations with Allende*, op. cit., p. 97.
75. *Breve Historia*, op. cit., p. 66.
76. Debray, op. cit., p. 104. The interviews took place the first week of January
    1972.
77. Ibid., pp. 82–83. Allende's comment about "class bias" is on p. 98.
78. Ibid., p. 178. The quotes are from Allende's first message to the Congress,
    May 21, 1971.
79. *La Payita*, as Mrs. Contreras was known, granted an extraordinary inter-
    view to the Italian journalist Gaston Salvatore, published in the Italian
    magazine, *Epoca*, January 10, 1988, and reproduced textually in *El Mer-
    curio* of Santiago, January 14, 1988. Mrs. Contreras had been living for
    many years in Paris, ironically as head of a Cuban travel agency, Habana
    Tours.

80. Robert Moss, *Chile's Marxist Experiment,* op. cit., pp. 54–55. Moss said the survey was done by the UNICOOP stores.

81. *Breve Historia,* op. cit., p. 113. The chronology of the Allende years appearing in *United States and Chile,* op. cit., pp. 373–395, put the number of demonstrators at five thousand (p. 380), and said the protest was also aimed at Fidel Castro, still governing Cuba from Chile, over four thousand miles due south of Havana. The chronology comes across as somewhere between sympathetic to and uncritical of Allende, perhaps because the sources were mainly so tilted (*New York Times, Washington Post, Christian Science Monitor,* Facts on File).

82. Sigmund, op. cit., p. 601.

83. Federico G. Gil, "Socialist Chile and the United States," in *Inter-American Economic Affairs,* Autumn 1973, as reproduced in *United States and Chile,* op. cit., p. 548. After months of negotiations, Chile reached agreement with the "Paris Club" creditor nations, including the U.S., for rescheduling an estimated $600 million in foreign debts, in April 1972. Nearly two-thirds of Chile's total $1.8 billion debt was owed to the U.S., and talks on that debt became snarled in the dispute over compensation for the seized copper companies, a dispute still unsettled when the Allende government was ousted.

84. *Breve Historia,* op. cit., p. 86. Martner spoke on September 14, 1971. His proposal came at a time when Latin American nations were struggling with their debts, but fully fifteen years before they would become so debt-burdened as to trigger similar "debt bomb" proposals.

85. The Nixon quote is from *United States and Chile,* op. cit., p. 376, the Allende quote from Debray, *The Chilean Revolution,* op. cit., p. 166.

86. Armando Uribe, *The Black Book of American Intervention in Chile* (Boston: Beacon Press, 1975), p. 75 (first published as *Le Livre Noir de L'Intervention Américaine au Chili* (Paris: Editions du Seuil, 1974), p . 75. The remark is from an official account of Allende's November 4, 1970, meeting with Charles A. Meyer, U.S. assistant secretary of state.

87. Soviet mining experts—dispatched by the Kremlin without cost to Chile—took a leading role in building the "excess profits" case against the U.S. companies. On July 8, 1971, though their consulting work ostensibly was done, it was announced that four of the Soviet experts would remain in the country—still without cost to Chile—to advise Chilean authorities on other mining matters. Their number eventually would reach fifty-five, and they would cost Chile plenty—see fn. 30, chapter 7. From *Breve Historia,* op. cit., p. 67. Interestingly, there is no mention of a Soviet role in a chronology prepared for the U.S. Congress on the very eve of Allende's overthrow by Virginia M. Hagen, Latin American Affairs analyst for the Library of Congress' Congressional Research Service, appearing as Appendix B, in *United States and Chile,* op. cit., pp. 397–415. But that analysis did ventilate uncritically such claims against the copper companies as that, prior to nationalization, the Chilean government had no effective control over the companies, as well as the spurious "excess-profits" claims, without noting that those "profits" were pre-Chilean tax (pp. 408–409). In "Chronology" (Appendix A), there is, at least, this: "He [Allende] cited a Soviet study and an investigation by the French Mining Society to prove his charges of mismanagement" (p. 377).

88. Testimony given by Assistant Secretary Meyer before the House Subcom-

mittee on Inter-American Affairs of the Foreign Affairs Committee, October 15, 1971, as reproduced in *United States and Chile*, op. cit., p. 34.

89. Henry Kissinger, *Years of Upheaval* (Boston: Little Brown & Company, 1982), p. 376.

90. The "big brother" quote is from "The Kremlin's Hand in Allende's Chile" by Professor James Theberge in *The Soviet Analyst*, August 15, 1974, as reproduced in *United States and Chile*, op. cit., p. 635. Theberge was then director of the Latin American Department of Georgetown University's Center for Strategic and International Studies, and would later serve as U.S. ambassador to Nicaragua, still later as ambassador to Chile. Chile's interest in possible cooperation with Comecon was conveyed by Foreign Minister Clodomiro Almeyda during a visit to Moscow, May 28, 1971 (*United States and Chile*, op. cit., p. 376).

91. Theberge in *United States and Chile*, op. cit., p. 637.

92. *U.S. Overseas Loans and Grants and Assistance from International Organizations; Obligations and Loan Authorizations, July 1, 1945–Sept. 30, 1978* (Washington: Agency for International Development, no date), p. 43. (Hereafter *U.S. Overseas Loans and Grants*.) In addition to $62.5 million in loans during that twenty-year period, the United States gave Chile $83.5 million in military grants, most of it surplus military equipment. But even that grand total—$146 million—was less than half in *twenty-two years* what the Soviets were offering in military aid in *one* year.

93. This apologia from Professor Gil was not untypical of "progressive" thinking that as Allende and his policies steered Chile towards bankruptcy, the U.S. should dump more dollars in: "Chile's policymakers are not facing easy choices either. The Allende government needs dollars to carry out many of its large-scale development projects. Chile's economy is so closely tied to the dollar economy that it cannot break out of this pattern of dependency without dislocating its entire financial system. Although United States economic pressure is driving Chile toward a search for alternative sources of foreign capital, it is doubtful that these sources in Eastern Europe, Japan and elsewhere in Latin America will have the capacity to meet all Chilean needs. At the same time, to surrender to the demands for compensation acceptable to the United States copper corporations would have disastrous political consequences and is simply not a viable alternative, for to do so would not only be a violation of the Chilean constitution and of the Unidad Popular program, it would also be considered by most Chileans as a betrayal of the sacred principle of national sovereignty." It should be remembered that Gil wrote those lines on the eve of Allende's overthrow, when the Chilean economy was already crumbling on all sides and inflation spiraling out of control. Gil, "Socialist Chile and the United States," in *United States and Chile*, op. cit., p. 556.

94. White House Communications Director Herbert G. Klein told reporters on November 30, 1971, that, based on conversations during a two-week visit to Argentina, Brazil, Peru, Ecuador, Honduras, and Mexico, he and White House counselor Robert H. Finch had "the feeling" that the Allende government "won't last long." The remark triggered a strong formal protest from Chile (*United States and Chile*, op. cit., p. 380).

95. James Theberge, who specialized in tracking Soviet affairs in the hemisphere, wrote: "The overthrow of the Allende government was a bitter but not entirely unexpected setback for Moscow's united front tactics in Latin

America, and had adverse repercussions for Marxist parties elsewhere in the West. Communists and Socialists in France and Italy who had earlier pointed to Chile as a model of the peaceful transition to socialism moved to disengage themselves from the Allende disaster. Instead of leading to socialism, united front tactics in Chile ushered in a period of unparalleled political violence, enormous suffering for Chile's workers and middle class, and the worst economic crisis in its history. Soviet designs for Chile to serve as the vanguard of the anti-U.S. front in Latin America ended in a complete fiasco and left a deep impression on the non-Communist political parties and the armed forces in the region. It reminded them of the grave risks of entering into an alliance with totalitarian parties. Despite protestations to the contrary, Marxist governments are driven inexorably to violate pledges to uphold the constitution, to destroy the private sector of the economy, and ultimately to install a totalitarian dictatorship." Theberge, "Kremlin's Hand in Allende's Chile," in *United States and Chile*, op. cit., p. 638.

96. Kissinger, op. cit., p. 669. As noted earlier, the bureaucracy managed to smother discussion of Chile so effectively that the Forty Committee dealt with it only four times in the twenty-one months before Allende's election. It was March of 1970 before a paltry $135,000 was approved for propaganda in support of democratic candidates, but even then "the State Department circumscribed the expenditure of these funds ... by a strong caveat to the effect that if any of the covert activities tended to endorse Alessandri, State Department support would be withdrawn forthwith. The concept of defeating one candidate without helping his principal opponent was rather original." As Kissinger also notes, this was in line with the prejudices of State's Latin American Bureau which "disparaged both the likelihood and the danger of an Allende victory." Ibid., pp. 665–666. It was June 27 before the Forty Committee would again take up the Chilean case, voting $450,000, but again, to be expended only in opposing Allende, and specifically not to help Alessandri, the one candidate with any chance of defeating Allende. Further, it was not only too little, it was too late, reaching Santiago during the last four weeks of the campaign, its use heavily hobbled by State Department constraints. As Korry's own anxieties of an Allende victory multiplied, he recommended a two-phase program: increase in funding for "spoiling" activities, and funds to influence the congressional vote, since it was certain that in the three-way race, it would be up to Congress to decide. The State Department opposed both proposals until Korry challenged opponents with the kind of on-the-dime, off-the-dime question bureaucrats despise: "If he [Allende] were to gain power, what would be our response to those who asked what we did?" Even then, State Department sabotage continued: Korry was advised through "backchannel" means that "it [State] opposed both pre-election and post-election programs on philosophical grounds, and it reiterated in the strongest terms its objections to using any of the approved funds to help Alessandri ..." Ibid., pp. 666–667.

97. Wrote Kissinger: "Ambassador Korry had no illusions about the consequences of an Allende victory. Responding to a query whether a modus vivendi might prove possible, he replied: 'A conscious effort to work out modus vivendi is a theoretical hypothesis without relation to reality. While the Allende government would move internally with initial prudence to seek to maintain a framework of constitutionality and legality, it would be committed, as Allende has stated, to policies that treated U.S. imperialism as "public enemy number one" in the hemisphere. Aside from [specific

actions including nationalization of U.S. industries, recognition of Cuba, North Vietnam, etc.] which in themselves would make a modus vivendi a practical impossibility for the U.S., the profound changes in the structure of Chile would probably necessitate an external "enemy" to justify an accelerating revolution . . . The Allende forces cannot escape the conclusion that if he is inaugurated the United States has admitted its impotence.' " Ibid., p. 668. Korry would prove prescient on every important point in that preelection cable.

By contrast, Nathaniel Davis, the man who succeeded Korry, makes plain repeatedly in his own memoirs, *The Last Two Years of Salvador Allende* (Ithaca: Cornell University Press, 1985), his personal fondness for Allende as well as his conviction that Allende was a sincere democrat and reformer, in direct contrast to his equally plain disdain for the forces of the Right; and particularly the Pinochet government. Examples abound: Davis "liked the president wholeheartedly" (p. 50); Allende "dreamed marvelous, soaring dreams. His aspiration was for a better Chile and for happiness and fulfillment for his compatriots . . ." (p. 53); Allende's last address "will go down in history as a moving statement of the aspiration of the Chilean Left . . ." (p. 255); he seems to express regret that he was unable to assist in spiriting out of Chile Carlos Altamirano, a man who by his words and deeds demonstrated repeatedly his vocation not for democracy but for radical violence (even the Communists distanced themselves from Altamirano, as, at the end, did Allende himself, commenting that when a Latin American ambassador asked Davis for help in getting Altamirano out after the coup, "I was not in a position to render this assistance . . ." (p. 368). Otherwise, Davis goes to lengths to show how assiduously he moved to block the CIA from aiding those desperate forces trying to bring Allende down—the truckers, p. 324, the shopkeepers, p. 327, his resistance to helping the paper company— *La Papelera*—from Allende's campaign of economic strangulation, p. 327, concluding, p. 327: ". . . I am confident that no elements of the U.S. Mission in Chile extended financial support to the strike movements of October 1972 and August–September 1973. Insofar as I know, no moneys or support of any kind were passed to *Patria y Libertad* at any time during my incumbency. I avoided opportunities to meet or know Cumsille of the shopkeepers, Bazán of the professionals (CUPROCH), Jara of the land transport federation, and Vilarín of the truckers . . ." Indeed, Kissinger wrote that despite unanimous votes in the Forty Committee in 1971 and 1972 for aid mainly to the political parties and media "threatened with extinction," and a small sum for the "private sector" (shopkeepers, labor unions, etc.), Davis "decided against disbursement" of the latter. Henry Kissinger, *Years of Upheaval*, op. cit., p. 382. One need only read his remarks on Pinochet, pp. 227–229—suspended disbelief laced with sly insinuations—to understand Davis's attitude toward the man who deposed Allende. Given Davis' prejudices, it is difficult to conclude that he was right and three presidents were wrong about Allende, both as to Allende as a democrat and the threat he posed to U.S. interests. This is particularly true when one remembers that the two U.S. administrations preceding Nixon's (Kennedy's and Johnson's) had backed their conclusions with an outpouring of money and activity to keep Allende from reaching the presidency that dwarfed anything Nixon did. As Kissinger wrote: "That an Allende government threatened our national interests was conventional wisdom when Nixon entered office." Kissinger, op. cit., p. 661.

98. On October 15, 1970, Kissinger arranged for Korry to present his views to Nixon directly, the conclusion having by then been reached that it was impossible to prevent Allende's accession to the presidency. Korry, the man who had earlier argued that modus vivendi with Allende was impossible, now seemed to do a flip-flop, urging U.S. "nonhostility in return for Chilean restraint." Kissinger reports that Nixon was "reconciled to Allende's accession but not to cooperation with him. He replied evasively and thereafter unfairly classified Korry as a 'softhead.' " Kissinger, op. cit., p. 678. Kissinger adds that he "did not [himself] focus on the dangers largely because the agencies with operational responsibility went through a complicated three-cornered minuet that kept the problem from high-level attention. Ambassador Korry took the position that an Allende victory was tantamount to a Communist takeover . . . But State's Latin American Bureau disagreed . . . the CIA tended to side with Korry but not to the point of asking the White House to resolve the difference; it knew that it could not effectively operate without strong State Department support . . ." Ibid., pp. 665–666.

99. Korry's role was examined microscopically not only in his own testimony, but that of other witnesses appearing during the year–long hearings (1975–1976) of the so-called Church Committee (named for its chairman, the late Sen. Frank Church, D-Idaho); U.S. covert activities in Chile are covered extensively in Volume 7 of the final report, and of particular value as to Korry's behavior is his opening statement, appearing on p. 31 of that volume: *Select Committee to Study Governmental Operations with Respect to Intelligence Activities, U.S. Senate* (Washington: U.S. Government Printing Office, 1976), pp. 144–209. (Hereafter: *Intelligence Activities.*) Korry's role also was extensively examined during the investigation of an earlier Church committee, set up in 1973 to probe the ITT affair: Subcommittee on Multinational Corporations, U.S. Senate. Its findings were in two volumes, *Multinational Corporations and United States Foreign Policy* (Washington: Government Printing Office, 1973). (Hereafter: *Multinational Corporations.*) As to Hersh, the *Times*, in 1981—seven years after the original articles—published a lengthy retraction saying that Hersh was wrong in claiming that Korry had known about alleged CIA efforts to overthrow Allende. The 1981 "corrective story," in the self-serving jargon used, noted that the original stories had destroyed Korry's career. Hersh owed his original fame to his exposure of the My Lai massacre incident in Vietnam. As to the Church Committee, Kissinger refers to the "tendentious report" in 1975 of Church's Senate Select Committee to Study Governmental Operations with Respect to Intelligence Activities in several passages: "There is no evidence," he wrote in one, "that the authors of the report tried to weigh the concerns about an Allende victory that we felt so acutely at the time." He later remarked that the committee "charged darkly that Chile had been 'for more than a year . . . on the 40 Committee's agenda,' " this on the basis of four meetings over eighteen months, only two of which made a decision; still later, that a plot to *kidnap* Chile's army chief, General Schneider, which "we had called off and to which we gave no support, no endorsement, no assistance, and no approval, is one of the featured events in the Senate Committee's investigation of *US Government* plots to *assassinate* foreign leaders" (emphasis in original). Ibid., pp. 658, 665, 677.

100. Gil, "Socialist Chile and the United States," in *United States and Chile,* op. cit., p. 544.
101. Which I so reported in a lengthy profile on Korry distributed by the Scripps-Howard Newspaper Alliance in the fall of 1971, and published in a number of Scripps-Howard newspapers at that time. Further light on Korry's behavior is shed in an extract from a letter to the editor of *Foreign Affairs,* published in the January 1975 edition, from Professor Paul E. Sigmund, in which he commented on in-fighting within the Nixon administration in opposition to those proposing to block Allende from reaching the presidency: "[Then-National Security Advisor Henry] Kissinger's chairmanship of a group which would normally have been chaired by the Assistant Secretary of State for Latin America was attributed in [the *New York Times'* article of September 15, 1974] to Assistant Secretary Charles Meyer's resistance to some of the anti-Allende measures adopted in mid-1970 at Kissinger's behest in the 40 Committee, which oversees the CIA. Meyer's opposition, as well as Ambassador Korry's determination, expressed at the time to the ITT representative in Chile, to 'try to live with Allende—not appease him—take a firm line, but attempt to negotiate at every turn,' cast some doubt on the 'roots-and-branches' theory of 'coordinated hostility' on the part of the American government toward Chile put forward to Richard Fagen elsewhere in this issue." Reproduced in *United States and Chile,* op. cit., p. 675.
102. Davis, op. cit., p. 28. In the preceding paragraph, Davis refers to Allende having "turned the other cheek" when the U.S., in 1971, spurned Allende's public invitation to have the nuclear aircraft carrier *Enterprise,* then in South American waters, call at Chilean ports, and added that "while the U.S. attitude sometimes looked churlish, Washington supported the Chilean military, and continued assistance to it." Davis defined "turning the other cheek" as refraining "from throwing out the U.S. Military Group [and continuing] to support military collaboration between the two countries." "Collaboration" actually meant continuing to accept U.S. military aid, and continuing to allow Chilean military to participate in joint exercises and training programs. But, as numerous commentators pointed out, this was more an expression of that consummate manipulator, Allende, massaging the military so as to neutralize it.
103. Kissinger, op. cit., pp. 678, 681. The issue of U.S. economic countermeasures against Allende is examined later in this chapter, and the subject of covert action in the Appendix. For the present, suffice to observe, as Kissinger did (p. 682), that "Chile under Allende remained one of the largest recipients of official American aid per capita in Latin America"; and, as to covert, as Davis himself observes (op. cit., pp. 308–327), the total expended during three years was a paltry $6 million, and it went to keeping opposition political parties and media alive, not to fomenting revolution.
104. Francisco Orrego Vicuña, "Some International Law Problems Posed by the Nationalization of the Copper Industry by Chile," published in the *American Journal of International Law,* vol. 67, 4, October 1973, reprinted in *Chile: the Balanced View,* ed. Francisco Orrego Vicuña (Santiago: University of Chile, Institute of International Studies, 1975). Reference to chief justice appears on 259, retroactive passage on 266, and majority view on 267.
105. As a result of the Anderson revelations, Allende, on May 12, 1972, pro-

posed a constitutional amendment, patterned after the copper company nationalization formula, to seize the 70 percent share of the telephone company remaining in ITT's hands. The Senate passed the measure on July 7, but the bill languished thereafter in Congress with no further action being taken. On September 29 of that year, ITT's $92.5 million claim stemming from loss of the company became active at the Overseas Private Investment Corporation (OPIC). The following April 1, Allende broke off talks with the U.S. on renegotiation of the $1.8-billion debt—stalled in any case because of hardening U.S. insistence on compensation for the $700 million in expropriated U.S. assets—ostensibly because of the charges of U.S. intervention in Chile aired at the outset of the Church Committee's ITT/multinational corporations hearings, then just getting underway.

106. Davis, op. cit., p. 25. OPIC's problem, Davis observes, was compounded because in the flush of U.S. government "enthusiasm for Frei's experiment in democratic progress . . . the U.S. government had granted investment guarantees in Chile without getting an airtight state-to-state agreement on compensation for the national enterprises." Among OPIC's "lucky breaks": Anaconda's decision, previously noted, to try to save on insurance premiums by putting part of its OPIC coverage on "standby," as well as working out its stock sale with the Frei government without full consultation and approval from OPIC. Ibid., pp. 25–26.

107. Nixon's statement—and the credit-worthiness quote—appear in the Virginia Hagen Congressional Research Service study published in *United States and Chile*, op. cit., p. 410.

108. ITT ultimately did collect: $34,706,917 in cash and $59,384,614 in OPIC-guaranteed Chilean government obligations. That 1975 cash settlement was, by far, the largest to that point in the eleven-year history of OPIC and its predecessor agency. But it would be eclipsed two years later by Anaconda's. That seven-year legal battle ended with a settlement of $47,504,034 in cash, $47,588,104 in OPIC-guaranteed Chilean government obligations. Those settlements would rank as one-two down to the present (through June 30, 1987), and alone account for better than a quarter of all the cash paid by OPIC in the two hundred claims involving cash settlements in the first twenty years of the agency's operations. Source: OPIC News Release, RJ/771, dated June 30, 1987, "Insurance Claims Experience To Date: OPIC And Its Predecessor Agency."

109. *Indicadores Económicos y Sociales*, op. cit., pp. 342–343 (exports), pp. 348–349 (imports). For those who dote on shock statistics: on December 4, 1972, it was revealed that the U.S., earlier that year, had agreed to *double* the size of its military sales to Chile. That's right, double—from a paltry $5 million to a piddling $10 million (earmarked, principally, for purchase of a C-130 transport plane, with leftover cash to buy armored personnel carriers, trucks and, possibly, tanks).

110. From a booklet published by the Chilean Embassy in Washington, entitled: *Chile: Speech Delivered by Dr. Salvador Allende, President of the Republic of Chile, Before the General Assembly of the United Nations, Dec. 4, 1972*, pp. 13–14, 17, 22–23.

111. Gil's remark is from *United States and Chile*, op. cit., pp. 551–552; Jarpa's from Lautaro Silva, *El Fin de Una Aventura* (Santiago: Ediciones Patria Nueva, 1974), p. 223.

112. Allende's UN speech, op. cit., p. 15.

113. Reference to 1971 IADB loans from Jonathan E. Sanford, analyst of international relations, Congressional Research Service, "The Multilateral Development Banks and the Suspension of Lending to Allende's Chile," *United States and Chile*, op. cit., p. 434, appearing as Appendix C; to World Bank behavior in earlier nationalization disputes, a World Bank white paper, also in Appendix C., p. 445; Chile as first Bank borrower, ibid., p. 441; lending criteria, ibid., p. 445, quoting then Bank President Robert S. McNamara.

114. Sanford, "The Multilateral Development Banks and the Suspension of Lending to Allende's Chile," in *United States and Chile*, op. cit., p. 424. Sanford notes (ibid.) that "the international economists suggested that the projected economic troubles be met by an increase in external lending to Chile rather than by international pressure for a reduction in the level of Chilean imports." In other words, the way to help a debtor in over his head is not to require that he spend less, but rather to lend him more.

115. Ibid., p. 423. Figures on debt service and debt appear on pp. 421–422, imports on p. 424.

116. Ibid., pp. 429, 430–431.

117. IDB white paper appears as an Appendix to the Sanford article, op. cit., pp. 440–441.

118. Ibid., pp. 440–441. When finally approved, on April 18, 1974, the Antuco project loan was for $75.3 million.

119. Ibid., p. 436. Sanford's critique of IDB performance appears on pages 430–434.

120. World bank white paper, in Sanford, op. cit., p. 444.

121. Ibid., p. 445.

122. Soviet bloc total in Theberge, "Kremlin's Hand in Allende's Chile," *United States and Chile*, op. cit., p. 635; the $91 million disbursement figure is in Elizabeth Farnsworth, "Chile: What Was the U.S. Role?" *Foreign Policy*, Fall 1974, as reproduced in *United States and Chile*, op. cit., p. 657; the $31 million figure in Sigmund, "Allende in Retrospect," as reproduced in *United States and Chile*, op. cit., p. 611; the Frei-year totals are in Sigmund, "Chile: What Was the U.S. Role?" op. cit., p. 665; figures for "other credits" in Sanford, op. cit., p. 430; IMF loans in "Chile: A Chronology," *United States and Chile*, op. cit., pp. 380 and 386; Chile's actual debt figures: $970 million on December 31, 1965; $2.2 billion, December 31, 1970, and $2.8 billion, December 31, 1973—all from *Indicadores Económicos y Sociales*, op. cit., pp. 312–313.

123. Quoted by Sigmund in "What Was the U.S. Role?" op cit., p. 663.

124. The letter came to light on July 23, 1973. *Breve Historia*, op. cit., p. 385.

125. Arriagada Herrera, op. cit., p. 49. He cites a man who would later serve in Allende's cabinet, Sergio Bitar: "La estructura económica chilena y la transición al socialismo," *Mensaje*, September-October 1971, p. 405; and Héctor Assael Bianchi and Sergio Molina: "El por qué y el como de las estatizaciones," *Panorama Económico*, May 1971, p. 5. Both magazines were edited in Santiago (*Mensaje* by the Jesuit order).

126. Ibid., p. 47. He cites Oscar Guillermo Garretón and Jaime Cisternas Pinto, "Algunas características del proceso de toma de decisiones en la gran empresa: la dinámica de concentración," *Convenio* SCT-ODEPLAN, March 1970, p. 8. (ODEPLAN is the government planning office.)

127. Figure for monopolies is in Markos J. Mamalakis, "The Allende Experi-

ment," *Chile: the Balanced View,* op. cit., p. 43. (The article originally appeared in *Res Publica,* vol. 2, no. 3, 1974, a public affairs quarterly published by Claremont Men's College in California.) For total number of Chilean companies actually expropriated: Genaro Herrera Arriagada, *De La Vía Chilena A La Vía Insurreccional,* op. cit., p. 323. On January 24, 1973, Allende expanded his original list of ninety-one companies specifically targeted for expropriation by twenty-four more. But, as we have seen, the number taken was actually much greater even than the 150 "monopolies" singled out for eventual seizure, never mind the ninety-one he bothered to identify. Furthermore, since Congress forbade expropriations without its consent, as the "legal" phase of takeovers was beginning, Allende resorted to presidential decrees. On ninety-five separate occasions, the controller general—who, under Chilean law, had to approve/disapprove presidential decrees and resolutions—disapproved Allende's decrees (forty-two of which "authorized" the seizure of companies). Allende then resorted to a 1927 (but dubious) constitutional device called the Decree of Insistence, whereby the entire Cabinet would sign the decree, overriding the Controller. He did that, through April 1973, a total of thirty-two times. As it happens, the Christian Democrats had paved the way for him in this matter, too: during Frei's six years as president preceding Allende, he used Decrees of Insistence sixty-three times in reaction to eighty-seven Controller disapprovals. By contrast, his predecessor, the conservative Jorge Alessandri, resorted to the Decree of Insistence once, and saw only three of his decree/resolutions rejected by the Controller. Source: *La Lucha Por La Juridicidad En Chile,* 1970–1973, op. cit., vol. 1, pp. 300–303. But, again, Allende and those around him, demonstrated repeatedly that they would abide by the law only when it served their purposes. His economy minister, Orlando Millas, said on May 11, 1973, that the government simply "does not recognize the right of the Controller and will not recognize the right of any person who has the audacity to arrogate to themselves the voiding of measures dictated by the President of the Republic himself" ibid., p. 310. In other words: Allende *was* the law in Chile.

128. Mamalakis, op. cit., p. 43. Deficits of state enterprises taken from table 14, p. 181.

129. Paul E. Sigmund, *The Overthrow of Allende and the Politics of Chile, 1970–1973* (Pittsburgh: University of Pittsburgh Press, 1977), p. 211. Sigmund cites the May 30–June 5, 1973, issue of *Ercilla,* 1976, p. 25.

130. Ibid.: agricultural output statistics, table 8; agricultural imports extracted from Sanford, "Multilateral Development Banks and the Suspension of Lending to Allende's Chile," op. cit., p. 437; Food-for-Peace reference from Sigmund, "Chile: What Was the U.S. Role?" op. cit., p. 660; amount of food-for-peace aid from Kissinger, op. cit., p. 681.

131. The 1970–1972 figures from Sanford, op. cit., p. 426; the 1973 figure from Raúl Sáez, "Chilean Short & Medium-Term Development Programs," *Chile: The Balanced View,* op. cit., table 1, pp. 230–231 (originally made as a statement before the Inter-American Committee of the Alliance for Progress [CIAP], February 5, 1974. Sáez was then minister of economic planning for Chile).

132. *Breve Historia,* op. cit., p. 207. The report appeared in *El Mercurio* July 29, 1972, six weeks after the deal was made.

133. Reference to 65 "requisitioned" firms in *Breve Historia*, p. 193. That Chamber of Deputies study revealed that to that point—June 13, 1972—263 companies had been taken over outright or "intervened" by the government, that those firms employed 185,000 workers; and that the government already controlled 47 percent of the country's industries, and 53 percent of the gross domestic product.

134. "Chile: A Chronology," *United States and Chile*, op. cit., p. 384.

135. *Breve Historia*, op. cit., p. 121 (the report was published January 2, 1972).

7

Time for Reckoning

ALLENDE: No, this is not a Popular Front, that has to be made quite clear.
DEBRAY: What should one call it then, a Workers' Front?
ALLENDE: A Workers' Front, a Patriotic Front, a Popular Unity, but with a backbone, in which the working class is indisputably the driving force, because although we do not have the hegemony of a single party, the Socialist and Communist parties are undoubtedly the parties which represent 90 percent of the workers—workmen, peasants, office workers, technicians, and professional people . . .[1]

LABOR'S LOVE LOST

It is impossible to know whether Salvador Allende believed this bit of bombast, uttered in the early days of his presidency. The line between reality and political theater in the world of Salvador Allende was always blurred, as it probably would finally become in his own mind.

What is clear is that there never was such a workers' juggernaut, marching shoulder-to-shoulder with him into the brave new world he said he was creating. Indeed, by April of 1973, Allende would confess that labor orneriness had twice pushed him to the extreme of considering resigning, a threat he verbalized during a particularly devastating strike at the nationalized El Teniente mine: "If the workers don't understand the process of change through which we are living, I'll simply go, and then you'll see the consequences." His exasperation exploded a few months earlier in another outburst: "Neither revolutionary consciousness nor morality exists among the workers."[2]

To begin with, though comparatively well organized by Third World standards, Chilean labor was weak and politically divided. Though the number of workers in unions had doubled during the Frei years as a percentage of the total work force, still the total of workers in unions stood at only 19.4 percent of the labor force when Allende came to the presidency, 22 percent at the end. Chilean unions traditionally had been dominated by the two Marxist parties, the Communists and the Socialists. Their principal bastion was the Central Federation of Workers (CUT, for Confederación Unica de Trabajadores), which, despite its double-speak name, never accounted for more than 60 percent of organized nonagricultural workers. The CUT was a direct descendant of the Chilean Labor Federacion (FOCH, Federación Obrera de Chile) which, in 1921, had become the very first labor federation in the world to join the Moscow-controlled Third Communist International. But by 1973, those two mainstays of the Popular Unity, the Socialists and Communists, were losing ground steadily and dramatically to the Christian Democrats, and not only in non-CUT unions, but in the CUT itself. In June 1972, the 560,000 members of the CUT voted to elect new officers. Despite elaborate efforts to rig the elections, the outcome, when finally announced, sent shock-waves through the Popular Unity coalition. The Communists polled 173,088 votes (30.9 percent); the Socialists 148,140 (26.46 percent); the Christian Democrats 147,531 (26.35 percent). Smaller, even more radical parties dominated the remaining 15 percent.[3]

The results were even less cheering for the Popular Unity in elections held in non-CUT unions. According to one usually reliable Chilean publication, the government coalition lost 80 percent of the union elections in 1973. Perhaps no setback on the labor front was more stunning than when, on February 10, 1973, workers at the country's biggest copper mine, Chuquicamata, ended thirty years of Marxist control of their union. That vote came just three weeks after it was reported that the now nationalized mine—the world's biggest open-pit copper mine—had lost money in 1972 for the first time in history. And it also came after a long period of verbal flogging of the mineworkers by Allende—who demonstrated, as he did, that he was the workers' champion only so long as the workers toed his line.

There was one other area in which the Allende government showed that, while it would claim to speak for workers, it was less prepared to listen to them: the campaign of nationalization of the companies which gave those workers their livelihoods. As one government labor leader put it: "We will not accept plebiscites. Nationalization will go forward—period." In almost every case, the "vote" whether to go from private to state ownership was done by acclamation, show of hands, or open ballot. Only once did the government accept the outcome of a secret ballot: at the large appliance manufacturer MADEMSA, where 925 workers voted for nationalization, 725 against.[4]

What is also clear is that the Allende years saw labor strife at levels never before witnessed in the country. The authors of a careful and restrained examination of the labor picture during the Allende years arrived at this conclusion: "Instead of support, the government received as many or more blows as it did support from the sector most friendly to it."[5] That sector was, of course, labor—in whose name Allende claimed to speak, to govern.

As shortages mounted, Patricio Palma, director of the government's Directorate of Industry and Commerce (DIRINCO), told his Communist party comrades at a party strategy session, October 2, 1972: "In every house of the grand bourgeoisie, there toils at least one comrade who knows the life and secrets of the masters of the house, and these comrades come from a working- or peasant-class background ... DIRINCO is in touch with these comrades and we are studying the concrete steps so that they can work with us in exposing those who have transformed their private storerooms into clandestine storerooms ..."[6]

It began disarmingly, early in that month of October, in the sparsely populated province of Aisén, a region of spectacular fjords and rugged islands almost too numerous to count, not much closer to Santiago (1,500 miles) than it is to the outstretched tip of Antarctica. Alarmed about reports that the government planned to establish a state trucking agency, the union of truck owners—made up almost entirely of owners of one or two trucks—went on strike in Aisén. Before it would end, a month later, that handful of truckers would be joined by hundreds of thousands of others, from shopkeepers to airline pilots, peasants to professors: 45 unions, including 400,000 peasants, 120,000 shopkeepers, 50,000 students. Hundreds of union leaders, truckers and workers would be jailed, radio stations seized by the government, others ordered off the air, trucks and small businesses "requisitioned," and martial law proclaimed in Santiago and a state of emergency in twelve of the country's twenty-five other provinces (which put virtually the entire population under military rule). The cost to an already sagging economy was put at $150–200 million, but, because the strike hit at the peak of the harvest season, the impact was even greater. The government at first attempted to crush it with force: Allende blustered that any shopkeeper who failed to open his doors within twenty-four hours would be deported, and DIRINCO Director Patricio Palma personally led police squads ordered to batter down shop doors and protective metal curtains, triggering a number of violent clashes. It was October 25 before Allende would agree to his first meeting with the strike leaders.

Viewing the violence, viewing the anger, former President Gabriel González Videla, a Radical, said: "The suffering and heroic middle class, today impoverished, humiliated, anguished, has brought strength out of weakness and gone from words to action as a last resort to make the

President understand that there is a majority, until yesterday silent, which will not one day more allow itself to be led like a sheep to be ruined by a sinister economic policy directed and administered by the Communist party."[7]

Beyond the rage, beyond the deep divisions, the October strike would leave another even more portentous legacy: as a condition of settlement, Allende was obliged to bring into his Cabinet flag officers from all three military services.

Chief among them was General Carlos Prats González, the man who had succeeded the murdered General René Schneider as army commander-in-chief. Prats, then fifty-seven, a man whose only experience outside of Chile had been as a student at the U.S. Command and General Staff School at Ft. Leavenworth, Kansas (1954–1955), and as military attaché in Buenos Aires (mid-1964 to early 1966), was destined to become, in the opposition press, the "most flogged" (*vapuleado*) military figure in Chile's modern history.[8] For some—the very admiring U.S. Ambassador Nathaniel Davis, for example—he "was the leader of the moment."[9] For others, he had already demonstrated either a stunning naiveté about the Allende government, or an extraordinary "go-along-to-get-along" attitude that went well beyond military subservience to civilian government. Few would remain dispassionate on the subject of Carlos Prats in the stormy months ahead as his involvement with the Allende government deepened.

On November 2, Prats was named to the key Interior Ministry post. In that role, he added to his command of the 32,000-man army, control also of the 26,000-man paramilitary Carabinero police forces and the heavily politicized nationwide detective force, Investigaciones. Joining the Cabinet with him were Rear Admiral Ismael Huerta Díaz (as public works minister), and air force Brigadier General Claudio Sepúlveda Donoso (as minister of mines). (The navy and air force commanders-in-chief had both declined the invitation which Prats accepted to join the Cabinet.)

The three were sworn in on November 2 together with the two top officials of the CUT: its president, Luis Figueroa (a Communist, named labor minister), and its secretary-general, Rolando Calderón (a Socialist, to Agriculture). Over the months ahead, Prats would develop a close and continuing relationship with the two. At the swearing-in ceremony, Prats strove to project his independence. The presence of representatives of the three armed forces in the Cabinet, he said, "is not a political commitment, but rather a patriotic collaboration at the service of social peace."

Prats and his military colleagues did, on November 5, succeed in ending the already weakening strike, pledging to leave trucking in private hands, take no reprisals against strikers, and return private property seized during the strike. But the government refused to accede to the demand which had become the rallying cry of the strike: a national plebiscite on the economy. With so little really settled—and so much unsettled—the October strike was a mere foreshadowing of labor strife yet to come.

FRIENDS AND FOES—BUT WHICH ARE WHICH?

Three weeks after the most convulsive month in Chile's modern history, Allende, on November 28, left the country for a two-week trip to Mexico, New York (for his United Nations speech, see pp. 333–334), Algeria, the Soviet Union, and Cuba (with brief pauses in Peru and Argentina). In what was then stridently anti-West Algeria, Allende said "future relations between Algeria and Chile will be those of revolutionary friendship because we have the same enemies." In Moscow, flushed with enthusiasm, he revealed the presence of five hundred Russian technicians in Chile, a comradeship he would affirm even more resoundingly on December 7, after meeting with Soviet Communist party chief Leonid Brezhnev, Prime Minister Alexei Kosygin, and President Nikolai Podgorny. Allende said he had reached "complete identity of points of view" with the Soviet leaders, describing the Soviet Union as "our big brother." Kosygin, responding to Allende's toast and remark that "we are no longer alone," said: "We shall always be with you." (Later that year, the Soviets awarded Allende the Lenin Peace Prize.) En route home, he made a triumphal stop at what Henry Kissinger would describe as "his spiritual home," Havana, receiving "an ecstatic welcome befitting the first head of a Latin American country to visit Cuba since Castro's rise to power" (more than a dozen years earlier). Before he left, he thanked Castro for his offer that the Cuban people "break off a piece of bread to give to the people of Chile"—a truly extraordinary confession, however indirect, of the unprecedently dismal descent of a once self-reliant nation in just two years to the status of international mendicant.

But his enthusiasm for these new alliances was not shared in Santiago. On December 14, the day of his return, Christian Democrat President Renán Fuentealba, writing on behalf of his party, directed eight stinging questions to Allende. The challenge was all the more remarkable because Fuentealba represented the left wing of the party which, only a few years before, had created the opening to Russia in establishing diplomatic relations with Moscow (see p. 170, chapter 4). Those questions included this one: "Is it the case that the credits which the Soviet Union would grant us in its role as 'big brother'—a role for the first time ever assigned by a president of Chile to a foreign power—would be of the tied, conditional and binding type which you and the parties of the Popular Unity have so harshly criticized in the past . . . ?" The letter spoke also of the "process of dependence upon the Soviet Union" which Allende was fostering, and "the captive markets dominated by Soviet imperialism." (The Chilean writer Joaquín Fermandois showed in a comparison of two loans made to Chile at that time how phony was the claim of "socialist solidarity"—and equally hollow the charges about hard-hearted capitalists. The first loan, in June 1971, came from the City Bank of New York, in the very heart of capitalism; another, six months later in January of 1972, from the Handlowy Warszawie Bank of Warsaw, the American loan was to help the debt service of the state steel company, the Polish loan to buy Polish industrial products—"the quintessence of a tied credit." That both banks also extended similar terms further demonstrated, Fermandois argued, that the notion that Socialist-bloc countries would help their developing brethren to liberate themselves from "dependence" was so much illusion.)[10]

Foreign Minister Clodomiro Almeyda would present the Soviets, a few days before Christmas, as a kind of Santa Claus for Chile. The Russians, he announced on December 20, had agreed to renegotiate Chile's $103-million debt and also grant Chile $30 million for the purchase of food and cotton and more than $180 million for the purchase of capital goods, including industrial equipment. Two weeks later, the newsletter *Latin America* claimed that Red China, not to be outdone by its Moscow rival, had granted $62 million to purchase food, medicines, machinery and equipment.[11] But, as we have seen earlier (pp. 338–339), neither the Soviet Union nor The People's Republic (Red China), nor the rest of the Communist-bloc countries, actually delivered on their promises.

As for Prats and his neutrality, during Allende's absence, as interior minister, he automatically served as de facto head of government as vice president (Chile has no elected vice president). In that role, Prats opted to use Allende's private gunslingers, the so-called Group of Personal Friends (GAP, Grupo de Amigos Personales), as part of his own corps of bodyguards. Challenged to explain why the army's commanding general would resort to a civilian security force of questionable legality, Prats answered lamely with a non sequitur: it would not have made sense, he said, for him to reorganize presidential security arrangements when he could avail himself of Allende's "most select personal permanent companions" (his phrase) for only fourteen days. Prats, who had a fair reputation as a writer (as well as painter), then used a colorful term (*zancadilla*, or "trap"), to make a promise that would come back to haunt him—and history.

"On the very day," he said, "when I realize that I have erred or failed—through personal stupidity or because I had fallen into a trap—I will present my irrevocable resignation to the President . . ."[12]

Events would demonstrate that it would take a good deal of evidence to persuuade General Prats that he had tumbled into a *zancadilla*. On December 28, responding to complaints of shopkeepers and others that the government had failed to honor the terms of the November 5 agreement ending the strike, the Chamber of Deputies voted 75–42 to suspend Finance Minister Orlando Millas as the person primarily responsible for the poststrike reprisals. Millas was the seventh Allende Cabinet minister ousted by act of Congress. (Impeachment of ministers first became a fixture of Chilean political life during the Frei years: fourteen ministers were impeached in that six-year space.) Allende countered by naming Millas economy minister and the economy minister (Fernando Flores) to finance. While legislators reacted angrily to the affront, Prats defended the president by arguing that the Chamber's action was "illegal and unconstitutional."

The new and momentous year of 1973 was only ten days old when the Allende government exploded its biggest bomb yet: the first-ever rationing in the country's history (though government spokesmen tried repeatedly to apply a different name to it). Further, rationing was to be accompanied by draconian measures which would give the state virtually total control over the very food Chileans would—or would not—have available to eat. In all, Finance Minister Flores announced twelve measures:

(1) Creation of a new National Secretariat of Distribution as part of the Economy Ministry. This Secretariat would enter into exclusive contracts with private sector firms producing basic goods;

(2) The creation of Committees of Vigilance to enforce compliance;

(3) Direct sale to the public of "basic goods" would be ended, as would bartering in them by private firms;

(4) State distributors would have sole and exclusive control of distribution of all "social area" production;

(5) Virtually all agricultural output would be marketed through state-run agencies;

(6) Direct control would be established over the quantity and the quality of all foodstuffs made available to each family, to be fixed "according to their real needs";

(7) Intensification of the work of the "organized people" to locate and root out black marketeers and speculators;

(8) Each family would be assigned a quota of basic foodstuffs, begin-

ning with cooking oil, sugar, rice, coffee, meats, up to a "basic basket" of some thirty staples; control of this process would be vested in the already established (and already highly controversial) Price and Supply Boards (JAP, for Juntas de Abastecimiento y Precios)—dominated, at local levels, by Popular Unity "Community Commands";

(9) Violations would be reported to the JAP;

(10) The number of JAP would be expanded until they covered each and every neighborhood in the country;

(11) Those who declined to work through the JAP "would cease to receive the concomitant benefits." (Those benefits meant discounted, government-subsidized prices, but they also meant much more: as private shopkeepers were quick to point out, JAP outlets hogged the dwindling supplies of vital staples, which meant that these items were increasingly not otherwise available, at any price, making a mockery of the "voluntary" character of participation in the JAP);

(12) Peasants would receive their foodstuffs through Rural Centers of Supply.

The JAPs were plagued by charges of corruption, illegality and favoritism from the first. Although the Allende government would continue its attempts to tighten control over food distribution, the JAPs never were able to achieve the goal of holding the population hostage to the UP for the food they would eat—in no small measure because of the growth of the black market which springs up everywhere when inefficiency, shortages and government intimidation efforts begin to run rampant.[13]

But none of this would still the firestorm of outraged reactions which followed Flores's announcement.

Former President Eduardo Frei branded the scheme "a clear and definitive action toward totalitarian control of the country ... The people of Chile," he added, "cannot tolerate that they be submitted to a dictatorship without escape." Fellow Christian Democrat Juan Hamilton said: "Those who have plunged the country into hunger would now impose a dictatorship of the stomach. He who does not submit to the JAP, to the Popular Unity, that person doesn't eat." The three principal federations of shopkeepers and merchants instructed their members to refuse to work with or form part of the Supply and Price Boards.[14]

But the public sound and fury paled in comparison to the invisible struggles touched off behind the scenes within the armed forces themselves, within Allende's fractious coalition.

On January 22, Allende signed a presidential order creating the National Secretariat of Distribution and Marketing (Secretaría Nacional de Distribución y Comercialización), and named air force General Alberto Bachelet Martínez to head it. The obvious purpose: to draw the military deeper into collusion with him, and into the vortex of an emotional and explosive controversy. To make matters worse, the three military ministers, in the face of civilian rage, announced their immediate support for the rationing measures, while claiming to distance themselves from the "political overtones" of the Flores announcement.

With both the army and air force under the control of generals supportive of Allende, the revolutionary pressure already boiling up in those branches would remain simmering below the surface. But in the navy, largely under the pushing and prodding of an improbable looking but steel-willed man named José Toribio Merino Castro, then the navy's second-ranking admiral, the pressure would lead to the first open break in military ranks. On January 19, only eight days after joining his colleagues in supporting the rationing plan, Admiral Huerta announced his resignation as public works minister, citing his disagreement with the policy. He was replaced by Rear Adm. Daniel Arellano.[15]

But for Admiral Merino, Allende's plan to put every Chilean man, woman and child at the mercy of the government for the food they would eat was the last straw. He made secret contact with a group of young economists and asked them to begin drawing up plans for a free market economy in a new government. In the army, a man Allende liked to mock as "Pinochito"—General Augusto Pinochet Ugarte—stepped up work on a harmless looking antisubversive plan he had ordered prepared shortly after taking over as chief-of-staff in December 1971. Soon, he would order work on an altogether secret—and much deadlier—plan. But then, so too would Merino.[16]

From the beginning, as we have seen in earlier chapters, two tendencies competed for power within the Popular Unity—and within the mind and emotions of Salvador Allende. One was *la vía institucional,* the institutional path, which argued that the "revolution" had already conquered the commanding heights of power. The task now, according to the *institucionalistas,* was to remake Chilean society into a Marxist-Leninist state, in which none of the vestiges of "bourgeois" power would remain—not private property, the *sine qua non* of political freedom; not the free press, without which no democracy can ever be secure; not an independent military, the one counterweight capable, in the last instance, of saving the country from totalitarianism; and, finally, not the political institutions themselves, those indispensable mechanisms which make government a servant of man, and not the other way around. This would be accomplished by making full use of the extraordinary powers vested in the Chilean presidency, and when those powers did not reach far enough, by stretching, bending—or just plain ignoring—the law, as Allende and his colleagues would do repeatedly. So long as the Communist party held sway in the affairs of the Popular Unity, the *via institucional* prevailed—if not as a fact of Chile's increasingly turbulent and impoverished daily life, at least as the dominant theoretical engine of change.

By early 1973, the *institucionalistas* could claim significant "success." With the pace of legal—and illegal—seizures of businesses, farms, industries, and financial institutions accelerating, the head of the cabinet-level Office of Economic Planning, Gonzalo Martner, could proclaim: "The bases of Chilean capitalism have been destroyed."[17] As for a free press, from his very first days in power, Allende waged an unrelenting campaign, not only to undermine the free press, but to expand government control of it. (The situation of the press will be discussed in greater detail in a following section.)

The JAP/rationing schemes aroused the powerful reactions they did because of the clear implications for freedom in Chile. Government control of business meant government control of livelihoods. The JAP—modeled on those long in place in the totalitarian Cuba of Fidel Castro—would mean life-and-death power. (Organization of them dated from July 1971; according to one account, by the end of 1972, 1,500 were operating in the country, 635 of them by mid-year in Santiago alone.)[18]

The *institucionalistas* could also feel smug about their "progress" in neutralizing the armed forces. Overtly, they were doing so by involving compliant military leaders in the web of government. Parallel with this—and here, in connivance with the radical elements—they were building up armed strength of their own, outside the law, while also working to split off noncoms and officers sympathetic to their cause from their a-political (or, more to the point, anti-Communist) commanders.

The country's vaunted democratic institutions were under frontal and flank attack. Frontally, Allende hoped to scrap the existing Congress in favor of a much more easily manipulated unicameral legislature, as well as to effect sweeping "reforms" of the courts and the constitution itself. From the flanks, he and his associates undermined the authority of the institutions by refusing to submit to the decisions, first of Congress, later and increasingly of the courts. Allende, and his associates, heaped verbal abuse on them, by way of attempting to undermine public confidence in them. One sample (among many): "We congratulate the workers who refuse to submit to a judicial order [based on] a mangled interpretation of the Supreme Court, the Congress, or the Comptroller-General. The will of our people stands above interpretations." The statement was made on August 1, 1972, by Carlos Altamirano, chief of Allende's Socialist party.

The other tendency striving for ascendancy within the UP—and within Allende—was the *vía insurreccional*, the path of armed violence, of open insurrection. Insurrection, obviously, not against the government, because the UP was the government, but insurrection against the country's "bourgeois institutions," its democratic past. By early 1973, because they had not been handcuffed, because they had not been jailed, because they continued to flaunt their power and their weapons and their violent aims, the *insurreccionistas* were gaining the upper hand.

It was Allende himself, after all, who had unleashed them in the first days of his presidency. Yet, from the very beginning, these men and women of violence had mocked Allende and his "legalistic" cohorts: mocked them with words, but much more importantly, with their polarizing deeds: seizing factories; swaggering across the southern ranchlands with their bandoleros and other guerrilla trappings while the government steadfastly denied their existence; and, later, by sparking ever more violent demonstrations among students and the inhabitants of the shantytowns ringing Santiago and other major cities. (Those shantytowns began to sprout up around major cities during the sixties, but expanded explosively once Allende reached power, many of their inhabitants lured by socialist promises of plenty. Nervous military commanders, viewing them as guerrilla redoubts, began plotting them on their maps.)[19]

But, with the exception of the turning-point murder of Pérez Zújovic, these self-styled revolutionaries were, for the most part, more nuisance than menace. Official patience with them, their patience with officialdom, reached a near-breaking point on August 5, 1972. On that day, hundreds of heavily armed Carabineros swarmed into Lo Hermida, a teeming slum on the southwestern outskirts of the city. For days, the area had been turned into a lawless redoubt where anarchy reigned so unchecked that among those taken captive by the rioters was Allende's nephew, Andrés Pascal Allende. The irony resided in that he was himself a leader of the Movement of the Revolutionary Left (MIR), which was spearheading the pocket "rebellion." In that fracas, one person was killed and eleven wounded (in characteristic revolutionary rhetoric, the event was immediately dubbed the "Lo Hermida Massacre"). In the aftermath, the two top officials of the political police, the Investigaciones, were briefly suspended, and Allende made a pilgrimage to the wake of the "murdered" martyr. Leaders of the revolt demanded that those responsible for the "massacre" be delivered into their hands to be executed as murderers, and an official delegation to the presidential palace went almost as far, demanding jail for the minister or deputy minister who gave the order for the raid.

In the months following, the MIR and Communist party leaders traded barbs regularly, and the rationing episode found them pitted in direct and bitter confrontation. In a communique calling the Flores rationing/distribution scheme a barely adequate point of revolutionary departure, the MIR—with a snarling aside directed at the Communist party (the "reformist sectors")—called for mass mobilization to seize those large industrial and commercial firms and farms still remaining in private hands, as well as the transport and distribution entities—and above all, "worker" control of the Supply and Price Boards. The "funda-mental task," the MIR communique added, is to develop and strengthen, throughout the country, neighborhood "worker" commands "as an alternative power center to the apparatus of the bourgeois state and independent of the government."

Just how profoundly deep—and ominous—the chasm dividing the *institucionalistas* from the *insurreccionistas* in the Allende govern-ment was would become evident eight days later. On January 24, MIR Secretary-General Miguel Enríquez, in a forty-five-minute harangue which included sharp attacks on "government reformists" and the "UP-Generals' Cabinet," said true popular power was on the rise in Chile. And, he said, when this power becomes dominant, we will dissolve Parliament and erect in its place an Assembly of the People. But no longer were these the mere rantings of a self-styled Chilean Che Guevara, tolerated by a vacillating government, because standing with him at this rally was Carlos Altamirano—secretary-general of the very Socialist party that was the senior partner in the coalition then ruling Chile.[20]

Nor did Altamirano stand alone in identifying with the apostles of violence. As noted earlier (p. 307), the 1972 Plenum of the Socialist party proclaimed flat-out that the "bourgeois state in Chile must be des-troyed," adding:

> To construct socialism, Chilean workers must exercise political control, must conquer all Power [capitalized in the original]. This is what is called the dictatorship of the proletariat. For revolutionaries, the solution is not in hiding or denying our objective, which is the taking of power. To flee from confrontation or abate the class struggle constitutes a very grave error.
>
> For socialists, each small triumph raises the level of the next fight, until we reach that inevitable moment of defining just who will hold power in Chile.

As Eduardo Frei would comment two years later, "once the objective value of the democratic system is denied and a nondebatable premise established that only one social class possesses truth and one party interprets it, the problem comes down to a strategy for the conquest of power."[21]

In February 1972, brushing aside appeals from their Communist partners to slow the pace of reform and mute the harsh (and polarizing)
revolutionary rhetoric, the Socialists responded with yet another defiant pronunciamiento. In it, they fumed that though progress had been
achieved, the bourgeois-capitalist character of the state remained
untouched. Worse, they said, true revolutionary transformation was
impossible so long as the government continued to respect "the existing
bourgeois democratic order." Instead, they said, Socialists would
encourage the outcroppings of People Power which had surfaced.[22] No
one in Chile doubted what was meant by those thinly veiled code words:
the MIR, the other armed brigades, the illegal seizures, the power to give
or withhold food itself, all of these must be brought to bear to break the
power of those who opposed the "revolution," and no mere laws or legal
institutions ought to stand any longer in the way.

Thus, the distance between the Communists, more cunning, more
cautious, and the Socialists, more strident, more impetuous, would
grow. The fight over rationing would exacerbate those profound differences, but it would take yet another event to escalate the conflict to the
level of the two senior partners of the rickety coalition. The rationing
announcement galvanized public opposition, but it was Allende's new
plan for nationalizations (creation of the so-called "Social Sector" of the
economy) which made the deep and bitter divisions between Allende's
own Socialists and the Communists all but irreparable. Announced on
January 24 by Economy Minister Orlando Millas, himself a Communist, it was immediately and sharply attacked by the hard Left as a
retreat from revolutionary principles because it seemed to indicate that
some companies, illegally seized, might be returned to their owners.
The ensuing fratricide revealed, starkly, the chasm which in the matter
of tactics separated the two senior partners.

The Socialists, now firmly under the control of the mercurial Carlos
Altamirano, wanted Allende to use the power he already had to destroy,
by whatever means, the power of all those who opposed the final triumph of the Marxist-Leninist state in Chile. The Communists sought
the same goal, but argued that it needed to be achieved by stealth, by a
process of cautious but relentless erosion of the power of the enemy,
avoiding those actions that would unite what they clearly understood to
be the majority of Chileans against them. With one eye on the hardening
alliance in and out of Congress between the Right and the Christian
Democrats, the other on rising public opposition, they argued that a
concession now to the Congress, the courts, and the Comptroller General on nationalizations would buy desperately needed time to build
their own strength, to divide the ranks of the enemy. Allende agreed
with them that a tactical retreat on nationalizations would serve as a

sop which would appeal to those in the opposition—and their number was considerable, their influence great—who argued that the rule of law was endangered but still intact in Chile.

The day after Millas's announcement, the Policy Commission of the Socialist party said the party not only had not been consulted, but did not share the government's three-tiered approach: state ownership, mixed ownership, and—the new wrinkle—"special cases." Those "special cases" clearly were the ones where Allende felt retreat was prudent. (The UP electoral platform called for a huge and dominant state sector, a mixed sector, and a small private sector.) When Allende attempted to defend himself as well as his (Communist) minister, claiming he had consulted in advance all the coalition partners, the Socialist party hit back even harder. In a January 29 statement, it, in effect, called its president a liar: "Neither the leadership of the Socialist party, nor its top economic figures, were ever consulted," the statement said. At a mass demonstration outside the Federal Courts building the next day, pamphlets were scattered urging that Chile be converted into another Vietnam.

Finally, on February 7, the Communists accepted Altamirano's suggestion that the intramural feuding stop, but did so with a parting shot: "It is not the phantasmagoric 'people power,' independent of the government and which exists only in the overheated minds of the MIR and its leaders, which should be supported, but the government of President Allende. But, as is known publicly, the suicidal demands of the MIR have found echo even within the Popular Unity . . ." (However sincerely a voice of reason then, the Communists, only five months later, would whistle a different and violent tune in support of "popular power.")

Lest there be any lingering doubts as to goals, the veteran party leader Luis Corvalán addressed those plainly: "In the matter of revolutionary transformations, there may be parties which would like to go as far as we; but none farther than we. NO" (capitalized in the original).[23]

The partners would never again fight in public, although another of the violence-minded partners was yet to weigh in with its own broadsides. In private, the tensions between them grew to the point that they refused even to speak to each other.[24]

So it was that Salvador Allende had become a general without an army, deserted by his own Socialist troops, and distrusted by those—the Communists—who realized they could no longer master events by manipulating him, because he was no longer in charge of events. As in ancient Greek tragedy, the noise, the commotion, the tumult would continue, but the catastasis had been reached. What remained was for the drama to come to the inevitable crashing end.

But along with the public bellowing, Allende listened to another voice, whispering in his ear. That voice belonged to a shadowy Spaniard named Joán E. Garcés Ramón. Garcés, though from Spain's rebellious Catalonia region, long a stronghold of Communist-Socialist-Anarchist thought, professed to despise violence because several members of his family had died in Spain's bloody civil war. Armed with a doctorate in political science from the Sorbonne, in 1970 this ascetic man then in his thirties wrote the newly elected Salvador Allende a letter praising Allende's ideas. Allende responded with an invitation to join him. Garcés did, becoming his chief speechwriter and political adviser. He would remain close to Allende to the very end, indeed sharing Allende's last supper, only then to exit Chile as mysteriously as he had entered. Early in 1973, Garcés wrote an article which, despite the typically convoluted style, was telling for what it revealed about the ideas he was passing along to Allende—a man who, as we have seen (see, e.g., p. 221), was not himself a font of original political wisdom.[25] There are, Garcés wrote, three grand strategies for the conquest of power: mass action, with its guerrilla variation; outright insurrection; and the political-institutional path. The three, he went on, "are not mutually exclusive and, in fact, given certain conditions, may converge." The third, he said, views the armed uprising as a possibility, not an inevitability. But, he made plain, power remains the goal—and if political-insitutional means won't do it, resort to one or both of the violent means clearly should not be excluded. By June of that convulsive year, Garcés no longer doubted that violence was coming; in a prescient June memo, he wrote that there was a need to organize the people "to resist a confrontation beginning in three to four months."[26]

Above the shouting, beyond the whispers, it would remain for Allende himself to make plain anew his resolve not merely to govern Chile, as had three score presidents before him, but to seize power, all of it, so as to create a new Marxist-Leninist order which would rule the country in perpetuity. On February 5, 1973, he announced the Popular Unity platform for the congressional elections the following month: the unicameral "people's assembly," court and constitutional "reforms" already alluded to, and added that since socialism in Chile was inevitable, "right-wing" attempts to block the revolution would only bring violence to Chile.[27]

Plainly, the revolution of wine and *empanadas* was rapidly deteriorating into an inferno of blood and bullets.

BOMBS, BALLOTS, BOOKS

The British journalist Robert Moss, who crisscrossed Chile frequently during the Allende years, reports that, in a heated exchange with military commanders over Admiral Huerta's resignation, Allende warned that should they turn against him, he would not commit suicide nor seek exile in Cuba. "I will take refuge in the Cordón Cerrillos," he said, "and you will never get me out."[28] Cordón Cerrillos, situated in the southeastern corner of Santiago, was one of the key bastions in a complex of industrial centers and slum areas ringing Santiago which, from the earliest days of Allende's government, the radical Left worked feverishly to transform into armed fortresses.

Indeed, on January 17—two days before Huerta did resign—Allende had moved the seat of his government for a few days to the huge Sumar textile factory. (Sumar, the country's biggest textile firm and one of the fifteen biggest industrial establishments in the country, was one of the very first of the Chilean-owned companies incorporated into Allende's "Social Area" of the economy.) There, he scolded workers for their lack of "revolutionary morality," and then offered them a model: "I give you," he told them, "the example of Cuba, where the organization of the people is exemplary. They have had to suffer rationing, even of sugar. But Cuba will, in eight or ten more years, be the people with the highest social level of Latin America." (Ten years after he so prophesied, Cuba, in 1982, again declined to provide statistics on most socio/economic indicators to international agencies; but what is known is that in 1980, the last time Castro would risk opening the floodgates, 125,000 Cubans uprooted their lives and fled, stripped of all possessions, to the U.S.)[29]

For Chile, Comrade Castro opened another kind of floodgate: of arms and men. Nor was he alone in pumping the instruments and practicioners of violence into a country which had, for so long, prided itself on its civility.

Allende had not even been confirmed by Congress as president, much less taken office, when he would present to a startled public his Grupo de Amigos Personales, his personal bodyguards—armed with submachineguns, speeding around the city in Fiat 125 automobiles (usually blue). Their number eventually would reach the hundreds, their armament as extensive as their training. From the first days of his presidency, hundreds, then thousands of sympathizers pilgrimaged to this new mecca of world revolution. Some were dilettantes, the romantic day-dreamers; others were case-hardened terrorists then on the run from their homelands: an estimated seven hundred Tupamaros from Uruguay, Montoneros from Argentina, Action for National Liberationists from Brazil (Argentina and Brazil were then under military rule, Uruguay beginning a tough and effective crackdown on the Tupamaros). But, there also came the "pragmatists" of revolution, including some 1,400 from the Soviet Union (among them, an elite of forty-six mining specialists earning many times the legal limit for public employees—and drawing it in dollars)[30]; and experienced military training instructors, guerilla fighters, and secret police experts from Cuba, Czechoslovakia, North Korea, and East Germany. At the end, the authorities would round up 14,000 foreigners without documents; many hundreds, perhaps thousands more, slipped across borders, escaped by sea, or passports in hand, left legally.

From the very beginning, the hot-heads Allende could never bring himself to silence bragged that they would create in Chile a "people's army" so powerful, so invincible, as to make the revolution irreversible.

Still, it was mainly dark shadows and sabre-rattling rhetoric until 2 P.M. on the afternoon of March 11, 1972. On that afternoon, a Cubana de Aviación plane touched down at Santiago's Pudahuel airport, and was shortly afterwards moved, over the insistent protests of two spunky customs agents (Manuel Sepúlveda Enríquez and Juan Saldías) to the remote southern end of the airport. Police Chief Eduardo Paredes insisted that the crates contained gifts from Fidel Castro for the president. No matter, retorted the officials, they must be inspected. Eventually, Interior Minister Hernán del Canto arrived on the scene. To his orders, the agents responded that when Brazil had made former President Jorge Alessandri the gift of an automobile, Congress had to pass a special law permitting him to bring it into the country—and that later he announced he would donate it to a charitable institution. The same was true when Queen Elizabeth of England made visiting President Eduardo Frei the gift of a silver tea service. Del Canto resolved the debate by ordering his armed men to load the thirteen crates into waiting station wagons and panel trucks from the police detective force, Investigaciones. In the ensuing furor, one official would claim the crates contained rum and other gifts from Castro to Allende. Allende himself claimed they contained mango-flavored ice cream, then modified that to paintings for an exhibit about to be inaugurated. What was clear was that the crates had been brought to Chile as the "luggage" of Dr. Eduardo (Coco) Paredes, then head of Investigaciones, a man very much plugged into the international switchboard of communist revolution.[31]

Shortly after establishing the Latin American Solidarity Organization (usually known by its Spanish initials, OLAS, for Organización Latinoamericana de Solidaridad) in 1967—over which Salvador Allende presided until becoming president of Chile—Fidel Castro persuaded his Russian patrons to expand an advanced school for subversion operating in Paris to include Latin Americans. Among those Castro dispatched to Paris as part of the Cuban cadre to work

with the Russian KGB "faculty," was the personal assistant to Manuel Piñeiro, then head of the Cuban secret police, the DGB. That
man—nicknamed "Gatillo Fácil" ("Easy Trigger")—was Luis Fernández
Oña, the operative generally credited with setting up the Neighborhood Committees of Vigilance in Cuba (which Allende would later
attempt to copy in Chile). Among those arriving in Paris for training: Eduardo Paredes. The two became friends, a friendship they
would resume when Castro assigned Fernández Oña to Chile (where he
not only became an Allende crony, but married the president's eldest
daughter, the political firebrand Beatriz). Paredes, implicated in the
activities of urban guerrilla groups which robbed banks and supermarkets and assaulted policemen between 1968 and 1970, was one of
Allende's first appointments, becoming one of the country's two top
policemen.[32]

Following the September revolution, police found in Paredes' home a
detailed inventory of what those thirteen crates actually contained:
forty-four sub-machineguns, hundreds of automatic pistols and other
handguns, two grenades, thousands of rounds of ammunition, cartridge
belts, gunmounts and other accessories. But the Paredes shipment was
the tip of the iceberg.

Between January 1971 and September 1973, Cubana de Aviación
planes carried out of Chile 10,793 kilograms of mail bound for Cuba.
But from Cuba to Chile, they carried 71,636.44 kilos of "mail." The
discrepancy between the "writing habits" of Chileans and Cubans
would later be cleared up when manifests and other documents—and
the seized war booty itself—would reveal that, via Cubana and other
means, enough Soviet, Czech and other types of guns and munitions
were smuggled into Chile to equip a division of over 15,000 men: 118
tons of explosives, ammunition, bombs, grenades; 120 units of heavy
war weapons, mortars, bazookas and antitank guns; 9,293 carbines,
shotguns and rifles; 6,945 automatic and semi-automatic pistols and
revolvers.[33]

To borrow from what came to be the key question in another investigation involving arms shipments*: what did the president know and
when did he know it?

In the case of Allende, the answer would appear to be plenty—and
very early on. In evidence: a document found in a safe near the presidential bedroom at La Moneda Palace after the September revolution,

---

* The question raised in connection with the diversion of profits in the mid-1980s from
the sale of arms to Iran to the Nicaraguan freedom-fighters, the *contras*: what did
President Reagan know about it, and when. It had become the battle cry of those railing
against President Nixon fifteen years before in the Watergate investigation which of
course did *not* involve arms shipments.

stamped "top secret" and addressed to "Companion" (the Chilean equivalent of "comrade") Allende, spoke of weapons furnished to MIR chieftain Miguel Enríquez: two 57 mm cannons, four 30-calibre machineguns, thirty-one Garand rifles, one sub-machinegun, two 22-calibre rifles and seventeen pistols. The memo was signed by José Rivero, a Cuban who served as Allende's chief of security, and was dated December 27, 1971.[34]

That Allende knew of—and encouraged—military training for factory workers was never in serious doubt. From the earliest days of his presidency, he would speak defiantly of his plans to turn the industrial clusters, the *cordones*, into redoubts, as he did in his January 1973 clash with the military commanders. So confident was he, in fact, that this Ring of Fire and Steel actually did exist around Santiago (and other major cities) that he would, at the very end, stake not only his government, but his very life on it.

As indicated previously, there was no shortage of instructors for the task. Between January 1971 and August 1973, 1,386 diplomatic visas and 1,294 official visas were issued in Havana to Cubans traveling to Chile. In the last seven months of 1973 alone, 633 Cuban "diplomats" arrived in Santiago. The Cuban Embassy in Santiago had an official roster of forty-two accredited diplomats (while the Chileans in Havana made do with six, a number much closer to usual custom and practice in the cases of such relatively small countries distant from one another and with relatively few normal diplomatic and commercial ties). The September revolution found 973 Cubans in Chile without proper documents.[35]

As British author Robert Moss wrote: "The finance for such goings-on was either borrowed from the capital of the state-run companies themselves (the government publishing house was a notorious donor) or taken from the secret budgets of various ministries. The foreign ministry alone disposed of more than $1 million a month in clandestine funds. Apprentice guerrillas looking for a job were given sinecures by state agencies like the municipal workers corporation, whose staff increased from 200 to 12,000 under Allende—although there was no notable increase in municipal works."

He also reported that military intelligence received reports early in 1973 that Cuban, Czech, and East German military instructors had been allowed access to state-run industries in the Cordón de Cerrillos, and that large quantities of arms (especially Czech-made) had been stockpiled.

In addition to the training and indoctrination, Moss noted, some factories were used for clandestine arms production. One example, the Madeco plant, which nominally made refrigerators but where workers on the night shift turned out "peoples' tanks," ordinary fork-lift trucks shielded by armor-plating and with heavy machineguns mounted on top. The Madeco work was under the supervision of a Brazilian exile named Sergio de Moraes.[36]

For the most part, illegal arms remained a ticking bomb—one which, when it blew, would blow up in the faces of those who created it. The detonator: the Arms Control Law, which not only limited possession to the armed forces and Carabineros of heavy weapons—everything from sub-machineguns and automatic weapons on up—but also made it a crime, punishable by prison, to "organize, belong to, finance, outfit, assist, train, incite or induce [others] in the creation and operation of private militias, combat groups or units militarily organized and armed" with the proscribed weaponry.[37] That law, which went into effect October 21, 1972, was not vigorously applied in the early days of timid military participation in the Allende government. Ultimately, disgruntled military commanders, mainly in the air force, would enforce the law themselves, until it would obliterate the secret planning and scheming and smuggling aimed at plunging Chile into the gro-tesquerie of bloody civil war.

Arms—how to get them, where to get them—were very much on the minds of the men in uniform, as well. Logically, the place to turn was the United States. For General Prats, there was another logical place to look: the Soviet Union. On the U.S. side, there was ambivalence reflect-ing a long tug-of-war between the Pentagon and the State Department. On the Soviet side, there was eagerness to extend its military axis all the way to the tip of the South American continent. Both magnetic fields were located within the context of the Chilean political and military past as well as the present. A word about the immediate past as it related to military matters:

Beginning in the immediate post-World War II years, there was an increasing closeness between Chilean and U.S. military forces, fostered in part by the developing Cold War between the U.S. and its European allies and the Soviet bloc. In 1947, the nations of Latin America com-mitted themselves formally on the side of the Western nations through the Rio Treaty of Mutual Assistance. Beginning in 1952, the United States became a major funding and supply factor in the moderniza-tion of Chilean military forces. As in the area of economic aid, Chile would receive, in per capita terms, the greatest outpouring of U.S. military assistance of any country south of the border—a total, be-tween 1946 and 1975, of $216 million. (Brazil, a country with ten times Chile's population and the only Latin American nation to fight alongside the U.S. in World War II, got $613 million in the same period; Argentina, with more than twice Chile's population, got $230 million.)[38]

Chile had yet another reason for wanting close ties with the United States: ever since the first days of its nationhood, Chile had faced frequent spasms of hostility from its neighbors on all sides, including the much more powerful Argentines.

Twin pressures converged to reshape U.S. military assistance programs in Latin America, including those with Chile. The first was a campaign in the late 1960s, headed by the late Sen. Frank Church (D-Idaho), to curtail sharply all forms of U.S. military ties with the region, including on-site training (Military Assistance Advisory Groups), arms grants and arms sales. (At the time, Latin American spending on arms was among the lowest in the world; with the restraining influence of the U.S. removed, not only did the U.S. lose much of its own influence, but Latin nations in the early 1970s went on an arms-buying binge without equal in the history of the region.) The second element was State Department pressure, particularly damaging in the case of Chile, which Henry Kissinger has labelled as "doctrinaire antimilitarism." "The theory," Kissinger wrote, "was to encourage a shift of resources from military expenditures to social and economic development, on the premise that these countries had no need for a defense establishment . . . Frei was encouraged to sponsor various demilitarization and disarmament schemes for Latin America. By October 1969 discontent in the Chilean military about lagging professionalism and inadequate pay erupted into an abortive coup against the government . . . [see pp. 190–192, chapter 4] The Nixon Administration inherited in Chile both a radicalized Christian Democrat Party and profound resentment on the part of the Chilean military against the United States as well as against the Christian Democrats. This almost certainly enhanced Allende's ability to 'buy off' or neutralize the military in the first years of his term . . ." Ambassador Korry, who represented the United States in Santiago during the last years of Frei and first Allende year, echoed Kissinger's judgment: "From 1967–1970, the U.S. initiated a policy which can only be described as unfriendly toward the Chilean military . . ." He added that during his first year in Chile (1968), "the Chilean armed forces put on a poor performance in their regular maneuvers because they lacked basic equipment and could not call up conscripts . . . because they didn't have enough shoes to shod them . . ."[39]

Still, as the following tables indicate, though military assistance authorized after 1968 dropped off sharply, deliveries of orders "in the pipeline" remained fairly strong during the Allende years, and U.S. military *sales* to Chile actually increased—Allende's "buy-off" tactic:

TABLE 32
U.S. MILITARY ASSISTANCE TO CHILE, 1966–1974

FISCAL YEAR	PROGRAMMED	DELIVERED
1966	$ 8,806,000	$ 8,366,000
1967	4,143,000	4,766,000
1968	1,801,000	7,507,000
1969	734,000	2,662,000
1970	852,000	1,966,000
1971	698,000	1,033,000
1972	870,000	2,227,000
1973	941,000	918,000
1974	912,000	619,000

Source: Covert Action, vol. 7 of the Report of the Select Committee to Study Government Operations With Respect to Intelligence Activities of the United States Senate, December 4 and 5, 1975, pp. 184–185.

TABLE 33
U.S. MILITARY SALES TO CHILE, 1966–1974

FISCAL YEARS	ORDERS	DELIVERED
1966	$ 1,057,000	$ 1,490,000
1967	2,559,000	1,690,000
1968	4,077,000	2,100,000
1969	1,676,000	2,147,000
1970	7,503,000	9,145,000
1971	2,886,000	2,958,000
1972	6,238,000	4,583,000
1973	14,972,000	2,242,000
1974	76,120,000	4,860,000

Source: Covert Action, vol. 7 of the Report of the Select Committee to Study Government Operations With Respect to Intelligence Activities of the United States Senate, December 4 and 5, 1975, pp. 184–185.

In one important area—one which did not require State Department assent—there was a sharp increase: training of Chilean officers at the School of the Americas in the (then) Panama Canal Zone, headquarters of the U.S. Southern Command. Those training experiences were especially valuable in the personal ties they forged between Chilean and American officers.

In September of 1972, Prats dispatched his second-in-command,

TABLE 34
TRAINING IN PANAMA

FISCAL YEAR	NUMBER OF PEOPLE	FISCAL YEAR	NUMBER OF PEOPLE
1966	68	1971	146
1967	57	1972	197
1968	169	1973	257
1969	107	1974	260
1970	181		

Source: *Covert Action*, vol. 7 of the Report of the Select Committee to Study Government Operations With Respect to Intelligence Activities of the United States Senate, December 4 and 5, 1975, pp. 184–185.

Augusto Pinochet, to Mexico, responding to an invitation from the Mexican Defense Department. En route back to Chile, Pinochet stopped off in Panama for a meeting with the commander of the U.S. Southern Command, General Underwood, "to talk over with him the problems of buying arms in his country. If the United States continued refusing to make available the materiel we needed," Pinochet said, "the Chilean government would be forced to accept offers from the Soviet Union."

"The practical results," he wrote, "were very poor."[40]

As early as 1971, the Soviets began dangling arms offers before the Chileans—$300 million in credits, by one account, greater by a wide margin than the total of U.S. military grants *and* sales to Chile over the preceding twenty-five years. To make the offer even more tempting, the Soviets in 1972 began furnishing the left-wing military regime then in power in Peru with advanced equipment, including T-55 tanks. The temptation resided in the reality that, since the War of the Pacific a century earlier, Chile and Peru had eyed each other nervously across their barren border. And to make the offer more tantalizing, the Soviets offered economically strapped Chile irresistible terms: a fifteen-year credit, no payments during the first five years, and 2 percent interest.[41] With Allende's active encouragement, senior Soviet military officials visited Chile, among them Soviet air force chief Marshall Pavel S. Kutajov. Conversely, the commanders of the Chilean air force and Chilean navy both visited Russia. On January 2, 1973, a first-ever group of students from the Chilean War and Army Polytechnical academies left on a trip to France, Spain—and the USSR.

But it was Prats himself who would raise the tension between East and West in the Chilean military to a crisis level. Prats had already demonstrated a fierce—some would call it blind—devotion to the preservation of democracy in Chile, no matter how much that democracy had deteriorated into a form with little substance. He also fretted in his diary about the perverseness of the United States, ascribing a good deal of Chile's economic difficulties to what he believed was collusion between official Washington and "transnational consortia."[42] Against that backdrop, Prats set out on May 2, 1973, on a month-long odyssey that would see him meet with senior military and civilian officials in Peru, the United States, Britain, France, the Soviet Union, Yugoslavia, Italy (including a private forty-minute audience with the pope), Spain, Brazil and Argentina. Given Prats' own leanings, and the attractiveness of the Soviet offers, Pinochet claimed to have larded Prats' official traveling team with officers he knew to be stoutly anticommunist.[43]

Washington's concern for events in Chile was reflected in the level of attention Prats got during his four-day visit: meetings with the chairman of the Joint Chiefs of Staff, the secretary and chief of staff of the army, and number two man at the State Department (as well as a meeting with Alexander Haig, minutes before the general took over as President Nixon's chief of staff—Prats remarked that Haig let him in on that "scoop").[44] If anything substantive occurred during the Washington visit, Prats made no mention of it in more than two printed pages of diary entries.

Not surprisingly, because the real centerpiece of the trip was his nine-day visit to the Soviet Union, May 10–19. There, he was received not only by the defense minister and chief of Soviet ground forces, Gen. Ivan Pavlovsky, but by Alexei Kosygin, president of the Council of Ministers. There, he visited not only Moscow, but also Leningrad and Volgograd (formerly Stalingrad), personally escorted by Pavlovsky. And there, he not only had talks, but was given VIP demonstrations of Soviet rock-etry—including the ABM installations ringing Moscow—as well as a look at basic training for army recruits and the chance to view a mock battle involving tanks, artillery and rockets. It was left to Defense Minister Grechko to tempt the visitor with Soviet wares, "at extraordinarily favorable financial terms." Prats himself gives no clue as to what he told his Soviet hosts before leaving "that grand nation" for Belgrade, but he did later tell his generals that he had agreed to buy "logistical" supplies from the Soviets. As to large-scale purchases of offensive or defensive weapons, the Chilean diplomat Jorge Edwards wrote that during his visit to Paris en route home, Prats confided that buying major arms from the Soviets, however attractive the idea, was impractical: "The tanks would never reach Chile," he was quoted as saying, because the officer corps felt so strongly opposed to entanglements with the Soviets that they would rise up in mutiny. "Nonetheless," comments the historian Fermandois, "Prats continued caressing the idea of buying arms from the Soviet Union."[45]

There were those who saw in Carlos Prats González "a tragic, poignant, and affecting figure," ultimately martyred because of his devotion
to democracy (U.S. Ambassador Davis, for example).[46] It is difficult to do
more than peruse his social calendar for the first week after his return
from his foreign travels and not conclude that, at the minimum, Prats
had a good deal of difficulty in distinguishing among the good, the bad,
and the ugly:

• The night after he returned, his first working dinner was a private
one at his home with the outgoing foreign minister Clodomiro
Almeyda (a man Kissinger described as "so far to the Left" that he
opposed closer ties with the Soviets only because he preferred the
then more radical Red Chinese of Mao Tse Tung").[47]
• The next afternoon, he met at his home—at their request, he says—
with the two Communists who headed the Central Workers' Federation; they told him the armed forces needed to close ranks with the
Popular Unity and the CUT to fight inflation and shortages.
• That evening, he dined at the home of Sen. Carlos Altamirano, by
then in firm command of the Socialist party, a man whose radical ways
all but guaranteed the final, violent collapse of Chilean democracy.
Four other leaders of the radical wing of the party were in attendance
(Carlos Lazo, Adonis Sepúlveda, Hernán del Canto and Rolando Calderón), but Prats makes it plain that most of the conversation was
between himself and Altamirano. Altamirano, evidently emboldened
that Prats was a soul-mate, said Socialists identified with *progressive*
military men, and that those "progressives" should join in backing to
the hilt a government crackdown on illegality (which, presumably,
meant the opposition who represented somewhere around two-thirds
of all Chileans). Prats told him there was an "ancestral aversion" for
Marxism in the armed forces. (Prats also confided to his diary that,
back from his travels, he had meditated on the situation in Chile and
arrived at the conclusion that a key to the problem was the psychological warfare under way to rouse the military against "the Marxist
threat." Prats put "Marxist threat" in quotation marks.)
• The next afternoon, Prats met with the equally radical leadership of
the tiny MAPU party.
• That night, Prats dined with the secretary-general and principal
ideologues of the Communist party, Luis Corvalán and Volodia Teitelboim, as well as with the Communist ministers, Hernán Millas
and Hugo Díaz.

Not until the next day, on the morning of his fifth day back, did Prats
get around to a brief meeting with a fellow officer, Pinochet. He told
Pinochet the army's Military Intelligence Service ought to act more
firmly against "extremists of the Right." (Prats routinely referred to
them as "fascists"; in the matter of the Left, he would demur—as he did

about the far-Left leaders of the CUT, for example—that while he did not share their points of view, he was convinced of their "intelligence, honesty and good sense.") Then, after another meeting with Allende, Prats reserved that evening's dinner for Radical party leaders.

That round of talks allegedly was undertaken after Allende asked him, at their first meeting after his trip, to return to the government with other military figures. Prats declined, but said he did agree to talk to Popular Unity and opposition leaders about various ideas for lowering the political pressure in the country. Several of those he met with (Almeyda, the CUT people, for example) were not "political leaders." More than a month would go by before Prats got around to trying to arrange a meeting with Christian Democrat leaders (and then with ex-President Frei, who gave him a cold shoulder). If he made any attempt to talk to the leaders of the conservative National party, there is no record of it.

Along the way, a friend told Prats that there had been a "dramatic change" in the attitude of younger officers, now persuaded that he was "glued" to the Popular Unity and was being "used" by the UP. Thus on Monday, June 11, back in his army role, he summoned the head of army intelligence, General Augusto Lutz, to ask him what he had on these reports.

"Oh, there've been a few 'whiskers' [pelambrillos], but nothing important, nothing serious," Prats said Lutz told him.

"That answer was enough for me to understand the attitude of the Military Intelligence Service: it was now clear to me that I could no longer count on that agency . . ."[48]

It was the first sign Prats gave that he sensed just how far he had moved from his comrades-in-arms and into what they, together with a rapidly growing number of disenchanted civilians, saw as the enemy camp.

On March 4, 1973, the largest number of Chileans in history would vote in elections which, although they didn't know it then, would be the last general elections to be held in the country for at least seventeen years. From the beginning, the campaign was pockmarked with violence.[49] And the elections themselves were no sooner held than they became the subject of a furious debate and a serious investigation to determine just exactly how many had voted.[50]

Although it was not obvious then exactly how many voted, nor exactly how they did vote, neither really mattered half so much as what those elections failed to settle, and what, little noticed in the heat of battle at the time, they did settle.

For the record, at stake were all 150 seats in the Chamber of Deputies and half of the fifty Senate seats. Official results gave Allende's Popular Unity 43.4 percent, the opposition, united in the Democratic Confederation (CODE, for Confederación Democrática), 54.7 percent.[51] Both sides claimed victory.

In later postmortems, the Christian Democrats, and to a lesser extent, the Radicals, would invoke virtually the identical objections to alliances with the Right which reverberate in the political debates of 1988, and which constitute now the same dilemma for finding a viable return to democracy as they did for preserving it. Postmortems notwithstanding, the democratic Left did, in 1973, what it did not do in 1970: it put aside its loathing of the Right long enough to prevent a legalized lynching of the country's dominant political, economic, and social traditions.

That election also marked the swan-song of U.S. covert spending in Chile during the Allende years: the so-called Forty Committee authorized $1,427,666 to be spent in support of democratic parties (chiefly the Christian Democrats) in that election. (A further secret outlay was authorized in August, but it was never used.)[52]

In terms of seats, under Chile's complicated system of proportional representation, the elections gave the UP a gain of six seats in the Chamber and two in the Senate, reducing CODE's edge in the Chamber to 87-63 and in the Senate to 30-20. The biggest single winner was the Socialist party, obviously siphoning votes from the left-wing of the now gutted Radical party.

Though comparisons of all kinds were made at the time to prove who "won," none was really valid because 1973 marked the first time ever in parliamentary elections voters had to choose between two coalitions rather than among a plethora of parties, each of which had its hard core of loyal followers. Furthermore, the rules favored "blocs" over individual parties in computation of seats.[53]

With that caveat, herewith the percentage figures of the vote for each of the parties in the 1969 and 1973 congressional elections:

TABLE 35

VOTE BY PARTIES, 1969 AND 1973 CONGRESSIONAL ELECTIONS (Percentages of total valid vote)[a]

PARTY[b]	1969	1973
Christian Democrats	31.0	28.5
National	20.8	21.2
Communist	16.6	15.9
Radical	13.5	3.7
Socialist	12.7	18.4
Radical Democracy	na	2.0

Table 35 (*continued*)

PARTY[b]	1969	1973
MAPU	na	2.5
Popular Socialist Union	2.2	0.3
PADENA	1.9	0.3
API	na	0.8
Independents	0.1	—[c]
Radical Left	—[d]	1.8
Christian Left	—[e]	1.1
Unified lists	—	1.8[f]

(a) Does not include void/blank votes.
(b) In 1969, each of the parties presented candidates under its own banner. In 1973, with the sole exception of the tiny Popular Socialist Union (USOPO), all ran either as UP or CODE candidates. But in each instance, the coalitions agreed in advance on which member party's candidate would contest each seat, and this was the basis for calculating the 1973 percentage results.
(c) None ran in 1973.
(d) Split off from the Radical party in 1971 over the Pérez Zúkovic assassination, breaking with the UP altogether in 1972 over shotgun expropriations issue.
(e) Formed by former MAPU leader Jacques Chonchol and far Left Christian Democrats in 1972.
(f) Divided evenly between the two coalitions.

(Sources: for 1969 figures, cf. Table 23, pp. 331–332; For 1975, Arriagada Herrera, *De La Vía Chilean A La Vía Insurreccional*, op. cit., p. 266.)

Overheated rhetoric, and even more so, the traumatic implications, also played a role in the outcome of those March elections, though not the oratorically intended one. Four days before the elections, former President Eduardo Frei—himself running for a Senate seat (he won handily)—said the opposition regarded the elections as "a morally binding plebiscite." If the opposition won "a clear majority," he said, then it would demand that Allende change course. But just as Allende made plain in the UP's electoral platform that a victory for his side would lead to a new order in Chile, the opposition also made plain its intention to impeach Allende if it succeeded in picking up the two Senate seats and eight Chamber seats it needed for a two-thirds majority in both houses.

But, as one commentator would put it, the electorate understood that though legal, it would not be a peaceful way out of Chile's dilemma. "Neither Allende nor the Popular Unity would give up the presidency of the Republic just because the Secretary of the Senate would hand him a piece of paper . . ."[54]

The electorate did not give Allende enough votes to erect his Marxist-Leninist dynasty, but neither did it give the opposition enough votes to impeach him. The opposition, however, already possessed a powerful legal weapon, and the outcome of March 4 was endorsement enough to put it to use: the long-smoldering issue of expropriations provided the ammunition.

Back on October 14, 1971, two leading Christian Democratic senators, Renán Fuentealba and Juan Hamilton, introduced legislation requiring congressional approval for any nationalization taking place after that date (see p. 342 in chapter 6). A few months later, on February 19, 1972, the Congress voted 100-3 to approve a series of constitutional amendments mandating it. On April 6, Allende vetoed the amendments, blustering that he would dissolve Congress (which he could not do) or call a plebiscite (which, in cases of such conflict, the Constitution required). He did neither; he decided instead to submit the dispute to the Constitutional Tribunal. On May 2, 1972, the opposition released a statement signed by every opposition member of Congress, including those Radicals who had now bolted the UP altogether over this dispute. Two days later, the UP responded with a statement signed by the presidents of all of the parties in the coalition. The opposition said the president was required either to sign the amendments or submit the dispute to a plebiscite. The UP said the law gave it the right to take it to the Tribunal. Given the gravity of the constitutional crisis, the Christian Democrats decided—against the repeated urging of the Right—to back off and await the 1973 congressional elections.

But it was Allende, and not the Christian Democrats, who took the initiative. On March 16, Allende resorted to a "decree of insistence" to compel the comptroller general to assent formally to the nationalization of forty-three companies which the comptroller had ruled were taken illegally. (The companies had been seized by presidential decrees. Under Chilean law, that unique institution, the quasi-autonomous comptroller-general, must approve all presidential decrees before they can take legal effect. That, of course, had not deterred the UP from de facto seizure of those companies; what remained was the hope of legalizing a series of fait accomplis. Under a practice of dubious constitutionality dating from 1927, the president could overrule the comptroller by obtaining the signatures of all of the members of his Cabinet for a "decree of insistence.")*

For the Christian Democrats, that was the last straw. On April 25, Congress voted to override Allende's year-old veto of the constitutional amendments limiting and defining expropriations, and gave him thirty days from May 7 either to approve or refer the matter to a plebiscite. On May 11, Allende submitted the matter to the Constitutional Tribunal which, although he had named three of its five members, ruled on May 30 that it had no jurisdiction in the matter. Accordingly, on June 2, the

---

* (For a discussion of the "Decree of Insistence" issue, see Note 127 Chapter 6.)

comptroller told Allende he had no choice: approve or submit the issue to a plebiscite.

For Allende, the choice was not to approve or go to a plebiscite—he knew he could not win—but whether to submit to the law or press ahead with his revolution outside the law. He chose lawlessness.

As the crisis neared a showdown, a leftist publication said of the fight between Congress and the president: "In the midst of the tense events of the past few two weeks, very few Chileans have noticed that the Christian Democrat leadership has activated a time-bomb very difficult to dismantle . . ."[55]

It would remain for Allende's cronies to render that bomb impossible to dismantle. Two days after the elections, the superintendent of education circulated plans for a unified national school system (known in Chile as ENU, for Educación Nacional Unificada). It was a week before word of the plan leaked, and when it did, it touched off the most emotional and explosive debate yet in a country already wracked by so many convulsions that yet another of this magnitude may have seemed inconceivable.

Inasmuch as the "radical transformation" of education was one of the cornerstones of the UP electoral platform in 1970, it cannot be said that the opposition was caught completely unawares.[56] Nor was there an audible outcry when, on January 30, 1973, Education Minister Jorge Tapia announced on national television plans for ENU. But the UP platform said the "New State" would not entrust this "radical transformation" to technocrats nor educators alone, but submit it to "study, discussion, decision and execution by organizations of teachers, workers, students, parents and guardians." There had been no such discussion.

Instead, the government exploded on a stunned public a plan that went far beyond anything contained in the UP platform, calling for a single nationwide curriculum with compulsory courses in socialism and work periods in factories. The aim, Tapia said, was to instill "values of socialist humanism" to achieve "harmonious development of young people's personalities." More than any single event, the plan galvanized Chile's military leaders into angry opposition to the Allende government. In an attempt to defuse that opposition, Defense Minister José Tohá arranged for Tapia to brief, on April 11, only three weeks before phase one of the program was to go into effect, some sixty top officers from each of the three branches on the proposal. Instead, the "confrontational . . . stormy" meeting laid bare the depth of the pent-up wrath and frustration of the military, focused now on what they saw as an assault on their own families: a program they saw as designed to indoctrinate the country's youth in Marxism. Tapia did not help matters, "reportedly admitting [during the meeting] that the school system of East

Germany had served as a model in drawing up the plan." Rear Admiral Huerta, who had quit the Allende cabinet in protest in January, led the attack from the floor—to "thundering," repeated, and rising applause. Not all the military leaders attacked the plan, however. One, instead, criticized his fellow commanders. That man was Carlos Prats González. ENU thus drove a deep nail in the coffin, not only of the Allende government, but of the one man who still had the power to avert a coup.[57]

When the government at first attempted to promulgate the changes by presidential decree, the comptroller general rejected the decree on the grounds that such a substantive matter required an act of Congress, thereby setting the stage for what might have become yet another constitutional crisis. Despite street demonstrations and solid political opposition, Tapia persisted, telling a Temuco audience on April 3: "ENU starts this year; have no doubt about that."[58]

Those street demonstrations would reach their peak on April 26, when thousands of pro- and anti-government students battled on Santiago's downtown streets, leaving 120 injured (and thirty-six windows of La Moneda Palace broken, which prompted Allende to appear on a balcony, megaphone in hand, to denounce the deed).[59] But by April 26—although the issue would continue to sputter through the bitter winter ahead—the fight was already over, because by then the Catholic church had joined the fray. On April 22, the bishops issued a statement saying they "oppose the thrust of this project, because its content respects neither human values nor Christian fundamentals." The next day, Allende said he had accepted the proposal made by Cardinal Raúl Silva Henríquez that the project be tabled pending a full-fledged national debate on education.[60]

Allende had overplayed his hand, badly. Until then, the Catholic church had been largely passive in the face of the mounting societal crisis in the country. Indeed, up to and including his Easter sermon, only a few weeks before, Cardinal Silva—while continuing to deplore violence—continued also to echo the rhetoric of the Popular Unity.[61] The school issue changed that.

But the school issue also galvanized into action right-wing organizations which, until then, had been limited almost entirely to keeping the flame of resistance burning through rhetoric, strikes, and demonstrations. These groups would now, increasingly, arm themselves. Chief among them was the Movimiento Nacionalista Patria y Libertad, founded in the desperate days of September 1970 by a young lawyer named Pablo Rodríguez Grez (see p. 301). Rodríguez first achieved national prominence in 1971 as the lawyer who defended Gen. Roberto Viaux Marambio, ringleader of the 1970 plotting that ended in the assassination of Army Chief Gen. René Schneider (see pp. 301–302 and, for details of that plot, the Appendix). During 1971 and 1972, the movement's principal activity was organizing landowners to defend themselves against illegal takeovers of their property. When the government announced not only food rationing, but clear signs of political controls over who would get food, and then followed with the unified school plan, the thoughts of these right-wing ideologues turned from words to revolution.[62]

They might have saved themselves the trouble. Because unbeknownst to them, ENU had also caused men far more powerful than they to decide that it could no longer be a question of whether—it could only be a question of when.[63]

THE PRESS UNDER FIRE

Around midnight on Saturday August 30, 1958, Salvador Allende— then making the second of his four runs for the presidency—made a campaign stop at the newspaper *El Mercurio*. While visiting with production workers in the "back shop," the candidate received an invitation to meet with the newspaper's top executives. "For once in my 25 years of public life," he told the *Mercurio* workers, "I have been openly and clearly discourteous. I have just declined that invitation . . ."[64]

The incident illustrates Allende's already strong antipathy toward Chile's leading newspaper. The feeling was mutual, and the episode might have signaled nothing more than the inevitable dislike of a politician of the Left for a newspaper of the Right. But the episode, quite apart from the depth of feeling his deliberate incivility would betray, was the first of many attempts Allende would make to split off *El Mercurio's* workers from its management, a prelude to seizing control of the hated colossus.

Allende was far from alone in seeing the significance of *El Mercurio*. Of the $6.5 million in covert U.S. aid to Chile during the Allende years, $1.6 million of it went to *El Mercurio*—slightly more than half of the total allocated to opposition media in order to enable them to offset advertising losses and, in the case of *El Mercurio*, to fend off government legal and tax assaults. (*El Mercurio's* editors were unaware of the clandestine support and would, for that reason, indignantly deny it when those reports first circulated.)

The attacks on *El Mercurio* and other opposition media also reflected Allende's philosophical disdain for a truly independent press, a disdain endemic to Communists and others on the far Left who saw the proper role of the press in a different light. The UP's electoral platform was brutally blunt: "These means of communication (radio, book publishers, television, press, movies) are fundamental for aiding in the formation of a new culture and a new man. For this reason, they must be imbued with an educational orientation and liberated from their commercial character, adopting measures by which the social organizations put these media at their disposal, eliminating from them the nefarious presence of the monopolies. The national system of popular culture will take special care to develop the filmmaking industry and the preparation of special programs for the mass media."[65] Allende would make explicit his own commitment to those views only a few months after taking office.

Inaugurating on April 9, 1971, the First National Congress of Journalists of the Left, Allende said: "Objectivity cannot exist in journalism. Journalists of the Left must share ever more in the struggle and must become the vanguard of revolutionary thought." On that same occasion, he defended his decision to bar access to one of his press conferences, a few days before, of a reporter from a conservative magazine and newspaper: "I am not willing to adopt an attitude of lack of virility and lack of dignity with those people, because they are delinquents and not journalists." As if to underscore his point, on April 15, Allende signed a decree which put government advertising under the tight political control of the dominant coalition partners—a measure fraught with significance inasmuch as the government already had a near stranglehold on the economy and was one of the country's principal advertisers.[66]

Over the next two and-a-half years, the Allende government would wage an unremitting campaign to expand state control of the media while muzzling the opposition press. It would be wrong to imply that the campaign succeeded. To the very end, Chile's press remained robust, irreverent, combative—and for some, even the indispensable catalyst for the coming revolution.[67] But, it would be equally wrong to underestimate the seriousness of the attempt, or the economic (and not infrequently, physical) perils it created for the country's free press. By 1972, the Inter-American Press Association, meeting in Santiago, denounced mounting official pressure on the press, taking particular note of official threats to jail journalists without benefit of court order. A few months later, the International Press Institute condemned the Allende government's "continuous campaign of intimidation and economic reprisals." Violence included a Molotov bomb attack on the newspaper *El Correo de Valdivia*, and shootings and beatings of individual opposition journalists. Nor was the international press exempted: on September 15, 1971, Allende ordered the closing of the United Press International in Chile (though he agreed to revoke the order ten days later); on September 15, 1972, Hernán del Canto, then secretary-general of the government, warned foreign correspondents that they would face expulsion from the country if the government found their reporting "tendentious" (none was).

In the matter of expanding state control: Allende was in power only three months when his government expropriated Zig-Zag, the country's largest publishing house (and one of the largest in all of Latin America). The pretext was a labor dispute, which had broken out after the September 4 elections. (Labor strife, usually contrived, was a device frequently used to justify government takeover of targeted companies.)

Thanks to access to the huge government advertising accounts, five UP daily newspapers and periodicals were published in Santiago alone. Among them: the biggest circulation newspaper, the Communist party's *Puro Chile*, which owed its "success" to a raucousness and increasingly bold use of pornography never before seen in the country. Help for propagating the revolution also poured in from abroad: *Punto Final*, the organ of the Movement of the Revolutionary Left (MIR), was Cuban-financed. Newsmen working for the Cuban "news" agency Prensa Latina helped to staff *Punto Final* and *Clarín*, another large circulation (and also raucous) radical-left newspaper. Documents captured after Allende's fall established that Allende himself bought that newspaper from his left-wing crony and business associate, Darío Sainte Marie, using $1.5 million in Czech, Cuban, and Swiss bank funds. Early in 1973, a Christian Democrat deputy, Mariano Ruiz-Esquide, claimed to have proof that the Communist party had acquired eleven radio stations, paying for some in dollars.[68]

Anxiety mounted so rapidly that, as early as September 16, 1971, the Christian Democrats—their entente with the UP though frayed was still intact—said press freedom was "under siege." Television, the document said, was in the hands of the government, since it not only operated the state channel, but the two university channels in that they were under the control of its followers; eight of the thirteen daily newspapers in the capital were also in the hands of the government or its allies; and moreover, 70 percent of the radio stations of the country were controlled by the government. (Other sources disputed those claims as to ideological line-up of the media.)[69]

The report also noted that despite such a suffocating presence in the media, the government continued to pursue control of the *El Mercurio* group (which published two of the five independent dailies in Santiago, as well as the leading newspapers in Valparaíso, the country's second city, and two smaller cities. Pressures ranged from efforts to foment labor strife among its 1,400 Santiago employees, to a tax investigation launched within Allende's first sixty days in office. That investigation led to a claim (which wound up in the courts) that the newspaper owed back taxes in the amount of 21 million escudos (at the then official rate, around $1.7 million). Ultimately, the Allende government would resort to a frontal assault: on June 22, 1973, *El Mercurio* was ordered closed for six days for publishing a communique of the entirely legal National party. It was the first time in its seventy-three-year history that the newspaper failed to appear. (The Supreme Court revoked the order the next day.) The National party's scrappy daily, *La Tribuna*, had to defend against no fewer than forty-seven government lawsuits by the end of 1972.[70]

If *El Mercurio* represented not only a burr under Allende's saddle, but the most powerful print media complex in the country, there was another target of great strategic value to the Popular Unity: the half-century-old *Compañía Manufacturera de Papeles y Cartones*, or the Papelera as it was known in Chile, headed by former President Jorge Alessandri. The Papelera was the one and only source of domestic newsprint in Chile; and it supplied 60 percent of the newsprint used. Nationalization of the Papelera was called for in the UP's electoral platform. To keep it free, executives of the firm had to wage a bitter fight that lasted nearly the entire three years of UP government. They could not have won it without the support of the majority of their 4,500 employees; indeed, reacting to the nationalization threat, the employees, on November 11, 1971, organized a fund to buy shares of any of the 16,500 shareholders who, for reasons of panic or otherwise in the face of government pressure, might wish to sell. Throughout, the Papelera also had the unflinching support of business groups, opposition politicians, non-UP labor groups, the Congress, and the military—all of which joined the fight. The main tactic was economic suffocation: the Inter-American Press Association, in its 1972 report, noted that while the cost of final products had risen nearly 100 percent—thanks largely to government-decreed wage and salary increases—the company had been permitted to raise the price of newsprint by only 19.6 percent. As a result, twenty-five top executives of the firm would tell Allende on June 7, 1972, that the company was losing 1 million escudos per day. (Military men in the Cabinet would, at the end of that year, persuade Allende to raise its prices somewhat, but the company's situation remained precarious, and the battle went on, down to the final days of Allende.)[71]

A third media target was the country's 170 radio stations, though the government never relented in its attempts to control and, when that failed, to intimidate the two nongovernment television stations. But the major target was radio, overwhelmingly hostile to Allende, and still more powerful than TV in Chile, particularly one station located just four blocks up the street from La Moneda, diagonally across Teatinos Street from Communist party headquarters. That station was Radio Agricultura, a station which, more than any other, became the voice of resistance to Allende. (By 1973, it had also become a key element in the secret planning of a group of feisty civilians and field grade officers.

The result was that on September 11, Radio Agricultura would become the voice of revolution.)[72]

From the time the first two radio stations were forcibly taken, on May 13, 1971, down to the very last days of the regime, attacks on radio stations—physical, legal and pseudo-legal—never ceased. The first showdown came on October 15, 1972, at the peak of the crushing October strike, when the government ordered the country's stations to join in a nationwide network, broadcasting government information office communiques. The comptroller general ruled that the mandatory network decree was illegal, and impeachment proceedings were started against Secretary-General del Canto.

That did not stop the government. Three days later, Radio Agricultura, Radio Balmaceda (owned by the Christian Democrats), and Radio Yungay were ordered off the air for pulling out of the network. The network was abolished only on October 27, by order of an appeals court judge. Seven months later, despite that ruling, the government would again order Radio Agricultura off the air, then defy still another court order to reopen it, following next with yet one more illegal order for another national network.

That case gave rise to what amounted to a government declaration of war on the courts. The Policy Commission of the Popular Unity announced plans to haul the justices of the Supreme Court before the Constitutional Tribunal, accusing them of "twisting the nose of the law." "The Supreme Court," the UP group charged, "has been transformed into just another redoubt of the Right and thus has lost its moral authority by converting itself into another bastion of reaction."[73] There was, of course, no provision in the 1970 amendment creating the Constitutional Tribunal for using it to "try" Supreme Court justices, and no such motion was ever brought.

The man who came to power promising to guarantee freedom of the press would now put himself on a collision course with the constitution itself because of his determined efforts to bend the press to his own purposes.

CARNIVAL OF MADNESS

This is, said Eduardo Frei, "a carnival of madness." The country is headed, he added, for "Marxist-type totalitarianism."[74] He did not exaggerate.

Even Allende's corevolutionaries recognized the wreckage their country had become. On February 28, *El Mercurio* published a confidential study done by the policy commission of the coalition party MAPU (Unitary Popular Action Movement)—a devastating inventory of the regime's economic catastrophes which concluded with an urgent call for infiltration of the armed forces as the only hope of staving off an armed showdown. Publication of that report would lead to yet another split in a party already so small that it would poll only approximately 100,000 votes in the March elections. Days later, *El Mercurio* published yet another secret report, this time of a senior official in the Office of Agricultural Planning. In it, Tomás Cox said the government had committed "enormous, profound and crass mistakes" in carrying out its agrarian reform, with the result that "food rationing will have to be implemented." But, as galling as those leaks may have been, they only confirmed what the outside world already knew: the Economic Commission for Latin America reported that once-vaunted Chile ranked second from the bottom in all countries of Latin America in terms of economic growth during 1972.[75]

The regime's closest allies in Latin America pitched in: Cuba with its (see p. 370 and end note #10, p. 426] 40,000-ton gift of sugar, Mexico with an emergency shipment of free fuel oil and gasoline (in response to a personal hat-in-hand appeal from Allende). Not all foreign aid proved beneficial: after a trial run, Chile had to send back to "Big Brother" Russia 125 earth-mover machines because of chronic mechanical break-downs.[76]

Amid the hardship, the telling revelations of special privileges for diplomats and others, and the internal feuding and polarization, came revelation after revelation of official corruption and abuse of power. Few rivaled that of illicit trafficking in automobiles, particularly since the UP platform had made ending official abuse in this area number five of the first forty measures it would take once in government (see note 30, this chapter). A congressional investigating committee reported in mid-1972 that Allende's private secretary (and mistress), Miria Contreras Bell de Ropert, had no fewer than twenty-eight automobiles registered to her name. Still later, it was learned that the state automobile monopoly had sold fifty-five Fiats to the MAPU party at the official price, and the far-Left party then turned around and resold them at the black market price—many times the official price. Greater still: a study early in 1973 showed that of 17,939 vehicles assembled in Chile during 1972, only 3,600 were accounted for by the state monopoly—meaning 14,339 had disappeared.[77]

But, as spring receded into what would become the bitterest fall and winter in the country's history, the caterwauling and the corruption, the economic catharses and even the elections themselves, all these were merely the sideshows in this carnival of madness. Statistics, who said what and when did they say it, the episodes large and small, those who claimed to reason why and those who behaved as though they knew only how to die, all these were, of course, the broken and scattered pieces of a puzzle that, even were it any longer possible to assemble, would no more a coherent picture form. Madness was abroad in the land during those darkening days of autumn, the madness of unbridled passions fired and fueled by resentments, anger, righteousness, hope-lessness, stupidity, and, yes, idealism, idealism run amok. Across the widening chasm which separated what were, by now, two irreconcilable sides, the adversaries shouted at and past each other as wittingly, unwit-tingly, they made ready to destroy each other.

"Civil war is imminent," declared the Popular Unity. We shall use every power within our means, the Christian Democrats shot back, to halt this totalitarian escalation. Confrontation is inevitable, said the country's top Communist, talk of *la vía institucional*, the institutional path, now gone to a pauper's grave.[78]

As the radical Left armed, the military stepped up its campaign to disarm them; between April and June, military strike forces staged an average of three arms searches per week. Beginning in June, the average was even higher.[79] By the end of June, even the *New York Times*, gener-ally sympathetic to Allende throughout, editorialized that Allende's policies had pushed the country to the brink of civil war.[80]

And, as the winds of the coming war whistled ever closer, on the upper floors of a drab office building, just a few hundred yards from the eye of the storm, hatches were battened down, lifelines to the outside world carefully reeled in, the course set: away from harm's way. The drab building housed the United States Embassy in Santiago.[81]

On April 19, the nine unions representing 11,500 workers at El Ten-iente, Chile's second largest copper mine, went on strike demanding wage increases sufficient to offset the 76.2 percent increase in the cost of living between October 1972 and March 1973. Chile would not again know labor peace under Salvador Allende; indeed, Chile would not again know real peace for many long years.

It would be July 2 before that strike would end, but before it did, the copper miners would be joined by doctors, teachers, students; there would be street fighting, and street dying, women would march and women would be beaten, and one woman would make history of sorts by sticking out her tongue. Chile's impoverished treasury would also be $60 million poorer in copper losses alone. And, in the midst of that developing anarchy, the country's retired admirals and generals would appeal to Allende: respect, please, the constitution, because if you fail to do that, in this trauma of contempt for law and order afflicting our land, then the compact which binds the armed forces to the civil authorities will be broken. "The time," the retired flag officers wrote, "to view events contemplatively, that time has past."[82]

The reply was not long in coming.

"Every factory, every farm, every union headquarters, every public office, must be converted into a bulwark of people power. Every industrial plant must be a fortress of the revolution." The speaker was Luis Corvalán, secretary-general of the Communist party, the same man who, a few months before (see p. 379) had hooted derisively at "people power" as the "phantasmagoric" invention of the MIR, the juvenile hotheads of revolution. For good measure, Corvalán told his audience in the Caupolicán Theater: "The legislative and judicial branches cannot remain unharmed, because they are enemies of progress . . ."[83]

There is an event in those pyretic days which stands apart, perhaps only because it fit so well the law of unintended consequences. On June 28, a handful of tanks and two trucks, with forty combat-equipped troops in each, rumbled out of the headquarters of the Second Armored Regiment and headed through morning rush-hour traffic for La Moneda Palace, about five miles distant as the crow flies, pausing for traffic lights as they made their way to the target. It was the beginning of the first military uprising in Chile in forty-two years, and it was over before the lunch hour. Twenty-two soldiers and civilians died, thirty-two were wounded and fifty prisoners taken. During the fighting, the tanks briefly shelled both La Moneda and the Defense Ministry, diagonally across the city's principal thoroughfare, the Alameda, then a huge open trench while a subway was being built. The uprising was supposed to be part of a larger rebellion involving other units—but none joined, thanks to the quick intervention of a number of generals, including Augusto Pinochet. General Prats, only the day before the object of national scorn, managed to redeem himself briefly by striding boldly into the Plaza Constitución under the guns of the tanks and assembled rebels, going from tank to tank, and ordering the crews to surrender. (They did.)

But the uprising was significant for yet another reason. When it erupted, Allende went on the radio from his residence: "I call on the people to seize the factories, the companies, to be alert, to pour into the downtown streets, but not to be victims; for the people to take to the streets, but not to be machinegunned, to do it, but to do it prudently, with whatever 'weapon' you have at hand." He added, "If the time comes, the people will have arms."

Factories were taken—more than two hundred additional plants were seized that day. In the aftermath, armed groups began openly patrolling the industrial *cordones* (clusters of factories), as well as the shanty-towns surrounding them. But there was no outpouring of supporters on the streets of the city.

Instead, the *tancazo*—as the rebellion came to be known—was an unexpected "dry run" for the military. Gen. Arturo Yovane Zúñiga, the

Carabinero general who would play a critical role during the September revolution, recalled: "(It) was not just a dramatic episode. It was the chance to see how the pro-government elements acted. I carefully noted what they did—the buildings they occupied, the sectors the industrial-belt workers sealed off, the number of people they mobilized, and everything else. The eleventh of September was very easy as a result, because they repeated exactly the same moves." As a result of events that day, Pinochet also ordered his secret plan of revolution revamped to reflect the lessons learned.

Five thousand miles to the north, National Security Advisor Henry Kissinger would report to President Richard Nixon: "All indications are that the coup attempt was an isolated and poorly coordinated effort. Most of the military leaders, including the commanders-in-chief of all three branches of the Armed Forces, remained loyal to the government."[84]

In victory, Salvador Allende had suffered a decisive defeat on June 29: he had asked the people to rally to his side. They had not.

Alejandrina Cox de Valdivieso neither looks the part of a heroine, nor did she seek the role. But, for one brief moment in those turbulent days, she was the toast of thousands in Chile. It happened on the morning of June 27—the day before the *tancazo*—on tree-canopied Vitacura Avenue, in the fashionable eastern end of the city. Mrs. Cox, driving into town with her son, looked up at a traffic light and there, reading the morning newspaper in the back of the car next to her, was Carlos Prats González, commander-in-chief of the army and already the *bête noire* of multitudes in Chile for his slavish support of Allende. Impulsively, Mrs. Cox stuck her tongue out at the startled general. He responded by drawing his service revolver and firing a bullet into the chassis of her car.

Frightened, Mrs. Cox took off, with General Prats in pursuit. Overtaking her, he ordered his driver to cut her off, and when he did, jumped from the car and pointed a gun at her head, demanding, "You apologize, you shit, or I'll shoot you." With that, a crowd of hissing, booing people gathered and—adding insult to the general's injury—took the air out of his tires and began berating him. Prats made his getaway in a taxi, while the crowd vented its wrath on his driver. Prats later compounded the damage by claiming that he mistook Mrs. Cox for a man (as one who interviewed her, I found that story singularly implausible).[85]

The incident was significant because it cost Prats dearly in the respect and esteem of his fellow officers—and his standing with them was already precarious. It would weigh heavily in his forced resignation two months later.

Down to the end of his Othello-like role in the Chilean tragedy, Carlos

Prats listened to the wrong whispers, until he would become a crucial accomplice in the murder of the Desdemona he professed to love most, his country's democracy. Oh, near the end, he did wonder—was, what he was doing, just "military ingenuity?"—but he did not doubt hard enough, or long enough, and so one can only speculate how differently the drama might have unfolded had the army been in the hands of one of sterner stuff, more suspicious of revolutionaries in democratic dress, less willing to lend himself to manipulative cynics and their *muñequeos*.

Instead, Prats lent himself ever more to Allende and his purposes, becoming ever more a politician while continuing to preach the necessity of keeping the military aloof from problems which are and ought to be managed as political.

On July 2, Allende asked Prats once again to join his Cabinet, together with navy and air force ministers. The next day, Prats met with the corps of generals. They voted unanimously against his rejoining the Cabinet. When Allende persuaded the chief of the navy (Admiral Montero) and an unnamed air force general to join the Cabinet, Prats tried again. This time, his fellow generals told him bluntly: go into the Cabinet, but resign first as commander-in-chief of the army. (Prats declined.) One general warned him: you have lost the confidence of the officer corps.

Still Prats did not get the message. He did not get it, either, when two generals (Oscar Bonilla and Carlos Araya) suggested to one of the few remaining generals still close to Prats—Brig. Gen. Guillermo Pickering Vásquez—that he ought to retire "for the good of the service." He did not get it, either, a month later, when at Military Academy graduation ceremonies, the audience "applauded exaggeratedly" when the nephew of Lieutenant Colonel Souper, the man who had led the *tancazo* rebellion, received his commission as a second lieutenant. Prats referred to it as "a discordant note."

Over the few weeks remaining to him, Prats concentrated not on fortifying his badly weakened military flank, but instead lurched ever deeper into the inner web of Popular Unity intrigue. His diary, for those weeks, reveals a private one-on-one dinner with Allende; another, at El Cañaveral (the suburban estate Allende had bought for—and where he frolicked with—his mistress), attended also by Luis Corvalán, the head of the Communist party, and Carlos Altamirano, the head of the Socialist party; a private meeting with the head of the violent Movement of the Revolutionary Left, Miguel Enríquez; as well as countless meetings with leaders of the Communist labor federation, left-wing congressmen, and leaders.

By then, those who had been closest to him in uniform, no longer doubted: "The Commander-in-Chief of the Army was the biggest obstacle we had to overcome, since he was totally addicted to Allende. I decided to speed up the preparations . . ."

The speaker was Augusto Pinochet.[86]

THE FINAL COUNTDOWN

To the very end, Salvador Allende attempted the impossible: to march to the beat of two very different drummers—at home, and abroad as well. As the crisis deepened, an elder statesman and wizened survivor of revolution, Communist China's Chou en Lai (Zhou Enlai, in the later Western usage), urged Allende "to go slower, to be less doctrinaire." The Chinese premier, "strongly sympathetic to Allende," warned him of risks, "but they didn't believe us . . . it was useless because the word of a foreigner meant nothing."[87]

Not quite. The Salvador Allende who enjoyed practicing firing machineguns with his son-in-law, Luis Fernández Oña—former chief of the secret police in Cuba before Castro dispatched him to assist Allende in his revolution—was more amenable to the advice of his old friend, Fidel Castro. On July 29, 1973, Castro wrote Allende a handwritten letter, hand-delivered by two of his top henchmen: Carlos Rafael Rodríguez, deputy prime minister and chief of the Communist party of Cuba, and Fernández Oña's successor as secret police chief, Manuel Piñeiro.[88] That letter—whose authenticity Cubans never denied—is so extraordinary as to merit quoting in full:

Dear Salvador: Carlos [Rodríguez] and [Manuel] Piñeiro are traveling there on the pretext of discussing with you questions related to the meeting of nonaligned countries [scheduled for early September in Algeria, and which Allende planned to attend]. The real purpose is to learn from you the situation and offer you, as always, our willingness to cooperate in the face of the difficulties and dangers hindering and threatening the [revolutionary] process. Their stay will be very brief inasmuch as they have a number of pending obligations here, and yet, not without sacrifice to their work, we decided that they should make the trip.

I see that you are now in the delicate question of dialogue with the Christian Democrats in the midst of serious events such as the brutal murder of your naval aide and the new strike of truck-owners. I well imagine the great tension and your wish to gain time, to improve the correlation of forces in case the fight does break out, and, if possible, to find a channel that enables you to push forward with the revolutionary process without civil strife, at the same time that you safeguard your historic responsibility for whatever may come. These are laudable aims. But in case the other side, whose real intentions we cannot evaluate from here, are embarked on a perfidious and irresponsible policy, demanding that the Popular Unity and the Revolution pay an impossible price, which, indeed, is more than probable, don't forget for a second the formidable strength of the Chilean worker class and the energetic backing that they have given you in every difficult moment; with the Revolution in danger, that force, at your summons, can paralyze the insurgents, shore up the support of the hesitant, impose their conditions and, if it is necessary, decide once and for all the destiny of Chile. The enemy must understand that it [the worker militancy] is alert and ready to swing into action. Its strength and combativeness can tip the balance in the capital in your favor even when other circumstances may be unfavorable to you.

Your decision to defend the process with firmness and honor even at the cost of your own life, which we all know you are capable of fulfilling, will rally to your side all the forces capable of fighting and all the worthy men and women of Chile. Your valor, your serenity and your boldness in this historic hour of your country, and above all, your firm, resolute and heroically executed leadership constitute the key to the situation.

Let Carlos and Manuel know how your loyal Cuban friends can cooperate with you.

I reiterate the affection and unlimited confidence of our people for you.

Fraternally,

Fidel Castro.[89]

As so often in his own career, Castro would describe for Allende in that letter a world that existed mainly in the revolutionary reveries of his own mind. The workers had not flocked to Allende's side, and as the days ahead would demonstrate anew, they were not with him—they were, by the tens of hundreds of thousands fed up with him, with what he had done to their country.

But by the time the letter reached him, Salvador Allende was himself little more than flotsam on the riptide of events. And yet, and yet . . . that summons to revolutionary heroics, immortality—"even at the price of your own life, which we all know you are capable of fulfilling . . ."—how could those words not reverberate six weeks later in the whiskied and ecstatic Walter Mitty-mind of a man who, submachinegun blazing, was then living out that lifelong phantasy as the fearless guerilla gunfighter.

Castro speaks of the truckers' strike. It exploded on July 25: 60,000 owners, 100,000 drivers and helpers, 75,000 trucks. The head of the Federation of Unions of Truck Owners of Chile, León Vilarín, himself a former Socialist, said the 198 member unions had agreed to the stoppage because "the government has not fulfilled a single one of the agreements" reached with General Prats ending the October 1972 strike. A few days later, on August 2, they were joined by 110,000 bus and taxi drivers. On August 16, the shopkeepers went out; they were shortly afterwards joined by the country's doctors; by the end of August, over 1 million Chileans were on strike, despite the calls of the Allende-allied Central Labor Federation (CUT) to its half-million members to counter the wave of strikes. As was inevitable in the escalating climate of violence and confrontation in the country, the new wave of unrest unleashed worsening episodes of arrests, street fighting, charges and countercharges. The worst—and most significant—events were triggered by the government's decision to seize trucks. A trucker was shot and wounded and five National party deputies beaten by Carabineros in one episode on the outskirts of Santiago on July 31.

On August 10, acting on orders of Deputy Transport Secretary Jaime Faivovich—from the MIR-addicted violent wing of the Socialist party—seven hundred Carabineros attempted to storm the El Monte trucker encampment and seize some of the 1,650 trucks and five hundred minibuses parked there. Using twenty-five Soviet-made tractors, guarded by three minitanks, they tugged and towed to no avail—largely because the truckers had all but buried their vehicles in the mud, removing key parts from others. It was later learned that Faivovich had acted in direct defiance of the orders of his brand new boss, air force commander-in-chief (and transport minister) César Ruiz Danyau. When Allende failed to back him and fire Faivovich, Ruiz, on August 18, resigned. Allende then demanded that he quit also as air force chief, raising disgruntlement to the level of crisis in the air force as a result of Allende's firing, a few weeks before, of the numbers two and four generals. Since both were known to oppose Allende, that move was widely regarded as a ploy by Allende to maneuver into position a general believed to have ties to the radical Left. (Appearing on a highly popular, and highly irreverent opposition television program August 19, Ruiz explained his reasons for quitting; General Prats, ever more critical of his fellow service chiefs as they distanced themselves from Allende, described Ruiz' performance as "a striptease.") Ruiz finally did step down on August 20, but only after satisfying himself that he had checkmated Allende against further attempts to coopt the institution. In his place, a decided hard-liner: Gen. Gustavo Leigh Guzmán. The first of the Four Horsemen was now in place.[90]

As the crisis deepened, so did the contradictions. On the one hand, extremist rhetoric and violence heated up—on both sides.[91] On the other, amid the escalating lawlessness, efforts to find a legal way out. On June 9, members of the newly armed Communist Ramona Parra brigade were the protagonists of the first open fire fight between a paramilitary organization and the military in a gun battle at Los Cerrillos airport. By July 14, an official report said that a total of 34,000 factories, shops, and service establishments had been seized by "workers" since the *tancazo*. In Greater Santiago, fortification of the eight industrial *cordones* was speeded up. Speaking at a Caupolicán Theater rally, MIR leader Miguel Enríquez defended the open emergence of "popular power": "The reactionaries will say that this is in violation of the laws, the constitution and the rule of law. Well, that *is* what it is!" One week later, the Socialist party clamored for even more: "The Socialist party is in a state of emergency throughout the country. Every party member should remain in constant contact with the regular agencies of the party . . . Take control of all companies . . . Stand guard, organize committees of defense, armed with whatever you can . . . Report to your committee of defense every meeting or suspicious movement of the fascists or 'mummies' [the mocking term for upper-class people]. Keep close watch on the reactionaries . . ."[92]

Never to be outdone, on August 22, around three hundred MIRistas in the city of Concepción demonstrated outside the headquarters of the Chacabuco Regiment, urging enlisted men to disobey their officers. When they were dispersed at point of bayonet, the MIRistas opened fire—the first armed clash involving the army. In Santiago, the day before, students demonstrating in support of trucker wives who had encamped (despite the cold) in the gardens of the Congress building, were fired upon by snipers in surrounding buildings. Six of them were wounded, many more clubbed and teargassed by police.

On the Right, Patria y Libertad stepped up its appeals for mass mobilization and urged private citizens to arm themselves, though mass arrests in May and the flight into exile of its top leader took a toll on the organization's effectiveness.[93]

One other violent incident requires brief mention. On July 26, as indicated in Castro's letter, Allende's naval aide, Capt. Arturo Araya Peters, was shot and killed just after midnight as he stood on the balcony of his home, an automatic weapon in hand. His wife said he went out to investigate what sounded to be a small explosion, and was cut down by machinegun fire. The Right accused the Left, hinting that Cubans may have been involved, avenging an alleged romantic liaison between Araya and Allende's daughter, the wife of Cuba's former secret police chief. The Left accused the Right, prompting the acting head of Patria y Libertad, Roberto Thieme Scheires, to offer to come out of hiding and surrender himself to naval authorities to clear himself and his colleagues of complicity. Two days after the killing, a self-styled munitions expert named José Luis Riquelme Bascuñán was arrested and confessed to Carabineros that he had participated in the murder with three Cubans and a member of Allende's private palace guard nicknamed "El Petizo." The Cubans were never detained, but the night of the murder, it was later learned, Alfredo Joginant, director of the Allende-controlled national detective force, Investigaciones, personally escorted passengers boarding a Cubana de Aviación flight. According to that report, the departing passengers had only minutes before obtained the needed travel documents. Riquelme, meanwhile, repudiated his earlier confession.[94]

Araya's murder had fallout closer to the core of the crisis. On July 27, the very day after Patricio Aylwin, president of the Christian Democratic party, accepted Allende's invitation for a dialogue, Carlos Altamirano, Aylwin's Socialist party counterpart, fired yet another of his rapport-shattering broadsides. The murderers of Araya, he said, were members of Patria y Libertad, but the intellectual authors of the crime were René Silva Espejo and Arturo Fontaine of *El Mercurio*, Sergio Onofre Jarpa (head of the National party) and—Eduardo Frei. Such a frontal attack on their revered leader, even coming from one famed for his blunderbuss style, was bound to dampen the conciliatory spirits of the Christian Democrats.

And there was yet another element of fallout. One of the men detailed to Valparaíso for Captain Araya's funeral was Gen. Gustavo Leigh. While there, he lunched with Navy Captain Arturo Troncoso, and a fateful meeting it would turn out to be. At it, agreement was reached on a matter weighing heavily on Leigh's mind: the navy's marines would protect and defend the air force's planes. As a result, the pride of the air force—forty Hawker Hunter jets, purchased by Allende as a gift to the air force—were moved from the vulnerable Los Cerrillos air base in Santiago to others as far south as Punta Arenas, as far north as Antofagasta. Two, redeployed to Concepción, would immediately begin low-level training missions over Coronel and Lota.[95]

Amid the bedlam, there would be one last stab at peace. On July 16, the Permanent Committee of the Catholic Bishops' Conference made an "extreme appeal to avoid an armed conflict among Chileans." "We represent no political point of view, no special interest nor group, but are moved only by [our concern for] the welfare of Chile and [our desire] to prevent the blood of Christ from being trampled underfoot in a fratricidal war." In that pastoral letter, the bishops called for peace talks. The very next day, Communist party chief Luis Corvalán said he was agreeable to such talks; on July 23, the Christian Democrats also agreed, while denouncing the "double dealing" of the Communists. On the one hand, PDC President Patricio Aylwin said, the Communist party speaks of its desire for peace, while on the other Luis Figueroa—high official of the party, former labor minister and again president of the

Central Workers' Confederation (CUT)—seeks the repeal of the peace-insuring Arms Control Law.

The talks opened and closed on July 30: Allende, flanked by his defense minister, Clodomiro Almeyda, and interior minister, Carlos Briones; Aylwin, accompanied by Sen. Osvaldo Olguín. Conspicuously missing: the party of the Right, the Nationals, not invited, even though in the March elections they had not only gained ground while the Christian Democrats continued to decline, but had emerged, by a wide margin, as the second largest political force in Chile; and the Socialists, still dominant in the coalition. Despite Allende's choice of two moderate Socialists to accompany him, the party itself, firmly in the hands of the radical wing, not only refused to participate but warned that it would "never accept" concessions made to the Christian Democrats. In such circumstances, the talks never had a chance. Even had Allende succeeded in driving a wedge between the Christian Democrats and their conservative allies, he still would have had to reckon with mutiny on the Left, revolution on the Right.

On August 3, the Christian Democrats said dialogue was dead. Five days later, Allende attempted yet one more *muñequeo*—the most dangerous one yet. He fired the all-civilian Cabinet he had sworn in only one month before, and named a new one that included all three service chiefs and, for the first time, the head of the paramilitary Carabineros, Gen. José María Sepúlveda. No longer could the fiction be maintained that the military were serving as "individuals," not representing their services, for all four of them insisted on remaining in command of their services as well. No longer could there be the fiction that the military should remain outside the political process: it was now only a question of which side they would take. To greater or lesser degree, all four of these military men believed they must support Allende. They didn't know it then, but it was a luxury of choice about to evaporate for them.

Allende's maneuver did succeed in winning a brief reprieve. On August 10, the Christian Democrats said they would give Allende their conditional support, but only provided he meet their basic condition: that the military not only sit in the Cabinet, but have real power to enforce the government's legality. Allende offered as a sop a compromise in the constitutional dispute over the "three areas" of the economy and nationalization of industries. But he could not and did not surrender to what would have amounted to giving his military ministers veto power over his acts. In that, against the clamor of the top generals who demanded even stiffer conditions as the price of military connivance, Prats sided with Allende, arguing that such "interdiction" of presidential powers would amount to a "bloodless coup" (*golpe en seco*).

Swearing in the new Cabinet of "national security," as he called it,

Allende said, "Chile is in danger; this is how civil wars start . . . this is Chile's last chance."[96]

He was right. There would be no further "dialogues." Indeed, the new Cabinet would last barely two weeks, and not three weeks later Aylwin would tell a Washington newspaper that if he had to choose between "a Marxist dictatorship and a dictatorship of our military, I would choose the second." The next day he would deny that the Christian Democrats—or the military, for that matter—wanted anything other than "a democratic solution to Chile's crisis." Yet, for many, he had sent a clear signal to the military.[97]

The legal ground beneath Salvador Allende was crumbling as rapidly as was the semblance of law-and-order in the country. On May 26, in an unprecedented communication signed by all fourteen justices of the Supreme Court, the Court warned of "an open and willful contempt of judicial decisions [by the executive] . . . which attitude further implies not only a crisis in the state of law . . . but also a peremptory or imminent breakdown of legality . . ."

On July 8, Senate President Eduardo Frei and Chamber of Deputies President Luis Pareto issued a joint declaration enumerating elements of a crisis which they said was not only creating a "brain drain" of desperate professionals fleeing the country but also included "an organized process of hate and violence . . . We are not enemies of changes . . . toward new ways of life and of new social and economic organizations," the manifesto said, "but we object strongly when they are carried out illegally and by means of violence . . .

"It is indispensable that the Government put an end to illegal take-overs [of farms and factories] and to armed groups that constitute a menace for the rest of the population and a parallel power to the police and armed forces . . . No people of any country can endure the tension created by the permanent insecurity [caused by] . . . armed groups with official backing . . ." The statement said the government itself bore the greatest responsibility for "a situation whose extreme dangers are impossible to hide . . ."

On August 8, the Bar Association, in a unanimous proclamation of its General Council, said, "the obvious fracturing of our legal structure can no longer be tolerated . . ."

On August 22 came the gravest blow of all: by a vote of 81 to 47, the Chamber of Deputies, in a "sense of the House" resolution, accused the Allende government of a pattern of systematic and chronic violation of the law and of the Constitution, resulting in "a grave breakdown [*quebrantamiento*] of the legal and constitutional order of the Republic." The document was replete with specific charges of illegality vis-à-vis the Congress, the courts, the comptroller general, the rights of individual and of other institutions of the society. As to Allende, the Chamber noted that Congress elected him only after he agreed to a set of constitutional guarantees, adding: "... it is a fact that the present government, from the very beginning, has persisted in seeking the conquest of total power, with the obvious purpose of submitting everyone to the strictest economic and political control of the State and achieving thereby the implanting of a totalitarian system absolutely opposed to the democratic and representative system established by the constitution ... That, to achieve this result, the Government has indulged not in isolated violations of the constitution and the law, but has made of these a permanent pattern of behavior, reaching the extreme of systematically ignoring and trampling the attributes of the other branches of government ... of not only permitting the creation of but protecting illegal parallel forces which constitute a most grievous danger for the nation ... "

Significantly, the resolution was directed not only to the president but also to the military members of the Cabinet. Indeed, the resolution said bluntly that it was the responsibility of the military—in light of the oaths they had sworn not only to uphold the constitution but also to be the ultimate guarantors of legality for all Chileans—to "put an immediate end" to lawlessness and "channel government action along legal paths and thereby assure the constitutional order of our country and the essential framework for democratic coexistence among Chileans ... " The resolution ended with a clear challenge to the very sense of honor of the military—those in the Cabinet, those, increasingly restive, outside:

"If they do these things, then those [military] ministers will perform a valuable service for the Republic. Failing to do so, they would gravely compromise the national and professional character of the Armed Forces and Corps of Carabineros, in open violation of the constitution and at serious damage to their institutional prestige."

Allende understood immediately the portents of the challenge. Two days later, he shot back that the Chamber was "promoting a coup d'êtat by asking the military forces to make governmental judgments independently of the authority and direction of the president." Terming the resolution "a political accord designed to disgrace the country abroad and create confusion at home ... [this] unworthy accord binds no one and lacks altogether juridical validity." Removing him, he said, would in any case require a two-thirds vote of Congress.

On August 25, even the Medical Asociation demanded that fellow physician Salvador Allende resign as president because "you have, to the present, shown no intention of submitting to the Rule of Law and respecting the law and constitution ... "

On August 31, the Bar Association threw down yet another gauntlet. The Bar invoked Article 43, Chapter 4, of the constitution, dealing with presidential incapacity, to argue that in the legal crisis, Allende had reached a point of "incapacity," and that therefore Congress should exercise its prerogative to oust him and call new elections.[98]

In days that followed, pamphlets and circulars demanding Allende's resignation appeared on city streets, and the Federation of Professionals, in a manifesto, added its voice to that clamor never before heard in a country which had so prided itself on the tensile strength of its institutions: that a constitutional president step down so as to put a suffering country out of its democratic misery.

Against such a backdrop of institutional disintegration, it was not surprising that more than a dozen professional and business organizations, including doctors, lawyers, teachers, engineers, and builders, would announce the formation of a patriotic front dedicated to the overthrow of Salvador Allende.[99]

In a very real sense, it was anticlimactic, but on September 9, the twenty-nine provincial presidents of the Christian Democrat party demanded that the party's executive seek not only Allende's resignation, but those of the entire Congress so that the badly smudged and besmirched slate of Chilean institutionality be wiped clean with new elections.

But there was far more than mere symbolism to this outpouring of protests and resolutions and proclamations emanating from so many of the most learned in the law of that land, those whose entire lives were intertwined with the latticework of the democracy they were now interring. Beyond the whereases and the wherefores, the legalese, there was etched an inescapable verdict: to the extent that it had ever existed, for tens of hundreds of thousands of Chileans, Salvador Allende's *vía institucional* was dead; indeed, democracy itself was so wounded that it would now slip into a long coma, longer than any dared imagine in that awful winter of discontent.

Allende was in office barely one month when Socialist party chieftain Carlos Altamirano told an interviewer that an armed showdown in Chile was inevitable, and that the "popular forces" would ready themselves for that day. By July of 1973, he said that the showdown not only was inevitable, but "the people are prepared to burn and blow up this country from Arica [on the northern border with Peru] to Magallanes [at the frigid southern tip], in a heroic liberating and patriotic offensive."[100]

He was wrong as to readiness. He was not wrong as to the efforts to create, to arm and train a revolutionary force in the farms, the factories, the slums, the schools and even in the presidential palaces themselves, so strong, so powerful, that not even the armed forces would dare defy them. That effort began when Allende, in those first weeks in power, pardoned the high command of the fire-breathing Movement of the

Revolutionary Left—one of whom, Joel Marambio, would be the first commandant of Allende's own private security force, the GAP (Grupo de Amigos Personales, Group of Personal Friends, as Allende so mockingly nicknamed those gunslingers).

From the earliest days, three of the parties of the Popular Unity—first the Socialists, then the MAPU, and then (though denying it until near the very end) the Communists—each fielded its own clandestine armed brigades. By mid-1973, even the Radicals had organized a guerrilla group. Nor was the Right idle: Patria y Libertad announced in August that it was going underground and would create as much havoc as possible so as to "accelerate the country's chaos and provoke a military takeover as soon as possible." (Though the organization did, as indicated, stage scattered attacks on power facilities and the like, even this display of bluster would soon boomerang: between August 22 and August 28, virtually the entire leadership remaining in the country—twenty-one persons—was arrested).[101]

But by mid-1973, the military was also making increasing use of the Arms Control Law, which gave commanders authority to conduct arms searches whenever there was a "presumption" of clandestine caches.

Although there had been numerous lighting raids on specific targets, the first massive military action—involving helicopters, planes and armored vehicles—occurred on August 6 in the southern city of Punto Arenas. In the course of the sweep through an industrial cluster built around the big, nationalized Lanera Austral plant, one worker was killed and one wounded. Mario Palestro, chief of the Socialist Parliamentary Brigade, raised military hackles when, in a remarkably bilious outburst, he called the commanding general of that region, Manuel Torres de la Cruz, "seemingly demented" and a "satrap who wanted or wants to convert himself into a kind of Caesar without crown or with the rank of general." The MIR added fuel to the fire by charging that the "reactionary and gorilla officer corps has placed itself in open illegality . . ." Not unexpectedly, Prats rebuked Torres, and warned his generals against excessive zeal in carrying out the arms raids, particularly since they had zeroed in only on the Left. But by then, no one was listening.[102]

Despite the outbursts, the raids continued. On August 30, the air force—which was the most aggressive in staging the raids—hit a MIR guerilla camp near the agricultural city of Temuco, rounding up twenty prisoners and uncovering a grenade factory "with as many as or more explosives" as at the nearby Maquehua air base.[103]

Subsequent accounts would frequently portray the drama of Chile during those dank and dreary days of August as though it had all been some kind of a courtly minuet of debates and verbal duels, a clash of abstractions and philosophical pirouettes. It was, instead, a time of anger and of anxiety, of violence and hardship, a time of hopelessness for many, desperation for nearly all—that dark wood of Dante, except one in which there is no Virgil leading the way to light, only the wild beasts and the darkness. Preserving the fiction of democracy in such a setting did not—could not—command so high a priority as preserving the nation state itself. Chile had been plunged into that abyss too familiar to the so-called Third World, one in which the struggle for life itself eclipses the rest of that trilogy: life, liberty, and the pursuit of happiness—a proposition incorrigibly elusive even for the fortunate inhabitants of those advanced countries such as the United States and Western Europe in which the accent is almost entirely on pursuit of happiness.

The legal system was in a tatters. Violence prowled the land. So, too, did labor strife. As the truck strike ground on, shortages multiplied, as did the violence linked to it. By August 17, the government described the strike's consequences as "catastrophic," claiming that the strike was responsible for loss of half the winter's green vegetable crop and half the country's milk output, and that planting was impossible in several provinces because of lack of seed deliveries. But by August 17, the truckers were not alone: on August 2, the owners of more than 110,000 buses and taxis went on strike; on August 16, 440,000 shopkeepers shuttered their stores, and they would later be joined by 3,000 striking doctors, 90,000 white collar workers, airline pilots, teachers; all told, by the first week of September, more than 1 million Chileans were on strike, united in a single purpose: Allende had to go.[104]

During an unprecedented visit to Castro's Cuba of the Chilean navy's training four-master, the *Esmeralda*, the chief of the Cuban secret police asked a Chilean official about the loyalty of the enlisted men. Told they were of modest birth, Manuel Piñeiro said the sailors would then represent no threat. How about the officers, he asked. "Petty bourgeoisie," came the reply. "For them," Piñeiro said, "you will have to install a political commisar." A bystander reportedly modified Piñeiro's remark: "For them, an executioner."

Apocryphal or no, what is beyond dispute is that by 1973, the hard Left openly, and the "sophisticated" Left more subtly, were both moving to infiltrate the armed services and drive a wedge between officers and enlisted men. By the end, not only were such appeals to mutiny appearing in pamphlets and occasional street demonstrations, they were also appearing in the radical press ("Soldiers: Disobey Your Officers," screamed one such headline in a left-wing magazine).[105]

Thus, it was not surprising that early in July 1973, officers at the Talcahuano naval base near Concepción should report to naval intelligence that they had detected the existence of political cells. The subsequent investigation exploded plans for a mutiny aboard two Valparaíso-based ships, the cruiser *Almirante Latorre* and the destroyer *Blanco Encalada*. The plan: seize and murder senior officers, set sail, and bombard the navy base. If successful, it would later be claimed that the plotters had quashed a right-wing conspiracy (by the now departed officers), and Allende would then be urged to close Congress and seize total power.[106]

The plot was denounced August 7. Four hundred sailors were rounded up for questioning, twenty-three held. Three weeks later, the navy said several of the plotters had fingered Miguel Enríquez, head of the MIR, Oscar Garretón, former under secretary of economy and head of the radical wing of MAPU, and Socialist party chief Carlos Altamirano, as the brains behind the plot. On August 30, Vice Adm. José Toribio Merino Castro, commandant of the First Naval District, asked the Court of Appeals in Valparaíso to strip Garretón and Altamirano of their parliamentary immunity so that all three could stand trial.

Before the brouhaha ended, at least one source would implicate Allende himself in the plotting, and the executive committee of the Popular Unity would accuse the navy of torturing the imprisoned marines. (Allende quickly disassociated himself from that charge, saying, on September 6, that it was "very harmful.")

Altamirano left no doubt as to his role. In a defiant speech on September 9, Altamirano admitted that he had met with the plotters at their invitation, but that it was to hear their charges of subversion against officers.

Army Commander-in-Chief Prats would leave no doubt, either, as to where he stood. In a diary notation commenting on the plot, he speculated that Altamirano and Garretón had perhaps been the victims of a clever ruse staged by naval intelligence or other anti-Allende forces. Prats' main concern was not with the possibility that the far Left might actually be doing exactly what they had been saying right along they intended to do—namely subvert the armed forces—but rather that the episode would be exploited to discredit Montero, the only other major service chief still committed to Allende.[107]

In the end—as in other decisive moments in Chile's history—it was not so much illicit arms and sinister plots but Chilean women who provided the powder of revolution. By August of 1983, the cupboards of Chile were bare, the country facing not economic crisis, but chaos. Bread was rationed, but there was little to be had at any price, and Allende himself said that there was, at the end, flour for only three or four days. The Central Bank had in its vaults a paltry 3 million dollars, barely enough to pay for two days' worth of food imports. Inflation had rocketed to an official 323 percent, but it was really zooming above a mind-boggling 500 percent. The Chilean escudo, quoted at twelve to the dollar when Salvador Allende took his oath as president, was not pegged at forty-six to the dollar officially, but almost no one traded dollars except on the black market, where they fetched 2,800 to three thousand escudos to the dollar. To make matters worse, the Allende government had created a byzantine mish-mash of multiple exchange rates, so that, depending on which one was used, a shirt cost either seventy-five cents—or ninety-five dollars. In such a topsy-turvy world, an empty flour sack cost more than one filled with flour. An egg cost twenty escudos, a hen sixty, or the equivalent of just three eggs, with the inevitable result that there were neither eggs nor hens. The government was shelling out for gasoline subsidies an amount equal to the cost of ten thousand taxis. A pack of cigarettes cost about the same as three movie tickets.[108]

In such a world, strikes were not merely strikes—certainly not for the wives of the strikers. So it was that on August 12, two thousand trucker wives demonstrated in the Plaza Constitución in front of La Moneda. Acting on direct orders from Santiago Mayor Julio Stuardo, Carabineros attacked the women with truncheons, clubs, and teargas. When the same thing happened five days later outside the Congress, many of the women took refuge on the grounds of the building—and would remain there, huddled against the winter cold in the corridors of the building, until the very end.[109]

These events were nails in Allende's coffins. Other demonstrations would entomb him inescapably. The first of them took place late in the afternoon of Saturday, August 18, at the main entrance to La Moneda. Prats was winding up a day-long series of meetings on the crisis provoked by Air Force General Ruiz' resignation as transport minister when he heard loud noises outside. His aide-de-camp, Maj. Roberto Sánchez, told him that around fifty wives of air force officers were demonstrating outside, and suggested that he agree to see a delegation. Prats agreed to receive two of them, professing his shock that these women would interfere so brazenly in service matters and use language such as "Marxist government." Prats assured them—wrongly—that Allende had not dismissed Ruiz but that it was Ruiz who insisted on quitting.[110]

That demonstration was mere dress rehearsal for what would come three days later. On the afternoon of August 21, the wives of three hundred officers, including those of seven general officers, congregated to present a letter of protest; summoned by (then) Interior Minister Orlando Letelier, visiting Prats at the time, Carabineros again used force to disperse the women. Prats viewed the event as an expression of "treason . . . cowardice." Others, principally his fellow generals who the next day voted 12–6 for his resignation, saw it as the last straw in his attempts to make the army an accomplice of a government they considered both lawless and Marxist. Two days later, Prats was out as army chief, Augusto Pinochet in.[111]

And then there was one . . .

That man was Adm. Raúl Montero Cornejo, then rounding out his third year as navy commander-in-chief. More than any of the other service chiefs, he was a Hamlet-like figure. General Ruiz, chief of the air force, remained faithful to his civilian commander-in-chief until he no longer believed that the president was himself honoring the constitution they had both sworn to uphold; General Prats, the army chief, never withdrew his support for Allende, even after he had been ousted (a week after his ouster, he met secretly with Communist party leaders to tell them of army plotting, and a few days before the revolution, he advised Allende to fire five or six generals so as to disrupt the command structure and thus gain more time to block a coup).[112] Admiral Montero, on the other hand, was never able to choose between his sense of loyalty to his branch and his constitutional duty as he saw it to submit to civilian authority. His unwillingness to break with Allende had already cost him first the trust, and then the support of his fellow admirals. His failure to act vigorously in the naval plot episode spurred his colleagues to demand his resignation. He gave it—but, down to the end, Allende maneuvered to keep him on the job, trying as he had in the air force crisis earlier in August to position commanders loyal to him in the services. At one point in those contortions, Montero, Admiral Merino and marine Commandant Sergio Huidobro sailed into a tempestuous postmidnight meeting with a "slightly drunk" Salvador Allende at which he would shout: "What you discovered at Valparaíso is only one tenth of what the Communists and the MIRistas are doing . . . I have declared war on the navy." He then reputedly boasted that the sprawling Tomás Moro estate—where they were meeting—was an "impregnable fortress," to which Huidobro replied dryly: "You should leave matters of security to the experts."[113] Faced with Allende's devious tactics, Merino and the other top navy commanders simply excluded Montero from the planning loop; when revolution came, Montero would, indeed, find himself incommunicado.[114]

There was one other force to be neutralized before it could be brought into the impending revolution: the 26,300-man paramilitary Corps of Carabineros. The top two generals—José María Sepúlveda Galindo and Jorge Urrutia Quintana—were "unconditionally loyal" to Allende, and the third-ranking general, Alfonso Yáñez Retama, thought to be sympathetic to the revolt, was sick in a hospital. (In fact, only seven of sixteen Carabinero generals were considered by the military chiefs to be trustworthy.) Only the day before the revolt would the fourth-ranking general—César Mendoza Durán—be formally brought into the plot and instructed to take command. Given the fact that the Carabineros were under the direct control of the Interior Ministry, to have done so any sooner was thought to be too risky.[115]

Twice in Chilean history, the military had intervened decisively in the political affairs of the nation. The first was in 1891, and in 1891 as in 1973, it was the navy that would take the lead to rescue the country from what it viewed as institutional collapse and chaos. (That bloody revolt included the sinking by forces loyal to the president of the pride and flagship of the fleet, the battleship *Blanco Encalada*—one of history's great ironies, remembering that the plot by noncoms loyal to Allende against their officers, eight decades later, involved a destroyer of the same name, *Blanco Encalada*. The 1891 revolt ended on September 19 with the suicide of José Manuel Balmaceda, a populist president viewed by many as a father-figure of Chilean Socialism, a particular hero for Salvador Allende. In the ugly atmosphere of early September 1973, when hatred ruled reason, Allende would hear taunts that he emulate his hero.)[116] Again, in 1924 and 1925, the armed forces intervened (yet another irony: the 1924 military manifesto ending nearly a century of virtually uninterrupted civilian rule was dated September 11). Those 1924 and 1925 uprisings were staged "against a background of political breakdown and economic chaos. . . ." In each, "a military junta assumed power to clean up the mess. . . ."[117]

The men who would head the new military junta—Pinochet, Merino, Leigh, Mendoza—were now in position, determined to "clean up the mess." Similarities with the past would end there.

In those last, tumultuous weeks, Allende swore in his twenty-eighth and last Cabinet (with four flag officers, but this time only one chief, Carabinero Commandant Sepúlveda); there were half-hearted peace talks, marches, and countermarches; more arms raids, more violence. General Viaux, having served nearly three years in prison for the kidnapping of Army Commandant René Schneider, left the country with something of a hero's send-off; American Ambassador Nathaniel Davis flew off to Washington to see Henry Kissinger and unleash countless conspiratorial post-mortems; the Chilean fleet set sail for a rendezvous with an American task force, while Soviet ships were also sailing in circles; Pablo Rodríguez sneaked back into the country vowing a fight to the finish.[118] None of it really amounted to much more than additional debris in an institutional avalanche no one could any longer stop or even much change.

*   *   *

Until those last days, Chile had come to be divided into two camps: the one that said that Chile's "democracy" must be preserved, meaning that Allende must stay—the institutions, in a word, must survive even as the nation itself perished. The other, and by then much larger mass of Chileans, cried out that the very survival of the country was at stake, and thus that Salvador Allende must go. In both camps, there were those who argued that the outcome must be determined "legally"—though their numbers had dwindled, their voices ever more muted in the din of an undeclared civil war. Now, in those stygian days of September, another force, long smoldering, exploded into the open: the MIR, the MAPU, the Christian Left, elements of Allende's own Socialist party—the hot-heads of the coalition he had never wanted or been able to dominate—met and decided that it was the revolution and not Allende that mattered. Accordingly, they resolved to break with the government and the Central Labor Federation (CUT) and, instead, launch a twin-pronged war strategy: mobilize the combat forces of the industrial belts and intensify efforts to stimulate mutiny within the armed forces. They, too, had no illusions about preserving "democracy"; they were wrong only about their strength, the determination of others to answer the call to arms (as virtually none of the leaders did). For, of the estimated number in the *cordones* available for combat, which ranged all the way up to 100,000, only a few thousand actually took up arms.

The die was cast during teatime Sunday, September 9, 1973, at a birthday party in Pinochet's home for his youngest daughter, Jacqueline Marie. Following his Friday marathon meeting with Allende, Merino drove the 120 kilometers (seventy-five miles) back to Valparaíso, now fully decided to give the order: execute Plan Cochayuyo (Operation Seaweed), the navy's secret plan to seize power, the following Monday. (Carvajal and others, who had been meeting with their army and air force counterparts, persuaded him to push it back a day to give the army time to organize). Merino communicated his decision to senior officers Saturday, then scribbled a fateful sixty-word note on a small piece of paper. It was addressed to Gustavo Leigh, the air force commandant, and army Commander Augusto Pinochet, junior (by three days) as a service chief to Leigh:

Gustavo y Augusto: Bajo mi palabra de honor el Día D será el día 11 y la hora H 0600.

Si Uds. no pueden cumplir esta fase con el total de las fuerzas que mandan en Santiago, explíquemelo al reverso.

El Almirante Huidobro está autorizado para traer y discutir cualquier tema con Uds. Los saludo con esperanzas de comprensión. Merino.

On the back, he added a dramatic postscript:

> Gustavo: es la última oportunidad. J.T.
> Augusto: si no puede toda la fuerza del primer momento, no
> viveremos para el futuro. Pepe.*

Admiral Huidobro stuffed the note in a sock for safekeeping and, accompanied by Capt. Ariel González, set out early Sunday afternoon for Santiago. Arriving at Pinochet's house, they found Pinochet and Leigh huddled in his study. Pinochet would later write that he had already given the order to the army to strike on September 14, and since the army—unlike the navy—was spread out from one end of the country to another, it was difficult to mobilize units in secret, particularly absent a pretext for doing so. Moving too quickly, without time to check loyalties up and down the chain of command, created another risk: "It would have been enough," Pinochet wrote, "that a single garrison refuse to obey to run the risk of polarizing the armed forces, plunging us into a fratricidal war." He was, therefore, reluctant to sign, deciding finally to do so out of belief that it would have been "suicide" for the navy to go it alone—and the navy, clearly, was determined to strike with or without the army. Spurning a preferred fountain pen, he took out his own and, on the back of Merino's note signed, as did Leigh, beneath a single word: "Conforme" (In agreement).[119]

Among those returning to Santiago that Sunday were Ambassador Davis, back from his hurried meeting in Washington where Henry Kissinger offered him a promotion, and Hortensia Bussi de Allende, back from a five-day visit to Mexico at the head of a Chilean delegation taking relief supplies to that nation after an earthquake. Davis's ultimate departure from Chile would be delayed by the events racing to an unseen climax all around him; Mrs. Allende would be back in Mexico far sooner than she might ever have imagined because of the same gathering storm.

There is one other event of that Sunday which requires further mention: Carlos Altamirano's fiery Estadio Chile (Chile Stadium) speech that afternoon. Reporting on the results of the just concluded meeting of the Plenum of the Socialist party's Central Committee, Altamirano

---

* "On my word of honor, D-Day is the 11th and H-Hour 6: A.M.

"If you cannot take part in this phase with all of the forces you command in Santiago, explain on the other side.

"Admiral Huidobro is authorized to bring up and discuss any topic with you.

"I greet you in the hope of understanding."

The postscript:

"Gustavo: This is the last chance. J.T. [for José Toribio]

"Augusto: If you can't [commit] full force from the outset, we will not live [to see] the future. Pepe."

put Salvador Allende on notice: the party did not and would not accept dialogue: "The Right can only be crushed by the invincible strength of the people, enlisted men, noncommissioned officers, and officers united to the constituted government . . ." Inasmuch as "dialogue" had been limited to the Christian Democrats—and not the Socialists' archenemies of the authentic Right—it was clear that the party was ruling out political accommodation of any kind. Indeed, Altamirano stopped just short of calling for the government itself to stage a coup, though he left little doubt that this was his meaning. "Let all know," he said, "that the United States is behind this conspiracy, stoking the flames of civil war, of counter-revolution, getting Brazil and Bolivia mixed up [in the plot]." In those circumstances, he told his shouting, bellicose audience, the Socialist party would support Allende only if he aligned himself squarely with "Popular Power," the code words for the arming and deploying of a parallel force of hard-line radicals. "Transformations," he said, "can only be carried out if the people take power . . . We serve notice that we will not accept arbitrary demands, from whatever source, armed or not armed. We will not submit to an illegitimate power. Chile will be converted into a new heroic Vietnam if the reaction tries to lord it over this country." He made it plain that he included Congress as well as the armed forces in referring to "illegitimate power." Of equal import: Altamirano not only acknowledged meeting with the navy plotters, but warned also of "revolutionary violence" should the appeals court lift his parliamentary immunity and that of Garretón at its scheduled hearing Tuesday. That warning gave Pinochet the pretext he needed to confine the Santiago and Valparaíso garrisons to quarters.[120]

Listening to the radio at home, Allende said:

"That madman is sabotaging me!"[121]

Notes

CHAPTER 7

1. Régis Debray, *The Chilean Revolution: Conversations With Allende* (New York: Vintage Books, Random House, 1971) p. 123.
2. The resignation quote is from *Latin America*, April 27, 1973, vol. 3, no. 17, p. 133; the morality quote from *Ercilla*, January 24, 1973, no. 1958, p. 8. Both are cited in Henry A. Landsberger and Tim McDaniel, "Mobilization As a Double-Edged Sword: The Allende Government's Uneasy Relationship With Labor, 1970–1973," July 1974, in *United States and Chile During the Allende Years, 1970–1973*, Report of the Subcommittee on Inter-American Affairs of the Committee on Foreign Affairs, U.S. House of Representatives, based on Hearings in 1971, 1972, 1973, 1974 (Washington, D.C.: U.S. GPO, 1974), pp. 624–625.
3. Genaro Arriagada Herrera, *De La 'Vía Chilena' a la 'Vía Insurreccional,'* (Santiago: Editorial del Pacífico, S.A., 1974), p. 222. Arriagada was one of the leading literary lights of the Christian Democrats—indeed, this book begins with a prologue by Eduardo Frei—and so was privy to the behind-the-scenes details of this crucial combat for control of the unions. In his book, he provides an abundance of detail (pp. 221–224) of the failed machinations to perpetuate government forces in undisputed control of the CUT. He also asserts (p. 220) that, far from demonstrating a newly awakened sense of proletarian power, the proliferation of strikes "seriously hampered" Allende's plans.
4. In the balloting on February 10, the opposition (mainly the Christian Democrats) won 7 of 10 seats on the union board, prompting the regional CUT secretary-general to brand the event as an "historic" defeat for his forces. Chuquicamata's 1972 losses—the first full year of government control—were put at $5 million by Christian Democrat Senator Juan de Dios Carmona, in a January 23 statement. *Breve Historia de la Unidad Popular* (Santiago: Editorial Lord Cochrane, S.A., 1974), Teresa Donoso L., ed., a chronology of key dates and events during the Allende years, 1970–1973, taken from the pages of *El Mercurio* and compiled by that newspaper, pp. 294, 286. The reference to government losses in non-CUT unions is in Landsberger and McDaniel, in *United States and Chile*, op. cit., p. 627. The assertion, which they remark "remains to be substantiated," appears in *Ercilla*. They also cite (p. 624) several examples of Allende's criticism of mineworkers. When Chuqui workers struck for a 70 percent wage increase a few weeks after his election, Allende denounced them as "a labor aristocracy." A year later, they report, during a visit to Chuqui, Allende "complained bitterly" of losses caused by unauthorized strikes. As an example of what he branded as "stealing," Allende said mineworkers demanded "60 days' wages for a job that took 20 days, left 30 minutes early at the end of a shift and arrived 15 minutes late."

5. Ibid., p. 620.

6. *Breve Historia*, op. cit., p. 227.

7. Data on the October strike: Origins of the strike, *Breve Historia*, op. cit., p. 230; number of strikers, ibid., p. 240; cost of the strike and other data, Prof. Paul E. Sigmund, "Allende in Retrospect," *United States and Chile*, op. cit., p. 605; Allende's threat to deport strikers, in Emilio Filippi and Hernán Millas, *Anatomía de un Fracaso (La Experiencia Socialista Chilena)* (Santiago: Empresa Editora Zig-Zag, 1973), p. 101; González Videla quote, *Breve Historia*, op. cit., p. 239.

8. The "flogged" quotation is from Patricio Dooner, *Periodismo y Política: La Prensa de Derecha en Chile, 1970–1973* (Santiago: Instituto Chileno de Estudios Humanísticos, no publication date). The book is a mainly hostile look at the performance of the conservative press during the Allende years: three frankly right-wing publications (the National party's newspaper, *Tribuna*, the newsmagazines, *PEC* and *SEPA*, and the "serious" press, *El Mercurio*. Dooner put the quotation marks around the adjective describing Chile's leading newspaper). On April 25, 1973, U.S. Ambassador Davis presented Prats with a diploma honoring him as a member of the Command and General Staff School's Hall of Honor for foreign officers who go on to top command of their home armies.

9. Nathaniel Davis, *The Last Two Years of Salvador Allende* (Ithaca: Cornell University Press, 1985), p. 115. Davis makes plain and explicit his great admiration for Prats throughout his book, covering the two years he served as American ambassador in Santiago.

10. The Algeria and "spiritual home" quotes are in Henry Kissinger, *Years of Upheaval* (Boston: Little Brown and Company, 1982), pp. 395–396. The balance is from *Breve Historia*, op. cit., pp. 264, 268–269. It was not, of course, "bread" which Castro would take from his people to give to Chileans, but sugar—40,000 tons of it. Despite the size of Cuban sugar output, even that staple was then rationed in Cuba, which meant that Castro's largess came at the expense of further hardship for Cubans. The loan comparison is from Joaquín Fermandois, *Chile y El Mundo 1970–1973; La Politica Exterior del Gobierno de la Unidad Popular y el Sistema Internacional* (Santiago: Ediciones Universidad Católica de Chile, 1985), pp. 440–441. (Hereafter *Chile y El Mundo*.) Fermandois, a professor of contemporary history at the Catholic University of Chile and the Catholic University of Valparaíso, has authored a volume of extraordinary documentation and painstakingly careful research.

11. *U.S. and Chile*, op. cit., pp. 386–387.

12. *Breve Historia*, op. cit., p. 270. Ambassador Davis makes no secret, by contrast, of his great admiration for General Prats, remarking to him at one point, for example, "If and when political progressives govern Chile again, Prats will be remembered." Nathaniel Davis, op. cit., p. 371.

13. *Breve Historia*, op. cit., pp. 278–279. As noted earlier, this publication was compiled by the editors of *El Mercurio* from the pages of the newspaper itself. *El Mercurio*, Chile's oldest and most influential newspaper, was in frank opposition to Allende throughout his career—and his government frankly hostile to the newspaper. In a letter-to-the-editor published by *El Mercurio* commenting on its handling of Flores's January 10 announcement, Allende described the newspaper's reporting as "lies," and took specific aim at the characterization of the principal measures Flores announced as "rationing" (though many other publications had used—and would con-

tinue to use—the same term). *El Mercurio* fired back with a quotation from the leftist magazine *Chile Hoy:* "The problem of rationing, of facing up to the need to fix quotas of consumption and not permit the market to operate freely, was a necessity which, three or four months ago, was politically discordant; it seemed then to be a policy for extremists. Today, no." The author of that statement: Fernando Flores. This exchange is found on pages 281–282. As early as January 5, 1973, Carlos Castillo, president of the Retail Commerce Purchasing Agency (CENADI, for *Central de Compras de Comercio Detallista*), said the government's distribution system already controlled 70 percent to 80 percent of all consumer goods. *Breve Historia*, op. cit., p. 277. Although official ration cards were never issued, Moss reported that on a visit to the vast (and violence-wracked) Lo Hermida shantytown, local commisars required inhabitants to produce their electoral registration cards as well as their identity cards in order to receive foodstuffs, and that some local JAPs had even begun to issue their own rationing cards. He also reported, as an example of lawlessness, the seizure of Agencias Graham, one of four state-operated distribution companies, by armed MIRistas. Since the takeover occurred only ten days before the March 1973 parliamentary elections, Allende declined to move against them, fearing an armed confrontation. Moss, *Chile's Marxist Experiment* (New York, Toronto: John Wiley & Sons, A Halstead Book, 1973), pp. 182–183, 173–174. Although military control was tenuous to begin with (Bachelet's staff consisted of only three army colonels and a naval captain), even that was not enough for the Allendistas. On June 7, 1973, Allende proposed legislation to create a new agency to replace Bachelet's Secretariat, on the grounds that the Secretariat's role was only "advisory." Allende gave his proposal an "urgent" label, which theoretically required that Congress act within thirty days or it would automatically become law, and said that if approved, he would name military men to the new agency—but it was still in hot dispute when he fell. *Breve Historia*, op. cit., p. 352.

14. Ibid., pp. 280 and 282.
15. Military men would remain in the Cabinet until after the March congressional elections, leaving on March 27. Ambassador Davis reports that they left only when Allende failed to meet a fourteen-point list of demands, including disarming of the paramilitary groups; promulgation of the nationalization amendments; efforts to improve relations with the United States; and more orderly public administration. Davis adds that "Altamirano and his left-wing Socialists regarded the officers' departure as a victory." Davis, op. cit., p. 146. Huerta, who had resigned already, would later lead the fight against government takeover of the educational system, and would still later become first foreign minister in the junta government.
16. Merino told me of his decision to begin work in January 1973 on an economic blueprint for the post-Allende future during an interview in Santiago, June 9, 1987. After the September 1973 revolution, Merino would, as junta member responsible for the economy, install many of those young technocrats in positions of power in the new government. As we shall see in chapter 8, this braintrust—known as "the Chicago boys," because so many of them had studied under or become disciples of free-marketer Professor Arnold C. Harberger and later also of Nobel Laureate Milton Friedman (who taught at the University of Chicago 1946–1982), would guide Chile out of economic prostration into perhaps the greatest period of economic prosper-

ity in the country's history. Details of Pinochet's plotting/planning—as well as of Merino's—are contained in my book, *Allende: Death of a Marxist Dream* (Westport, Ct., Arlington House, 1981), pp. 14–15, 56–58.

17. Martner made the statement on September 20, 1982. *Breve Historia*, op. cit., p. 220.

18. Robert Moss, op. cit., p. 66. Moss dates formation of the JAP from early 1972; I have taken the earlier date from Arriagada, op. cit., p. 204. Arriagada also says that by mid-1972, of 988 in the country, 675 were located in Santiago.

19. Augusto Pinochet Ugarte, *El Día Decisivo: 11 de Septiembre de 1973* (Santiago: Editorial Andrés Bello, 1973), 4th edition, pp. 57–58. Wrote Pinochet: "From the window of my office, I saw long lines of men and women with slogans spewing hatred. At headquarters of the [Santiago] garrison, we pinpointed on maps the locations of the new slums created by squatters and the jobless who, guided by Marxist leaders, were building a noose around Santiago which grew by the day . . ." These shantytowns, together with nationalized factories, made up the *cordones*, the bastions of hidden arms and paramilitary training.

20. *Breve Historia*, op. cit., pp. 282 and 287. The communique was issued on January 16, the Enríquez harangue took place on January 24.

21. Frei quotes the key points made at the Plenum and his comments on them in his "Prologue" in Arriagada, op. cit., p. 24.

22. Ibid., p. 293.

23. Data on the Socialist-Communist-MIR feuding from *Breve Historia*, op. cit., pp. 287–289, 292.

24. In her interview with *Epoca*, published January 10, 1988, and translated and re-published in *El Mercurio*, "Revelaciones de la Secretaria de S. Allende," January 14, 1988, pp. 1 and A8; *La Payita* recalled: "Discord reigned even in the government coalition. When Luis Corvalán, secretary general of the Communist party, and Carlos Altamirano, his colleague in the Socialist party, met with the president, they spoke solely through the president as intermediary: 'President, point out to Mr. Altamirano . . .' Allende, none-theless, had enormous confidence in himself and in his ability as a mediator. Though the situation did in fact worsen, he continued believing that he was in a position to overcome all crises . . ."

25. Former Communist Eudocio Ravines, for example, wrote: "Salvador Allende was not a Marxist, but a political opportunist, byzantine and garru-lous, of the sort which abounds within the leftist confines of Latin America. In the entire floodtide of his speeches, it is not possible to winnow out a single theoretical concept, a single philosophical direction. In the entirety of the farrago of his superficial verbosity, it is not possible to find a single original idea on the Chilean political process . . . Not even the most devoted of his partisans can cite a thought endowed with acuity or depth." Ravines's own bombast notwithstanding, the judgment he expressed was not only widely shared, but the passage also reflects a larger reality: the contempt of Chile's Moscow-lining Communists (and ex-Communists), with their bag-gage of structured, disciplined ideology, for the rag-tag style and intellectual disarray of the Chilean Socialists. Eudocio Ravines, *El Rescate de Chile* (Santiago: Empresa Editora e Impresora Edimpres Ltda., 1974), p. 127.

26. The Garcés article, entitled "Vía Insurreccional y Vía Política: Dos Tác-ticas," appeared in the magazine of the State Technical University, May-June 1973, #13–14, pp. 21–22, and is cited frequently by Arriagada, op. cit. The quotation used here appears on p. 98. Arriagada discusses this duality of

reasoning by Garcés and others close to Allende on pp. 281–289. Further background on Garcés is taken from my book, op. cit., pp. 42–43. The prescient June quote is from Davis, op. cit., p. 157.

27. Chronology, in *United States and Chile*, op. cit., p. 387. Allende was actually the thirty-first person to serve as president of Chile (including dictators) since Bernardo O'Higgins (himself a dictator) joined the Argentine-born José San Martin in liberating the country from Spanish rule.

28. Robert Moss, "Chile's Coup and After," in *Encounter* magazine, March 1974, as reproduced in *Chile: The Balanced View*, op. cit., p. 52.

29. The Allende quote is from *Breve Historia*, op. cit., p. 285. Statistics on Cuba are absent from such common reference sources as the World Bank's *World Tables*, and the International Monetary Fund's *International Financial Statistics*—placing Cuba in the company of such states as other Soviet-bloc countries, Chad, Mongolia, Iran.

30. On June 28, 1973, Christian Democrat Senator Juan de Dios Carmona said a contract with the Soviet firm Tsvetmetpromexport required that thirty-six Russian mining advisors and ten "interpreters" get thirty-day paid holidays, with their roundtrip air fares to the Soviet Union also paid by the Chilean government. The advisors were paid $844 monthly—in dollars—the interpreters $470, at a time when the legal limit for public employees in Chile was the equivalent of $30 monthly. When they first arrived, Allende boasted that their services would cost Chile nothing—see note 83, chapter 6. In a separate, August 28 report to Congress, the Comptroller General said 564 foreigners were officially on the public payroll, though it was later learned that the actual number was much higher. *Breve Historia*, op. cit., pp. 368, 409. The "pragmatism" of the Russians—and hypocrisy of the Allende regime—are particularly notable in light of the UP's electoral program, which included a section: "The First Forty Measures of Popular Government." Number Three promised "administrative honesty" ("no more favoritism," etc.), while Campaign Pledge Six was even more to the point: "The Public Treasury will not Manufacture New Rich People: We shall establish rigorous control of the salaries and perquisites of high public officials. The government will no longer serve as a factory [turning out] new rich people." Alain Labrousse, *El Experimento Chileno: Reformismo o Revolución?* (*L'Experience Chilienne* in the original French) (Barcelona, Mexico: Ediciones Grijalbo, S.A., 1973) pp. 474–475. But then, those same "First Forty" also promised "no more fatuous trips abroad" (#4) and "no more government automobiles for private purposes" (#5). Allende spent more time abroad in his three years than any Chilean president in history in a full, six-year term; his wife, Hortensia, was also a "fatuous" traveler; as for automobiles, Chile had never witnessed such wholesale diversion of public vehicles for private purposes, sinister (the GAP, with their Fiat 125s) and for profit (as we shall see shortly).

31. *Breve Historia*, op. cit., pp. 156–157, and Emilio Filippi and Hernán Millas, "Los Bultos Cubanos," op. cit., pp. 101–105. On March 17, the Senate asked the Supreme Court to appoint a judge to investigate, while the Chamber of Deputies opened its own investigation. On June 25, Congress completed action to impeach Interior Minister del Canto "as a common criminal" for his role in facilitating that "legal smuggling," and for his failure to carry out repeated court orders to arrest those involved in illegal *tomas* (takeovers) of farms and factories, thus failing to protect property and human rights. It was del Canto's second time in the dock: on January 26, he was adjudged

outside the law for ordering the illegal national radio hook-up during the October strike.

32. Details on Paredes in Manuel Trucco, "Foreign Armed Intervention in Chile," in *Chile: The Balanced View,* op. cit., pp. 90–91. Trucco was Chilean ambassador to the Organization of American States (OAS) at the time, and this article is taken from remarks he made on October 23, 1974, before that body. It is rich in specifics of arms shipments and foreign legionnaires who swarmed into Chile during the Allende years. Paredes was killed during the fighting on September 11, 1973.

33. Ibid., pp. 102–104. In making this statement, Trucco noted that on December 3, 1963, Venezuela had denounced before the OAS the discovery of several tons of arms and munitions smuggled ashore and subsequently traced to Cuba, intended for Communist guerrillas then operating in the country. As a result of Venezuela's complaint, the OAS would investigate and later vote severe sanctions against Cuba. Trucco asked that in light of Chile's complaint, those sanctions, then about to be lifted, be continued in force. But 1974 was not 1963, and the Chile of 1974 was under right-wing military rule while the Venezuela of 1963 was under a leftist democratic government—and so the OAS declined to take even symbolic action against Castro—even though the magnitudes in the Chilean case were much greater than those in the Venezuelan one. But, by 1974, the sanctions had been so ignored as to be meaningless. The case is worth remarking, nonetheless, because nonintervention is supposed to be one of the two sacred pillars of the hemispheric concordat (self-determination is the other), and a breach of either is supposed to trigger automatic outrage and action. As with so many "sacred" principles in international affairs, there is a good deal of moral elasticity involved; it really depends upon who is doing the intervening, and against whom, and what the particular "moral" climate happens to be when the intervening takes place.

34. Lautaro Silva, in *Allende: El Fin de una Aventura* (Santiago: Ediciones Patria Nueva, 1974), p. 322.

35. *Chile: The Balanced View,* op. cit., pp. 94–95, and *Anatomía de un Fracaso,* op. cit., p. 105.

36. *Anatomía de un Fracaso* op. cit., p. 146. Mention of foreign military instructors is in Moss, op. cit., p. 101. MADECO had been expropriated on September 17, 1971, ostensibly because of "internal problems."

37. *Breve Historia.* op. cit., pp. 237–238. Known as the "Carmona Law" (for its sponsor, Christian Democrat Senator Juan de Dios Carmona), it would become the most powerful weapon available in preventing the far Left from achieving its goal of arming and training a clandestine paramilitary force capable of forcing the military either to capitulate or fight what would have been a grim and bloody civil war. The left-wing Uruguayan writer Rama says that the law hit the books because of a technical error on the part of Allende, and "that it would be passed, promulgated and applied during the government of Allende is one of the gravest contradictions of the popular regime." Carlos M. Rama, *Chile: Mil Días Entre la Revolución y el Fascismo* (Barcelona: Editorial Planeta, S.A., 1974), p. 164. As effective as the law was, after the coup, a Communist leader would boast that "the generals discovered a small part of the arms we had." That unnamed leader, in an interview with the Italian newspaper *La Stampa,* published on October 26, 1973, said arms were not the problem: "Unfortunately, there were too few

who knew how to use them, because we had not had sufficient time to train the popular masses." Cited in Arriagada, op. cit., p. 25.

38. Joaquín Fermandois, op. cit., p. 91.

39. Henry Kissinger, *The White House Years* (Boston: Little Brown & Co., 1979), p. 664, and a presentation made by Ambassador Edward Korry at a symposium on Chile sponsored by Georgetown University's Center for Strategic and International Studies, August 15, 1974, as reproduced in *United States and Chile During the Allende Years, 1970–1973*, report on Hearings of the Subcommittee on Inter-American Affairs of the Committee on Foreign Affairs of the U.S. House of Representatives (Washington: U.S. Government Printing Office, 1975), pp. 640–641. (Hereafter *United States and Chile*.)

40. Pinochet, op. cit., p. 82.

41. Source for $300 million in credits, James A. Theberge, "Kremlin's Hand in Allende's Chile," in *The Soviet Analyst*, August 15, 1974, as reproduced in *United States and Chile*, op. cit., p. 635; for the terms, Pinochet, op. cit., p. 91.

42. Fermandois, op. cit., p. 91. Fermandois cites Prats' earlier diary, *Una Vida por la Legalidad* (Mexico: Fondo de Cultura Económica, 1976), p. 32. In the later memoirs, Prats tells of a conversation he had on June 7, 1973, with the Communist chieftains of the Central Workers' Federation, in which he told them that indispensable to solving Chile's problems was "arriving at a decorous understanding with the United States which heads off the suffocation of our foreign trade because the root of our economic ills is in that strangulation and in the collapse of internal production." Carlos Prats González, *Memorias: Testimonio de un Soldado* (Santiago: Editorial Antártica, 1985), 2nd edition, p. 398. The context makes it plain that Prats believed the United States was doing the strangling. If Prats harbored strong anxieties about the place of the Soviet Union as a menace to world peace or freedom, he does not evidence it in those memoirs. Rather, he discusses the U.S. and the USSR as opposing forces in a titanic struggle for supremacy. Unless otherwise indicated, Prats citations are taken from *Memorias*.

43. Pinochet, op. cit., p. 91. Writes Pinochet: "I managed to place officers opposed to making arms purchases in Russia as advisors [to Prats]. It [the Soviet offer] was an attractive but very dangerous proposition, since it would leave us tied to the Soviets, to their training instructors [who would teach not only how to operate the new equipment but also, Marxist-Leninist doctrine], to their parts and replacement chain, very 'plugged in' to any reactions of ours, as we knew had already happened in other countries . . ." Pinochet did not name the officers he "planted," but Prats did (p. 385), and apparently Pinochet was correct, for among them were two generals who were closest to Pinochet in plotting the September revolution: Oscar Bonilla and Raúl Benavides.

44. Prats, op. cit., p. 386. He said Haig let him in on the news minutes before he was to become White House staff chief.

45. Prats, *Memorias*, op. cit., pp. 388–390 (details of his Soviet visit) and Fermandois, op cit. (the Edwards and following quotations). Fermandois is right about Prats' "caressing" the idea of an arms deal with the Soviets. In *Memorias*, op. cit., p. 436, Prats records that on July 12, he was visited by the "affable" Ambassador Basov of the USSR. "We talked about some of the details underway on the logistical support agreement which I had worked out during my stay in that country [the Soviet Union]." Pinochet wrote that

Prats told the top army commanders of his Soviet purchases after his return—but only in response to a question from one of them. Pinochet adds that during the month of June, Prats was pressured constantly by Allende, Defense Minister José Tohá, and the Russian ambassador on the arms deal. He says that on June 20, Prats told him that the Soviet ambassador had complained that the purchases were strictly of logistical supplies and so limited in size; "The Soviet ambassador," Pinochet adds, "had reached the extreme of raising his voice and getting obstreperous [*violentarse*]." Pinochet, op. cit., p. 96. Two footnotes accompany Prats' travels, which stretched from May 2 to June 5, a time of mounting political strife and street violence in Chile (and a time Pinochet took advantage of, again as acting army commander, to advance his revolutionary contingency planning). At his audience with Pope Paul VI, Prats said the pontiff told him that, shortly after his inauguration, Allende had sent him a message promising that he "would not touch the Church, not even with the petal of a rose" (pp. 391–392). The other: back in Chile, Prats professed surprise (p. 395) at the storm of press criticism his trip had provoked, inasmuch as the other two service chiefs had visited the Soviet Union without any such criticism. That overlooked the fact, of course, that alone among them, Prats had agreed to serve Allende both as a cabinet member and constant confidante and advisor (not to mention the length and timing of his foreign travels).

46. Davis, op. cit., p. 371.

47. Kissinger, *Years of Upheaval,* op. cit., p. 680.

48. Prats, op. cit., pp. 397–493. Prats reports that, back in Chile, he learned of grave incidents while away, including clashes between "militants of the extreme Left" and Patria y Libertad, and that arms had been seized in raids on property of "the fascist groups." He reserves no such pejorative for the "elements of the extreme Left." To the contrary: describing a later meeting, on July 8, with Miguel Enríquez, leader of the Movement of the Revolutionary Left (MIR)—an organization with a record of murder, mayhem and rampant terrorism stretching back over five years—Prats says: "Although the enemies of the MIR regarded Enríquez as a satanic figure, I had long experience in dealing with people, and while true that I was in radical disagreement with the thought and methods of the MIR, I was still able to recognize that its leader was a young man of talent and sincerely convinced as to the justice of his cause—[however] mistaken in my judgment," (ibid.,p. 433).

49. Prats, then serving as interior minister, produced a report on electoral violence covering only the first weeks of campaigning, January 6–31, 1973: 449 arrests for putting up illegal electoral posters (241 Popular Unity persons, 208 opposition); 15 for carrying firearms (6 UP, 9 opposition); 30 violent attacks on party locales (12 on UP locales, 18 opposition); 3 deaths (one Communist, one member of the conservative National party, and one member of the right-wing Patria y Libertad); 5 serious injuries (2 Nationals, 2 Radicals, 1 Socialist); 4 less seriously injured (1 Socialist, 1 Christian Democrat, 2 persons without party affiliation); 41 light injuries (8 UP persons, 31 opposition, 2 unaffiliated). Cited in Prats, *Memorias,* op. cit., pp. 359–360.

50. The debate centered on the government's claim that between registration for the April 1971 municipal elections and for the March 1973 parliamentary elections, the number registered to vote had increased from 3.76 million to 4.51 million, a net increase of 750,000. To achieve that, there would

have had to be registration of 880,000 new voters, most of them in the 18–21 age group, because of the offsetting loss of voters in the same period (through death, mainly). In the face of widespread charges of fraud, the Law School at the Catholic University resolved to appoint an independent investigative panel, made up of three faculty members. Their report, released in July, concluded that a maximum of 570,000 new voters could have registered—or a quarter of a million fewer than the government claimed. There is a detailed discussion of this in Lautaro Silva, op. cit., pp. 195–210. The report itself appears in *Libro Blanco del Cambio de Gobierno en Chile; 11 de Septiembre de 1973* (Santiago: Editorial Lord Cochrane, no date), pp. 220–230; the 250,000 figure appears on p. 223. As a sidelight, Silva observes that in those polling places operating before 1970, CODE rolled up a 62–38 percent advantage over the UP—more or less the percentages forecast in preelection surveys. In the new polling places—those set up under UP auspices—the government managed to break about even with CODE. There was violence as well as an atmosphere of fraud about those elections: On January 17, Christian Democrat candidate Arturo Frei Bolívar escaped unhurt when his car was sprayed with nine bullets; a month later, he wasn't so lucky—a bullet pierced his brain. On February 17, another opposition candidate was wounded in Talca, and that same day an eighteen-year-old youth was shot and killed while painting opposition slogans on a wall. All told, political violence claimed five lives during the campaign.

51. CODE was formed in the spring of 1972, and made up of the Christian Democrats (PDC), Nationalists (PN), Democratic National party (PADENA), Radical Left (PIR) and Radical Democrats (PDR). "Who won" was largely a matter of which election one chose to compare with the 1973 voting: the one the opposition chose, 1971, in which case Allende's total had dropped sharply, or the one the Allendistas chose, 1970, in which case the UP total was up sharply. As we have seen, both comparisons are entirely spurious.

52. For those who would argue—and not without reason—that what Chile got instead was the legalized lynching of its democracy, this would, of course, be true—but only so long as "democracy" were understood to mean the determined efforts of a minority to impose its will and way of life on a majority, with or without benefit of law. That was the tragedy of Chile in 1973, and, to the extent that the non-Marxist majority finds itself unable to unite long enough to achieve power legally and construct a new framework for democracy, it remains the tragedy of Chile in 1987. Kissinger (*Years of Upheaval*, op. cit., pp. 376–377, 382, 395, 403), in explaining the unanimous decision of the Forty Committee to provide covert support to Chile's democratic parties (virtually all of it to Christian Democrats) and independent press, wrote: "Many developing countries provide a fertile ground for the network of political parties, front groups, pseudo-press agencies and so-called research institutes by which Communist and radical forces seek to dominate. Small, disciplined groups can have a disproportionate impact... our support for democratic forces in Chile was conceived as being justified only by special circumstances because important interests were truly engaged and all else had failed. The Soviet Union had no doubts that international issues were involved..." He notes that the two Democratic administrations preceding Nixon's had arrived at similar conclusions in shaping their decisions to pour (much larger) sums of covert support to essentially the same beneficiaries in Chile.

53. Arriagada Herrera argues (op. cit., pp. 258–261) that the opposition was playing with a stacked deck even going into the election. Since 1947, Chilean electoral law prohibited electoral pacts in congressional elections (though not in presidential elections). Once in power, and looking to the 1973 elections, the UP agitated for a change in the electoral law to permit blocs. Since both sides were confident, overconfident, really, that they could turn such an arrangement to their advantage, legislation to permit bloc voting—cosponsored by a Nationalist, a Communist, a Radical, and a Socialist!—was passed by the Senate in mid-1972. The risks were great: for the opposition to achieve its two-thirds majority in both houses, it needed to capture between 67 percent and 70 percent of the total vote. On the other hand, if the UP were to win in 1973 by the same one-tenths of 1 percent edge as it had in the municipal elections of 1971, under Chile's complex proportional representation formula, it would have won a commanding eighteen-seat majority in the Chamber. A one-vote edge—coupled with the corresponding one or two vote margin the same outcome would have given them in the Senate—would have presented them with the power, and the moral authority, to overhaul Chile's political system and way of life irrevocably. But 1972 was not 1971, and Allende, reneging on his earlier agreement, vetoed the bill on July 14, 1972, apparently gambling that if he could not yet get his way in Congress, at least he could prevent the opposition from amassing the two-thirds majority it needed in the Senate to impeach him. Next, in a curious twist, the Elections Tribunal, controlled by the UP but which included conservatives, ruled that whereas the parties could not present their own slates of candidates within an overall alliance (as provided in the vetoed legislation), there was nothing to prevent them from "merging" or "federating" with other parties. The effect: for the first time in Chile's modern history, voters had to choose between only two "parties": Unidad Popular and the Democratic Federation. (Parties making up each coalition decided among themselves which would contest each seat, which is why the later haggling over which party got how many votes was largely meaningless.) Christian Democrats later interpreted the veto and Electoral Tribunal ruling as perverse, aimed at embarrassing them, by forcing them to fuse into a single, blurred image with the Right. The claim is clearly self-serving when the frenzied fever of the time is remembered, and the conviction that Allende had to be stopped at all costs, reflected in the "morally binding plebiscite" appeal of Eduardo Frei who was, after all, the chief leader of the Christian Democrats.

54. The Frei quote is in *United States and Chile*, op. cit., p. 387. The impeachment observation was made by Arriagada Herrera, op. cit., p. 265.

55. Ibid., p. 270.

56. From the platform: "The profound transformations which are to be undertaken require a people socially conscious and in solidarity, educated so as to exercise and defend their political power, scientifically and technically apt to develop the economy of transition to socialism . . ." Among other points, the platform said, "the New State [capitalized in original] will take responsibility for the private institutions, so as to make possible the planning of education and of the unified, national and democratic school . . ." The first to be taken would be those schools "which select their student body on the basis of social class, national origin or religious persuasion. This will be done by incorporating into the [unified] educational system the personnel

and resources of private schooling." As quoted in Alain Labrousse, op. cit., pp. 469 and 471.

57. Paul E. Sigmund, op. cit., p. 606; Nathaniel Davis, op. cit., p. 13; and Carlos Prats, *Memorias*, op. cit., pp. 377–380. Prats—who had also defended the very unpopular Price and Supply Boards (JAP) a few months earlier (ibid., p. 356)—said the problem was not with the ENU law itself, but with a promotional brochure on the law. He does add, however, that neither Tapia nor Allende repudiated the brochure "even though they did not share its ideological partiality." Prats portrays Tapia as a man misunderstood at the meeting ("It was as if the minister had not spoken in Spanish . . ."), never losing his control as he responded to "dangerously . . . open accusations against the government, even to the extreme of branding it as 'Marxist.' " As others joined Huerta in attacking ENU—Gen. Javier Palacios, Col. Pedro Espinoza, Col. Víctor Barría, and unnamed naval officers—"each was supported by greater applause, while the patient and measured clarifications of Minister Tapia are met with silence." Prats said only one other officer spoke in defense of Tapia, Air Force General Gustavo Leigh, expressing the view that the real problem was a lack of clarity in explaining just what the ENU program would consist of. Prats says both Tohá and Tapia were "desolate" at the tenor of the meeting, which he said marked "the tolling of the bell of political activism [*deliberación*] in the bosom of the Armed Forces." The next day, meeting with six hundred officers in the Santiago garrison, Prats criticized the stands taken by senior officers at the previous day's meeting as frankly "political" [*deliberativos*]. That remark set off "coughs and harrumphs" among the officers, obliging Prats to bang the table "strongly" with his gavel. It was clear that Prats was a general rapidly losing his grip on his troops.

58. *Breve Historia*, p. 317.

59. Ibid., pp. 330–331.

60. Ibid., p. 325.

61. In his Good Friday, 1973, televised message Cardinal Silva spoke of "the suffering of thousands and thousands of our brothers who wander the streets of Chile aimlessly . . . they are the poor, the homeless, the weak. They have not chosen to be poor; that condition has been imposed upon them. The selfishness of a society based on profit has excluded them . . . Yesterday and today, they are mere pieces of a system, gears in a machine, doomed to produce goods for others which they will never enjoy themselves . . ." Later, in the same homily, the cardinal spoke of the "avalanche of hate and violence which seems to invade our country," but at no point did he attempt to fix blame, much less reproach the government. Still later, he speaks of Christ present "in the great current of social justice desired by ever larger groups of Chileans; in the wish for and the possibility of a world in which the workers participate in the decisions and the ownership of their companies . . . in the progress of the peasants who day to day become more responsible in producing food for Chile, organized intelligently and with their own labor leaders on the farms; in the great desire which moves all Chileans to construct with dignity the authentic sovereignty of Chile . . ." Though, in message after message during those tempestuous years, the cardinal repeatedly condemned violence, five months before Allende would reach power he was telling the country's bishops that "to achieve the profound transformations which Latin America now needs in the belief that there does not need to be violence is illusory. Many entrenched interests

have to be defeated, many situations of privilege have to be broken . . . All of that can never take place without a notable measure of violence . . . We must restrain ourselves from identifying the promotion of peace with indifference or coldness of commitment . . ." Cardinal Raúl Silva Henríquez, *La Misión Social del Cristiano: ¿Conflicto de Clases o Solidaridad Cristiana?* (Santiago: Ediciones Paulinas, 1973), pp. 119–120, 122; pp. 66–67. I have also carefully studied yet another volume containing church pronouncements during the Allende years, and find the same themes repeated in statements of the bishops and other church authorities. That volume is *Documentos del Episcopado: Chile, 1970–1973* (Santiago: Ediciones Mundo, 1974). But, as we have seen earlier (p. 160 and pp. 359–360), the intellectual leadership of the church in Chile had been captured years before by a group of far-left theologians, mostly Europeans, so it was not surprising that the church would find it hard to criticize Allende (or, subsequently, quick to condemn the Pinochet military government). Commenting on the Popular Unity's systematic campaign to prepare the way for ENU once in power, one Chilean educator remarked how Communist–front groups "gave a series of lectures at the University of Chile about the idyllic future of education, which all the nuns applauded with delight." Jaime Martínez Williams, "Education Under the Government of the Popular Unity," in *Chile: A Critical Survey*, ed. Tomás P. MacHale (Santiago: Institute of General Studies, 1972), p. 245. In addition to his careers as a lawyer and editor, Martínez was a past secretary-general of the Austral (Southern) University of Chile, and professor of law and journalism at the Catholic University of Chile.

62. Rodríguez, Benjamín Matte Guzmán and three other leaders of Patria y Libertad went into asylum in the Ecuadorean Embassy on June 29, 1973, when a pocket military uprising they had helped foment collapsed almost as quickly as it had begun. Their principal point of contact was a Patria militant whose brother was commander of the unit which revolted. On July 7, they left the country for Ecuador, though Rodríguez—thanks to his close ties with the Radio Agricultura-based group of civilians involved in the actual revolution—would be back in Chile on the eve of that event. (Matte was president of the National Agricultural Society, owner of Radio Agricultura and its affiliated stations.) Rodríguez had been arrested once, in March of 1972, accused of organizing a paramilitary force. There was truth as well as irony in his remark at the time: "The strangest part about this is that because they [the authorities] find 20 helmets, a few clubs and extinguishers, we are accused of having a paramilitary organization, while the MIR continues arming itself with impunity." By contrast with the Allende government's attitude of tolerance—and even of complicity—with the brazen build-up of illegal left-wing armed groups, including the MIR, Patria y Libertad was subjected to constant surveillance and harassment, without any conclusive evidence ever produced of its involvement in paramilitary operations or terrorism. A far-left author, Carlos M. Rama, makes a number of references to the "fascist" Patria y Libertad's "violence-prone history," and complicity in "a vast terrorist plan" during the October 1972 strike, but in two and-a-half pages of lurid prose offers not a scrap of specific evidence. Carlos M. Rama, op. cit., pp. 123, 126–127. Rama, an Uruguayan who also wrote a book praising his country's Tupamaro terrorist organization, was in Chile the last eighteen months of Allende's rule, teaching at the University of Chile and contributing to the government newspaper *La Nación* and the

equally radical *Clarín*. The translation of that book title: *Chile: A Thousand Days between the Revolution and Fascism*. Nathaniel Davis, U.S. ambassador to Chile during the last two Allende years, who barely disguises his own contempt for Patria y Libertad (and other anti-Allende forces of the Right), remarks nonetheless: "If truth be told, provocative wall slogans and grandiose schemes were probably Patria y Libertad's long suit—along with efforts to subvert rightist military officers." Davis, op. cit, p. 153. Davis also reports that Patria y Libertad received a grand total of $45,500 of the $7-million in covert U.S. spending in Chile during the Allende years—none of it after 1971 (ibid., p. 326). Patria y Libertad was suspected of involvement in one episode of violence, in late June, when bombs were exploded at several points around the city, including outside the home of a Cuban diplomat. Nobody was hurt in those incidents. According to Rama, "the top leaders of its armed militia were killed in a still unexplained shoot-out" in March of 1973 (ibid., p. 126).

63. Both General Pinochet and Admiral Merino told me, in extensive separate interviews in Santiago (Pinochet, October 22, 1974, Merino, October 18, 1974), that ENU was the final catalyst of their decision to oust Allende. That attitude was shared by a number of senior officers I interviewed for *Allende: Death of a Marxist Dream*, op. cit., and is reflected on p. 55 of the book.

64. "El Sr. Allende Vino a 'El Mercurio' Ayer a Medianoche," *El Mercurio*, August 31, 1958, p. 27. An accompanying photograph shows a jaunty, slender Allende, decked out in bow tie and, despite the midnight hour, dark glasses.

65. *El Mercurio* received $700,000 September 9, 1971, another $965,000 on April 11, 1972. Other media disbursements: $1,240,000 on March 28, 1971, to help the opposition acquire radio stations and newspapers; $77,000 to the Christian Democrats on May 10, 1971, to buy a press for their new newspaper. *Covert Action in Chile, 1963–1973; Staff Report of the Select Committee to Study Governmental Operations with Respect to Intelligence Activities*, United States Senate (Washington: U.S. Government Printing Office, 1975), pp. 59–61. (Hereafter: *Covert Action*.) As Henry Kissinger points out, "a monopoly of support to organizations financed, disciplined, and trained by our adversaries, many of them with direct links to the Soviet Union" is a recipe for the collapse of pluralistic democracy. *Years of Upheaval*, op. cit., p. 377. Ambassador Davis notes that the U.S. made no attempt to influence the editorial positions of the media it financed, and that to the best of his knowledge, *El Mercurio* editor-in-chief René Silva Espejo "was not even informed" of secret U.S. subsidies to his newspaper. *The Last Two Years of Salvador Allende*, op. cit., p. 344. Electoral platform data in Labrousse, op. cit., p. 472.

66. *Breve Historia*, pp. 48–49. The three largest UP coalition members each got a piece of the huge government advertising pie, as did API (Popular Independent Action), the tiniest member: the Communists through Agencia Territorio (which, among others, handled the account for Sumar, the biggest textile firm in the country seized in the early days of UP rule); the Socialists through Agencia Vanguardia (whose accounts included the state copper monopoly and the Banco del Estado); the Radicals through Agencia Latina; and API through Agencia Stentor. The foregoing is in Moss, *Chile's Marxist Experiment*, op. cit., p. 134.

67. Dooner, an openly jaundiced analyst of the behavior of the right-wing press,

postulates a "little-studied factor" which served as a trigger to revolution: "That was the destabilizing strategy of the press of the Right. In saying this, there is no crude suggestion that without this strategy, the same outcome would not have occurred. To the contrary, it is very probable that the outcome would have been the same. Nonetheless, it is our opinion that the time frame [*tiempos de maduración*] might have been otherwise." Dooner goes on to say that he neither denies the existence of real problems in Chilean society, nor that the rightist press was doing more than taking advantage of a style of political journalism created by the Left (though practicing it "much more efficiently"). Those caveats noted, he goes on to say that the conservative press helped "create the right atmosphere" for the coup. Dooner, op. cit., p. 9.

68. IAPA and IPI data are in Tomás P. MacHale, *La Libertad de Expresión en Chile* (Santiago: Ediciones Portada, 1973), pp. 9–10. The author attended that Santiago meeting and, as a member of IAPA's Committee on Freedom of the Press, participated in those discussions. The attack on *Correo de Valdivia* took place on May 5, 1973, and is in *Breve Historia*, op. cit., pp. 322–323. References to other acts of violence and del Canto's warning are in MacHale, pp. 10–11; data on foreign funding is in Manuel Trucco, "Foreign Armed Intervention in Chile," in *Chile: The Balanced View*, op. cit., p. 94. According to Trucco, $500,000 came from the Bank of Czechoslovakia, $280,000 from Swiss banks, and $780,000 from the Banco Nacional de Cuba. The Communist party charge is in *Breve Historia*, op. cit., p. 287.

69. *Breve Historia*, op. cit., p. 87. Chilean television spoke from a single angle even before Allende reached power. As U.S. Ambassador Edward Korry noted in 1970, "of the three TV channels in Santiago, in a still free society, one is totally controlled by the Marxist-Leninists of the University of Chile, another is controlled by a combination of Marxists and the very left-wing Christian Democrats of the Catholic University, and the third is the State's." Cited by Kissinger, *The White House Years*, op. cit., p. 659. As to the breakdown of newspapers and radio, the historian Vial Correa says that as of September 1973, eleven newspapers were published in Santiago: five pro-government, five opposition, and one neutral. (The discrepancy could be one of time-frames; the Christian Democrat report was issued two years before Vial Correa's count.) Gonzalo Vial Correa, "Decadencia, Consensos y Unidad Nacional en 1973," in *Política y Geoestrategia* (Santiago: Academia Nacional de Estudios Políticos y Estratégicos, #36, 1985), p. 18. Government sources claimed that as many as 80 percent of the country's radio stations were in opposition hands, and identified 45 of the 64 daily newspapers published in the country as opposition, 10 progovernment, and independent.

70. Davis, op. cit., p. 337.

71. During the 1972 regular session of Congress—May 21 to September 18—two former presidential candidates of the Radical party (Senators Baltra and Bossay)—teamed up with Christian Democrat Juan Hamilton to sponsor a bill to provide public financing and price guarantees for the press and radio. The bill was aimed in large measure at rescuing the Papelera from financial ruin. Allende vetoed the bill at the end of September. Sigmund, *The Overthrow of Allende and The Politics of Chile, 1964–1976* (Pittsburgh: University of Pittsburgh Press, 1977), p. 183. Data on the Papelera is from Davis, op. cit., p. 117, and the company's annual report for 1971–1972. An indication

of how intense—and prolonged—was the war to save the Papelera: the *Breve Historia* chronology of the Allende years, though by no means all inclusive, includes entries on thirty-four separate dates for the Papelera, stretching from August of 1971 to July of 1973. For background on Radio Agricultura and the role of its key figures in the secret plotting, see: Whelan, op. cit., pp. 32–34. As indicated therein, it was the government decision to silence Radio Agricultura in October 1972 that resulted in the first contact between the station's civilian rebels and the military man who would plug them into the planning to establish a secret communications command network.

72. *Breve Historia*, op. cit., p. 350. Though less significant in the overall picture, the pressure on the country's three independent television channels was no less severe. The government stood by, for example, in the early days of the Allende regime when a progovernment faction forcibly seized control of the Catholic University station, and throughout the Allende years, the government used a variety of means to block the station from beaming programing to a satellite station in Talcahuano (near Concepción, which would have enabled the station to expand its coverage not only to Chile's third city, but also to the rich agricultural region of southern Chile), finally defying court orders to do so. Despite harassment, the Catholic University station, alone among the four channels, managed to operate with relative independence. On August 30, 1972, "A Tres Bandas," the only truly opposition program on the government-run channel—the only one with nationwide broadcasting facilities—was ordered off the air, and a week later, Allende said, he issued the order personally: "I am not going to tolerate that they go around saying that a Cabinet officer steals from the people . . ." The principal University of Chile station (Channel 9) was forcibly held by Allende militants until police finally dislodged them under court orders three days before the coup. Less than forty-eight hours after a second University of Chile station (Channel 6) finally succeeded in going on the air, on June 19, 1973, police armed with sub-machineguns stormed the premises, smashing equipment, arresting thirty persons, and knocking the station off the air (ibid., pp. 218–219, 362).

73. *Breve Historia*, op. cit., p. 350.

74. Ibid., p. 314. Frei made that remark in an interview with the Milan newspaper *Corriere Della Sera*, reported in *El Mercurio*, March 30, 1973.

75. Ibid., pp. 300–301, 305. In its confidential study, covering the period October 1972-March 1973, MAPU spoke of the inflation, black market, food lines, shortages—none of which it ascribed to "internal and external aggression," as did official propaganda. The report also claimed that the country's foreign exchange reserves reached zero as of January 3, and that thanks to the Soviet bail-out (see p. 451-a), the regime had been given a four-month reprieve from bankruptcy. As a result of that study, Finance Minister Fernando Flores and Jaime Gazmuri—even though they had presided over the study—kicked out the hard left faction which had denounced it (and them), a faction headed by former Under Secretary of Economy Oscar Garretón and Eduardo Aquevedo. True to his radical colors, Garretón would be paired with Altamirano in what became the regime's final crisis, and which gave the military the pretext it needed for mobilizing troops for its revolution. Flores—denounced by his radical comrades for his "ambitions"—remained in the government he had so devastatingly badmouthed, and then ended his "service" to Allende by trying to cut a revolution-day deal with the military.

76. Ibid., pp. 338 and 328. Cuba's first shipment of donated sugar arrived on

April 11. Allende appealed for the oil products directly to Mexican President Luis Echeverría. Data on the Russian earth-movers is on p. 328, and the incident was April 20.

77. Ibid., pp. 306, 310. Cox's critique of the damage done by agrarian reform would not deter Allende from targeting, shortly afterwards, 2,500 more small and medium farms for expropriation: their size ranged all the way down to 10 hectares (124.7 acres), but most were in the 40–80 hectare range (98.8–197.6 acres). As Christian Democrat Sen. Rafael Moreno pointed out, those farms were then producing half of the country's dwindling output of farm products (ibid., p. 327). This gave rise to yet another constitutional fight: the opposition passed an amendment banning expropriation of farms under 40 hectares (just under 100 acres) and ordering the government to begin giving peasants, within two years, title to land already expropriated; the Allende government in common with so many leftist governments which come to power trumpeting the need for land "reform" had used a legal loophole to keep peasants on what amounted to state collectives rather than giving them title to the lands. There was one other indirect (but official) admission of failure: on March 16, the Foreign Ministry notified missions and international organizations in Chile that because of shortages, the government had decided to make special arrangements to provide them with nonperishable foodstuffs (such as sugar, cooking oil, rice, tea, coffee, etc.), as well as nonfood necessities (tooth paste, soap, toilet paper, detergents, matches, etc.), ibid., p. 309. Ibid., pp. 195, 351, 300. (For Miriá Contreras and automobiles scandals.)

78. Ibid., pp. 333, 339. The Christian Democrat quote is in Henry Kissinger, op. cit., p. 398. It was Communist party leader Luis Corvalán who, on May 16, said "the fatherland is in danger," adding that "confrontation is inevitable."

79. Davis, op. cit., p. 156. He reports that there was a "quantum leap" in the arming of the Left and attempts to infiltrate the military in the second quarter of 1973. He also said that at least eight new guerrilla centers were established in rural areas, as well as "significant" paramilitary training facilities developed in Santiago. The Communists, until then largely reluctant to commit to armed struggle, began "systematic efforts" to arm their Ramona Parra brigade, and the crude manufacture of weapons was also stepped up. As to the "marked increase" in reports of leftist infiltration of the armed forces, he wrote that leftist propaganda began appearing in barracks and on recruiting-station walls during the second quarter of 1973 and handbills passed around at military bases—some of them openly advocating insubordination.

80. Headlined "Chile Near The Brink," the New York Times editorial said that while Allende said that civil war must be avoided, "his Marxist-dominated coalition persevered with policies and tactics certain to accelerate the polarization that has pushed Chile close to the brink." The Times also said that were Allende to bring military back into his Cabinet, "it will be a confession of bankruptcy in leadership . . ." (he did). The editorial appeared June 25, 1973, and is in Henry Kissinger, op. cit., p. 400.

81. Kissinger and Davis both coincide in saying that the ambassador was three times given the final veto power over whether any covert funds provided to Chile would be diverted to private groups other than political parties and the opposition press—and all three times he refused to do it. (Kissinger, op. cit., pp. 382, 395 and 403.) The third time—August 20, 1973, when $1 million was authorized—was academic because the coup would occur

before any of those monies could be provided. The significant episode was in relation to the $1.427,666 authorized on October 26, 1972, for support of democratic forces in the March congressional elections. Of that, $100,000 was set aside for private sector use—the shopkeepers, the truckers, organizations such as Patria y Libertad—subject to Davis's approval. He refused to give it, although he would admit, to his chagrin, that through an inadvertence, the sum of $2,800 (two-thousand, eight hundred dollars) dribbled into the truck federation's coffers (unbeknownst to their feisty leader, León Vilarín, much as monies funneled to *El Mercurio* reached the newspaper without Editor René Silva Espejo or his other key editors' knowing until much later). Second-guessing Davis after the fact is, of course, inelegant and inappropriate. It is clear that had he embroiled the embassy even in discussions of coups, the United States would have been implicated in fact, as well as in the mythology of the Left. And, as he reports in his book, the opportunities abounded, at just about every social or official gathering he would attend in the final months of the regime. Instead, Davis steadfastly refused to be drawn, with the result that, "the gap between the desires of the Chilean opposition and the inclinations of our embassy widened," as he astringently describes the decision to turn a deaf ear to those, including Christian Democrats, who despaired of a peaceful way out (pp. 328–329). For that, Davis, obviously, is to be admired—but that admiration, for this observer, at least, must be tinged by the suspicion that the combination of his unabashed admiration of Allende and disdain for the Right figured importantly into his decisions. That suspicion is nowhere more powerfully fostered than in Davis's own book.

82. The retired flag officers wrote Allende on May 28. The miners' strike was punctuated with acts of violence—and growing displays of labor solidarity; on May 10, for example, 10,700 workers at the giant Chuquicamata mine walked off the jobs in sympathy with their El Teniente colleagues.

83. Corvalán spoke July 8 at the Caupolicán Theater. *Breve Historia,* op. cit., pp. 374–375.

84. Ibid., pp. 368–369; Davis, op. cit., p. 174 (the Yovane quotes); Whelan, op. cit., p. 14 (revamping of plans); Kissinger, *Years of Upheaval,* op. cit., p. 401. The abortive uprising also threatened Pinochet's personal plans: he had intended to have his own insurrection plan ready by the end of July, and in order to free himself of other responsibilities, had planned to send his wife and daughter abroad. They left on schedule for Panama, not returning until August 8. Pinochet took other measures in the aftermath of the *tancazo.* One was to order all army personnel to keep an automatic rifle and eighty rounds of ammunition in their homes, so as to defend against terrorist attack. Another—which would have important reverberations on the day of the revolution—was to assign two captains of his confidence to the demoralized armored regiment. With his insurrection planning temporarily paralyzed, he decided to wait until mid-July to reactivate it, this time in the guise of updating the army's internal security plan. Like Yovane, Pinochet regarded the *tancazo* as an unwanted uprising that nearly upset the revolutionary apple cart, but which, once it had happened, was a useful preview for the real thing. In a fifty-page pamphlet printed on plain newsprint which circulated in 1974 in Chile and which was widely believed to have been authored by Pinochet himself, General Pinochet is "quoted" as telling flag officers of all three services on the afternoon of the *tancazo:* "With everything negative that has been said about what happened this morning, it is

interesting to point out that there is a tremendously positive and satisfying side, and that is what is grandest of all about the army: its discipline, its training, its valor." Better than any maneuvers, the narrative goes on, the events of the morning had caused "the Marxists to reveal their equipment, their locations in [downtown] buildings and the industrial clusters surrounding the city, their plans and how they would move into action." *La acción del ejercito en la liberación de Chile (historia inédita)*, pp. 26–27. Pinochet reflected similar views in his memoirs of the revolution, *El Día Decisivo*, op. cit., pp. 98–102.

85. *Breve Historia*, op. cit., p. 367; Davis, op. cit., p. 155; and the author's interview with Mrs. Cox in Santiago, October 1974. The ambassador said he believed Prats, but as remarked earlier, Davis was also keenly admiring of Prats. Prats himself said he drew his gun only when the driver of the other car, now speeding along the Costanera with Prats alongside, repeated the "intolerable" offense. He indicates that he shouted at those in the other car to stop, and when they refused, fired at the front bumper of the car. (That he was evidently looking directly into the car alongside his not only at the stop light but also along the highway makes even more curious his failure to recognize the other driver as a woman.) He also says that the mob which surrounded him and his driver was on the point of assaulting him when the taxi driver—whom he identified as Carlos Rodríguez—rescued him. He said he tendered his verbal resignation to Allende that afternoon, but that Allende "in a thoughtful gesture" turned up at his house late that night together with two UP leaders Prats had become particularly close to (Fernando Flores and Jaime Gazmuri of the MAPU) to "express their support." Prats said the top generals also expressed their support when he reported the incident to them. He said he later wrote Mrs. Cox a letter of apology, and received one from her—neither of which she mentioned in my interview with her. Prats, *Memorias*, op. cit., pp. 415–417. Pinochet attributed the episode to Prats' visibly worsening state of nerves during June, "nervous in his behavior and abusive [*violento*] with his subordinates." Pinochet, op. cit., p. 96.

86. Prats, *Memorias*, pp. 452 (ingenuity), 425 (unanimous vote of generals), 428 (Pickering episode), 447 ("discordant note"), 423 (for example of this "a political problem"), and pp. 428–454 for details of his activities during July and leading up to Allende's renewed bid that he join the Cabinet on August 6. Prats singled out Generals Pickering and Mario Sepúlveda for special praise for their roles in putting down the June *tancazo* action, he said, which prevented the rebellion from spreading. The Pinochet quote is from *El Día Decisivo*, op. cit., p. 108. Like Prats himself, Pickering and Sepúlveda had become marked men for their revolution-minded comrades. Pinochet's first act when he took over command of the army on August 23 was to force both into retirement.

87. In Henry Kissinger, *Years of Upheaval*, op. cit., p. 405. Kissinger quotes Zhou from a conversation he had with the premier a few months after Allende's fall and death. Kissinger adds that, as to Allende's fall, Zhou remarked: "That kind of phenomenom was caused by itself." Zhou said he gave his advice in the only letter he ever wrote to Allende (see p. 436 and note 112).

88. With considerable justification, National party Sen. Pedro Ibáñez "The Chilean Crisis and Its Outcome," in the *United States and Chile*, op. cit., p. 594, would refer to Rodríguez as "this sinister person." Rodríguez had

served as a cabinet minister in the government of Cuban dictator Fulgencio Batista—the man Castro overthrew—reflecting Communist party (and Soviet) support for Batista. That support was withdrawn only a few months before Batista's fall (and when it was clear that the "correlation of forces" had shifted in favor of Castro). The Soviets then (and for a long time afterwards) distrusted Castro as an impulsive "romantic" revolutionary, which pretty much described their attitude toward Allende (before and after) as well. The unofficial Rodríguez visit came just three days after the mysterious murder of Allende's naval aide, Capt. Arturo Araya Peters. Rodríguez was the third senior Cuban to make a pilgrimage to Santiago: Castro, of course, and Foreign Minister Raúl Roa, who came in August of 1971, together with the Fisheries Minister of the Soviet Union.

89. *Libro Blanco del Cambio del Gobierno en Chile* (Santiago: Editorial Cochrane, S. A., 1973), pp. 101–102.

90. *Breve Historia,* op. cit., pp. 386, 388, 393, 399–400, 403, 409. The Chronology, in the *United States and Chile,* op. cit., p. 393, speaks of CUT's 1.4-million members—but then, as noted earlier, Chronology reflects a tilt to the left throughout. The fired air force generals were Lt. Gen. Germán Stuardo, second in seniority, and Lt. Gen. Agustín Rodríguez Pulgar, fourth. The fifth-ranked was Lt. Gen. Gabriel van Schowen, whose nephew, Juan Bautista von Schowen, was a top leader of the MIR. It was widely believed that Allende was attempting to leap-frog von Schowen to the top of the air force. General Ruiz had refused to join the Cabinet in October 1972, and resisted again in August 1973, agreeing to serve only when Prats, in defiance of the vote of his Council of Generals, persuaded Ruiz and a vacillating Admiral Montero to join him. Arturo Fontaine and Cristián Zegers, *Cómo llegaron las fuerzas armadas a la acción del 11 de septiembre de 1973?* (Santiago: *El Mercurio,* September 11, 1974), p. 14, and Carlos Prats, *Una vida por la legalidad,* pp. 70–71. General Prats revealed again during that truck strike just how far he had drifted from the thinking of his fellow officers, finding more to value in the behavior of the radical extremist Faivovich than in that of his fellow general officer, Ruiz. In a diary notation dated August 10, the day of the El Monte debacle, when Ruiz felt Faivovich had deliberately double-crossed him by ordering the attack, Prats wrote: "I am concerned at the incomprehensible attitude of General César Ruiz Danyau . . . who seems more a spokesman of the strikers than the representative of the government. If the problem preventing resolution of the conflict is Jaime Faivovich's continuance in office as subsecretary of transport, then Ruiz should replace him and energetically assume the responsibility personally of obliging the truckers to return to work" (ibid., p. 72). The "striptease" reference is in Davis, op. cit., p. 185. Ruiz was, of course, trying to oust Faivovich, and it was only when he discovered he could not that he quit; Prats also forgets that the strike erupted because of the failure of the government to keep the promises he had made to them months before when he did not "oblige" the truckers to end their strike, but achieved a negotiated settlement with them. As to the character of this final labor upheaval, while it is true that many of the strikers were professionals such as doctors, lawyers, and teachers, or self-employed (shopkeepers, truckers, taxi and minibus drivers), it is also true that their ranks were swollen by miners, postmen, airline employees, and many other "blue collar" workers. In *una vida por la legalidad,* Prats said of Ruiz's replacement by Leigh (p. 75) that a "sluggish, ambitious, mediocre coup plotter has been replaced

with another coup plotter who is intelligent, astute, and ten times more ambitious." No such reference—nor anything resembling it—appears in *Memorias*.

91. Although, in my opinion, it requires a kind of moral myopia to equate, exactly, the MIR on the Left and Patria y Libertad on the Right, that is exactly what Ambassador Davis did throughout. For example: "On July 17, two incidents reminded Chileans that extremists of both sides were traveling on parallel tracks. The publicity mouthpiece for the MIR, *Punto Final*, called for the 'dictatorship of the people.' On the same day, Roberto Thieme, acting head of Patria y Libertad, called on the radio for a 'total armed offensive' in a broadcast-and-run transmission. Neither event was of great importance, neither appeal met with mass response, and neither statement reflected a decisive change in the orientation of these extremist groups. But the two calls did signify that the MIR and Patria y Libertad were still augmenting each other's efforts in furtherance of the same goal—the destruction of the last fragile chance for Chilean institutional democracy" (Davis, op. cit., pp. 181–182). Although, as we have seen, virtually no significant leader outside of the government believed, by July of 1973, that much remained of "Chilean institutional democracy," much less that it could or even ought be saved, there is a good deal more to quarrel with here. First, of course, there is the objective record of MIR's long and well-documented history of crime and violence, before, during, and after Allende—a record which Davis occasionallay cites himself. By contrast, neither he (nor anyone else), cites chapter-and-verse of anything in Patria y Libertad's record vaguely resembling the MIR's, nor anything resembling parity in the size, scope, weaponry, or training of the two organizations; indeed, except for blowing up an odd transmission tower or two, broadcasting an inflammatory message or two (or, as the ambassador points out earlier as their "long suit," scrawling slogans on a wall or two), there is little evidence to connect Patria y Libertad to anything of consequence except the *tancazo* abortion. But, more importantly than any of this, equating the two fails to make the crucial distinction between a minority, determined by means legal or illegal, to fasten its way of life on a reluctant majority, and those who, in the name of the majority, fight to prevent a minority from getting away with it—even if that minority did use the devices of democracy to attain power in the first place. To do so is a little like equating police with robbers because both use guns. But, again, Davis demonstrates repeatedly his disdain bordering on contempt for the private sector in Chile (the shopkeepers, the truckers he refused to support and of whom he speaks disparagingly), as well as for Patria y Libertad. (Another example: he refers to P y L's "criminal hit squads," a rhetorical excess not only at odds with his usual aseptic style but which is nowhere supported by evidence.) The point here is neither to defend Patria y Libertad, nor to damn Davis, but to reveal something of the values and attitudes which would animate a man with extraordinary latitude in the management of American foreign policy toward Chile during those crucial times.

92. *Breve Historia*, pp. 379, 384, 401, 406.

93. Davis, op. cit., p. 154. He remarks that an arms-running operation from Argentina which Patria y Libertad was rumored to have established in the early months of 1973 in collusion with military officers in the Atacama district had "decreased in volume" by midyear. As yet another example of

P & L activity: "Collaborative ties were also alleged between Pablo Rodríguez, retired army major Arturo Marshall Marchesse—who had taken refuge in Bolivia after having plotted against both Frei and Allende—and Brazilian anticommunists" (ibid., p. 154). As a kind of "last hurrah," Patria y Libertad took out a newspaper advertisement on July 13 claiming credit for helping incite the tank uprising in June.

In urging disobedience, those MIRistas were echoing what, by then, had become a main tactic of the radical Left. For example, on July 12, Carlos Altamirano, speaking to industrial belt leaders, urged soldiers and sailors to disobey their officers should an uprising come. He also called on the *"cordón"* leaders to create a "people's court" to try "political and economic delinquents." *Breve Historia,* op. cit., p. 378.

94. *Breve Historia,* op. cit., pp. 387–388. Ambassador Davis chose to mock Thieme's surrender offer: "This offer was close to the last thing the admirals would have wanted, but—fortunately for them—nothing came of Thieme's grandstanding" in Davis, op. cit., p. 183. He doesn't tell us why that would have been so "close to the last thing the admirals would have wanted," nor, curiously, does he make mention of Riquelme's arrest and confession. He does, however, allude to the rumors of an affair between Araya and Beatriz Allende, married to Luis Fernández Oña. Christian Democrat Deputy Claudio Orrego said he "vouched for" the authenticity of Riquelme's confession, and speculated that the motive was to disrupt the peace talks about to open between the Christian Democrats and Allende. As for Rodríguez, confronted with the rumor during his visit, he dismissed it as "an infamy." *Breve Historia,* p. 390. Prats reports that when Army Intelligence Chief General Lutz told him Riquelme had recanted his confession only a few hours after making it, Prats ordered Riquelme turned over to the provost marshal. The very next day (Sunday, June 29), an intelligence officer told Prats that Riquelme stuck to his story, during night-long questioning, that he had confessed under duress. Prats adds that a physical examination by a military doctor failed to reveal any marks or bruises. That same day the Supreme Court named a special prosecutor, and—at Prats' suggestion—the navy also turned the case over to its legal arm. Prats, *Memorias,* pp. 447–449.

95. Davis, op. cit., p. 189, and Whelan, op. cit., pp. 128, 129.

96. *Breve Historia,* op. cit., pp. 379–380, 389–390, 392, 397; *United States and Chile,* op. cit., pp. 391–392; Prats, *Memorias,* op. cit., pp. 454–459. The Christian Democrats' basic demands: disarming of all armed groups, Right and Left; return to the owners of all illegally seized private enterprises; a constitutional amendment defining the three areas of property—private, mixed, and state; military participation in the government with "sufficient powers, at top and middle levels of government, to assure effective compliance with the decisions of Your Excellency, within the framework of the law and the constitution, applied equally to one and to all." On the three areas, Allende agreed to the amendment, provided the Christian Democrats would accept another that Congress could overturn a presidential veto of future amendments only by a two-thirds vote (instead of simple majority); as the March elections had shown, achieving a two-thirds majority in Congress was then—and was likely to remain—beyond the reach of the opposition. The Christian Democrats rejected that counterproposal as "dilatory." As to the military, Allende wanted it back—but only on the same, largely ceremo-

nial basis as when he had brought it in during the October 1972 truck strike. Prats, in his memoirs, says Allende first asked him to rejoin the Cabinet on August 6. Navy Commandant Montero, he said, had only one objection, which he then dropped the very next day, and that was that no military man serve as defense minister (the job Prats then, in fact, took). Ruiz was opposed to the service chiefs serving, though not to flag officers in the Cabinet. When he met on August 8 with his own generals, they expressed opposition to his accepting unless the Christian Democrat demands were met—which Prats said he could not accept because that would be a "bloodless coup" (*golpe en seco*). Prats and Montero finally persuaded Ruiz to go along with them, despite the added opposition of his air force generals. Ruiz was also already on shaky ground with his subordinates. One authoritative account relates that on the day of the *tancazo,* June 29, a group of air force generals were meeting with Ruiz, in his Defense Ministry office, when Allende summoned him to join with the other service chiefs on a balcony of La Moneda in a show of solidarity with the president. Returning, Ruiz was told the generals found that scene "humiliating." In the aftermath, a fifteen-member committee of top flag officers formed a committee to meet with the three regular service chiefs plus the Carabinero commandant to discuss future participation in the government. Out of these meetings, chaired by Adm. Patricio Carvajal in his capacity as navy representative as well as chief of the National Defense General Staff, would come a twenty-nine-point memorandum governing future military involvement—close in letter and spirit to later Christian Democrat demands in their peace talks with Allende. When it was finally ready, General Ruiz and Navy Commandant Montero took it to a scheduled meeting with Allende, expecting to meet Prats going in. Instead, they found Prats already closeted with an irate Allende and an indignant defense minister José Tohá; Prats obviously had spilled the beans and Allende tongue-lashed the startled navy and air force chiefs. That episode would be the last meaningful attempt at accommodation between the service chiefs and the president. Arturo Fontaine and Cristián Zegers Aritzía, *Como llegaron,* op. cit., pp. 14, 15.

97. Aylwin was quoted in the *Washington Post* of August 26, 1973, on Marxist vs. military dictatorship, and in the *New York Times* the next day on his party and the military seeking a democratic solution, according to Chronology in *United States and Chile,* op. cit., p. 393.

98. When similar resolutions had come to a vote in the past, the Popular Unity deputies left the chamber. This time, they did not because, as Sigmund notes, "there was some doubt until the last minute whether some of the Christian Democrats would vote for the resolution." That they stayed gave further legitimacy to the vote. Sigmund, op. cit., p. 233; *Libro Blanco,* op. cit.; Supreme Court, p. 215 (Allende would respond to that communique, triggering yet another Supreme Court manifesto, appearing on pp. 216–219); Frei-Pareto, pp. 235–236; Bar Association, pp. 237–238; Chamber of Deputies, pp. 239–242; second Bar Association, p. 243–247. Allende's response to the Chamber resolution is in *Breve Historia,* op. cit., p. 408; Medical Association, ibid.,p. 409.

99. Chronology in *United States and Chile,* op. cit., p. 391.

100. *Libro Blanco,* op. cit., pp. 34–35.

101. Chronology, *United States and Chile,* op. cit., p. 393. Allende claimed on August 3 that there had been 180 acts of terrorism against railroads, highways, bridges, pipelines, schools and hospitals in the week since the

murder of Captain Araya, which he linked to the truck strike and said was an attempt to isolate Santiago and other major cities. Although he implicated the Right in those events, it is interesting that four days later, a member of the MIR was captured following a dynamite blast which destroyed one hundred feet of pipeline near Curicó, killing two and injuring nine persons. In yet another incident, on August 13, a bomb knocked out power to Santiago, throwing the capital into darkness for fifty-five minutes and interrupting a televised address in which Allende was denouncing the striking truckers and the "fascists" of Patria y Libertad for the wave of terrorism. He also attacked "extremists" of the MIR for causing some of the violence. On August 15, bombs were discovered and dismantled in the gardens of the homes of three U.S. Embassy officials; the government assured Ambassador Davis such attacks would not be tolerated, while the left-wing press continued its attacks against the U.S. for its putative support of the strikes. On August 26, bombing attempts were made against the homes and automobiles of Cuban Embassy officers. No one was hurt in any of the diplomatic attacks (ibid., pp. 392–393, and *Breve Historia,* op. cit., pp. 395–396).

102. Prats labor federation cronies, the Communist Figueroa and the Socialist Calderón, went to his home on Sunday, August 5, to express their "indignation" at the methods used by troops under the overall command of Torres in the Punta Arenas raids. Two days later, Prats summoned Torres to Santiago, telling him that the excessive use of force was undermining confidence in the Arms Control Law, repeating similar sentiments in a subsequent meeting with the army's corps of generals. He said he was particularly concerned because there had been no raids on Patria y Libertad installations, although they had declared themselves in open rebellion. His authority was by then so weakened that two generals—Oscar Bonilla and Javier Palacios—told him to his face that they stood with General Torres. Since Torres was an air force general, Prats' already low standing in his own service now radiated into that service as well. Prats would lend himself to one more CUT maneuver. With the truck strike worsening, on August 15, CUT President Figueroa offered to make available men from his Communist-dominated organization to join the military in guarding such key installations as oil refineries, power stations, and the like, specifying that the CUT men would not be armed. When Prats relayed that offer to Admiral Carvajal, chief of staff of the Defense Ministry, Carvajal rejected the offer on the grounds that it would encourage the further formation of armed militia (Prats, *Memorias,* op. cit., pp. 453, 456–457, 466).

103. Ibid., pp. 394–395, and Chronology, *United States and Chile,* p. 391. Interestingly, the last major raid was staged in the night-time hours of September 7 at the sprawling Sumar plant in Santiago—where Allende had briefly installed the seat of his government for two days in January. As the raiding party approached, it was met by gunfire from within; three persons were wounded and twenty-three captured during the two-hour gun battle. The air force, in a communique the next day, said the big textile plant was not only an armed fortress, but that it was part of a well-rehearsed battle plan. As their men approached, the communique said, sirens sounded, followed by the firing of Bengal lights. Next, an estimated five hundred inhabitants of the surrounding shantytown, dressed in dark clothes and wearing sneakers, began lowering themselves stealthily from the rooftops of the

adjacent dwellings into the grounds of the plant. The raiding party withdrew to avoid a slaughter (*Breve Historia*, op. cit., p. 415). That event was also an unwanted dress rehearsal for what would become one of the bloodiest battles of the revolution, just four days later. As indicated already, raids were by no means limited to Santiago—cf., e.g., pp. 505–506.

104. After twice refusing demands that he fire Transportation Under Secretary Jaime Faivovich, the violence-prone Socialist who had ordered the August 10 attack on the El Monte truck encampment, Allende finally agreed to do so on August 18, installing army Gen. Herman Brady Roche in his place. It was too little, too late. Following the Sumar raid, Faivovich showed his temper once again: "The armed forces," he said, "are provoking the workers. They want to give the impression that they are the supreme authority of this country . . . the military coup is already underway." Data on the strikes and Faivovich quote from Chronology, *United States and Chile*, op. cit., pp. 391–392.

105. The incident was related by Jorge Edwards, then (early 1972) Chile's charge-d'affaires in Havana, in his book, *Persona Non Grata* (Barcelona, Buenos Aires, Mexico: Ediciones Grijalbo, 1976), p. 282, and is cited by Joaquín Fermandois *Chile y el Mundo*, op. cit., p. 100. The mutiny headline is cited by Paul Sigmund, op. cit., p. 608.

106. Robert Moss, "Chile's Coup and After," in *Chile: The Balanced View*, op. cit., p. 50.

107. *Breve Historia*, op. cit., pp. 395, 410, 414, 416. Moss mentions Allende in the above-cited article; he says that after the coup, he spoke briefly with an officer from the cruiser. Prats had told him that a petty officer aboard, named Maldonado, had told *him*, that he had taken part in a secret meeting with Allende in Santiago. Adds Moss: "That may well be the kind of thing that a frightened man says under pressure to please his interrogators, but whether or not Allende was personally involved in that plot, it is clear that his government was." Moss, op. cit., p. 50. For the diary notation: Prats, *Una vida por la legalidad*, op. cit., pp. 68–70. Interestingly, I can find no reference to entrapment in the later—and much fuller—version of Prats' memoirs. In that volume, Prats simply remarks that he was told of the sedition by a "worried" Admiral Merino, then acting commandant of the navy (while Admiral Montero, like Prats, served in the Cabinet). As for Prats, he demonstrates that he was far more concerned about the "excessive use of force" in military raids, particularly the just-concluded one (Aug. 4) in Punta Arenas (cf. pp. 447–458). Prats and his wife died in 1974 when a bomb shattered their automobile in Buenos Aires. *Memorias* was edited posthumously by his three daughters, Sofía, María Angélica and Cecília. Fermandois observes (op. cit., note 11, p. 105), that it was 1983 before Prats' daughters would deny the authenticity of the earlier book, *Una vida por la legalidad*, which, theoretically, would vitiate that book as a reliable source. However, given the fact it took them nine years to repudiate the book, Fermandois said he would use it insofar as it would reflect a mind-set (*mentalidad*). I have chosen to use it for the same reason. Davis offers no similar caveat about the Prats book—which he cites frequently—though it is possible he had not seen the later *Memorias*, since both his book and *Memorias* were published in 1985. It should also be observed that in *Memorias*, Prats' daughters included copies of numerous documents hand-written by their father.

108. *Breve Historia*, p. 415, for Allende on flour. The remaining economic data

from: *La Economía de Chile durante el periodo de gobierno de la Unidad Popular; la vía Chilena al marxismo* (Valparaíso: Escuela de Negocios de Valparaíso, Fundación Adolfo Ibáñez, March 1974), pp. 27–29, 76. As the following passages indicate, there actually was a multiplicity of exchange rates; rates for imports, for example, ranged from twenty to three hundred escudos to the dollar, but the majority of import transactions were at twenty-five escudos to the dollar (Fermandois, op. cit., p. 428).

109. *Breve Historia*, op. cit., pp. 400 and 406.

110. Writing of the event, Prats said he found "incredible" their "interference in service matters," and would find himself wondering: "Who, in such sinister fashion, is pulling the strings of this psychological conspiracy and is beginning to use as a diabolical formula the interposing as shields for their moral cowardice women of uniformed men?" It is true that Ruiz insisted on quitting as transport minister, but as Prats knew, it was Allende who then told him that, if he did, he would also have to step down as air force commandant. Prats claimed Allende offered a "grateful" General Leigh command of the air force but tied to the ministry job. Leigh reported back to him the next day (Aug. 18) that neither he nor any other air force general wanted either the ministry or commander's jobs. In fact, the Ruiz incident very nearly triggered air force rebellion. On August 18, the two principal bases near Santiago—El Bosque and Los Cerrillos—went to a "self-garrisoned" stage (confining themselves to base), usually the symbol of rebellion. To defuse that, Allende offered Leigh command of the air force, with no ministerial strings attached, which, Prats claimed, Leigh accepted, "moved . . . at the confidence the President would place in him." It was while all of this was going on (Aug. 18) that the wives' demonstrated. On Monday, the 20th, Ruiz—instead of showing up as scheduled for Leigh's swearing in—joined the "self-garrisoned" forces at Los Cerrillos. With yet another wives' demonstration taking place outside the Defense Ministry, tension mounted through the day as Leigh hurried to meetings with the rebellious air force officers, finally persuading Ruiz to step down and the officers to call off their pocket rebellion. Leigh would later reveal that he gave them assurances that revolt would come—but not quite yet (Prats, *Memorias*, op. cit., pp. 469–475, and the author's interview with General Leigh in Santiago, October 14, 1974).

111. The demonstration was led by a normally mild-mannered brunette named Maria (Maruja) Medina, who had played a key role earlier that year in mobilizing opposition to the Unified National Education Plan (ENU). But, as the wife of a retired colonel, she was technically "out-ranked" that frosty afternoon because the demonstrators included the wives of Generals Pinochet, Bonilla, Arellano, and Palacios—all destined to play vital roles in the forthcoming revolution—as well as those of Generals Contreras, Muño, and Viveros (whose brother, Air Force Gen. Mario Viveros Avila, would command the southern flank forces on September 11). Ambassador Davis, drawing on accounts of both Letelier and Prats, provides dramatic detail. He quotes Letelier, for example, saying that Prats, "his cheeks burning red, stood rigidly throughout the ordeal." Later: "Prats sat erect in his living room chair, his ironed Prussian-style tunic with polished epaulets tailored to fit his middle-aged body. 'I never thought,' he said, . . . 'that generals and colonels whom I have known since childhood would hide behind the skirts of their wives. I am sad for Chile because I have seen not only treason but a kind of cowardice that I did not conceive

of as possible' " (Davis, op. cit., p. 197). In *Memorias,* Prats makes no such reference to "hiding behind skirts" (other than his oblique reference to the air force women three days earlier). *Memorias*—which, again, Prats' daughters say was authentic, while repudiating *Una vida por la legalidad,* on which Davis drew, as spurious—casts some doubt of the authenticity of Letelier's account. In *Memorias* (p. 479), Prats said Letelier didn't arrive until 10 P.M., together with Allende, five or six hours after the demonstration started, and after a long list of others (including Pinochet, "to express his sorrow"). Prats did, however, refer several times with obvious sarcasm to "the distinguished ladies," and, at the end, made it plain that he believed that these women of "so many years of false friendship" were under the malevolent spell of right-wing voodoo. He believed he found in the demonstration at his house the answer to the question he had posed three days earlier—who is pulling the strings?—in the persons of a man and a woman. The man was Capt. Renán Ballas Fuentealba, who shouted at the demonstrating crowd, from the very doorstep of the general's house, that "Prats does not represent the army and is a traitor." The woman was the wife of army General Alfredo Canales (and Ballas Fuentealba was Canales' son-in-law). Canales had been forced into retirement a year before when Prats reported to Allende a conversation Canales allegedly had while under the influence of liquor in which he told an admiral of plans for a coup against Allende. The admiral had reported it to Prats (*Memorias,* op. cit., pp. 477–480, and Whelan, op. cit., p. 15, based on an interview with Mrs. Medina in Santiago, May 11, 1974). Following Prats' retirement, Pinochet agreed to the separation of Captain Ballas from the army, but after the revolution, the captain was hired as a foreign service officer, serving over the next dozen years in a number of countries. Prats also related (pp. 478–479) that General Bonilla was among the visitors on that fateful night, allegedly apologizing for his wife's participation in the demonstration—then telling his commander-in-chief that he had lost the confidence of the corps of generals. Prats says he told Bonilla that if he believed the "slanders" against him—that he had connived in Ruiz' ouster and later threatened Leigh—then he would never speak to him again. He then asked Bonilla to leave (ibid., pp. 478–479).

There is a discrepancy of much greater import between Prats' earlier and later memoirs; in the earlier one (pp. 76, 77–78), Prats says that the next morning, Wednesday, August 22, each of the generals, beginning with Pinochet, came to his office and reaffirmed his loyalty. In *Memorias* (p. 480), Pinochet is portrayed as expressing his regrets at what happened and promising to do what he could when the corps of generals met later, reporting afterwards that only a few generals were willing to sign a declaration of support. Prats insisted on seeing the generals himself, explained his position, and said he would wait twenty-four hours for their response. The next day, August 23, Pinochet announced that the majority was unwilling to back him (pp. 480–481, 484). He resigned that afternoon, after a two and-a-half-hour meeting with Allende (Fernando Flores being the only witness), Allende arguing that he shouldn't give in to political machinations, Prats countering that if he were to stay he would have to ask for the retirement of twelve to fifteen generals (those lined up against him), and that would lead to certain civil war. Both, he wrote, were guided in their arguments by "the national interest." We parted, Prats wrote, "grieving and with emotion," observing that "the noble Minister Flores" was also "profoundly moved" (ibid., pp. 485–486). In *Una vida por la legalidad,* the earlier version, Prats said that the vote against him was taken that same morning (Aug. 22) and that it was 12-6 against him, with Pinochet among those voting in his favor. There is no mention either of the vote or of Pinochet's position in *Memorias.*

112. Once again, a significant discrepancy between the earlier and later Prats memoirs: the meeting with Communist party leaders appears on p. 88 of *Una vida por la legalidad;* there is no mention of it in *Memorias* (although he does speak at length of his July 8 meeting with MIR chieftain Miguel Enríquez, whom he describes as mistaken but "a young man of talent sincerely convinced of the justice of his cause"). Enríquez brought him news of alleged subversive talk between army General Bonilla and ex-President Eduardo Frei), pp. 431–434. As to the report that he advised Allende to fire five or six generals, the source for that is the magazine *Ercilla,* March 13–19, 1974, pp. 12, 15. In *Memorias,* Prats also discusses at some length his luncheon meeting with Allende on Saturday, September 8, but makes no mention of such advice. The advice he says he *did* give Allende: on Monday, September 10, request congressional permission to leave the country for one year, and then, stability having been restored, "you will return in glory and majesty to finish your term." Allende said he would "never!" do such a thing. What he would do was announce on Monday that he would call a plebiscite on his presidency; Prats demurred that a plebiscite would take 30–60 days to hold, while he was facing a military uprising within ten days (ibid, pp. 509–510).

113. Merino and Huidobro gave me details of that August 29 meeting with Allende in separate interviews in Santiago, October 18 and October 24, 1974. Further details are from Moss, "Chile's Coup and After," op. cit., p. 51. In commenting on his reference to Allende as "slightly drunk," Moss says: he is, of course, not alive to testify as to the "accuracy of these quotations; my account is based on eye-witness reports gathered in Santiago." Allende met Merino twice following Montero's resignation on August 24, both times promising to name him to replace Montero, each time asking for more time. The first time was Monday, September 3, a meeting which was preceded by an emotional September 1 confrontation between Letelier (by now defense minister) and the entire group of admirals. Letelier gambled and lost: he asked each admiral, one by one, to give his reasons for saying Montero had to go; he hoped that so confronted, they would decline to embarrass their chief. But, one by one, beginning with Carvajal, they did. Letelier met with the admirals again on Monday; at that meeting, Montero fainted. Huidobro, a burly, bluff man who looked the part of a marine corps commandant, recalls that tears came to his eyes when he—at the direction of the other admirals—was compelled to tell a still wan Montero, his longtime friend and mentor, that, for the good of the service, he had to go. It was after these charged sessions that Montero, Merino, Adm. Pablo E. Weber Munnich, Huidobro, and Letelier went to see Allende. He then promised to turn over command of the navy to Merino on Friday, September 7. Instead, when Merino helicoptered to Santiago that day, Allende and Merino would lock horns in a six-hour marathon which ended in Allende putting off for yet another week the removal of Montero and his replacement by Merino. The negotiations

were now ended—for good. Back in Valparaíso, Merino met the next day (Saturday, September 8) with five hundred officers, lieutenant and up, and later with the fifteen top navy officers, and ordered Operation Seaweed activated. Details of those meetings from Fontaine and Zegers, *¿Como Llegaron las Fuerzas Armadas a la acción del 11 de Septembre de 1973,* op. cit., 19–20. One possible speculation for Allende's stalling: at lucheon late Monday afternoon, September 10, Allende was heard by a navy steward to tell Investigaciones chief Alfredo Joignant that he would be forced to name Merino on Wednesday—but that he wanted Joignant to "take care of him" before then (from Whelan, op. cit., p. 23). Data on the air force crisis from Prats, *Memorias,* op. cit., pp. 469–475, and Davis, op. cit., pp. 194–195.

114. Telephones at the homes of both Montero and Prats were among the first cut in the hours of darkness preceding the fighting, as part of Operation Silence within the overall revolutionary plan (Whelan, op. cit., pp. 76–77). Montero was not only "incommunicado" on September 11, he was thoroughly grounded. When his driver failed to turn up that morning, Montero called the Defense Ministry and was told they knew nothing about the driver. Finally deciding to drive himself, he found the official car wouldn't start. Neither would his own car. Nor would his son's. Deciding to hail a taxi, he found that the iron-grilled gate of his house was chained and locked. It was eleven that morning before he would reach his office, where he would be treated with respect, but made to understand that nothing was the same any more (*lo que usted nunca supo del día 11 . . . !,* a special supplement appearing in the Santiago newspaper *La Segunda,* September 10, 1974, p. 7). Prats remarks that when, on August 17, Carvajal gave him the new armed forces telecommunications plan to sign (as defense minister), he understood that although it was labelled as defensive, it had a double edge, but that he signed it anyway because of the need to be ready for anything in the face of the "sedition" then underway (*Memorias,* op. cit., p. 469).

115. Whelan, op. cit., pp. 17–20, 58–60, 73. Of the sixteen Carabinero generals, only seven (including Mendoza) were known to be sympathetic to the revolution.

116. For a brief discussion of Balmaceda's suicide and the events leading up to it, cf. p. 46, chapter 2.

117. Harold Blakemore, "Chile: Current Realities and Historical Perspectives," reprinted from the *Bank of London and South America Review,* March 1975, London, in *Chile: The Balanced View,* op. cit., p. 16. Blakemore, then secretary of the Latin American Institute at the University of London, notes that it was Balmaceda's "clearly unconstitutional behavior and alleged attempts to create a dictatorship" that led to that civil war—a situation clearly echoed in 1973.

118. The last Cabinet was sworn in August 28. The peace talks, which went nowhere, were held at Cardinal Silva's palace and brought together, first Allende with Christian Democrat President Patricio Aylwin, and later Aylwin with new Interior Minister Carlos Briones. As Ambassador Davis would remark, the talks foundered largely over PDC insistence on return to legality, and since "government by loophole and fait accompli had become so much a part of the UP program that a return to 'legality' would have required a virtual counterrevolution. This Allende was understandably unwilling to concede" (Davis, op. cit., p. 202). Viaux was sent on his

way September 4 by a crowd at the airport which included women bearing flowers; in a parting shot, he accused Prats of having been "a traitor" (*Memorias*, op. cit., p. 503). The demonstrations were held on September 4—Allende loyalists turning out on the anniversary of his election in numbers whose estimates ranged from a few thousand (the opposition) to a million (the presidential information office); anti-Allende forces held their rally the next day. Rodríguez allegedly returned in late August and, on September 9, was interviewed from the rural town of Cactin on Radio Agricultura. More on the Chilean—and Soviet—ships in the following chapter. But the event which would most fuel the fires of postcoup conspiracy speculations was Ambassador Davis' hurried trip to Washington to meet with Henry Kissinger, then about to leave his post as national security adviser to become secretary of state. Davis left Thursday night, September 6, and was back in Santiago Sunday, September 9. Davis was one of a number of top-recommended foreign service officers Kissinger invited to Washington in order to screen them for top jobs in the department once he took over (he offered one to Davis). Though Davis and Kissinger differ slightly on who said what during their one-and-only meeting, Saturday afternoon, September 8, they are both very plain on two essential points: (1) the United States knew little more about the specifics of the impending revolution than what experienced reporters were saying in their stories; (2) both were in emphatic agreement that the United States should stay out of it (Davis, op. cit., pp. 354–358, and Kissinger, *Years of Upheaval* op. cit., pp. 403–404).

119. General Augusto Pinochet Ugarte, op. cit., pp. 118, 121. The three far left groups met Saturday, September 8, and decided on the breakaway strategy. Altamirano would announce a modified version of it the following day in his war-like Chile Arena speech (more on that to come). Details of the tea are from Whelan, op. cit., pp. 23–24, and are based primarily on interviews with Pinochet and Leigh; estimates of the strength of the fighting forces in the *cordones*, ibid., p. 14. According to Fontaine and Zegers, the emissaries reached a toll booth as they were leaving Valparaíso when they realized neither of them had any money with them. They decided to use their enforced return to Valparaíso as an opportunity to convert Merino's oral mandate into a written one, and it was then that he would scribble the note to Pinochet and Leigh (Fontaine and Zegers, op. cit., p. 20). In his book, Pinochet writes that he settled on the September 14 date on September 5, and agreed to change because he saw the navy was determined to go it alone on the 11th, and that would have been "suicide" op. cit., pp. 118–121; details of Pinochet's description of the planning, as told to the author, are in Whelan, op. cit., pp. 13–15, 18.

120. Altamirano's speech from Ricardo Boizard, *El Ultimo Día de Allende* (Santiago: Editorial del Pacífico, 1973), pp. 131–136. Of the 130 finally accused in the navy plot, forty-five were convicted and sentenced. As to a Brazilian role, Davis describes reports of "coaching" Brazilians allegedly gave Chileans in 1973, and notes that in March 1973, the Brazilian ambassador to Santiago, Antonio Castro da Cámara Canto, "made a series of leading suggestions which I turned aside" (Davis, op. cit., pp. 331–334). No hard evidence—and certainly not of decisive or significant outside influence in bringing Allende down—has, to the best of this author's knowledge, yet surfaced.

120. "El Once, Hora por Hora," in *Que Pasa*, #177, September 10, 1974, p. 21.

8

September 11, 1973

THE WORDS OF WAR

At 8:10 A.M., Radio Agricultura was in the middle of a regular newscast when the voice of an announcer interrupted with a flash: "Here we have the voice of Salvador Allende, on a partial radio network. The president of the Republic has just said that the navy has isolated Valparaíso. Here are his textual words . . . [Allende's voice followed]:

" 'Speaking to you is the President of the Republic, from the Palace of La Moneda. Confirmed reports reveal that a sector of the navy has isolated Valparaíso [there was then a pause and a hum on the line], and that the city was occupied, which signifies a rebellion against the arm . . . against the government, the legally constituted government, which is shielded by the law and the will of the citizens. In this circumstance, I appeal, above all, to workers to occupy their places . . .' " That is as far as he got—except on three UP stations still not silenced by Operation Silence. On those, as he had done in June during the *tancazo*, he appealed to workers to assemble at their factory-fortresses and to prepare to defend the government, but to avoid provocations and await further instructions.[1]

Minutes after he spoke, two Hawker Hunter jets screeched low over the western sector of the city. Approaching Avenida San Martín, they fired rockets. When the smoke cleared, the transmitter towers of the three main UP radio stations were twisted ruins (Allende's own station, Radio Portales, was off the air for good; Radio Corporación switched to FM, though with a weak signal; Radio Magallanes activated a hidden emergency transmitter, and would, for several hours, remain the sole voice of a dying government).

At Radio Agricultura, in the last moments before dawn, an engineer worked feverishly to finish installing a "patch" linking the station to the Defense Ministry—and a secret command network painstakingly assembled by a group of civilian "ham" radio operators. Over that network

454

would flow the messages, the expletives, the uncertainties, and the surprises of revolution during Chile's most decisive day. From Radio Agricultura—backed up by Radio Minería, the two linked to a carefully selected group of other stations around the country—the people of Chile, and much of the world beyond, would learn of the most momentous events in the life of their country.[2]

It was 8:32 A.M., on that still frosty (44°F) morning, when the national anthem, followed by the words so long awaited by so many, so long dreaded by others, would reverberate from a hastily installed studio on the sixth floor of the Defense Ministry: [3]

> Santiago, September 11, 1973. In consideration of:
> (1) the extremely grave social and moral crisis afflicting the country; (2) the inability of the government to control the chaos; (3) the constant increase of paramilitary groups trained by the parties of the Popular Unity which will lead the people of Chile to an inevitable civil war; the Armed Forces and Carabineros of Chile resolve:
> 1. The President of the Republic must proceed to the immediate handing over of his office to the Armed Forces and Carabineros of Chile.
> 2. The Armed Forces and Carabineros of Chile are united to begin the historic and responsible mission of fighting for the liberation of the fatherland and to preclude our country from falling under the Marxist yoke, and the restoration of order and institutionality.
> 3. The workers of Chile can rest assured that the economic and social conquests which they have achieved to this date will not suffer fundamental modification.
> 4. The press, radio and television pledged to the Popular Unity must suspend their informative activities as of this instant. Failing to do so, they will receive air and land punishment.
> 5. The people of Santiago should remain in their houses so as to avoid unnecessary victims.
> [Signed] Augusto Pinochet Ugarte, General of the Army, Commander-in-Chief of the Army
> José Toribio Merino, Admiral, Commander-in-Chief of the Navy
> Gustavo Leigh Guzmán, General of the Air, Commander-in-Chief of the Air Force of Chile
> César Mendoza Durán, General, Director-General of Carabineros of Chile.

"Thus, in two minutes and twenty seconds, did an old order end and a new one begin."[4]

It was shortly after 4 P.M. Monday when a relieved Salvador Allende got word that the fleet had sailed from Valparaíso for its rendezvous with a U.S. squadron and the annual Unitas joint naval exercises. (At that time, the U.S. ships were just approaching Chilean waters, one thousand miles to the north, having sailed from the Peruvian port of Callao the day before.)[5] Altamirano and the other hard-liners of the Popular Unity notwithstanding, Allende had arrived at the conclusion that he had no choice but to risk all on a plebiscite on his presidency—and, according to one of his closest confidantes, was prepared to leave the presidency if the vote went against him.[6] He originally had intended to announce it in a radio broadcast that morning, but then postponed it until five that afternoon. News that the fleet had sailed persuaded him that he still had time; the fleet would not, after all, even reach Caldera, the rendezvous point with the Americans, for two days (it was about five hundred miles north of Valparaíso to that point). And so he decided, instead, to announce it the following day at an "anti-imperialism" exhibit at the extremist-infested State Technical University in Santiago. So that night he summoned to his estate Tomás Moro, Interior Minister Carlos Briones, Orlando Letelier (now defense minister), Foreign Minister Clodomiro Almeyda (he arrived back from the non-aligned conference in Algeria too late that night to attend), and Joán Garcés. They were joined at dinner by Mrs. Allende and his youngest daughter Isabel. After dinner, the four men retired to the first-floor study to discuss details of the plebiscite, and were just settling in with coffee and cognac when the telephone began bringing them news of mysterious troop movements in and around Santiago.

Though the reports were disquieting and information scanty, Allende remained convinced that the departure of the fleet amounted to a barrier to military action, particularly since the navy was unmistakably the focus of most revolutionary fever. And so, shortly after 1:30 A.M., he gave instructions to subordinates to continue to pursue the reports and sent the ministers home with instructions to rejoin him first thing the following day.[7]

"First thing" would come for all of them—and many, many more—very early indeed. Because the fleet had not sailed to its rendezvous with the Americans at all, but to a rendezvous with destiny. Ever since midnight, the ships—the cruiser Prat, the destroyers Cochrane, Blanco Encalada and Orella, the oiler Araucano, the submarine Simpson, and two escort craft—had lazed through fair seas just over the horizon from the coast. They were scattered along fifty-five miles of coast, from the copper port of San Antonio in the south, to Quintero, site of an air force base just north of Valparaíso. At midnight, the captains aboard each ship opened sealed orders: shortly after 5:00 A.M., the cold night air rang with the fateful "now hear this" from the public address systems of each of the ships. It was then that the three thousand men aboard those ships learned of the revolution, of their role in it. Although an estimated 10 percent of the men and a number of officers were believed to be loyal to Allende, there was no breach of discipline as the ships steamed back into sight of land. Their craggy silhouettes against the distant horizon were the first confirmation that the time for talk was past.[8]

At about that same hour, a coded message went out from the army's Communications Center on the eighth floor of the Defense Ministry:

EJERCITO DE CHILE
COMANDANCIA EN JEFE

SECRET: GRAL. DAG.
SANTIAGO, 11 de Septiembre de 1973.
R A D I O G R A M A

ASUMIR INTENDENCIAS Y GOBERNACIONES DE INMEDIATO Y OCUPAR coma EFECTIVAMENTE, PROVINCIAS Y AREAS JURIS-DICCIONALES coma TRANSMITIDO SIMULTANEAMENTE A COMANDO UU.OO. Y CDTES, GUARNICIONES PTO. ACTIVAR CAJSIS pto. ATTE.
CDTE. EN JEFE DEL EJTO.
POR O. DEL COMANDANTE EN JEFE DEL EJTO.
RIGOBERTO RUBIO RAMIREZ
CORONEL
Secretario General de Ejército

("Assume control and occupy immediately and effectively municipal and provincial seats of government, provincial offices, and dependencies; [order] transmitted simultaneously to commanders, operational units and commandants garrisons. Activate Internal Security Plan. Respectfully, Commander in Chief of the Army. For the Commander in Chief of the Army, Rigoberto Rubio Ramírez, Colonel, Secretary-General of the Army.")[9]

Allende had been asleep barely two hours when Carabinero General Urrutia, alerted by a telephone call from Valparaíso, roused him to tell him that the fleet had returned and the navy had seized Valparaíso. (In fact, the operation was carried out so surgically that Chile's second city was securely in the navy's hands before seven that morning, not a shot fired (and the only two casualties victims of accidents).[10] Allende dressed quickly, alerted a GAP guard to rouse the other "personal friends" (an estimated seventy-five were encamped at Tomás Moro, the opulent presidential estate). Together with Augusto Olivares Becerra—

perhaps his closest crony—Allende began working the telephones in an all but vain attempt to reach military leaders. (One call he did complete: to Gen. Herman Brady, newly named head of the Santiago garrison, who laconically told him there was nothing irregular going on.) Allende also awakened Letelier and Briones, both of whom also tried in vain to reach top commanders. Both then headed for their offices, Briones's in the northwest corner of La Moneda, Letelier's in the Defense Ministry diagonally across the Alameda.[11]

One call he might have completed: to Pinochet. After his second consecutive sleepless night Pinochet, at 5:30, worked out for forty-five minutes, as was his custom, showered and was dressing when, at 6:30, the telephone rang. Feigning a sleepy voice, he answered and was told that it was a presidential operator at Tomás Moro, that the president wished to speak to him. Since Allende apparently was then on another call, the operator said the president would call back later. The call never came. With a brief detour to the home of a daughter for a quick peek at his still sleeping grandchildren, Pinochet made his way to the army's communications center at Peñalolén, 7.5 miles east-southeast of La Moneda Palace.[12] Arriving, he broke the news; all present were "happy"—except the general's aide-de-camp. He was arrested.[13]

Of the five principal protagonists of the drama—Allende, the four military commanders—only one had ever experienced actual combat: José Toribio Merino, aboard the U.S. light cruiser *Raleigh* during World War II. (He bent the rules to do it; Chile was officially neutral in the war.) So it was that alone among them, he managed a decent night's sleep—but only after putting his private and official houses in order. The finishing touches having been put on Operation Seaweed—two pages which converted a defensive anti-insurgency plan into a blueprint for revolution—Admiral Merino gave orders Monday to move First Naval District headquarters temporarily to the Naval War College, situated in the port area itself and hub of navy communications. The pretext: avoid the Altamirano-related disturbances expected the next day. He then went home and told his wife, Gabriela, to take their three daughters and "hide." He first removed from safekeeping his life's savings—$135 in U.S. dollars—and turned them over to her. Next, he drove alone to the War College, summoned the top staff of some thirty officers, and broke the news, giving orders to instruct other naval bases to execute Seaweed at six the following morning. After sharing a glass of whiskey with the officers, Merino retired to his wardroom—and "slept like a log."[14]

Gustavo Leigh Guzmán—then nine days away from his fifty-third birthday and rounding out thirty-five years in the air force (including six in Washington)—gave similar instructions Monday to his wife (coincidentally, also named Gabriela): pack a few bags and take the children to the home of a close friend. But it had been a busy day for Leigh already, with abundant drama yet to come before his brief and restless repose. At eight-thirty that morning, he had summoned the twelve air force generals to his third-floor Defense Ministry office: "Gentlemen," he said, "the dice have been thrown. I move tomorrow, and I am going all the way, whatever the consequences. If any of you doesn't agree, say so and go home. There will be no reprisals." No one budged. "Most," he said, "were frankly jubilant." With that, he swore them to secrecy and ordered them to make ready to launch the air force's plan: Operación Trueno (Operation Thunder). (Pinochet swore in the six generals and a colonel he had selected for key roles in two dramatic ceremonies that Monday: using the sword presented to him when he was promoted to general, Pinochet invoked an old army tradition, that they swear an oath which was the equivalent of a death warrant, to be executed in case that man should betray the others. All seven swore the oath—without hesitation.)

Leigh joined Pinochet and four of the seven key army leaders for a final planning session at lunch. It was at that luncheon that the decision was made to bomb La Moneda if Allende resisted; another, if the revolution succeeded, to fly Allende and his family into exile, rather than hold him prisoner. It was also at that lunch that Pinochet added his signature to the revolutionary proclamation to be broadcast the next day, announcing creation of the junta and demanding that Allende resign.[15]

Before getting on with the war planning, Leigh would fight a private war of his own. That afternoon, he was visited by Alfredo Joignant, head of Investigaciones (Allende had given Joignant the police job the previous November after the Senate voted 32–14 to remove him as mayor of Santiago for his "repeated violations of the constitution"). Flanked by two police inspectors and three air force technical officers named to a commission Allende had created to investigate the spectacular air force-extremist shootout at the SUMAR factory the previous Friday, the tough-talking Joignant said he intended to order ballistics tests to determine who fired the first shots. In the sharp exchange that followed, Leigh cursed Joignant—and then threw him out of the office.

That afternoon, Leigh also signed up his first "recruits" for the revolution: four, five-man crews from the national airline, LAN Chile. When LAN pilots joined the nationwide strike the previous Friday, they took the precaution of ferrying the airline's fleet of planes to air force bases for safekeeping (and to protect against strike-breaking—an event that enraged Allende). Deciding those planes could be valuable for transporting troops, Leigh needed the pilots, copilots and flight engineers to fly them. He had no trouble in rounding up his "recruits," even to persuading them to spend the night at the air force. hospital—for safekeeping, too.

Before leaving his office that night, Leigh had one other important appointment. He had earlier summoned the commander of Group 7, based at Concepción, an eighty-minute hop from Santiago by subsonic jet. Leigh came swiftly to the point: "Crews under your command are going to be called upon to perform special missions tomorrow. They will receive their orders in the air. They are to use only rockets and machinegun ammunition—no bombs. You've got to be ready to carry out whatever orders you receive, even if it means bombing La Moneda or Tomás Moro, should that be necessary." The commander readily accepted, then headed back to Concepción to select crews for a mission never before assigned soldiers in that country.[16]

It was late when Leigh finally arrived at the home of Colonel Eduardo and Marisa Sepúlveda, where Gabriela Leigh and their two toddlers (aged three and four) were already settled in. While there, the secretary-general of the air force told him that Allende had been calling all over town trying to reach him. Leigh decided to wait until he reached his headquarters at the Air Academy before calling the president. "I had imagined just about everything—that Joignant had protested, that he [Allende] was on to something, anything—except what it turned out to be. He wanted to talk about the LAN planes." It was the last time the two men ever would talk.[17]

One man among the five had no plan at all. In fact, until shortly before noon on Monday, it could fairly be said that César Mendoza Durán didn't have a clue as to what was in store for him. Although Mendoza had been in touch with Brig. Gen. Sergio Arellano Stark and other key army plotters in recent weeks—as well as with a fellow Carabinero general deeply involved in the plotting—there had been no intimation until he arrived at General Leigh's office that forenoon that revolution was imminent. General Leigh was not a man to mince words: he removed the proclamation from a strongbox in his office, told Mendoza what was afoot, and asked him to sign. Recovering from his shock, Mendoza demurred that he believed Pinochet should sign first; Leigh agreed. (Pinochet signed at lunch, Mendoza returned that afternoon to sign.) What preparations have you made, Leigh wanted to know.

"None," Mendoza replied, reminding Leigh that his superiors, the two top Carabinero generals, were fiercely loyal to Allende, that only six of the sixteen of flag rank could definitely be counted on, and that the ranks of senior officers—a few majors, lieutenant colonels, and up—were rife with Allende sympathizers. But Mendoza exuded confidence, both because of his thirty-five years of experience, and also because he did have a few trusted people to work with.

One was the man who went to Leigh's office with him: Gen. Arturo Yovane Zúñiga. Allende had sacked Yovane from his job, as he had

Mendoza, because he aggressively enforced court orders against extremists. But, unlike Mendoza—who was exiled to an administrative job in Santiago (head of the Social Welfare department)—Yovane lost his administrative job as prefect of Valparaíso, but not his field command (chief of the Second Carabinero Zone). Over the preceding months, navy rebels felt him out cautiously, then began drawing him into their plans. He would prove invaluable in the hours ahead.

Back at his office, Mendoza dispatched a courier to yet another man he felt he could—and must—trust: Col. Mario Mackay Jaraquemada, head of the Carabinero garrison in the country's third city, Concepción, 325 miles southwest of Santiago. Concepción was of special importance because it was the birthplace and major stronghold of the MIR. (Mendoza was not the only commander with couriers abroad that day; not willing to trust all to communications networks, Pinochet had dispatched couriers in army planes to carry his orders to commanders at key garrisons.)[18]

In common with the other commanders, Mendoza realized the importance of maintaining appearances that day, and so he went ahead and attended a birthday party in his honor that night. Still svelte, Mendoza—an equestrian gold medalist in the Pan American games of 1951, bronze medalist in the 1952 Olympic games—was celebrating his fifty-fifth birthday on Tuesday, September 11.[19] The charade played out, he left the party around midnight and headed for a fateful meeting: the home of Col. José Sánchez, director of the seven-hundred-man School of Carabineros, the "West Point" of that organization. It was a stop Mendoza knew he had to make: he was at that point a general without an army. But if he could persuade Sánchez to join him, there was a chance they could neutralize the four-thousand-strong Carabinero force in and around Santiago, if not actually get them to join. Sánchez was understandably skeptical when, roused from sleep and dressed in a bathrobe, he was told by the fourth-ranking general that his unscheduled nocturnal visitor was about to assume command of the entire organization and join a revolution. But succeed he did. So, too, did General Yovane in a similar mission that night: at the eight-hundred-man Noncommissioned Officers School, and the elite, six-hundred-man Special Services force.

As Mendoza nosed his white Torino toward home close to 2 A.M., he realized that as important as were the pieces now in place, many more nerve-wracking uncertainties still remained. Although their posts around the country gave Carabineros unmatched geographic coverage of Chile, the stance they would take was so much in doubt until the very end that no arrangements had been made to include them in the secret command communications network. And that meant that César Mendoza was very much on his own.

Those thoughts still plagued him when his alarm went off at 5:50
A.M. Twenty minutes later, he was on his way to his headquarters in
downtown Santiago—but not before telling his wife to stay inside that
day, a message he also gave his twenty-four-year-old son and twenty-
year-old daughter. Then, quite alone, he started off for the Norambuena
Building where, over the crucial hours ahead, he would apply a mixture
of persuasion, rank, and personal magnetism to the job of bringing
26,000 men under his command—and into a revolution.[20]

Among the calls Allende did manage to complete: one to Admiral
Carvajal, who told him (as he had Letelier) that the troop activity in
Valparaíso was nothing more than routine arms control raids. (Allende
no more believed it than did Letelier; Isabel Letelier remembers that her
husband winked at her when he repeated the admiral's message). Still
another was to Carlos Altamirano, whose Sunday speech had created for
the military the smokescreen they needed to spring the trap.
Altamirano's wife of one year remembered that the telephone had been
ringing all night and that the call from Allende came around 6 A.M. (she
must have miscalculated by half an hour or so). "Carlos didn't tell me
what they talked about," she said. Instead, the man who had heaped
scathing abuse on the right-wing "scum" (the vulgarity he actually used
in his speech was *carajos*, or "pricks") and "cowards who hide in embassies, and seek asylum so as to flee from Chile and not have to face in a
manly way the consequences of their acts" would disappear into a long
and mysterious odyssey that would see him seek asylum in an embassy
in vain and finally flee from Chile . . .[20]

Awakening Briones, Allende told him to join him at La Moneda as
soon as possible. For Letelier, he had a different message: first a reproach
that so much military chicanery would catch a defense minister off
guard (Letelier had been on the job only two weeks), and then an order:
the place for the defense minister is the Defense Ministry. As a result,
Letelier would become the first cabinet minister to become a prisoner of
war; and the sight of him on television, leaving the ministry in custody
early that tumultuous morning, was a stunning confirmation of the
irreversibility of the revolution.[22]

There was another important detail: Allende told Carabinero
Director-General Sepúlveda to triple the guard at La Moneda and reinforce the palace with tanquetas, the rubber-wheeled armored cars used
as minitanks by Carabineros.

Two heavily armed convoys converged on Santiago within an hour of
each other that morning.

The first was headed by Allende himself. Wearing a gray tweed jacket,
woolen turtleneck sweater of the same color with dark gray geometric

designs, a sport shirt, dark gray trousers, and black shoes, Allende, ever the dandy, then added a finishing flourish: a blue silk handkerchief with red dots, tucked into the upper left breast pocket of his jacket. On his wrist, an expensive Galga Coultro automatic watch.

The convoy was made up of four Fiat 125s and a station wagon loaded with 30-caliber machineguns and three bazookas, and two tanquetas. Twenty-three GAP manned the vehicles (more than twice that number remained behind, already busily preparing the defenses for the presidential estate).

At 7:20, they careened onto already bustling city streets, hitting speeds of fifty to sixty-five miles an hour, and reaching the Morandé 80 entrance of La Moneda in just a little over ten minutes. Armed with a loaded and cocked AK-47 rifle, Allende alighted from one of the vehicles to a welcoming sight: more than a thousand Carabineros ringed the squat and sprawling palace. Also, as he had ordered, five strategically placed tanquetas, two heavy machineguns protruding from the pyramid-shaped turrets of each. Inside, he went quickly to the GAP guard room, took inventory of the weapons available; cursing the lack of a bazooka, he ordered the two top Carabinero generals Sepúlveda and Urrutia, already there, to arrange for more armament, and sent a similar message to the GAP at Tomás Moro. (Some Carabinero armament did arrive; an enterprising lieutenant made certain neither the GAP nor their weapons did.)

Those first arrangements made, he returned to the telephone: to his (mainly estranged) wife of thirty-three years, Hortensia ("Tencha"): "The situation is serious . . . I will remain here. You stay there. It is practically impossible for me to leave the presidency . . ." Other calls went out to CUT leaders Luis Figueroa and Rolando Calderón, with orders to mobilize the paramilitary shock troops of the industrial belts.[23]

The war, at this point, is a war of shadows, or telephone calls and radio appeals. Allende made several during that first hour in the palace, but they were heard by relatively few because of the effectiveness of Operation Silence; so long as they did remain on the air, the UP stations—Portales, Candelaria, Corporación, Magallanes—interspersed their broadcasts with "alerts" for the paramilitary groups as well as with cryptic coded messages. Top leaders of the government are photographed arriving at La Moneda, as on any other day: gaunt José Tohá, former minister of defense and of the interior, tells reporters as he enters the palace: "I haven't had a chance to assess the situation yet, but I can tell you this: we will turn over the presidency in 1976 . . ." Jaime Barrios, head of the Central Bank, arrives with his wife, Nancy Julien; a few minutes later, at 8:20, Carlos Briones, followed by Foreign Minister

Clodomiro Almeyda; at 8:50, Beatriz Allende, who claimed she bowled over a police barrier to get there and arrived pistol in hand; her late arrival seems to cast doubt on reports that her husband, Luis Fernández Oña, the Cuban secret police chieftain, had been tipped during the night that the revolt would break out at 7:45 A.M. Daniel Vergara—the gray eminence of the key Interior Ministry from the very outset of the regime—arrives in his blue Dodge Dart; Education Minister Edgardo Enríquez Froeden, father of the MIR leader, who put in a twenty-minute appearance, claiming as he left that he planned to work at his office; his extremist son, Miguel Enríquez Espinoza, who left after a brief visit; Fernando Flores, the brilliant young Socialist finance minister (who would later become a multimillionaire capitalist in the United States); two more Carabinero generals (Rubén Alvarez Oyarzún and Orestes Salinas, the latter, ironically, the man who headed during the Frei years the Grupo Móvil of Carabineros, the highly effective SWAT-type team so reviled by Marxists); presidential press secretary Carlos Jorquera, as well as Olivares and Joán Garcés; presidential secretary Osvaldo Puccio and his son, and yet another secretary, Frida Modak, and Allende's other daughter, Isabel; the president's naval, army and air force aides: Jorge Grez, Sergio Badiola and Raúl Sánchez; Radical leaders Hugo Miranda, Orlando Cantuarias and government Secretary-General Aníbal Palma; Eduardo ("Coco") Paredes (of the Cubana de Aviación arms shipments which Allende tried to palm off as mango-flavored ice cream, later as paintings); René Largo Farías (chief of the radio section of the Government Information Office, and the man who, shortly after midnight, called Tomás Moro with the first report of unusual troop movements); Agriculture Minister Jaime Tohá (brother of José); and five doctors, including Patricio Guijón Klein, who stumbled onto history's stage and would shortly discover his life forever transformed.

Less noticed: at the far eastern end of the palace, the part housing the Foreign Ministry, a single employee remained at his desk that day. Ernesto Espinoza made it to the office, only to find himself trapped there; for three Cabinet ministers, it was Providence that sent him.[24]

Yet another person made it to the palace that morning: Miria Contreras Bell de Ropert, *La Payita*. Then forty-six, round-faced, blue eyed, thick lipped, and (by most accounts) "singularly attractive," Mrs. Contreras had, for many years, been Salvador Allende's confidante, private secretary, and mistress. She had been awakened that morning by a call from an ex-army officer who later joined Allende's personal bodyguards, the GAP (only to be cashiered when it was learned he was a homosexual). "This time it's real," he told her. Dressing quickly, Mrs. Contreras collared her two sons and headed from El Cañaveral—the sprawling estate Allende had bought for her in the foothills of the Andes, east of

Santiago—for Tomás Moro, where she knew he had spent the night. By the time she got there, he had already gone; leaving her son Max, she and her son Enrique piled into their Renault 4 and headed for La Moneda, flanked by around eighteen GAPs she had persuaded to join her. At the Santiago prefecture, across the street from the palace, Carabineros would not let her proceed until she persuaded an officer to let her put in a call to the president. Rushing into the palace just as he was finishing his first radio speech, Allende asked her: "Tell me, truthfully, Payita: do you think they will actually bomb us? Will they have the courage to do it?"[25]

With the exception of a single youth leader—Enrique París—the Communist party was conspicuous by its absence from La Moneda that morning. The evidence is strong that alone among the coalition partners in this "carnival of madness," the Communists managed to learn enough, soon enough, to save their skins. Because, as it happened, the Communist party daily newspaper *El Siglo* was on the streets that morning with a huge red headline: "Every Man To His Battle Station" (*Cada Cual A Su Puesto De Combate*). The headline appeared over a story signed by Luis Corvalán Lepe, secretary-general of the party, calling on neighborhood commands, the industrial unions and paramilitary groups, the Supply and Price Boards (JAPs), to report for duty and make ready to defend the government to the end. The story, like the headline, was hastily subsituted for an earlier one during the night, while the presses were running, apparently after a warning reached the Central Committee from Valparaíso of what was afoot in the navy—hours before anyone else knew.

As a result, Communist leaders were also conspicuous by their absence on the streets of Santiago on that 11th day of September. Among the most conspicuously absent, the suave theoretician of the party, Volodia Teitelboim. Only two months before, Senator Teitelboim had responded indignantly to a Nationalist deputy's claim that he, Carlos Altamirano, and Erich Schnake had sought asylum in the North Korean Embassy when the abortive *tancazo* rebellion erupted June 29.

"Why would we take refuge?" Teitelboim shot back. "We are not rats. We will never abandon our fight for the people."[26]

When the fighting broke out on September 11, Teitelboim did run for diplomatic asylum cover, surfacing later in Moscow, where he became one of the principal voices of propaganda broadcasts beamed to Chile.

SANTIAGO UNDER SIEGE

The second armed convoy rumbled out of the Second Armored Regiment, home of the abortive June 29 revolt. Vincente Terreros Fernández looked up from his chores at his hole-in-the-wall but popular short-order restaurant, Sandwich Al Paso, just three blocks east of La Moneda at the northwest corner of Estado and Alameda. Observing the twin row of tanks straddling the huge subway construction trench in the middle of Alameda, one of the breakfast regulars cracked: "They must mean business this time. They're not even stopping for the lights." He was referring, of course, to the fact that the tanks had stopped for traffic lights on June 29. The patrons on all fourteen stools quickly agreed with the Tererros—father, mother, daughter María—that the prudent thing this time would be to lower the metal curtains, pronto![27]

Skepticism understandably greeted the infantry general, Javier Palacios, who arrived to take charge of an armored regiment at seven that morning; the men of the Second Armored had, after all, been led out on a limb June 29, and their top officers were then awaiting courts-martial. But anticipating just that, Pinochet had "planted" two captains from his staff in the regiment following the *tancazo* with the concealed mission of winning the confidence of other officers and men so as to tip the balance when the order to move out arrived. That time was now, as Palacios announced that he was assuming command under orders from Pinochet and Herman Brady, commander of the Santiago military district. At first there was silence, and then an officer (one of the captains?) spoke up: "Are you sure of what you are saying, my general?"

Mounting a tank, Palacios responded with a firm retort, "Now I run this show," and a wave of the arm. The others fell in behind him. By 8:30 A.M. the tanks were arrayed in enfilade position facing the south flank of La Moneda.

Yet another, smaller convoy—presumably headed by *La Payita*—made it to the scene of the action, but that's as far as it got. From a window in the Santiago Province government building, directly across from the presidential wing of La Moneda, Carabinero Lieutenants Patricio de la Fuente Ibar and Juan Martínez Maureira watched as carloads of GAP pulled into the garage wedged between their building and the Public Works Ministry. Although the two lieutenants were far outranked by a pair of officials just two floors above, they had already received radioed orders from Mendoza's headquarters to pull out. It was while debating what to do that the caravan arrived. That ended the indecision: they ordered the dozen men under their command to follow them into the garage where they surprised fifteen GAPs unloading submachineguns, antitank mines, bazookas, and boxes of ammunition— the heavy armament Allende had ordered delivered from Tomás Moro. The lieutenants marched their prisoners and war booty out of the garage and back into the provincial government building, locking the prisoners in the guard room. (As noted, Mrs. Contreras was allowed to leave—her son was not.) The young officers were barely back when the two officials above them were on the telephone, screaming orders to release the prisoners (the two were provincial Governor Julio Stuardo, notorious for his bare-knuckles handling of the striking truckers and their wives, and Carabinero Gen. Fabián Parada Hormazabal, prefect of the province). They refused. They refused even when ordered by higher authority. Salvador Allende telephoned from across the street in the palace, where their moves had been observed by, among others, his mistress, Miria Contreras. The action of the two was significant not only because of the loss of the reinforcements and the badly needed heavy weapons, but because the prisoners they took included one known as "Bruno"— wanted in connection with the murder of the presidential naval aide, Captain Araya—and another of special importance to *La Payita*, her son. Once again, the lieutenants refused. Instead, they called the crack Special Services unit for help; a bus was dispatched for the prisoners, removing them under intensifying sniper fire. (Allende had made the disbanding of the Carabineros' Grupo Móvil a campaign issue—the Left despised them because they were so good. Once in power, however, Allende couldn't bring himself to dispense with their services; he simply renamed them the Special Services.)[28]

Installed at his headquarters, Pinochet discovered that the Carabineros were out of the communications loop. (Because of a stubborn technical glitch, Pinochet and Leigh were also unable to communicate directly; they had to relay messages through a station set up, for reasons no one could later explain, at the Military Academy. There, the commanders-in-chief of the army and air force had an eighteen-year-old plebe named Dante Pino as the bridge between them.) Early that morning, the fighting not yet begun, the following would crackle over the rarely used low frequency (144.48 Mc):

"Station One [Pinochet] to Station Five [Carvajal, in the Defense Ministry]: Is Yovane working on Carabineros? [Evidently Pinochet meant to say Mendoza rather than Yovane.]

"Station Five to Station One: Yes, he commands the forces surrounding the Moneda."[29]

(Station Two was Leigh, Three was the Military Academy—though there was no command post there—and Four was not used.)

The obedience of the two lieutenants was an important confirmation that the Carabineros were, in fact, responding to the Mendoza/Yovane coup within the coup, as Carvajal had reassured Pinochet. But there had been another confirmation already, with two more yet to come.

At 8 A.M., a busload of Carabineros pulled up at Tomás Moro to relieve the night watch. The night watch boarded the bus, the day watch remained aboard, and the bus drove off—as per orders received that morning from their new commanders. Now, only the GAP remained to defend what Allende, only a few weeks before, had boasted was "an impregnable fortress." Indeed, only that morning he had told his wife to gather their daughters and grandchildren there, because he thought it would be the safest place to be. The presence of the guards and the tank unit "did add a note of security" for Mrs. Allende. Later, her driver told her: "Señora, there is no tank, nor for that matter, are there any military at the gate." The fortress was impregnable no more.[30]

But the rudest blows of all were delivered at La Moneda itself. It was close to 9 A.M. when a GAP burst into the president's second-floor office with the news: "Mr. President—the minitanks are pulling out!" By now wearing a helmet and carrying the 1,200 round-a-minute AK-47 submachinegun Fidel Castro had given him, Allende rushed to a small balcony overlooking the Plaza Constitución, just in time to see the last of the tanquetas disappear into Teatinos Street (and to be snapped in a famous photograph). Ten minutes later, the one thousand Carabineros ringing the palace also pulled out.[31]

Allende was now left with a handful of civilians and a palace guard of some fifty GAP—and, for at least a while longer, a force of some forty to fifty Carabineros still inside the palace. Facing him: a ground force of several thousand, and another unseen force, more terrifying yet.

As in most wars, paper, plans, and proclamations predominated over raw violence—for a time. But when the shooting did erupt, it was with stupefying fury. From his fifth floor perch at the American Embassy, kitty-corner across the Plaza Constitución from La Moneda, Public Affairs Officer Jim Halsema said he had not heard such intense small arms fire since World War II—and Halsema was no stranger to battle. (Indeed, his first brush with war happened when he was only three months old, aboard a train traversing revolution-ravaged Siberia; in the years ahead, he almost literally wandered into civil war in Spain, covered war in the Philippines and Indonesia as a reporter, and strayed into yet another, the Suez War, during what was supposed to be a holiday stopover in Cairo.)[32]

Considerable doubt has been cast on whether Pinochet was really committed to the September revolution, or simply stepped in at the end to take command of a revolution which subordinates had planned and were now ready to execute; or, as a variant of that theme, whether he wasn't also pushed by the navy (at the same time as he was being pulled by his own comrades-in-arms of the army); or, if he was committed, when did he finally make up his mind? Most of the doubts are based on conclusions extracted from the posthumous memoirs of his predecessor, Gen. Carlos Prats González, reinforced mainly by the observations of persons loyal to Allende.[33] That Prats himself was professionally and emotionally committed to Allende is beyond serious dispute; if there were no other basis for the conclusion—and such bases abound—his own memoirs demonstrate that. Extensive investigation for an earlier book which this author wrote on the overthrow of Allende has persuaded him that while Pinochet, together with many other leaders of the revolt, may have hoped for a political solution which would have made the revolution unnecessary, he did move steadfastly ahead with planning for the possibility of a coup from June of 1972 onward. Parallel with the planning for war, he played a skillful poker hand of fealty, first to his commander, General Prats, and secondly to the regime. (The first was easy, given a lifetime of obedience to higher authority; the second was more difficult, given a visceral loathing of communism, reinforced during six weeks of 1948 when, as a young captain, he was given command of the Pisagua detention center where some five hundred Communist leaders—rounded up under González Videla's "Ley Maldita" (Wretched Law)—were quarantined. "I learned there," he would later write, that "the Communist party was very different from what we had thought. It was not just another party. The differences were great and profound."[34]

Evidence not now available may later surface concerning Pinochet's role in the dangerous and conscience-scourging plotting to bring down the Allende regime. Until and unless such evidence does surface, what follows is a conscientious synthesis of the available evidence, in large measure the fruits of the aforementioned research for *Allende: Death of a Marxist Dream*, bolstered by close study of countless subsequent publications (including Pinochet's own):

One of Pinochet's first acts after taking over as army chief-of-staff in January 1972 was to review the army's contingency planning for internal security (all the services had such a plan). Concluding it was hopelessly outdated and inefficient, he ordered the elaboration of a new plan. As the situation worsened in Chile, on June 23, 1972, he ordered that defensive plan gradually transformed into an offensive plan, but so as to enhance security—and mask his real intentions—he broke the plan into several pieces, assigning different phases to each group without any of them connecting to any other. His original thinking: The army should be ready to strike, if events warranted, by late July 1973.

That decision, by mid-1973 now hardened, was upended by the June 29 *tancazo*—mainly because of the lessons learned during that abortive pocket revolt. In the aftermath, Pinochet ordered sweeping revisions in the plan, including provision for war games to test the army's ability to react to various internal security scenarios. His decision to do so openly proved fortuitous: alerted by Altamirano that Pinochet was involved in coup planning, Allende routed Pinochet out of bed at three-thirty one frosty morning in August and summoned him to a bizarre, black-of-the-night meeting at Tomás Moro. So certain was he that he was about to be assassinated—at the minimum, arrested—that Pinochet also awakened his wife and the two youngest (of his five) children still at home, and after an emotional farewell, took them to the home of his eldest daughter, Inés Lucía, for safety. Arriving at Tomás Moro, Pinochet's anxieties were heightened when he saw Carlos Toro, the Communist deputy chief of Investigaciones (and, still later, his ex-boss, Eduardo "Coco" Paredes). Also there, arrayed around the room, Pinochet reflected, as though the jury in a trial about to begin: Communist party chief Luis Corvalán, Finance Minister Fernando Flores, Orlando Letelier, and—yet another surprise—a high-ranking general. Finally, close to five in the morning, Allende made a dramatic entrance: dark suit, Russian-style lamb's wool cap, blue cape with red lining—looking for all the world, Pinochet would remark, like Mephistopheles himself. For the next thirty tense moments, Allende fenced and pried and poked at Pinochet in his engagingly sly style. Clearly, he knew something about Pinochet's frequent trips to the Army War College—including a prolonged one the day before—but clearly he needed to know more. As for Pinochet, since he did have a relatively "open" plan, he was able to speak about it and his activities openly—even to the point of inviting Allende to attend the war games when they were held. That "candor" allayed the suspicions of his inquisitors. At five-thirty in the morning, a greatly relieved Augusto Pinochet Ugarte made his way through the streets of the still darkened city back to his family.[35]

But beginning on July 16, there was also a second plan—like the first, code-named "Operación Alborada" (Operation Dawn), but, unlike the first, entirely secret. Working on it were two generals, four colonels and lieutenant colonels at the Army War College, all hand-picked, all sworn to absolute secrecy. By late August, it was ready: it called for the army to seize power on September 14, using the rehearsal on that day for the annual Armed Forces Day parade on the 19th as the pretext for moving troops. Conditions in Chile also enabled him to avoid moving troops, as he needed to, if he were to complete his double-ring of fire around the capital. At a September 5 meeting with Defense Minister Letelier, he said he could only use the Santiago garrison troops for the rehearsal because both food and fuel were too scarce to bring those from outlying garrisons into the city. Letelier agreed.

The double-ring consisted of troops converging on the center of the city for the crucial battles, while others moved secretly in from outside garrisons to surround the paramilitary forces in the industrial clusters before they had a chance to do the same to the army troops fighting on the downtown streets. It was the precipitative movement of two of them—the Yungay Regiment at San Felipe and the Old Guard Regiment, sixty and fifty miles north of Santiago, respectively—which triggered René Farías's first warning call to Allende, just after midnight; Pinochet, alerted even earlier, had already radioed the commander of one of the fidgety units to settle down, deciding that the risk of detection was less from the car radio than from the tapped telephones at his home and office. In addition to army units, marines dispatched by Merino were also converging on Santiago from Valparaíso.[36]

By 8:50 A.M. Gen. Washington Carrasco reported that Concepción, the country's third city, had fallen without a shot being fired. Furthermore, thanks to the work of one engineer and three telephone company technicians, the telephones of 1,800 top UP leaders were cut. In addition, he reported, the industrial *cordones* and the radical-dominated university had been neutralized. By noon, many of those top leaders were on their way to Quiriquina Island, in Concepción Bay, north of the city.[37]

Similar operations were carried out in Valparaíso; by 5:45 A.M., all twelve radio stations had been silenced (key crystals were removed under a carefully rehearsed plan), as were official and private radio transmitters. Since the telephone company was also in military hands, only the navy's own "green line" connected Valparaíso to the rest of the country. And by day's end—to Merino's later regret—"only" 260 persons had been taken prisoner. "I wish we had taken more," he would say later; ". . . we controlled the industrial strongholds . . . had we rounded up more activists, especially the leaders, we would have headed off a lot of trouble later."[38]

Under the command of Col. Julio Polloni Pérez, chief of army telecommunications and one of the key plotters, two hundred troops fanned out around Santiago during the predawn hours, divided into groups of twenty to thirty. Their mission, carefully worked out by Polloni, the civilian expert "César" who had worked with him, and others: silence as many as possible of the twenty-six commercial radio stations in Santiago (except those preselected as the voices of revolution), international cable and telex services, news agency lines, long distance and international telephone services, private radio transmitters—not the least of them, the powerful equipment installed in the warehouse of the state-run Development Corporation, which provided a twenty-four-hour radio link with stalwart ally Fidel Castro. That was phase one of the plan; phase two, the supersecret part, called for setting up the secret radio network which not only linked the commanders in Santiago, but also the military garrisons stretching the 2,700 miles from Arica near the Peruvian border in the north to Punta Arenas hard by the Straits of Magellan to the south. By 7 A.M., after weeks of planning and plotting, culminated by round-the-clock feverish, frenzied and frequently frustrating toil over the last few days, the job was done.[39]

The first, scattered shots were fired on army units as they converged on the downtown area. Even more than at the time of the June 29 *tancazo*, the paramilitary brigades had taken up positions on rooftops and strategically located windows throughout the downtown area, vastly augmenting the firepower protecting the fortress-like Moneda Palace. But over the hours ahead, much of that firepower would also be directed at other targets, including Radio Agricultura, the U.S. Embassy—and, quite by mistake, United Press International's too well-placed downtown offices. (The shooting would not prevent UPI from outfoxing Operation Silence and getting the big story out by a devious but effective channel.)[40] The entire Santiago operation was under the command of General Brady, one of the two close personal friends Pinochet had managed to maneuver into controlling the two crucial commands in the Santiago area, replacing Allende loyalists. Commanding the downtown area itself was Gen. Sergio Arellano—also one of the key plotters; indeed, he was putting the finishing touches on the combat plans until close to 2 A.M. Palacios was charged with the attack on La Moneda itself; and the other of Pinochet's two close friends, Gen. César Raúl Benavides, was given the job of capturing two (Vicuña Mackenna and Los Cerrillos) of the three *cordones de la muerte* ("belts of death," as the radical Left liked to call the heavily armed industrial strongholds flanking Santiago). The first two were south of the city; the third, Panamericana Norte, north of it; Col. Felipe Geiger and his Buin Regiment were assigned to that front.[41] The army troops took their orders directly, of course, from Pinochet, seconded by his deputy, Gen. Oscar Bonilla Bradanovic, installed at their Peñalolén headquarters. (At his last meeting with top generals the day before, Pinochet had designated Bonilla as the man who would take over should anything happened to him—an option Bonilla feared, for a few moments, he might have to exercise.) In claiming to follow strictly the order of seniority in naming Bonilla, Pinochet pointedly skipped over the actual numbers two and three men, Gen. Orlando Urbina and Gen. Ernesto Baeza, presumably because it was not clear whether they would tilt toward Allende or the rebels. (Baeza would not only become a key player on the eleventh, but quickly demonstrate his loyalty: he was named to the critical job of heading Investigaciones, the national police detective force, infested with Allende loyalists.) The incident is yet another demonstration of the institution-wrenching decisions so alien to the character and habits of the men who made them, yet another demonstration of the brother-against-brother ugliness unleashed on the bitterly divided land.[42] Coordination of the operations of the entire combined forces was in the capable and calm hands of Vice Adm. Patricio Carvajal Prado, installed on the ninth floor of the Defense Ministry and ably back-stopped by air force Gen. Nicanor Díaz, army Gen. Sergio Nuño, and others.

They would, that morning, be joined by another who would arrive to attend a routine meeting, only to discover he had walked into the command post of revolution: Gen. Ernesto Baeza. As indicated, Baeza had been omitted from the secret plotting, but he now found himself playing a pivotal role in that revolution.

On the fifth floor of the same building, about twenty officers, most assigned to Carvajal's Joint Chiefs' staff, manned the Armed Forces Operations Center (COFA). Until seven that morning, there was nothing unusual about appearances in the building—nor even outside: the guard had not even been beefed up. That would change at seven, when Díaz summoned the guard detail: "We are at war," he told them. "The armed forces have resolved to depose the government. Anyone not in agreement is free to leave." There was, he would recollect, but one question: "Has anything been done to protect our families?" a soldier asked.

The general said that was not possible. "Mine has no protection, either," he added.[43]

Diagonally across the Alameda, the scene in La Moneda was one of intense activity, too. While some prepared for battle, others shredded documents, still others inventoried armaments. Dr. Danilo Bartulín, the cardiologist Dr. Oscar Soto, and the other doctors went about setting up an infirmary in the administration offices of the palace, in the northeast wing of the building (they would later move to safer quarters in the basement.) Among those doctors: Patricio Guijón Klein.

A surgeon, Guijón was then forty-one, the father of four children, a man who lived modestly and inconspicuously with his family in a simple, DFL-2 (government-subsidized) house on Luis Carrera Street, and in common with most doctors in Chile at that time, compelled to work two medical jobs in order to make ends barely meet. Although attracted to Marxist ideas from his early youth, Guijón was not a political activist. In October 1972, Dr. Arturo Jirón, who had been Allende's surgeon, was appointed minister of health. He was succeeded by Dr. Patricio Arroyo, an Allende intimate and former classmate and close friend of Patricio Guijón. Arroyo asked Guijón whether he would like to join the presidential medical staff, a largely honorary appointment (he not only never got to examine his famous patient, he never even met

Allende; in fact, about all he got to do was join the other five presidential physicians at a weekly meeting).

At seven-fifteen on the morning of the eleventh, he got a telephone call from his friend and colleague, Dr. Alejandro Cuevas (nickname: Pelado).

"Pachi [Guijón's nickname since childhood], you've got to get to La Moneda—pronto."

"But Pelado, the meeting isn't until Wednesday. Today is Tuesday."

"Don't ask dumb questions, just get going," Cuevas responded.

Guijón's wife Silvia, listening in, said nothing but told their twelve-year-old boy to hurry—family rites included Patricio dropping the boy off every day at Colegio Alemán—while Silvia took the other two school-age children to their school at the eastern end of the city. Guijón was only halfway there when the brakes of the Fiat 125, the family's one luxury, gave out. As luck would have it, Silvia happened to be driving behind him in their battered station wagon. Patricio sent her back to the house for a tool to fix the problem. Half an hour later, she was back and he was on his way.

Fate handed Patricio Guijón yet another chance to escape the life-crunching happenstance still a few hours away. With no radio in his car, Patricio Guijón had no notion what was happening as he weaved his way around one Carabinero road-block after another, which were springing up to seal off the downtown area. Finally, he made it to within a short walk of the palace and "did the only intelligent thing I had done all morning": he pulled into an underground garage used by the U.S. Embassy where spaces were reserved for the former Braden Copper Co. (the Kennecott subsidiary, until its expropriation two years earlier). Guijón had been on the staff of the nationalized company for some time, and so he parked and left the keys in the ignition.

It was only when he finally reached the palace, around 8 A.M., that he learned of the momentous events afoot. One of his first thoughts was to let Silvia know where he had left the car; as Silvia, a nurse, was already at work at a hospital, he left word with his father, thus assuring the survival of "the family fortune." It would turn out to be a very lucky impulse, offsetting, perhaps, his unlucky determination to make it into La Moneda that September morning.[44]

A CHANGED MAN

Navy Commander Jorge Grez was among the first to see the change in Salvador Allende's mood.

"When I first arrived," he recalled, "I was shocked to see him with the helmet on and a sub-machinegun on his desk. But he was still in bold spirits. When I reported, he waved from his chair, and the first thing he said to me was: 'Once again, we have problems with your navy, Commander.' He had used those exact same words to me just two weeks before, and I was taken aback when he used them again.

"It was when someone on the OIR [the government information and broadcasting office] staff brought him the text of the proclamation that his mood changed. He had heard it, but now, reading it, he became much more somber, changed."[45]

Grez had taken over as naval aide-de-camp to the president only six weeks before, following the murder of Captain Araya. When he went off duty the previous evening, he had expected to spend the rest of the week relaxing. All that changed when he heard the radio reports of heavy Carabinero reinforcements around La Moneda earlier that morning, then learned that the president had left Tomás Moro for La Moneda. Arriving at the palace at around 8:35, a guard at first blocked his way; Grez persisted, and as he entered, was joined by *La Payita*—Miria Contreras.

At about that same time, Allende heard from two other military sources: Colonel Valenzuela, back from the Defense Ministry, reported that he had not only been unable to locate Letelier—he had also been barred access to his own office. Next, Allende received a telephone call from his air force aide, Col. Raúl Sánchez. According to one account, Sánchez said he was speaking on behalf of air force Lt. Gen. Gabriel van Schouwen Figueroa. Van Schouwen was then number two in seniority in the air force, and Allende regarded him as sympathetic to him, even though a few weeks before van Schouwen had incurred the president's wrath during the mid-August air force crisis. When Leigh balked at taking over from Ruiz Danyau, Allende offered the job to van Schouwen, who also turned it down. "No one wants to be commander-in-chief," Allende is reported to have exploded. "What do they want me to do—name Sánchez?"[46]

Now that same Sánchez was telling the president that the air force had a plane standing by to take Allende, his family and immediate associates into exile. "Tell General van Schouwen that the president does not flee by plane. The general should know how to act like a soldier, just as I know how to carry out my sworn duty as president of the republic." Hanging up the telephone, Allende is reported to have added: "The traitors, the traitors . . . they don't even have the guts to tell me this directly."[47] (With but a single line—the navy's green line—left into La Moneda, "the traitors" could not have told Allende anything directly. Regular telephone lines had been cut within the hour after Brady complained to Carvajal that Allende continued "pestering" him for information; some within the palace, however, did manage to make a few, sporadic outgoing calls through the morning.)

The combination of these events dashed any remaining hope Allende might have had that he was dealing with an isolated revolt involving the navy in Valparaíso and a few army units. Allende decided to take once again to the airwaves. Spinning the dial of a radio, seeking in vain to find stations still supporting him, he would find only one: Radio Magallanes, powered by an emergency transmitter.

"Next to his desk," Grez said, "he had three telephones with direct lines to the radio stations—Portales, Magallanes, and Corporación. He was jiggling the crank when an operator came on.

" 'This is the president,' he said. 'I am going to speak to the nation.' The operator said, 'Give me ten seconds,' and he waited, and then he went on." His voice was calm, his speech measured.[48]

"This will surely be my last chance to speak to you. The air force has bombarded the antennas of Radio Magallanes. My words carry not bitterness but disappointment. May there be moral punishment for those who have betrayed their oath: the soldiers of Chile, Commander-in-Chief Admiral Merino, who has proclaimed himself commandant of the navy, as well as Mr. Mendoza, that drag-along general who only yesterday affirmed his fidelity and loyalty to the government and who has now proclaimed himself director-general of the Carabineros. In the face of these deeds, I have only one thing to say to the workers: I am not going to resign!

"Placed in this historic juncture, I will repay with my life the loyalty of the people. I tell you that I am certain that the seed we have given to the worthy consciousness of thousands and thousands of Chileans cannot be rooted out entirely. They have the force, they can crush us, but social processes are not held back by crime or by force. History is ours, and the people will make it.

"Workers of my country, I have to thank you for the loyalty you have always had, the confidence you have placed in a man who was only the interpreter of a great yearning for justice, who pledged his word that he would respect the constitution and the law, and who has done so. In this definitive moment, the last in which I am able to speak to you, I wish to take advantage of the lesson: foreign capital and imperialism, united with reaction, created the climate in which the armed forces would break with their tradition, the one Schneider would teach them and Captain Araya would reaffirm,* both of them victims of the same social class that waits today at home while other hands reconquer power so that they can continue defending their profits and their privileges.

"I address myself, above all, to the modest women of our land, the farm women who believed in us, the worker who wanted more work, the mother who knew of our concern for children.

"I address myself to the professionals of the fatherland, those who continued working against the sedition sponsored by the professional societies, the classist societies, which also defended the advantages of a capitalist society of the few.

"I address myself to the youth, to those who sang and gave of their joy and their fighting spirit.

"I address myself to the men of Chile, the worker, the peasant, the intellectual, to those who will be persecuted, because in our country fascism has already been with us for a long while: in terrorist attacks, blowing up bridges, cutting railroad lines, destroying oil and gas pipelines, in the face of the silence of those who had the obligation to act. They were implicated. History will judge them.

"Surely, Radio Magallanes will be silenced, and the sound of my voice will not reach you again. It doesn't matter. You will continue to hear it. I will always be with you. At least my memory will remain with you: that of a worthy man who was loyal to the fatherland.

"You, the people, must defend yourselves, but not sacrifice yourselves. You should not allow yourselves to be cowed or mowed down, but neither should you be humiliated.

"Workers of my fatherland, I have faith in Chile and in its destiny. Other men will overcome this dark and bitter moment that betrayal would impose on us. Continue believing that, much sooner than later, once again the grand promenades will be opened on which free men walk to construct a better society.

"Viva Chile! Viva the people! Long live the workers!

"These are my last words, and I am certain that the sacrifice will not be in vain; I am certain that, at the very least, it will be a moral lesson that will punish felony, cowardice, and treason."[49]

It is not clear whether Pinochet heard that broadcast. It is clear how he reacted. Relaying the message through Cadet Pino, Pinochet asked Leigh to "study the possibility" of knocking out Radio Magallanes from the air. (As the day wore on, Pinochet's tone became more peremptory, his commands more unquestioned; Leigh's, strong throughout, did not yield ground so much as it was preempted by Pinochet.) The silencing job was given to Jorge Massa Armijo, a man who had won worldwide

---

* He was referring to Gen. René Schneider, the army commander-in-chief killed in October 1970, and his recently murdered naval aide.

fame on December 22, 1972, when he piloted a helicopter to a then unprecedented 16,500 feet in a daring rescue of the survivors of an Uruguayan air force plane that had crashed in the high Andes. Now, the thirty-nine-year-old squadron commander went aloft in another helicopter. He fired a single rocket from a distance of 1.2 miles (two kilometers). It was enough to do the job—Radio Magallanes was off the air for good. (Radio Corporación would sputter back on the air about an hour later, around 11 A.M., on the FM band. An air force major, firing an automatic rifle from the fourth floor of the Defense Ministry, blasted its antenna, situated on the roof of the State Bank Building across the street.)[50]

Allende had just finished speaking when the navy green phone on Commander Grez's desk began ringing. It was Admiral Carvajal, and he wanted Grez to convey word to Allende that he should leave the palace immediately—or shoulder responsibility for the consequences. Grez gave him a quick rundown on the situation inside La Moneda which Carvajal promptly relayed to Pinochet:

"I have just spoken to the naval aide-de-camp," Carvajal reported. "[He] tells me that La Moneda is being defended by around fifty GAPS and forty to fifty Carabineros, and that the president is running around with a sub-machinegun with thirty shots and saying the last two shots would be for himself."

"Pure fiction!" Pinochet exploded over the radio. "That lout wouldn't know how to shoot a tube of toothpaste."

Carvajal laughed and told Pinochet that he had instructed Grez to urge Carabinero General Sepúlveda to pull his men out or risk being bombed. Grez in fact talked to the lieutenant commanding that force, and he agreed to pull his men out at 10:30 sharp; hands in the air, they filed out the big Morandé doors then darted the fifty yards across the Plaza Constitución to the underground parking area of the Carabineros' Radio Patrol unit. When Allende discovered this, he once again vented his fury on the Carabinero generals. Unarmed, unguarded, and demoralized, they talked among themselves. "I did not see them again," Grez said. "They left the place."

"It was a hard blow to him," Interior Minister Carlos Briones remembers. "We believed the Carabineros would be loyal."

A navy steward adds: "It was about then that he started to drink—whiskey, Chivas Regal. By 10:30, he was pretty tipsy. Another military man inside the palace said he saw Allende down four whiskeys within one hour's time. Briones said he saw the president drink only one."[51]

* * *

Minutes later, Bando (Communique) Number Two:

"La Moneda Palace must be evacuated before 11 A.M. If it is not, it will be attacked by the Air Force of Chile.

"Workers should remain in their places of work, it being absolutely forbidden for them to leave.

"In the event they should do so, they will be attacked by land and air forces.

"The contents of Bando #1 are reiterated in the sense that any act of sabotage will be punished in the most drastic form possible on the spot."

Surrounded, virtually undefended, and facing aerial bombardment, Allende gathered all those in the palace for what amounted to his last large meeting. He selected the Toesca Salon, the largest conference hall at La Moneda (named for the Italian architect who, late in the eighteenth century, designed the neoclassic structure). Allende apologist Samuel Chavkin writes: "A huge chandelier lit up the unadorned, pale-yellow walls of the ceremonial chamber, usually reserved for high-level official functions. Allende sat down behind a huge table on the platform, at the head of the hall. Frida Modak [one of his personal secretaries] remembers that the president outlined the nature of the insurrection, reported on the latest developments, and spoke of his decision to fight it out at La Moneda. But, he explained, this was to be a political action, and should not be viewed in terms of personal martyrdom. Dispassionately, he went on to declare that the battle of La Moneda was only the beginning. 'This is how we write the first page of history. The next page will be written by the Chilean people and by all Latin Americans.' And once again he called on those in the palace who had no experience with firearms to get out and help develop the resistance on the outside. Also, he added, those who did not agree with his decisions to make a stand in La Moneda should leave, and should do so without guilt, without remorse: 'The struggle against fascism need not result in useless deaths; there will be plenty to do outside the palace.' " Next, Chavkin says, he turned to the matter of the nine women in the palace: his daughters Beatriz and Isabel, his "private secretary" (as Chavkin refers to his mistress Miria Contreras), Nancy Barrios, two UP newspaper reporters, two clerical assistants, the wife of an economist who decided to remain with him, and Frida Modak herself. After a prolonged and contentious exchange with the women—particularly Beatriz—"he rose and strode out of the room in the direction of his private office. There were no special words for his daughters or for anyone else. A short, steely silence followed. There was scarcely any time for us to react. Events were moving quickly and preparations for the defense of the palace took on a grim reality. As if to underscore the gravity of the moment, shots were heard from the direction of the main square in front of the palace . . ."[52]

And, indeed, the battle was heating up. Tanks of the Second Armored Regiment, situated on Teatinos Street in front of the newspaper *La Nación*, opened fire on the north facade of La Moneda—the side housing the presidential offices (as well as the Interior Ministry). One volley blew in the big double doors from which the Carabineros had fled moments before. Infantry School troops took up position at the corner of Agustinas and Teatinos, between the U.S. Embassy and the Hotel Carrera, the city's biggest. On the south side of La Moneda, the Tacna Regiment—the one General Viaux had led in bold rebellion four years before—deployed around the Plaza Bulnes (below the Defense Ministry and the United Press International offices). With them were the 1,200 men of the Noncommissioned Officers' School under Col. Julio Canessa Roberts, also one of the key plotters. Corp. Pedro Pizarro Mora, serving in that unit, remembers that when his company reached the plaza, they had to chase rubber-neckers off the streets, and at the plaza itself, although jeeps were already deployed, mounted with 30- and 50-caliber machineguns, they had to shoo away a couple holding hands and kissing.[53] There was no one holding hands and kissing when the shooting started.

From the Education Ministry diagonally across the Alameda, from the spindly ENTEL tower two blocks west, snipers opened fire. Pizarro hit the dirt and began firing while lying on his back. Eight men fell wounded around Canessa. The colonel and a major with him found themselves virtually cut off by heavy machinegun and rifle fire from three sides. "Some of my men practically shielded me with their bodies," Canessa said. Most of the shooting seemed to come from the Continental Theater building on the west side of Plaza Bulnes, a combination office/apartment building, whose tenants included the UPI on the ninth floor. A sweep of the building yielded a passel of prisoners; among the snipers, nine Hondurans. But because the sniping persisted, sharpshooters continued to rake the upper floors with fire for six hours. UPI manager Steve Yolen counted them as the longest six hours of his life: "it was," he said, "like the end of the world." When the smoke cleared, they counted four hundred impacts on the walls of the suite of offices, the gunfire so heavy at times that the offices were filled with the choking dust of concrete as bullets pinged off the walls. (Miraculously, none of the four UPI employees who remained throughout the ordeal was hurt.)[54]

From within the palace, the defenders opened up with everything they had. Dr. Bartulín narrates: "The noise of rifles and machineguns was deafening. Most of the shooting was aimed at the section of the palace which houses the president's private office. But out of that very office a bazooka was seen protruding from the window out of which a shot scored a direct hit at a tank as it neared the building.

"Momentarily it was heartening because our counterattack appeared to stop the junta soldiers. Two of their tanks had been destroyed and many of their men were in retreat. The commanding officer of the junta forces was enraged; he warned us by radio that unless we surrendered the air force would blow us to smithereens. . . ."[55]

Across that great divide that was the dug-up Alameda, Canessa was pulling his men back about 150 yards to escape the withering sniper fire.

Despite the shooting, the talking went on. Allende managed to get a call through to General Baeza at the Defense Ministry. He told the general he wanted the commanders-in-chief to come to La Moneda and negotiate with him. Baeza said he would relay the message, but believed Allende should simply surrender, as he had been advised to do.

"Allende told me that under no circumstances would he accept the ultimatum. He also said he didn't believe the air force would dare bomb La Moneda, and that, in any event, they could do whatever they wanted with him, he was not going to surrender.

"He was neither abusive nor excited as he spoke to me," Baeza added.

Baeza relayed the message to Pinochet. Baeza said Pinochet's reaction was "a flat no." Pinochet would express that "flat no" even more aggressively when he got on the radio to Carvajal. His voice rising, the words cascading ever faster, he veritably shouted into the radio: "I told you that creep is tricky. He is a liar. If he wants, let him go to the Ministry of Defense and surrender . . ."[56]

Carvajal was quick to comply with Pinochet's instructions—but he handled the assignment in the quiet, methodical manner befitting his pipe-smoking, very British style. Picking up the green phone, he called Grez, and told him that he wanted to talk to the president. The time was 9:25 A.M.

Going next door to the president's office, Grez noticed that the GAPs with him—outwardly suspicious of the military aides in the palace all morning—fingered their weapons menacingly. Grez relayed the message that Carvajal was on the green phone in his office. Without hesitation, Allende took the call.

"Carvajal began speaking," Grez reported, "but Allende interrupted him and began shouting and cursing at him. He was tremendously excited. When that flare-up passed, he quieted down, and Carvajal again spoke to him, but he didn't let Carvajal finish. He threw the telephone on the table and said: 'I am not going to permit them to speak to me in those terms . . .' "

Those "terms" were the first direct word to Allende: surrender or the palace will be bombed. Surrender and there is a plane standing by to take your party anywhere you want on the South American continent . . .

With tension mounting in the palace, Grez decided to consult with the other aides to coordinate their moves. The senior man, air force Maj. Roberto Sánchez—who had been with Allende throughout his presidency—finally reached La Moneda a few minutes later. When he did, Grez and army Maj. Sergio Badiola (who, as duty officer that week, had been at the palace since early morning) huddled and decided to request a private meeting with the president. Allende agreed, but several GAPs refused to leave the room, protesting that the *milicos* (the slang word for military) could not be trusted. Allende ordered them out, but when several still remained in a corner, "he got up and shouted: 'I want everyone out of here because I am going to talk to them!' Some," Grez continued, "still stayed in a corner, so we went into a small room. Altogether it took ten minutes for us to begin our conversation, and once we did, it didn't last but six or eight minutes.

"Each of us gave him our estimate of the military situation, and told him we each had a duty to fulfill in trying to persuade him. I pointed out to him the futility of a few armed guys attempting to hold out against the coordinated action of the entire armed forces, including an air force attack on the palace . . .

"He then told us he would not give up. He was not going to leave his office, and he was not going to negotiate with the commanders-in-chief on the conditions they demanded. . . . He told us, as the only representatives of the armed forces present at that moment, that his final decision was to stay in La Moneda, he was going to defend himself, and for that he had this, pointing to his sub-machinegun.

" 'I will defend myself,' he said, 'until the end, and if it is necessary, the last shot of this machinegun I will shoot here'—and with that he lifted his index finger and put it inside the roof of his mouth. The gun was then on his lap. . . .' "

Sánchez tried again to persuade him, but Allende was adamant. He authorized them to leave, "then he said a formal farewell to each of us. He shook hands with us, and then he got up and left. He called out in a very loud voice, to those outside, and told them of his decision to let us go." (Grez would recall later that of the four possibilities that ran through his mind before that dramatic meeting, he "never thought for an instant that he would order us killed.")

Each of the aides went to his desk, then they rounded up their assistants: Grez, the six or eight navy stewards, his driver and personal aide, made for the Morandé 80 door. It was 10:20 A.M. Then came the four hundred-yard dash across an area completely enfiladed by gunfire, "a tremendous amount of shooting."

Arriving safely at Defense, Grez reported directly to Carvajal: "He's not going to leave La Moneda."

"*Conforme*," said Pinochet, when Carvajal radioed Grez's report. "At ten to eleven I am going to give the order to bomb. Consequently, all units should withdraw at that time two blocks from La Moneda. . . ." After giving that order, he told Carvajal to make certain the last Carabinero guards not be fired upon as they left. And, betraying some of the nervous tension of the day, he wondered whether there was anything to a report that Allende had committed suicide, or to yet another that Allende might have sneaked out of the palace in one of the tanquetas. Carvajal assured him that the tanquetas had all pulled out before Grez and the other aides had their meeting with a very much alive Salvador Allende.[57]

If Grez had earlier thought Allende "a changed man," so too did another, a man who had known him as a close associate and political ally for twenty-five years, had served in his Cabinet, and, the night before, had shared his last supper. That man was Carlos Briones.

"He was a changed man that morning," Briones would observe later. Like the military aides, Briones, Foreign Minister Clodomiro Almeyda, and former Defense Minister José Tohá also met with Allende, trying to persuade him to surrender. " 'No, and that is final,' he told us," Briones said. " 'I will leave here dead.' "[58]

There would be other desperate attempts to find a peaceful way out in the hours ahead. None would succeed in doing more than to raise the hackles of Pinochet and Leigh and delay the bombing.

On one of those calls, Carvajal told Tohá that if Allende wouldn't surrender, "then take him by force." Tohá reminded Carvajal that the president was carrying a sub-machinegun.[59] As Carvajal was relaying that to Pinochet, Tohá was again on the line, asking for ten more minutes to attempt once again to reason with Allende. Pinochet interrupted: "This is Augusto. Confirm that you hear me, Patricio . . . this gentleman is buying time. He is trying to take advantage of us. I do not accept any negotiations. What 'conditions'? There are no 'decorous' conditions. What sort of crap is he trying to pull? Unconditional surrender! Is that clear? If he wants to go, accompanied by Sepúlveda [the deposed Carabinero commandant] to the ministry to surrender, good. If not, we are going to bomb."

Next, Pinochet called Leigh. "Gustavo, Augusto is calling you," Cadet Pino said, by now bandying the names of the top commanders as though they were old friends. Pino relayed to Leigh an account of the instructions Pinochet had just given Carvajal—the only time that day that Pinochet seemingly sought support for his decisions.

"Position Two to Position Three," Leigh said, aiming his message at the relay station. "It is nefarious to give delays and accept negotiations. All this talk is turning things around. Tohá, Almeyda, all of them, let's send them anywhere—except Argentina." (That was Leigh's first mention of a new restriction.)

"Do we or don't we attack La Moneda?" Leigh then demanded. His pilots were holding just south of the city. Static snarled communications, and to compound matters, Leigh was told that Pinochet could not come immediately to the radio because he was on the telephone. "To hell with delaying tactics, jeeps and women, I am going to attack now. Over and out."

Pinochet came back on the line: give them three minutes to get the women out, three minutes, he commanded. The attack was halted—but not for three minutes. It had been over two hours since the planes had streaked down the runway in Concepción headed for Santiago. They now had to return to Concepción to refuel.

"The air attack," Leigh said, "is now scheduled for 11:40. *Conforme?*"

"*Conforme,*" Pinochet responded.[60]

A TIME TO LIVE . . .

Realizing time was running out, Allende had put in a second call to Baeza at the Defense Ministry. Crucial minutes passed while an aide rushed to find Baeza, then meeting four floors above with Carvajal. More precious minutes were lost while Baeza returned and dialed Allende's number, only to find it busy, over and over again. Finally:

"General, I want to tell the commanders-in-chief I need ten extra minutes so that the women can leave the palace. One of them is my daughter, and she is pregnant. [That was Beatriz, then eight months pregnant; she had another three-year-old daughter at home; curiously, Allende did not mention that daughter Isabel was also there.] It is simple humanity. There are a great number of men here, but only the women will leave."

Baeza promised to do what he could, but warned that it would be difficult because the planes were already approaching.[61]

Allende had been having a very hard time persuading the women to go. Frida Modak recalls: "During a brief lull in the battle, the president rushed down to our shelter [he had stashed them for safekeeping in a small storage room] and began imploring us to leave. 'You are so young,' he said, 'and you have so much to contribute in the fight against the junta.' He addressed us individually, in turn, pointing up our value in the struggles ahead. . . ."[62]

Daughter Isabel remembers her father ". . . watchful by a window, encouraging members of his personal security force [the GAPs], and without losing his sense of humor in those miserable [*aciagos*] moments, firing his machinegun at the tanks of the rebels. When the fighting started someone said he should wear a bullet-proof vest. He refused, saying, 'Why should I? I'm a combatant just like the others.' " (Later, Allende expressed his amazement at "the coordination, precision and brutality of the military attacks," Isabel continued. "He felt disappointed at not having solved the problems with the navy . . . My father knew that the truck strike and the siege laid down by the attacking troops made it impossible for worker reinforcements to reach him, and from the very beginning of the attack, understood that help would not come from abroad, either.")[63] When he told the women—and a few men who had also decided to leave—that he had extracted a promise of a brief cease-fire and that a jeep would pick them up, Isabel protested: "Papá, you still believe in the word of a military man!" In fact, Allende very nearly derailed the truce talks when he let his temper briefly get the best of him. On the telephone with Carvajal, he said: "Take care, Admiral, that the fascists don't kill [the women]." "What fascists are you talking about, Mr. Allende," Carvajal shot back. "I know you," Allende said, "you are a sailor and not a fascist."

Hardest of all to persuade was Beatriz: closest to him in her revolutionary ardor, she was also his political confidante. First, she protested that if they left, they would be taken hostage. Still later, "They'll kill us." Allende said if the military did that, "history will judge them not only as traitors, but as murderers of women." Then:

"Please go. You have a mother to look after. You, Tati [Beatriz] have your husband; your duty is to be with him." Finally:

"If you don't leave, you'll force me to go into the street with you."

That ended the argument. The president escorted the group down to the Morandé side door.[64]

"I shall never forget that last time I saw Allende, his head covered by a helmet, his hand holding a machinegun," Frida Modak recalled. "There were no further last-moment embraces or farewells. We suddenly found ourselves out on the street, with the door shut behind us."[65]

The promised jeep was not at the door. Though the military did stop firing, the snipers—not privy to the Moneda-Ministry talks—continued. The jeep was forced to turn back. According to Modak's account, for the next four, harrowing hours, the women would wander from place to place, amid "a deafening roar of bullets," stumbling at one point into the lobby of a downtown hotel on Ahumada Street where a group was celebrating Allende's overthrow with champagne and merriment, until finally reaching the home of a friend of Nancy Barrios. The six of them would remain there for thirty-six hours.[66]

Six, because two had peeled off early in that stygian odyssey. And one never left at all: *La Payita.*

"I hid in a small cellar tunnel," she said. "I had decided to fight at his side to the very end. A little while later the president discovered me.

" 'I knew you would figure out some way to get around me,' he said. Soon after that, Bartulín asked me for the key to his car because he wanted to give it to a companion who had to go." (The "companion" turned out to be Beatriz; despite the shooting, the troops had already pulled back in anticipation of the imminent bombing, so the streets were deserted—except for two drunks whose reeling and gesturing added to the insanity of the scene. Beatriz decided to go back to the palace and pounded on the door until Dr. Bartulín opened it. He refused to let her and Isabel in, but did offer the use of his car. When the women reached the garage, they found it a shambles, and had to walk on.)

"A bit later," Mrs. Contreras went on, "I spoke again to the president. I asked him how he had convinced Beatriz and Isabel to leave. He answered: 'I told them they would be in charge of taking a personal message to Fidel.'

"Afterward, he called us all together in the Winter Garden. He gave new instructions, then spoke to his friend, Joán Garcés, asking him to go. 'This fight is not for you,' he said, 'because you are a foreigner. . . .' "[67]

Augusto Pinochet was not so much giving new instructions, as he was repeating the earlier ones. After Carvajal gave him a rundown of unit deployment, Pinochet said: "Good, because this cluck is not going to give himself up."

"We are attacking already," Carvajal told him, "we are surrounding and attacking with considerable intensity. Soon we are going to be able to take it [the palace]." (His optimism, as events would reveal, was misplaced.)

"O.K.," said Pinochet, "and as soon as we do, we drop him off at the airplane and send him on his way."

Carvajal reminded Pinochet that Allende had refused the offer of the airplane and wanted the commandants to come to the palace.

"What he wants," Pinochet said, "is for us to get there so they can stick us in a dungeon . . . so the answer is no. For now, attack La Moneda—hard!"

A few minutes later: "This is final, that he give up and hand in his resignation. This is the last time we will address him as president. He will be guaranteed his life and physical safety and sent abroad . . . resign and there will be no more bloodshed. Otherwise, to the last consequences!"

Carvajal: "In other words, the offer stands to take him out of the country."

Pinochet: "The offer stands to take him out of the country. But if the plane should crash as it is taking off . . ." (Nervous giggling followed this flash of gallows humor.)[68]

At about that time, Pinochet had another concern, closer to his bucolic headquarters. Stepping outside for a moment, he met the commander of the special paratroop unit, who told him Peñalolén itself was taking fire. Pinochet ordered an immediate sweep of the area, and returned to his post.[69]

As the war raged outside, Allende waged yet another of his own inside the besieged palace: "Let's give ourselves the pleasure of smashing the busts of all these old reactionaries," he told his companions. With a wave of the hand, he indicated the busts of the country's past presidents. "Respect only those of José Balmaceda and Pedro Aguirre Cerda, the only democratic presidents." (Aguirre Cerda had headed the first Popular Front government thirty-five years before and Balmaceda was, of course, Allende's special hero, the first Populist president, who ended his own life by suicide following an 1891 military uprising.) He then proceeded to lead the vandalism himself.[70]

Inevitably, a large number of civilians found themselves caught in the cross-fire of revolution. The largest number in one place was in the Hotel Carrera, facing the Plaza Constitución, diagonally opposite La Moneda. In addition to the strike-diminished staff of 240 (of a full complement of 465 employees), General Manager Miguel (Mike) Gallegos Dubost also had a full house of guests: 378, including thirty-seven foreign newsmen. At the first sign of trouble that morning, he had ordered the main doors opening onto the plaza closed. When the shooting started, he ordered the steel shutters closed over all windows on the second through fourth floors (the ground floor was solid wall except the door). Since a high percentage of his staff was Marxist and/or Allende loyalist, the first challenge was to win the staff to his side. "I appealed to their pride as Chileans, to be brave in this emergency," Gallegos said. It was an appeal he could make persuasively: he was then rounding out twenty-three years in hotel management, having risen through the ranks of three international chains, returning to his native Chile at the outset of the Allende regime to take over the Carrera. Next, he had the five telephone operators call all guests in their rooms and ask them to report to the lobby. "I told them [the guests] I had talked to the authorities—bullshit, I hadn't talked to anyone, of course—and they assured me they realized we were in an international hotel and no harm would come to us." When the tanks opened fire, "the whole building shook," Gallegos remembered. "Some people became hysterical and tried to run out. We had security at the door, blocking them, but it was a job ..."

The real test came when he learned of the impending air attack on a building located only two football fields away. Recruiting volunteers to patrol the corridors to prevent looting, he then led as many guests as would go to safety in the basement of the sturdy, thirty-five-year-old concrete building. As for the rest, he simply urged them to stay away from the windows. Most did: of the 620 persons in the building, only one—a newspaperman who caught shrapnel in his shoulder—was injured. That was all the more remarkable inasmuch as seventy-nine rooms in the building suffered damage; hardest hit were rooms 821 and 1121, the latter Gallegos' own suite, which took over 290 bullet impacts. The shooting was so intense that the hot lead set fire to curtains in the suite.[71]

Just a few blocks away, in the apartment of former president Jorge Alessandri, a maid could not resist the temptation to peek out the window overlooking the Plaza de Armas. "I had told her until I was sick of telling her, 'don't look out,'" the former president said. But she persisted, until a bullet lodged in her head, killing her.[72]

Hector Humeres was eight blocks from his office in the Contraloría when he heard the first military proclamation calling on Allende to resign. Humeres had headed that unique institution since 1967, the eleventh man to hold the job since its creation in 1927 (on the advice of an American, Edwin Walter Kemmerer). Although the Contraloría is located directly across Teatinos Street from the southeast flank of La Moneda Palace—and thus certain to be at the heart of the fighting, should it erupt—Humeres ordered his driver to go on. "I decided immediately," he would recall later, "that I must be at the office because Allende would need me as an adviser on legalisms, or as an intermediary of confidence [Ministro de Fe] should he agree to hand over power." The call he had steeled himself to handle never came, but a series of unforgettable scenes did await him as he watched the unfolding war through a crack in the heavy metal blinds of his ninth floor office. He watched the tanks opening up on La Moneda, the intense fire fights between troops below, the snipers in buildings all around (since none was in the Contraloría itself, only a few shots were fired at the building). As the hour approached for the bombing, Humeres prudently led the fifty employees who had made it to work that day to what they hoped would be the safety of the basement. There was no panic, even though that basement was situated no more than fifty feet away from the west wall of La Moneda.[73]

Half a block up from the palace on the eastern side, Vicente Garrido González—at forty-four, the chief pressman for the Christian Democrat daily newspaper, La Prensa—was wondering what to do when a detail of Carabineros settled the matter for him. The Carabineros ordered Garrido—and the others who practically fought their way to the newspaper that morning—to clear out. "I was scared, plenty scared, especially of the snipers," he said. "Most of the way I was in and out of doorways and so close to the walls, I almost became part of the masonry." Eventually, he made it home safely; he might have spared himself the ordeal; it would be two days before La Prensa would publish again.[74]

Yet another Christian Democrat made it only a small part of the way to his destination. Sen. Juan de Dios Carmona Peralta, a leader of the moderate wing of the party, was heading for Caracas that day. He learned of the Valparaíso uprising en route to the airport for his 9 A.M. flight. Since everything was still normal there, he decided to switch to an afternoon flight, just in case he should be needed. As he left the airport to head back to the city, air force trucks arrived to close the airport down. Domestic and international flights would remain grounded for several days.[75]

In his final radio speech that morning, Salvador Allende had spoken scornfully of the "seditious" professional societies. Although the bar and medical associations had both called for his resignation, he might well have had still another professional association in mind, because it was the first to say, Enough! That was the Chilean College of Engineers, representing eight thousand of the country's 9,500 engineers. In the association's elections that May, 92 percent of those voting were against the government, only eight for. On August 17, the college called flat-out for Allende's resignation, and more recently it had resolved to go out on a nationwide strike starting September 10 and stay out until Allende either changed course or stepped down. Eduardo Arriagada Moreno, president of the college, thought of that as he headed downtown that morning with a neighbor, Francisco Langlois. Reaching the college's building—flush against the Defense Ministry on the Alameda—they stowed the car behind the building and Arriagada headed for his ninth-floor office. His first act: send the staff home. Next: the nine directors of the association contacted the military General Staff next door and volunteered for duty, checking on the defense of basic installations—the waterworks, electric power company, etc. "That," Arriagada said, "was a day to remember."[76]

Timing was not turning out to be Jorge Alberto Braña's long suit. He had flown into Santiago from Buenos Aires only the afternoon before—his luggage laden with several items that at another time, in another place, would have been bizarre: six big loaves of bread, powdered milk and butter. Braña, a former major in the Argentine federal police, was security chief for Esso Standard Oil, with responsibility for Chile, Peru, Uruguay, and his native Argentina. He left the Carrera Hotel at eight that morning, scurrying across Plaza Constitución in the direction of the Esso offices, in the College of Engineers building. The walk over was easy; it was the walk back which would prove very nearly murderous.[77]

Nowhere was the tension greater, the activity more feverish than in La Moneda itself as the clock struck eleven. Allende led a group of GAPs to a small room in the basement, more like a medieval vault than a room. When Briones arrived with Almeyda, the Tohá brothers and Aníbal Palma, they discovered there was no room there. In panic and confusion, they fled through the open courtyard at the south wing of the building.

Ernesto Espinoza was barricaded in his first floor office when he heard the voices outside. Since arriving that morning, sniper fire had twice prevented him from leaving the palace, so after getting through a telephone call to his family, he decided to hunker down in that office.

"I looked out, and there was Almeyda, the Tohá brothers, Briones, and *el Pibe*, [the kid, nickname for Palma], and a newsman from the OIR office. They were all calm, and I invited them to join me in my office. We knew the bombing was coming, and each of them began telephoning his home. They had come to be with Allende and he had practically kicked them out of the basement.

"We debated where to take shelter, and first went to the vault of the Records Office, but I didn't know the combination.... Luckily, I remembered the boiler room, located in the basement. We went downstairs and pushed the door in. There we waited, thinking we were more or less safe. In any case, we had all said good-bye to our families."

Carlos Briones didn't feel so safe.

"I thought we would die there."[78]

At the other end of the palace, where Allende and some thirty others waited, the atmosphere was less somber. Allende had armed himself with a bottle of whiskey, "to while away the raid," as one of those present would later put it. *La Payita* would remember that every time the subject of the bombing came up, Allende said: "Don't be afraid, they won't dare." At one point, he toyed with the idea of a desperate dash to the presidential garage across the street, to link up with the large force of snipers in the Public Works Ministry. That idea was discarded, as was another: Allende said he would ask for a five-minute cease-fire and they could use the time to make their getaway.

"Mr. President," Jaime Barrios told him, "you can't ask for another truce."

"Don't you know, Jaimito," Allende answered, "that five minutes are sufficient to change history?"

With the acrid smoke of gunfire and the dust of blasted concrete filling the air, some arrived choking. "The president," Mrs. Contreras continued, "took off his mask and gave it to them."

At the Congress Building, just three blocks away, an officer shepherded the wives of the encamped truck drivers down to the basement of the Senate.[79]

The now deserted downtown streets grew ominously quiet.

THEY CAME OUT OF THE NORTHEAST

They came out of the northeast, circling San Cristóbal Hill in screaming descent from five thousand feet. The pilots of the two Hawker Hunters had only minutes before learned the identity of their target: La Moneda. Watching from the patio of his home in the eastern suburbs, Dr. Zoltán Bernath thought how lucky he was: ordinarily, he would have been at his office on the seventh floor of the building at Valentín Letelier #96, just a short block west of the target. From the garden of the U.S. Embassy residence, in those same eastern suburbs, Elizabeth Davis remembered it as "an eerily beautiful sight as they came from nowhere. The sun glinted on their wings . . ."[80]

The long delay in staging the attack was taking its toll on the commanders; part of it was the sheer anxiety of knowing the risks of attacking one building in a congested downtown area. Another was historic: not since June 4, 1932—the earliest days of Chilean aviation—had air force planes flown over the capital in anger and threatened La Moneda. (That first time, ironically, it was a leftist revolution, heralding the birth of the country's brief but crucial Socialist republic, the first in the Western Hemisphere.)

Now they came, at 480 knots (545 miles) per hour, each armed with eighteen rockets, some explosive, some detonating. Once the pilot lined up the target in a gyroscopic range finder, it took only four to eight seconds from the instant he pressed the button until the rockets streaked out at supersonic speeds toward the target.

The first pass was at 11:52 A.M., a brace of rockets released from a height of five hundred meters and a distance of eight hundred meters, approximately, as the plane passed over the Mapocho railroad station. The second plane was one minute behind.

Again and again they came back—four times, in all, each of them, each time raining stunning destruction on the palace. In all, nineteen rockets blasted the palace. Not one missed the target.

At 12:13 P.M., it was all over.[81]

"First, there was dark smoke," Jorge Braña observed from the Esso offices across the Alameda, "then white. Later, much later, I saw the flames begin to rise from the northeast corner . . ."

According to Chavkin's account, the survivors within La Moneda were "dazed, coughing, and choking from the noxious gas of the exploding rockets. Apparently the gas masks were not effective. Parts of the roof caved in. Splintered furniture, pieces of sculpture were scattered in all directions. But the most ominous was the wall of fire and smoke advancing from the left side of the palace, known as the Red Room . . . In a desperate effort to contain the fire, Allende ordered all faucets opened in the lavatories and in what remained of those in the kitchen. As one survivor described it, 'We were about to be burned to a crisp and drowned at the same time.' "[82]

Beatriz, Isabel—the other women—had pushed their way into *La Prensa*, now deserted except for a watchman who eyed the bedraggled women suspiciously. "He led us to the open stairwell," Frida Modak would recall, "saying that it was probably the safest place from whatever stray bullets might reach the building . . . No sooner had we sat down than the bombardment began. Our faces were drawn, eyes staring ahead. We were numbed with pain, and the radio kept jabbering away as rocket after rocket slammed down on La Moneda with thunderous explosion. From time to time our host would utter such philosophical comments as, 'Why don't those people in La Moneda give up? They probably aren't even there. They probably found a hiding place outside. And in the meantime—beautiful La Moneda will be destroyed.' " The women, glad the watchman had not recognized them, said nothing. Biting their tongues would prove even harder at their next temporary refuge.[83]

Over the heavy static on the command radio network:

"Direct hit. There is a large fire in the center of La Moneda." It was General Díaz, reporting to Pinochet and Leigh.

Just before the attack, Pinochet had remarked, "Killing the dog puts an end to the rabies." Next: "Tell me, Patricio, with everything that has been done so far, hasn't that gentleman reacted?"[84] He would now order a pause, in the hope that the attack Allende had said they would never dare make would end the fighting.

News of the half-hour cease-fire wasn't the only thing crackling over the airwaves. The commanders continued to crank out communiques, several prompted by Leigh, who, throughout, demonstrated a keen sense of public relations. The key one, at midmorning, was the 14-point *Bando # 5*, spelling out the reasons for the revolution. The text was hammered out between Leigh and Pinochet, with Cadet Pino brokering the conversation. Highlights:

1. The Allende government has incurred grave and demonstrated illegitimacy by violating the fundamental rights of freedom of expression, freedom of education, the right of assembly, the right to strike, the right of petition, rights of property, and the general right to a dignified and safe existence . . .
2. That this same government has shattered national unity, fomenting artificially a sterile and in many cases bloody class war . . .

. . .

6. That the mutual respect which must rule relations between the Powers of the State has repeatedly been violated, the decisions of the National Congress, the Judiciary and the Comptroller General ignored . . .

. . .

8. That the president of the Republic has shown, before the entire country, that his personal authority is conditioned to the decisions of committees and directing bodies of political parties and groups which support him, losing thereby the image of maximum authority which the Constitution assigns him . . .

. . .

10. That there exists in the country anarchy, suffocation of freedoms and moral and economic breakdown . . .
11. That the foregoing leads to the conclusion that the internal and external security of the country is in danger, that the survival of our independent State is at risk, and that the maintaining of the Government is inconvenient for the high interests of the Republic and its Sovereign People.
12. That these same antecedents are, in the light of classic doctrine which characterizes our historic thought, sufficient to justify our intervention to depose the illegitimate, immoral government no longer representative of the great national sentiment, avoiding in the process the greater evils which the present power vacuum could provoke . . .
13. That for all of these reasons, summarily expressed, the Armed

Forces have assumed the moral obligation that the Fatherland imposes on them of deposing the government which, although initially legitimate, has fallen into flagrant illegitimacy . . .

14. That, in consequence, together with the legitimacy of these measures, there falls to the citizenry, and of public officials in particular, the obligation of accepting and complying with these measures . . .[85]

But, man does not live by battles, nor even *bandos,* alone. In one after another of the centers of siege, thoughts would turn to food. Out of the basement, Allende asked *La Payita* to whip up a snack for him. "It's going to be a long day," he said. She found several chickens cooked by the navy stewards before they fled that morning. She was still assembling the snack when the shooting resumed; one shell opened a gaping hole in the kitchen. Once again, there was Salvador Allende, "firing from the windows with his AK, a gift of Fidel. We had to pull him by the legs to save him from being killed by the bullets." Later, she would say she saw him firing a bazooka on an attacking tank; Fidel Castro, "reporting" from Havana a month later, would claim Allende had knocked out a tank himself, a claim vaguely echoing Dr. Bartulin's less specific reference to the bazooka he saw firing with such deadly accuracy from the presidential office window (cf. p. 26, Chavilin).[86]

Allende would use the brief pause for yet another stab at saving his regime. He put in a call to Erick Schnake at Radio Corporación, in the sniper-infested State Bank Building across Morandé Street. It was, Schnake said, an "anguished" Allende who asked him to go on the air with an appeal to the worker brigades to swarm into the downtown area and save his embattled regime. But the voice of Radio Corporación was dead.[87]

At Radio Agricultura, Esther Hinojosa—an executive secretary who had worked at the station so long (thirty years) that she considered herself "part of the inventory"—cooked up plain noodles for the twenty persons there. Just a block or two away, retired Gen. Sergio Poblete Garcés, number two man in the Government Development Corporation (CORFO), sent his secretary, Eugenia Victoria Díaz, to scare up what she could in CORFO's cafeteria. She thoughtfully returned with a plate of lentils for him, but by then, the general had lost his appetite: he was one of two generals implicated in plots to subvert the air force, and his name was among those of ninety-five persons now being read on the radio in a new *bando.* The order: give up by four-thirty that afternoon, or face "serious consequences." Ms. Díaz persuaded her boss to go into hiding with her, which he did, for forty-eight hours.[88]

Cadet Pino was by now feeling his oats—though he had not yet had a chance to enjoy them. From the timid and scared occupant of a circum-stantial hot-seat at the beginning of the day, Pino's confidence had grown with the passage of the hours, so much so that on three or four occasions he even "improved on" messages from Leigh to Pinochet or vice versa. Not surprisingly, then, when hunger pains gnawed, he would be heard to demand imperiously over the high command network: "What's happened to our lunch? We ordered half an hour ago!" Later, after it apparently had been delivered: "How do they expect us to eat? There are no plates here."[89]

For months, CIA Station Chief Raymond A. Warren, then rounding out the third year of his second tour in Santiago, was under orders to stay close to the plotting all the world assumed was going on—but not so close at to get involved. Two cables went out to Warren in May containing orders. The first pointed out the likelihood of an opposition move against Allende "and the inevitability that the CIA would be blamed as the instigator of any coup." The Santiago station responded that if it were to meet its responsibility of predicting a coup—"ringing the gong"—then it would have to have a free hand to penetrate all conspiracies. Negative, headquarters said in the second cable: ". . . In a rather abrupt departure from CIA custom . . . this time, keeping CIA's record clean [is] more important than predicting a coup . . ." David Atlee Phillips, brand new in his job as head of the Latin American area of CIA's Clandestine Services Division, learned of this when he asked his prede-cessor whether the agency was helping the truck drivers, and discovered that, in order to keep the agency's nose clean, it was not.

Phillips was no stranger to Chile; a strapping man with resonant voice and intense blue eyes, he had served in Chile early in his twenty-four-year career as a spy (all of it in or on Latin America). Darkness had just settled over the sylvan tranquility of CIA's Langley, Virginia, head-quarters—5,015 miles due north of Santiago—when a clerk in the com-munications center tore a coded message off a teletype machine and rushed a copy to Phillips in his third-floor office. It was Monday night, September 10, 1973. Although there had been a number of false alarms in recent days, this one gave Phillips "a feeling at the back of his neck that this time it was for real." Phillips phoned his counterparts at the State Department and National Security Council, told them what he thought, and headed home for bed. So, too, did official Washington.

At 4 A.M., Tuesday morning, CIA headquarters received another tele-type message from a junior officer billeted at the Hotel Carrera, saying a coup was imminent. That officer—a young, attractive woman—had carried on a debate with Warren for weeks; she said a coup couldn't happen before Christmas, he said it could happen any time. When the bombs began falling on La Moneda that September morning, she walked into her boss's office, kissed him on both cheeks, and said, "Merry Christmas."

The U.S. Embassy did manage to maintain contact with Washington throughout much of the day, keeping an open telephone line to the Defense Intelligence Agency in Washington for several hours, though likely not from a telephone in the Embassy. The line eventually was cut, presumably by an operator in Peru.

But, like the CIA, there was little the Embassy could provide by way of insight: the CIA, because it was ordered to watch "from the margin," the embassy, because its ties were mainly with Christian Democrats—and Christian Democrats (with the possible exception of Carmona), were decidedly not people the military plotters trusted.[90]

The crucial action, inevitably, centered on La Moneda. But there were other battles that day, few more pitched than the one at Tomás Moro. The first attack on it from the air nearly ended in disaster. When Pinochet asked Leigh for help in "softening up" the intense resistance, Leigh at first attempted to send a helicopter. "But," he said, "the shooting was too intense—there were GAPs everywhere, on the rooftops, everywhere, and they were shooting even at the pigeons flying overhead. So I ordered a plane to attack, reluctantly because Tomás Moro is, after all, in the middle of a residential neighborhood."

With a rapidly lowering ceiling, the pilot missed. Sighting what he believed was the pathfinder helicopter, he fired. It turned out that the helicopter had moved away from the target area and was actually hovering near the Air Force Hospital, only ten blocks northeast of the presidential estate. Three times the jet swooshed over the "target," firing twelve rockets.

Luck was with him. The attack blasted a partly finished new wing and not the main hospital building, but fourteen persons were wounded. (No deaths were reported.)

Luck was also with Hortensia Allende. Half an hour before that first attack, Isabel Letelier, still trying to get a fix on what was going on, got through to Mrs. Allende at Tomás Moro.

"She was very annoyed because they wouldn't let her go to La Moneda," Mrs. Letelier remembered. " 'I'm going to get in a car and go by myself,' she told me. 'I want to be at Salvador's side.' "

At the downtown hotel where the four women had taken refuge, Isabel Allende sat slumped in a chair, "her eyes," Frida Modak said, were "flooded with tears." They had just heard a radio report that Tomás Moro was also under air attack. "Beatriz ran to console her, whispering that their mother might have gotten away before the bombing began."

She had.

Led by her driver, Carlos Tello, she made her way through a back gate in the wall into a British-run convent school, Sagrado Corazón. There, aided by the nuns, they obtained a car, setting out not for La Moneda but for the home of Felipe Herrera Lane, long-time president of the Inter-American Development Bank, a Socialist and self-styled Allende confidant. Once there, she called Mexican Ambassador Luis Martínez Corvalán, who picked her up that afternoon. A few days later she was in exile in Mexico.

The air force did not miss again. This time the attacking planes were coaxed onto target by a special spotter: Lt. Col. Julio Tapia, an air force accountant who volunteered for the job when he heard Leigh say he was sending his own helicopter aloft to handle the assignment.

"But, my friend," Leigh protested, "you are a bookkeeper and have no business buzzing around in helicopters. And do you have any idea of the risk you would run?" Tapia said he did—but he wanted to do it anyway.

"The pilot," Leigh said, "was a young fellow, young but very decisive, very aggressive. He and Tapia not only guided the planes, but also opened fire with the fixed .50-caliber machineguns on the chopper. I saw them from my command post. Later I saw them blasting away with the side machineguns."

Mission accomplished, Tapia reported to Leigh at the Air Academy Headquarters. He did not mention that they had taken a number of hits themselves, one a bullet that went through the floor in the space between Tapia's feet and the pilot's back.

Three rockets had smashed into the north facade of the mansion. Until then, the GAP defenders had fought fiercely; Corp. Iván Sáez Ayala remembers that they had more arms than men to fire them when they set out that morning from the Military Academy on what they were told would be "a routine patrol." The buses carried just a few soldiers and a couple dozen officer cadets from the academy; a 3/4-ton truck with them carried bazookas, rocket launchers, grenades, and .30-caliber machineguns.

"We came under fire even before we could see the wall around the place. They were shooting at us from an apartment building a little to the left of the place. We were approaching them from Pehuén Street, from the northwest, and were about to round the corner onto Tomás Moro Street when it started. A lieutenant ordered us to break for cover on a side street directly opposite the front wall. Most of the shooting was coming from machineguns mounted on watchtowers over the main gate."

The air attack broke the fighting spirit of the GAP defenders. They fled. Before the regular army unit under Col. Nilo Floody could move in, another "army" swarmed into the mansion: looters from a nearby slum, carrying off television sets, radios, and other appliances. They left behind: arms for two thousand men (Russian-made rockets, heavy machineguns, bazookas, recoil-less cannons, etc.), a cornucopia of food (for the up to 150 GAP housed there), and wine and liquor (for Allende and his guests).[91]

Far to the south, another kind of brigade was not at all on the defensive—yet. Commanded by a thirty-three-year-old former agronomy student who styled himself as "Comandante Pepe" (real name: José Gabriel Lliendo Vera), an eighty-man MIRista unit was laying siege to the Carabinero outpost at Neltume, in a heavily forested area of Valdivia province. Inside: Sgt. Benito Carrasco, Corp. Juan Campos Campos, two Carabineros (René Cáceres Aedo and Belisario Navarrete Sańchez), and the sergeant's wife, Rosa García.

For the past two years, Comandante Pepe had lorded it over an 860,000-acre zone of "liberated" farm and timberland in the mountain and lakes area south of Temuco—while Salvador Allende and his allies denied that there were any guerrillas operating in the country. As early as 1971, this small man with medium sideburns, black hair, black eyes, and black moustache saw Chile's future—and he liked it: "Civil war is inevitable," he told British author Alistair Horne. Now back in Chile after "post-graduate" training in Cuba, Pepe and his men encountered surprisingly stubborn resistance from within the rustic outpost, its log fences and wooden architecture vaguely suggesting a frontier fort. Inside, as Mrs. García loaded guns and distributed ammunition and water, the defenders—like figures in a Western movie—went from window to window, staving off the attackers. Help first came from the air; two air force helicopters strafed the attackers. Finally, a relief column arrived. Pepe and his men fled; captured a few days later, Comandante Pepe was tried and executed on October 3.[92]

North of Santiago, in the province of Antogogasta, a group of MIRistas from a nitrate mine attacked another isolated Carabinero post. A Hawker Hunter, patrolling in the area, was diverted to the scene. "They were so terrified," General Leigh recounted, "that they all started waving white handkerchiefs" when the pilot made a low pass over them. That was the end of the attack.

In that same region, at the Chuquicamata copper mine, the Communist general manager David Silberman rounded up one hundred men armed with sub-machineguns and hand grenades and, moving giant Wabco trucks into place, barricaded the entrance to the mine. (Silberman would later think better of it; with twenty of his men, he lit out for the Andes, and the big copper mine was taken without a shot being fired.)

"From one end of the country to the other," General Bonilla told Pinochet, "your orders have been followed, and though there are pocket actions, the fighting is being done by paramilitary brigades, and these have been almost entirely suffocated."

Pinochet's sense of relief was great. The one battle he had feared most had not materialized. From the beginning, he feared a beachhead in the strip of desert between Calama and Antofogasta, a thousand miles north of Santiago. If a government force had managed to seize and hold a piece of territory there, it would have been possible to reinforce them from the air—landing strips abounded—and that is exactly what Fidel Castro had said he would do. To make matters worse, both Peru and Bolivia to the north were then ruled by leftist-leaning generals. "That," Pinochet said, "would have been the beginning of a civil war."[93] But as morning slipped into early afternoon, that danger was behind him, and he could turn his attention to the final pockets of resistance in Santiago—and above all, to the man in that now smoking ruin of a palace.

. . . AND A TIME TO DIE

For twenty-two terrifying moments, they had huddled behind those four-foot thick walls. The walls shook, the walls shuddered, the air filled with choking dust. And then there was silence.

"Looks like it's over," someone cried out in the small vault where Allende and those closest to him crouched. Allende discovered he had been cut by flying glass; one of the doctors bandaged the cut.

A head count: Dr. Oscar Soto, one of the physicians, found only eighteen to twenty GAPs left to fight on. That number did not, of course, include Allende with his sub-machinegun (and, occasionally, bazooka), nor civilians such as the banker Jaime Barrios, also blasting away from the palace windows.

Allende seized on the opportunity to lead his small band back to the second floor to prepare for the inevitable ground attack. Though he did not know it, time was still on his side.[94]

"Gustavo, they are firing from the roofs of the Public Works Ministry and the State Bank. I think it would be a good idea to stage an air attack against the roofs in that area. I am going to send a parachute unit and special forces, but meanwhile, it would be a good idea to give them a going over from the air."

The voice was that of Augusto Pinochet, reacting to reports from his ground commanders that they were taking murderous sniper fire as they moved in for the final assault against the pulverized palace.

"O.K.," Leigh came back. "Just as soon as I can, in a few minutes, I am going to lay down some fire on those buildings."

Those "few minutes" would stretch into well over an hour before the two helicopters would finally appear, a delay with historic implications.[95]

The calm was broken by the roar of cannon fire, from the Sherman tanks firing on the exposed north and south facades of the palace, by 105-millimeter artillery pieces firing from Plaza Bulnes just a few hundred yards to the south. Then the machineguns and rifles opened up. Then the troops moved out. And that's when the ambush started.

"We had crossed there [Plaza Bulnes] before to talk to General Palacios," Sgt. Alfredo Leiva Lillo recalled, "but there was no shooting then. Now we were getting it from all sides. It was a scene from the movies."

Before it was over, perhaps half an hour later, seventeen soldiers had been wounded or killed, there in the Plaza Bulnes, two blocks west, in an ear-splitting crossfire from the big ENTEL (the government's international telephone company) and the Education Ministry. Lt. Hernán Ramírez Jald was next to Sergeant Toro, one of the most popular NCO school instructors, when he was mortally wounded.

"The bullet caught him on the top left side of his head," the twenty-three-year-old lieutenant said. "He was in a kneeling position when he got hit. The bullet went through his helmet, right through his head, and out the back."

Corporal Pizzarro, one of the last men to make it out of the Plaza Bulnes ambush, got a chance to avenge a fallen comrade before pulling back. "I saw a sniper pop out three or four times from a window below that Yoga sign [on the Continental Theater building]. Finally, the third or fourth time, I got him. He fell with his arms through the Venetian blinds. He stayed there all day like that, his arms hanging through the blinds."[96]

General Palacios' men, looping behind the Defense Ministry and crossing the Alameda at the University of Chile, got as far as the corner of Moneda and Morandé—within a stone's throw of their objective—before intense fire halted their advance, too.

Canessa, leading the attack from the south, and Palacios decided it would be suicidal to go on. That's when they called for an air strike.

Back inside the palace, yet another group of survivors—Almeyda, Briones, Espinoza, the Tohá brothers—emerged from their sanctuary. They couldn't believe what they saw. The entire northwest wing—Briones' Interior Ministry—was a smouldering rubble. Dashing across the Winter Garden courtyard to an office in the Foreign Ministry, they found an intercom connecting with the Defense Ministry.

Identifying themselves, they said they wanted to surrender. The officer who answered agreed to send a jeep. Minutes later, he called back: impossible, the sniper fire is too intense. Once again, they resigned themselves to waiting. About then, the tanks and the artillery opened up. Once again, they were in the jaws of death.

Incredibly, another persistent caller got through to them. It was Isabel Letelier. Almeyda answered.

"He was coughing," she said, "apparently still suffering the effects of the dust from the bombardment. He asked me where Orlando was and I told him at the Defense Ministry. He said they had been in the basement of the Foreign Ministry and had the impression that he was somewhere else—that something had happened to Orlando in La Moneda."

She reassured him that her husband was at the Defense Ministry. She had not seen his televised exit under guard from the Defense Ministry that morning; but she was right, he was unharmed. Death would stalk Orlando Letelier not in war-ravaged Chile, but on tree-lined Massachusetts Avenue, in the seeming safety of the capital of the United States.[97]

Almeyda offered reassurances of his own. "The president is all right. We don't know how the rest of the palace has withstood the bombing because we're at the other end, but the president is all right."[98]

The high command of the Christian Democrat party watched the bombing from the terrace of a secret hideout prepared for such emergencies. Party Vice-President Osvaldo Olguín Zapata put in a call to the Defense Ministry to plead for Allende's life.

"We have no intention of taking his life," he was told. "What happens to him now is strictly up to him."

Former President Eduardo Frei made a similar plea, and received an identical answer. It's strictly up to him.[99]

He made his move around 1:15 P.M. In a telephone call to Admiral Carvajal, Salvador Allende said he wanted to surrender and send emissaries to discuss surrender terms. The emissaries: Daniel Vergara, under-secretary of the interior (who had served longer in his post than anyone else in the senior ranks of the Allende administration); Fernando Flores, then secretary-general of the government; Osvaldo Puccio, Allende's private secretary. (They were joined by Puccio's nineteen-year-old son, also named Osvaldo, who insisted on accompanying his father.)

Carvajal ordered a cease-fire in the area, and managed to get a jeep to the Morandé entrance to pick up the four, who were taken under heavy guard to the main hall of the Ministry. Flores had a small bruise on his cheek; Vergara, though he appeared calm, looked all around him as he entered the dark and somber hall; Puccio appeared fidgety and nervous.

The chief of air force counterintelligence took charge of the group. They were shoved into an elevator and taken up to Carvajal's office.

Carvajal lit a cigarette slowly and deliberately, took a puff and then, with his characteristic calm, looked up at the men facing him: "Well, gentlemen," he said, "what brings you here?"

"We come," Flores said, "at the behest of His Excellency, the president of the Republic, Salvador Allende."

"The ex-president," Carvajal interrupted.

". . . at the behest of the president," Flores repeated.

"Ex-president, I say," Carvajal repeated, the smile leaving his face.

"We are here to discuss terms of the surrender," Flores finished.

"There are no terms, only unconditional surrender," Carvajal responded. Vergara said they would report back to the president. This time Carvajal let pass the reference to "president"; instead: "No, you'll stay here. We'll notify Allende."

Now prisoners, they were taken to the basement, stripped and searched.[100] There would be no more talk.

"Flores, Puccio, and 'Barnabas'* Vergara are here," Carvajal reported on the radio to Pinochet and Leigh. "Señor Puccio comes with terms from Allende. I told him they were not acceptable. I told them that the only terms were unconditional surrender. The only guarantee they would be given is that we will respect their lives."

"How about Allende?" Pinochet asked. "Has he or hasn't he come out?"

"No, he has not come out because, according to Flores, he wants to maintain decorous conditions for his surrender." Carvajal spoke slowly, in his drawling, calm cadence. Pinochet's reply was anything but calm.

"What 'decorous conditions'? There is no 'decorous condition'! What kind of a pipe dream is this? The only thing we offer him is respect for his life. In his entire life, he has never known decorum and now he comes around asking for it."

Pinochet was not yet president when he made his first foreign relations decision. Immediately following the negotiations exchange, he added: "Another thing. The Cuban Embassy is surrounded because they opened fire from inside with a machinegun. Call the ambassador and

---

* He used the nickname because Vergara's protruding chin was suggestive of a vampire, and also because the name was that of a character in a television show then popular in Chile.

tell him the following: they fired on our troops and so as to avoid an international incident, he should consider that he has at his immediate disposal a plane to take him to his country. Tell him that we break relations, that he should pack his bags and be ready to go within twenty-four hours. General Benavides gave me the information [about the shooting] and he would not lie to me."[101]

Just before the bombing raid, Augusto Olivares—Allende's closest crony—discovered René Largo Farías wandering aimlessly through the halls of the palace. It was Farías who had sounded the first alarm during the midnight hours which already seemed an eternity ago to him, to others. Someone offered him a gun; he declined, explaining he had never used one. Olivares told him he should leave; you can't help us here, you can do some good for the cause outside. Olivares practically pushed him out the Morandé Street door, into a no-man's land alive with the sound of gunfire. Farías walked slowly, with his hands in the air. Incredibly, he walked on, and on, to his house, a dozen blocks away.[102]

Now it was again Olivares's turn to take charge of events. He put in a call to the Defense Ministry. Colonel Pedro Ewing answered.

"Has Daniel Vergara arrived?" Olivares asked.

"Yes, with Puccio and Flores."

"Have they reached an agreement?"

"None worth talking about. Only unconditional surrender."

"Will Vergara, Puccio and Flores return to La Moneda?"

"No."

Such hope as he may have harbored drained out of Olivares with that call. He went down to the first floor, into a bathroom and, without bothering to close the door, began to urinate. Dr. Soto saw him and poked fun at him. Leaving, Soto heard a shot and rushed back. He found Olivares slumped over, a still-smoking pistol in his hand. Presidential press attaché Carlos Jorquera was the next to stumble onto the scene; seeing his close friend dead, Jorquera began crying uncontrollably.

Pulling himself together, Jorquera then went upstairs to tell Allende. Allende, *La Payita,* and a few others went downstairs.

"We saw Augusto on the floor," Mrs. Contreras remembered. "It was a depressing sight. I will never forget the look of anguish on the president's face as he saw his dearest friend dead."[103]

The fight went out of Allende. He decided to surrender.

But the men running the revolution did not know this, and so, as Palacios and Canessa pressed their pincers attack on the palace, Pinochet and Leigh occupied themselves with what seemed then to be significant matters. What follows is the full text of the conversations among the commanders over the command network during those crucial moments (roughly 1:15–1:45 P.M.; no times were given during any of the exchanges, and these times are extrapolated from what is known of the events themselves):

Carvajal to Pinochet: "The legal people and all advisers here, all of them, have recommended strongly that it would be advisable to give more thought to permitting him [Allende] to leave the country, because they tell me that his man is going to go from one socialist country to another insulting us. So it would be more convenient to keep him here." (In so saying, Carvajal was also reflecting the judgment of his boss, Admiral Merino. From the first instant, Merino was adamant: Allende should not be allowed to leave the country.)[104]

Carvajal had not finished his "over and out" before Pinochet's voice, unmistakably angry, boomed over the radio: "So, this champion is going to insult us, eh! Let him go to socialist countries. In other countries, they won't even receive him."

Carvajal attempted to interrupt: "These are, they're the requests of . . ."

Again, Pinochet cut him off: "Let him go!" he shouted, his voice filled with more emotion that at any other time that day. Again, Carvajal attempted to interject, and again he was cut off by an even-angrier Pinochet, his voice rising to a sharp rebuke: "Let him go!"

Leigh (who could hear Carvajal, but could not hear Pinochet), chimed in: "If he is in socialist countries, we needn't care less. But if he stays in this country, he is going to be a center of attraction and a focus for the masses and he is going to be exploited and . . ."

Pinochet again, unaware that Leigh was talking: "It's decided then. We are going to concentrate now on military problems." This time his words were carefully spaced, carefully emphasized.

From that instant forward, there would not again be any doubt that Augusto Pinochet Ugarte was the man in charge of Chile.

A pause, then the methodical voice of Patricio Carvajal: "Then we are going to proceed to arrest him, and his life will be respected, and he would be permitted to leave on the airplane with his family, and Mr. Puccio can accompany him . . ."

Pinochet: "And that he gets out of here immediately!"

Leigh to Carvajal: "The two helicopters are at this moment about to arrive. They are going to sweep the rooftops where the machineguns are, on the Public Works Ministry and State Bank. These helicopters are going to open fire within a few moments." (The helicopters were army Puma gunships, but for unclear reasons, they needed to be flown by air force pilots.)

Pinochet: "Please tell those pilots to make sure they fire only on the rooftops and let me know when they'll be there so we can coordinate their fire from the ground." (Leigh estimated another ten to fifteen minutes, since they were en route from Air Group Ten).

Carvajal (ignoring Pinochet's injunction to limit themselves now to military matters): "Second, that Fernando Flores and Orlando [apparently he meant to say Vergara but used, instead, the first name of Defense Minister Letelier] and that we send back [to the palace] as an emissary only Puccio, just Puccio . . ." Next followed another exchange between Pinochet and Leigh about the helicopter attack, and then, when Carvajal resumed, he brought electrifying news: "Augusto, they have just advised me they are ready to surrender unconditionally and have asked for a cease-fire."

Pinochet's gruff response: "From La Moneda to the airplane for the mister [he used the English word] and his family—and no other, no GAP."

That news came to Carvajal from General Baeza, Allende's chosen pipeline to the military that day. Baeza recollected: "Here they were, Puccio and Flores and Vergara, coming to us after the air attack, with a big part of the palace in flames and tear gas filling the air so as to force those still inside to leave without further destruction being done, and along they came with more or less the same proposition we had rejected that morning.

"Carvajal naturally would not accept, and so Puccio was named to take our answer back and the other two taken prisoner . . . Puccio was asking for paper and pen to write the answer, and while he was writing, the telephone rang; it was one of Allende's men, saying he had resigned and asking for a vehicle to get out."[105]

A cease-fire was ordered—but sniper fire continued from the surrounding rooftops. Crucial moments passed.

"We agreed," Baeza said, "to send a high-ranking officer to receive the president's surrender. But the fire was so intense that twenty minutes or more went by and they could not get through. So the attack on the palace was resumed."

Those twenty minutes would change the course of Chilean history.

Carvajal again, curiously directing his remark not to Pinochet but to Leigh: "Gustavo, Patricio here. Here in the command post of the garrison, we feel it would be convenient to demand of Allende, before he leaves, that he sign his resignation. I am in accord with that idea."

Then came the news that caused even the unflappable Patricio Carvajal to speak with obvious excitement: "Meanwhile, some people are coming out of Morandé 80. I suppose that Allende is among them. So for the moment, we are going to arrest all of them. I ask for your concurrence."

"Here, General Leigh for Patricio. Agreed, agreed. For me that is a detail. For me that is a detail that the Peruvians, when Belaunde left,[*] gave no thought to whatever. But O.K., if he signs, fine. But if he refuses to sign it, what are you going to do? The important thing is that he leave the country, at least in my judgment. Over."

"Agreed," Carvajal replied. "We'll see to it that he signs the resignation and then to Cerrillos so that the plane can leave. Good." Leigh added another "*conforme*" (agreed). Pinochet said nothing.

Carvajal: "I'm afraid that the departure of the plane cannot be so quick as all that if he is going to be given the opportunity of leaving with his family, because from the time Allende arrives and gets together with his family, I would imagine it will be at least an hour.[106] Over to you."

Leigh: "*Conforme, conforme.* I find we'll have to put a time limit on this, before night comes and we have problems. I can put a helicopter immediately at the Military Academy to embark all his people and take them to the airport. But let's not worry too much if, in the worst of cases, and in the end, if dark comes, this man gets aboard alone and the family stays in Chile. But with all this hanky-panky they can stall until dark to play whatever trick on us. I can put a helicopter in ten minutes. I can put a presidential helicopter in the Military Academy, and there the family can embark or he by himself immediately. Over."

Carvajal: "Agreed. I believe it would be convenient to set a limit in any case, because this is going to take a while. What time limit could we put?"

Leigh: "I calculate, Patricio, that the outside limit to take off with him should be four in the afternoon. And not one minute more. Over."

"Splendid. That's the way we'll do it. Finished as far as I'm concerned."

Suddenly, Pinochet joined in: "Do you read me, Patricio? Has Mr. Allende gone yet?"

"Some people are leaving now. I sent personnel of intelligence to find out the names of the principals who are leaving there."

Pinochet: "Listen, Patricio, another thing. I think that the three commanders-in-chief and the director-general of Carabineros have got to get together to issue a joint declaration. In that case, Señor Allende—out!"

Carvajal: "We are preparing the information to give out both by military communications and by radio, saying that Allende has surrendered and the others who give up, the principal ones who give up . . ." Again Pinochet interrupted, saying it should add that Allende had asked to leave the country.

Carvajal: "*Conforme.* Gustavo, Leigh tells me that he was going to

---

[*] In October 1968, the Peruvian army ousted President Fernando Belaunde Terry and set up a military junta; Belaunde left the country without formally resigning the presidency.

put a helicopter up to take Allende's family to Cerrillos so that they could take the plane and leave before four this afternoon."

Pinochet: "*Conforme. Conforme.* After four, I believe that around five or five-thirty, time for the meeting of the commanders-in-chief and director-general of Carabineros."

Carvajal: "What time do you want to hold the meeting?"

Pinochet: "I believe we should call it for four . . . around five or six—poof, old fellow!" (It was a rare flash of humor for Pinochet that day, and Carvajal chuckled appreciatively.)

Carvajal: "Good. We have a meeting of the commanders-in-chief in the ministry. Understood?"

Pinochet: "No. It has to be up here . . ."

Carvajal then slipped into what might have been a security lapse, naming for the first time that day the location of a command post: "You mean the meeting there in Peñalolén?" Pinochet confirmed that the meeting would be at his headquarters, and Carvajal said he would notify Admiral Merino—another first, the first mention of Merino's name on the radio that day. Carvajal said Merino would try to helicopter to Peñalolén from Valparaíso, adding that he would also notify Leigh. In an expansive mood, Pinochet added: "You, too, Patricio."

The network fell silent. The scene would now shift back to the embattled palace.

From the far end of the darkened corridor, Patricio Guijón heard the words clearly, resounding like a thunderclap. It was the voice of Salvador Allende:

"Give up everybody—this is a massacre!"

Guijón and the other doctors had spent most of that day in a small room in the basement. They were there during the air attack, "barricaded" behind a stack of papers and the mimeograph machine. Carlos Jorquera sat out the bombing with them there.

Then, around 1:15 P.M.—"the truth is I had lost any notion of time"—someone summoned the doctors to join the others in that second-floor corridor.

Guijón took up position about one-third of the way from the southern end of the group, some twenty-five to thirty persons in all. They were seated in a single row along the west wall. He did not see Allende, then in the spacious Salón Independencia, behind closed doors.

"I suppose we were there half an hour or forty-five minutes," he said. "There was no conversation. Each of us was lost in his own thoughts. I didn't even see the fire, although some closer to the other end did." (Much of the north side of the palace, facing the Plaza Constitución, was in flames.)

His reveries ended with Allende's words.

"*La Payita* goes first, I'll go last," Allende said.

Although bullets were not impacting in the area of that second-floor corridor, the sounds of gunfire outside were, the young doctor said, "deafening." So it was that, as the group began to make its way cautiously toward the circular staircase leading down to Morandé 80, someone said they ought to show a white flag as they emerged.

"I took off my doctor's apron and passed it along. For some reason, I also took off my gas mask and put it on the floor. Then I began crawling along the floor behind the others."

It was at that instant that fate dealt Patricio Guijón the third and final blow, the one that would obliterate the life he had known and substitute for it the melancholy one of reluctant witness to a history he despised.

"I was about to round the corner," Guijón said, "when I remembered my gas mask—even the lettering on it: U.S. Army. This was my first war, and I didn't have a souvenir for my boys. So I decided to go back for it."

Guijón was groping for it when some instinct made him look up.

The door to the Salón Independencia, the scene of so many grand state receptions, was now open, and light streamed through a huge open window of the high-ceilinged room. It sidelighted the figure of Salvador Allende, seated on a sofa, to the right of the window as Guijón faced in. In his hands was a weapon that Guijón—in his familiarity with violence and its artifacts would repeatedly refer to as a "shotgun"—gripped between his legs, the barrel pointed at his face.

For an imperishable instant, their eyes met, but no sign of emotion, no sign of recognition, crossed the president's face.

"I did not hear the shot—I SAW it," Patricio Guijón said. "Shot or shots, how could I tell with all that racket outside? When it happened, I ran to him and instinctively reached for his arm to take his pulse."

There was no pulse to take.

"Most of the top of his head was gone. Skin was folded over his eyes, most of his brains were on his lap and the floor. Brain fragments were also on the ceiling. But there was no blood. It was hard to recognize his face."

There was a small chair at right angles to the sofa. Guijón pulled it up close to the sofa.

"Then I looked around the room and realized that the military would be coming in any moment. I was afraid they might see the gun—it was still propped between his legs—and start shooting before they realized he was dead.

"So I got up and took the gun out of his hands. It was easy. If there is such a thing as a death grip, the president didn't have one on that gun. I then put the gun on the sofa and sat down again to wait."[107]

On the opposite side of the palace, Lt. Hernán Ramírez, with about fifty of the seventy men still fit for action in his company, reached the door of the Teatinos Street side when his walkie-talkie conked out. Unable to consult his commander, Ramírez hesitated a moment, then decided to plunge ahead into the palace.

"The door was open," Ramírez said. "I would guess that a number had made their escape by that door. We first occupied the south wing, where the Foreign Ministry is—the first, second and third floors. There was no resistance.

"Suddenly, in one room, I discovered these bigwigs: Briones, Tohá, Almeyda, and Palma and two officials who identified themselves as Investigaciones detectives, but I was sure they were GAPs. We opened the door and found them all seated, smoking cigarettes. The two Investigaciones guys had pistols. Tohá looked serious, but was very dignified. Palma seemed indifferent to what was going on, but I noticed he was nervous. Almeyda and Briones looked just plain deflated.

"I told them that if they resisted, we would shoot them. Otherwise, they were under arrest. I had them all lie on the floor, face down. After we searched them, we let them get up, and then I left two or three guards with them. By then the captain was there.

"We searched other rooms, but found no one. Then we made contact with troops from the Military Academy [Palacios' men] who had gone in on the Morandé side. I went from the second or third floor to the presidential rooms, and that's when I saw Allende."[108]

Patricio Guijón: "Maybe two, maybe three minutes passed before the soldiers came. There were three soldiers. A few seconds later, Palacios came in."

Palacios was leading the final assault, rounding the corner from Moneda into Morandé when he saw the white flag. He ordered his men to surround the prisoners, then had them lie face down on the sidewalk, except for one person, who was crying hysterically. That person was *La Payita*. Palacios ordered an ambulance to take her to the Military Hospital. (She would never reach there; the ambulance arrived a few minutes later, but unbeknownst to Palacios, the driver was an Allende loyalist who took her to a hiding place.)[109]

Then Palacios ordered Dr. Soto to go back into the palace and tell Allende he had ten minutes to give up. Soto would later tell authors Varas and Vergara that when he reached the second floor, he found Allende, machinegun in hand, surrounded by about fifteen men, dispensing orders. Soto said Allende seemed not to hear him.

"At last he said, as if from another world. 'Go down, go down all of you ... I shall go down last of all' ...."[110]

*   *   *

When the ten minutes pass, Palacios leads a platoon into the building. Two soldiers with him fall as GAPs blaze away in a tightening circle of resistance. Entering the long Gallery of Presidents—by now a bedlam of decapitated presidential busts (Arturo Alessandri, and even Balmaceda), broken glass, smashed furniture, discarded gas masks—Palacios finds himself face-to-face with a GAP no more than eighteen-years-old. The youth opens fire with a sub-machinegun. He misses, but a ricochet opens a gushing wound in Palacios' hand. A young lieutenant named Fernández wings the boy in the hand, then in the head, then pulls out a handkerchief and hands it to Palacios, who uses it to stanch the wound.

"Thank you," the general says.

The advance continues. Palacios nearly stumbles over the corpse of a GAP with eleven bullets in his body. Bodies are strewn everywhere, topsy-turvy. The few remaining GAPs—the most fanatic of all—fight on, ducking in and out of doorways, firing and cursing as they do. At least eight die in those last hideous moments, more are wounded.

Realizing that priceless relics are threatened by the flames, Palacios barks order after order: save this, roll up that rug, pull down those drapes. (One item he manages to save: the sword of the liberator, Bernardo O'Higgins.) A crate of ammunition catches fire and explodes, a roof caves in. A lieutenant calls out to him—over here, general.

Palacios first sees the figure of the dead man—seated on a red sofa, his head lightly resting on a shoulder, hands swollen and black with powder.

"There was not a single spot of blood, just his brains spattered all over him."—Patricio Guijón.

Next to him, a steel helmet and a gas mask. On the floor, spent shells. Everywhere in the room, a room dominated by a huge painting of the ceremony of the declaration of independence, furniture toppled, a whiskey bottle on the floor.[111]

To the trancelike man seated next to the body: "Who are you?"

"Patricio Guijón. I am a doctor, one of the presidential doctors."

"What"—the general demanded—"are you doing here?"

Guijón explained about the gas mask. And he told Palacios about moving the gun.

"And did you touch anything else?"

"Nothing else."

Palacios told him to put the gun back exactly as he had found it. Guijón complied. Palacios questioned him further, clearly suspecting that this quiet man might have murdered Allende.

"But he believed me when I told him I did not. And I did not."

Again, a sense of history seized Palacios. He sent word to have firemen, ballistics experts, report on the double. Nothing was to be touched. (He would later send also for a photographer. At 3:30, an officer marched into the newsroom of *El Mercurio*, three blocks away, and announced what few then knew: Salvador Allende was dead, and we need a photographer. Juan Enrique Lira and Hernán Farías were designated, but they never got to take their pictures. Arriving at the palace, they were told a photographer from Investigaciones was already there and they would not be needed; the Investigaciones photographer took twenty-seven photographs, none of which has ever been published.)[112]

"He stayed in the room the entire time," Guijón said. "Maybe an hour and a half, even longer. He never left."

In those first moments, Ramírez arrived with two or three cadets from the NCO school. He would describe the scene: "There were a few others—Lieutenant Catalán, from our school, Captain Rojas and Lieutenant Salgado from the Infantry School, and a few soldiers.

"The room was dark, and there was a stink to the place. The room was a mess, odds and ends lying all around the place, shells on the floor. General Palacios had moved a folding screen in front of the body of Allende. We peeked around it.

"His head was tilted to one side, his right hand was drooping. I recognized the moustache. Even though I looked for only a few seconds—it wasn't an inspection—I have a clear image in my mind. I remember his jacket. I saw a square-shaped whiskey bottle on the floor. I don't know what brand it was. There was smoke in the room. Then I went down to the street for instructions on what to do with our prisoners."[113]

Not even the imperturbable Patricio Carvajal could mask the explosiveness of the message he was about to transmit. The time was 2:38 P.M.

"There is a communication, information," he paused here, "from personnel of the Infantry School, who are now inside La Moneda. Because of the possibility of interference, I am going to transmit in English.

"They say dat," he pronounced the word in that fashion, "Allende committed sue-side," again, his pronunciation, "and is dead now."

Then, resuming in Spanish: "Tell me if you understand."

Pinochet: "Understood."

Leigh: "Understood perfectly. Over."

There followed a long silence.

The battle had ended, as unexpectedly as it had begun. Salvador Allende, Chile's twenty-eighth constitutional president, had been dead approximately thirty minutes. The months, the years ahead would increasingly cloud the question whether Allende was, in the larger war, the vanquished or the victor.

He remained seated on the sofa, clutching the weapon, AK-47, #1651, with a gold-plated inscription:

"To my friend and comrade-in-arms, Fidel Castro."[114]

It was Carvajal who would break the silence: "Uh, with respect to the airplane for his family, there would be no urgency, then, that the family leave immediately?"

His words trailed off into static. Back through the crackling came the hoarse voice of Pinochet: "Put him in a box and load him on an old plane together with his family! Let them bury him somewhere else—in Cuba! We're going to have a mess with the burial. This character, even to die, made problems!"

The calm, calming voice of Carvajal again: "Right. Uh, the information is going to be held in confidence, then . . ."

Pinochet: "Right. Patricio, the plane, put him in a box, embalm him, and send him to be buried in Cuba. Let them bury him there."

Pinochet's voice was, by now, calm. Though it was now beyond dispute that Pinochet presided over Chile's destiny, Carvajal appealed, unexpectedly, to Leigh: "Gustavo, I await your approval, your understanding."

Leigh chose to duck: "Patricio, it's all clear, all understood. I withdraw the helicopter [the one standing by to take Allende to the plane that would have taken him to exile] and await further news. Tell me if the meeting is still on for 6:00 P.M. at Peñalolén. Over."

Carvajal: "O.K., Augusto, from Patricio."

Pinochet: "I hear you."

"Merino reports that he can't make it by five-thirty and asks that the meeting be held at six."

Pinochet: "O.K., O.K. It is a good idea to consider that we have two possibilities: one that we bury him here secretly, the other that we send him off to be buried in Cuba or some other place."

Then, for Carvajal, an unaccustomed jumble of words: "I believe that this measure could be, could be kept, the situation, quiet, inasmuch as it is going, after the meeting, in the meeting at six."

Out of the mish-mash of words, Pinochet seized on one thought: "Agreed. Agreed. We keep it quiet."

Carvajal: "Good. As far as I'm concerned, that's all I've got."

Pinochet: "Me, too."

But it was not all that Gustavo Leigh had to say, nor, for any of them, would the subject of Salvador Allende's death go away quite so easily.

Perhaps it was the shock of that news, perhaps it was the heat of battle, but Leigh proposed—and Pinochet accepted—a grisly order that, however, was never passed on: "For each member of the armed forces who

suffers, who is a victim of attack, at any time, wherever, Marxist prisoners will be shot, those who are prisoners. Over." (The order that *was*
given: while martial law would last, anyone attacking military personnel or installations would be shot on the spot.)

Gustavo Leigh is a blunt, plain-talking man. He does not mask his
opinions. But he did now, resorting to a level of circumspection so rare
for him that it can only be understood in the context of the excruciating
tension of the moment. For the first and only time that day, he referred
to himself in the third person:

"The commander-in-chief says that it is indispensable that, as quickly
as possible, the chief surgeons of the Army Health Service, of the navy
and the air force and the chief of the Medical Service of Carabineros, as
well as the coroner of Santiago, certify the cause of death of Señor
Allende in order to avoid that later on the politicians charge the armed
forces with having provoked the death. This as soon as possible, and you
should pass the word to the various institutions" (that is, military
services). "Let me know if you have understood. Go ahead. Over."

It was Carvajal, not Pinochet, who responded to Leigh's realization
that the four service chiefs would soon find themselves on trial before a
jury of world opinion; a trial which, in the manipulated climate of
world opinion, would be dragged on for many years to come.

"Agreed. The doctors will be the heads of the medical corps of the
three institutions, plus the coroner of the Military Hospital. Right?"

"No," Leigh retorted. "Correction. Correction. The chiefs of the medical services of each institution, plus the Carabineros, and a fifth doctor,
who would be the coroner of Santiago, so that he would sign the death
certificate together with the military doctors . . ."

Carvajal: "Got it. Clear." Leigh repeated that time was of the essence;
Carvajal assured him he would move on it straightaway. (Apparently
Pinochet was away from his command post during this entire ex-
change.)

Leigh: "We've got to get out a communique. I don't know whether you
have done one there, on the cause of death. The way it happened at the
end. Do you have anything ready, or not?"

Carvajal: "Right. We are going to take something prepared to the
meeting of the junta of the commanders-in-chief" (that was the first
mention of "junta" since the morning proclamation).

Leigh was taking no chances that his ideas not be incorporated into
that communique, and he switched to the editorial "we" as though to
underscore his points: "We deem it necessary to be very careful to spell
out the facts well, because there are two successive aspects, and if they
are not well explained, they could easily appear contradictory: one, that

he [Allende] softened his stand and agreed to surrender, to give up; and, later, that it has been found he committed suicide. Also, there would be the incidence, the report of the doctors. But we do consider that this entire matter has to be very carefully laid out, in such a way that it doesn't end up vague or unclear and that it reflects the reality exactly to avoid later charges against us making it out that we intervened in this final decision."

Carvajal: "Agreed, understood. We will have all of those points in mind; we are going to make, to prepare a draft of the corresponding communique."

Leigh: "Fine, that statement should contain a general picture of the facts: for example, the action of the extremists that delayed the final denouement because of the fire from the neighboring buildings, and in fact, prevented the surrender or delayed it; the presence of a great number of foreigners, which has been proved; and, right after that, some background on the extremist pockets that still remain; and the general state of tranquility in the country as total. Thus, in general, we believe these ideas should give a general notion of the situation in the communique. Go ahead, over."

The death of Salvador Allende would not again be mentioned on the command network. But it would continue to haunt the rememberance of that day for many years to come, that day which *El Mercurio*, the country's leading newspaper, would call: "The Most Important Date In The History Of Chile In This Century."[115]

Redoubts there were and more bloody fighting would remain—relatively few of the estimated eight hundred snipers and paramilitary brigade fighters estimated to be in action in Santiago that day had yet been subdued. Around one hundred Socialist party brigade members, armed with rifles, bazookas, sub-machineguns and a 30-caliber machinegun, rendezvoused at a prearranged corner on Vicuña Mackenna street, then made their way to the Vicuña Mackenna industrial cluster on the city's southern flank. There, one of the most vicious battles raged through the afternoon and into the evening, first at the INDUMET metalworks and SUMAR nylon factory, spilling over then into the sprawling La Legua shantytown. La Legua—home to some 15,000 persons, "60 percent workers, 30 percent businessmen [a euphemism which covers everything from small shopkeeper to street-corner peddlers], and 10 percent criminals"—had been systematically built up as an armed camp over months. According to one eyewitness account, at least eighty paramilitary fighters were in action there that day. At least thirty Carabineros and sixteen civilians died in the fighting, which included the ambush of an ambulance. (In the following days and months, La Legua would be the scene of some of the bitterest, bloodiest and most controversial arms-and-subversives raids.)

It would be well into the next day before the well-armed brigades at the State Technical University (UTE) would surrender; a total of eight hundred persons (not all combatants) were taken prisoner. But, by nightfall, almost all other pockets of resistance, not only in Santiago, but the length of the land, had either been captured, or gone underground, to continue the struggle as hit-and-run guerrilla fighters.[116]

It was, then and for all practical purposes, a six-hour war. No authoritative death toll has ever surfaced. Estimates range all the way from ninety-three to eighty thousand (the figure ninety-three was issued by the junta on September 16; they would subsequently concede that the number was considerably higher—but without giving particulars). On the pro-Allende left side of the spectrum, author Chavkin says thirty thousand, Swedish Ambassador Harold Edelstam fifteen thousand—neither indicating source or basis for his estimates. First reports in the United States put the death toll at one thousand; most observors believe the true number killed in all combat, on the eleventh and during the not infrequent clashes with guerrilla or terrorist groups in the weeks following, to be somewhere around two thousand.

Pinochet himself, in an interview months after the coup, had this to say: "For all practical purposes, the fighting lasted four hours." He put the death toll then, and (apparently) over the six months following, at approximately 1,600, "including 200 of our own." The decisive impact on resistance of the air attacks was one reason he gave for a relatively low number of casualties. Another: the people understood that "this war is not against us," and they cleared out of the main combat zone—principally downtown Santiago—when the fighting erupted.[117]

What is beyond any dispute is that it was not the war anyone expected. The military leaders had braced for a war lasting at least three days and costing five thousand lives, and believed it to be a conservative estimate given their intelligence reports that as many as 100,000 had undergone clandestine paramilitary training during the Allende years. (Pinochet would later write that he expected at least ten days of hard fighting.) Allende himself had predicted that, should war come, it would claim 1 million lives. One strident, leftist writer, Laurence Birns, also predicted a continuing bloodbath, for workers would "bomb . . . kidnap and . . . assassinate," turning Chile into another Northern Ireland, because "no military force is large enough to prevent this." (He was, of course, wrong.)[118]

The air attacks, so stunningly executed, surely intimidated many from taking up arms, and persuaded others to lay down those they had.

Those attacks, including the helicopter sweeps, were also highly effective in neutralizing redoubts of resistance.

But at least three other factors explain the swiftness and relative bloodlessness of the coup: the secrecy and quality of the planning, and its surgical execution; the inadequacy of the planning and training of Allende's vaunted paramilitary brigades (which the far Left itself acknowledged); and the reality that even though armed, very many were just plain unwilling to use them, to die for Salvador Allende or his *"vía chilena al socialismo."*

And that should have been no more surprising than what was equally obvious: not surprising, because Salvador Allende never represented more than a minority, and even within it, there were many who never intended to follow him into the creation of a Marxist-Leninist state; equally obvious, because those who did intend that outcome were now a dangerous and determined enemy within the larger body politic. The social contract preserving the semblances of civility in Chile, already in tatters by September 11, was now torn beyond any hope of salvage or repair.

The blood spilled on September 11 represented redemption for the great majority of Chileans; for others, it had a different meaning. Words alone would no longer do, and even will was not enough, nor were ballots nor congresses the key—although each and every one could play a role in the struggle. But the crucial distinction was that it was no longer a clash of ideas, a contest of ideas, a competition to claim the hearts and minds of Chileans played out on the old and familiar level field of civilized engagement. It was now a war to the finish, a war that would be won, and vengeance done, only when the enemy was finally and irrevocably defeated, and all that he stood for crushed and smashed with him, for as long as it would take, by whatever means it would take.

LIFE AFTER DEATH

The battles with bullets all but ended, the war of words would begin almost immediately. Few events in that war would rival in intensity, in durability, the battle over Salvador Allende's death.

Volunteers from the Fifth Company of firemen, braving sniper fire, were the first civilians to reach the burning palace. The fire under control, they were followed, around four that afternoon, by a seven-man team from the Technical Section of the Homicide Squad, summoned by General Palacios. Headed by Inspector Pedro Espinoza, the team included a detective (Julio Navarro), two ballistic experts (Jorge Alman-zabal and Carlos Davison); a planimetry expert (Alejandro Ossandón); a photographer (Enrique Contreras); and a fingerprint expert (Héctor Henríquez). By six-ten, they had completed their work. The report, as it relates to the body:

"An external examination by the police revealed in the chin a star-shaped erosive-contused wound, representing the point of entry of the projectile, and on the borders of which was an appreciable amount of carbonaceous dust. In the right superficial zygomatic arch, another wound, apparently the point of exit of the projectile or of a bone splinter. In the left parietal region, a wound marking the bullet's point of exit producing the shattering of the cranial vault. There are fractures in the upper jaw, maxillary, the lower maxillary, the nose and the forehead. Lividity developing in the corresponding areas. Incipient rigidity at the maxillary level. Probable cause of death: cranial-encephalic trauma from a bullet wound of a suicidal nature."[119]

His death, as recounted by an Allende apologist:

"Allende listened to what Soto said and then ordered everyone to go down to give themselves up to the junta officers below. 'There is no point in useless deaths. I order you to go,' he told the men around him. Most of them obeyed. And so with their hands up in surrender, Dr. Soto and ten others began their walk down, single file. They were stood up against the wall, cursed and kicked by the soldiers who searched them for guns. In the meantime, a platoon of heavily armed soldiers rushed into the building and up the stairs. There was a brief exchange of gunfire. And then a perspiring, somewhat bedraggled but smiling officer rushed down to announce to other officers and soldiers at the door that Allende was dead.

"Allende was killed with five of his personal bodyguards, young men between the ages of eighteen and twenty-five, who would not leave their president . . ."[120]

With the passage of time, the versions would multiply, the accounts become more lurid, until it would become an article of worldwide faith that Salvador Allende had not taken his own life, but had been cut down, brutally and needlessly.

Nathaniel Davis, the American ambassador in Santiago at the time, devotes an entire chapter of his book, *The Last Two Years of Salvador Allende*, to six major versions of Allende's death, examining and dissecting each in considerable detail, before concluding: ". . . the weight of evidence in this case is strong. Pending undiscovered evidence to the contrary, it would appear that the Junta version is true in its essentials, and the five opposing versions are not."[121] The "Junta version" was, of course, suicide, the others, murder. Davis's conclusion is especially notable given his undisguised affection for Allende in this work, his undisguised disgust with the junta.

This author has arrived at a similar conclusion, based largely on painstaking research for the previously mentioned book, *Allende: Death of a Marxist Dream*. It is a conclusion reinforced by subsequent suicide evidence, undiminished by scrupulously examined subsequent assassination claims.

The earlier evidence came in two principal parts: the testimony of Dr. Patricio Guijón Klein, the only actual (or putative) eyewitness to the event itself, and a close listening, several times, to the tapes of the actual conversations among the senior military commanders over their secret command radio network the day of the revolution.

As to the first: although our philosophical and ideological paths have continued to diverge, nothing in the thirteen years since I first knew him has caused me to doubt, even slightly, the absolute integrity and honesty of Patricio Guijón. As the narrative in these pages demonstrates, fate dealt unkindly, even perversely with Patricio Guijón on that day, maneuvering him into a place in a drama which would make of him a melancholy captive of a history he did nothing to create. The accident of being there, the circumstance of his personal integrity, brought Patricio Guijón an accursed kind of fame: mocked, scorned, and reviled by the very persons and forces he most admires, those of the hard Left. Nor did it bring him fortune, as the very changed reality of Chile's booming and liberalized economy would for very many other doctors of his generation. He lived, in 1987, as he had in 1973: in modest, but slightly frayed, middle-class decorum. Worse, in all of these years, he would become a captive in a very real, physical sense: a witness too valuable to risk losing, he was barred by the regime from leaving the country.

The second source of certitude is those tape recordings. It is utterly inconceivable, at least to this author, that such an elaborate dialogue, spanning seven hours and so full of spontaneities, startled reactions, and human frailty, could have been scripted and then play-acted out after the fact. And no one listening to those tapes could doubt that it was never in the generals' plans to execute Allende, and that they barely knew how to react when they learned that he had taken his own life. This, of course, could be construed to mean that the leaders themselves may have been blameless as to the deed itself, but not necessarily rule out a cover-up for trigger-happy subordinates once it was discovered that, out of edginess or anger, those subordinates had, in fact, murdered Allende.

Possible, but improbable. Research for the earlier book included extensive interviews with a great number of persons who were with Allende that day, who saw a man unraveling before their eyes; and it also included probing interviews not only with Guijón, but with a young lieutenant (Ramírez) who was among the first on the scene, with *El Mercurio* photographer Enrique Lira, who was in the palace within a few hours of the event, when many of those first arrivals were also there. Further, other writers, other investigators—many quoted in these pages—have presented the eyewitness accounts of still other persons in the palace before and immediately after the event. With the single exception of a threadbare tale told by a seventeen-year-old GAP, who claimed to have witnessed a murderous end, all those eyewitnesses have coincided, through the many years, in two major conclusions: (1) Allende was not himself those last hours of his life; (2) it was not a bullet-riddled body that those there immediately afterward would see with their own eyes, but a man with half his head blown off, just as Guijón, just as the autopsy, just as the junta would assert. Such wounds are in no way consistent with those suffered in a desperate you-kill-me-before-I-kill-you shootout across a dimly lit but cavernous room.

Finally, there is another eyewitness of sorts, though because what follows is third person hearsay, it is introduced as little more than a tentative footnote: in June of 1987, Patricio Guijón would tell the author, within hearing of several other persons, that he had recently met in Santiago Carlos Jorquera, the former press secretary, back from exile in Venezuela. According to Guijón, Jorquera—also one of the last to leave the palace on the eleventh—said he knew Guijón was telling the truth. Because, he said, he too had seen Allende propping the sub-machinegun between his legs, pointed at his head, before fleeing himself. He did not see (or hear) shots, but he did witness this presuicide tableau. Why had he not made this public?—because, to do so, would have been to break ranks with what had become the universal party line, the one which said that Allende had been brutally murdered.[122]

The weight of the evidence points unmistakably in the other direction. Much as he had often said he would, Salvador Allende chose to end his own life, rather than accept surrender and captivity—just as his preeminent Chilean patriotic hero, José Balmaceda had done eight decades earlier.[123]

Long years after the fact, as this book was nearing completion, yet another—and highly credible—witness appeared to attest to Allende's suicide: Miría Contreras, his long-time mistress, and the only woman to remain with him to the very end on September 11.

Breaking fourteen years of silence, Mrs. Contreras gave an hours-long interview in 1987 to an Italian journalist, Gastón Salvatore. One can only speculate why this woman, pushed into the shadows for so many years, would choose to speak now. Pushed into the shadows lest she detract from the image of the "bereaved widow"—Allende's long-estranged wife—who toured the world constantly, fueling the Allende legend. Whatever her reasons, this is what, in the quiet of her Paris apartment, Mrs. Contreras told Salvatore about Allende's death: " 'It's turned out badly for you, Payita,' " Perro Olivares told me, blocking my way into the presidential office of La Moneda.

"Augusto Olivares [journalist, intimate friend of Allende as well as his life-long confidante] did not want me to see the body of Salvador behind the desk. He tried to cover my eyes with his jacket. I remember even now the sound of the coins and keys in one of the pockets. I struggled to get free. I went in and saw Salvador stretched on the floor in a pool of blood. He was dead. He had just killed himself with the Skorpio sub-machinegun Fidel had given him. He still had it between his legs . . ."

Salvatore: "When I point out that her story about Allende's death contradicts the version of the Chilean Left, which asserts that Allende was murdered by the military, she answers: 'That is what Fidel said in his famous speech in Havana, a few days after Pinochet's coup. He had at his side Tati [Beatriz Allende] . . . When I managed to get out of Chile and reach Cuba, no one liked my story of Salvador's suicide. I didn't even know that it wasn't supposed to be mentioned. The military and the Chilean Right were talking suicide. But I saw it, I saw him dead, a few seconds before the soldiers came in. Perro Olivares also killed himself at Salvador's feet, a little after talking with me. I have never understood which images altered the fact of his suicide. Salvador Allende had spoken many times of the possibility of suicide. "If they want to get me out of La Moneda before the end of my term," he often said, "they'll have to take me out feet first." He felt a great admiration for Chilean president Balmaceda, who committed suicide in 1891 after having been defeated in a civil war. . . .

"The bombardment of La Moneda continued . . . Then, through the window of the palace, I saw the City Hall [*Intendencia*] in flames. Enriquito, my son, was there. I thought: Salvador and Enrique, dead. Nothing else could matter . . .' "[124]

Alone, embittered, clinging stubbornly to his own ideals, his own illusions, Carlos Prats González would profess to worry that "my excomrades-in-arms will never recover in life peace of spirit . . . I think of the terrible responsibility which [they] have taken upon their shoulders, bowing down by force of arms a people proud of the full exercise of human rights and liberty . . ." He would ask why sincere democrats on both sides were not able to perceive, however dimly, the abyss before them. Carlos Prats was certain that he was among the few who did see that hideous abyss yawning before him.

One of those former comrades-in-arms—the usually reserved Patricio Carvajal—was not nearly so certain that Carlos Prats González saw anything clearly in those decisive, cataclysmic days before the abyss of the eleventh. Watching the smoke and flames issuing from La Moneda across the way, Carvajal said, in sorrow not in anger, of Prats, of the now deposed navy chief, Admiral Montero: "I believe that they were under the diabolical influence of that Satan [Allende]. They were hypnotized by him."[125]

"People were still looting when we came through the gates, but they started to run when we appeared."

Corp. Sáez Ayala had sat out the aerial attack on Tomás Moro on a bus, parked at a prudent distance, together with the other men of his unit. Now it was time to seize the mansion.

"The first thing I noticed was a pool with a stuffed crocodile alongside. That side of the house was half fallen down—it looked like maybe four rockets had hit the place.

"We saw three or four bodies, and then two women, a telephone operator and a nurse. The place looked like a palace even with all the destruction. A funny thing, there was no fire of any kind.

"I was one of the first guys into his [Allende's] office. There was a big desk with maybe eight drawers. In one of the drawers at the right, a big deep one, there was practically an entire bar. In the middle drawer were a lot of documents. I saw a lot of figurines, gold and silver. There was a closet full of clothes, and a TV and a fireplace, and two jugs filled with marbles.

"In his bedroom, everything was disorder, including elements that go against . . . well, you know, all kinds of deviate sort of things, pictures, but the pictures were the least of it. There were artificial penises and things like that, and all kinds of magazines with pictures.

"The artificial penises were on a glass shelf in the bathroom, not at all hidden or anything. There was also an exercise bicycle and some other things.

"Next to Allende's room there was a kitchen, and leading down from that a tunnel. Down there were not just bottles of whiskey but big carafes, and bottles of wine, hundreds of them—Casillero del Diablo and bad ones too. Behind the freezer we found a door. It was to a dark room, with armament in there, all kinds—rocket-launchers and grenades, all kinds of things, American, Russian, Czech. It was like a munitions dump."

Sáez also saw rooms for the GAP garrison: six bunks to a room, five or six telephones in each room, weapons racks, television sets in the rooms. In the GAP dining rooms, they found dishes with uneaten food.

"I didn't go upstairs to her [Mrs. Allende's] room, but I did see the strong box when they opened it—a notary, or whoever he was—and it was full of bills. I don't know whether they were dollars or what, but there were a lot of them. I was looking in through a window when they were checking that stuff. You can believe me or not. I don't care. I know what I saw, and that's what I've told you."

There was, indeed, a good deal more than would meet the corporal's discerning eye: "that stuff," for example, included $8,666 in U.S. dollars, and 5 million escudos (roughly $200,000 at the official exchange rate, $16,666 at the going black market rate). Notary Rafael Zaldívar would confirm Sáez' report about the abundance of pornographic materials, whiskey, fine wines, and extremely scarce foodstuffs. Official records would also reveal armament sufficient to outfit two thousand men. Official sources would also indicate that Tomás Moro housed between 120 and 180 persons, most young men rotated out after three to six months to make room for new recruits. Beginning July 24, 1973, they were put through a forty-two-hour intensive training program for offensive and defensive operations in the city. The instructors included two Cubans.[126]

Corporal Sáez saw two women. There was another he did not see: Laura Allende, herself a Socialist deputy, the sister who in life was emotionally and politically closer to Salvador Allende than anyone else. Unable to reach La Moneda that morning, she finally reached Tomás Moro just after the soldiers. A neighbor warned her off. Driving off in her tiny Citroneta, she remembered the eerie premonition which again and again had reduced her to wordless tears only two days before, that sunny, Sunday afternoon she had spent with her brother here at Tomás Moro. She thought of seeking asylum, but decided against it; she did not know it then, but she had yet another and more important rendezvous to keep.

Just under seven miles away, as the crow flies, others were discovering the only date they would keep would be with their jailers. Of the ninety-five persons named in *Bando # 10*, calling on them to surrender or "face the foreseeable consequences," twenty-six were already in custody at the Defense Ministry. All told, Col. Eduardo (Caco) Sepúlveda—on duty at the Ministry since the dark predawn hours—remembered seeing around two hundred prisoners seated on the floor of the main entrance hall of the Ministry that afternoon. Contrary to many published reports, the top officials of the deposed government were "well treated," according to one of them (Interior Minister Carlos Briones), even to the extent of being given a medical examination before being bused off to their first temporary prison, the Military School. (Much grimmer things would await them, even grimmer things for others. Already by evening, the first of what by month's end would be six thousand prisoners were being rounded up and hustled into the National Stadium and Chile Arena [Estadio Chile]; by early October, four thousand of them had been released; the number of prisoners taken in the rest of the country was about the same, the release pattern also similar. Already by evening, even more ominously, the first reports of summary executions would begin circulating.)

In those first hours, other "distinguished" prisoners would be packed off to the Tacna Regiment. Among them: Carlos Jorquera. While awaiting questioning with the other prisoners in the Ministry, Jorquera was recognized by a general.

"Aren't you the fellow who spoke so much about armed revolution?" the general taunted him. "How come you're not making a speech now?"

A group of Investigaciones detectives, captured during the fighting, argued that they were only following orders and ought to be released. General Palacios was not impressed: "To Tacna!" he ordered.

After questioning, Dr. Soto and the other doctors—who had been busy looking after wounded of both sides in the battle raging outside—were released. But Patricio Guijón was not.[127]

For most Chileans, the eleventh was a day of deliverance. For some, it was literally that. One such was León Vilarín, the feisty ex-Socialist who headed the truck federation, the man who had spearheaded the strike which had helped to make this revolution inevitable. For several weeks, there had been an order out for his arrest—an order he took delight in mocking. (On August 12, he even turned up as a guest on the popular "A Esta Hora Se Improvisa" television program. He evaded waiting police in a disguise prepared by his personal "spy" in La Moneda, Allende's own barber.) On the eleventh, he was in hiding at the home of a truck driver. Now he could go home.[128]

Many more were scurrying home that afternoon. At midafternoon, the military commanders announced a free transit respite from roadblocks so that those trapped downtown or in factories could make it home. At six sharp, a curfew would go into effect; anyone on the streets after that hour risked being shot on the spot. It would be noon Thursday before the state of siege would be lifted at all, and then only from noon until 6:30 P.M., so as to permit a limited return to normal activity. (The curfew would remain in effect for well over a year, though the hour was gradually pushed back; when it was finally lifted, many—particularly housewives—would say that it had worked wonders for family unity.)

U.S. Ambassador Nathaniel Davis made it to the embassy residence at seven minutes to six. His daughter, Margaret, would write that he reported the streets "so quiet it was eerie. No cars, no people—only police barricades. . . . they were still shooting down there. I asked him what had happened to Allende. He said he didn't have the faintest idea, but that there had been rumors. One was that he had taken asylum in the Mexican Embassy; another was that he had been seen taken out of the Moneda with his hands tied; another was that he was dead . . ."

Few persons did know what had happened to Allende at that hour. Indeed, it would be Thursday before an official communique was issued, and only then that more than a handful, including Davis, would know. Against that "reasonable certainty," Davis on Thursday penned a letter of condolence to Mrs. Allende (though he did not report it to the State Department at the time).[129]

One who clearly did not know the news: Erick Schnake, at Radio Corporación, across the street from the palace. When the station sputtered back to life briefly at 3 P.M., Schnake reported that the "anguished" president had not surrendered and "calls on the masses to prepare a countercoup." A rifle shot again silenced the station, for the last time, as it would turn out.

Others didn't know it—but they sensed it. Around 2 P.M., Dan Arzak (of the U.S. Embassy political section) turned to Jim Halsema and said: "Allende is dead. I feel it in my bones." (Jim Halsema was another not going home that day; he was part of a skeleton staff which would remain on duty at the embassy for three straight days. Thanks to the resourcefulness of a secretary, Norma Price, they would not dine in style, but they did remain provisioned with snacks.)

Another group did dine in style. Hearing the news that a military junta was now in charge of the country that evening, the women encamped in the National Congress Building in support of their striking trucker husbands "cheered and embraced and danced—except for the Allende people. They were furious." The speaker was Mrs. Silvia Díaz, one of the leaders of that long vigil of protest. She continued: "Until that moment, we were afraid this might be another *tancazo*. But with the swearing-in ceremony and all that, we knew this was for real. The military aide ordered a real banquet for us in the presidential salon of the Senate. And what a feast it was—ham, avocado, lettuce. Fabulous, because we hadn't seen ham for such a long time. We ate with silver service and uniformed waiters . . ."[130]

The spring-soft breezes of day were giving way to the grumpy cold of a fading day when Jorge Braña and a few others seized on the respite to make their way home. For Braña, "home" was, of course, the Carrera Hotel, which meant making his way across what had been the major battleground, in and around La Moneda.

"I walked slowly, very slowly, and carried my Argentine passport in my hand," he remembered. "Not that it would have saved me from getting shot, but I thought, if they do shoot me, at least they'll know who they shot."

Thanks to Manager Mike Gallegos' foresight, the 648 guests and employees of the Hotel Carrera would not want for sustenance that night—nor during the following days of virtual isolation. For weeks, the prudent Gallegos had been paying black-market prices to stockpile foodstuffs, using the ever-more worthless reserve of blocked escudos to do so (even though, at the end, he was able to charge his guests only three thousand escudos per day, meals included—roughly one dollar at the black market rate). That first night, Gallegos even decided to throw in a free glass of wine at dinner. A *Time* magazine reporter would later write: "Gallegos, upon whose thin breast every one of last week's guests would like to hang a medal, evacuated his charges to the cavernous second basement. It took on the atmosphere of a London tube stop during the blitz, but with a notable international flavor."[131]

The trip home was harrowing, too, for Frank Tonini, Halsema's sidekick at the U.S. Embassy.

"A corporal came back to our office and said it was O.K. to leave. He said it would be a good idea to go individually and not in a convoy as we had suggested. I asked him whether there were any guarantees of our safety. 'Of course not,' he said dryly.

"As it happened, we made it home without being shot at, but I can tell you that we did make a run for it from the door of the embassy to the garage next door when we first ventured out. We were stopped and frisked several times along the way. Apart from that, what I remember most was the number of Chilean flags flying from the windows of houses and apartments we saw along the way."[132]

Some few made it not home—but into hiding. One was the seventeen-year-old GAP, Luis Renato González Córdoba, who, from asylum in the Mexican Embassy, would later concoct a tale as full of holes as he said were in Allende's body. On the sidewalk outside the palace, González faked a fit and—like *La Payita*—was taken by a Popular Unity doctor not to the hospital, but into hiding. A few days later he made it into the embassy. So, too, did OIR boss René Largo Farías, and his deputy, Jorge Uribe, one of the last persons to leave the palace. Uribe got away by hanging three cameras around his neck, carrying another in his hand and posing as an *El Mercurio* photographer; the following Saturday, he was joined there by his wife and two sons.[133]

Some few went home reluctantly. Among them, Mario Carneyro, editor of *La Segunda*, afternoon tabloid in the *El Mercurio* group, and a constant burr under the saddle of Salvador Allende. Carneyro was one of the few—perhaps the only—newsman brought into the secret of the impending revolution in advance. Now, he would see his hopes of publishing the biggest scoop of his career dashed; no paper would be allowed to appear until Thursday, and the two selected were *El Mercurio* and Carneyro's archcompetitor, *La Tercera de la Hora*. Dejectedly, Carneyro called the Defense Ministry to arrange a jeep escort home for the staffers he had mobilized to report this story of the century.[134]

At yet another downtown hotel, the spanking new Tupahue, the revolution surprised a usually poised group of Russians: the 102 members of the Berioska Ballet Company. When the shooting first started, some—believing it was a celebration of some sort—rushed to their rooms and began waving small flags from the windows. An officer stormed into the hotel and warned the manager to keep his guests away from the windows, or risk having their heads blown off. It would be several days before they would continue on to Buenos Aires, and by then they were among 1,100 Russians leaving the country (a number far in excess of the 150 assigned to the bloated Soviet Embassy). Yet another group of twelve Soviet army officers and twelve technicians was deported. They were arrested September 11 at El Belloto, near Valparaíso, where they had been since 1972 ostensibly installing a factory to turn out prefabricated housing, actually involved in after-hours training of a cadre of "specially selected worker revolutionaries in the use of arms, street fighting, and urban guerrilla tactics."[135]

Some of the formerly privileged hierarchy of the "people's" government would end the day a good deal poorer than they had begun it. Former Education Minister Edgardo Enríquez (father of MIRista leaders Miguel and Edgardo Enríquez) was found with $50,000; at the home of former Economy Minister Pedro Vuskovic, authorities found three checks made out to him for a total of 60 million escudos ($2.4 million at the official rate, roughly twenty thousand at the black market rate); at the home of the Communist Deputy Luis Guastavino, $145,000 in cash; Alejandro Rojas, deputy and former president of the Federation of Students of Chile, was carrying "several thousand dollars" when captured.[136]

At five that afternoon, Senator Olguín, vice-president of the Christian Democrat party, takes a call from army headquarters. They bring him in on the secret: Allende has committed suicide. Olguín suggests that the autopsy be performed by the director of the Institute of Legal Medicine, a Dr. Vargas, in the presence of two Christian Democrat congressmen. (Neither he nor his caller is aware that the autopsy is already under way.) The general says he will get back to them. The call never came.

Pinochet: "They inform me that a distinguished political personality has called Second Division headquarters this morning to offer his services, leaving his telephone number." A little while later, the caller says he is moving to another location and leaves the new number. "When I receive that information, I limit myself to telling the [division] commander to thank him and tell him that he not continue offering his services, because they are not needed.

"Evidently, this fellow thought that we were going to turn the government over to him."[137]

The honeymoon with the country's political power-brokers—the Christian Democrats—had not yet begun, and already the first sour notes are sounded.

Enrique Urrutia Manzano, chief justice of Chile's Supreme Court, had over the preceding months found himself and the institution over which he presided locked in an ever-worsening and unprecedented combat with the executive branch. When he learned finally of the suicide, this tall, courtly man professed that the news had not surprised him. "Allende," he said, "must have realized how enormous his responsibility was for what he had done to this country. That does not justify suicide, but it does explain why I was not surprised when I heard the news."

Neither did the news surprise Pelayo Figueroa, the Senate secretary who had watched Allende at such close range for so many years and just three years before was the official who would officially notify Allende of his election by Congress as president of Chile. "I would have been surprised," he said, "if he had surrendered. That I couldn't imagine—he was too vain."[138]

Then, there were those who never made it at all.

When news of the coup reached Washington, a meeting of the Washington Special Action Group was convened in an underground conference room below the White House. Henry Kissinger, national security adviser and secretary of state-designate, presided. Among the reports: the U.S. flotilla was by then in Chilean waters off the northern city of Arica. Kissinger: "Turn them around." Someone protested the expense, the loss of face (the ships were supposed to continue around the tip of South America after the Chilean exercises, then up the Atlantic coast for further exercises with the Argentine and Brazilian navies). This time, Kissinger "listened not very politely and repeated, with a slightly-metallic edge to his voice, his instruction." The ships were turned around. Actually, they already had been alerted: Merino, that morning, had ordered a six-word signal radioed to the American flagship: "Motivos inesperados imposible realizar Operación Unitas." (Unexpected reasons impossible hold Operation Unitas.) Refueled later by the *Araucano*, the U.S. squadron reversed course and put in a few days later in Panama.[139]

Those were not the only ships to reverse course that day: food shipments from the Soviet Union and Eastern Europe were turned around on the high seas the day of the coup, leading Henry Kissinger to remark: "This gave dramatic proof of the political motivations of Soviet aid programs."[140]

Still another ship slipped away—but under the very guns of the Chilean navy. The Cuban freighter *Playa Larga* was unloading ten thousand tons of the sugar Fidel Castro had so flamboyantly donated to Chile when, on the tenth, it was moved from the dock in Valparaíso to make room for a ship unloading a perishable cargo. Throughout the day of the eleventh, the freighter remained unmolested at its anchorage not far from the destroyer *Blanco Encalada*. Around five that afternoon, the *Playa Larga* began to sail boldly out of the bay; there was some discussion of sending a volley across her bow from the guns of Ft. Vergara, an idea discarded because of the panic it might have set off in an otherwise becalmed city (and because of physical damage to windows and the like). Then the *Blanco Encalada* was dispatched in desultory pursuit, finally broken off so as to avoid an international incident. The *Playa Larga* sailed off, bearing most of the sugar. Speculation would continue, long afterwards, what other cargo—including human cargo—she might have also carried away.[141]

Rain began falling late in the afternoon, prompting Leigh to propose moving the locale of the commanders' meeting from Peñalolén—too close to the towering Andes for flying comfort with a falling ceiling—to the Military Academy. Pinochet agreed. Leigh—who had planned to close out his service career at the end of the year—headed for the meeting believing that it was to be a planning session. Arriving, he was greeted by Channel 7 television cameras, a cache of captured weapons, and the news that he was about to begin a new and grueling career, as a member of the government junta.[142]

César Mendoza, celebrating his birthday that day, had also expected to close out his military career in a few months. Like Leigh, he would find, instead, that he was about to embark on the most significant journey of his professional career, only in his case, catapulted suddenly from virtual exile in a petty post to center stage. Unlike Leigh, he did know what to expect, and so, in a caravan consisting of a minitank in front, three cars, and a minitank behind, Mendoza "made the run out to the academy at top speed."[143]

Admiral Merino didn't know, either, as he helicoptered over from Valparaíso. Seated next to him was his close companion and trusted confidant, marine commandant Adm. Sergio Huidobro. "Along the way," Huidobro recalled, "I couldn't help remembering that it was just forty-eight hours before that I had been racing to Santiago with the message Merino had scribbled, the one that really touched off the revolution. Now it was all over."[144]

Although "everything was well organized," in Leigh's words, it is not even clear just how much the man who planned it all knew himself. What is clear is that events would not turn out as Augusto Pinochet anticipated back in those first frenzied days, but then it would not be realistic, either, to imagine that anyone suddenly astride an inferno would see even the immediate present clearly, much less peer knowingly into the future.

Shortly after the coup, General Pinochet would have this exchange with authoress Florencia Varas:

"How were you designated president of the junta?"

"There was, in reality, a gentlemen's agreement. I do not intend to direct the junta for so long as it lasts. What we will do is rotate. First, me. Tomorrow it will be Admiral Merino, afterwards General Leigh and then General Mendoza. I have no interest in seeming to appear as the irreplaceable man. I have no aspiration other than to serve my country."

"And now?"

"End of this process, beginning of the reconstruction."

"How?"

"Restoring normality in the country."

"Will it be easy?"

"All the provinces are under control."

"A plan?"

"The second period is economic reconstruction. A national inventory has been ordered to show the chaotic state in which the nation finds itself."

"And later?"

"As soon as the country recovers, the junta will turn over the government to whomsoever the people wish."

"What kind of government will the junta exercise?"

"This is a national Chilean movement with no parallel with any other. The junta is not going to follow any model. We are a country which has lived in democracy. Here there are neither friends nor enemies. Here there are Chileans who ought to unite. Everyone united working for the reconstruction of Chile."

"Any intervention of the United States in the uprising?"

"Not even my wife knew about it. Neither the United States nor any other country had anything to do with this."

"How long have you waited?"

"Since January we waited [to see whether] a dialogue would take place between the Christian Democrat party and the government. Allende deceived us. He told us that he was the principal enemy of civil war, and [yet] our secret service had obtained photographs of the arsenals in La Moneda and Tomás Moro."

"And the Chilean Marxists?"

"Outlawed, the Marxist parties, because of their system, because of their style [moral], and their lack of ethics."

The authoress does not give the precise date of that interview, but inasmuch as the book, *Operación Chile,* was published in 1973, it had to have taken place within days of the coup. At the outset of the interview, she indicates it was held at Pinochet's headquarters at Peñalolén on the night of the coup itself—a possibility, but inasmuch as he was at the Military Academy until very late that night, it would not seem probable.[145]

There was other business before the junta could be sworn in. For one thing, Merino and Mendoza—who would now shoulder much of the burden for governing the country—had never met, and needed to be introduced. Then there was a round of backslapping.

"We congratulated each other on the outcome," Mendoza said, "and then we got busy. We were all happy, of course."

The first item of business was how to break to the country the news of Allende's death. It was decided to do it in a terse communique: his death and burial were condensed into 117 words. The next decision: to keep quiet until afterwards the decision about where to bury him.[146] (As indicated earlier, the communique was not made public until Thursday.)

At 10:00 P.M., before television cameras and radio microphones that brought the ceremony to a nationwide audience, the four, following the playing of the national anthem, spoke briefly. Pinochet said the junta was studying the naming of ministers, governors, and mayors. (The fifteen members of the Cabinet were announced the next day; all but two, the ministers of education and justice, were military men, although two of the military men were then retired.) Pinochet said the ouster of Allende was not a military coup, but rather a patriotic movement "to rescue the country from the acute chaos into which it was being plunged by the government of Salvador Allende."

He said the junta would maintain diplomatic relations with all nations except Cuba. (That very night, the ambassador of Brazil arrived at the Military Academy to tell Pinochet that his government recognized the new Chilean government; the Soviets and most other Soviet-bloc countries would break relations with Chile within the next few days.) Pinochet also said that while the Congress would be closed, the junta would respect the autonomy of both the courts and the *Contraloría*.

Leigh, speaking next, said the decision to act came "after putting up for three years with the Marxist cancer that brought us economic, moral and social disarray which could no longer be tolerated. In the sacred interests of the fatherland, we have found ourselves obliged to assume the sad and painful task we have undertaken."

Merino said that under Allende, the concept of a three-cornered state was collapsing, and in its place, the executive alone ruled. "Perhaps," he said, "it is a democratic tradition that has been broken. But when a state loses its meaning, there come forward those who, by obligation, assume the responsibility of maintaining its validity. That we do today. We are certain that all of Chile understands the sacrifice that this represents for us."

It would remain for Mendoza, the junior man among the four who, because of his training (as a lawyer) and experience (in a quasi-civilian organization, closest to the citizenry) would speak in the most conciliatory, and wistful, vein: ". . . it is not," he said, "a case of crushing ideological currents or tendencies, nor of personal revenge, but, rather, one of restoring public order and returning the country to the path of compliance with the constitution and laws of the republic. That, then, is the spirit of the junta, to return to the path of true legality. We expect from every citizen, without exception, your cooperation for the best success and best achievement of that goal."

The speechmaking done, Decree Law One was announced: creating the junta. The four then took their oaths of office. Pinochet was sworn by a man with an ironic last name: Gen. Enrique Montero Marx (soon to become deputy interior minister, serving for this occasion as minister of faith). Pinochet then swore in the other three.[147]

It had taken Chile forty-five years to rebuild democracy from the ruins of its last collapse. It had taken Salvador Allende just a little over one thousand days to shake the already tottering and rickety framework of institutional order so violently as to bring that democracy crashing down. On this 11th day of September, it had taken not quite fourteen hours for the new junta to consign the wreckage of that old order to the trash heap of history.

"The military have saved Chile, and all of us whose lives are certainly not as important as Chile's . . ."

The speaker was Eduardo Frei, the man the entire world had come to view as the very embodiment of what was so widely, so wrongly, perceived as the excellence of democracy in Chile. Those sentiments, voiced immediately after the coup, were shared by most in Chile, in those first, euphoric days.

It is possible, even, that in those first days, that too was the vision of the men of the junta themselves: that their job was to "save" Chile.

Soon, very soon, it would become increasingly clear to them, as it would to others, that the mission they would face, the one they would undertake, would go far beyond the mere destruction of an old order. With hardening resolve and an ever-clearer sense of purpose, they would set out to build a new order, an order such as Chile had never before seen. In reality, few countries ever had.

Darkness had fallen on the traumatized city. A light rain fell on streets deserted except for what would now become the familiar sight of military patrols. The sounds of gunfire from snipers, from the few remaining pockets of resistance, from nervous men, reverberated in the chill night air.

It was not quite 6:30 P.M. when the body of the fallen president, wrapped in a Bolivian poncho and laid out on a stretcher, was carried out of the Morandé side door of the palace.

Enter, briefly, from history's shadows, Jaime Grove Kimber, godson of Salvador Allende, grandson of the president's sister, Inés. His story:*

"It was around ten thirty in the evening, and we were all eating, when a navy captain came and told us what had happened, that Salvador had committed suicide. I was not surprised. I knew he would not surrender; it just wasn't his personality. He was a very strong person, and he would fight to the end.

"The captain said that since we were the closest family, they wanted us to take charge of the burial. He asked us where we wanted to bury him—in Santiago or Viña del Mar. He said they [the military] preferred Viña. We had buried my grandmother, Inés, at the tomb of my grandfather in Viña only three months before; in fact, my uncle [he used that term to refer to Allende] had attended. So my father said Viña, and the captain accepted immediately. Before he left, he gave us safe conduct

---

* Taken verbatim from *Allende: Death of a Marxist Dream*, op. cit. pp: 196–200: Based on the author's interview with Grove in Santiago, Oct. 23, 1974.

passes, for my father and myself—we had decided it would be better for both of us to go.

"The next morning [Wednesday, the twelfth], around 7:00 A.M., we started out for the house of my uncle, Patricio, on O'Brien Street in Vitacura, near the Vitacura Church. The streets were deserted [martial law was still in effect]. We were stopped by a patrol. They made us get out of the car and searched us. They asked for our documents, and my father showed them the safe-conducts. They searched the car. The safe-conducts were not stamped, and so they closed up the car and put us on a bus, me on the first seat, my father on the last, and two guards beside us. My father explained what we were doing, but it was to no avail, they wouldn't let him say more. We had no idea where they were taking us, only that we were heading out on Kennedy Avenue.

"Suddenly, a city bus came from the other direction, and a Carabinero lieutenant and two noncoms stopped us, talked to the soldiers, and put us on another bus. They took us to the Military Academy. It was around eight or eight-fifteen by then. We were there around an hour. They didn't tell us anything. My father went and talked to Col. Nilo Floody [director of the academy]. My father also had Carvajal's telephone numbers and called him. They gave us a new safe-conduct, stamped this time, and a military escort for our own car.

"We then went to Patricio Grove's house. There it was decided he would go get Laura [Allende's sister], and we would get Tencha [his widow]—I think Patricio told him where she was. And so we went to Felipe Herrera's house in Pedro de Valdivia Norte [just a few blocks west of Patricio Grove's]. It was around ten when we got there. We went in, to the living room. There were two other persons there. She [Tencha] came out, looking sort of sad. She had just found out and was sobbing. I said hello to her. She didn't say anything.

"We told her we had orders to go to the Military Hospital. We left around ten-fifteen. We had to go very slow, perhaps twenty kilometers [fifteen miles] per hour. It took us fifteen minutes [from Herrera's house on El Cerro Street to the hospital, only half a dozen blocks south on Providencia, it is normally a two or three minute hop]. We were stopped several times and asked who we were. They [the soldiers] didn't recognize her.

"The three of us got out at the hospital. She was wearing a dress with a lot of colors, a pink dress. At the hospital door, she asked to go in, and identified herself. The guards didn't want to let us in, they said they had no orders, that they didn't know anything.

"She was sobbing and pleading with them, for perhaps half an hour, saying she only wanted to see her husband. She asked to see the director of the hospital.

"After a while he came with a chaplain, and they advised us that the remains had been taken to Los Cerrillos, and we should go there. By then it was around eleven-fifteen.

"Along the way we were stopped several times. There was shooting all over the place [their route took them past two of the factory strongholds of paramilitary forces]. We weren't shot at, but we were scared to death. It was around noon or twelve-fifteen by the time we got there. Patricio Grove, Laura, and the air attache, Commander [Col. Raúl Sánchez Grove, were already there, plus a few guards, and some high air force officers.

"The two women were sobbing. It was very sad. The day was sunny, it was a springlike day, but it was a sad scene. We went to the plane, a DC-3 parked maybe fifty meters away. Before we got in, all five of us were searched, the men by parachutists, the two women by air force women in uniform. We went in, first my father, then me, then Tencha and Laura, then Patricio, then the aide. The first thing we saw were jump seats along both sides, ten or fifteen of them, round, metallic. In the middle was the casket, a light gray, covered with a blue-and-beige blanket and tied with cables. It was a very unpleasant instant. We were all silent.

"Tencha went forward with the aide and sat in the flight engineer's seat because she had a problem with her back. My father and I sat on one side, Laura on the other.

"Then the pilots came in. They were young and greeted us, but we did not answer. We took off around twelve fifty-five.

"We were all lost in our own thoughts during the entire trip, all silent, looking out the windows. I looked at the motor of the plane, and it sounds like a joke, but the plane—it was fifteen years old—the door, instead of being hermetically closed, it was a good ten centimeters [four inches] open, and the wind was coming in, and I looked at the motor through that crack.

"There were two high officers—admirals—and two Carabinero generals at the cemetery, but no one else. There was no indication they were going to bury Salvador Allende. Oh, there were around ten guards, too. The officers came up to us, and Laura and Tencha explained they were very sad and didn't want to talk. 'No problem,' the officers said.

"The hearse went to the vault, and we walked behind—six, ten persons, perhaps three meters behind. In the meantime, Diana Comber, who was married to my father's younger brother, Jorge Grove, had joined us. She lived in Viña, and my uncle Jorge was then in the United States. My father, Patricio, the aide, and I took the body from the back door.

"At the moment we were taking it, the top slipped off a little, about a couple of centimeters [about four-fifths of an inch] and I could see white bandages covering everything. We put the top back as best we could and carried it to the vault. There were about five gravediggers and others who work in the cemetery there. We tied the casket and lowered it into the first niche from the top, at the right—the tomb has six niches, and he was put in the first one from the top.

"No one spoke. Everyone was silent. The women were sobbing.

"At the instant we were putting the casket in the niche, Tencha said some words. 'Compañeros, here our compañero president leaves us. Let us hope that the people don't forget him. Look how he is buried, without so much as a floral wreath, and in complete anonymity.' She then threw a wild red rose she was holding in her hand on top of the casket.

"Then they closed the niche with a marble cover. We walked back to our cars, the same ones we had come in. We asked if we could go to the presidential beach house in Viña, and he [the aide] said O.K. She wanted to get some of their effects, his and hers. He said there would be no problem.

"It was around three when we got there. The household staff had no idea we would be coming. We took some of his clothes—pants, sweaters, the grandchildren's toys, some of her clothes—and put them all in two or three boxes, which we then put in the navy car.

"They took us from there back to the Quintero Air Base. When we arrived at Quintero, someone remembered that we hadn't eaten, and Sanchez invited us to eat. We had sandwiches, but ate them on the plane.

"Nobody in Viña knew we were there. The plane left at three-thirty— same pilots, and we all sat in the same places. We arrived in Santiago around four-thirty.

"My father, a naval officer, and I took Tencha to Herrera's house, and Patricio and Laura went to her house. The officer asked us if we could drop him off afterward at the Defense Ministry. The four of us went to Herrera's house. We all got out and said farewell to her. Then my father and I got back in the front seat and the officer in the back.

"That ride was the scariest of all. When we got to Alameda, we were the only car on it and snipers were shooting from the rooftops. We didn't go all the way—there was too much shooting—but left the officer around two hundred meters from the ministry. He got out and walked, and we turned around.

"We were stopped by three or four patrols on the way and one Car-abinero searched the car as well as us.

"It was around 7:00 P.M. when we got home. We were upset and nervous from what we had seen and been through and felt that day.

"We stayed home all that night and the next day too.

"I will remember, as I do now, detail by detail, what I saw that day for the rest of my life."

* * *

Two days later, his aunt Diana Comber was taken back to the cemetery to identify the body. She went with a high naval chief.

"They opened the niche," Jaime concluded, "and then the urn, for maybe two seconds, long enough for her to see.

"Then they took him and put him in the lowest niche, perhaps three and a half meters down."

Salvador Allende had returned to the seacoast land of his birth.[148]

Notes

CHAPTER 8

1. James Whelan, *Allende: Death of a Marxist Dream* (Westport, Ct.: Arlington House, 1981), pp. 96–97. Allende then went on to appeal to workers in the *cordones* and his other supporters to rally to his side, cautioning them, as he did, against reckless confrontation.
2. Ibid., p. 97. Details of "Operation Silence," pp. 80–82; for references to "César" and the other civilians involved, cf. pp. 27–31, 33, 47–48, 96, 136, 206.
3. "Resounded" is an accurate description, but it took a command, a curse and two false starts before the revolutionary proclamation would finally air. The command was given by Francisco "Gabito" Hernández, then acting manager of Radio Agricultura. Weeks before, a small but powerful transmitter had been installed in Hernández' one-story house to serve as the voice of revolution should regular communications be knocked out. When it came time to air the coup announcement, Hernández, from his home, ordered an incredulous station engineer to play the national anthem. "Are you crazy—they'll close us," the engineer answered. "That's an order," Hernández shot back. The engineer did, and Hernández followed it with the recording rushed to him that very morning, the one announcing the revolution. Nothing happened. The anthem was played again. Finally, midway through the second playing, from his standby, improvised studio on the sixth floor of the Defense Ministry, army Major Guillar stepped into the breach and began the historic announcement: "This is the network of stations of the armed forces and Carabineros of Chile . . ." The problem, it would later be discovered, was that in attacking the installations of the UP stations that morning, a rocket had also damaged a cable at the transmitter, necessitating the switch to the back-up system. Details from ibid., pp. 32–34, 82–83, 104, based largely on an interview with Hernández in Santiago, April 3, 1974, as well as with previously cited interviews with "César," "Mario," Colonel Polloni (October 23, 1974) and key Radio Agricultura figure Alvaro Puga (a series of interviews in October 1974), as well as details appearing in *Qué Pasa*, #177, September 10, 1974, pp. 27–28.
4. Whelan, op. cit., p. 105. Merino had not yet been named navy commander-in-chief, and, until then, Mendoza was fourth-ranking in the Carabineros. Further, until then, there had been no discussion of him—or anyone else—to take over as Carabinero chief. But then, this was war, and in war, the rule is to suspend rules.
5. One of three events which gave rise to much of the sterile speculation to "prove" U.S. involvement in the revolution; (the others were Ambassador Davis's lightning trip to Washington, a few days before the eleventh, to meet with Secretary of State-designate Henry Kissinger, and the impending visit of the U.S. air force acrobatic team, subsequently cancelled after consultations with the new Chilean government). Ambassador Davis discusses these alle-

537

gations in detail in his book, *The Last Two Years of Salvador Allende* (Ithaca-London: Cornell University Press, 1985), pp. 350–358, and there is further discussion of these issues later in this chapter.

6. Whelan, op. cit., p. 46, based on interviews with Briones in Santiago, May 13 and October 10, 1974.

7. Ibid., pp. 45–46.

8. Ibid., pp. 24–25, 57–58, 69–70.

9. Ibid., p. 70.

10. Allende continued to work on that speech after the ministers left, until 4 A.M. Source for two accidental casualties: "lo que usted nunca supo del día 11 . . .!," *La Segunda* (Santiago: Special supplement appearing September 10, 1974), p. 5. One was a sailor who accidentally fired his weapon, wounding himself; the other, a sailor wounded when a military patrol fired on the pickup truck he was riding in when the driver failed to heed the order (which they did not hear) to halt. The far-left propaganda campaign following the coup would portray Valparaíso as the scene of a bloodbath. For example, Samuel Chavkin would write that "Junta forces . . . overnight had executed hundreds of marines and sailors who refused to go along with the mutiny." He cites no source, but then if Chavkin made any effort to seek out or consult a single pro-junta source for his book, there is no evidence to that effect in the book: Samuel Chavkin, *Storm Over Chile* (Westport, Ct., Lawrence Hill & Company, 1982 & 1985), p. 24. Curiously, Ambassador Davis refers to Chavkin as "a pro-Allende scholar . . ." (Davis, op. cit., p. 236).

11. Whelan, op. cit., pp. 86–87.

12. Ibid., p. 71, based largely on an interview with President Pinochet in Santiago, October 22, 1974. Augusto Pinochet Ugarte, *El Día Decisivo* (Santiago: Editorial Andrés Bello, 1980), pp. 130–131.

13. Pinochet, op. cit., p. 131. Pinochet writes: "I accepted his position, and ordered his immediate arrest." Pinochet's detour caused him to arrive ten minutes past the seven-thirty deadline he had established, causing worry for General Bonilla, then in charge at Peñalolén and the man Pinochet had designated to succeed him in case he should be killed, imprisoned or incapacitated. It was, he wrote, a "worried" General Bonilla he found when he got there. As it happens, "Mario" was still struggling to finish the installation of the secret communications system at Peñalolén when Pinochet arrived. Whelan, op. cit., pp. 102–103. The number two and three army generals in seniority were skipped over and excluded from the planning process in the belief that they might be sympathetic to Allende.

14. Ibid., pp. 57–58, 74. Final revisions in the navy's plan had been completed only that day—Saturday, September 8—and until that night, only five officers on his general staff knew the new time and precise details for the navy's role in the coup.

15. Ibid., pp. 13, 16, 48–49, 50–51. The decision to bomb was taken in the belief—correct, as it turned out—that this would shorten the fighting and thus reduce casualties. As to exile, Leigh took a map and drew a line: "If he chooses Mexico, nothing doing. No farther than this" (pointing to Venezuela). The reason: Leigh was concerned for the safety of his flight crews, and thus did not want them to fly farther than they could reach in a single hop, so that they could then return immediately. Santiago-Caracas is 3,045 air miles, Santiago-Mexico 4,197 miles over water, 4,492 via a safer route

partially over land. Ibid., p. 21. Leigh served from 1960–1966 as Chile's air attaché in Washington.

16. Ibid., pp. 21–22 for Joignant anecdote, pp. 50–52 for the rest.

17. Ibid., pp. 50–53. After roasting Leigh as "seditious" that morning for refusing his order to return the planes, Allende had talked to the president of LAN Chile, who said that it was better, after all, to have the planes moved to a more secure place.

18. Ibid., pp. 17–20, 58–60, based mainly on an interview with Mendoza in Santiago, October 14, 1974.

19. Gabriela Leigh also had to keep up appearances; she went ahead with plans for a tea scheduled for the next day, September 11, in honor of the wife of Gen. Ruiz Danyau, the man Leigh had succeeded as air force commandant (ibid., p. 50).

20. Ibid., pp. 58–60, 73. Arriving at Norambuena that morning, Mendoza would discover that, reacting to reports of the Valparaíso uprising, General Urrutia had already placed Carabineros on alert—yet another anxiety Mendoza had to deal with.

21. Ibid., p. 78 (for Letelier), p. 79 (for Altamirano).

22. Ibid., p. 78, based mainly on interviews with Mrs. Letelier in Santiago, May 8 and 12, 1974.

23. Ibid., pp. 87–89, *Qué Pasa*, op. cit., p. 26.

24. *Qué Pasa*, op. cit., p. 25, and *La Segunda*, op. cit., p. 8.

25. Description of Mrs. Contreras from Florencia Varas and José Manuel Vergara, *Operación Chile* (Santiago: Editorial Pomaire, 1973), p. 97. Details of the morning from an interview Mrs. Contreras granted late in 1987 to the Italian journalist Gastón Salvatore, published in the magazine *Epoca*, January 10, 1988, and reproduced in its entirety in *El Mercurio*, Santiago, January 14, 1988, p. 1. The GAPs she persuaded to go with her—they balked at first on the grounds Allende had ordered them to remain at Tomás Moro, yielding only because of Mrs. Contreras' role as the unofficial "mother hen" of the GAPs—walked into a trap when they reached downtown with her. The decision to take her youngest son Enrique, a twenty-year-old student, with her would prove even more fateful. Mrs. Contreras' recent version seems to contradict earlier ones that it was Allende who had summoned the additional GAPs and their armaments from Tomás Moro to La Moneda. The 1987 interview is remarkable for many reasons, not the least of them that with it, Mrs. Contreras broke fourteen years of silence—during which time she had lived first in Havana, and then in Paris, dutifully remaining in the shadows while Allende's widow roamed the world adding to the legend of her late husband (hereafter *Epoca* interview). As noted earlier, Mrs. Contreras first met the Allendes in 1950, when she married an older man, Enrique Ropert, an engineer of "Socialist ideas," moving into a house on Guardia Vieja street in Santiago next door to #398—the Allende home. Ultimately, she would become his closest confidante, occupying an office which opened into his at La Moneda, making up a bed for his afternoon siestas, and spending riotous weekends with him at El Cañaveral where, among other things, she joined him in learning guerrilla warfare. At the entrance to El Cañaveral, there was a huge portrait of Allende, dedicated to "Payita, my best friend and grand companion, expressing through her affection which I have for her and hers. Affectionately, Salvador, September 5, 1970." Varas and Vergara, op. cit., pp. 97–98.

26. *Breve Historia de la Unidad Popular,* Teresa Donoso L., ed., (Santiago-Editorial Lord Cochrane, S.A., 1974), pp. 383–384.

27. Whelan, op. cit., pp. 99–100, 107–108, based on numerous conversations in Santiago, March through May 1974. I rented María's apartment while researching the book.

28. Ibid., pp. 114–115. Reference to the two captains "planted" in the regiment is in Pinochet, op. cit., pp. 100, 135.

29. Whelan, op. cit., p. 113. Unless otherwise noted, the source for all conversations over the secret radio network is a tape recording of actual traffic on the network during the seven hours when it functioned as main command link. The author was permitted to listen to the tape and make direct written transcriptions from it by the two civilians most responsible for creating the network. Fearing reprisals, both requested anonymity and are referred to in *Allende: Death of a Marxist Dream*—and in the present volume—by their pseudonyms, "Mario" and "César." Interviews with "Mario" began in Santiago May 4, 1974, continuing over the next ten days, resuming again on October 17, 1974; with "César," also in Santiago, October 17, 1974. Although it was intended as a command network, senior commanders continued to use it as a back-up system (and because of its relative security) for weeks after the revolution; indeed, according to one account, it would be September 25 before "Mario" would get to go home again (*Qué Pasa,* op. cit., p. 34). Neither of the two men made any such mention of prolonged service during our extensive conversations. Details of the work of the two men, and the military officers and technicians who worked with them, are on pp. 27–34, 47–48, 112–113 and 136 of *Death.*

30. Chavkin, op. cit., p. 122. Mrs. Allende told Chavkin that Allende gave her that message when he called her from La Moneda earlier that morning. But when she called daughter Beatriz, she discovered that she had already left for the palace to be with her father. Finally reaching Isabel, "Isabel, too, felt that she should be with him." Despite that, Mrs. Allende herself worked the telephones, trying to reach friends, trying to reach him ("every time I called, a different person would answer"), but made no effort to reach the palace in person. Either Chavkin—or Mrs. Allende—garbled events in this narrative, because she has the bombing of Tomás Moro taking place early in the morning, several hours before it actually happened. Her reaction is worth repeating, nonetheless: "Suddenly, the house was shaking as though from an earthquake. The *Junta's* air force pilots were on a reconnaissance overlight. . . . He (the driver) had hardly finished this sentence when the planes were over us again and this time they were dropping bombs. In seconds our lovely house was engulfed in flames, rubble and chaos. Coughing and choking from the pulverized masonry and staggering from shock, I recovered somewhat when our driver materialized at my side and said, 'Let's get out of here immediately. This is an inferno.' I owe my life to that driver." Ibid., p. 122.

31. *La Segunda,* op. cit., p. 13.

32. Whelan, op. cit., pp. 93–94, 123. Halsema's father was a U.S. army major, en route back to duty in the Phillipines after serving with Herbert Hoover's war relief mission to Russia. Halsema was in Manila when the Japanese bombed on December 8, 1941, and would be back four years later as a reporter covering the extremely bloody battle to liberate Manila. Based on interviews with Halsema in Santiago March 29 and May 2, 1974.

33. Ambassador Davis gives considerable credence to these doubts—see. e.g., pp. 227–229. Prats' actions in supporting Allende have been reflected in the previous chapter, and those actions spoke louder than any words. Still, for a sample of his thoughts on Allende, the man, the leader, see Carlos Prats González, *Memorias: Testimonio de un Soldado* (Santiago: Editorial Antártica, 1985), 2nd ed., pp. 374–375.

34. Pinochet, op. cit., pp. 23–29.

35. Whelan, op. cit., pp. 14–15 and Pinochet, op. cit., pp. 101–102. Pinochet's dramatic narration of the nocturnal meeting appears on pp. 108–112 of that volume. In that narration, Pinochet implies—but does not say—that the other general there present was Orlando Urbina, ultimately excluded from planning for the revolution. Months after that episode, he relates, army intelligence told him that Allende had been dining that night with UP officials when Altamirano called to alert him that Pinochet was plotting against him. Allende decided to have the second-ranking general (Urbina) present so that should Pinochet, when confronted, admit to anything, or fail to come across as convincing, the second-ranking general could immediately be put in his place as army commander-in-chief. Pinochet adds that after he left that dramatic encounter, Allende telephoned Prats to recount what had happened. Prats said he considered it was "impossible" that Pinochet might be plotting since "he is loyal to me and would have informed me of anything so serious" (cf. pp. 111–112). Prats confirms that he continued to attest to Pinochet's loyalty to the very end; Prats, op. cit., pp. 486, 510.

36. Pinochet, op. cit., pp. 129–130.

37. *Qué Pasa*, op. cit., p. 32. Prats remarks in *Memorias* (p. 469) that when Admiral Carvajal handed him a new communications plan for his signature on August 17, he understood that it was "double-edged"—that it could be used offensively as well as defensively—but that he signed it anyway because of the need to be ready for any seditious exigency in those stormy days.

38. Whelan, op. cit., p. 76, based largely on an interview with Merino in Santiago, October 18, 1974. Merino said that he had "deliberately" left one telephone line open to Santiago in the hope that someone loyal to Allende would use it, thereby "stampeding" Allende into La Moneda, where he would be an easier quarry for capture.

39. Ibid., pp. 28 and 79–88 (for Operation Silence), interview with Col. Polloni in Santiago, Oct. 23, 1974. Pinochet refers to Operation Silence as part of *Plan Hércules*, which he writes was finally modified Sept. 4, 1973 (op. cit., p. 136). He made no mention of *Plan Hércules* in his lengthy interview with me.

40. The twenty persons in Radio Agricultura came under intense and sustained fire from Communist party headquarters, diagonally across Teatinos Street (shots had been fired at the station from party headquarters even before the coup). At the U.S. Embassy, windows on the ninth and tenth floor—where the senior staff, including the ambassador, had their offices—were shot out; those on the fifth through eighth floor were not. Whelan, op. cit., p. 140. As did Dr. Guijón, pressman Garrido and a few others, Ambassador Davis refused to be deflected by the Carabinero roadblocks, and continued weaving and bobbing, finally walking the last three or four blocks amid the "crack of rifles, chugging teargas guns and the burping of automatic weapons." Davis, op. cit., p. 249. Details of the siege on UPI in Whelan, op.

cit., p. 139, based in large part on an interview with UPI man Roberto Mason in Santiago, April 17, 1974. UPI managed to get its story out when the news agency's correspondent in Mendoza, Argentina, got through on a forgotten private line. The line was kept open for eight hours, permitting Santiago's UPI to dictate a story directly from the scene of the action.

41. In the wake of Prats' resignation, Brig. Generals Mario Sepúlveda Squella and Guillermo Pickering Vásquez also resigned. To Allende's irritation, Pinochet insisted on accepting their resignations—while refusing to retire four generals Allende wanted out. In the cases of two of them—Bonilla and Arellano—Allende (correctly) complained that they were plotting against him. Squella and Pickering's resignations were key not only because these men were sympathetic to Allende, but with them out of the picture, Pinochet was able to appoint "two of my best friends" (as he would write) to the pivotal commands they held: the Santiago garrison and the Military Institutes (which included the Military Academy, the Non-commissioned Officers' School, the Infantry and Artillery schools, etc.). To the first: Gen. Herman Brady, to the second, Gen. Raúl Benavides. Pinochet, op. cit., pp. 114–115. Had this not happened, it is hard to see how the revolution could have occurred without immense bloodshed. It is worth observing what Pinochet had to say about those pro-Allende generals: "I wish to leave very clear that it is not my desire to stain their names; their attitude was due to blind obedience which they believed they owed to the government. I also believe today that only because of their stance were we able to fulfill destiny's mandate," adding that he found in it "the hand of God in such unexpected ways" (ibid., p. 115). It is interesting also to speculate whether Pinochet intended this observation to apply to Prats. What is clear is that another general—Arellano—would find himself persona non grata for a claim he made in a 1977 interview with Qué Pasa magazine (8–14 Sept., 1977, p. 31), in which he claims that it was he—and not Pinochet—who actually devised the operational plans for the eleventh, working through the tenth, indeed, to finish them. As to combat command assignments on the eleventh, cf., Whelan, op. cit., pp. 13–17 and Qué Pasa, op. cit., p. 25.

42. Pinochet, op. cit., pp. 126–127.

43. Whelan, p. 56.

44. Whelan, op. cit., pp. 35–36, 83–84, 101–102, based on numerous interviews and social meetings with Guijón in Santiago beginning April 4, 1974, and continuing over the next five weeks, resuming over a three-week period in October 1974, correspondence in the months following, and another meeting in Santiago June 17, 1987.

45. Ibid., p. 115. Based on an interview with Grez in Santiago, October 24, 1974. The "proclamation" was, of course, the one broadcast at eight-thirty announcing the formation of the junta and the demand to surrender. The reference to "trouble in your navy" was the in-fighting over the two preceding weeks over replacing Montero with Merino as navy commandant.

46. The "name Sánchez" anecdote is from Arturo Fontaine and Cristián Zegers Ariztía ¿Cómo llegaron las fuerzas armadas a la acción del 11 de Septiembre de 1973? (Santiago: El Mercurio, Sept. 11, 1974), p. 15.

47. Valenzuela-Sánchez in Chavkin, op. cit., pp. 21–22. Davis makes reference to the Van Schouwen telephone call, op. cit., pp. 245–246, citing as the source: Paul E. Sigmund, The Overthrow of Allende and the Politics of Chile, 1964–1976 (Pittsburgh: University of Pittsburgh Press, 1977), p. 242.

48. Grez in Whelan, op. cit., p. 117.

49. Ibid., pp. 117–118. I transcribed the text of that speech from a recording made available to me at Radio Agricultura.

50. Ibid., pp. 119, 122–123 (for excerpts from exchanges on the command network, and details of the Massa assignment). Massa, based on an interview with him in Santiago, October 10, 1974. In that earlier high Andes adventure, search parties had hunted for survivors for seventy days. It was later learned that the survivors had resorted to cannibalism to stay alive; the event would be the subject of numerous subsequent dramas.

51. Ibid., pp. 119 and 122 (based principally on aforementioned interviews in Santiago with Grez, October 24, and Briones, May 13 and October 10, 1974, and with the navy steward who witnessed the drinking). Although he requested anonymity, that interview, October 24, 1974 in Santiago, was tape-recorded.

52. Chavkin, op. cit., pp. 24–26. Davis, op. cit., p. 236, refers to Chavkin as a "pro-Allende scholar." It is hard to see how he arrives at that conclusion, certainly not justified on the basis of this book, in which Allende and his forces are uniformly virtuous (or victims), and Pinochet and his associates "fascist" villains. Further, if Chavkin made any effort even to listen to anyone opposed to Allende, there is no evidence of that in this book. The book jacket describes Chavkin as "formerly associate radio news editor at the United Nations," and adds that he spent five years in Latin America. The jacket itself says the book "spans a decade of fascist repression in Chile." Davis is not alone in his obvious admiration for Chavkin's "scholarship." The earlier version of this book—*The Murder of Chile*—was published to huzzahs from such congenitally left-wing commentators as Stanford's Richard Fagan and the Rev. Joseph T. Eldridge, director of the Roman Catholic church's Washington Office on Latin America.

53. Whelan, op. cit., pp. 114–115. Interview with Corporal Pizzarro in Santiago, October 14, 1974.

54. Ibid., pp. 23–24 and 139; Canessa interviews in Santiago, April 30 and May 1, 1974. UPI's Roberto Mason, news manager for Chile, would say later that a soldier in the Defense Ministry was among those ordered to fire at UPI, knowing that it was UPI—"but who would listen to a draftee in the middle of a war?" The draftee knew whereof he spoke; he was the son of a UPI employee (Mason interview, April 17, 1974).

55. Chavkin, op. cit., p. 26.

56. Whelan, op. cit., pp. 120–121. Interview with Baeza in Santiago, October 16, 1974. In his book, Pinochet (op. cit., p. 137) offers a somewhat milder and more abbreviated version of that episode. Mine is based on a close and repeated listening to the actual taped recording of command network traffic.

57. Ibid., pp. 121, 126–128. Question about Allende's tanqueta escape in Pinochet, op. cit., p. 137.

58. Whelan, op. cit., 126 (Briones interviews); the Tohá-Carvajal exchange from Varas and Vergara, op. cit., pp. 84–85.

59. Both Briones and Tohá would try again. At another point, after the bombing, Flores put in a call to Gen. Nicanor Díaz: "This is Minister Flores," he said. "Ex-Minister Flores," Díaz retorted. Flores told him that he, Under-Secretaries Puccio and Vergara had instructions to negotiate surrender terms. Díaz told them there are no terms—only unconditional surrender,

and to make their way to the Defense Ministry under a white flag. They did. Whelan, op. cit., p. 129, 132, 164; Fontaine and Zegers, op. cit., p. 23.

60. Whelan, op. cit., p. 132 (based on the tapes).
61. Ibid., p. 130.
62. Chavkin, op. cit., p. 27.
63. Isabel Allende, in an interview in Mexico with Régis Debray, published in the Dominican Republic magazine, *Ahora,* no. 518, October 15, 1973, as reproduced in Enrique Lafourcade, *Salvador Allende* (Barcelona: Ediciones Grijalbo, 1973), pp. 210, 212.
64. Whelan, op. cit., pp. 129–131, Varas and Vergara, op. cit., pp. 93–94. According to this report, Allende also used the argument that he wanted his daughters to take a personal message to Fidel Castro. Beatriz left Chile a few days later. In 1978, she committed suicide.
65. Chavkin, op. cit., pp. 28–29.
66. Modak's dramatic account of the escape appears in ibid., pp. 28–34. Reference to sniper fire preventing the jeep from reaching the women in Whelan, op. cit., p. 137.
67. *Las Ultimas Noticias,* Santiago, October 12, 1974: "La Payita Cuenta Su Versión del 11" (which the newspaper reprinted from an interview she gave to the Cuban magazine *Bohemia.* Journalist-authoress Teresa Donoso told me during a conversation in Santiago, May 7, 1974, that, a few days after the coup, she bumped into *La Payita*'s husband, Enrique, in Guardia Vieja Street. He told her that they (the UP) had expropriated his farm and that he hoped that the military would now give it back. A few days later, he was, in fact, arrested, after arms and military uniforms were discovered in a brother's house. The Contreras' were neighbors of the Allendes in Guardia Vieja Street; Enrique was ten to fifteen years older than his wife. Donoso had lived with the couple in Paris in 1961 while she was studying there. She described them as a "very bourgeois, very entertaining couple."
68. Whelan, op. cit., pp. 130–131. Pinochet stood fast in that offer even though he remarked at one point that his advisers were telling him that it would be a mistake to let Allende leave the country.
69. Pinochet, op. cit., p. 138.
70. *Las Ultimas Noticias,* op. cit.
71. Whelan, op. cit., pp. 125, 140–141, based largely on an interview with Gallegos in Santiago, March 14, 1974. As were the UPI offices, the Carrera was a mistaken target. Snipers were not shooting from the hotel—Gallegos made certain of that—but the offices of the government petro-chemical corporation (SOQUIMICH) were located directly across narrow Agustinas Street. As the first stray bullets from the troops below aimed at SOQUIMICH pinged instead off the crusty concrete of the hotel, smoke and sparks rose from the building, giving to the untrained eyes of the recruits below the sensation of return fire. So, the more pings there were, the more shooting there was.
72. Ibid., p. 125.
73. Whelan, op. cit., pp. 110–111, 141. Based on an interview with Humeres in Santiago, May 1974. None of the Contraloría people was hurt that day.
74. Ibid., pp. 66–67, 92, 141. Interview with Garrido in Miami, April 9, 1975.
75. Ibid., pp. 92–93. Based on an interview with Carmona in Santiago, April 7, 1974. Carmona enjoyed very close ties with the military, because of his service as Frei's first defense minister (1964–1968), but also because it was

he who had authored the Arms Control Law, so vital in checking the power of the paramilitary brigades. There is considerable reason to believe that Carmona was one of the few civilians taken into the military's confidence about the coup, and so it is likely that he was merely "keeping up appearances" by trekking out to the airport that morning.

76. Ibid., p. 185 Based on an interview with him in Santiago, April 15, 1975. Making his way home later that day, he moved from the frying pan to the fire: he lived a short distance from the Cuban Embassy, and the shooting there continued through the night of the eleventh and most of the twelfth.

77. Ibid., p. 101. Based on an interview with Braña in Santiago, April of 1974.

78. Ibid., pp. 142–143. The Espinoza quotes are from Varas and Vergara, op. cit., pp. 100-101.

79. Whelan, op. cit., pp. 143–144. Mrs. Contreras claims in that narrative that there was a young woman there singing softly, "Cuba, how pretty is Cuba." Inasmuch as all accounts agree that she was the only woman left there, she surely was taking poetic liberties for the benefit of her Cuban interviewers.

80. Ibid., p. 144. Based on an interview with him in Santiago, April 24, 1974. Ambassador Davis quotes from a letter his wife, Elizabeth, wrote, a day or two after the eleventh. The ambassador telephoned Mrs. Davis immediately after the attack to reassure her that the embassy—itself so close to the line of fire—had not been hit. She then relayed the word to the wives of other embassy officials (Davis, op. cit., pp. 263–264).

81. Ibid., pp. 144–145. Most of my information on the bombing raid was given to me by air force Commandant Gustavo Leigh during our extensive interview in Santiago, October 14, 1974, but important additional details were supplied by Col. Eduardo Sepúlveda, by then consul general of Chile in Miami, during numerous conversations stretching from the autumn of 1974 well into the spring of 1975.

82. Ibid., p. 144. Chavkin, op. cit., pp. 35–36.

83. Ibid., pp. 29–30. Fleeing *La Prensa* after the bombing, only to be forced to duck into a hotel when the shooting resumed. Mrs. Modak said the lobby was "jammed with joyous merrymakers, men and women, all obviously upper class, all celebrating the junta seizure of power . . . the revelers shouted themselves hoarse congratulating themselves that the Allende era was about over . . . each exclamation was like a dagger in our hearts. It was unbearable, suffocating." While they were debating how to get out, she said a man who seemed like the manager approached and said while he did not want them out, he felt that for their own safety—considering the situation in the hotel—it would be better that they did. Curiously, there are no luxury hotels within one block of the only street she mentions (Ahumada), and from the only one at all, there would be nothing resembling "a front-view seat on the bombing attacks on the palace . . ." From the hotel, they ultimately were able to hitch a ride, and though their adventures were far from over, eventually reach safety (ibid., pp. 30–32).

84. Ibid., pp. 145, 142, 126.

85. *Libro Blanco del Cambio del Gobierno en Chile* (Santiago: Editorial Lord Cochrane, S.A., 1973), pp. 249–250. Perhaps the best example of Leigh's public relations sense was in the *bando* which preceded that one: directed primarily to Chile's youth ("now, more than ever, the young should have confidence in the Armed Forces and superior destiny of Chile"), it also urged parents to "maintain the family nucleus intact"; and to the citizenry in

general: no demonstrations, not even in support of the new authorities. (That one would shortly be ignored.) It was also Leigh who suggested a *bando* saying the air attack on La Moneda had been necessary because Allende refused to surrender.

86. Ibid., pp. 158–159.
87. Ibid., p. 148.
88. Ibid., pp. 97–98, 157; based on interview with Mrs. Hinojosa in Santiago, April 3, 1974. Data on General Poblete, Ricardo Boizard, *Proceso A Una Traición* (Santiago: Ediciones Encina, 1974), pp. 59–60. General Poblete was implicated by First Sgt. Belarmino Constanzo Merino (code name: Galeán), in a MIR plot called "Plan September" which called for the seizing of the Air Academy and adjoining El Bosque Air Force Base. The original plot was to have been executed in September 1972 but had to be aborted. The new and expanded plan included infiltration and neutralizing as well of the Cerrillos Air Force Base in Santiago as well as the Quintero Air Force Base near Valparaíso. General Poblete was to have taken command of El Bosque; there, as at other bases, planes were to be blown up, anti-Allende officers and men imprisoned and arms distributed to MIRistas and other pro-Allende combatants. Tried in 1974, General Poblete was sentenced to be stripped of his Chilean nationality and sent into exile.
89. Whelan, op. cit., p. 158.
90. Details of the scene at CIA headquarters in Langley are from an extensive interview with a senior CIA official on June 2, 1975, in Washington (a retired officer, he requested anonymity). The exchanges between Phillips, his predecessor and the Christmas anecdote are in David Atlee Phillips, *The Night Watch; 25 Years Inside the CIA* (London: Robert Hale, 1978), pp. 237–238, 246–247; embassy communications, Davis, op. cit., p. 255. Davis observes that the call went out from the defense attaché's office; it is likely he is referring to U.S. army Col. Carlos Urrutia, chief of the U.S. Military Mission, whose office was situated on the eighth floor of the Defense Ministry itself, and which could explain how the "embassy" was able to communicate internationally. Urrutia himself told me that after trying without success to make it past the emerging Carabinero roadblocks that morning, he finally gave up and went home. Interview with Urrutia in Santiago, April 24, 1974.
91. Whelan, op. cit., pp. 145–146, 135. Telephone call, from interviews with Mrs. Letelier in Santiago, May 8 and 12, 1974. Chavkin, op. cit., p. 31; interview in Santiago with Corp. Iván Ayala, May 9, 1974; details Tomás Moro armaments, *Three Years of Destruction*, a booklet published by the Chilean Printers' Association (ASIMPRES), apparently in 1974, unnumbered page entitled ("No to Civil War"). That same source said that at Allende's weekend retreat, El Cañaverál, troops found a complete guerrilla training camp sufficient for sixty students, a factory for making high-explosive bombs, as well as armaments and ammunition.
92. *Septiembre de 1973: Los Cien Combates de una Batalla*, book published by the Chilean Armed Forces in 1973, pp. 23–24. Alistair Horne, *Small Earthquake in Chile* (New York: The Viking Press, 1972), p. 198. Horne recounts how, on a trip south to see for himself this area where Comandante Pepe— "a little like Strelnikov in Dr. Zhivago, was roaming the countryside at will"—he would meet an army major who told him that Pepe then "may have five thousand men. However, 'We could round them up tomorrow, if we

didn't have strict orders from the government not to' " (ibid., pp. 169 and 182). The five thousand figure was almost certainly an exaggeration. But I did have a similar experience on a reporting trip to Temuco area in the spring of 1972.

93. *Qué Pasa*, op. cit., p. 32, 36; Whelan, op. cit., p. 134; Pinochet, op. cit., pp. 140–141. Obedience to the new military authorities was virtually complete, but in Antofagasta, Carabinero Guillermo Schmidt Godoy shot and killed the precinct commander, Maj. Osvaldo Mario Núñez Carrasco, and deputy commander, Capt. José Héctor Dávila. Godoy was court-martialed and went before a firing squad the next day. Special international edition of *El Mercurio*, for the week of September 9–15, 1973, p. 7 (the first edition published after the coup).

94. Varas and Vergara, op. cit., p. 104.

95. Whelan, op. cit., p. 153.

96. Ibid., pp. 152–153, 154–155, based on interviews in Santiago with Corporal Pizzarro (October 14, 1974), Sergeant Leiva (May 12, 1974) and Lieutenant Ramírez (May 13, 1974).

97. A car bomb claimed the life of Letelier and a coworker at the left-wing think tank, the Institute for Policy Studies, on September 21, 1976. Letelier was, by then, an undercover agent for Fidel Castro. More on his murder in chapter 9.

98. Ibid., pp. 152, 153, based mainly on previously cited interviews with Briones and Mrs. Letelier.

99. Varas and Vergara, op. cit., p. 106.

100. The surrender episode is from Whelan, op. cit., p. 160, based in part on Briones interview, *La Segunda*, op. cit., p. 16 and Varas and Vergara, op. cit., pp. 125–126. Yet another wrinkle was added in Fontaine and Zegers, op. cit., p. 24: standing before Carvajal, Flores is said to have asked what they were accused of. Carvajal's reported answer: "Of having ruined the country." Chavkin, op. cit., claims the initiative for negotiations came from the military—not from Allende—and that Allende was "strongly opposed to such negotiations since he was certain that the junta would again demand his resignation, something he vowed not to do." Chavkin said he also feared "a trick, and that those undertaking the mission would never get back." It is conceivable Allende may have invented this version for the benefit of the hard-line fighters still with him; it is improbable that it happened. Carvajal made it plain from his first report on the radio network that the trio were en route at Allende's behest, and would at no time in the exchanges which would follow indicate anything to the contrary. The conditions the group carried with them: (1) Allende would surrender and resign the presidency; (2) a civilian would be included in the new government junta; (3) there would be a nationwide cease-fire; (4) negotiations between the military commanders and himself about the precise terms of surrender would take place. Some accounts also say he demanded that those with him in the palace be allowed to leave the country with him.

101. From transcription of the radio command network, previously cited. There was, indeed, shooting at the embassy—but disagreement as to who shot whom. The Cubans charged that they were fired upon, and that their ambassador, Mario García Incháustegui, was nicked in the hand. Eduardo Arriagada, head of the Engineering Federation, heard the shooting through the night of the eleventh and most of the twelfth from his home, just a few

blocks from the embassy. It continued, in fact, until Col. Pedro Ewing Hodar, then secretary-general to the Joint Chiefs (and about to become secretary-general of government in the junta administration) and Tobías Barros, chief of protocol of the Foreign Ministry, formally notified the Cubans late Wednesday, September 12, that diplomatic relations between the two countries were broken. Even before the huge official group left the country on the thirteenth, a Soviet Aeroflot jet left carrying the first 150 Cubans suspected of complicity in the illegal arming and training of the paramilitary brigades. Aboard that jet also: Beatriz Allende and her husband, Luis Fernández Oña (from numerous interviews in Santiago with Colonel Ewing February through May and October, 1974; interview in Santiago with Barros, April 11, 1974; and Arriagada, April 15, 1974). Interestingly, Sweden's Ambassador Harold Edelstam—vociferously pro-Allende, vituperatively anti-junta—confirmed that there was shooting from the Cuban Embassy. He said he was en route to his home Tuesday afternoon (the eleventh) when he discovered 150 soldiers advancing on the Cuban Embassy, two blocks away. Pushing his way to the officer-in-charge, he identified himself and demanded he be allowed to enter the Cuban Embassy, which he said was already pockmarked with bullet holes. Inside, he said he found the Cuban ambassador "with a huge bandage on his arm covering a gunshot wound from the first assault," and staff workers "cut by flying glass . . . with less serious bullet wounds destroying documents, packing suitcases, keeping vigil at doors and windows, and occasionally returning the fire with small arms." But Edelstam also claimed that the shooting subsided when he went in. Later that night, he claimed to have prevented a cannon assault on the embassy. The next day, he says, he was present when "a small man. . . . yelled that he was from the junta protocol office . . . [and] without further ceremony read a statement from the junta government that Chile had broken relations with Cuba and that he and the ambassador and all his staff were ordered to leave Chile by midnight." Without consulting with Stockholm, Edelstam on the spot agreed to assume representation of Cuban interests, putting the embassy and those within under the protection of the Swedish flag. Over the next few days, he would boast of smuggling refugees to "friendly embassies" (he names Mexico, Venezuela, Costa Rica, and Finland) and providing false names and identity documents, disguises, and other devices to get still others out of the country. One he boasts of rescuing: "Max Marambio, a young man who had been with Allende at La Moneda the day before . . ." He did not mention that Marambio was also a top leader of the very violent Movement of the Revolutionary Left, the first leader (and organizer) of the GAP, one of the fugitives, in fact, pardoned by Allende in the first months of his term. But then, Edelstam takes other liberties, as well: other accounts coincide that the shooting did not begin until the evening, and that Ambassador Incháustegui was wounded only superficially. After he finally left Chile, December 9, 1973, Edelstam's own very left-wing government (then headed by Olaf Palme, head of the Socialist International and then on an anti-American rampage over Vietnam), gave him extended leave so that he could conduct a worldwide propaganda campaign against the junta. Edelstam references from Chavkin, op. cit., pp. 131–136, 141. Chavkin titles this section: "Sweden's Heroic Ambassador Saves 1,300 Lives."

102. Varas and Vergara, op. cit.

103. Source for telephone call: Whelan, op. cit., p. 162, author's 1974 interviews with Colonel Ewing, during February, March and April. For the suicide scene, "La Payita Cuenta Su Versión del 11," *Las Ultimas Noticias,* op. cit. The story she told *Epoca,* fourteen years later, differs sharply from the earlier version. In the latter, she says Olivares shot and killed himself after discovering Allende dead; "*El Perro* [the Dog—his nickname] Olivares killed himself at Salvador's feet, a few minutes after speaking with me . . ." Chavkin had claimed (without attribution) that Olivares was killed in the air attack on La Moneda. But then, Chavkin also says there were about 25 sorties and that the attack lasted 40 minutes; actually, the two planes flew four sorties each, fired a total of 19 rockets, and the attack lasted a total of 21 minutes (Chavkin, op. cit., p. 35).

104. Ibid., pp. 162–163. Merino told me this during our Santiago interview.

105. Ibid., p. 164. Interview with Baeza in Santiago, October 16, 1974.

106. Actually, it would have been considerably more complicated than Admiral Carvajal could have imagined: Mrs. Allende was, at that hour, at the Mexican Embassy, and Allende's daughters Isabel and Beatriz were still in hiding after their postpalace ordeal.

107. Taken verbatim from Whelan, op. cit., pp. 167–169. Based entirely on the previously mentioned extensive conversations and tape-recorded interviews with Guijón in Santiago in 1974. Nothing I have read nor been told in the thirteen years since writing those lines has caused me to doubt the utter honesty of Guijón nor the complete accuracy of this account of Allende's death. For further insights into the personality and character of Guijón, see the Appendix to that book (*Allende: Death of a Marxist Dream*), pp. 201–204.

108. Based on previously cited interview with Ramírez in Santiago, May 13, 1974. I saw Briones later that same day and again the following October and was able to cross-check the lieutenant's account of the capture with him.

109. In her interview with *Epoca,* Mrs. Contreras says after Allende ordered everyone to surrender, she started down the stairs with a white cloth from the kitchen given her by Enrique Huerta, a member of the Socialist party's security force. First, she said, the doctors went down. Then, as she was starting down, Huerta asked her to go back upstairs to see why the others were not coming. She said she watched, from the top of the stairs, as the soldiers jumped Huerta, snatching the white cloth and striking him, shouting "Up with your hands!" She ran to Allende's office where Olivares tried to prevent her from going in. Seeing the dead Allende (and then Olivares, though she does not clarify how she failed to see him shoot himself at the fallen leader's feet), she next took the 1810 Proclamation of Chile's Independence and put it in a pocket of Olivares' jacket. Soldiers swarmed up the stairs. "They tore open the jacket and pulled me down to the street, putting me up against the wall with the others. I whispered to Huerta, next to me: 'The President is dead.' Others spread the word. The soldiers then ordered all of us to lie face down on the ground, hands on the back of our necks. A soldier told me: 'Get up and come over here closer to the wall. Cover your face with your hands to protect yourself against the ricochet of the bullets.' A sergeant appeared. 'And what are you doing here? Hands on the back of your neck.' The soldier told me again: 'Cover your face, lady.' I heard a voice I recognized. 'And you, what are you doing here?'

It was Jaime Puccio, an old friend, an army dentist, in army uniform. He was furious because he thought all the women had gone. I heard the siren of an ambulance . . . 'Make like you're dead,' Puccio said. Afterwards, to the male nurse: 'Take this woman—she's dying.' The sergeant reappeared. 'Dying? Hysterical, if you ask me.' 'Are you a doctor,' Puccio asked him. The nurse pushed me into the ambulance. I lost my shoes. Rounding the corner, there was an infernal amount of shooting. The driver stopped and the nurse said, 'speed up or they'll kill us.' At the emergency station, he discovered that the place was still in the hands of our crowd [*compañeros*]. With one leg in a cast, I was hidden in a house which until a short time before had been a house of prostitution. Other women also were in hiding there." Miria Contreras' room had a skylight. At night, men who were fleeing ran across the roof. She said she was "scared silly that one of them would fall through and land on my bed." *La Payita*, Salvatore remarks in an aside at this point in the narrative, was not afraid for her safety. Rather: "If that had happened, they no doubt would have accused me of being in bed with him." After ten days of absolute isolation, ten sleepless nights, in an apartment with no lights, unknown accomplices spirited her out to the Swedish Embassy. Two months later, she managed to leave the country clandestinely.

110. Varas and Vergara, op. cit., p. 131–132 and Fontaine and Zegers, op. cit., p. 24.

111. Whelan, op. cit., p. 170, and *La Segunda*, op. cit., p. 19.

112. But Lira would later get to see the body. He was one of a handful of Chilean newsmen allowed into the palace around six-thirty that evening, just before Allende's body was removed, and would tell an Argentina newspaper in an interview that night that he had seen Allende "with a bullet wound in his mouth." *La Segunda*, op. cit., p. 19, and interviews with Lira in Santiago, March 28 and April 8, 1974.

113. Previously cited Guijón and Ramírez interviews, from Whelan, op. cit., pp. 170–171.

114. Ibid., pp. 171–172.

115. Ibid., pp. 172–175; as throughout, these conversations were transcribed directly from the tape recording of the command network traffic. Leigh was only partially successful in insinuating his ideas into the final communique. The official communique read: "(1) At 1:30 P.M. on Tuesday, September 11, through the mediation of Fernando Flores and Daniel Vergara, Salvador Allende offered to surrender unconditionally to the military forces; (2) To bring that about, it was immediately decided that a patrol be sent, but whose arrival at the Moneda Palace was delayed because of the cunning action of snipers, particularly in the Ministry of Public Works, who sought to intercept it; (3) Entering La Moneda that patrol found in one of its rooms the body of señor Allende; (4) A commission of the Health Services of the Armed Forces and Carabineros and a forensic doctor certified his death; (5) At mid-day on September 12, members of his family held private funeral services." (As reproduced in the first edition of *El Mercurio* published following the coup, September 13, 1973, under a p. 1 headline: "Allende Died.") As spare as the communique was, it of course contained several misleading points, the most important of them that Allende had offered unconditional surrender through Flores and Vergara. As indicated earlier in this chapter, apparently he did later decide to do so,

but in his telephone call to General Baeza. Nor, of course, was it "that patrol" which found the body. But, at that point, the junta was still completing its own investigation, checking Guijón's story. They were also fighting a war. The reference to "most important date" is, as indicated at the outset of the chapter, from the subtitle of *El Mercurio*'s special supplement, published on September 11, 1974, the first anniversary of the revolution.

116. Details of many of these are in *Qué Pasa*, op. cit., pp. 34–36; Varas and Vergara, op. cit., pp. 226–227 (including the La Legua quotation) and Whelan, op. cit., pp. 175–183.

117. "General Pinochet: El Hombre del 'Día D'," in an interview in *Ercilla*, no. 2015, March 13–19, 1974, p. 12. I say "apparently," because the text is unclear. As published in the magazine, it reads, textually; " 'El combate duró practicamente cuatro horas,' contó el General Pinochet, con un saldo de muertos que, seis meses después, llegó a alrededor de 1.600 víctimas ('cerca de 200 de los cuales son de nosotros.')"

118. Outside limits and Birns quotation from Davis, pp. 368–370 (he quotes from *The End of Chilean Democracy* ed. Laurence Birns (New York: Seabury, 1974), pp. 67, 204–205; military predictions from Whelan, op. cit., p. 14, based on previously cited interviews in Santiago with the four military commandants; Chavkin, op. cit., p. 38; Edelstam is cited in Carlos M. Rama, *Chile: Mil Días entre la Revolución y el Fascismo* (Barcelona: Editorial Planeta, S.A., 1974), p. 224; *United States and Chile During the Allende Years, 1970–1973*, Report of the Subcommittee on Inter-American Affairs of the Committee on Foreign Affairs, U.S. House of Representatives, Based on Hearings in 1971, 1972, 1973, 1974 (U.S. GPO, Washington, 1974), p. 395; Pinochet in same, op. cit., p. 117.

119. Varas and Vergara, op. cit., pp. 153–154. I am indebted to Ambassador Davis for the translation, op. cit., pp. 273–274. Davis reports that Judd L. Kessler, a U.S. Embassy official in Santiago, played handball regularly with fingerprint expert Henríquez. Meeting at the Santiago YMCA shortly after the coup, "Henríquez confirmed the suicide account, including the head wound and the absence of body wounds. The Homicide Squad had examined the body carefully, and it is difficult to imagine Henríquez not having learned of multiple fatal wounds in the torso if they had existed. Kessler is convinced his friend was not lying to him." Davis adds that embassy intelligence reporting at the time, including "sources . . . not intended for American ears," were also consistent as to Allende's death being suicide (ibid., p. 304).

120. Chavkin, op. cit., pp. 37–38. Chavkin offers neither source nor clue as to the basis for his account, much less for the assertion that Allende "was killed." Cursing and even kicking, of course, are likely in the heat of battle, and Chavkin's account does not differ significantly from that of others— except, of course, in that all important matter of his unsubstantiated assertion that Allende "was killed." Varas and Vergara, op. cit., pp. 131–132, for example, relate that Soto had just put aside his sub-machinegun and was waiting with approximately thirty other persons, including the doctors, just inside the door of the Morandé entrance when suddenly it was pushed in and an officer shouted, "Surrender all of you shits" (cursing); Soto and the others were then pushed (kicking?) against the wall, hands over their heads, but no sooner had the frisking for weapons begun than

bullets began whistling overhead, leading the officer to order all, including the doctors, to "hit the dirt," lie on the floor.

121. Davis, op. cit., pp. 277–306 for the chapter, "Assassination or Suicide?" and p. 306 for the conclusion quotation.

122. Guijón related this during a conversation with the author, in the presence of several others, in Santiago, June 17, 1987.

123. For further insight into the character of Patricio Guijón, see Appendix in Whelan, op. cit., pp. 201–204. The young GAP—Luis Renato González Córdoba—told his story from exile in the Mexican Embassy in Santiago a week or so after the attack. Davis subjects it to dismembering analysis, op. cit., pp. 282–284.

124. *Epoca* interview, op. cit., "Revelaciones de la Secretaria de S. Allende," as reproduced in *El Mercurio*, January 14, 1988. Mrs. Contreras' version is at odds with Guijón's in two important respects: He says he was the last one to leave the corridor, and he says that after he actually saw Allende pull the trigger, he went in and remained with the president—alone—until the soldiers arrived. He, and others, including Mrs. Contreras herself, in her 1974 interview, also said that Olivares had taken his life earlier that day, during or just after the air attack. September 11 would be the last time Mrs. Contreras would ever see her son alive; she says in the recent interview that she learned that he had been shot five days later. Her elder son, Max, managed to get away, and years later, a doctor, was living in Cuba. Although in his late thirties, Salvatore said Max—visiting his mother in Paris during the interview—was completely white-haired, and claimed to have fought in Central America. Salvatore described him as fidgety and evasive about his work. Salvatore also reported meeting her husband, Enrique, remarking: "The old man appears serene. He could be one of those public pensioners who abandon the city for the life of the country-side . . ." Feeling responsible for what he had been through, including imprisonment in Chile, loss of his fortune, Salvatore wrote that Mrs. Contreras "treats him with a respectful timidity."

125. Prats, op. cit., pp. 512–513; Carvajal quote from Varas and Vergara, op cit., p. 163.

126. Whelan, op. cit., pp. 156–157, from an interview with Corporal Sáez in Santiago, May 9, 1974. Official data from Emilio Filippi and Hernán Millas, *Anatomía de un Fracaso: La Experiencia Socialista Chilena*, pp. 147–148, and (Santiago: Empresa Editora Zig-Zag, S.A., 1973), *Three Years of Destruction*, op. cit., section entitled "No To Civil War" (no page number). At the weekend retreat Allende had purchased for *La Payita*—El Cañaveral—the strong-box would yield $40,000 U.S., five refrigerators stuffed with imported goods, wine, whiskey, a private theater stocked with Vietnam war films and pornography, as well as photos of Allende "practicing as a guerrilla and others . . . more compromising yet . . ." Emilio Filippi and Hernán Millas, op. cit., pp. 147–148. That same source would allude to a report in an unnamed Ottawa newspaper to the effect that emissaries of *La Payita* had deposited in a bank there $6 million. El Cañaveral was also not only a heavily fortified and well-stocked guerrilla base, but it included extensive guerrilla training facilities. Tomás Moro training details from *Libro Blanco*, op. cit., pp. 171–175.

127. Number already in Ministry from Varas and Vergara, op. cit., p. 157, as was Briones quote, p. 161; Jorquera anecdote, p. 173, doctors, 174. Sepúlveda

from Whelan, op. cit., p. 182, as figures for total number of prisoners, p. 159. First reports said 220 persons were summarily executed in the first days of the coup; junta spokesmen denied those reports. There is no question that a number of such executions did take place, and that a good number of them were in accord with the published penalties under state of siege—in other words, legal. More on this in a subsequent chapter dealing with the entire human rights question. As for Patricio Guijón: around midnight, he too was taken to the Military Academy, and lodged there with senior officials of the Allende administration until Saturday, September 15. That day—without warning—he and the others were flown 1,500 miles to the south to a prison camp at the Marine base on Dawson Island, at latitude 54 degrees south, in the Straits of Magellan. He would remain there through the Southern Hemisphere spring, released (with a few others) on December 21, returned to Santiago to tell his story (for the first time) on national television, then join his family in time for Christmas. He would later tell the author: "Sylvia and I, from the bombing of La Moneda, me inside and her at home with the kids, had a kind of mental telepathy, and both of us never doubted that somehow I would live through the war" (Whelan, op. cit., p. 195).

128. Whelan, op. cit., p. 138, from an interview with Vilarín in Santiago, October 15, 1974.

129. Davis, op. cit., pp. 273 and 275. The ambassador said he reported the fact of the note afterwards, when "the U.S. government came under fire for having made no expression of condolence to Mrs. Allende." He noted that, in writing it, "I doubt that Mrs. Allende either welcomed my letter or believed me."

130. Ibid., pp. 140–141, 194, based on interviews in Santiago with Halsema March 29 and May 2, 1974, and Mrs. Díaz, May 9, 1974.

131. Ibid., pp. 185–187, based on previously cited interviews in Santiago with Braña and Gallegos, and *Time* magazine, "The View From the Carrera," September 24, 1973. Gallegos quickly realized how volatile liquor could be in such an emotionally charged situation, especially since most of his employees were Allende sympathizers. So, after that first round came prohibition: no more for two days. Gallegos not only provided for his own guests and employees, but for some seventy Carabineros holed up in the underground garage in Plaza Constitución in front of the hotel; he also provided some food and blankets for the U.S. Embassy staffers around the corner.

132. Ibid., p. 184, interview with Tonini in Santiago, March 29, 1974. Tonini was press attaché at the embassy.

133. Ibid., pp. 176–177. Among the many inconsistencies in González' "eyewitness" tale: he told Manuel Mejido, a reporter for the Mexican newspaper *Excelsior*, just a few days after the coup, that he was among those leaving when Allende ordered them to go. Once outside, he obviously could not have witnessed later events inside the palace. He also located Allende inside the palace differently than any other eyewitness—before and after the president's death. His tale: "We encountered a group of fascists under the command of Captain Mayor, in the halls near the Red Room. He shouted, 'Surrender, Señor Allende.' Our compañero said, 'Never, it is better to leave dead than surrender.' When he finished, we heard a shot from the military. It hit the Doctor. They opened machinegun fire, and we

fired against them. Twelve of our compañeros fell dead at the side of President Salvador Allende. Our firing became more intense. The officer and six soldiers fell. We approached the President's body. He was mortally wounded. He told us, 'A leader may fall, but still there is a cause. America will be free.' It was 1:50 P.M. when compañero Allende fell, assassinated by the bullets of the fascists and traitors. He had been hit by about six bullets; four in the neck and two in the thorax. . . . We picked up his martyred body and took it to its place, the Presidential Office. We sat him in his seat, put his presidential banner on, his gun in his arms, and embraced him. We found the flag . . . and covered him," from Birns, op. cit., p. 40, cited in Davis, op. cit., pp. 288–283. The elaborate ceremonial finished—in the midst of what was still a pitched battle—the young González would then "surrender." (There is no record of a "Captain Mayor," not in the palace, not in the Chilean army at that time.)

134. Whelan, op. cit., p. 185, based on an interview with Carneyro in Santiago, March 25, 1974. As with a number of others cited in this work, it was not actually one interview, but a number of interviews/conversations—and to few would I owe a greater debt of gratitude than to the late Mario Carneyro, a true gentleman of the press, a man who believed deeply in his ideals, fought for them, and was willing to die for them.

135. Ibid., p. 189, and *El Mercurio*, special edition of September 9–15, 1973, op. cit., p. 2, "Horas de Dramatismo y Tensión Se Vivieron en los Hoteles." As for the warning to stay away from the windows: *Time* correspondent Charles Eisendrath would report that as late as Thursday, September 13, he was typing in his room when a man knocked and asked permission to peek out the window to see whether his car, parked in the plaza below, had been damaged or destroyed. No sooner did the man part the curtains than a bullet banged into the room, and before Eisendrath could crawl over and pull the man away from the window, another bullet had thwacked into the room (*Time*, op. cit.).

136. *Libro Blanco*, op. cit., p. 47.

137. Varas and Vergara, op. cit., p. 175–176, and Pinochet, op. cit., p. 143.

138. Whelan, op. cit., p. 192, based on interviews in Santiago with the chief justice, on May 9, 1974; with Figueroa Toro, May 8, 1974.

139. Details of WASG meeting from Phillips, op. cit., pp. 248–249; Merino told me of the message during our interview in Santiago, October 18, 1974. It appears on p. 76 of *Allende: Death of a Marxist Dream*.

140. Henry Kissinger, *Years of Upheaval* (Boston-Toronto: Little Brown and Company, 1982), p. 410.

141. *La Segunda*, op. cit., p. 6.

142. "Tomás Moro, una aguja en el pajar," *La Segunda*, September 10, 1974, p. 14.

143. Whelan, op. cit., p. 190. Mendoza made the trip in a car other than his usual one, a different colored one.

144. Ibid., pp. 190–191.

145. Varas and Vergara, op. cit., pp. 207–208. I have presumed that it was Varas who did the interview because the book is a mixture of fact and allegory (the conversations of a mythical couple, echoing many of the real-life debates then raging in Chile); Varas is the journalist, Vergara a distinguished novelist.

146. Whelan, op. cit., pp. 191–192; reconstructed from interviews with all four

members of the junta, but these passages principally from the interview with Mendoza.

147. Ibid., pp. 193–194, and for Brazilian recognition, Pinochet, op. cit., p. 147. That first Cabinet: Interior, Gen. Oscar Bonilla Bradanovic (army); Foreign Minister, Rear Adm. Ismael Huerta Díaz; Economy, Gen. Rolando González Acevedo (army); Finance, Rear Adm. Lorenzo Gotuzzo Borlando; Justice, Gonzalo Prieto Gándara; Education, José Navarro Tobar; Defense: Vice Adm. Patricio Carvajal Prado; Public Works, Brig. Gen. Sergio Figueroa Gutiérrez (air force); Agriculture, Col. Sergio Crespo Montero (air force, retired); Lands and Settlements, Gen. Diego Barba Valdés (Carabineros, retired); Labor, Gen. Mario McKay Jaraquemada (Carabineros, retired); Health, Col. Alberto Spoerer Covarrubias (air force); Mining, Gen. Arturo Yovane Zúñiga (Carabineros); Housing, Brig. Gen. Arturo Vivero Avila (army); Minister-Secretary General of Government, Col. Pedro Ewing (army).

148. Whelan, op. cit., pp. 196–200, transcribed from a tape-recorded interview with Grove in Santiago, October 23, 1974. In Varas and Vergara, there is an account (op. cit., pp. 242–243) of the burial based, apparently, on interviews with Laura Allende and Navy Commander Jorge Contreras. Though not nearly so detailed as Jaime Grove's account, it coincides in all essential details—but adds one significant dimension. According to that account, Mrs. Allende asked permission at the gravesite to see her husband for the last time, saying she had been promised that in Santiago. When Commander Contreras at first demurred that the lead casket was sealed and could not be opened, someone observed that the top was, in fact, open a crack. Contreras then relented and allowed the widow to look briefly through the inner glass. Inasmuch as the face was totally bandaged, she asked that the casket be opened completely, but this time Contreras insisted that once opened, it could not be soldered shut again and denied that request. In Chavkin, op. cit., p. 123, there is a paragraph on the burial, apparently based on an interview with Mrs. Allende, in which the following appears: "The Junta guard refused to open the casket, despite señora Allende's insistence that she was entitled to see the body." (Chavkin apparently has garbled the timetable, claiming that she was already in the Mexican Embassy Tuesday, and that she would learn Tuesday of her husband's death when the junta announced it on radio and television; Jaime Grove was explicit on the point that she not only had been picked up at Felipe Herrera's house, but that she was returned to the same address.) Mrs. Allende then went into asylum at the Mexican Embassy and flew to that country on Thursday, September 13. Laura, who resolved to remain in Chile, was later detained briefly at the Defense Ministry when she went there in an attempt to locate *La Payita* (Mrs. Contreras) but allowed to go free because of her poor health.

9

Out of the Ashes

TAKING STOCK

For *Time* magazine correspondent Charles Eisendrath, "the break came Friday. Santiago, a city with a climate like Denver's and women like Paris', stretched out in the early spring sunshine like a cat cooped up too long in a closet. Thousands surged around the smoky ruins of La Moneda. People in their Sunday best jammed into El Tráfico bar, located in the shabby remains of the house where Chile's founding father, Bernardo O'Higgins, had met with the liberator of Argentina, José de San Martín. To the patrons swilling white wine and munching pork sandwiches, it seemed fitting to celebrate in a historic political monument—but there was no talk of politics, for the first time in memory . . ."[1]

It was a mood the new junta would quickly make its own: The country was choking on politics, and a respite was needed. *Bando* (communique) #29 closed Congress and vacated all congressional seats.

"Our people have been accustomed to living in a democracy," Sen. Juan de Dios Carmona would say later. Carmona, a leader of the moderate faction of the Christian Democrat party, added: "Yet we do not protest now, because we understand the danger we were in and that this sort of convalescence was necessary."[2]

Carmona's judgment was shared by the chief leader of the party, former President Eduardo Frei, who wrote, "Basic to the survival of a democratic society is a minimum of consensus among those who make up that society, and the acknowledgment, by all, of certain values which make possible the exercise of freedom and the rule of law. The truth is that in Chile, that consensus had been shattered." A leader of the political Right, Sen. Pedro Ibáñez, expressed even stronger sentiments: "Because of the irreparable decadence of which I was a witness, I must honestly admit that the democratic parliamentary system cannot work efficiently again in either the Chile of today or of the future. I say this with deep sorrow and even nostalgia. The Congress of Chile was the third oldest in the world."[3]

Inevitably, the Frei/Carmona view was not shared by the left wing of the party. Two days after the coup, fifteen top leaders—including Radomiro Tomic, the unctuous ideologue who had led the party to electoral defeat against Allende in 1970—released a communique "categorically condemning" the coup. The communique also called on the military to restore civilian rule "without delay."[4] But Frei and his followers, whose power had crested in 1972 and 1973 as disenchantment with Allende hardened into an angry and widespread public rage, held the upper hand. Tomic and Bernardo Leighton, the "boy-wonder" of Frei's administration, were expelled from the party in October 1973, and former party president Renán Fuentealba a year later.[5] It was an augury of bitter political warfare to come, within the once mighty party itself, in the larger drama of the new Chile emerging from the ashes of the old.

Frei was not the only ex-president to express support for the coup. Gabriel González Videla, the former Radical president (1946–1952), said he "does not have words to thank the armed forces for having liberated us from the Marxist claws." Asked what he expected for the future of Chile, González Videla said: "The best, because they have saved us and will permit us to live in democracy, inasmuch as the totalitarian apparatus which had been prepared to destroy us has itself been destroyed."[6]

Perhaps no quality about the postmortems over the "death of democracy" in Chile was quite so striking as the fact that few bothered to take into account how the Chileans—those *inside* Chile—were reacting. Thus, while much of the rest of the world was wringing its hands in consternation in the days following the coup, the dominant mood in Chile was one of jubilation. Wrote one foreign journalist: "Chileans will stop you on the street to say: 'How do you like our new Chile? We are free now. This is our second independence. The best of Chile is now in the government; be sure to tell people in North America that everything is fine in Chile.' " In Concepción—birthplace of the MIR terrorist movement—the mood the day following the revolt was one of carnival. That mood suddenly turned to terror late in the afternoon when one or more snipers opened fire on civilians promenading in the Plaza de Armas.[7]

Jubilation was, of course, both understandable and inevitable: Allende reached power with only a little over one-third the total vote, and only 28 percent of the total electorate. At no time did his coalition ever achieve a majority of those voting. And yet, as a major U.S. newspaper of decidedly leftist opinions noted editorially, "ever since he was elected

... Allende has acted as though he had a mandate to establish an out-and-out socialist society in Chile. In reality, no such radical consensus exists, and the fact that it doesn't goes a long way toward explaining the economic and political chaos into which the country has fallen."[8] A *New York Times* reporter, reporting from the scene, said "the revolt—the first break in civilian politics here in 40 years—came in the midst of an economic disaster and a class struggle that divided Chilean society as never before in this century."[9] It was across that great divide of strife, tension, hatred and chaos of an utterly polarized society that the battles of Chile would be fought in the months and years ahead. It is likely that, in the first days following the revolution, as many as 80 percent of Chileans were on the side celebrating what they saw as deliverance—a figure corroborated even two years later.[10] On the other side, many, perhaps 20 percent, were seething with anger and rage, in many cases taking up arms; many more were hounded, imprisoned, and not infrequently, brutalized. Chile was, truly, a country torn asunder, locked in the appalling grip of civil war. Most Chileans understood, accepted, what the "terrible simplifiers" of the outside world neither could nor would: It was no longer a matter of waving a wand and returning to a "democratic" past. That past, so little acknowledged when even noticed from afar, not only was "a dismal flop" (in the phrase of one experienced journalist[11]) but it had vanished in a hecatomb of demagoguery and doctrinaire fanaticisms. The task now, as the new military rulers saw it, as a great number of Chileans saw it, was to build a new political and economic structure. It was not so much a choice as it was an imperative—one which, inevitably, put the regime on a collision course with a substantial, vocal, and implacable minority of its own population, and with virtually the entirety of an uncomprehending world beyond.

A NEW BEGINNING

The shopkeepers, truck drivers, medical doctors, engineers, teachers, copper miners, and others who had—in desperation—brought the country to a standstill, immediately agreed to return to their jobs. Normality gradually settled over the embattled land. By September 18, the country's borders were reopened, internal flights resumed, and (non-Marxist) radio stations permitted to renew independent broadcasting. The dawn-to-dusk curfew was eased to allow workers to return to their jobs. At the country's biggest copper mine—Chuquicamata—production rose to 1,800 tons a day for September, the highest level in over three years. Thousands of Chileans from all walks of life put their money where their mouths were in those first days: voluntarily exchanging 9 million in dollars they had squirreled away, for their own currency, escudos. Newsmen, telephone workers, farmers, and others issued communiques pledging their support to the new government.[12] So, too, did political parties.

The national committee of the Christian Democrat party issued a statement the day following the coup stating the official position of the party:

> The events which Chile is experiencing are the consequence of the economic disaster, institutional chaos, armed violence, and moral crisis to which the deposed government brought the country, dragging the Chilean people into anguish and desperation.
>
> The facts demonstrate that the armed forces and Carabineros did not seek power. Their institutional traditions and the republican history of our country inspire confidence, that just as soon as they have fulfilled the tasks which they have undertaken to save the Chilean nation from the grave dangers of destruction and totalitarianism which threatened, they will turn over power to the sovereign people . . .
>
> Christian Democracy regrets what has happened. Faithful to its principles, it made every effort to achieve a solution through institutional political means . . .

By September 25, the PDC's Central Committee, in a brusque about-face, was describing the new government as a dictatorship and deploring repression. Augusto Pinochet had an acerbic response to that: "There were a number of politicians who imagined that we had made this revolution for them, that once we got rid of Allende, we were going to turn power over to them. They were wrong." Frei—and others in the party—continued for a good while longer defending the revolutionary government.[13]

The conservative National party, which rolled up the biggest vote of any single party in the 1970 elections, declared its "unrestricted support for any action designed to overcome the moral and material crisis in which Chile is living, and to restore to Chileans the security to live and work in peace, making possible progress and social and economic development in a climate of national unity." There was no mention in the National party's statement of a return to civilian rule.

The small and leftist PADENA (National Democratic) party—allied with the parties that had eventually nominated Allende during preelection skirmishing—issued the boldest statement of all:

> In recent months, we have waged a press campaign directed at the armed forces appealing to them to put an end to the state of economic

collapse into which the workers of our country had been sunk by the Marxists of the Popular Unity. We were one of the firmest contenders that only you could put an end to the state of misery and anguish and desperation in which the workers of Chile found themselves.

For more than 90 years, we have defended democracy and liberty and social justice. Today we feel proud of what you have done.

We are with you because you have interpreted [the wishes] of the great majority in our country. We feel proud of a tradition which you represent in these moments and we give our enthusiastic support to your patriotic stance.

Even Jorge Godoy, a Communist and long-time labor leader, who had served as one of Allende's last labor ministers, went on television to express his opposition to extremism in all its forms and the hope that Chileans could live in peace, justice and discipline.

Chief Justice Urrutia Manzano of the Supreme Court, on September 12, issued a statement—ratified by the full court the following day—expressing his "most intimate satisfaction" with the announced decision of the new government to respect the autonomy of the courts. He also called on all of the country's judges to "do your duty, as you have to the present." Later, the chief justice explained: "I did it, you see, because I have to give moral support to the junta which had just ended a situation of chaos in the country and—understand this well—to avoid the confusion, disorder, which the Popular Unity politicians hoped to produce."[14]

Amid the euphoria and confusion of those early days, the new government gradually took form. On the morning after the coup, Tobías Barros, the protocol chief of the foreign ministry, did what thousands of other conscientious Chilean career civil servants did that day, absent instructions to the contrary. He went to work, in his case at the still smoldering and ruined La Moneda Palace.

"I found on the stairwell leading in from the Morandé 80 entrance not a trace of human beings—no boots, no scraps of uniforms. It was the same in the corridors. My first reaction was that either someone had done a terrific cleaning job—or there were few deaths here.

"Then I went into the Salón Independencia. There were a few touches of him—his books, photos, that sort of thing. The room was intact. There was still a folding screen in front of the sofa—and stains from his brain on the ceiling. But otherwise, everything was intact." "Him" was, of course, Salvador Allende.

With three others, Barros then began to revive the Foreign Ministry, under the direction of a hastily appointed military minister: Rear Adm. Ismael Huerta Díaz (the man who had led the fight against ENU five months before). Barros's principal tool during those early days was a lined Orion notebook of the type schoolchildren use. In it, he recorded the main business of the ministry: Notes to Cuba and North Korea, advising them that Chile was breaking diplomatic relations with them. (North Korea was added to Cuba following Pinochet's speech the night before, for reasons that never were clear.) The text of a note advising all other diplomatic missions in Santiago officially of the change in government was also entered neatly in the notebook, as was the text of the circular advising those missions of Admiral Huerta's designation as foreign minister. In the notebook, too, went decisions on ticklish assignments, details of the arrangements for the departure of the Allende family to Mexico, and the notification to Cuban Ambassador Mario García Incháustegui, Barros's old crony from their United Nations days in New York, that he was ordered to leave the country.

"I went with Col. [Pedro] Ewing around 7 P.M. that [Wednesday] night," Barros said. "The ambassador had his right arm in a cast. I said to him: 'You say we shot you.' 'See for yourself,' he said, motioning to the cast.

"I told him that friendship was one thing, but duty another, and that it was my duty to tell him that an Aeroflot plane was ready to take him and the members of his mission out of the country. At that, Harold Edelstam [the Swedish ambassador, who later became one of the junta's most virulent hecklers], and the ambassadors of Peru and India appeared from the next room. He had called them, obviously to serve as witnesses.

"I told him he was free to take whoever he liked with him, but there was one man we believed in asylum in the embassy who could not go: Max José Marambio [the MIRista leader wanted on a murder warrant]. Ewing asked to see Marambio, because Edelstam said he was assuming responsibility for the embassy's affairs.[15]

"The ambassador said he wanted to take Allende's daughter and two Chilean secretaries, and we said we had no objections. Ewing and I both asked that they turn over any arms in the embassy to me. He said there were none, and invoked diplomatic right to prevent us from looking. We asked how it was that there had been so much shooting from the embassy if they had no arms, and he still refused to let us look."

(Edelstam, while still in Chile, would later confirm that there had been shooting from the embassy. He also would deny a published report in the United States quoting him as saying the Cubans had been given only three hours to clear out of the country. In fact, García Incháustegui and 160 members of his mission did not leave until the following day, the thirteenth.)[16]

The "Colonel Ewing" who accompanied Barros was destined to play a pivotal role in the emerging government: secretary-general, the cabinet-level clearing house job important in any presidential system, crucial in a government with four chiefs. A strapping, handsome six-footer, Ewing was tapped for the job because he was then serving in a similar role: military secretary to Adm. Patricio Carvajal, chief of the Defense Department's General Staff.

Once he had escorted the Cubans to the airport, Ewing reported back to the Defense Ministry, where Pinochet swore him in. "In those first days, everyone was piled on top of everyone else. With La Moneda burned out, the seat of government was, for all practical purposes, in the conference room of the Defense Ministry. The junta members—with the exception of General Mendoza [the Carabinero commander]—all had offices there anyway. Our office, in those early days, operated with only four or five persons in a small office with the foreign minister . . . Then someone remembered the big Diego Portales building, and after checking it out, we moved over there a few days later . . ."[17]

Offices they had; a plan of government they did not have. "Among the chiefs of the revolution of the eleventh, I wish to clarify, there was no concrete plan as to how we were going to govern." The speaker was Adm. José Toribio Merino, now the number two man in that government without a plan. So uncoordinated it was, that Pinochet said at the time that he came to head the junta through a gentleman's agreement which called for rotating leadership, first himself, then Merino, then Leigh, then Mendoza.[18]

The new government quickly promulgated a series of decree-laws to establish its legitimacy and legal framework. The first of them, Decree Law #1, signed before the television cameras the night of the revolution, constituted the junta as "the Supreme Command of the Nation with the patriotic duty to restore *chilenidad*,* justice, and the institutions which have broken down." The second said the junta would legislate through a series of numbered decree-laws. Another, on September 22, declared that Chile was under "a state of siege in time of war," which, among other things, had the effect of giving military courts ascendancy over civilian tribunals. Unlike civilian courts, military courts could (and did) decree the death penalty, and there was no appeal from their decisions.[19]

On September 12, the junta named the following to the Cabinet:
Army Gen. Oscar Bonilla Bradanovic, Interior Minister
Rear Adm. Ismael Huerta Díaz, Foreign Minister
Army Gen. Rolando González Acevedo, Economy**

---

* Literally "Chilean-ness," this would translate, roughly, as Chilean values, traditions.
** The ailing General González was out within the month, replaced by a civilian, Fernando Léniz. Of the others, Crespo Montero and Barba Valdés were retired officers.

Rear Adm. Lorenzo Gotuzzo Borlando, Finance
A civilian, Gonzalo Prieto Gándara, Justice
A civilian, José Navarro Tobar, Education
Vice Adm. Patricio Carvajal Prado, Defense
Air Force Brig. Gen. Sergio Figueroa Gutiérrez, Public Works
Air Force Col. Sergio Crespo Montero, Agriculture
Carabinero Gen. Diego Barba Valdés, Lands and Settlements
Carabinero Gen. Mario McKay Jaraquemada, Labor
Air Force Medical Service Col. Alberto Spoerer Covarrubias, Health
Carabinero Gen. Arturo Yovane Zúñiga, Mining
Army Brig. Gen. Arturo Vivero Avila, Housing
Army Col. Pedro Ewing Howar, Secretary-General of Government

An authoritative source wrote at the time: "The political makeup of the fifteen-man Cabinet is somewhat left of center, more or less along the lines of the Christian Democratic party which ruled Chile before Allende's election. The Cabinet is decidedly not right wing, and among the junta's first decrees was one outlawing right-wing extremist groups as well as those of the Left . . ." Yet another noted that Pinochet himself "was generally regarded as favorably disposed toward the Christian Democrats and was said to have supported Tomic in the 1970 election."[20]

The new stewards of Chile's government confronted a country still engaged in a shooting war—indeed, the bloodiest battles were fought in the days following the coup itself, and it would be five months before relative peace would reign.[21] Chile's economy was in ruins and the country faced an uncertain future.

Roberto Kelly's first problem was entirely unexpected: what to do with the eighteen or so Soviets he found on the payroll at the government's Office of Planning (ODEPLAN). The big, bluff and balding Irishman had retired from the navy as an admiral in 1967 after thirty-five years' service. Admiral Merino, directing economic affairs under the division of labor worked out by the junta members, already had Kelly in mind, and asked him to take a job which amounted to helping devise a master plan for a new Chilean state. Kelly was on the job first thing Wednesday morning in the bullet-scarred ODEPLAN offices facing Plaza Constitución, just a few yards from the still-smoldering palace.

By day's end, those Soviets had received their "pink slips." Within a few months, Kelly had trimmed the ODEPLAN staff to four hundred, half the number he found when he arrived. It was a process being repeated throughout the government. "In December," Kelly recalled, "we found 300,000 uncashed checks—a relic of Allende's tactic of piling more and more of his people onto the public payroll." A study done in the early months of junta rule showed that, by mid-1972, the size of the public payroll had increased under Allende from 414,618 to 626,943—with the biggest buildup yet to come, in 1973.[22]

Merino was, in fact, the only member of the junta who brought not only a plan but a team to his new job. (He actually brought two plans, one for the economy, another, still being developed, for education.) The new economic program had been blueprinted by a small group of young economists who began informal discussions in 1972 concerning what the economy of Chile might look like if, by some miracle, someone should one day ask them to take charge. One person they shared their thoughts with: Adm. José Toribio Merino.[23] Thus, what began largely as an exercise in frustration and whimsy, coalesced finally into a tightly reasoned, empirically supported thesis designed to transform the most state-dominated economy in the hemisphere (after Cuba) into one with, arguably, no equal as a free market economy. Those ideas were contained in a 187-page mimeographed study entitled "Policies of Development." Copies were closely guarded and distribution carefully controlled (each copy was numbered).[24]

The study traced the origin of Chile's economic ills to the economic collapse of 1930 and subsequent rise of socialist thought and content in economic affairs. It then proposed action plans in twelve general areas (everything from taxation and income redistribution to capital markets, price policies, and industrial and agrarian policies). Because many who worked on that plan had studied at the University of Chicago, the plan became known as the work of "the Chicago boys." Around twenty-five to thirty of those young economists—their ages ranged from twenty-six to thirty-five—went to work even before the shooting had stopped. In the event, where specific proposals embodied in the plan were not followed, the general free enterprise and inflation-fighting philosophy of the plan was.

Among early measures which were adopted:

- A temporary wage freeze and suspension of the 200 percent wage hike which had been scheduled to go into effect October 1;
- Prices were unfrozen so as to stimulate the sagging supply of goods. But, the junta also warned, on October 3, that profiteers would be jailed, and many were. When prices rose sharply in October, the junta reacted by decreeing special bonuses and pension and family allowance adjustments. The largest bonuses were ordered for poorer workers—the first of a number of measures the junta would take through the years to create an effective "safety net" for Chile's poorest;
- The work week was extended from forty-four to forty-eight hours;

- Within a month, the government returned to private owners more than three hundred enterprises that had been illegally seized, and announced plans to sell off around 260 other government-operated enterprises. Agreement was quickly reached with the owners of many of the fifty American companies that had been seized, and a high-level commission was named to begin immediate negotiations on compensation for seized American properties, including the big copper companies;
- Agricultural output, which in 1973 had actually plunged to 1936 levels, when Chile's population was one-half that of 1973, was stimulated just as the fall sowing season was underway through sharp price increases and guarantees to small and medium-size farmers against expropriation;
- The escudo was abruptly devalued from artificial low levels (forty-six to the dollar in the open market, twenty to three hundred to the dollar for imports) to an immediate 850. In the last days of Allende, the black market rate had soared to three thousand to the dollar, and, as noted in chapter 7, bankers and importers were forced to decipher a bewildering array of official exchange rates. After the coup, three rates were introduced: one for imports, one for copper, one for general exchange purposes;
- Import duties were greatly simplified and streamlined;
- To deal with the problem of official debt—Chile was then, in per capita terms, the most heavily debt-burdened country in the world after Israel, the bloated public sector alone owing more money than was in the hands of the entire private sector[25]—the junta announced severe austerity measures. These included an announced cutback of 100,000 jobs from the government payroll. As a first step, all government jobs with the exception of those in the judiciary and the controller-general's office were declared "temporary."

The program had some immediate successes. Foodstuffs and other long-scarce goods suddenly blossomed on shop shelves. Copper production, already climbing in September, reached record levels in October and November after plunging to ruinously low levels under Allende. Farm output picked up rapidly. Three weeks after the coup, one reporter wrote: "Already the signs are in the air, as unmistakable as the budding trees that proclaim the arrival of spring in this grey, grimy capital: a renaissance of the local stock market; suddenly renewed advertisements and commercials for restaurants, discotheques, boutiques and bake shops; the reappearance of taxis on downtown streets . . ."

Said Chilean businessman Andronico Luksic: "I am laughing for the first time in a long time. I sing in the shower and my days are full of plans."[26]

But it was only the beginning, and the road ahead was harder, much harder than any of the military commanders had imagined. Viewing the task ahead, an official in the Economy Ministry said: "It's a monster, an absolute monster."[27] (More on the junta's economic planning in the next chapter.)

> We should say, with all frankness: Any man who shoots against our forces, dies. Any man who shoots innocents, dies. And we will not rest until we clean these traitors from our country, be they foreigners or Chileans.
>
> —Gen. Gustavo Leigh, member of the junta,
> at a news conference in Santiago,
> September 19, 1973

Within the spindly borders of the tormented land that was Chile, forces more sensed than seen inexorably commanded events. Columnist William F. Buckley sensed those forces in the first days following the revolt: "There is a heavy penance exacted of those who treat democracy frivolously," he wrote. "The Greeks are paying that price, as are the Brazilians. Portugal and Spain have paid it for over a generation of time.

"Democracy is a fragile institution, and people who are careless with it should simply not be surprised if, having convulsed their countries, they are themselves inconvenienced."[28]

Within two days of the coup, Pinochet announced the penance for those who had treated democracy frivolously in Chile. The junta, he said, was determined to "exterminate Marxism" from Chilean life. Leigh's words, a week later (echoing similar stern thoughts expressed over the secret radio network during the heat of battle), amounted to war without quarter.

The junta never did say how many were executed summarily under the martial law edicts announced the day of the revolution. Summary executions were officially terminated on October 24. But military courts continued to try prisoners and, in some instances, to decree the death penalty. As of October 24, official sources said eighty-one persons had been executed after trial by military courts. An undetermined number more were reported killed while trying to escape. At least twelve were killed in one such instance on October 24, and six more were reported slain in similar circumstances September 24. The Commission on Human Rights of the Organization of American States, citing "reliable sources," said 220 persons had been summarily executed in the first months following the coup. The Chilean government reacted angrily, saying the commission had failed to cite a single specific case or even name names or places. The commission subsequently reported in detail on four separate incidents involving the collective executions of a total of forty-four persons.[29]

As part of its campaign to "exterminate Marxism" legally, the junta, on September 21, outlawed the Communist and Socialist parties, and four Marxist and pro-Marxist miniparties which had backed Allende. Non-Marxist parties were declared in indefinite "recess." The Congress, also in "recess," was formally dissolved as part of that same series of measures. At the same news conference announcing those measures, Pinochet gave the first solid indication of long-range military rule.

Democratic, civilian government, he said, would be restored "as soon as the country . . . forgets the chaos it was living in." Asked how long that could take, Pinochet said: "When a sick person has to have an arm amputated, it is very difficult to say how long he will take to recuperate." Leigh softened the impact of that somewhat by disclosing that a commission had been named to draft a new constitution, and that it would be submitted to the electorate in a referendum.[30]

Next, the junta zeroed in on the Communist-controlled Central Workers Confederation (CUT). On September 25, it was declared illegal "for having been transformed into an organization of political character, under the influence of foreign tendencies and devoid of national spirit." Individual unions were not affected; only the loosely knit and highly politicized CUT. But, the power of unions was sharply curbed by new rules reshaping labor courts and banning industry-wide strikes.

To make its political control complete, the junta also fired all mayors and city councilmen and appointed known anti-Marxists to replace them.

Education was the next target. Describing the university system as "a focus of Marxist teaching," the junta, early in October, fired the rectors at all seven campuses of the state-run University of Chile and replaced them with military men. (The distinguished scholar Paul Sigmund, although scarcely sympathetic to the junta, noted that "there remained only one group of institutions which might provide a center of resistance to military rule, the universities.")[31] Air Force Gen. César Ruiz Danyau, whose resignation in August had paved the way for one of the coup leaders, General Leigh, to assume command, replaced Christian Democrat Dr. Edgardo Boeninger at the main, Santiago campus. Military delegate-rectors were also named for the country's two Catholic universities. Thousands among the 128,000 students and hundreds of faculty members were suspended because of suspected leftist ties, and a number of courses cancelled pending review. Many among the students were later expelled, and a number of teachers fired.[32] Textbooks used in grade and high school classrooms were reviewed and Marxist-tinged works pruned out.

Though most of these measures enjoyed the support of the decisive majority of Chileans who had clamored for the coup, one measure did not: An official attack on miniskirts, then in vogue.[33]

But another did: so popular was the 11:00 P.M.–5:30 A.M. curfew with many Chilean wives that it became known—joshingly—as The Family Protection Act.

The Catholic church—long allied with the Christian Democrat party (PDC), and mainly with its leftist leadership—took a position of passive-aggressive hostility to the junta from the outset. Roman Catholic bishops, led by the Catholic primate, Raúl Cardinal Silva Henríquez, issued a statement two days after the coup deploring "the blood which has reddened our streets, our settlements, and our factories—the blood of civilians and of soldiers, the tears of so many women and children. We ask respect for those fallen in the struggle, and, first of all, for he who was until Tuesday September 11th, President of the Republic." The statement also expressed hope that the "advances achieved by the former government for the working and peasant class, will not be reversed," and that "institutional normality" would soon return to Chile.[34]

The cardinal, who had paid a courtesy call on Pinochet and the other military chieftains in the first days after the coup, agreed to celebrate the traditional *Te Deum* Mass on September 18, Independence Day, but shifted it from the Cathedral to the Church of National Thanksgiving. Pinochet, in his memoirs, recalled that the cardinal agreed to offer the junta the same support he had given the previous government, "but nothing more than that."[35] All three living ex-presidents attended the mass, as well as the chief justice of the Supreme Court and other high political and church leaders. As two commentators on church-junta relations observed, relations between the junta and the church were, from the outset, "bad."[36] (More of the role of the church in the following chapter.)

THE WORLD REACTS

Swedish Ambassador Edelstam was far from alone in taking pot shots at the new government. The British writer David Holden observed: "Salvador Allende died a lucky man. In life he was a failure. Both his policies and his country were shattered long before the end. But in death he achieved success beyond his dreams. Instantly canonized as the Western world's newest left-wing martyr, he became overnight the most potent cult-figure since his old friend, Che Guevara." Yet another, author Robert Moss, wrote sardonically: "It was a bit boy scoutish of them, but the soldiers who overthrew Salvador Allende thought that they had earned the gratitude of the American people, and of the West in general. For one thing, they had prevented the transformation of Chile into a sort of Latin American Czechoslovakia, complete with Soviet bases ... Alas, how little these soldiers understood the mood of the times in Washington or London. With the spirit of Helsinki* about, it is not done to attack Communists too stridently. Since the intellectual defense of capitalism has become a minority cause in most of the countries that owe their present affluence to it, these disciples of Adam Smith and Milton Friedman were a positive embarrassment . . ."[37]

From Mexico to Moscow, a howl went up that would frequently border on hysteria—when not outright cynicism. Cried one, ". . . the Chilean military will haul the nation back to the Stone Age, where a primitive and simplistic warrior village will be bedded down for a long sleep awaiting the fantasied attacks coming from every direction." Another said, "civil war surely will be the central fact of Chile in the years to come."[38] The commiseration of the outside world was usually in direct contrast to the mood of celebration of most Chileans.

Fidel Castro, whirling around the world after attending the conference of "Non-Aligned" Nations in Algiers—a conference Allende had also expected to attend—flew into New Delhi on his first official visit to India and was given a warm welcome by Mrs. Indira Gandhi. (Castro had just won the affection of the "non-aligned" Arab states by announcing at Algiers that Cuba was breaking diplomatic relations with Israel.) In Hanoi, a day later, Castro called the coup "a hateful act . . . perpetrated by stooges of North American imperialism." He added, in words Moscow had initially rejected but because of the new lessons of Chile came increasingly to make its own, "There is no longer any alternative except a revolutionary struggle."

The coup seemed to have caught Moscow off balance. Only a few days before the revolution, the Soviets had signed a new scientific and cultural agreement with Chile, and reports appearing in the Soviet press in the days preceding the eleventh gave no hint of imminent doom.[39] Thus, Moscow's first reactions were more bluster than slashing. On the day after the coup, Radio Moscow proclaimed Allende a martyr and said he "was not the sort of person" to commit suicide, the first prong of a propaganda offensive that would endure through the years. On September 14, the Central Committee of the Communist party of the Soviet

---

* Moss refers to the agreement reached in Helsinki between the United States and the USSR calling on the Soviets to liberalize their control over the lives of their own citizens in return for tacit Western acceptance of permanent Soviet control of the captive nations of Eastern Europe.

Union issued a mousy statement proclaiming "solidarity" with the Chilean working classes, adding that "neither reprisals nor terror can break the will of the people or close the road to economic and social progress."[40] Russian floundering continued until September 21, when the Soviets broke diplomatic relations, blaming alleged persecution of Soviet officials by the junta for the break. But by then, the Soviets had already launched "a sustained and well-orchestrated propaganda campaign aimed at isolating and discrediting the regime." *Pravda,* on September 26, reported that "the streets of Santiago were flowing with blood." On September 28, Moscow Radio said women and children were being shot by the junta in an effort to intimidate people, and a month later, on October 28, added that "tens of thousands of Chilean democrats" had been killed. Moscow Radio also stated that Allende had been "murdered in cold blood," and that his residence had been "wiped off the face of the earth." Premier Leonid Brezhnev expressed horror at the "monstrous, completely open violation of a country's constitution, the unceremonious flouting of the democratic traditions of an entire nation."[41]

On November 30, a Soviet Committee for Solidarity with Chilean Democrats was formed to establish "contacts with national committees in other countries and jointly with them take actions aimed at all-round isolation of the Chilean military junta." (Those efforts to isolate and undermine the junta included fomenting a protest campaign to prevent the sale of arms to Chile.[42] The campaign found echo in the United States: on October 2, 1973, Sen. Edward M. Kennedy [D-Mass.] proposed a total ban on arms sales to Chile, and a $25 million ceiling on all aid to Chile. More on the U.S. response later in this chapter.)

Adverse reaction was not limited to avowedly Marxist countries. In Mexico, President Luis Echeverría, close to Allende since his own days as a student in Chile, ordered three days of official mourning. It was the first time Mexico had so honored a fallen foreign head of state since the assassination of John F. Kennedy. Meeting at Blackpool for its annual conference, Britain's Labour party gave a standing ovation to Allende's former ambassador in London—the first nondelegate to address a party conference since two Spanish Republicans were invited to do so in the 1930s.[43] In Paris, a crowd of thirty thousand marched through the streets shouting, "down with the murderers and the CIA."[44] In Rome, where the Communist movement was second only to that of France in the Western world (and ahead of what was then the number three country, Chile), billboards and wall scrawling eulogizing Allende appeared throughout the city. In West Germany, governed then by Willy Brandt's Social Democrats, the government expressed "deep dismay." In neighboring Argentina, the leftist government of Juan Perón decreed three days of official mourning. Venezuela, where leftist politics had dominated political thought and discourse for fifteen years, also declared official mourning; and the leftist-controlled Latin American Labor Confederation, based in Caracas, accused "imperialist powers" of staging the coup. To Chile's north, Peruvian President Juan Velasco Alvarado—heading a leftist military dictatorship—sent a message of "deepest sympathies" to Allende's widow. The Christian Democrat party in Peru, on September 19, issued a communique reflecting the wobbly ideology of the leftist wing of the Chilean party. The statement blamed both the Left and the Right in Chile for Allende's death, condemned the military coup, and protested what the party said were signs it had detected that the new military rulers were attempting to woo the support of the Right.[45] In Rome, the Italian Christian Democratic party—heading an uneasy coalition of mostly leftist parties—said it was "difficult to understand" how its Chilean counterparts "could expect an early return to constitutional and democratic methods." The far left wing of the Italian party was particularly miffed, inasmuch as it had been plumping for a coalition with the Italian Communists similar to Allende's coalition.[46] Responding in part to the Italians, more generally to the fusillades of his putative political allies around the world, Frei directed a letter to Mariano Rumor, president of the Christian Democracy International, in which he said the military coup was necessary because "a cancer requires major surgery, and not an aspirin."

That scholarship and research transcend ideology and political boundaries is a hallowed—and loudly proclaimed—cornerstone of academic freedom. Nonetheless, in the aftermath of the coup, the Ford Foundation ended grants to anyone working inside Chile, and the University of California severed its links with the University of Chile.[47]

Allende's former envoys around the world quickly joined the counterattack. In Rome, the respected anti-Allende Chilean journalist Nena Ossa remembered strolling down a street late Tuesday afternoon when she saw a headline announcing a coup in her native Chile. Because of the six-hour time difference, the newspaper contained only scant details of the outbreak of the revolt.

"That night," Mrs. Ossa said, "there was very little news on the radio. So the next morning, I telephoned our ambassador, Carlos Vasallo. Although he was a Communist, we were on reasonably good terms. I asked him what was going on.

" 'I don't know,' he told me. 'All I know is I have lost my president and many of my friends. All communications to Santiago have been cut and there are no airplanes.'

"Later, around noon, I was with a German journalist and he suggested we go to the embassy. The ambassador said a radio station [presumably clandestine] was transmitting to Bahía Blanca, in Argentina, and from there, reports were being sent out. The ambassador started to say that the Christian Democrats were to blame, because they had refused to reach an understanding with Allende. Then a secretary came in and whispered something in his ear. The ambassador said he had a visitor. We asked him whether we should leave and he said no. Then he received the visitor and the two of them talked in a far corner of the room.

"We overheard them saying that it couldn't have been suicide, that Allende must have been murdered, they spoke of murders [apparently referring to Augusto Olivares as well as Allende], and the Christian Democrats.

"As we were leaving, my German friend told me that the visitor was the most important Communist party journalist in Italy. That afternoon, the party newspaper trumpeted a story about the 'murder' of Allende.

"By late afternoon, the plazas were full of graffiti: 'Chilean Fascists-Murderers,' and that sort of thing."[48]

Thus—in Moscow, in Rome, elsewhere, far from the scene, long before any serious evidence could exist—one of the two canards of the Chilean revolution was born: That Allende had been murdered. (Ironically, a few days later, Allende's widow "confirmed" that her husband had committed suicide, a version she would later repudiate. Daughter Isabel, not only asserted that her father had been murdered, but even named his murderer. But, then, she also said there was another witness, the "seriously wounded" Miria Contreras.)[49]

The other canard was not far behind. On September 18, Allende's former ambassadors to China, East Germany, Hungary, Yugoslovia, and Rumania, called a press conference in Rome to accuse "North American imperialism" of "coldly planning the death of Allende and the ruin of the country." Their statement appealed to "men of goodwill" to do all possible, "with the greatest urgency, to stay the hand of murderers and to put an end to the bloodbath in Chile."[50]

OF PLOTS AND PRISONERS

In his previously cited October 1973 interview with the Madrid newspaper *ABC*, former President Eduardo Frei spoke of the discovery of "armament superior in number and quality to that of the Army: armament for 30,000 men . . ." (He noted also the boast of a Communist leader that "the generals have found only a small part of the arms we had. . . .")[51] In light of later reports, that estimate almost certainly was an exaggeration. But what was no exaggeration at all was the war footing of the far Left in Chile. That Allende knew about this and connived in it is virtually beyond dispute. His own residences, Tomás Moro and El Cañaveral, were themselves among the most awesome arsenals of illegal arms.

As noted earlier, discovery of arms on a significant scale began in July, when the military began applying the Arms Control Law in earnest. But the precoup discoveries paled by comparison with what was found afterwards. Conservative estimates said five thousand men could be armed with weapons uncovered in the first days. Even before the Communist leader's boast, the military estimated that, on the basis of documents they had found, they had located less than a quarter of the arms smuggled into Chile by air and sea, and over wilderness land routes. Chilean military intelligence said it had found evidence that approximately 100,000 Popular Unity men had undergone some kind of military training in the years between 1969 and 1973.[52]

Seven training schools were discovered—one of them at El Cañaveral, the country estate Allende had bought for his personal secretary and mistress, Miria Contreras. Situated at the edge of the Andes, a few miles east of Santiago, El Cañaveral was Allende's favorite weekend retreat. Facilities there included an obstacle course, gunnery ranges, and housing for 130 "students." (Tomás Moro, the palace Allende provided for himself in Santiago, had quarters for 150 irregulars.) At both complexes—as at the training camps—the military found antitank guns, sub-machineguns, bazookas, mortars, mines and grenades, as well as rifles and revolvers. The cost of this clandestine arsenal—obviously not the paraphernalia of a "peaceful road to socialism"—ran into the millions.

The military also discovered extensive documentation—including a list in the safe of Daniel Vergara, the long-serving undersecretary of the interior—of 14,085 foreigners who were in the country illegally. Among those foreigners captured almost immediately: twelve Soviet army officers who had been training worker-revolutionaries at a Soviet-installed factory at El Belloto, near Valparaíso. Naval intelligence had had them under close surveillance from the time of their arrival a year before, and they were arrested on the morning of the revolution—along with eight Soviet engineers and technicians working with them—and expelled several days later.[53]

But the most startling secrets came from a safe in Allende's office at La Moneda—the outlines of a plot to stage a preemptive coup. Those

documents revealed that the plan was to liquidate top military commanders en masse when they gathered for the September 18 Independence Day ceremonies, murder or jail six hundred opposition political
and opinion leaders, and clamp a "people's democracy"–type dictatorship on the country. Pinochet said the military intelligence service
(SIM) had picked up rumors of the plot before the coup, but that the full
details were not discovered until afterwards. In early press reports,
existence of the plot—called Plan Z—was invoked as a pretext for
staging the revolution. Pinochet, in an interview with the author, disputed that claim. His disclaimer that discovery of the plots (there were
several, including one in the air force) was the trigger for revolution
rings true since none was ready for execution.[54]

Chile was a country where consensus had been incinerated in the
hatreds of class warfare. It was a country where Right and Left were
plotting how to annhilate each other's future franchise. It was a country
where many were arming and scheming to murder one another. It was a
country where foreign legionnaires by the thousands, swarming in during the Allende years in response to the siren song of revolution, added
to the din, to the divisiveness, to the danger. (The junta claimed to have
identified more than 13,000 of them, including: 4,178 Bolivians, 2,139
Argentines, 987 Cubans, 1,297 Brazilians, 3,266 Uruguayans, 580 Col-
ombians, and 148 Mexicans—though that number would apparently be
disputed by United Nations officials.)[55]

It was against that chaotic and high tension background that the junta
moved to consolidate its control of the country. Several thousand persons, including many foreigners, were rounded up in the first days after
the coup, many herded into makeshift detention centers such as the
National Stadium and the indoor Arena Chile in Santiago. A reporter
who was part of a group of newsmen taken to the National Stadium said
the prisoners were given blankets, "appeared to be well fed, and Red
Cross personnel were being allowed to see them." He said 240 foreigners
were among the approximately 3,500 to four thousand then being held
there.[56]

Although the number imprisoned—just as the number of those who
died in the revolution—was far fewer than, to take one example among
many, those who would die and suffer long imprisonment in the Nicaraguan revolution a few years later, Chile was almost instantly converted
into a pariah state castigated for human rights atrocities.[57] Nicaragua
never was. The point needs to be made because it reveals much about
the elasticity of the rules of indignation as they apply to regimes of the
Right, and those of the Left. As Henry Kissinger wrote: "Was there not
involved a double standard that continued to be demonstrated at an
ever-accelerating pace throughout the 1970s? No radical revolution, no

matter how bloody—one thinks of Cuba, Iraq, Algeria, many African states, Vietnam's occupation of Indochina, Khomeini's Iran—has confronted the worldwide press campaign and the global indignation evoked by the clumsy authoritarians of Santiago. Was its crime in its methods, or its position on the right of the political spectrum? Was its sin the lack of civil freedoms, or the abandonment of the leftist embrace? Why is the argument so widespread that left-wing governments like Nicaragua's are supposed to be moderated by economic assistance while conservative governments like Chile's must be reformed by ostracism? The socialist government of Sweden cut off aid to Chile on September 13, within forty-eight hours of the coup, before its implications could possibly be known. Had it ever acted with such alacrity, or at all, against left-wing tyrants? Indeed, it had lavished aid on Hanoi throughout the Vietnam war and afterward."[58]

Within three weeks of the coup, Chile released the last six of the twenty-five Americans who were among the foreigners detained. Two of them, first at a press conference in Miami, later in testimony before Sen. Edward Kennedy, would tell lurid tales of mass executions which reverberated around the world; less noticed was their later admission that they had actually seen nothing, only heard the sounds of shooting which they supposed must be firing squads.

Two other Americans never came back. One—allegedly involved in the navy mutiny plot against the high command that was one of the triggers for the revolution—would later become the hero of a major movie, *Missing*. A *New York Times* reporter, writing from Santiago at the time, described the two as "deeply committed to the Allende cause [but] pacifists and gentle intellectuals not involved in Chilean politics."[59]

Within weeks of the coup, the junta had granted safe-conduct passes out of the country to 1,729 foreigners and their families. By the first anniversary of the revolution, that number had risen to 8,416, virtually all the foreigners who wished to leave, leading to a commendation from the representative of the UN High Commission for Refugees for Chile's handling of the problem.[60] Unnoticed in the exodus, of foreigners and Chileans, was the return of approximately twenty-thousand Chileans who had fled during the Allende years. That number was approximately equal to the number of Chileans who left following the coup.

Many top leaders of the Allende government and of the Socialist and Communist parties managed to evade capture, most taking refuge in embassies. Among them was the most hunted of all: Carlos Altamirano. He ultimately reached Paris with a Cuban diplomatic passport, issued by the consulate of Cuba in East Germany. Others evaded capture, despite a $14,000 reward the government offered for information leading to the arrest of any of the thirteen most-wanted Allende leaders.[61] One among them was lucky: Volodia Teitelboim, chief ideologue of the Communist party, was out of the country on the eleventh. He never came back. Surfacing shortly afterwards in Moscow, he began a new and enduring career as chief commentator of an ambitious series of radio programs beamed to Chile (and Latin America), by transmitters so powerful that, in parts of Chile, they were almost the equivalent of local broadcast stations. (Teitelboim was the man who, on July 19, had said defiantly: "Why were we going to seek asylum? We are not rats. We will never abandon our fight for the people.")[62]

With the exception of Allende, no high-ranking government or party official died in the fighting, on the eleventh or afterwards. But a number were captured and questioned at the Defense Ministry and Military Academy. On September 14, the new justice minister, Gonzalo Prieto Gándara, met with the prisoners and offered them a plane to fly into exile. To a man, they refused, demanding instead to be tried. The next day they were taken on a twenty-one-hour air and boat journey to Dawson Island, a remote naval base, 1,500 miles south of Santiago. A few—Interior Minister Carlos Briones, considered a moderate; Dr. Patricio Guijón, the presidential physician who saw Allende shoot himself; and the former defense minister, José Tohá—were released in December. (Tohá, a gangling 6 foot 6 inch man of forty-seven, lost sixty pounds during his confinement; hospitalized in Santiago, he died a few weeks later. The official version was suicide; others attributed his death to cancer; still others charged murder.)

Those who remained behind spent their first two months on Dawson Island in crude barracks they promptly dubbed "The Sheraton" (no doubt since Santiago's two leading hotels were then both Sheratons). For the balance of their eight-month confinement there, they were in roomier and more comfortable quarters constructed for them. (Another group of lower-ranking prisoners—485 men and forty-nine women—held on wind-swept Quiriquina Island in Concepción Bay—were taught carpentry and bricklaying so they could build their own quarters. On arrival, they had to make do in dilapidated barracks at Fort Rondizzone, originally built to guard against pirates.) The Dawson prisoners also were put to work erecting dozens of telephone poles along thirty-five miles of the island's territory, building roads, digging tunnels, and hauling timber. In their free time, they gave each other courses on everything from international finance to English, cybernetics, and neurology.[63] Except for complaints about the food and early harassment by some of their jailers, there were no reports of serious mistreatment of the Dawson prisoners. Among the many Chilean and foreign newsmen (and Red Cross officials) to visit the island, the Brazilian journalist, Antonio Alberto Prado, reported two serious problems: the raw cold, and, quoting a prisoner, "the lack of freedom, with no charges to defend against, because none has been made against us."[64]

The Dawson Island prisoners—thirty-five in the first batch, a few more later—included Clodomiro Almeyda, the foreign minister; Orlando Letelier, former ambassador to the U.S., defense minister at the end; Luis Corvalán, Communist party secretary-general; Fernando Flores, General Prats' close friend, who years later would become a multimillionaire in the United States in his esoteric field of computers, cybernetics; the Puccios, father and son, who had been in the palace with Allende; Radical party President Anselmo Sule; chief presidential physician Dr. Arturo Jirón; Education Minister Dr. Edgardo Enríquez (father of the MIR chieftain, who would be killed a month later in a shoot-out with soldiers); Dr. Enrique Kirberg, president of the Technical University, the most radical of all the campuses (and scene of some of the heaviest and most prolonged fighting of the revolution).

Orlando Letelier was among those brought out of the Defense Ministry around 8:30 A.M., on the morning of the revolution, before the heavy shooting started. Elizabeth Davis, wife of the American ambassador, saw the scene on television and reported that the Orlando Letelier she saw was a changed man. (She could not have known that in addition to the trauma of sudden capture, the defense minister was a "changed man" for another reason: the afternoon before, he had undergone painful root canal work.)[65] But Mrs. Letelier did not see that television program, nor did she hear about it. She dialed number after number throughout the day attempting to learn of his whereabouts until finally, late in the day, she got through to General Leigh. " 'Don't worry,' he told me. 'Your husband's situation is going to be clarified soon. He is very well, and there is nothing for you to worry about.' " Mrs. Tohá received similar reassurances that day from a Commander Merrick, and the next day, received a call from the Defense Department telling her to pack a bag for her husband. (When an officer came to pick it up, he gave her a note from her husband, in which he asked her to include a coat, some cigarettes, some sweets, and above all, some warm clothing, because it was extremely cold where he was going. Mrs. Letelier, the day after the coup, managed to talk on the telephone to her husband.) A few days later, Pinochet received a delegation—the wives of Almeyda, Letelier, and Tohá—and after reassuring them that their husbands were all right, delivered "a harangue" about their husbands' collusion with Marxists.

He also agreed to forward mail to their husbands. For most, it would be four months before they would see them again.[66]

Efforts to free the high-ranking prisoners began almost immediately. Kurt Waldheim, then secretary-general of the United Nations, and Ecuadorean Ambassador Leopoldo Benites, then president of the UN General Assembly, responding to pressure from the Soviet bloc, made an appeal for Corvalán's life. The Chileans responded that Corvalán would be court-martialed for high treason, adding, "We are telling everybody to mind their own business."[67] (No such appeal, Kissinger noted, was made later for the victims of Iran's revolution, "who were far more numerous and far more badly treated.") Ultimately, and largely through the efforts of the United States, Corvalán was freed in a swap for the Soviet dissident leader, Vladimir Bukovsky. (That the Soviets would release a man who had denounced the practice of committing political dissidents to psychiatric wards, and thus acknowledge that he was, in fact, a political prisoner, was a measure of the importance they attached to the Chilean communist movement.) Thanks, also, to U.S. intervention, both Almeyda and Letelier were released in 1975.[68]

Nor were such appeals confined to those outside Chile. Bernardo Leighton, one of the leaders of the left wing of the Christian Democratic party, filed for a writ of habeas corpus for several of the imprisoned ministers, including Briones and Almeyda. The Appeals Court rejected the petition on a technical ruling that would fester at the heart of many legal controversies yet to come. Leighton later left Chile himself, setting up a well-financed and well-staffed headquarters in Rome to organize and foster opposition to the junta—one of several such in Europe.[69]

Another man, central to the Chilean cataclysm, was free to leave. On September 12, Carlos Prats González called his former second-in-command, Augusto Pinochet Ugarte, to say that he wanted to leave Chile. He was already the focus of new rumors. One set said right-wing hit squads planned to assassinate him. Another said he was commanding counterrevolutionary forces in the south of Chile.

Two days later, Pinochet returned his call. While agreeing that he knew the counterrevolution rumors were false, Pinochet said it would be difficult to authorize Prats' departure unless he would agree to make a televised statement "clarifying his position." Unbeknownst to Prats, Pinochet was then looking at a report of the Army General Staff, recommending against exile for Prats, at least until he explained what he knew about: (1) Marxist plans to destroy the armed forces; (2) misappropriation of government funds to benefit extremist groups or individuals; (3) the presence of foreign Communists in Chile to organize paramilitary forces; (4) the existence of illegal armed groups in government offices themselves. Pinochet decided to accede to Prats request out of respect, he said, for his rank; he agreed to fly him to the Argentine border in a military helicopter. On September 14, Prats taped his brief remarks, saying that from the moment of his resignation, he had removed himself from all public activity, that he would never lead a rebellion which would only shed more blood among brothers, and that his only wish now was to leave the country—as he had intended to do even before the revolution.

At 6:30 A.M., on Saturday, September 15th, having said farewell the night before to his daughters, grandchildren, and wife (who would join him later), Prats left his home, bound for Argentina. He would never come home again.[70]

THE WAR OF WORDS, THE SEARCH FOR MEANING

But the existence of the clandestine arms, and the fanatical resistance of a cadre of extremists clustered mostly in the MIR, accounted for much of the bloodletting in the weeks following the coup. The bloodletting never, however, approached the proportions portrayed in lurid accounts in much of the world's press. One, which continued to be quoted long after it had been refuted, and which was instrumental in creating the mythology of mass murder and mayhem, appeared in *Newsweek* magazine in the October 8, 1973, issue.

It was written by an English correspondent for the magazine, John Barnes, who was flown out from London to cover the aftermath of the coup—presumably because of his prior experience in Latin America (though not enough experience to learn to speak Spanish).

The title of the article was chilling enough: "Slaughterhouse in Santiago." The article began dramatically—and inaccurately: "Pablo Neruda, Chile's Nobel Prize-winning poet, was dead of cancer, and even as his body was lowered into its grave, his countrymen set about trying to murder his words. Books of all kinds, not only Neruda's but those of Mao and Marx and Marcuse, were seized by the tens of thousands from homes, bookstores and libraries and then fed to bonfires in the streets of Santiago.[71] Chilean universities, once proud bastions of independence, were purged of suspected leftists, and ordinary people learned to dread the midnight knock on the door. All this was bad enough, but *Newsweek* correspondent John Barnes discovered last week that the reign of terror has already gone much further than most people thought."

What followed was more political harangue than journalism. In the article, Barnes, reporting on fighting in the shantytowns, ascribed the "terror" in them to a lust for vengeance, because it was in those "*poblaciones*" that Allende had had his greatest support. There was a good deal of fighting in the *poblaciones*, but for the more obvious reason that, as at La Legua, the far Left had long since invaded them and converted them into lawless bastions of armed terrorists.

It was when Barnes attempted to get specific that he marched into his own journalistic slaughterhouse. "Workers at the morgue," Barnes wrote, "have been warned that they will be court-martialed and shot if they reveal what is going on in there. But I was able to obtain an official morgue body-count from the daughter of a member of the staff: by the fourteenth day following the coup, she said, the morgues had received and processed 2,796 corpses.

"No one knows," Barnes added, "how many have been disposed of elsewhere."

The trouble is that Barnes was dead wrong. Among those who sprung to challenge him was Luis H. Diuguid of a sister publication, the *Washington Post* (which owns *Newsweek*): "The number of violent deaths in the Chilean capital over the three weeks since the military coup appears to have been approximately 750, on the basis of checking today at the central morgue. This contrasts both with latest official count of 284 for the whole country and with a report by John Barnes in the current issue of *Newsweek*, saying that the total number of deaths registered at the central morgue in the two weeks after the coup was 2,796.

"This reporter visited the morgue today and was told by the woman who has kept records there for several years that 2,796 was indeed an accurate count—of all the deaths recorded by the morgue from January 1 to September 25, rather than during the brief period after September 11.

"Assuming that to be accurate, and it would apparently be hard to falsify if the system is as foolproof as was explained to me, then there have been about 750 more bodies processed through the morgue so far this year than one would normally have expected."

Diuguid—despite his own clearly discernible pro-Allende, antijunta proclivities—went on to bury also Barnes' lurid tale of a grave-digger who allegedly told Barnes that he had heard reports of helicopters gathering bodies at the emergency first-aid center in Santiago and then carrying them out to sea to be dumped. "Under normal circumstances," Diuguid wrote, "all violent deaths in the Santiago metropolitan area must by law be processed through the central morgue." Diuguid obviously operated on the assumption that, in a country steeped in bureaucratic reflexes, bureaucratic rigamarole continued to rule even in the aftermath of a revolution.[72]

These events are worth recalling not just because of what they reveal of the tone and tenor of reporting on the coup and its aftermath, but because the myths created in those early days became the premises on which so many permanent conclusions were formed. Barnes' figures (and phony book-burning claim) continued to surface for months afterwards in paid advertisements, newspaper and magazine articles.[73] In the U.S. Congress, Senator Edward Kennedy read the Barnes article into the *Congressional Record*. On October 8, 1973—six days after the *Washington Post* (among others) had challenged the validity of Barnes' reporting[74]—his figures were repeated matter-of-factly in a full-page ad in the *New York Times* and other major U.S. newspapers, under the headline: "Chile: The Massacre Continues." (The ad was paid for by the Chile Emergency Committee, a who's who of leftist causes which included among its several hundred signers singer Joan Baez; the revolutionary priests, Daniel and Philip Berrigan; Daniel Ellsberg [the man who leaked the "Pentagon Papers"]; actress Jane Fonda [fresh from her pilgrimage to Hanoi in support of the North Vietnamese enemies of the United States]; writers I.F. Stone and Kurt Vonnegut, and historian Henry Steele Commager. That ad was the committee's second. In the first, on September 23, the signers proclaimed that "the streets [of Santiago] are red with blood . . . thousands are reported to have been killed . . . Having dealt a death blow to the constitutional order, the right-wing *junta* has launched a reign of terror . . . the U.S. government and certain large corporations bear major responsibility for what has happened in Chile. . . .")

Most of the first press reports conceded that Allende had brought the country to chaos, and many even acknowledged that in those circumstances, revolution was inevitable. Tolerance of the revolutionaries evaporated rapidly when the new rulers made plain they had no intention of returning to the status-quo-ante. As the weeks wore on, almost no charge was too improbable, no matter how improbable the source. Four months after the coup, newspapers, and radio and television stations around the world featured a report by a "woman's delegation" just back from Chile, reporting that "80,000 persons have been killed and 150,000 thrown out of work as a result of the *junta* takeover . . ." News agencies described the organization, the Women's International Democratic Federation, as "leftist"; actually, the federation was a well-identified Soviet front organization, set up in 1945 as a key component of the well-funded Soviet "disinformation" and propaganda network.[75] Such reckless reporting would, increasingly, become the rule, in a pattern that contained three main elements.

(1) Rumor, unverified charges, and flamboyant claims found ready forums.

(2) Allende was portrayed, in the worst of cases, as a Don Quixote, more often as a martyr; his government, invariably, as "democratically elected."

(3) Conspicuous left-wingers dominated the commentary on events in Chile.[76]

Yet not all of the commentary glorified Allende and vilified the junta. Sociologist Emanuel De Kadt, of the far leftist University of Sussex Institute of Development Studies, wrote that "the military intervened when the legality and constitutionalism which Allende continued to proclaim as the essence of the *Vía Chilena* was becoming, or had become, a figment of his imagination." MIT Professor Paul N. Rosenstein-Rodan wrote that Allende "died not because he was a socialist, but because he was incompetent." The *Economist*, in an editorial September 15, 1973 ("The end of Allende"), said that "the temporary death of democracy in Chile will be regrettable, but the blame lies clearly with Dr. Allende and those of his followers who persistently overrode the constitution." A similar theme was evoked by James D. Theberge, director of Latin American studies at Georgetown University's Center for Strategic and International Studies. The villains, he said, were the "fanatical, radical Marxist elements in Chile, tolerated if not encouraged by Allende, that bear the ultimate responsibility . . ." By the end of September, Theberge said he had already detected "a concerted campaign . . . by leftists, ultra-leftists and irresponsible anti-American politicians in Latin America and certain circles in the United States to capitalize on the tragic end of Allende in Chile . . ." (Theberge's analysis was echoed several months later by the Chilean Communist party, which said Allende's coalition had failed to solve "correctly" its problems, blasting the extreme Left for a "dogmatic approach which eventually turned into enemies 'whoever was not a proletarian.' ")[77]

Even such a conspicuous liberal commentator as Selden Rodman—writing in a distinctly liberal publication, the *New Leader* ("The Lessons of Chile," October 15, 1973)—wrote of "a pattern of legal deception . . . established throughout the country" as early as January 1971. "Once in power," Rodman wrote, "Allende and his intolerant followers did everything they could to antagonize the less radical elements of the population." As to outside manipulation of the coup: "Nothing, in fact, would have more surely influenced the Chilean military to refrain from acting than evidence of CIA meddling in its country's affairs."

From the Right, William F. Buckley—who had observed events in Chile first-hand during the Allende years—wrote that "it is inexplicable that those who in the mid-fifties welcomed the military revolt against Juan Perón, who was elected by a majority greatly exceeding that which voted for Salvador Allende, should now regret the overthrow of Allende. Perón had taken to demagogy, to authoritarian practices, to the persecution of journalistic enemies. He had gutted the Argentinian economy which has not yet returned to the pre-Perón rank among Latin American economies.

"Allende," Buckley continued, "spread a barmecidal banquet among his people, offering everybody everything. The laws of nature quickly overtook him, and everyone's cupboard was bared, and the country was taken along the road to Weimar, while Allende, between speeches, boozed and debauched, in his regal quarters, with Faroukian devotion—finally interrupted by his patient colonels."[78]

But these were voices in the wilderness; in the main, cant and bombast and withering abuse was hurled at those who defied the rapidly emerging mythology.

Wrote Henry Kissinger: "Within weeks of Allende's overthrow, his incompetence, corruption, and violation of democratic procedures—all widely-acknowledged while he was alive—disappeared from public comment . . ."[79]

The first of the canards—that Allende had been murdered—was quickly emblazoned in the world press.

Time magazine, in its September 24, 1973, cover story on the coup, said: "The military claimed that Allende had killed himself rather than surrender. Allende's supporters insisted that he had been murdered. In a sense, the manner of his death was irrelevant. Almost overnight, he became an instant martyr for leftists the world over—and a legendary specter that may well haunt Latin America for years." (The manner of his death was, in fact, an important element in keeping the specter alive.)

As to the second, the U.S. press also was quick to echo the charges. The *New York Times*, on September 15, gave three-column display on page one to a Belgrade dispatch—"Tito Hints That U.S. Is To Blame in Chile"—reporting on "an angry speech" made by President Tito. In it, the eighty-one-year-old Communist dictator "charged . . . that imperialist reaction—an apparent allusion to the United States—had instigated 'hireling generals' to overthrow and murder" Allende. The *Times* story cited no evidence offered by Tito to support his charges.

Two days later, James Nelson Goodsell of the *Christian Science Monitor* wrote from Buenos Aires that "in much of Latin America, the United States is being assigned the villain's role in the military rebellion . . ." In the next paragraph, Goodsell noted that "the Latin American reaction against the United States seems less based on fact than on deep-seated suspicion flavored by history." Disclaimer notwithstanding, the story was printed—also without benefit of a single source of supporting evidence to substantiate the "villain" charge.

Much of the Latin suspicion was fired, Goodsell wrote, by the "lightning weekend visit" to Washington of Ambassador Davis immediately before the coup. That Davis was one of several ambassadors summoned to Washington by Secretary of State-designate Henry Kissinger was not mentioned in the dispatch. (As remarked in chapter 8, following his designation as secretary of state on August 22, Kissinger drew up a list of outstanding career diplomats he wanted to interview for top jobs in the department, and Davis was among them. As a result of that meeting, Kissinger decided to appoint Davis director-general of the foreign service.)[80]

The press was not alone in the U.S. in firing speculation of an American role. In the Congress, Senator Kennedy issued a statement "in which he expressed hope that Secretary of State-designate Kissinger would testify in public before a Senate committee on the American role in Chile." Within a few weeks, Kennedy blasted a decision to lend Chile $24 million (at commercial rates) to replace wheat shipments from Eastern Europe and the Soviet Union that had been turned around on the high seas on the day of the coup. In what would become a foretaste of his unrelenting hostility to the Pinochet regime, Kennedy called that food loan "the latest symbol of our willingness to embrace a dictatorial regime which came to power in a bloody coup and which continues to conduct summary executions, to burn books, to imprison persons for political reasons, and to deny the right to emigrate."[81]

But it was more than merely a war of words that was unleashed against Chile. On September 13, demonstrators attacked the Chilean Consulate in Córdoba, Argentina—traditional stronghold of the far Left in that country—smashing windows and raising Chilean and red flags. In Madrid, two days later, demonstrators clashed with police in the downtown area and hurled Molotov cocktails into the offices of the Chilean airline, LAN-Chile.

Over the next three months, the Chilean government would document many more attacks on Chilean missions—four of them in France, three in Argentina, others in West Berlin, the Netherlands, Paraguay, Brazil, Venezuela, and Italy.[82]

Beyond the bullets, bombs, and propaganda barrages, the Communist world was making a quieter, more serious assessment of the lessons of Chile.

Rumanian President Nicolae Ceausescu, touring Latin America at the time, arrived quickly at the same conclusion as Fidel Castro: Chile, he said, demonstrates "that a democratic path to socialism is not possible."[83] Chile had thus sparked anew the long-smoldering debate in the Communist world about peaceful-vs.-violent means to power—a debate which had driven the Russians and Chinese apart, and one in which Castro had sided with the Chinese Maoists until reined in firmly by his Soviet masters. Ironically, Allende's election had vindicated Moscow in its dispute with Castro over the right means to achieve power in Latin America. Allende's overthrow now strengthened Castro's hand. (Moscow ultimately would accept Castro's arguments, and back to the hilt his armed adventures in Central America, one of which brought to power the Sandinistas in Nicaragua.)

Orthodox Communists—including Volodia Teitelboim, the ideologue of the Chilean party, writing from exile in Moscow—insisted on the validity of the "peaceful" path to revolution, but said the concept had been badly applied in Chile. Specifically, Teitelboim and several Soviet commentators, in their analyses, singled out the alienation of the regime from the middle class. But these analyses were coupled to warnings that revolutionaries must be prepared to resort to arms if counter-revolution threatened. Still later commentators—A.I. Sobolev, for example—criticized Allende's "pedantic" adherence to constitutionality, and some said Allende should have staged a preemptive coup to liquidate his enemies. On May 1, 1974, following a meeting of leftist groups in Rome and Paris, a declaration was issued saying that the biggest failing of the Allende regime had been its inability "to induce the majority of the population to support it." The declaration ducked the question of means to employ in the future, saying "the character which the struggle to overthrow the dictatorship will assume in the end cannot be defined at this stage."

In the Soviet view, the main challenge was to construct a "United Antifascist Front" made up not only of Popular Unity parties, but also of all "forces advocating a restoration of democratic processes within the country." That front should seek to recruit the Chilean Catholic church as well as the "entire" Christian Democratic party, and "the patriotic section of the armed forces."[84]

The left wing of the Christian Democratic party (PDC)—not unexpectedly—ultimately took the bait. In July of 1975, two former presidents of the PDC joined two former presidents of Allende's Socialist party and a former president of the atomized Radical party in signing a declaration of intent to work together for restoration of a "just and socialist democracy in Chile." The signers were perennial leftists Bernardo Leighton and Renán Fuentealba for the PDC (although both had been expelled from the party); Aniceto Rodríguez and Clodomiro Almeyda for the Socialists, and Anselmo Sule for the Radicals. They were among fifteen former political leaders attending a symposium in Caracas, Venezuela, sponsored by a West German-funded Social

Democratic foundation. Orlando Letelier—released from imprisonment thanks in large measure to the quiet intervention of Henry Kissinger[85]—said "this can be an important first step toward restoration of democracy in Chile." The same news dispatch noted that "among those known to be pressuring for a reconciliation of the Christian Democrats and the parties that backed Allende are the Catholic Church hierarchy in Chile and Cuban Prime Minister Fidel Castro." Although the Communists were not invited to the Caracas conference, the agenda and the strategy devised there dovetailed perfectly with their own prescriptions.[86]

(In agreeing to close ranks with other "non-fascists," the Caracas conference chose to overlook the explicit goals for government of their putative partners. On October 11, 1973, the Chilean Communist party issued an appeal: "The people will return to power again, and naturally it will not be forced to restore all previous institutions . . . A number of institutions in which many people sincerely believed proved now to be rotten. Who would conceive of supporting the existing juridical system or parliament which buried itself through its participation in the antigovernmental conspiracy?" By May 1, 1974, the parties of the hard Left were even more explicit in a "Popular Unity Declaration": "Our objective is not the simple restoration of the democratic regime which fell on September 11, nor the mechanical repetition of the experience of the peoples' government. The old structure showed that it was incapable of defending itself successfully against fascist aggressors and of adequately generalizing the will of the vast majority of the country which demanded profound social changes. A new state must therefore emerge from the antifascist struggle. . . .")

For the Communists, drawing the right lessons from the Chilean experience was more than simply an autopsy to determine the cause of death. The Communist movement around the world faced unusual opportunities in the months following the fall of Allende—and scored impressive gains—in a number of places. In March of 1974, Portugal's long-standing right-wing dictatorship was toppled and, a month later, Communists were in the provisional government. By the end of the year, they were the dominant force (although ultimately dislodged). In Greece, following the overthrow of the military regime in 1974, Communists were allowed to operate legally for the first time in twenty-seven years; the first time, in fact, since, in the immediate aftermath of World War II, they had attempted, with Soviet backing, to seize power through force of arms. In France's general elections that May, the Socialist-Communist alliance achieved the greatest success the Left had experienced in that country since 1946, falling only 400,000 votes (out of 26.3 million cast) short of capturing the government. In Italy, the

Communist party—the country's second biggest—offered to ease the political instability (which it had, in large measure, fostered) by sharing power with the Christian Democrats, pledging to work within the framework of the Common Market and NATO. In Britain, the Conservative government fell and was replaced in March by a weak Labour government; in the midst of the economic and political crisis, Communist influence increased when it gained a position on the General Council of the powerful Trades Union Congress.[87] In Spain, Franco fell ill in the summer of 1974, and the Communists moved aggressively to build alliances, dangling offers of working within a broad political coalition.[88]

The Chilean experience echoed throughout all of these maneuverings. Communist strategists saw that their best hope of success in each resided in stilling anxieties of potential partners about their capacity to "cooperate" in coalition governments. In January, four months after Allende fell, Western European Communist leaders met in Brussels and reaffirmed the need of Communists to forge alliances with democratic and progressive forces.[89]

In July of 1974, *Latinskaia Amerika*, the major Soviet journal on Latin America, and the Soviet-front World Labor Movement (WLM), cosponsored a symposium to evaluate events in Chile. A.A. Galkin, of the WLM, related developments in Europe to the efforts of the Right to frighten people with the excesses of the extreme Left. "In light of this," he said, "the danger is evident of looking on the Chilean experience as a denial of the possibility of the peaceful path of solving basic social problems." (Six years later, after the Sandinistas shot their way to power in Nicaragua, Soviet analysts were singing a different tune.)[90]

But, in all of these analyses based on the Chilean experience—designed mainly to coach comrades in other countries, particularly in the then-effervescent European countries, how to take better advantage of their opportunities—there was no suggestion that Allende was brought down by external forces. Rather, the analyses concentrated on x-raying the internal weaknesses and contradictions that had brought about his collapse.

WASHINGTON: A HOUSE DIVIDED

On September 13, the White House said flatly that "the president had no advance knowledge of any specific plan for a coup."

"Our embassy," White House spokesman Gerald L. Warren said, "had instructions in the event that any elements in Chile came to them with any plans for an uprising not to have anything to do with them. And these instructions were followed carefully."

State Department spokesman Paul J. Hare said there had been numerous rumors of a military revolt throughout the year. In the days before the actual coup, he said, the embassy in Santiago relayed word that an uprising would occur on September 8. When none happened, the embassy said it had learned of a coup planned for September 18. Then, around midnight of September 10, the embassy "did receive reports that September 11 was to be the date, and this," Hare added, "turned out to be correct."

"There was absolutely no way of knowing beforehand," Hare said, "that [on] any of these dates, including the September 11 date, a coup attempt would be made." In the same statement, Hare expressed official U.S. "regret over the loss of life in Chile, particularly of the Chief of State, President Allende."[91]

On September 14, a representative of the junta told U.S. Ambassador Nathaniel Davis that the military commanders had "deliberately" kept the United States in the dark about their revolt plans so as to prevent any possibility of U.S. involvement. Rumors of the coup reaching the embassy—including the one which proved to be right—came from lower-level officers not directly involved in the plotting. Pinochet said that not only were no foreigners brought in on the coup plotting, "not even my wife knew what I was going to do."[92]

> In 1969, individuals in State were allied with some in ISA [the Pentagon's International Security Agency] in an almost messianic mission of social reform in Latin American countries. Essentially, this meant removing the military from positions of authority, with the resultant ascendancy of left-wing forces. Contacts with the military were minimized, and Defense was substantially removed from any role in the formulation of U.S. policy. It was as if there were no national security interests south of the border.
> —Richard A. Ware, then number two man in ISA[93]

Although he did not know it then, Richard Nixon had only eleven months left in his own presidency when Salvador Allende fell. Neither Nixon nor his new secretary of state had any illusions about Allende, about the need to support the new military regime. But Nixon was then fighting a rear-guard action to save his presidency as the Watergate crisis deepened. Kissinger was consumed by far more massive foreign policy concerns: the collapse of the Vietnam peace process in the ruins of North Vietnamese treachery; new fighting in the Middle East, followed by enervating shuttle diplomacy; the modern world's first energy crisis; deteriorating relations with the Soviet Union; improving relations with Red China. In those crucial first days there was yet another: preoccupation with his Senate confirmation hearings as secretary of state.

Chile thus became easy prey in Washington for the messiahs of social reform.

On the morning after the coup, General Pinochet contacted the head of the U.S. Military Assistance Advisory Group in Santiago. In his report to President Nixon on the secret meeting, Kissinger said Pinochet stressed that "he and his colleagues had not even hinted to us beforehand of their planned action and said he thought it had been better that way." Kissinger added that the junta's fundamental desire was to restore the traditional ties of friendship with the United States. Chile needed help with food and one year's debt relief. The report concluded:

> Pinochet understands and is relaxed about the matter of recognition. He volunteered that obviously the U.S. should not be the first to announce its intention to continue relations with the new Chilean Government. He also recognized the advisability of avoiding too much public identification with us for the moment.[94]

Deep beneath the White House, in a room about the size of a two-car garage, the Washington Special Action Group (WSAG) met on the morning of September 12 to assess the coup and the U.S. reaction to it. The biggest substantive issue: what to do about the American flotilla then in Chilean waters for the Unitas exercises? Kissinger, chairing the meeting, was firm: "Turn them around." Very expensive, loss of face, everyone would understand, came the remonstrances. Impatiently, and "with a slightly metallic edge to his voice," he repeated the order. Kissinger then peppered the group with a series of questions on economic matters, for which no one had an answer (and which, one participant confessed, "were beyond my comprehension"). Kissinger then excused himself briefly, went upstairs to the Oval Office to consult with Nixon, and returned with a series of decisions.

Kissinger recalls: "The consensus of the WSAG undoubtedly was relief at Allende's overthrow (though not his death). We were conscious of the danger that we might be blamed for both. In the post-Vietnam, Watergate atmosphere, the United States had to bend over backward to avoid charges of American complicity in an event that everyone in the room considered in our national interest." Against that backdrop, it was decided to "mute" the issue of U.S. recognition of the new government; wait, in other words, until Latin American and European governments had moved. Wrote Kissinger: "Such a course, I argued—with wild optimism—would 'defuse any charge of our implication which would not only be damaging to us but more importantly to the new Chilean government.' " Ambassador Davis was instructed discreetly to notify the junta through an intermediary that "our basic disposition was favorable."

Two other important decisions emerged from the meeting. The first was to anticipate Chile's economic aid requests and propose suitable responses. The second, to defend against expected charges of complicity in the coup, to prepare a list of all CIA activities in Chile over the preceding three years. "The list," Kissinger wrote, "would enable us to rebut inaccurate charges and to assure ourselves there had not been any unauthorized action that might be used to implicate the United States. The CIA turned up no such event. This did not, however, prevent the charges."[95]

It was September 24 before the United States would formally recognize the new government. By then, twenty-two other countries had already done so, including Austria, Denmark, France, Switzerland, the United Kingdom, and democratic Venezuela—as well as the military governments of Brazil and Uruguay. Even so, Ambassador Davis could not disguise his queasiness. Although he had by then been notified of his new assignment, the man who had been so averse to clandestine aid to those opposing Allende was now privately urging clandestine support for "democratic parties . . . particularly to the Christian Democrats." The ambassador also managed to choke off a "back-channel" between top Chilean businessmen close to the junta and American counterparts with White House links. "For a few days," Davis wrote, "it looked as if the Chileans would be able to use this link to short-circuit the embassy, the Department of State, and the U.S. policy process in their ongoing effort to achieve an unrestrained and unconditional U.S. embrace."[96]

On September 14, the WSAG met again—and had the answers to some sixty economic questions Kissinger had raised. Kissinger resisted pressures to use the coup as "a bargaining point" to win concessions on the expropriation and debt issues. Another issue would distract their attention: Plan Centaur.

Arriving in Mexico City from Santiago, Mrs. Allende was the house guest of the former Chilean ambassador who, in late July, had received the unannounced visit of a black American, described as about thirty-five and slim, who claimed to be a defector from the CIA. The man told the diplomat he was a code expert and had with him secret documents and microfilms which only he could decipher and which detailed a CIA program to overthrow the Allende government. The ambassador bought the story. By September, the CIA had learned the true identity of the "defector": an American parole violator with a criminal history. He had since flown to Cuba using a false Chilean passport supplied by the ex-ambassador. Nonetheless, the ex-diplomat told Mrs. Allende about "Plan Centaur," and shortly afterwards, in an interview with the British news agency *Reuters*, she recounted the story. The story was then splattered around the world.[97]

The United States "muted" its behavior toward the new regime in other ways.

On September 20, the WSAG "sidestepped" a Chilean request for one thousand helmets and two thousand flares for night fighting. Even more incredibly—and despite an earlier determination to honor military agreements reached with the Allende government—the administration delayed for several weeks the delivery to Chile of three destroyers, which, as Kissinger notes, had been "promised to Allende!" (Emphasis in original.) Reflecting on these and other pending issues between the two countries, Kissinger added:

> All of these maneuvers obscured the fundamental problem: How was the United States to reconcile its geopolitical interests and its concern for human rights? It would be idle to deny that we felt a sense of relief at Allende's collapse. The new Chilean government, whatever its faults, would not assault our interests in every international forum as its predecessor had done. It would not be a haven for terrorists from all over the world threatening to solidify totalitarianism in Chile and to subvert neighboring Western Hemisphere governments. We could not convince ourselves that undermining the new government would serve either the cause of human rights or our own security. Yet there was no blinking the fact, either, that the very opposition parties and newspapers that we had attempted to keep alive under Allende were suppressed by the *junta*. The imposition of an authoritarian regime in a country with the longstanding democratic tradition of Chile was a special pity—but the circumstances that brought it about were extraordinary, too.

Philosophizing notwithstanding, "the issue arose in America at the worst possible time ... In the domestic anguish through which we went, it was impossible even to pose such questions. We were being driven much further on a course of isolating Chile than we thought wise ..."[98]

There were a few small gestures in those first days. On October 11, Kissinger agreed to include Chilean Foreign Minister Ismael Huerta in a luncheon given for Latin foreign ministers in New York for the opening of the UN session. Kissinger found "a naval officer of great courtesy but no experience in diplomacy ... genuinely baffled on how to deal with this strange country whose press and Congress were increasingly antagonistic to a friendly government in Santiago while they had largely ignored, or been mildly sympathetic to, a Marxist predecessor explicitly whipping up anti-American radicalism throughout the Western Hemisphere. He was convinced that the Chilean military had saved Chile from a totalitarian regime and the United States from an enemy—and he was right in both judgments. When I warned that Chile would pay a heavy price in its international image if it resorted to brutal repression, he replied that his government's first priority was to control the 'internal situation.' I stressed that we considered the new government basically in our interest but that I would feel free to call to his attention actions by the *junta* that might weaken its international standing—a delicate way of raising the human rights issue."[99]

Kissinger did not mention it, but there was one other important way in which the new regime differed from the old: drugs. The junta moved immediately to crush illicit drug trade between Chile and the United States. According to one account, during the last year of the Allende regime, $309,048,000 worth of cocaine from Chilean laboratories was seized by U.S. authorities. Within seven days of the coup, the new government agreed to a U.S. request to extradite known Chilean smugglers to American authorities. Chilean authorities reported that Popular Unity parties had been receiving monthly payoffs of $30,000 from international drug operatives.[100] Little notice of this was taken in either the U.S. press or official Washington; Ambassador Davis devoted two sentences to the matter: "After the coup a *junta* spokesman alleged that the Mafia had paid Allende's police authorities $30,000 a month. It should be added, of course, that not everything the *junta* spokesman asserted was true."[101]

The first foreign aid to reach Chile came not from the United States, but from the Inter-American Development Bank. On September 18, the bank announced approval of a $68 million credit for the Antuco hydroelectric project. Left-wing commentators around the world seized on this event to "prove" that there had been an economic blockade of Chile, but that it was now being rapidly "dismantled." The problem with that jejune theory—advanced, among others, by Elizabeth Farnsworth in *Foreign Policy* magazine—is that it ignores altogether the ponderous decision-making procedures of such international institutions. As pointed out in chapter 7, that project, which had been working its way through the IDB since November 24, 1972, had not been approved by an IDB project committee until July 26, 1973, and would not actually win final IDB approval until April 25, 1974.[102]

*   *   *

On September 26, the U.S. Agriculture Department granted Chile a $24 million credit to buy 4.4 million bushels of U.S. wheat, replacing Soviet and Eastern European shipments turned around on the high seas the day of the coup. In November, the Commodity Credit Corporation followed up with a $28 million loan to buy feed corn. On December 12, a Chilean economic delegation arrived in Washington for talks on the $124 million debt past-due U.S. creditors (for the period November 1971, when Allende unilaterally suspended payments, through December 1972). Nine days later, agreement was announced in accord with a creditors' nation agreement of April 1972. Negotiations also were opened on compensation for nationalized American companies.[103]

In January 1974, Chile reached agreement with the watchdog International Monetary Fund—the *bête noire* not only of the Allende regime, which refused to deal with it, but of radical regimes everywhere. Under that agreement, Chile pledged to maintain strict financial and monetary policies. As a result of that agreement and the $95 million standby credit that went with it, Chile reached accord the following month with the Club of Paris nations for rescheduling of the $1 billion 1973 and 1974 debt, improving on the 5 percent cash offer proposed by the Allende government during the July talks.[104]

Noting these developments, a business newspaper in New York, the *Journal of Commerce*, said, "bankers and businessmen here are encouraged by the economic policy and actions of the ruling military *Junta . . .* Bankers here believe Chile once again will be a good market for foreign capital and private investment . . ."[105] It was in that setting that private banks in Europe and the United States announced the reopening of loan facilities for Chile. In November, Manufacturers Hanover Trust granted the first major loan, $24 million, to the Banco de Chile.

In January of 1974, Chile agreed to pay $8.1 million in past debts to the World Bank. In return, the bank, in February, approved a $5.25 million loan for preinvestment studies (and, in what amounted to a bookkeeping operation, $8.3 million for power and highway projects). Since this was the bank's first new loan to Chile since the pre-Allende years, this too became part of the "economic blockade/dismantling" conspiracy theory. Except: the loan had reached the board of directors one week before Allende's fall, and as the bank's 1974 White Paper reflected (see chapter 7), "staff continued to work on the assumption that both the loan amendments and the Technical Assistance project would eventually be approved."

But the loan that attracted the greatest fire was $22 million to help restore Chile's shattered agriculture. An international team which visited Chile late in 1973 concluded that agriculture and energy were Chile's two most pressing aid priorities. On the assumption that if money for agriculture were to help, it would have to be in hand in Chile in time for the 1974 growing season, the IDB's staff at mid-March described the loan application as "an emergency situation . . . requiring prompt action." Several countries protested that the loan was being considered too rapidly; the United States did not support the loan, but said it did not oppose it, either. Approval was announced on March 30, as the bank's directors gathered for the annual meeting, this time in Santiago. (Announcing loans in host countries is a bank tradition.)

Wrote Farnsworth: "The IMF and the Inter-American Committee on the Alliance for Progress, recognizing that a massive rescue operation is necessary to keep the Chilean economy afloat—and the *Junta* in power—have called on the international financial community to provide a mini-Marshall Plan for Chile. In effect, the loans granted since the coup represent phase two of the U.S. counterinsurgency program in Chile—they prop up a brutal dictatorship which rules through terror but promises good investment opportunities for American businesses. Questions of creditworthiness are not even raised . . ."[106]

But the U.S. noose around Chile's neck had begun to tighten even before the shooting stopped. Having already denounced even food credits for Chile, Senator Teddy Kennedy, on October 2, 1973, proposed a "sense-of-Congress" amendment to the Foreign Assistance Act calling on the president to cut off aid, other than humanitarian assistance, "until he finds that the government of Chile is protecting the human rights of all individuals, Chilean and foreign—provided in the Universal Declaration of Human Rights." As finally approved in December 1973, that provision did not appear, but Kennedy was back again in 1974. In December of that year, both houses voted to end all American military aid to Chile "unless the President reports to Congress that Chile is making fundamental improvements in the observance of human rights." That vote came despite testimony by a three-man panel of scholars who made an eleven-day visit to Chile in July, interviewing more than seventy-five persons across "a broad political cross-section," including government officials, religious leaders, students, teachers, and lawyers. The panel, headed by Dr. Ernest Lefever, a foreign policy specialist at the prestigious Brookings Institution, reported that the Chilean government, "in attempting to clear away the devastation of the Allende period . . . has made some mistakes, and has not been as diligent as it might have been in preventing the abuse of suspects, including torture and summary executions, by overzealous soldiers." But, he said, they found no "serious abuse" of prisoners in Chile since "last April."[107] Their words were lost in a whirlwind of condemnation of Chile. By

1976, all U.S. aid to Chile was ended, a step the United States had never taken against the Marxist-Leninist, Salvador Allende.

> Mike Wallace: And all of this done in the name of what? In the name of keeping Chile from going the way of Castro's Cuba, no?
>
> Former U.S. Ambassador Edward M. Korry: That's right. The specific line was to prevent Chile from becoming a second Soviet bridgehead in the Hemisphere.

Korry had just finished telling the 25 million-or-so persons tuned into CBS's "60 Minutes" of the massive—and illegal—efforts of the Kennedy and Johnson administrations to keep Salvador Allende from reaching power.[108] Now, eight years later, the brother of the president who ordered those activities was leading the fight against those who had removed Salvador Allende from power.

Not that he was alone. Senator J. William Fulbright (D-Ark.), the powerful and very liberal chairman of the Senate Foreign Relations Committee, told the Senate he was impressed with the "unprecedented" unanimity of the opposition to the coup. He and others in Congress reported receiving thousands of telegrams, letters, and phone calls from universities and church groups, expressing concern for those imprisoned in Chile; and strong suspicions of U.S. involvement. Those protests fell on fertile ground in a Congress not only dominated by liberals, but at the moment caught up in the euphoria of Watergate-inspired investigations. Chile would become the target of numerous congressional investigations and hearings, culminating in the long (and sensationalized) Church Committee hearings of 1975–1976. (Those hearings and related questions dealing with U.S. involvement in the overthrow of Allende are dealt with in the Appendix.)

More often than not, those hearings were, by far, more sound and fury than significance. For some, such facts as were developed were not allowed to stand in the way of theory. One such was the ultraliberal congressman Michael J. Harrington (D-Mass.).

A few days before he left Chile, Ambassador Nathaniel Davis had a visitor from Washington. It was Congressman Harrington, who later complained publicly that the only opportunity he had to talk with Davis was in the presence of "three or four Chilean generals." (Those three or four generals were three of the four members of the Chilean junta.)[109]

His three-day visit ended, Harrington told the *New York Times* that he went with a "bias" and that his visit had reinforced that bias. He said he was convinced that U.S. economic policies of "deprivation" had set in motion a string of events that led to Allende's overthrow.[110] A few months later, Harrington began to pressure Chairman Lucien Nedzi (D-Mich.) of the House Armed Forces CIA subcommittee for a detailed review of CIA operations in Chile. Nedzi countered that he and his committee had been thoroughly briefed, but since Harrington was not a member of the committee, Nedzi declined to give him details. In the face of Harrington's persistence, Nedzi agreed to call a new, closed-door hearing on April 22, 1974. Special security was ordered since CIA Director William Colby planned to reveal all the details of CIA involvement in Chile. The transcript of that hearing, made by a congressional court reporter, was stored (as was customary) at a vault in CIA headquarters in Langley, just outside of Washington. In June, Harrington—"a vocal, hostile critic" of the CIA, in the phrase of the usually restrained David Phillips—demanded to review the transcript. Believing the matter was on hold until Monday morning, Phillips went home for the weekend, only to learn that Harrington had finagled a copy of the transcript late Saturday. In sending the transcript to Harrington, the House committee took "extreme precautions" such as Phillips had never seen before: Harrington was required to sign a statement in which he acknowledged his obligation to hold the contents closely.

Harrington, who reviewed the transcript twice, later wrote a letter summarizing its contents to Rep. Thomas E. Morgan, chairman of the House Foreign Affairs Committee. That letter leaked simultaneously to the *Washington Post* and the *New York Times*, on September 8, 1974. In both accounts, Colby was quoted as saying the "goal of the clandestine CIA activities . . . was to 'destabilize' the Marxist Government of President Allende."

Colby insisted he had said no such thing. So did Phillips, who was there. But Phillips did not trust to memory alone—as Harrington insisted on doing. Phillips reviewed the transcript a dozen times. There was no such thing as "destabilization" in it. Harry Schlaudeman, then deputy assistant secretary of state, remembered hearing the term for the first time in his life when Harrington himself used it repeatedly in badgering questioning of Schlaudeman on June 12, three months before the leaks.

In the short term, Colby was riled because the leaks came in the middle of a Soviet-sponsored worldwide propaganda campaign, Solidarity With Chile Week.[111] In the longer term, Colby became wrongly associated with a term he had not used and which would come to epitomize what the CIA had not, in fact, done: orchestrate the overthrow of Salvador Allende in Chile. But Colby understood all too well: catchy terms are the stuff of which Big Lies are made.

*   *   *

Former Ambassador Edward Korry had all but been run out of Santiago in 1971 by the liberal media-foreign policy axis in Washington, ostensibly because, as a cold warrior, he could not communicate with Marxist Allende. If communications compatibility was on the mind of anyone in the foreign policy establishment in the years of military rule in Chile, it would rarely reflect in the choice of ambassador to represent the United States in Santiago. On November 1, 1973, the liberal Nathaniel Davis left Santiago. He was replaced by another career foreign service officer who, on the record at least, was even more liberal than he: David H. Popper. As the experienced Chile watcher Robert Moss observed, Popper's past— "and the fuss that was made about it at the time of his appointment—did not exactly help him to find his feet on the rather Manichean terrain of present-day Chile." Although, Moss went on to remark, Popper's "relations with the *Junta* are notoriously frigid," there were no calls in the *Washington Post* or *New York Times* for his removal.[112]

Gerald Ford was rounding out his first month in the White House when the story broke. He walked right into the trap. Attempting to justify the CIA action, he instead seemed to be confirming the worst-scenario allegations that the CIA had engineered Allende's ouster. Crowed one academic critic: "Ford's defense of the CIA dirty tricks against a democratically elected government in Chile indicates that far from learning from and rejecting his predecessor's Watergate ways he proposes to extend the practices into the international arena."[113] Those "revelations," now seemingly confirmed by a bewildered new president, set in motion a frenzy of media, academic, and congressional inquisitions—one of which (the Church hearings) would leave the CIA severely wounded, all of which would lay waste the hope of a reasoned, reasonable relationship between the United States and the even more bewildered, but very determined, new rulers of Chile.

THE NEW PORTALIANS

Despite the excesses of the Chilean generals ... I still suspect that their concept of the ideal leader is not Mussolini or Franco but de Gaulle. They have all read the memoirs of de Gaulle, they know what he did for France in the 1950s, and they admire him.

MIT Professor Paul Rosenstein-Rodan, in the year following the coup[114]

The judgment was correct—but incomplete. Chile's new rulers looked more, far more, to their own past than abroad for inspiration.

The source was Diego Portales Palazuelos. To know Diego Portales, to know his ideas and their impact on Chilean history, is to possess the most important single key to understanding the rationale for what would follow in Chile. Knowing these things, it becomes incomprehensible, in fact, that any inside or outside Chile should profess surprise at what the generals did or why they did it.

> *In accord with the Portalian inspiration which guides it, the Government of the Armed Forces and of Order* will exercise with energy the principle of authority, punishing drastically any outbreak of indiscipline or anarchy.*
>
> Article 3, "Declaration of Principles of the Government of Chile," March 11, 1974

Six months would go by before the new government would enunciate in a systematic and comprehensive fashion its goals and principles. But the example of Portales was already vivid in the mind of Augusto Pinochet when, one month to the day after the revolution, he delivered his first State of the Union report to the country. He spoke from the Great Hall of Santiago's tallest office building, now the seat of government and renamed by the new regents the Diego Portales Building. That speech reverberates with the principles Portales had preached and practiced, nearly a century and-a-half before, to rescue Chile from anarchy, to lay the foundations of a strong and flourishing society.[115]

Chile was, in 1830 as in 1973, a shambles. In the twenty years since declaring its independence from Spain on September 18, 1810, the country had been the scene of endless infighting, reconquest by the Spaniards, and four years of increasingly autocratic rule by its liberator, Bernardo O'Higgins, before he, too, was driven into exile. In the five years leading up to 1830, there had been ten governments, and a bloody civil war; in the south, the three Pincheira brothers and their marauders looted, murdered and plundered at will. Begging and lawlessness were rife on the streets of the cities. In 1828, a deputy rose in Congress to say that in just one year, there had been eight hundred murders on the streets of Santiago, then a city of 48,000. An armed escort was needed to traverse many areas on the outskirts of the capital.[116]

It was into this shambles that Diego Portales arrived, drawn not by ambition but by circumstance, declining the ultimate prize, the presidency, when it was offered to him, leaving on Chile an imprint very likely without equal down to modern times. Born in Santiago on June 15, 1793, of a monied family, Portales was trained as an assayer of metals (*la docimasia*), never in the art of government or statecraft. To one

---

* "Forces of Order" is the name frequently given Carabineros.

Chilean historian, that "lack" was part of Portales's strength: ". . . it was precisely the political theoreticians who had brought the country so much trouble. Juan Egaña with his Moralist Constitution of 1823, José Miguel Infante with his federal organization of 1826, had brought nothing but anarchy . . . those who followed, Pinto and Mora, also theoreticians, had done no better. . . ."

It was business, and specifically doing business with the government, that pushed Portales into politics in the first place. His company had a state-franchised monopoly for tobacco trading. In 1824, the company became embroiled in a dispute with the government over repayment of British loans granted for the trade in tobacco. Ultimately, those talks would become politicized, leading Portales to organize a small—but influential—political group of his own, and to launch a satirical newspaper called *El Hambriento* (*The Hungry One*). Following the 1829 revolution, in which he played an important role, Portales was tapped by the new government, April 7, 1830, to become minister both of foreign relations and of war and the navy. He brought to those tasks such energy that he became the true dynamo and guiding force of the government, given extraordinary powers by Congress to carry out his program.

The task Portales faced was not unlike the one the revolutionaries of 1973 believed they faced: to give the state an organization which would enable it to guarantee peace and work. "Portales understood this," historian Galdames wrote, "and plunged wholeheartedly into the endeavor. Most urgent, as he saw it, was to bring calm to the country and stability to public administration. To do that, it was necessary to put an end to the revolutionary spirit and deal with the disfigurers [*transformadores*] of order as implacable enemies of all progress."

Portales took aim first at the military caudillos whose jockeying for power over the preceding two decades had brought such bloodshed and strife to the country, firing every officer who declined to swear loyalty to the new government. (Pinochet and his associates performed similar surgery: firing the politicians, of Left and Right, and dismantling the political system which, in their view, had brought similar bloodshed and strife to the modern Chilean nation.) Next, Portales moved to create a professional civil guard—forerunner of Chile's Corps of Carabineros—and bring professionalism to the armed forces as well, creating the Military Academy. Inevitably, those moves generated subversive plots. Portales "repressed them with an iron hand."

But Portales's greatest legacy, broadly speaking, was the sense of order, discipline and morality that he brought to government and the citizenry at large. Chile would not again know serious political upheaval for sixty years, sixty years which saw it grow into one of the most prosperous and stable states in the world.

In a more formal sense, his great legacy was the constitution of 1833, the document which would remain as the legal framework of Chile for ninety-two years. The constitution was the work of a Constituent Assembly, which worked two years on drafting it; but it was, in large measure, the expression of Portales's ideas. The new constitution created a regime of "force and authority": a strong president, subject to a minimum of control. Municipal and congressional elections were under his control and that of his appointees, mayors, and provincial governors. The president appointed not only all judges, but all public employees. As commander-in-chief of the armed forces, he had supreme command of them, as well as of the police forces. What emerged was the "autocratic" or "Portalian Republic." Nor did these ideas spring suddenly from the mind of Portales; they had found expression a dozen years earlier in terms that would many years later find powerful echo in Pinochet's own public statements.[117] (Not unexpectedly, either, the revolutionaries of 1973 quickly realized that Chile's problems were deep and organic, and curing them would require a new Portalian constitution. By September 24, 1973, a committee was already at work laying the groundwork for drafting a new constitution; the Supreme Decree #1,064 of November 12 formalized their work, declaring the "need to reconstitute, renew, and perfect the fundamental institutional system of the Republic for the full attainment of the goals set forth in the act of Constitution of the Government *Junta*.")

The constitution of 1833 survived intact and completely unchanged until 1870. That year, during the era of the "Liberal Republic" (1861–1891), Congress hotly debated a complete overhaul of the document but finally enacted a single amendment limiting the president to one, five-year term. The great overhaul of the document occurred in the aftermath of the calamitous civil war of 1891 against the president Allende most admired, José Manuel Balmaceda (1886–1891). (Curiously, in that civilian-inspired and directed revolution, the last significantly bloody one Chile would experience until 1973, the navy backed the forces fighting to retain the Portalian system while the army supported the populist president.) At that time, a vindictive Congress amended the constitution to gut the presidency of its powers, erecting in place of the presidential system a sterile and fractious parliamentary arrangement. It lasted until the 1925 half-hearted (and, because it was so enfeebled, self-destructive) attempt to restore the former presidential system. (From 1891 until 1925, politics was so fragmented that there were no fewer than 121 changes of Cabinet, involving 530 Cabinet ministers, reeling and spinning from one crisis to the final one, the collapse of democracy in 1925.)[118]

The parallels between pre-Portalian and pre-Pinochet Chile are reflected in these lines written by historian Galdames (*before* the 1973 revolution, it should be noted, for those quick to impute base motives to ideas inhospitable to their own):

> Portales's system of government relied on a realistic concept of politics, distant from the utopia of those who drafted the plan for a democratic republic which, in the short term, would raise the cultural level and lead to the enjoyment of widespread economic well-being . . . The liberalism of the time dreamed of the implanting of social reforms to put the entire population of the country in tune with democratic institutions. A vain illusion. By contrast, Portales, a cool observer of the social panorama of Chile, without failing to acknowledge the advantages of democratic values, insisted that first need come an institutional adjustment, characterized by a strong, centralized government, distant from partisan influences. . . .
>
> What has been classified as the Portalian concept of the State should be evaluated in the context of the time in which it was applied. Anarchy had found bloody expression in the revolution of 1829 and threatened to plunge the fledgling republic into a theater of new trials. The genius of Portales consisted of interpreting with realism the historic moment of his country and then demonstrating the will to change the direction of events. Order had to be imposed on chaos, even at the expense of all manner of sacrifices and misapprehensions. . . .[119]

Misapprehensions there were, more would come, recalling Oscar Wilde's observation that the worst tyranny of all is to be misunderstood, a pain the Portalian Pinochet would know only too well. But praise there was, too. On September 24, 1832, Congress passed a resolution on the occasion of Portales's first departure from government: "Don Diego Portales," it read, "took up his duties in the most anguished moment for the country, when the rule of law had been destroyed and the flame of civil war lit, when anarchy and disorder threatened the nation with political ruin, displaying in those lamentable circumstances an extraordinary zeal, vigor and patriotism; he managed, with the wisdom of his counsel and correctness of the measures which he proposed, to reestablish gloriously public tranquility, order and respect for national institutions. . . ."[120]

In one important area, Portales was, no doubt, at odds with the thinking of those around Pinochet—at least initially in their government—and that was in his view of the United States. Learning of the new Monroe Doctrine proclaimed by President James Monroe, Portales wrote: "Careful not to escape from one domination to fall under another! One must be skeptical of these gentlemen who very nicely approve of our champions of liberation, without having helped us in the slightest. . . ."[121]

Honest and efficient public administration was another legacy of the

Portalian era—just as Pinochet and his associates made it a hallmark of their own administration. Portales demanded not only integrity, but public accountability, requiring that every public servant respond in writing to any criticism, "under pain of dismissal."

Even in death, Portales impacted on the fate of his country. In 1836, the Bolivian president, Andrés Santa Cruz, seizing on internal divisions in Peru, invaded that country and formed an alliance with forces there with the clear intention of seizing Chile as well. Though Chile's forces were greatly outnumbered and though it faced armies more recently blooded in war, Portales viewed the threat as too dangerous to be evaded. Congress quickly acceded to his request for a declaration of war. He was deeply involved in war preparations when, on June 6, 1837, he was kidnapped by mutinous troops and executed in cold blood. His death, viewed first as a national calamity, served to galvanize support for the war, and on January 20, 1839, at the battle of Yungay, Chilean forces decisively defeated the Confederation. Decisively, except that, down to modern times, Chile has faced a number of threats from its neighbors.[122]

This lengthy parenthesis was necessary because "Portalian inspiration" were not mere words or hollow slogans for Pinochet and his associates. Portales incarnated for them the hope and promise which Chile had lost, and which they intended to restore. Pinochet proclaimed:

> For the first time in this century, Chile has an authentically-national government ... A national government is the counterpoint to government of parties or of classes, such as have dominated in our country virtually since 1891. For such governments, national objectives do not exist, giving way to hazy "Programs of Government," generally of paltry achievements and weighted down with foreign ideological dogmas, when not actually claiming to speak for one sector of the citizenry arrayed against the rest of Chileans. ...
>
> Chile was in the past a great nation, precisely when it consolidated its political independence; and, under the inspiring seal of the Portalian Republic, it had governments of true national sense and objectives, directed by men with a deep spirit of public service. And its [Chile's] decadence coincided with the advent of partisan or demagogic governments, in which the country was criminally divided in the sterile and petty struggle for private advantage. ...

This reverence for the principles and the achievements of the Portalian Republic was at the essence of Pinochet's vision of Chile, leading inevitably to the conclusion:

The political and party recess will, then, have to be prolonged for many years more, and could only be responsibly lifted when a new generation of Chileans, formed with healthy civic and patriotic habits and inspired in an authentic national sense, are able to assume the direction of public life. Those who try to break this recess in any way at all will collide with our implacable decision not to permit it. . . .[123]

Another man had said almost exactly the same thing before: Diego Portales, in 1822 (see endnote 117).

There was another powerful native strain influencing the behavior of the generals and admirals who made the 1973 revolution: their own military traditions, and, in a larger framework, the traditions of the military in Latin America.

Unlike the revolution in the United States, the first great revolutions of Latin America owed their origins far more to external than to internal events: specifically, the American Revolution (1776), the French Revolution (1789) and, most importantly, Napoleon's seizure of the Spanish throne (1808). This latter event called into issue the legitimacy of the colonial regimes in the Americas and gave immediate impetus to revolutionary movements. Thus, from the beginning, those movements were more military in character and leadership than civilian, conferring a legitimacy on the military in national affairs which it did not possess in Europe or in North America.

Thanks to a combination of factors, Chile's military escaped deteriorating into *caudillismo*—the free-booter guerrilla or bandit types plundering the rich as well as the ordinary populace—which afflicted most of the rest of Latin America through the nineteenth century (and, in some cases, well into the twentieth). Chief among those factors were Portales's vision in laying the groundwork for a professional military organization and the constant threat of external aggression. Contrary to the facile image of military "gorillas," the advanced armies of Latin America—Chile's in the vanguard—developed a highly sophisticated corporate ideology; for Amos Perlmutter, distinguished scholar of world military history, it was, in fact, "among the most sophisticated among modern militaries anywhere . . ." Perlmutter goes on to remark that, as a result, "the Latin American military's contributions to the modern state are considerable," bringing for over a century "organization, ideology, and managerialism" to the bodies politic of their countries.

But, despite the influence of European philosophy and European instructors in their academies, "from its outset, the Latin American military . . . was conscious that it was *designed* to achieve and maintain political order . . ." This concept was, indeed, embodied in the very first decree law of the junta: the armed forces, it said, was "the organization

which the State has been given for the safeguarding and defense of the
moral and physical integrity of its historic cultural identity ... its
supreme mission is to assure, above all other considerations, the survival of said realities and values, which are the highest and most permanent ones of Chilean nationality."[124]

This conceptualization of the military—the ultimate arbiter not only
of the constitutional fidelity of the regime, but of the integrity of
nationhood itself—transcended even the more widespread concept of
"the pratetorian army." Yet, such a notion was anything but an historic
given in Chile, for no other major military establishment in Latin
America had remained so subordinate to civilian control as had the
military in Chile. Following the period 1925–1932, when the Chilean
military ruled directly or indirectly (and, in most reckonings, effectively), it abided by the Portalian constitutional diktat that it be "essentially obedient."[125] But in Chile, as elsewhere in the world, the long-
developing cracks in the facade of professional aloofness from the
dramas of the larger society would crumble when civilian rule itself
crumbled. Noting military coups and countercoups in all Latin American republics, in most independent Arab states, in most African states,
in several Southeast Asian polities, in Pakistan, in Greece, and in Portugal in recent times, Perlmutter wrote: "These events confirm the historical and political fact that when civilian government is neither effective
nor institutionalized the executive is unable to control the military.
The collapse of executive power is a precondition for praetorianism."[126]
In Chile, in September of 1973, little remained of either constitutionality or executive power. In the Portalian vision of Pinochet and his
associates, the ethical and moral integrity of their country was also in
dire jeopardy.

In common with the military of most major Latin states, Chile's went
through a long process of professionalization, first under the tutelage of
Europeans (mainly German and British), then, for a quarter of a century
following World War II, of Americans. Professionalization at first was
easily understood: preparing to defend the homeland against foreign
aggression. But as the perception of external threats receded, professionalization, increasingly, meant joining in the work of nation-building. "Progressive" thinkers prodded the military to believe that they
needed to arm themselves intellectually for wars on poverty and underdevelopment as well for traditional battle. That trend created an inevitable paradox: at what point did the application of these skills and energies
constitute an invasion of the civilian sphere of influence? There was yet
another paradox: socioeconomic development involves profoundly
political choices. How, then, to claim political aloofness in such cir-

cumstances? (Interestingly, few would be more adamant about the socioeconomic imperative for the military than Salvador Allende, and also Carlos Prats González, the general who most loudly proclaimed the need for distance between garrison and governance.)[127]

Parallel with professionalism came another development: an increasing tendency to revile the military, portraying them as the agents of powerful oligarchs, blocking change and progress. The stereotype was as wrong as it was superficial.[128] Yet, as we shall see, it was an idea with powerful consequences for Chile (and for much of the rest of Latin America, as well as for U.S. security interests in the hemisphere).

Although universal military service in Chile was mandated in 1900, the upper classes generally managed to evade conscription and increasingly shunned voluntary service. A 1969 study done by the Chilean high command makes the point: 90 percent of the officer and noncommissioned officers of the army were drawn from worker and peasant class families, and the remaining 10 percent from the middle class. In political terms, 80 percent were classified as center-left, the rest divided among conservatives and Marxists. There was yet another strain, hinted at in the study, made explicit by other commentators: a powerful, old, and "visceral anticommunism" in the Chilean military.[129]

Since the military was scorned by the intellectual Left and snubbed by the aristocratic Right, beginning in the 1930s there developed "a profound schism between the civilian and military worlds," in the phrase of one Chilean military analyst. The writer, Genaro Arriagada, adds: "Important relations between the two did not exist. The military world developed its cultural and social world completely apart from the civilian one." Pinochet, years later, summed up the attitude of many top leaders toward the "oligarchy": "These gentlemen congressmen, from the best families, instead of investing the riches which nitrate gave the country, took the first ship to France to squander their fortunes."[130]

In 1933, partly because of the Depression, partly because of the inevitable political backlash against military rule in the years preceding, the new civilian rulers began hacking away at the size and perquisites of the military. By 1940, with much of the world already at war, the army was smaller than it was in 1930. But the heaviest blows—fiscal as well as to the military's self-esteem—came in the mid-1960s. In the United States, which the armies of Latin America had come to depend upon for material, training, and collegial support, an antimilitary reform movement in the Congress led to a series of legislative moves that all but uprooted the U.S. military presence in the region. The thrust of these measures was to compel the military establishments south of the border to settle for "constabulary" status, with a narrow responsibility for securing their own frontiers. Such patronizing paternalism was bitterly resented among the Latin American military, and far from engendering restraint, the "reforms" set in motion the greatest binge of arms buying in the history of Latin America.[131]

But if the military resented these measures, they found warm welcome among the "progressives" surrounding President Eduardo Frei. As the Frei government systematically neglected military pay and other needs, ominous signs of military discontent began to surface. Beneath the surface, an even more ominous process of politicization began which reflected alienation and a weakening of military confidence in and commitment to civilian rule.[132] The year 1969 saw the first serious military uprising in more than forty years.

The debate over what "essentially obedient" and "non-deliberative" meant, in relation to Chile's military, was a sterile and largely irrelevant exercise. In practice, there never had been the kind of clear separation between civilian and military prerogatives in Chile such as existed in the U.S. and the most advanced nations of Western Europe. Sergio Miranda Carrington, former director of the Center for Law of the University of Chile, spoke witheringly of the "precipitate ignorance or undisguised haughtiness" of those who, for two generations, claimed that the only role of the armed forces was to guard the country's frontiers. He then went on to enumerate a number of traditional "nonmilitary" attributes of Chile's military: supervising elections; operating their own educational institutions down to high school levels (the military schools' diplomas have the same standing as those issued by civilian secondary schools); running various industrial operations that supply civilian as well as military needs; controlling all civil aviation, including air terminals; operating shipyards serving civilian needs, as well as controlling yacht clubs. Even the National Administration of Sports is under the Defense Ministry. And beginning in the war-time year of 1942, when "zones of emergency" were legislated for the first time to deal with the danger of imminent invasion or grave acts of sabotage, military involvement in "civilian" activities was extended even more widely, for military commanders were given charge of such zones. Following the horrendous earthquakes of 1960, the law was expanded to allow the president to declare zones of emergency for up to six months in cases of "public calamities." Constitutional rights were restricted in the areas covered for so long as the decree was in force. Although clearly not intended for use in putting down labor disputes, Allende used the law to do just that, culminating with the great strike of October 1972 when virtually the entire country was placed under such states of emergency—which meant under military control and governance. Inevitably, those military governors were called upon to make a great number of political decisions: to "deliberate," in other words.

If there was still standing a conceptual wall of any kind separating the country's military from a decision-making role in the deepening crisis in the country, that wall came tumbling down with the ever-increasing level of internal tumult, with the corresponding increase in active military participation in the Allende government. As noted in chapter 7, on the day following the June 1973 *tancazo* rebellion, five flag officers from each of the three armed services formed an unprecedented, ostensibly informal "Commission of Generals." The stated purpose was to analyze the internal crisis and harmonize the behavior of the services. Their work culminated—publicly—with a July 2, twenty-nine-point memorandum outlining the views of the high command as to what needed to be done to preserve constitutionality in the country. But, privately, the "Commission" continued to meet—increasingly, in private homes. Gradually, "almost imperceptibly," according to Gen. Sergio Arellano Iturriaga, one of the key participants, those talks drifted from joint political analysis to joint conspiracy planning.[133] The major details of that activity and participation were dealt with in chapter 7, and further observations on General Prats' role will be made in the following chapter.

What is clear is that by 1973, Chile's military leaders rejected out-of-hand the notion—to paraphrase Tennyson—that theirs was not to reason why, but to sit and watch their country die. A secret analysis prepared for the army high command just two weeks before the revolution made explicit how far they had come in their thinking from disconnected "professionalism": "The essence of the existence of the Armed Forces is rooted in the survival [*supervivencia*] of the nation. This fact alone concedes to them . . . a moral authority above political parties, trade unions, professional and/or religious associations, when these have failed in the fulfillment of their national tasks . . ."[134]

What is also clear is that the senior commanders had already spurned the demand of General Prats that they owed their allegiance only to the president. One of the leaders of the impending revolution dared to challenge Prats in a crucial moment: "It is not enough to respect the constitution; we must also make sure that it be respected."

Nor, by 1973, were the commanders any longer willing to accept a role as mere "uniformed employees"; they saw themselves, in Ortega y Gasset's phrase, as "not a brute force, but a spiritual force."[135]

They were, in a word, the new Portalians.

There are those who argue that Augusto Pinochet was a latecomer to the revolution of 1973, consenting only when he realized how adamant were the other service chiefs, how far along the planning was in his own backyard. His immediate superior, Carlos Prats, insinuates as much;

and the then U.S. ambassador in Santiago, Nathaniel Davis, repeats reports that "Pinochet continued to show signs of cold feet" right up to September 9. Prats claims that he—and not Pinochet—gave the order in April of 1972 for the updating of the internal security plan. Nothing I have read nor learned in the fourteen years since my exhaustive research in 1974 for my own book on the revolution has caused me to alter significantly the conclusions reached then, and reflected in earlier chapters of this book: Pinochet realized as early as 1972 that a day of revolutionary reckoning might come, and by July of 1973 he was actively preparing for one. But, so, too were others, principally in the navy, and it is very likely that the navy, under Admiral José Toribio Merino, finally forced Pinochet's hand. If he was experiencing "cold feet" on September 9, there are at least two plausible explanations: the awesome responsibility he was about to assume, and the sheer logistical nightmare of amalgamating two or more highly detailed plans of revolution in the twenty-four hours or so available—from the time the decision to strike was made to the time when fleet and troop deployments had to begin.[136]

In the perspective of time, when he took command of the plot fades into unimportance contrasted with the indisputable fact of his rapid takeover of the revolutionary government.

> The priesthood and the military are not careers for earning a living, but vocations for serving God and Country.

Father Santiago "Cuico" Urenda was fond of drilling those concepts into the minds of his students at Sacred Heart Junior High School in Valparaíso. One of them was Augusto Pinochet Ugarte. For him, the advice was unneeded. From his earliest youth, young Pinochet was so fond of playing with his lead soldiers, that he "never went to bed without first changing the guard." Years later, he would write that reading tales of heroism and the history of Chile, were possibly what awakened in him the idea that "the goal of my life had to be to become an officer of the army."[136] Born November 25, 1915, in Valparaíso, he was the eldest of six children of Augusto Pinochet Vera and Avelina Ugarte Martínez de Pinochet, and was his mother's favorite until her death. His father was a general customs agent in that port city, and the family lived on the third floor of an old commercial building owned by the Roman Catholic archdiocese—shops on the first floor, a boarding house on the second. "Tito"—the nickname his mother gave him—began his education as a boarding student at San Rafael Seminary, but was expelled for breaking windows. A rambunctious lad, he continued to have his share of "visits"—as the prefect of discipline liked to call his disciplinary sessions. But he also benefited from the large cadre of French priests teaching at Sacred Heart. Though he excelled at math, French gave the boy fits; classmates remember how he wrenched his face out of shape in a futile attempt to pronounce the language.

He was a strapping seventeen-year-old when, on his third try, he finally was accepted at the Military School, "counting the hours" before starting his four-year career there on March 11, 1933. Beginning that Depression year, cadets graduated not as lieutenants but as warrant officers (*alférez*). The first promotion, to second lieutenant, came in 1938; four more years passed before the next, four more to captain (on the long and slow climb of that era) and (in 1981) on to a rank not used since the days of the liberator Bernardo O'Higgins: Captain-General of the Army.[137]

It was while serving as a young infantry second lieutenant that Pinochet had his first brush with leftists. He was stationed at Concepción when the 1939 earthquake hit and he saw socialist militiamen, wearing khaki uniforms and berets. Pinochet said they helped themselves to foodstuffs and other emergency supplies intended for earthquake victims, leaving him with "an image of rotten thieves." Six years later, while serving in the northern garrison at Iquique, he first experienced civilian importuning of military men. It was in the months following the 1945 election of Gabriel González Videla, who won with Communist support, as president. "Wherever we went, there was but one topic of conversation . . . that his victory with partners like them was going to bring about great upheavals of all kinds in Chile." Pinochet adds that neither he nor his army friends attached much importance to such talk—politics was for politicians. But the passing months brought worsening conditions—long lines of men and women outside shops increasingly barren of basic necessities. Then, in 1947, González Videla rammed through Congress a law outlawing the Communists (the Law for the Defense of Democracy, or the *Ley Maldita*, the Wretched Law, as the Left dubbed it). "It was," Pinochet wrote, "a moment of great happiness for the people of Iquique, for all Chile, when the president decided to do that." On October 23, after elaborate secret precautions, the president declared a state of emergency and ordered a massive roundup of Communists. Pinochet, then a captain, was among the officers assigned to detain Communists in that northern area of nitrate mines and transport them to the remote and virtually deserted port of Pisagua. The following year, he was back at the prison camp he had helped build, this time as commandant. The fourteen months he spent there hardened Pinochet's conviction that Communists were "not just another party . . . I confess that from that moment, I felt a profound desire to penetrate and study those concepts . . . since it worried me greatly that such pernicious and contaminating ideas would continue being spread across Chile. . . ."[138]

Pinochet was embarked on his first serious military training, at the Infantry School, when he met Lucía Hiriart. She was then fifteen, he ten years her senior. The year was 1940. She had gone out with a friend to collect funds for some charity, when they met the girl's father, Guillermo Barros, commandant of the school, accompanied by a young second lieutenant. Guillermo gave her five pesos "for the two of us." The young officer neither introduced himself nor spoke. She thought he looked poor. She was right—he later confessed that he hadn't spoken because he didn't have a red cent to his name at the time.

Her school was located across the street from the officers' club, and the young lieutenant missed no opportunity to see her—but, because of her tender years, he did not speak to her. Noting his interest, his fellow officers accused him of "infanticide." It was later, after being formally introduced, that they began dating, marrying two years later. Described in one biographical sketch as "charming, attractive and socially at ease,"[139] she was no stranger to politics: her father, Osvaldo Hiriat Corvalán, had served for eight years (1937–1945) as a Radical party senator, and, during that same period, as minister of the interior; he was also acting labor minister in the presidency of Juan Antonio Ríos. The couple has five children—two boys, three girls. In common with most military wives, Mrs. Pinochet remained in the background through the years prior to 1973, emerging to play an active role in organizing youth and womens' organizations following the revolution.

Pinochet was a thirty-one-year-old major when detailed in 1956 to the Chilean Military Mission in Washington, his first foreign assignment. That one lasted only a few months, dovetailing into another as a guest instructor at the Military Academy of Ecuador. (Interestingly, he makes no mention of his Washington experience in *El Día Decisivo*, nor in any other of his writings or interviews I have been able to find, but his 1973 biographical sketch does list English as a second language. Yet in two, extended interviews, I have never heard him speak it, nor—diplomatic friends tell me—have they. One offered an explanation: Pinochet is a perfectionist, and what he does he will do only if he does it well, particularly in the presence of others.) Apart from the visits of American military officers to Chile, Pinochet had at least four more contacts with U.S. military people: visits to the U.S. Southern Command in the (then) Panama Canal Zone in 1965, 1968, and 1972, as well as an official tour of the United States in 1968. Such contacts notwithstanding, Pinochet gave no indication of being "pro-American," even before the roughing up at the hands of the United States following the revolution. But, then, Pinochet is not an easy man to read: taciturn with all but his intimates, he is fond of invoking the Spanish axiom that "one is master of what one does not say, slave to what one does." A man who has known him many years at close range told me: "Pinochet is a *huaso* [a Chilean cowboy], pure and simple. Although he likes to read, and particularly history, the history he reads is mainly Chilean, because he is, to the marrow, intensely of this land. He is not a cosmopolite, and so his ideas and attitudes have their roots in this soil." He describes himself as "a man of few friends, reserved in character . . . affectionate, detached [*desprendido*]. My wife and I have always been very close, doing things together . . ."[140]

His wife chides him: when you speak, you always look annoyed. That, he retorts with an impish grin, is because I was raised that way.[141] (It is, nonetheless, a quality which adversaries have used to powerful advantage against him. Although he is a doting father and perhaps an even more doting grandfather, capable of great warmth, the photograph most routinely published abroad shows a prune-faced Prussian, not infrequently wearing dark glasses.)

Federico Willoughby, the man most responsible for burnishing Pinochet's image during the early years of the junta, describes him as "very human . . . pleasant with those he considers his equals or superiors, rougher with his subordinates." Contrary to most images, Willoughby describes Pinochet as "the most intelligent and politically sophisticated of the four [junta members], a man of greater character and courage to face the trials of government."

To improve his speaking style—extremely rigid and wooden at first—Willoughby coaxed him into appearing before small-town groups, Centers of Mothers and the like.

As with most of his friends, Pinochet tilted—at least in the sixties—to the Christian Democrats, Willoughby said, adding that Pinochet had told him he had voted in 1964 for Frei. His favorite daughter, Lucía, was enrolled as a PDC party member.

When he assumed power, Willoughby said, Pinochet expected the revolutionary government would last no more than ten years, concluding later that it would take an entire generation to achieve the changes he envisioned for Chile. "We never spoke of time frames [*plazos*], but of goals. Our first horizon was 1980. Later, a dynamic set in that made it very difficult to let go of power."

Willoughby said Pinochet was an avid student, taking classes in economy, geopolitics, foreign policy—even, in 1978, four or five classes in economy from Milton Friedman himself, the man whose ideas were so significant in charting the junta's economic strategies.

"At the beginning" Willoughby said, "he wanted to listen and learn. Later, he lost that capacity to listen to those who might have brought him good ideas . . ."[142]

Augusto Pinochet, in 1973: ". . . tall, ramrod straight, and powerfully built. His green eyes are warm and friendly, disarmingly so, for they peer out from a no-nonsense face crowned by an abundant shock of black hair, graying at the temples, parted in the middle and brushed straight back. Thick eyebrows, a leonine nose and puffed cheeks, streaked lightly by veins, a thin moustache and bulldog chin . . . Despite his fifty-seven years, [up] at 6:00 A.M., exercise a customary forty-five minutes . . ."[143]

Though Pinochet stands a little over six-feet tall Allende liked to call him—behind his back, to cronies—"Pinochito" ("little Pinochet"), confident that he would be able to manipulate him. General Prats, his immediate superior, made not a single judgmental remark about Pinochet in his extensive memoirs (516 printed pages, exclusive of epilogue), except to pay repeated tribute to his demonstrated loyalty. It was his confidence in that loyalty that caused him to recommend Pinochet so strongly to Allende when, during his two and-a-half-hour meeting on August 23, 1973, Prats insisted on his own resignation.

That very afternoon, Allende summoned Pinochet to inform him of his appointment as new commander-in-chief.

The meeting took place at La Moneda Palace, in a small room named "Diego Portales."

It doesn't say so on his official biography, because officially it never happened, but José Toribio Merino Castro had seen combat long before September 11, 1973. During World War II, although his nation was officially neutral, he finagled his way aboard the U.S. light cruiser *Raleigh*, first as an "observor," finally as a regular officer. During his year aboard (1943–1944), he saw action in the Pacific.

This was written of the number two man in the junta, a year following the revolution:

"At first glance he might strike the observer as a popinjay, strutting and posturing and puffed up with self-importance, because he does tend to prance, and there is something of the dandy about him. But upon closer inspection the image of vaingloriousness gives way to a more beguiling one, that of a pixyish person full of deviltry. Neither image captures the reality of Merino, but it is true that there is an impishness about the [man] with the Groucho Marx moustache that rules out putting him down as a pompous man. While the casual observer might be forgiven momentary confusion between those two images, few familiar with him would fail to remark other qualities: spontaneous warmth, an affectionate, generous personality, deep love of the sea—and the inner strength and resolve of a man of profound convictions.

"José Toribio Merino was born on December 14, 1915, in the hometown of his mother, the charming four-century-old city of La Serena, without peer in all of Chile for its colonial character, and famed for its sweets, which may account for Merino's lifelong weakness for them. His father, grandfather, and great-grandfather before all bore the name of José Toribio, and he was set to follow in his father's footsteps as commander-in-chief of the Chilean navy. And, like his father, who had been a thorn in the side of Chile's dictatorial president, Carlos Ibáñez del Campo, back in the late twenties, he was at irreconcilable odds with his president. He became the senior service chief who most defiantly confronted Allende . . ."[144]

Alone among the men who made the revolution, Merino had, in fact, confronted Allende even before he became president, seeking assurances that, if confirmed by Congress, Allende would respect the independence of the armed services. Those September visits annoyed the army and air force chiefs—and very nearly precipitated the resignation of Frei's defense minister. History can only speculate how such an event might have impacted on the intricate and volatile webwork of negotiations, conspiracies and anxieties in those tense and explosive days preceding Allende's ascendancy to the presidency.[145]

Even more than most naval officers, Merino was a cosmopolite. And, in common with many of his generation, he was very pro-American, an affection that, though battered, survives down to the present. (He quite frequently managed to slip into the United States incommunicado, while a member of the junta, often to indulge one of his great passions—golf—with old American military cronies in the Washington area.)

Like Pinochet—born just one month before him—Merino was the eldest child, in his case, eldest of four. To his family, the boy they knew as "Pepe" revealed a generous streak from his earliest days. Once, while still living in La Serena, the young child saw a barefoot boy walking down the street. He proceeded to throw his own shoes out the windows to the boy. From his earliest days, too, he revealed a restless spirit, an active, inquiring mind: hobbies ranged from raising birds to hunting, painting, photography and, later, stamp collecting.

Most of his youth was spent in Viña del Mar, the resort city immediately to the northeast of the seaport city where Pinochet was growing up. Merino, too, studied with Sacred Heart priests (though at their newly established school in Viña). Those studies were interrupted for two years in 1927 when strongman president Carlos Ibáñez, in order to rid himself of the navy chief who was giving him so much trouble, dispatched Merino's father to Geneva as Chile's representative at the League of Nations. That city was then (as now) so expensive that the family rented a house in Paris, where they had the opportunity to mix with the self-exiled President Arturo Alessandri. The first year of their European stay, Merino and his brothers were placed at a boarding school in London. A daughter recalled that the school had so few showers that her father, fond of bathing daily, paid out of his own pocket to have one installed for himself. The following year, 1928, the boys transferred to the American High School in Paris. Back in Chile, Merino finished his high school career at Sacred Heart with distinction: third in his class, with prizes for comportment, French, physical education, English, arithmetic, and geometry. It was a performance he would not repeat at the Naval School, which he entered the following year, 1931: he was, he would confess, "busy chasing girls" (*pololeando,* in the delicate Chilean usage). Among the lifelong friendships he formed at that school: Patricio Carvajal, who would play such a decisive role in the September 11 revolution, and Ismael Huerta, in the events leading up to it, when he was first foreign minister of the new revolutionary government.

His graduation cruise as a cadet, aboard the oiler *Maipo,* took Merino in 1936 to San Francisco, the first of many, many visits he would make to the United States over the years. Three years later, in 1939, he was back in northern waters, this time in Tampico, Mexico, aboard yet another oiler, the *Rancagua.* He got his first command—the corvette *Papudo*—in 1952, the same year he married Gabriela Margarita María Riofrío Bustos. A sister recalls: "My mother was very fond of her, but she never told Pepe. That, with him, would have been the kiss of death." As it was, the dashing bon vivant, so fond of motorcycle racing and fonder yet of wine and women, was ready to settle down.[146]

It was very likely inevitable that the first man to speak openly of a junta would later be the first to leave it. Even before it was formed, this strong-willed man—Gustavo Leigh Guzmán—had clashed with another strong-willed man, Augusto Pinochet. Pinochet tells the story. It was at the fateful September 9 tea on the occasion of his youngest daughter's birthday. Leigh asked to speak to him in private. Once in the study, Leigh told Pinochet that the four services, united, could topple the Allende government, and if they were to do it, a junta would be named. Leigh added that although he had two days' more seniority than Pinochet as a service commander, he would accede to Pinochet as president of the junta. Pinochet interrupted him to say that he was mistaken; the commanders-in-chief ranked in the order of the standing of their respective services, and that was army, navy, and then the air force. "Since he accepted what I said and because it wasn't the time for argument, I then confined myself to hearing him out," Pinochet added.[147]

Gustavo Leigh Guzmán was, on the day of revolution, just eight days away from his fifty-third birthday, and, after thirty-five years in the service, only three and-a-half months away from hoped-for retirement. Retirement would have to wait—but Leigh had learned to wait. When it did finally come, it was a reward submerged in bitterness.

Just as Merino loved the sea, so too did Leigh love the skies, the adventure of flight, and particularly, the freedom of military flight. "Military flight is marvelous," he told an interviewer. "One flies for oneself, the pleasure is one's own. You don't have 100 passengers, making 200 demands, nor the flight plan controls."

But, if he loved the skies, he loathed cold water. Fellow cadets remember a moment of crisis during his Military School career when, in Santiago's Cousiño Park, he balked when ordered to follow other cadets off the high diving board into the pool.

"I don't know how to swim, my lieutenant," Cadet Leigh told Donald MacLean, the officer in charge.

"Dive in," MacLean ordered.

Leigh repeated his plea three times. MacLean persisted in his order three times. Leigh's classmates watched silently as he slowly scaled the ladder. Suddenly there was a loud splash: the entire water polo team had plunged into the pool and formed a circle beneath the diving board.

"I think we grabbed him before he even hit the water," a classmate remembered. Leigh climbed out of the pool and presented himself before MacLean.

"Your order carried out, my lieutenant," the shivering cadet said.

The second of four children of Hernán and Laura Leigh, he became so enamored of aviation as a small child that playmates took to calling him "the swallow," when not "Pilot Leigh." The loss of his father when he was only six meant the boy had to make his way without the role model he said he always missed. He also had to work hard to defeat a dangerous enemy for one planning a career in aviation: mathematics. It took a good deal of tutoring and coaching, but he finally made it, winning a scholarship to the Military School. (Water again: a Military School humor magazine said Cadet Leigh, in charge of the baths, was so honorable, he never took a single one.)

If he had an aversion to cold water, he loved the beach, and especially the one at Llolleo, where his family vacationed at a house his grandfather had bought. There was horseback riding on the beach—and there were the girls.

"With their fathers looking on, right?"

"Come on, we weren't stupid. Besides, there were those great sand dunes . . ."

Doubtless some of the intense anticommunism of President González Videla rubbed off on him: Leigh was, for a time, the president's pilot. He also was a pioneer helicopter pilot.

By 1960, Leigh was a widower with two children. A fellow officer who was also a widower, Sergio Crespo (later minister of agriculture in the junta), introduced him to Gabriela García. When he was assigned that year as air attaché at the embassy in Washington, the couple considered a quick wedding. They decided to wait. A long wait it would be: Leigh remained in Washington for six years. They finally married in 1966, when he returned to Chile.

Those years in Washington not only gave him a command of English unequalled by other members of the junta—doubtless a factor in the judgment of many foreign correspondents who found him the "most articulate" member of the junta—but also a solid affection for the United States. He also developed a number of friendships with U.S. officers he would strengthen through repeated return trips to the U.S. in later years.

Where and how he developed his fierce anticommunism is less clear. What is clear is that, even more than Pinochet, he was regarded as the hardest of the hard-liners among the top commanders. His behavior in later years would call into question the accuracy of that image.

Junta press spokesman Federico Willoughy agreed with the characterization of Leigh as a "man of facile expression," adding that he also had "a great deal of charisma." But Willoughby also said he found Leigh to be a man of "changeable opinions, with an up-and-down character, euphoria and then depression."[148]

For the fourth member of the junta—César Mendoza Durán—September 11 always had been a special day, as far back as 1918. Mendoza was born on that day, in that year—a native of Santiago, like Leigh. The ninth of eleven children, Mendoza grew up on what were then the countrified outskirts of the city. An avid reader of history and the classics, math was for him the same nemesis it was for Leigh. He entered the Carabineros School in 1938, the year after graduating from the city's prestigious Instituto Nacional high school. Commissioned a second lieutenant in 1941, in the years ahead he almost literally rode to the top. An outstanding horseman, he spent four months in 1949 in New York, participating in the Sixty-first Equestrian Exhibition there. Two years later, he captured the gold medal at the Pan American Games in Buenos Aires; it was pinned on his chest by a very irritated Evita Perón (the Argentines had expected to sweep the competition; instead the Chileans stunned their hosts and the favored Mexicans, capturing nine medals, including four gold ones). He was back in the United States for competitions in 1957, then for the 1959 Pan American Games at Chicago; finally, in 1960, once again in the Olympic Games, in Rome. When the revolution came more than a dozen years later, he retained, at fifty-five, the svelte physique and agility of movement a lifetime of physical activity would suggest.

Though his role in the junta was low key, Mendoza—perhaps because Carabineros bore the brunt of so much public ire during the Allende years—was among the first to say plainly that the junta was determined not only to build a new polity, but to root out the old one.[149]

PINOCHET TAKES COMMAND

QUESTION: Mr. President, you will remember that in Communique [*Bando*] #5, it says that the *Junta* will remain only as long as needed to return to normality. What changed later?
PINOCHET: Gen. Mendoza, Gen. Leigh, Adm. Merino and I did sign a document which said that. But you forget that we signed that when the movement [he used that euphemism for the revolution] had just ended. When we began to study things, when we began to analyze the problems . . . we arrived at the conclusion that the problems were *much, much* profounder than we had imagined. [Emphasis in original.][150]

Someone asked Augusto Pinochet, some years later, whether he believed he still had behind him the "consensus" of support that he enjoyed at the time of the revolution.

"Consensus—what a magic word!" he retorted. "There's never been anything such as total consensus in this country. Why, Pedro de Valdivia was in this country only a short time when he had to hang his partner Pedro Sánchez de la Hoz, because he had rebelled against him. . . ."[151]

Consensus, in 1973, they had. But it was a narrow consensus, one which said only: deliver us from this Allende evil. Nor—except for their visceral anticommunism, greatly strengthened by the society-traumatizing Allende experience—was there consensus among the four members of what was, after all, a makeshift junta. And so, they began their journey without maps, groping to make rule by committee work, to create a plan of their own. To the dismay of the Right and the Left it was a plan that excluded the traditional programs and personages of both.[152]

The first step in forging such a plan was taken on October 4, with the formation of an Advisory Committee. Significantly, it was, at first, made up only of army officers—and advised only the president of the junta, Pinochet. When the others protested, it was rapidly broadened to include representatives from the other services, some thirty in all, as well as a handful of civilians. And, as the Advisory Committee of the Junta, it was now charged with advising all four members. But it served as such mainly in name only, and was, in fact, headed by one of the army officers closest to Pinochet in coup plotting: Julio Canessa, one of the first colonels to achieve flag rank after the revolution. Six months after its creation, Canessa described it as a "Presidential General Staff."[153] In

keeping with the spirit of the new regime, it was a youthful organization: ages ranged from thirty-five to forty-eight. Key among the civilian
young turks: Jaime Guzmán Errázuriz, a brilliant, bookish former president of the Law Center at the University of Chile, and one of the most
brazenly outspoken voices against Allende. This man of small physique
and almost monastic life-style would loom large among those charting
ideological directions for the new junta.[154]

As 1973 drew to a close, it was clear that Pinochet and his associates
were settling in for a long campaign. Decree Law #128, on November
16, clarified the scope of the expression "Supreme Authority of the
Nation" used in Decree Law #1: "... from September 11, 1973, the
Government *Junta* has taken on the exercise of the constituent, legislative and executive powers." That decree law (DL) said the judiciary
would continue to function with the independence and authority conferred by the constitution of 1925—for many a legal anomaly, since DL
#128 was so sweeping that it supplanted that constitution. (That same
month the electoral rolls were declared invalid.) The belief was reinforced by the promulgation of another DL abolishing the Constitutional
Court (created by the 1970 reform to hear strictly constitutional questions). Another DL in December banned elections in unions and established regulations governing them. Under Decree Law #5, in effect
since September 12, the country was in a state of siege defined as the
equivalent of "state of war," which provided, among other things, for
summary execution (although, as noted, these were officially ended as
of November 1973).

Against this were the first signs of economic recovery. An American
correspondent, viewing the scene, wrote:

> There is still a depressing mood of fear in Chile. Armed troops patrol
> Santiago's streets, and gunfire is frequently heard at night . . . Despite
> all this, Chileans, if they had the choice, would probably reluctantly
> vote for the *Junta* as the lesser of evils. Though the *Junta* is hardly
> popular, it does have the country running again. Chileans chafe under
> its totalitarian restrictions, but they also remember the chaos and
> strife of Allende's regime. For the moment Chile's citizens appear
> content to get back to work and the rhythms of an orderly society. But
> with their long democratic tradition, they are not likely to tolerate
> *junta* rule indefinitely.[155]

At 6:00 P.M., on March 11, 1974—the day, coincidentally, when
classes resumed in Chile—Augusto Pinochet presented what, until
then, was the most important thesis of his career: the Declaration of
Principles of the Government of Chile. The scene was the Plenary Hall

of the Diego Portales Building, crammed with foreign diplomats, government figures, judges, media and labor leaders. With his three junta colleagues joining him at the podium, each resplendent in beribboned dress uniform and flanked by unblinking aides-de-camp, Pinochet, over the next forty-five minutes, spelled out what, in its essentials, would be the ideological framework of Chile's government until the adoption of a new constitution six years later. The message, like the ceremony itself, reverberated with patriotic themes, a summons to build a new Chile based on the traditional values of the past.[156] It was divided in three parts: (1) Chile in a world context (brief); (2) man and society (long); (3) the nationalist, realistic, and pragmatic inspiration for the revolution (longer). The first two were preambles, premises for the third.

1. There are, the statement said, two options available to developing nations: the socialist path, inspired in Marxism-Leninism, and the one typical of advanced Western nations where economic development and social justice exist in harmony. The first, of course, was rejected. The second path was found also deficient. While market economies are "incomparably more acceptable" than the others, the junta's ideologues rejected the materialism they engendered; the materialism of "consumer societies" which "spiritually submerge and enslave man." It was, they noted—recall, the time was the mid-1970s, the twilight of the hippie and radical protest eras, the onset of the environmental and earth mother movements—a materialism that stimulated youthful rebellion, nostalgia for the simpler and more serene world of yesteryear. And yet, their economically prostrate land was not to pine for a fictitious pastoral society, but to build. Chile, then, "must seek to achieve simultaneously and harmonize in a balanced fashion, freedom as a form of life with accelerated economic development, progress with social justice."

2. As to man in society, the document spelled out five major principles: (a) the rights of man were natural, and superior to those of the state; (b) the state must be at the service of man, and not vice versa; (c) the reason for being of the state was to secure the common good; (d) the state must assume only those functions which individuals, families, or natural groups of individuals cannot undertake themselves (national defense, police, foreign relations); (e) this principle also presumes the right to private property and free enterprise.

3. Inspiration, aims: National unity was presented as the most highly valued objective of the new nation the military intended to build, a unity that would leave behind "the long period of ideological messianics and preaching of miserable hatreds." To achieve it, there was a call for a return to the "spiritual integration" which was the cornerstone of "our founding fathers, heroes, teachers and statesmen." The document called for a reawakening of "that true patriotism which is a visceral love for

Chile and a desire to see it once again great and united." The guiding force would be "an authoritarian, impersonal and just government," characterized by the personal effort, example, seriousness, and austerity of those who lead, the apolitical character of public employees. They would work through a system of comprehensive national planning.

In the field of human rights: a juridical order expressing respect for freedom of conscience and the right to dissent—with a sharp exception: "The experience of recent years indicates the need to place admissible limits to that dissent. Never again, in the name of a pluralism badly understood, can an ingenuous democracy be permitted that allows to operate within it organized groups which sponsor guerrilla violence to reach power, or while pretending to accept the rules of democracy, sustain a doctrine and a morality whose objective is to construct a totalitarian State. In consequence, Marxist parties and movements will not again be allowed in the public life of the country. Chile is not neutral in the face of Marxism ... this government is not, then, afraid to describe itself as anti-Marxist. Doing so is not to adopt a 'negative' posture, since it is Marxism which, in truth, denies the most fundamental values of every authentic civilization. . . ."

There will, the statement said, be a new and modern institutionality, one which decentralizes political and social power. Since the creation of such "solid stability" requires "purging our democratic system of the vices which facilitated its destruction," the military government "fixes no limit for its undertaking ... because the task of reconstructing the country morally, institutionally and materially, requires a profound and prolonged action. . . . This government has been categorical in declaring that it has no intention of being a government of mere administration, a parenthesis between two similar governments of parties; or, in other words, that it's not a case of a 'truce' for regrouping so as to return power to the same politicians who bear so much responsibility, through their acts of commission or omission, for the virtual destruction of the country . . . Notwithstanding this, the *Junta* will hand over political power in the opportune moment to whomsoever the people elect in universal, free, secret and informed elections. The Armed Forces will assume, then, the role of institutional participation which the new Constitution assigns it, and which will be that which must correspond to those charged with safeguarding the National Security . . ." A cornerstone of the new political order would be decentralization, a reinvigoration of local and municipal government.

In the social sphere, the junta said it would work to depoliticize and then rebuild labor, student, professional, and business organizations— redirecting them to fulfill the nonpolitical but specific purposes for which they were originally created. Family, women, youth, these were to the pillars of the traditional new society.[157]

Those ideas echoed, profoundly, a modern adaptation of the vision of a philosopher of singular significance to some of the key architects of the new order: Thomas Aquinas. But the statement also reflected, profoundly, the Portalian vision, modernized in later years by such eminent Chilean conservative thinkers as Jorge Prat Echaurren. Years before the 1974 Statement of Principles, Prat advocated such ideas—patriotism, regionalization, national planning in a free market setting. Significantly, he also envisioned a circumstance in which the armed forces might, one day, be called upon to leave their "glass house" or "glass showcase."[158]

That statement also contained important clues for the future—not only as to the durability of the new regime, but as to the proposition that, for as long into the future as their reach would extend, the military of Chile would not again remain impassively in a glass house, indifferent to the fate of their nation.

On June 17, 1974, Decree Law #527 codified the nature and organization of the junta. More importantly, it signaled the end of rule by committee. The law said the junta would continue to exercise the constituent power and the legislative power through decree laws, while the president of the junta would henceforth exercise executive power. Theoretically, decisions would continue to be taken only by unanimous consent. In reality, as press reports indicated at the time, the practical effect was to establish Pinochet as the undisputed number one. No longer could the junta designate the president; the decree established a hierarchy that would rule thereafter. First, the commander-in-chief of the army, next, of the navy, followed by the air force and finally Carabineros. Unless prevented by "death, resignation or any kind of absolute incapacity," the man already in the job would remain there so long as he remained commander-in-chief of the army. Nor was any time limit set for his term. To make it explicit, he was given the title "Supreme Chief of the Nation," while retaining the title "President of the Junta." Theoretically, the other junta members retained certain power: their approval was needed for appointing ministers, ambassadors, governors and mayors, but only if these enjoyed the "confidence" of the president. The statute also formalized the division of labor among the junta members: the economy for the navy (including the Central Bank), social areas for the air force, while Carabineros got agriculture, and lands and settlements.

On December 17, 1974, the shift of power away from committee to one-man rule became final: Pinochet was named President of the Republic. His power was now almost complete.[159] It would take another event, nearly four years later, to make it so.

According to some conspiracy theories, Pinochet had set out shortly after assuming power to purge the army of generals "disloyal" to him. "Disloyalty" was defined as having engaged in coup plotting before—or separately from—Pinochet, upstaging him, in a sense. Among such generals, Manuel Torres, Arturo Viveros, and Sergio Nuño—the latter two, very junior generals—went to early retirement within a year. Another, Oscar Bonilla, died in an airplane crash in 1975. Arellano, as noted already, was out in 1976, followed into early retirement by an even more junior general, Javier Palacios.[160] It is possible that Pinochet forced them out, and it is also possible that he forced them out for that reason. But if he did, the secret of it remains shrouded in institutional secrecy. There is little reason to doubt that, once he had fixed on a long-range goal of creating a new nation, for which he needed to assume absolute power, he would have demanded a high degree of personal loyalty from the senior members of his inner circle.

It is clear that, once embarked on that course, he brooked little dissent within the junta itself, and what there was tended to come from a single source: Gustavo Leigh. From the very beginning, on the eve of revolution when he challenged Pinochet's very right to rule, this mercurial and strong-willed man had been a burr under the saddle of the hard-charging Augusto Pinochet.

The breaking point came in a June 1978 interview Leigh gave to the Italian newspaper *Corriere della Sera* of Milan. He was asked what he would do if he were to learn that the government of Chile had had a hand in the murder, two years earlier in Washington, of Orlando Letelier, Allende's last defense minister (and former ambassador to Washington). (More on this in the next chapter.) Leigh responded that were that to be the case, he would have to reconsider his position in the junta, because such an event would dishonor the armed forces.

Learning of this, Pinochet said Leigh had to go.

In an interview with the author, Leigh said that it was, in fact, only the culmination of a long period of tension between them. At bottom was a profoundly different vision of military rule.

Leigh said Pinochet repeatedly brushed off his questions about creating new electoral rolls to replace those voided in 1973; about his insistence that work be speeded up on drafting the new constitution. "He always got annoyed when I brought these things up," he explained.

"From the beginning, in 1973," Leigh said, "I believed we should govern no more than three to five years, that that would be time enough to clean things up, to disinfect the country. All organisms wear out, and governments are no exception. They create their own capital of resentments, of incomprehensions, of rivals. My idea was that we should give way to someone like a retired military officer during a transition period back to full civilian rule." But, he went on, Pinochet made short shrift of his ideas.

On July 24, 1978, a decree was promulgated removing Leigh from the junta. But even in this, Leigh said, the junta tripped over its own rules. Under the June 1974 code, a member could be removed only in case of physical or mental "absolute" incapacitation, and Leigh was of sound mind and body. Further, when the decree was sent to the comptroller for his necessary assent, he sent it back because it contained only three signatures and all four members needed to sign. Leigh refused to sign what he described as his "self-expulsion." The impasse finally was resolved by quickly swearing in Leigh's successor, Gen. Fernando Matthei Aubel, and having him sign.[161]

There would not again be serious public dissent within the junta until 1987.

Nevertheless, as Pinochet moved to consolidate his power, most Chileans still seemed to approve. A journalist of notoriously hostile views toward the junta (and other military governments), wrote at the time: "In spite of such privation, the majority of Chileans appear to welcome the new stability and to accept the military regime, at least passively."[162]

Notes

CHAPTER 9

1. *Time* magazine, September 24, 1973, p. 21. Eisendrath either knew little about Santiago's weather, or Denver's—or both. It never snows in Santiago, for example.
2. Based on an interview with Carmona in Santiago, March 27, 1974. At that point, Carmona, in common with many other Christian Democrats (beginning with Frei) who had supported the coup, still believed that the military would soon return rule to civilians.
3. Frei made that observation in his preface to Genaro Arriagada Herrera, *De La Vía Chilena A La Vía Insurreccional* (Santiago, Editorial del Pacífico, Instituto de Estudios Políticos, 1974), p. 23. Ibáñez, "The Chilean Crisis and Its Outcome," *The United States and Chile During the Allende Years, 1970–1973,* report of the Subcommittee on Inter-American Affairs of the Committee on Foreign Affairs, U.S. House of Representatives, hearings held July 1, October 15, 1971; September 11, 1972; March 6, September 20, 25, October 11, 31, December 7, 1973; August 5, September 17, 18, 1974 (Washington: Government Printing Office, 1975), p. 596. (Hereafter *United States and Chile.*) Frei also made a moving statement—alluded to in the preceding chapter—in an interview with the Madrid newspaper *ABC,* October 10, 1973: "The military have saved Chile and all of us whose lives are certainly not as important as Chile's but they are human lives, and many, and all of them are not yet safe because the armed forces continue discovering hideouts and arsenals. A civil war was being prepared by the Marxists. And that is what the world does not know, refuses to know."
4. Quoted in Florencia Varas and José Manuel Vergara, *Operación Chile* (Santiago: Editorial Pomaire, 1973), pp. 233–235. Sigmund notes (Paul E. Sigmund, *The Overthrow of Allende and the Politics of Chile, 1964–1974* [Pittsburgh: University of Pittsburgh Press, 1977], p. 249), that the dissident declaration did not appear in the Chilean press until over a year later, finally published by the Santiago newspaper *La Segunda* on November 29, 1974.
5. Michael Fleet, *The Rise and Fall of Christian Democracy* (Princeton: Princeton University Press, 1985), p. 178.
6. Augusto Pinochet Ugarte, *El Día Decisivo, 11 de Septiembre de 1973* (Santiago: Editorial Andres Bello, 4th ed., 1980), p. 152.
7. Frank Blatchford, "Chile: Mixture of freedom, police state," *Chicago Tribune,* September 24, 1973. The "police state" part referred to heavily armed patrols in the streets during those first weeks, as well as the roundups of suspected extremists. Blatchford said, "many of the Chileans I have talked to say they find the military presence reassuring. But for others, especially for Leftists and foreigners, a knock on the door provokes shivers of terror." The Concepción incident is in *Septiembre de 1973: Los Cien Combates de Una Batalla* (Santiago: Editorial Gabriela Mistral, apparently late 1973), p. 46.

624

The magazine-style book was a publication of the armed forces and Carabineros, highlighting scenes of heroism and battles during the revolution.

8. "Chile's Plunge Into Chaos," *Los Angeles Times*, August 29, 1973, one week before the coup. Given the *Times'* conspicuous leftist stance on virtually all issues, the editorial was particularly significant. The following day, yet another liberal American newspaper, the *Miami Herald*, expressed an identical sentiment in an editorial, "Noose of Crisis Is Tightening Around the Throat of Chile": "The wonder of Chile is that the government still stands . . . President Salvador Allende's determination to bring socialism to Chile has driven the country into so deep a political cleavage that civil war threatens."

9. Johathan Kandell, "Chile's Military Imposing Strict Standards on Nation," Santiago-datelined dispatch in *New York Times*, September 28, 1973.

10. Writing three months after the coup, *Time* magazine correspondent Charles Eisendrath, noting hardships and repression of the early days, said ("The Price of Order," *Time*, December 31, 1973): "Despite all this, Chileans, if they had the choice, would probably reluctantly vote for the *junta* as the lesser of evils . . . Chileans chafe under its totalitarian restrictions, but they also remember the chaos and strife of Allende's regime." Nearly two full years after the coup, a June 1975 Gallup Poll showed 76 percent of those responding supporting Pinochet, only 20 percent opposed. Cited in Fleet, op. cit., p. 181.

11. The experienced journalist was William Montalbano, then chief Latin American correspondent for the *Miami Herald*, and a man of strong "progressive" enthusiasms. The complete phrase ("There's Optimism in the Air in Chile Despite Massive Problems for *Junta*," Santiago-datelined dispatch, *Miami Herald*, October 1, 1973, p. 20-A): "And so the dust settles on a social experiment that was audacious, divisive, and by most yardsticks, a dismal flop." Montalbano makes it plain he is talking about the Allende experiment. The *Economist* expressed a broader view, in a "leader" (editorial) in its September 15 issue: "Few people believe that Chile can now return to its old way of doing things . . . There must be no confusion about where the responsibility for Chile's new tragedy lies. It lies with Dr. Allende and those in the Marxist parties who pursued a strategy for the seizure of total power to the point at which the Opposition despaired of being able to restrain them by constitutional means . . . the military-technocratic government that is apparently emerging will try to knot together the social fabric that the Allende government tore apart. It will mean the temporary death of democracy in Chile, and that is to be deplored; but it must not be forgotten who made it inevitable." Quoted in *Noticias*, September 19, 1973, p. 4. *Noticias* was a weekly digest of hemisphere news published by the National Foreign Trade Council, Inc., headquartered in New York.

12. Source for resumptions: *Bolsa Review*, vol. 7, #82, October 1973, p. 496, and for copper output, vol. 7, #83, November 1973, p. 561. Source for currency: *Chile*, #359, for November 25–December 10, 1973, p. 2, a publication of the Organization of American States in Washington. The *Review* was a publication of the Bank of London and South America. As to newsmen, the congratulations came from those not immediately sacked (or jailed) as Marxists. Notes I made in talks with news executives in Santiago at the time indicated 560 of 1,850 professional newsmen lost their jobs in the weeks following the coup; two were executed.

13. In an interview with Pinochet in Santiago, October 22, 1974. Frei, in an

interview with the author in Santiago, May 7, 1974, spoke critically of certain aspects of the junta's economic policies, and of human rights abuses, but did not believe the time was yet ripe for a return of constitutional democracy. In fact, he did not speak out publicly against the junta until twenty-one months after the coup.

14. From a special, postcoup edition of *El Mercurio,* September 13, 1973: PDC: "FF.AA. Merecen la Patriótica Cooperación de Todos los Sectores," p. 4; National party: "Partido Nacional Llama a Respaldar a *Junta* Militar," p. 6; PADENA: "Declaración del PADENA," p. 3; Godoy: "Ex Ministro Comunista Declara su Rechazo a Todos los Extremismos," p. 4; Urrutia Manzano: "Complacencia del Poder Judicial," p. 1. The follow-up explanation was from his interview with the author in Santiago, May 9, 1974.

15. Marambio was in hiding at the Cuban Embassy. Edelstam later recounted how Marambio—"a young man who had been with Allende at La Moneda the day before"—became his first refugee at the Cuban Embassy. Although Edelstam did not specifically say so, it is probable that the Mirista leader was among the nine hundred persons Edelstam boasted of getting out of Chile, many of them surreptitiously and illegally, in the three months following the coup before he himself left the country. Marambio incident in Samuel Chavkin, *Storm Over Chile* (Westport, Ct.: Lawrence Hill & Company, 1985), p. 136. Years later, Italian journalist Gaston Salvatore reported that Marambio was, together with Allende's former mistress, Miria Contreras Bell de Ropert, directing Coralfilms, a movie production company in Paris. According to Salvatore, the great Colombian writer (and Communist) Gabriel García Márquez was one of Coralfilms' principal scriptwriters. Salvatore referred to Marambio as "another hero of the Chilean resistance." "Contreras, yo, la amante de Allende," in *Epoca,* January 10, 1988, as reproduced in *El Mercurio* of Santiago, January 14, 1988, p. 1, "Revelaciones de la Secretaria De S. Allende."

16. Interview with Barros in Santiago, April 11, 1974. Barros had known García Incháustegui ten years earlier, when both were serving at the United Nations. This was not García Incháustegui's first expulsion experience: in 1961, the very democratic government of Uruguay, kicked him out because of his alleged role in organizing strikes. The Cuban Embassy which he headed in Santiago was, by far, the largest of the Latin American missions in Chile. There were forty-eight persons accredited from that embassy, thirty-nine of them Cubans. (By contrast, Brazil—the continent's biggest country with around thirteen times Cuba's population—then had fifteen persons in its Santiago embassy.) In the year 1973, a total of 633 persons had come to Santiago from Havana on official missions. Edelstam, an even older acquaintance of Barros's, bears further special attention. In contrast to what he said while still in Santiago, once outside the country a few months later, he embarked on what amounted to a vendetta against the junta, frequently travelling with and sharing platforms with Allende's widow. By December 12, 1973, *Le Monde* of Paris was quoting him as saying there were 15,000 dead, 35,000 jailed, and 30,000 orphans in the Chilean revolution. (Quoted unabashedly, in his Allende-eulogizing book, by Carlos M. Rama, *Chile: Mil Días entre la Revolución y el Fascismo* [Barcelona: Editorial Planeta, 1974], p. 224.) The level of Edelstam's "reporting" did not much improve. Barros first met Edelstam in wartime Berlin when Edelstam, then a dashing young diplomat (third secretary of the Swedish Embassy) and married to a very pretty young noblewoman, was a lion of the social circuit. When

Edelstam turned up in Chile years later, it was sans wife, although Barros said he understood there had been later marriages. Barros remembers that Edelstam, even though a diplomat of a neutral country during World War II, was aiding members of the Norwegian underground at the end of the war and later had adventurous postings in Southeast Asia and Guatemala (when guerrilla warfare was peaking there in the early 1970s). Barros said Edelstam, from the time of his arrival in Santiago in 1972, had "the style and air of superiority of many European diplomats in countries they think of as inferior." In a kind of reverse snobbery, Edelstam threw himself, passionately, into the cause of Allende's "revolution." It cannot be over-emphasized, either, that Edelstam represented a government that was, after all, socialist itself, and one which strongly supported Allende. As late as August 31, 1973, the Swedish government had pledged a 40 million kroner credit (roughly $7.7 million) to Allende. The socialist, pro-Allende proclivities of the Swedes were rarely mentioned in press accounts of their later "moralizing" about events in Chile. For further insights into Edelstam's eulogy of Allende and his role in the immediate aftermath of the coup, see Samuel Chavkin, op. cit., pp. 131–157.

17. Interview with then General Ewing at his office in Santiago, June 10, 1987. Located only a few blocks east of the ruined palace on the Alameda, the twenty-two-story building—then Santiago's tallest office structure—had been opened in April of 1972, just in time to house the United Nations Conference on Trade and Development (UNCTAD). It would remain the headquarters of the junta, and serve as the seat of the presidency until March 11, 1980, when restoration of La Moneda was completed and Pinochet moved the presidency back to the palace—seven years and six months to the day after the revolution.

18. Interview with Merino in Santiago, June 9, 1987. Pinochet is so quoted in Varas and Vergara, op. cit., p. 209. They quote him as saying: "I have no interest in looking like the indispensable man." (. . . *una persona irremplazable*).

19. Sigmund, op. cit., p. 250.

20. *Noticias*, September 19, 1973, op. cit. That judgment would shock those who reflexively equate military with right wing, an error in many Latin American countries, unquestionably so in the case of Chile of 1973. More on that subject later in this chapter. For that phase of its report, *Noticias* drew on published reports in *Time* of September 19, *Journal of Commerce*, September 18, *Wall Street Journal*, September 17, *Christian Science Monitor*, September 19, and *Financial Times* September 17. Pinochet's pro-PDC disposition from Fleet, op. cit., p. 179. As Fleet notes, that would not, however, prevent him from quickly siding with those who viewed the Christian Democrats as primary agents of the crisis.

21. Wrote Pinochet: "Casualties were much greater in those clashes [patrol actions] than in the fighting on September 11. Armed clashes began to diminish gradually only after the fourth month. In the raids which were carried out after those bloody encounters, an immense quantity of arms, propaganda and extremist pamphlets normally would be found." Pinochet, op. cit., p. 148.

22. Interview with Kelly en route from Santiago to Miami, June 21–22, 1987. Kelly came by his Irish name and ruddy looks from his paternal grandfather, who was posted to Chile in 1870 as an advisor to the Chilean navy, liked the place, and stayed. The employment figures are from a report, "Rol del Sector

Público en Economía," *El Mercurio*, May 4, 1974, p. 2. Davis notes that Allende larded the payrolls of government offices and nationalized companies with Popular Unity loyalists. Among examples: the SUMAR textile plant went from 2,500 to 3,500 employees after nationalization; Cervecerias Unidas, the Santiago brewery, more than doubled its work force; the El Teniente copper mine added four thousand workers to the eight thousand already on the payroll. Yet another: the Municipal Works Corporation (CORMU) reportedly ballooned from two hundred to twelve thousand under Allende. Nathaniel Davis, *The Last Two Years of Salvador Allende* (Ithaca: Cornell University Press, 1985), p. 17.

23. Merino told the author, during an interview in Santiago, June 9, 1987, that because of those contacts, he had not only a team but an entire economic program ready to unveil when he took over. In that interview, he specifically mentioned "Léniz and Kelly"—Fernando Léniz, then general manager of *El Mercurio*, destined to become first civilian economy minister under the junta, and the aforementioned Roberto Kelly. Other authors of the plan included Emilio Sanfuentes (journalist-economist who died a few years later), Sergio de Castro, later minister of finance, Alvaro Bardón, and Sergio Undurraga.

24. Mine, given to me by one of the key authors of the plan, is number 188. The study contains neither names nor dates, but in his June 9, 1987, interview with me, he said the plan was ready by March 1973.

25. Joaquín Fermandois, *Chile y El Mundo, 1970–1973; La Política Exterior del Gobierno de la Unidad Popular y el Sistema Internacional* (Santiago: Ediciones Universidad Católica de Chile, 1985), p. 435. The public-private sector comparison is from *El Mercurio*, May 4, 1974, op. cit. The newspaper reported that as of December 31, 1974, the public sector debt stood at 288 billion escudos; money in the hands of the private sector at that same point totaled 210 billion escudos.

26. The "signs" quote from William Montalbano, *Miami Herald*, October 1, 1973, op. cit. "Laughing" from "A future for business in Chile," *Business Week*, September 29, 1973. Luksic had reason to laugh: his Luchetti Spaghetti Factory in Santiago was the first industrial plant returned to its owner by the junta, but they had to fight to do so. Seized by workers three months earlier and later "intervened" by the Allende government, one hundred of the plant's five hundred workers occupied the plant during the revolution and fought a pitched battle with soldiers on September 12. Among the American firms which reached quick understandings with the junta to resume operation of their holdings: Dow Chemical, whose two plants had been seized in 1972 over protests of the comptroller general. Dow faced a problem of many returning owners: damage to the plants under incompetent management was so great it was estimated it would cost $2 million to repair. Budd Venable, Dow's president for Chile and Argentina, also lamented: "They didn't even keep books." By November 14, 1973, Chile and the U.S. had already reached agreement on the basis for compensating the copper companies. Additional sources: (Dow), "Chile: An uphill struggle to revive business," *Business Week*, November 17, 1973; (compensation), a Santiago-datelined Reuter dispatch "Copper firms: topic for U.S., Chile," *Christian Science Monitor*, November 14, 1973; "Dow Picks Up the Pieces in Chile." Herbert C. Meyer in *Fortune* magazine, April 1974; *Dow Latina*, vol. 1, January 1974 (company publication published by Dow's Latin American Headquarters, Coral Gables, Florida.

27. Quoted by Everett G. Martin, "After Allende: Chile's Rulers Face Huge Economic Woes, Make Some Progress," *Wall Street Journal*, October 4, 1973.

28. Buckley, "From Way Out in Left Field Come 'Executions' in Chile," column in *Miami Herald*, September 28, 1973.

29. Figures from "Chile Orders End of Summary Executions," Santiago-date-lined dispatch, *New York Times*, October 25, 1974. The same story reported the slaying of Chilean journalist Carlos Berger Gurainik and eleven others. They were shot, allegedly after breaking loose from their guards while being transferred from jail in Calama to Antofagasta. Berger's wife said she had been officially notified her husband and twenty-five others had been shot October 19 "for trying to flee." Earlier, on September 24, military authorities reported the death of six prisoners during what they described as an escape attempt in the port city of San Antonio ("6 Chile 'extremists' slain in escape bid," Santiago-datelined story, *Chicago Tribune*, September 25, 1973). The report on the *Status of Human Rights in Chile* (Washington: Organization of American States, 1974 [CP/doc.381/74, November 21, 1974], p. 21), quoted Santiago newspaper accounts detailing a total of thirty-one summary executions through October 11, 1973. But on p. 152, the commission cited "reliable sources" as the basis for the statement that "approximately 220 persons" were executed without trial. This brought from the government of Chile, in its *Observations* on the report, a sharp retort: "It is truly surprising that such a grave accusation as this should be put in such vague terms on just half a page . . . the report not only fails to mention a single specific case of such shooting but it even fails to mention as a beginning of the evidence the names or the places where such executions took place. It makes a serious and gratuitous statement that the Government of Chile rejects most categorically . . ." *Observations by the Government of Chile on the 'Report of the Status of Human Rights in Chile'* (Washington: Organization of American States, 1974), p. 34. (Referred to hereafter as "*Observations by the Government of Chile*".) It was published as a mimeographed reprint (CP3 85/74), dated December 4, 1974. In its 1985 *Report on the Situation of Human Rights in Chile*, the commission reported on four cases, all by then investigated by Chilean authorities: the discovery of fifteen badly decomposed bodies in two vaults of a limestone quarry near Lonquén; the execution of five peasants at Mulchen, early in October 1973; the discovery of five more bodies in a field near El Carmen y Maitenes—five men who had been ". . . forced to fight one another" before being killed; and the discovery of nineteen bodies at Laja, former employees of the Paper and Cardboard Manufacturing Company (*La Papelera*), arrested and executed during the first week of fighting. In all cases, charges were brought against military men, and in each, the charges were dismissed under amnesty provisions covering the state of war period in Chile (Washington: Organization of American States, 1985), pp. 55–57.

30. All indications are that neither Pinochet nor anyone else in power had any idea, during those first chaotic days, how long military rule would last. Although they give no date for the interview, authors Varas and Vergara quote Pinochet as saying the first objective of the junta was a "process of reconstruction," to be followed by economic reconstruction, "and then, as soon as the country has recovered, the junta will turn the government over to whomsoever the people desire . . ." *Operación Chile*, op. cit., pp. 209–210. Indications are that the interview took place in the first days after the coup.

31. Sigmund, op. cit., p. 254.
32. Johathan Kandell, "Purges of Chilean Left Shakes Colleges," Santiago-date-lined story, *New York Times*, November 14, 1973. Kandell said that at the University of Concepción—birthplace of the radical MIR—about 6,000 of 16,000 students and hundreds of professors had been suspended. About 1,500 students in the University of Chile's schools of fine arts, music and architecture, as well as about 100 of their professors, were suspended; 44 of 360 professors and about 70 students at the university's law school were also suspended. Course censorship centered on the social sciences, he said. Except in back-handed fashion, nowhere in that lengthy dispatch did Kandell note—as did Sigmund—the very real revolutionary tinder quality of the campuses.
33. It was also a reform that went to an early grave. The Education Ministry, two months after the coup, issued an edict requiring that students acquire "habits and attitudes of austerity, cleanliness and order." School administrators interpreted that, among other things, to mean lower hemlines for girls. In 1973, miniskirts in Chile were among the world's shortest. Although the edict fizzled, by 1975 fashion had decreed lower hemlines—and that edict did prevail. "Chilean *Junta* Bans Miniskirts in Schools," *Washington Post*, November 19, 1973.
34. *Documentos del Episcopado de Chile, 1970–1973* (Santiago: Ediciones Mundo, 1974), p. 174.
35. Pinochet, op. cit., p. 152. Pinochet said the military commanders returned that protocol call two days later, and it was there that the cardinal informed him of his plans for the eighteenth.
36. Enrique Correa and José Antonio Viera-Gallo, *Iglesia y Dictadura* (Santiago: Centro de Estudios Sociales), p. 93. (Like so many books published in Chile, no publication date is given, but the book apparently came out late in 1986.) The *Centro* is a Christian Democrat think tank, and the authors make plain their support for the "progressive" (and antijunta) behavior of the church.
37. David Holden, "Allende and the Myth Makers; Political Realism & Revolutionary Romance," *Encounter*, January 1974, p. 12. Robert Moss, "The Tribulation of Chile," *National Review*, October 10, 1975, p. 1105.
38. Laurence Birns, "Chile: A Bloody Fall," *WorldView*, November 1973, as reproduced in *United States and Chile*, op. cit., p. 531; Carlos M. Rama, op. cit., p. 211. Birns was then professor of Latin American studies at the New School for Social Research in New York City.
39. Leon Gouré and Morris Rothenberg, *Soviet Penetration of Latin America* (Miami: Center for Advanced International Studies, University of Miami, 1975), p. 108. James A. Theberge, then director of the Latin American Department of Georgetown University's Center for Strategic and International Studies, wrote shortly after the coup that "Moscow was deeply disturbed but not especially surprised." He based that on Allende's failure to heed Moscow's repeated go-slow admonitions, but failed in his analysis to make a convincing case that Moscow actually expected such a sudden, decisive blow. Theberge, "Kremlin's Hand in Allende's Chile," *The Soviet Analyst*, August 15, 1974, as reproduced in *United States and Chile*, op. cit., p. 638.
40. Gouré and Rothenberg, op. cit., p. 120.
41. In breaking relations, the Russians accused the Chileans of "arbitrariness, lawlessness and mockery" toward Soviet institutions in the country. The statement cited a number of examples of alleged offenses against Soviet

citizens and agencies, including crew members of the Soviet ship *Eklip-tika*, newsmen, and performers. The statement also accused the junta of "bloody terror directed against . . . the entire Chilean people," and of "anti-communist hysteria." Robert G. Kaiser, "Soviets Cut Relations With Chile," Moscow-datelined dispatch, *Washington Post*, September 22, 1973. The "sustained and well-orchestrated" quotation in *Pravda*, and remaining Radio Moscow citations are from James D. Theberge, *The Soviet Presence in Latin America* (New York: Crane, Russak & Co., 1985), pp. 81–82.

42. Gouré and Rothenberg, op. cit., p. 122. Report of the Committee for Solidarity from Radio Moscow, December 1, 1973, the arms campaign, April 21, September 2, 1974.

43. Holden, op. cit., p. 13. Holden reports that within twenty-four hours of the coup, Ron Hayward, general-secretary of the British Labour party, was writing one of Allende's former colleagues to say it was difficult to express the sense of horror and anger felt by the British Labour movement "as the aspirations of the working people of Chile—shared by so many others around the world—are destroyed at the hands of a few arrogant and ignorant officers acting at the behest of those who believe their right to rule is unchallengeable." The party conference passed resolutions not only condemning the coup but also the "precipitate action" of the British government in recognizing the junta, demanding that the British ambassador be recalled from Santiago and all aid, loans and credits be cut off.

44. *Time*, September 24, 1973, op. cit.

45. "Demócratas Cristianos Condenan Golpe en Chile," *La Prensa*, Lima, September 21, 1973.

46. The Italian Christian Democrats, in common with many European leftists, equated the Chilean Socialist party with European Socialists or Social Democratic parties—a serious error. As we have seen, the Chilean "Socialist" party had little "social" content, a great deal of radical and violent content, all of which placed it to the left of the Communists. The quote is from "Italy's Reaction Strong," Rome-datelined dispatch, *New York Times*, September 15, 1973.

47. Moss, "The Tribulation of Chile," op. cit., p. 1107.

48. Interviews with Mrs. Ossa in Miami, over several days, in July 1975. I had known Mrs. Ossa during previous reporting trips to Chile.

49. Isabel was among the women in the palace on the eleventh, leaving before the aerial bombardment. In an interview with Régis Debray from Mexico City, published just four days after the coup, the now exiled daughter said she "is sure my father did not commit suicide. Who killed him? One of his companions, who remained behind with him, but who could not leave afterwards, told me that it was a captain he could not identify. A radio station identified him as one Garrido or Gallardo. But the name doesn't matter. There is another witness to Allende's last moments, and I can mention her name: his secretary, Miria Contreras, seriously wounded, who was taken to the military hospital. We haven't heard from her since." From an interview published in the Dominican Republic newspaper, *Ahora*, #518, September 15, 1973, quoted by Enrique Lafourcade, *Salvador Allende* (Barcelona: Ediciones Grijalbo, 1973), pp. 210, 214. Although she did not know it then, Isabel obviously was repeating a widely quoted report originating with a left-wing Chilean writer named Robinson Rojas Sanford, later contained in a book he authored (*The Murder of Allende*; New York: Harper

& Row, 1976). Ambassador Davis, no friend of the junta, in his careful analysis of the six major versions of Allende's death, has this (inter alia) to say about Rojas: "Rojas claims to have talked with 'eyewitnesses,' but he provides no indication of his sources. Although the English version of Rojas's book has over 40 pages of endnotes for 220 pages of exposition—a full page of notes for every six pages of text—the crucial discussion of the staged 'suicide' and the 'contradictions" in the junta version carries no endnote or citation of any kind . . . Rojas's account has a quality that is not characteristic of real-life situations . . . There are significant differences between Rojas's original 1974 Spanish text and his 1976 English version . . ." Nathaniel Davis, *The Last Two Years,* op. cit., pp. 292, 294, 296. But, as seen in the preceding chapter, all of this is irrelevant, because in addition to the entirely credible Guijón version of Allende's suicide, and the impressive corroboration of it, there was another witness. Although Isabel could never have guessed that *La Payita* had actually witnessed the suicide, much less that—fifteen years later—she would publicly tell what she had seen, that is exactly what did happen. (And she was not, of course, "seriously wounded," or wounded at all, though Isabel could not have known that at the time, either, because Miria Contreras was still in hiding in Santiago.) All of this is resurrected solely because the "murder" versions were not only propagated (and very uncritically so) by major publishers, but in newspapers, magazines, radio and television around the world. By contrast, there has been almost total silence about the final confirmation of what was actually fully evident then: Allende committed suicide.

50. "U.S. Backed Coup, Allende Envoys Say," *Baltimore Sun,* September 19, 1973, Rome-datelined dispatch by the paper's Kay Withers. Chile's own Communist party, in its first official communique, on October 24, blamed the U.S.—but did not offer any evidence either. The statement also conceded that "grave errors had been made."

51. Frei's prologue in Arriagada Herrera, op. cit., p. 25. Frei does not name the Communist leader, but quotes from an interview published in the Italian newspaper *La Stampa,* October 26, 1973. In his book, *El Día Decisivo,* Pinochet says that in the first month after the coup, authorities seized 45,000 revolvers of various calibers, 40,000 pistols, 10,000 machine-pistols, 12,000 combat rifles, 500 bazookas (*lanzacohetes*), 70 antitank weapons, and 20 flamethrowers (op. cit., p. 217).

52. Cited by Augusto Pinochet Ugarte, op. cit., pp. 217–218.

53. Cited by Theberge, op. cit., p. 79. Theberge cites *Ercilla,* October 10–16, 1973, and his own interviews with the Chilean military in December 1973. The factory was KPD, ostensibly set up in 1972–1973 to manufacture prefabricated housing. Theberge wrote that after working hours, the Soviet officers instructed a hard-core of specially selected recruits in the use of arms, street fighting, and urban guerrilla tactics.

54. While acknowledging that "Plan Z" was a factor in the decision to revolt, Pinochet indicated that it was not a decisive factor—revolutionary plotting had begun long before anyone got wind of "Plan Z." The interview took place in Santiago, October 22, 1974. For details of "Plan Z," see *Libro Blanco del Cambio de Gobierno en Chile: 11 de Septiembre de 1973* (Santiago: Editorial Lord Cochrane, no date), pp. 39–65; Emilio Filippi and Hernan Millas, *Anatomía de un Fracaso: La Experiencia Socialista Chilena* (Santiago: Empresa Editorial Zig-Zag, 1973), pp. 149–153; Lautaro Silva, *Allende: El Fin de una Aventura* (Santiago: Ediciones Patria Nueva, 1974),

pp. 277–322. My own assessment, after diligent effort to put together a coherent, cohesive image of just what "Plan Z" might have involved, is that there doubtless was a plan called "Plan Z"; indeed, there were a number of different plans for decimating democratic opposition, in various stages of development. But, there was no final, finished, overall master plan for staging a preemptive coup. It is equally clear, however, that many around Allende—and probably Allende himself—were moving in that direction. For details of plotting involving government officials in contact with military men, see Ricardo Boizard, *Proceso A Una Traición* (Santiago: Ediciones Encina, 1974). Sigmund professes "wonder . . . how they [the military] believed that a paramilitary force that was ill-equipped and untrained, and could not have numbered more than 3,500 to 5,000 men, could destroy armed forces totaling 87,000." He writes also of "the fanatical search for arms," and "military paranoia," and describes the Plan Z found in Vergara's safe as "either a forgery or a document produced by the left wing of the Socialist Party of the MIR." Sigmund, op. cit., pp. 256–257. Two years after his book was published, a vastly outnumbered and outgunned Sandinista force seized power in Nicaragua, thanks largely to external pressure on the government. Eighteen years earlier, an even smaller rag-tag band headed by Fidel Castro defeated a much larger—and much better equipped—army in Cuba. In the case of Chile, putting aside the matter of numbers available for combat, estimates of soldiers and sailors loyal to Allende in the military ran as high as 10 percent. The combination of the government's own power, plus those factors, give great credibility to the hypothesis that a preemptive coup, involving mass assassination of the military high command, might well have worked.

55. Source for break-down: *Chile,* #357 (a publication of the Chilean Embassy in Washington) September 24, 1973, p. 3. In a Santiago-datelined story, *Baltimore Sun,* January 30, 1974, "U.N. was deluged with Chile refugees," Richard O'Mara quoted officials of the United Nations High Commission for Refugees' office in Santiago as saying they had, to that point, registered only 3,200 such aliens. He added that approximately half had been relocated then: 474 to Sweden, 287 to France, 139 to Switzerland, one hundred to Cuba. He added that West Germany was expected to fulfill its agreement to receive up to eight hundred refugees. A substantial part of the discrepancy might be accounted for by the number of foreigners who slipped across borders into neighboring countries, sought asylum in embassies (hundreds did), never bothered to register, or simply went underground.

56. Frank Blatchford, op. cit. Blatchford said the reporters "were unable to talk to the prisoners except to shout to them over a distance of about 10 yards. They yelled for us to throw them cigarettes and some complained that they had been held there for days without questioning." He reported that at one stadium entrance, prisoner-barbers were cropping the locks of long-haired inmates "under the watchful eye of army nurses and guards." He also wrote of "an underground team dressing room [that] looked like a dungeon with a dozen men peering from behind the barred door at the entrance," reportedly foreigners. But neither Blatchford, nor any of the other reporters whose eyewitness accounts of visits to the stadium I have seen, wrote of any prisoners denouncing executions, torture or other flagrant abuses.

57. The Sandinista revolution and its aftermath cost forty thousand lives, at least ten thousand of them killed in the Sandinista drive to power, in a country with less than one-quarter Chile's population. There were nu-

merous, confirmed reports of summary executions, including mass executions; one Sandinista defector said five thousand had been slaughtered in the first months of Sandinista rule. Within the first year, 100,000 refugees streamed out of the country and into neighboring Costa Rica, Honduras, and El Salvador. Nine years after they seized power, the regime continued to hold an estimated seven thousand political prisoners, many of whom had never been tried. As early as 1982, Amnesty International reported that at least 3,174 prisoners had been illegally convicted. Source for death toll and refugees: *Encyclopaedia Britannica Book of the Year, 1980* (Chicago: Encyclopaedia Britannica, 1980), pp. 560, 593; the Sandinista leadership has repeatedly used the 40,000 figure in public statements. Source for executions and illegal convictions: James R. Whelan and Patricia B. Bozell, *Catastrophe in the Caribbean* (Ottawa, IL.: Jameson Books, 1984), p. 56. The authors cite (for executions) report "Los Derechos Humanos y Su Vigencia en Nicaragua," *Comisión Permanente de Derechos Humanos de Nicaragua*, December 4, 1982, p. 2; and (for illegal convictions), UPI dispatch "Dice 'Amnistía Internacional' Que Están Presas 3,174 Personas por Colaborar con Somoza" *Diario Las Américas* (Miami), June 24, 1982.

58. Henry Kissinger, *Years of Upheaval* (Boston: Little Brown & Company, 1982), pp. 412–413. Kissinger goes on to say that while he neither condones all the actions of the junta, nor the humane motivation of many of its critics, it is also true that the generals faced near civil war conditions.

59. The two of the lurid tales: Adam and Patricia Garrett-Schesch. On the basis of claims, Senator Kennedy blasted the Nixon administration's "policy of silence," and later proposed his cut-off of U.S. aid to Chile. The two who never came back: Frank Terruggi, a twenty-three-year-old economics student from Chicago, whose remains were identified in the Santiago morgue on October 2; and Charles Horman, a thirty-one-year-old filmmaker from New York, whose body was never found. Marvine Howe, "2 Americans Slain in Chile: The Unanswered Questions," *New York Times*, November 19, 1973. Ms. Howe reported that both men were associated with North American News Sources, "a group of young Americans who published a small nonprofit magazine on the United States for the local leftist press. The articles were often critical of the negative United States position on the Allende Government." She said Horman had gone to Chile in June 1972 with his wife, Joyce, and had written a script on the history of imperialism in Chile and was doing research on a book for Chile's "transition to socialism." She said the two had, until recently, lived in "a large, comfortable house in Las Condes, a fashionable Santiago suburb . . . a permanent open house for Chilean and foreign artists, Marxist-Leninist discussion groups and other intellectuals and their children . . ." Teruggi had been studying at the University of Chile since his arrival in Santiago a year and a half earlier. She said most who knew him "say he was a loner, quiet, monklike and completely dedicated to the cause of socialism." Horman's parents later sued eleven U.S. officials, including Ambassador Davis, alleging their complicity with Chilean authorities in their son's disappearance, finally dropping the suit eight years later. Davis and his colleagues counterfiled, charging defamation. Since the movie *Missing* purports to be a "true story," Davis says, he devoted three-and-a-half pages of his book to answering claims in the episode (Davis, op. cit., pp. 379–382).

60. The figures, and reference to the commendation, are from Pinochet's report

to the nation on the first anniversary of the coup, September 11, 1974, p. 10, of the mimeographed copy made available by the presidential press office to foreign journalists and others. O'Mara, *Baltimore Sun*, op. cit., applied convoluted logic (and writing) to describe the UN refugee program in Santiago as the biggest ever mounted by the UN. It was not the biggest in terms of refugees, he clarifies; those honors went to such countries as Uganda, in the expulsion of Asians the year before. Rather, it was the biggest in the number of UN people working on it: thirty to forty, locally recruited from other agencies, volunteers ("wives of UN officials," for example), whereas in Uganda the UN had to make do with only three or four persons. From this came a headline: "U.N. was deluged with Chile refugees." (Again, for comparative purposes, Nicaragua, with one-quarter the population, produced over 100,000 in the first year alone after its revolution.)

61. Ambassador Davis said Altamirano "was probably spirited out of the country under the aegis of a Latin American embassy. The ambassador of that country approached me, in fact, asking my help in this operation, but I was not in a position to render this assistance." The visa information is from Manuel Trucco, in "Foreign Intervention in Chile," made originally as a statement before the Organization of American States, October 23, 1974, where Trucco was then serving as Chile's ambassador, reprinted later in Francisco Orrego Vicuña, ed., *Chile: The Balanced View* (Santiago: University of Chile, Institute of International Studies, 1975), p. 100. Trucco said French police took note of Altamirano's visa. The reward is from *Noticias*, October 3, 1973, p. 4.

62. By the mid-1980s, Moscow beamed several hours of radio programming to Chile per day. The Teitelboim quote is from *Breve Historia de la Unidad Popular* (Santiago: Editorial Lord Cochrane, 1974), p. 383. The book is a chronology of the Allende years compiled by *El Mercurio*.

63. Chavkin, op. cit., p. 103. Quiriquina prisoners from an AP, Concepción-datelined dispatch, "Leftist Chile Prisoners Build Their Own Jail," *Miami Herald*, December 21, 1973. Of the estimated seven thousand persons imprisoned in the first weeks, others were held at such places as Pisagua (the desert camp created by President González Videla in 1947 to house Communists), aboard the naval training ship, *Esmeralda*, moored at Valparaíso, as well as two other vessels (the *Lebu* and *Mappo*), and various military installations.

64. Prado, "O limbo gelado de Dawson," *Visao*, February 25, 1974, pp. 38–40. Letelier named the island: "the frozen Limbo of Dawson."

65. Davis, op. cit., p. 249. Information on the root canal from interviews with Mrs. Letelier in Santiago, May 8, 12, 1974.

66. Whelan, *Allende: Death of a Marxist Dream*, pp. 181–182 (based on the previously cited 1974 interviews with Pinochet, Leigh, and Mrs. Letelier), and, for the meeting with Pinochet, Chavkin, op. cit., pp. 124, 128–130. Chavkin claims the letters were not delivered for four months; this does not square with what Mrs. Letelier told me during our interviews. In Chavkin, she is represented as much more hostile, sarcastic about Pinochet, both during the two Defense Ministry meetings immediately following the coup, and about him personally. When I interviewed her, Letelier was still in custody. Chavkin evidently interviewed her several years later, not only after her husband's release, but given the publication date of the book (1982), presumably after his murder in Washington in 1976.

67. Santiago-datelined dispatch, "*Junta* to Try Communist Chief," *Washington Post*, Oct. 4, 1973.
68. Kissinger (*Years of Upheaval*, op. cit., p. 412) notes that the Corvalán appeal was "a symptom not of Waldheim's sympathies but of the double standard of the dominant group in the United Nations." Ambassador Davis records that he opened his campaign for the release of Almeyda and Letelier at his farewell call on October 23 to Interior Minister Oscar Bonilla. He said he also urged friends in the State Department's Bureau of Inter-American Affairs to intervene, and they did so—Deputy Assistant Secretary Harry Shlaudeman suggesting to Davis's successor, David H. Popper, on March 4, 1974, that he ask the Chilean government for Letelier's release. Then, he said, came a lucky break: McGeorge Bundy, a former Harvard faculty colleague of Kissinger's and then head of the Ford Foundation, asked Kissinger, then secretary of state, to intervene on behalf of both men. Kissinger agreed to do so, despite his description of Almeyda as "so far to the left that in the past he has opposed Soviet positions out of admiration for the more radical Chinese Communists and Cubans" (*White House Years*, Boston: Little Brown & Company, 1979, p. 680). Because of his service as Allende's ambassador in Washington and earlier as a high-ranking official of the Inter-American Development Bank, plus his own engaging personality, Letelier had many friends among the elites of Washington's liberal power centers, and so his cause was particularly popular, even though he, too, belonged to the radical Socialist party in Chile. As the other former Allende officials were released, Davis continued to intercede for those who came to the United States: "I was able," he writes, "to recommend a few for academic and other jobs." Davis also became a circumstantial actor in the Corvalán-Bukovsky swap in December 1976. In July 1975, Davis resigned as assistant secretary in charge of African affairs in protest against covert U.S. intervention against the Soviet-backed regime in Angola. Kissinger persuaded him to accept a new post as U.S. ambassador to Switzerland. It was there, at the airport in Zurich, that the actual exchange took place. Davis accepted Soviet demands that Corvalán be turned over to them in full view and with full honors, while Bukovsky would be picked up behind a truck servicing their aircraft, out of sight of the press and bystanders. He further made sure that Chile's ambassador was also kept in the background; the Chilean ambassador had demanded a place in the exchange equal to that of the Soviet ambassador—logical, since it was his government, and not the U.S., which was releasing a prisoner in exchange for one held captive by the Soviets (Davis, op. cit., pp. 384–390). Moss (op. cit., p. 1108) reports a spy-story subplot to the Corvalán-Bukovsky exchange. In 1975, Victor Louis, "the mysterious Moscow-based journalist who always seems to know what the KGB wants to know," Moss writes, arrived in Santiago, ostensibly on a reporting mission. But, "after much bureaucratic confusion, Louis was permitted to fulfill his real mission, which was to interview . . . Corvalán in jail and discuss terms for his possible release."
69. For writ, Sigmund, op. cit., pp. 249–250; for Leighton in Rome, Moss, op. cit., p. 1110; Moss reports that Leighton had a staff of sixty Chilean exiles working with him there. Similar, handsomely funded operations were set up in London, East Berlin, Paris, and other capitals. The legal controversy revolved around Article 72 of the 1925 constitution, which empowered the president to order the arrest and indefinite detention of persons during time

of "state of emergency." The provision granted far greater powers to the president in case of external attack or emergency, far fewer in case of internal crisis. The junta nominally acknowledged the applicability of the 1925 constitution at the outset. But it also said (Decree Law #128 of November 12, 1973) that the constitution would continue in effect *except* that "The Constituent Power and the Legislative Power shall be exercised by the Government Junta through decree laws bearing the signatures of all of its members ... [and] The provisions of the decree laws that amend the Political Constitution of the State shall form part of its text and shall be considered embodied in it" (Article 23, DL 128). One such decree law was #5, of September 12, 1973, which greatly expanded the scope and meaning of "state of siege" so as to permit the government to suspend a number of rights, including *habeas corpus.* Legalistic criticisms of junta actions in the earlier years centered on the language and meaning of the 1925 constitution, and not on the express acts of the legal government of Chile to change that document—as though it is not and has not been a commonplace of governments that come to power by revolution to suspend, amend, abridge, or discard existing constitutions. It should also be noted that the junta announced at the very outset its intention to draft a new constitution and submit it for voter approval which, in 1980, it did.

70. Prats and his wife were murdered in Buenos Aires on September 30, 1974, when a car bomb exploded. More on their murder in a subsequent chapter. Details of his departure from Carlos Prats González, *Memorias: Testimonio de un Soldado* (Santiago: Editorial Antártica, S.A., 1985), 2nd ed., pp. 513–515, and Pinochet, *El Día Decisivo,* op. cit., pp. 148–149. Prats reproduces in *Memorias* (p. 508) a letter from Pinochet, dated September 7, in which Pinochet expressed "the firm conviction that I address not just a friend but, above all, the *Señor General* who, in every assignment which he was called upon to perform, did so guided solely by a higher sense of responsibility, for the Army as well as for the country." Pinochet added that he remained "unconditionally at your service, both professionally as well as personally." That letter does not appear in Pinochet's memoirs. Pinochet reproduces in his book (p. 151) a letter from Prats, dated September 15, in which Prats said "the future will say who was wrong. If what you have done brings general well-being to the country and the people really feel that a true social justice has been implanted, I will be happy to have been wrong, in seeking with such zeal, a political solution to avoid the coup.... I thank you for the facilities which you provided so that I could leave the country ..." Prats coupled that with an appeal for the release of Fernando Flores, the young Cabinet minister he had become so attached to. The Prats letter was not reproduced in his memoirs. The Prats affair continued to stick in Pinochet's craw through the years. In an interview with the author, June 11, 1987, mention of Prats name evoked from Pinochet an emotional response that it was an outrage that there should be even an insinuation that he was a party to that assassination. To the contrary, he said, he had risked the wrath of his fellow commanders, before his own position was consolidated, to facilitate Prats' departure from Chile.

71. This part of Barnes' reporting was as lurid as the rest. Far from widespread ransacking of private homes and burning of tens of thousands of books, there was, as Sigmund noted, but one such case: "A single instance of book-burning, widely reported in the foreign press, took place during the searches

[for arms] of the San Borja apartments, where many foreigners with government connections lived" (Sigmund, op. cit., p. 253).

72. Barnes, "Slaughterhouse in Santiago," *Newsweek*, October 8, 1973, Diuguid, "Chile Death Toll Said 750," Santiago-datelined dispatch, *Washington Post*, October 3, 1973, p. 1. Contrary to Barnes' assertion about lifelong Communist party activist Pablo Neruda, the junta had actually declared two weeks of national mourning following Neruda's death (two weeks, in turn, before the *Newsweek* article appeared). Pinochet himself paid tribute to Neruda, calling him "one of the sources of pride in our national culture." In point of fact, Neruda's books remained on full view and sale in Santiago; several months after the coup, for example, Santiago newspapers carried heavy advertising for a handsome, new bound edition of the complete works of Neruda, selling for around $125.

73. Davis, op. cit., p. 368, observes that some reporters "clearly overestimated the loss of life," and then refers to the Barnes report, adding: "Other journalists later corrected Barnes . . ." Sigmund, op. cit., p. 253, while accepting the ambassador's "more reliable" estimates of those killed (between three thousand and ten thousand), seems to credit one of the most lurid and preposterous claims to come out of the revolution: bodies of those executed floating down the Mapocho River through Santiago. The "river" is actually a rivulet, and in September of 1973 (as is usually the case), had a flow so limited that not much more than a twig could "float" on it. Even fifteen years later, taxi drivers and others old enough to remember would, invariably, call the attention of visitors to the "river" and remark on the absurdity of those claims.

74. The Barnes article triggered a journalistic donnybrook with few parallels. On November 2, the *Wall Street Journal* published an article by the Chilean journalist and sociology professor Pablo Huneeus which was an outright rebuttal of the Barnes story. (Huneeus was anti-Allende, but not nearly the "right winger" critics would later attempt to make him out to be.) In that same issue, the *Journal* also published a companion article by its own (and very competent) Latin America correspondent, Everett G. Martin. Martin criticized Barnes' body count as one that "seems to have been based on events which didn't happen and figures that were misinterpreted." On November 15, the *Journal* gave over a large segment of its opposite-editorial page to a reply from *Newsweek* executive editor Kenneth Auchincloss, in which he gamely defended Barnes, while ducking many of the specific points raised by Huneeus, and fuzzing the central issue of Barnes' trip to the morgue. Huneeus was back in the *Journal* on December 11 with a reply to the reply. The debate eventually fizzled, but was memorable in a profession which then, at least, so infrequently held one of its own publicly accountable for the integrity of his or her reporting.

75. "Women report Chiles death toll," an AP story, datelined United Nations, N.Y., in the *Rocky Mountain News*, January 24, 1974. For the Federation's pedigree, see, e.g., Richard H. Shultz and Roy Godson, *Dezinformatsia: Active Measures in Soviet Strategy* (Washington: Pergamon-Brassey's, 1984), p. 25. The authors note that the Federation was attached to the International Department, believed to be the most important of three "active measures" departments working directly under the Secretariat of the Communist party of the Soviet Union. The ID is charged with liaison with nonruling Communist parties and revolutionary movements in furthering Soviet policy and propaganda objectives.

76. Examples of the first: Under the headline, "Two Assert Chilean Junta Is Killing Many Prisoners," Terri Shaw reported in the September 25 *Washington Post* on the allegations of two self-professed American radicals, graduate student Adam Garrett-Schesch, thirty-one, of Madison, Wisc., and his wife, Patricia, thirty. The two had been arrested briefly in Santiago, then ordered out of the country. Garrett-Schesch was identified in the story as a founder of a radical political party known as the Wisconsin Alliance. Despite such obvious bias, the *Post* gave prominent attention to the couple's claim that they had seen what literally hundreds of others also would have had to see: the execution of four hundred to five hundred persons in Santiago's prison, crammed not only with prisoners but also, from the very earliest days, with diplomats and other international observors. Still another: Marlise Simons, a Dutch journalist taken into custody shortly after the coup because of what the junta regarded as her slanted reporting, left the country late in September. From Buenos Aires, she wrote a "news analysis" attempting to link Patria y Libertad, a right-wing organization involved in scattered acts of sabotage, with the top leadership of the junta government. Ms. Simons peppered her sprawling "analysis" with pejoratives for persons with conservative or right-wing views. Despite Ms. Simons' obvious point-of-view, the *Post* devoted thirty-six column inches in its October 3 editions to her "analysis:" "Neo-Fascists Close to Chile Military Junta." Yet another: the *Baltimore Sun*, in its November 11, 1973, issue, allowed its Latin America correspondent the latitude to refer to the three top junta members as "in a sense, fanatics." The fourth, Carabinero Gen. César Mendoza, was dismissed as "less rabid."

As to the second, the "canonization" of Allende as British writer David Holden put it: the day after the coup, the *New York Times* published a heavily tilted assessment of the Allende years written by Israel Shenker ("Power Elluded Allende, Then Slipped From His Grasp," September 13, 1973). The final crunch in Santiago was reduced to a contest between "Dr. Allende talking increasingly of 'people power,' while conservative parties demanded his resignation," which, of course, overlooked the role of the dominant and mainly left-wing Christian Democrat party. In the same assessment, Dr. Allende "found himself embroiled in a prolonged politically motivated strike," which, of course, had the effect of exonerating Allende of blame for precipitating the strike(s). By Sunday, September 16, the *Times* weighed in with yet another "assessment," this one done by former reporter Bernard Collier, under the headline: "A Devastating End for a Unique, Troubled Venture." Collier, a reporter of notably leftist enthusiasms and a reputation at the *Times,* according to *Newsweek,* of "sloppiness and inaccuracy," put together a unique and conceptually troubled account, long on sloppiness and inaccuracies, short on resemblance to Chilean reality. (The *Newsweek* reference is from "Private Lives," October 20, 1975, p. 96.) Within three days of the coup, Lewis H. Diuguid, writing in the *Washington Post* ("Allende's Legacy: The Workers Feel They Participated," Sept. 14, 1973), advanced the theory reflected in the headline—one difficult to reconcile with the sheer numbers of workers, including mineworkers, who joined anti-Allende strikes, as well as the decline of Popular Unity strength in union elections.

As to the third, in the media's mephitic handling of the Chilean revolution, the choice of witnesses: the first opinion article to appear in the *New York Times* written by an outsider was the work of the French Communist and Allende crony, Régis Debray. It appeared on September 26, 1973, under the headline: "Salvador Allende: In Memoriam." To make the message even more poignant, the *Times* published, on the same page, a poem ostensibly written by Pablo Neruda, just before his death. According to the newspaper, the poem was "broadcast" to the Asia News Service of Berkeley, California, by *Prensa Latina*, Fidel Castro's propaganda/press agency. (Asia News Service was not otherwise identified, but it did not appear in the 1973 edition of *Editor and Publisher International Year Book*, the authoritative compilation and standard reference work on the American publishing industry. There was, at that time in Berkeley, a Pacific News Service, created with the help of the far-left Institute for Policy Studies of Washington.) The *Times*— while taking the trouble to list characters identified in the poem—identified Neruda simply as the "Chilean poet and 1971 Nobel laureate." There was no mention of his lifelong Communist party activism, nor his service as Allende's ambassador to France. Though not finding space on its commentary pages over the succeeding months for opposite views of Chilean reality—and they did abound—the *Times* did, on December 27, clear space for "Chile's Lesson For Leftists," by Max Gordon. Gordon was identified simply as "a writer on scientific matters [and] former editor of *The Daily Worker*." Presumably, some few *Times* readers might have known themselves that the *Daily Worker* was the name of the official Communist party newspaper of the United States, until the paper folded in the late 1950s. Further examples: *Atlantic* magazine, in February 1974, offered its readers a sophomoric essay written by Harvard undergraduate Robert F. Kennedy, Jr., an essay not only riddled with inaccuracies, ideological rhubarbs, and non-sequiturs, but distinguished also for a novel economic theory regarding Chile's runaway inflation: "The government," Kennedy wrote, "was content with inflation. It was an inflation which improved the position of the very poor through certain selective controls, by reducing the value of debts owed to creditors, and by undercutting the power of the rich. It was one way of redistributing wealth, but a costly way." (By contrast with Kennedy's benevolent hindsight, Allende himself, in his electoral program, said inflation "creates havoc in people's homes, especially for the housewife. According to official statistics, the cost of living has risen almost 1,000 percent in the last 10 years. This means that every day Chileans who live from the proceeds of their work are robbed of part of their salaries or wages . . ." In his first message to Congress as president, Allende described stopping inflation as "the axis of our redistributive policy." By contrast, too, with Kennedy's "analysis," the Inter-American Economic and Social Council said Chile's hyper-inflation, by 1973, had become "the pivotal short-range problem of the Chilean economy, because of its extremely-ruinous effects.")

Harper's, the second of the two major magazines appealing to upper-middle class Americans, provided its readers with a different kind of reporting. In its March 1974 issue, it published an article by Gabriel García Márquez. It told its readers that García Márquez "was the author of 'One Hundred Years of Solitude,' and 'Leaf Storm and Other Stories,' and that he was working on a novel entitled 'The Fall of the Patriarch.' " *Harper's* did not tell its readers that the great Colombian novelist was a former member of the Communist party, who continued to define himself as a Communist "without pinning myself down." He had, however, pinned himself down to the extent, the previous October, of donating the $23,000 he had won in a Venezuelan literary competition to a Marxist-Leninist party which he said he hoped would "one day make the revolution in Venezuela." And he did pin himself down to the extent of joining exiled Spanish Communist poet Rafael Alberti and Allende's former ambassador to Peking, Armando Uribe, on the "Bertrand Russell Tribunal" (nee: "U.S. War Crimes Tribunal"), held in Rome just one month after the *Harper's* article appeared. Characteristically, the "Tribunal" expressed concern only for the situation of human rights in four right-wing countries of Latin America: Bolivia, Brazil, Chile, and Uruguay.

77. James Theberge, "Chilean Leftists are blamed for coup against Allende," op-ed article, *Miami News*, September 26, 1973. Dr. Theberge was not alone in that judgment: The Chilean Communist party, in a position paper prepared in Santiago in June 1974 and released to the Associated Press in Buenos Aires, said the coalition failed in "solving correctly the problems faced by the popular government," and blamed the extreme Left for a "dogmatic approach" which eventually turned into enemies "whoever was not a proletarian." The Communists said "active resistance" against the military had already started, but insisted that the loss of political democracy still didn't mean violence and civil war were the only roads left. The statement then weaseled on the violence issue: "Violence is intrinsic to any way of conquering power by the working class and the popular forces," the paper said. "This violence can express itself with or without weapons" ("Chile Reds Begin 'Active Resistance,' " AP story datelined Buenos Aires, *Miami Herald*, June 22, 1974).

78. Buckley, *Miami Herald*, September 28, 1973, op. cit.

79. Kissinger, *Years of Upheaval*, op. cit., p. 411.

80. James Nelson Goodsell, "Latin America points finger at U.S.," *Christian Science Monitor*, September 17, 1973. The only "source" Goodsell cited in that story was inveterate Yankee-baiter Juan Domingo Perón, the Argentine dictator then back in power in Buenos Aires. Kissinger and Davis coincide in their memoirs that Kissinger offered Davis another date if September 8 were too volatile a moment in Chilean affairs; Henry Kissinger, *Years of Upheaval* op. cit. pp. 403–404, and Davis, op. cit., pp. 354–358. That Davis agreed to make the grueling trip to Washington that weekend (roughly twelve hours each way) is further indication of how little *firm* intelligence was available on the imminence of revolution at that point. Indeed, in his column, September 22, 1973, *Washington Post* ("No Direct U.S. Role Seen in Chile Coup"), columnist Jack Anderson had this to say about the coincidence of Davis's trip: ". . . on the contrary, we have learned that Davis chose that weekend for his visit because he expected it to be comparatively calm in Santiago . . . Davis, of course, knew about the stirrings within the Chilean Armed Forces. But he had emphasized in his secret cables that 'events move slowly in Chile, or perhaps better said, Chileans have great ability to rush to the brink, embrace each other, and back off . . .' When Davis met with Kissinger, according to our sources, they spent no more than five or ten minutes reviewing the Chilean situation. Most of their discussion was devoted to internal State Department matters." Anderson's sources told him—also accurately—that Kissinger wanted to size up Davis, among others, for promotion. Davis himself wrote in his memoirs (pp. 375–376) that the decision to appoint him was not made until after a follow-up meeting with Kissinger the weekend of September 21, and not announced until October 11.

81. Kissinger, *Years of Upheaval*, p. 410, and Sigmund, op. cit., p. 260. Most of

Kennedy's charges were pure hyperbole, and to the extent that there was truth to any of them, they largely reflected the chaos, confusion, and excesses, that occur during a state of war.

82. These attacks—and forty-one others through October 11, 1974—are recorded in *Observations by the Government of Chile, op. cit.*, pp. 54–61.

83. "Ceausescu Dijo que a Allende le Faltó Firmeza Para Aplicar el Socialismo," *La Prensa*, Lima, September 21, 1973. Ceausescu said in that September 20 press conference in Lima that when the "popular forces" are in power, "they must act with complete firmness against internal and external reactionary forces." Interestingly, Ceausescu tempered his revolutionary oratory as to the future of Rumanian-Chilean relations. That, he said to insistent questions, was a matter he would study once back home. His hedging was understandable: The very next day, the Soviet Union—then very much more in command of its satellite states than in later years—broke diplomatic relations with Chile.

84. This summary of the Soviet assessment was extracted from Gouré and Rothenberg, op. cit., pp. 108–125. The specific citations: Teitelboim, "For a Victorious Revolution," *World Marxist Review*, #11, November 1973, and "Prelude to Victory," ibid., #3, March 1974, cited on p. 109; A.I. Sobolev, "Revolution and Counterrevolution: The Experience of Chile and Problems of Class Struggle," Rabochii Klass i Sovremennyi Mir, #2, March–April 1974, p. 14, cited on p. 115 (Sobolev was then deputy head of the Department of International Communist Movement of the Marxist-Leninist Institute under the Central Committee of the Communist party of the Soviet Union); the reference to the May 1, 1974, declaration is from pp. 121, 125, reference to the July 1974 symposium from pp. 109, 110, 118, 125, and reference to the "Antifascist Front" is from p. 123. Goure and Rothenberg offer as their sources for the foregoing a Radio Moscow broadcast, February 10, 1974, Radio Moscow, June 27, 1974, an article in the Italian Communist party newspaper, *L'Unita*, June 15, 1974, p. 15, and Teitelboim, *World Marxist Review*, #3, March 1974, p. 88.

85. Even Davis, at frequent odds with his former boss, acknowledges Kissinger's role in freeing Letelier. Davis said he urged Kissinger to intervene with the Chilean government on behalf of Clodomiro Almeyda, Allende's long-time foreign minister and a leading Socialist, and Letelier. ". . . to the secretary's great credit," Davis writes, "he did so, skillfully and effectively. I am confident that his action was a contributing factor in effecting these men's release in 1975. Considering Orlando Letelier's subsequent murder, the U.S. government's humanitarian intervention in 1974 takes on a bittersweet taste" (Davis, op. cit., p. 386).

86. Lewis H. Diuguid, "Leaders of Chilean Parties Vow Effort Against *Junta*," Washington Post Service story datelined Washington, published in *Miami Herald*, July 22, 1975.

87. David Holden, chief foreign correspondent for the *Sunday Times* of London, wrote in the January 1974 issue of *Encounter* magazine ("Allende & the Myth Makers: Political Realism and Revolutionary Romance") that the British Labour party reacted almost hysterically to Allende's overthrow. Within twenty-four hours of the coup, Ron Hayward, general secretary of the party, wrote one of Allende's former colleagues to express shock that "the aspirations of the working people of Chile—shared by so many others around the world—are destroyed at the hands of a few arrogant and ignorant

officers acting at the behest of those who believe their right to rule is unchallengeable." Judith Hart, who held several top posts in Harold Wilson's government, then a member of Labour's National Executive, said, "for Socialists of this generation, Chile is our Spain," and "this is the most vicious fascism we have seen in generations." At the Labour party's annual Blackpool Conference, early in October, Allende's former ambassador to London was given a standing ovation when he became the first nondelegate to address a party conference since two Spanish Republicans were allowed to do so in the 1930s. Holden added that resolutions were passed condemning the coup and asking for the recall of the British ambassador from Santiago and the withholding of all aid, loans and credit; and calling on the Labour movement to campaign for the restoration of democracy in Chile, and to offer financial and other assistance to the Popular Unity movement. No sooner was Labour back in power, in March 1974, than it announced a dramatic cutoff in all aid to Chile (a pittance), and a ban on new arms sales to Chile (but, on a more concrete level, they did not cancel delivery of two submarines and two frigates built in Britain for Chile at a cost of $150 million). Judith Hart, back in government as minister of foreign aid, also announced that Chilean students studying in England—mostly Allende loyalists—would continue to receive scholarship aid. In February 1975, the Labour government, one of the most outspoken groups in the world about the supposed effects of an "economic blockade" against Allende, announced that it would not give Chile more time to repay its overdue debts. Chile, at that time, owed the United Kingdom $77.4 million—8.5 percent of its total debt to the U.S. and fourteen other Club of Paris members. The government said it would stay away from a meeting of Chile's foreign creditors in mid-March, scheduled to discuss an easing of Chile's overseas debt repayments. (West Germany, another Socialist-tinged government outspoken about the "economic blockade," also suspended aid to Chile at the end of 1974.)

88. This summary of developments in Europe is taken from "Communist Movement," *1975 Britannica Book of the Year* (Chicago, Encyclopaedia Britannica, Inc., 1975), p. 185, as well as individual articles from that volume on France (p. 314) and Portugal (pp. 561–562).

89. Gouré and Rothenberg, op. cit., p. 110. Speaking specifically of the Portuguese case, G. B. Ardaev of the World Labor Movement warned of the dangers of moving too fast, especially in extending economic benefits to the lower classes, arguing that this was one of the causes of the economic crunch discrediting the Allende regime. Two Soviet commentators (I.N. Zorina and Iu. F. Kariakin, "A Political Chronicle of the Chilean Revolution," *Latinskaia Amerika*, #5, September–October 1974, p. 148) also seemed to have their eye on Portugal when they traced the consequences of the Chilean Communist party's failure or inability to play a vanguard role in the revolution. Sobolev (in the previously cited work, p. 22) wrote that "it is extremely important to pose the problem that, within a bloc where the parties are considered equal, the Communist party, using its theoretical armament and organizational unity, is always required to play an innovative and unifying role." Goure and Rothenberg note (p. 119) that Sobolev's use of "innovative" and "unifying" seems to be his Aesopian way of saying "vanguard."

90. For example, the authoritative publication, *Soviet World Outlook*, noted the year following the Sandinista victory that "an upsurge of theoretical

writings [in Soviet publications] on the meaning of Nicaragua include indications of a turnabout in Soviet assessments of Che Guevara's theories of armed struggle hitherto condemned by Moscow" (*Soviet World Outlook*, vol. 5, #4, April 15, 1980, published by the Advanced International Studies Institute, Washington, D.C., in association with the University of Miami). In characteristic Soviet-style double-speak, by 1981 armed struggle was fully endorsed, and those who rejected the violent path to power were put down as backward. The June 1981 issue of *World Marxist Review,* an international Communist journal, reported, for example, that a "study commission" had concluded that, "far from impeding armed struggle, as some petty bourgeois theorists contend with reference to the experience of the 1960s, the present international situation largely predetermines its favorable outcome" ("Latin America: A Continent in Struggle," *World Marxist Review,* June 1981, p. 47, cited by Morris Rothenberg in *Central America: Anatomy of Conflict,* Robert S. Leiken, ed. [New York: Pergamon Press, 1984], p. 137).

91. "U.S. Expected Coup But Decided Not To Act," Washington-datelined dispatch, *New York Times,* September 14, 1975. That headline, twisting the substance of the story below out of all reasonable shape, was also at odds with reality. An appendix of this book contains a fuller discussion of what the U.S. did—or did not—know about the September revolution. A close and meticulous reading of the memoirs of the three U.S. principals who would have known—plus exhaustive investigation of my own with Chilean and U.S. sources—has persuaded me that the White House and State Department reports, issued in the first days after the coup, were painstakingly accurate: The U.S. had general knowledge about coup talk, but no specific, pinpoint information until the eve of the action. (My own research convinced me that the message that the coup was coming was flashed to Washington around 8 P.M. on September 10, and not at midnight as the State Department report indicated, a relatively minor discrepancy explained mainly by the delay in getting the message from the CIA to anyone in authority at State.) The three U.S. officials, and the relevant pages of their memoirs: then U.S. Ambassador Nathaniel Davis, op. cit., pp. 354–361; then Secretary of State Henry Kissinger, *Years of Upheaval* op. cit., pp. 403–404; and the man who then headed the Western Hemisphere Division of the CIA, David Atlee Phillips, *The Night Watch: 25 Years Inside the CIA* (London: Robert Hale, 1977), pp. 247–248. Of the three, Davis attaches the greatest significance—in hindsight—to just how solid U.S. advance information was when the coup actually and finally did come. Yet he offers nothing concrete to justify the conclusion that he really knew, and my own research showed that those overnight reports flashed from Santiago were so inconclusive that top policy makers were not alerted. Furthermore, Ambassador Davis's own movements on the morning of the coup, as well as those of other key embassy officials—putting themselves in danger by driving into the very eye of revolution, the American embassy—does nothing to suggest *certain* knowledge.

92. "Chile *Junta* Says It Kept U.S. In Dark," Washington-datelined dispatch, *New York Times,* September 15, 1973. Ambassador Davis makes no mention of any such incident in his memoirs, but then the main thrust of the ambassador's reportage of postcoup events is to distance himself from the Washington hard-liners (President Nixon and Secretary Kissinger) and show himself as blameless both for the coup and its bloody aftermath. He devotes

several pages, for example, to speculations as to whether the United States should have "warned" Allende, even when it is clear that Allende himself knew at least as much about the developing danger of revolution as did U.S. intelligence services (Allende's Saturday warning from General Prats, for example, cf. chapter 7). Davis remarks (op. cit., p. 364) that had he proposed warning Allende, "my Washington superiors would no doubt have concluded that I had gone around the bend." The Pinochet quote is from a press conference he gave in Santiago on September 21 and reproduced in *El Día Decisivo*, op. cit. p. 156.

93. Richard A. Ware, *The Pentagon's Office of International Security Affairs, 1969–1973, or Two Citizens Go to Washington*, brochure published by the American Enterprise Institute for Public Policy Research, Washington, D.C., 1986, reproducing the G. Warren Nutter Lecture in Political Economy given by Mr. Ware, January 22, 1986. Ware was then principal deputy assistant secretary of defense in the International Security Agency. The quote appears on p. 12. Ware notes that "the case of Chile loomed large during our watch . . . We were concerned about the danger to stability in the Western Hemisphere should Chile and Cuba become partners in communism. Chile also is of strategic importance because of (1) its long border with Argentina and other countries; (2) its long coastline with the only three deep-water ports on the west coast; (3) its control of both shores of the Straits of Magellan; and (4) its control of Easter Island in the South Pacific." He adds: "Fortunately, Chile stepped back from the brink."

94. Kissinger, *Years of Upheaval*, op. cit., pp. 408. Kissinger attributes his "preoccupation" with the Senate hearings as the probable reason for his delay until September 19 in reporting this to the president.

95. David Atlee Phillips, pp. 248–249. Phillips attended as chief of the Western Hemisphere Division of the CIA, backing up CIA Director William Colby, who gave the opening briefing at the meeting; and, Kissinger, *Years of Upheaval*, op. cit., pp. 406–407. Kissinger wrote that Colby "correctly predicted that the military would insist on fundamental changes in the political system. Their distrust of civilian politicians made early elections highly unlikely." Colby also predicted that while the junta would not reverse all of Allende's social programs, it would permit a gradual return to private ownership; in foreign policy, a shift away from antagonism toward the U.S. and "a mellowing of Allende's Third World stance." Kissinger also notes that it was decided to leave up to the Chileans whether to call off the imminent visit to Chile of a U.S. Air Force stunt-flying team. (They decided against it.) The WSAG was, in Phillips' description, "an after-the-fact type of Forty Committee, with a slightly larger composition."

96. Davis, op. cit., p. 376. Davis writes that the question of "ongoing covert support for the democratic parties" came up at a Washington meeting the weekend of September 22–23 with Assistant Secretary of State Kubisch. Kubisch, he said, wanted an immediate cut-off of all such aid, expressing his unease about covert programs. "I was concerned at the beleaguered state of the democratic parties in Chile, already facing the *Junta's* antipathy. Foolishly, perhaps," Davis continued, "I expressed myself as less convinced than he was of the need to cut off support immediately, particularly to the Christian Democrats. Kubisch was probably right; in any case, we discontinued this support without delay." In Davis's view, "relations between the *Junta* leaders and the Christian Democrats were crucial to the prospects of

the regime but it appears that the generals did not understand the fact" (ibid., p. 372). Obviously, "the generals" did not view that as a "fact." Queasiness on the recognition question shines through in his comments on the complications produced by "our precipitate act" in quick recognition of the Brazilian military government in 1964. "We had good reason to be careful," he then wrote of 1973. "Reuters was reporting pointedly on the sixteenth that the first to recognize the Chilean regime were 'two of Latin America's right-wing military governments'. . . ." (ibid., p. 374). This would seem to suggest the novel notion that a British news agency should be a factor in shaping U.S. foreign policy behavior. As to the "back-channel," Davis said when a Chilean businessman friend of his tipped him off, "I sent Washington a meticulous, deadpan account of the goings on and asked for guidance. My telegram was EXDIS [exclusive distribution], which ensured that fifty to a hundred copies were sprayed out to key Washington offices. I received a somewhat embarrassed reply, relayed from the White House, and these back-channel activities ceased." Davis had gone to Washington that weekend for a follow-up interview with Kissinger on the two or three jobs Kissinger had in mind for him. On October 11, Davis's appointment as director general of the foreign service was announced, and he left Chile on November 1, 1973.

97. Kissinger, *Years of Upheaval*, op. cit., p. 408, and Phillips, op. cit., pp. 240, 250. Kissinger said to use the economic issues "might make the new government appear to be the tool of the economic interests of multinational companies." Regarding Plan Centaur, Phillips writes, "I have no doubt that the Cuban DGI [the intelligence service] was soon aware that this parole violator was an impostor; nevertheless he flew on to Chile on a Soviet airliner." He adds: "I certainly understand why Mrs. Allende, whom I know to be a fine person, might readily accept the fabricator's story. But, I can assure her now, there was no truth to it, and the evidence provided by the envoy was spurious." The "60 questions" is also from Phillips, who relates how resourceful the embattled (literally) embassy in Santiago was in digging out the answers (ibid., p. 250).

98. Kissinger, *Years of Upheaval*, op. cit., pp. 410–413. I have quoted from Kissinger at length because of the post-Allende conceit that the United States coddled the Chilean government during the Nixon and Ford years. However much Kissinger—and others—believed in the *wisdom* of such a course, they were never able to sustain such a policy, or to begin it, really. Instead, from the very beginning, the United States became the new regime's most serious international tormentor.

99. Ibid., pp. 409–410.

100. Cocaine and extradition from a prepared statement given by Dr. Ernest W. Lefever, then senior fellow, Foreign Policy Studies, at the Brookings Institution in Washington, D.C., on Monday, August 5, 1974, before the Subcommittee on Inter-American Affairs of the House Foreign Affairs Committee, as reproduced in *United States and Chile*, op. cit., p. 195; government report in *Chile*, #258, October 23, 1973, p. 2. Lefever says that for his "swift and unprecedented" cooperation, the deputy secretary of Chile's Interior Ministry was given a citation by the United States. *Chile* reports that General Ernesto Baeza, then director of the nationwide detective police force (Investigaciones), was apprised of the payoffs while attending a world meeting of Interpol in Vienna. Draft legislation to tighten control of

the drug traffic was approved on March 14, 1973, by the Chilean Chamber of Deputies and was still awaiting Senate approval when the revolution took place.

101. Davis, op. cit., p. 342.

102. Elisabeth Farnsworth suggested the "blockade dismantling" theory in an article, "Chile: What Was The U.S. Role? More Than Admitted," *Foreign Policy*, #16, Fall 1974. Her article was, in large measure, a response to one by Prof. Paul Sigmund in the January 1974 issue of *Foreign Affairs*; Sigmund authored the second of the two in this issue of *Foreign Policy*, his entitled, "Less Than Imagined." It is a reflection of the intellectual (dis)temper of those times that Sigmund would come under attack in yet another *Foreign Affairs* article in its January 1975 issue, authored by Prof. Richard R. Fagen of Stanford, entitled "The United States and Chile: Roots and Branches," an article which, in turn, provoked in that same issue an extraordinary exchange of letters written by Sigmund and Fagen.

103. Chile agreed to pay the U.S. $60 million over a four-year period, and an additional $66 million at 6 percent interest over a six-year period, beginning in 1975. Chile also agreed to pay the Overseas Private Investment Corporation $7.8 million to cover obligations incurred because of the Kennecott and Bank of America expropriations. As to compensation, as indicated in chapter 7, the last of the agreements with the major companies—the copper firms and ITT—was reached in 1977. Details of 1973 talks from Sigmund, *The Overthrow*, op. cit., p. 261, and Kissinger, *Years of Upheaval*, op. cit., p. 410.

104. The complex agreement was in two parts: 80 percent of debt acquired before December 1973 was rescheduled into fourteen semi-annual payments beginning January 1977; the balance was due in three installments: 5 percent in 1974, 5 percent in 1975, and 10 percent in 1976. "Recent Bank Loans to Chile: A Chronology," *United States and Chile*, op. cit., p. 436; and, for July terms, *Bolsa Review*, op. cit., vol. 7, #83, November 1973, p. 569. As to the IMF, Plank #31 of the Popular Unity's Platform of its "First Forty Measures" said: "No more links with the International Monetary Fund. We shall renege the commitments with the International Monetary Fund. We shall put an end to the continual shameful devaluation of the escudo." From J. Ann Zumwalt, ed., *The Chilean Road To Socialism* (Austin: University of Texas Press, 1973), p. 280. It was one of the pledges the UP kept.

105. George W. Telfer, "Eximbank Weighs Chile Action," *Journal of Commerce*, January 10, 1974.

106. Farnsworth in *Foreign Policy*, op. cit. The article is a mish-mash of misstatements, misrepresentations, and distortions. For example, she speaks of the IDB granting Chile a $65 million credit for a hydroelectric project on September 18, 1973, and then, seven or eight sentences later, of an IDB grant of $75.3 million for construction of a hydroelectric plant—as though they were separate loans. Quoting from the March 1974 issue of *Noticias*, she said that the coup loans and credit lines opened to Chile—from the United States, Brazil, Argentina, the IMF, the World Bank, the IDB, the Andean Development Corp.—amounted to $468.8 million. But that "arithmetic" fails to recognize that the $75 million ultimately approved for Antuco was for a project the Allende government itself had characterized as "of the highest priority" for Chile; and that the $95 million in

IMF credits were conditioned by complying with certain stringent conditions and targets—"creditworthiness," in other words—and granted by an agency which the Allende government not only refused to deal with, but reviled, repeatedly. But even more to the point is the assumption that there is something morally wrong about concluding that there is, in international affairs, a distinction to be made between friends and foes; or that banks, bankers, and even international banking agencies are wrong if they are wary of economic chaos and gross management incompetence, and responsive to those who are seemingly willing to work with them in restoring fiscal order. As it happens, by the late 1980s, when Chile had become one of the most attractive investment opportunities in the world, U.S. businessmen were slow to take advantage of those opportunities.

107. Phil Gailey, "Don't Withhold Aid from Chile *Junta* Because of 'Mistakes,' Panel Is Told," Washington-datelined dispatch, *Miami Herald*, August 6, 1974, p. 12-B. Lefever was accompanied to Chile by Dr. Riordan Roett, director of Latin American studies at Johns Hopkins University, and Dr. Albert Blaustein, a Rutgers University law professor. The three testified on their return before the House Inter-American Affairs Subcommittee.

108. From the transcript of "60 Minutes," vol. IX, #16, January 9, 1977, pp. 8–9. Asked by interviewer Mike Wallace who had committed "tens of millions of dollars in AID [Agency for International Development] monies for covert electoral purposes in 1963 and 1964," Korry responded: "The Kennedy White House, to defeat Salvador Allende in the 1964 election, and to elect Eduardo Frei and the Christian Democrats. That is one thing. The second thing is that millions and millions were given to Jesuit-led organizations in Chile by the Kennedys and the Johnson Administration in response to appeals for monies from the American taxpayer—quote—'to oppose laicism, Protestantism and Communism.' Both these actions are violations of U.S. laws. The third thing that President Kennedy did, which they want to hide, is that he personally asked—and this was legitimate—David Rockefeller [head of Chase Manhattan Bank], in the spring of '63, to organize the [sic]—a group of multi-nationals to support American policies in all of Latin America." Korry evidently misspoke when he referred to appeals from "the American taxpayer." He went on to say that the United States was still paying yearly "hush money" through the CIA to Chilean politicians for their roles in the 1963–1964 electioneering when he arrived in Chile in 1968. He also accused of "hypocrisy" "liberal democrats," including Walter Mondale, Hubert Humphrey, and the AFL-CIO leadership—all of whom, he said, were fully informed about the covert and illegal activities, but who would later become "great moralizers" (ibid., pp. 9–10).

109. Davis (op. cit., pp. 383–84) notes that Harrington's pique apparently began when he was unable to pick the congressman up at the airport because of a prior appointment, and that Harrington then rebuffed suggestions that they meet later at the embassy residence or office, as well as subsequent suggestions. At one point, Harrington demanded that Davis meet him early on the morning of October 27 at the entrance to the National Stadium in order to inspect that detention facility. Despite contrary advice from his staff, Davis agreed; Harrington then decided to withdraw the request.

110. "Lawmaker Visiting Chile Links U.S. Economic Policies To Coup," Santiago-datelined story, *New York Times*, October 28, 1973.

111. Phillips, op. cit., pp. 252–254. Phillips recounts that Schlaudeman telephoned him after testifying to tell him that he had been " 'really roasted by Michael Harrington. He kept asking me about the "destabilization" of the Allende regime. Have you people given Congress anything to indicate that "destabilizing" was part of the plan?' I assured Harry that I never heard of the term and soon forgot the conversation." He would remember it when the leaked stories exploded three months later, and "a new word [entered] the political arena" (ibid., p. 254).

112. Popper had served in the 1940s on the editorial board of *Amerasia*, which became the center of a much-publicized (and congressionally investigated) furor. *Amerasia* was part of a tightly-knit Leftist clique, urging American support for the Chinese Communists led by Mao Tse-tung in their life-death struggle against the Kuomintang Nationalist government headed by Chiang Kai-shek. The quotation is from Moss, op. cit., p. 1108. Within a year of his appointment, Popper did draw a sharp rebuke from Secretary of State Kissinger for "lecturing the Chilean regime on democratic practice." Reports at the time said that after word of the rebuke leaked, Kissinger refused to allow an official expression of confidence in Popper. The event which triggered the incident was a report Popper had filed describing a July 22, 1974, meeting he had had with Chilean officials concerning the impending visit of Army Secretary Howard Callaway. During that talk, Popper reportedly brought up the concern of some members of Congress over the lack of democracy in Chile. When Kissinger saw the telegram—similar to several others Popper had previously sent—he scribbled in pen: "Tell Popper to cut out the political science lectures." It was not the first time the two had clashed; shortly after becoming secretary of state, Kissinger had removed Popper as assistance secretary for international organizations ("Kissinger Rebukes Diplomat in Chile," AP story, *Miami Herald*, September 28, 1974, p. 26-A).

113. Ford said (accurately) that the CIA activity was designed "to help and assist the preservation of opposition newspapers and electronic media and to preserve opposition political parties. I think this is in the best interest of the people of Chile, and certainly in our best interest." Sigmund, *The Overthrow*, op. cit., p. 259. Sigmund goes on to say that "the statement was widely criticized both for its assumption of a unilateral right by the United States to intervene in free elections, and for its lack of complete candor about where some of the CIA financial support went (for example, to the *gremios* and to Patria y Libertad)." The academic was James E. Petras, a sociology professor at the State University of New York at Binghamton, in testimony September 18, 1974, in *United States and Chile*, op. cit., p. 308. Testifying just ten days after the "destabilization" leaks, Petras invoked as fact that "we further know that the CIA was not stabilizing a democracy but in their own language destabilizing it." Professor Sigmund, although certainly one of the most thoughtful commentators on Chile, had in his commentary lurched into egregious error. As to the first part: in a polarized world, the United States has an obligation to assist democratic forces fighting for their very survival against despotic ones with far greater funding and even less fastidious outside assistance. As to the second, the truckers, the key *gremio*, got the princely sum of $2,800, and that by inadvertence; Patria y Libertad got a grand total of $45,700, all of it in the first year of Allende—long before it went "violent." The vast bulk of the $6 million, itself a piddling sum, went to opposition media, facing gov-

ernment strangulation, and to political parties, principally the Christian Democrats. Farnsworth remarks that Sigmund is "a Christian Democrat advocate." In his admirable work, while waxing indignant about the crumbs given a right-wing organization and a feisty labor group, he evidences no such indignation about the huge sums covertly disbursed to elect the Christian Democrats in 1964. That is dismissed in two sentences: "Over half the cost of the campaign, a total of $2.6 million, came from the U.S. Central Intelligence Agency through various intermediaries and without Frei's knowledge as to its source. Considerable CIA money also went to the Liberals and Conservatives, who could pull out all the stops in making anti-Communist appeals without compromising the Christian Democrats as a party" (ibid., p. 34). The actual amounts furnished the Christian Democrats then—and again in the 1969 and 1970 elections—were much greater than that.

114. Paul N. Rosenstein-Rodan, "Why Allende Failed," p. 617.
115. Pinochet's October 11, 1973, speech is reproduced, inter alia, in El Día Decisivo, pp. 159–168. In it—explicitly rejecting "the Marxist conception of man"—Pinochet described public service as "a mission . . . requiring efficiency, honor and loyalty," adding that the government's own acts must reflect "strict public morality, so as to initiate, with its example, a profound change in the mentality of the country"; "Respect for the honor and dignity of the person . . . the sense of duty and a mystique of labor developed in each one of us must become the essential norms for the spiritual rebuilding of the country. The moral purging which the Fatherland will experience will be reflected in order, the cleanliness of our cities, discipline in our acts. The Government will complement and safeguard the foregoing through the integral reestablishment of the principle of authority, which will be brought to bear without hesitation against all those minority or extremist groups seeking to disrupt the peaceful coexistence of Chileans, as it will also against all forms of crime. Never again will a small group of the audacious find official tolerance to proclaim and practice their violent purposes, or suppose that they can break the unity of those born on this soil, sharing as we do a patriotic formation and cultural ancestry and common history which form the monolothic foundation of 'Chilenity' " (ibid., pp. 1166–167).
116. Luis Galdames, Historia de Chile: Prehistoria a 1970 (Santiago: Productos Raval, 1974), pp. 307, 316; Walterio Millar, Historia de Chile (Santiago: Editorial Zig-Zag, 1973), 29th ed., pp. 221–227.
117. As early as 1822, Portales wrote a friend from Peru: "Political things do not interest me, but as a good citizen, I can express my opinion with complete freedom, even to censuring the acts of the government. The democracy promoted by so many illusory people is absurd in countries such as the Americas, full of vices, where the citizens lack all the virtues needed to establish a true republic. Nor is monarchy the American ideal . . . The republic is the system which we ought to adopt, but, do you know how I understand it for these countries? A strong, centralized government, whose men are truly models of virtue and patriotism so as to channel citizens along the path of order and virtue. When they have become moral, then let come the completely free, liberal government, full of ideals, in which all citizens take part . . ." Quoted by Bernardino Bravo Lira, De Portales A Pinochet: Gobierno y Regimen de Gobierno en Chile (Santiago:

Editorial Jurídica de Chile, Editorial Andrés Bello, 1985), pp. 67–68. As we shall see shortly, Pinochet used almost identical concepts, if not words, in his address to the nation on the first anniversary of the revolution.

118. Galdames, op. cit., pp. 299, 300–301, 320; Millar, op. cit., pp. 226–227; Jordi Fuentes & Lía Cortés, *Diccionario Político de Chile, 1810–1966* (Santiago: Editorial Orbe, 1967), p. 390; Francisco Javier Díaz Zalazar, ed., *Nueva Enciclopedia de Chile* (Santiago: Ediciones Copihue, 1974), vol. 1, pp. 87–90; for 1891–1925 period, Eduardo Frei in *Reforma Constitucional 1970* (Santiago: Editorial Jurídica de Chile, 1970), pp. 24. *Reforma* has six authors (but no editor is listed): Frei; Sergio Molina; Enrique Evans; Gustavo Lagos; Alejandro Silva, and Francisco Cumplido.

119. Galdames, op. cit., p. 321.

120. *Pensamiento de Portales* (Santiago: Colección Ideario, 1974), pp. 138–139. That slender volume, made up mainly of excerpts from Portales's letters, was brought out early in the Pinochet regime, and, to further underscore its significance, with a forward written by Rear Adm. Hugo Castro Jiménez, then minister of education.

121. Ibid., pp. 75–76. Portales went on to say that he feared the Monroe Doctrine was the first stage of a plan for the conquest of America, "not by force of arms, but by [extending its] influence in every sphere, if not today, tomorrow." By the 1960s and early 1970s—before the U.S. became one of the military government's most acerbic and stinging critics—most top military officers in Chile were strongly pro-American.

122. Galdames, op. cit., pp. 337, 339–340. Galdames notes that "the manifestations of mourning and the funeral pomp accorded him had no precedent in Chile . . . The war which Portales had declared became more popular with his death, because it was presumed that the assassins had been instigated and even paid by Santa Cruz." (They had not, and in fact, it was a mindless and pointless barracks rebellion which created Chile's greatest martyr.) Galdames also notes, as do other historians, that in the aftermath of Yungay, Chile came to be viewed by European powers as one of the strongest—if not *the* strongest—military power to emerge from Spain's colonial empire.

123. Pinochet's speech to the nation on the first anniversary of the revolution, Sept. 11, 1974 (pp. 5–6, 8 of mimeographed version distributed by the presidential press office, and titled, *Palabras del Jefe Supremo de la Nación, Augusto Pinochet Ugarte, Al Conmemorarse El Primer Aniversario de Gobierno*).

124. Amos Perlmutter, *The Military and Politics in Modern Times* (New Haven: Yale University Press, 1977), p. 167. He defines that ideology as Comtist positivism, and credits it with "enormous" influence on the militaries of Brazil, Argentina, Peru, "and even Chile." In passages aimed mainly at Spain, but which he says suggest wider generalizations, Perlmutter observes that military intervention "at least in its early stages is instigated by disgruntled civilians and power-seeking politicians . . . In seeking the support of the military, politicians threaten the constitutional and political practices to which they are dedicated and on whose behalf they have recruited military support. Furthermore, once the officer-politicians have assumed civilian characteristics and expectations, they lose their hold over the army . . ." (ibid., p. 169). That, of course, is precisely what happened in Chile when, in 1972, Allende first drafted the military

to prop up his government, and it is precisely what happened to General Prats in 1973 when he behaved increasingly as a political figure. It is also a measure of the unanimity of opinion about the need for a Portalian renaissance among Chile's military leaders that the "civilian" Pinochet never did lose the support of the country's armed forces. The comments about maintaining political order and disengagement appear on pp. 178 and 173, respectively; *designed* emphasized in the original.

125. The 1833 constitution contained that language. The 1925 constitution—adopted, ironically, while Chile was ruled by a military-dominated junta—added the following: "The armed forces cannot deliberate" ("Ningún cuerpo armado puede deliberar."). In the Jan. 9, 1971, Statute of Guarantees which Allende was required to sign as a condition of indispensable Christian Democrat support for his assuming the presidency, that language was amended to specify that the "public force" was made up solely and exclusively of the armed forces and the corps of Carabineros, "institutions essentially professional, hierarchical, disciplined, obedient, and not deliberative." The intent, obviously, was to forestall the creation of parallel paramilitary forces which, of course, is exactly what the Popular Unity would then go about doing. As noted previously, the National party—which had polled one-fifth of all the votes in the 1969 congressional elections, and whose candidate trailed Allende by a razor-thin margin in the 1970 presidential elections—was excluded from the drafting process for these amendments, and thus abstained in Congress when they were voted on.

126. Perlmutter, op. cit., p. 89. That finding is echoed and reinforced by Solaun and Quinn: "... we have established three indicators of governmental ineffectiveness and illegitimacy in the coup setting (although others are surely possible): (1) acute congressional-presidential conflict; (2) high levels of civilian violence or direct action; and (3) overt civilian-military coalition against the government." The first two were powerfully present in the Chile of 1973. Mauricio Solaun and Michael A. Quinn, *Sinners and Heretics: The Politics of Military Intervention in Latin America* (Urbana: University of Illinois Press, 1973), p. 62.

127. Among many examples, one might cite Allende in March of 1971: "The Armed Forces exist to defend the physical and economic frontiers of the country"; again, at graduation ceremonies for the Military School, July 31, 1973: "To be a soldier today signifies not only having prepared oneself through the hard years of training in the Military School, but also constantly improving oneself not only in those disciplines appropriate to one's speciality, but also across the wide range of human knowledge. One does not conceive today of a limited soldier, however outstanding, limited only to mastery of the techniques of war ... This means, and so it must be, the incorporation of the Armed Forces into the great process of collective effort, through knowledge of the economic and social reality of the country, through a profound and deep internalization of all that which implies serving the country on the frontier of industry, the University, the farm, the sea, the air ..." Cited by Sergio Miranda Carrington, "*Las Fuerzas Armadas en el Ordenamiento Jurídico de Chile*," *Fuerzas Armadas y Seguridad Nacional* (Santiago: Ediciones Portada, 1973), pp. 40–41. Or this, from General Prats: "The defense of the national patrimony is today a dynamic 'geoeconomic' conceptualization, by which it becomes necessary

for the Armed Forces to have an active and permanent participation in the great tasks of socio-economic development ..." From a May 2, 1972, interview with the Santiago magazine *Eva*, cited in Carlos Prats González, *Memorias: Testimonio de un Soldado* (Santiago: Pehuen Editora, 1985), 2ND ed., p. 262.

128. As Perlmutter (op. cit., p. 89) observes, "... some social scientists did not believe military rule as worthy of study as civilian rule. This prejudice had a variety of causes, ranging from ignorance to antagonism toward war and the military profession." As to the stereotype, Charles D. Corbett writes: "Recent research tends to undermine the image of a region-wide nine-teenth century alliance between the oligarchy and the military, and cer-tainly in this century the various officer corps have been largely middle class in composition ... Viewing this phenomenon [military interference in political processes] against 'western' traditions, U.S. analysts have most often conceptualized a predatory group acting upon rather than within its society, positing the choice for U.S. policymakers between support for 'high-handed military dictatorship and struggling civilian democracy.' " Corbett, *The Latin American Military As A Socio-Political Force* (Miami: Center for Advanced International Studies, University of Miami, 1972), p. 4.

129. The study was done by the Defense Department's General Staff, then headed by General Prats, and presented to the commanders-in-chief of the three armed services on December 30, 1969 (Prats, op. cit., p. 141). The study noted that among conscripts, "there are, in general, none from the upper classes." The study describes the 80 percent as "of not Marxist proclivities." Genaro Arriagada H., an assiduous student of Chilean mili-tary affairs (albeit from a decidedly Christian Democrat perspective), writes that the Chilean military's "visceral anti-communism" was "not a consequence of the propagandistic campaign of the Right in the 60s and early 70s, but a deep-seated tradition" (Arriagada, *La Política Militar de Pinochet* [Santiago: Impresor Salesianos, 1985], pp. 46–47). The Defense analysis, incidentally, contained an uncannily close forecast of the out-come of the presidential election the following September: Popular Unity (candidate yet to be named), 38 percent; Alessandri, 35 percent; Tomic, 27 percent. (The actual totals: Allende, 36.2; Alessandri, 34.9; Tomic, 27.8.)

130. Arriagada, *La Política*, p. 39. The Pinochet quote is from a remarkable hour-and-a-half interview he gave three top editors of the Santiago maga-zine, *Qué Pasa*, #785, April 1986. Pinochet was referring to the "parlia-mentary period" between the collapse of the presidential system in 1891 and the creation of the pseudo-presidential system of 1925.

131. Even Prats, scarcely a hard-liner, wrote of the "general negative reaction in Latin American military circles against North American 'paternalism.' " Military leaders, he continued, began to argue for the need to "indepen-dence themselves" from foreign military tutelage. As a parting shot, he added a sarcastic complaint that "the obsolescence of the equipment sup-plied by the United States" offended the dignity and self-respect of the military in any case (Prats, op. cit., pp. 100–101). The reform movement was spearheaded by Sen. Frank Church (D-Idaho), then chairman of the Senate Subcommittee on Western Hemisphere Affairs, and the even more powerful Sen. J. William Fulbright (D-Ark), chairman of the Senate Foreign Relations Committee. Legislation passed in 1967 put a cap of $150 million

on U.S. military assistance to the entire (then) twenty-one nations of Latin America, half that in grants, half in sales. Sales of sophisticated weapons, such as advanced fighter planes, was banned (Latin Americans were told they could have the short-range F-5 "Freedom Fighter," or nothing; they thus turned to Europe, and particularly France, for the sophisticated Mirage fighter jets, some eventually acquiring MiGs from the Soviets). Subsequent measures killed off Military Assistance Advisory Group missions in the region, thus creating a double-headed monster: the cycle of supply-maintenance-resupply was broken, and the close working bonds between U.S. and Latin military developed through the MAGs was also fatally weakened. Before the U.S.-imposed "reform," Latin arms spending was the lowest of any region in the world; freed of the restraining U.S. influence, Latin America went on an arms-buying binge in the late sixties and early seventies without precedent in history.

132. Arriagada H., an articulate and outspoken Christian Democrat critic of the Pinochet government, while dismissing the Viaux uprising as lacking in a larger political significance, does agree that by 1968, ". . . groups of officers and generals began more and more to defy the principles of subordination to the political power and those of non-deliberation . . . even graver, the questioning of the High Command also began . . ." (Arriagada, *La Política*, p. 38). As noted, in April 1968, the entire eighty-man graduating class of the Military Academy resigned in protest against conditions in the military. Wrote Prats: ". . . what happened in the Military Academy was an institutional temblor which facilitated the sowing of a bad seed which, with the passage of time, would grow poisonously" (Prats, op. cit., pp. 110–111). In the wake of that crisis, on May 6, 1968, the defense minister assembled the entire corps of generals and the officer corps of the Santiago garrison to ask for time to address their grievances. It was, in a very real sense, the onset of "deliberations" among senior commanders. But, as significant as that was, of even greater significance were the formation of secret military lodges and societies, and of clandestine meetings involving retired generals and active duty officers—a polarization within army ranks. Increasingly, many concerned not only about their own precarious situations, but about the leftward slide of their country, rallied around the strongly conservative Gen. Roberto Viaux.

133. Sergio Arellano Iturriaga, *Más Allá del Abismo* (Santiago: Editorial Proyección, 1985) p. 43.

134. Cited by A. Pineda de Castro, *Pinochet: Verdad y Ficción* (Madrid: Vasallo de Mumbert, 1981), p. 117. The study was prepared by the army's Operations Division and submitted to the high command August 27, 1973—three days after Prats' resignation.

135. For the Ortega y Gasset quote (from his "España Invertebrada") I am indebted to Miranda Carrington, op. cit., p. 36. The challenge to Prats came from Gen. Oscar Bonilla, on September 13, 1972, and is cited by Prats, op. cit., p. 290. Prats' reply was that for the army to do that would be "to stuff the Constitution in our pockets." But, as the months went by, it was increasingly apparent that, for Prats, "constitution" meant only the president, and not the other powers of state, and that however sincere he might have been, he followed Allende blindly because he was in deep and abiding sympathy with the goals and aims of Allende's government.

136. Nathaniel Davis, op. cit., p. 219. Davis, who makes plain a dislike for

Pinochet rivaling his esteem for both Prats and Allende, adds in an endnote that the contrast between the description of an agitated Pinochet given by Gen. Sergio Arellano Stark and the one given by Pinochet himself of his "quietude . . . is close to incredible" (ibid., n. 45, p. 438; Prats, op. cit., p. 256). Prats said he ordered updating of the internal security plan on April 4, 1972, a few days after an automobile accident on March 31, 1972, in the town of Curimón, led to the accidental discovery of munitions, a hand grenade and propaganda leaflets in the possession of the MIRista occupants of the vehicle. He took Gen. Mario Sepúlveda Squella, then chief of army intelligence, to a Tomás Moro meeting with Allende to brief him on the extent of the MIR subversive apparatus uncovered in Chile's major cities. Pinochet said he had first ordered the plan updated shortly after taking over as chief of staff, earlier that year, then a new version done in June of 1972. In his book, El Día Decisivo (p. 121), Pinochet speaks of his anxiety when confronted on September 9 with what amounted to Merino's ultimatum: revolt on the eleventh and not the fourteenth, as he wanted. If a single garrison were to disobey, he said, it could have meant polarization of the armed forces and a fratricidal civil war. Still, he felt that in the face of Merino's determination, he had no other choice but to accede. Pinochet also offers an explanation in that book as to why he did not take part in such interservice plotting as the Commission of the Generals' meetings: the ouster, in September of 1972 of General Canales—a man for whom he said he had "special regard"—after Admiral Justiniano reported to Prats on Canales' subversive talks with him. Pinochet said, what "I got out of that experience was that the revolution must be prepared in a very tight circle and only with persons of our Army, without mixing in anyone else, not even for purposes of informing them" (ibid., p. 82).

137. The lead soldiers quote was attributed to his wife, Lucía Hiriart de Pinochet, in a special section of the Sunday magazine of El Mercurio, February 3, 1974, p. 8: "Infancia y Juventud de la Junta"; Pinochet's quote is from his book, El Día Decisivo, p. 17. Pinochet was in the presidency only a few months when he would decorate his old teacher, Father Urenda, with the Order of Merit for his lifelong service as a teacher.

138. In his Qué Pasa interview, op. cit., Pinochet speaks of twelve years of professional studies; the 1973 mimeographed biography seems to indicate nine, including three—not four—at the Military Academy, and two postgraduate courses. Pinochet himself seems confused on this point: in his El Día Decisivo (p. 11), he speaks of "four years of hard work," graduating in 1936. In the mimeographed biography, his years of study are given as 1933–1936. Promotion was slow in the army of Pinochet's service: he was seven years in grade as a captain (1946–1953); seven as a major, six as a lieutenant colonel. In 1966, he made colonel, three years later, brigadier general; in 1970, the only other flag officer rank then available, general of division, before, in 1973, becoming general of the army, the rank reserved for the commander-in-chief of the army. In the years since Pinochet, there has been both grade inflation (from 25 generals in 1973, to 39 in 1980, to 54 in 1984), and a great speeding-up in promotion time-tables; it took Pinochet a typical thirty-two years to make flag rank. By 1984, the average for generals had dropped to twenty-eight years. But, in 1979, a new law restored the warrant officer rank and stipulated minimum time in grade, so that thirty years minimum would again be needed to make general. There was

a spectacular increase in the size of the army from 1970 onward: In 1970, continuing a trend which began in the 1930s, the navy was the largest service: 17,821 men and women, against 12,144 in the army. Under Allende, that trend was dramatically reversed: by 1973, the army had grown to 32,000 against 18,000 for the navy. An authoritative source would show that by the late 1970s, the army numbered 50,000 and the navy 24,000. Sources: for 1970, Arriagada, op. cit., p. 103 (his figures square with those used throughout by Prats); for July 1974, *Britannica Book of the Year, 1975* (Chicago: Encyclopaedia Britannica, 1975), p. 212. For late 1970s, John Keegan, *World Armies* (New York: Facts on File, 1979), p. 127. Growth continued in the 1980s; the 1988 *Britannica Book of the Year* (p. 263) put the army's strength in July 1987 at 57,000, the navy at 25,500. Although it should be obvious, I will observe, nonetheless, that both grade inflation and substantial growth in the size of the military became inevitable in the measure that the military—and military commanders—assumed a great number of formerly civilian functions in running the government. (* I have chosen the translation "warrant officer" rather than the more conventional "ensign" for *alférez* because in the United States, at least, ensign is an exclusively naval rank, and is actually the equivalent of second lieutenant. *Alférez* was used in Chile for all armed services, and ranked below second lieutenant.) Federico Willoughby, who served as press spokesman for the junta during its first three years, said Pinochet did, in fact, take formal classes in Marxist theory after becoming president. Willoughby said this during an interview with the author in Santiago, June 16, 1987.

139. Pinochet, *El Día Decisivo*, pp. 20–29.

140. In an interview with Blanca Arthur, "1986: El Balance de Pinochet," *El Mercurio*, December 28, 1986, p. D-1.

141. "Chile's Strongman, Augusto Pinochet Ugarte," *The New York Times*, September 13, 1973.

142. Interview with Willoughby, op. cit. Willoughby left the junta in 1976 after suffering severe health problems. At first, he worked for all four junta members, and was among those who urged having a single strong leader. Willoughby was firm in his belief that Pinochet was that man. Willoughby's outspoken opinions have cost him heavily in recent years, his access to the junta blocked—with all that signifies in terms of lost business opportunities for a public relations practicioner.

143. From my earlier book, *Allende: Death of a Marxist Dream* (New Rochelle: Arlington House, 1981), p. 10. The description was drawn from my first private interview with him, October 22, 1974.

144. Ibid., pp. 22–23. Based largely on my first interview with Merino in Santiago, October 18, 1974.

145. The first of those meetings took place on September 12, 1970. Having secured the permission of the then navy commander-in-chief, Admiral Porta, Merino went with three other senior admirals (Buzeta, Weber, and Poblete) to demand of Allende assurances that if Congress were to elect him, he would respect the traditional independence of the armed forces. Merino, this time with Admiral Montero, had a follow-up meeting with Allende a few days later. Merino did not attend a third, on October 1, involving Admirals Weber and Eberhard. When Prats, informed by Porta, reported on them on September 21 to General Schneider, Schneider said this would now trigger a "contacts race" among military rushing to see the

two finalist candidates, Alessandri and Allende. On October 2, Schneider protested to Porta that these meetings violated the compact among the military commanders-in-chief to eschew contacts with the candidates. Porta defended them on the grounds that his admirals had merely briefed Allende on technical matters facing the navy. But, as Prats noted, the real purpose was to exact the guarantees of independence. Schneider's fears apparently were not realized; as far as is known, no other top commanders entered into such substantive negotiations with the candidates. Defense Minister Sergio Ossa apparently didn't learn of them until October 8, at which time he summoned the three service commanders and said he viewed those talks as a vote of no confidence in him and that he therefore should resign. Arguing that the meetings were not really consequential, Schneider and Air Force Chief General Guerraty talked him out of it. Details in Prats op. cit., pp. 172, 176, 180–181.

146. Details from *El Mercurio*, "Infancia y juventud de la *Junta*," pp. 10–11, and mimeographed biographical sketch dated September 27, 1973, and furnished by navy headquarters. Merino had already been head of household for ten years when he married, following the death in 1942 of his father. But, as his sister reports, that didn't slow down his enthusiasm for motorcycle racing; it would take a serious accident during a 100-mile race in 1949 to do that. The Merinos have three daughters.

147. Pinochet, op. cit., p. 120. He said it was while they were engaged in that conversation that Merino's messenger arrived with the summons to revolution. It should be remembered that of the four revolutionary leaders, only Pinochet and Leigh were, at the time, officially heads of their services. Allende had continued to stall on giving Merino the top navy job, and Mendoza was catapulted to his post by fiat of the other three.

148. *El Mercurio*, "Infancia y Juventud de la *Junta*," op. cit., and Willoughby interview, op. cit. Willoughby used the English words "up-and-down" in describing Leigh. Early in the life of the revolutionary regime, one correspondent wrote: "At times, General Leigh, the most articulate and right-wing of the *junta* members, has appeared to have a more domineering personality" (Jonathan Kandell, *New York Times*, "Chilean Assumes Full Leadership," June 27, 1974). Kandell was, of course, right about Leigh's "domineering" personality; it happens that Pinochet's was more so. As indicated, English-language fluency did not alone account for Leigh's reputation for "articulateness." As early as grammar school, he was tapped because of his budding oratorial skills to deliver the farewell speech fifth graders traditionally gave sixth graders as they moved on to junior school.

149. Ibid., and mimeographed biographical sketch distributed by Carabinero headquarters in September 1973; also a lengthy interview with him published December 3, 1973, in the Santiago newspaper *Tribuna*, "Carabineros no es el pariente pobre de la *Junta*." In that interview, Mendoza said Chile "will return to constitutional normality when the new Constitution takes effect, by which time we expect that Chile may be considered free of the danger of falling in hands of persons of a system or doctrine which preaches hatred, envy and violence . . ." Evita Perón, according to Mendoza, was heard to murmur as she pinned medals on the Chilean victors, "They brought me out here for this crummy role" (*papelón*).

150. *Qué Pasa* interview, op. cit.

151. *Qué Pasa* interview, op. cit. History-buff Pinochet was referring to the

execution of de la Hoz after he attempted to seize power while Valdivia was off to Peru to enlist support for the struggling colony. The conquistador Francisco Pizarro had named the two coequals in settling the virgin lands which would become Chile in order to settle competing claims to a royal warrant for colonization.

152. Since it is true that the Right did share with the military a basic tenet—anticommunism—it is also true that the Right continued to support the junta for a much longer time than did the Left. But, by the early 1980s, most people of the traditional Right—represented chiefly by the old National party—were in opposition, and were replaced on "the right" by a new generation of technocrats and ideologues roughly analagous to the neoconservatives and New Right in the United States. Pinochet alluded to this in a 1986 interview when asked about opposition from the Right of those who had so long supported the revolution: "What happened," he said, "is that the Right imagined that we made the revolution for them. And that just wasn't so" (Blanca Arthur, "1986: El Balance de Pinochet," in *El Mercurio*, December 28, 1986, p. 1-D). Pinochet and the others had, of course, long before said the same thing about the Christian Democrats—they hadn't made the revolution for them, either.

153. In an interview with the author in Santiago, April 3, 1974. Canessa further characterized it as a coordinating rather than a directing or planning agency—roughly akin to the White House staff. But, in Santiago as in Washington, those lines frequently blur. In an interview with the Santiago magazine *Qué Pasa*, Canessa said one of its major projects was formulating basic policies by ministry and by sector of activity (" 'Estado Mayor' Técnico Para La Junta," #152, March 22, 1974, pp. 32–36).

154. Notes I made at the time of my interview with him in April of 1974 referred to the "spartan, barren" look of his apartment. Guzmán, who seemed to have virtually unrestricted access to Pinochet during the early years, was also one of the influential figures in the first round of efforts to draft a new constitution. In the 1980s, he formed a miniparty devoted to supporting and perpetuating the ideals of the Pinochet revolution.

155. Charles Eisendrath, "The Price of Order," *Time* magazine, December 31, 1973.

156. My notes, taken in the hall at the time, record how "lustily" the audience joined in the singing of the national anthem, the slow flag-raising ceremony, the big military band playing. Pinochet launched immediately afterward into his speech, reading from the text, "occasionally bouncing on his heels and looking up briefly . . . his voice with the resonance of a baseball bat, not flat, more like cracking out words, and, in typical Chilean fashion, occasionally rising an octave or so to make a point; not an increase in decibels, but up an octave."

157. As part of the "depoliticization" of social organizations, a DL was issued banning elections in all such "intermediary" organizations. I have quoted here from a blue booklet issued by the junta's Division de Comunicación Social, "Declaración de Principios del Gobierno de Chile"—at least four years after the speech promulgating the "Principles" was given. At the beginning of the booklet are photos of the four junta members, the last of them of Air Force Gen. Fernando Matthei, who didn't take over his job until 1978, following the minicoup which ousted General Leigh. There are, however, no discrepancies between that text and the one published by

El Mercurio both the day after the speech, and again in a special section published September 11, 1974, "El Alcázar Asediado," pp. 20–23.

158. Although he authored no detailed theory of government, Aquinas did adapt Aristotle's formulation of the polity to a Christian framework, particularly in *De Regno*, and *In Libros Politicorum*, as well as in several volumes of his masterwork, *Summa Theologiae*—works much studied and revered by the Catholic-educated technocrats of the new regime. Prat, president of the youth wing of the Conservative party in the 1940s, later president of the Bank of the State and finance minister under Alessandri, created his own party for a run at the presidency in 1964. He withdrew from the race out of fear of dividing the non-Marxist vote even further and thus assuring the election of Allende. But he was a fecund writer and teacher, and his ideas left a strong imprint on many of the technocrats who would become the brain trust of the junta. In a television interview on May 1, 1964, he responded to a questioner who recalled that in an earlier interview he had said the "the armed forces could not remain as in a showcase [*vitrina*] indifferent to the social, economic and political processes of Chile." After noting that he believed the military understood very well their basic mission was to defend the national territory, he added: "Naturally, in that mission, the armed forces are not in a showcase and are necessarily thinking people . . . If a government, to take a hypothetical example . . . would attempt . . . to turn over [to a foreign power] what is today ours, I believe our armed forces would leave that showcase. And, insofar as the defense of our institutions and laws is concerned, if these were attacked, if these were placed in danger, they [the military] also would have to leave that showcase. But if a government fulfills its mission of maintaining the territorial integrity and the dignity of the nation, and abides by and makes others abide by the laws of the republic and respects its institutions, I am certain that there can never be a *coup d'état* and that our armed forces will never go beyond their specific mission . . ." Three further examples, among many, taken from a book on him done by a man who was himself an influential ideologue in the new government, Mario Arnello: "The government of national unity is the only one which can get underway that most genuine motor of progress, pride in country. The country's advance is slowed because no one points the way to bold and historic goals which . . . light the love of country as the fire in which they are forged . . ."; "Oligarchic governments, those dominated by social or economic groups, or political parties which have become slaves to their great electoral clients, these give us a very different image of our country . . ."; "If parliament functions badly, or the Executive functions badly, then it is evident that the State will not fulfill its mission. Scholars, sociologists, economists can produce all the statistics they like, write the books and cite the most convincing facts: but, if we do not possess the right instruments . . . to produce the unavoidable changes, we will reap nothing but frustration, desperation, chaos and rebelliousness" (Mario Arnello, *Proceso a una Democracia: Pensamiento Político de Jorge Prat*, pp. 333–334, 141, 127, 173). (As so often happens with books edited in Chile, particularly in earlier years, there is no publication data, only—in my yellowing copy—Inscription #29177. Inasmuch as the documents included were derived from Prats' 1963–1964 presidential campaign, I would deduce that the book was published at about that time. It is notable that Prats said

these things even before the divisive and unbridled partisan dogmatism of the Frei years, the bedlam of class warfare, and the chaos of the Allende years.)

159. Jonathan Kandell quoted one source as telling him: "History has shown that collective leaderships simply do not work. We need a one-man rule" (Kandell, "Chilean Assumes Full Leadership," *New York Times*, June 27, 1974).

160. Arriagada, *La Política*, develops this theory, pp. 58–61 and 100. I am indebted to him also for the very useful tables he developed listing the composition and service dates of the army's corps of generals for the years 1966, 1973, 1980, and 1984, pp. 189–197.

161. Interview with the author in Santiago on June 16, 1987. I have never seen Leigh's version of his ouster as recounted here published elsewhere. Leigh then ran a small—and apparently modest—real estate business ("apparently" because his offices were small and quite humble in their furnishings and appointments). Leigh said that following his firing, his security guard was gradually removed, but added: "What difference does it make? If they want to kill you, they'll kill you anyway." It is remarkable in itself that, given his visibility, he not only survived unscathed, but was the target of no terrorist attacks in all of those years; five years' service on the junta inevitably meant that he had accumulated a significant number of blood enemies. Leigh said he had not again seen nor talked with his former colleagues of the revolutionary junta.

162. James Pringle, "Chile: Stability of a Sort," *Newsweek*, March 11, 1974, p. 49. In that article, Pringle echoed the familiar syndromes about the high level of Chile's democracy, pre-Pinochet, disdain for its "draconian anti-leftist rule," and scorn for the economic policies.

10

Into a New World

THE ENEMY WITHIN

On June 14, 1974, the National Intelligence Agency (*Dirección de Inteligencia Nacional*, known almost exclusively by its initials, DINA), came into being. Its stated purpose was to put an end to anarchy—and many of the abuses—which had reigned in internal security matters following the September revolution. Security responsibilities had been formerly scattered among at least six agencies: the intelligence services of the three armed services, the Carabineros and its intelligence arm, and the national police detective force, Investigaciones. All of them experienced rapid growth, and they acted not only separately from each other, but often at cross-purposes and even as rivals. When the government responded to insistent demands that it produce prisoners or missing persons, it frequently did not because it literally could not find them in the maze. DINA was supposed to bring order out of that chaos, combining all internal security activities in a single agency. (Several weeks earlier, on April 27, the forty-seventh anniversary of its foundation, the Carabineros had been moved out of the Interior Minister, home since its creation, to the Defense Ministry. The move had the effect of making it the fourth armed service.)

DINA was patterned, to a large extent, after the intelligence agency set up by the Brazilian military regime after it seized power in 1964. According to one, well-placed source, Brazilians—who had worked in close harmony with the revolutionary government from the outset—advised the Chileans in setting it up. That source said DINA's essential mission was "to eliminate the *violentistas,* the violent ones."[1]

DINA was nominally responsible to the full junta; in practice, it became increasingly an all-army operation, responding only to Pinochet. After only one year of operation, it had a military staff of some two thousand, bolstered by another two thousand civilian employees. Its network of informers was said to be at least eight times as large, including many defectors from the MIR and other radical elements of the Popular Unity.[2]

During its three-year existence, DINA became—in the phrase of one antijunta commentator—"the spinal column of the regime . . . in Chile, during that period, no other organism would have greater influence over the national life."[3] Ultimately, it became a rogue elephant, and its runaway deeds did more to indict the regime before the court of world opinion than anything else. To head it, Pinochet selected Colonel (later, General) Manuel Contreras Sepúlveda. Pinochet first knew him as an engineering officer in the southern city of Osorno. He caught the eye of his superiors while commanding the regiment at Tejas Verdes.

Federico Willoughby, a man then high in the government, described Contreras as "a perfectionist. If, instead of DINA, he had been put in charge of highways, we would have the best highway system in the world." Willoughby said he and others opposed Contreras' plan for a comprehensive secret intelligence service which would include operations as well as intelligence-gathering. They lost.

Increasingly, this close observer said, Contreras—in a tactic reminiscent of longtime FBI head J. Edgar Hoover—gained Pinochet's complete confidence.

"Following the assassination of Adm. Carrero Blanco [in Spain], he persuaded the president that he had to tighten up his personal security. So, he took to picking up the president in the morning with his security escort, and on the way downtown, he regaled him with the latest gossip the intelligence service had picked up."[4]

That blind trust—if it was that—cost Pinochet dearly. But, whatever the price, it was one he paid, never backing down in his refusal to offer up Contreras as something of a "sacrificial lamb" to appease foreign pressure, coming chiefly from the United States. (More on this subject in a subsequent section.)

According to author Robert Moss, an exceptionally credible observer at that time, DINA was given three assignments at the outset. They were, in descending order of priority:

1. Destroy the Movement of the Revolutionary Left (MIR).
2. Prevent the Christian Democratic party from reorganizing as an effective force.
3. Destroy the clandestine networks of the Communist party.

In the first, DINA clearly succeeded.

In the second, DINA "succeeded" in the short term only—but at frightful cost to the regime in backlash, mainly from abroad. Moreover, should the Christian Democrats return to power at any time soon, it could trigger the kind of retribution against the former military rulers visited upon the military in neighboring Argentina in the mid-1980s.

In the third, while inflicting unquestioned damage on the Communist power base, the campaign failed.

They called it "the miracle of Concepción." Chile's third city, stronghold of the MIR, fell to the military on September 11 in a matter of hours. Only two soldiers died, both killed accidentally; but more than one thousand persons were rounded up and an estimated four hundred foreigners attached to the University of Concepción were expelled from the country. The MIR, which never numbered more than ten thousand, never recovered.

Early in November 1974, Miguel Enríquez—who had come to prominence when he confronted the visiting Robert F. Kennedy—was killed in a gun battle with security forces. A few days later, his successor, Humberto Sotomayor, fled to asylum at the Italian embassy, and was expelled from the MIR. Leadership passed to Allende's nephew, Andrés Pascal Allende, but he, too, had taken asylum at the same embassy. The following year, the top two commanders in Chile, Dagoberto Pérez and Alejandro de la Barra, were killed in gun battles, and a series of raids netted authorities at least half of the MIR's cached arms. By early January 1975, a veteran American correspondent wrote: "The only important guerrilla organization ever to operate in modern Chile, the self-styled Movement of the Revolutionary Left, is on the run today, its potential for future activity probably hopelessly crippled."[5]

Marxist political parties* were banned from the first days of the new regime, the others declared "in recess." On March 12, 1977, all others were banned as well and their property confiscated. (They remained outlawed until promulgation of a new law on political parties, early in 1987, but, in fact, non-Marxist parties began operating openly as early as 1983.)

Of all the non-Marxist parties—and in many ways, even more than the Marxist parties—none was held in greater contempt by the new rulers than the Christian Democrat party. They blamed the Christian Democrats not only for paving the way to Chile's collapse into Marxist-Leninist chaos, but as serving, before and after the collapse, as "useful fools" of the Communists.[6] The participation of top exiled Christian Democrats, including two former presidents of the party, at a Caracas conference in 1975 organized by former leaders of Allende's govern-

---

* Those parties were the Communist, Socialist, MAPU, Radical, Christian Left, and API—all part of Allende's Popular Unity coalition, and a tiny radical party called the Popular Socialist Union. The non-Marxist parties outlawed later included the PDC, National, Radical Democratic, PIR and National Democratic.

ment, fueled that antagonism. The conference adopted a resolution calling on Christian Democrats to work together with Popular Unity forces to restore a "just and socialist democracy in Chile."[7]

According to former Christian Democrat President Andrés Zaldívar—himself exiled for three years—one of three of the party's activists, at one time or another during junta rule, had suffered detention or imprisonment. Another former party president, Gabriel Valdés Subercaseaux, said confiscations had cost the party the loss of properties worth $8 to $9 million. Party ideologue Jaime Castillo Velasco was roughly seized by persons who declined to identify themselves and shown his order of expulsion only when en route to the airport.[8]

The party's principal radio station, Radio Balmaceda, was silenced several times in the first years of junta rule, and the party newspaper, *La Prensa*, forced to close in February 1974 when government advertising, the lifeblood at that time of newspapers, all but evaporated.

Despite harassment, the Christian Democrat party did, in fact, continue to function—holding caucuses, issuing manifestos, electing officers.

By contrast, the Communist party—fully legal only nineteen of its fifty-one years of existence prior to 1973—once again went underground, deeply underground. Not a single one of its important leaders remained at large in Chile following the revolution. Nearly two years later, security forces had to confess that they still hadn't been able to discover the name of a single new member of the central committee. Press reports at the time referred to "an initial mood of despair and self-criticism."[9] The party emerged rapidly from its gloom, however, drawing on the lessons learned during earlier clandestine sieges. Top priority was given to penetrating every possible apparatus of power, including the armed forces and the labor unions. To make themselves "respectable," they sent out orders to their activists: "dress correctly, wear your hair short, work harder than everyone else in your office, arrive early, and leave late." One of their early union successes: capturing control of the newsboys' union, which, as Robert Moss noted, "provides a perfect pretext for strolling into anyone's front yard." Though the intelligence services purged their own ranks relentlessly, some Communist cells remained active: air force intelligence, in 1975, managed to photograph a group of its noncommissioned officers in a clandestine meeting with Communist leaders. But, then, infiltration of the armed forces had long been a tactic of the party in Chile, mindful of Lenin's command: "There has not been, nor can there be, any great revolution without disorganization of the Army." From Moscow came orders for a "radical change" in tactics, including "stepping up work in the army."[10]

By June of 1974, the party began to invoke again the "non-negotiable" element of Communist doctrine: the use of violence. But because the principal tactic continued to be to lure the Christian Democrats into a united front, it was muted.[11] At that point, moreover, the party had scant resources for a "violent" confrontation; it had only begun building its Manuel Rodríguez paramilitary brigades a few months before Allende's overthrow, and these were now badly decimated.

Hope of an alliance with the PDC discarded for the moment—it would surface again and again—the party began to speak more openly of violence. In a Radio Moscow broadcast in 1976, party ideologue Volodia Teitelboim spoke of the need "to rethink the military problem." While still eschewing violence, Teitelboim urged efforts to change the "false social consciousness" and "false conception of public duty" of soldiers. Communists, he added, in a slap at their legalistic tack during the Allende years, cannot be "Gullivers bound hand and foot by legality." On April 5, 1977, a group of cashiered Chilean military men in exile announced the formation in London of the "Front of Democratic Armed Forces of Chile in Exile"; a second was formed the same day in Brussels, a third shortly afterward in East Berlin. On April 6, Jaime Estévez declared in a Radio Moscow broadcast that the purpose of these Soviet-organized entities was to build on such "basic concepts as fatherland, sovereignty and national security" to lead the fight "for the overthrow of the fascist *Junta.*" In August of that year, the Central Committee of the Chilean Communist party, in a plenum celebrated in Moscow, constituted itself as "The General Staff of Revolution."[12]

One month after the victory of the Sandinistas in Nicaragua, the Communists vacillated no more: Chile "could become the second Nicaragua," party General Secretary Luis Corvalán said in an August 28, 1979 broadcast, warning the next month that "if fascism is not eradicated and proscribed, terrorism would find in Chile a wide open field for its action." On September 3, 1980, Corvalán proclaimed a new era of "popular rebellion" and "acute violence." A few days later, the party's Manuel Rodríguez Command (later Front) staged its first terrorist actions. While still insisting that unless they could subvert the armed forces and police in "national mobilization" the revolution could not succeed, the party served notice from Moscow that, henceforth, "the fight is on all fronts . . . with a responsible, bold, decided and decisive armed response. . . ." Corvalán defined those fronts and stages as guerrilla warfare, mass resistance, terrorism, and, finally, a massive armed uprising.[13]

Countermeasures against the Communists cost a junta member his job. General César Mendoza Durán, director of Carabineros, resigned on August 2, 1985, following revelations implicating members of the service's intelligence agency in the decapitation murders of two Communist leaders and a left-wing dissident, and later the kidnapping of five members of a teachers union. Fourteen members of Carabineros' *Dirección de Comunicaciones y Informaciones* were charged in the murders, five in the kidnappings. Mendoza was succeeded that same day on the junta by his deputy, General Rodolfo Stange Delckers, who proceeded to dissolve the intelligence agency.[14]

Once committed to violence, the party grew ever bolder. Overestimating its strength, it declared 1986 "the decisive year," stirring up hit-run protest demonstrations and labor strife, and issuing defiant manifestos. Its armed cadres struck again and again—holdups, sabotage, random murders of Carabineros and other government forces. Although it did not organize the *Demanda de Chile*—sponsored by most anti-Pinochet political groups—the Communists were active in that bloody two days of protests, leaving six dead and at least six hundred injured. (Among the dead, a Chilean with a U.S. resident card, Rodrigo Rojas Denegri, and among the injured—badly disfigured when doused with kerosene— Carmen Gloria Quintana. That event brought already tense relations with the United States close to the breaking point.) The regime was shaken, but still solidly in command. Finally, the Communists overplayed their hand, badly. They tried (and very nearly succeeded) in assassinating Pinochet himself. It was a desperate gamble. In one informed Chilean analysis, the Communists risked all "because they believed that the only way of finishing off the regime was by finishing with the 'dictator' himself. . . . the Communist Party believes that the regime has a chance of making its constitutional framework stick, which would mean that they would be out of the political picture, not for years, but for decades."[15]

It was a gamble they lost. In the crackdown following that assassination attempt—in September 1986—the security forces devastated the party's armed wing. But, by then, the Manuel Rodríguez Front had become a loose cannon, out of control of party tacticians seeking desperately, in the changed political climate of Chile, once again to show a "democratic face" so as to win legitimacy even if not, in the short run, formal political alliances.[16]

The party which nominally dominated Allende's government—the Socialists—remained a contradiction in search of a reason for remaining whole. On one side were the "traditional" socialists, on the other the Leninists closely aligned with Fidel Castro's Cuba. In 1979, the inevitable rupture finally came. By 1987, there were thirteen discernible factions—ten of them Leninist, three "moderate"—this in a party which, when it came to power at the head of the coalition in 1970, had only sixteen thousand card-carrying members. With heavy financial support from the Socialist International and Venezuela's Democratic Action party (*Acción Democrática*), former party Secretary-General Aniceto Rodríguez returned to Chile intent on uniting non-Leninist factions into a viable electoral force taking part in the 1988 plebiscite. The principal obstacle was the formidable head of the Leninist factions, former Foreign Minister Clodomiro Almeyda (the man Secretary of State Henry Kissinger, prodded by then U.S. Ambassador Nathaniel Davis, fought so hard to pry out of prison following the revolution).

TURNING DEFEAT INTO VICTORY*

Shortly after arriving in Mexico City, Allende's widow enjoyed a resurrection not unlike that of her late husband. Just as he would "soar on the wings of the Western press" to achieve instant folk hero status, Hortensia Bussi de Allende was transformed from a woman scorned to the valiant widow. Supplanted in the late president's affections years earlier by another woman, she now began a new and peripatetic career as a bereaved widow fighting to preserve and restore the legacy of her late husband. (As noted earlier, the woman who supplanted her—Miria Contreras Bell de Ropert—sulked in silence for fourteen years, first in hiding in Santiago, later in Havana, still later in Paris; see preceding chapter. By the time *La Payita* finally spoke her peace, Mrs. Allende's usefulness had all but ended.)

The sixty-one-year-old widow was barely settled in Mexico when she was whisked to Moscow. There, according to one account, "she was feted as the latest of a long line of revolutionary heroines" at the October 1973 World Congress of Peace Forces. She met several American Communists attending the meeting, and they persuaded her to make a speaking tour of the United States.

"Mrs. Allende," wrote noted anti-Communist author Victor Lasky in his booklet, *Turning Defeat into Victory*, "had no trouble getting a visa to visit the United States for a two-week lecture tour, despite her well-known international Communist connections. For example, for some time she had held the office of Vice President of the Women's International Democratic Federation, a Soviet Front group." According to Lasky, that alone should have made her ineligible for entry under then

---

* From the title of a booklet authored by Victor Lasky and published by the American-Chilean Council, New York, September 1975. The publication was subtitled: "The Soviet Offensive Against Chile." It is my understanding that the council was later dissolved when it was learned that some of its funding came from the Chilean government; Lasky has told me he was not aware of it at that time, and I believe that, in any case, the authenticity and accuracy of work produced under its aegis ought be the issue, not the now-known source of its funding.

existing national security provisions of the U.S. visa law. She listed as her principal American contact a Milwaukee man identified in sworn congressional testimony as a member of the Communist party, and a delegate to the same World Peace Forces Congress she had attended in Moscow.[17]

Lasky writes that accompanying Mrs. Allende on her tour as personal secretary and translator was Fernanda Navarro, "a former leader in the youth movement of the Communist Party of Chile. A fiery orator herself, Ms. Navarro substituted for Mrs. Allende at a Town Hall rally in New York arranged to protest 'the U.S.-backed fascist coup in Chile,' and as a memorial tribute to Allende and the Chilean Communist poet Pablo Neruda." (The State Department later claimed it could find no record of issuance of a visa to Ms. Navarro, but as her appearance at Town Hall and elsewhere in the United States demonstrates, the fact that she was in the country was scarcely a secret.)

Mrs. Allende began her twelve-day lecture tour in the U.S. December 7, 1973, in California. Speaking at the Los Angeles Convention Center, she called for a major campaign to force the Nixon administration to "abandon its financial policy of support for the *Junta*," and asked the American people for the same help for "oppressed Chileans and their courageous struggle" as had been mounted in support of "the Vietnamese people." The tour included stops—and similar speeches, with similar supporting casts of characters—in Chicago, Detroit, and Cleveland. (In Cleveland, her visit was sponsored by a group called "Catholics, Lutherans, Episcopalians and Methodists for Social Action (CLEM)"; her host was the Rev. George Hrbek, whom she had met in Moscow.

That was far from her only U.S. visit. She was back on February 19, 1974, for a ten-day stay, although this time restricted to a twenty-five-mile radius of midtown Manhattan. While there, according to the Communist party newspaper, *The Daily World*, she met with "more than fifty trade union leaders representing more than one million workers." In April 1975, she was back, this time at a "public inquiry into the CIA" held at Battell Chapel on the Yale University campus at New Haven, Connecticut. Among those joining her were the man who had leaked the "Pentagon Papers," spelling out U.S. strategic options in Vietnam, Dr. Daniel Ellsberg; the authors of an "exposé" book on the CIA, Victor Marchetti and John Marks; attorney Leonard Boudin, identified with many radical causes before (and since); and Michael Harrington, the congressman whose leak of the spurious "destabilization" testimony of CIA Director William Colby had caused the House Armed Service Committee to deny him further access to its secret files.[18]

"Exactly who is paying her bills," Lasky wrote of Mrs. Allende's travels, "can only be surmised. But wherever she goes, she is put up at the finest hotels and she dines at posh restaurants, befitting a former First Lady of Chile known for her expensive tastes."

While Mrs. Allende was on the hustings, former Sen. Gladys Marín—and former chairwoman of the Young Communist League of Chile—was finding warm welcome on Capitol Hill. Sen. Daniel Inouye (D-Hawaii) invited her to testify before his Senate Subcommittee on Foreign Operations. Meeting with then Sen. James Abourezk (D-S.D.), she "launched into a typical Communist diatribe against the CIA," Lasky reported. "According to a *Daily World* correspondent who accompanied Ms. Marín, Abourezk nodded in agreement, saying, 'Many people, and they were not leftists, were very disturbed by what the U.S. did in Chile.' " Rep. Herman Badillo (D-N.Y.) came off the House floor to greet Ms. Marín, promising his "full support for the people of Chile." Rep. George Brown (D-Calif.) said he was "totally opposed" to U.S. foreign aid to Chile.

Welcoming several hundred delegates to a Legislative Conference on Chile, then Rep. Bella Abzug (D-N.Y.) called for an end to U.S. economic and military aid to "the fascist *junta*." Rep. Ronald Dellums (D-Calif.) received a standing ovation when he said, "The U.S. is the world's Number One gunrunner, the Number One counter-revolutionary force." (That conference's roll-call of luminaries included Angela Davis, author Studs Terkel, and Harry Bridges, long-time president of the International Longshoremen's and Warehousemen's Union.)

In New York City, the National Coordinating Center of Solidarity with Chile swung into operation from headquarters in a five-story building it shared with the New York State Communist party, the U.S. Committee for a Democratic Spain, the National Committee to Reopen the Rosenberg Case, and others.

Thus, the revolution was still in infancy when powerful forces in the United States pronounced sentence on it, and began mobilizing to crush it. Those efforts would never end.[19]

Although the United States was the number one target of antijunta agitation, it was by no means the only theater of operations. The previously cited World Congress of Peace Forces, organized by the Prague-based Soviet front, the World Peace Council, brought together 3,200 delegates from 144 countries. According to *Pravda*, the delegates represented 1,100 political parties, national organizations and movements, as well as 120 international organizations. General Secretary Leonid Brezhnev pledged the Soviet Union's "complete solidarity with the democrats and patriots of Chile." The head of the modern world's most comprehensive and enduring totalitarian despotism also declared "the firm belief that the just cause for which they struggled and are struggling now in such difficult conditions, the cause of independence, democracy and social progress cannot be defeated, cannot be exterminated, and the defense of these lofty values, their translation into life, the struggle against those who threaten them and seek to destroy them, is unbreakably linked with the struggle for ensuring lasting peace on earth." Brezhnev was speaking about Chile.

In July 1974, the World Peace Council's Secretary-General, Romesh Chandra, led a delegation to Mexico, Venezuela, Colombia, Ecuador, and Argentina, to stir up antijunta sentiment. The cause was a popular one; in the aftermath, he wrote in the Communist party's weekly *New Age* in India that the WPC had never before "enjoyed the prestige and authority which it commands today." By December of 1974, Chandra said that the Chilean government was facing "growing opposition at home and total isolation abroad."

That same year, the International Commission Investigating the Crimes of the Chilean *Junta* was organized; it held meetings in Helsinki and Copenhagen during the first year, and in Mexico City in February of 1975. Writes Lasky: "worldwide publicity including a lengthy article in *The New York Times* without any mention of the Commission's communist origins" was part of the bonanza reaped.[20]

The Mexico City meeting was given an important boost because of the presence of many of Allende's former senior associates. Two of the key ones had been released by the junta from prison—former Foreign Minister Clodomiro Almeyda, and former Defense Minister Orlando Letelier. (Other participants included Carlos Altamirano, who had finally surfaced in Havana, where he had been given "a hero's welcome"; Mrs. Allende; and Pedro Vuskovic Bravo, more than any other the architect of Allende's disastrous economic program, and by then head of the *Casa de Chile* in Mexico.)

The twenty-nine top Allende officials still at Dawson Island had been moved in May 1974 to considerably more congenial confinement near the seashore resort town of Quintero. Letelier was released a few months later, Almeyda early in 1975.

By then, the government was moving to thin out the ranks of those it was still holding: human rights sources put their number in May 1975 at 3,100 (reports abroad were still reaching as high as ninety thousand). Only two hundred remained prisoner in Santiago, all of them at the Estadio Chile, according to an official report. The government was also moving to speed the paperwork needed to begin trying those held. To demonstrate its openness, it agreed to permit openly jaundiced international observers, such as former U.S. Attorney General Ramsey Clark (identified with a long succession of left-wing causes through the years;

he came as a member of the U.S. "Fair Trial Committee"). Typical of those early trials, a group of more than fifty MIRistas in Temuco were sentenced early in 1975 to terms ranging from sixty-one days to twenty years.[21]

Yet another U.S. mission took a look at the human rights situation in Chile at that time; Ralph Dungan, appointed by President John F. Kennedy as ambassador to Chile, was sent on his inspection trip to Chile by the younger Kennedy, Sen. Edward M. Dungan reported that the country seemed "to be moving along normally," and that he had enjoyed the junta's full cooperation in his fact-finding mission. As a result, he said, he had held absolutely private conversations, without interference, with "dozens" of political prisoners. At the conclusion of his trip, he reported: "In large measure, one must recognize that life is taking shape there as the people—not all the people, but almost the majority of the people—want it to, and that is good."[22]

On the first anniversary of the coup, Pinochet announced that with the exception "of especially grave cases, those prisoners who so wish are free to leave the national territory once and for all [*definitivamente*]. . . . But our love for liberty and our respect for the natural rights of man does not allow us to turn a deaf ear to the dramatic lamentations of millions of human beings who live today oppressed by communist tyranny. In those countries, regimes fully consolidated and which do not live as does Chile in a situation of emergency, have constructed an entire system of violation of all freedom and human rights. For that reason, we consider it our moral duty, before the decision just announced materializes, to challenge the Soviet Union and Cuba, under the supervision of the International Red Cross, with headquarters in Geneva, to proceed to allow the same number of prisoners as will benefit by our decision to leave their countries."

There was, of course, no corresponding response from either of those countries. Still, although not all countries were eager to receive those allowed to leave, within a few months, the first two hundred were on their way out of Chile. By 1977, virtually all of Chile's political prisoners had been released.[23]

It would, of course, be a wrong verging on insanity to imply—much less assert—that all those who opposed the junta around the world in those tumultuous times were Communists, or Communist stooges. It would be equally insane to ignore the role of the Kremlin in stoking the fires of antijunta fury. Chile was crucial to the Kremlin's *vía pacífica*—burrow-from-within—strategy for Latin America. Yet another measure of just how important it was: the ambassador the Kremlin assigned to Allende's Chile, Aleksandr V. Basov, was a member of the Central Committee of the Communist party of the Soviet Union, and had been a high official of the motherland, the Russian Republic, before his Santiago posting. Years later, explaining their 1979 invasion of Afghanistan, Soviet ambassadors in Europe were saying the Kremlin "could not permit another Chile."[24]

Within two months of the coup, Radio Moscow initiated its half-hour program beamed to Chile, "Listen Chile," repeated four times daily. (The schedule was later expanded.) Through those broadcasts, through the numerous congresses and front organization activities already indicated, Moscow made explicit its goal of isolating, suffocating and finally destroying the junta.

EMBATTLED BORDERS

When Augusto Pinochet and his associates came to power, they found themselves under siege not only from afar, but also along all three foreign borders. Partly for reasons of history, partly for reasons of ideology, Argentina, Bolivia, and Peru all viewed the new regime in Santiago with attitudes ranging from antipathy to outright hostility. There was a certain irony in this: all three of the men currently in power in those countries were themselves military men, and all three had come to power (at least originally) through violent revolution. But there was an important difference: two of the three—the "populist" Yankee-hater in Buenos Aires, Juan Domingo Perón, and the one-legged general, Juan Velasco Alvarado, in Peru—were dedicated leftists. The third, Col. Hugo Banzer Suárez, presided over a country with a long-standing grudge against Chile.

Already in a declared war against communism, this prostrate and shattered country thus also faced the very real possibility of a shooting war with one or more of its neighbors. That it did not happen was a tribute to luck, dogged diplomacy, and steady nerves. In the case of Chile, an argument could be made—Pinochet makes it—that a civilian government might have blinked at a fateful moment, plunging the country into just such an inferno.[25]

PERU:

"Key U.S. diplomatic and military observers have concluded from actions of the Peruvian military *Junta*, including massive arms purchases from the Soviet Union and the presence of Russian advisers, that Peru may be preparing to make war on Chile to recapture territory seized by Chile nearly 100 years ago." So read the "lead" on a front-page story in the *Washington Star-News*, August 4, 1974. It was written by the newspaper's veteran Latin America correspondent, Jeremiah O'Leary, known for his excellent sources in the defense and intelligence communities in Washington.

At the time he wrote, Peru had deployed two-thirds of its armed forces in the south, near the Chilean border. Those formidable forces included many of the estimated 150 Soviet T-54 and T-55 tanks Peru had already received (at least two hundred more were yet to come). The tanks were only a fraction of the arsenal which the Soviets began shipping to the Peruvians following the fall of Allende. By accepting those shipments on the same, "concessionary" (virtual giveaway) terms Chile's military had spurned, Peru became the first country in the Western Hemisphere, after Cuba, to receive Soviet military assistance.

As this was happening, the U.S. Congress—prodded chiefly by Sen. Teddy Kennedy—slapped an absolute arms embargo on Chile.

A commentator wrote at the time: "We [the United States] spent billions of dollars and tens of thousands of lives in an effort to keep Vietnam free from Communist oppression. . . . We lost the battle in Vietnam. The battle was won in Chile. And yet, we deny anticommunist Chile the help they need to survive. . . ."[26]

In July 1974, the Velasco Alvarado government in Peru published its Plan Inca, a clear and explicit blueprint of what was already implicit, the regime's socialist aims: nationalization of airlines, banks and finance, insurance and shipping companies, as well as total control of the mining and petroleum sectors. Among confiscation targets that year: a number of foreign companies (mainly American), completing a cycle of nationalizations begun almost immediately after the military coup in 1968. During that year, the government also seized all national daily newspapers.[27]

There were, of course, no reprisals from Washington; on the contrary, there was an impassioned plea from Secretary of State Henry Kissinger to Congress for arms sales to the stridently anti-American regime in Lima.

Nor were there, of course, any demonstrations protesting the Lima regime's assault on American property, or on its own people's right to know. Nor were there protests of rampant militarism, such as had prompted the paternalistic policy of denying U.S. arms to Latin America, when Peru, despite severe economic problems, lavished $1 billion on an arms build-up during the first five years of military rule.[28] Nor, for that matter, was there an outcry against Peru's then six-year-old denial of its peoples' political liberties.

Early in the Allende regime, the ever witty Henry Kissinger was said to have remarked that "Chile is a dagger—pointed straight at the heart of Antarctica." It reflected, of course, an attitude of disdain, indifference and ignorance about Latin America common to the power brokers in Washington and European capitals, and it was a remark Kissinger would soon come to rue as Chile forced its way onto the American foreign policy agenda. Military planners knew better; during both World Wars, Britain and the United States found it necessary to patrol the area with heavy forces. An article in the January 1975 issue of a specialized publication, *Defense and Foreign Affairs*, pointed out that Chile controls and borders the Straits of Magellan and Beagle Channel, the only two alternative routes through which ships can cross from the Atlantic to the Pacific, and vice-versa, other than the vulnerable Panama Canal. Destruction or temporary disabling of the Panama Canal would divert all maritime traffic between the two oceans to the Cape Horn area.

"A friendly Chile would permit the passage of her allies through the straits," the article noted, "while her enemies would have to take the Drake Sea route . . . not as dangerous as in the days of sail . . . but the absence of friendly shores around it, the threat of air attack . . . from the South American mainland cannot be so easily dismissed. . . ."[29]

Evidently these considerations were on the minds of Pentagon planners as they pressed—in vain—for assistance to the imperiled anti-Communist regime in Santiago. As Jeremiah O'Leary noted in the previously cited August 1974 article:

> Military reasoning, amid the implication that it is shared by Kissinger, is that the chances of armed collision would be reduced if Chile had access to a reasonable number of modern planes such as the F5 and some armor more recent than World War II vintage. Beyond that, the Nixon administration is not enchanted with the Russian military presence in Lima and holds to the general theory that Washington had more political influence with countries tied to American resupply than countries with no such requirement. . . .

But Richard Nixon's views had long since ceased to matter; he resigned as president five days after those lines were published. A few fought a rear-guard action; on the same day that O'Leary's article appeared, scholar Ernest W. Lefever added his voice in testimony before Congress:

> A week ago, on July 29, in the Peruvian Independence Day parade, 54 Soviet T-55 tanks, with 100 MM guns were shown, along with three batteries of Yugoslav 105 M-M howitzers, 8 truck-mounted surface-to-air missiles, and other missile support equipment. Peru also has 60 M-4 Sherman medium tanks, and 100 AMX-13 French tanks with 106 M-M guns.

In contrast, Chile's 76 M-5 Sherman tanks are no match. With this undisputed superiority, Peru may well be tempted to attack Chile to recover the territory it lost to Chile in the 1878-1883 war, possibly with the encouragement of Moscow. . . .

Fourteen senators joined Sens. Strom Thurmond (R-S.C.) and Jesse Helms (R-N.C.) in a letter to Secretary Kissinger: "[The] cut-off of military aid to Chile has led to a very serious imbalance between the forces of anti-communist Chile and those of Soviet-supplied Peru," which could lead to "open warfare." Larry P. McDonald, a conservative Democratic congressman from Georgia, wrote an appeal based in part on his own fact-finding trip to Chile, "Let's Help Our Friends—Not Our Enemies."[30]

But the likes of Lefever, Thurmond, Helms, McDonald, and a disorganized and feeble Ford administration, were no match for the powerful liberal coalition by then firmly in control of Congress. Chile received many lectures and little help from the United States. Later in 1974, Congress tightened the 1973 restrictions even further by banning all future U.S. arms deliveries to Chile beyond those negotiated before July 1, 1974.

Evidently strategic considerations were uppermost on the minds of Soviet analysts, for they, by contrast, rushed immense amounts of military aid to Peru, including:

- 50,000 Kalachnikov rifles;
- two batteries of SAM-3 and SAM-6 missiles, as well as an unknown quantity of SAM-2 and SAM-7 missiles;
- 30 MI-8 helicopter gunships;
- Soviet advisors to instruct in their use, estimates ranging from 15 to two hundred.

Theberge observed:

The potential importance of the Peruvian revolution was not lost on the Soviet leaders. Moscow realized that the Velasco regime, by preparing the road to Socialist development and pursuing a foreign policy with strong anti-American overtones, could help to weaken American influence in Latin America. Peru is viewed by Moscow as a harbinger of a powerful anti-imperialist and anticapitalist trend within the Latin American military. Ambitious generals in Bolivia, Ecuador and Panama have already been influenced by the Peruvian model. . . .[31]

The Soviet armament was added to Peru's force of 12 French Mirage supersonic fighter planes, 12 light bombers (Chile had none), 200

Yugoslav 105 mm mortars, 7 Czech-made 122 mm field guns, and 6 operational submarines.

More was on the way—from the United States. President Ford requested $20 million in military credits to Peru for 1975, plus $900,000 for training. Sales included: 36 A-37-B planes, 2 "Guppy" class submarines, 150 APC-113 armored cars, 9 Grumman Tracker planes, and up to 16 F-5 jet fighter planes, as well as 100 tank transport vehicles capable of operating in the kind of mountain country characteristic of eastern Chile.

All of this to a poor country which, even before this massive build-up, had from 1964 to 1973 outspent its traditional adversary Chile by more than three to one on new military hardware.

Though slightly superior in numbers of soldiers, and arguably superior in seapower, the Chileans realized they were badly outgunned and moved rapidly to defuse a potentially fatal situation through diplomacy. While tensions continued to mount behind the scenes, both countries issued public statements in March of 1974 blaming war talk on outsiders; the Chileans named it flat-out—"international communism."[32]

But a pair of events in 1975 brought a temporary halt to the atmosphere of crisis: the ailing Velasco Alvarado was removed in a peaceful coup on August 29 and replaced by a more moderate general, Francisco Morales Bermúdez. The coup came after months of rioting and strikes (in one strike in February, more than one hundred were killed and six hundred injured).

The other was the result of a Pinochet initiative that produced a brief period of détente with Bolivia—Peru's partner in the War of the Pacific, a century earlier, and its probable ally should new hostilities erupt.

BOLIVIA:

Bolivia, alone, had neither the military power nor the disposition to attack Chile. Indeed, the government of General Hugo Banzer was the very first to send aid to revolution-stricken Chile, a planeload of medicines and plasma. But Bolivia did have a grudge, a one hundred-year-old grudge, nurtured in the education of Bolivians ever since the War of the Pacific, based on the belief that land-locked Bolivia was "entitled" to recover its land bridge to the Pacific Ocean.

So central is the issue to the psyche of Bolivians that even their telephone directories bear the legend: "Bolivia demands access to the ocean." Although it has no coastline, noted a report in the British newsmagazine *The Economist*, the country has a navy of 3,600 men, "who patrol Lake Titicaca and splash about in rivers. On the nation's annual Day of the Sea, naval officers stand at attention, on trucks dressed up as ships, solemnly rolling through the streets of La Paz."[33]

It would be funny except that it is not; it is a wound that has never stopped festering, breaking out frequently into bitter and ugly ruptures between the two countries.

Pinochet was in power only one month when he took the first step toward rapprochement; during a visit to the northernmost city of Arica, Pinochet expressed the wish to meet with Banzer. It was easier said than done; Bolivia had broken diplomatic relations with Chile in 1962 (when Chile diverted the waters of the River Lauca, spilling down out of the Andes into a tiny swatch of Bolivia, to build the Chapiquina hydroelectric plant).

Banzer faced a particularly knotty problem. Like Pinochet, he was anti-Communist. Indeed, Banzer came to power in 1971 amid worldwide charges that the CIA had engineered his ouster of the "nationalist-leftist" military government that had seized power in 1970. (Banzer's accession put an end to not-so-secret Allende initiatives to reach a new understanding with the like-minded Bolivians, based on "revolutionary understanding." Revolutionary fervor notwithstanding, the talks had splattered off the same wall that had separated the two countries ever since the War of the Pacific).[34]

Pinochet and Banzer found the chance to meet, however, a few months later when both were in Brasilia for the inauguration in March 1974 of President Ernesto Geisel. Pinochet described his talk with Banzer as "a talk between soldiers, without rhetoric of any kind."

Two months later, a beaming Banzer said there was no reason to suppose that there would be a new War of the Pacific, but he added, "Bolivia cannot remain unjustly cloistered, subject to the good will [of neighboring countries]. We are a peaceful country, we do not seek vengeance, and we do expect understanding."[35]

That talk paved the way for a personal meeting between the two presidents on February 8, 1975, in the tiny Bolivian border town of Charaña. There, amid much fanfare, the two presidents signed the Act of Charaña, calling for a renewal of diplomatic relations, for negotiations on a new nonaggression pact among Bolivia, Chile, and Peru, and for continued talks in respect to Bolivia's long-craved corridor to the sea.

Pinochet did, of course, demand a quid for his quo.

The Chileans believed they had already been generous to Bolivia: they had built a railroad linking La Paz to the sea at Arica, allowing Bolivian products free transit; they had also paid the Bolivians 6 million pounds sterling as an indemnity (a very hefty sum in the late nineteenth century). In the after-glow of the "Embrace of Charaña," Bolivian soldiers were allowed to supervise the transport of Bolivian imports on the railroad. Pinochet also was said to have agreed to build a new port north of Iquique for exclusive Bolivian use.

In exchange for granting Bolivia roughly two thousand square kilometers of Chilean territory stretching from mountains to sea across Chile's northern frontier, Pinochet wanted a similar slice of Bolivian soil; sources at the time said the idea was his. In the process, Chile would not only get back about the same amount of space it lost, but would acquire a buffer between itself and Peru, an old geopolitical ambition. (Peru's southern border area approaching Chile is fairly populated; by contrast, in the entire 58,072 square kilometer Tarapacá region of northern Chile, there dwelled a total 174,981 souls, and 90 percent of them were clustered in the small cities of Arica and Iquique; hence the Chilean sense of the indefensibility of the northern region.)[36]

The ink was barely dry on the act when Banzer recanted and Peru protested. The Peruvians, invoking their 1929 treaty with Chile, said that if there were to be territorial concessions, then they were an automatic party, particularly since the corridor in question had been amputated from them. They demanded that Arica—Chile's northernmost city—be converted into an international city and that the three countries share sovereignty over a sixty-six kilometer area.

Relations once again turned sour. There was talk of a massive march of Bolivians across the Andes, down into the desert and on to the sea. Hope sputtered briefly when Pinochet, Banzer, and Peruvian president Morales Bermúdez met in Washington in 1977 for the signing of the Panama Canal Treaty, reopening talks on the corridor question. But on March 17, 1978, charging insincerity on Chile's part, Bolivia again broke diplomatic relations and dispatched troops to the Chilean border. In 1979, Bolivia expelled thirty Chileans on charges of espionage. Culminating an intense diplomatic offensive, Bolivia succeeded in 1979 in getting the Organization of American States—consistently hostile to the Pinochet regime—to stipulate, by a 25-1 vote, "that it is of permanent hemispheric interest that Bolivia be given sovereign and useful access to the Pacific Ocean." President Jimmy Carter had already begun pressuring the Chileans, noting in 1979 that the problem was "a cause of conflict on the continent." (Years later, the United Nations Conference on Law of the Sea found that of the landlocked countries, Bolivia was among those that enjoyed the greatest rights of access to the sea.) Chile's persistent position that the issue was not a multilateral one finally found echo when the OAS, in 1980, called for bilateral talks between Chile and Bolivia. In 1983, the conference of self-styled Non-Aligned Nations, meeting in New Delhi, approved a resolution offering its "categorical backing to the legitimate and just demand of Bolivia" that it recover what it had lost in a war a century earlier.

In 1985, Chile offered new negotiations. Once again, the talks collapsed on the same negotiating terrain. When in June 1987 Chile announced it was withdrawing from the talks, Bolivia reacted angrily; Banzer, by then an ex-president, demanded a break in commercial relations.

However much of a united front of international opposition Chile faced on the issue into the early 1980s (when those positions softened), it was an issue on which there was unity at home. Gabriel Valdés Subercaseaux, then president of the Christian Democrat party, and perhaps the most acidly outspoken critic of the junta in Chile, said following the collapse of the latest round of talks, "To resurrect problems of sovereignty dating from the 19th century is totally out-of-date [*extemporáneo*] and does not fit in [*no se compadece*] with modern times." Asked about concessions to Bolivia, junta member Adm. José Merino said, "I would say no; I do say no; there will be no outlet to the sea given to Bolivia."[37]

As noted, the new Peruvian government headed by General Morales Bermúdez was regarded as more moderate, and, as one authoritative source wrote, "was expected to take some strain off the Chilean government. Despite denials in Lima, many hemispheric observers had believed the Velasco regime was intent on a military effort to recover territory lost to Chile nearly a century earlier. . . ."[38] There did, indeed, follow a period Heraldo Muñoz would describe as "the tender idyll." Although Chile, in November of 1976, rejected Peru's proposal for tripartite sovereignty over the proposed "corridor," relations continued until January 1979, when Peru expelled Chile's ambassador on grounds of espionage, and relations were reduced to an envoy level. The new civilian government of President Fernando Belaúnde Terry, who inherited a wrecked economy when he took office in 1980, was interested in borrowing ideas—and Chilean advisers—so as to implement a replica of the Chilean economic model in his country. Yet another factor contributed to his desire for improved relations with his neighbor to the south: Peru's brief—but ominous—armed clashes with Ecuador over old border problems with that country. Diplomatic relations were resumed in April of 1981.

Curiously, diplomatic relations improved even more following the inauguration in July 1985 of the leftist and mercurial Alan García as president of Peru. Although he pointedly invited a number of Chilean opposition leaders to his inauguration, he also dispatched one of his closest advisers to Santiago to convey his wish for "the best possible relations with Chile." Still, beneath the surface, tension remains, reflecting a reality cited by Chile's leading newspaper, *El Mercurio*, on March 8, 1985: relations between the two countries have developed "within an historic negative framework of suspicions and distrust." Those two characteristics, the newspaper went on to say, were accentuated with the ascendancy of the rightist Pinochet regime in 1973.[39]

Argentina:

Seen from afar, much of the developed world smugly assumed that there was something Gilbert and Sullivan in the notion of war between nations such as Argentina and Chile. Yet historically the tensions between them have been as real as between many other neighboring nations or imperial systems around the world, and the danger of those tensions exploding into war equally real. Although both countries have faced other neighbors in war, they have never fought each other. But beginning in 1978 and continuing over much of the four years following, the danger was white hot at times.

> I believe there were people there [in Argentina] who wanted to attack, and others no. There was an internal struggle. Finally, those who wanted to negotiate won out.

The speaker was Gen. Fernando Matthei Aubel, commandant of the Chilean air force, and third-ranking member of the junta. He referred to the Beagle Channel crisis of the late 1970s.[40] Actually, the crisis for the Pinochet regime started even earlier. The day it came to power, it faced a hostile government across the Andes. It was headed by Juan Domingo Perón.

Juan Domingo Perón began his rise to power in 1943, an obscure colonel in a relatively minor post, labor minister, in a divided and aimless military government. He exploited the confusion to build a power base for himself through a series of demagogic measures popular with the left-dominated unions, adding goon squads reminiscent of tactics used by Hitler and Mussolini in their rise to power. In the 1946 elections, with the traditional parties fragmented and fractious, he narrowly won the presidency.

> Argentina exemplifies how a superior, educated, wealthy and religious nation, possessing virtue and great mental and physical assets for over three decades, has suffered a deluge of evils as her government sank into the depths of degradation, corruption, venality and irresponsibility. Murder, torture, kidnaping, terrorism and guerrilla warfare ensued.
>
> The cause of all this was the breakdown in morality and communist infiltration.

> As far back as 1945 . . . the then vice president and dictator, Perón, while pretending opposition to communists, actually was intriguing closely with them; they had replaced the Nazis in his esteem.
>
> Simultaneously, he, his mistress, later wife, Evita, and his henchmen, enriched themselves on a vast scale. When Perón died, his third wife and heir, Isabelita (a former bar girl) suddenly found herself the nominal head of a government which had fulfilled 85% of the program laid down by Karl Marx and Friedrich Engels. Presently she is imprisoned for stealing public funds.

That encapsulated version of thirty years in the life of a country obviously suffers the imperfections of all severe condensations of complex reality. It suffers the second disadvantage of explicit anticommunism, no longer fashionable, and the author of those lines was, in fact, outspokenly anti-Communist. But the author of those lines came to his anticommunism through the vast experience in international affairs that confers authority on his judgments. The speaker was Ambassador Spruille Braden, who began his career in Latin America in 1917 in Chile, representing the copper company bearing his name (and which would later become Kennecott Copper), later serving as United States ambassador to Argentina, Bolivia, Colombia, and Cuba. He was in Argentina when Perón came to power.[41]

Ousted in a military coup in 1955, the aging Perón was allowed to return in November 1972, after seventeen years of accelerating social and political disintegration. His Peronista movement, firmly in control of the country's big labor unions, won the elections in March 1973. Two months after his inauguration, President Héctor Campora was pushed aside by Perón himself. When Perón died the following July 1, he was succeeded by his second wife, Isabelita. Since she had problems in abundance in consolidating her own hold on power—greatly aggravated by the growing boldness and violence of the radical left Montoneros guerrilla/terrorist organization—it was a time of respite for Chile. (She was ousted in a military coup in March 1976.)

More than respite, it was a time of yet another "tender idyll," albeit a brief one, between two military regimes with a common denominator: severe measures to combat internal subversion from the Left. The similarity—dissimilarity, really, since Argentina's prolonged "dirty war" against internal opposition far surpassed in human rights violations anything seen in Chile—ended there. As Theberge had observed about the tendency of the Latin American military to look increasingly to Moscow after being scorned by the U.S., the ruling Argentine military—like Peru before them—were rapidly expanding their ties to the Soviet Union, which Perón had cultivated. Trade between the countries shot up from $30 million in 1970 to $634 million in 1979, to $1.5 billion in

1980. Argentina also ignored President Jimmy Carter's 1980 call for a worldwide boycott of wheat shipments to the Soviet Union in retaliation for its invasion of Afghanistan. The Argentines, taking up the slack left by the U.S., shipped 7.5 million tons of wheat and other grains to the Soviets via East Europe.[42]

But there was that one, brief moment. In November 1976, the Argentine president, Lieutenant General Jorge Rafael Videla, spent four days on an official visit to Chile. It is likely that his visit exceeded for euphoria anything by way of presidential visits seen before or since in the annals of the two countries. The two "first couples" took a sightseeing drive together along the coast, with Pinochet at the wheel; the presidents mixed—"without benefit of police lines"—with passersby at the resort city of Viña del Mar; they attended Mass together, both receiving Communion, both reading passages from the Bible; they witnessed a performance of horsemanship at the army's riding academy; they wined and dined at the seldom-used presidential seashore retreat at Viña del Mar; they rode in nineteenth-century carriages to flower-bedecked colonial San Isidro.

At the end of the visit, Videla promised to sell Chile 500,000 tons of wheat per year, 1977–1979. It was, a leading Chilean newspaper noted in an editorial, "without exaggeration . . . the beginning of a new era. . . ."[43]

The "new era" foundered shortly afterward on the rocks of an old problem: the Beagle Channel dispute.

The continent, far down near the tip of the dagger, is as capricious as the howling winds and the raging seas that have made this place, Cape Horn, a setting of matchless hardship, of heroics and legend in the annals of seamanship. On the Argentine side, the land is a fairly solid block, chiseled to a final point at Cape San Diego. On the Chilean side, it is a scourge of inlets and jagged islands and islets too numerous to count, of gulfs that go nowhere, of bays so navigationally treacherous that one is called Useless Bay and another Desolate Bay, of fjords and ice floes, of mountains climbing nearly eight thousand feet out of the water, of reefs and shoals and shallows—and of channels. One of them, roughly two hundred miles south of the Straits of Magellan, seventy miles north of the Cape, is the Beagle Channel, slicing in a fairly straight line across the tip of South America between meridian 68*36'38.5" to 66*25' meridian longitude west of Greenwich. Discovered by the British naval survey sloop *Beagle* during her voyages of 1830–1834, the channel is 120 to 150 miles long—depending on where measurements are taken—averaging three to 3.5 miles wide.

In common with most countries emerging from colonial rule and sharing common borders, Chile and Argentina from early on had differences of opinion about theirs, and particularly those of the remote south. In 1843, Chile took control of the Straits of Magellan and claimed everything to the south, in 1847 locating a settlement at Punta Arenas. The Argentines protested, and over the ensuing years, desultory efforts were made to reach a settlement. In 1878, both countries ordered their fleets into southern waters, and war was only narrowly averted. The Boundary Treaty of July 23, 1881, resolved all points at dispute—except the Beagle Channel question. In accord with a General Treaty of Arbitration signed in 1902, His Britannic Majesty was named arbitrator; in 1938, under a second protocol, U.S. Attorney General Homer S. Cummings was named to arbitrate; in 1960, a third protocol referred the dispute to the International Court of Justice. But none of these protocols was ever ratified and negotiations went nowhere.

Finally, invoking the 1902 treaty, Chile, on December 11, 1967, invited the British government to intervene as arbitrator. Balking at first, on July 22, 1971, Argentina agreed, and as before, a court was impanelled by the arbitrator: one Briton and four members chosen equally by Argentina and Chile from the International Court of Justice at the Hague. By September 1976, oral pleadings began, and in November, the court began its deliberations.

Queen Elizabeth announced the finding in London, April 18, 1977—granting to Chile perhaps the most disputed real estate of all: Picton, Nueva and Lennox islands, "and the islets and rocks adjacent to them." Argentine president Videla's reaction was to send a personal letter to his genial host of the year previous, proposing an exchange of views to work out details of the award. By January 6, 1978, it was plain to Chile that what Argentina wanted was not just the aforementioned islands, but *all* the islands situated south of the Channel to Cape Horn. Although Pinochet had hopped across the border to Mendoza on January 18 for a private meeting with Videla, Argentina, nonetheless, announced on January 25, 1978 that the six-year arbitration process was "incurably void" (*insanablemente nulo*).[44]

Hoping to head off war, Pinochet agreed to meet Videla again, on February 20, 1978, in the southern Chilean city of Puerto Montt. There they agreed to 180 days of additional negotiation. Pinochet said later that, given the widespread and strong feeling in Chile that the Argentines were bullying his country, it took all of his considerable authority, in and out of government, to impose his will. By November 2, 1978, Chile announced that the negotiations had been "exhausted." Both countries immediately went on a war footing.

More than at any time since assuming the presidency, Pinochet found himself with a country united behind him. Former President Eduardo Frei said he and the Christian Democrat party offered their "unrestricted support"; even the Socialist party—through the far left Clodomiro Almeyda, and the even farther left (and official fugitive) Carlos Altamirano—declared its backing for the Chilean position and asked for urgent United Nations intervention to avoid war.

Pinochet faced war fever at home and a vastly more powerful enemy along the two thousand mile border.

> Based on intelligence that the Argentines would attack in the south, I moved my headquarters to Puerto Montt. At the same time, I sent Hernán Cubillos [the foreign minister] to Buenos Aires with instructions: keep a cool head. We don't want war because you lose your head. When Cubillos called from Buenos Aires and said how difficult it was, I told him again: stay calm. Yes, we avoided war—but, we did not yield, either.

President Pinochet related the above in an interview with the author in Santiago, June 11, 1987. He spoke the last words slowly, repeating the last phrase (his customary technique for achieving emphasis).[45] In that same interview, he also revealed something of the internal dissensions within the junta as war fever escalated. He said the navy wanted to send two squadrons to southern waters, but he countermanded that order, saying it would be a red flag to the Argentines. (In an interview with Admiral Merino two days earlier, the admiral said flat-out: "I deployed two squadrons south.") Pinochet said he did the same thing with the air force, restraining it so as not to aggravate tensions. (Air Force Chief General Matthei, in a June 15, 1987, interview with the author said, "I want to tell you that I controlled very rigidly the air force of Chile. We made no moves anyone could interpret as provocative.")

Said Pinochet: "Not a horse moved anywhere near the border without my approval."

During the Buenos Aires sessions, Cubillos proposed that the two countries either take the dispute to the International Court at the Hague, or agree on a mediator acceptable to both. On December 12, Argentina proposed Pope John Paul II, and Chile immediately accepted. No sooner was that agreement reached than the Argentine Military Committee—made up of Videla and other members of his junta, as well as senior military commanders—stipulated a condition: the two countries must first agree on the question of limits. As one observer commented, "they wanted to win the game before it was played."[46]

Despite the overwhelming evidence that the Pinochet government had not only abided strictly by the rules of arbitration, but had gone the extra mile to avert war, the international community declined to support Chile. (Indeed, in San Francisco, with an Argentine attack on Chile imminent, the leftist-dominated International Longshoremen's and Stevedore's Union refused to load eleven tons of bomb parts Chile had ordered in 1974, ostensibly to protest the labor situation in Chile.) But there was a flurry of resolutions, meetings and hand-wringing. President Carter sent a private message to Pinochet offering to "help develop a prompt mediation by some other party." Carter made clear that "the United States does not want to inject itself into the substance of this complicated matter. . . ." He also said that "if aggression were to occur because of the Beagle Channel dispute, we would speak out strongly against it."[47]

When Chile asked for an urgent meeting of consultation of the Organization of American States under the Inter-American Treaty of Mutual Assistance (the so-called Rio treaty), the OAS voted to explore possible consultative mechanisms. The European Economic Community urged both countries to seek a peaceful solution. Even such traditional allies as Uruguay, Paraguay, and Guatemala, declined to express public support for Chile.

Into this dangerous breach stepped Pope John Paul II. On December 22, he dispatched Cardinal Antonio Samore on a good will mission to both countries. After what was described as "exhausting" negotiations over the Christmas holidays, Cardinal Samore persuaded the two countries to sign, on January 8, 1979, the Act of Montevideo, which agreed to an immediate military stand-down, and to a request for papal mediation. Nearly two years later, on December 12, 1980, the Vatican showed both countries a draft agreement. Although not favorable to Chile, Pinochet promptly accepted. Argentina did not, requesting a series of clarifications. While this was going on, in January 1982, the Argentines renounced the 1972 treaty, not due to expire until the end of that year. The Vatican eventually managed to paper over that crisis as well—but only after nine more months of saber-rattling tension along the border. (Yet another measure of the antagonisms Chile faced: when, early in 1981, Chile and Argentina both detained military officers of the other country, and Argentina unilaterally sealed off the Chilean border, West Germany—under Chancellor Helmut Schmidt's shaky coalition government headed by Willy Brandt's Social Democrats—retaliated against Chile. The government suspended the sale to Chile of two submarines being built for it. Brandt, and the Social Democrats, were among the most strident voices in Europe decrying alleged outside interference, including blockades, against Allende.)

Finally, with a civilian government (Raúl Alfonsín) once again in Argentina's Casa Rosada, hope rose in 1983. It took longer than was expected, but on October 4, 1984, the Vatican announced a final agreement. It was signed in Rome on November 29, 1984. General Videla, chief of the Chilean delegation through the long mediation process, remembers tears unashamedly staining the cheeks of those present.

The new agreement confirmed Chile's right to the land awarded in 1977, established new boundaries for the eastern mouth of the Straits of Magellan, stipulated navigational rights, and created mechanisms for arbitration (through the government of Switzerland).

A few more hurdles remained—principally in Argentina. In Chile, all major political parties expressed their support, although the navy had some reservations. After two months of study, the junta approved the treaty on May 11, 1985. In Argentina, Alfonsín submitted it to a popular referendum on November 25, 1984; better than 80 percent of those voting expressed support for the treaty. Finally, with the Argentine Senate voting 23-22 to approve, it was ratified and signed in the Vatican, May 2, 1985.

Other problems would arise between the two countries, but for the most part, what analyst Heraldo Muñoz would describe as "the worst relations" between the two countries in decades were now history.

Pinochet, looking back on it, said: "It is remarkable, isn't it, how little was really known abroad about this crisis, and about the very remarkable fact that a supposedly martial-military government would show not muscle-flexing *machismo*, but serenity and restraint in the face of international hostility and incomprehension and bellicosity at our borders."[48]

OF POLLS, PILGRIMS AND POGROMS

In 1977, Mary McGrory—possessor of perhaps the most invective pen of any major columnist on the Left in America—described President Pinochet as "the Chilean dictator who is perhaps the world champion violator of human rights."

As she wrote, Pol Pot was concluding the butchery of roughly one-third of the population in Cambodia, in what would come to be known as "the murder of the gentle land"; in Uganda, a rampage of atrocities included those attributed to the sadistic dictator Idi Amin himself; in the People's Republic of China, the deaths of Mao Tse-tung and Chou En-lai led to new purges in a country that had already seen 35 million perish on the altar of revolution; in Panama, the dictator Omar Torrijos Herrera was in the eighth year of his long and brutal reign (he died in 1981 and was succeeded by the even more brutal, corrupt, and thoroughly anti-American Manuel Antonio Noriega); in Nigeria, military dictatorship was rounding out its eleventh year of iron rule which included the virtual extermination of the Biafran minority which had sought to win independence*; and this does not, of course, mention the world's most pervasive totalitarian state, the Soviet Union, and its far-flung and sinister satrapies.

But more than mere punditry, there was scholarship to support the inquisition. A study done by two political scientists and published in 1977 showed that, among the twenty Latin American Republics, Chile had plummeted from number two to number eighteen on an index of democracy. The Cuba of Fidel Castro—then celebrating his eighteenth year of absolute power in the most thoroughly totalitarian regime in the hemisphere—ranked fourteenth. Paraguay, ruled by a right-wing strong-man, and Haiti, a perennially hopeless case, ranked behind Chile.

It is a further sign of the times that the *New York Times*—never at a loss for reasons why openings to the world's left-wing regimes ought not be exploited through patience, accommodation and flexibility—would write that Chile ought to be denied aid "even for projects helpful to the poorest Chileans."[49]

While the rest of the world commiserated over Chile, Chileans saw their plight differently. A 1975 Gallup Poll showed that 64 percent of the Chilean people believed they were better off than when Allende fell, and only 13 percent felt they were worse off. Seventy-three percent believed conditions were continuing to improve, 11 percent that they were deteriorating. The results in 1976 were even better: 76 percent expressed support for Pinochet, only 20 percent hostility. It was a similar story in 1977, with an important new wrinkle: 65 percent support, only 12 percent demanding immediate elections—and 71 percent said the junta's free-market economic policies were favorable for the country.

There was another poll in 1977 which got little notice in the din of condemnation and grieving over Chile. The Gallup organization surveyed residents of fifteen nations, asking this question: "Which of these do you think is likely to be true of 1977: a year of economic prosperity or a year of economic difficulty?" Fifty-one percent of the Chileans were optimistic, 44 percent pessimistic. Only Uruguayans were more optimistic: 52 percent looked to better times that year (Uruguay's government was then military-controlled). Chileans, in that survey, were more optimistic than citizens of Great Britain, Italy, France, Spain, Holland, Australia, Canada, Brazil, Switzerland, Japan, India, West Germany, and the United States—the governments of all of which (with the excep-

---

* It is a measure of the elasticity of standards, if not of consciences, that Nigeria, having taken the first tentative steps toward a return to civilian rule in 1977, would, the following year, welcome such champions of human rights as Helmut Schmidt of West Germany and Jimmy Carter of the United States. In the first ten years of its military rule, despite a number of at least equally important steps, only five foreign leaders visited Chile, all of them from South America.[50]

tions of Brazil, Japan, and Spain) had, in greater or lesser measure, taken harsh measures to protect the citizens of Chile.

Such evidence could not, of course, go unchallenged. The *Washington Post*'s Karen De Young, who later professed her public enthusiasm for the Sandinista dictatorship in Nicaragua, located an unnamed Santiago sociologist who disputed the Gallup findings.

One poll did manage to command substantial media attention—a Gallup Poll, at that. People of sixteen countries were asked whether they thought the people of Chile were better off or worse off since the September revolution. By a margin of more than two-to-one, people outside Chile thought in 1975 that people inside Chile must be worse off (although a very high percentage, ranging from 26 percent in South American countries to 50 percent in Europe) said they just plain didn't know.[51]

Given the massive bombardment of hostility to Chile—in the media, from academics, from governments—it is not unreasonable to express wonder that so many still didn't "know."

> This government reiterates its determination to maintain international relations with all countries whose governments do not attempt to intervene unduly in our internal problems. . . .
>
> I am capable of making a pact with the devil if he attacks my enemy.

The first phrase belongs to the new Chilean government's Statement of Principles, announced on March 11, 1974. It would prove to be a vain hope. The second belongs to Dudley Thompson, then (1976) foreign minister of the (then) socialist government of Jamaica, and it illustrates, to a certain extent why the hope was vain. Chile was the wrong kind of "devil," because the enemy it attacked was communism. And, in an age of détente, on the eve of a U.S. president's pronouncement that "an inordinate fear of communism" was passé, it was like flogging a horse that, if not dead, was at least no longer a bucking bronco menacing life and limb. So it was—to develop the example—that the Michael Manley government in Jamaica, which was busily dismantling the economic viability of its country according to the most enlightened canons of nationalism and socialism, could embrace next-door neighbor Fidel Castro, but could not embrace Augusto Pinochet's Chile.

Jamaica, accordingly, cast one of the two votes against holding the annual meeting of the Organization of American States in Santiago in June of 1976. The other was cast by Mexico, which had already broken diplomatic relations with Chile, but—in defiance of an earlier OAS decision—never with Cuba.[52]

Jamaica at least turned up for the meeting; Mexico boycotted it. But hundreds of delegates—and some 530 journalists—were on hand when the Sixth General Assembly opened, Chile's first important moment on the international stage since the revolution. The conference was three days old when the superstar, Henry Kissinger, arrived aboard Air Force Two, flanked by bride Nancy and an official party numbering 120. Treasury Secretary William Simon had preceded him in Santiago by a month, but Kissinger was, otherwise, the first high-level member of the American administration to visit Pinochet's Chile. Although he wasn't there to hear Pinochet's welcoming speech, he surely had been informed that it included not only a blast at Mexico for a boycott that "was a form of ignoring the principle of non-intervention," but also that "in the face of an ideological war which puts at risk the sovereignty of free nations and the essential dignity of man, there is no place for comfortable neutralities which contain within them the germ of suicide."

Although Kissinger would take pains in that U.S. election year to distance himself from Chile, his remarks at the conference echoed Pinochet's. While defending the process of détente with the Soviet Union then underway, Kissinger also took note of the dangerous tendency toward the export of communist doctrine and the growing military power of Soviet client states. The United States, he said, had the will and the power to guarantee that there would be no more Angolas— certainly not in the Americas. He spoke three years before the Sandinistas would create just exactly that in Nicaragua. Ironically, it was the example of Chile that led the Soviet Union to accept once again Fidel Castro's insistence on armed struggle as the route to power in the hemisphere, the key to the Sandinista triumph.[53]

On June 8, the day after his speech, Kissinger met with Pinochet for an hour and ten minutes. (Missing from his small entourage at that meeting: U.S. Ambassador David Popper, by then not only a *persona non grata* to Pinochet, but also to Kissinger—see preceding chapter.) Before going into an official luncheon, Kissinger excused himself for a private chat with Pinochet. Neither side has ever divulged what transpired during those five minutes.

That conference was the last major international event Chile would host for many years to come. No other Cabinet-level American would visit the country for another seven years, and when she did, she found herself indirectly—but plainly—repudiated by her own State Department.[54]

President Allende represents an attractive figure, new in America; with his parliamentary background, his prudence and political wisdom, his agility and breadth of criterion, he is a guarantor of democracy.

François Mitterand, then first secretary of the Socialist party of France, and later president of France, expressed that judgment as he ended a visit to Chile one year into Salvador Allende's presidency.[55] Chile was, in fact, an obligatory mecca during the Allende years for dozens of conspicuous pilgrims of self-styled "progressive" thought and politics. Unsurprisingly, many could never understand why such an experiment had to end, why a man they judged so prudent, so wise, had to go. Thus, while Allende lived, many closed their ears to the clamor of Chileans from three living presidents on down who said Allende was dragging Chile into a black hole, just as they would not listen when told the military had saved Chile. Later, even more closed their eyes to the evidence of a new and sturdy country emerging from the ashes of the old.

Nor is this to suggest that the very real errors and excesses of revolutionary government were not a factor in the wall of hostility which rose up around Chile. They were. But it becomes suspect when one views the contrast between the reflexive and ritualistic outrage generated by Chile's wrongs as against the silence or, worse, muffled sniveling over the far more egregious wrongs committed by regimes such as Cuba or Nicaragua or Zimbabwe or Panama—much less the horrors of the truly murderous ones, such as Vietnam, Ethiopia, Iran, or Kampuchea (Cambodia).

There was, of course, the Soviet-orchestrated campaign to crush Chile. But even without that, Chile's new rulers would remain stigmatized until/unless they made peace with the Christian Democrats and, to a lesser extent, the Radicals and Socialists—and that, of course, they would not do. Each of these parties is plugged into a powerful international switchboard, above all, the Christian Democrats, with formidable allies in Venezuela, Italy, El Salvador, West Germany, Great Britain, the Scandinavian countries, and in the U.S. liberal wing of the Democratic party.[56] When the military took power, Socialists or Social Democrats (or Socialist-minded Labour governments) were in power in Sweden, Norway, Denmark, Holland, the Federal Republic of Germany, and Britain; France, Greece, and Spain joined the list a few years later. Italy had been governed by the Christian Democrats since the war, and Christian Democrats alternated in power with the Social Democrats in West Germany. The implacable, visceral hostility of many of those intensely ideological governments cannot be underestimated.

What follows is not intended as a comprehensive survey of Chile's foreign relations under military rule; it is a highlighting of what, taken together, was the unremitting hostility of most of the outside world of governments and international agencies during the first dozen years of military rule in Chile.[57]

Chile has no friends in the world today. We do not have friendly [*armoniosas*] relations with the countries of the Western Hemisphere. In fact, exceptions noted, the situation is the same throughout the Western world. . . .

> General Gustavo Leigh, one of the original
> revolutionaries, following his ouster from
> the junta.[58]

Although General Leigh, himself sternly anti Communist, was not among them, there were those who argued from the early days that part of the problem was that Chile's basic message—anti-communism—no longer "sells." A corollary, it was argued, was that Chile wasn't paying sufficient attention to diplomacy, particularly in the Third World. Under Pinochet, Chile never retreated from the first. As scarce resources permitted, Chile did move to remedy the second.[59] But in the end, it was money that talked: as Chile became one of the undeniable economic success stories of the world and had more to spend, formerly insurmountable barriers began to drop. There were, of course, other factors as well, not the least of them steady moves toward a return to democracy in Chile. (The emergence of conservative governments elsewhere, particularly that of Margaret Thatcher in Great Britain, produced some easing in tensions; relations with the United States under Ronald Reagan, by contrast, showed only brief improvement, before descending rapidly to the Carter level—or lower. Chile's relations with the United States will be the subject of a later section.)

In the Western Hemisphere—apart from the previously discussed border state problems—the two principal antagonists were Mexico and Venezuela. Mexico's foreign policy has, for many years, contained two immutables: calculated antagonism toward the United States; undisguised loathing of regimes of the Right. Venezuela has gone through two principal phases since its return to democracy in 1960. It was the first important target of Castro-inspired subversion in the early 1960s, and while ridding itself of its internal Communist security problem, it took a number of "hits" from human rights organizations for abuses (although the international human rights apparatus was far less developed in the sixties than in the seventies.) Venezuela, in fact, provoked the first hemispheric sanctions against Castro, after proving that Cuba was the source of an illicit 1963 arms shipment discovered before it could reach its Castroite guerrilla and urban terrorist forces. But having overcome its own internal security problem, Venezuela embarked on a foreign policy course more congenial to the ideology of its two dominant parties, COPEI (Christian Democrat) and Acción Democrática (more akin to Social Democrat). Both are parties of the Left. Venezuela's foreign policy, ever since the mid-sixties, has veered ever more to the Left.

Venezuela's pressures—until the mid eighties, when it became a principal source of funding for Christian Democrat and Radical party politics—were mostly symbolic. It was one of the first countries, and among the most adamant, in demanding the release from prison of key Allende regime figures such as Foreign Minister Clodomiro Almeyda and Communist party chief Luis Corvalán. Later, at the 1976 OAS meeting, Venezuela demanded a full amnesty for all political prisoners (which it had declined to grant during its own internal security wars a decade before). Venezuela, Mexico—and Cuba—are, in fact, the only Latin American states to have voted against Chile at every United Nations session at which they were present from 1975 through 1985 when the human rights situation came up.

Mexico, inevitably, became the principal base camp in the hemisphere for the most radical Chilean opposition. But the Mexicans did not break relations with Chile before luring them into what many Chileans believe was a trap. In May of 1974, Mexican Foreign Minister Emilio O. Rabasa traveled to Chile with the names of seventy-two refugees the Mexicans wanted freed. Securing safe conducts for all, Rabasa proclaimed it "a triumph for both nations, thereby putting an end to an area of friction between them." He added that Mexico would now "fulfill its previous commitments" made to the Allende government, specifically, to sell fertilizers and sulfur which were badly needed for the country's farms. Suddenly, and without warning, Mexico announced on November 27 that it was breaking diplomatic relations with Santiago. No explanation was given, and relations have never been renewed. Indeed, President Miguel de la Madrid made the nonrenewal of diplomatic relations one of his campaign pledges.[60]

In Mexico, as elsewhere, political tension did not preclude commercial relationships: in only two of the nine years, 1974–1982 inclusive, would Chile's exports to Mexico dip below the *highest* level ever reached under Allende, and at their peak (1981) they were nearly nine times higher than the Allende peak year of 1971.[61]

Britain's Conservative government fell on February 28, 1974. The New Labour government lost no time in taking aim at Chile, hardly surprising given the stridency of its attitude at its Blackpool Conference the previous October, when the shooting was still going on in Chile (see preceding chapter). On March 27, Whitehall announced it was suspending aid to Chile and would grant no more permits for the sales of arms. The first was a matter of small importance, the second was not: between 1970 and 1974, Chile had become one of Britain's best overseas customers for arms, to the extent of 70 million pounds sterling ($160 million). Furthermore, at the time, British shipyards were finishing work on two submarines (the *Hyatt* and *O'Brien*) and two frigates (the *Condell* and *Lynch*) ordered in 1968 by the Frei government. Work on the *Condell* was so far advanced that a Chilean crew had already begun sea trials aboard her. Foreign Secretary James Callaghan declined to say whether Britain would honor the deal. (Days later, the Foreign Office said they would, influenced no doubt by the reality that failure to do so would have meant incurring heavy indemnization penalties. Britain made the deliveries on schedule.)[62]

Two days after the British announcement, Mines Minister General Arturo Yovane Zúñiga said he would propose to the junta the suspension of Chilean copper sales to Britain. It never happened, but the flap did produce a windfall of sorts for Chile. Prices on the London Metals Market for copper jumped sharply to a record level.[63]

Early in March 1975, the Labour government announced it would give Chile no more time to pay its overdue debts; nor would it attend the Club of Paris meeting later that month (at which the other industrialized nations agreed to a rescheduling of Chile's foreign debts). The following year—acting on the pretext of the alleged mistreatment a British physician—Britain reduced diplomatic relations with Chile to the *chargé* level. Relations were restored to ambassadorial status when Margaret Thatcher came to power in 1979.[64]

As happened in other countries that were officially hostile, the private sector in Britain reacted to Chile's booming economy in the late 1970s; a number of trade missions visited the country, new export credits were authorized. By 1980, the Thatcher government felt secure enough to lift the embargo on arms sales to Chile. Thus, comments Muñoz, "economic reasons explain in part the decision of the Thatcher government to lift the embargo." Besides British investor interest, he notes, "Great Britain, which gets 30 percent of its earnings from exports, needs foreign markets." Those Thatcher policies paid off quickly: British exports to Chile rocketed from $65.6 million in 1978 to $171 million in 1981. Not surprisingly, the government's arms decision came under immediate attack from church groups, including the archbishop of Canterbury, Cardinal George Basil Hume, head of the Roman Catholic church. The government backed off to the extent of cancelling a $21 million order for small arms and weapons which could be used for "repressive" purposes, but remained firm on big ticket items, including a destroyer, a frigate, eighteen Jaguar jets, Hawker-Hunter fighter bombers, and others.[65]

Warmer relations with the U.K. were not without problems for Chile, particularly during the 1982 fighting between Britain and Argentina over the Falklands Islands (Malvinas, to the Argentines). Chile remained officially neutral during the crisis, but in all of its moves toward rapprochment with London, it had to keep a weather eye on its wary and edgy Argentine neighbors.

As Chile moved even more resolutely than Prime Minister Thatcher herself to create a free market economy, building on privatization of formerly state-operated firms and activities (as she had), relations continued to improve. By 1982, Great Britain led the fight in the United Nations to end the special "prosecution" of Chile on human rights charges.[66]

Relations with other major European countries proceeded on similar, dual tracks. Late in 1974, the Federal Republic of Germany announced it would no longer provide financial assistance to Chile because of the "political situation"; the next year it was modified somewhat—West Germany declined to release a DM 21 million credit to Chile until former Foreign Minister Clodomiro Almeyda was released from prison. Four years later, in 1979, Chilean Foreign Minister Hernán Cubillos was submitted to a series of snubs in Bonn—just a few days before Prime Minister Helmut Schmidt received Allende's widow. Two years later, as noted earlier, West Germany suspended the sale of two submarines to Chile, when Chile came under attack from Argentina. (Not until 1984 did Chile finally get the first of them, the second the following year.) But again, despite those tensions, commercial relations blossomed, by 1980 reaching nearly $1 billion. Even more impressively, Chile's exports to the Federal Republic were nearly double the volume of its imports that year ($612 million vs. $308 million). In 1980, West Germany was Chile's second trading partner in the world, after the long-dominant United States. German businesses also became one of the principal sources of investment capital in Chile, and Chile's economic programs attracted high praise from sources ranging from the president of Volkswagen-Brazil to the German Industrial Federation. Nevertheless, as late as 1987, Chile found itself a political football in the in-fighting between the Christian Democrats and their Bavarian sister party, the Christian Social Union.[67]

> We've got to find a friendly way—or one not so friendly—to get rid of Pinochet.

Italy's Socialist Prime Minister Bettino Craxi may have been feeling his oats when he uttered those words in March 1985, having survived two years in the prime ministership, and thus bidding fair to become the longest-serving Italian prime minister in modern times. (He succeeded, although he would not, ultimately, get to serve as long as he expected.)

Craxi's remarks would have been brazen and intolerable interference in the internal affairs of another state at any time.[68] Coming at a time when Chile's economy (unlike Italy's) was making a solid comeback, when the country was moving decisively toward a return to democracy, the remark might have earned universal condemnation. There was none.

The episode dramatized a new reality in Chile's tormented foreign affairs: just as relations were gradually improving with other Western European states, they suffered severe damage with three—for reasons quite beyond Chile's control. In 1981, the Socialist François Mitterand was elected president of France; in 1982, the Socialist Felipe González was elected president of Spain; in 1983, the Socialist Craxi began his four-year reign at the head of the Italian government. (In 1982, the Socialist Andreas Papandreou took over in Greece, but that country was far less relevant to Chile.)

For three years following the death of Generalísimo Francisco Franco in 1975, Spain was supportive of the new regime in Chile. By 1978, it began to alter, but following González's win, it changed dramatically. Just how profoundly ideological differences influenced relations was demonstrated in September 1983 when the vice president of Spain, Alfonso Guerra, said in a public speech "that the only legitimate President of Chile is called Salvador Allende." But, in one important area, there were even closer ties: Spain's aeronautical industry cooperated actively in building Chile's new—and burgeoning—state-run National Aeronautical Enterprise (ENAER, from the Spanish *Empresa Nacional de Aeronáutica*).[69]

Although the Gaullist Valery Giscard D'Estaing presided over France during the first seven years of junta rule, relations with that country were none too cordial, either. Chile's distinguished ambassador—Jorge Errázuriz Echeñique—found himself listening to a Giscard lecture on human rights as he presented his credentials in 1975. In 1979, Chile's foreign minister was forced to meet "furtively" with his French counterpart during a visit to that country because of a well-orchestrated protest campaign (in which future President Mitterand played a conspicuous role). Still, the French—by then Chile's biggest arms supplier—continued to sell arms, most importantly, Mirage 50 jet fighters, part of a $160 million package.[70]

With Mitterand in power, "conflicts have been permanent" between the two governments, Muñoz wrote. Serious problems started during the presidential campaign, when Giscard's prime minister, Raymond Barre, secured an embargo on the hefty Chilean arms purchases. Those deals (some already consummated) included: AMX 30 armored tanks, AMX 13 armored cars, 16 Mirage jets, 155 mm cannons, "Milan" antitank rockets, "Puma" helicopters, 68 mm, armored carrier-mounted antitank shells, and "Exocet" surface–to–surface missiles. Of fifty AMX-30s ordered, the Mitterand government blocked delivery of the last twenty-nine.[71]

Relations with Italy were bad from day one. On September 11, 1973, Italy reduced relations to a "de facto" level, and it was May 19, 1981, before they were raised even to *chargé* level. Italy, of course, has been ruled since the war by Christian Democrats in combination (extremely volatile and shaky) with Social Democrats and small splinter parties. With the decline of the Communist party in France, Italy's became the largest in the Western world, polling 30 percent of the vote in the early 1980s. In such an environment, union, academic, and other political groups were able to maintain constant pressure on their government to maintain a stern hostility to Chile. But, as the Craxi remark demonstrates, they did not need to work overtime to do so.

But, as with Britain, all three of those countries—Italy, Spain, and France—continued to expand their commercial ties with Chile, including investments in Chile.

There were smaller vexations in Chile's international path. In the first nine months of the revolution, Chile recorded fifty-six attacks on its diplomatic missions or diplomatic entities overseas, ranging from flag burnings to a mob attack (in Paris) on the Chilean airline offices which caused $5 million damage. In the climate of antijunta sentiment fanned by the Socialist government of Sweden—perhaps the most vituperative of all the Western governments—police needed to deploy almost two battalions of riot police to protect the Chilean team competing in a 1975 Davis Cup tennis series.[72]

On March 23, 1980, President Pinochet was in the air en route across the Pacific for a visit to the Philippines when President Ferdinand Marcos abruptly cancelled the visit (which was also to have included stops in Fiji, Hong Kong, and New Guinea). The official reason given was the discovery of a plot to kill both. Marcos' decision, it was learned later, came about under pressure from President Jimmy Carter, via the U.S. State Department. Back in Santiago on March 24, Pinochet announced he was breaking diplomatic relations with the Philippines; Marcos, a week later, sent a special emissary to explain privately to Pinochet and the incident was closed (except for Foreign Minister Cubillos, fired as the scapegoat for the incident).

In 1983—ostensibly out of concern for human rights violations—even Zambia broke relations with Chile, even though the two were the cornerstone countries in the International Committee of Copper Exporting Countries. (It was little noted in press reports at the time, but Zambia was the pot calling the kettle black. In its tenth annual survey, the respected and independent organization Freedom House ranked Zambia exactly where it ranked Chile: partly free. Actually, in terms of civil liberties, Chile was in the fifth group of nations, Zambia in the sixth.)[73]

Not everyone was content merely to hector. As noted, Communist parties in countries now charier than ever of including them in "democratic" coalitions sought to draw on the lessons of Chile to make themselves more "acceptable." Chilean Communist party leader Luis Corvalán—as noted, released from prison in exchange for Soviet dissident Vladimir Bukovsky, following an international pressure campaign—went to a hero's welcome at the Kremlin. There, Nikolai Podgorny, president of the Soviet Union, pinned the Lenin Peace Prize on him. Corvalán, in his January 4, 1977, speech, sounded the new siren song: "There is no doubt that today, much less tomorrow, Chile will not be what it was yesterday. And although circumstances have changed and continue to change, there are Communists, Socialists, Radicals, Christian Democrats, and other trends in Chile, and they will be there after the Pinochet dictatorship has gone. The events in Portugal and Spain show that these trends are mighty rivers that fascism has been and is unable to dry." Then, and again in a television interview a few days later on the state-run British Broadcasting Company, Corvalán predicted a coalition government "excluding the fascists." Sweetening the message, he spoke of a mixed economy when this "grand coalition" should come to power.

Corvalán and other Communist leaders had reason for concern. An Associated Press survey of Communism in South America at the time reported that "repressed by governments and torn by factional disputes . . . the once-influential pro-Moscow communists in Latin America now face exile, public apathy, and isolation. . . ."

Out of this emerged the new Communist message: antifascism based on "international solidarity." It was, as noted, a message that found resonant and rapid echo.[74]

Two major Communist states never broke relations: the Peoples' Republic of China, apparently on the premise that Chile's principal enemy, the Soviet Union, also was theirs; and Romania, because of the high level of commercial relations between the two countries, and probably more importantly, because of the eccentric nature of the Nicolae Ceausescu dynasty in Bucharest.

There was one other group abroad that did not join in the chorus of condemnation: those who had themselves lived under communism. Few were more vocal than the Cuban exile community in the United States. In 1975, two such groups called on their fellow exiles to support Chile. Said one, in a message to Pinochet: We "identify fully with the government and the people of Chile in their titanic struggle within and without their national frontiers, in an effort to protect our Western and Christian civilization, now facing the most tragic threat in its history. . . ."[75]

OF HUMAN RIGHTS AND HUMAN WRONGS

No radical revolution, no matter how bloody—one thinks of Cuba, Iraq, Algeria, many African states, Vietnam's occupation of Indochina, Khomeini's Iran—has confronted the worldwide press campaign and the global indignation evoked by the clumsy authoritarians of Santiago. Was its crime in its methods, or in its position on the right of the political spectrum? Was its sin the lack of civil freedoms, or the abandonment of the leftist embrace? Why is the argument so widespread that left-wing governments like Nicaragua's are supposed to be moderated by economic assistance while conservative governments like Chile's must be reformed by ostracism? The Socialist government of Sweden cut off aid to Chile on September 13, within forty-eight hours of the coup, before its implications could possibly be known. Had it ever acted with such alacrity, or at all, against left-wing tyrants? Indeed, it had lavished aid on Hanoi through the Vietnam war and afterward.

> Henry Kissinger, writing from the
> post-government vantage point of
> 1982[76]

The answer to those rhetorical questions is obvious and, indeed, relieved of the requirement of diplomatic restraint, Kissinger goes on to answer the last one. (Had he been writing later, Kissinger might have gone on to observe that Sweden—together with most West European critics of Chile—continued to lavish aid through the eighties on Nicaragua, a regime with a human rights record that was truly appalling.)

One of the very first international human rights authorities to visit Chile—Luis A. Reque, executive secretary of the Inter-American Commission on Human Rights—made a point not dissimilar to Kissinger's: "It can be stated," he wrote in the immediate aftermath of battle, "that a number of prisoners were subject to harrassment, abuses, maltreatment, and, in some cases, torture. However, it should be noted that reports appearing in the international press on maltreatment and torture are exaggerated."[77] Reque's words disappeared in the din (I can find no reference to them for example, in literally hundreds of press clips from newspapers the world over covering the years immediately following the coup).

Reque arrived in Chile one month after the revolution. But he was not the first international human rights representative: within a few days of the coup, the United Nations High Commission on Refugees was in action. The International Red Cross was allowed to begin visiting detention centers on September 25 and quickly developed a program of biweekly visits to all detention centers around the country.[78]

Within six months, the UN commission reported that the emergency phase of its work was finished. High Commissioner Ernest Schalatter of Switzerland expressed his gratitude for the high level of cooperation accorded the agency, noting that in six months the commission, working with two other international agencies, had relocated more than 5,900 persons of fifty nationalities to thirty-eight countries. (A report in the *Washington Post* at the time noted that Communist countries were not among those welcoming refugees, a fact causing "some bitterness among Latin American leftists" since "many Chileans seeking new homes are loyal members of the Communist Party, which has supported the Soviet Union since the party was founded some 50 years ago.")[79]

Less than one week after the coup, Amnesty International and the International Commission of Jurists complained to the Inter-American Commission on Human Rights (ICHR) of "reports of mass arrests and in some cases summary execution of political opponents as well as refugees of other countries." Those organizations asked the OAS to intervene. In the absence of ICHR's chairman, Executive Secretary Reque met on September 27 in Washington with Chile's acting representative to the OAS, requesting permission to visit Chile. He got it one week later, and was on his way in a little over two weeks.

Chile gave similar facilities to many other international organizations. One which it gave—and then revoked: permission for a special panel of the United Nations Commission for Human Rights, created at the commission's March 1974 meeting in Geneva. The five-member panel, headed by Pakistani Ali Allana, was already in Lima en route to Chile, when President Pinochet abruptly cancelled the visit, calling his decision "the second defeat for the Marxist-Leninists. . . . How many human rights commissions," he said, "have been sent to Cuba, the Soviet Union, and recently to Vietnam, Laos or Cambodia and other parts of the world where the most horrendous crimes are committed? . . . because they have the Marxist-Leninist shield, they are exempt."

Press reports at the time described it as a "surprise move." They should not have. Earlier that year, one astute correspondent wrote that, in the face of repeated condemnations, "Chile's military *junta* may be changing the relatively liberal policy it has followed up to now in allowing outside commissions and delegations to witness its military trials and investigate conditions of human rights in the country. . . ."

The Chileans, he said, were particularly irate for two reasons: the international campaign "orchestrated by the Soviet Union and Cuba, both countries with long and unrepentant histories of human rights violations that continue to this day; criticisms that don't take into account the pre-civil war condition of political and institutional crisis that prompted the military's bloody uprising on Sept. 11, 1973." The first organization to find the door slammed was the Swiss-based Interparliamentary Union, which had planned to send two parliamentarians to visit former Chilean congressmen then being held prisoner. (Only a small handful of members of Allende's coalition fit that description.)[80]

Chile was stung first by a January 1974 report filed by Amnesty International asserting that, while diminished, political arrests and executions were continuing, and "there is substantial evidence of a persistent and gross violation of the most fundamental rights." The Chilean government hit back that the Amnesty team reached its conclusions after a week-long visit limited to Santiago. Still later came a sharply critical report issued by the Geneva-based International Labor Organization; the *Miami Herald* used it as the basis of an editorial, but made no mention—nor did other press reports—that Congress in 1970 had cut off funds to the ILO for two years because of its anti-American, pro-Communist line, nor that top AFL-CIO leaders had complained that the ILO "is rapidly being captured by Iron Curtain countries."[81]

But, more than anything else, it was the report of the OAS Human Rights Commission in November of 1974 that stuck in the craw of the Chileans, particularly as their attempts to rebut key points were virtually ignored in press reports.

Though denied entry to Chile, the five-member UN Working Committee—made up of representatives from Austria, Ecuador, Belgium, Pakistan, and Sierra Leone—filed a 132-page report in October 1975. The report asserted that "chaotic and inhuman brutality" following the coup had been replaced by "more systematic methods" directed against selected individuals. The authors said they based their findings on "all sources" outside Chile. One week later, the Chilean foreign ministry said Chile "categorically rejects the claims . . . as inexact and lacking foundation," and pointed out that the report acknowledged that its claims could not be verified. Defending its own behavior, the Chilean statement added that the junta had applied "with prudence" measures "conforming to legislation in existence before this government came to power . . . to confront the emergency situation in which the country lives, and as a consequence of rebuilding the nation and re-establishing its institutional normality." (The government later claimed it had denied the ad hoc group entry because it refused to give "minimal guarantees" that Chile would have an opportunity to review and rebut "concrete charges.")

When the UN General Assembly voted in December 1974, the tally was ninety-five in favor of the report, twenty-three abstentions, eleven against. The United States abstained; not a single Western European country supported Chile.

Commenting later on the UN report, Sen. Daniel P. Moynihan (D-N.Y.), said Chile's refusal to admit the ad hoc group was "true. But it is only part of the truth. The whole truth would include the fact that Amnesty International and the International Red Cross were permitted to visit Chile. Moreover, if the visit of the Working Group had gone through, it would have been the first time in history that any government had permitted such a visit." That part of the "truth" never managed to make its way into any press report I have ever seen, at the time or since.[82]

Eventually, as the United Nations Human Rights Commission added Israel and South Africa to what became known as the Iron Triangle of abuser nations, there were second looks at the integrity of the organization itself. The *Washington Post* noted in a 1977 article that almost three-fourths of the thirty-two countries on the commission were themselves accused of violating the rights of their citizens. Walter Kovey of B'nai B'rith told the *Post* that the commission's resolutions in recent years had almost totally ignored the individual's right to freedom, redefining human rights to embrace "economic rights." Observing that the commission had ratified an amendment that enabled governments to restrict emigration for reasons of "national security" and "public order," Kovey said, "in the hands of a totalitarian regime, these resolutions become a device for whitewashing repressive policies." Walter Laquer wrote in the May 1977 *Commentary*: "The old League of Nations showed weakness and cowardice, but even in its worst moments it never reached the depths of degradation achieved by the United Nations. Western representatives on the Human Rights Commission and other such bodies say in mitigation that they have succeeded in preventing even worse outrages. This does not change the fact that by playing the evil game and adhering to the perverted rules, they confer respectability on institutions whose main function is to prevent the implementation of human rights, and to justify their suppression."[83]

Others, heretofore conspicuously absent from human rights front lines, joined the worldwide pogrom. In May of 1975, the presidents of Harvard and Brandeis universities as well of the Massachusetts Institute of Technology told the OAS's Human Rights Commission that they were concerned about reports of "violations of the most elemental human rights in Chile." "This is a problem of fundamental decency," the academics said. (By contrast, another academic, Nobel laureate Milton Friedman, went to Chile and, in a letter to the *Wall Street Journal*, reported: "On the atmosphere in Chile, it is perhaps not irrelevant that at two universities, the Catholic University and the University of Chile, I gave talks on 'The Fragility of Freedom,' in which I explicitly characterized the existing regime as unfree, talked about the difficulty of maintaining a free society, the role of free markets and free enterprise in doing so, and the urgency of establishing those preconditions for freedom. There was no advance or ex post facto censorship, the audiences were large and enthusiastic, and I received no subsequent criticism."[84]

No subject in international affairs lends itself to more emotionalism—or manipulation—than human rights. All but the most depraved or demented favor human rights, for themselves, for others. Consensus as to exactly what human rights consist in, and how they are to be secured, tends to end there. U.S. founding father James Madison, in *The Federalist* (#51), wrote, "If men were angels, no government would be necessary . . . in framing a government which is to be administered by men over men, the great difficulty is this: you must first enable the government to control the governed; and in the next place oblige it to control itself." Controlling the governed amidst chaos and civil war— the case of Chile without serious question in the early years of revolution, arguably so in the years since—is a riddle for which there is no easy answer. Yet, through its role as instant trivializer, the mass media of the world—in Solzhenitsyn's phrase, "the greatest power within Western countries"—fosters distorted images and encourages stampedes into snap judgments, its own, and others. Judgments in the modern world, once made, tend to harden rapidly into "truth." But, as the distinguished American journalist Tom Wicker noted, "journalism, with its focus on events rather than character, is ill-equipped for such a judgment," by which he meant distinguishing between "the quest for power to do good . . . [and] the simple quest for power."[85] The history of the world in modern times is replete with examples showing that when the brokers of world opinion determine that a leader—or regime—means well, that it intends to exercise power "to do good," there is no end to the forbearance shown. For the many reasons submitted here into evidence, international consensus formed early—very early on the part of some— that the Pinochet regime could see no good, hear no good, do no good.

That, among other things, the regime also did evil, there is no serious dispute, either.

As the attacks on Chile increased in intensity and ferocity, the regime gradually conceded that some mistakes had been made. Sergio Diez, Chilean delegate to the United Nation's social committee, said late in 1975 that the authorities at times had to "muddy their hands" to keep order. Earlier that year, President Pinochet reacted to charges of mistreatment of prisoners by ordering the release of the names of twelve military men he said had been jailed for abuses. A reporter for the *Washington Post* obtained private interviews with nine of the twelve still in jail, and concluded: "None of the crimes they were jailed for [were] related to political prisoners.... According to the men interviewed, none of the crimes had occurred during interrogation of prisoners and none involved the deliberate, graduated violence associated with torture. Further, the men all said they knew of no torturers who had been jailed. Confronted with her [the reporter's] finding, a government spokesman then said that must mean that no torturers were serving prison terms in Chile."[86]

It is a subject which invites a first person digression.

His name was Fernando Salas, this chain-smoking—and unmistakably anguished—young priest seated before me in the shabby, cluttered old chalet on a street of old chalets. The time was late April of 1974 and the place the headquarters of the Committee on Cooperation for Peace in Chile, known popularly as the Committee for Peace, with Father Salas its first executive director. Beginning shortly after the coup, churchmen began collecting data on missing persons, allegations of abuse of prisoners, executions, disappearances. As a result the Committee for Peace was set up on October 9, 1973, by an interdenominational group of Roman Catholic and Lutheran bishops and the grand rabbi of Chile.

I made my first visit to the committee on April 30, 1974, returning twice in the days ahead, at various times over the intervening years, and most recently (to its successor agency, the Catholic church's Vicariate of Solidarity, as well as to the Chilean Commission on Human Rights, established in 1978), several times in 1987. I have met and talked not only with officials of these organizations, but with persons off those premises who say they were tortured, or that members of their families had been shot or disappeared. I do not know how many of these stories are true, but I have no doubt that many of them are. I have no doubt that such organizations, by their very nature, attract many activists fiercely opposed to a government such as that of Augusto Pinochet, and that not a few of them will be manipulative exploiters of such situations. But neither do I doubt the earnestness and humanity of many working long hours in that melancholy, harrowing, officially persecuted, ghoulish field.[87] I am not indifferent to human suffering. Nor do I believe that even the most noble of ends justifies evil means. The problem is knowing which facts are true, which truths matter most when one is in conflict with another.

> Q: Don't you believe that errors may have been committed during his time in the matter of human rights?

A: You people are in glory in this country . . . You take your children to school without problems, walk the streets, you don't have to stand in line to do your shopping . . . you're tranquil. But, in '73, there were 30,000 firearms scattered around Santiago. Do you think that those people who fought, who participated in that attempt at communist revolution were just going to remain quiet? We did not find ourselves facing saints on September 11. Extremist documents have been found showing authentically, for example, that a son-in-law was charged with killing his father-in-law . . .

Augusto Pinochet, responding to
a question in April 1986[88]

Father Salas had been ordained as a Jesuit priest only two years when he received a summons to report to the archbishop's palace in Santiago. He was told to begin work immediately helping victims of the civil war. He began work the next day.

"Why you?"

"I don't know," he said, pausing to puff his Belmont cigarette. "Maybe because I had no political connections or ties."

From parish priest in the Los Nogales shantytown one day this thirty-two-year-old man with the brown curly hair and no-nonsense manner went the very next day into what would become one of the most gruelling and embattled jobs in Chile. "At first," the bespectacled priest said, "I was absolutely alone, but it didn't take long to see the many dimensions of the problem. I thought then the job would take three or four months. We've been here seven, and some problems still exist." Support, he said, came rapidly, from the churches in Chile, from the World Council of Churches. His first month budget of $10,000 grew rapidly to $40,000 ("and is still growing"), almost all of it from the United States and Europe.

"The responsibility for Chile is on their [the military's] shoulders," he said. "The church is only trying to help the government to be just and work to the benefit of all citizens. We give them social facts, it's up to them to correct the problems, to investigate and verify, to take measures."

At this point—early 1974—church and state were not yet in collision; that would come later. But they were on a collision course, and that began much earlier.

Father Salas himself symbolized that "disaster in search of a place to happen." Although he had no overt "political" affiliation, in common with many Jesuits in Chile, he had a clear ideological creed. It was known popularly as "liberatation theology" which, beginning in the early 1960's, progressively radicalized the Church in Chile. Eighteen months after this interview, he was in jail, charged with hiding members of the underground guerrilla organization, the Movement of the Revolutionary Left, from security forces.

Raw statistics, from the committee's files, to March 5, 1974:

Prisoners: 3,100

Relocated: 4,100

Behind raw statistics, Father Salas speaks:

"They've come to us to tell of all kinds of abuse, of torture—electric prods, beatings by people with black hoods over their heads. Some people have been made to stand in water forty to fifty centimers (roughly fifteen to eighteen inches) deep, forcing them to sleep standing up in it; there have been cases of sexual abuse, and stubbing out cigarette butts on all parts of people's bodies ... worse things ... mice crawling over people's naked bodies."

Beyond statistics, from the committee's case files:

"Case #66: Prisoner: Serrrano Galaz, Roberto Esteban. Identity #45072. Date of birth: 2 Sept. 1939. Nationality: Chilean. Civil status: Married. Number of dependents: Four. Place of detention or arrest: His home: Settlement on Paine Road. Date of detention: October 16, 1973. Who arrested: Soldiers from the San Bernardo Infantry Regiment. Circumstances of detention or arrest: At the time of the arrest, his wife was beaten, with the result that she lost the child she expected. She was seven-months pregnant. The soldiers said they were taking him in for questioning, and that he would be back at 9 the next morning. Subsequent inquiries: His wife has requested information from the Defense Ministry, National Office of Detained Persons, the San Bernardo Prison, Rancagua, Buin, Talagante garrisons, the Red Cross International, without positive results. Other information: His wife has the following problem. Since he was employed on the [agricultural] settlement, he has until May 1 to return to his work, or failing in that, the family must give up their housing at the settlement."[89]

As indicated earlier, the first extensive outside investigation was carried out by the Inter-American Commission on Human Rights (IACHR), from July 22 to August 2, 1974. It was also the last. Numerous other groups—some private, some quasi-official, some self-anointed— carried out "investigations" of one kind or another, particularly in the first two years, but continuing through all the years of junta rule. But there was never such a thorough on-site investigation as that conducted by the OAS's human rights arm, although in 1978, Chile finally relented and allowed a UN mission to conduct a two-week on-site inspection. Just how conflictive the human rights question can be, or is, can be gleaned from the bitter recriminations exchanged through the years by the government of Chile on the one hand and the IACHR on the other.

Just how much perspective can influence findings can be gleaned from reports filed by different groups at approximately the same time.

What is beyond challenge is that Chile has been subjected to a scrutiny and a public pillorying without equal. Both have been far out of proportion to the magnitude of the crimes seriously even *imputed* to it, and grotesquely out of proportion by comparison with the international silence, connivance, or rhetorical shrugs in the face of the far more heinous human rights crimes of so many other regimes.

Five of the IACHR's then seven members, supported by three professionals and three secretaries, traveled to Chile in 1974 for that on-site survey. Their findings, contained in a 177-page report,* were submitted to the OAS Permanent Council on October 31, 1974, and to the OAS General Assembly on May 1975. The report, it should be noted, contained a number of allegations of torture more graphic and gruesome than those recited by Father Salas.[90] The ink was barely dry on the report when the fireworks started.

On December 4, Chile filed an eighty-three-page response, the last thirty-four pages chronicling various incidents of violence directed at soldiers, policemen, or Chilean official installations abroad.

Chilean and other observers pointed out that "at least" seven of the ten categories of human rights violations cited by the commission were a matter of interpretation of Chilean law. Since civilians and other innocent persons always suffer in wartime settings—as do civil liberties—nothing galled the government of Chile more than the commission's refusal to consider the situation in Chile prior to September 11, and its denial that a "state of war" existed in Chile.[91] For the Chilean authorities, the fact that the commission said it "cannot, nor does it seek to, make a comparative study of the political systems that have succeeded each other in Chile" meant a refusal to credit the causes of the events which took place after September 11. As to whether a "state of war" existed afterward, the Chileans argued: "The writers of treaties [sic] on Military Criminal Law in general and the Chilean authors in particular agree that the state or time of war may be: (a) real or effective, or (b) imminent or virtual. . . . The real state of war in the period immediately following September 11, 1973, having been proven, this is also valid as regards the imminence of a situation of war in the period in which this commission visited the country . . . It is not necessary to be in Chile to hear daily the Moscow and Havana radio programs in which they periodically incite to subversion; or to verify the public collections

---

* It should be noted, however, that the first sixty pages covered procedural matters and the report of the commission's executive secretary during his aforementioned fact-finding visit in October of 1973. It is also germane to note that perhaps half of the report itself consisted of depositions—of necessity containing a number of unsubstantiated allegations—of prisoners, including lengthy statements made by former top officials of the Allende government who had been held on Dawson Island.

in many sectors of the world for the purpose of financing the purchase of arms and aiding the Chilean subversion. . . ."92

The report said that during its stay in Chile, "commission members were accompanied in all cases by military authorities. It should be stated that the accompanying officials did not hinder or disturb the commission's work. They always stayed discreetly apart while the commission members interrogated the prisoners, who therefore could speak more freely." The report then went on to complain that the commission was denied access to five sites where a number of reports seemed to coincide that torture had been practised before prisoners were shifted to other detention centers. The government declined on the grounds they were "military" establishments; two of the five clearly were not, one was an annex of the Santiago Investigations Bureau, the other a property at #38 Londres Street known as "The House of Terror," or "The House of the Bells" (for the tolling of the bells of a nearby church).93

The Chileans also accused the IACHR of using "deliberately dramatic" language in accepting at face value claims of torture: ". . . for instance, of the 109 persons whose statements are included [in the report], 44 state that they were not subjected to maltreatment . . . 46 state that they suffered maltreatment at the time immediately following September 11, a circumstance which, on the other hand, appears to be justified by the commission itself . . . only 19 persons state that they have suffered whippings in recent times, and of these, only three can exhibit marks on their bodies that might have been caused by this sort of maltreatment . . ."

The wounds of this war of words between Chile and the IACHR have never healed. Acting on instructions of the full OAS General Assembly, the commission prepared special reports on Chile again in 1976 and 1977 (both noting improvements in human rights conditions, but urging more); and, beginning in 1977, it required an ongoing special section on Chile in its annual reports.

On May 6, 1981, Chile pulled out of the commission and refused to respond to any further communications from it. Acrimony over the reports backfired onto the commission itself. In March of 1976—two months before the OAS meeting in Santiago—three of the seven commission members decided to resign, saying they were disheartened by lack of stronger OAS action against Chile. Two said they doubted that hemisphere governments really wished to protect human rights, which they charged were flagrantly violated in several countries. Two months later, Executive Secretary Luis Reque, the Bolivian who had held the job from the inception of the IACHR sixteen years earlier, accused Chile of conducting a long campaign to force him out. One press report said the uproar was without precedent in the commission's history.94

Not everyone, however, saw the situation in 1974 so bleakly as did the

IACHR. Two experienced scholars on Latin America, accompanied by a law professor, went to Chile one month before the commission did. While there, they interviewed seventy-five persons, among them church leaders, former President Frei, four members of Allende's Cabinet, defense lawyers in political trials, and International Red Cross and UN human rights officials. They reported that, "according to the testimony of many Chilean and foreign observers, serious abuse was virtually eliminated by late April of 1974. . . ."[95]

The year 1982 was one of worldwide recession. The economies of Latin America were particularly hard hit. For Chile, it was a catastrophic economic earthquake.

In the aftermath, opposition political figures—led by the Christian Democrats—capitalized on rising public discontent to set in motion a series of massive demonstrations, monthly "days of action." The first was a nationwide strike called by the Confederation of Copper Workers on May 11, 1983, which boiled up into huge demonstrations in August. Pinochet responded by sending the army into the streets. Sixty persons died and hundreds were injured before late that year a political truce brought calm. Among those arrested and held incommunicado for several days: Gabriel Valdés, president of the Christian Democrats, and Rodolfo Seguel, president of the copper workers' union.

Those turbulent events produced the first serious cracks in the ruling coalition since 1973, for the air force and navy distanced themselves from the army's heavy handed tactics. Those events also produced a new worldwide wave of anti-Chile reaction. Seven European countries—France, West Germany, the Netherlands, Italy, Denmark, Belgium, and the United Kingdom—signed a petition to Foreign Minister Miguel Schweitzer expressing "live concern." French Foreign Minister Clause Cheysson described President Pinochet as a curse upon the country.[96]

Those events also brought the Organization of American States back into the picture. Reacting to what it called "the persistence of the problems reported and even of the worsening of the state of human rights" in Chile, the IACHR decided in May 1984 to do a new and comprehensive report on human rights in Chile. It asked for permission to visit Chile. Hearing nothing for six months, it asked again. On January 16, 1985, Chile responded: no. It appended a series of allegations against the commission, beginning with a protest that its response to the 1974 report, its "point by point" rebuttals, had been "utterly ignored." "Events and circumstances that are commonplace in the countries of our hemisphere are violations of human rights only if they occur in Chile ... It is not my intention," Chile's foreign minister continued, "to deny existence of a number of human rights problems in my country, just as there are in all nations of the world. . . . But that is no reason for the commission . . . to give the impression of the presence of a vast number of problems, as it does in the special chapter of its most recent annual report, [which] is full of frivolous statements. . . ." The commission reacted with a sharp retort of its own, concluding: "Up to now, no American state in which a state of law exists has questioned, as your government has, the procedures used by the commission . . . I should inform you, however, that even if the government of Chile does not remove the obstacle it has set for the commission, this will not prevent it from continuing to prepare a report on the situation of human rights in Chile."[97]

Nor did it. On October 1, 1985, the commission released its report, 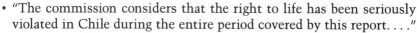 covering the entire period of junta rule to that time. Highlights:

- "The commission considers that the right to life has been seriously violated in Chile during the entire period covered by this report. . . ."
- ". . . torture has been a continuous, deliberate and systematic practice through the entire period which began in 1973. . . ."
- ". . . the right to personal liberty . . . has suffered a marked and sustained deterioration during the period covered by this report. . . ."
- "It is in the exercise of political rights that the commission finds the synthesis that makes it possible to explain both the serious situation characterizing human rights in Chile and the alternatives that will make it possible to change it. To a very large extent, the violations of human rights . . . have stemmed from the disproportionate measures used by the government to achieve the goals it has set itself. Regardless of the value judgment those goals merit, none of them justifies their achievement at the cost of sacrificing the inalienable rights of the human person. . . ."[98]

> Terrorism is the maximum violation of human rights.
>
> In Chile, there are not, nor have there been, violations of human rights. We, the men who grew up in these armed forces, are not cruel. . . .
>
> This government has never denied that there have been conflictive situations which may have translated as problems of human rights. . . .

The first statement, in large measure, underpinned the rationale of the junta, as it confronted the reality of violence: violence directed first at the society at large during the Allende years, directed later at the government and its agents.

The second was made by President Pinochet in the early days of revolution, in an interview with *La Tercera de la Hora* of Santiago (March 7, 1974). It reflected an earnest and strongly felt self-image.

The third reflected what happened when men who were not cruel came to grips with the problem of the first. It was made by Mario Calderón, the Chilean Foreign Ministry's adviser on human rights, in 1987 (and quoted in *Hoy* of Santiago, in its decade-spanning special edition of May 1987).

All three statements were "true."

Hoy headlined the table: "To Live in Danger." It summarized major human rights violations for the period 1979 through 1986, using figures supplied by the Roman Catholic church's Vicariate of Solidarity. The government sharply challenged the authenticity of those figures. They are presented in the belief that they are probably more true than untrue:

TABLE 36
HUMAN RIGHTS VIOLATIONS, 1979–1986

YEAR	ARRESTS	DEATHS	INTERNAL EXILE	TORTURES
1979	1,325	14	1	143
1980	1,129	17	106	91
1981	911	33	60	68
1982	1,789	24	81	123
1983	15,077	96	130	434
1984	39,440	74	170	205
1985	9,116	66	171	168
1986	33,665	58	—	255
TOTALS	102,452	382	719	1,487

(The Vicariate defines "deaths" variously as those executed, or killed in armed clashes, by political homicides, torture, unnecessary violence, abuses of power, and more. Arrests include persons held for only a few hours. Street demonstrations, a resurgence of terrorism, and the 1986 assassination attempt on Pinochet explain the sharp jump in arrests.)

Source: Hoy, special edition, May 1987, p. 36. *Hoy* is itself aligned to the Christian Democrats and thus outspokenly critical of the junta.

The decision to allow a human rights team into Chile in 1978 earned for the government a brief respite from United Nations hectoring. Late that year, the UN commission's special Chile Working Group was disbanded and replaced by a special observer. A fund set up that year to provide financial and legal aid for "politically persecuted Chileans and their families" was, two years later, converted into a fund for political refugees of all nationalities. But, by 1980, the UN commission said conditions in Chile had worsened—a decision undoubtedly influenced by the intense internal political opposition to the plebiscite that year on a new constitution. In July 1981, Amnesty International, which enjoys official observer status at the UN, published a report purporting to show evidence of systematic torturing of political prisoners.

Just as it had with the OAS, in 1983 Chile balked at further cooperation with the United Nations. Despite efforts by Great Britain and other nations to stop singling out Chile year after year for special scorn, the UN General Assembly in 1987 voted its thirteenth consecutive condemnation of Chile—every year, that is, since the junta had taken power. (Only one other country in the world received comparable attention: South Africa.)

Despite those votes, the UN's special observer, Fernando Volio Jiménez, conceded during his second visit to Chile in March of 1987 that "advances have been made." Among them: an agreement with the Red Cross International to give their representatives access to persons within five days of their arrest. Yet another: progressive scaling back of the number of exiles barred reentry to the country (down to fewer than one hundred by early 1988). Thousands, including such prominent Allende figures as Clodomiro Almeyda, took advantage of the opening and returned, in Almeyda's case to take command of the ultraleft wing of the Socialist party.

Of all the international organizations involved in human rights in Chile, none was more intimately and constantly involved than the International Red Cross. In March of 1988, a team of scholars from the Heritage Foundation in Washington made a week-long fact-finding visit to Chile. An internal memorandum, prepared after their return, reported on conversations with Dr. Jean-François Bonard, serving his second tour of duty for the Red Cross in Chile. According to the report, Bonard said the earlier agreement had been expanded, so that "he could go into any prison in Chile, at any time, to see any prisoner. He did not have to make an appointment, or let them know he was coming." He also said Red Cross doctors were permitted immediate and unqualified access to any prisoner, except those held incommunicado.

Following the disbanding, in June 1987, of the Centro Nacional de Informaciones—the state security agency that succeeded DINA and attracted most human rights fire—such prisoners were held by the civilian Investigaciones police force. By statute, they could be held incommunicado only five days, although in certain circumstances, that could be extended for up to thirty days. At the time of the Heritage visit, only one person was being held incommunicado in the country.

According to the Heritage report, "he [the Red Cross representative] stated categorically that the government appears to be dedicated to stamping out abuses. . . ."[99]

RENDER UNTO CAESAR . . .

No discussion of human rights in Chile during the Pinochet years would be complete without examining the role of the Roman Catholic church in Chile. No discussion of the equation of power in the politics of Chile would be complete without an examination of the role of the church.

Although Fundamentalist religions have been enjoying strong growth in Chile in recent years, somewhere between three-fifths and three-quarters of all Chileans in most recent studies profess to be Catholics. The church in Chile—as in most other countries—is heavily politicized. As in most other Western countries, the politics of the church in recent years have veered ever farther to the left.

Inevitably, that political outlook has influenced the attitude and behavior of the church in Chile toward the right-wing regime in residence since 1973 in La Moneda Palace.

> When Chile and the world pass judgment on Allende, he will be judged as a revolutionary. Will his work at La Moneda have meant a decisive step toward the appearance of that New Man—sound, free, responsible, creative and involved? Will the antivalues fomented by the capitalist system have fled in the face of the collapse of the structures sheltering them today? Allende knows what is expected of him, and he is willing to deliver. . . . As the government of the Popular Unity advances toward [the creation of] that New Man, a Christian cannot but march at its side, since that New Man is none other than the same one which Christ came to install upon this earth.

That "New Man" was, of course, the eternal figment of Marxist-Leninist poppycock, the one Allende claimed he would raise up from the ash heap of injustice, inequality, and economic depravity of the "capitalist"* Chile he inherited in 1970. The quotation is not from one of his campaign speeches, nor a Communist or Popular Unity broadside. It is from issue #194, November of 1970, of *Mensaje*, the publication of the Jesuit order in Chile—the order historically vaunted as the "Defenders of the Faith" in the Roman Catholic church.[100]

Mensaje, the Jesuits, were at the cutting edge of that shift to the left in Chile, as Jesuits were in much of the rest of the Western world. (Years later, reining them in would become an early priority of a pope attempting to recapture for Rome control of a radicalized and all but runaway church.)[101] By the early 1970s, that shift had progressed to the point where 78 percent of all priests in Chile identified themselves as on the left politically. By then, in Chile—as in virtually all of Latin America—the ends for the church were a given, only the means were debated. On one side, the "clerical radicals," on the other the "radical pastors," all working to further the same "revolutionary" goals.[102] The leftward

---

* I have put "capitalist" in quotation marks because there was very little "capitalist" about the economy of Chile in 1970; the state already occupied most of the commanding heights, and the private sector was still in transition out of feudalism.

move has today the potential for producing a deep and serious schism in the church.

As the historian Gonzalo Vial Correa notes, "the Chilean Catholic church has actively and constantly intervened in Chilean politics." As early as 1901, José María Caro Rodríguez, a theology professor who would later become the number one ranking figure in the church in Chile, warned the faithful that to vote for one of the two candidates for president that year would be to commit a sin.[103]

In 1925, formal church-state separation was imposed by President Arturo Alessandri on a reluctant Vatican and the archbishop Crescente Errázuriz Valdivieso;[104] the "friendly separation" was written into the 1925 constitution, putting an end for the moment to a long series of church-state conflicts. (It should be noted that, unlike the U.S. Constitution, the Chilean constitution of 1925 explicitly subordinated religion to itself and such laws as Congress would enact.)[105]

Neither church nor state long observed the separation.

In the wake of the political upheavals of 1932—including the brief "Socialist Republic" of Marmaduke Grove—the Bishops' Conference in 1933 ordered young Catholics in the National Association of Catholic Employees to join en masse the Conservative party. Many balked, and the Vatican stepped in, with a letter written in 1934 by Cardinal Eugenio Pacelli on the express instructions of the pope (Cardinal Pacelli five years later became Pope Pius XII). The letter instructed the bishops "to distance themselves from the vicissitudes of militant politics . . . and allow the faithful the freedom . . . to form political entities." The letter also urged "activity designed to improve the economic situation of the working class inspired in the principles of Catholic social doctrine."[106] Thus, the Vatican simultaneously directed the bishops to remain aloof from politics, but to become active in economic policy; since the two are inseparable, the contradiction inevitably drove the church even deeper into politics. To complete the contradiction, the faithful were henceforth free to support the party of their choice, which meant the bishops no longer had the authority to point the "correct" political path as, for example, for achieving those improvements in the economic situation of the working class. It did not, however, inhibit the bishops from doing precisely that.

Until the 1940s, the Roman Catholic church in Chile was closely tied to the Conservative party because the party defended traditional church prerogatives against encroaching secularism on such controversial matters as marriage, burials, and education. Taking a cue from the Vatican's lead of the year before, a group of dissident Conservative youth leaders bolted in 1935 to form a new party, the Falange National party. Among them were men who later dominated the Christian Democratic party: Eduardo Frei, Radomiro Tomic, Bernardo Leighton, Manuel Garretón, and Ignacio Palma. Inspired by the ideas of the French Catholic philosopher Jacques Maritain, these men argued for a "communitarian third position" between capitalism and communism, based (at first) on fealty to church social doctrine. Their refusal in 1938 to support Gustavo Ross, the official candidate backed by the Conservative party, was regarded as an important factor in Ross's razor-thin loss to the Popular Front coalition including Radicals, Socialists, and Communists and headed by Pedro Aguirre Cerda.

Interestingly, from his tiny northern outpost of La Serena, then Bishop Caro fired off a telegram of congratulations to Aguirre before his victory had been made official by the Congress. Despite the new emphasis on social reform he brought to the church's agenda—part of the same strategy of winning converts among the alienated working classes which prompted his telegram to the radical Pedro Aguirre— Chile's first cardinal drew the line at accepting communism in theory. In 1947, Caro publicly rebuked the Falange for defying his authority in three ways: refusing to acknowledge that the Catholic church was completely opposed to communism; favoring diplomatic relations with the Soviet Union; opposing the Spanish ruler Francisco Franco.[107] (Frei, the leader of the party which in 1957 became the Christian Democrats, responded the following year by declaring: "There is something worse than communism; anticommunism.")

By the time it shed its Falange skin and emerged as the Christian Democrat party, the PDC had also shed one of its basic premises: that of a frankly religion-based ("confessional") party. Instead, it created an intellectual cotton candy that was vaguely Christian, aggressively "humanistic," and decidedly secular. Ironically, much of the new ideology flowed from a Jesuit institute called the Belarmino Center, established in the late 1950s and headed by a Belgian priest named Roger Vekemans.

> When I asked people in Chile a standard question, "Who runs this place?" I heard some standard answers—Frei, copper, Congress, women, the United States, "a gang of do-gooders," the fire department, and "the people." Then came one unexpected, "The University of Louvain."
>
> John Gunther, writing after an extended visit to Chile in 1965[108]

Gunther went on to explain that the response was a reflection of "the wide local prestige" of Father Roger Vekemans, educated at Louvain.

Gunther went to some length to argue that Vekemans—who had gone to Chile ten years before—was not the *eminence grise* behind the Frei government, then added: "... but his influence is pervasive on the highest level. Time and again we heard ideas formulated by him repeated by others, even if they did not fully appreciate where the ideas had come from." Gunther described this "tall, lean, craggy man with the pale spellbinding eyes" as "a most remarkable man, one of the most exciting I met in South America. He has drive, logic and determination."

Gunther did not so state, but Vekemans also was a man with a very strong and very leftist social agenda. That agenda found expression in the pages of *Mensaje*, the bridge linking the religious "progressivism" spawned by Belarmino with the political messianism of the Christian Democrats. Even Frei's electoral slogan—"revolution in freedom"—was believed to have come from Belarmino, as did much of the conceptual framework for his "noncapitalist path to development."

In a December 1962 special issue entitled "Revolution in Latin America," *Mensaje* openly embraced the Christian Democrats' "third position." An editorial written by the Jesuit Hernán Larraín Acuña described revolution as a movement "in progress," and called for a zero-based overhaul of society: uprooting as rapidly and as profoundly as possible the political, economic, and social structures then in place. "Nobody can know exactly where a revolution ends," the editorial said, "but life is a risk and Christianity is not a religion of bland security but rather of generous frenzy. . . . only through unity with Christ can we 'Christianize' the revolution in progress. . . ." The editorial added that "the revolution is reform. But not this or that reform, but integral and radical reform. [What is needed is] unbreakable resolve to break radically with the existing order, of finishing with the past, and taking off from zero, construct a totally new order." Those words, it should be noted, were written at a time when Chile was the toast of the world's cognoscenti as one of the two most advanced and stable democracies in the Southern Hemisphere.[109]

That same year, Chile's Catholic bishops issued two pastoral letters echoing many of the same themes, but with one important difference. Christians, one pastoral said, have an obligation to support institutional changes, such as authentic agrarian reform, tax, administrative and business reforms. The exception, which for only a short time would distinguish the church from its chosen political handmaiden, the Christian Democrats,[110] was the flat statement: communism is "diametrically opposed to Christianity." The pastoral described it as a "system which offers no remedy for the ills that we must erradicate. . . . Communism has never won out through reason, or the value of its doctrine, but always as a result of the feebleness of states and [political] parties which call themselves democratic, and has risen to power only to become the implacable foe of all who do not think alike, including those who made its ascension possible. From the triumph of communism in Chile, the church and all of its children can expect only persecution, tears and blood."

That message of anticommunism (as noted) helped defeat in 1964 the Marxist candidate Salvador Allende and elect the Christian Democrat Eduardo Frei. But Frei and his Christian Democrats had personally rejected anticommunism; and so too had the man who, for the next two crucial decades, would serve as the primate of the church in Chile: Raúl Silva Henríquez.

In May of 1961, Cardinal Silva Henríquez, one year in his post, said in an interview with the Santiago newspaper La Nación: "It is stupid to reject everything Communist just because it is Communist. They have done positive things in that most delicate of all areas, public morality." It was the first known case of a Catholic prelate in Latin America imputing legitimacy to the Communists, a position at odds not only with that of the Vatican, but also (to that point) with his own fellow bishops in Chile. That same year, he issued a nine-thousand-word pastoral letter which Gunther (among others) noted as reflecting the reformist or "revolutionary" wing of South American Catholicism. Read to every congregation in Chile and given a 200,000-copy printing, it called for land reform, punishment for tax evaders, the "curbing of the big monopolies," and a vastly expanded program of education. He criticized "those wealthy Chileans who deposited their money abroad while millions were in misery at home . . . One-tenth of the Chilean population receives almost half of the national income. This bad distribution of Chile's riches is paid for in malnutrition for the people. . . . Social injustice and poverty foster communism. . . ." To underscore his own social commitment, the cardinal donated fifty thousand acres of church-owned farmland to tenants, later adding thirteen thousand more, and was photographed at the plow. While emphasizing social doctrine, he also warned against "excessive veneration" of and "sentimental devotion" to the Virgin Mary. It was part and parcel of the religious Left's mocking of "popular religiosity." (Ironically, years later, the church would clash with the junta when the authorities banned the newly popular annual pilgrimages to the country's leading shrine.)[111]

The Catholic church in Chile has traditionally looked to the outside world for support, both financial and human. The human support included many radicalized priests from France, Belgium, Holland, Spain, and even the United States. Money traditionally had come from Europe. During the Frei years, as the church moved ever leftward, money poured in from the United States, a reflection of the diffuse euphoria in Washington for the "progressive" government in power in Santiago. Some of the U.S. money was illegal. Edward M. Korry, who served as U.S. ambassador to Chile from mid-1967 to late 1971, told the story:

> Question: Who committed those "tens of millions?"
> Answer: The Kennedy White House, to defeat Salvador Allende in the 1964 election, and to elect Eduardo Frei and the Christian Democrats. That is one thing. The second thing is that millions and millions were given to Jesuit-led organizations in Chile by the Kennedys and the Johnson administration in response to appeals for monies from the American taxpayer—quote—"to oppose laicism, Protestantism and Communism." Both these actions are violations of U.S. laws.[112]

The Belarmino Center, busy churning out ideas for the revolution "already in progress" to root out free enterprise and traditional values in Chile, was, presumably, one such beneficiary of those illegal millions from the American taxpayer. Belarmino's ideas, as indicated, found expression in the publication *Mensaje*; they would scarcely have found favor among American taxpayers. In issue #147 of *Mensaje*, 1966, for example, the Jesuit Father Hubert Daubechies wrote of the "sad and noble end" of the Colombian priest Camilo Torres, killed while a member of a marauding Communist guerrilla force in that country. To Father Daubechies, Father Torres "sincerely loved his people and gave himself fully to their redemption. A life given to a great cause, such as that of Camilo Torres, radiates a singular magnetism." (Shortly before he was killed in an ambush, Father Torres had written: "As a Colombian, as a sociologist, as a Christian, as a priest, I am a revolutionary. I consider that the Communist party has genuinely revolutionary elements, and thus ... I cannot be anti-Communist ... because, although many of them may not know it, many of them are true Christians. The Communists should be well aware that I will not join their party ... However, I am ready to fight with them for common aims; against the oligarchy and the domination of the United States, to seize power for the people. ... The Revolution can be peaceful if the minorities do not offer violent resistance. ... Revolution is not only allowed to Christians but is obligatory for those who see in it the only effective and large-scale way of carrying out works of love for everybody.")[113]

Another Jesuit, Gonzalo Arroyo, wrote (in issue #167), that the "guerrilla hope for Latin America culminated in 1967" with the death of the Argentine-Cuban guerrilla Ernesto (Che) Guevara.

"Until now," wrote yet another priest, "social structures have been based on faith. That must change, and man must use his reason."

In 1964, *Mensaje* came out in favor of progestogen contraceptive pills as being no more than a substitute for "the natural dynamism of nature"—that, in a country that already had the highest abortion figures in South America, and, moreover, at a time when the Vatican was cranking up a major campaign against the Pill.[114]

It would be impossible to disentangle the influence of outside events from the internal forces at work in transforming the church in Chile into a bastion of radical social thought. What is beyond dispute is the role played by the revolutionary papacies of John XXIII (1958–1963) and Pope Paul VI, during his fifteen-year reign (1963–1978). Of crucial significance was the Second Vatican Council (1962–1965), which battered down virtually all the barriers marking the boundaries of authority, religious rites, and even the outlook of the ancient church, and encouraged a new wave of reform. Twenty years later, the Vatican was fighting a losing battle to contain the wild whirlwind sown at that council.

These were echoes of the "progressive" thinking shaking the church in Europe, ideas that questioned the very permanence and solvency of traditional church teaching. And they were the precursors of what, beginning at Medellín, Colombia, in 1968, would come to be known as "Liberation Theology."

The old church in Chile was dying. Control was passing to a new generation of bishops, elevated to their posts in the sixties, appointed by the reformist popes, "their thought formed in the times of progressive and transforming optimism." Abetted and encouraged by the reformist doctrine emanating from the Vatican II Council, the Chilean church changed even more rapidly and radically than did others. As two authors sympathetic to the radicalization of the church wrote, Vatican II "left its mark on the church [in Chile] for decades. . . . Under the direction [*impulso*] of Pope Paul VI, the hierarchy made their modern advances which squared accounts with the old Christianity." More than half of the five thousand nuns in Chile left their church schools and other agencies to work in the slums and rural settlements during that period. Between 1960 and 1971—while the population of the country grew from 7.3 million to 8.8 million—the number of priests in the country stagnated: 2,528 in 1960, approximately 2,600 in 1971. Bishops purported to approve of the radical changes; ordinary priests, nuns, and lay workers far more so. Ordinary Catholics seemed less enthusiastic: those calling themselves Catholics dropped from a high of 86.6 percent of the population in 1970 to either 60.1 percent in 1979 or 74.4 percent in 1986 (depending on which poll you believed). In the same period, those identifying themselves as "Protestants" increased from 5.5 percent to 12.2 percent. Growth among Protestant religions was strongest among Fundamentalist groups—generally supportive of the junta.[115]

In 1968, nine priests, three nuns, and two hundred lay persons seized the Metropolitan Cathedral in Santiago, protesting the church's prohibition of the Pill, and the decision of Pope Paul VI to attend the Eucharistic Congress in Colombia that year (because in Colombia, "a capitalist system exists, which converts the Pope into an accomplice of the exploitation of the people"). They protested also the building of a new and grander Shrine to the Virgin of Carmen at Maipú, a stand with strong antimilitary undertones. The Liberators, José de San Martín and Bernardo O'Higgins, had declared the Virgin Patroness of the Army, and following the decisive battle of independence at Maipu, April 5, 1818, had ordered a shrine built there. The protesters objected to a new shrine replacing the modest original one.

For twenty-four hours, the invaders sang protest songs and celebrated a mass, having first adorned the cathedral's altar with images of the guerrilla-priest Camilo Torres and of Che Guevara. Clotario Blest, speaking for the protesters, said: "We are hand-in-hand with our Marxist brothers, on the barricades of the people against capitalism, following the example of Camilo Torres. We are members of the Young Church. We revere Che Guevara. We admire him." Cardinal Silva, responding to public outrage, first threatened to excommunicate the rebels, but said later: "I went to see the priests involved, I was with them, and we had a very open dialogue, and I have sensed the goodness in them. I believe that it is very positive that there be these tensions." Monsignor Ismael Errázuriz, auxiliary bishop of Santiago, later echoed those sentiments when he said, "we believe in dialogue and practical action with the Marxists, not at the academic level but in action, with the people."[116]

A few Catholics fought back, through the pages of their publication, *Fiducia*, later through an organization they founded called The Chilean Society for the Defense of Tradition, Family and Property. They argued that the Frei government's "reforms" ran counter to church doctrine because of their socialist and confiscatory character. Only one (among thirty) of the bishops supported them.[117]

In September of 1969, the Young Church organized a mass at the University of Chile's Pedagogic Institute "to pray for the victims of persecution and repression, in particular for comrade Jorge Silva Luvecce." Silva Luvecce, a member of the very violent Movement of the Revolutionary Left, was then in jail for robbing banks. The mass was celebrated by the Argentine priest José Ruiz Guinazu. In his sermon, Father Ruiz said, "the worst charge they have against Jorge Silva is his having chosen the path of violence, but violence has other authors who have not appeared in this process, and who, to the contrary, are today his judges: the most illustrious and solemn justices of the Supreme Court. . . ." It was the beginning of a continuing involvement of many other priests and nuns with the MIR, particularly following the fall of Allende.[118]

Two other events late in 1969 bear brief mention.

The year was ending, political fever rising in anticipation of the following year's presidential elections, when Cardinal Silva said: "If a Christian votes in conscience for a Marxist, I understand it." Later, Father Hernán Larraín, editor of *Mensaje,* said on television: "I see no reason that would prevent a Christian from voting for a Marxist. Marxists and we Christians can reach agreement." (Father Larraín, and another Jesuit who was a leading contributor to *Mensaje,* Father Gonzalo Arroyo, traded in their pens for activism, abandoning the Jesuit center in Santiago to work in the politically charged atmosphere of the shantytowns springing up around the capital.)

On December 12, 1969—reacting to the abortive military uprising led by General Viaux—the Bishops' Permanent Conference issued a pastoral letter on the role of the armed forces in a democracy. It was signed by all five Chilean archbishops, as well as by the presidents and executive secretaries of the Permanent Conference. The bishops said they were speaking out so as not to be criticized later for silence in the face of threats to the dignity of man and his liberty. It was, in other words, a warning to the military to keep hands off should the Marxist Salvador Allende win the forthcoming elections. "Political authority proceeds from the people who elect their representatives. It would be inadmissible that a group within our armed forces would try to divert them from their true mission. . . . When the dynamic of force is unleashed, no one can guarantee its final control. The imposition of a policy by terror, by dictatorship, or by force of arms, brings with it brutal repression of those who oppose it and the suppression of all freedoms considered dangerous for those who hold power. The country would find itself on the path of political trials, forced exiles, flagrant injustices, suppression of a free press, of the impossibility of defending oneself from suspicions and lies, and, in the end, of the firing squad [*paredón*]."[119]

There were those who found prescience in that message. There were also those who found augury in the failure of the bishops to warn against the coming to power in Chile of a Marxist-Leninist government, as they had in the past, including the previous presidential election of 1964. "It is not an easy task to know to what point the church's silence was due to such apprehensions [as being linked to a "campaign of terror" waged by anti-Communists], or to what point by a desire to avoid favoring [the rightist] Alessandri . . . The only sure thing is that the church kept silence."[120]

It kept no such silence when Allende did bring Marxism-Leninism to power. Allende had not as yet been confirmed by Congress when the bishops made plain their implicit support for him: "We have cooperated, and we want to continue cooperating in bringing about changes, especially those which favor the poor," they said in a September 24, 1970, statement. "We understand that change is difficult and brings with it great risks for all. We understand that it is difficult to give up some privileges. . . . The Chilean people want to continue with the regime and style of liberty for which they have been fighting for the past 160 years. . . ." Cardinal Silva was not far behind: even before the inauguration, he told Allende, "Mr. President, count on me." Allende was barely in office when, at a reception at the Soviet Embassy, Cardinal Silva told newsmen: "The basic reforms contained in the program of the Popular Unity are supported by the Chilean church; we look upon this with immense sympathy." He made his reasons evident in another statement: "There is more of the gospel's values in socialism than in capitalism."[121]

Unsurprisingly, Sen. Volodia Teitelboim, principal ideologue of the Communist party, told newsmen later of talks between his organization and church authorities, singling out for special praise Jesuit priests and the Young Church for their attitude toward communism.

Times had changed, principles as well. Completely. In 1958, on the eve of the presidential election that year, a Jesuit of an earlier generation—Father José Aldunate, then editor of *Mensaje*—wrote: "Communism as a doctrine and as a movement is an evil in society. The moral problem of cooperation with communism is nothing but a particular case from the more general case of cooperation with evil."[122]

In April of 1971, the bishops repaired to the rustic southern city of Temuco to draft a formal position paper on the new regime. While they were meeting, eighty priests gathered in Santiago under the direction of the prolific Jesuit writer Gonzalo Arroyo for a symposium entitled, "The Collaboration of Christians in the Construction of Socialism." Economic and social backwardness, they proclaimed, "has a clear and precise cause: the capitalist system, product of foreign imperialism maintained by the dominant classes of the country. . . . We confirm the hopes," the priests continued, "which the coming to power of the Popular Government, with its resolute action in favor of the construction of socialism, signifies for the working masses. The intuition of the people is not mistaken. Socialism . . . opens the way to a new economy which makes possible an autonomous and accelerated development and the termination of the division of society into antagonistic classes. . . ." Twelve members of the Theology Department of the Catholic University supported the statement; one who dissented agreed that "the capitalist system is inhuman and execrable," but accused the eighty priests of confusing "socialism and Marxism, social ownership of the means of production with state ownership, and cooperation with Marxists in specific projects with collaboration with them in building a Marxist state."[123]

The bishops, in their pastoral (*Gospel, Politics and Socialisms*), made plain, beginning with the deliberate use of the plural, that they had no quarrel with socialism, while making explicit their quarrel with capitalism. But it also attempted to blunt the stampede of "The 80" and other priests toward *the* socialism of Salvador Allende, arguing that there were many forms of achieving the aims of socialism. They also warned that "a Christian who desires to keep his faith may not—in his enthusiasm for political collaboration—adhere to the Marxist picture of the universe and man or, as Pope Paul VI says, 'to its atheistic materialism, to its dialectics of violence, and to the manner in which it interprets individual liberty within the community, while at the same time denying all transcendence to man and his personal and collective history.' " Cardinal Silva attempted to make a similar distinction, in a letter to the executive secretary of The 80: "There can be many points of contact with Marxists," he wrote, "but I believe it is indispensable that Christians not renounce their Christianity, and [instead] bring the spiritual values that it has to the fight for liberation. . . . For the drafters of the report, there is no other formula of liberation but 'revolution,' and 'the revolution,' according to them, is but one: 'The one now underway in many countries of Latin America, with the coming to power of the proletariat. . . .' " On April 26, 1972, he wrote twelve priests and seminarians just back from Cuba: "We ask priests and aspirants to the priesthood, Chileans and foreigners, to limit themselves to their strictly ministerial functions; should anyone believe that his vocation is political, we ask that he reconsider his priestly vocation." He also wrote 150 "progressive" Latin American priests, and the bishop of Cuernavaca, Mexico, Sergio Méndez, officially distancing the Chilean church from a revolutionary church gathering in Mexico.[124]

It was too little, too late. And besides, the prelate's words did not square with his deeds. He explained the murder of Army Commander-in-Chief Gen. René Schneider by telling Allende: "Schneider died so that you could happily occupy your position." On May Day 1971, he did what no other Catholic bishop had ever done before; he attended the rally organized by the Communist-controlled Central Workers' Federation, and the following December attended the federation's annual congress. This, of course, gave the impression of a church imprimatur for Communist domination of the labor movement. In November 1971, he granted a lengthy interview to visiting Prime Minister Fidel Castro of

Cuba—a despot who had brutally persecuted the church in his own country. Defending his action, the cardinal said the interview had been requested by Castro, and that "the church reaffirms its willingness to participate in any sincere and respectful discussion; and its readiness to consider any suggestion or project aimed at promoting a more just coexistence and fraternal peace. . . ."[125]

Thus it was that, from the early sixties onward, the church in Chile marched ever more to the beat of a socialist drummer, embracing Allende and his objectives, if not his Marxism itself. To the very end— the cardinal's desperate attempt in July of 1973 to bring the Christian Democrats and Allende together—the church's ranking prince in Chile fought to preserve the socialist experiment (and/or, in Pinochet's view, the Christian Democrats from the coming cataclysm).[126] The bishops, in 1969, had already made plain their rejection of military intervention. The most visible and vocal priests had already made plain their overwhelming embrace of the ideas of "the radical church."

A year after Allende fell, the church, for the first time, condemned what he stood for: not a "Chilean path to socialism," but a variation on a familiar Marxist theme, the pursuit of total power through manipulation of democratic means. The following year, the bishops issued an even stronger statement, *Evangelio y Paz:* "We recognize the service performed for the country by the armed forces in liberating it from a Marxist dictatorship which seemed inevitable, and that would have been irreversible, a dictatorship which would have been imposed against the majority in the country and which afterward would have crushed that majority. . . . In that sense, we believe it just to recognize that the armed forces interpreted, on September 11, 1973, the majority yearning, and in doing so, rid the country of an immense obstacle."[127]

These were, however, small parentheses in a larger and persistent pattern of church-state clashes. Once again, external forces played a role. Pope Paul VI issued his first statement on Chile September 16, 1973, asking "will be possible to prevent civil war and restore concord among the citizens?" A few days later, on October 7, the pope spoke of "violent repression. . . . with each passing day, the irrational and inhuman resort to murderous arms to establish order becomes more evident or, more precisely, the repressive domination of some men over others." The following April, as the bishops were hammering out their first pastoral on the new regime, the pope sent a cable urging them to provide "aid to the needy, especially among the poor." The Vatican demonstrated its tilt later when accrediting Chile's new ambassador—compelling him to tone down his ceremonial remarks—and even more pointedly later when Pope Paul VI granted a private audience to the widow of Chile's Marxist-Leninist president. Correa and Viera-Gallo note also that Cardinal Silva Henríquez had a number of audiences with the pope in those early months, and that the cardinal's remarks became progressively "clearer and more critical" following them.[128]

The document the bishops produced on April 24, 1974, marked a decisive break with the new regime—although it was not nearly so inflammatory as was the reporting of it abroad. In it, *La Reconciliación en Chile,* the bishops said there was rule of law in Chile, the right to dissent existed, and that they did not doubt "the righteous intention nor the good will of our governors." But they also referred to "obstacles to reconciliation," including: "the climate of insecurity and of fear . . . the increase in joblessness and of arbitrary dismissals for ideological reasons. . . . we are concerned, in some cases, about the lack of effective juridical safeguards for personal security which translates as arbitrary and excessively prolonged detentions in which neither those affected nor their family know the concrete charges behind their arrest; questioning with physical or moral pressure. . . ." The bishops also expressed reservations about the pace and direction of the new government's frankly free-market economy, judging that it would "place an excessive burden of sacrifice on salaried persons. . . ."[129]

By the first anniversary of the revolution, the church was in open opposition. By 1975, coinciding with increasing antijunta activity among Christian Democrats, the church was in open confrontation. News stories published abroad took note of the developing conflict; the political character of the church itself was not part of the reportage. The major collision occurred in 1980, when the bishops condemned the plebiscite which approved Chile's new constitution. In 1980, five bishops announced that anyone practicing torture in their dioceses, or who ordered it, or who failed to prevent it when it was in their power to do so, would be automatically excommunicated. In 1981, Cardinal Silva described the government as "totalitarian." Despite such public broadsides, which continued the intensifying barrage begun within months of the revolution, the bishops said in a 1982 pastoral, *Renacer de Chile,* that they had "exhausted the way of private negotiations." In that document, they made plain their support for "a political alternative" to the present government. By the following year, public demonstrations and violence were rife in the land—although the economic crisis was a greater causative factor than the encouragement of the church to political agitation.

In *Renacer* and their subsequent manifestoes, the church leaders developed a fourteen-point scenario for Chile's political future: (1) There is a grave national crisis; (2) It demands a political solution; (3) Democracy is that solution; (4) Democracy is integral to Chile's past and future; (5) The church is committed to the democratization of the country; (6) The distinction between church and state spheres must be maintained, although the church cannot limit itself to a mere "tolerance" of the state, but must stand in judgment of it; (7) The church favors mass mobilization, the defense of human rights, and efforts to persuade the rulers of the necessity for democratization; (8) Violence is to be rejected as a solution; (9) The Bishops Conference rejects the form in which the 1980 plebiscite was carried out, and the text of the constitution approved by it (while ducking the thorny question of whether it also rejected the legitimacy of that document; the church would insist, however, that on the return to civilian rule, the constitution ought to be removed should the people wish it); (10) The episcopacy promotes national unity and reconciliation; (11) But alongside that, the bishops recognize the right to dissent and peaceful protest; (12) The church favors a minimum social and political consensus on ground rules for a return to normalcy; (13) The church demands that the government establish a timetable for a return to democracy (the government had, but it was unacceptable to the churchmen); (14) The church stands with its people in their journey back to democracy.[130]

Two events—one external, one internal—played crucial roles in the policies and practices of the church.

The internal one was the retirement, in 1983, of Cardinal Silva Henríquez, and his replacement by Juan Francisco Fresno. Although his public behavior was not markedly different from that of his predecessor, he did not bring the baggage of long and close association with the leadership of the Christian Democratic party, nor of a prominent figure in church relations with Allende. Nor had he been in the forefront of the attacks on the Pinochet government. For all of those reasons, he was clearly more responsive to the winds blowing from far beyond the country's borders.

Those winds came from the Vatican, and were the critical external factor. On August 6, 1978, liberal Pope Paul VI died, followed by the sudden death on September 28 of his successor, John Paul I. The new pontiff, Karol Cardinal Wojtyla—John Paul II—was the first non-Italian pope in 455 years. Forged in the fires of World War II and the subjugation of his native Poland by the Soviet Union, John Paul II was cut from a more conservative cloth. Within a year, he had censured Hans Küng, perhaps the most widely known among liberal theologians, prohibiting him from teaching. Similar actions were taken against Jacques Pohier, a French Dominican, and Edward Schillebeeckx of the Catholic University of Nijmegan was "closely questioned." By 1985, Joseph Cardinal Ratzinger—head of the pivotal Sacred Congregation for the Doctrine of the Faith—was saying in a series of interviews, that Vatican II, in effect, needed to be rolled back. He spoke of the need for a "restoration of preconciliar values."[131]

But Pope John Paul II had another stake in Chile, from the earliest days of his papacy: mediating the explosive Beagle Channel dispute between Argentina and Chile. The Vatican hoped that this peace-making role, the first one undertaken by Rome in many years, would give it heightened authority to attempt similar endeavors in other conflicts, such as in the Middle East and Central America. There emerged a "triangular relationship": the still-belligerent Chilean church, the Chilean government, Rome. Rome occasionally prevailed, and certainly managed to exercise a restraining influence on the Chilean church; despite its ideological divergences, the Chilean church—at least at the top—was still inclined to submit to the authority of Rome.[132]

Perhaps nothing would demonstrate that more than the pope's six-day visit to Chile in April of 1987. There is no clear evidence that the Chilean church flatly *opposed* it, and if it had, it no doubt would not have taken place. But there are abundant signs that many of the bishops would have preferred that it not happen, in the measure that it could be interpreted, as it was, by many, as legitimizing the government which they had so long opposed. For the pope, the Chilean visit—his thirty-third foreign trip—was undoubtedly simply another phase of the peripatetic mission he had set for himself early in his papacy, and which had seen him throw himself again and again into the jaws of controversy, in his native Poland, in Haiti, in Nicaragua, in the Phillipines, in Holland. The ultimate impact on the present and future of Chile may never be known.[133]

What was beyond dispute was the sense of his messages, then, and in an anniversary message a year later: eschew violence, work patiently within the system. Whether influenced by the pope or the rapidly evolving situation in Chile—economic progress which could no longer be ignored, political freedom expressed ever more boisterously—the fact is that Cardinal Fresno's messages were less combative, as well. Indeed, by 1988, he worried aloud less about attaining freedom than whether his fellow Chileans could accommodate peacefully to it.[134]

The cardinal's concerns may well have begun in his own backyard, the Catholic church in Chile. By 1988, both Left and Right agreed: the church in Chile, in 1988, was torn as never before. From without, the urging of the Vatican to minister first and foremost to souls. From within a long-radicalized church, the demand that the church must occupy the ramparts of revolution. One observer has predicted that, following the 1988 presidential plebiscite, there is a strong probability that at least five bishops could break away from the established church—a phenomenon not dissimilar to the emergence of the so-called "Popular Church" in Nicaragua by churchmen/Sandinistas unwilling to submit their zeal for the "gospel" of Marxist-Leninist revolution to the discipline of Christ's Vicar on earth. The fact that "progressives" had won control of the Bishops Conference at the end of 1987 heightened that possibility.[135]

From the beginning, voices have been raised in the church against the leftward march, against the implacable attack on the attempt to build a new Chile. Among them: Bishop Augusto Salinas Fuenzalida, who on its third anniversary called the revolution "an historic event, whose transcendental importance needs to be measured in all of its grandeur. Our country had been invaded by ideological forces alien to its historic characteristics and its Christian faith was already at the edge of being enslaved." And, on December 1985, Bishop José Joaquín Matte (vicar general of the army), who said: "Twelve years ago, the rosary was recited without rest and Mary performed the miracle: the second independence of Chile." Even in that April 1974 statement of the bishops, so widely portrayed beyond Chile as a declaration of war against the junta, there were lines not reported: "We wish to emphasize to anyone abroad who reads this declaration that it reflects a situation that concerns only the people of Chile who, we are certain, in spite of our differences, will know how to resolve our own problems . . . the governmental authorities, informed of the contents of this declaration, have assumed the noble attitude of respect for our liberty which constitutes the best proof of the right to dissent that exists in Chile and of the maintenance of the rule of law in our fatherland. . . . we feel it is most important that the outside world know that the Chilean situation is incomprehensible if one fails to take into account the chaotic state and the enormous and passionate exacerbations that existed under the previous government." In July of 1985, theologians from nine countries—including the former president of the Latin American Bishops' Conference, Cardinal Alfonso López Trujillo of Medellín, the city which had given its name to the birth of Liberation Theology—gathered in a tiny Chilean town and produced a stunning rebuttal of that dogma.[136] But, as one of the most conspicuous leaders of the Left in the church hierarchy, Bishop Carlos Camus, pointed out: "no one should deceive themselves as to the majority and official position of the Catholic church. . . ."[137]

In such an intellectual climate of revolutionary ardor, it was, of course, inevitable that many churchmen would cast their lot with men and women who fought with guns and bombs for the "gospel of revolution." Foreigners, including a number of Americans, were conspicuous among them. At the beginning, the authorities were circumspect, as when they expelled the Rev. Robert Plasker in September of 1974. Father Plasker, a member of the Congregation of the Holy Cross, was an instructor at the exclusive St. George's School in Santiago. In ordering him out, the government simply said it was because of his "antigovernment" activities. Later, the charges became more specific. The government also acted against the American-born priest Gerard Whelan, ex-rector of St. George's. Authorities said he had hidden in his house the number three leader of the MIR: fugitive Martín Humberto Hernández Vásquez, a member of the MIR Policy Commission, later burying Hernández' AKA rifle, two grenades, and an automatic pistol in a vacant lot. Father Whelan, who had renounced his American citizenship in 1972, was one of several clergymen and nuns caught up in that dragnet. Four Americans—Father John Devlin, a Holy Cross priest, and three nuns, Sisters Paula Armstrong and Barbara Nelson of the Notre Dame order, and Peggy Lepsio of the Maryknoll Order—were also implicated. (There were reports that Father Devlin had helped Andrés Pascal Allende, the top MIR leader, to make his getaway from Chile.) Another American priest, Father Daniel Panchot, also a member of the Holy Cross Order, was arrested subsequently. The Americans were all deported, but only after the government accused the U.S. Embassy of helping the nuns to hide while negotiations were underway for their safe conduct out of Chile. It was that investigation which also led to the arrest of the British Dr. Sheila Cassidy, center of a subsequent furor and cause for reprisals by the Labour Government in London against Chile. Father Whelan and three Chilean Jesuit priests—including Father Fernando Salas, first director of the Committee for Peace—were held for trial. In the wake of this round-up, the regime pressured the church to disband the committee, then released the four priests (and 160 political prisoners) in a conciliatory gesture.[138]

Outside of Chile, church groups were in the vanguard of the fight against the military regime. Isolated examples: On May 16 and May 17, 1976, the National Coordinating Center in Solidarity with Chile—a self-avowed Communist-front organization—organized a "National Legislative Conference on Chile" at the Jesuit Gonzaga High School in Washington. The principal speaker was the recently released Orlando Letelier, Allende's last defense minister, who told the gathering that "resistance in Chile is alive." The Religious Sisters of Mercy, Province of Chicago, presented a resolution at the April 1977 meeting of the Bank of America, demanding that the bank cease loans to Chile. In October 1975, representatives of thirty-five Roman Catholic and Protestant church groups importuned General Motors—then considering resuming operations in Chile—to ensure that its workers have the right to choose a union, and to seek the release of then jailed union leaders.[139]

With the economy still wobbly in the aftermath of the 1982 collapse, a new wave of violence and political agitation, and the failure of previous attempts at achieving political dialogue, Cardinal Fresno began in 1983 to push the country's political leaders to band together in a grand alliance demanding a return to full democracy. In his Easter message that year, the cardinal said: "It would seem in these moments that our national aspirations have managed to unite behind a single name: democracy. That is what all sides want for Chile. What's missing, nevertheless, is a clearer consensus as to what kind of democracy we want to achieve and the changes and timetables to reach it . . . The problem, as I see it, is not in the differences of opinions, but in the attitudes of intransigence with which those attitudes are presented."

He set out to overcome them. It was nearly midnight on August 25, 1985, when two men arrived at the cardinal's palace bearing a document signed by the heads of eleven political parties (of the fifteen engaged in the negotiations). It was the National Accord, spelling out that "minimum consensus": direct election of the president and Congress; reestablishment of full exercise of freedoms, including unrestricted political activity; constitutional reforms, including elimination of a post-1989 role of permanent preeminence for the armed forces. The Communists, after years of urging broad-based alliances to confront the junta, wrote Cardinal Fresno on September 6 declining to participate. (To participate, they would have had to pledge to renounce any behavior designed to undermine the institutions of democracy; they had already, however, committed themselves to the violent conquest of power.) In their letter, the Communists did offer to cooperate in achieving the goals of the accord, and held out the possibility of participating in future negotiations.

Since the document amounted to telling Pinochet that he should abandon the society and institution-building measures he had been embarked upon for a dozen years, he rejected it out of hand. His three junta colleagues expressed varying degrees of support for the accord. Rumblings were heard in the army.

On September 24, 1985, Pinochet agreed to meet with Cardinal Fresno, even though the cardinal declined to celebrate a mass as part of the meeting. The meeting lasted less than twenty minutes. When the cardinal attempted to raise the subject of the accord, the president interrupted him: "Better to turn that page," he said. The accord was dead—buried decisively later under an avalanche of new political jockeying and bickering, a new wave of violence, a resurgent economy. By the time the church would again attempt a mediating role, political parties were operating at full tilt, and the race was already on to the plebiscite.

For the past quarter of a century, Chile's Roman Catholic church leaders have, increasingly, waged war against the evils of the market or "free enterprise" economy—and not just the caricature of it as it then existed in Chile, but on capitalism as a more universal concept. In that, they reflected church doctrine which, in economic matters, became increasingly more critical of capitalism following Pope Leo XI's ground-breaking encyclical, "Rerum Novarum," an 1891 tract which included an attack on the abuses of capitalism. Subsequent papal pronouncements, and particularly Pope Paul VI's "Populorium Progressio" in 1967, expressed lessening resistance to socialism, heightened antagonism to capitalism. In countries such as Chile, where the church had strong links to liberation theology and other radicalizing movements, criticism of capitalism evolved into rejection of it.

Beginning in the first days of the Pinochet revolution, the church was locked in mortal combat on yet another battlefield fraught with ideological and political as well as altruistic implications: human rights.

Dogmatism on economic policy led church leaders, from the first, to reject the new market-based strategies of the government as fashioned to favor the rich, punish still more the poor. In this, the world's media—overwhelmingly committed to the same vision of deliverance from want via "progressive" Marxist formulations—lionized the work of the church, as in this not untypical, entirely tendentious *Washington Post* article: "In response to Pinochet's rule, the church, which until several decades ago was identified largely with the economically-privileged and politically conservative, has intensified ties with the persecuted and impoverished. . . . Going beyond the denunciations issued periodically against government economic and political policies, the church has widened its presence in Chile's urban slums where resistance to Pinochet is strongest. . . . Many wealthy Catholics find the church's new emphases on social awareness and lay initiatives distasteful, out of place or directly threatening. . . ."[140]

Homilies against the market economy continued long past the point when its success could no longer seriously be disputed—including its success in providing *real* (as opposed to rhetorical) protection and opportunities for the poor of Chile. Indeed, as *Forbes* magazine would observe in December 1987, "In many instances the Chilean economic model could be broadened to alleviate human suffering in the impoverished Third World." A World Bank study on poverty in Latin America found: "The Chilean case is particularly interesting because it represents a successful attempt to focus government social spending on the poorest segments of the population. By slashing government spending on upper-income groups and targeting expenditures on the poorest, it has been possible to provide the most urgently needed social services in spite of the grave economic crisis. . . . Chile's performance in targeting social spending is unequaled in the region, and substantial improvements in efficiency have been achieved in the delivery of social services to the poor. . . ."[141] (As we shall see in the following chapter, Chile's performance in creating unprecedented economic opportunities for the population at large have also been unequaled in the region.)

There has, nonetheless, been no visible evidence of church acknowledgment that capitalism is producing the prosperity socialism only promises. Inevitably, the contrast between the messages of the pulpit and the palpable realities of the marketplace has contributed to an erosion in public confidence in the church. Even taking Huneeus' optimistic data bases for religious membership and commitment in modern Chile, we would find the following:

TABLE 37

EVOLUTION OF THE DEGREE OF CITIZEN SUPPORT FOR THE LEADERSHIP/ORIENTATION OF THE CHURCH, 1979–1986 (In %)

QUESTION: Do you agree or disagree with the present leadership (*orientaciones*) provided by the Cardinal and Bishops of the Church?

	1979*	1986
Agree	82.9	73.7
Disagee	10.4	14.1
No opinion	6.7	12.1

Source: Carlos Huneeus, *Los Chilenos y la Política: Cambio y Continuidad en el Autoritarismo* (Santiago: Salesianos, 1987).

* He cites Renato Poblete, etc., *Imagen de la Iglesia de hoy y religiosidad de los chilenos* (Santiago: Centro Belarmino, 1980, Table #83).

Yet another study provided an important insight into the behavior of Chilean Catholics in recent years. Under church law, attendance at Sunday mass *every* week is compulsory. While claiming in this (and many other surveys) that religion occupied a high level of importance in their lives, and a corresponding high level of respect/support for the church's prelates and their positions, when Chileans were asked how they manifested those views in their own and actual behavior, i.e., frequency of attendance at mass, the results indicated otherwise:

TABLE 38

FREQUENCY OF ATTENDANCE AT MASS

FREQUENCY	NUMBER OF RESPONDENTS	PERCENTAGE
Never	184	30.0
Few times a year	241	40.0
2–3 times per month	53	9.0
Every Sunday	87	15.0
More than once per week	34	6.0
TOTALS	599	100.0

Source: Survey performed among six-hundred persons of both sexes and all socioeconomic strata, in Greater Santiago, between November 21 and December 6, 1985, by the Latin American Faculty of Social Sciences (FLACSO, from its Spanish initials), "Encuesta sobre la realidad sociopolítica chilena" (FLACSO: Santiago, 1986), p. 14, cited in "La Cultura Política Chilena Según Las Encuestas de Opinión Pública (1983–1986)," Patricio Chaparro Navarette, ed., *Seminarios* (Santiago: Instituto Chileno de Estudios Humanísticos, 1986), table 40, p. 47. (There was one no-response to this question, one of twenty-eight in the survey.)

There has been a persistent discrepancy between the view of outsiders of the level of concern of Chileans on the other main area of church activity and concern: human rights. Survey after survey showed verbal support for the work of the church in this area. Survey after survey showed a majority of Chileans expressing the view that the church ought to stick to "strictly spiritual" matters.[142] When asked, however, what they thought, not about the one (the church's work in human rights), nor about the other (what the church should be doing), but about what concerned *them* personally, Chileans had a very different view of what matters in their country than have outsiders. Example, the following "unaided" question from a 1987 national Gallup Poll, using a very large sample base:

TABLE 39

PUBLIC PERCEPTION OF NEGATIVE EVENTS, 1987

QUESTION: Chile in common with every country has problems. Which, in your opinion, were the two principal negative events in the country during 1987?

	PERCENTAGE	ESTIMATED POPULATION REPRESENTED
Natural catastrophes	79.8	6,502,583
Terrorism	78.2	6,372,205
Inflation	67.1	5,467,711
Unemployment	58.9	4,799,525
Lack of democracy	21.3	1,735,652
Human Rights violations	15.8	1,287,479

Source: "Encuesta de Gallup-Chile: 'Sí,' 39.4%, y 'No,' 26.6%," *El Mercurio,* January 14, 1988, pp. 1 & C-2. The survey included ten questions and a sample of 8,878 persons of seventeen years or older, representing 8,148,600 citizens (or virtually the entire adult population of the country). "Unaided" means the respondents were not given a list of "events" and asked to choose from them, but simply to say themselves which two they considered the most negative.

Two important asides about this survey: (1) Contrary to usual glib reporting, the greatest level of concern about terrorism was expressed by women (83.4%), persons forty-five-years of age and older (80.6%), and poorer persons (78.8%)—the inhabitants, in other words, of those shantytowns where radical terrorists were encamped and which they used as their bases of operation. Concern about terrorism is rarely mentioned in press reports about Chile; (2) This clarification concerns "natural catastrophes": northern Chile suffered the worst earthquake since 1862, the heavily populated Santiago area the worst flooding of this century, leaving thirty-two dead, 100,000 homeless, and property damage estimated at more than $100 million. These disasters also were little reported outside the country—and there were, of course, no massive relief operations mounted by the U.S., church groups, or others to help stricken Chileans; they helped themselves.

Bread-and-butter and personal safety are, of course, issues uppermost on the minds of people everywhere. It is also true that there had been a dramatic improvement on the civil and human rights fronts in Chile (although in earlier surveys using unaided questions, Chileans also ranked human rights concerns among the lesser of their priorities). But there is yet another factor which may play a role in the attitude of many Chileans: the perception that the church's handling of human rights has had a heavy ideological/political content.

In a press conference on September 30, 1975—a few months before the Committee for Peace was ordered disbanded—Bishop Carlos Camus acknowledged that "there are many officials of the Committee with Marxist ideas, because that is logical." While arguing that its activities were of a "genuinely religious character," political scientist Michael Fleet observed that "the *Comité* became a symbol and rallying point for those wishing to oppose the dictatorship because of their own circumstances or in connection with broader issues. . . ." As noted in the preceding chapter, the committee's first executive director, the Jesuit priest Fernando Salas, was implicated in November of 1975 in efforts to shield the wounded number two leader of the MIR terrorist organization.[143]

No sooner had the committee been dissolved than, in January of 1976, the church announced the formation of a new one, the Vicariate of Solidarity. In the years since, vicariate lawyers have filed more than eight thousand *habeas corpus* writs, and visited more than twenty thousand prisoners. The vicariate said despite their efforts, the courts had honored very few of their *habeas* petitions. (Coincidentally, eight thousand was the number the government had cited years before as the number of judicial orders flouted or ignored by the Allende regime.) In 1978, the United Nations conferred an award upon Cardinal Silva Henríquez and the vicariate for their human rights work. In 1987, the very left-wing Americas Watch described the vicariate as "the flagship of human rights groups in Latin America, the class act."[144]

It would be a grotesquerie to imply that the vicariate's work has been motivated by or limited to a political/ideological agenda—just as it is a grotesquerie to fail to acknowledge that political/ideological considerations do play a role (which most of the press and outside observers routinely do). Though church-state skirmishing continues, the level of conflict has diminished sharply in recent years, and with it, the perception of two forces in a trance of implacable animosity.

During, as well as after the Allende years, the Communist party targeted the Catholic church as a key factor in the Trojan Horse coalition it would build to reach and then monopolize power. In that, it failed. It would not, however, stop trying. On April 24, 1987, in the course of a symposium in Buenos Aires sponsored by the "South American Commission for Regional Peace, Security and Democracy," Communist party leader Luis Guastavino Córdoba proposed the eighty-year-old Cardinal Raúl Silva Henríquez as the right man to head a provisional government in 1989. Others present, including former Allende officials Oscar Garretón and Rolando Calderón, joined in seconding the proposal. The cardinal, also there, was quoted as saying that he would accept the "nomination" "only if it would serve to unite the opposition and lead definitively to democracy." During a visit to New York a month later, the cardinal publicly declined the "nomination"; by then, the country's bishops, in a demonstration of new political caution, were spurning all proposals to thrust themselves into the middle of the political maze. Although other political leaders, mainly of the hard Left, continued to tout the idea, it sputtered out in the political effervescene of 1988.[145]

The caution reflected a growing uneasiness with radicalization on the part of those still precariously in command of church destinies in Chile. The radicalization had found its first institutional expression in 1971 when the church sanctioned the creation of these "distant daughters of the [Second Vatican] Council," Grass Roots Ecclesiastic Communities (CEB, from the Spanish name *Comunidades Eclesiales de Base*). These were the field outposts of the new wave of radical priests, nuns and religious laity, in shantytowns, in peasant settlements and farm collectives. Manned by "Christians for socialism," formerly limited to criticizing a church still doing penance for its ties to fetid capitalism, these would now be church-supported bastions for spreading not merely the gospel, but also the good news of "politics, democracy and social change."[146] The decision to create them, given official sanction by the 1968 Second General Conference of Latin American Bishops in Medellín (the progenitor of officially sanctioned liberation theology), marked formal acknowledgment of "the end of an era," the era of the traditional church. The Rev. Tom Connally, a Columban priest working in one, expressed the revolutionary euphoria of the liberation theology animating the CEBs. He described it as a combination of sociology, economics, political science, philosophy and Christian precepts, using Marxist class analysis as a base for attempting to help the poor. "Nobody gives liberty," he said. "It has to be taken. . . . There are two classes of people, oppressors and the oppressed. People up in the States always have trouble understanding this. It's very simplistic, they say. But poor people never have any problem understanding." Father Connally, and another American priest, Father Mark Mengel, said they and others like them carried out formal religious functions—but it was social work that occupied most of their time.[147] Born of radicalism, these CEBs increasingly challenged the very authority, structure and doctrine of the church itself. But, as less aggressive church ideologues joined newly queasy church elders in questioning the efficacy of mixing Marxism and Christianity, even the CEBs—by 1987 numbering some 1,500 in Greater Santiago alone—were not enough. New and even more radical "grass roots" organizations sprang up beginning in the late 1970s: Popular Christian Communities (CCP, Comunicades Cristianas Populares), taking their cues, in part, from ideas of Fidel Castro and the Nicaraguan revolutionary/priests. When the bishops, bowing to the wishes of the Vatican, began expressing reservations about the rambunctious and rebellious mavericks in their midst, they found themselves rebuked. Asked whether there wasn't a contradiction between these two "forms" of the church, one of the principal spokesmen of liberation theology in Chile, Ronaldo Muñoz, said: "No . . . what there is is a great wound in our church, produced by some sectors of the clergy and the bishops who remain far from our people. . . . Our pain is that the Vatican, for several years now, is listening almost exclusively to that [more moderate] sector of the Latin American hierarchy. . . ."[148]

The battle lines have been drawn.

THE BOMBS THAT WOULD NOT DIE

Chile became too small for him. Contreras connected with intelligence people in Europe, and the first thing you know, he wanted to build his own KGB. I think that's what happened. But he's not bitter now. I think he still has a contract with the CNI, doing things others can't. They're not going to punish him.

Federico Willoughby, spokesman for the junta during the first two years, in a June 16, 1987, interview with the author[149]

"Contreras" is General Manuel Contreras Sepúlveda, the man who created and then directed Chile's National Intelligence Agency (DINA, Dirección de Inteligencia Nacional) during the three years it existed. CNI was its successor agency, the more euphemistically named National Information Center (Central Nacional de Informaciones). (In 1987, it, too, was dissolved, those internal security functions restored to civilian agencies, a key element in the transition back to democracy.) Willoughby was responding to questions about murders, bombings which incinerated hopes as well as lives.

The first of those bombs exploded at 12:40 A.M. on September 30, 1974, on an ominously darkened street of a swank section of Buenos Aires.

The second exploded at 9:35 A.M. on September 21, 1976, in a traffic circle of an equally swank section of Washington, D.C.

In between, on October 6, 1975, there was another bloody episode, this one a "cold-blooded" shooting, in Rome.

Those incidents—and particularly the first two—would very nearly become the gallows of the Pinochet revolution.

In the first, a bomb placed on the underside of the chassis, almost directly below the driver's legs, exploded with such force that the roof of the 1973 Fiat 125 landed on the balcony of an eighth-floor apartment across the street. Sofía Cuthbert de Prats, seated in the front passenger side of the car, died, mutilated. Her husband, Carlos Prats González, fifty-nine, the former commander-in-chief of the Chilean army, who was about to enter the car on the driver's side, died, hemorrhaging internally, externally.

In the second, a bomb similarly placed in a four-door blue Chevrolet Malibu, killed the driver and a front-seat passenger, and slightly injured the passenger's husband, seated in the back seat. The driver was Orlando Letelier del Solar, forty-four; killed with him was Ronni Karpen Moffitt, twenty-five; injured was Michael Moffitt, twenty-four, Ronni's husband of not quite four months.

In the shooting in Rome, Bernardo Leighton Guzmán, sixty-six, suffered gunshot wounds to the head, and his wife, Anita Fresno, wounds which left her temporarily paralyzed from the waist down, when they were ambushed as they returned to their apartment after dining with friends.

The Chilean government steadfastly denied a role in any of these events. The name of one man echoed through all three: Michael Vernon Townley, an American who had lived in Chile since the late 1950s, and was said to have had ties in the sixties to anti-Castro Cuban exiles in Florida, and later, in the early 1970s, in Chile with the anti-Allende Patria y Libertad organization. In 1974, he became an agent of the DINA.

In June of 1976, George W. Landau, then U.S. ambassador in Asunción,

Paraguay, got suspicious about visa applications presented by two individuals bearing official Chilean passports: one Juan Williams Rose and one Alejandro Romeral Jara. He revoked the visas that would have allowed them to travel to the United States, but took the precaution of copying the photos and documents and sending them off to the FBI in Washington. There, someone recognized one of the photos as that of an individual known to have frequented anti-Castro Cuban circles in Miami. A quiet request went to the Chilean police to investigate the real identities of "Rose" and "Romeral Jara." FBI agent Robert Scherrer, who since 1970 from his Buenos Aires base had covered six South American countries, had earlier offered his services to Argentine authorities investigating the Prats murder (they politely spurned the offer). He was now assigned to look quietly into the visa applications. He developed enough to persuade Assistant U.S. Attorney Eugene M. Propper in Washington to request permission of Chilean authorities to interview "Rose" and "Romeral Jara." That was in February 1978.

When, on March 21, a Supreme Court judge in Santiago declared he lacked jurisdiction in the case, it was turned over to a military prosecutor, General Héctor Orozco.

That same day, General Contreras announced that he had asked for early retirement—only seventeen months after attaining flag rank. After a noisy farewell, which included rumblings of severe discontent in military ranks, Contreras dropped briefly from sight (though not only would his name loom ever larger, but he himself would be heard from again and again). On March 30, General Orozco interviewed "Rose"— Michael Vernon Townley. "Romeral Jara"—army Captain Armando Fernández Larios—had already been questioned by a judge. The next day, Propper got to see Townley, who gave him his name, period. One week later, the government decided to expel Townley, and he was off the following day, over the loud protests of the chief justice of Chile's Supreme Court that his expulsion violated the law. Federal agents were awaiting Townley in Miami. A few days later, General Orozco, accompanied by the deputy director of the CNI, flew to the U.S. and obtained permission to meet with Townley, by now being held at the Quantico Marine Barracks, thirty miles south of Washington. A key element of the three-cornered deal (actually signed by Propper's boss, U.S. Attorney Earl J. Silbert, and Enrique Montero, Chile's under-secretary of the interior): Townley would not be accused in the U.S. of any other crime which had taken place anywhere, at any time prior to the Letelier murder. (According to one source, Chile later denied signing any such deal.) Townley now began talking.[150]

But not to the press—at first—so little was known about him. Veteran Latin American specialist Virginia Prewett wrote:

"Townley has talked little to newsmen ... but his Chilean wife,

Mariana Callejas de Townley, has talked a lot. News reports say she, too, was a DINA agent, and 'knew of the DINA order to kill Letelier.'

"She told Santiago journalists that she had earlier been a Socialist. She said Townley was hiding 'from the MIR,' Chile's Socialist terrorists, who would kill him because he knew too much. Then she said that, if in the hands of U.S. authorities, Townley 'would say anything they wanted him to.'

"U.S. papers have reported that Mariana told Chilean journalists she had been a 'Communist, a Socialist, a Zionist, and while residing in the U.S., a supporter of Eugene McCarthy' [the hapless and very liberal Democratic presidential hopeful in 1968]...

"She is described as the stronger character of the two, and it was she who finally persuaded Townley, interviewers say, to tell the story U.S. prosecutors hoped to hear ... There are curious apparent similarities between Townley and Lee Harvey Oswald [the man who murdered President John F. Kennedy]. Behind his drooping walrus moustache, Townley's photographs reveal the same 'loser' look. His background of apparent ambivalence between Leftist and Rightist political extremes is similar to Oswald's ..."[151]

Townley was quoted on November 15, 1978, as saying all three assassinations—the two which succeeded, the one which did not—had been ordered by his DINA boss, General Contreras, and that he, Townley, had played a "starring role" in all three. In court, he was described as a "bald-faced liar," an "animal," "a man who talks about eliminating people as if they were bugs."[152]

From the moment they learned the news of their parents' murder, during the predawn hours of September 30, 1974, the three daughters—Sofía, María Angélica, Cecilia Prats—began a dogged and unrelenting crusade: first to preserve and project the image of the life's work of their parents through publication of their father's memoirs (they succeeded, eleven years later); second, which they waged in Chile, in Argentina, in the United States and Italy, to bring the perpetrator or perpetrators of the murder to justice. Events such as the revelations of Townley galvanized them again and again to action. Again and again, they splattered against indifference, bad luck, international complications, the law itself.

The Letelier trial opened on January 9, 1979, before U.S. District Judge Barrington Parker in Washington. Security in the court room was heavy—there had been at least one death threat—and jury selection took four days, the longest selection process since the Watergate trial in Washington in 1974. The trial was over on February 21, 1979. There were four defendants present, five missing. The four were Townley, and three Cubans (members of the U.S.-based Cuban Nationalist Movement, as intensely anti-Communist as it was anti-Castroite). The missing included two Cubans who managed to escape arrest and three Chileans. Townley, who allegedly recruited the Cubans and provided the plan, as well as planting the radio-operated explosive device itself, had plea-bargained immunity from some charges and reduced sentences for others in return for turning state's evidence against his Cuban accomplices. He was sentenced to forty months to ten years in prison; he served nearly five years of that sentence, a year more than he had been given to understand he would. Two of the three anti-Communist Cubans, Guillermo Novo and Alvin Ross Díaz—charged with actually activating the bomb (Townley was in Miami when it went off)—drew life sentences. The third, Guillermo's brother, Ignacio Novo Sampol, was sentenced to eight years in prison for lying before the grand jury and concealing knowledge of the crime. In sentencing them, Judge Parker said that never before in his ten years on the bench had he seen "as monstrous and cold-blooded" a murder. (On appeal, the convictions of the Cubans were reversed in April 1981 on the grounds that the trial judge had erred in admitting testimony from "government informants" held in the same jail as the Cubans. Tried anew in May of 1981, the two were found innocent on the murder charges, although Guillermo Novo was again convicted of perjury. Townley, following his release from prison in 1983, was allowed to change his name and assume a new identity under the U.S. witness protection program.)[153]

The Leightons, recovered, returned to Chile in May 1978 to the cheers of one thousand supporters awaiting them at Pudahuel Airport. Leighton was, of course, one of the founders of the Christian Democrat party, a top leader of its left wing, and, during his three years in exile in Rome, an outspoken critic of the junta.

Indicted with Townley and the Cubans were three others: General Contreras, his deputy, Colonel Pedro Espinoza Bravo, and Captain Fernández Larios, accused of working with Townley in plotting the Letelier assassination. Once he had Townley in U.S. custody and talking volubly, the U.S. attorney prosecuting the case, Eugene Propper, returned to Santiago (June 1978) and moved for the extradition of Contreras, Espinoza, and Fernández Larios. Never before had the United States asked any country to deliver up to its courts top officials of its secret intelligence agencies. Chile's Supreme Court refused. The three were indicted anyway. The U.S. recalled its ambassador for "consultations," Chile retaliated in kind, and relations between the two countries, already tense, were described as "severely strained." They would remain so, as the extradition fight continued into 1988, with frequent hints that handing over his former intelligence chiefs was the price Pinochet would have to pay for good relations with the United States. As Heraldo Muñoz observes in his authoritative study of Chile's foreign relations in recent years, "the murders of Orlando Letelier and Ronni Moffitt have been, without question, the most critical and delicate development in recent Chilean-American relations." So delicate, in fact, that when a member of President Reagan's Cabinet would say in 1981 that the case was closed, all legal avenues having been exhausted, another government official proclaimed that it was not. It wasn't.[154]

Though Chile had fought hard (and successfully) against U.S. efforts to extradite both him and General Contreras, Fernández Larios, in 1987, managed somehow to make his way to the United States where he, too, in a plea-bargaining deal, confessed to being an accessory in the assassination of Letelier. He insisted after arriving in the United States that President Pinochet did not know of the plan to kill the former cabinet minister and diplomat, and if he had known, would have fired General Contreras. Those charges set in motion a series of new U.S. punitive moves against Chile. Chile subsequently charged Fernández Larios with desertion, and indicated it would request his extradition once he finished serving his twenty-seven-month-to-seven-year sentence in the U.S.[155]

Letelier—who had served as Allende's ambassador to the United States, then as his last defense minister—was director of the Transnational Institute of the far-left Institute for Policy Studies (IPS) in Washington at the time of his murder. Mrs. Moffitt worked at the IPS as a fund-raiser, and her husband Michael as an assistant to IPS cofounder Richard J. Barnet on a project called "Global Reach," aimed at uncovering wrongdoing by multinational corporations. Months after his murder, the report of a preliminary FBI investigation was leaked, showing that at the time of his death, documents in his briefcase identified Letelier "as a Soviet agent operating under the direction of the Cuban DGI" (the Cuban security agency, Dirección General de Inteligencia). His control agent was Julián Torres Rizo, the top Cuban intelligence agent in the U.S.; in addition, Letelier was in direct contact in Cuba with Beatriz Allende Fernández, who, on at least one occasion, was his paymaster, sending him a check for $5,000. (Allende's daughter Beatriz was married to Luis Fernández Oña, number two in the DGB). The story was not only dismissed at first by major newspapers, but three of them refused to publish even a paid advertisement affirming Letelier's Cuban/Soviet ties. Though busy at the time investigating efforts of ally South Korea's intelligence agency to influence U.S. congressmen, Congress declined to investigate leads suggested by the documents of enemy Cuba's efforts, using Letelier and others, to do the same: among numerous examples, one of the documents showed that Letelier had paid part of the expenses to attend a Mexico conference of Rep. Michael Harrington (D-Mass.), the originator of the "destabilize" fiction involving the CIA and Chile. Inasmuch as Chile was a "pariah" nation with virtually no friends—but many powerful enemies—in Washington, the Justice Department dropped its own investigation at the close of the Carter administration, claiming "lack of evidence."[156]

(By contrast, at the time of the murder, Sen. Edward M. Kennedy [D-Mass.] called immediately for a complete investigation, as did Democratic presidential candidate Jimmy Carter. Sen. James Abourezk [D-S.D.], joined in the call, adding that Chile was responsible for the deaths of "thousands" of political opponents.)

Until the Townley extradition, there had been no real light shed on the Prats murder. The general and his wife died as a virtual civil war was beginning in Argentina; on the same day they were killed, leftist guerrillas seriously wounded two high-ranking Argentine army officers and the driver of their jeep just outside Buenos Aires. There were ninety-five political assassinations in Argentina in the first three months of 1974, a total of 814 by the end of 1975, 354 in the first six months of 1976. For the Prats, the aging President Juan Domingo Perón represented security; his death on July 1, 1974, stripped away that protective mantle, as a frenzy of Left-Right violence ensued. Perón's widow, María Estela Martínez de Perón, inheriting the presidency, said it was as though "the four horsemen of the Apocalypse had been loosed on our land." She lacked the political strength to continue her husband's leftist policies or to retain in place those sympathetic to them. Among the first to go was the commander-in-chief of the Argentine army, a man who, like Prats, had served a leftist presidency at the peril of his standing with fellow officers.[157] With him gone, with Perón gone, there really was no shield left as those four horsemen of death and destruction roamed the land, respect for law a casualty for a long time afterward.

In such a setting, the investigation into their deaths was cursory. Case #289-74 was closed "temporarily" on November 25, 1975, no arrests, no leads. Four years later, as the Townley trial was ending in Washington, Argentina's foreign minister said, "under no circumstances" would the Prats investigation be reopened; Argentina and Chile were then locked in a tense and volatile border dispute. In the wake of the trial—and Townley's statements about his and DINA's complicity in the Prats and Leighton crimes—investigators from both Argentina and Italy arrived in Washington, attempting to learn what they could. Townley, of course, would tell them nothing; lawyers for one of the convicted Cubans said his client might know something about the Prats murder, but wanted to know what guarantees Argentina would give their client if he did cooperate. Plea-bargaining is unknown in Argentina; the Argentines said nothing. They got nothing. The daughters persisted, hiring lawyers in Argentina, in the United States. Then a spy case exploded in Buenos

Aires, involving DINA people also believed linked to the Prats murder; the Prats case was again pushed to the back burner.

Sensational new charges: on August 10, 1979, *El Mercurio* reported from Santiago that Letelier's murder was part of "Operation Condor," a coordinated action involving intelligence services of Argentina, Bolivia, Paraguay, Brazil, Uruguay, and Chile—all then ruled by anti-Communist military governments—designed to neutralize the Left. According to the newspaper, "Operation Condor" included plans to liquidate leftists in France and Portugal, but the CIA got wind of it and tipped the French police in time to squash these plans.

Time passes. In 1982, a new and more vigorous prosecutor, Oscar Mario Salvi, satisfied himself after extensive investigation that Townley had slipped into Argentina on a false U.S. passport twenty days before the Prats murder, and left the day of the bombing. Since Townley was due to be released from prison in the U.S. any day, Salvi began a frantic race against time to press extradition proceedings. After a series of misadventures, he finished in the nick of time—to assume his own promotion to the federal bench in Buenos Aires, as well as to secure a hearing just as Townley was said to be packing his bags to leave prison. In July 1983, Federal Judge Albert V. Bryan held two hearings on the extradition request. In that Alexandria, Virginia, courtroom Townley would cringe for the first time ever under the unforgiving stare of María Angélica and Sofía Prats. The women said they felt confident the judge was tilting toward granting the petition, the one which would force Townley to respond for the murder of their father. A few days before what was to have been the crucial hearing, Judge Bryan died of a heart attack. Judge Harris Grimsley, who took over the case, ruled against extradition on the grounds that the pretrial "plea bargain" was binding. As he did so, he said: "A murderer goes free."[158]

In 1984, democracy having returned to Argentina, a new and vigorous investigation was opened. Four years later, there were still no arrests.

Taking the stand on January 17, 1979, in U.S. District Court in Washington, Townley showed no remorse over Letelier's death: "Orlando Letelier," he said, "was a soldier, and so was I."

Ironically, on the day Orlando Letelier died, Pinochet's finance minister Jorge Cauas arrived in Washington for talks with Treasury Secretary William Simon, the hoped-for centerpiece of a full-fledged partnership for economic recovery. Wrote Latin commentator Virginia Prewett: "The murder, of course, wiped out the [Cauas] press conference and aborted Chile's long-prepared global economic 'take-off.' "[159] If Orlando Letelier was a soldier, then this man, who only a week before his murder had been stripped of his Chilean citizenship for his antigovernment work, had, in death, won an important battle.

Notes

CHAPTER 10

1. The source was Federico Willoughby, press secretary for the junta during the first years, in an interview with the author in Santiago, June 16, 1987. In his job, Willoughby was in close and daily contact not only with Pinochet, but with other senior personages in the government. Willoughby, who had worked before 1973 for the United States Information Agency and the Ford Motor Company, was forced to resign in January 1976 because of severe health problems. Former U.S. Ambassador Nathaniel Davis devotes four pages to a discussion of "The Brazilian Connection and Other Ties," in precoup planning, citing considerable evidence of Brazilian links to the military before the coup, including the claim of his predecessor, Edward M. Korry, that "the actual technical and psychological support" for the coup "came from the military government of Brazil." (It can be nothing more than a claim; Korry had left Chile—and government service—two years before the coup.) Davis recounts that in March of 1973, the Brazilian ambassador in Santiago, Antonio Castro de Camara Canto, "made a series of leading suggestions (which I turned aside), trying to draw me into cooperative planning, interembassy coordination, and joint efforts looking toward the Allende government's demise. . . . All in all there is no real doubt in my mind that allegations of a Brazilian connection are true." Nathaniel Davis, *The Last Two Years of Salvador Allende* (Ithaca: Cornell University Press, 1985), pp. 331–334. Korry made his statement—cited by Davis—in the *Los Angeles Times*, "Confronting Our Past in Chile," March 8, 1981, sec. 6, p. 5. Davis left Santiago two months after the coup, too soon to have any direct knowledge of a Brazilian role in DINA (or much of anything else, post-Allende). It is not improbable that there may have been one; the then Brazilian military government, as noted, was the very first to recognize the junta, and remained a staunch ally of the Pinochet regime during the early years, working closely with Santiago on a number of fronts.
2. Although the air force had only four full-time operatives among the two thousand military, the number three man of DINA was an air force officer charged with counterintelligence. According to Willoughby, op. cit., the number two man was air force, and the administrative chief of DINA was from the navy. These would be relatively small discrepancies; of larger import was Willoughby's assertion that he believed the junta was "aware of [al tanto de] what was going on in DINA." It needs be remembered, however, that Willoughby left government service in 1976, and it appears that he was speaking of their being "aware" during the early stages of DINA. But, even that token force was withdrawn. General Leigh, in his June 16, 1987, interview in Santiago with the author, said he did so when he realized he could exert no control over DINA. He made a similar statement to Florencia Varas, in her book: *Gustavo Leigh, El General Disidente* (Santiago: Editorial Aconcagua, 1979), p. 78. Statistics on the size of DINA (and MIR defectors) from Robert Moss, "The Tribulation of Chile," *National Review*, October 10, 1975. pp. 4–5. Moss notes that among the civilians there were eighteen economists

in a special section responsible for reporting on the likely effects of new economic measures—giving its power yet another dimension.

3. Genaro Arriagada H., *La Política Militar de Pinochet* (Santiago: Impresor Salesianos, 1985), p. 155. A formidable scholar and specialist on Chilean military matters, Arriagada was also a leading Christian Democrat writer and thinker, and approached issues from that adversarial vantage point.

4. Willoughby, op. cit. He refers to the assassination late in 1973 of Adm. Luis Carrerro Blanco.

5. "Miracle," MIR size estimate, and university references from Lewis H. Diuguid, "Stronghold Calm After Chile Coup," a Concepción-datelined dispatch in the *Washington Post*, November 11, 1974. Diuguid quoted the zone army commander, Gen. Washington Carrasco, as saying of the university, the birthplace and the most important bastion of the MIR: "Would you believe it? There were a thousand students of sociology [in the 8,000-strong student body]. Now I ask you, how could this country need a thousand sociologists?" It was at that university that students, led by Enríquez, booed and spat upon Robert F. Kennedy on November 1, 1965, when he attempted to debate them. "Crippled" quotation and arms seizures data from David F. Belnap, "Top Chilean Rebels Routed by *Junta*," a Los Angeles Times Service dispatch datelined Santiago in the *Miami Herald*, January 7, 1975, p. 16-A.

6. Pinochet was still saying it, with even greater conviction, in late 1986: "For example, what serious person can believe in those who call themselves democrats yet walk hand in hand with the Communists? Can anyone deny that the attitude of the Christian Democrats has been permanently useful to the Communists? If you look back, you also find that Christian Democracy, with its collectivist policies, its indecisiveness, and very definitely, the leftism imprinted on it by its leaders, facilitated the advance of Marxism to power in 1970." Blanca Arthur, "1986: El Balance de Pinochet," a lengthy interview with him published in *El Mercurio*, December 28, 1986.

7. Lewis H. Diuguid, "Leaders of Chilean Parties Vow Effort Against *Junta*," a Washington-datelined Washington Post service dispatch in the *Miami Herald*, July 22, 1975, p. 8-C. Less radical members of the party in Chile, though by then in open opposition to the junta, nonetheless denounced the signers and concept of such a pact.

8. In interviews with the author in Santiago, Zaldívar, January 29, 1987, Valdés, January 30, 1987; data on Jaime Castillo from *Report on the Situation of Human Rights in Chile*, General Secretariat, Organization of American States, 1985, p. 134. Zaldívar, then chairman of the Christian Democratic party, was traveling in Europe with his wife in October 1980 when notified that he would not be allowed to return to Chile. The reason given was an interview he had given to a Mexican newspaper in which he allegedly said that "in Chile a government with military participation different from the present could be established." He denied making the statement, as did the newspaper itself. The government then said the action was "preventive," and based on a past "systematic course of behavior."

9. Joseph Novistki, "Chile's Embattled Left Split," a Buenos Aires-datelined story in the *Washington Post*, May 5, 1974. Novitski, then a special writer for the *Post*, betrays in that story a mind-set reflected in most major media stories at the time. Referring to the three common tenets of the Left, he described the third thus: "The short-term aims are to restore democracy in Chile and to try to defend the working class, the power base of the Left, against the drastic effects of the military government's austerity program."

The Reds were, in a word, the Robin Hoods, defending the downtrodden poor against the rapacious rich. Quite apart from the fact that he (and so much of the rest of the media) were wrong—the junta's economic policies provided for the poor of Chile as the rhetoric-ridden claims of the past never had— there is a basic assumption built into the assertion: the Marxist analysis of economic problems and solutions is the correct one, and in the measure that a government deviates from that, it must work to the disadvantage of the "poor." The tone, tenor and text of that reportage, in common with so many others at the time, make plain that Novitski was not merely reporting on what someone else thought, but accepting the validity of the claims themselves.

10. Moss, "The Tribulation of Chile," op. cit., p. 1110. Official ignorance of central committee members from the same source. Infiltration targets from Juray K. Domic, *Destrucción de las Fuerzas Armadas por el Partido Comunista* (Santiago: Editorial Vaitea, 1975), 4th ed., p. 32. As Juric points out in that quote from Lenin, "disorganization" can take various forms, from divide and conquer, to internal sabotage and assassination. The "radical change" quote is from a series of articles written by Domic on the military policies of the Communist party for the government newspaper *La Nación*, this one published on June 21, 1986, "Política Militar del PC (II)." In it, Domic quotes Soviet analyst Kiva Maidanik, writing in *Latinskaya Amerika*, # 2, 1975, p. 126. Domic is one of the most lucid and knowledgeable authorities on Communist party movements and strategy I have ever known.

11. In a June 1974 "position paper" ostensibly prepared in Santiago and made available to the Associated Press in Buenos Aires, the party said its chances of returning to power legally have "considerably narrowed," but that "active resistance" had already begun. The manifesto warned party members against "individual terrorism and adventurism," because it would provoke countermeasures, adding that "the cancellation of political democracy doesn't necessarily make civil war the only road open to the people." But it added: "Violence is intrinsic to any way of conquering power by the working class and the popular forces. This violence can express itself with or without weapons" ("Chile Reds Begin 'Active Resistance,' " AP dispatch datelined Buenos Aires in the *Miami Herald*, June 22, 1974, p. 24-A). Several months later, the party issued a call to the Christian Democrats to join in "the construction of a broad, anti-fascist front where all the men, women and youth of our people are included" ("Chile Communists Seek United Front With Nation's Largest Political Party," Santiago dispatch in the *Miami Herald*, December 28, 1974, p. 20-A). The following year, another twelve-page communique, claiming that "objective conditions for developing the mass struggle . . . are much more favorable now," demanded amnesty for political prisoners, permission for exiles to return home, and dissolution of DINA. But it carefully avoided mention of violence, saying, "nothing nor anyone will cause us Communists to deviate even a millimeter from the struggle's objective, which is to isolate the fascist military *junta* and replace it with an anti-fascist democratic government" ("We'll Keep Up Fight in Chile, Says Report Attributed to Reds," an AP dispatch datelined Santiago in the *Miami Herald*, December 25, 1975, p. 13-A).

12. Domic, *La Nación*,; Teitelboim also from Davis, *The Last Two Years*, p. 393. Reference to the exiled armed forces front and Estévez are in the third article in the Domic series, "Política Militar." (By 1980, having served their propaganda purpose, those fronts had vanished without a trace.) Of Estévez,

Domic writes that "the Soviet functionary of Chilean birth [is] now happily back in the country after having performed services for so many years to the cause of international communism." By 1986, when Domic was writing, many avowed Communists had not only been permitted to return, but had chosen to do so—a commentary in itself on the level of repression in the country. Data on the plenum is from articles 4 and 5. That plenum was presided over by long-time Communist party chieftain Luis Corvalán, by then rescued by Moscow in the swap for Vladimir Bukovsky. In the course of it, he boasted that in the few short months of organization of paramilitary brigades, mainly in expropriated factories, the Communists had managed to enroll, arm, and begin training ten thousand men.

13. Domic, op. cit., article 5; Teitelboim on guerrilla warfare from Davis, *The Last Two Years*, p. 393.

14. *1986 Book of the Year* (Chicago: Encyclopaedia Britannica, 1986), p. 574. The Carabineros were arrested on information developed by the *Central Nacional de Informaciones* (CNI), the successor agency to DINA. The three Communists—José Manuel Parada, Manuel Guerrero, and Santiago Nattino—were found decapitated on March 30, 1985, in Quilicura. Presenting his resignation, Mendoza said he was quitting "because he felt like it, period." (*"porque se me antojó, nomás"*). A native of Puerto Montt in Chile's spectacularly picturesque southern lake region, home to many German-descended settlers, General Stange was born September 30, 1925, and educated at the *Instituto Alemán* (German Institute) and *Liceo de Hombres* (Men's High School) of Puerto Montt. He joined Carabineros on March 16, 1947, reaching flag rank on November 27, 1977. Fluent in German, he spent six months in West Germany in 1966 on a scholarship (and was later decorated by that country). Stange became one of the top experts in Chile on the drug traffic, representing his country at a number of conferences abroad, including the United States, Panama, and Brazil.

15. *Qué Pasa*, June 11–17, 1987, p. 7.

16. On Sunday September 7, 1986, a Frente Manuel Rodríguez (FMR) commando group, involving a total of seventy persons (thirty of them at the scene), staged a rocket and machinegun ambush of a presidential caravan as it traversed a lonely stretch of rural road in a canyon southeast of Santiago. Five members of Pinochet's escort, including his driver, were killed, eleven seriously wounded. Pinochet escaped with minor wounds to his left hand. In the crack-down following "Operation Twentieth Century," an estimated 40 percent of FMR cadres were captured, including at least thirty involved in the operation. The FMR, which had ratcheted up its organization that year from "cells" to "columns"—larger and more visible, organized for large-scale urban terrorism—were forced to scale back sharply. Shortly afterward, security forces—alerted by a tip from Gen. John Galvin, the departing commander of the U.S. Southern Command*—dealt the FMR a colossal blow: the capture of 70 tons of arms and munitions, as well as secret caches, plans, and at least thirty-six key personnel, obliterating an operation that had been painstakingly planned over at least a year. The armament and related facilities and equipment, worth an estimated $20 million, was believed to have been shipped from Cuba and Nicaragua, and included: 3,400 M-16 rifles; 117 Soviet rocketlaunchers; 179 antitank rockets; 3.5 million rounds for automatic rifles; as well as machine guns, FN-FAL assault rifles, sub-machine guns, two fishing vessels used to transport them, various vehicles, "safe-houses," and underground storage facili-

ties. In an August 1987 postmortem of the Communist party Central Committee in Buenos Aires, the FMR leadership was severely criticized for inadequate planning and training (the attack on Pinochet failed, in no small measure, because only three of the six LAW antitank missiles fired, and because of inadequate training of some participants). The party ordered the FMR to cut back on its activities while the party pursued contacts with amenable political leaders to solidify broad-based support—if not actual alliances. But by then, the rebellious FMR was not taking orders from its political partners; it continued to stage a series of bombings, kidnappings, and assassinations which not only brought new counterattacks, but heightened voter (and political leadership) resistance to the far Left. The Communists themselves at no time renounced violence, nor would they instruct their loyalists to take part under whatever guise in the 1988 presidential plebiscite; but they *were* engaged in delicate balancing-act talks with politicians on the leftist fringes of "legitimacy" to gain legitimacy for themselves. (*While visiting Santiago on his farewell trip, the U.S. general alerted Chilean security to satellite intelligence obtained by the U.S. sources which led to the seizure of the arms shipments at Carrizal Bajo, a tiny fishing village on a stretch of virtually deserted coast at the edge of the Atacama Desert.) Data for the foregoing taken from *Carta Confidencial*, # 10, September 15, 1987, pp. 12–24. The publication is said to have access to government security services and to reflect many of their viewpoints. Information on General Galvin's tip from the magazine *Hoy*, special edition, "La Década de Hoy, 1977–1987," May 1987, p. 15.

17. Victor Lasky, *Turning Victory Into Defeat: The Soviet Offensive Against Chile*, an American–Chilean Council booklet, September 1975, p. 12. Lasky said the man, John Gilman, had been so identified in March 1955 testimony given before the House Committee on Un-American Activities.

18. Foregoing from Lasky, op. cit., pp. 10–15. On Harrington, Lasky quotes syndicated columnist James J. Kilpatrick as writing, "If Mr. Harrington's brazen contempt is not cause for expulsion [from Congress], no cause will ever be found." Congress declined to do that, opting instead for denial to one committee's secret files. Ibid., pp. 8–9.

19. Ibid., pp. 10, 15–17.

20. Ibid., pp. 5–9.

21. The 3,100 figure was given to the author on May 3, 1974, during a series of visits to the Committee for Peace, a church-organized group set up to deal with human rights problems. Number of Santiago prisoners from *El Mercurio*, March 9, 1974, p. 22, "En El Estadio Chile Existen 200 Detenidos"; data on *MIRista* trials and Fair Trial Committee from "In a Shadow Country," *Time* magazine, April 22, 1974, p. 44. Among those transferred from Dawson Island were Luis Corvalán, Letelier, Daniel Vergara, Osvaldo Puccio, Enrique Kirberg, Carlos Jorquera, and Jaime Tohá. Data from *El Mercurio*, May 5, 1974, "Desde Dawson," in Weekly Round-up section, p. 21.

22. "Informe de Dungan," *El Mercurio*, May 5, 1974, p. 21. Since Mr. Dungan presumably presented his report in English, which *El Mercurio* then translated into Spanish, and which I am now translating back to English, there unquestionably is slippage—but having seen other English-language references to his report, I am confident the essence of it has survived intact here.

23. "Palabras del Jefe Supremo de la Nación, Augusto Pinochet Ugarte, al Conmemorarse el Primer Aniversario de Gobierno," a mimeographed version of

his first anniversary speech provided by the presidential press office, pp. 30–31. In that speech, Pinochet also said that safe conducts out of the country had already been granted to 1,729 foreigners with ties to the Allende government, and to 8,416 Chileans who took refuge in embassies. Data on 1977 from *1978 Book of the Year* (Chicago: Encyclopaedia Britannica, 1978), p. 247. In December 1974, Chile offered to send an additional two hundred persons to Mexico, among them, Allende's sister, Laura. Several weeks later, Mexico still had not responded. Among the "unwelcome" ones: her son, Andrés Pascal Allende, by then head of the MIR. He was allowed to leave asylum in the Italian Embassy in 1976 and emigrate to Costa Rica. Gonzalo Facio, foreign minister of that impeccably democratic country, described the MIR leader as "not a desirable guest. That's why we pressured him [*apuramos*] to leave." He went to Cuba. Facio made the statement while in Santiago for the 1976 annual meeting of the Organization of American States: *Qué Pasa, # 268,* June 10, 1976, "Los que vinieron a vernos," p. 10. It is interesting to note that of the hundreds of top Popular Unity leaders who fled to embassies when the shooting started on September 11, only a handful of them chose communist embassies.

24. Flora Lewis, "Kremlin's European Policy," the *New York Times,* April 22, 1980, p. A14, cited by Nathaniel Davis, *The Last Two Years of Allende,* op. cit., p. 393.

25. In an interview with the author in Santiago, June 11, 1987, Pinochet cited several specific instances where, during the prolonged and explosively tense crisis with Argentina, war was only a misstep or temper tantrum away. A civilian government, he said, might have felt compelled in such circumstances to prove its "machismo" to the electorate, a consideration not faced by an authoritarian military regime. In his meticulous but openly hostile analysis of Pinochet's military policy, the Christian Democrat scholar Genaro Arriagada H. refers to a war threat as obviously strengthening the hand of the government, not only with the populace, but with the military as well. In one sarcastic (and inconclusive) passage, he writes that "the idea of the regime, actively divulged in the barracks, that Chile has been at the edge of war or in war during these nearly twelve years of dictatorship, undoubtedly has played a fundamental role in the process of control of the army." He goes on to refer to the "imminent risk of war against Peru and Bolivia (1976–1979) or Argentina (1979–1983)." The crisis with Peru actually began earlier. Arriagada, *La Política Militar de Pinochet,* p. 32.

26. Scholar and diplomat James D. Theberge wrote: "The overthrow of the Allende government in September 1973 focused Moscow's attention on Peru as the most promising member of the 'anticapitalist' and 'anti-imperialist' front in South America. . . . Moscow and Lima had been discussing the subject for nearly two years. But it was reportedly only after the fall of Allende that the Soviet Union agreed to provide an estimated 200 T-55 medium tanks, heavy artillery, and other equipment to the Peruvian Army on extremely generous, concessionary terms." Theberge, *The Soviet Presence in Latin America* (New York: Crane, Russak, 1975), p. 87. The battle quotation is from a September 1975 promotion blurb of Victor Lasky, *Turning Victory Into Defeat.*

27. *1975 Book of the Year* (Chicago: Encyclopaedia Britannica, 1976), p. 545.

28. Theberge, *The Soviet Presence,* p. 88. Theberge noted that Peru, having consolidated "superiority in numbers and quality of weapons and warships,

it favors a ten-year arms freeze in Latin America to solidify its position in the Andean region" (ibid). The Peruvians, in common with many other Latin nations, reacted to the U.S. arms cut-off by simply shifting their orders to the French, Italians, British, and Swedes, and ultimately, to the Iron Curtain countries as well. Unlike the United States, those countries needed foreign arms sales to underwrite huge research and development costs for weapons systems. Unlike the United States, those countries had no continuing interest in internal stability in Latin America. The result was an arms-buying binge without precedent in the history of a region which—under U.S. tutelage prior to the "new morality"—had one of the lowest levels of arms spending in the world. Peru was one, egregious example.

29. Cited in an undated publication of the American-Chilean Council entitled *Chile's Defense Needs,* apparently issued early in 1975, pp. 2–4.

30. Lefever testified on August 5, 1971, before the House Subcommittee on Inter-American Affairs; cf., *United States and Chile During the Allende Years, 1970–1973,* report of hearings before that subcommittee July 1 and October 15, 1971; September 11, 1972; March 6, September 20, 25, October 11, 31, December 7, 1973; September 17, 18, 1974 (Washington: Government Printing Office, 1975), p. 190 (hereafter *United States and Chile During the Allende Years*); senatorial letter from Lasky, op. cit., p. 17. McDonald visited Chile during the first week of July 1975 and noted in his article that "Chile is moving toward greater freedom ... while Peru is moving toward the opposite." His article was published in *Conservative Digest,* February 1976. McDonald was among those killed in 1982 when the Soviets shot down the Korean airliner. Lefever paid a heavy price for his defense of the Chilean revolution during those early years as being, if not a perfect government, better than most in the world. That was one of the indictments against him when, in 1981, he went before the Senate for confirmation as assistant secretary of state for Human Rights in the new Reagan administration (he was forced to withdraw). Lefever was, in 1974, a senior fellow on the Foreign Policy Studies staff of the Brookings Institution in Washington, a member of London's International Institute for Strategic Studies, the Johns Hopkins University Society of Scholars, and a widely published author.

31. Theberge, *The Soviet Presence,* p. 88. Data on Soviet arms from Moss, "The Tribulations of Chile," p. 1107. (He is also the source for other arms data in the following paragraphs.)

32. On March 27, two senior Peruvian officials issued a statement in which they said Peru had no intention of harming Chile, and that the common enemy of both was underdevelopment ("Perú Alude a Situación con Chile," an AP story datelined Lima in *El Mercurio,* March 28, 1974, p. 14). The officials were Air Minister Lt. Gen. Rolando Gilardi and Gen. José Graham, chief of the presidential Advisory Commission. The next day, Chilean Foreign Minister Vice Adm. Ismael Huerta reacted with a statement blaming tension on "an evil-intentioned campaign of international communism"; he referred also to the report of an unnamed French journalist—presumably Régis Debray—in which he claimed Velasco Alvarado had told him that he would not rule out the possibility of war with Chile. Huerta said that the journalist "has ideas clearly opposed to [this] *Junta*" ("Canciller Huerta Denuncia Campaña Del Comunismo," *El Mercurio,* May 28, 1974, p. 1). The next day in Lima, Velasco told a news conference he "rejects any

possibility of a clash with that brother people" ("No Existe Conflicto Entre Chile y Perú," AP story datelined Lima in *El Mercurio*, March 29, 1974, p. 1).

33. "Sea seek again, señor?," *The Economist*, September 5, 1987, p. 40.

34. Allende dispatched Communist party ideologue, Sen. Voloidia Teitelboim, on a confidential mission to La Paz early in 1971. The Bolivians rebuffed his overture for a renewal of diplomatic relations, saying that could only happen when Chile recognized Bolivia's minimum demands, i.e., a corridor through Chilean territory to the sea. Later, Bolivia's leftist President Juan José Torres himself said he believed that "reconquest" would yet be achieved without "chauvinism," but through "revolutionary understanding" (Joaquín Fermandois, *Chile y El Mundo 1970–1973; La Política Exterior del Gobierno de la Unidad Popular y el Sistema Internacional* [Santiago: Ediciones Universidad Católica de Chile, 1985], pp. 146–147, hereafter *Chile y El Mundo 1970–1973*). Reference to first aid and Pinochet's Arica speech from Heraldo Muñoz, *Las Relaciones Exterior del Gobierno Militar Chileno* [Santiago: Ediciones del Ornitorrinco, 1986), p. 38.

35. Pinochet quote, Muñoz, *Las Relaciones Exteriores*, p. 38; Banzer, "Acceso al mar," *El Mercurio*, May 4, 1974, p. 1.

36. Soldiers and new port from Moss, "The Tribulation of Chile," p. 1107; Pinochet's idea from Muñoz, *Las Relaciones Exteriores*, p. 38. Area of the buffer from "Los Laberintos del corredor," *Análisis*, 8–14 June, 1987, p. 20; and population/area the Tarapacá region, 1970 census figures, from *Atlas Regionalizado de Chile* [Santiago: Instituto Geográfico Militar, 2nd ed., 1981), p. 47. The idea of swapping something in exchange for the corridor was an old one; *Análisis* relates that President Harry Truman was believed to be the inspiration for 1950 negotiations undertaken after Chilean President Gabriel González Videla had visited him in Washington; the idea then was for Chile to give up a corridor in exchange for irrigation waters for northern Chile's arid wastelands from Bolivia's immense Lake Titicaca (ibid., p. 21).

37. Sources: Muñoz, *Las Relaciones Exteriores*, pp. 60–61, 142–147; *1980 Book of the Year* [Chicago: Encyclopaedia Britannica, 1981), p. 243 (expulsions); the Santiago magazine *Hoy*, June 8–14, 1987, # 516, "Con la mirada en la historia," pp. 6–8 (Chilean generosity, Truman proposal, Law of Sea conference, Merino response); " 'Minuto de la Reafirmación' Hubo en Bolivia," *El Mercurio* June 12, 1987, p. 1 (Bolivian reaction); in Santiago newspaper *La Epoca*, June 9, 1987, "Gabriel Valdés dice que resucitar problemas de soberania no es propio de los tiempos modernos," p. 9. The Law of the Sea conference alluded to was held in 1987.

38. *1976 Book of the Year* [Chicago: Encyclopaedia Britannica, 1976), p. 190.

39. Muñoz, *Las Relaciones Exteriores*, pp. 151–154; the *El Mercurio* citation, ibid., p. 151.

40. In an interview in Santiago with the author, June 15, 1987.

41. Braden made these remarks in a speech "Soviet threat to the Panama Canal" February 28, 1977, before the Belair Council of the Navy League of the U.S.A.

42. Muñoz, *Las Relaciones Exteriores*, p. 156. Again: although there were rumblings in the 1970s and early 1980s about human rights violations in Argentina, there was never anything approaching the U.S. and international campaigns to isolate and punish Chile.

43. "Videla puso fin ayer a su visita a Chile," UPI story datelined Santiago in *La Prensa Gráfica* of San Salvador, El Salvador, November 15, 1976, p. 4. The

Chilean newspaper, cited in that dispatch, was Santiago's *La Tercera de la Hora.*

44. Background of crisis from *Canal Beagle: Laudo/Award 1977,* official publication of the government of Chile, in English and Spanish, on the controversy, published in 1977, pp. iv-xxii; Muñoz, *Las Relaciones Exteriores,* p. 158. *Laudo,* a 498-page document in addition to the fifteen-page introduction, includes the full original language texts of the awards, including Queen Elizabeth's April 18, 1977, statement, and reproductions of the official maps, as well as a Spanish translation. Although the Queen announced the award April 18, it was dated May 2—the date when it was officially presented to representatives of both governments.

45. In that same interview, Pinochet clarified "yield nothing": we gave up no territory, he said, only rights to navigation, and that we were willing to do.

46. From a lengthy interview in Santiago June 19, 1987, with General Ernesto Videla, for several tension-fraught years, chief of the Chilean delegation in the various bilateral and mediation sessions with Argentina; the quotation is in Muñoz, *Las Relaciones Exteriores,* and attributed to the writer Luis Jerez Ramírez, from his book, *Chile: La Vecindad Difícil* (Holland, no date), p. 265. The Spanish phrase is "se trataba de ganar el pleito antes de iniciarlo."

47. Text of Carter's December 15, 1978, letter was furnished to the author in Santiago. I believe it had not heretofore been made public.

48. Muñoz, *Las Relaciones Exteriores,* pp. 155–164; author's interviews with Pinochet and Ernesto Videla, op. cit.

49. McGrory's column was published September 9, 1977, in the *Washington Star-News,* and is cited in *American-Chilean Council Report,* September 29, 1977, p. 2. McGrory now writes for the *Washington Post.* Reference to the *New York Times* editorial appeared September 11, 1977, and is from the same source. The study is cited by Muñoz, op. cit., p. 22, who gives as his source: Kenneth F. Johnson, "Research Perspectives on the Revised Fitzgibbon-Johnson Index on the Image of Political Democracy in Latin America, 1945–1975," in James Wilkie and Kenneth Rudle, eds., *Quantitative Latin American Studies* (Los Angeles: University of California, 1977), p. 89. The Fitzgibbon-Johnson Index contained five criteria: (1) Freedom of expression; (2) Free elections; (3) Free organization of political parties; (4) Independent judiciary; (5) Civilian dominance (over military). Costa Rica was ranked number one in 1975, Venezuela and Colombia numbers two and three; fourth place went to Mexico, a country then celebrating fifty years in which no national or state election had ever been won by any party except the ruling one.

50. President Alfredo Stroessner of Paraguay was the first, in September of 1974; the presidents of Uruguay came twice, Juan Bordaberry in September 1975, Gregorio Alvarez in March of 1982; President Videla of Argentina visited twice, the second time to discuss whether the two countries would go to war; and Brazilian President Joao B. Figueiredo visited in October 1980 (Source: Muñoz, *Las Relaciones Exteriores,* p. 137).

51. 1975 data in William F. Buckley Jr. column, "Clouds Are Slowly Lifting, Post-Allende Chileans Believe," as published in the *Miami Herald,* April 20, 1975, p. 3-E. As Buckley noted, "the poll . . . has been widely ignored—mostly because it tends to interrupt the lucubrations of American opinionmakers saying only unpleasant things about the government of Chile"; 1976

data from Michael Fleet, *The Rise and Fall of Chilean Christian Democracy* (Princeton: Princeton University Press, 1985), p. 181; 1977 from *American Chilean Council Report*, op. cit., October 31, 1977, p. 1; 1977 world survey data from ibid., February 28, 1977, p. 1; De Young's article appeared in the September 21 *Post*, and is cited in the October 31 issue, op. cit.; the freedom survey is from the *Miami Herald*, "Reaction to Chile Freedom Unfavorable," October 13, 1975, p. 3-AW (by contrast to those favorable to Chile, this one was splashed under a large headline across five columns at the top of the page). In that story, the Gallup Organization makes an observation which was still then (1975) defensible, but which continued to be repeated by rote long after there was a scrap of validity remaining: "that the new government has support—particularly among the middle and upper classes," and, by implication, that its policies were designed to benefit the rich at the expense of the poor. Buckley, op. cit., pointed out that even at the onset of that year, survey data showed that "among laborers and farmers, over 80 percent believe that their living conditions are improving and will continue to improve." Writing a few months after the coup, former President Eduardo Frei Montalva said it was not true, "as attempts have been made to depict it abroad," that opposition to Allende and support for revolution came only from "the middle classes." See Frei's prologue in Genaro Arriagada Herrera, *De La Vía Chilena A La Vía Insurreccional* (Santiago: Editorial del Pacífico, 1974), p. 22; even Jonathan Kandell of the *New York Times*, writing immediately after the coup, spoke of "the large lower-middle and middle class that virtually demanded military action . . . in the midst of an economic disaster and a class struggle that divided Chilean society as never before in this century." "Chile's Military Imposing Strict Standards on Nation," a Santiago-datelined dispatch in the *New York Times*, September 28, 1973. It is worth harking back to this because years later, European and American leaders would still be decrying the coup as illegal, some even going so far as to dismiss the legitimacy of the new regime.

52. Thompson was interviewed after arriving to attend the OAS meeting in Santiago; unlike Mexico, which boycotted the meeting, Jamaica attended. In that interview, Thompson indicated which "enemy" Castro had attacked: speaking of Cuba's growing military presence in Africa as a surrogate of the Soviets, Thompson said, "I believe that came about because Cuba was so beholden [*comprometida*] to Russia that it had no choice but follow its orders. I don't believe that Africa is going to be transformed into a communist continent. They are very nationalistic. Now what does give me great pleasure is to see that there is at least one country in the world which attacks my enemy, and that is the one which practices 'apartheid,' because that goes against my race" (quoted in *Qué Pasa*, # 268, June 10, 1976, p. 11). When the OAS General Commission met December 11, 1975, to decide on Chile's invitation, the vote was 14-2 with seven abstentions. Abstaining were the United States, Barbados, Colombia, Costa Rica, Haiti, Trinidad-Tobago, and Venezuela. When the higher permanent commission voted on December 18, the vote was 17-2, with five abstentions (the United States still abstained, but Costa Rica and Haiti decided to support the bid). The "inordinate fear" remark was from President Jimmy Carter's famous Notre Dame speech, a few months after assuming the presidency in 1977.

53. This account, including paraphrase of Kissinger's remarks, from *Qué Pasa*, op. cit. Kissinger, in his memoirs, says only that he "delivered a major

speech on human rights" (Henry Kissinger, *Years of Upheaval* [Boston: Little Brown & Co., 1982], p. 413). It should be noted that *Qué Pasa* has been generally projunta in its editorial policies. It should also be noted that Kissinger could not be held accountable for the "new Angola" in the hemisphere, Nicaragua, which came about during the presidency of Jimmy Carter, whose policies were decisive in shaping the Nicaraguan outcome.

54. Visiting the country in August 1981, Jeane Kirkpatrick, then U.S. ambassador to the United Nations (a Cabinet-level post at the time), said the Reagan administration had decided to put the Letelier case behind it, all legal procedures having been exhausted. Seven months later, Assistant Secretary of State Thomas O. Enders said during a Santiago visit that the United States expected "prompt action" against those responsible for the murder (cited in Muñoz, *Las Relaciones Exteriores*, p. 33). Details on conference opening from William Montalbano, "Leader of Chile's Military *Junta* Urges Human Rights in Americas," Santiago-datelined dispatch in the *Miami Herald*, June 5, 1976, p. 20-A. To reinforce his call for new mechanisms to safeguard human rights in the Americas, Pinochet ordered the release of some 400 political prisoners in the weeks before the conference— a move also said to be taken partly in response to pressure from U.S. Treasury Secretary William Simon. During his visit to Santiago the month previous, Simon had said such an easing was needed as a condition for American aid. At that OAS conference, Panama's Foreign Minister, Aquilino Boyd, fired a salvo presaging a stepped-up Panamanian campaign to wrest control of the Canal from the United States, referring to Republican presidential contender Ronald Reagan as "a racist extremist." Candidate Reagan had strongly opposed U.S. surrender of the Canal, ibid.

55. *Breve Historia de la Unidad Popular*, a chronology of the Allende years compiled by Teresa Donoso Loero, an editor of *El Mercurio* and taken from the pages of that newspaper, published in Santiago shortly after the fall of Allende in 1973. The Mitterand citation appears on p. 106.

56. Muñoz points out that in 1948, for example, Chilean opposition figures— Allende's widow, two former Christian Democrat presidents (Gabriel Valdés and Andrés Zaldívar)—met, among others, with the chancellor of West Germany, the king of Belgium, the prime minister of Greece, the president of France, the president of Argentina, the president of Colombia, the president of Venezuela, the president of the Council of Ministers of Italy, the president of Spain. Comments Muñoz: "various opposition leaders have a much more expeditious access to the foreign ministers and foreign chiefs of state than the Foreign Minister himself and other high officials of the military regime," *Las Relaciones Exteriores*, p. 139.

57. The Chilean scholar Heraldo Muñoz' book, frequently cited here, is a brilliant and painstakingly comprehensive study of Chile's foreign relations during the junta years, the fruit of five years of labor. Although it is an invaluable trove of well-documented data, it is also sharply adversarial. Muñoz, who did his masters and doctorate at the University of Denver, studied also at Harvard and the University of Chile, where he now teaches. Although he takes note of the ideological prejudices of many of Chile's international antagonists, he persistently—in the opinion of this author— undervalues their importance, while accepting on what amounts as face value the proposition that Chile got what was coming to it case-by-case (in other words, the altruistic motivations of those who did the punishing, the

unwarranted offensiveness of the punished). Even in a narrow sense—viewing Chile in isolation from all other countries—that stretches the credulity, at least of this observor.

58. Florencia Varas, *El General Disidente* (Santiago: Editorial Aconcagua, 1979), pp. 96, 99–100, cited in Muñoz, *Las Relaciones Exteriores,* p. 172.

59. Muñoz notes that as early as November 1974, an article in *El Mercurio* reported the meager resources allocated to the foreign ministry; a week later, the newspaper criticized the "excessive anticommunist orientation" in Chile's foreign policy, and the lack of professionalism (due, of course, to the number of military who replaced purged careerists). Four years later, another influential publication, *Economía y Sociedad,* echoed the same theme, saying "the anticommunist cause as a fundamental parameter in international relations lost impact [*vigencia*] . . . it's time to re-think our strategy. . . ." Muñoz, *Las Relaciones Exteriores,* pp. 41–43. Muñoz cites two different official sources as saying in 1984: (1) in 1973, Chile maintained relations with fifty-three countries and had thirty-two ambassadors abroad, while in 1984, it had diplomatic relations with 106 countries and had sixty-two ambassadors abroad; (2) the other source said in 1973, Chile had relations with fifty-five countries, and diplomatic relations with 107 countries (ibid., p. 138). The differences seem too small to quibble over.

60. "Chilean Diplomats Begin Packing After Mexico Severs Ties," Mexico City-datelined story in the *Miami Herald,* November 28, 1974, p. 14-C. Campaign pledge from Muñoz, *Las Relaciones Exteriores,* p. 291.

61. *Indicadores Económicos y Sociales, 1960–1985* (Santiago: Banco Central de Chile, 1986), p. 343. The Allende high was $15.4 million; in 1981, Chile's exports to Mexico totalled $86.8 million. When the bottom fell out of the Mexican economy in 1983, exports dropped to a paltry one million dollars, but by 1985 had bounded back up to $51 million. Though generally higher than during the Allende years, Chile's imports from Mexico peaked at $55.7 million (in 1979).

62. "Inglaterra Suspende Ayuda," London-datelined AP story in *La Segunda* of Santiago, March 27, 1974, p. 1; "Londres: Suspendida la Ayuda a Chile," London-datelined AFP dispatch in *El Mercurio,* March 28, 1974, p. 1; "Fuerzas Armadas: Entrega de Naves," *El Mercurio* April 14, 1974, p. 1-B. It is, of course, one of life's continuing ironies that a government such as that of Great Britain would spend billions to defend itself against the Soviet Union, while also being willing to sell all manner of arms to a regime (that of Allende) purposefully allying itself with the Soviet Union—and then would refuse to sell arms to a regime vigorously opposing the Soviet Union and all that it stands for.

63. "Suspensión de Entrega De Cobre a Inglaterra; Sugerencia del Ministro de Minería," *El Mercurio,* March 29, 1974, p. 1; "Precio Record Del Cobre," London-datelined AFP story in *El Mercurio,* March 31, 1974, p. 50. Prices for current deliveries jumped from $1.280 to 1.321 pounds sterling; for three-month future deliveries, 1.666 to 1.845 pounds. While criticizing Chile's reaction as "severe," the London newspaper the *Daily Telegraph* also called the Labour government move "an unjustified affront," commenting acidly, "Chile is not, to put it mildly, worse than the Soviet Union" ("Critican Política Ante Caso Chileno," AFP dispatch London-datelined in *El Mercurio,* March 31, 1974, p. 50.

64. "Britain Rejects Chile Debt Plea," the *Miami Herald,* March 1, 1975, p. 3-B.

The doctor was Sheila Cassidy, a thirty-eight-year-old physician at a Roman Catholic mission hospital, then training to be a nun. She was arrested on November 1, 1975, on charges of treating a guerrilla leader wounded during a shoot-out with authorities. After her release on December 30, she charged several weeks later in London that she had been stripped naked, tied to a bed and given electric shock treatment. She later repeated her charges before a United Nations panel in Geneva. The Chilean government produced a handwritten declaration and several prepared forms she had signed, all saying she had never been subjected to any maltreatment (She said they had been dictated to her by a guard holding a sub-machine gun on her). The Chilean government said it "decisively rejects that Sheila Cassidy has been the object of tortures, not only because of the inopportuneness of the accusation made by her on arrival in England, but also because of the moral cowardice constituted by the fact that she had not made any complaint, be it through English diplomatic agents, be it through competent tribunals." The explanation given was that no such denunciation was made "in order not to hamper her departure from the country"—a claim which flies in the face of dozens of similar denunciations filling page after page of human rights reports compiled by international organizations starting as early as October 1973, and the fact that Chile had, by then, released *all* aliens who wanted to leave. In some cases, their release was conditioned on a promise that they would not be allowed to leave the host territory for at least sixty days, so as to give Chile time to present extradition papers for those wanted on specific, criminal charges. Muñoz quoted the very left-wing *Guardian* newspaper as saying Chile had, in 1979, "apologized" for mistreatment of her, as a precondition for a restoration of full diplomatic relations (Muñoz, *Las Relaciones Exteriores*, p. 105). Remaining background all from articles in the *Miami Herald:* "Chile Denies M.D.'s Claim of Torture," a Santiago-datelined dispatch, January 4, 1976, p. 10-C; "Britain Vows U.N. Protest Over Torture," AP London story, January 10, p. 28-A; "U.N. Panel Hears Torture Charge," AP Geneva-datelined story, January 20, 1976, p. 6-B.

65. Import statistics from *Indicadores Económicos y Sociales, 1960–1985,* op. cit., p. 349. Balance from Muñoz, *Las Relaciones Exteriores,* pp. 104–105, 107–108. Britain was far from alone in reneging on such deals: in 1980, the Austrian government cancelled the sale of one hundred tanks and three hundred machine guns after Prime Minister Bruno Kreisky's Socialist party protested; in 1983, the Swiss government cancelled the sale of twenty mm cannons to Chile when news of the sale was published.

66. Muñoz notes that during the early 1980s, all manner of rumors circulated alleging secret agreements between Great Britain and Chile for bases, landing rights, and other arrangements—in the Antarctic, at the southern naval base of Dawson Island, and elsewhere—in exchange for arms deals allegedly including the aircraft carrier *Hermes.* Both governments steadfastly denied the reports. One obstacle to improved relations was finally removed by act of God: the death in a Santiago hospital on May 14, 1984, of accused Nazi war criminal Walter Rauff. Britain (and other countries) had been demanding that Chile expel him so that he could stand trial for war crimes.

67. 1974 from "West Germany Cuts Chile Aid," the *Miami Herald,* November 9, 1974, p. 7-B. Egon Bahr, minister of economic cooperation, was quoted as saying, "We are confirmed democrats and if something anti-democratic occurs in prolonged fashion, such as something against humanity, against

our convictions, then we are free to decide to offer no more aid." Trade statistics from *Indicadores Económicos y Sociales, 1960–1985*, op. cit., pp. 343, 349. Chile's imports from West Germany suffered the same sharp drop following the 1982 economic crisis as they did in general with the rest of the world. After visiting Chile in 1981, Wolfgang Sauer of Volkswagen said, "the Chilean economy is a model for Latin America"; the Industrial Federation said in 1983 that the recovery programs adopted in Chile were "the best and the right ones," cited in Muñoz, *Las Relaciones Exteriores*, pp. 287–288. The 1987 flap involved political asylum for fourteen Chileans jailed on charges of committing violent crimes. During a July 1987 visit to Chile, Norbert Blum, West German labor minister and a deputy chairman of the Christian Democrats, said Bonn should offer the fourteen asylum and told Pinochet to his face to "stop the torture." Franz Josef Strauss, head of the Christian Social Union, called Blum's conduct "scandalous." As *The Economist* pointed out, the issue reflected squabbling over tactics: the Christian Democrats wanted to move left and prove their credentials by "taking a harsher line against far-right regimes." The Christian Social Union wanted to woo back conservative voters ("Friends like these," *The Economist*, August 8, 1967, p. 36).

68. Muñoz, *Las Relaciones Exteriores*, pp. 179–180. A Chilean foreign ministry spokesman said Craxi's remarks evoked memories of Mussolini's intervention in Ethiopia. It was a month before tempers cooled on both sides—but relations remained cool to frigid as they had been. After extraordinarily convuluted, Byzantine maneuvers, Craxi was finally nudged out in 1987.

69. Muñoz, *Las Relaciones Exteriores*, 130–132.

70. "Giscard desea Liberación de Reos Políticos en Chile," AFP story datelined Paris in *El Centroamericano*, León, Nicaragua, October 24, 1975, p. 1. Giscard said the events of 1973 in Chile had "provoked emotion in the French people," adding that he wished for the prompt "liberation of political prisoners." Errázuriz, who had served as president of his Liberal party, as professor of law, for sixteen years as a deputy in Congress (including chairman of the Foreign Relations Committee), as well as ambassador to Peru (1961–1965), responded that because of his experience, "I can affirm that Chile will return to normality when the circumstances permit and in the measure that the rules of non-intervention are respected." Biographical data from Lia Cortes & Jordi Fuentes, eds., *Diccionario Político de Chile, 1810–1965* (Santiago: Editorial Orbe, 1967), p. 170. The "furtive" visit is in Muñoz, *Las Relaciones Exteriores*, p. 281, who notes that Mitterand went on television to rebuke any official contact with Chile. Nonetheless, it was during that visit that Cubillos concluded the $160 million deal for purchase of the Mirage planes, as well as tanks and missiles, and received assurances that the French would complete work on Santiago's subway system.

71. Muñoz, *Las Relaciones Exteriores*. In 1984—to keep the sales pipeline open—the French did sell Chile one Mirage III for training purposes.

72. Source: *Observations by the Government of Chile on the "Report on the Status of Human Rights in Chile" Prepared by the Inter-American Commission on Human Rights*, Organization of American States Document CP/385.74, December 4, 1974, pp. 54–61; "Swedes Bracing For Violence at Chile Net Play," Stockholm-datelined UPI dispatch in the *Miami Herald*, September 11, 1975, p. 7-D. Chilean players in the semi-finals in the southern town of Baastad received death threats, and provincial police chief Hans

Fjelner said in deploying 1,555 heavily armed policemen, "We have to regard this as a military action with the possibility of attack." He was right: some seven thousand screaming demonstrators tried to lay siege to the stadium, held at bay by the heavy security forces. Back home, Chile ultimately defeated South Africa in the American Zone finals.

73. *Freedom at Issue; Freedom Around The World, 1982*, published by Freedom House, New York; cf pages 8–9 for table of comparative measures of freedom, p. 11 for ranking of nations by political rights and by civil liberties. In terms of civil liberties, Chile found itself in 1982 ranked *ahead* of the great bulk of (unmolested) countries on the African countries, as well as such other "untouchables" as People's Republic of China, Egypt, Jordan, and Saudi Arabia, and in the same bracket as Argentina, Morocco, Pakistan, Singapore, Tunisia, and Turkey, among many others. Altogether, fifty-eight countries ranked *below* Chile on the civil liberties totem pole—which ought to (but does not) put the incessant "human rights" attacks on Chile in focus.

74. James D. Theberge observed that "Communists and Socialists in France and Italy, who had earlier pointed to Chile as a model of the peaceful transition to socialism, moved to disengage themselves from the Allende disaster. Instead of leading to socialism, united front tactics in Chile ushered in a period of unparalleled political violence. . . ." Theberge, *The Soviet Presence in Latin America*; Corvalán and AP survey from *American-Chilean Council Report*, February 28, 1977, pp. 1–2. Corvalán was referring to the rapid emergence from decades-long clandestineness of strong Communist parties following the deaths of long-time right-wing rulers Salazar in Portugal and Franco in Spain. At least one British writer was not gulled by Corvalan's soothing message: Hella Pick, writing in the *Manchester Guardian*, January 23, 1977, said, "Corvalan did not dispel the suspicion that his democratic road to socialism remained only a means to an end: the establishment of communist rule. The Chilean Communist leader, as the full transcript of his [BBC] interview shows, is highly-equivocal on democracy. He evaded a question about a free press and free elections by saying: 'It must be a different democratic regime from the past.' " The same *Report* cites an indepth article in the *Free Nation*, which it identified as "a bi-weekly newspaper published by the National Association for Freedom in England," on the "Chile Solidarity Campaign." According to that article, among those affiliated with the "Chile Solidarity Campaign" were the International Marxist Group, the Young Communist League, the International Socialists—and Britain's ruling Labour party. The *Report* adds that, with such backing, the campaign's "unsurprising" early successes included: half of Chile's Hawker Hunter jet fighters grounded for lack of engines because Rolls Royce workers in Scotland refused to service them; demands by workers in the British copper industry that management cease using Chilean copper.

75. Hilda Inclán, "Exile groups praise Chile," the *Miami News*, July 31, 1975, p. 4-A. The exile groups were the Cuban Nationalist Unitarian Commando of New York and the Cuban Masons in Exile (Masons, from colonial times, have been a powerful force in Latin American affairs). The Masons were particularly pleased because Pinochet had revoked Chile's Order of Merit that Allende had conferred on the brothers Fidel and Raúl Castro, and Cuban president Dr. Osvaldo Dórticos.

76. Kissinger, *Years of Upheaval*, p. 413. As noted in the preceding section, while still in government, as Gerald Ford's secretary of state during the election year of 1976, Kissinger had himself already joined the chorus of condemnation against human rights abuses in Chile. Indeed, in the passage immediately following the one cited, he goes on to say that he does "not mean to condone all the actions of the *junta*, several of which I consider unnecessary, ill-advised and brutal. Nor do I question the human motivation of many of its critics. . . ."

77. "General comments," in Reque's report of October 21, 1973, to the full commission, based on "very intensive activity" (language appearing in the report), during his October 12–17 visit to Chile: *Note Dated October 31, 1974, Addressed to the Chairman of the Permanent Council by the Chairman of the Inter-American Commission of Human Rights Transmitting the "Report of the Status of Human Rights in Chile" Prepared by the Commission (OEA/Ser.L/V/II.34/doc.21)*, Organization of American States Document # 381/74, November 21, 1974, p. 20 (hereafter *OAS 1974 Human Rights Report*).

78. Ibid., p. 68.

79. "Comite de refugiados de la NU terminó período de emergencia," *La Tercera de La Hora*, Santiago, March 12, 1974, p. 4. The other organizations were the Intergovernmental Committee for European Migration (ICEM), and the National Committee for Aid to Refugees, an interdemoninational church organization; Terri Shaw, "Communist Nations Reluctant to Accept Chilean Refugees," the *Washington Post*, January 5, 1974, p. 1. The story noted that while Cuba had offered to take more than one hundred non-Chilean refugees, and East Germany about seventy, "the Soviet Union . . . has not responded to the U.N. appeal." ICEM statistics for 1973-December 1982, showed that a total of 20,646 persons had been relocated, of whom the Soviet Union took sixty-two—or three-tenths of 1 percent of the total. Sweden took the highest percentage, 15.6, followed by France, 10.6, and the United States, 8.8. Cited by Muñoz, *Las Relaciones Exteriores*, p. 24. The Chilean government chided the Inter-American Human Rights Commission for failing to take note, in its 1974 report, of "the words of praise that [UN High Commissioner] had for the Government of Chile for the loyal, timely, and fair manner in which it had at all times cooperated in his functions. It is regrettable to have to record this oversight." *Observation by the Government of Chile on the "Report on the Status of Human Rights in Chile" Prepared by the Inter-American Commission on Human Rights*, OAS Document 385/74, December 4, 1974, p. 3 (hereafter *Chilean Response to 1974 OAS Human Rights Report*). As early as March of 1975, ICEM reported that it had relocated more than seven thousand Chileans and citizens of thirty-four other nations to forty-five nations. It also noted that it had relocated back to Chile three hundred "Chilean professionals" who had fled during the Allende years. ICEM was founded in 1951 as a nonprofit group based in Geneva, and during its twenty-three years of operations until then had relocated more than 2 million refugees ("7,000 in Chile Relocated After Coup," UPI story datelined Santiago, the *Miami Herald*, March 3, 1975, p. 16-A).

80. All from the *Miami Herald:* "Chilean Leader Cancels U.N. Panel's Inspection," a Santiago-datelined story, July 6, 1975, p. 6-AA; "Chile's Action in Barring U.N. Commission Hailed as a Defeat for Marxist-Leninists,"

August 22, 1975, p. 5-B; David F. Belnap, "Chile May Change 'Open Door' Trial Policy," a *Los Angeles Times* service dispatch datelined Buenos Aires, February 6, 1975, p. 4-B. Belnap said while the government denied torture reports, "torture continues, according to neutral diplomatic observers in the Chilean capital . . . and the number of persons claiming to have been tortured and willing to speak about it to interviewers is increasing every day." He also noted that because of its "legalistic outlook," Chile had allowed such human rights groups to conduct investigations, while other Latin American countries, notably Cuba and Brazil, had refused.

81. Kathleen Teltsch, "Chile is Accused in Report to U.N.," United Nations-datelined story in the *New York Times*, January 20, 1974, p. 1; "ILO Indicts Chile for Cruelty," editorial in the *Miami Herald*, June 4, 1975, p. 6-A. It is worth singling out because the *Herald* had the reputation of being closer to Latin American affairs than perhaps any other American newspaper; "End Torture, Labor Asks Chile," Geneva-datelined AP story in the *Miami Herald*, June 25, 1975, p. 10-A. That story (among others) offered no characterization of the ILO, but did note that the United States, back in by then, abstained because the resolution contained some provisions going beyond the scope of the inquiry on which it was based. The vote at the ILO meeting was 236-0, with 106 abstentions. Data on the 1970 congressional cut-off and AFL-CIO quote from Lasky, *Turning Victory into Defeat*, p. 18.

82. All from the *Miami Herald*: "Chile *Junta* Accused of Repression," United Nations-datelined AP story, October 15, 1975, p. 1; "Chile Rejects Report on Repression," Chile-datelined report, October 22, 1975, p. 1; Moynihan from William F. Buckley Jr. column, "Chile Sí, But Cuba No; The Violation of Rights Paradox," December 5, 1975, p. 7-A. Buckley points out that among the sponsors of the condemn-Chile resolution were Algeria, Bulgaria, Cuba, Czechoslovakia, and Poland, adding: "There isn't an Algerian, Bulgarian, Cuban, Czechoslovak, or Pole, who would not consider as idyllic, in comparison with his own, the life of a typical Chilean"; "Chile Denounces U.N. Resolution as Slander," AP story datelined Santiago, December 14, 1975, p. 13-C. Although the uniqueness of the UN action against Chile and the nature of so many of the key accusers was not "newsworthy," the following *did* appear in a "news brief" reporting on the UN General Assembly's Social Committee to consider a Chilean human rights initiative calling for a UN system for monitoring human rights violations *everywhere:* "Chile's resolution was widely seen as a tactic to counter charges of human rights violations by the government of Gen. Augusto Pinochet. . . .," the *Miami Herald*, November 28, 1975, p. 4-A.

83. The *Washington Post* article appeared April 19, 1977, and both it and the *Commentary* quotes are from *American-Chilean Council Report*, op. cit., May 26, 1977, p. 2.

84. "Preocupa Harvard Situación Chilena," New York-datelined AP dispatch in *El Caribe* of Santo Domingo, Dominican Republic, May 13, 1975, p. 10-C-1. The presidents were Derek Bok, Harvard; Jerome Weisner, MIT; and Marvin Bernstein, Brandeis. They were joined by Nobel laureate Linus Pauling, who early on aligned himself with the most radical antijunta organizations; Friedman quote from William F. Buckley Jr. column of December 3, 1975, "Chile Sí, But Cuba No," op. cit. The presidents professed to be particularly concerned about the imprisonment of Enrique Kirberg, rector of the State Technical Institute, the most radical of the higher educational institutions

in Chile, and scene of some of the bloodiest fighting during the first three days of revolution.

85. The Soviet Nobel Laureate, in his 1978 commencement address at Harvard University, said: "Such as it is, however, the press has become the greatest power within the Western countries; more powerful than the legislature, the executive, and the judiciary." Wicker, columnist for the *New York Times* (and the newspaper's former Washington bureau chief), made the observation in a commentary he wrote on the play, *All the King's Men*, the Pulitzer Prize-winning "docu-drama" play on the life of the late Huey Long of Louisiana.

86. "Some Hands Got 'Muddy,' Chile Admits," United Nations-datelined story, November 9, 1975, p. 11-F; Joanne Omang, "Torturers in Chile? None Imprisoned," Santiago-datelined *Washington Post Service* story, May 22, 1975, (eight columns across the top of) p. 5-A A, both in the *Miami Herald*. Though persistently hostile to the junta in her reporting, Omang appeared in this story to have done painstakingly thorough reporting in arriving at her conclusions. She says in her story that when confronted with her conclusions, "a government spokesman concluded that there were no torturers serving sentences in Chile." She adds: "The finding contradicts Pinochet's repeated statements that security personnel guilty of excesses in their treatment of political prisoners are punished. Last week, he agreed to allow this reporter to interview prisoners to support his claim." With his authorization, the Ministry of Justice provided the names of the twelve prisoners in two Santiago prisons, all of them convicted of crimes including rape, murder, assault, and robbery—but not torture or mistreatment of political prisoners.

87. The Committee for Peace was dissolved as of December 31, 1975, on express orders of President Pinochet, who accused it of being "a means that is made use of by Marxist-Leninists" to create problems that disturb "the peace of the public and the necessary calm. . . ." By the time its work was done, the committee had given assistance in 6,494 cases of what it described as political persecution in Santiago, 1,908 more in the provinces, medical assistance to 16,922 persons, plus assistance to 6,411 persons who lost their jobs allegedly for political reasons. In his letter responding to Pinochet, Cardinal Raúl Silva Henríquez acknowledged that "the purity of the service rendered has occasionally been clouded by the interposition of elements alien to its original intent," but rejected the overall Marxist-Leninist indictment. One year earlier, in October 1974, the government prohibited the return to Chile of the Lutheran Evangelical Bishop Helmut Frenz, then copresident of the committee. As the committee was winding down its work, in November 1975, two of its lawyers were arrested and held in prison for three months; one, José Zalaquett Daher, was subsequently expelled from the country. The following August, human rights lawyers Jaime Castillo and Eugenio Velasco were picked up by agents who refused to identify themselves and, en route to the airport, were told they were being expelled. After his return in 1978, Castillo was appointed president of the Human Rights Commission; on August 11, 1981, he was expelled again, but allowed to return afterward. Yet another, Hernán Montealegre, lawyer of the church's Vicariate of Solidarity, was arrested on May 12, 1976, and held for six months. On Christmas eve, 1984, Germán Valenzuela, president of the Chilean Human Rights Commission, was arrested with two other

officials of the organization and sent into forced relocation. In August 1985, Dr. Pedro Castillo, president of the Chilean Commission Against Torture, was sent into internal exile on sparsely populated Melinka, an island in the remote southern Los Chonos archipelago. There were several other instances of actions against leaders or officials of human rights organizations, but following dissolution of the Pro-Peace Committee, not against the organizations themselves. When the government repeatedly charged human rights lawyers with being Communists, the Bar Association, on August 27, 1984, adopted a resolution defending those lawyers and their work. Source for foregoing: *Report on the Situation of Human Rights in Chile* (Washington: Organization of American States, 1975), pp. 242–251. According to the Chilean Human Rights Commission, in 1986, there were 169 incidents involving attacks on human rights activists: 43 arrests, 3 kidnappings, 14 involving "cruel treatment," and 109 incidents of bully tactics (*amedrentamientos*) (*Informe de la Comisión Chilena de Derechos Humanos Sobre la Situación de los Derechos Humanos en Chile Durante 1986*, February 1987, p. 7).

88. "Chile y Su Futuro," in *Qué Pasa* magazine, #785, April 1986, pp. 14–15.

89. All of the foregoing was based on interviews at the committee office April 30, May 1, and May 6, 1974. I have taken a few liberties in translating data from the Case card, but not with any part of the substance of it. It was one of a number of *fichas* I was permitted to transcribe, all of which tell similar stories of arbitrary arrest, and the inability later to locate loved ones. In yet another, #102, Bernarda Pinto Caroca reported on March 5 how her cousin, José Hugo Alfredo Vidal Arenas, and three family members, together with other peasants, were routed from their homes at three in the morning of October 3 by soldiers with their faces painted black. None had been heard from since. (Smudging grease or other materials to darken their faces is, of course, a long-standing practice for soldiers on night operations, but its psychological impact on civilians, particularly peasants, unfamiliar with the practice would doubtless be great.)

90. Reporting, for example, on a July 31, 1974, visit to the Santiago Public Jail, "in sight of the jail personnel, without being molested": Prisoner #1 "they tore off two of his toenails and injured his fifth lumbar disc. Electric shock was applied to his eyes, causing cataracts...." #3, "electric shock in the Air Force War Academy. Blindfolded for 75 days." (Others, including one man accused of having shot and killed a Carabinero, said they were not mistreated at all.) Although the report says torture took "the most aberrant forms" (p. 138), in the case of women, only one of twenty-eight women interviewed—all at the "Buen Pastor House of Correction" on the outskirts of Santiago—specifically charged sexual abuse. The report describes the establishment, under the supervision of nuns, as "tranquil; conditions in the dormitories appear to be good; there is a television set...." Thirty-seven of the thirty-eight prisoners there were charged with political crimes—five had already been sentenced, thirty-two were being prosecuted. All said they had done nothing. Of specific allegations, two of the most graphic: #15, "they tortured her with electric shock, beatings on the lower part of her body, the use of the electric bed, etc., for the first two days. The last four days she was placed with other persons in a ditch full of excrement...." #7: "She was tortured in Investigaciones, where she was disrobed, subjected to electric shock, and made to witness the torture of other prisoners...." That

section of the report concludes with the observation that "at the express request of some of the prisoners, who stated that they had been subjected to serious torture, all references to their particular cases has been omitted, because they expressed fear that their attitude would provoke reprisals." Since twenty-eight of thirty-seven did speak freely, and since "there was no obstacle to speaking directly with the prisoners," and since the circumstances of their arrest could have been camouflaged while circumstances of the abuses made explicit, that assertion seems gratuitous. Names were not used for most such summary depositions, male or female (*OAS 1974 Human Rights Report*, op. cit., pp. 125 and 91–96).

91. A perusal of press clippings in the months preceding and following the commission's report would support the frustration of the Chileans: "Arsenals Seized, Chile Junta Says," the *Miami Herald*, October 1, 1974, p. 19–A (the story reported on the seizure in Valparaíso of a cache of Soviet and Cuban arms sufficient to equip one hundred men); "Band of Extremists Captured in Chile," the *Miami Herald*, June 26, 1975, p. 2-C (reporting on the capture of twenty-five guerrillas after they had slipped into southern Chile from Argentina); "Detenidos Otros Trece Extremistas en Chile," *Novedades*, Managua, October 8, 1975, p. 18 (reporting on the capture of thirteen members of the Socialist party secret cell in the northern city of Arica); "Chile: Foiled Invasion by Argentines, Cubans," the *Miami Herald*, November 11, 1975, p. 5-B (reporting on the foiling of an "invasion" by 1,200 guerrillas from Cuba and Argentina, due to have taken place November 15); "Se Enfrentan en Chile, policías y extremistas," *La Prensa*, Managua, October 17, 1975, p. 3 (reporting on a prolonged gunbattle between Carabineros and an assault group twenty-five kilometers north of Santiago); "Extremistas Ametrallan Carro de Industrial Chileno," *Novedades*, Managua, October 19, 1975, p. 23 (reporting on the machinegunning of an industrialist by five hunted MIR guerrillas trying to escape a dragnet); "Revelan Plan De Secuestros y Asesinatos," *Novedades*, October 22, 1975, p. 20 (reporting on the capture of five members of the Argentine terrorist group, Revolutionary Army of the People, who revealed a plan to kidnap or murder a number of prominent Chilean figures.

92. *Chilean Response to 1974 OAS Human Rights Report*, op. cit., pp. 6–7; *OAS 1974 Human Rights Report*, op. cit., pp. 1–2. The report said, "A normal observer would not have imagined that he was in a country in a 'state of war.' " The word presumably should have been treatises, not "treaties."

93. *Report*, op. cit., pp. 137–138. In its response, the government brushed aside the commission's suggestion that if it could not visit those places, then a high-level and independent investigating team designated by the government ought to be able to, and then render its report. The commission described this as its "only—but serious—reservation that must be made regarding the cooperation given . . . to enable it to perform its duties. . . ." In its response, the Chileans did nail the IACHR for one request which it said "shows the haste with which the report was prepared": listing as one of those off-limits sites the Chilean training ship *Esmeralda*, one of the places where reports coincided that tortures had taken place. Chile pointed out that during most of the commission's visit, the *Esmeralda* was, in fact, on its annual training cruise at Pearl Harbor in the Hawaiian Islands, some five thousand miles away.

94. The *Miami Herald*, both articles datelined Washington and written by

Lewis H. Diuguid of the *Washington Post:* "Three Members of Rights Commission Quit Over Inaction on Chile Report," March 6, 1975, p. 18-A, and "Chile Is Chief Target Of Rights Commission," May 2, 1976, p. 34-A. The three who decided not to seek reelection were Justino Jiménez de Arechaga of Uruguay, Genaro R. Carrio of Argentina, and Robert F. Woodward of the United States. They also cited OAS "inaction" as "a factor" in their decisions. Arechaga and Carrio expressed disillusionment about the IACHR's effectiveness. Reque added his voice to theirs in criticizing Chile.

95. Testimony before the subcommittee on Inter-American Affairs of the U.S. House of Representatives' Committee on Foreign Affairs, of Dr. Ernest W. Lefever, August 5, 1974, in *United States and Chile During the Allende Years, 1970–1973,* a compendium covering hearings before the subcommittee July 1, October 15, 1971; September 11, 1972; March 6, September 20, 25, October 11, 31, December 7, 1973; August 5, September 17, 18, 1974. Dr. Lefever was then a senior fellow on the Foreign Policy Studies staff of the Brookings Institution, Washington; he was reporting on a fact-finding mission to Chile involving himself, Dr. Riordan Roett, director of Latin American Studies at the School of Advanced International Studies, Johns Hopkins University, and Dr. Albert Blaustein of the Rutgers University law school. The mission was funded by the American Enterprise Institute for Public Policy Research of Washington. While saying that the junta leaders were "somewhat tardy" in acknowledging the problem of abuses in the early days and "slow in taking corrective measures," he also said that the junta had been "conceived in desperation and brought forth in anguish." Those portions of his testimony cited here appear on pp. 182, 184–185 of the report, referred to hereafter as *United States and Chile During the Allende Years.*

96. Information on the protests from *Hoy* magazine of Santiago, Special Edition, May 1987, "La Década de Hoy," May 1987, "De protestas a propuestas," p. 11; *1984 Book of the Year* (Chicago: Encyclopaedia Britannica, 1985), pp. 232–233; tensions in the armed forces, *Transición a la Democracia,* Augusto Varas, ed. (Santiago: Asociación Chilena de Investigaciones para la Paz, 1984), p. 40.

97. *Report on the Situation of Human Rights in Chile* (Washington: Organization of American States, 1985) (OAS Document 17), pp. 291–293; 304–305. At one point in its rebuttal, the commission described as "astonishing" Chile's observation that the annual reports had included none of the favorable reports on Chile's socio-economic progress rendered by various international agencies. That, too, seemed gratuitous, in light of the previously mentioned increasing emphasis on socio-economic considerations by the UN Human Rights Commission. It would also seem particularly gratuitous inasmuch as much of the IACHR's information comes to it from the Chilean Commission on Human Rights. The February 1986 report of that body includes this: "Among the principal factors which influenced the situation of those rights in Chile during 1985 was the economic and political situation of the country. . . ." The next four pages contain several tables of economic indicators (*Informe de la Comisión Chilena de Derechos Humanos Sobre la Situación de los Derechos Humanos en Chile Durante el Año 1985,* pp. 24–28).

98. *Report on the Situation of Human Rights in Chile,* op. cit., pp. 287–290. It should be noted that the IACHR has done special and/or comprehensive reports on human rights conditions in other countries of the hemisphere.

Among them, one covering the first twenty-five years of Fidel Castro's rule, another on four years of military rule in Argentina (1976–1980), one on Panama (1969–1978), as well as others on Uruguay, Suriname, Paraguay and Haiti.

99. Internal Heritage memorandum dated April 12, 1988, prepared for the president and other top officers of the foundation.

100. Cited by Jaime Guzmán Errázuriz, "The Church in Chile and the Political Debate," in *Chile: A Critical Survey* (Santiago: Institute of General Studies, 1972), p. 297. (The book was originally published earlier that year in Spanish as *Visión Crítica de Chile*. I have taken a few liberties in what I trust is the burnishing of an otherwise stilted English translation).

101. In 1981, Pope John Paul II, disregarding custom, removed the vicar general and created the office of "Personal Delegate of the Holy Father to the Society of Jesus." The Society's top authorities had named New Yorker Father Vincent O'Keefe as vicar general when the incumbent, Father Pedro Arrupe, suffered a disabling stroke. To the newly invented office, the pope named an eighty-year-old, nearly blind Italian priest, Father Paolo Dezza. In the circumspect phrase of author-journalist Peter Hebblewaite, "it appeared that the pope was trying to take control over the world's 26,000 Jesuits, whose political commitment in Latin America had caused offense." *Book of the Year* (Chicago: Encyclopaedia Britannica, 1982), p. 602. Americans old enough to remember will recall the "political commitment" in the late 1960s of the Jesuit Berrigan brothers, whose anti-Vietnam war activity "caused offense" through a number of law-flouting activities.

102. The survey is cited by Arturo Navarro Ceardi, "The Christians and the Triumph of the Popular Unity," in *The Chilean Road to Socialism*, Dale L. Johnson, ed. (Garden City, N.Y.: Anchor/Doubleday, 1973), p. 304. Significantly, it is taken from the Feature Service of the official Cuban "news" agency, *Prensa Latina* (ES857/70). Navarro Ceardi was then with the Catholic University in Chile. He quotes from a study done by the Office of Religious Sociology of the Jesuit Center, published in *Mensaje* (No. 193, Oct. 1970), in which 78 percent of young priests identified with the so-called "Young Church," 18.7 percent with the conservative Chilean Society for the Defense of Tradition, Family and Property. The author adds: "In other words, more than three-fourths of the Chilean priests identify themselves with the Left." *Carta Confidencial*, op. cit., in issue #9, August 27, 1987, offered these statistics (without attribution): 1,652 priests committed to various branches of the radical church, 223 leaning in that direction, and 325 "traditionalists." The terms "clerical radicals" and "radical pastors" is from Ivan Vallier, "Radical Priests and the Revolution," pp. 21–23, in *Changing Latin America: New Interpretations of Its Politics and Society*, Douglas A. Chalmers, ed. (New York: The Academy of Political Science, Columbia University, 1972), vol. 30, #4. Writes Vallier: "Thus, the basic conflict in the Latin American church is between the manifest, one-step style of the clerical radicals and the latent, extended-linkage style of the radical pastors, or between those who insist that the church must move directly and bodily to the side of revolutionary change and those who believe that Catholicism's most significant contributions to change have to do with latent meanings. . . ." The first reflected the style of those priests and nuns who actually took up arms and/or directly aided and

abetted those who did, the second those who, through teaching and preaching sought to change the nature of the church, the attitudes of the faithful. In the first, it meant broadening the role of the church to embrace political and social issues as well as merely spiritual ones, so as to expand the "appeal" of the church, its ability to satisfy a greater range of "needs." In the second, to "collapse the boundaries between religion and the world," arguing that "the political-economic arena of society . . . [is] the real world [and] the only place in which Christian experience can be gained." In other words, to give "religious meaning to new social and economic responsibilities." (I have here deliberately "collapsed the boundaries" between Vallier's two formulations, since both seek the same goal.) Although continuing to pay lip service to the idea that both capitalism and communism were "evil," the dominant forces in the church in Chile made increasingly explicit their support for Allende's Marxist-Leninist revolution.

103. Gonzalo Vial Correa, "Historic Factors and Their Influence in Chile," an address before the Chamber of Commerce of the United States in Santiago, August 1986, pp. 4–5, of mimeographed text. Father Caro was then (in 1901) a professor in the seminary when Germán Riesco and Pedro Montt— "both alike like two drops of water," according to Vial—were contesting the presidency. Father Caro warned against a vote for Riesco, a warning which led to a bizarre episode: candidate Riesco was refused absolution in the Santa Ana parish because he was a "Riesquista." Vial describes Caro, who became Chile's first cardinal in 1946, as "probably the most important figure of the Catholic church in this century and one of the most venerated figures because of his wisdom, modesty, humility and conciliatory character."

104. Alessandri negotiated directly with Pope Pius XI, Cardinal Pietro Gaspari, the Vatican secretary of state, and Monsignor Errázuriz. Although opposed, the Vatican caved in because of the favorable experience in Brazil following church-state separation in 1891—and the unfavorable experience in other Latin American countries where that separation had not occurred. Since the church had for so long depended on state subsidies, the laity in Chile had never developed the habit of supporting the church themselves—nor would they, in the years ahead. Thus the church's new "independence" would ultimately force it to look to foreign sources for its livelihood.

105. "Freedom of religion" was guaranteed in the second paragraph of the first article conferring "constitutional guarantees" of the 1925 constitution: The constitution guarantees "the expression of all beliefs, freedom of conscience and the free exercise of all religions which are not contrary to morality, good custom or public order, permitting, therefore, the respective religious denominations [confesiones] the right to erect and conserve churches and their dependencies in conformity with the conditions of security and hygiene fixed by laws and ordinances. The churches, denominations and religious institutions of whatever belief [culto] will have the rights with respect to their properties which present laws authorize and recognize; but they will be submitted, within the guarantees of this constitution, to common law for the exercise of the control [dominio] of their future properties." As can be seen, the explicit and implicit legal restraints on religious freedom in this constitution are quite distinct from the "Congress shall make no laws" language of the U.S. Bill of Rights—a reflection

of the reality, so often missed, that Chileans created legal norms for themselves like and unlike those of other democracies, according to their own lights and needs, long before Pinochet reached power and began to construct legal norms according to the lights of that government.

106. Gonzalo Vial Correa, "Perfil Histórico de la Democracia," p. 58, in *Política*, vol. 1, January 1987 (Santiago: Instituto de Ciencia Política, University of Chile), a special edition devoted to a discussion of "bases for a democratic regime."

107. Cited by Gonzalo Vial Correa, "Perfil Histórico de la Democracia," op. cit., p. 58. On the subject of relations with Russia, Cardinal Caro noted that the Falangistas argued in favor of them because of the "economic benefits" for Chile, to which he said: "Whatever the ballyhooed [*sonadas*] economic advantages, the religious and moral interests of our beloved people were going to suffer immense damage with those relations."

108. John Gunther, *Inside South America* (New York: Harper & Row, 1966), pp. 274–275. This was the eighth of Gunther's extraordinarily researched and comprehensive "Inside" books.

109. Guzmán, "The Church in Chile," pp. 282–283; *Carta Confidencial*, op. cit., #12, October 15, 1987, pp. 32–33. By 1968, *Mensaje* had abandoned the Christian Democrats and the "third position," coming out ever more plainly and insistently for a more immediate and radical revolution.

110. Enrique Correa and José Antonio Viera-Gallo, *Iglesia y Dictadura* (Santiago: Centro de Estudios Sociales, approximately 1987), pp. 86–87, write, for example: "In 1962, the Bishops' Conference released two important documents where one can see the strength achieved by democratic ideas favorable to change, which had their political expression in the Christian Democratic party . . . the second of them ('Social and Political Duty in the Present Moment'), in condemning communism, gave indirect aid to the candidate of the PDC, Eduardo Frei, who won the presidency in 1964."

111. Correa and Viera-Gallo, op. cit., p. 192, make reference to a revived interest twenty years later on the part of radical churchmen in such "religiosity," so "scorned by the Christian intellectuals of the Left in the 60s." Renewed interest was part of a search for new ground on which the radical church could unite with Marxism. The authors do not disguise their own enthusiasm for the ideas and programs of the radical church. The clash occurred in 1975 when the authorities said they acted on information Marxist elements planned to sow disorder during the annual pilgrimage to the shrine of the Virgin of Carmen Church at Maipú. As many as thirty thousand of the faithful by then participated in those pilgrimages. "Church in Chile Cancels Major Rites in Protest Move," AP dispatch datelined Santiago in the *Miami Herald*, December 6, 1975, p. 5-B. The headline referred to the church's decision to cancel all religious ceremonies in reaction to the government ban on the procession.

112. Korry was interviewed on the CBS Television program, "60 Minutes," January 9, 1977. The quotation is from p. 8 of the official transcript of that program. There was, as far as I have been able to ascertain, no follow-up to that revelation, not in the media, the Congress, or elsewhere.

113. Cited in Alistair Horne, *Small Earthquake in Chile* (New York: The Viking Press, 1972), p. 39.

114. Horne, op. cit., p. 231. He observes that the magazine had its knuckles rapped by the Vatican for that stand. He adds that in 1961, abortions in Chile took one life for every two live births.

115. Correa and Viera-Gallo, op. cit., pp. 75, 73. The "decades" quote appears on p. 223. The authors cite a 1975 survey done by Brian H. Smith in which 50 percent of Chile's bishops said they approved of social teaching as matters of doctrine, while 60 percent of clergy, nuns, and lay workers wanted more social doctrine in the church. "Social doctrine" are buzzwords for grafting Marxist ideas onto loose "Christian" values. Smith, *The Church and Politics in Chile: Challenges to Modern Catholicism* (Princeton: Princeton University Press, 1982); number of priests from *Nueva Enciclopedia de Chile,* Francisco Javier Díaz Zalazar, ed., vol. III (Buenos Aires: Ediciones Copihue, 1974), pp. 344–345. Church affiliation statistics from Carlos Huneeus, *Los Chilenos y La Política: Cambio y Continuidad en el Autoritarismo* (Santiago: Salesianos Printers, 1987), Table 34, p. 142. The higher church affiliation statistics from Carlos Huneeus, the lower ones from a Gallup poll done in 1979 and cited by Huneeus, p. 140. That Gallup poll showed 28.4 percent as professing not to belong to any religion. Huneeus claims (p. 139) that "the Government has actually encouraged the development of the Evangelical Churches" through access to television and economic facilities. The flip side, according to Huneeus (who writes, it should be noted, from a Christian Democrat perspective), "there has been a sustained effort on the part of the Government to erode the social and cultural bases of the Catholic Church." The study was funded by a grant from Germany's Konrad Adenauer Foundation, and undertaken by the Centro de Estudios de la Realidad Contemporánea, an organization allied to the Christian Democrats. The surveys reflect 889 interviews carried out in the Greater Santiago area of persons eighteen years of age and older during the month of June 1986.
116. *Carta Confidencial,* op. cit., #12, October 15, 1987, pp. 34–35.
117. Guzmán, op. cit., p. 285.
118. *Carta Confidencial,* op. cit., pp. 41–42.
119. Correa and Viera-Gallo, op. cit., p. 87–89.
120. Guzmán, op. cit., p. 286.
121. September 24 statement from Correa and Viera-Gallo, op. cit., p. 89; Cardinal Silva from *Carta Confidencial,* #12, op. cit., pp. 36–37. Speaking to journalists following that Soviet Embassy reception, Cardinal Silva said, "the majority of the reforms proposed by the Popular Unity coincide with the desires, with the proposals of the Church, so that there is a clear support [for them]." The "more than" quote is from Paul E. Sigmund, *The Overthrow of Allende and the Politics of Chile, 1964–1976* (Pittsburgh: University of Pittsburgh Press, 1977), p. 145.
122. *Carta Confidencial,* #12, op. cit., p. 37; Guzmán, op. cit., p. 298.
123. Guzmán, op. cit., p. 292; Sigmund, op. cit., p. 145. Guzmán notes that Father Arroyo was then being rumored as a candidate for the post of minister of agriculture in Allende's cabinet; Father Arroyo was then a militant in the far-left MAPU party, which had split off from the Christian Democrat party. Guzmán also said that when he later criticized the policy of the church "not to sanction anybody canonically," Cardinal Silva said the complaint appeared to have "a touch of monarchism, or at least of authoritarianism hardly in accordance with the present concept of a pastoral government."
124. Guzmán, op. cit., pp. 288; Cardinal Silva made his comments in a March 3, 1972, letter to the Group of 80, which continued to operate and continued to produce position papers of its own. Quoted in Cardinal Silva Henríquez,

La Misión Social del Cristiano:¿ Conflicto de Clases o Solidaridad Cristiana? (Santiago: Ediciones Paulinas, 1973), pp. 102–103; the response to the twelve priests and Mexican bishop from *Nueva Enciclopedia de Chile,* vol. III, op. cit., p. 345. If the Chilean church had become radicalized, the Mexican one was more so. In 1984, Monsignor José Salazar, president of the Bishops' Conference of Mexico, was quoted as saying that "the only valid revolutionary alternative has to be inspired in Marxist principles . . . violence is the only way given the violence which the oppressed today face . . . one must seek the strategic alliance of revolutionary Christians with Marxists in the process of liberalization of the continent, and proclaim socialism inspired in Marxist principles as the only acceptable alternative . . . the only theological profoundity which fuses faith and the revolutionary commitment is the theology of liberation . . . therefore, I reject outright the institutional church as it exists today, inasmuch as it has made Christians 'ideologized,' kidnaped, domesticated, deformed, twisted, degraded, confused, manipulated, depoliticized, isolated, and monopolized. . . ." Cited in César Hidalgo Calvo, *Teoría y Práctica de Propaganda Contemporánea* (Santiago: Editorial Andrés Bello, 1986), p. 244–245.

125. Guzmán, op. cit., p. 293. As Guzmán notes, the Schneider explanation was gratuitous, not only because it went beyond the merely protocolar expression of condemnation or hope for quick solution of the crime, but because it amounted to a leap to political judgment before much was yet known about the murder.

126. Wrote Pinochet: "After the collapse of the Allende-Aylwin conversations, the Chilean episcopacy believed it opportune to intervene to save the Christian Democrats. To do that, they believed it necessary to create anew conditions favorable to a renewed dialogue with the Popular Unity and the Christian Democrats, without wanting to understand that the situation had already reached an extreme that had no political solution." Augusto Pinochet U., *El Dia Decisivo: 11 de Septiembre de 1973* (Santiago: Editorial Andrés Bello, 4th ed., 1980), p. 105.

127. Correa and Viera-Gallo, op. cit., pp. 94–95. The undated 1974 document was entitled *La Iglesia y la Experiencia Chilena Hacia el Socialismo.* The second was issued September 5, 1975.

128. Ibid., p. 98. They recite that the Vatican secretary of state "rectified" remarks prepared by Ambassador Héctor Riesle because they implied an identity of purposes between Santiago and the Vatican contrary to the pope's thinking. The reference to the "clearer" criticisms is in Endnote 19, p. 169. As a further indication of Vatican thinking, they note that both the bishops' April 1974 pastoral and the cardinal's Easter sermon were published in the official Vatican newspaper, *L'Osservatore Romano.*

129. "Cardenal Raúl Silva: 'En Chile impera el Derecho,' " *La Segunda,* April 24, 1974, p. 1. When he finished reading his statement, the cardinal waved off questioners and left. Correa and Viera-Gallo quote one of the leaders of the left wing of the hierarchy—Bishop Carlos Camus of Linares—as saying the bishops had first made private contact with the junta following their December 1973 plenary assembly, but were "coldly received" when senior bishops personally presented their still-secret communique. But he hints at what might have raised junta hackles when he remarks that right up until the time of their April 1974 meeting, "we expected an announcement from the government, promised to the cardinal, which could have

radically changed the situation." Clearly, the bishops were already privately importuning the generals to hand over power to civilians, a position they would argue publicly and vigorously thereafter. The *New York Times* exemplified the kind of coverage given that document in a front-page story April 25, headlined: "Chilean Bishops Accuse *Junta* of 'Climate of Fear.' " In it, reporter Jonathan Kandell used the word "torture" and spoke of six thousand political prisoners. The word "torture" does not appear in the two-thousand-word statement; the Spanish word used was *"apremios."* The Dictionary of the Royal Academy defines the verb as "to hurry, or compel someone to do something quickly; to oppress, or squeeze; to compel or oblige with a command of authority that someone do something...." The equivalent "torture" does not appear. *Diccionario de la Lengua Española* (Madrid: Real Academia Española, 1970), 19th ed., p. 106. Kandell attributed the six thousand figure to "church sources concerned with legal aid for political prisoners ...," yet I have in my possession a note given me that very week, during one of several interviews at the Committee for Peace, indicating they then knew of three thousand prisoners. On May 3, the *Times* followed with an editorial, "The Bishops Speak," in which they dismissed as "nonsense" the response of junta member Gen. Gustavo Leigh, "I have great respect for the church but, like many men, without realizing it, they are vehicles for Marxism." The editorial repeated the reference to "torture" (twice), and set the tone for countless similar press reactions. Bishop Camus apparently was less concerned about the accuracy of the reporting than the extent of it: the document, he said, "had gone round the world and occupied the front pages of the most important newspapers" (Correa and Viera-Gallo, op. cit., pp. 92–93.

130. Extrapolated from ibid., pp. 157–165.
131. Comments on Pope John Paul II from the 1980 and 1986 *Book of the Year* (Chicago: Encyclopaedia Britannica), pp. 602–603, and 366, respectively. That Cardinal Ratzinger's views were causing consternation among Chile's church radicals was reflected in the comment of liberal writers Correa and Viera-Gallo that, should such views persist, they could force "substantial modification" in the policies of the church hierarchy, since they draw on Vatican II as justification for their ideology (op. cit., pp. 224–225).
132. Correa and Viera-Gallo record, for example, that with treaty negotiations in their final and most delicate stage, the papal nuncio, Monsignor Angelo Sodano, is believed to have persuaded the bishops to drop a reference in their July 16, 1984, pastoral, *Evangelio, Etica y Política,* to a provisional article (#24) of the 1980 constitution. During the transition to the constitution entering into full force in 1989, that article gives the president virtually unlimited power to order the arrest of persons, restrict rights of assembly, ban persons from entering the country, or order their expulsion, either abroad or to internal exile. Once the treaty with Argentina was finalized, the bishops, on May 14, 1985, called on Pinochet to pledge never again to invoke it. He refused. The immediate cause of that May statement was the decapitation murder of three Communist party professionals, one of whom worked for the church's Vicariate of Solidarity (an event which led to Gen. César Mendoza's departure from the junta; he headed Carabineros, responsible for the murders). They also note the pope's repeated

stress on the need for "reconciliation," e.g., in November 1984; in June of 1985, the bishops said reconciliation alone was not enough; the guilty parties also had not only to acknowledge their wrongs, but insofar as possible, repair the damage (*Iglesia y Dictadura,* pp. 124, 131, 136–137).

133. There was ammunition for all sides. Flying into Santiago on April 1, the pope told newsmen aboard his plane that Pinochet was "a dictator." Once there, he spoke of encouraging moves toward a return to democracy. The international media—to the ire of many Chileans—gave lavish attention to an obviously orchestrated leftist demonstration which disrupted the centerpiece of the Santiago visit, a huge open-air mass in O'Higgins Park. That drew a sharp rebuke from the Rev. Pasquale Borgomeo that the media "indulges the dramatic aspects rather than the significant ones. . . . demonstrations here and there, with the corresponding intervention by the forces of order, risk keeping off center stage the passionate and moving reception for the pope by the people of Santiago." But the *Washington Post*—and other newspapers around the world—also recorded Pinochet's words as the pope arrived, defending his rule as necessary to save Chile from "the hate, lies and death culture" of communism. And, in the aftermath, the Chilean government widely circulated publications such as its *Chile Today,* with a cover picture of a smiling pontiff and a smiling president walking side-by-side in the bright sunshine. In advance of the pope's arrival, the bishops' Permanent Council went to great lengths to emphasize the pastoral character of the visit, its president telling *El Mercurio* he didn't see how the pope's visit could "favor anything bad or postpone anything good." Among the sources: the *Washington Post,* "Gen. Pinochet, Welcoming Pope, Denounces Communist 'Lies,' " April 2, p. A27; "Pope Tells Chile's Bishops To Press for Free Elections," April 3, p. A-1; "Chileans Trade Blame For Violence," April 5, p. A-1; "Chile: As the general said to the Pope," *The Economist,* April 4, 1987, pp. 32–33; "Pope Pleads Again for Chileans To Be Reconciled, Shun Violence," the *Buffalo (N.Y.) News,* April 5, 1987, p. 2; international edition of *El Mercurio,* week of April 9–15, 1987 (devoted almost entirely to the papal visit); *Chile Today,* June 1987, #54 (published by the Embassy of Chile in Washington); Correa and Viera-Gallo, (op. cit.) 148–149.

134. In his message, the pope rejoiced that the encouragement he had given to "living together in peace" (*convivencia*), had triggered "study . . . reflection . . . so as to translate it to action in your daily lives." "Love" for each other, he said, was, then, the message he wanted to repeat, "for each Chilean during this year in which the nation prepares to decide on events important for your future . . . Love is patient, it seeks to serve, and not to do harm to our brother, but rather to do good for him . . ." He also repeated his earlier admonition, significantly from the Mass of Reconciliation he had celebrated in Santiago: " 'Violence is not Christian, it is not evangelical, it is not the path for solving the real difficulties of individuals, or peoples . . .' " In his Easter homily, Cardinal Fresno expressed the hope that his countrymen, "as we travel the important route of 1988, may share ideas, initiatives and valid principles, while, at the same time, respecting the ideas and principles of those who do not think as we do . . ." I fear, he said, that "the tensions, confrontations, hatreds and breakdown of communication into which we have sunk, may become ever more uncontrollable once the stages we are to traverse in 1988 are completed." We must, he said,

revive a sense of learning to live together in a more brotherly and Christian way. "We must do so while there still is time, and we don't have much time to do so . . ." Both the papal and cardinal's messages from international editions of *El Mercurio*, the first for the week of March 24–30, 1988, pp. 1–2, taken from the March 28 editions of the paper; the second from the week of March 31–April 6, pp. 1–2, taken from the April 4 editions.

135. Correa and Viera-Gallo—after claiming that Pope John Paul II's papacy has produced no change in the character of bishopric appointments—express dual concerns: Rome's "tendency to modify the composition of the Latin American bishops' conferences in a conservative direction"; that if the revisionism of Vatican II continues, "many bishops, theologians and pastoral workers may draw closer in greater measure to those who identify with the most advanced and politically committed post-Council theological currents. This current is the one which has directed the Chilean church in recent years and is responsible for the rupture between [the church] and the conservative bloc in the sixties. It was they who approved and drove the political and social reforms of the era, looked with attention [sic] at the first year of Allende's government, became enthusiastic about the Alliance for Progress, and experienced an intense affection for Paul VI." Stripped of its protective and convoluted rhetoric, these leftist authors are saying that if the church moves right, many of those who have pushed it down the leftist path in Chile in recent years will join forces with the most radical "Catholics," abandoning the establishment (op. cit., pp. 167, 225). *Carta Confidencial*, op. cit., #20, April 5, 1988, p. 35, identifies five "breakaway bishops": Fernando Ariztía, Jorge Hourton, Tomás González, Carlos Camus, and Alfonso Baeza. According to this analysis, their position is that if the junta's candidate wins the plebiscite, they will denounce the outcome as fraudulent; if the opposition candidate wins, they will exploit that opening as a "detonator" to bring the entire Pinochet-constructed system down immediately. And, if they don't get their way within the Bishops' Conference, they would break away. Elected to head the conference in December of 1987 were Bishops Carlos González Cruchaga, president, and Sergio Contreras, secretary-general. During his twenty years as bishop of Talca, one of Bishop Cruchaga's closest advisers was the Belgian priest Joseph Comblin, a leading architect of liberation theology (who was expelled from Brazil in 1971 for ties to terrorists, from Chile in 1974, and later allowed to return). On private property, Bishop Cruchaga said: "Sacred it is not." On the difference between civilians and military: "Two scales with distinct values. The problem is that the military man is trained for war, to defend himself, to attack." On the new market economy in Chile, he branded it as "individualist," and thus a "social sin" (*Carta Confidencial*, op. cit., #16, January 15, 1988, pp. 9–13).

136. Among the highlights of their "Declaration of Los Andes": "Liberation theology . . . claims to be 'a new way of making theology,' through the lens of the 'oppressed' . . . demanding an essentially political rereading of the Word of God, interpreting the entire Christian existence, faith and theology in political code"; "Theology can and must make a fruitful use of social science. But, there is no room for accepting the subordination of theological discourse to the discourse of any positing science"; "Jesus Christ is presented to us as 'the subversive from Nazareth,' intentionally committed in the 'class war' of his time, and they describe for us his life

and liberating death as that of a simple martyr to a popular cause, crushed by the ruling Judeo-Roman 'establishment.' . . . Surely our Lord did move within the social context of his time and place. But that image of 'historic Jesus,' who died for the poor and against the rich as classes, does not come from the message of the New Testament, but, a priori, from the dialectic of conflict and contrasts deeply with the faith of the church on fundamental points"; "With respect to the church, without ignoring the love for the poor which one can discover in some liberation theologians, we must add with pain that in the figure of a 'Popular Church,' such as these theologians present, we cannot recognize the face of the true Church of Christ." (Correa and Viera-Gallo, op. cit., pp. 235–246). The document contains a great deal more of value, but unfortunately has been given only a fraction of the attention as pronouncements of those it seeks to combat. Other signers included the archbishops of Bahia, Brazil, and Arequipa, Peru, as well as the pro-tem grand chancellor of the Catholic University of Chile, Monsignor Jorge Medina Estévez. Among lay persons attending: Humberto Belli, ex-editorial writer for *La Prensa* of Nicaragua, who had fought the Somoza regime in his native country only to see it fall under the tyranny of the Sandinistas.

137. Bishop Fuenzalida from "Movimiento 11 Septiembre nos salvó de la esclavitud," *La Segunda,* September 13, 1974, p. 1; Bishops Matte and Camus from Correa and Viera-Gallo, op. cit., pp. 10–11, 93.

138. Sources, all the *Miami Herald:* "Chile Hunts Priests, Nuns Who Aided Leftists," November 5, 1975, p. 1-A; "2 Catholic Priests Surrender in Chile," November 16, 1975, p. 4-D; "Chile Expels Priest Charged With Link To Leftist Guerrillas," November 26, 1975, p. 16-A; "Charges in Chile Denied by Cleric," November 27, 1975, p. 12-D (a South Bend-dated story); back in the United States, Father Panchot's superior denied the priest was involved with guerrillas, saying that he had simply worked for the Committee for Peace "to give assistance to families of political prisoners"; "Chile Plans Trial Of Four Priests," December 17, 1975, p. 9-D; "Rift of Church and State Widening in Chile," December 19, 1975, pp. 25-A; the *Miami News,* "Chile boots out three nuns," November 8, 1975, p. 1. The allegation against Father Devlin is from *Carta Confidencial,* op. cit., #20, April 5, 1988, p. 42. That issue notes that among other Chilean priests arrested were Father Martín Garate, chief of a MIR cell at the Nueva Palena shantytown; Father Rafael Maroto, a MIR "sympathizer" in 1968, who, by 1985, was the official spokesman for the Democratic Popular Movement, a Marxist terrorist group; and Father Renato Gianio, pastor of La Victoria, who admitted having hidden an arsenal in his house.

139. "Chile, Communism and the NCCB," in *The Mindszenty Report,* vol. XVIII, #11, November 1976, p. 1; "Loans for Chile Will Be Continued," the *Miami Herald,* April 24, 1977, p. 17-B (the bank's shareholders rejected the Mercy Sisters' resolution); "GM Urged to Give Chile Unions Help," the *Miami Herald,* October 12, 1975, p. 1, Section BW. *The Mindzenty Report* (p. 3) identified a number of Catholic priests and nuns who joined at the Chile Coordinating Council's Washington meeting in May of 1976, along with such luminaries of the Left as Father Dan Berrigan, Angela Davis, Communist party presidential candidate Charlene Mitchell, and convicted Soviet atom spy Morton Sobel. There have been a number of solid studies of the leftward movement of mainstream churches over the past

two decades. A recent and excellent one: Edmund W. Robb and Julia Robb, *The Betrayal of the Church: Apostasy and Renewal in the Mainline Denominations* (Westchester, IL., Crossway Books, 1986).

140. Details of the finalization of the accord, junta reaction and the September meeting from Special Tenth Anniversary edition of the magazine *Hoy,* "1977–1987: La Década de *Hoy,*" May 1987, pp. 13–14, 19; cardinal's 1983 homily from Correa and Viera-Gallo, op. cit., p. 146. Bradley Graham, "Chilean Oppressed Turn to Vicariate," the *Washington Post,* a Santiago-datelined dispatch, May 2, 1987, p. 61-C. The pejoratives ("economically privileged," "politically conservative," "wealthy Catholics") reveal far more of the writer's prejudices than they do the reality of the church in Chile (or Latin America). Viera & Gallo acknowledge, op. cit., p. 181—and they write from a leftist perspective—that even liberation theologists recognize that "the poor in Chile and Latin America have always been in the church." (The liberationists claim that the difference is that now, under their tutelage, the poor "form part of the decision process.") There have also been countless studies showing that most resistance to the radical changes in church practice following Vatican II came from blue-collar faithful, not the elites. It is, of course, true that the church was allied with the "politically conservative"; they were Catholics, the "politically liberal" not only non-Catholics, but until Marxism became theologically acceptable, the enemies of the church. As for opposition to Pinochet, it is also true that armed opposition has centered in the shantytowns, because it is there that the MIR (and, in more recent years, the Communist party's armed wing, the FMR) has chosen to encamp. But, just as the notion of "peasant" radicalism of the sixties proved to be so much revolutionary rhetoric and media hot air, surveys in Chile show that far and away the greatest opposition to Chile comes from university students and the hard Left (Communists, the even more radical Socialists, etc.).

141. "Poverty in Latin America: The Impact of Depression," a World Bank Publication (Washington: The World Bank, 1986, p. 20).

142. Huneeus, for example, says that in his survey, 37.3 percent gave the very highest rating to the work of the church's human rights organization, the Vicariate of Solidarity, 20.1 gave it the next highest rating, and only 9.3 gave it bad ratings. Yet, he observes at the same time that 51.6 percent want the church to limit itself to "strictly religious and moral" matters, 46.2 percent that it should involve itself in political matters affecting the entire country but without favoring or harming any specific political party. Huneeus, op. cit., pp. 151 and table # 27, p. 114.

143. Bishop Camus quote from *Carta Confidencial,* op. cit., #20, April 5, 1988, p. 43; Father Salas from "Chile Hunts Priests, Nuns Who Aided Leftists," AP Santiago-datelined dispatch in the *Miami Herald,* November 5, 1975, p. 1-A; Fleet, op. cit., p. 189. Fleet says the church's "unprecedented visibility" since 1973 has led to a sharp increase in religious vocations: from 100 seminarians enrolled in 1973, to 208 in 1977, to 659 in 1979. How much of that is explained by the appeal of "revolutionary activism" will remain to be seen. Father Salas and the American nun Sister Helen Nelson took Nelson Gutiérrez to the convent of Notre Dame where he remained under medical treatment from October 18–24, 1975, for two bullet wounds in the leg received during a gun battle with security agents at a farmhouse where he was in hiding. Two American nuns also were accused

of collaborating in that operation and were also deported from the country. Gutiérrez was first given medical treatment by British physician Dr. Sheila Cassidy, who herself then sought refuge at a rest house in Santiago of the Columban fathers, an Irish Roman Catholic order. Security agents were met with a hail of automatic weapons fire that wounded one agent and killed a woman servant caught in the crossfire when they went to arrest Dr. Cassidy. Her arrest and subsequent imprisonment triggered the previously discussed attack on Santiago by Britain's Labour government.

144. From the beginning, the Vicariate broadened its base to include social work in the slums, no doubt responding in part to the need to assert an official church presence alongside the multiplying missions of the "Popular Church" radicals. The first vicar, Father Precht Banados, thirty-six, referred to it in his announcement of its formation, saying it would also offer "popular eating places, polyclinics and work subsidies for unemployed persons." "Catholics Form New Unit to Aid Chile Prisoners," AP Santiago dispatch in the *Miami Herald*, January 17, 1976, p. 21-A. The eight thousand figure is in *Chilean Response to 1974 OAS Human Rights Report*, op. cit., p. 3; America's Watch quote from Bradley Graham, the *Washington Post*, op. cit., who describes it—as do most reporters—as "the U.S.-based [organization] which monitors human rights violations in the region." Given the unmistakable and persistent left-wing bias of Americas Watch, that would be akin to describing the fox as monitoring abuses in the chicken coop. For a documented example of that bias, see Allan C. Brownfeld and J. Michael Waller, *The Revolution Lobby* (Washington: Council for Inter-American Security, 1985), pp. 51–53.

145. As Soviet analysts Gouré and Rothenberg observed, "the main thrust of [post-coup Soviet] strategy for Chile is to build the widest union of possible forces opposed to the junta . . . [including] the Chilean Catholic church, as well as the 'entire' Christian Democratic party." Leon Gouré and Morris Rothenberg, *Soviet Penetration of Latin America* (Miami: University of Miami Center for Advanced International Studies, 1975), p. 123. They cite Radio Moscow broadcasts of February 10 and June 27, 1974; "De Simpatizante a Candidato," *Carta Confidencial*, op. cit., #12, October 15, 1987, pp. 39–40. According to that newsletter, the idea of the cardinal's candidacy was first floated on February 24, 1985, in the Madrid newspaper *El País*, later actively picked up in Chile by the Democratic Popular Movement (MDP), the umbrella organization of ultra-Left parties; "Presiones a los Obispos," #5, June 4, 1987, pp. 26–27. The latter article asserts that the MDP sent the Permanent Bishops' Conference a nine-page letter shortly after the Buenos Aires meeting asking that the church "make possible the path of reconciliation in our country" by leading the fight for a Provisional Government headed by a candidate acceptable to "all democratic forces." The bishops politely declined, as they also declined a similar appeal from the Christian Democrats—and an internal demand that the bishops oppose any move to exclude the MDP from any pre-electoral alliance or accord.

146. Correa & Viera-Gallo, op. cit., p. 178. Gone now, they write, was the "cosmic vision" of a detached, celestial-pointing church, in its stead "the lively and boundless enthusiasm for progress in this world and of faith without restrictions. . . ." Overboard, too, foul capitalism. They quote Fernando Castillo, "the theologian closest to the CCPs," on the need of the

church to draw nearer the poor. This implies, Castillo says, "the recognition of an historically-crystallized guilt in the form of connivance or complicity [of the church] with the powerful. . . ." Ibid., p. 184.

147. "Distant daughter" and "end of era" from Correa & Viera-Gallo, op. cit., pp. 177–178; Connally-Mengal from Charles A. Krause, "For U.S. Priest in Chile, 'Liberation Theology' Means Bringing Dignity to Poor," Santiago-based story in the *Washington Post*, February 14, 1979. That story was one of a spate of similar ones which appeared following the Puebla, Mexico, conference shortly before where the Latin bishops, under the guidance of the new pope, John Paul II, tried to role back some of the radicalism of Medellín. This story, like so many others, set up an irresistible equation: liberation theology, now under attack, embodied the "Roman Catholic church's relatively recent commitment here to the poor. . . ." This new ersatz Marxism and "Christianity" represented "commitment to the poor"; rejection of it meant rejecting the poor in this class warfare vision of the world. Father Mengel was then pastor of a parish with eighty thousand Catholics; around four hundred attended the special International Labor Day mass Krause used as the focus of his story. Then thirty-five, he had gone to Chile in 1971, at the onset of the Allende government. Krause noted that numerous Columban priests from Ireland, the United States, Canada, Australia, or New Zealand were living in CEBs scattered through Father Mengel's parish.

148. From Correa and Viera-Gallo, challenge to authority, pp. 181, 197; CCPs, pp. 193 ff; Muñoz, p. 196 (Muñoz was editor of the magazine *Pastoral Popular*); number of CEBs, "Predominio de la Corriente Liberacionista," *Carta Confidencial*, op. cit., #9, August 27, 1987, p. 28. Faced with stiffening church resistance to alliances with Marxists, radical theologians began fashioning a new framework for cooperation, building (inter alia) on "the traditional sympathy of progressive Christianity for the Cuban revolution" and "communion with the Nicaraguan experience." One problem: what to do about violence, "not rejected in principle" by the communities. One clear area of consensus: "real democracy" must be the goal, an aggressive fight for human rights, social change, popular action, the means (ibid., pp. 206–207). (The enthusiasm for democracy would seem odd, for some, coming from those otherwise committed to the defense of one of the longest lasting totalitarianisms in the Western Hemisphere, Cuba, and one of the bloodiest dictatorships, Nicaragua.)

149. Edwin Harrington and Mónica González, in their book, *Bomba en una calle de Palermo* (Santiago: Editorial Emisión, 1987), p. 309, quote former U.S. Attorney Eugene M. Propper as saying Willoughby went to see him in Washington in 1978 to offer a deal: Chile would hand over Brig. General Contreras—whom Propper was trying to have deported to the United States as the "brains" behind the assassination of Orlando Letelier—if the U.S. would lay off one of Contreras' young subordinates, Capt. Armando Fernández Larios, also implicated in that murder. According to this account, Willoughby was sent as the emissary of Gen. Sergio Covarrubias, chief of staff of the presidency. The story seems highly improbable. Willoughby had left government service after two years as press secretary because of severe health problems, and has never again worked in government. If he did make such an "offer" to Propper, it would have more probably reflected what appeared, in his interview with this author, to be

his own antagonism toward Contreras. Further, as he indicated in that interview, Pinochet has, through the years, taken many "hits" from abroad rather than surrender Contreras, and it is even less likely that he would have even considered such a plan then, when he was dealing with severe rumblings within the military.

150. The assertion that Chile denied having signed such an agreement appears in Harrington and González, op. cit., p. 291. Propper disclosed the deal during a bench conference in the Letelier trial with Judge Barrington Parker. Under it, he said, "any information which we had . . . would be used only in the U.S. courts, or given to the government of Chile. That is, we would not spread it to the press, and Chile, in turn, said if it came up with any information on the Letelier case, it would give it to the U.S." Silbert himself later defended the deal, saying that "if one is going to uncover a tight-knit conspiracy," it is "virtually indispensable" to have the testimony of an insider. *Facts on File 1979 Yearbook* (New York: Facts on File, Inc., 1980), pp. 74–75, 234. Propper would himself later—and egregiously—"spread it out," coauthoring a book about the case (rare, though not entirely unheard of for former prosecutors), and speaking out publicly on what was learned in the course of a supposedly confidential investigation. Indeed, his public disclosures at a conference in Caracas, on February 22, 1983, were instrumental in the decision of the government of Italy to inquire into the possibility of extraditing Townley, and the government of Argentine actually to file for and get (a very nearly successful) extradition hearing.

Details of Townley's expulsion from Harrington and González, op. cit., pp. 257–259, 287–288, 290–292. The authors write from a decidedly leftist perspective, and are quite selective about what they emphasize, what they omit, in what is otherwise a painstakingly detailed journey through the subterranean mazes of intelligence services in many countries. They assert that at the farewell for General Contreras, President Pinochet's wife made a surprise appearance, and is alleged to have said, "an injustice has been committed against you, and I don't know how it can be repaired"— "evidence" of an alleged repudiation of her husband's action. They also claim that the only active duty general to attend was Gen. Herman Brady Roche, then defense minister and one of Pinochet's closest collaborators (and rumored heir apparent), who self-destructed for appearing to side with Contreras. (He did not; indeed, General Brady was named only the month before to the newly created rank of lieutenant general, which enabled him to remain in uniform beyond the limit for compulsory retirement, and he continued to serve for several more years.)

151. Virginia Prewett, "The Mysterious Letelier Affair: Another Rush To Judgment?" a Special Report published in September 1978 by the Council for Inter-American Security, Washington, D.C., p. 19.

152. In an interview with Jeremiah O'Leary, published in the *Washington Star*, November 15, 1978, cited by Harrington and González, op. cit., p. 315. The description was given by lawyers for the Cuban defendants fingered by Townley as the actual perpetrators of the murder, in an effort to discredit him as a witness. *Facts on File 1979 Yearbook*, op. cit., p. 114.

153. Data on the trial, sentencing, and Judge Parker's remark from *Facts on File 1979 Yearbook*, op. cit., pp. 19, 234, 369. (Propper reported receiving death threats immediately before the trial.) Townley talked more than even he

knew while in custody. Among other things, he claimed that the DINA had developed for possible use in case of war with Argentina or Peru a lethal gas named "Sarin," which paralyzed the nervous system. He also said he had brought a cylinder containing that gas to the U.S. in 1976 for possible use in the Letelier murder. The Chilean government denied the story, but in January 1982, Senator Kennedy made available to the press further details about the gas he had obtained from the FBI. In February 1982, the FBI also made available copies of fifty-two letters written by the presumably unsuspecting but very cooperative witness Townley to his wife, friends, and officials of the government, containing all manner of allegations about his former security service chiefs and colleagues, as well as the claim that his own legal expenses had been paid by the Chilean government in 1978 and 1979. Extensive excerpts from those letters are reproduced in *Bomba en una calle de Palermo*, op. cit.

154. Muñoz, op. cit., p. 28, and for case closed, p. 33. As indicated previously, the case closed remark was made by Jeane Kirkpatrick, then U.S. ambassador to the United Nations, during an August 1981 visit to Santiago. The following March, Thomas Enders, assistant secretary of state, said on his visit to Santiago, that the U.S. expected "a decision in the near future in respect to the trial of those responsible" for the murders as a precondition for a U.S. resumption of military arms sales and assistance to Chile. On May 14, 1979, Chief Justice Israel Bórquez of the Chilean Supreme Court rejected the extradition requests for the three officers, saying that the evidence against them was insufficient because it was based "on a paid accusation"; the U.S. temporarily recalled its ambassador, and on June 14, Pinochet followed suit, recalling his. On October 1, the Supreme Court ruled similarly in a second U.S. extradition request, again citing inadequate evidence and provisions of Chilean law, and the dance of the ambassadors was repeated. In 1981, a Chilean military court which had heard evidence in the case over a three-year period, found the three officers innocent. Refusal to deport the three—in accord with Chilean law—was not the same as noncooperation; as early as 1978, Chile had pledged its full cooperation in the investigation. How much it actually gave will remain for future inspection of secret records in the case. In November 1980, the case took yet another turn when a federal judge in the U.S. ruled that the Chilean government should pay $2.9 million and the three ex-DINA officers another $2 million directly to the families of Letelier and Ronni Moffit. The Chilean government argued immunity from the jurisdiction of a foreign government; before that matter was finally resolved in its favor (though not accepted by Congress, as we shall see), another period of tension ensued concerning the possible seizure of Chilean assets in the U.S. to satisfy the judgment.

155. On January 21, 1987, Fernández Larios, by then a thirty-seven-year-old major, resigned his commission, and sometime that day or a few days thereafter, left Chile, apparently in the company of two FBI agents. On February 4, 1987, he appeared before U.S. District Court Judge Barrington Parker in Washington, pleading guilty to two charges of being an accessory after the fact in the Letelier-Moffitt murders. After his mysterious trip to the United States, Fernández Larios had, on January 29, signed a plea-bargaining agreement under which he would agree to plead guilty to those reduced charges in return for telling what he knew about the planning and

execution of the crime. On May 6, he was sentenced, and on September 10, following a petition for reduction of sentence, the sentence was set aside and Fernández Larios was released. Under the plea-bargaining agreement, he was given a new identity and allowed to remain in the United States under the witness-protection program. In an interview with *El Mercurio*, following his court appearance, Fernández Larios said he decided to skip to the United States "to clear his name." In response to a question, he said that "General Pinochet did not know about the murder of the former foreign minister Orlando Letelier. I believe that he only knew the cover story which was invented later." " 'Pinochet Ignoraba Plan Para Asesinar a Letelier'; Dijo Fernández Larios a *'El Mercurio,'* " February 13, 1987, p. 1. The newspaper put the English-language words "cover-up" in parenthesis next to the Spanish "historia falsa." *El Mercurio* reporter Jenny del Río had submitted written questions, and Fernández Larios's lawyer Axel Kleiboemer telephoned the answers. The major also told the newspaper he knew nothing about the murder of General Prats in Buenos Aires. In his appearance before Judge Parker, he said that when DINA chief General Contreras briefed him on the murder mission he said he instructed him that he "should never say that he went to see Mr. Letelier, because if General Pinochet should find out about that, he would kick me out of the army." "Interrogatorio del Juez Parker a Armando Fernández Larios," February 22, 1987, p. 1. That assertion would fit with what Federico Willoughby told the author during our previously cited interview in Santiago, that when Pinochet learned of DINA's complicity, he was overheard in his office shouting at Contreras, who immediately afterwards requested retirement.

156. The "Soviet agent" quote is from the late Rep. Larry McDonald (D-Ga.), "Extensions of Remarks," *Congressional Record*, June 24, 1977, p. E 4057. The eleven documents introduced by McDonald (pp. E 4057–4063) reveal a wide-ranging and worldwide webwork of activities involving Letelier, many in direct concert with the DGI, others through contacts with Beatriz Allende; Clodomiro Almeyda (the very radical former foreign minister then serving as executive secretary of the Popular Unity in exile); Carlos Altamirano, from his East German base and his worldwide travel as well as his work with individuals and organizations in the U.S. Columnist Jack Anderson broke the briefcase story on December 20, 1976; a few months later, Senate sources leaked another set of documents to columnists Rowland Evans and Robert Novak. The *Washington Post* published a "rebuttal," discounting the importance of the revelations, then declined to print a second Evans and Novak column answering the "rebuttal." The *Post* also refused to publish a letter from a media-monitoring organization, Accuracy in Media (AIM). The *Post*, the *Washington Star* and the *New York Times* then published a full-page paid ad prepared by AIM. Veteran Latin America writer Virginia Prewett, whose syndicated column did not appear in Washington, obtained a full set of the "Briefcase Papers," offering them to Washington newspapers, radio and TV stations as well as to two Washington magazines—without success. Only the *Star* did limited reporting of the issue, but as Prewett observes, "there was never a press firestorm over Letelier's 'Briefcase Papers' to compare with the firestorm accusing Chile at the time of the murder." Prewett, op. cit. McDonald's Congressional Record insertion—which included his call for an investigation—was

the first full Washington exposure of the "Briefcase Papers." It is illustrative of the nature and commitment of the left-wing establishment's pro-Allende, anti-junta zeal already in 1976 that the State Department moved quickly to waive visa impediments for Allende's widow, Hortensia, so she could attend Letelier's funeral. Bishop James S. Rausch, secretary-general of the Catholic Bishops' Conference in the United States, officiated at the requiem funeral mass at Washington's St. Matthew's Cathedral; Joan Baez sang; and Sen. George McGovern (D-S.D.) was among those who gave eulogies. Ambassadors of more than twenty countries attended the funeral services. "Asistieron 2,500 Personas A Una Misa En Honor De Orlando Letelier," AP dispatch datelined Washington in *La Gaceta*, Tampa, Fla., October 1, 1976, p. 17.

157. Argentine President Juan Carlos Onganía, deposed in 1970 after four years in the Casa Rosada, had enunciated a doctrine of "ideological frontiers"—identifying communism as an interloper which should be as much excluded from the Americas as a physical intruder. At the Tenth Session of Commanders of the Armies of the Americas in Caracas early in 1974, Gen. Jorge Raúl Carcagno, head of the Argentine army, repudiated that concept. Much to the chagrin of the U.S. delegation, he was supported by Gen. Edgardo Mercado Jarrín, commander of the very leftist Peruvian army. As Harrington and González observe, he faced a situation not unlike Prats' as he, like Prats, made clear his ideological as well as formal support for a leftist president, in his case, Juan Perón: "Not all [Argentine] officers, not even the majority, shared Carcagno's thinking." Carcagno was Prats' principal protector; with Perón dead, Carcagno was among the first ousted, and Prats' security responsibility shifted. Those authors wrote: "Transferring the security of Carlos Prats from the Army Intelligence Service to the [civilian] State Intelligence Service was like giving the lettuce to the canary to watch...." Harrington and González, op. cit., pp. 174–175, 182–183.

158. Harrington and González, op. cit., pp. 457–459, 461–463. For the Prats women—understandably—the notion of letting someone go on a technicality was pure and simple injustice, or callousness, or both. The concept of "plea bargaining"—a choice between the lesser of evils distasteful even to Americans—is unknown under the Napoleonic code in Latin countries.

159. Asked by Judge Parker at his sentencing on May 11, 1979, if he had any regrets or remorse, Townley said he felt "a great deal of remorse for the death of Ronni Moffitt." *Facts on File 1979 Yearbook*, op. cit., p. 369.

Prewett, op. cit., p. 4. Simon had become the first U.S. cabinet-level official to visit post-Allende Chile, arriving there for a ten-hour meeting on May 7, 1976. He said the junta's policies "are clearly laying the foundation for viable economic development," but warned that "there is an extricable relationship between our economic freedoms and our personal and social freedoms." Before leaving, the secretary said he was "pleased" by the government's decision to release forty-nine prisoners on the eve of his arrival and to take other ameliorating steps. Despite his findings, Congress voted a month later to forbid all military aid to Chile and limit heavily conditioned economic aid to $27.5 million—which Pinochet later spurned. Careful cultivation of contacts over the following years—and a number of important steps announcing easing of restrictions announced by Pinochet earlier in 1979—were to have culminated with the Cauas visit.

11

Mission Accomplished

To rebuild is always slower and more arduous than it is to destroy.
For that reason, we know that our mission will not be so fleeting as
we would like, and that is why we specify no timetables, fix no time
frames. Only when the country has achieved the social peace neces-
sary for true progress and social development to which it is entitled,
and Chile no longer shows a face reflecting hatreds, will our mission
be accomplished. To achieve those goals, we ask for the help of God,
we ask our people for their self-denial and patriotism, and to those
with responsibility for governing, we ask their unlimited devotion,
all to the benefit of the cause which we have embraced.

Augusto Pinochet, in an address in The Diego Portales Building,
October 11, 1974

Some months before those lines were spoken, General Carlos Prats
González, rushing as though by premonition to complete his memoirs,
wrote that the essential error of the Allende regime was that it
attempted to cram into three years what, legally, it had a six-year franchise for. The error, he wrote, was even graver inasmuch as in the course
of that first term, Allende could have succeeded in uprooting the institutional forces arrayed in such stubborn ideological inflexibility against
him: a parliament "relatively opposed"; a judiciary "under the unrestricted control of the bourgeoisie"; a comptroller-general of "capitalist
mentality"; and a writing and electronic press whose dominant elements were also opposed to him. The general did not add that, based on
the election results that put Allende in the presidency, he also did not
have with him in his revolutionary fervor somewhere around 65 percent
of the Chilean people. Nonetheless, General Prats wrote, Allende should
have presided over a six-year transition which would have led to a full-
fledged Socialist regime in 1976.[1]

Once the dust of battle settled, Augusto Pinochet and his associates
also set out to create a revolution. Like Allende, they faced formidable
internal opposition. Unlike Allende, they faced external hostility from

780

all sides. Very few, anywhere, were willing to suspend disbelief—as most of the world had for Allende—about the path they had chosen, the means they sought to apply, their chances of success.

But this is a very particular, very special fascist regime. The economic policy, for instance; in that field you have the extreme application of the free law of the market. Of course, in a very monopolistic economy that means a system in which the industrialists are free to compete—what they call to compete—at the level of prices they wish and, at the same time, salaries are established by decree. This, then, is a free market for a small segment of the population, the owners of the monopolies, the owners of the land, a small segment of the Chilean population. The general policies applied in the economic field are those supported by the so-called Chicago school. That has not been applied in any other capitalistic society. . . . Every day the civilian group against the junta is increasing and, at the same time, some sectors of the armed forces—of the families of the armed forces—are becoming the victims of the economic policies applied by the junta. That would create a deterioration of the position of this group of generals serving the interests of a very small group of the Chilean population and would create some kind of new objective condition which would open the road for a political change in Chile.

Orlando Letelier, a short time before his murder in 1976[2]

Socialist economist Letelier was, of course, reflecting not only his own personal loathing of the regime which had held him prisoner for 364 days, but also conventional socialist wisdom about economic development. He was wrong on every major conclusion, but he was right on one premise: not even the generals who presided over Brazil's economic "miracle" of the 1960s and 1970s had dared apply true market economy strategies as were the Chileans. Since that conventional wisdom also happened to be the dominant orthodoxy about economic development, few were willing to accord the Chilean experiments a patient hearing, either.[3]

Nor did the largely isolated Chilean leaders resort to the traditional Latin American fall-back: of blaming others, and principally the United States, for their failures, their short-falls. Since it was the tradition in Latin America—and, in recent years, among the intelligentsia of the United States as well—to impute much of the burden of responsibility to the United States for success/failure within Latin societies, it would be that much longer before anyone would be willing to recognize what the Chileans did achieve by themselves.

THE SUPREME COMMANDER

I will die and the person who succeeds me will also die. But there won't be elections.

Augusto Pinochet, then fifty-nine, as quoted in an AP Santiago dispatch published in U.S. newspapers, June 23, 1975

That was a reckless promise Pinochet did not keep. But the message implicit in it—the one that said anything less than a profound revolution would have meant that the blood of September had been shed in vain—that one he did set out to keep. Once goals were clarified, Pinochet moved rapidly to do what such far-reaching goals demanded: end rule-by-committee and install himself as the unquestioned leader of his regime of "liberty in authority." Definitions were the first step. Pinochet coined "liberty in authority." Other junta members expressed variations on that theme, all agreeing on three fundamentals: (1) Chile's political past offered no viable ground on which to rebuild; (2) nor did Chile's economic past; (3) nothing of lasting value could be built which would reintroduce into the body politic the errors of the past, and above all, the insidious cancer of Marxists-Leninists committed to manipulating the system so as eventually to devour it. In short, as the junta said boldly in its March 11, 1974, "Declaration of Principles": "it is essential to change the mentality of Chileans." With the passage of the years, and in the measure they believed they were closing on that goal, their thoughts turned increasingly to life beyond the junta, to the "guided democracy" they believed they were building. Said one of the second wave of junta members, air force General Fernando Matthei Aubel: "We are democrats at heart. The admiral [José Toribio Merino] and I have known other countries, and I have lived in England, in the United States. We both speak fluent English. I speak German as well, and we drew nourishment from Western philosophy. The president, as well, has drawn on Christian philosophy, and he is the conductor of this process."[4]

Pinochet, the man who ordered politics into a deep sleep in Chile, became "conductor of the process" by, in effect, politicizing the military as perhaps never before in the history of the country. As a result, when internal opposition did flare up within the military—and there were three such identified flare-ups—he was able to extinguish those flickerings of rebellion virtually effortlessly, the surface image of junta solidarity barely singed.

On September 21, 1973—ten days after the coup—Decree Law #33 suspended the operation of the Examining and Appeals Boards governing promotions of army officers, shifting that authority exclusively to the army commander-in-chief: Pinochet. On Christmas Eve 1973, yet another Decree Law gave him sweeping new powers over promotions and retirement. This decree—though effective that day—was not published until ninety days later. In September 1975, some concessions were written back into the rules, but none which seriously diminished Pinochet's power, and one which radically transformed past practice. In the past, general officers sat on the Examining Boards for senior army officers, but disputed cases went to a different and broadly based Appeals Board. Now, the generals on the renamed Selection Boards were both judges and juries, themselves handling appeals from their selections. (Just how important that separation of powers could be was illustrated by a case with historic portents: the experience of Herman Brady Roche, a key figure in the 1973 revolution and one of Pinochet's closest collaborators thereafter. In 1971, then Colonel Brady was ordered into retirement by the Examining Board. On appeal, there were two votes against him—Generals Prats and Schaufauser, the two army representatives. His career was saved by the three other votes—Allende's defense minister, and the navy and air force commanders-in-chief who served on that board. Brady later not only got his star but went on to become one of the first lieutenant generals in the Chilean army, enabling him to serve on many years past normal retirement.)

Parallel with these moves, there was another: grade inflation. When Allende came to power, there were nineteen army generals, separated by only four years of active service. Under Allende, the number jumped to twenty-five, the spread to nine years between the most senior general (Prats, date of service, 1934) and the newest (Lutz, Palacios, and Carrasco, 1942). By 1980, there were thirty-nine army generals, and by 1984, fifty-four; from the most senior (Pinochet, 1937), the spread now extended twenty years to the most junior (1956). Since the 1980 constitution empowers Pinochet to remain as army chief for eight years beyond the end of his presidential term in 1990, it is conceivable that, by the time of his retirement, thirty-four years of service would separate Captain-General Pinochet from the most junior "colleague" among his generals. Wrote military historian (and junta critic) Genaro Arriagada: "Naturally, such an explosive increase in the number of officers who enjoy this rank has to have ended by affecting negatively their dignity and influence . . . [In a similar vein,] in that picture of differences of age, the very idea of 'corps' or of 'equals' has disappeared. General Pinochet is assured of heading a group of generals who not only owe him their promotion, but in which the youngest among them will react as a captain would in the presence of a general."[5]

On September 19, 1978, a new army flag rank was created: lieutenant general (and *generales de division* were renamed *mayores generales*, and *generales de brigada, brigadier generales).* The next day, three major generals were promoted to the new rank: Herman Brady, Raúl Benavides Escobar, and Carlos Forestier Haengsten. Since all three were then serving in presidentially appointed jobs, and since all three were past mandatory retirement age, it meant that all three would continue to remain on active duty solely and exclusively at the pleasure of the president. It bears noting that, until the return of Vice Admiral Patricio Carvajal as defense minister in 1983, all of those who served in that post after 1978 (Benavides, Forestier, and Washington Carrasco) were lieutenant generals whose continuance in the military depended on the president keeping them in that job. There was one other important change involving general officers: In September 1979, General of the Army Pinochet (the traditional title for the army commander-in-chief) referred to himself for the first time as "Generalísimo." In June 1981, the arrangement was formalized and a new wrinkle added: for the first time since colonial times, the commander-in-chief of the army also held the title: Captain-General. Thus, as president, he was "Generalísimo" of the armed forces, in his army role (which he never abandoned), General of the Army and Captain-General. (Pinochet himself, in a 1985 interview, said assigning the title "Generalísimo of the Armed Forces" to the presidency was a means of demonstrating that the military remained subordinate to the political power— roughly the equivalent of the U.S. concept of the president as "Commander-in-Chief.")

There was an even more draconian move made regarding colonels: Decree Law #624 of 1974 required that colonels serving in that grade for three years submit their resignations, which would then be considered by the Selection Board. But since, in order to achieve a general's star, colonels needed at least four years in grade until 1979, five thereafter, the practical effect was that colonels had to enjoy the good opinion not just of their peers (as before), but also of the government (since government and military high command were now one and the same) to reach flag officer rank. This, junta critic Arriagada argued, was contrary to "the highest moral values of a leader of troops . . . [and] overlooked the fact that the military serve the interests of the nation, whatever may be the form of government or persons who make it up."[6]

Figures are not available, but there was one other significant element in the strategy of subordinating the military to the goals and purposes of the revolution: purging the armed forces, from top to bottom, of the very considerable number of hard leftists, as well as a number who had openly collaborated with the Allende regime, or demonstrated their distaste for the junta. Several generals and admirals were quietly allowed to take retirement, and a number of them went into exile. Of two charged with high crimes, one of them died while in imprisonment, another was sent into exile and stripped of his citizenship. At one detention center, ninety-five military men were discovered among the prisoners in the first year after the coup, thirty of them officers. At least two officers were identified as under sentence of death.[7]

Through a series of such moves, Pinochet ultimately concentrated in his hands power over the lives of senior officers formerly shared, under the 1925 constitution, by the president, the Senate and the army commander-in-chief. Curiously, while his power over the army reached (and probably exceeded) a level not seen since the Ibáñez dictatorship four decades before, his power was less, in one important respect, than that of the elected presidents who preceded him: the power to appoint the commanders-in-chief of the other armed services, including Carabineros.

Under one interpretation, the sitting members of the junta at the time of the 1989 presidential elections could remain in their posts for eight years thereafter, beyond the power of that first openly-elected president to remove. Wrote Arriagada: "That political aberration . . . means that a president elected by the opposition, for example, could have as commanders-in-chief, immovably during his entire term of office, sirs Pinochet, Merino, Matthei and Stange."

Although Pinochet did, in fact, share this and other key powers with his colleagues of the junta—and they, too, acquired comparable control over their own services—he also steadfastly moved to locate himself clearly above them. In that, he succeeded beyond any serious discussion—although not nearly to the extreme hecklers claimed, as in this: ". . . from mid-1976 onwards, one stopped almost completely talking about Merino and Leigh as the men in charge of the economic and social sectors. General Pinochet held executive power entirely in his hands."[8]

There were formal steps, as well as the symbolic, informal ones. Decree Law #527 of June 26, 1974 (Statute of the Government Junta) formally ended the concept of Pinochet as "first-among-equals" in collegial rule: order of precedence was established, with him as number one, Merino two, Leigh three, and Mendoza four. That statute also mandated the requirement that junta decisions be adopted by unanimous vote.

As of December 17, 1974, Pinochet became President of the Republic, and as such, the supreme authority of the nation. He had, of course, until then been titled President of the Junta of Government. He remained as the presiding member of the junta. Decree Law #1426 of 1976 insulated the junta against mandatory retirement, stipulating only three grounds for retirement: death, resignation, or permanent disability. Under Decree Law #537, the president exercised executive authority, subject to junta agreement (though he exercised it solely in regulatory matters and appointment of mayors; his powers would subsequently be greatly expanded under the 1980 constitution, as we shall shortly see). Legislative power was exercised by the junta, decree laws requiring the signatures of all four members. (The Judiciary remained intact, although with the country living continually under a state of emergency—or more—from September 11, 1973, until early 1988—the power of military courts was greatly expanded, that of civilian courts commensurately circumscribed.)

There matters rocked along more or less in equipoise until early 1978. Two events changed the equation. The first was President Pinochet's seemingly petulant reaction to the 1977 United Nations condemnation of Chile for human rights violations, the fourth consecutive, calling, as had the earlier ones, for a quick return to democracy. On December 21, 1977, the president called for a "consultation," so that "every man, every woman, and every youth in this country will have to decide, in the secrecy of his conscience, whether he supports the president in his defense of the dignity of Chile and reaffirms the legitimacy of the government of the Republic . . . or whether, in contrast, he supports the resolution of the United Nations and its pretension to impose our future destiny on us from abroad . . ." Angry reaction to such outside sermonizing was not limited to Pinochet; in August of that same year, General Gustavo Leigh had angrily denounced U.S. President Jimmy Carter as a "hypocrite," for a human rights policy which condemned Chile at the same time his government was seeking rapprochement with the Castro dictatorship in Cuba, then in its eighteenth year of totalitarian rule. But Leigh was troubled by the tone and tenor of the "consultation," and what he perceived to be the growing imperiousness of the president. Joined by other air force generals and admirals, he urged Pinochet to call it off—only he went public. Héctor Humeres Magnan, for ten years the comptroller-general and the man who, from that post, had repeatedly rejected as illegal Allende decrees, ruled illegal the calling of the "consultation." He was fired. In the balloting on January 4, 1978, three-quarters of those voting backed Pinochet. Although he had insisted the "consultation" had no internal significance, in its aftermath an elated President Pinochet said the outcome demonstrated that no other elections would be needed in Chile for at least ten years. Hyperbole notwithstanding, the outcome greatly strengthened the claim to legitimacy of his government—and of Pinochet's paramountcy within it.[9]

The second public event—series of events, really—came a few

months later with the U.S. accusations, followed by the Townley revelations, that Orlando Letelier had been murdered at the instigation and direction of Chile's security service and chiefs (detailed in the preceding chapter). Leigh—and right-wing leader Pablo Rodríguez Grez—supposedly called for dissolution of the junta. But behind the scenes, tension had already reached the breaking point between the two strong-willed men, Leigh and Pinochet (see preceding chapter). The last straw was Leigh's previously cited interview with Milan's *Corriere della Sera* in which he called for a return to normalcy in Chile within five years. On July 24, 1978, the junta declared Leigh's "absolute impossibility" of serving, and when he refused to resign voluntarily, fired him. Eight air force generals declined to replace him, and—as per established practice—when one junior to them (General Matthei) accepted the commander-in-chief's baton, they went into retirement. Other officers resigned in protest.[10]

This "coup-within-a-coup" died out almost as quickly as it had flared up. There were later rumblings of discontent within the military, far and away the most serious ones over the ouster of General Contreras as head of the state security agency the following year,[11] and again, in 1985, when President Pinochet summarily rejected the political opening proposed under the church-mediated National Accord. But there never again was an open challenge to his authority, and never again any question about the power he wielded.

As noted earlier, in September 1979, Pinochet referred to himself for the first time as "Generalísimo of the Armed Forces." During the annual independence celebrations in September of that year, there was an event fraught with symbolism: the president and his defense minister placed the first floral wreath at the "Altar of the Fatherland," the resting place of the remains of the liberator Bernardo O'Higgins. They were followed by the vice-commander of the army and chief-of-staff of the army; then, in third place, the navy, followed by the air force, and then by Carabineros.[12] Thus, not only did Generalísimo Pinochet outrank all the others, but the armed service he simultaneously commanded—the army—came next in order of precedence and authority. That arrangement was solidified in the 1980 constitution by transitory article 14, under which Pinochet no longer remained a member of the junta, but had, as his substitute, the next-in-line in army seniority. And that man served at the pleasure of the president.

The destinies of Chile were now firmly in his hands. But to the very end, the three nonarmy members of the junta continued to exercise their legislative function and to guard jealously their second prerogative, as the constituent body for the transition to democracy. In June 1987, all three said publicly they believed the next president should be a civilian and a "younger" man. Having gone on record to that effect, none of them again raised the subject as the deadline approached for them to make their final choice as to the junta's presidential nominee.

A NEW CONSTITUTION

The framework of "rebuilding the country morally, institutionally, and materially" began to take shape as of September 24, 1973, with the appointment of a commission created to study, prepare and propose a preliminary draft of a new constitution. Preeminent among the members in the early days was Jaime Guzmán Errázuriz, a young law professor at the Catholic University of Chile, and a leading conservative activist dating back to his student days. His pen (and voice as a commentator at feisty Radio Agricultura) had been among the most potent weapons in the war of words and ideas against Salvador Allende. To one observer sympathetic to the junta, this "tiny conventicle of civilian advisors of a *franquista* tendency that sometimes verges on the theocratic" achieved influence that went "almost unchallenged." In later years, the commission's chairman, Enrique Ortúzar Escobar, emerged as the dominant figure—much to the chagrin of his former boss. A lawyer, Ortúzar had served President Jorge Alessandri as minister of the interior, secretary-general of government, foreign minister, and, finally, as justice minister. He was not quite fifty-nine when Pinochet appointed this man who was as stubborn in his convictions as he was relentless in pursuing them.

The record of the commission's deliberations is spotty, mainly because of the secrecy they decided was necessary to conduct their work effectively; but it also seems clear that they tapped into deep "theocratic" and Portalian yearnings that were latent among the revolution's leaders, particularly Pinochet.[13] Made up initially of seven men and one woman, it was originally (and erroneously) named the Constituent Commission. In 1976, the name was changed to Commission for the Study of a New Constitution. In the first years—over the strong objections of at least one member—the commission advised the junta and cabinet ministers on the drafting of some laws as well. Altogether, eleven persons served on the commission—including former top Christian Democrat leader and senator Juan de Dios Carmona (expelled from the party for "collaboration"). Their work continued uninterruptedly from September 24, 1973, until October 5, 1978, producing a 301-page conceptual framework followed by a 104-page detailed draft constitution. That draft included a preamble and fourteen chapters with 123 permanent constitutional articles and eleven transitory articles (covering the period from the time the new constitution would take effect until the return to civilian rule).[14]

While that task was underway, the junta moved to broaden its support base. One of the most persistent criticisms—leveled even by those congenial to the revolution—was the "blunder" of failing to seek an accommodation with former President Eduardo Frei Montalva. During a one hour and fifty-minute speech preceding a huge torchlight rally in downtown Santiago on the second anniversary of the coup, Pinochet announced plans for a Council of State.[15] Among those who would be invited to participate, he said, would be the three living ex-presidents of Chile. When the council came into being, on July 15, 1976, it was presided over by former President Jorge Alessandri Rodríguez; former President Gabriel González Videla was one of the other seventeen members of the blue-ribbon (and decidedly conservative) panel. Eduardo Frei declined to participate.[16]

That Jorge Alessandri should preside over this council was both a supreme irony and a supreme guarantee of rectitude. His father, the former President Arturo Alessandri Palma, had not only been forced out in what amounted to a military coup, but had returned to the presidency long enough to preside over the creation of the constitution of 1925. As to Jorge Alessandri's integrity, not even his deadliest enemies ever called that into account.[17]

The council was created by the first of four constitutional acts, drafted by the Study Commission and announced on September 11, 1975. Commission chairman Ortúzar said the intention was to put an organic juridical floor under the new political, social and economic reality of the country, and to do so by stages. "Traditional democracy," President Pinochet said a few days later in explaining and defending the new strategy, "is defenseless to protect liberty, the law, mutual respect and [the opportunity] to live in progress and justice. It will be necessary to create new legal mechanisms whereby to give a more efficient and a more authentic backing to the will of the people . . ."[18] On the following anniversary, September 11, 1976, three more constitutional acts followed: the first abolished Chapter I of the 1925 constitution,* substituting a statement of the "Essential Bases of the Chilean Institutional System," stipulating the legality of past and future junta laws, decrees and regulations. Sovereignty, it said, resides in the nation, and—in one paraphrase—"does not recognize any limitation other than respect for

---

* The four articles of that chapter define the state, the source of its sovereignty, its inviolability, and this: "No magistrate, no person, nor gathering of persons, can attribute to itself, not even on the pretext of extraordinary circumstances, any other authority or rights other than those which are expressly conferred on them by law." Clearly the abrogation of this article and its substitution were indispensable if the junta's acts were to be legally defensible.

the rights emanating from human nature."[19] Constitutional acts three and four defined rights and duties of the person and limitations to which those rights may be subject under states of emergency. Putting an end to patchwork constitution-building became one of the Council of State's early orders of business.

Inaugurating the work of the council, Alessandri said: "For years, I have been pointing out with tireless insistence that the constitutional regime in force and prevailing political practice were counterproductive to the ends each sought . . . The phenomenon we lived was not that of a sudden and chance [ocasional] breakdown of the constitution," of a legal system "merely betrayed"; far from that, he said, what Chile had experienced was "the complete breakdown, from its very bases, of the juridical institutionality in force . . . such a disaster carries within itself, inevitably, the necessity of constructing a new [institutionality], also from the foundation up."[20]

As the institution-building process went forward, the junta members moved resolutely to counter rising political opposition—and quash rumors of internal fissures. In separate speeches early in the new year 1976, the four members of the junta said military disunity rumors were the work of a Soviet-inspired international conspiracy. And, for the first time—although they did not mention him by name—they directed fire at former president Frei, accusing him of a "treasonous attempt" to divide the armed forces.[21]

Pinochet spelled out the precise "itinerary" for the creation of the new Chile at a speech delivered on July 9, 1977, at a hill in Santiago called "Chacarillas," site of an annual Youth Day commemoration. Under "The Chacarillas Plan," as it came to be known, there would be three phases to the itinerary: the first, "recovery," would end by December 31, 1980; the second, "transition," would last until 1985; the third, "normalization," would begin in 1991. During the first, the armed forces would control the political process during the drafting and promulgation, subject to plebiscite approval, of a new constitution. During the second, civilian participation in the government would be expanded; the power of the junta would be transferred to a Council of State, and an unelective legislative body created. The third would begin with presidential elections and a return to civilian rule—except that the armed forces would continue to exercise a newly institutionalized "vigilance" over national affairs. In his presidential message on September 11, 1979, Pinochet spelled out his government's specific goals, "the seven modernizations," he called them: a new labor code; overhaul (privatization, really) of the social security system; incentives for great agricultural expansion; educational, public health, judicial and administrative reform. (In that speech, while outlining other significant foreign policy aims, he also took the first public poke at the United States.[22] On November 10, 1977, Pinochet followed up his Chacarillas speech with a letter to the Study Commission in which he spelled out these and other principles as worthy of their consideration as they crafted the new constitution.

With the economy moving rapidly out of the anarchy and collapse the government had inherited in 1973, and into a period of boom without precedent in the country's history, the regime also relaxed a number of restrictions: on March 9, 1978, the state of siege was lifted, replaced by a much milder "state of emergency"; on April 1 of that year, the overnight curfew was lifted for pedestrians; on April 19, a general amnesty was declared for all political prisoners, and that same month, a cabinet reshuffle for the first time made civilians a majority in the Cabinet. In the first two years of the revolution, a total of 7,500 persons had been arrested; in the next two years, the number dropped to one thousand. A confident government—buoyed in no small measure by the outcome of the January "consultation"—reversed itself on July 12 and agreed to allow a special United Nations human rights committee access to Chile.[23]

The 1925 constitution—as much admired outside Chile as it was almost universally discredited within—was drafted over a three-month period by a commission which included some two hundred persons, representing all the then existing political parties. All were, by present standards, center to center-right on the political spectrum, and the traditional conservative parties dominated the mix. Further, as Eduardo Frei would write years later, the real work was done by a small subcommission. President Alessandri, "who had in his hands all the levers of power," Frei added, "using flattery or threats . . . [and] the most varied resources . . . managed to impose his thesis." The new constitution was approved overwhelmingly in an August 30, 1925, plebiscite—that is, by 127,483 citizens, or barely 3 percent of the population. Indeed, only 45 percent of those eligible to vote, in a tiny electorate that still did not include women, bothered to do so, and yet that constitution would acquire the character of divine writ in the fulminations of those who later mourned, not the internal collapse of democracy in Chile, but "the death of democracy."[24] The new 1925 constitution borrowed copiously from the language of the 1833 original—but profoundly altered the balance of power. A presidential system (intended to be strong, but it wasn't) replaced the anarchy of a strong parliamentary system. The ink was barely dry before the first attempts at reform began. It would take the advent of the "machine politics" of the Christian Democrats in the 1960s to achieve the first significant changes (discussed in chapter 4). Frei justified the need for reform on grounds clearly reflecting Christian

Democrat ideology: the emergence of "scientific" techniques which demanded central state planning of the economy. Frei, who said the reform fight began in the first months of his government, described the use of the plebiscite device to effect constitutional reform in the face of an obstructionist congress as the "most significant" constitutional change to emerge from the long congressional skirmishing. Frei wrote those lines ten years before the debate over the plebiscite to ratify the 1980 constitution;[25] in their arguments against the 1980 document and the technique used to approve it, Christian Democrats rarely again referred to the imperfections of the 1925 document.

But they were not alone in rejecting it. In his May 21, 1973, message to congress, Allende had said the constitution no longer met the needs of the nation, and the Popular Unity was preparing a draft for plebiscite vote which would permit the transfer of power to the "proletariat."

It is unlikely that there was—that there could have been—a man who would better understand Chile's constitutional dilemmas in all of its dimensions than Jorge Alessandri. His own father had been ousted from the presidency in a military coup because of the paralysis of the political system produced by the rotting away of an earlier constitution. On August 16, 1978, President Pinochet turned over to the council the Study Commission's first set of conceptual recommendations, and then, on October 31, the draft constitution itself. Although the Study Commission had worked in secret, a number of outside constitutional scholars and others had been invited to offer recommendations. The Council of State now undertook to broaden even further the input base as it began the task of refining it for later consideration by the junta. More than 150 proposals were received by the December 15, 1978, deadline in response to the council's call for public comment. Organizations responding included the National Press Association, College of Journalists, Association of Broadcasters, College of Architects, and others. Between November 1978 and July 1980, when it completed its work, the council held numerous plenary and committee meetings, often inviting outside experts to appear.

Jorge Alessandri was, from the beginning, opposed to the idea of creating a "new" constitution, a process he likened to "a leap into the void." Instead, he worked for reform: "They [constitutions]," he wrote in a letter to Sergio Carrasco Delgado, "must be reformed, because however perfect they may be, habits grow up through the years which denature them . . ."[26] He was as good as his word. On July 8, 1980, in a special audience, former President Jorge Alessandri delivered the council's draft to President Augusto Pinochet. Pinochet promptly turned the document over to a seven-person working committee.

There were twenty-seven important changes between the Study

Commission and the council drafts. In one after another, what came to be known as "the Alessandri constitution" urged returning to the precepts of the 1925 constitution, and in one important case—involving the role the armed forces could play in the country's political processes—that of 1833. The changes were literally from beginning to end; even the preamble was eliminated as too "doctrinaire."

Those amendments are analyzed in detail in Jorge Carrasco's excellent book, *Alessandri: Su Pensamiento Constitucional; Reseña de su Vida Pública* (pp. 128–133). What follows are a few highlights:

—The commission proposed an eight-year term for presidents, and qualifications equivalent to those needed for senators. The council said six, and two qualifications: to be born in Chile and to be at least forty years of age, both as in the 1925 constitution.

—In case of death or disability, the commission proposed that the president's successor be designated by the Senate and serve until the next congressional election. The council wanted new elections called within ten days.

—The commission would have left to the commanders-in-chief of the services the organization of the armed forces. The council said that was inconsistent with efforts to create a strong presidency, since it would subordinate the authority of the president to the service chiefs in that important area.

—The commission proposed a 150-member Chamber of Deputies, leaving base of representation to be defined by a later Electoral Law. The council wanted 120 deputies, elected by districts.

—For the Senate: commission, thirty members, elected from a single national list; council, unanimously, elected by regions, thus to "maintain a political tradition more than a century old."

—The commission wanted to add derelection of duty to the causes for removal of generals and admirals. The council argued for leaving matters where they stood under the 1925 constitution—up to the president whether to oust his flag officers.

—The commission proposed two annual legislative sessions, lasting a total of six months. The council believed it would be better to leave it at a single session, May 21-September 18 of each year.

—The commission proposed language expanding the political reach of the military: "They are also not deliberative save for matters relative to their specific functions and in accord with their internal regulations. In structure and action, they are to submit to the juridical order and exercise the attributions which the Constitution and Law confer on them." Again unanimously, the council recommended going back to the 1833 language: obedient and nondeliberative.

—On designation of the service chiefs, the commission proposed that the president be compelled to select from the top two in seniority, and that they could not be removed from their posts. Promotions and retirements would be only as proposed by the respective service chiefs. The council said appointments should be up to the president, retirements and promotions as governed by law and regulations.

—National Security Council: The council wanted to add the ministers of interior, foreign affairs, defense, economy, and finance—so as to assure civilian domination of the NSC.

—The commission proposed that constitutional reforms be enacted as under the 1970 legislation, raising, however, the vote required to three-fifths (instead of a simple majority), and two-thirds to activate the "insistence" mechanism which put strict time limits on executive branch compliance. The council wanted the simpler 1925 rules to apply, and also greatly to limit the use of plebiscites for constitutional reform.

—The council balked at the creation of an "economic superpower," a Central Bank president and board appointed by the president to serve fourteen years. The council wanted six-year terms, a requirement that all serve exclusively in those posts, and to give a vote as well as a voice in their deliberations to the finance minister.

Above and beyond those changes, Jorge Alessandri had some ideas of his own, and one of them involved one of the most controversial—and misrepresented—political issues of modern times in Chile: the prolongation of Pinochet's power during a transition period. Alessandri identified himself as the author of the idea of a transition period, although his proposal—and then the council's—was dramatically different from that which would emerge. The highlights, as proposed by the council:

1. The transition would last five years from the date the new constitution entered into effect which, in turn, would be 180 days from the date of the plebiscite.
2. During the transition period, and for ninety days beyond, the new constitution would be in full force, except as noted below.
3. Pinochet would remain as president during the transition period.
4. The junta would remain, though with sharply curtailed power, the principal among them to designate a successor to fill out the transition term in case of death or disability of the president. As to themselves, once the transition period ended, junta members would become members for life of the Senate.
5. A bicameral appointed Congress would be created to serve during the transition period: a 120-member Chamber named by the junta, and a Senate as follows: living ex-presidents; twenty senators designated by the president from a preestablished slate, and twenty-one he could name freely. The first elections, for president

and senators, would be held within ninety days of the end of the transition period, the first for senators four years later.

6. Members of the Constitutional Tribunal, with oversight of the entire process, would be elected at least ten days before the transition period began.

7. The Election Qualifying Board (*Tribunal Calificador de Elecciones*) would begin to operate at least thirty days before the first election of president and deputies.

8. For the first three years under the new constitution, mayors would be delegated by the president (and elected thereafter).

9. Pending a new organic law governing the operation of Congress, the internal rules which governed Congress until 1973 would apply to the extent that each was compatible with the new constitution.

10. The Central Bank also would continue to operate under existing rules until new ones were legislated.

Alessandri had other important recommendations. One, which also would later become controversial, "that in the plebiscite on the new constitution, a norm should be included that would prolong in his office the present President of the Republic until the end of the transition period. Experience demonstrates that there is nothing more disturbing for national harmony that a premature presidential election." But just as he believed it important to continue with a strong executive during the transition period, so, too, he believed it was vital to have a functioning Congress, even if appointed. He gave three reasons; it would: (1) assure the faithful interpretation of the new constitution; (2) provide for public discussion of new laws, the sooner the better; (3) make possible an adequate and proper representation of the diverse democratic currents of opinion in the country.

His textual words on transition, from a letter to Carrasco dated July 21, 1980, bear close attention. Jorge Alessandri was then eighty-four-years-old. He was writing not for himself, but out of a deep knowledge of his people and their governance, out of his concern for them, for their future:

> I have proposed something for the transition period which is compatible with reality. Those who impugn the proposed mechanism forget that Mr. Pinochet is in the government with full and absolute power, and that it is forthcoming on his part to want to place himself within constitutional norms. Those of us who live with our feet on the ground are obliged to facilitate his way, proposing measures compatible with reality. The present government, to establish itself, had to oppose the force of the out-of-control [*desorbitado*] government of Allende with force. The use of this force generated suffering and

injustice, which then translate as hatreds and designs of vengeance and getting even. Those who have participated in these events are not unaware that difficult situations will have to be faced in the future. What's more, Pinochet's remaining in office [*permanencia*] is a guarantee of order and tranquility.

To propose a designated Congress is not a novelty in our country. We take pride, properly, in our "140 years" of democracy, during which half the time, through an electoral farce, Congress was designated by the President of the Republic. The sacred rights of the people have been mocked by the political parties every chance they got. They were the authors of the "Thermal Congress"* and they tried to do the same with the one which preceded it. Furthermore, through ad hoc electoral laws, the people in fact have been limited simply to ratifying [*consagrar*] as their representatives those the party directorates impose upon them. It was for that reason that I maintained, and got, a constitution that, instead of leaving this to a law with whatever name, established norms which would prevent such abuse from continuing.[27]

At this point, believing his work now done, the old man tucked a confidential note for President Pinochet in a sealed envelope and handed it to the executive secretary of the council. He instructed him to deliver it to the president the day after the plebiscite, but only in case the vote approved the new constitution. If the vote went the other way, the emissary was to await new instructions.

Before delivering the text of the council's draft to the president, Alessandri received Interior Minister Sergio Fernández, the justice minister, Miss Mónica Madariaga, and General Santiago Sinclair, chief of the presidential staff. He told them he would send along as soon as possible a comparative analysis of the two texts, commission and council. A few days later, he said that would not be necessary; he had read in the newspapers a detailed version of the proposed constitution, and it contained very important changes.

Don Jorge Alessandri—as was his custom—then repaired to the shadows to await history's verdict. Repeated efforts to get him to speak out were rebuffed; to do so, he said years later when long after the fact he finally did, would only have influenced the outcome, and he believed the decision now should repose in the hands of the Chilean people.

No one knows with certainty what happened next, in the month between the time the council finished its work and the junta produced

* He referred to a back-room deal between party bosses and de facto President Ibáñez in 1930 at the Chillán hot springs—hence the name. They agreed among themselves on who would serve in the new Congress, taking advantage of a legal technicality which said that when the number of candidates was the same as the number of vacancies, no elections were needed. President Ibáñez had his summer home at Chillán.

its version of the constitution. It is known that the junta appointed a seven-person working group, but they have never published the minutes of their meetings, nor discussed their work. Since at least two laws require such disclosure, presumably the essence of those deliberations someday will be known.[28] Speculation inevitably has centered on the assertion that Pinochet himself blue-penciled the radical changes.

What is known is that the text presented to the voters was radically different from the one drafted by the council. Carrasco has identified 175 changes in the permanent articles, eighty-five of which he classifies as important, fifty-nine as fundamental.[29] At the beginning, most rage and indignation centered on the twenty-nine transitory articles governing the transition period; as that period finally neared an end (1988–1989), attention switched to the 120 articles in the permanent constitution itself—as will be discussed in a later section.

On August 8, 1980, the junta published Decree Law #3464 approving the text of the proposed constitution. That same day, Decree Law #3465 called for a plebiscite to be held on September 11, 1980. All Chileans aged eighteen or older, including the blind and the illiterate, were obliged to vote; foreigners legally resident in the country were permitted to vote if they chose. Since there were no electoral rolls, an identity card was required to be able to vote. Mayors were charged with setting up polling places, opening no earlier than 7:30 A.M., no later than 12 noon, remaining open for eight hours.

Before the voters—on a simple ballot with a gummed edge easily sealed for secrecy—was a simple proposition: "National Plebiscite. New Political Constitution of the Republic of Chile. 1980. Yes. No." Voters were to put an "x" in the box of their choice.

But the plebiscite involved more than the constitution itself, as awesome as this alone was. It also involved the rules under which Chileans would live until 1990, including one (Article 14), which identified by name and title the person who would preside over those destinies: "the present President, General of the Army don Augusto Pinochet Ugarte."[30]

The political pot, bubbling with increasing energy in recent years, now reached a full boil.

POLITIC OR PERISH

Politics in the post-Allende period subdivide in time and space. The spaces are familiar: the hard Left, occupied by the Communists and the Socialists, and their lesser partners in Marxist-Leninist revolution; the Left-Center occupied by the Christian Democrats; the Right, after the coup, a space more of personalities than of identifiable parties. Evolution would occur in all three spaces.

In the space occupied by the parties of the hard Left, shock and cowering switched around the middle of the seventies to a declared violent war. But, as the country's return to democracy neared, belligerency gave way to schizophrenia: a refusal for reasons ideological as well as practical to renounce violence as against the hard reality of the need to design a new Trojan Horse in order to aspire to a place in the new order.

The Right as an identifiable party vanished into a diaspora of its own creation: its overwhelming support for the revolution. Through the seventies and most of the eighties, the Right remained reluctant to turn its back on the revolution. But, beginning in 1982, the men of the Right began to regroup in a multiplying plethora of miniparties as they, too, faced the dilemma of how to be viable in a post-Pinochet world.

The Christian Democrats (PDC)—and many who tagged along with them—lurched more than marched through four identifiable phases. The first, from 1973 until 1975, was mainly one of support for the revolution, albeit with increasing sullenness. The second, a period of aimlessness, exploded into the third, political activism and renewed alliances with the far Left. This focused on the fight before and immediately following the 1980 plebiscite. Economic crisis, beginning in mid-1981, became the *deus ex machina* that again rescued the party from its lassitude and confusion. Feeding on the popular discontent and anxiety fostered by the crisis, the party once again made common cause with the far Left (though not, formally, with the Communists), in what was confidently believed would be a movement to force the Pinochet government from power. The notion that Pinochet could be unseated by popular pressure died hard, and, in the end, was overtaken by events. By early 1987, the transition back to democracy—however imperfect— was, in fact, happening. The last phase for the PDC began early in 1987; it concentrated on political mobilization, internal and external, designed to position the party as the catalyst of a coalition capable of capturing power. On the axiom that if you cannot beat them, it is better then to join them, the Christian Democrats and a gaggle of lesser counter-revolutionary parties joined the process. Since so many in the PDC, and those stragglers allied with them, despised both the designers of the process and the machinery they had designed, the "joining" was surly and played out uncertainly. PDC fortunes in the post-Allende period, as the scholar Michael Fleet has observed, have clearly risen and fallen as the economy has risen and fallen—they prosper most in times of hardship.

But by late 1987 and early 1988, it was politick or perish, and so the Christian Democrats looked and sounded and acted increasingly with the cockiness and *prepotencia* which, many years before, had caused even the admiring *New York Times* to refer to "a stiffness that many considered to be arrogance."[31]

Since only the Christian Democrats pursued a coherent, above-ground strategy—although by no means a monolithic one—we shall focus mainly on their journey from 1973 to the political moment of truth of 1988.

It is true that the party as a whole did not break openly with the junta until after the party plenum in April 1975. But, as noted in chapter 9, the principal left-wing leaders of the party *never* accepted the coup, and skirmishing began within a few months of the coup.[32] Official party policy remained, however, one of "constructive" cooperation, which meant that while party members were forbidden to take policy-making jobs in the government, they were allowed to fill "technical" jobs in areas of their expertise. Some went well beyond those bounds; Jorge Cauas, a lifelong Christian Democrat who had headed the Central Bank under Frei, joined the Cabinet as finance minister on July 11, 1974, in the midst of a sharp exchange between party and junta leaders; he was among the first civilian cabinet ministers following the coup, and became, for a time, the economic "czar" of the junta.

Staunch anti-Communists from the party's more moderate ranks banded together over strong objections from the leadership to sign a letter in November 1974 published in both Chilean and leading foreign newspapers. Drafted by Frei's former defense minister, Sen. Juan de Dios Carmona, these "collaborationists" defended the junta and its goals, including the political "purification" process and outlawing of the hard Left, as necessary to rebuilding the country. This led to a new phase, "critical independence," which meant avoiding all-out confrontation, while viewing the junta as an evil to be extirpated.

Two events in 1975 sharply dramatized the dilemma facing the party. Despite public opinion polls showing overwhelming public support for the junta, the party's April plenum, bringing together about five hundred leaders and activists, voted overwhelmingly for outright opposition. That decision alienated the moderate elements in the party. In July, two former party presidents—both from the left wing of the party—joined in Caracas, Venezuela, with leaders of Allende's Popular Unity in forming a united front against the junta. That idea was flatly rejected by party leaders in Santiago; and although the powerful left wing of the party was alienated, the Caracas dissidents were not disciplined. Explanations at the time centered on the fact that the party had only specifically ruled out alliances with the Communists and they were not present at the Caracas meeting; but Socialists, even more radical than the Communists, were present, and the Socialists' last secretary general was then calling for armed struggle against the junta.[33]

When party president Patricio Aylwin argued that the party must work with enemies of Allende as well as of the military to restore democracy, he was sharply rebuked by the military. In a September 25, 1975, statement, the junta said they had not made the revolution to hand over power to old-style politicians, but rather to build a new type of democracy—without political parties. It was the clearest indication yet to the PDC and others—those willing to "endure" a one-to-three year military interregnum—that the military was settling in for a long siege, and without them.[34]

Central to the junta's strategy was the "depoliticization" of the myriad of grassroots organizations—labor, trade, guild, university, social, sports, cultural, professional, peasant, quasi-religious and others—a politicized universe which historian Gonzalo Vial has described as "that mortal menace to national consensus." More than any others, the Communists and the Christian Democrats had "invaded" and politicized these entities, weaving them into their own ideological patterns, stitching them together into the fabric of their very essence and strength. With the single exception of the unbreakable church-PDC bond, which was actually strengthened during the early years of junta rule, the depoliticization campaign was succeeding.[35] (Labor, the subject of a later discussion, was not "depoliticized," but cut off from party funding; while radicalized, it did become more "independent," and, in many ways, more labor-oriented.) No party suffered the consequences of the traumatic depoliticization surgery more than did the PDC; only new elections will reveal the true extent to which the party has succeeded in rebuilding its broad base of special interests. The same is true for the Communists, despite their vaunted ability to regroup underground; they have never before in Chile been forced so far underground, so thoroughly, for such a long time.

Although analyses of the Chilean economy routinely ignore it, the entire world suffered economic depression in 1974 and 1975, caused, in large measure, by the energy crisis precipitated by the sudden and sharp increases in oil prices decreed by the Organization of Petroleum Exporting Countries. In Chile, the crisis was aggravated by two factors: the first was the need to apply shock treatment to a mortally sick economy; the second was the credit strangulation of the country by an increasingly hostile world (in the four years, 1974–1977, Chile's public debt remained all but frozen at $3.5 billion, actually declining slightly). To make matters worse, copper prices fell disastrously.[36] In that setting of suffering, Christian Democrat maneuvering—if not political fortunes—expanded briefly. But, for most of the period, 1975–1980, the PDC was a party in jeopardy of withering away, a prospect magnified on March 12, 1977, when the junta outlawed all political parties and began seizing their assets.[37] It did, however, possess one asset of incalculable value which no one could seize and which, more than any other, held it together.

That asset was Eduardo Frei Montalva—although for a time, there was a question about his physical capacity to lead. There was no question, however, that he towered over all others in Chile who might be expected to lead opposition to the junta. But, since at the outset he offered support and not opposition, it was argued that Frei did so because he had been given to understand that new elections would be called within the first year after the coup, elections he almost certainly would have won.[38]

Such a narrow view does not seem to square with the fervor Frei brought to countering the cant surrounding Allende and September of 1973. Because it contains so much of that spirit of indignation in the face of a Big Lie, one such communication bears full inspection. It was an extraordinary letter Frei wrote on November 8, 1973, to Mariano Rumor, president of the World Union of Christian Democracy. The letter is all the more significant because Rumor, then premier of Italy, was himself presiding over a Christian Democrat coalition then "enjoying" the active support of the free world's largest Communist party, itself panicked into attempting to make common cause with its longtime rivals precisely because of the ouster of Allende in Chile. The text of Frei's letter:

> I believe it is my duty to write you, and through you, the directorate of the World Union of Christian Democracy, so that you may know our thoughts in respect to what has happened in Chile and its repercussion abroad.
>
> What happened in Chile?
>
> This country has known more than 160 years of practically uninterrupted democracy. It is worth asking then who and what are responsible for its break-down.
>
> In our judgment, the entire responsibility for this situation—and we say it without euphemisms—resides with the regime of the Popular Unity which was installed in this country.
>
> On what do we base this affirmation?
>
> That regime was always a minority yet was never willing to recognize it. It won the presidential election with 36 percent of the vote. That rose to 50 percent four months afterward in municipal elections, continuing an old Chilean tradition that the people give their support

to the recently elected government. In the congressional elections of 1973, that percentage dropped to 43 percent despite [the government] having exercised an intervention unknown in the history of Chile and having used the entire machinery of the state, enormous financial resources and pressures on individuals and organizations, unleashing a violence which caused a number of deaths and many more wounded by gunfire. Beyond that, fraud involving at least 4 to 5 percent of the vote was later proved; public agencies, among other things, falsified thousands of identity cards.

What, at bottom, was the problem?

The essence of the problem is that this minority government, presenting itself as a legal and peaceful path to socialism—that was the slogan in its national and international propaganda—was absolutely determined to install in the country a totalitarian dictatorship and was taking progressive steps to bring about that outcome, so that by 1973, there no longer was room to doubt that we were in the presence of an absolutely abnormal regime, and that few were the steps that remained to be taken to install fully a totalitarian dictatorship in Chile.

I am attaching several documents related to this point.

To the political picture must be added two facts which have been decisive in the Chilean process.

The first is that, once this government was in office, several thousand representatives of the extreme Left, of guerrilla forces, of extreme-left revolutionary movements of America, began converging on Chile. Tupamaros came from Uruguay, members of extreme or guerrilla organizations from Brazil, Bolivia, Venezuela and all other countries, committing numerous serious crimes not subject to parole [inexcarcelables crímenes]. The Embassy of Cuba was transformed into a veritable Ministry, with a larger staff—just the Embassy of Cuba in Chile—than the entire staff of our Foreign Ministry in 1970. That gives you an idea of the scope of the situation. Beyond that, we found ourselves being invaded by North Koreans and other representatives from the Socialist world.

Men known on this continent for their guerrilla activities found immediate employment in Chile, posts in the public administration, but many of them devoted their time to paramilitary training and to setting up guerrilla schools, in some cases on terrain which not even representatives of the armed forces or Carabineros were allowed to penetrate. The second fact was the accelerating importation of arms. The Christian Democrat party repeatedly protested against this. There are more than fifty articles published by the party and made known in Parliament relating to the illegal arms trade. The government always denied that assertion. Driven by its concern, the PDC introduced an arms control bill, a bill which once enacted into law served as the basis for staging raids which revealed the existence of heavy quantities of imported arms.

An objective analysis of the facts reveals that the fundamental reason why this old democracy suffered such a blow was because the government of the Popular Unity brought the country to a situation which none could any longer endure, and that it was endured so long as it was bespeaks the admirable solidness of Chilean democracy.

All of this suggests a basic reflection.

Why has what happened in Chile produced an impact so disproportionate to the size, location, population and importance of the country? Why has the reaction of the Soviet Union been so violent and extreme? Why has world communism launched this campaign to judge what has happened in Chile and to attack Christian Democracy? The reason is very clear.

Its [the Allende government's] fall has represented a blow for communism in the world. The combination of Cuba and Chile, with its 4,500 kilometers of Pacific coastline, and its intellectual and political influence in Latin America, was a decisive step toward domination in this hemisphere. That is the reason for the violent and disproportionate reaction.

This country served them as a base of operations for the entire continent. But that is not all. This gigantic publicity campaign tends to hide a basic fact: the failure of a policy which they had presented as a model for the world.

We ask only one thing: come and see for yourselves. We have the right to ask this of our friends. That's what Christian Democrat Union leader Bruno Hechk did, and he could see the truth for himself.

See for yourselves if there is a bombed-out house in any shantytown. In all of Chile, there are only two such misfortunes: La Moneda and the presidential residence acquired by the Popular Unity government. Come and see for yourselves if there is a factory or a mining center where so much as a single bomb has fallen.

We are not part of the present government. We do not defend the errors it may commit, some of them inevitable in such a terribly difficult situation.

But we cannot either accept that lies be transformed into something systematic, while the causes of the situation are hidden, thus concealing the responsibility of those who ruined and destroyed Chilean democracy.[39]

Such strong views did not spring full-blown from Frei's mind after the coup. During the last six months of Allende's government, Frei had served as president of the Senate, raising his voice frequently and powerfully against what he perceived as the wanton destruction of democratic institutions. And because he did believe so strongly that the villains were Salvador Allende and his associates, and that the damage they had done was so great that it could not be quickly mended, he kept his silence for the first twenty-one months of junta rule. Finally, in mid-1975, he spoke out at length in a magazine interview, followed by a sixty-five-page essay, "El Mandato de la Historia"; war stories of censorship notwithstanding, even a government-backed newspaper in Santiago gave coverage to "Mandato." In that tract—"notably defensive" in its first part, an apologia for his own administration—Frei attacked both the economic and social policies of the junta, arguing that the military was repeating the very errors that had led to the discrediting and overthrow of Allende. As Fleet observes, in expressing regret that he had not sought out "a broader consensus from other political and social sectors," Frei "certainly did not mean the Left."[40]

Although "Mandato" received wide coverage in and out of Chile, Frei did not thereafter exert the strong leadership many—and particularly those clamoring for confrontation—were seeking. In very real measure, that was because he no doubt understood far more than many of his tempestuous and doctrinaire coreligionists how readily the party could disconnect itself from the reality of support for the junta. Fleet quotes one-time party president Andrés Zaldívar as saying that in 1980, the party's "support from the masses is minimal"; Frei, at the same time, told of an experience he had during a visit to Chile's south. He said all of the one hundred or so people with whom he spoke indicated a preference for life under the junta, even under the existing conditions, to a return to Allende and the Popular Unity. Further, when Frei asked the same question of Christian Democrat party delegates, 80 percent responded similarly.[41]

It was, then, Frei who managed to give the confused and squabbling party a sense of point and purpose—and to keep it from straying too far to the left, a position many of the most vocal of its leaders instinctively preferred. The clamor for a more antagonistic style was reinforced as the junta cracked down on party activists.

Where did it start—the PDC sniping drawing junta fire, or vice versa? The answer is far from clear; what is clear is that the very strong and latent animosities on both sides had boiled up to the surface by 1975, and the mutual recriminations intensified thereafter.

Moss, for example, reported that a leading Christian Democrat leader told him during a 1975 return visit that of 242 party activists at the Chuquicamata copper mine, only eleven were left. Other sources have asserted that more than one-third of the top Christian Democrat activists had, at one time or another since 1973, been imprisoned, if only briefly.[42]

Whoever fired first, by the time of the 1980 plebiscite, the two sides were clearly facing each other from opposing trenches in a war needing only a reason for happening. The plebiscite provided the reason.

THE PLEBISCITE

Eduardo Frei was in the midst of a triumphal tour in newly democratic Brazil when news of the convocation of the plebiscite reached him. He went over to an immediate attack, firing broadside after broadside while still in Brazil, assuming personal command of the counterattack when he returned to Chile. Whether he willed it or not, the plebiscite became, to a large extent, a contest in which Chileans were asked to choose between Eduardo Frei and Augusto Pinochet. From the first instant, the former president made plain his complete and bitter rejection of the plebiscite, and he fought hard and tirelessly in what would become his last major battle.[43]

Support came quickly from two of the party's left-wing leaders abroad. In Caracas, former PDC President Renán Fuentealba described the plebiscite as a "farce" and "illegitimate," and said "the dictatorship will win by means fair or foul" (*por las buenas o por las malas*). From Geneva, Radomiro Tomic, the party's losing candidate in the 1970 elections, cabled Frei to express his "total support . . . in your repudiation of the farce of a plebiscite."[44]

But on this one issue, one which threatened the very essence of its hope of a franchise on power, few in the PDC—of the Right or the Left—failed to close ranks behind Frei in what became a titanic battle.

Commentators of the Left and the Right in Chile agree that the country became thoroughly politicized during the decade of the sixties. They disagree on the causes. But they agree that the beneficiaries of the process were the Christian Democrats, the Communists, and, to a lesser extent, the Socialists.[45] They prevailed because these were the parties of ideas, discipline and organization, whereas the Right disintegrated as a cohesive political force because it had come to rely on personalities, and the Radicals flew apart because they had neither the one nor the other.

Pinochet, and those around him, agreed that the parties had come to exercise excessive power in the society. But they parted company with the ideologues of the Christian Democrats as to how and why that had happened, and—obviously—what had to be done about it. Their solution was "protected democracy," the mechanism the "Constitution of Liberty" they now were putting to the vote.[46]

Whatever else might be said about the constitution of 1980, it cannot be said that it was approved in the shadows. From the moment the draft submitted by the Council of State was made public in July, Chile was buried beneath an avalanche of statements, interviews, articles, analyses, propaganda, paid advertisements, clandestine leaflets, pamphlets and periodicals, bombastic headlines and impassioned claims and counterclaims.[47] (More on the controversial subject of the terms and extent of freedom of the debate in a moment.) The Christian Democrats made plain their dismay at the prospect of having Pinochet remain in power for five more years as soon as they read the proposed transitional rules, and submitted the entire draft to study by the Group of 24, made up of constitutional and legal experts headed by a former justice minister in Allende's Cabinet, Manuel Sanhueza Cruz. "The Council of State," PDC President Andrés Zaldívar said, "has taken almost two years to produce its draft . . . We believe it is our obligation to analyze these propositions with the greatest care so as to avoid a hurried judgment that would make more difficult the debate on a subject of such importance for the future of Chile." Among the early reactions was one by a former member of Frei's Cabinet, Enrique Kraus Rusque, who characterized as "a flagrant sin of arrogance" the assertion of former presidents (Jorge Alessandri and González Videla), by way of justifying the transition period, that "save for honorable exceptions, citizens of the greatest ability and rectitude prefer to distance themselves from all political involvement."

But if the Christian Democrats were alarmed in July, they were apoplectic in August when they saw the junta's version of the proposed constitution and call for a plebiscite only thirty days later. They were particularly furious at first that the plebiscite, as they saw it, gave the citizenry only two choices: return to the chaos of 1973 or approve a new constitution and with it the permanence in power of Pinochet until 1990, and even possibly until 1997. And, early on, they attempted to raise both Pinochet and junta member Gen. Fernando Matthei on the petards of their own earlier words. On December 27, 1977, Pinochet was quoted in *El Mercurio* as saying: "To hold a plebiscite or a referendum, it is necessary to have voter registration rolls [*registros electorales*], election laws, polling places, etc." (The president had said that in explaining why the 1978 "consultation" was not a "plebiscite.") On July 29, 1979, Air Force General Matthei was quoted as saying: "If the constitution were to be submitted to a plebiscite without there being full debate and information, it would become a farce. A new constitution must go to a plebiscite at all events, but only after the political parties are operating so that they may express their opinion." Despite repeated taunts, both the president and the general remained silent on the five major objections to the plebiscite:

1. The voters were being offered no real choice. Among many who made this argument was an ad hoc citizen group, in a full-page ad: "What," they asked of the stated alternative to voting "Yes," "does return to September 10, 1973, mean? That the country collapse into chaos, since the man who was then president of the Republic

is dead and the parliament dissolved? Is that what General Pinochet would give us to understand?"[48]

2. There was no real opportunity for proper debate and discussion since the country was living under a state of emergency that restricted right of assembly, and the government was armed with unusual punitive powers.

3. There was no real electoral machinery in place: no registration rolls, no established polling places, no opposition participation in monitoring the vote and vote-counting processes; no election tribunals to fix rules and mediate disputes.

4. The opposition did not have adequate access to the mass media, and particularly to television.

5. Those who drafted the proposed constitution represented only one shade of ideological opinion: the Right.

But if these were the long-range and philosophical concerns, the immediate and emotional one was how to escape the prospect of having to live under a greatly strengthened Pinochet presidency for ten more years, perhaps seventeen. For, no matter how draconian it may appear, how difficult to amend, how gloomy the prospect of life under it, a constitution is a piece of paper, and with political will, it can be changed. By contrast, if Pinochet should triumph in the plebiscite, he would have not only the strength but a mandate—however much it may be disputed—to remain in the presidency beyond the likely lifetimes of any of the country's old-line politicians.

From all sides came opinions, analyses, calls for action, proclamations. The far Left, already committed to taking power by violent means, was divided. The Communists ultimately decided to join the Christian Democrats in urging a "No" vote; the Socialists and small MAPU party urged abstention. The Christian Democrats, while attacking the process with increasing ferocity ("the greatest fraud in the history of Chile"), had at first wavered as to what to do about it. At one point, PDC chief Zaldívar appeared to invite the outlawed Communists and other Marxist-Leninists to join them in "a national understanding"; he later repudiated the idea of such an alliance while defending the right of the Communists to participate in the process. At another point, the party appeared to be opting for mass mobilization as an implied means of thwarting the plebiscite. In the end, it decided to take part, warning again and again that "dictatorships don't lose elections" (while defenders of the junta retorted that dictatorships don't hold them). The decision to participate was also likely tinged with a note of optimism; with less than two weeks to go, even a group of right-wing former congressmen thought a "No" vote might prevail.[49]

The country's leading newspaper—consistently supportive of the junta—expressed support for the plebiscite, but with grave reservations. Editorialized *El Mercurio:* the next decade will not be one in which law rules man, but man rules law, and thus "will not be a State of Law." To try to convince ourselves otherwise, the newspaper said, "would be to deceive ourselves and play a false role before the country."

Organized labor, reemerging with a distinctively left-wing cast in the wake of liberalization measures adopted in 1979, lined up squarely against the plebiscite. Christian Democrat youth leaders called it a "pseudo-plebiscite" and said the constitution to emerge from it "will be valid only so long as force sustains it." But, apart from calling on youth leaders to "organize so as to liberate Chile from oppression," they also were not able to decide whether to vote or stay at home.[50]

Law school professors at the Catholic University, headed by their dean, Sergio Gaete, said the plebiscite was legal. The Lawyers' Guild of Santiago said it was not. Former junta member Gen. Gustavo Leigh said he would vote "No," but it would do no good because "in these kinds of dictatorship, the results are controlled. They are never going to give out real figures." For his brother, former lawmaker Hernán Leigh Guzmán, the right vote was "Yes"; "only future generations," he said, "will have sufficient perspective and serenity to realize in all of its magnitude what Chile owes to its armed forces." Luis Alegría, president of the National Federation of Plastic Workers, said vote "No"; Héctor Peña Cabrera, president of the Labor Front of the Bank of the State, said "Yes." León Vilarín, the ex-Socialist whose truck owner/drivers played such a vital role in the fight against Allende, said, "I fought for a government of the armed forces where all Chileans would have access to it, and not to install one controlled by the extreme Right"; Germán Riesco, president of the National Agriculture Society, another thorn in Allende's side, said he would vote "Yes," because Chile needed more time "to correct the vices and vacuums of the past"; former Conservative deputy Julio Su-bercaseaux said "No" ("They're trying to imitate in Chile the experience of General Franco with his twenty-three years in government. That's dangerous."); Enrique Campos Menéndez, director of the National Libraries, Archives and Museums, said he would vote "Yes," because it was enough to contrast the "chaos" of the Allende years with "social, economic and cultural recovery under the protection of a regime both orderly and just, which grants all Chileans a future of personal liberties and true national sovereignty."[51]

There were, of course, voices from afar. The *New York Times* said in an editorial that Chileans were going to the polls to vote for any president of their choice, so long as that choice was President Pinochet. In Quito, the newly formed Latin American Association of Human Rights—identified only as "nongovernmental"—denounced the plebiscite as an "antidemocratic fraud." The then governing party of Spain, the Union of the Democratic Center, cabled a message of solidarity to the Christian Democrats. In Caracas, Communist party leader José Cademartori, one-time economy minister in Allende's Cabinet, claimed Chile's "democratic forces" had united behind former President Frei's proposal for a civilian-military transition government. He also warned that after the "fraud," the struggle in Chile "is going to be radicalized. There is no other hope." As the voting was actually starting, Allende's widow, Hortensia, told newsmen in Mexico that opposition to the plebiscite had brought together Popular Unity parties with the Christian Democrats. She added that, although she would never forget what she called Frei's silent complicity in the fascist coup, "Frei can be and must be used."

Outside voices also were heard inside Chile. Eduardo Ríos Arias, president of the labor union "Group of 10," said he had talked to several Santiago-based labor attachés of Western countries, and "two or three of them . . . have told me, unofficially, that this is a fraud . . ." Ambassadors of Holland, France, Great Britain, Switzerland, Denmark, Italy, and Belgium met with representatives of the antiplebiscite Group of 24 and reportedly told the Chileans the plebiscite was contrary to every political advance of this century (although that version was later denied).[52]

"The word of the church," proclaimed the pro-Christian Democrat magazine *Hoy*, "will be of key importance." As it turned out, not quite. There was a new pope in Rome, a new caution in the Chilean church, fearful not only of rankling Rome, but also of deepening the divisions within its own ranks at home. Just how great those divisions might be was reflected even before the bishops met when one of their senior members—Archbishop Emilio Tagle of Valparaíso—expressed his complete support for the plebiscite.

On August 23, the Episcopal Conference released a statement that neither endorsed nor opposed the plebiscite nor the proposed constitution itself. "Both the plebiscite and the juridical norms which could emanate from it will have the moral authority and will enjoy the respect of the citizenry in the measure that they are an authentic expression of national feeling," the statement said. Five conditions must be met for that to happen, the bishops added. One was clear: that the vote be secret. One was not: that different subjects not be lumped together (approval of the constitution with continuation in power of the junta). The other three were debatable: sufficient information for the electorate; a clear and legal statement of what the choices were and their consequences; full guarantees of the honesty and correct execution of the process. Pinochet brushed the statement off with a remark that it grieved him that the Catholic church apparently distrusted the honesty of the armed forces.[53]

It was Frei, then, who spearheaded the attack; and it was an old political arena that became the scene of the biggest counteroffensive. By early afternoon of Wednesday, August 27, the streets around the Teatro Caupolicán on San Diego Street were teeming with banner-waving people. By 6 P.M., with Caupolicán bulging with more than seven thousand persons, Carabineros closed off access to it. The opposition estimated that 100,000 persons were gathered outside, listening to the proceedings over radios and loudspeakers (but the newspaper *La Tercera* said the next day experts estimated the number was closer to fifteen thousand). Tens of thousands more, the length and breadth of Chile, tuned in to a twenty-one-station nationwide radio hook-up (only Arica in the far north, population 93,000, was excluded). It was "The Gathering of Free Chileans."

Actor José Manuel Salcedo emceed, and inside the cavernous hall *lolos* and *lolitas* (attractive young people from the better neighborhoods), wearing yellow arm-bands and carrying walkie-talkies, handed out white carnations to the ladies, confetti to all to scatter on signal. But that was mainly on the ground floor, where the well-manicured and neatly tailored elite of the Christian Democrats took their places. In the galleries, blue jeans were the motif, the angry young faces of Popular Unity militants the look. They soon got a chance to vent their feelings. When a women's folklore group sang a song of the late Violeta Parra— Communist heroine of folk music—the gallery exploded in cheers. They did again when a group of actors, all Allende sympathizers, gave a reading evoking past national luminaries; when they alluded to Nobel Laureate (and life-long Communist) Pablo Neruda, and to Luis Emilio Recabarren (founder of the Communist party in Chile), a new round of shouting and sloganeering ensued ("Pinochet get out"; "Pinochet murderer"). When the national anthem was sung, omitted from it was a passage referring to "valiant men, valiant soldiers."[54] Among the celebrities looking on: old party war-horse Bernardo Leighton, fully recovered from his Rome wounds. (Healed, too, were the wounds inflicted during the in-fighting immediately after the coup, which Frei supported and Leighton bitterly condemned, and for which he and others were expelled for a time from the party. Frei reserved his first *abrazo* [backslapping embrace] for Leighton.) Others present included the writer and polemicist Genaro Arriagada Herrera, PDC secretary-general; Hugo Zepeda de Barrios, former Senate president, one of a handful of prominent conservatives firmly opposed to the plebiscite and a member of the Group of 24; Allende's first Mining minister, Orlando Cantuarias; Daniel Sierra, president of the heavily politicized Theology Center of the Catholic University; and the noted philosopher Jorge Millas.

The star of the evening arrived at 7:15 P.M. as Manuel Sanhueza, head of the Group of 24, was speaking. Frei took his place in the front row in time to hear Millas refer to the plebiscite as "an act of intellectual oppression." It was 8:10 when Frei mounted the podium; from high in the hall came a shout, "Viva Salvador Allende," followed from the floor by cries of "Frei, Frei . . . *El pueblo unido/jamás será vencido* (The people united, will never be defeated). Through the continuing shouts Frei finally managed to interrupt: "The hope of Chile does not have the name of a person," he said. "The hope of Chile is represented by this event, which reflects the historic will and immense majority of Chile." During the sixty-eight minutes he spoke, Frei called for:

1. The immediate formation of "a government of civilian-military transition," which, over a period of two to three years at most, "will establish the conditions to stanch the wounds of the past, reestablish unity and peace among Chileans, restore the full functioning of a democratic regime, and guarantee internal and external security for Chileans. During this period of transition, the government will retain legislative functions."
2. Popular elections to be held, once this government was constituted, to choose members of a Constitutent Assembly, or similar body, which would draft a constitution and submit it to a plebiscite "under a system of absolute guarantees, with options clearly defined and full freedom of expression."
3. The rapid reestablishment of basic liberties, including repeal of the state of emergency, and the return of exiles.

In addition, or "in any case," Frei called for the immediate reestablishing of full freedom of the press and speech, the promulgation of electoral and political party laws, labor liberalization, and an end to intervention in the universities. "Democracy," he said, "is not chaos." Noting that at that very time, President Jimmy Carter and Republican challenger Ronald Reagan were engaged in a series of televised debates in the United States, Frei challenged President Pinochet to debate him on television—at the minimum, make television time available for this one occasion in order to present the opposition view on the plebiscite. Rejecting the plebiscite as "lacking validity," he claimed that "the country now awaits [the government's] response" to his and other alternative proposals. But, he said, "if all doors are, unfortunately [*por desgracia*], closed, on September 11, we will vote 'No.' "

As he concluded his speech, Frei called on those inside and outside the hall to return to their homes quietly "as an example of responsibility." He then made his way quickly out the rear of the hall, passing tigers, camels, and elephants from the circus due to open immediately afterwards in the Caupolicán arena.[55]

The government gave Frei's remarks short shrift. A relatively low-level agency—the National Division of Social Communications [*Dinacos*]—said in a press release that the idea of a televised debate was a publicity stunt. There was no comment on Frei's substantive proposals. Pinochet, on the stump to drum up support for the plebiscite, said that at Caupolicán, those in the opposition "dropped their mask . . . We have always warned that Marxism is deceiving them and we have had the opportunity of seeing a group of perfectly mated [*mancomunado*] Marxists and pseudo-Christian Democrats. I never believed this could have happened . . . because they said they were defenders of freedom, and here they are joining with the totalitarians." To those who say the plebiscite is false, he said, "I answer: no plebiscite in which the people take part, where they follow their consciences, can be called false. False were those hidden assemblies where they prepared and selected candidates and adopted their resolutions behind the backs of the people."[56]

Pablo Rodríguez Grez, head of the hard right-wing organization Patria y Libertad, said of Caupolicán: "History repeats itself. Today the Communists help them, and tomorrow they will pave the way for the Communists. It happened yesterday, it will happen in the future." The proplebiscite organization Nueva Democracia, linked to the conservative ideologue Jaime Guzmán, said: "He who yesterday would come before the country as an alternative to communism presents himself today as an alternative with communism." Gen. Sergio Badiola, secretary-general of the government, told three thousand labor and guild leaders that the armed forces would guarantee that the plebiscite would be "absolutely crystal clear" and clean. Frei continued to hit hard in speeches and interviews, and on September 9, he once again addressed the country over a national radio network. (Paid announcements in newspapers called on "free Chileans to gather together and listen with their family and friends . . . record this talk and pass it around . . .") Only a few days before the plebiscite, the Group of 24 proposed that the plebiscite be suspended for sixty to ninety days so that voters could be given two choices: the government's proposal and one hammered out by the opposition. In the meantime, they urged that the Election Review Tribunal envisioned in the 1925 constitution be set up to supervise the plebiscite. That proposal embodied the main points of the Frei proposal—except that it said that should the government win the plebiscite, the draft constitution proposed by them would be adopted, and a transition government would be established only in the event the opposition should win.[57]

In those last weeks, tempers flared, indiscretions multiplied. Edgardo Boeninger, former rector of the University of Chile and member of the Group of 24, told three hundred students at the university that the overthrow of Allende was "a tragedy," the destruction of Chilean democracy. Patricio Aylwin, who headed Boeninger's Christian Democrat party in 1973 (and would head it again as the time approached for the 1988 elections), told a different group at the same university that in light of conditions in the country, military rule was necessary—but the transition period should not be prolonged more than three years. Having said that, he also said that if the government won the plebiscite, the PDC would not recognize the outcome, but if the government lost, it should step down immediately. When a number of Christian Democrats went public in support of the plebiscite, the party sharply attacked them as "persons long since eliminated from the rolls of Christian Democracy," or persons "who never were" real members.[58]

At least two PDC objections were dubious at best, spurious at worst. One concerned the absence of voter lists. Frei himself, in his previously quoted 1973 letter to Italian premier and world Christian Democrat leader Mariano Rumor, had said that in Chile's last elections before the coup, there was massive fraud, and government agencies, "among other things, falsified thousands of identity cards." Identity cards were, of course, used for registering, so that the lists which the junta had ordered destroyed in 1973 were vitiated. The second concerns the monolithic character of those drafting the constitution. A top Christian Democrat, Juan de Dios Carmona, had, as noted earlier, participated in the first constitutional working group—for which he was banished from the party. Frei himself was invited to join the Council of State—an invitation he spurned. It is true that the junta made radical changes in the council-drafted constitution, but it is equally true that the Christian Democrats chose to boycott the entire process.

As the date for the elections neared, one highly qualified voice was not heard. True to his lifelong vision of rectitude, Jorge Alessandri refused repeated requests that he express an opinion on the plebiscite. Although the former president harbored serious misgivings about the radical changes made in the constitution the Council of State under his direction had drafted and which now would go before the people, he kept these to himself, convinced that it was the people of Chile who now should decide. To intimates, he said that for him to do otherwise would be unduly to affect the free choice which he believed belonged to them.[59]

September 11 broke sunny and warm in Santiago. Before the day was ended, the greatest outpouring of Chileans in history would cast their ballots at 30,255 polling stations. Among them, Eduardo Frei: "I came to vote," he told a phalanx of Chilean and foreign newsmen gathered at Escuela Argentina just before two in the afternoon, "because I recommended a 'No' vote at the Caupolicán, and I could not remain in my house availing myself of a privilege forbidden to other Chileans.* I feel humiliated and used [vejado] by having to take part in this event, and I energetically reject the validity of this plebiscite." As he was about to climb into his car, the former president added: "Sad, isn't it?" Former President Alessandri, voting three hours earlier at the Instituto Nacional, declined to make a statement.

TABLE 40
VOTE IN THE 1980 PLEBISCITE

Yes	4,121,067	65.71%
No	1,893,420	30.19%
Blank	83,312	1.33% *
Void	173,569	2.77%
TOTAL	6,271,368	100.00%

* Blank vote totals were, as had been announced previously, counted as though they were "Yes" votes, although they were also shown separately. The decision to do that was intended to discourage a protest vote of blank ballots.

Source: Control Nacional de Escrutinios (National Vote Tally Center), Interior Ministry, as published in El Mercurio, October 16, 1980. (Preliminary figures released September 12 showed insignificantly small variations in all totals.)

The total voting was more than double that of the 1970 election which put Salvador Allende in the presidency; the "No" vote in this plebiscite was 700,000 votes more than Allende polled in winning, and the "Yes" vote very nearly four times what he received. The 1980 vote also eclipsed by 700,000 the previous high vote tally, recorded in the 1978 "consultation."

Contrary to some forecasts, women voted far more overwhelmingly for a continuation in power of the junta than did men: 2,242,072 for, 821,156 against; for men, the tallies were 1,878,995 for, 1,072,264 against. The highest "Yes" totals were recorded in the southern Araucanian region (77.76 percent), the highest "No" in far south Magallanes and the Santiago metropolitan area (37.25 percent and 35.92 percent, respectively); the "No" vote was also slightly above the national average in the second city, Valparaíso (33.2 percent), and higher yet in the traditional leftist stronghold Concepción, the third city (40.9 percent; the Eighth Region as a whole, however, posted 30.5 percent).

The next day, the Santiago stock market—a "bull market" for most of the period beginning in 1978—shot up sharply. The president of the

* Frei referred to the fact that this vote, as all others in Chile, was obligatory. Based on the National Statistical Institute estimate that 6,753,656 were eligible to vote, it would appear that half a million stayed home.

exchange said the rise reflected investor confidence that business in Chile "will remain a free market for eight more years."[60]

In Washington, the State Department criticized the plebiscite, saying the opposition not only had been intimidated, but prevented from expressing adequately its opinions. In Bonn, the Social Democratic government headed by Helmut Schmidt said conditions still did not exist for recognizing the validity of elections in Chile. The twenty-one-nation Council of Europe voted to condemn the plebiscite in one of its plenary sessions. In London, *The Observor* said a detailed report showing massive fraud was in the offing.

Meeting with foreign correspondents the next day, an exultant President Pinochet had a message of his own for Washington: "Let us work in peace [*tranquilos*]. So that you [newsmen] know it, it did not cost the United States one dollar, one bullet, one life, to get the Communists out of Chile. And when we have needed something, instead of helping, they have beaten up on us [*nos han golpeado*]." He also said he would welcome working with the opposition, but it would have to come to the government. He also announced a scheme of civilian-military government of his own: grassroots assemblies at the municipal level (promptly denounced by PDC chief Zaldívar as destined to become one-party rule cut from a "fascist" mold).

From his command post in Moscow, Communist party Secretary-General Luis Corvalán Lepe said the results reaffirmed the need for "rough [*aguda*] violence."

There was a familiar pattern of "selective indignation" operating in the reaction of the Western world to the Chilean plebiscite and process for adopting a new constitution. It would be enough to recall remarks made by Dr. Mark Cannon, executive director of the Commission on the Bicentennial of the U.S. Constitution: "Nearly two-thirds of the world's 160 national constitutions have been adopted or revised since 1970, and only fourteen predate World War II . . . 53.5 percent of the independent states of the world have been under more than one constitution since the Second World War. The average nation has had two constitutions since 1945, and two states, Syria and Thailand, have each had nine constitutions over the past forty years . . . The Constitution of the United States has proven remarkably durable." Clearly, most of the constitution-writing and/or "reforms" Cannon alluded to were carried out under processes considerably less pristine than that of Philadelphia in 1787—or, for that matter, Santiago in 1980. Yet, there was rarely a protest, much less the worldwide outcry that accompanied the Chilean plebiscite.

Nor was there, to take another example, any such outcry several years later when Cory Aquino—"the Jimmy Carter of the Philippines, full of good thoughts and words . . . innocent of the wicked skills of governance but thought to be able to bring about a new era of good feeling"—set about creating a new constitution for her country. To quote Dr. Ray S. Cline, a scholar of rich experience in international affairs: "President Aquino has decided to stake her future on a new constitution drafted by a commission she hand-picked in such a way as to put it under left-wing, anti-Establishment lawyers and political ideologues. She has approved their draft without opportunity for review or amendment. This constitution provides for 1987 elections of legislators but, simply by fiat, puts Cory Aquino in office as president until 1992, with no opportunity for any opposition to come forward. Even Vice President Laurel balks at this procedure as high-handed, though he is slated to remain as vice president on the same provision . . . Voters will have only a 'Yes' or 'No' vote on approving the constitution, and if they vote 'Yes' they put Cory in office for a six-year term . . ." The U.S. response was to rush $1 billion in military and economic assistance to the Philippines, and later to announce plans for a $5 billion to $10 billion multinational assistance program over the 1988–1993 period. To take one further example, from a world reeking of double standards: On April 12, 1980, Master Sergeant Samuel K. Doe literally shot his way to power in Liberia: the country's president was killed in his bed, and thirteen government officials were executed on a nearby beach. The United States responded, during Doe's first five years in power, by lavishing $500 million in aid, the largest amount in per capita terms given to any African nation (and since the country has only 2 million very impoverished inhabitants, the equivalent for each of more than six months' total income). In 1985, amid bloodshed and intimidation of opponents, Doe won the presidency in an election independent observers said he had lost. U.S. aid declined (from a high of $93 million) but continued ($37 million in 1988). Meanwhile, corruption in the tiny country became so rampant that Doe consented to import seventeen U.S. technicians—paid by American taxpayers—to cosign all government checks. Well, almost all: of the $220 million annual budget, Doe managed to squirrel away $65 million which Doe and others used for "extrabudgetary expenditures" such as Mercedes automobiles. By contrast, Chile has received nothing—zero—in U.S. economic and military assistance in the entire decade, virtually nothing since the ouster of a Marxist-Leninist government in 1973, during which time there has been no serious episode of corruption of any kind.[61]

As he had said he would the month previous, former President Alessandri resigned from the Council of State on September 12. Former President Frei retreated into the shadows. PDC President Zaldívar took up the cudgels of opposition—with increasing fury. In an interview with the Mexican magazine Visión just before the plebiscite, Zaldívar had warned that if there were no peaceful opening to democracy, Chile "will be dragged into seeking violence and force as the means of ridding ourselves [*derrocar*] of a regime that tries to stay on against the majority will of Chileans." Labor leader Hernol Flores chose sarcasm: "We exceeded our expectations; I thought they would only give us 25 percent or so." Christian Democrat leaders Genaro Arriagada and Enrique Krauss were just plain bitter. Krauss said the plebiscite "adds nothing to the process of recovery of institutionality." Arriagada said, "there has been no electoral process here. What there has been is a fraudulent process."

But, more than any other, it was Zaldívar who led the attack. Finally, in an interview published mid-October in the Mexico City newspaper *Uno Más Uno*, Zaldívar was quoted as saying that if the Pinochet regime maintained its authoritarian posture, "anything can happen in the future, including a civil war." He said his party remained firmly opposed to violence, but extended an invitation to all—including the Communists, but excluding those who have "thrown in lock, stock and barrel, with the junta" [*comprometidos a ultranza*]—to join in forming a military-civilian transition government which would be headed by "non-fascist . . . rescueable" military men. (Interestingly, in that interview, he was called upon to explain why Christian Democrats in El Salvador were willing that year to join in a civilian-military government which came to power through force of arms—largely under U.S. tutelage—but were unwilling to do so in Chile.) Zaldívar was traveling in Europe with his wife when the story broke. A few days later, the government announced that he would not be allowed to return to Chile.[62]

Many of the attacks in the early days following the plebiscite centered on the opposition's lack of media access—which really came down to access to television. With the exception of news clips—and those were limited—the opposition was not allowed time on either of the university-operated television stations (both of which, through repeaters, then reached most major urban areas), nor on the state-run TV network. By contrast, progovernment spokesmen appeared frequently and extensively. The government never did respond directly to Frei's request to be given network television time—but the hard-hitting (and thoroughly projunta) tabloid, *La Segunda*, did. The newspaper recalled that in February 1967, Frei's government had refused a similar request from the Senate that its president be allowed nationwide radio time (television was still insignificant in Chile) to respond to a sharp Frei attack on Congress. That attack came during what Frei described as "not a political crisis, but an institutional crisis." At stake was a sweeping overhaul of the constitution which Frei had been attempting to ram through Congress from the very beginning of his presidency; the reforms, he argued, were needed to give the presidency the broad planning powers it needed in a modern world and to be able to govern efficiently in the face of a fractious Congress. Those remarks stirred a hornet's nest in Congress, and led to the call for nationwide network time to answer. In a message responding to the Senate resolution, Frei's acting interior minister, Juan de Dios Carmona, said "radio networks were the exclusive domain [*facultades*] of the executive, and for that reason it would not yield to the Senate, inasmuch as that branch has [access to] other means of expression." Interestingly, the Senate president then was a man named Salvador Allende.[63]

But, asked *La Segunda*, how significant was television anyway? Radio, the newspaper pointed out, was far and away the dominant medium in Chile: 14 million sets in use, or 1.3 per inhabitant. (By contrast, in 1980, there were only forty-eight TV sets per one thousand inhabitants, and TV signals did not reach entire areas of the country.) On radio, *La Segunda* asserted, opposition views were given very extensive time—quite apart from a pro-opposition "spin" given to many radio news reports. The newspaper published a full page of excerpts from radio programs it had monitored over a fifteen-day preplebiscite period to make its point.[64]

As to the printed word, as indicated previously, there was a plethora of opposition viewpoints in print—as well as sharp attacks on the government.

Claims of fraud also abounded, before and after the plebiscite. One study purported to show fraud in 39.7 percent of the polling places in the Santiago metropolitan area. The National Verification Board (Colegio Escrutador Nacional), headed by Comptroller-General Osvaldo Iturriaga Ruiz and including a Supreme Court judge and a court officer, said the board made an exhaustive review of complaints before releasing its final figures on October 16.[65]

Despite those claims—muted in later years—from the very beginning the opposition picked over the figures to find signals of strength and hope. One such analysis pointed out that—fraud or no—the number of those voting "No" had increased by 67.7 percent between the 1978 "consultation" and the 1980 plebiscite (up from 1,131,115 in 1978, or 20.32 percent of the total, to 1,891,332, or 30.17 percent in 1980); the "Yes" vote, meantime, increased only 26.55 percent (from 4,177,064 to 4,203,615).[66]

Though the charges of fraud would never cease, they were later muffled for two reasons: the Christian Democrats knew that, with or without fraud, the regime had clearly won an unmistakable victory, one which, in the view of an outside expert observer (Michael Fleet), "greatly strengthened Pinochet's hand." The second was that, as early as

1975, Frei himself recognized that the military had broader support among the public at large than politicos might wish to acknowledge. According to one PDC internal analysis made in the aftermath of the plebiscite:

> For the next four or five years it [the opposition] won't be able to change this government. At first we thought that in Chile such crude authoritarianism would never stand a chance. Then, during the 1975–1976 economic crisis, people said: It won't survive. Then we thought that international pressure would bring it down. In September it managed to quash such dreams entirely.

> From now on we have to set long-range objectives, try to get society to evolve in depth—in universities, factories, neighborhoods, army barracks—while patiently working to renew and reinvigorate party doctrine and organization. That's not defeatism, it's realism. Politics is the art of the possible, not a way to compensate for the dullness of daily life by dreaming.

Among those on the hard Left, as well as the PDC, "the prevailing mood was of confusion and discouragement that bordered on despair . . . for the next eighteen months the party languished in indecision and inactivity as it searched for ways to oppose a hypersensitive but otherwise impervious and seemingly unstoppable government . . ."[67]

"OUT OF THE WAY—HERE COMES CHILE!"*

That slogan, adopted early in 1981 by the *gremialistas*, the corporate state ideologues around Pinochet, reflected the exuberance of the administration in winning the plebiscite. With the economy booming, the administration promulgated a series of significant measures:

—On January 3, a new General Law of Universities was adopted, designed mainly to encourage "privatization" of higher universities (though subject to strict governmental controls). Among other things, it included a means-test for university students; those able to pay all or part tuitions were required to do so. This was, in itself, revolutionary: in Chile as elsewhere in Latin America, free college education for anyone wanting it was regarded as a "right"; in practice, it favored middle- and upper-class individuals, usually at the expense of the poor.[68] Pious and repeated protestations that the Pinochet government favored the rich at the expense of the poor notwithstanding when their own ox was gored, the well-off university student and faculty communities raised a howl

* The Spanish phrase: *"Abran cancha, viene Chile."*

of protest. The pro-PDC magazine *Hoy* characterized the law sarcastically as having "introduced higher education into the market economy." As part of its design to encourage private universities, the new law narrowed to twelve main vocational areas the courses offered in the eight state universities, downgrading philosophy, journalism, and sociology to nonuniversity level. Campus political activity was banned. (It continued anyway, both in the form of electioneering, and using the universities as redoubts of antigovernment activities; indeed, shortly after the law was announced, a group of students occupied the Santiago headquarters of UNESCO to protest the law and the arrest of student leader Patricia Torres.)

—On February 4, membership in professional associations was made no longer obligatory, and the associations were stripped of their control over codes of ethics and qualifications of professionals. The measure was part of the "depoliticization" of interest groups. It met with fierce resistance from professionals.

—On March 10, Decree Law #3648 abolished the special Labor Tribunals, assigning jurisdiction over labor disputes to the ordinary civil courts. The Inter-American Commission on Human Rights said that, in its view, the measure "deprived the workers of the special protection afforded them by a special proceeding for rapidly dealing with the conflicts that arise daily in employment matters."

—On March 11, 1981, the new constitution formally went into effect. Pinochet was sworn in for an eight-year term and celebrated the occasion by transferring the presidential offices from the Diego Portales Building back to the fully restored La Moneda Palace. In his inaugural speech, he reaffirmed his government's plans for reforms in seven areas: labor, social security, education, health, the judiciary, agriculture, and administration. Action had already begun on the first three. A new labor code had been enacted in 1979. On November 4, 1980, radical changes were introduced in the social security system—rickety and unreliable in Chile as in most of the rest of Latin America. As of March 1, 1981, all workers were required to put aside a fixed percentage of their earnings, and were given the choice of doing so either in the state system or in the private plans created several years earlier. (The results, to be discussed in a later section, have been one of the most phenomenal success stories in the world.) Education reform has already been discussed.[69]

Exuberance had its dark side. Perhaps no provision of the new constitution aroused so much anxiety and wrath as Article 24 of the transitory articles, those governing until the return to democracy in 1990. That article permits the president, on his own authority, to declare the existence of the danger of disturbance of internal peace for renewable periods of up to six months. During these periods he could order the arrest or enforced exile of persons, bar entry to others, and decree restrictions on right of assembly or of information. In March of 1981, Gerardo Espinoza, one-time interior minister under Allende, was arrested and expelled from the country under Article 24. In August, Jaime Castillo Velasco, president of the Commission on Human Rights, followed, as did former Allende ministers Carlos Briones and Orlando Cantuarias. Although the commission he headed was a burr under the regime's saddle—and unquestionably a haven for many hard-line revolutionaries—Castillo Velasco himself was an intellectual, widely respected in and out of Chile. Briones was a constitutional lawyer, the moderate legalist in Allende's final Cabinet; both, and in particular Briones, would return to Chile a few years later much more implacable in their opposition to the regime.

Article 24 drew probably more fire than any other provision of the new constitution. Unlike changes made in other council transition articles, Article 24 was added in its entirety after the council had submitted its draft.

The changes made by President Pinochet and/or the junta in the draft constitution prepared by the Council of State were so sweeping that they not only "greatly strengthened Pinochet's hand," but also placed him—literally—above the law itself during the transition period.[70]

In so heavily rewriting the council draft, Pinochet and the junta sought to reshape the constitution to achieve seven major aims:

1. Create a presidency of practically unfettered powers;
2. Reduce, greatly, the power of Congress;
3. Strengthen safeguards for private property and, in the process, virtually institutionalize the market economy system;
4. Enshrine traditional values, beginning with family protection, while banishing from society "any person or group propagating doctrines injurious to [atenten contra] the family, promoting violence or a conception of society, [or] the state of the juridical order of a totalitarian character, based on the class struggle . . ." Such individuals, groups, parties or other organizations were declared unconstitutional;
5. Give the armed forces a permanent tutelary role over society (although the government denied this);
6. Reduce the power and scope of political parties;
7. Make it virtually impossible to change the constitution.

To achieve that, the junta made fifty-nine "fundamental" changes in the draft submitted by the Council of State. Of equal importance were the council proposals which the junta chose to ignore—most significantly, the creation of a bicameral legislature to replace the junta which, although appointed, would have served as a sounding board for public opinion.

In a sense, an examination of those changes is an exercise in futility, since the opposition, from the center-Left Christian Democrats to the hard underground Left, have never accepted the legitimacy of the 1980 constitution at all. Furthermore, the opposition also rejected many of the council's proposals, although most were those governing the transition period. Presumably, given the opportunity, opponents would simply declare the constitution null and void in its entirety and begin anew. Indeed, one of the original drafters wrote afterwards that "constitutions are not revealed truth, and, therefore, can be modified." Still, as the transition period neared its end, responsible opposition leaders such as PDC President Patricio Aylwin said grudgingly that the "illegitimate" constitution was, all the same, a fact.[71]

Of the fifty-nine changes in the permanent articles which Carrasco Delgado identified as "fundamental," herewith some of the highlights:

1. A positive one, in Article 1. For the first time in a Chilean constitution, it is specified that the state is at the service of the individual.
2. Military personnel on active duty were given the vote; traditionally, that had not been the case in Chile, and both the Council of State and Study Commission wanted to keep it that way.
3. An "equal rights amendment"—specifying equal rights for men and women—was eliminated from the final text.
4. The possibility of requiring payment of full or partial premiums for public or private health care plans was written into Article 19, as was the statement that local communities should share with the state primary responsibility for education. Both are truly revolutionary formulations in Latin America.
5. The final version—in Article 19—actually went beyond the council in liberalizing provisions governing press freedom; the revised text also facilitates private access to radio and television ownership.
6. Conversely, that same article extends the possibility of censorship from motion pictures to "other artistic activities."
7. While wanting to end obligatory membership in professional associations, the council sought to retain it for university professors. The final version eliminated that exception.
8. Article 19 was also amended to permit expanded mechanisms for the earmarking of federal tax revenues to local governments.
9. Article 19, as approved, broadens property rights in such a fashion as to make more difficult a return to a statist economy, and streamlines procedures for paying, in cash, for properties expro-

priated by the government (though, in the process, possibly opening the way for protracted court battles to resolve disputes).

10. The council wanted to reserve oil, gas, coal, copper and other types
of extractive industries exclusively for the state. The final version
opens the door to concessions—although not for the big copper
mines, the so-called Gran Minería. A concessionaire acquires the
same constitutionally protected rights as any other owner.

11. Article 25 extends presidential terms from the council-proposed
six years to eight years.

12. Article 29 empowers the Senate to name a successor to serve out
the entire term in case of death or disability of the president; the
council wanted new elections within sixty days.

13. As approved, Article 32 gives the president the power to fire all
public officeholders—not simply presidential appointees. Conversely, another clause restricts the power of the president to
designate or remove commanders of the armed forces.

14. Article 41 removed the council- and commission-proposed stipulation that once a state of "exception" (siege, emergency, etc.)
ended, those sent into exile or denied entry to the country would
be eligible to return. As now written, their exile could be
extended indefinitely.

15. Article 44 raises from a grade school education to a high school
education the requirement for election as a deputy, and adds that
candidates must reside in the district which they seek to represent.

16. The Senate would be made up of twenty-six elected members,
two from each region; the council proposed thirty-five, so as to
allow greater representation from the more densely populated
Santiago, Valparaíso, and Concepción regions. (Both the council
and the final draft provide for nine other Senators: two of them
would be appointed by the president, four would be ex-service
chiefs appointed by the National Security Council, two would be
ex-Supreme Court justices elected by the court, and the ninth
would be a former comptroller-general also elected by the court.)

17. The number, qualifications, and terms of senators to be named by
the president was changed in Article 45, and a residency requirement was added for Senators.

18. Article 60 greatly restricts the legislative jurisdiction of Congress,
retaining, for example, the language from the 1925 constitution
"solo son materias de ley" ("the only subjects for legislation are").
Alessandri and the council found that language "dangerously"
restrictive. Congress is further limited to decreasing the president's spending proposals, but cannot alter his revenue forecasts;
nor is Congress permitted to legislate spending without showing
how and where the money will come to pay for it.

19. Article 63 raises from simple majority to a three-fifths vote the
requirement for enacting "basic" or "organic" laws.

20. In Article 76, the council proposed a system of wide competition for judgeships; that language was eliminated. The final draft also made retirement of all judges, save for the chief justice of the Supreme Court, obligatory at age seventy-five. The council proposed a mechanism for creating exceptions. The council's proposed Article 80, which would have introduced a new concept of unconstitutionality of laws, was eliminated altogether.

21. As approved, Article 81 greatly downgrades qualifications—and, by implication, the authority—of the Constitutional Tribunal. Article 84 does the same for the Election Review Tribunal.

22. Article 93, as proposed by the council, would have reestablished the unquestioned subordination of the military to the civilian government. As rewritten, once appointed to four-year terms by the president, the commanders of the armed services and Carabineros could not be removed until their terms were ended.

23. In defining the National Security Council (NSC)—first created during Allende's last year in the presidency—the council sought to assure civilian domination: eight members drawn from civilian posts, five from the military. As approved, Article 95 stipulates four from military ranks, three from civilian.

24. Perhaps no clause in the new constitution has caused greater apprehension and criticism than Article 96, defining the attributes of the National Security Council. As proposed by the council, the NSC would render its opinions to the president on any matter which, in its judgment, affected national security. As approved, the NSC could convey its opinion to *any* legally constituted authority, and not simply on national security matters, but on matters "which in its judgment gravely endanger [*atente*] the bases of institutionality." The practical effect is, of course, to make the NSC—controlled by the military—the supreme arbiter of national life, empowered to stand in judgment, and thus interfere in, any matter it might choose. Alessandri observed that this power would make governance especially difficult for a civilian president. Article 96, added after the council's draft, also empowered the NSC to require any public official to provide information it deemed affected internal or external security. To make matters even more draconian, the council had proposed that the NSC be regulated in all of its aspects by an organic constitutional act of Congress; as written, the NSC would establish its own rules and regulations for its functioning.

25. Of equal concern are the final mechanisms for constitutional amendments—mechanisms which make it virtually impossible to alter the 1980 document. The council proposed a simple majority vote in each house of Congress for a proposed constitutional amendment; as written, Article 116 requires a three-fifths vote of both houses. But, if the president vetoes the proposed amendment, it would take a three-quarters vote of both houses to over-

ride. (The council had proposed a two-thirds vote to override.) Since nine members of the thirty-five-member Senate are de facto, and the president appoints two of them directly, those presumably like-minded Senators would need to round up only one more vote to block any such reform. Finally, Article 118 makes it even more difficult to amend Chapters I, VII, X, and XI of the constitution; these govern general principles of institutionality; the formation and attributes of the Constitutional Tribunal; the organization and scope of the armed forces; and the National Security Council. The Council of State had required special procedures only for Chapter I. As written, to amend any of the four chapters, Congress would have to approve the amendment by a three-quarters vote; the amendment would then await the next session of Congress. For it to become law, Congress would then need to approve it intact by a two-thirds vote, no changes permitted. The president could refer the amendment to a plebiscite if he still did not like it. (The plebiscite escape clause was in the council draft as well.) Even a former president of the Conservative party and an ex-senator—Francisco Bulnes Sanfuentes—was moved to observe: the constitution has been converted "into a wall of steel blocking the natural evolution of institutions."[72]

In addition to ignoring the council's proposal for creation of an interim legislature, the junta extended the transition period from the five years the council proposed to eight years. And, through the addition of Article 24, the junta vitiated the council proposal that constitutional guarantees would apply as soon as the constitution took effect.

In fairness, it should be observed that the junta insisted it had not created a "tutelary" role for the armed forces through the mechanism of the National Security Council. Patricio Carvajal, back in as defense minister, said in an extensive 1988 interview, for example, that the language in Article 96 (B) that the armed forces could "represent" their viewpoints meant "advise," not stipulate. But, asked interviewer Raquel Correa, what's the sense of "represents" when you have the tanks, the planes? Carvajal: "... It's an escape valve so that they [the military] don't have to use the tanks and the planes ... President Allende, very proud of his manipulative abilities [su 'muñeca'] called the commanders-in-chief one by one, patted them on the back [los palmoteaba] and told them, 'you, general, you are responsible for saving the country and so you have to do this and that ...'" Now, it will be a council, made up of important personages, which will give the president its estimates [lo que estima]." The interviewer insisted: "And with a military majority what effect do you think that 'estimate' will have?" Carvajal held fast: "It's representing a point of view [*es una representación*]. The president listens and makes his decision."[73]

Jorge Alessandri held his tongue for three years. Finally, on November 8, 1983, in a speech before the Fifth National Entrepreneurial Meeting, he spoke publicly for the first time of his serious misgivings with the junta-drafted constitution. He made plain that when he saw how radically the council's text had been changed—particularly the elimination of an interim Congress, the prolongation of the transition period, and Article 24—he decided to step down as president of the council. But, above all, it was a speech in which he appealed for harmony and a positive approach to building rather than tearing down. He had sharp words, too, for those who sought support abroad to further their political ambitions at home. "Now," he said, "we receive the visits not only of the international organizations to which we belong, but also of 'inspectors' from foreign governments, which is absolutely contrary to our national honor and which cannot be reconciled with the self-esteem which was one of the most outstanding characteristics of Chile as a nation."

In the aftermath of that speech, there were those who attempted to bait him, asking why he had not revealed his reservations before the plebiscite. He responded that he had acted out of what he believed was a sense of honor, of patriotism; to speak out then, he said, would have risked defeat of the plebiscite proposals, "and that, in my judgment, would have led to an extremely grave situation." Besides, he added, the council's text was published on July 9, the junta's one month later, so that there was more than ample time before the plebiscite, which took place the next month, for anyone who really wished to see for himself or herself the very different and contrasting perspectives animating the two. If, he said, more effort had been devoted to that analysis—"which would have demanded a good deal less effort than the rally at the Caupolicán Theater"—the opposition's work would have been more fruitful.

On January 18, 1984, Alessandri met with a group of independent youth leaders. It was his last public appearance. Four days later, he suffered a disabling stroke.[74] Jorge Alessandri died on August 31, 1986, at the age of ninety.

For Eduardo Frei, the end came sooner: at 5:11 P.M., on January 22, 1982, in Santiago's Clínica Santa María. He was eleven days past his seventy-first birthday. His son, Eduardo, said his father "died as a dissident." Five years later, one of his disciples—former party president Andrés Zaldívar Larraín—wrote: "With each passing day, an immense majority of Chilean men and women, young and old, manual laborers and intellectuals, professionals and businessmen, realize that his absence makes it more difficult to find the path we have lost."[75]

Chile was, indeed, bereft now of the two giants from its democratic past. They were two men of a very different vision of their country, of a very different prescription for its governance, for the organization of the society itself. But in one respect, they were identical: each was a man of great integrity, and of a boundless love of his country. Each, in very different ways, left a great void.

DOWN—BUT NOT OUT

The Santiago stock market, established in 1893, is one of the oldest in the world. Beginning in 1978, it began to rise as never before in its history. On May 4, 1981, an event occurred that signaled serious trouble. On that day, trading was halted in shares for the giant Viña del Mar Sugar Refining Company (CRAV, from the Spanish Compañía Refinería de Azúcar de Viña del Mar). Though little noticed at the time, it was the forward edge of an economic storm that very nearly capsized what had begun to appear as an unsinkable ship of state. (The economic situation will be discussed in a subsequent section.)

Wrote Michael Fleet: "With collapse, fragmented and near despairing opposition parties, including the Christian Democrats, won a new and unexpected lease on life. They regained their badly shattered confidence and began to consult and coordinate with one another. Although divisions remained, a new openness on the part of virtually all groups was apparent. *Mapucistas*, Left Christians, Socialists of varying orientations, even the Communists discovered new merit in democratic politics and began to speak of the Christian Democrats and other 'bourgeois' forces in positive terms. Christian Democrats, in turn, hailed the new democratic tendencies of the Left, and some even endorsed Tomic's view of a decade earlier, i.e., that the party could not and should not govern except in alliance with popular (read 'left-wing') forces."[76]

With Frei gone, Zaldívar in exile, and still later, with the death of moderate leader Claudio Orrego, there was, in fact, no significant barrier remaining to restrain the party from following the southern star (i.e., leftist) which had always mesmerized the bulk of the party's elites. Following Zaldívar's ouster, his rival, Tomás Reyes—who had fought for an alliance with the illegal Popular Unity forces—seized control and, for a few months, radicalized the party even more. In party doxology, the power struggle between *chascones* and *guatones** was resolved through

---

* *Chascones*, or "long hairs," were mainly younger and more leftist party members; *guatones*, or "fat bellies," more moderate elements, including *freistas*. The *chascones* sought alliances only on the Left; the *guatones* a center-right alliance.

"consensus." In reality, the election of Gabriel Valdés in April 1982 represented not so much "consensus" as the triumph of the mainstream Left over the Reyes' ultra-leftists, the party's moderates too disorganized and disoriented seriously to challenge either.

Valdés, whose leftist sympathies were evident even during his tenure as Frei's foreign minister, quickly steered the party on a dual-track course: rhetorical and then active confrontation with the regime, accommodation with forces to the PDC's left. Valdés even found words of warmth for Allende. While insisting that the party would not enter into any formal alliances with either the Communists or violence-fostering elements such as the MIR, Valdés did publicly call for legalization of the Communist party—the first time anyone of consequence had done that in Chile since the September revolution. He also sponsored the creation of a Private Political Committee (CPP, Comité Político Privado) to serve as a semiclandestine liaison with the outlawed Marxist-Leninist coalition known as the Popular Democratic Movement (MDP, Movimiento Democrático Popular).[77]

As the economic crisis deepened—by 1982 the official unemployment rate had ballooned to 19.6 percent—cracks appeared in the facade of unity surrounding President Pinochet. A small group of former members of the National party deserted to form the antigovernment Republican party. The National party itself moved to distance itself from Pinochet (and never again would support him as a political leader, although expressing lukewarm support for his policies). Wrote Christian Democrat ideologue Jorge Olave: "instability in the government coalition set off a progressive isolation of Pinochet on the part of his followers, who fattened the ranks of a growing semiopposition . . . The opposition began, then, a 'unilateral' transition, activating political parties and electoral processes in virtually the totality of the professional associations, university student federations and other intermediary organizations, triumphing in all of them."[78]

On May 11, 1983, the opposition took to the streets, in what was to become a series of monthly "days of action." The first event was an ingenious echo of one of the most widely publicized auguries of the end of the Allende regime: a march of the "pots and pans," women parading through the streets of Santiago to protest shortages. The first, by one account, involved 700,000 protesters in Santiago alone and became the model for an annual Day of National Protest.[79] Under the leadership of Christian Democrat Rodolfo Seguel, the Copper Workers Confederation led the first nationwide strike since the onset of junta rule. Lucy Blackburn, a British economist, wrote in the *Encyclopedia Britannica's Book of the Year:* "demands for an acceleration of the timetable for a return to democracy became widespread . . . Opposition to the regime came not only from the workers, who attempted a general strike in June 1983, but also from large sections of the middle class, who felt betrayed by the collapse of their country's economy. Many industrialists and farmers who previously had backed the regime wholeheartedly switched their allegiances and became eager for change. Even within the ranks of the army, discontent was alleged to be rife. In July, a group of army officers issued a document calling upon soldiers 'in the interests of our fatherland and with honour and responsibility . . . to make imperative a change in the helm of the government and in the supreme command of the armed forces . . . Few commentators believed that President Pinochet would complete his full term of office and remain in power until 1989 . . ."

Wrote Olave: "Opposition political leaders concluded that the authority of Pinochet was seriously weakened and his abdication imminent . . ."[80]

On August 22, 1983, a coalition of mainly leftist parties stitched together by Valdés and Socialists Julio Stuardo and Hernán Vodanovic issued their Democratic Alliance (AD, for Alianza Democrática) proclamation. It called for Pinochet's immediate resignation, the formation of a provisional government, and a return to full democracy within eighteen months. Three weeks later, on September 10, the hard Left announced the formation of the Popular Democratic Movement (MDP) made up of the Communist party, the MIR, the far left Socialists headed by former Allende minister Clodomiro Almeyda, and three revolutionary minigroups. They, too, called for an end of Pinochet's rule, but insisted that it be forced through violence, street demonstrations, strikes, and sabotage. Incidents of violence did rise sharply beginning in 1983, peaking in late 1986. On January 15, 1984, the Communist party high command announced via Radio Moscow that 1984 would be "The Year of the General Strike to finish off the dictatorship."[81]

The opposition had overplayed its hand, and Pinochet was about to get a better grip on his. "There they are," he fumed, "democrats who call themselves Christians, together with Socialists or Communists. What impudence, gentlemen, what lack of morality, lack of a concept of honor!"

Until then, he had relied mainly on a mailed fist: for the August "day of action," there were eighteen thousand army troops in the streets of the cities, and labor and other protest leaders (including Seguel) were jailed en masse, a curfew reinstated. During the protests, which lasted through the end of the year, a total of sixty persons died in clashes, hundreds more were injured, thousands arrested.

Now, Pinochet switched to a velvet glove.

On August 10, he reshuffled his Cabinet, increasing the number of civilians from nine to twelve. Key among them: Sergio Onofre Jarpa, sixty-two-year-old former senator and president of the National party. Onofre's charge: political dialogue.

Parallel with that, Pinochet announced a series of conciliatory measures: on August 26, the state of emergency was lifted (but the Public Disturbances Law, due to expire at the end of the month, was extended for six months); a list was published naming more than one thousand exiles who would be allowed to return; and three top Christian Democratic leaders were released from jail.[82]

With the political opening came political pettifogging, the bastard progeny of long-suppressed rivalries, frustrated ambitions, thwarted ideals. In the phrase of sociologist Carlos Huneeus, the opposition had for too long operated as "elites," dwelling in policy "catacombs," developing, debating theories and day-dreams behind the backs of the people. The challenge now was to articulate answers, in the open, to broad-based problems. It remained an elusive goal. Although the political opening in Chile did not, as Olave wrote, match the experience of Spain, where—following Franco's death—122 political parties and groups of one kind or another sprouted, new parties no sooner appeared than they divided and subdivided. One after another added a hyphen to the name of an existing party, followed by the name of the new caudillo of that particular variant of political inspiration to differentiate his from everyone else's. Pacts, accords, blocs, assemblies, multiplied almost as fast.[83]

As talks with the Democratic Alliance sputtered, Jarpa concentrated on a different task: forging an alliance of conservative groups. On July 1, 1984, Jarpa announced success: the formation of a powerful coalition of eight conservative parties. Juan de Dios Carmona was rumored to be the man who would head the new federation. The deal fell apart one month later.[84]

While the politicians wrangled and finagled, violence continued. With the Communist party's own armed wing—the Frente Manuel Rodríguez (FMR)—now fully operational, more than 130 bomb attacks were recorded in the first three months of the year. On April 1, the FMR claimed credit for a series of explosions that cut off electric power to two-thirds of the country. On March 23, a ninety-day state of emergency was restored, Santiago was placed under a curfew for two days, and by month's end, more than six hundred arrests were made. Continued bombings led, on May 15, to a new and tougher antiterrorist law, which reinstated the death penalty for those guilty of terrorist murders. Days of national protest were organized anew in March, April, May, September, and October. On November 5, the Cabinet resigned to give President Pinochet greater freedom to deal with the worsening situation. He promptly ordered an even tougher crackdown, declaring another state of siege, the first in over seven years. More than five hundred persons were seized in a series of lightning raids on Santiago shantytowns, traditional havens of far left terrorists.

The regime came under siege from two other quarters. On May 24, opposition leaders filed suit accusing the president and his family of corruption; on May 25, an Appeals Court judge ruled that he lacked constitutional authority to try the president. Still later, a group of lawyers tried to bring a related case against Pinochet, claiming the state had been cheated of $30,000 in a land deal near the president's home. That case, too, was voided on the same grounds.[85]

Equally ugly confrontations occurred between the church and the regime. In January 1984, the hierarchy enlisted the support of Pope John Paul II to obtain the safe conducts for four members of the MIR who had sought asylum in the Vatican's diplomatic mission in Santiago. The four, accused of murdering the military governor of Santiago in August 1983, were permitted to leave for Ecuador following the pope's personal plea. In February, four hundred protesters took shelter in the cathedral of Punta Arenas while Pinochet was visiting that southern city. The president angrily accused the church of organizing the protest and turning young people against the government. Against the backdrop of mounting violence, the church accused the regime of responsibility for a fivefold increase in reported torture cases during 1983. Months later, in September, church-state relations sank even lower when, during one of the "days of action," a French priest was shot and killed.

Behind the scenes, Jarpa worked with the Council of State through most of 1984 to create the machinery for the transition to democracy. Those proposals were unveiled in September and included draft legislation governing voter registration, as well as the legalization and regulation of political parties. He tried also to persuade President Pinochet to move the date for the presidential plebiscite forward from 1988 or 1989 to 1987, to put into effect the political parties' laws in 1984, and the election of Congress in 1985. He also fought for another proposal emanating from the conservative "Group of 8": foreswearing the use of Article 24. The Christian Democrats and their allies of the Democratic Alliance, meanwhile, produced proposals of their own in August, including one that the laws regulating political activity be hammered out in talks between the government and opposition instead of unilaterally.

The president gave his answer in September: he intended to serve out the entirety of his term, not due to expire until March 11, 1989. On October 29, he followed with an announcement that legalization of the political parties was on hold, and that no elections would be held except under the timetable envisioned by the 1980 constitution. On January 11, 1985, the president accepted Jarpa's resignation, and that same afternoon swore in Ricardo García Rodríguez as interior minister.

The days of "political opening" were at an end. The opposition would try again and again to force a speedier timetable, to compel changes in the institutional framework. But the brief window of opportunity for forcing a weakened and defensive president to step down was now firmly shut, and would not be reopened. By the end of 1984, political risk analysts Frost and Sullivan gave Pinochet a 55 percent chance of surviving the next eighteen months—though they also predicted that he would be replaced within the next five years, i.e., before the end of his term in 1989.[86]

Pinochet was once again in command, in no small measure because the opposition was leaderless and in disarray. Further, with the signing of the Vatican-mediated peace accord with Argentina, the country faced no serious threats on its borders for the first time since the junta had come to power. Finally, though it was little noticed then—and when it was, dismissed with what amounted to a good deal of wishful political thinking—the Chilean economy was already on the road to recovery.

The problem was that the opposition refused to believe that it lacked the power to work its will on the regime, and so politicians continued to hatch plan after plan in smoke-filled rooms, while the acrid smoke of teargas and the angry sights and sounds of confrontation continued on the streets.

Through the waning months of 1984 and first months of 1985, the Group of 24—the opposition's constitution-drafting group—toiled to bring forth a new transition plan of its own. In the end, it died stillborn. The Communists declined to sign because it would have required that they renounce violence; as recently as their January 1985 Central Committee plenum, the party had concluded that the times called for violence because "a revolutionary situation is rapidly maturing" in Chile. The Christian Democrats balked at entering into any kind of agreement with the Communists so long as they espoused violence. Party President Gabriel Valdés, in an April 1985 letter to the Communist party's Central Committee, said the PDC rejected violence as a matter of principle. But, he said, the PDC also believed that the Communists were playing into "the dictator's" hands by resorting to violence, a war he said the opposition could only lose.[87] No sooner had the Group of 24 proposal died than another arose, on April 16, 1985. This group called itself Democratic Intransigence (DI) and lumped together groups as disparate as Communists, humanists, and dissident rightists of the Republican party. DI advocated a campaign of civil disobedience and implacable opposition to bring the regime down. Although the Christian Democrats had been preaching the same thing as far back as 1980, once again they declined to take part, and another antigovernment scheme fell apart.

Finally, under the sponsorship of Cardinal Juan Francisco Fresno, the opposition managed to unite in principle as never before in a National Accord, signed on August 25. This one brought together eleven parties, including the six of the PDC-led Democratic Alliance, and, significantly, two rightist parties, the National party and Jarpa's National Union. Toning down the earlier demands which had splattered off a wall of solid junta resistance, the National Accord demanded relatively few immediate changes—the most important, the abandonment of Article 24. The only change demanded in the ground rules governing the elections, as provided for in the 1980 constitution, was direct presidential and congressional elections in 1989 instead of the presidential plebiscite, followed a year later by elections of congressmen to serve staggered terms. As indicated earlier, junta member Gen. Fernando Matthei said, "if the Accord did not exist, we would have to help to create it"; the new Carabinero commandant (and junta member) Gen. Rodolfo Stange agreed, and after first indicating reticence, so did Admiral Merino. But one person did not: President Pinochet rejected the proposals out of hand, arguing that he was not going to negotiate away instruments for which he had achieved 67 percent popular support in the plebiscite.

Once again, there were rumblings of military rebellion. On November 7, the president notified the junta that he had ordered eight generals into retirement, including junta member Lt. Gen. César Raúl Benavides. Benavides, the number two-ranking general behind Pinochet, had been promoted only the year before to the newly created rank of lieutenant general. Lt. Gen. Julio Canessa was named to replace Benavides as head of the army and the army's representative on the junta. Although not nearly so public and explosive as the challenge he had faced eight years earlier from Gustavo Leigh, the Benavides episode presented Pinochet with the second—and last—direct threat to his rule at the level of the junta.[88]

Chile suffered more than man-made violence in 1985. Although it was far less reported in the international press than the street violence, the country was wrenched on March 3 by a calamitous earthquake registering more than 8 on the Richter scale, causing at least 177 deaths and more than $1.8 billion worth of damage to the tottering economy. Port facilities in Valparaíso and other major sea terminals were severely damaged.

Having quashed the internal challenge, Pinochet now moved to face down the external one. In the aftermath of tumultuous protests September 4–6 which left ten dead and 120 injured, Pinochet reimposed a state of emergency, and the church denounced what it called an "escalating spiral of madness." Attempting to check that spiral, the cardinal invited government figures to join signers of the National Accord at the traditional Te Deum Mass celebrating the country's independence on September 18. According to one report, the government responded by surrounding the cathedral with its supporters, who harassed the cardinal's guests as they left the mass.

Still, the cardinal persisted in seeking to persuade Pinochet to reconsider the accord's proposals. Finally, a month after the cardinal had requested the meeting, the president received the prelate on December 24. The meeting lasted less than twenty minutes. When the cardinal attempted to raise the subject of the accord, the president brushed it aside with a wave of the hand: "No, no," he was quoted as saying, "better turn the page."

In the phrase of the Christian Democrat-supporting magazine *Hoy*, if 1985 was the year of peace talks, 1986 would be "the year of the rifle."[89]

And so it was.

Believing the "correlation of forces" was right for them, Communist party leaders designated 1986 "The Decisive Year," the year they believed they could drive Pinochet from power through a combination of terrorism and mass demonstrations. The party's military arm, the Manuel Rodríguez Front (FMR), felt sufficiently emboldened to expand the size of its terrorist units from cells to larger "columns." According to a report in *Berliner Morgenpost*, many of those terrorists learned their lessons—including "silent assassination" and bombing techniques—at a secret terrorist training camp at Naumburg (on the Saale River in East Germany, near Leipzig). In just two years—January 1984 through December 1986—more than six hundred Chileans died or were wounded in terrorist acts.[90]

Strikes were a key part of the campaign to bring the regime down. Manuel Bustos, top leader of National Labor Command (CTN, for Comando Nacional de Trabajadores), said at the time: "We will call as many strikes as are needed to finish with Pinochet and his regime."

It was during that wave of violence that one of the most widely publicized human rights events took place. With the National Accord now a dead letter, the fifty-six-year-old head of the Medical Association, Dr. Juan Luis González Reyes, decided to move into the vacuum. In April 1986, he created the Assembly of Civility; bringing together many of the earlier dissidents but also including the clandestine Communist party. The assembly's moment of truth was centered on the Demand of Chile—two days of public protest, strikes, and rallies intended to paralyze the country. (They largely succeeded.) During those two days—July

2nd and 3rd—six persons died and more than six hundred were injured. Among the dead: Rodrigo Rojas de Negri, Chilean-born but then a legal resident of the U.S. and who had lived most of his nineteen years in the United States. Among the injured: Carmen Gloria Quintana, then eighteen. Rojas, visiting Chile, had gone with Quintana to Santiago's Nogales shantytown to take part in an antigovernment demonstration. When soldiers appeared, the crowd scattered, but Rojas and Quintana were detained. At the time, Rojas was carrying a Molotov cocktail. According to Quintana, the soldiers took them to another street, beat them, then doused them with gasoline and set them on fire. She said that when Rojas tried to smother the flames, they hit him again. After the flames died down, she said they were taken in a truck to the outskirts of the city and dumped in a ditch, left for dead. But they managed to crawl to a road, where they were found. Rodrigo died four days later. Quintana suffered third-degree burns over two-thirds of her body. In the first two years after the incident, she underwent a total of thirty-six operations; two more years of operations would be needed to reconstruct her face and body, although doctors have told her there will always be scars on her face, as well as her legs, arms, and part of her back. A few months after the incident, her family moved to Canada, although they later returned to Chile, and Carmen Quintana herself plans to return to resume her university studies (she was a freshman engineering student at the University of Santiago when the episode happened).

In the aftermath, the twenty-five members of the army platoon involved were turned over to military justice, but finally only Lt. Pedro Fernández Dittus was jailed (for six months), accused of "unnecessary use of violence with a resulting death and serious injuries." He later was released on bail pending the possibility of further action on a reduced charge (the "quasi-crime of homicide," which some attacked as implying the incident was "an accident").[91]

The Rojas-Quintana incident created new tensions in relations between Chile and the United States and joined the Letelier case as a point of attack for anti-Pinochet forces in the U.S. Congress.

For Dr. González, the Demand of Chile earned him forty-five days in prison—and, the following year, a medal presented by the Department of Human Rights of the U.S. Academy of Sciences, as well as honorary membership in that body.[92]

By September, after a year-long wave of bombings, hit-run attacks on policemen and public installations, and other sabotage, the FMR activated "Plan Twentieth Century," their boldest operation of all: a plan to assassinate President Pinochet. As seen in chapter 10, the nearly successful September 7 attempt backfired badly. It not only led to a new—

and highly effective—crackdown on the terrorists themselves, it galvanized public support behind Pinochet and precipitated the collapse of the most ambitious opposition political coalition yet, the National Democratic Accord (ANDE).

ANDE arose from the ashes of the moribund Assembly of Civility. The center-right National party—by then, a hollow echo of its once robust self—had been in a *paso doble* with the Christian Democrats since 1984: dramatic movement forward, dramatic spin, and then movement backward. In October of 1984, party leaders believed they had reached agreement on a document of consensus with the PDC, drafted jointly;[93] suddenly, the PDC pulled out, sent the Nationals a polite letter calling the document very important, but declining to sign.

The following year came the National Accord, which the National party signed—but with misgivings. Pedro Correa, secretary-general of the National party, said the problem was that two "extreme" parties were included: on the Left, the Christian Left ("in common cause with the Communists"), and on the Right, Union Nacional ("too tied to the government"). Although rejected by Pinochet, there remained one ray of hope, one incentive for trying again: The fact that the heads of eleven parties consented to sign such an accord, as ex-PDC President Andrés Zaldívar put it, showed that agreement could be reached on fundamental points among parties from the Left to the Right.[94]

Building on that spirit of broad consensus, the so-called "Group of 13"—thirteen parties from the center-right National party to MAPU on the hard left, and this time including a newcomer to the political scene called the Humanist party—negotiated a revised version of the National Accord. Called the National Democratic Accord (ANDE), it contained ambitious "Bases for the Sustaining of a Future Democratic Accord." ANDE enjoyed one brief moment of success: the coordinators (headed by Correa) managed to arrange a meeting to discuss their plan with junta members Admiral Merino and General Stange. Finally, on September 8, 1986, the plan was unveiled.[95] The timing could not have been worse. September 7 was the date of the attempted assassination of President Pinochet. On September 8, the country was once again under state of siege, the after-shock of the four hundred bullets fired at the presidential caravan decimating dialogue.

Though there were those who still did not or would not acknowledge it, the time when the political opposition could imagine it might create its own rules and timetables was past.[96] For a few, violence remained an option. For both the Right and the Left, it was a time to pursue more realistic alliances with those of similar ideological outlook. For the Christian Democrats, it was a time to rethink their choices of strategies, of leaders. For all those political actors of greatest visibility—though not necessarily of greatest real popular support—a single imperative would gradually, haltingly emerge: to unite long enough, credibly enough, to defeat Augusto Pinochet.

JOURNEY'S END

I tell you that it [the assassination attempt] has strengthened my will to fight to the last moment of my life for the defense of the values which set Chile apart as a nation.

President Pinochet, looking back on the assassination attempt[97]

If there had been any doubt in anyone's mind before, there could be no excuse for doubt any longer: the days of "dialogue" were over.

"The opposition made the wrong diagnosis, and so they had the wrong strategy," Pinochet said early in 1987. The diagnosis was that the government was weak, and that it could be ousted, by force, by persuasion, by the combination of both. As a result, the opposition did not so much oppose the government as make war on it. "That," concluded the newsmagazine *Qué Pasa*, "was their first mistake—that they were capable of overthrowing the regime." Now they would have to slug it out on the terrain of electioneering, of votes. But, the magazine added, the public had less and less confidence in politicians. And so there was only one viable strategy left: to unite in saying "No." More, they could not agree on, and as the months passed, it became plainer that the fractious and disputatious opposition could barely agree on that.[98]

On New Year's Eve, 1986, Pinochet announced an end to the state of siege, the virtual end to banishment of radicals and all but a handful of self-styled revolutionaries, and the imminence of the third of the laws setting the stage for the transition back to democracy: the law regulating political parties. (The Election Qualifying Court Law had been enacted early in 1986, the Election Registration Law on October 1, 1986.) Buoyant and confident, the president then went on vacation.

Politicians, by contrast, went almost immediate into orbit.

"The law," fumed Social Democrat Arturo Venegas, "establishes so many obstacles for the formation and functioning of a party that, given the authoritarian characteristics of the regime, it makes impracticable the right of association."

Trabas—obstacles—there were. They were put there in fulfillment of the junta's long-standing conviction that the unregulated and unrestrained activities of political parties, infiltrating and politicizing every sector of the society, were among the chief causes of polarization and chaos in the country in the years leading up to 1973. But the law had not been formed in haste. Work on it had begun in June 1984. In October 1986, Pinochet ordered Interior Minister Ricardo García to invite comments. A number of political groups presented ideas; many did not. García consulted with law professors and constitutional scholars, traveled from one end of the country to the other sounding opinions. In all, twenty presentations were received. On January 15, 1987—two weeks after Pinochet had dispatched the draft to them—the junta, in its role as legislature, approved the law and sent it to the Constitutional Tribunal for final review and approval. Main features of the new law:

- In order to limit proliferation of miniparties, the law required that for a party to qualify as a national party, it must enroll at least one-half of 1 percent of the registered voters in at least eight of the country's thirteen administrative regions; purely regional parties could be created under similar ground rules. Until after the first election of deputies (in 1990), arbitrary minimums were established for each region, ranging from two hundred signatures in the Eleventh Region (Aisén, in the far south, population 65,000) to thirteen thousand for Metropolitan Santiago. To qualify nationally: 33,550. Timetable for qualifying: 210 days, beginning thirty days after the party petitions for legal recognition when it is declared a "party in formation." To survive as a party, it must poll a minimum of 5 percent of the total vote in congressional elections every four years. A party could also be dissolved if more than one-half of its members resign—a familiar phenomenon in Chile during the sixties and seventies.
- By contrast with past practice, a party's officers and presidential candidate must be chosen openly, by the full membership. The membership must also approve mergers with other parties. To foster decentralization of the leadership—and, specifically, to cut down on the power of the traditionally overweening capital region—no one region can have more than twice as many representatives as any other region on the party's general council. (The council is the policy-making caucus of its members in the Senate and Chamber of Deputies.)
- No party can accept funds from abroad, and all party financial records must be open to public audit.
- Party membership rolls are public record. (Party leaders at first objected heatedly to this provision; later, when registration was well along, they discovered the advantages—for direct-mail and other proselytizing purposes—of buying those lists from the Electoral Service. The very first to do so, in fact, were those who had protested most strenuously, the Christian Democrats and a Socialist group, Popular Party for Democracy, paying 200,000 pesos for

microfiches of the full 4 million then registered, 500,000–700,000 pesos for the computerized lists [roughly $825 for microfiches; $2,050–$2,870 for computerized lists].)[99]

Particularly galling to the old-line parties was the prohibition, in Article 2, against party participation in unions, and in community and other "intermediary" organizations. The law also required that cabinet ministers, ambassadors, the president and his personal appointees could not, during the time of their service, remain active in or be subject to the discipline of parties.

Eugenio Ortega, secretary-general of the Christian Democratic party, said the new law should be ignored. Party president Gabriel Valdés said, under the new law, all social leaders would have to resign as party activists—and that, he was not about to accept. "Why should I lose the entire social mass that we have? Who would I be left with? All the social leadership is of my party: the presidents of student federations of the University of Chile, the biggest; of the Catholic University, of the University of Valparaíso, of the University of Concepción; the presidents of all of the big unions—copper, oil, textiles, railroads, telephones, electricity—they're all in my party. The presidents of the professional associations—the bar, engineers, architects, doctors, agronomists, sociologists—they're all Christian Democrats. I do not accept this rule of Pinochet's, because it violates the rights of association." On January 24, the expanded National Council of the party, numbering some ninety persons, met to debate the level of participation on its governing board of precisely those "social" leaders, as well as the make-up of the national directive and regional organizations. Party Vice President Claudio Huepe said the party would resolve these questions according to their own rules, and that no government law would dictate their structure.

On January 29, five opposition legal scholars filed a ten-page brief with the Constitutional Tribunal in which they asked that the tribunal declare the law unconstitutional. Interestingly, they framed their petition within the precepts of the 1980 constitution, referring to rights "consecrated" in that document. The tribunal rejected their petition, and on March 11, the law became effective.[100] Defiance thereafter gave way to a blend of compliance on the basics—the ground rules for qualifying as a legal party—evasion elsewhere.

Fund-raising was a conspicuous example of evasion. Opposition political figures logged 652 foreign trips in the space of two years (1986–1988); former PDC President Andrés Zaldívar posted forty-two himself (though many were in his interlocking capacity as president of the Christian Democrat International organization). Even church figures—conspicuously linked to the Christian Democrats—made frequent trips abroad, both raising money, and (not infrequently) the hackles of the government with their anti-Pinochet statements. Favorite destinations were Washington, Bonn, Madrid, and Caracas—all bastions of support for the Christian Democrats. Top PDC leaders, including labor leader Manuel Bustos, lionized by the AFL–CIO, maintained a virtual shuttle to Washington, meeting with administration figures from President Reagan and Secretary of State George Schultz on down.[101] Increasingly, and in increasing amounts, foreign funding flowed to Chile to finance "studies," and "political consciousness-raising"—almost all of it for parties or groups on the center-left or farther left. In one spectacular case, a massive sum of money was earmarked from Washington without the Chileans even asking for it. But money and moral support were not all the pied pipers of Chilean politics sought abroad; at one point early in 1987, PDC President Valdés even floated the idea of asking former President Jimmy Carter—a favorite of the Christian Democrats—to head a U.S. committee for free elections in Chile[102] (Carter declined then, but later, in 1988, joined former president Gerald Ford as honorary co-chair of an elections watchdog group engineered by implacable Chile-basher Teddy Kennedy.) (The foreign dimension in the final stages of the political process will be examined in a subsequent section.)

While most Chileans were still enjoying their summer vacations, the political process took another giant step forward on February 25, 1987, when registration of voters began. Within one month, 333,000 had signed up. As registration continued, the source of the anxiety of political leaders became more evident. In Chile, as in most other democracies, a relatively small number of voters are political "activists," but in Chile the number of those enrolled in specific parties had never exceeded 10 percent of the total electorate. That 10 percent tended to come largely from the ranks of the "social leadership" which was the backbone, in particular, of the Christian Democrats and which the parties were not, theoretically, barred from organizing and taking over. (This is one of the provisions of the new party law most flagrantly ignored.) Despite a proliferation of public opinion polls—mostly commissioned by the political parties or institutes allied to them—purporting to "prove" high levels of allegiance to the parties, reality showed otherwise as the country neared its long-awaited rendezvous with democratic elections. Fifteen months after registration began, a record 6.5 million Chileans (of an estimated 8 million eligible) had already registered to vote. Of that number, 233,245 had signed party cards—not even 3 percent of the electorate.[103] (The final tally, when registration rolls were closed on August 30, 1988: 7,435,913, or 92.11 percent of the country's voting age population.)

Elaborate safeguards were built into the voter registration system—

beginning with the unimpeachable integrity of the man named to head it, Juan Ignacio García. Long-time professor of constitutional law at the University of Chile, García had first joined the Election Registration Service in 1964 as a young lawyer, rising to the level of deputy director during the Frei and Allende years. Many of the provisions used in past elections were built into the new legislation, with some add-ons: for example, to vote, persons will need not only their registration card, but personal identity card as well. Further, since the lists are computerized, detection of double-registration and other fraudulent practices has been made more efficient. At the polling places themselves on election day, every party legally qualified will have the right to post observers, as well as the five official monitors (*vocales*) assigned to each polling place.[104]

On the same day that the new political parties law went into effect, March 11, the opposition went over to the long-delayed electoral counteroffensive. On that day, Sergio Molina Silva—Frei's first finance minister and a top PDC strategist—formed a "nonpartisan" Movement for Free Elections (later, the Committee of Personages). Molina himself rapidly became the anointed instrument for official Washington, and his movement one of the principal beneficiaries of foreign "investment" in the Chilean electoral process. As shall be seen in a subsequent section, not since 1964 had foreign intervention in Chilean internal affairs reached such levels of financial and institutional activity. Now—as then—the Christian Democrats were the principal beneficiaries, and now—as then—foreign interference was met either with media silence or approval, in stark contrast to the outcries that surrounded the far more modest levels of intervention in the 1970 election that put Salvador Allende in power.

Genaro Arriagada, former secretary-general of the Christian Democrat party, now serving as secretary-general of the Coordinating Committee for Free Elections, observed:* "In the matter of foreign money, the opposition has pangs of conscience—in the sense that we don't like it. But, on the other hand, we also know that, in a picture of such disproportions as to include spending for publicity, to reject that money—provided its sources are clear and public—would signify accepting the continuation of a regime which is a disgrace to the country. It's a complex situation. I don't know of anyone in the opposition who doesn't have doubts of conscience about it . . ." But, then, Arriagada spoke more than a year after the money began to cascade into Chile.[105]

---

* Late in 1987, Molina's group reconstituted itself as the Committee of Personages so as to claim the "moral high ground" of appearing to fight only for clean elections—and thus be eligible for the U.S. funding unavailable to a purely partisan group. The battle for the "No" was then entrusted to a fellow Christian Democrat—Arriagada—and hence the "new" Coordinating Committee for Free Elections.

With the visit of the pope to Chile, April should have brought a pause in the rapidly heating-up political process. It did not, for two reasons. The first was the decision of the underground Left—chiefly the long dormant and atomized Movement of the Revolutionary Left (MIR)—to attempt to disrupt the pope's huge outdoor mass in Santiago's O'Higgins Park. Wearing masks and throwing rocks, the attackers provoked disturbances that left 260 persons injured. In the aftermath, virtually the entire political leadership, including all but the extreme left of the Christian Democrat hierarchy, joined in blasting the MIR and the above-ground umbrella organization of the outlawed parties, the Democratic Popular Movement (MDP, for Movimiento Democrático Popular). The effect was to chill enthusiasm for alliances with the far Left, all but assuring the isolation of the Communists.

The second was the message that the pope introduced on his return to Rome, that, at the minimum, there might be danger to the church from the Left as well as from that more familiar church villain, the Right: "The Catholic church cannot remain indifferent," he said, "to the anti-religious aspects of Marxist ideology." Monsignor Angelo Sodano, the papal nuncio in Santiago, later reinforced that message: "Christians everywhere," he said, "should meditate on what the pope said about the church in Latin America not ignoring Marxist attacks on it. Marxist criticism of religion—and not criticism, but condemnation of religion—is another matter to which we cannot remain indifferent." (One year later, after serving ten years in Chile, Monsignor Sodano was appointed to the number three post in the Vatican, secretary of the Council for Public Affairs—giving greater importance yet to the place of Chile in the papal scheme of things.) For his pains, the pope found the walls of Rome plastered with posters attacking his performance in Chile.

At all odds, the papal message produced an almost immediate thaw in state-church relations. Cardinal Fresno not only turned up at La Moneda to accept a medal from President Pinochet with the nuncio looking on, but embarked on a tour of military bases, including the air force base in Antarctica in company of junta members Generals Matthei and Gordon. "None of this," Carta Confidencial, a staunchly progovernment publication commented, "could have happened if his Holiness John Paul II had carried away a negative impression of the Chilean government."[106]

With the pope's message still ringing in their ears—and besieged from all sides with appeals to take one or another side in the developing political denouement—thirty bishops gathered in June for the Episcopal Conference's Extraordinary Assembly. Their meeting also took place just a few weeks after Communist party leader Luis Guastavino's stunning proposal that the aged Card. Raúl Silva Henríquez agree to serve as head of a provisional government (an idea the retired prelate toyed with briefly, before rejecting it at the end of May). The document the bishops produced, *The Challenges to Reconciliation,* resembled previous ones in that it lent itself to multiple interpretations. But on one point it was crystal clear: "It is our wish that not one Chilean Catholic fail to register or to vote when the time comes. We should be examples of good citizens." Furthermore, they urged registration "as soon as possible." In their April 1988 plenary, the bishops ratcheted up the intensity of their message (*In Justice and Peace*), saying that while the forthcoming plebiscite would not solve all the problems of the country, "it will determine in grand measure the conditions for getting along with each other" (*convivencia*).[107]

In a church so long radicalized, it was inevitable that many would reject the notion that the real enemy of reconciliation in Chile was on their left. The bishops themselves, in their reaction to the O'Higgins Park disturbances, declined to mention the MIR as responsible for it. Msgr. Jorge Hourton was quoted in the clandestine Communist party publication, *El Siglo,* as saying he found it difficult to believe the Communists had planned the disorders. With the plebiscite only a few months away, a church-connected group—backed by more than $1 million in funding, most of it from the United States and ostensibly set up to assist in informing and registering voters—was forced by a public outcry to back off when it was discovered they were actually mocking a "Yes" vote, while advocating a thumbs-down "No" vote. Militants of the "popular church" continued to take part in antigovernment acts; an American nun and a French seminarian were among a religious group arrested in a protest at La Moneda commemorating the third anniversary of the decapitation murders of three Communist leaders. But the most spectacular episode of all was reserved for the eighty-one-year-old Card. Raúl Silva Henríquez. When his successor, Cardinal Fresno, received his medal at La Moneda, Cardinal Silva—who had locked horns with Pinochet from the very beginning—was conspicuous by his absence. Then, as 1988 dawned, Cardinal Silva made plain, in a series of interviews given in Spain and Italy, just how strong his anti-Pinochet passions were. Among his statements:

- The situation is bad because General Augusto Pinochet does not want to leave. In part, because he has nowhere to go. Where can he go where they won't kill him? a Spanish journalist who interviewed me recently said, and I believe that he was right. That man's [Pinochet's] days are numbered if he leaves there.
- It's very difficult to know whether a dictator has public support. I don't believe so. What he has is the backing of the armed forces, and

the support of the rich class [*la alta burguesía*], but not all of them. I don't know whether even 30 percent of the electorate will vote for Pinochet . . .

- First there have to be elections. Fair elections, without fraud. If Pinochet is elected legally, we must respect him.
- The military will give the country back its lost liberty [after the plebiscite]. If the vote count is respected, the Chilean people will vote against Pinochet.
- The opposition can win the plebiscite convoked by the regime so as to assure its remaining in power for eight more years if at least three conditions are met: that a sufficient number of persons register, that the voting be free, informed and secret, and that the vote count is clean.
- Military men are not made to govern. At least not in my country.
- The coup of 1973 initiated an undesirable situation in breaking with the administration of Salvador Allende which, although imperfect, was a democracy . . . The de facto government was born because the totality of human rights were [*sic*] not respected in time. The military did not want power, but the majority of the people asked their intervention to put an end to the stupidity [*torpeza*] of some Communists and Marxist-Leninist socialists, who divided the Allende government so as to install a dictatorship of the proletariat.
- The best way to assure the future democracy is to abandon every kind of vengeance against the military, including Augusto Pinochet.
- On torture and justice: It is a usual situation, and the fault of Pinochet, and he and the torturers ought to be punished.
- On Communist strength: They are more powerful than before. It's incredible. These military came to finish off the Communists and what they have done is to make them stronger.
- The military have stained their hands with blood. They thought everything goes against communism. Unfortunately, they did not achieve it [the defeat of communism]. In the time of democracy, the Communists never got more than 19 percent of the vote. Now, after fourteen years of dictatorship, they get 30 percent in the university. We [the church] have not protected the Communists as such, but as persons persecuted who merit the support of the church.
- I did not say in Madrid that communism was the principal enemy of Chile. I maintain that the government of Chile is the enemy of communism, in the same way that communism is of the military regime. And that if you look at the reality of the country, it can be said that communism has increased its presence, which is the equivalent of a defeat of the regime.
- I believe that the military will hand power back. The army, I am sure of it, is going to understand that it's time to go. The problem is where to put Mr. Pinochet. The Chilean military did not want to

enter government, but Chileans, a majority of them, demanded it and pushed them into it. The stupidity of the socialists and Communists contributed to that as they tried to install their dictatorship of the proletariat.

- On church unity: It is pretty united, although there are dissensions. I wouldn't know how to tell you how many church members support Pinochet.
- On the Christian Democrats: In this moment, it is, without question, the majority party and it is campaigning for a 'No' in the plebiscite.

In the wake of the storm his remarks provoked in Chile, Cardinal Silva told an interviewer in Turín: "I've said what I think. I didn't want to bother the government. I have had to speak, and I have said what I think. Perhaps I'm wrong. But that's what I think and I cannot lie."

Bishop Carlos Camus of Linares—who earlier had said that the time might come when those who had tried to assassinate President Pinochet in the 1986 attack which left five dead would be thought of as heroes—offered immediate support. "Cardinal Silva Henríquez," he said, "speaks immense truths in a country accustomed to live with lies for some time now."

The reigning church hierarchy was more circumspect. Cardinal Fresno said he joined in the sentiments of the president of the Episcopal Conference, Bishop Carlos González, that it would not be "prudent to comment because we do not know the entirety of what the cardinal may have said, and it might have been distorted." Asked about a strong government protest to the Vatican, the nuncio's office declined comment.[108]

On April 8, 1987, the ban was lifted on public meetings by political parties. The race was on.

Coalition-building was uppermost in the minds of political leaders once they realized that it was a plebiscite—or nothing. Already in late 1986, the U.S. National Endowment for Democracy (NED) had bank-rolled a meeting of eleven opposition parties in Caracas, Venezuela, in an effort to form a united front. A year later, an opposition leader complained that throughout most of 1987, Chile's political parties spent their time staring at their own belly buttons, while the government monopolized the agenda of issues.[109]

That same leader, Genaro Arriagada, believed that Chilean politicians needed to borrow from the lessons of Venezuela, Spain, Portugal, Uruguay, Brazil, and Argentina, where political parties were able to retain their separate identities yet could agree on broad programs for a return to civilian rule after military dictatorships. The problem in

Chile, he said, was "maximum-ism": holding out for unattainable, overly ambitious and detailed goals and programs. The answer for Chile, he argued, was simply to agree to defeat Pinochet in the plebiscite by registering enough voters and then persuading them to vote "No"; ideological differences, competition among candidates, that could come later, in the ensuing direct election of a president.

Arriagada knew whereof he spoke; the year had witnessed an endless series of coalition marches and countermarches.

The first one was easy; no sooner had the political parties law been approved by the junta than three conservative groups—Jaime Guzmán's Democratic Independent Union (UDI), Andrés Allamand's National Union (NU), and Sergio Onofre Jarpa's National Labor Front—agreed to fuse in a new party called National Renewal (Renovación Nacional). They were joined shortly afterwards by Juan de Dios Carmona's Social Christian Movement. The group immediately made overtures to the former bulwark of the Right, the National party. On February 16, in the course of a forum in Santiago, leaders of those parties, plus two other small rightist parties, proclaimed unity on a basic point: "Never Again a '64' "—a reference to the unconditional support the Right had given Eduardo Frei in 1964 in order to block the election of Salvador Allende. (The Christian Democrats rewarded them then by freezing the Right out of their government altogether, then refusing to join with them in a 1970 alliance to defeat Allende.) Union seemed near. But, when the colorful Patricio Phillips Peñafiel replaced his wife, Carmen Sáenz, as president of the National party in May, the climate for fusion chilled noticeably. Finally, on June 6, the National party broke off the talks. Observers, noting that the National party had initiated talks with parties as far to the left as the pro-Marxist Christian Left (IC, for Izquierda Cristiana), concluded that Phillips' strategy was to attempt to challenge the Christian Democrats for dominion over the big centrist vote. Said Phillips of National Renewal: "I'm flying in a jet, while they're still in a prop plane. The democratic Right is the National party, five times bigger than National Renewal and everything hanging off it . . . I'm going to take the Right where it ought to be. If they see me hesitate or not do what I say am going to do, then it's time to criticize me. In the meantime, don't destroy what we are building. Don't stick priests in politics, because later we're not going to know what to do with them. You can't put priests in bed or in politics." Boasting and colorful style notwithstanding, one year later the Renewal party had signed up 48,291 members, the National party—which had been the first to begin a membership drive—9,563 members.[110]

Although Phillips may have been willing to talk to the Christian Left, they were not—period. Echoing the line of their political mentors, the

Communists, the IC made plain its contempt for the process in the early stages. Said Luis Maira, leader of that ultraleft breakway faction from the PDC: "If Christian Democracy, which is the largest party in the country, decides to apply for recognition in accord with the norms of the Law of Political Parties, then the totalitarian regime will have been legitimized, and the PDC will have removed itself irremediably from any possibility of an opposition united front." The IC never did attempt to win legal recognition for itself, but remained a political battering ram of sorts because of its strong following among the feverishly active priests and nuns of the "popular church."[111]

Leaders of the old-line parties, bluster and bravado apart, had plenty to worry about as electioneering got underway. A major survey published in June of 1987 showed political parties ranking second from the bottom in public esteem (church leaders got the highest marks, terrorists and guerrillas the lowest).[112]

Spurned by the Left, continuing to spurn their kindred spirits on the Right, the Nationals could not turn their backs altogether on the government. But they could and did slight Pinochet, finally requesting a private meeting to present him with a list of ten civilian candidates of "consensus" they believed could head off defeat in the plebiscite. Snorted *Carta Confidencial:* "Here's a party which cannot even collect enough signatures to qualify as a national party arrogating to itself the right and reason of proposing to the maximum authorities of the country a 'candidate of consensus!' " Spurned now by La Moneda as well, the party looked increasingly to the Left—and to allying itself with the forces of the "No."[113]

But so long as the Christian Democrats remained under the leadership of "the abrasive Gabriel Valdés," the party would have no truck with the Nationals, nor any other group on the Right. Roared Valdés: "Why are we going to make an alliance with the Right? To lose our entire 'social' support base, and convert Chile into another El Salvador or Nicaragua? What's the point of an alliance with their Right? To insert ourselves into a government which is falling? Who needs them? What are we [the PDC] in the middle class? 64 percent! How much support on the center-left? 46 percent! How many are with us on the center-right? 40 percent! The other parties of the Right don't amount to 10 percent." Not only were his numbers inflated, his own days at the helm of the PDC were numbered as fall edged into winter in 1987.[114]

One group managed to overcome severe internal squabbling long enough to unite under the leadership of Allende's former foreign minister, the sixty-four-year-old Clodomiro Almeyda Medina, who had slipped into the country early in 1987. The Christian Left, Radicals-Luengo, MAPU, Historic Socialists, Socialists-Almeyda, Communists, and MIR, agreed in June of 1987 to band together in a Front of the Left. It was, in reality, a union more of form than of substance. The Communists reiterated that month that there could be no meaningful elections in Chile so long as Pinochet remained in power; in that, they were echoed by Christian Democrat leader Fernando Castillo Velasco, former rector of the Catholic University. In that same month, by contrast, the ultraleft Socialists headed by Almeyda were grudgingly urging their faithful to register.[115]

Reluctantly, haltingly, the leadership of the Christian Democrat party came to the conclusion that its strategy of confrontation had failed. They realized also that they had no hope of prevailing alone—in the plebiscite, in the elections beyond. And that meant that Valdés, the man who had headed the party since 1982, had to go. There were those who saw in that conclusion the invisible influence of the State Department: disenchantment with him because—to quote a hostile observer— "despite the greatest financial, journalistic, and diplomatic aid within memory in contemporary Chilean history," he had not only failed to budge the regime, but hardened its resolve. Washington had also made plain a preference Valdés could neither swallow nor credibly represent: a consensus candidate pledged to preserving intact the free enterprise economic model now so indisputably successful in the country.[116] That the Christian Democrats kept a wary weather eye on Washington was obvious: their Santiago-Washington "shuttle diplomacy" was a reflection of their conviction that drumming up international financial and moral support—and acute pressure on the regime—was central to a strategy of success. Washington was the catalyst of those ambitions. Clearly, Gabriel Valdés was not the man to forge alliances; indeed, Social Democrat leader Carlos Neely publicly accused Valdés not only of responsibility for the collapse of previous coalition-building efforts, but also of being "the decisive sponsor" of funding for far left parties. "Be more moderate?" he asked rhetorically, when challenged on the subject of his intransigence. "Moderate with a dictatorship? I was not born to be a Chamberlain. Nor my party, either. If I decide to run, I am going to win." When it was clear he would not, Valdés switched his support to Ricardo Hormazábal, a man Valdés said "had more votes in the party than anyone else."[117]

The decision process in the Christian Democrat party, in common with other Chilean parties, had never been "democratic" in the usual sense of open and broad-based. Beginning in 1973, it became, perforce, less so, with power concentrated almost entirely in the hands of the National Directorate. On January 24, 1987, partly to defuse Pinochet's taunts about the secrecy and clannishness surrounding party decisions, and partly in tacit compliance with the new political parties law, the ninety-member Expanded National Council (Consejo Nacional Ampliado) agreed to new rules of openness, including direct election for the first time of delegates to the annual plenum. Backstairs skirmishing for control of the party began in March, formal campaigning on April 15, and by June had become so intense that the party leadership clamped a lid on the three who by then had emerged as candidates to preside over the party in the two crucial years, 1987–1989: on the left, Hormazábal; in the center, Arturo Frei Bolívar; on the right, old party war-horse Patricio Aylwin Azócar, then sixty-eight.[118]

As decision time neared, Valdés maneuvered implacably to prevent the party from moving right. Of the major force on the Right, National Renewal, Valdés stormed: "RN ... has to accept responsibility [*tiene que asumir por*] for 13 years of dictatorship. Who do they think they are fooling calling themselves Center-Right! Why don't they want to say they are on the Right? Bad conscience? Chile needs a democratic Right. The Center is taken. National Renewal seeks to prolong the regime. We are for substituting for the regime."[119] On June 19, he proposed yet another grand political accord, which would contain three levels: one constitutional, one on human rights, a third on social justice. All three presented a clear opening to the hard Left. Valdés professed to see great "progress" toward the only kind of accord he could ever warmly embrace—one heavily tilted to the left—when, on June 29, the Socialist party-Almeyda called for exploiting "breaches" in the junta's legal and moral defenses. The regime, the outlawed Socialists said, was trying to perpetuate itself by restricting access to the vote. The task, they said, was to encourage the widest possible registration and vote in the plebiscite.[120] It would now remain for the PDC rank-and-file to decide whether they shared Valdés' vision of this as an opportunity, or felt it was merely a confession on the part of an important segment of the hard Left that it could no longer hope to shoot or bully its way into the political arena and therefore must piggy-back on legal political entities congenial to it.

On July 4, they got that opportunity—26,000 voting in the first ever party election to select delegates to the plenum. (Snorted Pinochet afterward: "really special, these democrats"; they hold an election in which "no one knows how many voted, nor the results.") But, in his analysis of the voting, Aylwin was so confident that he had the election locked up that he spent the weekend before the plenum with his family at their Algarrobo beach home rather than continue the arduous campaign he had launched on May 22. Those hopes were buoyed further on the day the convention was to open, July 31, when Adolfo Zaldívar announced he was throwing his support to Aylwin.

Through that Friday, the 239 delegates began arriving at Punta de

Tralca, on the rugged Pacific Coast roughly sixty-five miles west of Santiago. Their destination: a rambling building formerly part of the Santiago Seminary, situated at a place called Vaticano. Once used for religious retreats, it was a favorite now for business meetings. The business at hand: elect the five members of the key directorate, the fifteen national counselors, as well as the man who would lead the party for the next two years. Democracy or no, they met behind closed doors. Aylwin's turn at the podium finally came, it would be learned subsequently, at 4 A.M. on Sunday, August 2. When he sat down, an hour and-a-half later, the weary delegates gave him a standing ovation. Two hours later, he was elected president for the sixth time (some accounts say the seventh). The vote: 132, Aylwin; 94, Hormazábal; 14, Arturo Frei. The party elite had not only rejected the Left, they had also rejected the traditional "play-safe" option of the "consensus" centrist candidate, Frei, choosing instead the unmistakable center-rightist Aylwin. Given the precariousness of his mandate—55 percent of the vote—of equal importance was the national directorate elected with him: Gutemberg Martínez, secretary-general, and Andrés Zaldívar, first vice president— both clearly allied to Aylwin; Edgardo Boeninger, third vice president, a center-leftist in the party. Only Narciso Irureta, second vice president, belonged to the party's ultraleft wing.[121]

Aylwin went to work almost immediately to execute his three-pronged mandate:

1. Seek dialogue with the military chiefs on the junta;
2. Vigorously promote voter registration;
3. Construct a socio-economic program to offer voters as an alternative to Pinochet's.

If all else failed, there was a fourth: forge the broadest possible coalition to defeat Pinochet in the plebiscite.

The military chiefs indignantly rejected "dialogue" on the terms proposed: direct election of the president and Congress, to be followed by "reform" of the 1980 constitution. The constitution, the transition process it envisioned, these, the military leaders said unanimously, are not negotiable. They accused the Christian Democrats of trying to divide them; given the PDC's announced strategy of conducting these talks privately, informally, using a "subtle and indirect style," they may have been right.

On voter registration, the goal Aylwin now set as the minimum needed was 5 million to 6 million; during the party presidency campaign he had spoken of registering 8 million. (At that point, six months into the voter registration process, and with other parties then cranking up their own registration drives, 1.6 million were already registered.)

Comparing 1987 with 1973, he said: "Then, the task of democrats was to calm passions; today, we need to mobilize the country. There is apathy, and people are desperate . . ."

On the socio-economic program, Aylwin made plain from the start that the Christian Democrats still had no intention of buying into the program of the "Chicago Boys." "We do not," Aylwin said, "want Pinochet-ism without Pinochet." As to Valdés' three-tiered proposal, Aylwin said he agreed with the sloganeering, not the substantive point. Yes, he said, there is a need for wide consensus on constitutional and human rights issues: "More difficult will be to put together a socio-economic pact that will bind us [the opposition] together during the transition to the first democratic government."[122]

As had happened so often before, the PDC believed it faced a divided and vulnerable enemy. For one thing, both Admiral Merino and General Matthei on the junta had reacted positively to the PDC decision to join the electoral process—and its move to more moderate leadership. (The Aylwin-Merino honeymoon would be short-lived.) But of much greater import to their calculations was a stunning series of statements made by three of the four junta members in June: that they thought the candidate for president in 1989 ought to be a civilian. Admiral Merino got it started in an interview with Roland Dallas of *The Economist;* he told Dallas he did not believe Pinochet would be a candidate, and that he believed the candidate should be a civilian, of the center-right, about fifty-two or fifty-three years old, and sufficiently strong and qualified to preside over the transition back to full democracy. Those remarks touched off an immediate sensation and a wave of speculation to find the Cinderella who fit the mystery slipper. Next, returning from a trip to the United States, General Matthei celebrated his sixty-second birthday by saying he agreed with Merino. And next, Carabinero General Stange said he agreed with his junta colleagues. Pinochet said nothing, but his defense minister, Vice Admiral Patricio Carvajal, said he couldn't agree less; he thought Pinochet was the right man for the job.

Exulted Valdés: "There is a profound division in the government."[123]

The reports of the death of junta unity, as it turned out, were altogether premature.

On July 4, 1987, Pinochet announced an economic program known as "the seven modernizations." On July 7, he reappointed Sergio Fernández to the key Interior Ministry, one of seven changes the president made in his twenty-member Cabinet in July. Another, two months earlier, had put Sergio Melnick in as the cabinet-level director of economic planning. The changes had deep significance—and long-range implications. Fernández, who had served as the first civilian interior minister from

1978 to 1982, was regarded as the overseer of the process leading up to the final adoption of the 1980 constitution. He was also regarded as one of the chief exponents of corporatist political thinking for the government. Melnick was a charter member of the Chicago Boys group that created the free market economic revolution; he joined in the Cabinet a kindred spirit, Hernán Büchi, firmly ensconced as finance minister. Melnick was known at the University of Chile as a "futurist," a skilled communicator as well as planner. In yet another change, Army Brigadier Manuel Concha was named economy minister, replacing businessman Juan Carlos Délano.

As a result of these changes, the dark days of exile for the old triad—the political philosophers, the economic dreamers, the armed forces modernizers—were over. They had hit bottom two-and-a-half-years earlier with the ascendancy of Sergio Onofre Jarpa in Interior and Luis Escobar Cerda in Finance. In the years since, the long latent animosities of many traditional conservatives, and protectionist-spoiled businessmen, to the revolutionary political and economic ideas of these groups had found vocal expression in government press offices and on state-controlled television. But with these changes, with the new "modernizations" program, Pinochet was serving clear notice: he was firmly committed to those ideas, and he wanted to strengthen and consolidate them so as to carry Chile along on their momentum well into the twenty-first century. "At bottom," commented *Hoy*, "they [the reformers] seek nothing more nor less than to preserve indefinitely the package of neoliberal reforms . . . Defenders of the model believe that 'persons come and go, institutions remain.' In other words, they have in mind the possibility that General Augusto Pinochet may not win the plebiscite and may then have to negotiate what follows . . ."[124]

To read the newspapers in Chile during 1987—certainly to read foreign newspaper reports about Chile—one might easily have been forgiven for imagining that there was but a single concern: politics. It was not. Mother nature, so long the country's tormentor as well as benefactress, went on a rampage in July when a Pacific storm overflowed river banks, washing out roads and bridges and flooding low-lying residential areas in central Chile. At least thirty-two died, and as many as 100,000 persons suffered damaged or destroyed homes. Property damage was estimated at more than $100 million.

Realizing that talking their way to power was firmly blocked, the Christian Democrat leadership concentrated on shoring up alliances abroad and at home. Foreign alliances and the campaign to "internationalize" the Chilean political process were given a huge boost at the second International Parliamentary Assembly, held September 4–6, at Santiago's Hotel Tupahue. The sudden appearance, however, of the fugitive Communist party leader, Luis Guastavino, ruffled the proceedings briefly, triggering a walkout by National party President Patricio Phillips and other delegates. But for the most part, this assembly—as the first one the year before—was mainly a rally of anti-Pinochet ideologues from around the world. According to *Carta Confidencial*, opposition figures managed to corral foreign financial commitments of $2.6 million for their various electoral programs at that conference. Among U.S. participants was Rep. Theodore Weiss (D-N.Y.), who has been, together with Sens. Ted Kennedy (D-Mass.) and Tom Harkin (D-Iowa), among the principal congressional antagonists of the Pinochet government in Washington. (Conversely, Weiss has argued for a "normalization" of relations with Cuba, and criticized the U.S. military operation that rescued Grenada from a Communist dictatorship.) Yet another American attending was Carl Gershman, president of the supposedly neutral (and taxpayer-funded) National Endowment for Democracy. A surprise visitor to the assembly was former Socialist Deputy Erick Schnake— the last voice in Chile to call publicly on Popular Unity militiamen to rally to the aid of their embattled president Allende on September 11, 1973. Schnake crossed into Chile from Argentina on the last day of the conference and stunned many with a hard-hitting attack on Communist party insistence on armed struggle against the regime, a complete role reversal from 1973. His remarks contrasted with those of Christian Democrat labor leader Manuel Bustos, who deplored the decision of his party to eschew alliances with the Communists, a decision he branded as "dumb, inapplicable and incompatible with the Declaration of Principles of the PDC."[125]

Through the balance of 1987—despite the misgivings of many in the PDC—talks with other opposition figures centered on agreeing on a candidate to serve as the standard-bearer of the "No" vote in the plebiscite. By October, the PDC had settled on a name: Eduardo Frei Ruiz-Tagle, a man who though inexperienced in politics was possessed of a matchless asset: his name. A forty-four-year-old civil engineer, he was the eldest son of the late president. Until 1983, when he took over the presidency of the Eduardo Frei Foundation, he was a stranger to public life and did not make his first important speech until December 1986. Thereafter, he became a regular on the oratorical circuit. Interestingly, among the other names floated early on was that of his sister, Carmen Frei Ruiz-Tagle, eldest of the seven Frei children and the only one who had been long active in public life. (In 1971, when she rolled up the largest margin of victory in the country in municipal elections, defeating the then kingpin of the National party, Sergio Onofre Jarpa, her father rushed to PDC national headquarters following a televised debate and, bursting with paternal pride, exclaimed: "Did you see how well Carmen did?")[126]

But candidacy was not to be in the cards, for either—at least not yet.

Viewing the political fandangos of those first months of election-eering, the feisty and unconventional political analyst (and Social Democrat) Carlos Neely wrote: "The opposition has boxed itself into a dead-end street trying to identify a 'candidate' or a 'leader' of impossible qualities if he were to satisfy the demands of all those participating in the game. They [the opposition] continue to be ruled by folkloric ideo-logies either messianic or of a tenant mentality. Forty years of political frustration has taught them nothing. They imagine they can fabricate a miraculous program which has as its common denominator liberalism, classical social Christianity, liberation theology, social democracy, and warmed-over Marxism."[127]

Among the many foreign interests increasingly involved in Chilean politics, few would play a more instrumental role during late 1987 and early 1988 than Zune Associates, International Consultants. Headed by Jean B. Zune, this Caracas-based company served as an adviser in vir-tually all Christian Democrat political campaigns in Latin America, and had been hired by Andrés Zaldívar, now number two in the PDC hierarchy, to consult on the Chilean campaign. Ms. Zune, during early 1988, was described as a virtual commuter between Caracas, Ecuador, and El Salvador (her efforts in the latter were hardly auspicious; Chris-tian Democrats there were routed in the March parliamentary elec-tions). Her report to the PDC, delivered the last week of December 1987, sent shock waves through the party. One of her principal recommenda-tions: present no candidate at this time. On February 15, 1988, the National Directorate accepted the recommendation, withdrawing the candidacy of Eduardo Frei. (Frei himself had never waxed enthusiastic about serving as a stalking horse in the 1988 or 1989 plebiscite; given his youth, many argued that he should "save" himself for the presiden-tial elections of 1990, should Pinochet lose the plebiscite, the 1997 elections otherwise.) The Zune Associates argument was that putting forth candidates now would only jeopardize opposition unity, as well as give the government a clear and clean target for their electoral fire. Candidacies, the firm argued, should come after the plebiscite. The task now was to create the broadest possible alliance of democratic parties under a common banner which would commit none of them ideologi-cally. There would be but a single common denominator: "No" to Pinochet remaining in power. (In a January 31 interview with *La Ter-cera*, PDC President Aylwin had already backed off on this: "A candi-date," he said, "was necessary if we were going to have free elections, but if we are going to a plebiscite, then I see no need to designate one now." He—and others in the opposition—then began speaking of a "standard-bearer" rather than a "candidate," a distinction of arcane delicacy.) Other important Zune recommendations:

- Create an opposition umbrella organization to coordinate—internally and externally—the "No" vote. On January 18, 1988, such a shell was in place, the "Campaign for the 'No,'" under the command of Christian Democrat Genaro Arriagada. On the external front, apart from communiques, trips abroad, and the increasing deluge of delegations and missions to Chile, the opposition announced in March 1988 that it intended to add more than three hundred foreign observers from "the parliamentary democracies of Europe, Latin America, Central America and the United States" to the potpourri of academics, intellectuals, teachers, trade unionists, politicians and others already cascading into the country.
- Stop referring to "fraud" in connection with the plebiscite—at least, at home. Chileans simply did not believe it. Less than two months later, Zaldívar, in a February 1988 interview, was among those who said, "to speak of fraud in the plebiscite is another error of the opposition." That, of course, neither did—nor would—preclude trumpeting the "fraud" theme outside of Chile.
- Work even more closely with church leaders in developing a joint strategy, "and to obtain its [the church's] full support, both internally and externally."
- Of paramount importance: calm the anxieties of the military that, with the advent of civilian rule, they would face wholesale inquisition, as in neighboring Argentina (where military chiefs, including the former president, were imprisoned). Zune Associates urged private contacts with military officers at all levels to project a seven-point understanding: they would not be persecuted; those guilty of excesses would be tried only by military courts; a soldier's duty to obey orders would be recognized; it would also be recognized that much of what was done was done in the name of national defense and to confront the Marxist danger the country had faced; the armed forces, in turn, could demonstrate their will to rectify their own mistakes; the important role the armed forces must play in the transition to democracy would be stressed; and finally, the armed forces would themselves transmute into "armed institutions of the democracy." Nothing else, the report said, should be contemplated until and unless civilians were able to achieve complete control over the armed forces, as President Raúl Alfonsín had in Argentina.

The report also had recommendations for the party's Basic Program of Government, then being drafted. One of them recommended that only passing reference be made to the swollen size of the military budget, a topic of increasing prominence in the political debate.[128]

The summer of 1987–88 was unlike any other of modern times, a period of little pause for the country's leaders, when as much heat was generated by the political cauldron as by the warm Southern Hemisphere sun. Going into the year, a Gallup Poll published in *El Mercurio* on January 31 showed Chileans closely divided on the plebiscite: 44.3 percent of the women said they would vote "Yes" for continuing with Pinochet, 17.9 percent no; men, on the other hand, said they would vote 34.2 percent yes, 35.9 percent no.

While opposition politicians struggled to mobilize cohesively, other civilians weighed in with their views. In late January 1988, the Confederation of Production and Commerce—the country's top business and retail organization—left the sidelines and joined the fray with an unprecedented announcement of full support for the plebiscite process. Confederation president Manuel Feliú told a press conference that the transition needed to be carried out without violence, but within the framework of the 1980 constitution, "which sets out the procedures already approved by the citizenry." "A democratic form of government," the statement said, "profoundly reflects the sentiments of our community and is the best for the perfecting and development of a system which respects and encourages private initiative, the basis of every free society. We business executives adhere to the process of advance toward full democracy, in the belief that the vices which led to the political, social and economic crisis of 1973 will not again be present." Looking on as Feliú spoke were top leaders of the national manufacturing association (SOFOFA, for Sociedad de Fomento Fabril), the National Agricultural Society, the National Chamber of Commerce, the Chamber of Construction, the Association of Banks and Financial Institutions.

On January 29, 1988, another important piece was added to the legal framework when the Constitutional Tribunal announced the names of lawyers elected in secret balloting to serve on it. Tribunal Secretary Rafael Larraín also announced that as of February 23, the tribunal would begin work on the plebiscite law itself.

Meanwhile, Pinochet himself looked and acted every day more like a political candidate, touring the country inaugurating new housing and other public works projects, making speeches. In one, on January 16, 1988, he uncorked a surprise: work was underway in Valparaíso on the site of a former hospital to house the future congress. Heading up the $40 million project—a powerful example of decentralization of the government—was Modesto Collados, minister of Housing under Frei, minister of Economy (1984–1985) in the Pinochet government. The project consists of a central building housing three assembly halls—one each for the Chamber of Deputies, the Senate, and Plenary Sessions, covering a total of forty thousand square meters of floor space. A congressional library (six thousand square meters) and parking for five hundred vehicles were also included, as well as two adjoining six-floor office towers to provide working space for legislators, committees and staff. The complex is expected to be ready by March 1990, when the first elected Congress assembles.

The Christian Democrats—serving as the "respectful big brother" (Aylwin's phrase) of a six-party grouping—tried yet another negotiating ploy in January: to persuade Pinochet to scrap the plebiscite in favor of elections for a civilian-military government that would serve during a transition period lasting no more than four years, during which time institutional changes would be debated. The government still said no. Labor Minister Alfonso Márquez de la Plata, in a January 31 interview with María Eugenia Oyarzún in *La Tercera*, said: "Incredible . . . they want to immobilize the country for four years . . . it's an insult to public opinion." De la Plata also took aim at economic proposals in the package, which he said amounted to "a return to a Socialist society."

In January, the political wars exploded on the country's television screens for the first time since 1973. The University of Chile network led the way with a ninety-minute program, "Currents of Opinion," aired in prime time on Sundays and featuring debates among leaders of all strains of legal political groups. The Catholic University's television corporation announced that it would follow suit several weeks later with a competing round-table program hosted by three top journalists. In addition, the government announced new plans to provide thirty minutes of free air time daily for political announcements during the 30 days of official campaigning. Opposition and government supporters each would get fifteen minutes.

Those government supporters were having problems of their own. Feuding within the National Renewal party (RN) broke out over whether to commit to support whichever candidate the junta selected. The feud took a dramatic turn early in April with the expulsion from the party of Jaime Guzmán, one of the founders. Guzmán immediately gathered up most of the forces of his Independent Democratic Union (UDI) into a new group: "UDI for a 'Yes.' " *El Mercurio*, noting that RN had rolled up the biggest registration of any of the four parties that had achieved legal status as such, tried to put a brave face on it: the Left, the newspaper said, had never been able to unite in a single party, either. Besides, with mitosis continuing among the political entities of the Left, it would only serve to fortify the public image of the a-political Pinochet. But, in the end, the newspaper's editorialists made it plain that this schism among the principal civilian forces supporting Pinochet was a serious setback, only somewhat mitigated by the success of yet another progovernment group in securing legal status. It was a setback not only in the short term, the newspaper said, but also sowed dangerous seeds of dissension among those who ought to be the civilian backbone of any new government, should he win.[129]

On February 2, thirteen "parties" announced they had joined in a "Concentration for the 'No.' " "Parties" is in quotation marks because, when put to the test of proving they had any real support, only two in the concentration—or "command," as it was also called—managed to scare up enough signatures to qualify as a legal national party. They were the Christian Democrats and the Humanists; a third, the more leftist Party for Democracy (PPD, Partido por la Democracia), was aggressively "No," later joined the concentration, which eventually included 16 "parties." (The PPD appeared to be the chosen vessel for participation of the outlawed Marxist-Leninist parties, including the hard left Socialists and Communists.) Although attempts were made to describe the concentration as broad-based—and it was routinely portrayed as such in foreign press accounts—it managed to attract no significant conservative parties; the National party continued with its stance of seeking a consensus candidate, tilting toward a "Yes" vote, and the other rightist parties were all committed to a "Yes."

The thrust of the sixteen was, from the start, a variation of the "Philippinization" stratagem: if "No" were to triumph in the plebiscite, then demand immediate presidential and congressional elections and constitutional overhaul. Under this formulation, the "Yes" vote would need to win by a margin of at least 6 percent, or the outcome would be denounced as fraudulent, and worldwide pressure would generate to force new elections—if not actually force the government out. On the other hand, a "No" win by so much as a single vote would be sufficient for the "detonator" of mass protests, rallies, riots, and foreign pressure to demand repudiation of the procedures called for in the 1980 constitution. Even the moderate Christian Democrat leader Andrés Zaldívar insisted that defeat of the junta's candidate meant defeat of the government's "institutionality" as well. "In practice," he said, "that [a 'No' vote] would mean that the armed forces would have to bow to the expression of the citizen majority of this country. If the 'No' wins it is because people want and accept the position of the opposition, that is, that the constitution has to be modified in all those areas which make it antidemocratic." Zaldívar was equally adamant on another point: waiting a year for presidential elections, as the 1980 constitution provides, would be "inoperable . . . Think what would happen. I ask the working people and businessmen of this country if they believe that during that year there would be peace or any kind of investment, or would it be a seismic movement, because we would have a defeated government in power?" (To moderate politician Zaldívar, moderate junta member Fernando Matthei shot back with equal firmness: "This constitution, gentlemen, is not at stake. We respect it, and we will see that it is respected."[130]

Quite apart from the fact that the opposition had never conceded the converse—that should "Yes" win they would desist in their demands for constitutional reform—there was another and ominous aspect of the unfolding strategy: The government (and major parties of the Right) had all said they would respect the outcome of the plebiscite, no matter who won. Of the opposition parties, only the Humanists and the miniscule Chilean Socialist party had also unequivocally agreed. (The Humanists reversed course only a few weeks before the Plebiscite saying "yes" could win only by "fraud," so they would not accept a "yes" outcome. But, with little more than a month to go to the plebiscite, the Humanists suffered a mysterious internal crisis and lost their standing as a legal party when they ousted their top leadership.) The Christian Democrats not only hedged, depending upon which of them was speaking, but even waffled individually from week to week. And since they had never "accepted" the legitimacy of the 1980 constitution, but only agreed to compete under its electoral ground rules when it was clear they had no other option, the stage was clearly set for a collision course—amply supported through aggressive advance propagandizing abroad. That collision course hardened when the Christian Democrats embraced this "rupture-ist" or "detonator" strategy originally propounded by the underground Communists and the ultraleft "popular" Catholic church groups. The plebiscite thus would be "legitimate" only if those in the opposition won; if they did not, they had made plain their rejection of the constitution, and remained ambiguous about respecting the plebiscite.[131] The goal, then, would be to seek a Philippines-style implosion produced by internal and external pressure. This would force the government either to resort to massive repression to enforce the outcome, or to surrender.

As indicated earlier, it was a dual-track, "heads-we-win, tails-you-lose" strategy. Abroad, the message was to undermine confidence in the plebiscite. On March 20, for example, "concentration" coordinator Genaro Arriagada told the prosocialist Madrid newspaper *El País:* Pinochet "only can win via fraud, and if he does it, this can touch off a national and international repudiation which can destroy him." In New York, another Christian Democrat—Sergio Molina, head of the U.S.-bankrolled Committee of Personages—said a month later that "conditions are not in place [*dadas*] for an electoral process, inasmuch as there are restrictions on personal freedom and press freedom is restricted." Interestingly, he made that statement the day after the leftist leader Ricardo Lagos was engaged in an explosive antigovernment harangue viewed by a Chilean television audience estimated at 2 million.[132]

At home, the Christian Democrats continued to develop a parallel strategy of confidence and optimism. Arriagada told interviewer Raquel Correa that Pinochet had created a self-fulfilling prophecy: there was, in his entourage, no other viable candidate, and for the opposition, "Pinochet is no problem. According to our analyses, Pinochet is an essentially unpopular man." But, said Arriagada, if Pinochet were "easy," a civilian selected by the junta "is more easily defeated yet." By mid-May, Arriagada was predicting the opposition would assemble 200,000 volunteers throughout the country to monitor the plebiscite and assure that it be clean and fair. He made the statement in the popular prime-time television program "Face the Nation" ("De Cara al País").[133]

Arriagada may have been whistling in the dark. Gallup polls showed a steady rise in support for the "Yes" vote. In March, the break-out was 47.2 percent for "Yes"; 29.4 percent "No"; and 23.4 percent still undecided. Of even greater concern for the opposition as this heretofore-untested electorate emerged: 80.9 percent said they did not feel represented by any political party.[134]

Against that backdrop it was not surprising that many on the left now regretted joining the process in the first place. Commented the far left weekly *Análisis* in May (#223): "There can be no doubt that the shortest, easiest and neatest path to defeating Pinochet and his nightmare of a government should have been massive and peaceful abstention . . . a refusal to register and adhere to its political laws. If we Chileans had not registered, if only the narrow band of addicts of the Totalitarian Regime had done it, by this time—without the slightest cost or social effort— the Dictatorship would be totally isolated and its Constitution . . . torn totally to pieces . . ." As the magazine wrote, 5.7 million were already registered (and those who had not were on notice that they faced fines of 25,000 pesos, around $90, if they failed to do so); and sixteen parties were in various stages of attempting to win certification.[135]

On the seventh anniversary of the 1980 constitution, Pinochet expressed his views on the meaning of the plebiscite, the life of the country beyond it:

> Chile seeks to eradicate all vestiges or dangers of moral disintegration, violence and totalitarianism. This constitutional task reflects our patriotic effort to integrate the principles of authority, freedom and justice, essential for healthy and fruitful coexistence and the common welfare. The upcoming plebiscite is part of the process . . . After [it], Chile will [have] . . . a new government, different from the one we had until 1973 and from the one we have had since . . . The new institutional order establishes ample channels of participation

for those who disagree with government policy. They will be able to help govern the country from the Senate and the Chamber of Deputies, either by cooperating with the Executive or by promoting amendments or political alternatives . . . We demand that the opposition respect the Chilean people, and that its proposals be objective and not promoted by ideological or partisan objectives . . . Our opponents have repeatedly stated their interest in reducing the institutions we are attempting to establish to ashes. If the political and ideological concepts of such politicians win, all sectors of Chilean life will soon return to the backwardness prevailing in the country prior to 1973. I must also point out and stress the importance of defining in the plebiscite the kind of institutional phase we want . . . [and] the profound democratic ideals motivating the military men all these years [which] has had no other goal than to lay the basis for the all-encompassing and increasing development of our country under a true democracy . . .[136]

A few weeks later, in a speech before 4,500 women in Viña del Mar, he all but proclaimed his candidacy: "Is there any dictator who, on his own accord, and with all the power of force and law in his hands, would have curtailed himself? None. Nonetheless, this constitution established that the citizenry would decide whether this government continues or does not continue for eight more years. That is the question, and there is no other: you want President Pinochet to continue or you do not want him to continue? Later . . . the commanders-in-chief will respond if he who has been president of the Republic has done a good or a bad job. They will know how to respond."

Crowed Gabriel Valdés in the same city the next day: "Now we clearly know the meaning of the plebiscite. Pinochet himself said it clearly. He has notified the commanders-in-chief of his decision . . . what he said is very important because it demonstrates, as he himself said, that to vote 'Yes' is to vote for Augusto Pinochet, approve his fifteen years of government and accept that he continue governing until the end of the century. Therefore, and with absolute logic, to vote 'No' signifies rejecting what has been done during these fifteen years, to vote that Pinochet not be the candidate, and change the regime." Valdés added, with customary irony, that it appeared "inconceivable" that a presidential candidacy should have been announced in "a gambling casino." Former Socialist Sen. Erich Schnake called the president's remarks "unheard of; they resemble a little the old proclamation, 'The State Is Me . . .' " Interior Minister Sergio Fernández fired back that the opposition attacks were "dogmatic, vengeful and seditious."[137]

On May 5, *El Mercurio* published the twenty-one-point economic and social program of the thirteen "parties" clustered in the Concentration of the "No." The signatories* reaffirmed their insistence that a "No" vote meant "the people of Chile defeat Pinochet, his regime and his institutionality," clearing the way for their negotiating a quick deal with the armed forces that would put them—and their ideas—in power. Most of the points in the program were pure electoral platform boiler-plate (reduce unemployment, improve public health, bring "dignity" to peasants, etc.). But some were very substantive, signaling the opposi-tion's unmistakable intention to restore a central role for the state in the economy and the repoliticization of citizen groups (labor legislation reform, "strengthening" professional associations). Two were partic-ularly odd: one called for scrapping the thirty-year-old home mortgage-support system (a complex system called Units of Development [Uni-dad de Fomento], which had become an increasing political football because of a handful of foreclosures); the second called for "reprogram-ming" the foreign debt. Chile had built an enviable reputation as the only major debtor country in Latin America never to have defaulted on its debt; in phrases of familiar class-struggle demagoguery, the docu-ment spoke of canceling "the overdue debts of the poor in the same way that the state has taken charge of the debts of the big banks and corpora-tions." Fernando Agüero, president of the National Manufacturing Soci-ety (SOFOFA), said the proposals "seem to have been put together by an advertising agency," and added: "No one tells us where the money to pay for all this will come from." Pinochet, on the campaign trail in Copiapó, denounced "a new alliance between a party that styles itself as Chris-tian and a Marxist group, for the purpose of reviving programs and recipes already tried and which failed."[138]

But, by then, there was a real question as to who was in charge in the opposition camp. That question arose on April 25, when Ricardo Lagos Escobar, who until then had played a supporting role in the campaign, electrified the country by arguing, on the popular television program "Face the Nation," that the goal in Chile is to build socialism, "the socialism which Allende tried to build." He hinted as well at the possi-ble return to state ownership of many of the huge companies privatized during the Pinochet years. He also challenged Pinochet to acknowledge that he had not been sufficiently forthcoming with the country, that his promises had not been kept, and that there were 12 percent more poor people in Chile in 1988 than in 1973. (The next day, reacting to sharp government counterattacks and the veiled threat of an official slander action, Lagos said he had no intention of offending anyone.) Not only

---

* The signers were Patricio Aylwin, PDC; Clodomiro Almeyda, "his" Socialist party; Enrique Silva Cimma, Radical party; Ricardo Núñez, "his" Socialist party; Luis Maira, Christian Left; José Tomás Saenz, Humanist party; Amador Navarro, Social Democrat party. The PPD was "studying" the document, as were the remaining mini-"parties" allied with it.

was the Left ecstatic, so too were top Christian Democrats: labor leader Manuel Bustos said that while many were "frightened" as they listened to Lagos' blunt talk, "he only spoke the truth, what has been on the minds of millions." PDC President Aylwin said his party shared Lagos' political views, though not all his economic ideas. Rightist leader Jaime Guzmán called Lagos "the new Allende," and said by his action, the Christian Democrats had lost leadership of the opposition. National party leader Patricio Phillips attacked Lagos sharply, and said, "if the military are in power today, it is because you [socialists] brought us collapse." Economist Ricardo Recabarren accused Lagos of "an astonishing number of inaccuracies, half-truths and downright falsehoods," including his claim that Chileans were poorer now than in 1973.[139]

Ricardo Lagos Escobar is the quintessential international technocrat, and thus is not only plugged into a far-flung international network of friends and supporters, but enjoys also the benediction of the U.S. State Department, which views him as "a viable moderate." He also is the quintessential salon socialist, of an ilk the American writer R. Emmett Tyrell, Jr., has described as "Beverly Hills Bolsheviks," or "Bolsheviks in Guccis," although he should by no means be confused with a dilettante of socialism. Armed with a doctorate from Duke University, he taught at the University of Chile, headed various U.S.-Chilean organizations, and served as a consultant to international organizations. Academic Lagos became "apparatchik" Lagos with the arrival in power of Salvador Allende, serving him as special ambassador to the United Nations with responsibility for a number of the regime's torturous financial negotiations. In 1973, Allende appointed him ambassador to Moscow, an appointment aborted by the September revolution. After ten years in the shadows, he emerged in 1983 as the head of the Democratic Alliance, representing the Carlos Briones branch of the Socialist party (a pastiche of Marxists and non-Marxists). The extent of his international connections was demonstrated in 1986 following the attempt on President Pinochet's life. He was among those detained in the massive round-up. During his nineteen days in jail, Santiago was bombarded with cables, telephone calls and letters demanding his release. Described by *Hoy* as representing the hardest line within Chilean socialism, Lagos pulled the Briones faction out of the Democratic Alliance in 1986 because he feared the alliance was veering too much to the center-right. Curiously, this forty-nine-year-old lawyer/economist/politician would later claim that the only way to win in the elections was to achieve opposition unity under a single banner. "The most important thing is to gain the right to elect a candidate. If we get that, then the Cory Aquinos will appear spontaneously."[140] His April 25 television appearance scarcely enhanced that purpose.

The immediate loser was Ricardo Núñez, a hard-line socialist. (Following the Soviet invasion of Afghanistan in 1979, Núñez was among those in the mainstream party who joined chieftain Carlos Altamirano in supporting the Soviets. Others bolted, the beginning of the modern fragmentation of the party.) Of the above-ground socialists, Núñez was, until then, the strongest. Now it was Lagos.

But of even greater consequence was the impact of his remarks on the overall "correlation of forces," and the fragile harmony of the Christian Democrats. Lagos himself sensed he may have played into the junta's hands by evoking images of a return to Allende-ism. In backpedaling remarks a few days later, he said the experience of the Popular Unity began and ended with Allende, just as other political moments had come and gone. To say that there are certain broad policies or general principles that you wish to maintain, he added, does not mean you want to replay an entire historic episode. PDC leader Valdés, seeking to capitalize on the excitement Lagos had stimulated on the far left—while blunting Allende-again fears—attempted to blame the government for the furor, "What they want," he said, "is to put before us the quarrels and divisions that destroyed democracy eighteen years ago, because they are afraid of the unity and maturity that we democrats demonstrate today. They want to remain in power forever, block the way to the future, because only the past justifies them." Privately, he was said to have argued within party circles that the Lagos experience proved the party had committed a grave mistake by letting others claim the leftist terrain.[141]

Once again, the Christian Democrat party was rent by the struggle between those pulling the party to the right and those pushing it to the left Andrés Zaldívar, while joining in those ostensibly applauding Lagos, said the political future of the opposition was in the center. "Neither the Left nor Ricardo Lagos are going to lead the 'No,' " he said. "He said so himself. Besides, anyone with a certain amount of knowledge and political sensitivity knows that there can be no transition from a government such as this one—military, of force—and a government of the Left. . . . to lead the country to democracy the transition has to be poised on a balance in the center." Having said that, Zaldívar moved out of the limelight. To some, this signaled yet another subtlety of the process: those with postplebiscite presidential ambitions could not "burn" themselves out in this fight.

The Christian Democrats attempted to recapture the initiative, proposing a Council of Presidents as a means of shoring up unity in the sputtering Concentration for a "No." In it, Aylwin suggested, the PDC would act as "first among equals." The idea found no takers. Meanwhile, behind the scenes, the intraparty fight heated up to where the national directorate meeting scheduled for mid-May had to be pushed back one month. *Chascones*—the ultraleft—were demanding a full-fledged evaluation of Aylwin's stewardship at that meeting.[142]

Amid the sound and the fury, on May 6, Law #18,700, "The Organic Constitutional Law on Popular Voting and Tallying," was promulgated—the last major piece of legislation clearing the way for the plebiscite (and, as intended, for future elections). The law contained 177 permanent and ten transitory provisions, and was based largely on a 1962 election law. As with the Political Parties Law, this one stipulated that only funds of national origin could be used for electoral purposes. Although campaigning had, in fact, been going on for months, the law specified that the formal period for campaigning was from thirty-one days to three days before the plebiscite. Electioneering was banned in movie theaters, video centers; banned, too, was the use of mobile or stationary loudspeakers, except in connection with public rallies. Painting slogans on walls, bridges, and the like was forbidden, as was attaching posters to them (the exception: on the facades of offices of political parties or independent candidates).

At that point, the best guess was that the plebiscite would be held in October, later, that the date would be December 11; part of the reasoning behind this date is that by December, the United States—likely to be the most meddlesome of foreign states in the process—would be fully distracted with its own postelectoral transition to a new government. Long-time antagonists, such as Assistant Secretary of State Elliott Abrams, would either be gone from office or be deprived of significant clout. At all odds, the junta had to give the citizenry at least thirty days advance notice. That they did on August 30: ending the long suspense, they set the plebiscite for October 5, 1988. Despite rumblings of junta disunity in the days leading up to decision day, Pinochet was named as the candidate at a meeting lasting just a little over an hour.

A few months before, on June 1, fellow junta member Admiral José Merino had robbed the opposition of one of its international wailing walls: the electoral process, he said, would be carried out without any restrictions in place on citizen rights. In other words, for the thirty days leading up to the voting, for the first time since 1973, Chile would live without a "state of exception" of any kind.[143] On September 24, the state of emergency was lifted, for the first time in 15 years, Chile lived under a normal rule of law.

It was September of 1987 before anyone got around to noticing—certainly to taking seriously—the appearance of an unexpected wild card in the political process: the emergence of a strong, tightly disciplined, and thoroughly enigmatic, Humanist party. By mid-1988, everyone was taking it seriously; only the enigma remained, though somewhat resolved. Although the Humanists were far from the first to start signing up members, they were the first to cross the finish line and qualify as a legal national party. As of June 1, 1988, their party ranked second only to the National Renewal party in number of signatures formally presented. Altogether, it was estimated that by June of 1988 they had signed up 100,000 in their (by then) two parties: the Humanist party (PH) and the Green party (formed to attract otherwise apathetic voters responsive to environmental and ecological issues). At the time, they were both formally committed to a "No" vote; after that, no one could be quite certain what they intended. In February, they themselves had said they would commit to going along with the status quo for no more than the four years of transition the opposition was then proposing; later, the Humanists ruled out in advance the possibility that the "yes" vote could win cleanly.

In the southern area of South America, the humanist movement dates from May 4, 1969, when Mario Rodríguez Cobo, leader of the SILO movement, gave a talk at the Argentine border town of Punta de Vaca in which he expounded his views on human suffering, its causes and cures. That conclave, attended by thousands, gave rise to loosely organized groups in Argentina and Chile—in the early years, mainly hippie communes dedicated to the drug culture and to the denial of traditional family or educational bonds. Later, in Chile, came the Community for Human Development, rejecting the drug culture and announcing devotion to the eradication of violence from the world. Paradox one: the Rodríguez Cobo disciple who implanted the movement in Chile was Werner von Erhemberg Pincheira, a student at the University of Concepción. He was later one of the founders of the very violent Revolutionary Vanguard, still later of the equally violent but more successful Movement of the Revolutionary Left (MIR). An attempt to investigate a SILO-MIR link in 1971 was thwarted when the MIRista leaders, sheltered by the Allende government, refused to appear in court. The Christian Democrat newspaper La Prensa said on October 9, 1971: "The same threads which pull the MIR manage SILO." Paradox two: The man who would later preside over the movement fought against the Allende regime. SILO disappeared in 1973; in 1975, the Community for the Equilibrium and Development of the Human Being appeared in its stead, later achieving legal status on October 13, 1981, as the Movement for the Development of the Human Being, or more simply, "The Community."

In 1975, on the Greek island of Corfu, a worldwide gathering of humanists assembled as the Movement for the Development of the Human Being, decided to launch political parties. By 1988, the Movement operated in fifty-two countries, with political parties established in forty. In 1981, the Chilean group managed to collect 300,000 signatures in breathtakingly short time, calling for a Permanent Treaty of Peace between Argentina and Chile. On May 26, 1984, the Humanist party was organized; in August, the party used the early peace lists to undertake careful research to identify probable members. Using as its theme the existence in the world of a moral-existential crisis between excessive materialism and personal alienation, the movement culled from its research six hundred persons inducted as electoral "missionaries." Once trained, they were charged in turn with training six thousand recruiters. Under the supervision of the missionaries, those recruiters had, by 1987, enrolled 67,000 persons in the Humanist party (although only 45,000 signatures were presented to the election board).

Until September 1987, no one paid much attention. That changed when José Tomás Sáenz, a real estate broker serving as the party president, called a festive press conference in Santiago. With two hundred party faithful cheering his every announcement, Sáenz disclosed that the party had collected 19,000 signatures in the metropolitan Santiago area (half again the number needed); five thousand in two other regions where they needed only 3,800. Looking on as Sáenz spoke were presidents of Humanist parties from Canada, Switzerland, West Germany, Ecuador, Peru, and England, as well as leaders from Venezuela, France, and Argentina. Sáenz also unveiled the party's interim platform: (1) unity of all opposition forces which eschew violence, in practice as well as in theory; (2) prompt election of a single opposition candidate. ("If they don't," observed *Carta Confidencial*, "then the Humanist party will present one of its own, a man of perhaps middle age, moustachioed . . ."—Sáenz, of course.)

Analysts scrambled to learn more about this new phenomenon. Some parties courted them; others attacked (Carlos Cruz Coke, secretary-general of the hard right National Vanguard [Avanzada Nacional], said categorically that the majority of the PH's signatures were those of Communists, using the party as a Trojan Horse). Friend and foe alike were given sharp pause by one reality: unlike every other political force in Chile, the Humanists had never suffered a single division. Further, in their statutes, there is no distinction between men or women, youths or seniors; all are simply Humanists, and the candidate with the most votes—man, woman, or youth leader—wins. A key point: political activity is subordinate to the movement. For promotion in the movement, there is a highly developed point system that discourages outside infiltration for all but the most patiently, perversely dedicated.

Humanists are not only younger (average age: 20–22), but better educated than the rank-and-file of most other parties. Little is left to chance. The point system is calibrated and stored in computers. The movement's Chilean Institute for Humanistic Studies does constant tracking of political, social and economic trends. The PH uses the color orange for virtually all of its propaganda materials; militants are asked to wear bright and distinctive colors at public rallies. Members greet each other with the left arm raised, three fingers extended upward, signifying peace, happiness, and strength.

Among the point-building "good works" expected of Movement activists is to pitch in in political campaigns. Thus, while other parties were importing—and spending—millions to build their political constituencies, Sáenz could boast that it cost the Humanists only 95,000 pesos (roughly $330) to collect 24,000 party signatures in three provinces. Though they charge their members no dues, they do require that each unit pay its own way—which each unit does by collecting bottles for refunds, selling newspapers, organizing neighborhood dances, and the like. Also in contrast to the record of contentiousness in other parties, the Humanists' Disciplinary Tribunal is unique: as of early 1988, it had yet to handle a single case.

Despite what many might characterize as their priggish view of the world, Humanists are not averse to a good celebration. On the third anniversary of the party's founding in Chile, they assembled two-thousand guests for a noisy gathering at Santiago's Cariola Theater. There, Sáenz criticized both the government and the opposition, calling on those "same opposition politicians of today who contributed to the defeat of '73 to step aside and make way for younger and more effective leaders." Referring to obstacles in the way of creating a single opposition party for the plebiscite, Sáenz said, "paradoxically, those who probably enjoy the least backing tend to be those who stipulate the greatest number of conditions."

In common with humanist movements everywhere, the party proclaims five overarching principles:

1. The value of the human being as the measure of all things [the flashpoint of conflict for those who hold that man is subordinate to God];
2. Gandhi-style active "non-violence";
3. An economy based on cooperatives, with the state in a tutelary role, retaining ownership of basic resources and large enterprises. On private property, Sáenz said in a January 1988 statement, "We don't favor it, but we respect it." He added that in advocating cooperatives, they were not pushing for stripping either the state or private owners of enterprises they already had. Said Sáenz in that statement: "The State should coordinate economic, social and political functions, but we are for minimizing the action of the State in favor of cooperatives;"

4. Free choice based on access to full, unfettered information. [As an expression of member "free choice," during the 1987 rash of strikes, humanists were left to decide for themselves whether to take part; since opposition leaders had not yet gotten around to taking them seriously, no one asked them officially to join in, and had they been asked, Sáenz said, their minimum demand would have been the adoption of measures to assure the least possible risk of harm coming to participants through violence];
5. Simultaneous transformation of individuals and society.

Sáenz was reelected president of the Humanist party in an April 15, 1988, party election in which he faced no opposition. That party consolidated, "The Community" moved to form the Green party (which the right-wing National Vanguard mockingly calls "The Tomato party.") The first interim president was a U.S. citizen, Sharon Brown Barton, who arrived in Chile in June 1968 as a tourist, staying on and obtaining her permanent resident card in 1970. Among the first enrolled was her brother, Zbigniew Edward Korysma Zep, also a U.S. citizen. Later, the two hundred Community members who made up the party's initial cadre elected Andres Korysma as president, Katrin L'Homme Ungerer as vice president. At the first party convention, March 27, 1988, the guest of honor was Wilhelm Knabe, a Green party federal deputy from West Germany. Shortly afterwards, the far-left Green party of the Federal Republic pledged full cooperation with the Chilean party, especially on environmental, demilitarization and disarmament issues. The party expected to enroll forty-thousand members of its own in time for the plebiscite, which would give it, too, certification as a national political party. Thus, the two Movement parties were certain to become a major force not only in the plebiscite itself, but in the formation of a new congress.

The Movement enforces not only strict discipline internally, but is tightly knit internationally, holding international congresses every six months. (The most recent ones were in West Germany in July 1987, and Spain in January 1988.) The two Chilean general delegates are Sáenz and Wilfredo Alffen Ovando, who report, in turn, to SILO's original founder, Mario Rodríguez Cobo. An example of international networking: leaders of the Chilean Group of 600 "missionaries" have been busy helping Peruvians organize a political party in that country.

The enigma: who are they? As late as May 26, 1988, *El Mercurio* was referring to them as "a mystery, still not entirely revealed." In most of Western Europe, humanist Green parties have been at the forefront of opposition to NATO, nuclear force modernization, and related defense issues. In Argentina, the Humanist party joined forces with the Communist party in 1987 provincial elections. So far in Chile, they have muted their international views and been both moderate and demure on national issues.

What they are is easier: a political force clearly to be reckoned with, now and likely for years to come.[144] [In a bizarre series of events on the eve of the Plebiscite, Sáenz and other top leaders resigned their posts mysteriously on September 5. In the disarray, the party then failed to complete the legal paperwork, and on September 12, was disqualified as a party.]

There were twenty-six identifiable political entities operating in Chile when party registration began in 1987. By June 1988, only sixteen had filed for certification as national or regional parties, and, of those, only twelve had presented signatures. Most had no chance of ever going anywhere. On the far right, two hundred members of the illegal Nazi party gathered in Santiago's General Cemetery in 1987; nothing further was heard of them. On the far left, MAPU—the self-styled "brain trust" of the Popular Unity which, despite its proletarian professions, chose to sweat out exile in Paris—was now divided into three minuscule splinters. The once proud National Democratic party (PADENA) sunk to such depths that, in 1985, water and electric service to party headquarters was shut off for nonpayment of the bills; in 1988, it was a faction in search of even a handful of signatures, in the meantime pledging its "support" to the "No" forces. The Republican "party," praised by Christian Democrats as a model of a "responsible Right," did not even bother to seek certification. A number of tiny groups continued to mill around at the stage door of the political arena: a Theocratic Movement, the Chilean branch of the worldwide Religion, Family and Tradition movement; a Trotskyite party (radiating new respectability in the reflected light of Gorbachev's *glasnost*), and a Magic party of the People. Commented *Carta Confidencial* of these miniparties: "These fervent calls for a Single Opposition Party, or a Party for Democracy, are formulated by leaders who realize with panic that their public appeal is barely sufficient to fill up a few rows of the balcony at the Cariola Theater."[145]

Three others among the smaller parties bear mention. One is the Social Democratic party. The party was founded in 1972 by then-Senator Luis Bossay Leiva, who broke away from the Radical party, then in Allende's coalition, charging that the government was under Communist control. He then created the Radical party of the Left (PIR), the following year rechristened the Chilean Social Democrat party. In theory, it should be rich: Social Democrat parties in early 1988 dominated governments in Argentina, Ecuador, the Federal Republic of Germany, Israel, Peru, Portugal, Spain, Switzerland, and Venezuela, and are significant in Mexico and Uruguay. But the Social Democrats in Chile, although among the first to seek certification, eleven months into the process had managed to scare up a reported six thousand signatures—less than one-fifth of what they would need to qualify as a national party. Part of their poverty was due to the decision of the International Socialist movement not to recognize the Social Democrats, but the Radical party, and the West German party, richest of the ruling SD parties, decided to support the Christian Democrats. In intense infighting, the SD leadership which ultimately prevailed had all but subordinated itself to the Christian Democrats. That leadership was headed by Amador Navarro. The losing faction, headed by Arturo Venegas, was drummed out altogether for arguing that if "No" won in the plebiscite, still the opposition should play by the rules of the Constitution and wait another year before open presidential elections.

The second is the Radical party—it, too, weakened by chronic feuds and fissures. Finally, on May 5, the Electoral Tribunal ruled that the group headed by Enrique Silva Cimma, sixty-eight-year-old former Comptroller-General (1959–1967), president of the first Constitutional Tribunal (1970–1973), was the only one entitled to use the Radical party name. Less than one month later, Silva Cimma and his secretary-general, Ricardo Navarrete, marched into election service headquarters bearing nineteen bulging folders containing 52,783 names, though too late to meet the June 5th qualifying date for the plebiscite. The Radical party, arguably the oldest political party in Latin America (though a tenuous argument it is) was very much back in the picture, joining the Christian Democrats, the Party for Democracy, and the Humanists as the fourth major partner of the "Concentration for 'No.' "[146]

The third party is a moderate Socialist party—above-ground, legal, and therefore roundly castigated by the various underground and radical socialist "parties." Headed by Juan Carlos Moraga, it had, by late May, secured seven thousand signatures and was inclined to join the "No" forces.

On May 28, 1988, funeral services were held at the Recoleta Franciscan Church in Santiago for Laura Allende Gossens, sister, confidante, and political colleague of the late president. On May 23, 1981, she had committed suicide in Havana (as had one of Allende's daughters, as had Allende himself). Telegrams were read at the service from her son, Andrés Pascal Allende—long-time MIR leader; her other children, Pedro, Denisse and Marianne; and from her sister-in-law, Hortensia Bussi de Allende. Roman Catholic Bishop Jorge Hourton, presiding at the services, said "in life, in death, in the repatriation of her ashes, Mrs. Laura Allende Gossens reveals a tragic destiny, just as this last quarter of the twentieth century in the history of Chile probably will be understood as a profoundly tragic century."

Shortly afterwards, former Allende ministers Carlos Briones, Sergio Bitar, Gonzalo Martner, Mireya Baltra and former Senator Rafael Agustín Gumucio announced plans for a week of homage to Allende, June 20–26, in advance of the eightieth anniversary of his birth. With his widow still residing in Mexico City, plans were also announced for commemorative events there; Ricardo Lagos, basking in his new prominence as a putative heir-apparent to the Allende mantle, was among those planning to attend.[147]

WAR TO THE FINISH

It was not quite 7:15 A.M., on the frosty morning of Friday, May 20, 1988, when Carlos Arturo González Valenzuela, a thirty-one-year-old flautist in the Carabinero band, said goodby to his wife and two small children and set off for the bus that would take him to his job. Minutes later, three masked men pumped six bullets into Sergeant González' body, finishing off the job with shots fired from his own service revolver.

He was the fifth Carabinero murdered in cold blood in 1988.

At 9:40 that evening, Carabinero Corporal Jaime Orlando Sandoval Mendoza was seated near the rear of a small minibus, en route home to his wife, when three men suddenly surrounded him and opened fire. Six bullets penetrated his body. The gunmen then ordered the driver to stop, and they fled through the rear door. The driver roared off in a vain attempt to rush the dying man to a hospital. Sandoval was dead before they got there.

He was the sixth Carabinero murdered in cold blood in 1988.

On May 28, two young men on a motorcycle overtook a car in which military prosecutor Fernando Torres Silva was riding and attached a device to the trunk of the car. They were seen by Torres' escort, who warned him by radio, while opening fire at the speeding motorcycle. The object was a bomb. The terrorists managed to escape, thanks largely to a homemade iron shield rigged to the back of the motorcycle. It was the third attempt on the life of Torres Silva, the man who had led the prosecution of those captured in connection with the huge Communist arms smuggling operation uncovered in August 1986 at Carrizal.

On May 31, the government announced that the state of emergency was being extended for ninety days.

On June 6, 1988, Army Lieutenant Colonel Miguel Rojos Lobos paused at the wheel of his red Citroen, at the driveway leading to the street outside his office. He was waiting for a chance to pull into traffic and head home after a long day at the office. He never got that chance. Two men wearing woolen caps pulled down over their faces blocked his way, then opened fire at point-blank range with 12-gauge sawed-off repeater shotguns. Three shells blasted into his body. He was dead-on-arrival at the hospital.

On June 7, 1988, the U.S. State Department communicated to the government of Chile its "concern": If it had noticed the killings, the State Department did not mention it. It was concerned about the state of emergency. Although the airwaves and the printed pages bristled with politics, the State Department said: "We are concerned and profoundly disillusioned. For a democratic decision-making process to occur, it is necessary to create, several months in advance of the forthcoming plebiscite, an atmosphere of respect for human and civil rights. As we pointed out in our Statement of Support for Democracy in Chile, of December 17, 1987, states of exception which limit the rights of association and of expression are not compatible with a legitimate electoral procedure." The State Department had thus aligned itself anew with opposition political forces in serving notice that, should the opposition fail to win the plebiscite, its very legitimacy could be at issue.

Chile's Roman Catholic bishops could not, either, bring themselves to express their concern about the terrorist killings. But, in a statement issued the very day after the murder of Colonel Rojas, the bishops did express their "concern" that although progress had been made, preparations for the plebiscite did not fulfill entirely their expectations.[148]

> Let the record show that the Manuel Rodríguez Patriotic Front (FMR) will only respect in the plebiscite the triumph of the "No," because as all Chileans know, "Yes" could only triumph through fraud. We will never reconcile ourselves to, nor will we ever capitulate to, this regime.
>
> A communique issued by the Communist party's terrorist wing, May 1988

Back in October of 1987, the Central Committee of the party met and decided on its three-pronged strategy: (1) instruct its members to register for the elections and step up infiltration of democratic organizations; (2) continue to apply terrorist pressure to the regime; (3) when the regime reacted to the attacks, mobilize international pressure denouncing "repression" and the stifling of free expression. On March 18, 1988, the FMR had announced a fourth option: Augusto Pinochet remained an assassination target.

Violence was to come in three forms:

(1) Murder, sabotage
(2) Strikes, mass demonstrations
(3) Disruption of university and high school activities

To placate party hot-heads angry that the party would take any part in the "fascist" electoral process—a theme that consumed two days of Central Committee debates—the party resolution, in the tortured, convoluted style so typical of Communist pronouncements, said: "We believe that, with different shades and forms of opinion, there is agreement in the sense . . . [that] . . . a campaign for free elections not underpinned by military struggle to eliminate the dictatorship borders on the absurd. All Communists share the idea that combat must be first in order of priority. The simple fact of registering resolves no problem by itself. The only thing that can change the picture is [armed] struggle and we do not accept postponing it until '89."[149]

But registering would play to the eternal yearning of Christian Democrats and others to see them back in the process, if only they would again show their "democratic" colors.

> *The progress made in Chile in the field of human rights has not been sufficiently recognized; this failure could lead to discouragement among those who work in Chile to better their country's record on human rights. We need to recognize, among other things, that Chile has a functioning and active opposition press and that many in the political opposition travel freely to meetings, such as the one in Geneva, where they criticize President Pinochet's government, and return to Chile.*
>
> U.S. Ambassador Patricia M. Byrne, in a statement to the UN Economic and Social Council, May 19, 1987

Part of the reason for the "failure to recognize" progress was to be found in media reporting of the situation. Part was in the way in which the UN itself handled the information available to it. The special UN rapporteur on Chile, Fernando Volio Jiménez, complained that the UN's 1986 resolution "did not take into account my reports." Volio, former foreign minister of Costa Rica, said, that "annoys and discourages me . . . the resolution was political on the part of those who drafted it and also on the part of those who approved it. I would have expected more objectivity—for example, they should have taken the terrorism into account."[150]

To "remedy" that lack of objectivity—presumably—Panama and Cuba were added to the UN Commission on Human Rights in 1988, a commission that already included some of the most egregious human rights offenders in the world.

Early in May 1988, former Socialist Senator María Elena Carrera slipped into the country illegally from Argentina. In so doing, she joined a growing list who did, although by so doing, they risked prison (or exile) sentences of 541 days. On May 31, the government published another list of twenty-five persons—mostly former Communist or Socialist party officials of Allende's government—permitted to return to the country. Chief among them was MAPU leader Jacques Chonchol, ideologue of Frei's agrarian policies, later Allende's highly controversial agriculture minister. At that point, only 430 names remained on the still-proscribed list, most of them top Communist leaders or known terrorists. Commented *Carta Confidencial* acidly: "While hundreds of thousands annually flee 'royal socialisms,' and millions more are prevented from doing so . . . the most dedicated enemies of the Chilean 'tyranny' fight for the right to live within its borders. . . ."[151] On August 31, the ban was lifted completely; among those who would then stream back into Chile: Allende's widow, Mrs. Hortensia Bussi de Allende.

If the Communists were adept at exploiting "democracy's rotten freedoms"—in Lenin's phrase—they were also long experienced in the practice of violence. Internationally, Chile's terrorists belonged to three Latin American terror rings: the Revolutionary Junta of the South, financed by the Soviet Union and Cuba, the America's Battalion, sponsored by Libya, and the Nicaraguan-supported Coordinating Committee. According to Chile's Investigative Director Fernando Paredes, the Soviet Union provided the financial and logistical support, as well as coordinating international propaganda, and Cuba provided the bulk of the training (at camps in Punto Cero, Piñar del Río, Trinidad, and Havana), though Chileans also underwent training in Nicaragua, Libya, East Germany, and Czechoslovakia. (Nearly a year after he made those revelations, Cuban Vice President Carlos Rafael Rodríguez publicly acknowledged Cuban support for Chile's "guerrilla movements.") That terrorist junta also includes Peru's Shining Path and Tupac Amaru, Colombia's M-19 and Popular Liberation Army, Argentina's Montoneros, Uruguay's Tupamaros, Venezuela's Red Flag, and El Salvador's Farabundo Martí National Liberation Front. The junta generally meets in Bolivia.

Cuba coordinates its subversive network from its big intelligence operation in Buenos Aires. In 1987, the Cubans were believed to have trained three hundred and fifty Chilean terrorists; in 1988, they planned to double that number.

Support abroad allowed the Communist party apparatus to impose order at home. The first task confronting the Communists in 1988 was to fuse or at least mastermind cooperation between the two feuding terrorist organizations, the MIR and its own (and rebellious) FMR. The second was to rebuild both. The MIR had been badly weakened in 1983 through effective action of Pinochet's security forces and internal bickering; the FMR had also been hit hard following its 1986 Carrizal arms shipment and botched assassination attempts, and was further shattered on June 15, 1987, when security forces discovered eight of its "safe houses." Eleven terrorists were killed in a pitched gun-battle at one (leading to immediate local and international human rights protests). Documents seized in those raids led to further FMR arrests.[152] Acting through a cover organization calling itself the United Left (IU, for *Izquierda Unida*), the Communists appealed in late 1987 to Castro for help. In a series of meetings, first in Havana, later in Montevideo, from December 17–19, and, at the same time in Buenos Aires, Castro said he would help if he were allowed covert participation in the plebiscite process, if the FMR were more prudent in its operations, and if it coordinated them with the political leadership of the party.

Differences with the Communist party leadership patched up, the FMR, from its Buenos Aires headquarters, embarked on a new campaign of subversion and violence in 1988. To protect its "image" flank, the FMR opened propaganda offices in Spain, France, Belgium, Italy, and Venezuela. At home, rebuilding its depleted ranks was accompanied by an arms build-up, much of the new weaponry flowing in from neighboring Argentina. In January, Military Prosecutor Fernando Torres Silva said new arms caches—M-16 rifles and explosives—had been found in the areas of Temuco, Concepción, and Chillán. He also said he had established a clear connection between the groups involved in the Carrizal arms shipment, the attack on President Pinochet, and the Santiago "safe-house" which was the scene of the bloody June 15, 1987, shoot-out. He said he had also discovered that the Carrizal group had used a small plane to distribute arms around the country before their operations had been discovered.

The FMR began 1988 with a series of "bangs": four bombs went off the night of January 28 in Concepción; the next night, two branch banks in Santiago were hit; four other bombs were discovered in time in Coronel and Calama. One, on January 31, blew up prematurely; the three FMR terrorists manipulating it died. In line with their announced plan to disrupt public transport, two minibuses were burned over the last weekend of the month in Santiago, another in Valparaíso.

The MIR, despite a new division of terrorist "labor" which ostensibly put it in charge of rural operations, planted a bomb of its own in La Cisterna, on the outskirts of Santiago, early in February; that one claimed the life of Carabinero Major Julio Benimeli, chief of the Special Operations Branch in the Metropolitan area. On April 2, Carabinero Corporal Alfredo Rivera Rojas, thirty-five-year-old father of two, was shot in the back by three youths as he was about to board a bus to return home from duty. Rojas, carrying groceries he had picked up minutes before, was climbing on the bus when the first shots were fired; his assailants threw him from the bus and shot him dead as he lay on the pavement.

Around two-hundred persons were picked up for questioning. They would be recorded in human rights statistics. Corporal Rivera would not be.

The Communists and their allies of the hard Left—including, on occasions, Christian Democrat labor leaders—were far less successful in strikes. Under the Communist party 1988 "Plan for National Uprising," the first of a series of general strikes was to have begun March 5, building to full-scale confrontation on Labor Day, May 1. Those fizzled; only railroad workers went out, and that strike was settled eighteen days later, on April 29. On May Day, only twelve thousand turned up in Santiago for the traditional Labor Day rally—and that became an even greater fiasco when masked Miristas attempted to burn a U.S. flag and created other incidents as Manuel Bustos Huerta, president of the National Workers' Command, was speaking. Later, the same group insulted and menaced Bustos, who had to be escorted to safety by a squad of supporters. Similar incidents occurred in Valparaíso, Iquique, Concepción, and Temuco, but the Santiago incident created the greatest reverberations, driving a new wedge between the hard Left and the emerging labor movement. Given the presence of a who's who of ultra-left leaders at the rally—including new hero Ricardo Lagos—the episode recalled the backlash generated by FMR antics during the papal visit, suggesting that the radicals might again be out of control.[153]

If the Mirista purpose was to restore to Bustos the revolutionary backbone which, in its view, he had lost, then it failed—miserably. Bustos announced after the May Day episode that a general strike scheduled for May 11 was off—indefinitely.

The Communists flubbed their labor initiatives, and they didn't do much better on yet another front: a series of planned seizures (tomas) of urban lands. Under their plan for insurrection, "vanguard" cadres were to lead fifteen thousand shantytown dwellers in seizing some thirty parcels of unoccupied land between March 30 and May 1 in Santiago, Valparaíso, Concepción, Temuco, and Puerto Montt. They actually managed to grab three in metropolitan Santiago, one in Viña del Mar, and one in Puerto Montt; a total of around 350 family groups took part.[154]

On the third front—student agitation—the Communists were much more successful. The first serious problems surfaced in 1987 at the University of Chile and were directed, ostensibly, at the university president, a Pinochet appointee. Rumblings of trouble also were heard in secondary schools, in no small measure fostered by teachers long disgruntled with the 1981 education reforms and capitalizing on the new openness in the Chilean society.[155]

On January 20, 1988, *El Rebelde,* the clandestine publication of the MIR, published a scathing attack on the University of Chile rector and warned that with the resumption of classes in March, universities would be targets of all manner of demonstrations. Classes were barely underway when virtually every major campus in the country was hit by student strikes; by then, coalitions of ultra-left groups controlled most student federations. Viewing the situation of strikes and demonstrations, Héctor Herrera Cajas, rector of the Metropolitan University and professor at the Catholic University of Valparaíso, said that it was "undeniable" that universities and the Catholic church itself were "infiltrated by Communists."[156]

But more ominous yet were Communist efforts to mobilize high school students. Former Communist party Senator Julieta Campusano, awaiting trial on charges of having returned illegally to the country, called on students at mid-May to take to the streets in protests against "the imperialist octopus." The fight, she said, "is not of a year, nor a decade, and those of us who are revolutionaries now, must remain so forever." Following her speech—one of a number of such rallies and seizures of schools—high school youngsters, with their faces covered, marched along one of the city's principal thoroughfares, then erected flaming barriers to traffic. Commented *Carta Confidencial:* "Faced with the failure of their 'social mobilizations' . . . what they are seeking is a victim. . . ." They were seeking that "martyr" among children twelve to fifteen years of age—"militia detachments," they called them.[157]

If, as it would appear, the Communists had lost their ability to summon huge strikes, rally slum-dwellers, it was equally true that they had lost none of their ability to murder, maim—and manufacture martyrs. Thus was Chile, in 1988, divided between those who sought support for their views through ballots and those who sought to impose theirs through bombs and bullets.

Notes

CHAPTER 11

1. Carlos Prats González, *Memorias: Testimonio de un Soldado* (Santiago: Pehuen Editores, 1985), pp. 531–32. Prats made plain that he did not locate the blame entirely with Allende, nor with those who accompanied him. Prats' daughter, María Angelica, visiting her parents in August 1974, just a month before the murder, said her father worked intensely on his memoirs, determined to finish before the end of September. "It seemed that he sensed something," she recalled later. (Quoted by Edwin Harrington and Monica González, *Bomba en una calle de Palermo* [Santiago: Editorial Emision, 1987], p. 210. Toward the end, Prats was increasingly moody— and embittered. To Moy de Tohá, widow of Allende's defense and interior minister José Tohá, he wrote early in September 1974: Pinochet "is a good professional, but personally a mediocrity . . . As to his behavior, I can tell you that his treason has no paragon in the history of Chile. . . ." In a March 16, 1974, letter to Allende's widow, "Tencha," he wrote that he had steered clear of politics in exile, observing that "much effort has been displayed in Chile to find a clue that could affect my honor or that would permit them to exhibit me as 'the general at the service of Marxism' . . ." (ibid., pp. 215–16).

2. Laurence Stern, "Slain Statesman Still Held to Hope for Chile's Future," *Washington Post* service story in the *Miami Herald*, September 26, 1976, p. AW 25-A. Stern quoted from a tape-recorded interview with Letelier done shortly before his death by Washington free-lancer Richard Pollock for a public radio documentary on Chile. Letelier knew, of course, that talk of "monopolies" as applied to Chile was largely Marxist mumbo-jumbo (or demagoguery); despite the return of many companies to original owners, the state in Chile still owned outright the giant industry, copper, and controlled the lion's share of the balance of the economy.

3. One, among many, examples of a rush to judgment by academics: James F. Petras, prolific writer/commentator on Chile and Latin America, professor of sociology at the State University of New York at Binghamton, and member in 1971 and 1972 of the executive council of the Latin American Studies Association, in testimony before the House Subcommittee on Foreign Affairs, September 18, 1974: ". . . A sense of social justice and popular participation is so firmly implanted among the populace that junta efforts to impose a Brazilian type economic development model based on coercion will certainly face severe challenges and will ultimately fail . . . Chile lacks the internal market and industrial export potentialities which made Brazil so attractive to foreign investors in the late sixties and early seventies and which formed the basis for its externally-induced expansion . . ." *United States and Chile During the Allende Years, 1970–1973*, report of hearings before the Subcommittee during 1971, 1972, 1973, 1974 (Washington: U.S. Government Printing Office, 1975), p. 301. As we shall shortly see, Professor Petras was wrong about the internal market, exports and foreign investment—although it is likely that if Chile had continued with approved, "progressive" economic policies, he would have proved right.

One example, among many, many of media doom-saying: William Montalbano, "Chile Struggles, Still a Chaotic Economic Lab," *Miami Herald*, November 19, 1975, p. 8-D. "The minority rich are best off now by government intention and the gap between them and everybody else is growing. The poor are suffering worst, and the middle class, close to a majority, legitimately can claim to have been battered from pillar to post by both the extreme Left and the extreme Right in the space of five years. The difference now is that the new policies—if they work—may one day produce a healthier country—for the survivors . . . The social side of the picture is grim . . . *Mensaje*, a Jesuit magazine, estimates that an average working-class family of five has lost half its purchasing power since the coup . . . In short, Chile is experiencing a deep recession, or a mild depression . . . radical overhaul being undertaken by The Chicago Boys . . . certainly is not winning the generals any new friends in Chile . . ." The glib Montalbano had significant reverberative power, not merely because his articles were widely printed in the many Knight-Ridder Newspapers and many subscriber newspapers, but also because American correspondents tended to look up to him as a savvy trendsetter. Quite apart from dropping *Mensaje* in without qualification as a source, Montalbano was also egregiously wrong in pronouncing last rites over an experiment still in its crib. Not only did the new policies succeed, they expanded the rolls of "survivors" and created many friends; public opinion polls in the mid-1980s onward showed Chileans overwhelmingly favoring a free market economy.

4. Interview with the author in Santiago, June 15, 1987. As indicated earlier, General Matthei joined the junta on July 24, 1978, replacing dissident Gen. Gustavo Leigh. There has been only one other change in the remarkably stable personnae of junta personnel: Carabinero Gen. Rodolfo Stange Oelckers, who replaced Gen. César Mendoza in August 1985.

5. Genaro Arriagada H., *La Política Militar de Pinochet* (Santiago: Salesianos Printers, 1985), p. 204. I have drawn extensively on that book, including information on the number of generals, changes in the regulations, the Brady anecdote. It needs to be remarked again that there were two factors partially explaining the great increase in the ranks of senior officers—the army itself had grown, from somewhere around 25,000 in 1973 to 57,000 in latest-available statistics—and that a number of generals were, inevitably in a military government, serving in posts formerly reserved to civilians. Given the long record of external threats from Peru, Argentina, and (to a lesser extent) Bolivia, discussed earlier, plus the long stagnation in force levels and materiel allocations during the 1960s, a build-up in the military was logical.

6. Arriagada, op. cit., p. 186. He quotes Gen. Ernesto Medina Fraguela, *Nuestra Defensa Nacional Frente a la Opinión Pública* (Santiago: Imprenta Benapres y Fernández Ltda., 1941) as commenting on a similar measure adopted by Col. Carlos Ibáñez del Campo during his four-year, de facto presidency (1927–1931). The scholar Francisco Orrego Vicuña argues—although not convincingly for this observer—that the armed forces have remained "hierarchically and in terms of discipline subordinated to the structure of the state as government." He adds that the Chilean military readily submit to the state, not always to the "government." Francisco Orrego Vicuña, "El Papel de las Fuerzas Armadas en la Redemocratización de Chile," pp. 17–18, paper prepared for the Centro de Estudios del Desarrollo of Santiago. Orrego Vicuña, a professor at the

Institute of International Studies of the University of Chile, took his doctorate at the London School of Economics and Political Science.

7. Those charged were Air Force Brig. Gen. Alberto Bachelet Martínez, named by Allende (because of his known sympathies for the Popular Unity government) to head the National Secretariat of Distribution early in 1973; and retired Air Force Gen. Sergio Poblete García, number two man in the Government Development Corporation at the time of the coup. The Distribution Secretariat was widely viewed as a smokescreen to use rationing to bend opponents to the will of the regime; General Poblete was charged with participating in the MIR-inspired plotting to subvert the air force. General Bachelet died while awaiting trial; General Poblete was one of nine persons stripped of their citizenship during the early years of the junta. Information on the imprisoned soldiers and officers, and the death sentences asked for Captain Carlos Patricio Carvacho and a "Captain Vergara" is from the OAS 1974 Human Rights Report (Washington: Organization of American States CP/doc.381.74, 1974), pp. 85, 88.

8. Arriagada, op. cit., p. 145. The sardonic quote is from the same author (a leading Christian Democrat literati), p. 153.

9. The Leigh-Carter quote is from Heraldo Muñoz, Las Relaciones Exteriores del Gobierno Militar Chileno (Santiago: Ediciones del Ornitorrinco, 1986), p. 102; Leigh spoke of his reaction to the "consultation" in an interview with the author in Santiago, June 16, 1987. The "consultation"—Pinochet was careful not to describe it as a "plebiscite"—was held on January 4, 1978, only twelve days after Pinochet first announced it. Chileans were asked to vote "yes" or "no" on this statement: "In the face of the international aggression unleashed against the government of the homeland, I support President Pinochet in his defense of the dignity of Chile, and I reaffirm the legitimacy of the republic to conduct in a sovereign way the process of the institutionalization of the country." To aid illiterates, "yes" was identified with a Chilean flag, "no" with a black flag. The result: 4,177,064 yes; 1,131,115 no; 258,169 blank or invalid votes. Humeres was rapidly replaced as comptroller by Sergio Fernández. Rhetoric notwithstanding, Pinochet was, in fact, already planning another election on the constitution then being drafted. Source for consultation text and "no other elections": 1979 Book of the Year (Chicago: Encyclopaedia Britannica, 1979), p. 24.

10. The call for dissolution of the junta is in Edwin Harrington and Mónica González, op. cit., p. 292; details of the reaction to Leigh ouster in special edition of Hoy magazine, "La Década de Hoy," May 1987, pp. 7–8. Leigh's impatience now contrasted with his attitude as expressed less than a year before: "... This psychological war," he told an interviewer, "will have to continue whatever government may come. A pure civilian government, with criteria such as those which we had since the 20s, would be a profound mistake ... We have underway a constitutional reform commission, working efficiently for the future, but its work must necessarily be slow and meticulous [acuciosa]. We cannot make the suit before we have the man who is going to wear it. ...." "En Un Año, Otro País," interview with Leigh published in Qué Pasa, #178, September 17, 1974, p. 35.

11. Disagreements in Santiago over how to handle the Letelier investigation revealed a sharp split between hard- and soft-liners within the regime. The "soft-liners" argued that failure to yield to U.S. pressure could bring the regime down, and urged granting the U.S. request to extradite the three DINA officers. The "hard-liners" said to do so would destroy the military

cohesion and loyalty essential to sustain the regime. The in-fighting first broke into the open in 1977 when DINA leaked details of a scandal in a major financial institution ("La Familia"), so as to discredit the government's economic team and other perceived soft-liners. Retired Gen. Odlanier Mena, who succeeded Contreras as chief of the DINA successor agency, the CNI, was said to have cooperated actively with the FBI in its investigation, producing new tensions. He also was said to have linked Contreras to fraud involving the IVA fund (the Spanish initials for Value Added Tax). When Mena resigned in July 1980 following the murder of a high army officer, hard-liners accused him of failing to curb terrorism; soft-liners—chief among them, former Foreign Minister Hernán Cubillos and former Education Minister Gonzalo Vial—expressed support for him. In June 1979, Contreras and his former deputy, Col. Pedro Espinoza, filed suit against Cubillos, Vial, and Interior Minister Sergio Fernández, claiming that an Education Ministry lawyer assigned to defend the three DINA officers against extradition had been pressured by Vial, backed by Fernández and Cubillos, to drop the case. Pinochet and his junta colleagues dismissed the suit. Contreras reacted angrily: "The only thing I say is the following: General Pinochet has judged that this situation is completely finished [superada]. As a military man, I am once again willing to follow the orders of my general, despite the ignominious attitude of some of the lackeys who presently surround him." Heraldo Muñoz, op. cit., pp. 30–32. At one point, Contreras threatened to go public with what he knew about CIA operations; the CIA reportedly responded, fire when ready. Nothing happened. From Harrington and González, op. cit., p. 307.

12. Arriagada, op. cit., p. 160.
13. Robert Moss, "The Tribulation of Chile," in *National Review*, October 10, 1975, p. 1113; the rebuilding quote is from the junta's March 11, 1974, Declaration of Principles.
14. Details of the commission's work from Sergio Carrasco Delgado, *Alessandri: Su Pensamiento Constitucional; Reseña de su vida pública* (Santiago: Editorial Jurídica de Chile, Editorial Andrés Bello, 1987), pp. 117–118. The original commission was formally created by Supreme Decree #1064, October 25, 1973, and was made up of: Enrique Ortúzar Escobar, its chairman, Sergio Diez Urzúa, Jorge Ovalle Q., Enrique Evans de la C., Gustavo Lorca R., Alejandro Silva B., and Alicia Romo R. Silva, Evans, and Ovalle were replaced in 1977 by Luz Bulnes A., Raúl Bertelsen R., and Juan de Dios Carmona P. All but three of the eleven were professors of constitutional law (Mrs. Romo, Carmona, and Ortúzar the exceptions). Professor Silva maintained throughout that the commission should limit itself to working on the constitution.
15. "Crearán Consejo de Estado," and "33 aplausos durante el Mensaje de S.E.," from *La Tercera de la hora*, Santiago, September 12, 1975, p. 6. Virtually the entire front-page of that edition of the tabloid was given over to a picture of the huge torchlight really centered in the Plaza Bulnes. Among those seated on the podium during Pinochet's speech were Cardinal Silva and former President González Videla; Frei did not attend. During the speech, Pinochet also announced a one-step reduction in the state of siege, from "internal defense" to "internal security": the essential difference, that military courts would resume functioning as in time of peace and their decisions could be appealed to the Supreme Court. But, military law "as in time of war" continued to be applied to acts of sabotage or terrorism.

16. The council was created by Decree Law #1319 of January 9, 1976, and its membership followed the lines outlined by Pinochet in his speech the preceding September. In addition to the two former presidents: Enrique Urrutia M., ex-president of the Supreme Court; Héctor Humeres M., former comptroller-general; Gen. Oscar Izurieta M., ex-commander-in-chief of the army; Adm. Ramón Barros G., former navy commander; Gen. Renato García V., ex-air force commander; Gen. Vicente Huerta C., ex-Carabineros director-general; Juan de Dios Carmona, ex-minister of defense (under Frei); Hernán Figueroa A., former ambassador; Professor Ortúzar; Carlos F. Cáceres C., professor of the School of Economics; Julio Philippi, representing professional organizations; Pedro Ibáñez, representing business interests; Guillermo Medina G., representing labor; Mercedes Ezquerra B., women's organizations; Juan A. Coloma, youth; and, during the early part of the council's work, Juvenal Hernández J., former rector of the University of Chile, representing education. Carrasco, op. cit., pp. 120–123. The "blunder" quote is from Moss, op. cit., p. 1109. The problem with that thinking was, of course, that it assumed: (1) the country's political past was worth returning to; (2) the Christian Democrats were the worthy stewards of that return to the past. The junta believed neither.

17. Alessandri demonstrated that sense of integrity and independence early on, and would, in fact, continue to demonstrate it down to the very end. Pinochet heeded Alessandri's first protest, but not the second. In 1977, General Raúl Benavides, then interior minister, and General Sergio Covarrubias, then chief of staff of the presidency, appeared before the council to propose additional constitutional acts on regional government. Alessandri protested to Pinochet that the junta should stop creating a constitution piece-meal, and concentrate on creating a complete constitution. Pinochet agreed, and asked the council to review and react to the work of the Study Commission once it was ready. Carrasco notes that Alessandri revealed that exchange in his very last public speech, on November 5, 1983, at the Fifth National Management Meeting (*Encuentro Nacional de la Empresa*): "Reclamo para mí el honor de haber obtenido que se pusiera término a las Actas Constitucionales, así como que se llegase a redactar una nueva Carta Política" (ibid., p. 120). The second concerned changes made in the constitutional text finally approved by the council, as we shall now see.

18. Carrasco, op. cit., p. 119, and, for quote, "Pinochet: Chile construye una nueva democracia," AP-dispatch datelined Rio de Janeiro reporting on an interview with Pinochet published in the newspaper *O Globo* of that city, and published in the *Miami News*, September 23, 1975, in its Spanish-language news section.

19. "The Political Organization of the State in the Chilean Legal System," in *Report on the Situation of Human Rights in Chile* (Washington: Organization of American States, 1985), OAS Document 17, September 27, p. 14. Indicative of the attitude of the authors was a reference to "the constituent power it [the junta] had *allegedly* assumed ..." (emphasis added), p. 13. Reference to chapter 1 is the author's translation of Article 4 from Luz Bulnes Aldunate, *Constitución Política de la República de Chile: Concordancias, Anotaciones y Fuentes* (Santiago: Editorial Jurídica de Chile, 1981), p. 154. That useful volume contains not only the texts of the 1925 and 1980 constitutions, but also the text as proposed by the Study Com-

884 OUT OF THE ASHES

mission, concurrences/dissents of commission members to specific articles, the decree law convoking the plebiscite for the 1980 constitution, and a break-down by regions and sex of the vote in the plebiscite.

20. *Una Salida Político-Constitucional Para Chile*, Gutemberg Martínez Ocamica, ed. (Santiago: Instituto Chileno de Estudios Humanísticos, 1985), p. 69. The book is a compendium of remarks made by nine leading figures from the far (but legal) Left to the Right, at a seminar of the same title held in Santiago, July 27–28, 1984. Those participating included two former ministers in Allende's Cabinet, a former comptroller-general, a former (and now present) president of the Christian Democrat party, and a member of the commission which drafted the original text for the 1980 constitution. The latter (Sergio Diez) offered the Alessandri quote cited here.

21. "Chile Junta Leaders Proclaim Their Unity," Agence France-Presse dispatch datelined Santiago in the *Miami Herald*, January 29, 1976, p. 10-C-2. The rumor apparently originated in a front-page article in the *Sunday Times* of London, which reported that it had reliable information that ten generals had demanded Pinochet's resignation. The newspaper apparently based much of its speculation on the resignation of General Sergio Arellano Stark, identifying him (erroneously) as number-three ranking; actually, he was number twenty-two (of twenty-five in 1973, at that point approximately number fifteen). "Chile Quiet on Reported Call for Chief's Ouster," an AP story datelined Santiago in the *Miami Herald*, January 7, 1976, p. 10-B, refers to the London report and Santiago reaction. Arriagada, in his thorough work on the military under Pinochet (op. cit.), makes no mention of any such plot.

22. "Chacarillas" from Alvaro Pineda de Castro, *Pinochet: Verdad y Ficción* (Madrid: Vasallo de Mumbert, 1981), pp. 164–165; "El camino de Pinochet," special May 1987 edition of *Hoy*, op. cit., p. 17. Chacarillas commemorates the heroism of seventy-seven young soldiers killed in the battle of La Concepción during the War of the Pacific. The 1979 remarks from "Mensaje al País de S.E., el Presidente de la República, General de Ejército, D. Augusto Pinochet Ugarte, Al Conmemorarse el 6th Aniversario del Gobierno," mimeographed copy of the September 11, 1979, speech issued by the presidential press secretary's office, pp. 20–24. In his extensive review of foreign policy events and plans, Pinochet not once mentioned the U.S. by name, but did lump the U.S. with the Soviet Union in opening remarks referring to superpower "interventionism . . . open or subtle expressions of imperialist ambitions." The Soviets, of course (though not named either), were blasted for subversion and armed "interventionism"; the U.S.—"although inspired in noble principles of freedom and human dignity which we share fully"—for "not calculating the risks of exporting systems [*esquema*] alien to the reality of other nations, and which also applies its new doctrine with a selective and discriminatory character which deprives it of all moral force" (ibid., p. 5). He was referring to (new) President Carter's highly capricious "human rights" policies, directed mainly at punishing right-wing regimes. In that speech, he spoke also of Chile's new foreign policy initiatives with Third World countries, efforts to overcome the breach in relations with Western Europe, and, significantly, new initiatives with Japan, the beginning of Chile's "Pacific Basin" awareness. He referred to an invitation extended during a recent

visit of Japan's foreign minister to Chile to visit that country—a trip he has never made.

23. Number of prisoners from *Report on the Situation of Human Rights in Chile*, op. cit., p. 113. The report uses Vicariate of Solidarity figures and refers to those cases that "entailed the intervention of the Vicariate," which, therefore, were mainly (but not entirely) political cases. Recapitulation of 1978 events from *Book of the Year* (Chicago: Encyclopaedia Britannica, 1979), p. 247.

24. A total of 134,421 voted in the plebiscite, only just under seven thousand voting against the new constitution. Former National party senator (and top leader) Francisco Bulnes Sanfuentes noted that the basic document was drafted by the president, his justice minister, José Maza, and his son, Fernando, ramming it first through an eleven-man commission named by the president, and then through a one hundred-member consultative assembly over the strong objection of radicals, conservatives, and many liberals. He adds that President Alessandri had also said repeatedly that he would submit the draft to a constituent assembly, deciding instead at the last minute to refer it directly to a hastily convoked plebiscite. The principal parties of the day—the conservatives and the radicals (as well as some of Alessandri's liberals)—objected strenuously to the validity of the plebiscite. In *Una Salida Político-Constitucional Para Chile*, op. cit., p. 132.

25. Eduardo Frei, "La Reforma Constitucional en su Contexto Histórico-Político," in *Reforma Constitucional 1970* (Santiago: Editorial Jurídica de Chile, 1970), pp. 34, 41, 45. Since the 1925 constitution unleashed the ever-expanding power of political parties, the Christian Democrats were generally pleased with the document. The 1970 reforms reflected their earlier confidence that they would rule for another thirty years, and their wish therefore to adapt the document to the dominant socialist strain in their economic policies. Even though they controlled Congress, Frei was not able to muster the votes he needed to get all he wanted. He did call the plebiscite innovation "the most transcendental of the reforms approved [in 1969] by Congress," just as he described state economic planning as "the indispensable tool for economic development." The 1925 constitution, he wrote, had become so quickly out of date because it emerged "only seven years after the First World War had ended and eight years after the socialist system had been installed in Russia."

26. Carrasco, op. cit., p. 126. From a letter Alessandri wrote to Carrasco on July 21, 1980. He had expressed very similar terms as he was beginning the task, in an August 22, 1978, letter.

27. Discussion of commission-council differences, Alessandri's additional thoughts, and foregoing quote from Carrasco, op. cit., pp. 126–138. As the foregoing clearly indicates, Alessandri shared the deep distrust of many of restoring to political parties the power they formerly retained which perverted congressional elections into the rubber-stamp procedure he describes.

28. That working group was made up of: Interior Minister Fernández; Justice Minister Madariaga; the judge advocates (*auditor general*) of the army (Gen. Fernando Lyon); the navy (Adm. Aldo Montagna); the air force (Gen. Enrique Montero); the Carabineros (Maj. Harry Grunwald), and the legislative secretary of the junta, Mario Duvauchelle. The laws governing dis-

closure were Decree Law #991, and Law No. 17.983 of March 28, 1981, the only exceptions being national security.

29. Carrasco, op. cit., pp. 147–223, for his detailed comparative analysis. Also useful is Luz Bulnes Aldunate's *Constitución Política de la República de Chile: Concordancias, Anotaciones y Fuentes*, op. cit. Carrasco points out (note #253, p. 140) that Alessandri was particularly peeved that Study Commission Chairman Ortúzar was among those consulted by the working group, with the result that he "put back many of the ideas which the council had rejected . . . objecting also to his [Ortúzar's] lack of vision in political matters." Given that President Alessandri had appointed Ortúzar to no fewer than four different cabinet posts, the put-down seems gratuitous.

30. Details of the plebiscite from Luz Bulnes Aldunate, op. cit., pp. 399–402.

31. "Another Blow to President Frei," *New York Times*, April 17, 1967, p. 26, cited by Weston H. Agor, *The Chilean Senate: Internal Distribution of Influence* (Austin: University of Texas Press, 1971), p. 159.

32. For example, party leaders leaked to the international news media a letter from two top officials to Pinochet in which they accused the junta of human rights violations, mistreating labor, and trying to suppress all political activity. See, e.g., Jonathan Kandell, "Chile's Big Party Criticizes Junta," a Santiago-datelined dispatch in the *New York Times*, February 8, 1974, p. 1. Within a few months, there was a spate of similar stories revolving around a sharp exchange of letters between party President Patricio Aylwin and Interior Minister Gen. Oscar Bonilla. Many Christian Democrats had assumed they would enjoy a special relationship with Bonilla since he had served as military aide to former President Frei and was believed especially sympathetic to them (as, it was assumed, were such generals as Sergio Arellano and Herman Brady). Reacting to repeated closings for censorship violations of the party-owned radio station, Radio Balmeceda (flagship of a national network of stations), Aylwin said the junta was denying Christian Democrats "the right to represent our points of view." Bonilla, in a letter the PDC leaked, retorted, "please do not write to me in any terms that are not those of an administrative authority of a recessed party respectfully addressing the government of the nation." See, e.g., James Nelson Goodsell, "Chile's politicians regret support of military junta," *Christian Science Monitor*, July 29, 1974, and "Chile's Christian Democrats Defying Junta on Censorship," an AP story in the *Miami Herald*, July 19, 1974, p. 28-A. The party's newspaper, *La Prensa*, had been forced to shut down in February 1974 because of financial problems—the drying-up of government advertising, but also the inability of the party itself to provide subsidies, plus the general climate of economic depression.

33. The results of the poll at the April plenum were: full collaboration with the junta, 4.6 percent; critical collaboration, 28.8 percent; active critical independence (the then-party policy), 68.2 percent; outright opposition, 9.1 percent, and "resistance" (presumably armed), 1.5 percent. Cited in Michael Fleet, *The Rise and Fall of Christian Democracy* (Princeton: Princeton University Press, 1985), p. 181. He notes that a June gallup poll showed 76 percent supporting Pinochet, 20 percent opposed. The "Declaration of Caracas" was signed by former PDC presidents Bernardo Leighton and Renán Fuentealba; for the Socialists, Aniceto Rodríguez and Clodomiro

Almeyda; for the hard left wing of the Radical party, Anselmo Sule, who was the main organizer of the meeting (and who had his citizenship revoked for that and other "actions abroad which directly attack the basic interests of the state"). The meeting was paid for by "a West German-funded Social Democratic foundation," and also included Orlando Letelier and former PDC cabinet minister Sergio Bitar, then a fellow at the Harvard Institute for International Development (one of numerous Popular Unity and antijunta Chileans who found quick sinecures at U.S. universities). Lewis H. Diuguid, "Leaders of Chilean Parties Vow Effort Against Junta," in the *Washington Post*, July 22, 1975, p. 8-C. Peru's President Alan García in 1988 instructed his vice president, Luis Alberto Sánchez, to raise the question of Sule's citizenship during a visit to Santiago; Pinochet declined. García, like Sule, is a member of the Socialist International, except that Sule, deprived of a political base back home, had also recently lost his SI regional vice-presidency to Enrique Silva Cimma, head of one of the less radical Radical factions in Chile. From *Carta Confidencial*, #22, May 9, 1988, pp. 21–25.

34. *1976 Book of the Year* (Chicago: Encyclopaedia Britannica, 1977), pp. 189–190. Fleet, op. cit., p. 177, is among those to observe that most civilians, including top Christian Democrats, were willing to accept military rule for a transitional period of one to three years.

35. Gonzalo Vial Correa, "Decadencia, Consensos y Unidad Nacional en 1973," in *Política y Geoestrategia*, #36 (Santiago: Academia Nacional de Estudios Políticos y Estratégicos, 1985), p. 27. "Invaded" is from the same source. Vial served during 1979 as the junta's education minister. As to church-state ties, Fleet, op. cit., p. 186, notes that many on the Left who had drifted away from the party in the 1960s and during the Allende years because they considered it too bourgeois made common cause with it in the church-run human rights organizations.

36. Taking 1974 and 1975 together, the *developed* countries in the Organization for Economic Cooperation and Development experienced a decline in their GNP of about 2.5 percent compared with 1973; in the U.S., the drop was 5.1 percent; ". . . in 1975, as in the previous year, the less developed countries faced enormous problems because of the world economic slowdown. Only the oil-producing countries were able to escape the cruel effects of the recession . . ." *1976 Book of the Year*, op. cit., pp. 275, 288. To make matters worse for Chile, copper prices fell between May 1974 and early 1975 from 1,400 pounds sterling per ton to five hundred a ton on the London Metals Exchange (ibid., p. 293). Debt statistics from *Indicadores Económicos y Sociales, 1960–1985* (Santiago: Banco Central de Chile, 1986), p. 313. During the same period, private lending to Chile did increase significantly, but given the still overpoweringly dominant role of the state in the economy, it was small palliative, indeed. Fleet (op. cit., p. 193) quotes from a secret plenary session of the PDC in April 1980, at which "they acknowledged that things were, in fact, at an all-time low." Fleet, taking no note of external economic pressures, recites (p. 184) several indicators of the crisis, asserting that "many families were reduced to begging for a living and forced to live on survival diets of low-grade wheat bread and other grains. Soup kitchens and food distribution programs sponsored by the Catholic Church and other institutions kept many alive who would not otherwise have survived."

37. The then president of the party, Gabriel Valdés Subercaseaux, in an interview with the author in Santiago, January 30, 1987, said the party had lost "between 80 and 85 buildings ... newspapers, radio stations, theaters, furniture, equipment ... all without compensation." He put the value of the expropriated property at between $8 million and $9 million. Fleet, op. cit., p. 184, says the hard times of 1975–1976 opened a window of political opportunity because of increased political activism, agitation and maneuvering, but that Frei failed to exploit it properly.

38. A report published in a Madrid newspaper in January 1976 said Frei was then awaiting surgery for cancer at a clinic near Bonn (and, to make matters worse, that party president Patricio Aylwin had suffered a brain tumor). If true, Frei lived on for seven more years—and Aylwin not only lived on, but in 1987, once again was elected president of the party. The report was published in the Madrid newspaper El Alcázar, January 8, 1976, "La Democracia Cristiana Chilena, Sin Dirigentes." Latin American newspapers rarely reveal cause of death for notable figures (I have never seen natural causes so discussed in print in the region), so there is no way of knowing whether those events actually happened. As to the prospect of elections, Fleet, op. cit., p. 176, refers to an article by Christopher Roper in the Washington Post, September 15, 1973, in which "Frei is said to have written to his son of military assurances of new elections within six months of the coup."

39. The letter is quoted in César Hidalgo Calvo, Teoría y Práctica de la Propaganda Contemporánea (Santiago: Editorial Andres Bello, 1986), pp. 350–352. The British scholar P.A. Allum noted that "in reaction to the overthrow of the Marxist Salvador Allende in Chile, the Communist party secretary, Enrico Berlinguer, spelled out his proposal for a 'historical compromise' between Communists and Catholics." Allum, "Italy's Political Crisis: Transition or Disruption?" special report in 1976 Book of the Year, op. cit., p. 444.

40. Fleet, op. cit., p. 183, and American-Chilean Council Report (a publication of American-Chilean Council, New York City) February 26, 1976, pp. 1–2.

41. Ibid., pp. 193, 194; Fleet quotes Ercilla, no. 13, of 1980, for both the Zaldívar quote and the Frei anecdote.

42. Robert Moss, "The Tribulation of Chile," National Review, October 10, 1975, p. 1110. Jorge Olave ("La oposición al pinochetismo," in the special tenth anniversary edition of Hoy, "La Década de Hoy," May 1987, p. 19) says a June 1985 survey of the National Board of the PDC revealed that 36.7 percent had been detained, tortured, and sent into external or internal exile.

43. Frei traveled to Brazil to inaugurate an international symposium in the southern city of Canelas on the report of the so-called Brandt Commission on North-South worldwide problems—named for Willy Brandt, the former Socialist premier of West Germany. According to the pro-PDC Santiago magazine Hoy (week of August 20–26, 1980, "Cara y sello de un viaje"), leading Brazilian newspapers such as Jornal do Brasil, Folha da Tarde, and O Globo hailed Frei as "the most genuine representative of democracy in Latin America." Frei said the Brazilian media treated the plebiscite as "a joke in bad taste. They laughed ... they howled [se reían a carcajadas] and I felt myself blushing, to think that such a thing could happen in my country." As he made his way around Brazil, Frei gave numerous inter-

views. In one, in Sao Paulo, he said that whatever the outcome of the plebiscite, "the military regime will not manage to remain in power for eight more years" ("Opiniones de E. Frei Sobre El Plebiscito," AFP dispatch datelined Sao Paulo in *El Mercurio*, August 13, 1980); in another, he said the plebiscite "is not a formula for transition for democracy but a prolongation of the regime," and that if the military insisted on remaining in power, "it will produce a radicalization of the country" ("Eduardo Frei no Cree en el Plebiscito," AP story from Sao Paulo in *Ultimas Noticias*, August 14, 1980); in yet another, he accused Pinochet of maintaining himself in power "by force of arms and with the support of the Right," adding, "I do not recognize the new plebiscite as valid." In that interview, he also had words of praise for the Communist party, saying that "it is working splendidly well in Chile" (from an interview with the Brazilian magazine *Veja*, as reported in an AP dispatch datelined Rio de Janeiro, published August 18, 1980, in *La Tercera*, "Dicen en Brasil: Frei critica al Plebiscito y elogia al PC"). In an interview weeks later, Andrés Zaldívar Larraín, then president of the PDC, was asked whether the plebiscite had come down to a contest between Pinochet and Frei. While answering that he believed it was more than a clash of personalities, a battle between two political alternatives, Zaldívar added: "Clearly, after the plebiscite this confrontation will continue because our formula [the PDC proposal] has produced a convergence of grand social forces. In that sense, it is indisputable that Frei will be the standard-bearer [*mantendrá la bandera*] of the opposition alternative" (editorial in *Ultimas Noticias*, September 11, 1980, "El Sí Apoya a Pinochet; El No Respalda a Frei?").

44. "Renán Fuentealba," AP dispatch datelined Caracas, in *El Mercurio*, August 13, 1980; "Tomic Apoya a Frei," AFP dispatch datelined Geneva in *La Tercera*, August 29, 1980.

45. The Christian Democrat scholar and ideologue Carlos Huneeus, for example, speaks of "the excessive presence of the parties in Chilean public life" as a *consequence* of the country's political problems, not a *cause* (emphasis his). In what appears to this author as a strained syllogism, he writes that the weakness of political institutions was the cause that permitted the parties to expand their power, and that those "political weaknesses" had their roots, in turn, in the "abrupt and intense politicization of the society during the sixties as a result of the late extension of political citizenship—especially the right to vote—to wide areas of the citizenry." He notes that between 1912 and 1957, the ratio of registered voters to total population remained constant, whereas between 1958 and 1964, it doubled, taking another leap forward in 1970. The benchmarks were women's suffrage, beginning with the parliamentary elections of 1949, then with the presidential election of 1952; the active political recruiting of previously excluded rural and industrial workers; and, finally, giving the vote to illiterates and lowering the voting age from twenty-one to eighteen in 1970. Carlos Huneeus, *Los Chilenos y La Política: Cambio y Continuidad en el Autoritarismo* (Santiago: Salesianos Printers, 1987), pp. 182–184 (hereafter *Los Chilenos y La Política*). The book was made possible through a grant from West Germany's Konrad Adenauer Foundation, the statistical studies underpinning it through a Ford Foundation grant, and was executed by the Center of Studies of Contemporary Reality (CERC) of the Academy of Christian Humanism in Santiago.

46. As early as his first anniversary speech, Pinochet had said that "except for the isolated efforts of a few enlightened public figures, Chile had been governed since 1891 by class and party governments, characterized by 'politicking and demagoguery' " (cited in Paul E. Sigmund, *The Overthrow of Allende and the Politics of Chile, 1964–1976* [Pittsburgh: University of Pittsburgh Press, 1977], p. 273). In a key speech made on April 6, 1979, inaugurating the academic year at the University of Chile, he said, "the country has been the slave and victim of its Congress until 1925. Now it was the slave and victim of the political parties . . . Universal suffrage does not, in and of itself, have the quality of being the only valid means of expression of the will of the Nation . . . Indeed, our country directly proved that neither formal democracy nor popular suffrage, understood as operating formulas by themselves, are sufficient to effectively address contemporary conditions . . ." There were, he argued, two intrinsic enemies of an effective and real democracy in Chile: the demagoguery created by the emergence of unbridled political parties, and communism, the cancer within (*Report on the Situation of Human Rights in Chile, 1985*, op. cit., pp. 259–261); on his vision of a "protected democracy," he told foreign correspondents in May of 1977: "Democracy must, then, exercise all the necessary and just authority so as to preserve the values on which it rests, and to foresee and overcome successfully those emergency situations which could affect national security. Only in a regime of authority, just and impersonal, which assures order and tranquility, can a people achieve its development and well-being"; on his conception of freedom, "For us, freedom is a value which goes well beyond the mere exercise of a political right. We regard as essential, as well, economic and educational freedoms, the right to work, of unionization, social security and health, inasmuch as these are vital expressions from moment to moment in the daily lives of people . . ." (A. Pineda de Castro, *Pinochet: Verdad y Ficción* [Madrid: Vassallo de Mumbert, 1981], pp. 201, 204).

47. The author has in his file more than one hundred such clippings, from a wide variety of publications, including several (such as *Hoy*) decidedly tilted to the Christian Democrats. A perusal of them will disclose words such as "dictator," "dictatorship," "fascist," "illegal," "invalid," and many more scarcely characteristic of a state of censorship.

48. Zaldívar's quote from "Declaración de Zaldívar Sobre La Constitución," in *El Mercurio*, July 12; Krauss in a lengthy opinion article bearing only his name in *La Tercera*, July 13; the paid ad, "Grupo de Ciudadanos Se Dirige A La Junta De Gobierno," in *La Tercera*, August 24, 1980. Among the 118 signers were Felipe Herrera Lane, a Socialist and former president of the Inter-American Development Bank; Raúl Sáez, a Christian Democrat who, in 1963, headed the Alliance for Progress; the Radical leader Luis Bossay L.; and León Vilarín, the feisty head of the truck drivers' federation so pivotal in the fight against Allende. The signers called on the government to delay the plebiscite until adequate election machinery was in place, full access to the media and right of assembly restored, and viable alternatives put to a vote. Significantly, they addressed the message to Pinochet as "Chief of State," and then the members of the junta—which reinforced the suspicion that the authors were attempting to split off sympathetic members of the junta (if there were any) from the man they clearly targeted as the villain.

49. In its first formal statement, dated August 14, Zaldívar and the four other top party leaders said, "in these conditions, the so-called [*supuesto*] plebiscite is completely lacking in validity and, in consequence, the text to be voted on, as well as all future actions executed in the exercise of powers emanating from that text, are likewise illegitimate and without value" ("A La Opinión Pública," in *La Tercera*, August 17, 1980). (The other signers were Jaime Castillo, Raúl Troncoso, Tomás Reyes and Carmen Frei—the former president's daughter and only one of his seven children to take an active role in politics until that time). The government newspaper *La Nación* mischievously headlined Zaldívar's press conference announcing that statement: "Zaldívar: Buscamos unidad con los sectores marxistas," August 15; *Ultimas Noticias* headlined it the same day: "Plebiscito: Ex DC Fijan Posición." Reference to an alliance of any kind was not in the two-page statement, but rather in response to a reporter's question. What he said on the subject was: "We seek a national understanding [*encuentro*] with all sectors of opinion, including with the Marxists if they so desire." That remark played into the hands of the very many Chileans who wanted nothing to do with another era of Marxist-Leninist path to anywhere. On August 30, Santiago newspapers printed a lengthy statement from Zaldívar in which he said, ". . . we are not today, we are not tomorrow, in favor of political alliances with the Communist party, but with the same clarity, we believe that ideas are not prohibited by law . . ." Zaldívar was quoted on "worst fraud" in *La Segunda*, September 9, "Denuncias hizo Andrés Zaldívar." Among the events he protested was the refusal to allow Frei to address mass meetings in Concepción and Valparaíso, while—by contrast—seven trains were reserved to take proponents of the plebiscite to a Pinochet rally in Valparaíso. While still undecided as whether to participate or boycott the plebiscite, Zaldívar called for "mass mobilization" to express "in the manner each can" a rejection of the plebiscite as "illegitimate" ("Llamado a Movilización Contra el Plebiscito," *El Mercurio*, August 15, 1980). Optimism was reflected, for example, in the prediction just ten days before the voting of a group of former National party congressmen that "the majority of the country was inclined to vote no"; former Senator María de la Cruz predicted that 80 percent of all women would vote "No" (they actually voted "Yes" by a margin of nearly three to one) ("Movimiento de colosos," *Hoy*, week of August 27–September 2, 1980).

50. *El Mercurio* editorial quoted in "Las dudas del plebiscito," *Hoy*, week of August 20–26, 1980, p. 13; PDC youth, "JDC no vota ni Sí ni No," *La Segunda*, August 20. Interestingly, Frei had his last preplebiscite meeting with a youth group made up mainly of students; noting that most were no more than seven years old during his government, twelve during Allende's, he urged them to reorganize the PDC, to be men and women of ideals of peace and service to the country ("Reunión de Frei Con Grupo Juvenil," *El Mercurio*, September 10). The largest labor group—first called the Group of 10, at that time the National Labor Coordinator—called for a "No" vote in a communique that made plain its contempt for the government's free market economic policies ("a socio-economic model based on minority interests and linked exclusively to powerful economic groups"); in another: "We have no doubt that the constitution which would enter into force in 1989 will bring prosperity, security, progress and justice to the

rich ..." The organization, headed by Manuel Bustos, cited Pinochet's 1977 remark about a plebiscite requiring voter lists, to mock the 1980 plebiscite as "a mere consultation." A smaller and even more left-wing organization, the United Workers Front (FUT), fulminated against the plebiscite as "invalid and immoral," but like so many others, took no position on whether to vote or to abstain. Not surprisingly, the National Organization of Public Employees (ANEF)—hard hit by the junta's systematic paring down of the bureaucracy—urged a "No" vote ("La Coordinadora Nacional Sindical A Los Trabajadores Y A La Opinión Pública," paid ad in *La Tercera,* August 22; "Declaración del 'Grupo de los Diez,' *El Mercurio,* August 20; "Grupo de los 10 Responde a la 'Nueva Democracia,' " *La Tercera,* August 22; "Ni Sí Ni No," *Ultimas Noticias,* August 22; "La ANEF fundamenta rechazo," *La Tercera,* September 6).

51. "Luces para el debate, Plebiscito III," *Hoy,* September 10–16; "El 'Sí' de los ex DC y el 'No' de Vilarin," *Ultimas Noticias,* September 2; "Hay Clima Electoral Pero Falta Ambiente," *La Segunda,* September 9, 1980.

52. "Las cartas sobre la mesa," report of an article published in issue #163 of *Hoy,* as it appeared in *Ultimas Noticias,* September 7 (Spanish support and meeting of ambassadors); *Hoy,* September 10–16, "Reunión con diplomáticos" (denial that they had taken a stand); *Hoy,* "Movimiento de colosos," August 27–September 2, pp. 12–13 (*New York Times,* Ecuador and labor attachés); "Comunismo reconoce acuerdo con la DC," *La Nación,* September 3 (Cademartori); "Viuda de Allende dice que 'hay que utilizar a E. Frei,' " *La Segunda,* September 18 (Hortensia Allende in Mexico interview).

53. "Las dudas del plebiscito," *Hoy,* August 20–26, p. 13; " 'Queremos un consenso mayoritario que respete la minoría,' *Hoy,* September 3–9, pp. 26–27. Cardinal Silva was in Europe when the Episcopal Conference met; on his return, he expressed the fear that "a stable institutional order cannot be founded on this plebiscite" ("Por que SI, por que NO," *Hoy,* September 10–16, p. 9).

54. Rally scenes from "Desarollo del Acto en Teatro Caupolicán," *El Mercurio,* August 28, 1980; "Frei: Es alternativa?" *Qué Pasa,* September 4–10, 1980, p. 7; "Fuerte Presencia Marxista En Acto De Ayer En El Caupolicán," *La Segunda,* August 28, 1980; data on radio coverage from "Cuestión de Medios," *Hoy,* September 2–9, 1980, p. 12.

55. Frei's remarks from a text published in APSI, #84, September 21–November 3, 1980, "Discurso del ex Presidente de la República Eduardo Frei, el miércoles 27 de agosto en el Teatro Caupolicán," pp. 57–59; departure from hall from *Qué Pasa,* September 4–10, op. cit., p. 7; shouts and Frei's reaction, "Rechiflas y aplausos en reunión del Caupolicán," *La Tercera,* August 28, 1980. Those attending heeded Frei's appeal; there were only a few incidents following the rally, with seven civilians and five Carabineros treated for minor injuries and no arrests. By 11 P.M., Prefect Juan Alegría reported all calm downtown (*El Mercurio,* op. cit., p. C-4).

56. "Las cartas sobre la mesa," *Ultimas Noticias,* op. cit. (for Dinacos reply); *Hoy,* op. cit., August 27–September 2, p. 12, and September 3–9, p. 10 (for Pinochet). Pinochet referred to the practice of selecting candidates and staking out policy strategies in small and secretive party caucuses.

57. "La Estrategia de Caupolicán," *Ercilla,* September 3, 1980, p. 9 (for Rodríguez and *Nueva Democracia*); *Hoy,* September 3–9, p. 10 (for Group

of 24); *El Mercurio,* September 9 (for ad, eight columns by four and-a-half inches deep). The Group of 24, tilted Left though including some dissident figures from the Right, had been operating for several years as an alternative to the junta-appointed constitutional drafting groups.

58. "Edgardo Boeninger Reiteró Su Posición," *El Mercurio,* August 22; "Reveladoras declaraciones de Aylwin en Escuela de Derecho," *La Tercera,* August 26, 1980; "Democracia Cristiana descalifica a ex militantes que votarán 'sí,'" *La Tercera,* September 11. Even before the September 11 statement, Genaro Arriagada, PDC secretary-general, issued a statement that "in every party, there are desertions. But in ours, you could count them on the fingers of one hand ... more numerous are those Chileans who, having occupied posts in the government, have gone over to the ranks of the opposition" ("Existe el Derecho a Cambiar de Opinión," *Ultimas Noticias,* August 30, 1980). Among the "defectors" was former PDC deputy Blanca Retamal, who reacted to Frei's Caupolicán appearance by saying it puzzled her "that he wants to convert himself into the leader of the Left" ("El 'Sí' de los ex DC y el 'No' de Vilarín," op. cit.). Most of the fire was, however, directed at former Senator (and cabinet minister under Frei) Juan de Dios Carmona, then serving as ambassador to Spain. When Carmona said on television that those opposing the plebiscite were not true democrats, Aylwin responded with a public challenge to a debate on prime-time television, adding "that with your influence as a man of confidence of the government, I believe it will enable you to get the time we need" ("Aylwin acepta desafío de Juan de Dios Carmona," *La Tercera,* September 4, 1980).

59. Carrasco Delgado, op. cit., p. 143. Alessandri's taciturnity did not prevent his former campaign manager, Eduardo Boetsch G.H., from saying the former president would vote "Yes," and furthermore that for the same patriotic reasons, "he has asked his friends to work with enthusiasm and patriotism for the approval of the plebiscite" (ibid., pp. 143–144).

60. Frei voting from *Ultimas Noticias,* September 12, " 'Triste Cosa, No?' " and *El Mercurio,* September 12, "Frei Concurrió A Las Urnas"; stock market from "Cuando las aguas se calman," *Hoy,* September 17–23, 1980, p. 12.

61. Allan C. Brownfeld, "Constitution Was A Spectacular Success of Founding Fathers," *Human Events,* July 18, 1987, p. 12 (Cannon quote); Ray S. Cline, "The Ballad of Cory and Johnny," *Conservative Digest,* February 1987, pp. 107 (Carter) and pp. 108–109 (constitution). In legislative elections following the February 2, 1987, constitutional plebiscite—which Aquino won by a more than three-to-one margin—her hand-picked slate won twenty-two of twenty-four Senate seats, 162 of two hundred House seats at stake. Dr. Cline, a professor of International Relations at Georgetown University, and cofounder of Georgetown's Center for Strategic International Studies, is a former deputy director of the CIA. Data on U.S. aid from Richard D. Fisher, Jr., "A Strategy For Keeping The U.S. Bases In The Philippines," a *Heritage Foundation* Asian Studies Center Backgrounder, #8, May 20, 1988, p. 2. The new constitution also suggested a nuclear-free zone for the Philippines, site of the last remaining military bases in a vast ocean area of increasing Soviet presence and encroachment. Since Mrs. Aquino came to power in 1986, Communist insurgents have seized control of an estimated 20 percent of the nation's territory. Data on Liberia from Blaine Harden,

"Liberia, in Grip of Graft, Puts Americans at Treasury's Helm," a Monrovia-datelined dispatch in the *Washington Post*, May 29, 1988, p. A-20, and the 1981, 1986, and 1988 *Book of the Year*, op. cit., pp 490–491, 462–463, 642 (per capita income), respectively. The American technocrats are from the U.S. Agency for International Development.

62. "Declaración de dirigente del ex PDC," *La Tercera*, September 17 (Zaldívar on grass roots organizations); "Los Perdedores Quedaron Contentos," *Ultimas Noticias*, September 12 (labor leaders); "Entre el Silencio y Algunas Denuncias," *Ultimas Noticias*, September 12 (Krauss and Arriagada); "Movidas fuera de tablero," *Ercilla*, #2356, September 24, 1980, p. 8 (Corvalán and Zaldívar in *Visión*); "Amenaza de guerra civil, la última infamia de Zaldívar," *La Nación*, October 17, 1980, the complete text of an AP dispatch datelined Mexico City reporting on the *Uno Más Uno* interview. According to the Inter-American Commission on Human Rights, in their *1985 Report On The Situation of Human Rights in Chile*, op. cit., p. 137, the newspaper later denied that Zaldívar had said that. If he did not say it in 1980, he said it plainly in 1987, in an interview in Santiago with the author, June 29, 1987. Speaking of the forthcoming plebiscite in late 1988 or early 1989, he said: "If Pinochet should go so far as to stay on beyond '89, I am one person who is convinced, absolutely convinced—and not just me but many leaders in this country, and for that matter, many close to the government are also convinced—that the reelection of Pinochet beyond '89 will necessarily plunge [*conlleva*] the country into confrontation. Not the confrontation of guerrilla warfare, but yes of terrorism . . ." It would be three years before Zaldívar would be allowed to return to Chile following his October 1980 exile. In that same Mexico City interview, Zaldívar said the civilian-military government proposed for Chile would be different from the one installed a few months earlier in El Salvador. The Christian Democrats in El Salvador joined in a government that came to power in a military coup induced—if not actually engineered—by the United States. His convoluted answer essentially defended the Salvadorans on the grounds that the situation there had reached its breaking point.

63. "La Historia Le Pena A Frei," *La Segunda*, August 25. Frei had made his first request for TV network time on August 22. The newspaper quoted extensively from a speech Frei had made in the town of Castro, February 12, 1967, in which he recalled numerous examples of congressional obstructionism of presidents, with ruinous results for the country. He said he headed a government "with a coherent program," but needed the legal instruments to enable it to do the coordinated planning modern times demanded; Congress, he said, refused stubbornly to give him that leeway (although his party had controlled both houses of Congress throughout his presidency): "It is necessary to bring about the institutional reforms so as not to frustrate the country, because it is not possible that the people exert themselves [*se movilice*] to elect a government which afterwards finds its hands tied by a minority which makes its action impossible." The speech stirred up a hornet's nest in Congress, and the Senate, on February 15, voted to request radio network time. *La Segunda*, beginning with its huge page one headlines, was, of course, drawing a direct parallel between what Frei did in a time of full democracy in Chile and the behavior of the Pinochet authoritarian government thirteen years later. As to news clips,

for example channel 13 of the Catholic University, they did devote five minutes to the Caupolicán Theater event, but Frei's speech was limited to two passages—and the station broadcast a follow-up "analysis" by the conservative leader Jaime Guzmán. The University of Chile channel gave twenty seconds to Frei's speech and, according to the pro-PDC *Hoy*, seventeen minutes' rebuttal time to hard-liner Pablo Rodríguez. The state-run channel devoted a total of thirty seconds to the event, none of it on Frei's speech ("Cuestión de medios," *Hoy*, September 3–9, 1980, pp. 11–12).

64. "Se informa sobre el 'No'?" *La Segunda*, September 8, 1980.

65. The fraud findings were reported by Eduardo Hamuy—a Christian Democrat sociologist, working with six hundred volunteers and screening 981 polling places in the metropolitan Santiago region. Those findings are reported in "Origen, Contenido y Práctica de la Constitución Política de 1980; Su significado desde la perspectiva de los Derechos Humanos," a publication of the Chilean Commission on Human Rights, Santiago (no date), p. 9; "Definitivo: mayoría del Gobierno fue de 67.04%," *La Nación*, October 16, 1980. The system used was: first count done by the officials at each polling place; then at the town or city (*comuna*) level by the mayor and his aides (mayors were, of course, appointed by Pinochet); next, at the regional level, a commission made up of the regional administrator, the senior-ranking member of the Court of Appeals for that region, and the official charged with oversight for real estate property in the region (*Conservador de Bienes Raíces*). At the national level, the board was made up of the comptroller-general, a Supreme Court justice, and the secretary of the Supreme Court.

66. "Cuando las aguas se calman," *Hoy*, September 17–23, 1980, p. 13. The magazine was using the preliminary figures reported September 13.

67. Fleet, op. cit., pp. 195–196. Fleet ascribed the "sharp terms" used by "normally circumspect" Andrés Zaldívar in reacting to the plebiscite as an indicator of that mood of discouragement and despair. Fleet cites as the source for the internal analysis Jean Pierre Clerc, "Chile: A Second Wind for the Dictatorship," *Manchester Guardian-Le Monde Weekly*, March 29, 1981, p. 12.

68. In a study of public spending in Latin America, Guy Pfeffermann notes: ". . . education expenditure is heavily slanted in favor of middle classes. Considerable efforts were made on secondary and university education while the quality of primary education often remains appalling, especially in the rural areas. Except in Chile, no attempt has been made at collecting user charges, so that even the children of relatively well-off families have access to university without payment. At the same time university entry has been broadened enormously and the number of students has exploded when the poor seldom enter, let alone complete, secondary school . . . One of the most progressive policy changes is the elimination of free university education. Ten primary school pupils can be trained for the cost of one university student. In some countries (Brazil and Colombia, for example), the ratio is thirty-to-one. Yet only a minority of university students come from poor families and they can be protected by a system of scholarships or student loans . . ." Guy P. Pfeffermann, "Public Expenditure in Latin America: Effects on Poverty," *World Bank Discussion Papers*, #5, 1987, pp. 15, 19. Pfeffermann is the chief economist of the Latin America and the Caribbean Regional Office of the World Bank.

69. "El Camino de Pinochet," special anniversary edition of *Hoy*, op. cit., p. 9 (slogan, first measures); *1982 Book of the Year*, op. cit., p. 239 (education, labor, and social security reforms, and UNESCO protest); IACHR comments, *1985 Report on the Situation of Human Rights in Chile*, op. cit., p. 231.

70. That there is no constitutional provision making the president accountable for his acts during the transition was affirmed by a Santiago Appeals Court judge on May 25, 1984, in ruling on a criminal case instituted by private individuals against the president. That ruling was subsequently confirmed by the full Appeal Court and by the Supreme Court, cf., *1985 Report on the Situation of Human Rights in Chile*, op. cit., pp. 19–20.

71. During a 1984 seminar on constitutional/political options, for example, Aylwin said: "Like it or not, that Constitution is in force [*rigiendo*]. That is a fact which forms part of reality, and I accept it [*lo acato*]" (*Una Salida Político-Constitucional Para Chile* [Santiago: Instituto Chileno de Estudios Humanísticos, 1985] p. 149). The "revealed truth" remark was made at that same seminar by Sergio Diez Urzúa, a member of the original constitutional drafting committee, and appears on p. 69. The book contains the proceedings of a symposium held in Santiago July 27–28, 1984, bringing together nine men representing all shades of ideological opinion save for those of the Communists. Aylwin was reelected PDC president for the sixth time in July 1987.

72. Comparisons from Carrasco Delgado, op. cit., pp. 147–202; Bulnes quote from *Una Salida Político-Constitucional Para Chile*, op. cit., p. 132.

73. Raquel Correa, "Un Consejo Que 'Aconseja,' " excerpted from the text of a longer interview with Carvajal, "Las Fuerzas Armadas y . . . La Política," *El Mercurio*, May 22, 1988, as reproduced in the newspaper weekly international edition for May 19–25, 1988, p. 6.

74. Speech excerpts and "baiting" from Carrasco Delgado, op. cit., pp. 225–227, and 144–145. On November 30, 1983, Alessandri responded in *La Segunda* to a pair of attacks on him by Jorge Ovalle Quiroz.

75. The "dissident" quote from a booklet published by *Hoy:* "Frei: La Vida de un Demócrata," inserted in its edition #548, January 18–24, 1988, p. 1; the Zaldívar quote from a booklet he authored, *Eduardo Frei: Pensamientos* (Santiago: Ciceros, 1987), p. 1. Zaldívar was one of several PDC exiles who flew to Santiago for the funeral, only to be barred entry at the airport. Others included former President Renán Fuentealba, Jaime Castillo and Belisario Velasco. Among foreign dignitaries who came: former Italian Premier Mariano Rumor and former Venezuelan President Rafael Caldera. Jorge Alessandri had asked no special honors; the government nonetheless decreed three days of mourning, and as in the case of former President Frei, tens of thousands of Chileans paid their last respects.

76. Fleet, op. cit., p. 198.

77. Valdés, in an interview with *El Mercurio*, cited by Fleet, op. cit., p. 201, was quoted as saying he "respected the memory of Salvador Allende, but believed that the policies of the Popular Unity government had been 'profoundly mistaken.' He added that the Communist party should be legal because 'every idea has a right to exist,' insisting that parties should be judged by their actions and not their ideas alone." Fleet refers to Valdés as a "compromise candidate," and the pro-PDC magazine *Hoy* refers to the "strong debate over ideological renovation, policy of coalitions and leader-

ship characteristics" being "resolved by consensus, facilitated by the dramatic flop [desborde] of the economic model applied by the Chicago Boys." Special edition, May 1987, op. cit., p. 18. Reference to the CPP is in *Carta Confidencial*, César Hidalgo Calvo, ed., #9, August 27, 1987, p. 38.

78. Jorge Olave, "La oposición al pinochetismo," *Hoy*, op. cit., pp. 18–19. So tiny was the Republican Right party, as it came to be known, that in a March 1986 survey of potential voters in Greater Santiago, it was not even mentioned when those surveyed were asked to name the parties then existing, and then, in response to a specific question—which party or political bloc do you think is "most attractive"—it ranked dead last, with 1.4 percent. "Encuesta de Opinión Pública: Partidos Políticos. Qué Saben Los Chilenos?" *Qué Pasa*, #780, March 20–26, 1988, pp. 17–20. It is one measure of the level of dogmatism—if not fanaticism—in the upper reaches of the PDC that those who attempted to defect from the ranks of government supporters were spurned by the party, while being castigated by the government as "traitors." Olave speaks euphemistically of their not being accepted by "the opposition," but there was, of course, no "opposition" available for defectors to join other than the PDC. Obviously, the hard-line Marxist-Leninist parties would be no more interested in them than they would be in Marxist-Leninists. Olave himself offers another measure of the same phenomenon when he writes that "unlike other authoritarianisms, the Chilean knows no case of relevant figures of the opposition joining with the regime." That judgment supposes that those very significant Christian Democrats—such as Carmona, Cauas and others—ceased to exist as *"figuras relevantes"* once their consciences led them to "join the regime"; or, that one did not qualify as "opposition" unless one was on or to the left of the PDC itself. Among others who "joined the regime" were former National party President Sergio Onofre Jarpa and many others of the Right who, while generally supporting the government, nevertheless managed to retain their own political personalities.

79. Fleet, op. cit., p. 202. He says that the "largest" of the monthly demonstrations took place in August, when seventeen persons were killed in clashes with troops deployed to keep order.

80. *1984 Book of the Year*, op. cit., p. 232, and *Hoy*, op. cit., p. 19. Ms. Blackburn was identified as an economist in the Group Economics Department of Lloyds Bank of London.

81. Data on these groups from *Análisis*, June 15–21, 1987, pp. 35–36. The *Alianza* was made up initially of the PDC, the Radical, Socialist, Social Democratic, and Republican parties. On September 6, 1983, the formation of yet another group was announced: the Socialist Bloc (Bloque Socialista), composed of the Socialist party, the MAPU, the Christian Left, the MAPU-Worker/Peasant party, the Socialist Convergence Group, and the University Convergence. It was an attempt, launched in 1979, to reunite the badly splintered Socialist party, by then split into six identifiable factions, by 1987 so fragmented that *Carta Confidencial* referred to them as the "13 island archipelago." *Carta Confidencial*, #9, August 27, 1987, pp. 15–20. Radio Moscow quote from Juray Domic, "Política Militar del PC (XXXIV)." *La Nación*, January 31, 1987, p. 4.

82. Data on protests and Pinochet's response from *Hoy*, special edition, op. cit., p. 11, and *1984 Book of the Year*, op. cit., p. 232. According to Vicariate of Solidarity figures, the number of those arrested in 1983 and 1984 jumped

up sharply to the highest totals since the immediate aftermath of the revolution: 4,537 in 1983 (3,802 of them in mass round-ups, virtually all quickly released), and 5,343 in 1984 (divided equally between individual and collective arrests, reflecting stepped-up terrorist and other antigovernment violence).

83. Olave, op. cit., p. 19, for the atomization reference and Huneeus. To illustrate, the Socialist party (PS), for example, spawned these mutants: PS-Briones, PS Mandujano, which later became the PS-Histórico, PS-Luengo, PS-Almeyda PS-Núñez, not to mention the Movimiento de Acción Socialista (MAS), the Unión Socialista Popular (USOPO), and the Grupo Convergencia Socialista. The MAPU, insignificantly small to begin with, was followed by the splinter group MAPU-Obrero Campesino. The Radicals were similarly fragmented.

84. Hoy, special edition, op. cit., p. 13. Carmona, together with William Thayer who had also served in Frei's Cabinet, had formed a party called the Movimiento Socialcristiano para Chile (PSD). The party attracted a number of disaffected moderates from the Christian Democratic party. Just how far apart they had grown from their former fellow partisans was shown when they spurned the Democratic Alliance for being under the leadership of "well-known Marxist-Leninists." According to Hoy, Jarpa's deal foundered when it was learned that two of the more populist elements in the coalition—Jarpa's own Unión Nacional and the Movimiento de Acción Nacional (MAN)—had cooked up a plan binding all coalition partners to speak in a single voice.

85. 1985 Book of the Year, op. cit., pp. 583–584. The accusations did not involve Pinochet directly, but two of his children, and the amounts involved were relatively puny. As indicated earlier, even Pinochet's most impassioned enemies grudgingly concede that the administration has been singularly free of corruption.

86. Cited by Fleet, op. cit., p. 207, FN #43; he refers to Latin American Weekly Report, 1984, 12.

87. "Crónica de una oposición desencontrada," Análisis, June 15–21, 1981, p. 36; Valdés' letter from Democracia Cristiana y Partido Comunista (Santiago: Editorial Aconcagua, 1986), pp. 203–213. The book is a compilation of articles, speeches, letters and analyses, including those of Eduardo Frei, Radomiro Tomic, Jaime Castillo, Genaro Arriagada, and Valdés. The January Communist party plenum quote is from Ricardo Núñez, writing as secretary-general of the Socialist party. Núñez, Carta Abierta A Los Dirigentes Y Militantes De La Izquierda Chilena, mimeograph copy of an advertisement published December 29, 1986, pp. 3–4. In it, Núñez explained why his party rejected an alliance both with the Communists and the MDP, which included the Communists. Those who advocate or practice violence, he argued, "are not uniting the Left, and much less the people . . ." but by their divisive tactics "would only prolong the popular defeat of 1973." In his letter, Valdés—in impassioned terms—argued that the Communists were playing into "the dictatorship's" hands in two ways: ordinary citizens do not know how to use gelatin bombs and the like— these are the tools of terrorists trained in international terrorism schools, "be they of the right or left, who, at times, interchange their own terrorist agents"; on the other side, there was the superior power of the armed forces. Further, Valdés argued, such warfare would enable Pinochet to

persuade the military that the end of his regime would spell its own annihilation, as also the regime's allies "of the economic and financial Right, in the United States and Europe," that they needed to support him to the end because the choice was "between the present dictatorship and a future dictatorship of pro-Soviet character" (op. cit., p. 206).

88. It was not, however, the last time Pinochet would reshuffle the corps of generals in reasserting his authority. Following the attempt on his life in September 1986, he once again moved eight generals into retirement, replacing General Canessa on the junta with Gen. Humberto Gordon.

89. *Hoy*, special edition, op. cit., pp. 13–14; *1986 Book of the Year*, p. 574. Benavides' rebelliousness was far less threatening, too, because—unlike Leigh—he was not a coequal by any stretch of the imagination, but a clear subordinate of Pinochet. As president, Pinochet was commander-in-chief of all of the armed forces, but in addition, he had never surrendered his role as commander-in-chief of the army, and the 1980 constitution clearly empowered him to remove the army representative on the junta at will.

90. *Carta Confidencial*, op. cit., #12, October 15, 1987, pp. 41–46, quotes at length from an interview in the West Berlin newspaper, published August 14, 1987. The account was based on the revelations of a Capt. Dieter Zirkel, who had escaped to the West after ten years in prison. According to Zirkel's account, groups of twenty Chileans had been sent by the Communist party to each of the one-year training sessions over a period of several years. Their training included weapons training from small arms to light artillery, as well as firing antiaircraft and antitank rockets; radio communications; camouflage; physical and psychological toughening up; and, of course, political indoctrination. Once their training had been completed, according to Zirkel, they were expected to return to Chile to train others so as to build a broad base of revolutionaries ready to strike when conditions were ripe for civil war. The terrorism casualty count was given by Attorney General Ambrosio Rodríguez in announcing plans for a "National Reparations Fund" to compensate victims of terrorism, and reported in *Chilean Review*, vol. 1, #4, May 1987, p. 4.

91. Carla Hall, "Carmen Quintana's Personal Holocaust," the *Washington Post*, March 26, 1988, p. C-1. She was interviewed during a number of public appearances in Washington, escorted by a translator from the ultra-leftist *America's Watch* organization. Since the burning incident, she had spoken in Canada, Geneva, Sweden, Holland, East Germany, West Germany, and Belgium, and was then about to travel to Australia. She also had been back to Chile twice, once testifying seven hours before the civilian court hearing the case.

92. "Asamblea a la vista," *Hoy*, #517, June 15–21, 1987, p. 10.

93. The party's 1984 proposals—spelled out in a paid ad published October 11, 1984, in *Las Ultimas Noticias* (p. 14)—revealed just how far it had moved from its strong projunta stance (and why it had, in the process, become a hollow shell of its former self, the conservative terrain it had abandoned seized by new rightist parties). Among other things, it called for laws governing elections, political parties and the like no later than the first quarter of 1985, elections for Congress during the first half of 1985, and constitutional changes to restore to Congress the powers it had under the 1925 constitution, while scaling down presidential powers to the same baseline. The proposals also called for "modifying" constitutional Article

8 (which outlawed Communist and other "totalitarian" parties); replacement of the junta by the Congress; and direct election of the president at the conclusion of the transition period. As to "hollow," the National party was the first to register under the 1987 Political Parties Law. Yet, as of June 1, 1988, seventeen months later, the party had managed to sign up only 9,663 supporters, far fewer than the number needed to qualify as a national party (Blanca Arthur, "Entre el Mito y la Realidad," *El Mercurio* international edition, week of May 26–June 1, 1988, p. 6).

94. Based on interviews with the author in Santiago: Correa, January 28, and Zaldívar, January 29, 1987.

95. Running six printed pages, the document differed from earlier pronouncements in that it contained no demands—only statements of principles. Among them: a call for university autonomy, a separation of powers clearly intended to enhance congressional powers at the expense of the presidency, a central role for political powers, and the principle of "not excluding any political party" from democratic participation. Notably missing this time: Jarpa's National Union, which had signed the National Accord. As saccharine as this one was, and the internal security climate notwithstanding, this agreement, like the others, fell apart within a few months as the signatories began proferring their own "interpretations" as to its meaning. In an accompanying statement, the document's three principal authors—Eugenio Ortega, Pedro Correa, and Jorge Molina—said the assassination attempt "and numerous terrorist acts" then occurring demonstrated that "only a rapid transition to democracy opens the way to social peace . . . This agreement has as its principal objective to guarantee confidence in the future of Chile" by showing that diverse political groups could unite on basic principles.

96. The National party was still trying to resurrect ANDE in December 1986. In a statement issued following a December 13–14 meeting of its "expanded leadership group" ("Voto Político del Partido Nacional"), the party referred—curiously, it would seem—to the previous pacts as a union of "democratic political forces with which we have formed *a single party*" (emphasis mine; the Spanish: ". . . intensificar la gestación de la unidad de las fuerzas políticas democráticas con las que antes integramos un solo partido . . .").

97. Blanca Arthur, "1986: El Balance de Pinochet," *El Mercurio*, December 28, 1986, p. 1-D. In that lengthy interview, Pinochet said his first thought when the shooting began was to cover his grandson, who was traveling with him, but he himself believed "that my time had come . . . Later, when we reached home, I gave thanks to God for having kept us from harm in an attack of such magnitude . . ."

98. "Qué lío!" *Qué Pasa*, #844, June 11–17, 1987, pp. 6–7, 11.

99. "Las Garantías para el Plebiscito," *El Mercurio*, January 24, 1988, pp. 1–2. Party-only lists were also available, at a paltry 4 cents per page; the first to take advantage of that opportunity was the sagging National party, though by January of 1988, all but *Avanzada Nacional* had bought the lists of one or more of their competitors.

100. Venegas and Ortega quotes from "Confusiones ante Ley de Partidos," the government newspaper *La Nación*, January 31, 1987, p. 3; details of the law from "Nuevo Avance: Ley de Partidos," *Ercilla* (the progovernment magazine) #2686, January 21–27, 1987, pp. 8, 11; Valdés quotes from interview with the author in Santiago, January 30, 1987; Huepe from "Partido

Decidirá Sus Estatutos Soberanamente," *El Mercurio*, January 25, 1987, p. C-3; appeal from a typewritten copy of the petition filed with the court. The litigants were Germán Urzúa, Jorge Ovalle, Mario Verdugo, Alejandro Jara, and Mario Papi. Defiance notwithstanding, the PDC at that meeting of its "Consejo Nacional Ampliado" decided that henceforth the party's highest governing body, the National Board, would be elected by the full plebiscite vote of its membership.

101. The 652 figure is from *Carta Confidencial*, #17, February 11, 1988, p. 22; Valdés' from Raquel Correa, "A la Altura de los Liderazgos," *El Mercurio*, international edition, May 5–11, 1988, p. 6, an in-depth interview with Zaldívar. As indicated in an earlier note, *Carta Confidencial* is widely believed in Santiago to enjoy special access to military intelligence sources, so it is likely that its figure came from airport passport checks. Though ostensibly retired, Cardinal Silva was a frequent traveler abroad, stirring a major hornet's nest in 1988. Others included Archbishop Bernardo Piñera, president of the Episcopal Conference, who as he was leaving for Chicago in June 1987—invited by Cardinal Joseph Bernardin—said he hoped to raise money while there to fund diocesan projects ("Monseñor Piñera Viajó a EE.UU.," *El Mercurio*, June 11, 1987, p. C-2).

102. Valdés—who generally can muster few words of praise for the United States—described Carter in his 1987 annual report to the party as that "admirable fighter for his profoundest moral convictions." In that same speech, for example, Valdés referred to the United States as "a great nation," but one which, "nevertheless, is 'an imperial republic,' in Raymond Aron's phrase; and, as such, one which has structural difficulties in the way of coherently pursuing an international policy in certain areas, especially relative to the peripheries of Africa, Asia and Latin America." As to Ronald Reagan, Valdés remarked dryly that his administration "has continued the general lines of said [Carter] policy," but added that the "ruling power circles" in Washington wanted to perpetuate the neoliberal economic model then in place in Chile. Valdés said, while respecting their viewpoint, he found such an idea "too simplistic. . . . completely unworkable and ethically unjustified . . ." (*Política y Espíritu*, #328, September 1987, pp. 12–13, containing the text of Valdés' report to the PDC National Board, July 31–August 1, 2, 1987).

103. Blanca Arthur, "Entre el Mito y la Realidad," op. cit. Ms. Arthur notes in her article that the number enrolling in parties could that week (first week of June 1988) jump to 305,000; that would still be under 5 percent of the total.

104. Within the first fifteen months, two thousand such cases of double-registration were detected and reported to the courts. "Detectan Dos Mil Registros Dobles," *El Mercurio*, international edition, May 19–25, 1988, p. 5.

105. Raquel Correa, "La Campaña por el 'No,'" *El Mercurio*, January 24, 1988, p. 2.

106. Quotes and mention of posters from *Carta Confidencial*, #3, May 2, 1987, pp. 6–8; as to the Communist-MDP link, as that "insider" publication noted (p. 9), the Communist party was widely known to be "the big brother" of the MDP. Monsignor Sodano's appointment was announced on May 30, 1988. "Monseñor Sodano a la Santa Sede," *El Mercurio*, international edition, May 26–June 1, 1988.

107. Five distinct currents were visible at the conference, ranging from open

participation in the political process on one side to the strictly evangelical mission on the other. The MDP urged the bishops to call for the installation of a provisional government. The Christian Democrats wanted the church to join—again—"in a common front against the regime," serving as mediators in the creation of a new political alliance promptly dubbed "the Philippinization Formula," after the new constitutional process implemented in the Philippines earlier that year, largely engineered under church auspices. Within the church, the most radical proposals came from the staff of the Permanent Conference of Bishops, and particularly one from a group of three far-left ideologues encrusted within the Santiago archdiocesan organization: the priests Antonio Lagos and Oscar Jiménez, and the nun Margarita Westwoot. Among other things, they said, "Christian people oppose a center-right political opening," and also any alliance which would include the MDP. Reconciliation, they added, would not be possible so long as the dictatorship continued. In Chile—as in the United States—the executive secretariats of church organizations tend to be well to the left of the church rank-and-file. Quote on registration from *Chilean Review*, vol. 1, #5, June 1987, back page; balance from *Carta Confidencial*, #5, June 4, 1987, pp. 24–27; 1988 message from *El Mercurio*, international edition, April 21–27, p. 1.

108. The church group, Civic Crusade for Citizen Participation, headed by a priest, is an offshot of Civitas; according to an exhaustive study of foreign funding done by *El Mercurio* ("Platas Negras, Blancas ... y Políticas," January 24, 1988, pp. 1, 4–5 D), Civitas gets most of its funding, indirectly, from the U.S. Agency for International Development ("laundered" through the Coordinating Committee for Free Elections). Ostensibly, the crusade was set up to train twelve thousand volunteers in voter registration and vote-monitoring techniques. But, when it became known that the priest running it served also as a director of the leftist Assembly for Civility and other top jobs were held by Christian Democrat activists, a backfire started which led to a hold on further work pending a review. That review was further enforced when it was learned that, reassurances of neutrality notwithstanding, the crusade was actively promoting a "No" vote (*El Mercurio*, international editions: "Cruzada Cívica," March 31–April 6, 1988, p. 3, and "Reestudio de Estrategia," April 21–27, p. 3). Arrests, "21 Detenidos En Acto Frente A La Moneda," *El Mercurio*, March 31–April 6, p. 5; Cardinal Silva's remarks and reactions from *El Mercurio*, January 31, 1988, pp. 1–3 D; Camus quote from "As the General said to the Pope," *The Economist*, April 4, 1987, p. 33. It is true that the Communists had never polled more than 19 percent in *popular* elections in Chile; it is not true that they never exceeded that total in *university* elections. Bishop Camus made his remark following the arrest and alleged "psychological torture" of an eighteen-year-old niece, a short time before the pope's visit to Chile.

109. Raquel Correa, "La Campaña por el 'No'," op. cit., p. D-3, interview with Genaro Arriagada, then serving as secretary-general of the Coordinating Committees for Free Elections, attempting to become the command post of the "No" vote. The phrase he used was: "Durante el Año que pasó se dedicó [la oposición] prácticamente a girar sobre su propio ombligo." NED contributed $67,000 for the Caracas meeting.

110. Details of the merger from "La UDI Acordó Fusión con UN," *El Mercurio*, January 25, 1987, p. 1, and "Jarpa: 'Estamos de Acuerdo en Una Unión sin Condiciones,' " *El Mercurio*, January 25, 1987, p. C-3; Phillips quotes from

Mónica González, "En 1973 debiera haberme tomado el gobierno," interview in *Análisis* magazine, June 15–21, 1987, pp. 24–27. The PN communicated its final decision on June 6 in a seven-page letter to Ricardo Rivadeneira Monreal, then president of RN; the main issues separating the two groups were Phillips' insistence on demanding constitutional reforms in any new government, and what Phillips perceived to be the RN's lack of frank commitment to democratic ideals. But, underpinning the impasse were personality clashes between Phillips and some PN leaders expressed in the insistence that those (like Jarpa and Guzmán) who had served in the government should not now serve in political leadership, and his caustic criticisms of "Chicago Boys" economics. It was a measure of his gruff style that at the party's May 1987 national convention at which the question of alliance was thrashed out, delegates to what was formerly mocked as a *momio* ("mummy," for ossified, upper-class) party were served for lunch an *empanada*, a ham sandwich and an apple—in a plastic package.

111. *Carta Confidencial*, #3, May 2, 1987, p. 13.
112. "Encuesta: Lo que Piensan los Santiaguinos," *El Mercurio*, June 14, 1987, p. C-2. The study was done by the Center for Public Studies—the only rightist institute of its kind then operating in the country, and was funded in part by the National Endowment for Democracy through a contract with the University of South Carolina's Institute of International Studies. A total of nine hundred persons in the Santiago metropolitan area aged eighteen and older—three hundred each from upper, middle, and lower classes—were interviewed between December 9, 1986, and January 15, 1987, for the study. The Gallup Organization provided technical assistance. On an ascending scale of one to seven, bishops and priests got a 5.3 percent ranking, followed by professional organizations, student federations, labor unions, non-Catholic pastors (4.8 percent), businessmen, military (4 percent), political parties (3.7 percent), and the violent at the bottom (2 percent). A previously cited study done by the Christian Democrat-oriented Center for the Study of Contemporary Reality (CERC) published at approximately the same time reflected a better light on political parties, in response to two different questions: "Do you think political parties, in general, are indispensable to govern the country?" and, "Do you agree, more or less agree, or disagree, with the following phrases: Without political parties there cannot be democracy; Political parties are useless [*no sirven para nada*]." The first drew an overall 60.3 percent for indispensable, 23.7 percent not indispensable, and 16 percent no opinion/answer. Older persons rated parties much higher than eighteen-to-twenty-five year-olds, a factor of considerable significance inasmuch as fully half of those who will vote are under thirty-five. Only half the young group rated parties as indispensable, while all other age groups gave them at least a 61 percent indispensable rating. To the first of the second brace of questions, the answers were: 56.9 percent agree, 16.3 percent more or less agree, 17.3 percent disagree, and 9.5 percent no answer; to the second, 17.3 percent, 17.9 percent, 56.4 percent, 8.4 percent. That same survey showed a drop, from 68.5 percent in 1973 to 60.3 percent in 1986, of those who believed parties were indispensable for governance; a slight drop in the number who thought they were not indispensable, and a big jump (from 4.8 percent to 16 percent of those who said they did not know or who did not answer). Carlos Huneeus, *Los Chilenos y La Política* (Santiago: Salesianos Printers, 1987), pp. 68–70. That study, backed by a Ford Foundation grant, involved

889 interviews in June 1986, and the findings were first released in May of 1987. Publication of the book was aided by a Konrad Adenauer Foundation grant.

113. "PN Entregará Nombres de Candidatos a S.E.," *El Mercurio*, international edition, March 31–April 6, 1988, p. 4; *Carta Confidencial*, #21, April 20, 1988, p. 11. That publication identified three strains by then in the party: one, headed by Phillips, pushing for a "consensus candidate"; one, headed by Juan Eduardo King of Concepción, pressing for an "understanding" with the PDC: and the "silent majority," opposed to both of these positions but remaining in from nostalgia for what the party once was. *Carta Confidencial* (p. 12) noted that on March 13, 1988, Valdivia provincial leaders said they wanted the party to go on record once and for all in support of the junta candidate, and that in the forthcoming party convention, only those regions where the party had achieved legality be allowed to participate. (At that point, the number was five, including King and Valdivia.) King emerged publicly at mid-April advocating a "constructive 'No' " in the plebiscite (" 'Se Deberá Optar por Un "No" Constructivo,' " *El Mercurio*, international edition, April 21–27, 1988, p. 4).

114. His remarks from the previously cited January 30, 1987, interview in Santiago with the author; "abrasive," from "Prising out Pinochet," *The Economist*, April 11, 1988, p. 16. Valdés had been hand-picked by the party's top leadership in 1982 following the exile of party president Andrés Zaldívar and death of Eduardo Frei. At the party plenum in June 1985, the first since 1973, Valdés had very nearly been ousted. The first-round voting gave him 110 votes, Juan Hamilton 83, Adolfo Zaldívar 25, and one other a blank vote. On the second round, he won—by a single vote.

115. "Acuerdo en Frente de Izquierda," *La Tercera*, June 14, 1987, p. 8. Almeyda was followed into Chile on June 21 by Aniceto Rodríguez, former secretary-general of the Socialist party, and a personage more palatable to "progressives" in the Christian Democrat party already wooing the relatively more moderate socialist, Ricardo Núñez. The effect was to force Almeyda even farther to the left in virtual lock-step with the Communists. Shortly after his illegal return, Almeyda was sent into internal exile in Chile Chico, a charming but thoroughly remote village 1,300 miles south of Santiago. Numerous national and international political figures pilgrimaged there to see him while his trial on charges of violating the antiterrorist law made its way through the courts. By a vote of 2–1, the Fifth Court of Appeals, on May 13, 1988, upheld Almeyda's sentence to 541 days in prison, without possibility of parole. Rodríguez was escorted from Caracas, where he had lived during his thirteen years of exile, by three Venezuelan deputies, as per a vote of the Venezuelan Congress. No sooner back in Chile, he called for a congress at year's end of the five major branches of Chilean socialism in the hope of bringing about reunification. It did not happen. He also registered to vote, saying: "With six million persons registered, there is no possibility of fraud." A week after his return, Almeyda's group did soften its stance on taking grudging part in the plebiscite ("Ahora en el re-exilio," *Hoy*, #524, August 3–9, 1987, pp. 12–13). The Communist party position was spelled out in its underground newspaper, *El Siglo:* There can only be free elections, it said, "without Pinochet . . . without the [1980] constitution . . . without exiles . . . without the proscription of the popular parties . . ." Castillo Velasco was quoted

as expressing similar sentiments in an interviews with *El Siglo*; both references are from *El Mercurio*, June 11, 1987, p. C-2: "PC Reitera Posición Frente a 'Elecciones Libres' "; "Fernando Castillo: 'Con Pinochet No Podrá Haber Comicios Libres.' "

116. "Definiciones en Punta de Tralca," *Hoy*, #524, August 3–9, 1987, pp. 6–8. Assistant Secretary of State Elliot Abrams told Congress early in 1987 that the U.S. was pressing Chile for early, direct presidential elections, and favored a consensus candidate committed to the free market economic model. Valdés never concealed his rejection of that model. Finally, when junta member Fernando Matthei challenged the opposition, on July 28, 1987, to define their views on the economy and private property, Valdés responded at a breakfast meeting with newsmen three days later: the present economic model, he told them, could only work in a dictatorship. As noted, he expanded on those views during his annual report to the party's plenum.

117. The "support" quote is from *Carta Confidencial*, #9, August 27, 1987; Neely, "Informe Político #2," May 1987, p. 5 (a ten-page typewritten report on legal size paper); Valdés, previously cited interview. Neely's report leaked to the press, and its publication led to his ouster as vice president of his party and other disciplinary action; the Social Democrats were then in delicate alliance talks with the PDC. In that report, he described Valdés' stewardship as "disastrous." "With a very able and tenacious international effort, G. Valdés convinced the 'political classes' of the United States and Europe that he, personally, was the providential man, qualified to succeed Pinochet in some critical development provoked by 'social mobilization,' backed by external pressure. He was the unquestioned leader of the only party great both in quantity and quality, closely intertwined with the mostly leftist Catholic church and, apparently, the only one who could count on the compliance of the ex-Popular Unity one-third [of the electorate]. He did a good job of selling his stratagem and received generous financial aid for his party and related organisms, and was the decisive sponsor of funds lavished on the Socialist party, the Christian Left, MAPU, and even for the Radical party . . ." (Valdés' mention of "Chamberlain" was, of course, a reference to the prewar British prime minister Neville Chamberlain who believed he had succeeded in averting war through a series of pacts with Adolf Hitler.)

118. "A Tres Bandas," *Hoy*, #517, June 15–21, 1987, pp. 11–12. Party ideologue Jaime Castillo Velasco had complained that the infighting, exploited by the anti-PDC press, was creating "a horrible image" for the party. On June 9, the national directorate asked all three candidates to restrain themselves and their supporters. A few days later, the three agreed to keep their debates out of the press and stick to issues only—agreements which were, of course, honored in the breach. Hormazábal, an ex-deputy, advocated a broad-based coalition which would include the Communists on the left, National Renewal on the right; he rejected the 1980 constitution outright, but was willing to bend if the armed forces would agree to open elections for president, and a Congress granted constitution-writing powers. Frei, also an ex-deputy, rejected an alliance of any kind with Communists, but was for other alliances which would enable the party to recapture the political center. Like Frei, ex-Senator Patricio Aylwin rejected both alliances with Communists and violent confrontations, arguing instead for a

three-pronged strategy of pressure on the government (generated internally and externally), an acceptable alternative plan of government, and direct negotiations with the armed forces. At mid-June, a fourth candidacy was put forward—Adolfo Zaldívar Larraín, representing a party "renewal" faction. He is a younger brother of the former party president, and was said to be willing to "abdicate" in favor of his older brother if circumstances were right to do so. Early skirmishing centered mainly on the struggle between elder brother Andrés Zaldívar and former Sen. Juan Hamilton to take up the mantle of Eduardo Frei in the moderate tradition. When neither could prevail, Aylwin emerged as the compromise choice. Among other names floated were those of Gutemberg Martínez, rival of Arturo Frei Bolívar for leadership of a younger generation of anti-Communists in the party; Claudio Huepe; and Alejandro Foxley (backed by Valdés as a possible alternative to Hormazábal). But they rapidly merged into the three candidacies expressing the three major strains within the party.

119. "Al calor de la contienda electoral," *Qué Pasa*, #837, April 23–29, 1987, p. 17. Like Valdés, Hormazábal also rejected an alliance with the RN; another long-time party leader and ex-senator, Osvaldo Olguín, said flatout he favored such a tie; Adolfo Zaldívar, Juan Hamilton and former University President Edgardo Boeninger expressed varying degrees of reservations.

120. "Definiciones en Punta de Tralca," *Hoy*, August 3–9, 1987, p. 8.

121. "El Derrotero del PDC," *Hoy*, #525, August 10–16, 1987, pp. 6–8; "La Definición de la DC," *Qué Pasa*, #852, August 6–12, 1987, p. 38. *Qué Pasa* and other sources I have seen describe this as Aylwin's sixth presidency; *Hoy*, closer to the PDC than most other publications, puts it at seven. *Carta Confidencial*, in an analysis not otherwise explained, claimed that in the voting the "Aylwin Line" got 42 percent of the vote, the "Hormazábal Line" 38 percent, "Renewal" (Zaldívar) 7 percent, "Frei" 6 percent, and "Consensus" 5 percent. A possible explanation: delegates voted those "tendencies," which were then lumped together to give Aylwin his 55 percent (Zaldívar and Frei) (#9, August 27, 1987, p. 38).

122. "Como entenderse con las FF.AA.," an interview with Aylwin, *Hoy*, #525, pp. 8–9; "La Definición de la DC," *Qué Pasa*, op. cit., both postconvention interviews with Aylwin. In his remark about Pinochetismo, Aylwin was responding to an *Hoy* question: "There are sectors of the regime and the U.S. Department of State that propose a consensus candidate who preserves the economic model. Would you accept that formula?" The "subtle, indirect" reference is from the same issue of *Hoy*, noting Valdés' claim that in the 1983 "peace talks" with Sergio Jarpa, the PDC had been drawn into a trap: the opposition, believing the regime was weak, demanded everything. Jarpa, meantime, in that view, was only interested in lulling the opposition into a demobilization without offering anything in return. "The lesson was learned," the magazine wrote. . . . "This time it will be the opposition that chooses its opposite number [*interlocutor*]. It will not be with the executive branch, nor its representatives. The dialogue must be with the junta for two reasons": because it is the legislative body, and because the opposition wants constitutional reforms. "The styles will be subtle and indirect. The [party] leadership will not negotiate, nor will there be public understandings. What there is will be private . . . Personal contacts, also, will prevail. More than knocking on the door of the junta as

such, it will be a matter of sounding out the commanders-in-chief . . ." The 8 million figure was from a speech made June 10 in Osorno, "Aylwin Pidió 8 Millones de Inscripciones," *El Mercurio*, June 11, 1988, p. C-2.

123. "Aylwin: 'Merino Me Ha Ofendido Injustamente,' " *El Mercurio*, international edition, March 31–April 6, 1988; "El dilema de un candidato civil," *Hoy*, #517, June 15–21, 1987, p. 6; "Civiles," in La Semana Nacional, *La Tercera*, June 14, 1987, p. 3; "General Matthei," and "Valdés," in Revista Noticiosa Semanal, *El Mercurio*, June 14, p. D-13. On March 29, 1988, Merino said Aylwin "lied" when he, and other political leaders, said the purpose of the plebiscite was to approve or reject the constitution. Aylwin said Merino had "caricatured" his views; he understood that the plebiscite was to approve or disapprove the candidate named by the junta, but that it also had a deeper political significance. Admiral Merino himself, he averred, had said that should the "Yes" vote win, it would be "a backing of the action which the government has undertaken"; by the same logic, Aylwin said, a "No" vote meant the rejection of that same set of policies, and thus a mandate for change. As for General Matthei, he clarified in his remarks that he intended to step down as air force chief in 1989 to make way for younger commanders, and thus had no intention of remaining in government thereafter whatever the plebiscite outcome. Although those June remarks were cited repeatedly in foreign press accounts, none of the junta members ever again referred to a civilian—or any other—alternative candidate to Pinochet.

124. "Chicago 'boys' miran al 2000," *Hoy*, #524, August 3–10, 1987. According to Alvaro Vial, director of the National Statistical Institute, the "7 modernizations" included: internal and external security for Chileans; expanded employee stock ownership programs (ESOPs) for workers; intensified initiatives to expand Chile's links with the outside world; increased and broader public access to consumer goods; stepped-up regionalization and decentralization of government; a modernized justice system with increased access for all; rationalization of the public sector; increased investment in key sectors; intensified export growth; better pay and improved employment opportunities; sustained economic growth; and a more intense war on poverty. Reference to Fernández' constitutional role from *Chilean Review*, vol. 1, #6, July-August 1987, p. 1.

125. *Carta Confidencial*, #10, September 15, 1987, pp. 1–4. Weiss had co-sponsored several measures to sanction Chile, including one to end Overseas Private Investment Corporation programs in Chile—although Chile had long since become one of the few countries on earth amicably to satisfy all of its OPIC claims. Those claims had been created by Allende's confiscation of American companies, and, as noted previously, threatened to drive OPIC into bankruptcy. But, as one authoritative publication has noted, Weiss' "ideological views . . . are about as leftish as those of any House member." Michael Barone and Grant Ujifusa, *The Almanac of American Politics 1986* (Washington: National Journal, 1987), p. 945. Schnake was at Radio Corporación across the street from La Moneda on September 11. When the station was able to resume broadcasting briefly at three that afternoon, Schnake broadcast an appeal for help which Allende had given him three hours earlier; Schnake did not know that Allende had already been dead for more than an hour when he did so. He had lived in exile in Spain, and returned to Chile on September 6. In 1973, the Social-

ists were the violent ones, the Communists only near the end. In marching out of the conference, Phillips said "he would not remain in the same assembly with the kidnappers of [Lieutenant Colonel Carlos] Carreño," a reference to the kidnapping several days earlier of an army officer by a Communist commando group of the FMR. Though that event shocked Chileans, it did not seem to perturb other delegates; though Guastavino, as coordinator of the party's Central Committee, was the most conspicuous Communist at the assembly, he was far from the only one.

126. Biographical data on both from "Los Presidenciables," a series of biographical sketches published by *Hoy* in June 1987, pp. 40–43. Carmen Frei cut her political teeth accompanying her late father in his 1964 presidential campaign. In 1963, she married sociologist Eugenio Ortega, who would later become secretary-general of the PDC under Valdés; Carmen herself had been elected a vice president of the party in 1982 together with Valdés, and both she and her husband were identified with the *"chascón"* (leftist) wing of the party. During the three years her husband worked for the United Nations in New York (1976–1979), Carmen worked in a U.S. federal program for Latin children (she had taken her degree in specialized education for disadvantaged children). In June 1987, Graciela Bórquez, director of the party's women's department, said she believed Carmen Frei was the one person the opposition could unite behind as a presidential candidate ("Proponen Canditura de Carmen Frei a Presidencia," *El Mercurio*, June 11, 1987, p. C-2). Nothing further came of that proposal. Her brother, Eduardo, was thought to be closer to the moderate views of their late father. He was the keynote speaker in December 1986 at a seminar, "Consensus and transition to democracy; the experience of Spain," and it was that speech which lifted him to public attention.

127. Carlos Neely, *Informe Político #4*, September 1987, p. 2 of a thirteen-page typewritten report Neely prepared for the leadership of his Social Democrat party.

128. *Carta Confidencial*, #18, March 2, 1988, pp. 19–29. Plans for foreign visitors from *Chilean Review*, vol. 1, #13, March 1988, p. 4. The announcement was made by Luis Pareto, coordinator of the International Assembly of Parliamentarians, who said a coordinating commission would be formed with Christian Democrat Sergio Molina's Committee of Personages. That group had already begun inviting intellectuals from around the world. Meanwhile, María Rozas, national director of the University Professor's Association—also controlled by the Christian Democrats—said academics from Germany, England, France, and the United States would also act as observers during the upcoming plebiscite. She said teachers' groups had shown an interest in meeting in Chile, "before, during and after the plebiscite."

129. The newspaper published two major editorials in the week following the 4–3 vote of RN's disciplinary tribunal to oust Guzmán ("Crisis en Renovación Nacional," Saturday, April 23, and "El 'Sí' y la Crisis," April 24, both from *El Mercurio*, international edition, April 21–27, 1988, p. 3). The fight mainly pitted Guzmán against Sergio Jarpa, who remained in command of RN, and revolved around Guzmán's insistence on early and unequivocal support for the junta candidate, Jarpa's insistence on preserving the party's negotiating flexibility. The blow was softened somewhat by the fact that on April 4, the National Vanguard Party (Avanzada Nacional), headed by

Benjamín Matte and to the right even of the RN, announced that it had secured a sufficient number of signatures for legal recognition as a national party. Though split over tactics, both wings of RN remained firmly committed to a "Sí" vote in the plebiscite.

130. The 6 percent theory is in *Carta Confidencial*, #21, April 20, 1988, p. 1; Zaldívar in an interview with Raquel Correa, "A la Altura de los Liderazgos," *El Mercurio*, international, May 5–11, 1988, p. 6; Matthei, "Lo que No Está en Juego," *El Mercurio*, international, May 26–June 1, 1988, p. 3. It is interesting to observe that whereas the Christian Democrats saw nothing "inoperable" about a four-year "lame duck" government—their January transition proposal—they did profess to be worried about the viability of a one-year lame duck government. As to political "parties," as noted previously, as of late May 1988, only five parties had presented enough signatures to qualify as legal national parties. By then, the "concentration" embraced somewhere between fourteen and sixteen "parties," depending on how the various splinters were counted.

131. In March 1988, both PDC President Aylwin and Zaldívar, the party's number two man, said they would respect the outcome, provided it was a clean plebiscite (*Chilean Review,* vol. 1, #13, March 1988, p. 4). But, in his May 8 interview with Raquel Correa, Zaldívar, for example, was hedging. Question: "But you have said publicly that you would respect it." Answer: "If it is the result of a clean plebiscite, of course we will accept it. But the campaign already is not clean, because there is inequality in the matter of media; the government is abusing fiscal resources; mayors are pressuring the people; the regime is trying to buy the conscience of the people giving away everything from houses to bicycles . . . If the plebiscite is not absolutely clear, clean and transparent, no one is going to believe in it nor legitimize it. And if this government stays on for eight more years, I believe the country is going to fall into a process of increasing confrontation . . ." If a leader of the "moderate" wing of the party was already stipulating conditions of purity inexistent in the history of the country (and found in few, if any, less developed countries anywhere) while also decrying pork barrel politics common even to the most advanced democracies, the leader of the party's Left was even less circumspect. Said Gabriel Valdés, in a May interview: "The triumph of a 'Yes' vote is a utopia, and I don't believe in utopias" (issue #303, *Cosas*, quoted in *Carta Confidencial*, #23, May 25, 1988, p. 6).

132. Arriagada is from an AP story dated March 20 and Molina a UPI story dated April 26, both reproduced in *Carta Confidencial*, the first, issue #20, April 5, pp. 10–11, the second, #22, May 9, 1988, p. 13. Molina, former finance minister under Frei and listed among the presidential candidate possibilities by the pro-PDC magazine *Hoy* (in its previously cited "Los Presidenciables" series, #2, pp. 61–63), had created the Committee for Free Elections, which then became known as the Committee of Personages (or Personalities in some translations; the Spanish word is *personalidades*).

133. Comments on Pinochet from Correa interview, op. cit., p. D-3; volunteers from " 'Oposición Reunirá 200 Mil Voluntarios,' " *El Mercurio*, international edition, May 5–11, 1988, p. 4. Commenting on the volunteers' plan, *Carta Confidencial* (#23, May 25, 1988, p. 2) said it was a long way from reality, and that, in fact, the only actual force already mobilized in opposi-

tion was the church. On that same program—carried on the Catholic University's television network—Arriagada acknowledged that "some progress" had been made in clearing television time for the opposition, but complained that he expected "nothing" from the third network, the government channel.

134. "Un 47.2% Cree Que Es Mejor que Gane el 'Sí,'" *El Mercurio,* international edition, March 31–April 6, 1988, p. 5. That survey was done between February 22 and March 12, and was based on a sample of 2,400 voter-age persons, equivalent to 6.3 million persons in the voter-eligible population. "Untested" because, as pointed out earlier, nearly half of those registering were thirty-five-years-old or under, meaning they had never before voted in a presidential election. The continuing pro-yes Gallup curve was consistent with findings in the 1985 survey done by the left-wing FLACSO organization in Santiago: 76 percent of those surveyed located themselves from the center to the center-right. Cited in "La Cultura Política Chilena Según Las Encuestas de Opinión Pública (1983–1986) (Santiago: Instituto Chileno de Estudios Humanísticos, 1986), p. 55. In introducing the work, political scientist Patricio Chaparro noted (p. 5) that the FLACSO study, although based on a relatively small sample (six hundred persons), was "a serious study." With the Christian Democrats clearly abandoning the center once again in 1988, it was not surprising that such a high percentage would say they felt no party represented their interests.

135. Cited in *Carta Confidencial,* #23, May 25, 1988, pp. 1–2; the 5.7 million figure is from *El Mercurio,* international edition, May 19–25, op. cit., p. 5; fines, "Establecen Multas Para Ciudadanos Que No Voten," May 5–11, p. 5.

136. *Chilean Review,* vol. 1, #13, March 1988, pp. 1–2.

137. " 'Comandantes en Jefe Dirán Si lo He Hecho Bien o Mal,'" " 'Ahora Ya Sabemos Quién Es el Candidato,'" and " 'Crítica de la Oposición Es Dogmática y Revanchista,'" *El Mercurio,* international edition, April 21–27, 1988, pp. 1, 6, 5. The Pinochet speech was made April 22, in the Municipal Casino in Viña del Mar, traditional scene of large meetings in that seashore resort city.

138. *El Mercurio,* international editions: "Cambios de Fondo Propone Programa Económico Opositor"; " 'De Donde Saldrán los Recursos,'" May 5–11, p. 5; "DC y Marxistas Quieren Revivir Receta Agotada," May 12–19, p. 1. There was something especially ironic about the statist/socialist Christian Democrats and their Socialist allies including "bringing down inflation" in their program: it was precisely under their governments that inflation had soared progressively to levels rarely seen in human history. The UFs (Unidades de Fomento) were, in fact, established to encourage the availability of mortgage money in economies with runaway inflation. Basically, they guarantee to lenders principal, plus a built-in mechanism for interest-plus-inflation. During the Frei-Allende years, when "the state" paid everybody's bills, scant attention was paid to delinquencies. But, with the emergence of a market economy in the 1980s—and specifically, with the reprivatization of banks and other financial institutions—there was a small number of foreclosures in the wake of the 1982 economic collapse. By 1985–1986, UFs began to surface as a political rallying cry. On June 11, 1987, the National Association of Fiscal Employees (ANEF) protested that from 1981 to 1987, UF had shot up by 204 percent, while base salaries for public employees had increased by only 69.2 percent. According to *Carta*

Confidencial (#15, December 11, 1987, pp. 23–24), only 1.2 percent of UF holders were then in arrears; 1,580,000 were current in their payments. The real target of the political pressure would appear to be Chile's highly successful privatized social security system, since so many of those pension plans had significant investments in banks, insurance companies and other financial institutions which held the UF "paper." For socialists and the statists of the Christian Democrats, a pension program over which they had no political control was an abomination—no matter how successful. One government bail-out idea then being floated, according to *Carta Confidencial,* would cost the state $120 million.

139. From *El Mercurio,* international editions: " 'Meta Es Construir el Socialismo de Allende,' " and " 'Crítica de la Oposición Es Dogmática y Revanchista,' " April 21–April 27, 1988, p. 5; " 'Lagos Interpretó a Millones de Chilenos' "; " 'Compartimos Críticas Políticas de Lagos' "; " 'Ese Socialismo No Corresponde a Chile,' " April 28–May 4, 1988, p. 7; "PDC Perdió Liderazgo De Oposición Chilena," May 5–11, 1988, p. 4.

140. Biographical data from "Los Presidenciables," op. cit., vol. 2, pp. 55–57. Why he would form a new party of his own rather than join forces with either of the established and ostensibly more leftist socialist parties (those of Almeyda and Ricardo Núñez) is in intriguing question. Long before the April 25 speech, *Carta Confidencial* postulated a theory (#15, December 11, 1987, pp. 18–19): "The principal force behind the PPD has challenged President Pinochet to prove that he is a communist. Any person of average culture, who had studied the writings of Lenin or [former KGB chieftain] Beria, understands clearly the role and interference-running function [*puente de plata salvador*] that Mr. Ricardo Lagos is performing on behalf of the Chilean Communist party. Unmistakably, Lagos intends to constitute himself as the Allende of 1952, when the Communist party was illegal [and Allende ran interference for them]. On a personal level, it would appear that Mr. Lagos is convinced that he is the successor to Allende . . . Ricardo Lagos has demonstrated, repeatedly, his cleverness and subtle ability to favor the Communist party . . ."

141. Núñez' support of the Soviet invasion is in Patricio Tupper, ed., *89/90: Opciones Políticas en Chile* (Santiago: Ediciones Colchagua, 1987), p. 305. *El Mercurio,* international editions, "Experiencias de la UP," April 28–May 4; " 'Gobierno Quiere Revivir Las Divisions y Querellas De Hace Dieciocho Años.' " Lagos made his follow-up remarks on April 27. Valdés clarified that he did not mean it was Allende's attaining power that had destroyed democracy, but rather "the quarrels and visions" of democracy's last years. Valdés' private opinions from *Carta Confidencial,* #23, May 25, 1988, p. 14.

142. "A la Altura de los Liderazgos," op. cit.; Zaldívar's move from the limelight from *El Mercurio,* international edition, May 19–25, 1988, p. 2, " 'Primus Inter Pares.' " In that May 22 editorial, the newspaper wrote: ". . . until a few days ago, Andrés Zaldívar had appeared in the press as the head of the Coordination for the 'No.' But, since he expressed in his recent interview his full availability [*concordancia*] for a possible presidential candidacy, he has not again been seen in charge of said coordination." In-fighting from *Carta Confidencial,* #23, op. cit., pp. 26–28.

143. *El Mercurio,* international edition, May 5–11, 1988: "Promulgada Ley sobre Votaciones y Escrutinios," pp. 1–2; " 'Lo Más Probable Es que el Plebiscito Sea en Octubre.' " The latter story quoted junta member Gen.

Fernando Matthei as saying October was "the most probable" date. " 'Plebiscito Será Sin Estados De Excepción,' " May 26–June 1, p. 5. *Carta Confidencial* (#23, op. cit., pp. 4–9)—which had earlier predicted it would be between October 17 and October 21 (#20, p. 7)—now speculated on the December date. Among its reasons: the election would be preceded by three days of rest because of the December 8 religious holiday and probability of a Friday "bridge" into the weekend; the Washington factor; the proximity to summer and Christmas, both times of general buoyant spirits. The publication warned that the only risk was that the well-to-do would repeat their 1970 mistake: spending the long weekend at the beach instead of voting.

144. Most of the data for this summary of the Humanist and Green parties have been extracted from two issues of *Carta Confidencial*, #15, December 11, 1987, pp. 26–36, and #22, May 9, 1988, pp. 36–48. As to "moderate and demure," while the pages of *El Mercurio's* international edition during 1987 and 1988 have overflowed with political bombast, charges, counter-charges, alliances, alliances come unstuck, the Movement is rarely mentioned at all. Sáenz was so underrated that *Hoy* did not even include him among the seventy or so possible candidates in their June 1987 "Los Presidenciables" series.

145. "Los Micro-Partidos," *Carta Confidencial*, #11, September 30 1987, pp. 15–26. Editor/Publisher Cesar Hidalgo Calvo could be forgiven for under-estimating Lagos' PPD in December 1987; it was the following April before he would achieve political prominence.

146. "PR Completó Presentación De Firmas en Todo el País," and "Partidos Políticos en Formación," *El Mercurio* international edition, May 26–June 1, 1988, pp. 5–6; the first story was from the June 1 edition, the second May 26. Faced with the loss of the Radical name, the faction headed by Luis Fernando Luengo dropped out of the legal picture and linked arms with the underground parties of the radical Left.

147. *El Mercurio* international editions, "En el Cementerio General Sepultaron a Laura Allende," May 26–June 1, back page; "Recordarán Natalicio de Salvador Allende," June 2–8, 1988, p. 5. Allende was born July 26, 1908.

148. *El Mercurio* international editions: "Extremistas Asesinaron a 2 Carabineros," May 19–25, p. 1; "Fiscal Torres Salvó Ileso De Emboscada Terrorista," May 26–June 1, p. 1; "Asesinado a Tiros Oficial de Ejército"; "Chile No Subordina Decisiones al Exterior," pp. 1 and 5, respectively, June 2–8, 1988: and, "Obispos Expresan Inquietud Por Marcha del Proceso," June 9–15, 1988, p. 1. In a sharp response to the U.S. note, Chile's foreign ministry said the government based its decisions on facts and circumstances as it sees and evaluates them; "Chile," the statement added, "is a sovereign nation and no Chilean will accept that its institutional process toward democracy may be blocked by foreign interference." Ibid. PDC President Patricio Aylwin, meantime, said the Interior Minister was "prejudging" when he accused Communists as responsible for the murders, adding that "the murder of Carabineros did not happen during times of democracy" ("Ministro de Interior Está Prejuzgando al Acusar a Comunistas," *El Mercurio*, May 19–25, 1988, p. 5). The MIR and other terrorist organizations were, as indicated in previous chapters, formed during the Frei government, began their violent careers then and were especially violent during the Allende "democracy." In their statement, the bishops based their "concern" on two specifics: the relatively low level of registration of younger voters—a form of youthful apathy scarcely limited to Chile; and

lack of total access to the media, particularly to the government television network. That network was, in fact, the only medium the opposition was not exploiting fully and riotously, and the bishops' statement overlooked the fact that under Chilean law, electioneering—and with it access to that channel—was not supposed to begin officially until one month before the election, and a date still had not been set for the plebiscite. In a June 12 editorial, *El Mercurio* noted that when the opposition had only limited, if any, access to media, then the bishops' pronouncements filled a need. "But today, to the dozens of groups which daily issue political pronouncements must be added the interference of diplomats, organizations or special emissaries of foreign governments, performing artists and intellectuals brought to the country for electioneering purposes and, on top of that, the many associations, union and student pronouncements derived from the progressive politicization of the various organs of press . . . But the pastors have failed to refer to a danger much greater and which would have been timely to underscore, in view of the murder of an Army officer the very day before the bishops' communique: that of political criminal violence, which week after week claims the lives of Chileans . . ." Ibid., p. 3.

149. Editions of *Carta Confidencial:* proclamation and Pinochet assassination, #23, May 25, 1988, p. 5 (the publication cites a letter published by the MAPU magazine *Análisis*, #226); Central Committee meeting, #22, May 9, 1988, pp. 26–27 and #18, March 2, 1988, pp. 11–12. "Manuel Rodríguez Patriotic Front" refers to that terrorist organization's "political" commissariat; I have used the "FMR" initials for simplicity. Presenting two faces to the world was, of course, old hat for the Communists, just as was creating overt and covert organizations. At the Second Congress of the Communist International, held in Moscow in July 1920, Lenin laid down the twenty-one conditions for membership in the Comintern. Communists, Lenin told them, "should not be doctrinaire but flexible. They should not spurn the opportunities that the capitalist state affords through its rotten freedoms. Thus the Communists ought not to reject the chance to use parliaments, and to work through the trade unions; if an occasion warrants, they should join in a bloc or even enter the opportunist Socialist parties." A Communist "struggled through both legal and illegal means and so the American or Swedish Communist, though he lives in a society so different from the Russia of 1895, is told that his Party must (emphasis in original) have an illegal as well as a legal apparatus. . . ." Adam B. Ulam, *The Bolsheviks* (New York: The MacMillan Company, 1965), pp. 497 and 501. In the first quotation, Ulam was paraphrasing from Lenin's pamphlet, *Left Communism— Childish Disease of Communism*. 1895 was the year of Lenin's imprisonment; the two years 1893–1895 were regarded as the years of his emergence as a leader of Bolshevism, and the latter year for orthodox communism is commemorated as the true advent of the revolutionary process.

150. *Chilean Review:* Vol. 1, #5, June 1987, p. 4 (Byrne statement); Vol. 1, #1, February 1987, p. 4. The UN continued to ignore Volio's findings: On November 27, 1987, the General Assembly voted 81–5 (with 47 abstentions) to express its "deep concern" over human rights violations in Chile, Afghanistan, and Iran (although only 58 nations could bring themselves to condemn abuses in Iran). Volio, commending Chile for "exemplary" cooperation, said his first-hand observations enabled him "to verify the disposition of the Government of Chile to improve its behavior in the field of political freedom, with ambient conditions favorable to life without fear

among the citizens and with respect for each one of them, as well for the development of a harmonious, integral and enlightened society." Preparations for the plebiscite itself, he said, represented "an advance in the field of human rights" (*Chilean Review*, Vol. 1, #14, April 1988, p. 5).

151. Besides Almeyda, among others returning illegally were Communist leaders Julieta Campusano and Mireya Baltra (also in 1987). *El Mercurio* international editions: "Ex Senadora María Elena Carrera Quedó Libre Bajo Fianza," May 12–18, 1988, p. 1; "Autorizan Ingreso De 25 Exilados," May 26–June 1, 1988, p. 1; *Carta Confidencial*, #4, May 18, 1987, p. 18.

152. "Chilean Terrorists Belong to Transnational Terror Rings," *Chilean Review*, Vol. 1, #5, June 1987, p. 3; "Cuban Official Admits Training Guerrillas," *Chilean Review*, Vol. 1, #15, May 1988, p. 4. Commenting on Rodríguez' admission in an April 1988 interview with the Brazilian magazine *Veja*, Santiago's *La Tercera* said that "while Gorbachev hypnotizes the West, he has handed Cuba the task of pressing the attacks on countries south of the Rio Grande." Terrorist meetings, plans: *Carta Confidencial*, January 15, 1988, pp. 20–22. Referring to the MIR, the magazine notes that following the murder of Santiago Mayor Carol Urzúa Ibáñez and two of his guards, August 30, 1983, security forces captured seven top MIR leaders, including Arturo Villavela Araujo. According to the magazine (p. 29), Villavela was considered the best planner of urban terrorist actions on the South American continent, leading Castro to decree three days of official mourning following his death. In April 1987, Castro had to intervene to restore order in the MIR, ordering Andrés Pascal Allende (Allende's nephew)—accused of making a "fetish" of armed actions—to turn over leadership of the organization to Nelson Gutiérrez and Hernán Aguiló Martínez, (pp. 29–31). As for the FMR, in 1987, it engaged in three spectacular actions—and a number of sabotage incidents and at least one Carabinero murder—before being reined in: disrupting the Pope's open air mass; engineering the escape of four of their number being held in connection with the attempted assassination of Pinochet from the Valparaíso military prison; and, kidnapping Army Lt. Col. Carlos Carreño on September 1 (he was released in Sao Paulo December 2, 1987). All three, in one fashion or another, were fiascos: the first, because of the public opinion backlash; the second, because it was said to have cost the hard-pressed organization $700,000; and the third, because they had originally demanded a $2-million ransom but, in the face of relentless pressure on them internally and public condemnation, later scaled back to $50,000. They were so weakened, in fact, that they were unable to carry through on their threat of disrupting the World Youth Soccer Cup championships in Chile in October of 1987—an event that attracted some 300 foreign journalists and would have given them guaranteed worldwide publicity.

153. "Acto de los Trabajadores Fue Transformado en Mítin Político," *El Mercurio* international edition, April 28–May 4, back page. Among those present were communist leader Fanny Pollarolo; former Socialist leader Aniceto Rodríguez (now nominally affiliated with Lagos' PPD); MAPU leader Víctor Barrueto, and Luciano Valdés of the also-illegal Almeyda wing of the Socialists. International labor leaders were on hand from Italy and Spain, and observers from a number of other countries. One person suffered gunshot wounds in Santiago; in Valparaíso, two were wounded, 94 arrested; 30 were arrested in Iquique, four injured, six arrested in Concepción, where the disturbances were quickly linked to the MIR.

154. According to *Carta Confidencial* (#23, May 25, 1988, pp. 37–46), the MIR acted when it got wind of Bustos' intention of suspending that strike call anyway. On the one hand, he was said to have come under heavy pressure from his own party to scale down confrontation as a tactic because of the furor generated by the Ricardo Lagos television speech in April. For another, closely tied to the first, foreigners bankrolling the PDC and others were pressuring them to concentrate on beating Pinochet in the plebiscite, not—as before—toppling the regime. Bustos was said to have been given similar advice during his frequent trips to AFL-CIO headquarters in Washington. At first, the MIR tried to weasel out of blame, with a May 5 public letter in which it implied that it may all have been a government trick. Bustos, in a May 21 article in the ultra-left daily *Fortín Mapocho* was not buying, and for good measure, said that from now on, there would be no more hooded individuals permitted at Workers' Command rallies. Data on *tomas* from same issue, pp. 30–31. In issue #15, December 11, 1987, *Carta Confidencial* published a revealing report (pp. 43–44) on how the Communists intended to use the La Victoria shantytown as a prototype for this phase of their insurrection. La Victoria was the oldest of the shantytowns in the Santiago metropolis, established 30 years before. Communist organizers—aided according to the publication by Father Pierre Dubois— seized control of several community organizations, until 500 of its activists were able to exercise iron rule over the lives of the 25,000 inhabitants.

155. In 1981, two radical reforms were introduced: to teach, one no longer needed a university teaching certificate, but could be drawn from other professional backgrounds. The other, in decentralizing education, made teachers private instead of public employees, and thus subject to the forces of the private market, including job security and wages. Communists and other political groups were quick to roil those already troubled waters, provoking labor trouble wherever and whenever they could. At the university level, a radical change was introduced, as well as at the eight state campuses: for the first time, "outsiders" made up one-third of the boards of those institutions (academics one-third, and government officials one-third). During the transition period up to 1989, Pinochet appointed university rectors as well; beginning in 1989, those boards would present slates from which the president would have to choose.

156. *El Mercurio* international editions: "PC Infiltró Universidades y Iglesia," May 12–18, 1988, p. 5. In elections, for example, for a new Student Federation at the University of Chile, a slate headed itself by the very leftist Christian Democrat Youth polled 61.5 percent of the votes; but that slate included representatives of two ultra-left organizations, the Christian Left and the Socialist Party-Núñez, as well as of the "mysterious" Humanists. The rest of the votes were divided among Communists, Socialists-Almeyda, and other hard-leftists. The Right, charging the elections were rigged, called for a boycott; abstention was an impressively-high 36.8%. Taking office a few days later, the new slate made plain how politicized was their agenda; besides demanding the resignation of the rector, they called for a fight for the "No" vote, university "autonomy," an end of efforts to collect fees from students in arrears, etc. "Ganó Nómina Encabezada por la JDC," May 19–25, back page; "Asumieron Nuevos Dirigentes de FECH," May 26–June 1, 1988, p. 5.

157. "Ex Senador Comunista Arengó a Niños Liceanos," *El Mercurio* international, May 12–18, 1988, back page. *Carta Confidencial*, #23, op. cit., p. 9.

12

The New Nation

THE HEROIC DAYS

In January of 1980, The World Bank published an exhaustive study of the Chilean economy covering the first five years of military rule. The study was done by a fourteen-member team of experts of different specialities, bolstered later by written contributions by five other experts, and refined through subsequent research and discussions with Chilean government figures. The first of the summary observations of that report bears repeating:

> Under extraordinarily unfavorable circumstances the Chilean authorities have engineered an economic turnaround without precedent in the history of Chile. When the military took power in September 1973, inflation had reached an annualized rate of around 1,000 percent, net international reserves were negative, the foreign debt in arrears, and production was declining for the second consecutive year. The deficit of the central government alone exceeded 20 percent of the GDP, the money supply was out of control, the financial system in shambles, and the exchange rate grossly overvalued . . .[1]

The man called upon to pick up the pieces of the shattered economy recalled: "Things had gotten so bad that we were importing potatoes from Poland and pork from China—but you couldn't find those on shop shelves, either."[2]

As the authors of that World Bank study noted, "few economies in the world have been as much studied, argued over, and prescribed for. Chile has continuously been at the center of international debates regarding the causes and effects of inflation; the proper role of government in promoting development; the dependency of developing on developed economies; the instability arising from reliance on a single export com-

916

modity; and the implications for economic growth of democratic decision-making, welfare programs, agrarian reform, foreign investment, and import-substitution industrialization."[3]

This is not the place to fan the flames of that debate, nor to argue the merits of market versus statist economies. It is, however, the place to point out that most academic and journalistic critiques flow from premises clearly prejudiced in the direction of a larger rather than a smaller role for the state as an engine of progress and social justice. Those critiques are the ones, then, which largely influence the perceptions and behaviors of government policy-makers, becoming, in turn, the fodder of further journalistic/academic discernments. A corollary of that, running through so much of the serious scholarship and more ephemeral media reportage on Chile, is the presumption that policies that seek to stimulate business growth and development are, *ipso facto*, designed to favor the "rich" at the expense of the poor. One widely respected American reporter managed to get through an entire, lengthy "analysis" of the 1975 crash without once mentioning external factors, but did manage to echo (wrongly) the prevailing orthodoxy: "The minority rich," he wrote, "are best off now by government intention and the gap between them and everybody else is growing."[4]

That is, of course, a caricature—at best—of what was happening, but it reflected a mind-set brought to analysis by serious analysts, as well: zeroing in on the amount of government spending to prove/disprove the regime's purity and social conscience.

Chile is not, and has not been, however, an easy subject for analysis. Quoting, again, from the World Bank study:

> Chile is an economically underdeveloped country as that term is normally understood. Among its identifying characteristics are a heavy dependence on a single primary export commodity, low productivity in agriculture, a high rate of infant mortality, high chronic unemployment and under-employment, and significant absolute poverty. In contrast, however, its per capita income, extensive manufacturing sector, and high degree of urbanization rank Chile among what has come to be treated as a middle tier of nations, while its moderate population growth, early introduction of social security and other public welfare programs, and the literacy and sophistication of its people place it close to the ranks of developed countries. To complicate the image further, although prosperous in comparison to the subject countries of most World Bank reports, Chile's relative position has eroded steadily for the past several decades. While development began to accelerate in many Latin American and Asian countries, Chile experienced slow growth, extreme price instability, and recurrent balance of payment crises. . . .

During the 19th century, Chile was one of the leading economies of South America. Its markets and people were open to both trade and ideas; and Chilean statesmen and institutions had a great influence throughout Latin America. . . .

In the four decades that followed the Great Depression, successive governments accepted increasing responsibility for promoting economic development and achieving a more equitable distribution of its fruits. . . . The results of these efforts, as evidenced by economic performance over most of this period, did not match the intent. Because of failures in execution or design, the increasingly large and complex governmental machinery required to administer these policies was often diverted to the service of private individual or group interests. Policies invoked to accomplish one end—e.g., hold down the cost of living of urban workers—frequently conflicted with other objectives—e.g., increased domestic food production and external payments viability—and a new set of taxes, subsidies or controls and/or a new public agency would have to be added to repair the damage. Support of these activities required a substantial shift of resources from the private to the public sector. Given the political inability to cover all the costs via taxation and the weakness of the domestic capital market, the transfer was accomplished via inflation and foreign borrowing. . . ."[5]

The military government did not create "the high chronic unemployment and under-employment," nor the "significant absolute poverty" nor the myriad of other problems cited in the preceding recital—though you would rarely know this from a reading of press or even scholarly accounts of the period. But this was the statist mold, forty years in forming, that Augusto Pinochet and his associates set out to break. He brought to the task a profound conviction:

"Without incurring in determinist excesses," he said, "we can point out that in the inter-relationship between the economic and the social and political orders, economic freedom is a necessary requisite for the existence of a truly free political system."[6]

To break that mold meant breaking forty years of deeply ingrained psychic and social as well as economic deformities. Ordinary citizens—from farmers to bankers and businessmen, from students to housewives, churchmen to union leaders, and even sportsmen—had come to look to the state as Big Brother, the arbiter, the catalyst, the court of last resort for all problems. It meant overcoming the resistance of a bloated and entrenched bureaucracy, not only opposed ideologically to the radical ideas of a market economy but (understandably) fearful of the menace the new strategies of a diminished state apparatus posed to their own power, their very jobs. It meant restoring the rationality of the market to prices, and that inevitably meant sharp price increases, some of them shockingly so. To break the mold meant, too, ending import substitution strategies that, in effect, built a high tariff wall around the Chilean economy. Those strategies had created not only business fortunes, but tens of thousands of jobs in industries that were inefficient, expensive. A 1969 study revealed some of the implications of these policies for consumers—and industrialists:

TABLE 41

CHILE: PRICE COMPARISONS, SELECTED METAL-MECHANICAL
PRODUCTS (First Semester, 1969) (US Dollars)

PRODUCT	PRICE IN CHILE[a]	INTERNATIONAL PRICE[b]
Electric sewing machine	366	120
Automatic washing machine	510	200
Home refrigerator	498	80
Gas stove	177	63
Air conditioner	1,156	150
TV set	415	110
Bicycle	133	27
Disc for farm implements	17	10
Industrial abrasive wheel	281	95
Electric drill press	593	140
3-phase motor, $1/2$ HP	101	33

[a] Ex-factory or wholesale, with exception of washing machine, which is priced at the consumer level.
[b] CIF Valparaíso

Source: Adapted from *Chile: An Economy in Transition*, p. 34, citing a survey by Chilean Steel Institute, in Edmar Bacha and Lance Taylor, "Growth and Trade Distortions in Chile and their Implications in Calculating the Shadow Price of Foreign Exchange." *Analysis of Development Problems: Studies of the Chilean Economy*, North-Holland, Amsterdam, 1973, p. 129.

Clearly, tearing down those walls, bringing Chile fully into the world economy, was risky. And it was bound to be painful. There could be but one justification: that the Chile that would emerge would be better than the mess the country was in when the revolution began.

Chileans, by the thousands, began to bet that it would be better from the earliest days. Just as thousands fled or were forced to leave the country, so, too, did many voluntary exiles return: an estimated twenty thousand in those first few years. The World Bank study indicates that in 1974, more than $12 million of foreign exchange was sold to the

Central Bank by private individuals, "indicating substantial capital repatriation." Upper-class Chileans showed their confidence in yet another way in the early months of excruciating crisis, when the government's vaults were very nearly empty: in the first six months, the Central Bank reported receiving 46,331 units of jewelry, works of art, watches, gold and silver coins—citizen donations to the work of rebuilding the shattered country.[7]

Economies are, of course, more than a matter of growth rates. But, pending closer inspection of key elements in the socio-economic picture in succeeding sections, growth rates are a valid point of departure. As the following table demonstrates, once the hemorrhage was brought under control, Pinochet's "Chicago Boys" created a more robust economic corpus for Chile than had any of the three preceding regimes. (The table takes into account only the last four years of Alessandri, and the period up until the 1982 crash, which will be examined in a later section.)

TABLE 42

CHILE vs. LATIN AMERICA: AVERAGE ANNUAL GROWTH RATES, GROSS DOMESTIC PRODUCT, 1961–1981 (Alessandri, Frei, Allende & Pinochet administrations) (Percentages)

YEAR	CHILE[a]	LATIN AMERICA[b]
THE ALESSANDRI YEARS		
1961	4.8	4.3
1962	4.7	3.5
1963	6.3	7.3
1964	2.2	5.1
THE FREI YEARS		
1965	.8	4.7
1966	11.2	4.5
1967	3.2	6.0
1968	3.6	7.1
1969	3.7	6.8
1970	2.1	6.7
THE ALLENDE YEARS		
1971	9.0	6.8
1972	−1.2	7.0
1973	−5.6	8.3

TABLE 42 (*Continued*)

YEAR	CHILE[a]	LATIN AMERICA[b]
	THE PINOCHET YEARS	
1974	1.0	7.0
1975	−12.9	3.8
1976	3.5	5.4
1977	9.9	4.8
1978	8.2	5.1
1979	8.3	6.5
1980	7.5	5.9
1981	5.3	1.7

Source: Banco Central de Chile; Adapted from Jorge Rodríguez Grossi, ed., *Perspectivas Económicas Para La Democracia: Balance y Lecciones Para La Experiencia Chilena* (Santiago: Instituto Chileno de Estudios Humanísticos, 1984), p. 32.

Admiral José Toribio Merino Castro, the man in overall command of the economy during those first days, brought to his awesome task the discipline, dedication, and relentlessness he would bring to a major military campaign. For months after the September revolution, he and every other top naval officer involved with economic affairs virtually barricaded themselves in Santiago at what came to be called "the house of the admirals." "We visited our families Saturdays and Sundays— visited, that is, when the workload allowed it. Otherwise, every night after work, we dined together and then went on well into the night, discussing the problems of the various ministries under our responsibility, adding in the process hours and hours of fruitful labor and coordination. It was," said the commander-in-chief of Chile's navy, "the longest 'cruise' of my life."[8]

The times called for steady nerves and strong medicine. They called those "the heroic days."

Merino also brought to the task "The Brick." This was the name the authors gave to their blueprint for a new Chilean economy. Since August of 1972, ten, mainly young, economists had been striving, under the overall "command" of the retired admiral, Roberto Kelly, to prepare for the day, if ever it would come, to rebuild their divided and disintegrating country. Finally, in May of 1973, with work on the plan snarled, Kelly summoned the group to the Hotel San Martín in Viña del Mar. There, they smoothed over their differences, and Emilio Sanfuentes Vergara was assigned the job of producing a five-page summary. Among that original core group of ten were a number who would occupy cabinet posts in the new administration. Besides Kelly—who himself would hold two ministerial posts—the "elder statesman" among them was Sergio de Castro, in one sense the original "Chicago Boy" in Chile. De Castro was then forty-three; none of the others was older than thirty-eight. All, in one fashion or another, would go on to play key roles in the future of their country; de Castro, for example, would go on to serve from 1975 to 1982 in the Cabinet, first as economy minister, then as finance minister. The others: Alvaro Bardón Muñoz, later President of the Central Bank; Manuel Cruzat Infante, founder of one of the most dynamic financial conglomerates in Chilean history; Juan Braun, who became one of his top executives; Pablo Baraona Urzua, also a Central Bank president and economy minister; Andrés Sanfuentes Vergara, academic, and his brother, Emilio, a business executive (and protégé of both Baraona and de Castro, "rescued" from his career as a sociologist and sent to study economics at Chicago); Sergio Undurraga Saavedra, who would run the State Development Corporation office in New York; Juan Villarzu Rohde, later the budget director; José Luis Zabala Ponce, director of research for the Central Bank. On September 11, the day of revolution, the photocopying machines of *El Mercurio* worked overtime to churn out numbered copies of the 187-page document, *Políticas de Desarrollo* (cited in the preceding chapter).

On September 14, a navy car pulled up at de Castro's house on Oxford Street in Santiago to inform him that Admiral Merino wanted to see him—pronto. Arriving, he was escorted to the fifth floor by a guard pointing a submachine gun at his gut. Merino, totally unknown to him, burst in, informed him that he had been named to advise the new economy minister, General Rolando González Acevedo, and left as abruptly as he had come. Shortly afterwards, the minister appeared. He had "The Brick" under his arm. The next day, they went to work.[9]

"Be Brief—We're Three Years Behind." That sign was everywhere to be seen in government offices spartan to the point of shabbiness during those early, intense days of free market revolution. Differences—and there were strong ones—were mainly muted in the spirit of camaraderie so common to acute crisis.[10] The economic team of free-marketers assembled by Merino quickly agreed on goals. There was never any doubt as to the first priority: tame inflation. Emilio Sanfuentes, one of the key Chicago boys, would, in fact, describe inflation as the "number one, number two, and number three priority."[11]

Substituting the market for the state in the economy meant high priority for monetary policy, traditionally given short shrift when not ignored altogether in Chile. That meant declaring war on the practice of using printing press money to cover mostly government deficits, but also on the Byzantine credit needs of the private sector. (Despite a number of tough measures and false starts, the regime was unable to slow growth in the money supply during the early years.) It meant, also, creating rational exchange rates and rules, and in this, they mostly succeeded—though also with a few false starts. As to goals, Merino blocked out three large ones:

(1) Exploit the country's farm, timber, mineral, and off-shore resources as never before. The result would be to develop a broad-based export economy, ending the tyranny of dependence on a single export commodity subject to the whims of foreign demand and pricing practices.

(2) Substitute private enterprise for state enterprise, returning illegally seized companies to their legitimate owners, selling off others (the word "privatizing" had not yet become fashionable).

(3) Allow the market rather than the state to dictate prices and control production and distribution decisions. This meant scrapping the patchwork of regulations that led to such insanities as a full sack of subsidized cement during the Allende years costing less than an empty sack would cost on the free market.

To achieve many of these goals, two other conditions needed to be met: belt-tightening in government, and an about-face on attitudes towards foreign investment. After nearly a decade of harassment, foreign investors now found themselves being courted.

The new stewards of Chile's economy enjoyed a "breather" lasting not even one year. Copper prices, which began a steady climb after skidding to a 1971–1972 low, hit a record high of $1.52 per pound on April 2, 1974. Copper production also rose to record levels: from 735,000 tons in 1973 to 902,000 in 1974. Agricultural output showed a phenomenal 16.7 percent increase over 1974, construction 20 percent. Overall, in real terms, 1974 gross domestic product rose 5.7 percent over 1973.* By September, a buoyant Admiral Merino was describing the economic situation as "very promising . . . there is confidence, confidence at home, confidence abroad. There is investment and there is a dynamic which leads us to believe that the economic recovery of Chile is already well underway."[12]

He spoke too soon—nearly two years too soon.

* This figure reflects GDP change in real terms, and is taken from *Chile: An Economy in Transition*, op. cit., p. 95. According to that study, the 1974 growth rate was 5.7; 1975, − 11.3; 1976, 4.1; and 1977, 8.6.

THE DARK YEARS

High copper prices and increased resource flows from foreign lenders helped to sustain a mild recovery in 1974, but both sources of support collapsed in 1975 with a combined resource loss to the economy equivalent to about 12.5 percent of the 1974 GDP. Since that time, the copper price has remained at its lowest level, in real terms, in more than two decades, while foreign official lenders have been substantial net extractors of resources from the economy.

Chile: An Economy in Transition,
op. cit., p. 164

Since there is no conceivable combination of external circumstances which could wreak comparable havoc in the much more broadly diversified and dominating (as opposed to dependent) U.S. economy, there is no easy way to project the consequences of an externally produced jolt to the U.S. economy equivalent to 12.5 percent of gross domestic product. But it does give some sense of the magnitude of the calamity to understand that the year-to-year fall in the Chilean economy which it engendered (17 percent, in real terms) was as though the United States economy had plunged that year by an amount roughly equal to the combined value of all U.S. agriculture, mining, construction, and transportation/communication sectors.

The steep fall in copper prices cost the country $826 million in 1975, equivalent to 10 percent of the previous year's GDP. To make matters worse, 1974 was the first year of the world-wide "oil shock." Oil imports which cost Chile $148 million in 1973 cost the country $481 million in 1974, $257 million in 1975 (down not in price but in volume, as the economy itself all but collapsed), $392 million in 1976. Wheat and fertilizer prices jumped sharply; even sugar prices, through cartel pressure and a fluke buying decision in Japan, skyrocketed (from $4 a ton in 1972, to $10-$12 by December 1973, to $26 early in 1974). The combination of lower copper prices and higher prices for imported goods meant the terms of trade effect equalled about 12 percent of GDP.[13]

Inflation was slowed somewhat during 1974—but it was still a staggering 376 percent. Massive wage increases during the year failed to keep up with the inflation they were helping to fuel: 500 percent cost-of-living adjustment in January, again in July by 20 percent to 40 percent, and in October, by 24 percent. In 1975, inflation began to career seemingly out of control once again in the first half of the year; it was only through severe austerity measures that it was reduced to single-digit numbers beginning in July, but the price rise for the year still averaged

341 percent. Open unemployment reached 20 percent of the labor force in Greater Santiago despite an emergency government program giving jobs to about one-third of the unemployed. Michael Fleet wrote of "many families reduced to begging for a living and forced to live on survival diets of low-grade wheat bread and other grains." Per capita food consumption dropped 4.8 percent in 1974, and 14.8 percent in 1975. Wrote the World Bank study mission: "It would be hard to overstate the enormous material sacrifice endured by the Chilean people through this period. The loss of real income and employment brought severe and widespread hardship, particularly for the urban unemployed who lacked a cushion of accumulated savings to fall back on."

It was Chile's worst depression since the 1930s. By the time full recovery was achieved, the various shocks suffered since 1970 had, "in a global sense, cost the nation a full decade of economic growth."[14]

I think of the counter-inflation policy as the performance of a pilot trying to dip under a dense fog, bringing the plane closer and closer to the ground in order to regain vision—at the risk of not having enough space to pull out of his perilous dive.

> Author/journalist Robert Moss, writing early in the war to rescue Chile's threatened economy from yet another collapse.[15]

Nobel laureate Milton Friedman, one of the intellectual mentors of the regime's "Chicago Boys," was summoned to Chile early in 1975 to advise on shock treatment.[16] On April 14, Economy Minister Fernando Léniz was replaced by Sergio de Castro. Even more importantly, another "Chicago Boy," thirty-nine-year-old Jorge Cauas Lama, who had joined the Cabinet on July 11, 1974, as finance minister, was given control over virtually all spending and financing decisions throughout the public sector. The perilous dive beneath the dense fog had begun.

Cauas, a lifelong Christian Democrat who had served as one of the original members of the team of young technocrats devising Eduardo Frei's economic program, and later as number two in the Central Bank under Frei, had agreed to give up a lucrative—and "safe"—job as director of the World Bank's Studies Department in 1974 to return to embattled Chile as an advisor to Raúl Sáez, himself then in a pivotal advisory role. In common with a number of other so-called Chicago Boys, he had not studied there, but at Columbia University (as did another later kingpin of the economy, Hernán Büchi Buc). But he did buy into the Chicago school ideas, and was now given virtual *carte blanche* control over nine ministers. Pivotal to it all was a newly created Monetary Council which he chaired. Members included the minister of economy, the minister-director of the National Planning Office (ODEPLAN), the president of the Central Bank, and a member representing

President Pinochet. The Council set personnel limits as well as peso and foreign currency spending levels for each ministry and decentralized agency. CORFO, which remained the holding company for state-owned companies still dominant in the economy, was subordinated to the "super-minister" Cauas as well. Viewing the calamity on all sides, Cauas said his first job was "to neutralize the bombs buried in the system." He defined those "bombs" as the distorted price system, monetary supply and demand, lack of discipline (and with it low productivity in the workplace), and the chaotic exchange rate system. He set a goal of reaching a growth rate above 7 percent by 1977, 10 percent by 1980. The first was reached, the second narrowly missed.

Among Cauas' immediate targets for shock treatment was the government itself, on both the revenue and spending sides. On the first, he was able to build on important steps already taken to increase government revenues. Central to these were tax reforms implemented beginning late in 1973 and early in 1974. One was revaluation for tax purposes of agricultural and nonagricultural real estate, by factors of thirty and ten respectively. Severe penalties were introduced for tax evasion. Corporate tax rates were raised, and there was a one-time collection on corporate net worth. Corporate tax rates, on the other hand, were lowered from 62.2 to 48.6 percent. Elimination of the black market, the shift of import activity back to the private sector, the abolishing of the tariff exemption granted public agencies, and improved tax administration also contributed to enhanced tax collections. Important, too, was the return of copper taxes: in 1973, the federal treasury had collected negligible receipts from copper. All told, those measures produced a 62 percent increase in tax collections in 1974 over 1973—all the more extraordinary in the years immediately following, remembering that the economy was flat on its back. On December 31, 1974, these and other measures were incorporated in a sweeping tax reform law; among its innovations was a 20 percent value-added tax (VAT) in place of a long-standing "cascading" sales tax. Income and property taxes, and the excise taxes on luxury goods, were all jacked up another 10 percent as part of the April 1975 austerity program, and exemptions to the VAT eliminated on all but a few basic commodities (milk, wheat, bread, fresh fruits and vegetables, books and magazines).[17] The World Bank study found that the effect of those changes "has undoubtedly been an improvement" in the system's fairness: "equal treatment of equal incomes and probably an increase in the direct tax system's overall progressivity as well." Although some of these were textbook market economy measures designed to stimulate business, the bulk of them were aimed at increasing collections from the upper-income sectors of Chilean society; not at benefitting the rich, but soaking them. One searches press reports of the time in vain for even a mention of this.

What one does find is a plethora of stories such as the *Washington Post* service article that inspired this headline: "Chile Shifts Fiscal Policy—But Will It Aid Poor?"[18]

On the spending side, Cauas and his colleagues took aim at the public enterprises still in state hands. Although by 1975, the government had divested itself of most of the companies illegally seized under Allende, one in four persons in the work force was still on the government payroll. Of Chile's 100 largest nonfinancial enterprises, by book value, the companies in which the state still owned 50 percent or more of the shares as late as the end of 1976 accounted for 79 percent of total assets and 81 percent of net worth. All ten of the biggest and twenty of the twenty-five biggest enterprises were in state hands. Under Allende, those companies were forced to increase their work forces greatly—enabling Allende to boast, thus, of how he had lowered unemployment. Conversely, their prices were frozen. In the period mid-1972 to mid-1973, the consumer price index rose sevenfold. During that same period, the prices charged by the state steel company declined in real terms by 80 percent; electric company rates lost 90 percent of their real value; despite rising international oil prices, the inflation-adjusted price of petroleum sales fell 79 percent. Obviously, those companies could remain alive only so long as money remained in the treasury to bail them out. By September 1973, there was none. Furthermore, those public companies had built up a debt larger than all the money then in the hands of the private sector. Early in the Pinochet government, virtually all prices and interest rates were freed to find their own levels. The government moved to restore economic health to the companies under its control: petroleum prices were raised elevenfold, steel and electricity prices sixfold, and telephone rates more than doubled. Simultaneously, state enterprises were put on a pay-your-own-way-basis. Deprived of subsidies (and, increasingly, the protection of high tariff barriers), a number of companies went bankrupt: among those which went under were such giants as SUMAR and MADECO. Inevitably, these radical and rapid moves into a market economy set off a number of price "shocks." No price-support decision was more controversial than removing the subsidies for bread; bread prices tripled in the first six months of junta rule. The flip side of that: bread subsidies were, by the end of Allende's rule, costing a government whose own financial cupboard was very nearly bare 7 billion escudos per month—and no bread was to be found, except in the black market. But the poor had precious little—if any—access to the black market. (If city dwellers were the losers, small farmers, and particularly the poorest and most traditionally neglected among them, were the winners, a topic for later discussion.) By mid-1975, all but two of the important public enterprises were operating at a profit.[19]

The bloated government bureaucracy itself was another target. Admiral Merino had estimated that 37 percent of the government's own payroll was redundant; by April 1976, it had been cut by 30 percent. A case in point was CORFO, created as a development agency but which, under Allende, became a giant holding company for the companies swallowed up by his government. By the time he fell, it had 6,200 employees. By late November, that number was down to 1,600—and heading for half of that.

As a result of the increased revenues and deep spending cuts, the federal budget was in the black in 1975 (in current dollars) for only the second time in twenty-five years.[20] Even more remarkably, it stayed in the black until the 1982 crash; remarkable not only because of the severely adverse terms of trade, and politically motivated foreign credit squeeze, but because Chile rapidly began also once again to honor its international debt obligations. Those policies also enabled a government which inherited a treasury bereft of cash reserves—and thus defenseless in the face of the agonizing crunch on the economy and Chile's people—to build back its foreign reserves to $455 million by 1976. The following table, using 1976 dollars as a common denominator, reflects the spending/income trends:

TABLE 43
EXPENDITURES, REVENUES, AND FISCAL DEFICIT
(Millions of 1976 Dollars)

	1972	1973	1974	1975	1976	1977
Total Expenditures	3.576	4.858	3.536	2.607	2.540	2.699
Debt Service	122	145	483	447	566	435
Total Revenues	2.082	2.187	2.391	2.360	2.313	2.499
Direct Taxes	486	566	623	674	515	564
Indirect Taxes	1.280	1.172	1.243	1.388	1.384	1.553
Non-tax Revenues	145	158	277	105	62	68
Customs Duties/ Adjustments	126	260	—	—	—	—
Copper	45	29	248	193	352	314
Deficit	−1.494	−2.672	−1.146	− 247	− 227	− 200

Source: Indicadores Económicos y Sociales 1960–1985 (Santiago: Central Bank of Chile, 1986), p. 47. All figures have been rounded to nearest whole number. Expressed in current dollars, the surplus in 1975 was $111 million, in 1976, $85 million, and 1977, $24 million. (See table on p. 45, same report, for current dollar figures.)

Merino was, himself, one of the "casualties" of the 1975 crisis. Ailing, he was forced to step aside for several months, turning over command to Vice Admiral Patricio Carvajal.[21]

Other elements in the move into a market economy—and then out of the cauldron of depression—bear brief examination:

MONETARY AND EXCHANGE POLICY

Over the years, the government exerted control over monetary policy chiefly through its power to fix reserve requirements on commercial bank deposits, to set limits on credit expansion on a bank-by-bank basis, to rediscount commercial bank loans, and to fix interest rates. That power had become progressively subordinated to political ideology, culminating under Allende with the enforced incorporation of virtually the entirety of the private banking system into the state sector. For most years beginning in the 1930s, the maximum legal interest rate rarely exceeded the annual rate of inflation. Even with taxes and other charges added, the cost of borrowing money was "far below the real cost of capital." The result, for those fortunate enough to have access to the credit system, was to provide "a substantial subsidy" to borrowers. As the World Bank study also notes, "the allocation of credit became a function of administrative decision rather than of price and relative rates of return." The new government set about almost immediately to relax credit controls, and, two years later, to shift the banks back to private hands as well as introducing greater competition into the banking system. Interest rates, locked in at between 19 percent and 24 percent between 1966 and 1970, were raised to 60 percent late in 1973, to 90 percent in March 1974, and to 200 percent in May 1974, finally freed from all controls in May 1975. New financial institutions blossomed to meet the profit opportunities thus created. With the drop in inflation beginning at the end of 1975, real interest rates within Chile were extremely high compared to international rates. The result was to create a new profiteering situation in which a number of companies were willing to import goods at or even below cost so as to lay hands on foreign exchange trade credits which could then be turned over to the local money market. This had the further effect of stunting the development of an authentic domestic capital market, and of diverting funds away from productive investments. "Cheap" dollars also would later encourage a binge of consumer buying abroad, much of it on tenuous lines of credit. This policy, coupled with a stubborn insistence on maintaining an artificially low exchange rate was, arguably, the only serious policy blunder made by the regime's financial technocrats.[22]

With the elimination of the fiscal deficit, the private sector claimed an expanding share of credit, leading to the ending of quantitative credit controls in May 1976.

The administration's goal of curbing printing press money ran counter in the early days to the effects of the freeing of prices and government efforts to maintain employment and restore purchasing power. The result was that the money supply grew by 107 percent in the last quarter of 1973 alone, then dropped to the mid-20s percent through the first half of 1975, hitting 50 percent-plus levels twice during the crisis years of 1975–1976 before a brief respite in 1977–1978.

On May 26, 1975—fifteen years after Chile abandoned its inflation-ravaged peso for the escudo—the government announced that, as of September 1, the escudo would be junked in favor of a revived peso. At the time of the 1960 switch, the peso was trading at 1,000 to the dollar. The new peso, Central Bank President Pablo Baraona Urzúa said, would be worth 1,000 escudos. The escudo had been devalued 38 times since the revolution, 10 times in 1975 alone—the latest only a few days before, when the rate for imports and exports went from 4,100 escudos to 4,300 escudos to the dollar. The bank rate for changing money went from 4,500 to 4,800. At the heart of exchange policy was systematic devaluation, using a crawling peg system, which achieved its goal of stimulating exports during the time it was in place. After revaluations in July 1976 and March 1977, the peso again began a slow fall until it reached 39 to the dollar on June 30, 1979. The Central Bank kept it at that level until May of 1982—deep, too deep, into the financial crisis of that year.

Overall, monetary policy was clearly a conspicuous blot on the economic picture during the first ten years of junta rule.

DEBT

The International Monetary Fund (IMF) and the Inter-American Committee on the Alliance for Progress, recognizing that a massive rescue operation is necessary to keep the Chilean economy afloat— and the Junta in power—have called on the international financial community to provide a mini-Marshall Plan for Chile. In effect, the loans granted since the coup represent phase two of the U.S. counter-insurgency program in Chile—they prop up a brutal dictatorship which rules through terror but promises good investment opportunities for American businesses. Questions of creditworthiness are not even raised.

Elizabeth Farnsworth, writing in the
Fall 1974 issue of *Foreign Policy*[23]

The international community did not rally and mount a rescue operation. The IMF did grant a number of credits to Chile between 1974 and 1976 (as it had done eleven times before), but despite its own awesome economic problems, by 1978, Chile had repaid virtually every last dime of those credits. If there has been a U.S. counter-insurgency program in Chile, it has been, almost from the very beginning and down to the present day, designed to drive Augusto Pinochet from power, and, failing that, to undermine his government by every available legal means. American businesses, until very recently, were among the last to recognize and react to the investment opportunities in Chile. Questions of creditworthiness were not asked; Chile, as the World Bank study notes, was simply cut off by the international lending agencies, in keeping with the previously cited view expressed by the *New York Times* that "the time to restore economic aid, even for projects directly helpful to the poorest Chileans, is after the Government has revived the rule of law. . . ."[24]

In March 1974, the rich countries that make up the Paris Club did agree to reschedule 80 percent of Chile's debt due that year, and agreed to a smaller rescheduling the following year. It is hard to see how they might have done otherwise: of its total foreign debt of $4 billion, Chile owed $830 million in principal and interest in 1974, more than one-third of it unpaid bills carried over from the previous year. To pay that amount would have consumed 37 percent of the country's total merchandise export earnings. In 1975, when the bottom fell out of those earnings, payments would have claimed fully 48 percent of export income. Even with the concessions granted, the bill still came to 32.7 percent of merchandise export receipts. In 1976, Chile met its full debt service obligations without rescheduling for the first time since 1970—even though, to do so, the country had to pay out 36.5 percent of its export earnings. Although capitalist countries had continued to provide lending to Allende's Marxist-Leninist government, socialist countries suspended lending to capitalist Chile (without, of course, a deluge of articles in newspapers and learned journals about an "economic blockade").

The result of all of this, as indicated by the following table, is that far from benefiting from a helping hand from abroad, Chile—struggling to its feet—actually funneled more money into the vaults of the international agencies and rich countries than it got from them:

TABLE 44
RESOURCE FLOWS BETWEEN CHILE AND FOREIGN LENDERS, 1973–1977
(Millions of US dollars)

		1973	1974	1975	1976	1977
A.	Commitments	328	748	404	483	960
B.	Disbursements	316	540	287	433	570
C.	Repayments	−120	−199	−345	−548	−651
D.	Net Disbursements	196	341	− 58	−116	− 81
E.	Interest	− 37	− 79	−157	−209	−201
F.	Net Resource Flow	159	262	−214	−325	−282

Source: *Chile: An Economy in Transition*, op. cit., p. 110.

As the bank noted, the lending picture—favorable through 1974—
"changed abruptly in 1975, as foreign lenders were disenchanted by
Chile's deteriorating balance of payments situation, project pipelines
were exhausted, and external political attitudes hardened towards the
Pinochet Government." Private banks—less susceptible to political
pressure—took up some of the slack, providing $120 million in 1976,
$826 million in 1977. Thus, the report continued, "in 1977 private
banks accounted for 86 percent of total loan commitments to Chile, as
compared to less than 20 percent, on average, over the previous decade."
As to the mini-Marshall plan: "The international lenders withdrew
$214 million in foreign exchange in 1975, contributing significantly to
the foreign exchange crisis and the resultant economic contraction."[25]

TRADE AND FOREIGN INVESTMENT

In July 1974, the junta promulgated Decree Law 600, a new foreign
investment statute, designed to attract foreign investment and technology by guaranteeing foreign owners the same legal rights as national
investors. Between October 1974, when the Committee on Foreign
Investment began work, and August 1978, some 319 projects worth $2.5
billion were approved. Disappointingly, only about one-fifth of that
amount had actually entered the country to that point. "Decision 24"
was a major part of the problem.

The law specifically stipulated that all such investments would be
subject to the decidedly antiforeign investment Decision 24 of the
Andean Pact. Chile was one of the founders of the five-nation Andean
Pact, created on May 26, 1969. The other members were Bolivia, Colombia, Ecuador, and Peru, with Venezuela added later. The Pact represented an attempt to increase the integration process among these countries within the larger framework of the eleven-nation Latin Amer-

ican Free Trade Association (LAFTA), on the assumption that their economies were more compatible, thus facilitating a speedier dismantling of trade barriers. On July 1, 1971, Decision 24, a common investment code governing foreign investment in the five nations, went into effect, reflecting the ideas then in vogue among developmental economists that foreign capital threatened both sovereignty and genuine economic growth. The code severely limited the amounts and types of new foreign investment in the region, and contained a fade-out provision requiring either merger with local interests or outright sale to them.

No sooner had Chile's decision been announced than two of the member nations objected. After numerous diplomatic pirouettes, Chile finally withdrew from the pact in October 1976,[26] and in March 1977 announced a new and much more liberalized foreign investment law: the ownership fade-out requirement was eliminated, limits were removed on profit remittances and the only restriction on capital repatriation was that it could not begin for three years. The only other restriction governed access to local credit, which was limited by the state. The Investments Committee was streamlined and its procedures simplified. Results followed quickly.

As of December 1976, CORFO had sold or disposed of 439 of the 494 firms it had come to control. Of those remaining, government policy was that CORFO would retain control of twenty-three of them, including the national petroleum company (ENAP), the sugar industry (IANSA), electric company (CHILECTRA), steel company (CAP), and Petrochemical company. With Chile's exit from the Andean Pact, Argentine and Brazilian investors quickly announced plans to acquire some of them. The first major break-through came early in 1978, when Exxon Corporation concluded a $107 million deal to acquire the La Disputada copper mine. Actual investments flowing into—or out of—the country from 1973 to 1979 looked like this (in millions of dollars):

TABLE 45

DISINVESTMENT/INVESTMENT IN CHILE, 1973–1979

1973	1974	1975	1976	1977	1978	1979
−4.8	−556.8	+49.8	−1.2	+16.3	+177.8	+232.6

Source: Economic and Social Progress in Latin America, 1980–1981 Report (Washington: Inter-American Development Report, 1982), p. 432.

Of the $2.5 billion in investments approved between 1974 and August 1978, 89.5 percent were in mining ($2.2 billion); 6.7 percent were in industry ($168 million); 2.7 percent were in services ($64 million), and the rest were in energy/fuel, transport, agriculture, and construction.

Along with attracting new investors, the government set out quickly to mend fences with old investors. The first among them was the Dow Chemical Company, which had come to Chile in 1967 in a joint venture with the Chilean government. On September 25, 1972, Petrodow employees went on strike, and three weeks later, the Allende government "requisitioned" the plant—despite a "counter-strike" by supervisors and professional staff against the takeover. Two days after the revolution, Dow was invited to return, and on January 4, 1974, Dow's Concepción and Santiago plants and other properties were formally returned to the company. In rapid order that year, Chile settled claims with Cerro Corporation ($3.2 million in cash, $38.6 million in seventeen-year notes), Bank of America, and International Fibers. On October 24, 1974, Chile reached agreement to settle Kennecott Copper Company's claim for expropriation of its El Teniente mine for $68 million: $6.5 million in cash, the balance in sixteen semi-annual payments at 6 percent annual interest. As indicated earlier, Chile had settled all outstanding claims by the end of 1977—saving American taxpayers tens of millions of dollars, since virtually all of the expropriated companies were insured by the U.S. government's Overseas Private Investment Corporation.

Nor were investment opportunities limited to foreigners. The new economic frontiers opened up by the revolution brought out the entrepreneurial spirit in a whole generation of Chileans. One such group, called "The Piranhas" for their nontraditional business enthusiasm, included thirty-nine-year-old Javier Vial Castillo, an agronomist. Discussing his investment plans early in the revolution, Vial said: "We are playing double or nothing now. . . . I want to be rich in a rich country. I'm not at all interested in being rich in a poor country."[27]

Perhaps in no area was the new government's success more immediate or spectacular as it was in trade. Foreign trade operations were resumed fifteen days after the revolution, with top priority at first given to food and medicine imports. Financing of trade, formerly a monopoly of the Central Bank, was rapidly decentralized, with all national banks assigned quotas for carrying out operations.

Under Allende, imports had been subject to a rat's nest of duties averaging 94 percent and rising to in excess of 500 percent. By June 5, 1974, the average had been chopped to 67 percent, the maximum to 140 percent; by August 13, 1975, those figures were 44 percent and 90 percent, respectively; by March of 1978, 15 percent and 20 percent, and, finally, in June of 1979, to a flat 10 percent for all but a handful of imports (automobiles chief among the exceptions).

From mid-April of 1974, the government ended import controls on about 2,400 different products—a process of simplification that continued in the years following. The new rules yielded dramatic results: in just the first five months of 1974, imports totalled $963.6 million—up 356.3 percent over the same period in 1973.

In a free market environment, exports showed similar improvements. As the World Bank study observed—"consistent with its general policy of assigning the role of price determination and resource allocation to the marketplace"—the government did not offer major subsidies or special incentives to exporters. Instead, progress came mainly from rationalization of the exchange rate, lowering of import restrictions, and elimination of administrative and bureaucratic obstacles. In March 1974, the report adds, the large tax drawbacks provided by the Allende government were reduced to zero. The result: "Despite the generally sluggish world economy, non-copper exports grew rapidly . . . non-copper exports doubled in value from 1973 to 1974. From 1974 to 1977, industrial exports doubled again, while agricultural exports almost tripled in value. . . . By 1978, the share of industrial exports in the total had risen to 31 percent, compared with only 8 percent in 1973. . . . Chilean exports were shipped to 90 major different countries in 1977, double the 1973 number. . . ."[28] Admiral Merino spoke of the opportunities early in the process: "There are 200,000 possible crewmen the length of Chile's coasts, enough for a 1,000,000-ton fishing fleet. Riches of fabulous potential, so well exploited by Denmark and Norway, for example. . . . But in few areas of the world can a boat leave port in the morning, as in Chile, and return in two hours with 120 tons of fish aboard." As indicated earlier, developing the country's latent forest products industry was given high priority. Said Merino: "While we've been dying of hunger in Chile, we've been sitting on a treasure chest of gold, and only needed the key to open it."[29] The following two tables vividly reflect the success of the export policy:

TABLE 46

NON-COPPER EXPORTS, 1971–1978 (Millions of dollars)

YEAR	OTHER MINING	AGRICULTURE[a]	INDUSTRIAL	TOTAL
1971	116	39	140	295
1972	105	21	103	229
1973	127	25	103	255
1974	157	57	308	523
1975	185	86	391	662
1976	197	119	520	836
1977	216	160	628	1,003

[a] Includes primary forest and fisheries products.

Source: Adapted from Chile: An Economy in Transition, op. cit., Table III.8, p. 108.

TABLE 47
SELECTED NON-COPPER EXPORTS, 1970, 1973, AND 1977

	1970	1973	1977P
Agricultural:			
Fresh fruit	11.8	14.0	63.6
Beans, onions & garlic	7.0	4.8	30.7
Wool	6.4	0.0	15.0
Manufactures:			
Fishmeal	15.5	13.6	86.5
Frozen shellfish	6.2	1.8	26.2
Sawn pinewood	3.7	2.5	54.6
Other wood products	5.4	2.1	15.8
Paper and pulp	31.5	29.8	134.4
Chemicals/petrochemicals	7.3	4.6	77.9
Basic metals	23.5	28.3	103.2

P provisional. *Source:* Ibid., Table III.9, p. 108.

Thus it was that an economy which, until 1974 had generated no more than 10-13 percent of its gross national product from exports, was well on its way to reaching a 30 percent-plus figure—one of the basic elements in the success stories of the "miracle economies" of the Pacific Rim.

The economy responded rapidly to the new strategies. By the first quarter of 1976, the depression bottomed out. In 1976, gross domestic product grew by 4.5 percent; in 1977, by 8.6 percent. Unemployment, which had peaked at 19.1 percent in the Greater Santiago area in August 1976, was down to 12.2 percent in November (9.2 percent of the people were out of work, the rest were entering the job market for the first time). Underemployment fell sharply during 1977 as well. Inflation, cut in half from 1975 to 1976, was more than halved again in 1977, to 63.5 percent.[30]

The man who had presided over the turn around—Jorge Cauas—was given an important new assignment going into 1977: ambassador to the United States. Now with Jimmy Carter in the White House, the United States was more hostile than ever, but still vital to Chile's hopes of full recovery. In his place went those battle-scarred Chicago boys: Sergio de Castro, from his post as economy minister, while Pablo Baraona left the presidency of the Central Bank to take his place as economy minister.

Looking back on it, the World Bank team wrote:

> These policies (orthodox monetary and fiscal policies, devaluation of the exchange rate, drastic cut in public spending, tax increases and

credit tightening) have been widely criticized for having caused the steep recession that followed. While one may argue the relative merits of different approaches to managing the crisis, however, it is clear that the massive foreign exchange constraint made recession inevitable, whatever the policies adopted. . . . Given the magnitude of the crisis faced and resource constraints that strapped the system, one views the Chilean situation in 1975 with a profound sense of helplessness. There were, perhaps, additional measures that might have been taken to shift more resources toward reduction of the worst suffering, but it is difficult to visualize a major change in the picture without considerably more outside assistance than the international community was evidently prepared to offer. . . ."[31]

Both because it sheds light on a little-noted aspect of the severe recession/depression scenario, and because of the implications for the future of Chile, brief discussion of the social safety net created by the government is in order.

Those measures gave the lie to the careless and common charges about policies designed to favor the rich at the expense of the poor. As the World Bank study showed, "the squeeze placed on middle- and upper-income groups generally is illustrated by the real increases on taxes on income and property that occurred during the fall in output. In relative terms, it is perhaps these groups whose net incomes suffered the most from the austerity program *per se.*" Then, in yet another passage: "Another impact of the freezing of prices was the sharp explosion of wholesale relative to consumer prices, suggesting a substantial squeeze on the earnings of retail merchants. . . ."[32] Obviously, as the report goes on to note, the rich are in a far better position than are the poor to ride out economic tempests; the point is whether the government, in trying to make the best of a horrendous situation, compounded the plight of the poor or tried to help them.

Much of the argument centers on the freeing of prices, particularly of foodstuffs. The case of bread has already been discussed. It is pointless to boast of how caring a government is because it provides subsidies with money it no longer has to support a product that disappears from the marketplace anyway. But there is yet another hidden aspect to this: the significant shift of income produced by the freeing of prices toward the traditionally poorest segment of the country's employed workers— farmers. The report notes that prior to 1965, "it was clearly the larger farmers who benefited most from the administered price and subsidy system. Access to subsidies was opened to the land reform beneficiaries during the 1965–1973 period, and they have undoubtedly been hurt by their elimination. Most *minifundistas* [small farmers] and tenant farmers, on the other hand, remained at the end of the subsidy line historically and have probably benefited from the recently improved

prices of the goods they market. . . . [Thus,] while the freeing of prices
. . . of 'basic' commodities may on balance have been regressive from a
distributive standpoint, the many other benefits and controls that have
been removed had clearly been benefiting primarily the middle- and
upper-income groups. It was the latter who were the principal users of
subsidized electric power, gasoline, credit or capital goods. Indeed, to
the extent that such subsidies encouraged the substitution of capital for
labor, the resultant loss of jobs and absolute income was concentrated
among lower-income groups. . . ."[33]

Between 1965, when large-scale expropriations began, and 1973,
when they ended, almost 10 million hectares of agricultural land was
expropriated—almost half of Chile's arable land—and 60 percent of the
irrigated land. Under Frei's government, most beneficiaries were located
on nine hundred cooperative settlements (asentados), and it was only in
1970 that the first of the 20,000–30,000 families on them were offered
title to the land. Allende greatly accelerated the takeover pace, but
offered no titles. Under Allende, a huge bureaucracy scattered through
twenty-seven independent agencies was involved in agrarian "reform."
The Pinochet government halted expropriations, returned illegally
seized land to owners—and granted titles to 45,000 farmers. The
bureaucracy was largely dismantled. Overall, the agriculture sector
grew rapidly and constantly. Though the jury was still out on the impact
on individual farmers, the World Bank mission concluded that "these
changes in structure and policy have laid the basis for a more rapid and
efficient long-term growth of agricultural output and income, enabling
Chilean agriculture to become in the near future a net earner of foreign
exchange after decades of rising deficits. . . . The few surveys that have
been done indicate a healthy tendency toward the more intensive use of
both land and labor in the reformed sector. Moreover, reform beneficiaries have demonstrated a high propensity to use modern inputs,
despite the removal of subsidies, and a high level of industrialization.
On the other hand, output is constrained by serious undercapitaliza-
tion, medium and long-term financing is extremely scarce, the institutional supports previously provided both by cooperatives and by
government agencies have been weakened, and a rising proportion of the
titled parcels are reportedly being sold or otherwise transferred to persons from outside the reformed sector. . . ."[34]

To meet the crisis in the cities, the government, in March 1975,
launched a Minimum Employment Program (PEM), financed by the
central government but administered by local governments. Preference
was given to heads of households; wages were set at approximately 75
percent of the monthly minimum wage. Although then ineligible for
other benefits, an estimated 50,000 workers received food rations dis-

tributed monthly under a program funded by the U.S. Agency for International Development. By the end of 1975, PEM gave work to 125,000 workers; by the end of 1976, that number had swollen to a quarter of a million, or almost 7 percent of the labor force. By December 1978, that number was down to 118,000 workers. Cost of the program rose from $34.8 million in 1975 to an estimated $84 million in 1977.

On still another front, the government in 1974 made sweeping reforms in the unemployment insurance program, "including bringing the manual work force within a true insurance program for the first time." Progress it was; perfection it was not: only about one-seventh or one-eighth of those reported as unemployed in 1976 qualified for benefits under it. Yet another strong commitment was made in job training: as of January 1977, employers were given income tax credits to provide special training for their workers. During 1977, more than 300 enterprises took advantage of the program, providing training for 55,000 workers. An additional 40,000—in the fields of agriculture, forestry, and fishing, as well as some PEM workers—received training under National Training and Employment Service scholarships. Finally, so as to stimulate employment opportunities for youth and seniors, in April 1978, President Pinochet ordered gradual elimination of the minimum wage for persons under age twenty-three or over age sixty-five (and gradual reduction in real terms for others).

Other measures included a transportation allowance, which the report noted "resulted in a substantial improvement of low-paid blue-collar workers relative to those at the bottom of the white-collar pay schedule"; and the rapid improvement in the real minimum wage. Taken together, the report said, while "it is difficult to draw clear-cut conclusions about the redistributive impact of wage policies within the working class . . . the only statement that can be made with any degree of confidence is that employed, manual, minimum-wage recipients have improved their position relative to any other broad grouping of wage or salary earners."

Two other programs bear mention: a 1975 wage subsidy program was put in place, providing employers with benefits equal to one-half the minimum wage for each worker hired over and above the number employed at the end of a base month. By December of 1977, 42,000 workers were being subsidized under the program.

Steps were also started in the early days of the revolution to modernize the chaotic social security system—subject for a later section. When the Pinochet government came to power, thirty-five different social security institutions administered more than two hundred different funds. Recognized as suffering "serious deficiencies" for at least twenty years, efforts at "reform" had, until then, made the system less workable. Under political pressure, the ratio of pensioners to active contributors to the system rose from 10 percent in 1955 to 31 percent by 1975. Despite reductions, social security payroll taxes in 1977 still averaged 40 percent of the taxable payroll. Evasion, inevitably, was widespread. To make matters worse, the system had long discriminated against manual workers, the lowest paid group covered by the system.[35]

Often overlooked in reports on the new economic strategies is the obvious: however grand the slogans, a poor economy impoverishes all. Only through growth, genuine growth, are benefits available for distribution. The World Bank report took note of that: "Apart from progressively reducing the regressive inflation 'tax,' the greatest contribution of the new strategy to the long-term improvement of income distribution will perhaps derive from the enhanced prospects for employment generation derived from faster growth and more rational pricing. . . . The principle of the new approach is sound. A large proportion of past subsidy programs, financed to a considerable degree by inflation, went to the benefit of the middle-income groups while dealing very inefficiently with the relief of poverty. . . ."[36]

BRIGHT DAYS

Chile should lend us its economic team. Economists who can simultaneously cut inflation, tariffs and unemployment, will be welcome in Washington.

> Wall Street Journal, in an 1980 commentary on Chile's economic recovery[37]

The "Chicago Boys" did all of that and more.

Measured from December to December, the consumer price index in Chile had shot up 163.4 percent in 1972; 508.1 percent in 1973; 375.9 percent in 1974; 340.7 percent in 1976. By 1977, it was down to a manageable (by Latin American standards) 65.3 percent increase; the next year, 30.3 percent; in 1979, 38.9 percent, in 1980, 31.2 percent, and in 1981, 9.5 percent.

Import duties, as noted, which had soared as high as 700 percent for some goods under Allende, were all but flattened at 10 percent in June 1979.

Unemployment,* which had peaked at 19.8 percent in the second quarter of 1976, was down to 12.8 percent by the end of 1977—and there

---

* All figures are for Greater Santiago which, as noted earlier, are the only reliable figures for employment/unemployment until very recent years.

was reason to believe that may have been overstated. Average annual rates over the next few years were in the same range: 14.2 percent for 1978, 13.8 percent for 1979, 11.8 percent in 1980, and 10.9 percent in 1981. But, to say how many were unemployed tells only half the story. The other half is how many were working—and even then, there is an important footnote to both: how many were coming into the labor force. Four principal factors explain the sharp increase in the number of job seekers. The first of them was the explosive growth of the metropolitan population itself beginning in the 1960s. Other factors included the youthfulness of the population; the reality that hard times drive many to seek work who would not otherwise; and, finally, changing social attitudes (the feminist movement created more two-income households in Chile as well as in the northern industrialized nations). Thus, as the following figures (expressed as thousands of persons) show, the number seeking employment for the first time shot up sharply beginning in 1971:

TABLE 48

NUMBER OF PERSONS ENTERING JOB MARKET, 1971–1981

1971	1972	1973	1974	1975	1976	1977	1978	1979	1980	1981
12.7	15.6	11.5	31.4	45.5	56.4	35.3	42.5	43.0	37.8	32.1

The total work force in the metropolitan region ballooned from 1,052,000 in 1971 to 1,480,000 in 1981; the number of those working jumped from 1,012,200 to 1,280,500, reaching record levels every year but one (1975) along the way. That meant a 27 percent increase in the number of persons working in 1981 compared with a decade earlier. Furthermore, the indices of real wages and salaries—which had gone into a steep nose-dive during Allende's last year—finally nudged into levels above 1970 in July 1977, and then, in 1978, began a sustained sharp climb above them. Again, contrary to the prevailing mythologies, blue collar workers fared far better than did white collar employees. The index of real receipts of minimum-income blue and white collar workers, 1970–1977, showed that the former went from a baseline 100 in 1970 to an average high-low range of 173–163 by the end of 1977. Minimum wage white collar workers never managed to recover from the sharp slump that began in 1971, so that by the end of 1977, their index had climbed back to only 87–83 percent of its 1970 levels.[38] Overall, wage/salary levels 1970–1978 looked like this:

TABLE 49
INDEX OF AVERAGE REAL WAGES AND SALARIES, 1970–1978
(Average 1970: 100)

YEAR/MONTH	WAGES	SALARIES
1970 (average)	100	100
1971 (average)	118–119	119–120
1972 (average)	100–113	94–106
1973 (January–July	61–94	52–80
(October)	52–40	39–30
1974 (October)	71–67	73–69
1975 "	"	"
1976 "	85–80	82–78
1977 "	96–91	97–91
1978 "	113–107	110–104

Source: Chile: An Economy in Transition, op. cit., adapted from Table III.22, p. 149. In July 1977, the indices stood at 103–97 and 106–100, respectively; in 1978, for January, at 106–100 and 107–101; April, 109–103 and 110–104, and July, 116–110 and 115–109.

Only a strong, vigorous—and growing—economy could have overcome such a myriad array of adversities to provide for such a demand for jobs, while improving wage levels in the process.[39]

Allende had called copper "Chile's salary." If it was, then, given economy-wrenching fluctuations in world market prices, Chile's exertions represented more a form of indentured servitude than the dignity of free labor. Fortunately, the Pinochet government had set out purposefully to free Chile from that vassalage. The policy not only worked, but paid handsome dividends: between 1973 and 1977, copper fell from 82.3 percent of Chile's exports to 53.1 percent. In the same period, farm, fishery, and forest exports more than tripled as a share of exports, from 2 percent to 7.3 percent; industrial exports did even better, rising sixfold, from 3 percent to 18.7 percent. As a result, the country's gross national product was able to bound back from the 1975 crash, growing by a phenomenal 52 percent in the six-year period 1976–1981, inclusive—despite the fact that copper prices remained at their lowest average levels in a quarter of a century.[40]

That export picture got even better in the years ahead: By 1981, copper was producing more money for Chile than ever before in history—thanks to greatly increased output—but had dropped to 43 percent of total exports. Once-humble farm, fishery, and forest products now stood at 9.25 percent of the total (and the dollar totals were even more impressive: $25.5 million in 1973; $365.4 million in 1981); industrial exports were up to 32.28 percent of total exports ($89.4 million in 1973, $1.3 billion in 1981).

(In one of those ironies of the Law of Unintended Consequences—though one so common to international boycott experiments—the U.S. arms embargo slapped on Chile forced the country to develop a munitions industry of its own. By 1987, the country was exporting $400 million worth of military hardware, and the United States was accusing Chile—very implausibly—of arming Panama and Nicaragua.)[41]

Cheap dollars and low import duties inevitably fueled a dramatic increase in imports in an economy long denied not only the tools for growth but also creature comforts. Imports shot up from $2.046 billion in 1977 to $6.512 billion in 1981. A healthy chunk was in capital and intermediate goods needed to drive growth. Those imports increased nearly two-and-a-half fold during that period, and together accounted for more than 70 percent of the total. But consumer goods figured importantly in the mix, too: up nearly four times in the same period. Chileans, who had spent a paltry $3.5 million on imported cars in 1975, paid $427 million for them in 1981.

David Belnap, a keen-eyed *Los Angeles Times* correspondent, wrote as the boom was first gaining momentum late in 1977: "Mayonnaise from Argentina and television sets from Japan have something in common in Chile today. Both cost the consumer less than the same products made locally. The same is true of a long list of imports, ranging from power tools to textiles. Moreover, all are available in the local marketplace, which is not the case anywhere else in the Southern Hemisphere." Nor was there any reason for caution. As Belnap noted, Chile "today boasts one of the world's best credit ratings" among international bankers. When Chile sought to borrow $50 million that year on the Eurodollar market, the loan was quickly oversubscribed by 100 percent. An Associated Press story, widely distributed, reported in 1977 that Chile's economy had turned the corner, and "a rosy economic future is on the near horizon."

Scotch, observed *Hoy* dryly, replaced *pisco* as the national drink.

During these heady years, Chile once again became the pacesetter for Latin America, as the following table demonstrates:

TABLE 50
AVERAGE GDP GROWTH RATES, CHILE AND LATIN AMERICA, 1977–1981 (In Percentages)

YEAR	CHILE	OVERALL LATIN AMERICAN AVERAGES
1977	9.9	4.8
1978	8.2	5.1
1979	8.3	6.5
1980	7.5	5.9
1981	5.3	1.7

Source: Adapted from *Perspectivas Económicas Para La Democracia, op. cit., Table 7,* p. 32.

Not surprisingly, the foreign buying binge soon impacted on the country's trade balance. In 1978, the country's merchandise trade balance
inched into the red; by 1981, the deficit was $2.7 billion—and much of it
was financed by foreign credits. Even more ominous was the current
accounts deficit of the balance of payments: from $1.2 billion, or 5.7
percent of GDP in 1979, to $4.7 billion, or 14.5 percent of GDP, in 1981.
When Allende fell, 80 percent of the country's debt was owed by the
government. In 1981, the government's share was down to 35.3 percent.
But private debt had skyrocketed from $1.2 billion in 1977 to $10.1
billion by December 1981.

Danger flags were flying. They were largely ignored—until too late.[42]

FROM "BASKET CASE" TO CORNUCOPIA

*Chile's so-called "economic miracle," which was heralded domes-
tically and abroad as proof of the wisdom of the "monetarist, supply-
side" economic theories of the University of Chicago's Milton Friedman and those of the Reagan Administration, began to come apart in
1982, and come apart it did with explosive force in January 1983. . . .
Chile is now considered an economic basket case. As one top American bank official, who did not want to be identified, declared, "Chile
is in ruins, its industrial base is virtually blitzed out, physically
obliterated. . . ." A Chilean economist, who also refuses to be so
identified, viewed these developments as "shattering . . . body
blows" to the well-being of the country. Even "under optimum conditions, with generous availability of foreign financing, and a takeover
by a government dedicated to reversing the nation's plight, it would
take years to restore Chile's production levels to what they had been
in 1969." . . . Most observers agree that the Junta is tottering and
Pinochet is on the ropes. Just how the demise will be brought about is
the most debated question. . . .*

Samuel Chavkin, in a 1985 retro-
spective on the 1981 crisis[*]

Although more lurid than most, Marxist apologist Chavkin's report of
the death of the free market in Chile was premature, to say the least.
Still, his barely disguised glee at capitalism's "collapse" in Chile was not
altogether unlike funeral dirges playing in much of the popular press
then—and afterwards. Even the conservative journal, *Policy Review,*
published by the Heritage Foundation, spoke ominously of "The Coming Crisis in Chile" in a Fall 1985 article (replete with other egregious
gaffes and inanities).[44]

* Samuel Chavkin, *Storm Over Chile: The Junta Under Siege* (Westport, CT.: Lawrence
  Hill & Co., 1985), pp. 238–239. The book, which features on the cover "foreward by
  Hortensia Allende," is a warmed-over version of his earlier *The Murder of Chile.*[43]

As it happens, quite apart from the obvious implausibilities—those anonymous "experts," for example—Chavkin and other doomsayers were wrong on every significant count. Indeed, by 1985, the evidence of recovery was abundant, but ideological fanatics refused to see it, just as they had refused to believe it in 1977.

They underestimated then, just as now, the soundness of economic planning predicated on a free market. They underestimated then, just as now, the grit and vision of the men and women who, from 1975–1981, had made such an "heroic attempt to restore free markets to what had long been one of the world's most inefficient economies." Having come so far, they had no intention of sliding back into that quagmire of inefficiency.

Experts saw the crisis differently than did the ideologues. To begin with, they saw it in a global context, which few press pundits did or would, fewer yet among the ideologues. In 1982, the industrialized world was struggling to emerge from the deep 1980–1981 recession triggered by the second great oil price shocks of 1979. In the United States, it was the worst economic slump since the Great Depression. The unemployment rate—10.8 percent at the end of December—was the highest in three decades, car sales the lowest since 1961. In Latin America, there was a delayed reaction. As the rich countries fought to lessen the blows to their own economies, demand for Latin American exports dropped. Interest rates shot up, new capital flows dried up.

When crisis hit, it did with a fury approaching that of the Great Depression: at least 30 million persons lost their jobs in Latin America. Debt built up and manageable during the years of "cheap" dollars suddenly reached explosive proportions, creating what came to be known as the "Debt Bomb" crisis. A 1985 World Bank study noted that, "beginning in 1982, the region [Latin America as a whole] began to transfer resources to the rest of the world on a massive scale representing between 25 and 30 percent of exports of goods and services, not including capital flight." First came a sharp drop in output: Argentina in 1981; Bolivia, Chile, and Costa Rica in 1982; Brazil, Ecuador, Mexico, Paraguay, Peru, Trinidad and Tobago, Uruguay, and Venezuela in 1983. Then came steep falls in personal income. The study concluded that "under optimistic assumptions" some countries were likely to find themselves in 1990 with per capita GDP barely exceeding the level of 1970. In that group were Argentina, Chile and Peru. Bolivia, the study said, was likely to show a lower per capita GDP in 1990 than in 1970. "Except in Brazil and Colombia," the study reported, "Latin America's development has been set back by more than a decade."[45]

As it turned out, even that sober assessment would prove to be excessively gloomy in the case of Chile—even though, of all the Latin American countries, none appeared in more dire straits.

Overall, in the face of the sharp increase in interest payments and sharply worsening terms of trade, per capita income in Latin America fell by 11 percent during 1981–1983. In 1982, in Chile, the fall was 15.5 percent. In 1983, it fell by another 2.4 percent. For Latin America as a whole, the decline continued in 1985, as well, by 1.5 percent.

In an economy not only expanding, but changing tone, tenor, and direction so rapidly, and doing so at the outset in a war setting, there were, of course, blunders. What is truly remarkable is that there were not far more of them.

With the rapid expansion in demand for credit, the government in 1974 chartered financial institutions that specialized in high-interest and short-term (as few as four days) loans. Until late 1975, when a few of them failed, they operated under buccaneering rules: not only were capitalization levels low, they were not subject (as banks were) to rigid rules governing ratio of reserves to loans. Although they could not offer checking accounts, they could accept third-party deposits. After 1975, they were put under rules similar to those governing banks. Between 1975 and 1981, the number of banks and financial institutions in Chile rose from nineteen to fifty-nine. The following table gives a sense of the change in the banking system from Allende to the crash of the Eighties:

TABLE 51
STRUCTURE OF LIABILITIES, PRIVATE COMMERCIAL BANKS
(Percentages)

	1970	1983
Time and demand deposits	49.5	22.1
Capital and reserves	7.1	5.5
Undistributed profits	0.3	− 2.1
Foreign loans	5.2	31.7
Owed to Central Bank	4.2	16.6
Other	33.7	27.2

Source: Juan Foxley R. & Pablo Piñera E., "Sistema Financiero y Política De Crédito en Chile," in *Perspectivas Económicas Para La Democracia*, op. cit., Table 2, p. 87. They cite the 1970 Statistical Bulletin and 1983 Financial Report of the Superintendency of Banks and Financial Institutions.

In Chile, as in the United States, it would take the hard experience of bank failures in the unfamiliar environment of the roller-coaster economy of the late seventies and eighties to force a rewriting of the rules.

For many, the first blunder was made in 1979, when a medium-sized bank—*Banco Osorno y La Unión*—failed and the government moved in to guarantee depositors and creditors against losses. It also shielded banks and finance companies against losses following the May 1981 collapse of the big sugar company, CRAV—the event, as indicated in the preceding chapter, was seen by many as the leading edge of the coming economic hurricane. The big storm started to hit in November, when four banks and other financial institutions began to totter.[46]

Once again, it was a time for steady nerves and bold measures. On August 31, 1982, Rolf Luders Schwarzenberg, a confirmed monetarist of the Chicago school himself, had been brought in to take charge of the economy: minister of both Finance and Economy.[47] Luders recalled later that, as the crisis boiled up, Pinochet took personal command. When it became apparent that however contrary it might be to free-market convictions, the government either would have to intervene with the banks or risk a cataclysmic collapse of the entire banking system, Pinochet moved with resolve—and stealth. Three laws were needed to permit the government to intervene with the banks. To bring them before the junta in normal fashion would have required a time lag of several days—and risked a confidence-shattering leak that easily could have precipitated a full-scale bank panic. Pinochet resolved the problem by summoning the junta to his "Monday office" at the Defense Ministry, where he could be assured of complete security in adopting the needed measures. On Thursday, January 13, 1983, the government took over five banks and liquidated two others.[48]

At first, the government sought to have creditors—domestic and foreign—absorb the losses of the two banks being liquidated; international pressure forced that policy to be scrapped forty-eight hours after it was announced. Ultimately, both foreign and domestic creditors collected what was owed them; depositors in the failed banks, however, recovered only 70 percent of their money.

Altogether, the state was forced to liquidate and/or intervene sixteen institutions accounting for 42 percent of the financial system's banking assets. Fully 20 percent of the banking system's assets were classified as "unproductive" by the end of 1984—meaning either past-due or acquired in cash by the Central bank. (The Central Bank was not, however, a "soft touch"; beneficiary banks were required to repay those obligations out of future profits before they could pay a dime's dividend to their ultimate shareholders.) By April of 1984, the Central Bank had extended emergency credits to the intervened and/or liquidated banks equivalent to one and-a-half times the entire private sector money supply. To statist economists, these events proved "the failure of the economic model"—not that it needed adjustment, but that it had "failed." Crowed two economists critical of the free market system: "The solution developed by the government [intervening with the banks] does not resolve the problem . . . [but] reflects the unwillingness of the government to recognize the gravity of the crisis, and to give the appearance that banking remains private. It would have been very difficult for the Pinochet administration to recognize after eleven years of applying a model which gives priority to private property as its central element that it would wind up with the financial system in the hands of the State because of its own insolvency."[49]

They spoke too soon.

The crisis was barely over when Pinochet remarked: "This intervention was not the result of a socialist ideological zeal. To the contrary: we did it to protect the common weal while making possible the maintaining of an economy sustained by individual initiative." He meant what he said.

Out of that wreckage would come an entirely new banking system. By 1984, the government had already begun a scheme of recapitalization and reprivatization of the banks. Only this time, ownership was broad-based. Not two years after the gloating and doomsaying of the statists, in March of 1987, bank reprivatization was completed with the sale of the *Banco de Chile* and the *Banco de Santiago*—the largest and third-largest in the system. Before the crash, *Banco de Chile* had 17,700 shareholders; now it had 39,222. *Banco de Santiago* had fifteen; now it had 15,781. (The second largest bank, *Banco del Estado*, was government-owned—and solvent—and therefore not a candidate for intervention.) No single shareholder was permitted to own more than 2.5 percent of the stock. Thanks to a series of imaginative and innovative financial measures, banks which in 1983 had uncovered losses equivalent to 200 percent of their capital by July 1986 had provisions against losses well above the total capital and reserves of the system. In the four years between January 1983 and December 1986, the total capital of the banking system grew by 47 percent.

A postscript: the system, of course, was not scrapped. But the rules were rewritten, on November 27, 1986, with a new banking law, replacing old laws in force for thirty years. Central to them: "the distancing of the state from the system."[50]

Virtue can sometimes prove to be a vice. In one important aspect, it did in the Chilean crisis. From 1979 until the second half of 1982, wages had been indexed. The good news was that with that floor in place, while Chile's gross domestic income was falling by 19 percent, wages fell by only 3 percent in real terms. The bad news was that unemployment—"by far the worst in the region"—got worse as a result of the high wage level. From a 10–11 percent average in 1980–1981, it shot up to an official 19.6 percent in 1982. This time, blue collar workers and those on the lower end of the income scale were hit hardest: by the end of 1984, when overall unemployment was down to 14 percent, unemployment among the poor was still at 22 percent. At the beginning of 1982, 162,878 persons were enrolled in the government's Minimum Public Employment program (PEM); by year's end, that number more than doubled, to 336,469, reaching an absolute high of 396,277 in May of 1983. As the crisis deepened, the government created yet another program for unemployed heads of household. That program, roughly akin to the Public Works Administration program in the U.S. during the 1930s Depression, started in October 1982 with 54,187 enrolled, hitting a high of 228,491 in November 1983. By one reckoning, the jobless rate in 1982 reached 27 percent.[51]

Many attempted to read into the management of the crisis a deadly backstairs war between Chicago-school *blandos* (soft-liners) and military *duros* (hard-liners), seeing in the June 14, 1982, decision to devalue and once again "float" the peso proof of a victory of the *duros*. A similar interpretation was given to Pinochet's ouster, on April 2, 1984, of the Finance and Economy ministers, both "free-marketers," or *blandos*. Differences over tactics there were, but insiders insist that Pinochet himself never wavered in his firm conviction that the road to success was paved with free market ideas.[52]

But the crisis also fostered the belief that Pinochet could be pushed from power. Viewing the strikes, public demonstrations, and rallies at their peak, Pinochet told Frederick N. Nunn, a decidedly hostile U.S. academic, that the street disorders were economic in origin, and manipulated by politicians who needed power in order to justify their existence. He added a third category: hypocrites whose 1973 support had waned when they had not been returned to power. He made equally plain his determination to do whatever was necessary to put an end to civil strife.[53]

This time—unlike 1975—Chile did receive international help, though to be sure, not from the United States. (Despite the severity of the hardship, the United States ended even its Food for Peace program in Chile in 1983, though still dumping millions of dollars' worth into countries such as Cambodia—by then a Hanoi client state called Kampuchea—and Uganda.)[54] Working closely with International Monetary Fund and World Bank specialists, the Chilean authorities devised a hard-nosed recovery program which came to enjoy their "full support"—expressed in a billion-dollar assistance program ($750 million in IMF Special Drawing Rights and $250 million bridge financing from the Bank). Those agreements cleared the way for $1.09 billion in fresh commercial bank credit in 1985 to cover the balance-of-payments gap. Among those measures: moving away from a fixed exchange rate to a flexible peso. The exchange rate had been locked in at thirty-nine in

1979 in the hope of tying Chile's inflation rate to world rates. For a time, it worked. Freeing it now helped to contribute to the opposite effect. Between 1982 and 1985, the peso went from thirty-nine to the dollar to 160 to the dollar; From a low of 9.5 percent in 1981, the consumer price index jumped to 20.8 percent in 1982, and kept right on climbing until it peaked at 30.5 percent in 1985. (As bad as Chile's inflation was, in 1985 only one country on the South American continent—oil-exporting Venezuela—was in the official "moderate" inflation category. Mexico, Peru, Brazil, and Argentina were running inflation rates from not quite twice Chile's to more than twenty-one times higher.)[55] Import duties were jacked up from 10 percent to 20 percent, causing imports to drop by 21 percent in 1983. Forecasts were starkly realistic, assuming a continuing hardship level in terms of trade, and particularly in world copper prices. (To underscore the hardship point: the Economic Commission for Latin America estimated that, by 1983, Chile's terms of trade had deteriorated 63 percent since 1970, which, as David Gallagher observed, meant that "one ton of copper could, by 1983, buy only one-third of the imports it could buy 10 years before.")

But, as Gallagher noted, Chile enjoyed a solid advantage as the country moved to meet the staggering crisis: "All the economic reforms of the 1975–1981 period are still in place, and they provide an appropriate legislative infrastructure from which to take off. Unlike any other Latin America country, Chile now has a simplified economy, untrammeled by useless rules and artificial subsidies. The country's finances are in order. Entrepreneurs have gradually learned that their long-term interests are served by competition in the marketplace, unlike their counterparts in other Latin American countries, for whom doing business means doing deals with the government. Chile's rigid old labor laws are a distant nightmare. Each worker knows where his future pension is to come from. Finally, there are no legal obstacles to foreign investment."[56]

Gallagher was not simply blowing smoke. Chile suffered two crippling setbacks in 1984 and 1985. Copper prices in the country's financial plan had been projected at 70 cents—a price 45 percent below the average for the previous 25 years. In 1984, the price fell to 62 cents, and that cost the country a quarter of a billion dollars in lost revenues. In 1985, it crawled up to only 64 cents—representing somewhere around $180 million in lost revenues. Then, early on the evening of March 3, 1985, an earthquake registering more than eight on the Richter scale struck near the seacoast village of Algarrobo, seventy miles west of Santiago, leaving 177 dead and damage of more than $1.8 billion.[57]

Nonetheless, the sturdy foundation Gallagher described proved more than adequate to the challenge. In 1984, real gross domestic product grew by 6.3 percent, well above the projected 4 percent. Despite steeply higher costs, imports rose much faster than had been expected; the government reacted by pushing duties even higher, from 21 percent to 35 percent. Still, the trade surplus stood at $300 million (and in the years ahead, would grow to monumental Pacific Rim proportions). Long-range development of the country's rather meager oil reserves paid dividends: by the mid-1980s, Chile was one of a handful of Latin countries which had succeeded in insulating itself against catastrophic oil shocks. Unemployment dropped from 1982's 19.6 percent to 12 percent in 1985.[58]

It was the beginning of a sustained—and spectacular—growth in Chile's economy which would surpass even the performance of the tide-turning late seventies. Finance Minister Hernan Büchi B.—whose mod hair styles make him look more like a rock star than a finance minister, but whose policies were strictly free market and monetarist—spelled out two major goals when he took over February 12, 1985: reduce the current-account deficit and pep up production—thereby improving employment opportunities. In both, he succeeded handsomely.[59]

In its mid-year publication in 1987, *Finance and Development*, a quarterly published by the International Monetary Fund and the World Bank, reviewed Chile's efforts in the postcrisis years. Gallagher was not alone in his judgment: "The recession was so deep that unemployment reached 25 percent and the financial sector was virtually bankrupted . . . trade reform survived the crisis and the rationalization it had fostered left Chile's industrial sector in a far stronger position to withstand the shocks of the 1980s. In recent years the economy has grown strongly, and unemployment has come down to under 10 percent. Economic liberalization clearly contributed to this recovery."[60]

Even painstakingly researched publications—such as *National Geographic* in its July 1988 issue—when they acknowledge progress in Chile at all, tend to portray it as the rich getting richer and the poor either neglected altogether, or when looked after at all, looked after by church groups. The truth is otherwise.[61]

Noting that Chile was one of seven (among twenty-three) Latin American and Caribbean countries that had continued success in bringing down infant mortality, the Inter-American Development Bank, in its 1987 report, added: "Almost all of these countries have a good health record going back a number of years or have been making a noteworthy effort recently; this may be the case of Chile, which has maintained a vigorous food-distribution program and expanded drinking-water and sewerage services. . . ."

The World Bank, in its study of "Poverty in Latin America: The Impact of Depression," was even more explicit, and because it is so radically at odds with the careless press image of Chile, bears quoting at length:

> The Chilean case is particularly interesting because it represents a successful attempt to focus government social spending on the poorest segments of the population. By slashing government spending on upper-income groups, it has been possible to provide the most urgently needed social services in spite of the grave economic crisis ... per capita social expenditure increased by 36 percent in dollar terms between 1980 and 1984, with a slight dip in 1983, while total social expenditure increased by 46 percent during that period. The fastest increase (140 percent) was in social welfare, including the government make-work programs; social welfare programs account for 24 percent of total government social spending. Social security spending almost doubled as part of a drastic reform which initially increased the burden on public finance. But education spending (which in 1984 accounted for one-quarter of social spending) increased by only 8 percent and public health spending went down by 19 percent. The overall increase in government social spending is all the more remarkable because total government spending was reduced during the crisis as part of the adjustment effort. Success in targeting social spending on the poorest groups was achieved at the expense of the groups immediately above the poverty line. There has been little investment in facilities catering to the lower middle classes in recent years. Nevertheless, Chile's performance in targeting social spending is unequaled in the region, and substantial improvements in efficiency have been achieved in the delivery of social services to the poor. . . .
>
> In Chile, there has been continuous progress through 1984 [later data was not available when this report was written] in general mortality, infant mortality, and neonatal mortality (infants who die at less than twenty-eight days old). Nutritional surveys show a declining trend in malnutrition among children under six years old (as well as for each of the subcategories: slight, moderate, and advanced malnutrition), with a slight increase in 1983 and a subsequent improvement in 1984. Rates are among the lowest in the developing world, with total malnutrition affecting 8.4 per thousand children in 1984. Education statistics, however, show a reduction in primary school enrollment rates in 1982 since 1980. Because school drop-out rates are far higher for the poor than the rest of the population (evidence exists for 1979), it can be that the lower primary enrollment rate is related to poverty. . . .

Observed *Forbes* magazine in December 1987: "In many instances, the Chilean economic model could be broadened to alleviate human suffering in the impoverished Third World. . . ."[62]

*   *   *

Much is made in critiques of the Chilean economy of the claim: (1) that per capita income in 1988 was lower than it was in 1981 (and, in some entirely erroneous assertions, lower even than 1970); and (2) that under Pinochet, the country has become saddled with one of the largest debts, in per capita terms, in the world.

The boom—in contrast to continuing crisis and recession in other major Latin countries—continued uninterrupted in 1988. Gross National Product was up 5.2 percent in the first quarter of the year, fueled largely by steady growth of exports. However, there was no question whatever that in 1988, Chile was into the fifth consecutive year of strong and sustained economic growth. At mid-year, on the basis of preliminary figures, *El Mercurio* reported that the economy was already 10 percent higher than the peak 1981 level. Should that prove out, then it would no longer be true, also, that per capita income was lower than that historic high—reached under Pinochet.[63]

Debt is another matter. To begin with, as noted in the preceding chapter, Chile was, in 1973, second in the world to Israel in the per capita size of its foreign debt (and first in per capita terms in Latin America; in 1987, Chile ranked eighteenth among the nineteen Hispanic countries of the hemisphere in the percentage increase of its debt 1970–1987). Next, when discussing debt—as when discussing incomes—it ought to be remembered that the economy of Chile was not jolted during the Allende years—it was shattered. It had to be rebuilt with a minimum of outside help and a maximum of outside hostility. Thirdly, that all of Latin America went on a borrowing binge in the 1970s, and did so in the context of a rapidly expanding world economy. As the World Bank poverty study observed, "between World War II and the depression of the 1980s, Latin America was one of the fastest-growing areas in the developing world. Indeed, between 1960 and 1980 only a few developing countries, including the successful Southeast Asian economies, expanded at a faster rate." With banks awash in petrodollars, and the Latin countries eager for rapid change, borrowing patterns shifted from international agencies and their long-term—and longer lead-time—loans, to private commercial banks and shorter-term loans. From 1970 to 1980 alone, Latin America's public debt leaped from $20.7 billion to $160.3 billion (and then nearly doubled again in just the next five years).[64] But borrowing by itself does not necessarily "fuel growth"—a term frequently used by those attempting to explain away Chile's success. Witness, indeed, the economic miseries of the region's (and the world's) three biggest debtors: Brazil, Mexico, and Argentina. In one of its frequent looks at the debt problems of Latin America, *The Economist*, on January 9, 1988, headlined its article: "Brazil and Mexico: Which is worse off?" On September 26, 1987, the magazine asked:

"Argentina: Worse to come?" A few months later, in an April 1988 article, it provided the answer, describing Argentina and Peru as "the two worst economies in the world." In yet another—"Nuts to Brazil?" August 29, 1987—*The Economist* opined: "Thanks largely to the suffocating incompetence of its government, Brazil is not the economic powerhouse it could so easily be. Instead, it remains the biggest current threat to the stability of the world's financial system." For much of 1987, Brazil refused to pay even the interest due on its foreign debt, "saving" $3 billion in interest payments. Less noticed was the fact that six other Latin American countries had also adopted "can't pay, won't pay" policies in 1987: Bolivia, Costa Rica, Cuba, Honduras, Nicaragua, and Peru.[65]

There is yet another point which ought to be taken into consideration when discussing the growth of debt: inflation. If no such allowance is made, the raw figures would indicate that Chile's debt rose from $3.9 billion when Allende fell to around $19 billion in 1987. But, applying 1987 dollars to both figures so as to adjust for inflation, the real figures would become $9 billion in 1973, $19 billion in 1987. Furthermore, it is important to consider what the borrowed money was used for. In the case of Chile, $4 billion went to pay interest alone on the debt left behind by Allende. Another $2 billion went to finance the working capital needed to build up the export sector.

Finally, much of it was needed to help offset the revenues Chile lost through lower copper prices, the higher prices Chile had to pay for imported oil—taken together, a staggering $40 billion over the 14-year period. Expressed differently: if copper prices had remained at 1973 levels, Chile in 1988 would have had no foreign debt at all, but a huge foreign reserve surplus. The same, of course, could be said for any country suffering adverse terms of trade; as it happens, coming out of the crash of the eighties, only one other South American country endured worse terms of trade than did Chile.[66]

At all odds, Chile was not among the countries reneging on its debts, however painful their payment had become. (The Christian Democrats, in their electoral platform, viewed debt waffling as a political opportunity, serving notice that if back in power, they would "reprogram accumulated debts.") In the wake of the 1982 crisis, the government moved quickly to restore confidence within the framework of the IMF/ World Bank bail-out. Because the government was willing to guarantee private debt, it was able to roll over substantial portions of the total in successful negotiations with foreign private banks in 1983, 1985, and 1987. So high was Chile's credit standing that all 407 banks agreed to the terms of the 1987 arrangement in record time. Signed in New York on June 17, 1987, the deal postpones the first payment on the old stock of debt until 1993 and the first principal payment on the 1983 and 1984 new monies until 1991. That agreement covered $10.6 billion of Chile's $19 billion debt, and saved the country $448 million in 1988 interest charges.[67]

Central to the debt strategy has been a highly innovative and highly successful program of "debt swaps." Professor Steve H. Hanke of Johns Hopkins University has commented that "Chile has been the only country that has been able to make good use" of them. Chile's program (unlike neighboring Argentina's, for example) has succeeded because it met two fundamental conditions: (1) attractive investment opportunities; (2) good design. Since they were introduced in 1985, Chile's debt swaps have reduced the country's foreign debt from $20.2 billion to $18.7 billion in June of 1988. In line with a surge of interest in Chile on the part of other Pacific Basin countries, a New Zealand investment company in 1987 made the biggest single debt-to-equity conversion: $165 million. Writing of the 1987 performance, *Friedberg's LDC Debt Comments* said: "Last year, Chile alone among the principal 32 less developed debtors in U.S. Treasury Secretary [James] Baker's original initiative reduced its foreign debts...." *The Economist*, on July 11, 1987, wrote: "If Brazil could match Chile's record, its US $110 billion debt would shrink by US $16.5 billion and its interest bill by some US $1.5 billion a year...." In fact, about the only international financial forum not to take note of Chile's success under the Baker Plan was Mr. Baker's Treasury Department, in keeping with the Reagan administration's policy of studied hostility towards Chile. This incited *International Currency Review* to chortle: "Poor Mr. Baker! With everyone decrying the failure of his 'plan' announced in Seoul in the autumn of 1985, the Treasury Secretary has been unable to convey his satisfaction about the one success story the so-called 'Baker Plan' has to its credit—Chile. For the Chilean Government, being a dictatorship—which is the crucial background factor contributing to stabilization—has consistently pursued sensible economic policies for three years, as a result of which its superbly managed economy is now achieving substantial growth. Moreover, this is happening despite heavy dependence on copper—the real price of which is now lower than in 1930."[68]

TRIUMPHANT DAYS

In talks to students, U.S. Education Secretary William J. Bennett liked to invoke what he called the "gate" test as one measurement of peoples' attitudes towards their governments. If a country's gates were opened and people fled, it was a pretty good indicator of widespread discontent—and that has, of course, described Communist dictatorships down to the present day. It also describes many—but not all—right-wing dictatorships. In the case of Chile, it is instructive to note that, once the gates began to open in the early eighties for the estimated twenty thousand Chileans officially or voluntarily in exile, they and their families began streaming back into the country. Except for hunted criminals and terrorists, there has been no significant exodus in a number of years, although with a tiny handful of exceptions, Chileans have been free to leave the country if they so chose. And, as noted in the preceding chapter, many left-wing figures returned even before the gates were officially open to them, knowing as they did that they were walking into almost-certain prison or internal exile sentences.

Many Chileans who, for reasons of career or personal circumstances, have remained abroad, cast their "gate" votes on the country in another—and dramatic—fashion: sending their money back into the country. As early as 1986, the American economist Steve H. Hanke, noting that flight capital was a "foul-weather barometer for debtor nations," cited a Morgan Guaranty analysis that for every dollar in foreign loans that has poured into Latin America, flight capital has drained seventy cents out. "Chile," he wrote, "is one Latin American debtor nation in which the capital-flight phenomenon has been reversed; Chileans have actually been repatriating capital and earnings from abroad." By early 1987, less than two years after the promulgation of Chapter XVIII of the Central Bank's "Rules for International Exchange," overseas Chileans had invested an estimated $850 million of the 2 to 3 billion dollars said to be stashed abroad.[69]

There was a good reason for such a reverse flow: few, if any, equity markets in the world rival Santiago's, thanks to a privatization program probably unequalled in the world. In the weeks following "Black Monday," the 1987 stock market crash, the world's top ten stock markets bottomed out anywhere from 18.38 percent below their peak (Tokyo) to 44.15 percent (Australia). Santiago's slid 15.22 percent. But, even more revealingly: placed against four of the world's hottest markets (Hong Kong, Italy, Singapore, Australia), November 1986-November 1987, Santiago left all four far behind. Three of the four showed declines, Australia's gained 2.1 percent, while Santiago's shot ahead 65.57 percent. Over the longer haul—1975–1986—the record is even more impressive. During that period, Standard & Poor's index of U.S. stocks rose to 449 percent from a base of 100 percent; Morgan Stanley's index showed worldwide stock prices up 567 percent; in Santiago, similar calculations showed shares up 2,060 percent. Small wonder: of 155 companies listed on the small (but old: 1893) Santiago exchange, 23 showed income yields of 50 percent or higher from January 1 through

May 31, 1987. Nor did the trend change following "Black Monday"; while all four of the other "glamor" markets showed year-to-year declines, Santiago's market shot up another 43 percent from November to late June 1988.[70]

Such long-term, sustained results obviously are not flash-in-the-pan phenomena, reflecting no more than market manipulation and speculation. The essence of the market strength is at the very core of the Pinochet revolution itself: the sea change from an economy dominated by the state to an exuberantly free enterprise one. By early 1988, fewer than a dozen of the 530 companies under state control in 1973 remained entirely under government ownership. The privatization process was carried out in three phases: 1973–1975, return to their rightful owners of the roughly 350 companies illegally seized; 1975–1981, privatization of banks and other financial institutions; 1983 onward, sale of the bulk of the remaining companies in CORFO's hands. Those sales not only poured $1.3 billion into the treasury through mid-year 1987, but had made "popular capitalists" out of an estimated 250,000 Chileans. Furthermore, by contrast to 1973 when the state ran those companies and piled up losses in that one year of $500 million, all of them were now profitable. Clemente Martínez, a supervisor in one of the biggest pellet plants, the Pacific Steel Company (CAP, for *Compañía de Acero del Pacífico*), three hundred miles north of Santiago, described for the *New York Times* a recent "collective bargaining" request: that workers at the plant have access to information on how their shares in the company were doing on the stock market without having to wait for the next day's newspaper. "What is happening here," said Martínez, a member of the worker delegation, "is that workers, both blue collar and management, are developing what I call a shareholders' culture." Those steelworkers had abundant reason for feeling good about what was now, in significant measure, truly "their" company: in 1987, CAP more than doubled its profits over the 1986 level. Of 6,500 employees, four thousand had bought stock in that booming company. To the distress of Marxist-minded politicians and old-style union bosses unaccustomed to such genuine worker independence, similar stories were being played out in a number of major companies privatized in recent years—with workers in those companies joining local and foreign investors in buying shares under Employee Stock Ownership Programs (ESOP) backed by government loan programs. Others have included the local and long-lines telephone companies, the big nitrate company, the electric utility serving Santiago and Valparaíso, a sugar refinery, the state-airline, and even such unique cases as the University of Chile's engineering school, hospital and television station. María Teresa Rosende Gaete, general manager of a computer service company, recalled that it was the union that originally proposed employee stock purchase. With the aid of ten-year loans from CORFO, 114 of the company's 120 employees participated in the $1.5 million purchase. "For the majority of us," she said, "the initial reason was job security, but now people have begun to see it as an investment."[71]

The following table indicates highlights of the program:

TABLE 52

PRIVATIZATION, 1985–1987

COMPANY	% TO BE SOLD	% SOLD 12/30/87	% SOLD TO WORKERS	% SOLD TO PENSION FUNDS
CTC (Tel. Co.)	45	30	6.4	4.2
ENTEL (long-lines)	49	33.03	—	18
CHILGENER (electric generation)	100	65.30	6	14
SOQUIMICH (nitrate)	100	82	12.5	4
EMEL (electric distribution)	100	100	100	—
CAP	100	100	34	—
IANSA (sugar)	49	49	16	—
CHILMETRO (electric distribution)	100	100	31	24

Sources: "Dispersal of Ownership," *Chile Now,* #62, March–April 1988, p. 16 (A publication of the Chilean Ministry of Foreign Affairs, Santiago).

As the program gathered momentum, the trend was to offer even larger shares of these companies for sale. The original plan, for example, called for selling only one-third of what is in most countries a sacred cow: the state airline, LAN-Chile. In May of 1988, Decree Law 18,400 raised the share available for sale to 60 percent.

There has been one other key element in "popular capitalism," and more recently, in powering the build-up of the private sector and with it the continuing stock market boom: privatization of the country's social security system. Under the reform, unveiled on November 4, 1980, eligible workers were given five years to decide whether to stay with the hodge-podge of government-run pension plans, or move into private plans called AFPs—Administrators of Pension Funds. Organized as private companies, their only function is to administer pension funds. Under the private option, each worker contributes 10 percent of his salary for retirement and between 3 percent and 4 percent for disability. Each member has his own account that grows with his contributions.

Each of the ten funds operating by 1988 was under strict scrutiny and guidelines governing investments: no more than 50 percent of these funds can be invested in government bonds, and the bonds must be diversified. Otherwise, for the first four years, the AFPs were limited to investments in such "safe" instruments as mortgage bonds, bank certificates of deposit, and private companies' debentures. As the above table indicates, under new rules which went into effect in 1986, the funds are now permitted to invest up to 30 percent of their portfolios in blue-chip stocks and shares of the privatized companies. By late 1987, the AFPs had developed a $2.5 billion pool for investment, with $3.3 million in fresh money flowing into the system every month. That AFP investment pool is equivalent to nearly 10 percent of GDP, an immense source of added strength and solvency for the economy. A stronger and more vigorous economy, in turn, means dividends and growth for the investors, in this case the pension funds. And that means that those pension funds—unlike Social Security in the United States—have continued to grow at an average 10 percent per annum real rate of return. That growth has been through return on investment, of course, not recourse to new taxes. Further to safeguard the funds, the AFPs are required to maintain 90 percent of the financial instruments that make up their portfolios in custody of the Central Bank.

Unlike Social Security funds in the U.S. and other industrialized countries, the size of the individual's ultimate retirement is tied to the amount of his contribution. Low-income workers enjoy special protection: if a worker's pension savings are not enough at the legal retirement age to buy a specified minimum annuity, the government makes up the difference from general tax revenue. Others, on retirement, can keep their money in the AFP they have always used, making limited, regular withdrawals; or, they can use the accumulated capital in their accounts to buy an annuity from an insurance company (with provisions for beneficiaries).

Under the old, government system, since benefits were only loosely tied to contributions, pensions became political footballs. Special interest groups muscled legislators to grant ever greater advantage for their constituents. The result was "a labryinth of different and unfair pension provisions, with some powerful groups able to retire their members with nearly full benefits after as few as 25 years of work." In Chile, as in many countries, pension funds were also "open to use, and mostly abuse, by government bureaucrats not accountable to the ultimate beneficiaries," leading to "gross waste and mismanagement."

As happened in the U.S., when individuals were (briefly) given the right to choose building private pension protection through IRAs rather than being held captive entirely to the wobbly Social Security system, the sale of tax-deferred IRAs boomed. In Chile, not only did the over-whelming majority choose the private plans, but coverage expanded to more than half again as many workers as had ever before been covered: roughly 2.9 million in the private plans as of mid-1988, only half-a-million in the old government plans.[72]

Viewing this massive shift from reliance on Big Brother government to self-reliance, a Christian Democrat policy strategist moaned: "After we take over, we will find a dwarfed state." The party official, Raymond Briones, chairman of a committee examining and critiquing fiscal policy, added: "It might work in Japan, Korea, or Taiwan, but not here. If you remove the state as the motor of development in Chile, then you will be left with foreign control because there is no internal capacity to generate development."

A Chilean banker saw it differently: "Any future government that starts playing with the profits of companies, either through price controls, negative interest rates or something else, will have an immediate impact on the pension funds. And when you play with people's pensions, you get them upset." As the date for elections neared, the radical Left politicians made plain their intention, at first chance, to roll the changes back to the good-old-days of Allende socialism. Christian Democrats, on the other hand, reflected the eternal divisions within the party between the dominant statist thinkers and the party's more moderate wing. But the opposition's electoral program, with the Christian Democrats playing a leading role, took clear aim at the new Social Security system, and left little doubt that, should they reach power, they would also overhaul the business system.[73]

Sergio Bitar, former Allende cabinet minister back from his exile sinecure at Harvard University, called flat-out for renationalization of banking. Edgardo Boeninger Kausel, former rector (president) of the University of Chile and a leading Christian Democrat theoretician, proposed that the state take back "traditional services" (such as electric power) and resume a dominant role in steel, chemical, electronic and large industrial projects, and take minority positions in a variety of other enterprises so as to assure "democratic orientation and control." Such views collided head-on with those of the once-cautious (and formerly state-pampered) National Manufacturing Association (SOFOFA). Its president, Ernesto Ayala, said it would be "solemn stupidity" (disparate) for any government in Chile to implant a "populist" economy. "All populisms are false and demagogic and lead to nothing but distaste, as happened with Argentina's Austral Plan and Brazil's Cruzado Plan, both of which proved to be fiascoes. The Chilean people are smart enough not to believe in phony demagogueries."[74]

This economy which is incapable of generating development did, nonetheless, manage to generate one million new jobs from September of 1982 to May of 1988. By the latter date, it was generating new jobs at the rate of six hundred per day. Manufacturing, long the mangy dog in a state-run kennel, had now become the largest single sector in the national economy (21 percent), growing faster (at 6.5 percent a year) than the economy itself. In 1987, manufacturing provided jobs for a record high 562,000 persons, and was selling more than 1,100 different items to seventy-five different countries. Manufacturing exports, 11 percent of Chile's total in 1970, were now 35 percent of the total, worth $1.8 billion in 1987. With such explosive growth, by the first quarter of 1987, unemployment was down to 8.5 percent; by May of that year, at historic lows in eleven of the country's thirteen regions—and that without inventing jobs in state-run companies that were systematically bankrupting the country. Real wages during 1987 increased by 0.5 percent. Yet another powerful indicator of recovery: at year's end, only 100,000 persons remained in the government's minimum employment program. This country incapable of generating development, in just the first four months of 1988, pushed its exports to yet another record high; higher, indeed, in just four months ($1.725 billion) than for all of 1973. But then, in 1973 exports contributed only 12 percent to the GNP; in 1987, the figure was 28 percent, putting Chile in a class with the "miracle economies" of the Pacific Rim. Fruit exports alone—a piddling $14 million in 1973—continued to climb: up 24 percent in the 1987/1988 season over the same period in 1986/1987, to a thumping $550 million. Finally, this country incapable of generating development managed to achieve in 1987 the highest level of domestic savings in twenty-eight years (32.8 percent of GDP, measured in 1977 pesos).[75]

So strong was the surge in the economy, in fact, that the government moved aggressively to slow growth in 1987 so as not to re-ignite inflation. Still, growth in 1987 set an all-time record: up 5.7 percent, propelled chiefly by the highest volume of exports in the country's history ($5 billion). So conservative are the economic planners that, while welcoming a $400 million windfall coming from the highest copper prices in seven years, they refused to build higher prices into their forecasts. "Rest assured," said Finance Minister Hernán Büchi, "we are not going to turn our back on policies designed to diversify exports, and depend gradually less and less on copper, at the first signs of a bonanza which experience tells us is likely to be temporary."[76]

Chile is the only country in Latin America in which U.S. businessmen can count on political stability. Despite the ... coming plebiscite, I believe that the Chilean economy will continue being good and will continue working adequately. Whether Pinochet stays or does not stay, I believe that those who head the government will realize how crucial agriculture exports are for bringing in hard currency. That they would not jeopardize.

Former Secretary of State Henry
Kissinger, in May 1988

Presumably, Kissinger—so long critical of the Pinochet regime—was now saying the same thing to the blue chip companies he advised on the politics of international investments. A few days before he spoke, the U.S. Commerce Department—in contrast with the continued animosity of the White House, Treasury and State Departments—said Chile's economic prospects continued to be "very positive" despite plebiscite uncertainties. "The firm free market policies of the Chilean government have enabled local and foreign companies to take advantage of new and profitable opportunities." The respected publication, *The International Economy*, in a 1988 "country risk" survey of twelve developing nations in Latin America, Europe and Asia, showed Chile well positioned vis-à-vis the others; the publication also gave Chile its highest "social-political index" rating, meaning the social/political situation in the country allows the adoption of appropriate economic programs.[77]

Even more significant were the judgments of those with a great deal of money at risk. One such was Susan Segal, of New York's Manufacturers Hanover Trust Company, who chaired the twelve-bank committee negotiating Chile's debt with 407 commercial banks. Chile's financial plans, she said, were "an example of how new ideas should be brought to the negotiating table." Of even more significance was the judgment of John Reed, the dynamic young head of the U.S.'s largest bank, Citicorp. Citicorp alone among them had resisted accepting Chile's proposals. In May of 1987, Reed stunned the financial world when he announced that Citicorp intended to increase its reserves by 150 percent to $5 billion as a hedge against losses on its huge portfolio of Third World loans. Commented *The Economist* at the time: "The common sense in the Citicorp decision is that it ends the fiction that a dollar lent to Peru's government or some Marcos-corrupted company in the Philippines is worth the same as a dollar lent to the United States Treasury, or IBM." But the magazine also observed that Reed "must tread carefully" so as not to signal retreat from his steady resistance to letting Third-World debtors off the hook with concessionary interest rates or writing off loans. A month later, Citicorp joined the other banks in agreeing to a new package which saved Chile $1 billion. Then, following a visit to Chile in August, Reed said: "We think the Chilean economy is working very well and should begin to think of a return to the voluntary loan market . . . The Chilean economy is at the best level in Latin America."[78]

Not surprisingly, new investments have cascaded into Chile. Economist José Piñera has divided Chile's postwar period into three stages:

(1) 1954–1970, when foreign investment averaged $200 million yearly, 60 percent of it in the mining sector
(2) 1974–1986, $250 million yearly average; mining still dominated—60 percent—but another 28 percent was in services, such as banking and insurance
(3) 1987, $1 billion in one year; 60 percent in debt-equity swaps, and $400 million in new investments.

If Piñera had been writing a few months later, he might have added a fourth period: 1988. In just the first four months of 1988, new projects totalling $1.430 billion were approved, of which $273.5 million actually entered the country. For the same period in 1987, the corresponding figures wee $327.5 million and $146.5 million.[79]

Some American firms, such as Exxon's mining division, weighed the possibility of developing a copper mining operation to the tune of more than a billion dollars. But after a year's investigation and expenditure of $100 million, the venture came to a halt, with little likelihood that it would continue . . .

The Marxist apologist and prophet Samuel Chavkin, writing in 1985[80]

Mr. Chavkin was, alas, engaging in still more wishful thinking. By 1987, Exxon Minerals had increased its stake for expansion of *Los Bronces* and *El Soldado* mines of its *Disputada* holding to $720 million; $36.8 million of that entered the country in the first quarter of 1988. In 1986, the mines produced 72,000 tons of copper. In fact, although there has been a surge of new investments from Asia and Oceania, the U.S. still leads as a source of investment capital. Among major newer projects: $350 million for a methanol plant at Punta Arenas, in the extreme south (a U.S. consortium), and an Amax investment of $300 million for non-ferrous metals.

But the grand-daddy of new copper investments was being pulled together by a consortium made up of Broken Hill Proprietary of Australia, Río Tinto Zinc of the United Kingdom and Mitsubishi of Japan: in the first quarter of 1988, they added $55 million to a previously invested $85 million to develop the *La Escondida* project. Investment is forecast to reach $1.1 billion, and the mine to produce 330,000 metric tons of high-grade copper annually. Meanwhile, besides the respite in 1987 after the long slump in copper prices, Chileans got more good copper news early in 1988: the discovery of new reserves at the state-held *El*

Salvador mine estimated at 350 million tons, enough to prolong the life of that mine another twenty years.

Over its fourteen years in power, the Pinochet administration had, in fact, invested $4 billion itself into the four *Gran Minería* (Big Mining) operations the government retained—a key factor in the doubling of output from 1973 to 1986 (from 743,000 tons to 1.4 million). Despite low prices, copper and other mining outputs paid $11 billion over that period into the national treasury—more than 15 percent of the country's income.

Foreign investors were active on a wide range of other fronts: Australia's Bond Group acquired 30 percent of the old ITT-owned telephone company (and pumped $123.8 million into the country in actual outlays in the first quarter of 1988). A thirty-one-year-old Brazilian entrepreneur, Eike F. Batista, announced plans early in 1988 for a $180 million investment in a gold and silver mine in the high Andes; together with previously announced investments (involving Shell Oil, Westfield and Citibank), this would push Chile closer to its goal of becoming one of the world's ten largest gold producers by the end of the decade. Japan, which had displaced traditional European markets as Chile's second largest trading partner (after the U.S.), had also become increasingly important as a source of investment capital, including a toehold investment by the KOWA group in the Chemical and Mining Society of Chile (SOQUIMICH). The New Zealand Dairy Board planned a $40 million investment in dairy farming, while Fletcher Challenge of that country earmarked $120 million in a private forestry company. Others, in various stages of processing, included Chile veteran Anaconda Corporation ($65 million for exploration and feasibility studies at a new copper mining site), Anglo American Corporation of South Africa, $70 million for expansion of a copper mine and concentrating plant; Foote Mineral of the U.S., $50 million to exploit lithium reserves.[81]

José Piñera, who had held two cabinet posts under Pinochet, may not be an entirely objective observer, but he is unquestionably an astute observer. In the previously cited talk to fellow entrepreneurs, he spoke of the enormous economic but also social strides made in Chile. They were, he said, the fruits of "a society not obsessed by the State and by political power." Because it reveals so much about the potential that yet remains in the country, the next passage in his remarks bears repeating:

> What has caused this extraordinary transformation? The answer is clear: a coherent socio-economic policy deeply committed to liberty, brought to bear on a potentially wealthy country at a time of great technological progress. Chile is probably one of the countries of the world with the greatest mineral resources per square kilometer of territory. In addition to having the world's largest copper and lithium

reserves, it has important reserves of molybdenum, nitrate, coal, iodine, rhenium, manganese, gold, sulphur, barite and zinc. Its coastline, one of the largest in the world, grants it access to thousands of marine species, which feed along the Chilean seaboard because of the Humboldt current, thus allowing it to create "farms" at sea. Its rich soil permits the production of the best fruit and vegetables and its climate is particularly suited to forestry. Whereas in Sweden or in the United States, the pine grows, respectively, at a rate of 5 and 7 cubic meters per hectare/year, in Chile the growth rate is 22 cubic meters per hectare/year. The country also has important energy resources, mainly hydroelectric, but also in hydrocarbons and other forms of energy. However, only a development strategy based on the country's comparative advantages could have transformed this potential wealth into real wealth.[82]

There are, of course, those who believe that what is good for business—and particularly if it U.S. business—must be bad for "the people." In a commentary on a new UNICEF study of the impact of economic adjustment programs on the poorest in society, *The Economist* said that adjustment programs imposed by the International Monetary Fund (IMF) have "few admirers in rich-country universities, think-tanks and charities. The currently-fashionable complaint is that its 'adjustment programmes' put a needlessly heavy burden on the poorest people— either through incompetence (say the moderates) or by design (as class warriors insist). . . . The charge that the IMF puts the greatest burden on the poor must be taken seriously . . . [but] the IMF is already much closer to being right than its critics allow. Painful adjustment is not always avoidable. When commodity prices fall by the 30% they have done in the 1980s, it is purlblind to suppose that exporters of commodities will not be squeezed. Without the IMF bridging loans, the squeeze would have been far tighter. Anyway, some of the policy changes urged by the Fund are of greatest help to the poorest. . . ." Then, in a discussion of the study itself, this key observation: "The study's second main prescription is that help should be targeted on the poorest people while adjustment programmes are under way. This is more questionable— however inoffensive it sounds. Targeting usually depends on governments. But nothing in this book inspires confidence in the ability of developing-country bureaucrats to hit targets of any kind. . . ."[83]

Yet, as the World Bank study on poverty pointed out, the Pinochet government **did** succeed in "targeting" the needs of the poor. But it did so within an ever-expanding concept of free enterprise. In the process, it created a solid infrastructure for sustained growth, as well cushioned against external shocks as any small and developing country could hope to be in what is a global village.

Building a sturdy, diversified export economy is one facet of this. In a study done by *El Mercurio*, it was shown that between 1964 and 1970, exports grew by only 1.3 percent; during the Allende years, they actually declined by the same percentage; between 1973 and 1987, the annual growth rate averaged 7.4 percent. Even more striking are the comparisons involving nontraditional exports. Between 1964 and 1970, their growth rate averaged 3.7 percent; between 1973 and 1987, 16 percent.[84]

Creating a truly "new Chile" is yet another facet. Nowhere has this been chronicled more powerfully than in a new book by the Chilean economist Joaquín Lavín. Entitled *Chile: A Quiet Revolution,** in 174 fact-packed pages, it recites example after example of what would otherwise become quickly apparent to all but the most casual visitors to Chile who knew the country before and after. The Chile Lavín describes is a country of choices. It is a modern country.

A quick sampling, from Lavín, of the first:

> We were accustomed to retiring from the pension fund for public employees, the Social Security [fund] or the pension fund for private employees; our health was entrusted to the National Health Service, or to the National Medical Service; we studied at the University of Chile, Catholic University or Technical University; we watched TV on channels 13, 11 or 7. Nowadays, things are very different. We can retire from the pension fund that we choose, out of a selection of more than 10; we can entrust our health care to our favorite health insurance fund from a choice of about 20; pursue higher studies at any of the 25 public or private universities or professional institutes; we can choose between 5 TV channels in Santiago, four cable TV channels, and an increasing number of families are doing their own programming by renting films at any of the 87 video clubs in the main cities throughout the country. In 1974, a housewife doing her shopping at Almac supermarket had a choice of 5,500 different products. At present, it is possible for her to choose from among 15,500 various items. . . .[85]

Such a smattering is, of course, far more meaningful for Chileans than outsiders, because Chileans—certainly those old enough to remember—know the distance that separated the promise of socialized medicine in Chile from its realities; they understand how regimented was the fare on those three official television channels (either state- or university-run). Above all, they knew that while Almac may have had 5,500 items in its inventory, the shelves told a much different story.

"Modern" is, in some ways, easier to demonstrate in capsule form. Chile is, for example, the most computerized society in Latin America,

---

* *Chile: A Quiet Revolution* (Santiago: Editorial Zig-Zag, 1988). The book went through four printings in one year in the original Spanish—*Chile, Revolución Silenciosa*—before the first English-language translation.

with over 35,000 in the workplace, another 80,000 in homes. Possessed of the largest proportion of computers per student, it is also the largest exporter of software programs: over $1 million, and growing rapidly. Though dwarfed in population by Brazil and Mexico, and significantly smaller than Argentina, Peru, Colombia and Venezuela, Chile generates the second highest level of computer traffic from the region to the United States. There are more than 1,500 telefacsimile machines in the country; in 1975, international telephone traffic was 4.5 million minutes per year. By 1986, the figure was 40.2 million. Chile is very definitely plugged into the world beyond.

But it is a modern country in many other ways, as well: for example, there are now four thousand hectares of computerized drop-irrigated vines growing in what was, a few years ago, a desert. This is one of the reasons why Chile has become the world's number one exporter of table grapes.

Chile is a new country—in ways subtle, in ways dramatic. One of the dramatic ones is a 1,941-kilometer Austral Highway which now connects Chile's most remote—and until now, mainly isolated—southern regions with the rest of the country. Work on that highway began in 1976, and was officially finished on March 2, 1988, when President Pinochet dedicated a two-ton monument symbolizing the labor of the two thousand workers who toiled to build it. The highway cost $300 million. Before the highway, there was little reason for anyone to live there; in Aysén, population density was only 0.6 persons per square kilometer. Now, there are twenty-three sawmills. Three years ago, there were only four small fishing industries in Puerto Chabuco; now there are eleven, and 3,500 people travel daily from Coyhaique and other inland points to work in them. As the road progressed, so, too, did tourism into that area of gorgeous fjords and stunning glaciers. And, with increased tourism, the number of hostelries and inns increased astronomically. All of this, of course, is but a beginning: The road has opened up 1.6 million hectares of formerly isolated pastureland for livestock breeding. But already, it has changed the lives of the people in that region. In 1972, infant mortality there was 107.9 per thousand, high even by Chilean standards; in 1986, it was 19.7 percent.[86]

It used to be that all roads led to Santiago, because that's where power began and ended. As indicated in the preceding chapter, the next Congress will sit not in Santiago, but in Valparaíso. Projects such as the Austral Highway in other areas of the country have produced "a quiet revolution," too. Between 1974 and 1984, per capita GDP increased in the northern and southern regions; the Santiago metropolitan region's share of gross domestic product fell from 46.5 percent in 1970 to 41.5 percent in 1984. The Valparaíso region, long number two, has been displaced as an economic powerhouse by the Bíobío region to the south

(Concepción as its hub). Decentralization is a reality in another way: municipalities increasingly are able to stand on their own tax-based feet, for the first time. In 1970, the budgets for all municipalities in Chile was $40 million; by 1986, it was up to $700 million, enabling cities to take on such tasks as garbage collection, aid programs for the poor, running 6,800 schools, as well as health care centers, clinics, and even hospitals. Decentralization plus mechanization/modernization— plus a reduction of 208,963 persons employed by the state between 1977 and 1986—means less red tape, a simpler life for average Chileans. It used to take four days to get a birth certificate. It now takes thirty minutes. A passport was a one-week undertaking, and it is now done in less than twenty-four hours. José Piñera observes what transferring power into the provinces has done in another important way: health care. In 1970, none of the "provinces" had an infant mortality rate lower than the national average, then 79.3 per thousand, except for Santiago, which was 53.3 per thousand. By 1983, four regions had rates lower than the national average which itself was down dramatically. In 1970, the National Health Service had a ratio of medical consultation per person of 1.5 in the regions, a figure lower than that of Santiago. By 1983, the ratio had increased to 2.3—slightly higher now than for the capital.[87]

The quality of life in Chile has improved in many other visible—and important—ways. Piñera points out that "these advances have benefited mostly middle and lower-income segments of the population, since those in the higher-income brackets already enjoyed access to these goods by 1970. A few such statistics: in 1970, there were 920,000 home owners. In 1982, there were 1,550,000. Furthermore, the houses they live in are much better. In 1970, 21.3 percent were of adobe, mud, refuse, or similar construction; by 1982, that figure was down to 14 percent. In 1970, 24.6 percent of them did not have electricity. In 1982, 15.3 percent did not. Then, 52 percent had neither shower nor bathtub. In 1982, the figure was 38 percent. The number of television sets increased from 335,400 in 1970 to 1,932,500 in 1982 (and the number of households owning a TV set increased from 19 to 78 percent); refrigerators went from 499,000 to 1,202,900; washing machines, not even counted in 1970 because they were so few, numbered 800,000 by 1982. In 1976, there were 262,000 cars; in 1985, more than 600,000; in a country with so many cities hard by mountains, this has inevitably had a serious downside: severe air pollution problems. The number of telephones per inhabitant rose from 4.5 in 1973 to 6.7 in 1987." It should be emphasized that most of these figures were taken from the 1982 census—before the long and sustained economic take-off. More recent statistics in one area show, for example, that under a $600 million program, 77 percent of the urban population now has sewage systems and 97 percent has drinkable water. Seventy percent of the rural population has drinkable water. By

1990, that was to be increased to 82 percent. And, more recent statistics in yet another area reflect important progress. Between 1973 and 1986, ownership titles to either agricultural or urban land were delivered to 143,628 families, turning 1,453,795 hectares of agricultural land and 32,746,464 square meters of urban land into private property. Many of those beneficiaries were long-neglected Mapuche Indians. Inevitably, this brought some cries that the policy was undermining their culture by fragmenting them; nothing, it would seem, is ever perfect.[88]

> Since the early 1920s, Chile has created an endless number of institutions, enacted laws and channeled public resources toward social development objectives in an effort to upgrade the standard of living of the people, especially those living in poverty.
>
> Public expenditures per capita increased more than 30 times between 1920 and 1970. Early in the 1970s it reached some 15 percent of the GNP. Even so, the contrast between efforts undertaken and results obtained was shocking. The reason was insufficient economic growth and the inefficiency of some of those social programs, the benefits of which did not reach the poorest sectors.
>
> A World Health Organization study singled out Santiago in 1967 as the western hemisphere's most unhealthy city. In the early 1970s, Chile's infant mortality rate was one of the highest in Latin America. The 1974 "Map of Extreme Poverty" prepared by the Catholic University of Chile utilizing 1970 census data, showed 21 percent of the nation's population living in abject poverty.
>
> From 1940 to 1970 the rate of GNP growth per capita was approximately 1.14 percent per year. At that rate, doubling the GNP required 61 years.
>
> Higher education, which benefited 4 percent of the student population, absorbed 50 percent of education resources. Meanwhile, 41 percent of the poorer children did not attend school. Social security system benefits were allocated in accordance with the political power of recipient groups. The poorest of the poor, the independent workers, were completely outside the system. . . .
>
> From a Chilean government working paper discussing the macroeconomic program for 1988 and beyond.[89]

The Pinochet government launched a two-pronged attack on these old and very stubborn problems. The first—building a strong and vibrant economy—has now been widely acknowledged. The second—committing energy, imagination and money to the problem—has not. The record does not justify the verdict. The following three tables put the spending of the Chilean government on social welfare, education, and health in the context of similar spending by Latin America's largest democracies:

TABLE 53

CENTRAL GOVERNMENT SOCIAL EXPENDITURES, 1980–1985
(Percentage of Gross Domestic Product)

COUNTRY	1980	1981	1982	1983	1984	1985
Argentina	5.2	5.2	4.0	5.3	4.9	5.9
Brazil	8.6	9.3	10.6	9.5	8.7	n.a.
CHILE	16.8	20.0	25.3	20.8	20.4	19.4
Colombia	4.5	5.0	5.0	5.1	5.5	n.a.
Mexico	3.8	4.4	4.9	3.6	3.6	3.5
Peru	5.5	5.6	4.9	4.9	4.8	4.6
Venezuela	8.3	9.4	10.0	9.8	9.4	9.8

Source: Social and Economic Progress in Latin America, 1987 Report, Table IV-5, p. 64.

TABLE 54

CENTRAL GOVERNMENT EXPENDITURE ON EDUCATION, 1980–1985
(Percentages of Gross Domestic Product)

COUNTRY	1980	1981	1982	1983	1984	1985
Argentina	1.9	1.8	1.4	1.8	1.7	1.6
Brazil	0.7	0.8	1.0	0.8	0.6	1.2
CHILE	4.1	3.5	3.8	3.3	3.4	3.3
Colombia	2.3	2.3	2.7	2.8	3.0	n.a.
Mexico	3.3	3.8	3.6	2.7	2.6	2.7
Peru	3.6	4.0	3.5	3.5	3.4	3.3
Venezuela	4.3	5.1	4.6	5.0	4.3	5.0

Source: Ibid., Table IV-6, p. 64.

TABLE 55

CENTRAL GOVERNMENT EXPENDITURE ON HEALTH, 1980–1985
(Percentages of Gross Domestic Product)

COUNTRY	1980	1981	1982	1983	1984	1985
Argentina	0.5	0.4	0.3	0.4	0.4	0.5
Brazil	1.3	1.5	1.7	1.5	1.5	n.a.
CHILE	2.1	2.9	3.6	3.0	3.0	2.7
Colombia	0.8	0.9	0.7	0.8	0.7	n.a.
Mexico	0.5	0.5	0.3	0.2	0.3	0.3
Peru	1.3	1.4	1.1	1.3	1.3	1.1
Venezuela	1.1	1.5	1.4	1.3	1.2	1.3

Source: Ibid., Table IV-10, p. 68.

Expressed differently: Chile's social expenditure is about 60 percent of the fiscal budget—four times the rate it was before the Pinochet government came to power. And the results:

> Acute malnutrition, which affected 7 of every 1,000 children in 1975, has practically disappeared.
>
> Infant mortality, 65.8 per 1,000 in 1973, one of the highest rates in Latin America, has dropped to 18.6 per 1,000, one of the lowest in the hemisphere.
>
> Life expectancy at birth grew from 65.1 years in 1973 to 71.48 in 1986.
>
> Acute poverty, measured by the same standards, was reduced from 21 percent in 1970 to 14 percent in 1982.
>
> The number of children from poor families not attending school was reduced from 41 percent in 1970 to 9.9 percent in 1982.
>
> City sewage system coverage grew from 31.1 percent in 1970 to 77.4 percent in 1986.[90]

Life is, of course, the greatest human right of all. Lavín points out that today's young Chileans are better educated and better integrated with the world around them. But, thanks to the kinds of health improvements reflected in the above statistics, "every Chilean born [today] can live 35,000 hours more than those born in 1970."

The Chile they are being born into is a very different Chile from the one the present rulers found fifteen years ago. Pinochet spoke to those born into the new country, the country largely created by him and those who journeyed with him out of the wilderness of unwanted revolution. No longer is it a country, he told them, in which a handful of bureaucrats shape your lives for you. In this talk (at the opening of the fifth annual session of the Economic and Social Council, in May of 1988) he expressed what undoubtedly is the greatest legacy of his government, whatever history's final judgment. The country you build, he told them, will be the one you yourselves design, because the system we have created, the one we leave behind, is one where the state is the servant, the individual the master. In your hands, and no one else's, is the future.

Notes

CHAPTER 12

1. *Chile: An Economy in Transition,* a World Bank Country Study (Washington: The World Bank, 1980), p. 164. Though copyrighted 1979, the study was published in January 1980. The group did its original on-site research in Chile during March-April 1977.

2. Adm. José T. Merino Castro, commander-in-chief of the Chilean navy and "czar" of the economy during the first days of the revolution, in an interview with the author in Santiago, June 9, 1987.

3. Ibid., p. 14.

4. William Montalbano, "Chile Struggles, Still a Chaotic Economic Lab," Santiago-datelined story in the *Miami Herald,* November 19, 1975, p. 8-D. Montalbano cast the entire drama, as the headline indicated, in terms of economic "experimenting," managing the extraordinary feat of getting through an entire story splashed across all eight columns of the newspaper without mentioning external factors. "In theory," he wrote, "the short-term effect of concentrating more wealth in fewer hands will have long-term benefit by stimulating new investment and promoting genuine economic growth. The social side of the picture is grim." He quoted—without further identifying—the "Jesuit" magazine *Mensaje* on the impact of the recession on poor families. Interestingly, he was re-cycling the identical example taken from *Mensaje* by Joanne Omang of the *Washington Post,* and printed in his newspaper six months before: "Chile Feels Shock Treatment," May 30, 1975, p. 24-A. Omang, however, referred to *Mensaje* as "the respected Catholic Church journal." As we have seen, *Mensaje* was a radical-left publication, and a favorite of American reporters eager to make their own points, even if it meant copying the same example from it six months later.

5. *Chile: An Economy in Transition,* op. cit., pp. 1–2. Nor should it be supposed that statism was a phenomenon that came of age during the Allende years. As detailed in chapter 4, the greatest transformations took place during the Frei years. As this report notes (p. 39): "The growth of the public sector accelerated under President Frei, total expenditures rising 16 percent per year in real terms from 1964 to 1968, or from 31 to 37 percent of GDP. Government explicitly assumed primary responsibility for promoting economic and social development."

6. Quoted in A. Pineda de Castro, *Pinochet: Verdad y Ficción* (Madrid: Vasallo de Mumbert, 1981), p. 187. The author does not indicate the circumstances of the statement, but it resembles many similar statements Pinochet made during the early years of his government.

7. *Chile: An Economy in Transition,* op. cit., p. 110; "Cuantiosos Aportes a Reconstrucción," *El Mercurio,* March 7, 1974, p. 1. The donations were valued at 1,508 millions escudos—about $1.5 million at the then-official

exchange rate. About 20,000 of the donations were rings. The most valuable objects were auctioned off internationally.

8. In an interview with *Qué Pasa* magazine, "Habla El Almirante Merino," #152, March 22, 1974, p. 9. As pointed out in chapter 9, Admiral Merino had already begun working with his economic team in March of 1973; among them were Léniz, the first civilian economy minister, retired admiral Roberto Kelly, who took over the State Planning Office (and in 1979, also served as economy minister).

9. Arturo Fontaine Aldunate, *Los Economistas y el Presidente Pinochet* (Santiago: Editorial Zig-Zag, 1988), pp. 18–20 and 39–40. Fontaine relates that the day after the revolution, Merino had summoned Kelly—an old friend and sailing companion, as well as fellow officer—to give him names for the new economic team. Kelly began with the names of the group, adding more as he went along. As he was about to leave, Merino informed him that he was to take over the cabinet-level Office of State Planning; Kelly had to look up the address of this unfamiliar agency in the telephone book before he could start work. Kelly remained in that post until 1979, serving for another year as economy minister. De Castro had enrolled in 1952 at the Catholic University's School of Commercial Engineering (as the business school was then called). In June 1955, four University of Chicago economists arrived in Chile to negotiate an exchange agreement—funded by the U.S. "Point Four" program, forerunner of the Agency for International Development—with Catholic University that included setting up a Center for Economic Studies (*Centro de Investigaciones Económicas*). The group was made up of T.W. Schultz, chairman of the Chicago Economics Department and a later Nobel laureate; Professor Earl J. Hamilton; Professor Arnold C. Harberger (future dean and the spiritual mentor of the Chileans in the years ahead); and Professor Simon Rottenberg. The 3-year agreement was concluded in 1959, later extended to 1964. It was the beginning of the Chicago Boys era. De Castro, one of the interpreters for the visitors, was later one of the first selected for post-graduate study at Chicago, and still later returned for a doctorate. Ibid., pp. 23–25. Baraona, who also did his graduate studies at Chicago, formed a close friendship with de Castro while he was serving as dean of the Catholic University School of Economics and de Castro headed the Center for Economic Studies. In 1966, they "discovered" Emilio Sanfuentes and persuaded him to do graduate work at Chicago. Cruzat took his master's degree in economics at Chicago, his doctorate at Harvard. Bardón also studied at Chicago—where his classmates included Emilio Sanfuentes and another later economy minister, Sergio de la Cuadra (who served briefly, in 1982); others who knew each other at Chicago included Miguel Kast Rist, state planning director and labor minister (1979–1982); Juan Carlos Méndez (budget director since 1975).

10. The first serious dispute within the economic team was over the dizzying price rises which followed freeing prices and devaluating the peso. At a stormy junta meeting October 2, 1973, Admiral Merino stormed at Rear Adm. Lorenzo Gotuzzo, the first finance minister: "Admiral, you have been deceived. I order you to stop that devaluation (to 850 escudos to the dollar)." Gotuzzo refused. After a tense silence, Pinochet recessed the meeting to allow tempers to cool. General Leigh then proposed summoning Raúl Sáez as an adviser. Sáez, who had arrived only a few days before from Caracas, agreed to serve first as an adviser to Pinochet, playing a key role in the first

U.S. and European debt renegotiations; he later (in July 1974) was named minister of economic coordination, finally leaving government in 1976. On October 15, the compromise was announced: three rates, one for tourists (850), one for foreign trade (280), a temporary one for copper (115). It was Sáez who proposed Fernando Léniz Cerda, then general manager of the *El Mercurio* group, as the first civilian economy minister. Like Sáez, Léniz was not an economist but an engineer—one of several who would occupy key positions in the Pinochet economic brain trust. Sáez, whose own father had gone from army enlisted man to general officer, had, in the devastating 1960 earthquake, attracted the attention of a young air force officer for the job he did of clearing a landslide-blocked river near Valdivia. That officer was Gustavo Leigh. Sáez went on to become one of the original "nine wise men" of the Alliance for Progress, and served briefly as finance minister under Frei (quitting when political ideologues around Frei gutted his plan for fighting an inflationary crisis). Although steeped in the "developmental" ideas so in vogue in and around the Alliance, which made the state the centerpiece of development, Sáez became a team player in the challenge of rebuilding the country. Notes the author made while awaiting an interview with Economy Minister Fernando Léniz, May 8, 1974, reflect the "spartan" theme: "The only 'decoration' in the spacious but starkly-plain reception room was the ubiquitous 'Sea Breve—Estamos Atrasados 3 Años' [Be brief, etc.] sign on the glass door leading to his private secretary's office. Scattered around the room: cheap, imitation leather chairs, a small lamp with a dirty white shade, and some old provincial telephone books, the only 'reading' materials." The confrontation scene from Fontaine, op. cit., pp. 53–57.

11. Robert Moss, "The Tribulation of Chile," *National Review*, October 10, 1975, p. 1111.

12. Figures from *Chile: An Economy in Transition*, op. cit., pp. 93, 95, 104; Merino, "Almirante Merino; análisis de doce meses," *Ercilla*, #2041, September 11–17, 1974, p. 14. Record high copper price in *1975 Book of the Year* (Chicago: Encyclopaedia Britannica, 1976), p. 489. Merino was far from alone in his optimism: I spent a good part of 1974 living in Chile, interviewing scores of persons in and out of government, Chileans and foreigners, of all stations. There was a generalized optimism, much of it doubtless the continuing after-glow of the widely felt sense of deliverance from the Allende cataclysm. As early as March 24, 1974, *El Mercurio*, highly responsible and authoritative in its economic reporting, was headlining an ODEPLAN report at the top of its business page (p. 43), "Notable Recuperación de la Economía Chilena," (Notable Recovery of the Chilean Economy).

13. *Chile: An Economy in Transition*, op. cit., p. 106 (total cost oil drop and percentages); wheat/fertilizer, p. 144; terms of trade, p. 112. Actual oil import figures, *Indicadores Económicos y Sociales 1960–1985*, op. cit., p. 344; sugar from "Crisis en la Política Económica," *Qué Pasa*, #152, March 22, 1974, pp. 10–11. When sugar prices rose sharply in 1973, Japan decided to protect itself, covering its 1974 needs with a single, 500,000-ton purchase, which triggered the sudden explosion of the world price. An example of the careless (or perverse) reporting which has characterized so much media reportage on Chile: William R. Long, then an Associated Press writer stationed in Chile, wrote late in 1976 of "periodic dips in world prices of copper." In the same Santiago-datelined dispatch, he wrote of "highly favorable world copper prices in the middle months of the year" as a contributing

factor in the country's trade surplus. Copper prices in 1976 averaged 59.9 cents a pound, barely one-half the highest Allende year average, and as the 1980 World Bank study showed, for the entire period of 1971–1978, the average real price for copper was 40 percent below that of the years 1971–1973 (op. cit., p. 104.) He also wrote that triple-digit inflation began with Allende; actually it began in the last two Frei years (1969 and 1970). "Chile Economic Plight Improves, Figures Show," the *Miami Herald*, October 19, 1976, p. 18–A.

14. Wage adjustments from Paul E. Sigmund, *The Overthrow of Allende and the Politics of Chile, 1964–1976* (Pittsburgh: University of Pittsburgh Press, 1977), p. 268. *Chile: An Economy in Transition*, op. cit., pp. 144–145 (inflation), p. v (unemployment and worst depression), p. 96 (lost decade), p. 164 (hardship). Michael Fleet, *The Rise and Fall of Chilean Christian Democracy* (Princeton: Princeton University Press, 1985), pp. 184–185. For food consumption figures, he cites James Wilkie and Stephen Haber, eds., *Statistical Abstract of Latin America*, Vol. 18 (Los Angeles: UCLA Latin American Center, 1981), p. 7. Fleet credits the Catholic church for setting up life-saving soup kitchens and food distribution programs, but makes no mention of the government's jobs and other emergency welfare programs.

15. Robert Moss, "The Tribulation of Chile," *National Review,* October 10, 1975, p. 1112.

16. It was a measure of how far "Fried-mania" had advanced in Chile that *El Mercurio*, on May 11, 1974, reprinted on page two the entire text of a paper Friedman had co-authored in 1946 on rent control. The irony is that the *real* intellectual godfather of Chile's economic "miracle" was *not* Friedman—who made only one or two lightning trips to Chile at the peak of his U.S. fame—but his Chicago colleague, Professor Arnold C. Harberger, who has known Chile intimately for over 30 years. The media assumed "Chicago" must mean Friedman—and another media myth was born.

17. "Defuse bomb" and goals from "El difícil cambio de rumbo," *Ercilla*, #2041, September 11–17, 1974, p. 19. *Chile: An Economy in Transition*, op. cit., pp. 119–121. The 5 percent surcharge on income tax was removed in September 1976, and other reductions went into effect on January 1, 1977. The VAT exemptions remained in force until 1977. Other features of the new law were introduction of a tax on undistributed corporate earnings, previously untaxed; elimination of taxes on capital gains; unification of the tax base and rate schedules, thereby abolishing a large number of special rates, exemptions, and loopholes; the extension of indexing to the valuation of all business assets and liabilities. The assessed values of agricultural and non-agricultural properties were raised again, by factors of three and four, and income tax rates also raised again, as were such user taxes as road tolls. As the study notes (p. 161), the elimination of the tax on capital gains has theoretically reduced the progressiveness of the tax structure. In reality, assessing and collecting the tax had always been difficult in Chile, and it had never yielded significant revenues. The study's authors had reservations only about reduction of corporate and other business incomes, and the elimination of the tax on net wealth. But they added that if the government was right—that those measures would stimulate savings and investment and, thus, economic growth—then they could prove beneficial to the entire society.

18. Joseph Novitsky, in a Santiago-datelined story published in the *Miami*

Herald, October 28, 1974, p. 8–D. Reporters and correspondents are not responsible, of course, for the headlines on their stories, but Novitsky's handling of the data clearly justified this one. In it, for example, he speaks of "a recent shift that benefited only the well-to-do. . . . For a year, the country's military government has enforced an economic austerity program that has squeezed those two million [poorest] hardest, driving down already insufficient diet levels and leaving people hungry and politically unhappy." This story did not even include the usual perfunctory aside about the military inheriting a country in a mess; perfunctory because the writers would then routinely ignore the implications of what it means to inherit a country in a mess. Quite apart from that egregious deficiency, this writer also errs wildly in asserting that the policies were designed to "benefit only the well-to-do." As the World Bank study notes (p. 118), "government spending continued to grow rapidly in nominal terms, rising more than 5½ times from 1973 to 1974. A major element in this increase was the Government's effort to partially restore and maintain employee purchasing power through a series of large wage adjustments. . . ." That this policy was not altogether successful does not detract from the intent of its design. Obviously, in an economy in ruins, the poor do suffer—greatly. But it makes no sense to impute their plight to those who are trying to solve the problems created by others. These observations are important because such news stories, published in Washington and other key cities and capitals, played an important role in shaping the perceptions of policy-makers and others towards Chile.

19. *Chile: An Economy in Transition,* op. cit., pp. 116–117, 121, 123, and 155. State company debt from "Rol del Sector Público en Economía," *El Mercurio,* May 4, 1974, p. 2. The debt was 288,920,447,000 escudos; money in the private sector as of that date, December 31, 1973, was 210,373,000,000. Bread subsidy figure from "Crisis en la Política Económica?" *Qué Pasa,* #152, March 22, 1974, p. 10. The state nitrate and coal companies (SOQUIMICH and ENACAR) and the national airline (LAN) were the only major state companies still receiving operating subsidies in 1977. One of the few exceptions to the no-subsidies policy was in the forest area: an ambitious reforestation program to quadruple Chile's long-fiber forest resources by the late 1990s. As we shall see, that policy has paid extremely handsome dividends already.

20. Merino, "Habla El Almirante Merino," *Qué Pasa,* #152, March 22, 1974, p. 8. He added that "we cannot just throw these people into the street," but he spoke before the depression hit. The 30 percent figure is from *Chile: An Economy in Transition,* op. cit., p. 116.

21. Fontaine, op. cit., p. 87. This heretofore unreported episode—as are so many in Fontaine's excellent and fascinating book—took place beginning early in 1975. Fontaine says merely that "the [serious] indisposition of the Admiral appears to reflect the anxieties of the moment."

22. *Chile: An Economy in Transition,* op. cit., pp. 45–47, 132, 136. The report noted (p. 137) that the problem was compounded in February 1977 when new regulations designed to restore confidence in finance companies— raising to the equivalent of about $1 million the capital and reserve requirement for loans without commercial bank guarantees—had the effect of inhibiting access to credit of small and medium firms.

23. Reprinted in *United States and Chile During the Allende Years, 1970–1973* (Washington: Government Printing Office, 1975), p. 659; a compilation of

testimony and documents assembled by the Subcommittee on Inter-American Affairs of the Foreign Affairs Committee, U.S. House of Representatives. Ms. Farnsworth's overheated rhetoric was typical of commentary on Chile appearing at the time in even respected international journals.

24. *Chile: An Economy in Transition*, op. cit., p. 114. As the study notes, "Chile's long history of balance of payments difficulties have made it a frequent and heavy user of IMF credit facilities"—from the very inception of the Fund. *New York Times* editorial, published September 11, 1977, cited in *American-Chilean Council Report*, #3, September 29, 1977, p. 1. The Council, now defunct, was based in New York City.

25. Ibid., p. 110. As the report notes, the denial of credits was a major factor in aggravating the 1975 downturn. Professor Paul N. Rosenstein-Rodan had been among those urging the Committee of the Alliance for Progress to support Chile's recovery efforts. He told the committee that Chile deserved such support because of its demonstrated determination to develop a well-coordinated economic policy, develop agricultural production, and stimulate copper and non-traditional exports. He predicted that with outside support, Chile was likely to restore per capita wages and salaries to 1970 levels within two years' time. Even with the unforeseen depression, he wasn't far off the mark; the wage and salary indices both exceeded 1970 levels by July 1977. "Statements made by Fernando Léniz, Jorge del Canto, Walter Sedwitz and Paul Rosenstein-Rodan to CIAP Subcommittee Meetings in Santiago, a booklet published by Editora Nacional Gabriela Mistral, 1974, pp. 26–27.

26. The decision to withdraw was actually based on a refusal to ratify the Pact's Decision 100 of April 10, 1976, which would have postponed crucial deadlines and altered certain negotiation procedures. By withdrawing then, Chile was released from the requirement in the original Pact to adhere to most Pact commitments for five years. As important as the foreign investment law was to Chile's decision, the Pact's policies on external tariffs was important too, running counter to Chile's decision to break the protectionist mold. The Pact had been floundering already; it had succeeded in approving only two industrial programs in six years, and only one country (Peru) had ratified one of them (dealing with petrochemicals). Furthermore, fully half of Chile's imports from member countries were petroleum products and other raw materials outside the Pact's rules. Source for foregoing: *Bank of London & South American Review*, Vol. 10, November 1976, pp. 611–613. In 1972, only 13.7 percent of Chile's exports were sold to the eleven LAFTA nations (the ten South American countries, plus Mexico); by contrast, it bought 21.8 percent of its imports in those countries. Source: *Economic and Social Progress in Latin America*, 1973 annual report (Washington: Inter-American Development Bank, 1974), p. 85.

27. Quoted by Joseph Novitsky, "Chile Shifts Fiscal Policy—But Will It Aid Poor?" op. cit. Vial was president of the Banco Hipotecario. Novitsvky reported that he had stayed in Chile during the Allende years, trying to defend in the courts his properties—the bank and two appliance factories. He lost, but shortly after the revolution, got them back, as did other owners whose properties had been seized illegally. Vial told Novitsky his group planned to double its output of appliances, double the output of a small copper mine, and build three new Holiday Inn hotels in Chile—a planned investment of $164 million over six years, which would create five thousand

jobs. Vial and his one-time associate Manuel Cruzat built two of the highest-powered international consortia ever to arise in Chile. Both the Grupo Vial and the Grupo Cruzat Larraín became over-extended in credit; the first collapsed in the 1982 crash, and the second was able to negotiate a rescue operation with the government. Many prominent figures in the government had, at one time or another, been closely associated with one or another of these two men—leading to inevitable charges and insinuations of wrongdoing. But, as we shall see, when the moment of truth came, at least one top government official—Rolf Luders—would put his sense of duty ahead of allegiance to his former associates.

28. *Bolsa Review,* Vol. 7, #83, November 1973, p. 560 (resumed operations), and Vol. 8, #89, May 1974, p. 280 (import controls); Roberto Zahler in *Perspectivas Económicas Para la Democracia: Balance y Lecciones Para La Experiencia Chilena,* Jorge Rodríguez Grossi, ed. (Santiago: Instituto Chileno de Estudios Humanísticos, 1984), p. 23 (duties) (referred to hereafter as *Perspectivas Económicas Para la Democracia*); "Espectacular Desarrollo Del Comercio Exterior," *El Mercurio,* September 11, 1974, p. 48 (imports); *Chile: An Economy in Transition,* op. cit., pp. 101 and 108.

29. In an interview with *Qué Pasa* magazine, "Habla El Almirante Merino," #152, March 22, 1974, p. 9. Spurred by subsidies—the only important ones retained—forestation in Chile expanded rapidly. The prerevolution high was in 1972: 24.8 thousand hectares under the National Forest Corporation, 6.3 thousand in private hands. By 1976, the state share was 54.1 thousand hectares, the private 53.6, for a total of 107.7 thousand hectares—more than triple the previous high. Source: *Estudio Económico de América Latina 1977* (Santiago: U.N. Economic Commission for Latin America, 1978), pp. 178–179; unemployment figures from *Bolsa Review,* Vol. 11, January 1977, p. 30. The World Bank study (p. 139) shows unemployment peaking at 19.8 percent in the first quarter of 1976.

31. *Chile: An Economy in Transition,* pp. 94–96 and 154. The report reinforces caveats entered several times earlier in this book as to the reliability of statistics, particularly in the precomputerization and highly inflationary years. For example, the report notes (p. vi): "Caution is called for in the use of Chilean economic statistics. The rapid changes that have occurred in recent years have made their interpretation subject to a wider than normal range of error. Despite such caveats, however, the mission believes that it has been possible to identify correctly the fundamental trends of economic policy and performance in Chile over the past several decades and that conclusions of the report are supported by the evidence. . . ." (p. 9): "There are, unfortunately, no reliable national unemployment data for Chile, either historical or current. Systematic, regular labor force surveys are carried out only in the Santiago metropolitan area. . . ." (p. 158): "Several important caveats are required when discussing the wage share data from the national income accounts. The first is the already noted unreliability of the national income accounts themselves under the weight of the enormous statistical problems of the past decade. Second, the division of income into labor and non-labor income is misleading, inasmuch as the latter includes the earnings of all self-employed persons in unincorporated enterprises. . . ."

32. Ibid., pp. 154 and 156.

33. Ibid., pp. 155–156. Farmers in the so-called "reform" sector made up approximately 12 percent, and minifundistas 42 percent of the total farm population in 1976. (Ibid., p. 185).

34. Ibid., pp. 171–172, 174, and 190–191. Under Allende, the Agriculture Ministry payroll alone grew from fewer than 11,000 to more than 27,000 employees.

35. Ibid., pp. 142–143, 151–153, 157, and 159. The report notes that evasion was also encouraged by the fact that actual benefits were unrelated to the level of earnings reported over most of the lifetime of a contributor. "Double-dipping"—working in another job while collecting a pension—had also become common—and legal.

36. Ibid., pp. viii and 163.

37. As quoted in *Hoy*, Special Edition, "La Década de *Hoy*," May 1987, p. 40—with apologies to the original writer for slippage in translation.

38. *Chile: An Economy in Transition*, op. cit., Table III.21, p. 148. The 1971 averages were 137–141 for blue collar workers, 108–110 for white collar workers. In 1972, those averages were 115–130 and 80–91, respectively. In the first quarter of 1973, the bottom really fell out, the indices standing at 58–91 and 38–59, respectively; the massive wage adjustments at year's end pushed minimum wage blue collar workers to a high (155–137) not reached again until the last quarter of 1976, and their white collar counterparts to a level (78–70) they would not either see again until the end of 1976. The study speculates that the differences between average and minimum wages and salaries happened because of "a significant narrowing of pay differentials among blue collar workers, at the same time that scales were stretching out in the case of white collar workers." (Ibid., p. 148.)

39. *Indicadores Económicos y Sociales 1960–1985*, op. cit., pp. 152 (CPI figures), 264 (labor force/employed figures), 266 (those entering work force); *Chile: An Economy in Transition*, op. cit., p. 139 (1976–1977 unemployment); *Orden Económico y Democracia* (Santiago: Centro de Estudios del Desarrollo, 1985), p. 207 (1978–1981 unemployment averages). The inflation rate for all of Latin America in 1976 averaged 64 percent, though it dropped in 1977 to 41.8 percent; still, for countries with "high inflation" that year, of which Chile was one, the overall rate was 126.5 percent (Source: *Estudio Económico de América Latina, 1977*, op. cit., p. 29). The province of Santiago's population increased from 2,237,425 in 1960 to 3,320,790 in 1970—a significant percentage of whom (17.4 percent) had no education, and thus obviously represented a severe challenge for any government seeking to incorporate the newcomers into the productive economy, further complicated by the fact that many were Araucanian Indians or peasants with no experience in urban living. (Source: "La Población se Ha Incrementado en 32.55%," *El Mercurio*, February 9, 1975, p. 28.) The metropolitan population of Santiago, defined somewhat differently, had grown at an annual rate of 3.4 percent beginning in 1961, a growth rate that slowed significantly only in 1975 as the rural economy began to pick up. By the 1980s, it was down to annual growth rates of 2.4 percent, but by 1980, the metropolitan population had risen from 2.087 million in 1960 to 3.763 million in 1980. The World Bank report notes (p. 141) that "there may, in fact, have been an increase in the importance of self-employment during the economic crisis despite the failure of the statistics to record it. For labor force reporting purpose, some individuals who have lost their jobs may be considered by their family members, as well as by themselves, to be unemployed, even though they have solicited and performed some remunerated work in a self-employed capacity. Since they are not employed in their customary status, they view and report themselves as unemployed. We

would be inclined to believe that some greater measure of such irregular self-employment has escaped the survey enumerators and that, as a result, the number of self-employed workers has been understated. If so, the rate of unemployment, as defined for the purposes of the survey, has been overstated."
40. *Estudio Económico de America Latina, 1977,* op. cit., p. 197; David Gallagher, "Chile After The Fall: Free-Market Policy Gradually Vindicated," the *Wall Street Journal,* May 31, 1985, cited in *Chile: An Appraisal of Investment Opportunities in the Equity Market* (Toronto: Friedberg Commodity Management, Inc., 1986), p. 15. The author had done limited consulting work with that firm in 1987.
41. Export figure from José Piñera, "A New Chile," reprint of an April 1988 article in *Economía y Sociedad,* p. 2. On October 28, published reports claimed the U.S. had "reliable intelligence" that Chile had provided cluster bombs to Panama for use by the Sandinista government of Nicaragua against the *contras.* Chile issued a formal denial the next day. John M. Goshko, "U.S. Says Chile, Panama Help To Arm Nicaragua," the *Washington Post,* October 28, 1987, p. A–23, and "Chilean Denial on Bombs," October 29, 1987, p. A–40. The story was an absurdity to begin with: Panama and Nicaragua are two of the hemisphere countries which have been most aggressively hostile to Chile—and which Pinochet and his government have repeatedly singled out as examples of what governments should not be. Furthermore, the original story included this: "Spokesmen here for the three countries said they had no information about such a sale but that the story sounded improbable." The original story was published at the top of the page, under a bold, two-column headline; the denial appeared in a news-briefs column under the smallest type-size headline the *Post* uses for news stories.
42. *Indicadores Económicos y Sociales 1960–1985,* op. cit., pp. 339 and 341 (exports), 344 (make-up of imports); *Economic and Social Progress in Latin America,* op. cit., 1980–1981 and 1986 Annual Reports, pp. 426 and 419, respectively (import figures); *American-Chilean Council Report,* op. cit., September 29, 1977, p. 4 (Belnap, Eurodollar and AP references; the *Los Angeles Times* story was published August 8, and the AP story August 14, in (among others) the *Chicago Sun-Times*); Zahler in *Perspectivas Económicas Para La Democracia,* op. cit., Table 6, p. 28 (debt figures). *Hoy,* special edition, op. cit., p. 40 (*pisco*/scotch). The 1981 import figures, and corresponding extrapolations, are approximations, inasmuch as they were based on Customs Service figures and not directly comparable to the other Central Bank-based figures. Most of the international press continued to ignore and/or explain away Chile's spectacular success story. Despite a GDP growth rate which more than doubled the average for Latin America as a whole in 1977, even the *1978 Book of the Year* (Chicago: Encyclopaedia Britannica, 1978), while taking note of major indicators, wrote (p. 248): "The slow recovery of the economy continued."
43. It is a further measure of Chavkin's point of view that he ascribed "much of" Chile's foreign debt to "shady speculative ventures by several powerful conglomerates which also controlled Chile's principal banks." The book is mainly a series of stenographic records of rambling recitals by Mrs. Allende and other Popular Unity figures. As to the need for "anonymity," fully eight years earlier, columnist Jeffrey Hart wrote in the *Los Angeles Herald-Examiner,* while on a reporting trip to Chile: "In the real world, you know when people are living in a state of 'fear.' In the Soviet Union chance acquain-

tances will not talk with you. They are genuinely afraid. One of the hazards of social life here in Santiago, however, is that when you ask someone what he or she thinks of the government you are likely to get a half-hour disquisition. People here argue heatedly about current government policy. . . ." Another, Michael Padev, a member of the Washington bureau of the *Indianapolis News*, wrote about the same time: "Nobody can fool me into believing that a government is democratic when it is dictatorial, or that a regime is popular when it is not. I found the Pinochet regime genuinely popular though, like in most countries including our own, I heard a lot of criticism against its policies, especially in the economic field." Both cited in *American-Chilean Council Report*, op. cit., October 31, 1977, pp. 1–2.

44. Mark Falcoff, "The Coming Crisis in Chile," Policy Review, #34, Fall 1985. Falcoff was then a resident fellow at the American Enterprise Institute—yet another nominally conservative organization—and associate director of its Center for Hemispheric Studies. Among the gaffes were to speak of the bank takeover as "Pinochet's socialism," this fully a year after the reprivatization program was well underway. He spoke also of "a brief if remarkable economic recovery" from 1978 to 1981, "fueled by high prices for copper, its principal export, and by a flood of new foreign loans"—managing, in a single sentence, to get both cause and effect wrong, and the time frame in which they occurred, to boot. Falcoff further demonstrated his depth of understanding when he wrote of "the unlikely event that the debtors can find a way to retire their loans"; his superficiality when he repeated the tinny cliché that "until 1973, [Chile] possessed the most stable and established democratic system in Latin America, with a political culture, at least superficially similar to Italy or Fourth Republic France." (!) Altogether, I enumerated twenty-four such examples of speciousness in the six-and-a-half pages of that article. The basic thrust of his "argument" was that the U.S. ought to use Chile's debt and need for further capital as bludgeons to pummel Pinochet out of power. It needs be remembered that this folderol was published in the fall of 1985, well into the second consecutive year of strong economic recovery.

45. David Gallagher in the *Wall Street Journal*, op. cit. ("heroic attempt"); *1983 Book of the Year*, op. cit., p. 632 (impact on U.S.); *Hoy*, special edition, op. cit., pp. 40–41 (Latin American unemployment); *Poverty in Latin America: The Impact of Depression* (Washington: The World Bank, 1986), pp. 3–4 and 6 (referred to hereafter as *Poverty in Latin America*). Gallagher, a former fellow at St. Anthony's College, Oxford, was then a business consultant in Chile.

46. *Poverty in Latin America*, op. cit., pp. 4–5 (Latin America statistics); *Indicadores Económicos y Sociales 1960–1985*, op. cit., p. 116 (Chile per capita); *Perspectivas Económicas Para La Democracia*, op. cit., Juan Foxley R. and Pablo Piñera E., "Sistema Financiero y Política de Crédito en Chile," p. 86 (number of banks/financial institutions), and Roberto Zahler, op. cit., p. 31 (*Banco Osorno* and CRAV).

47. Luders received both masters and doctorate degrees from Chicago. In 1971, he left Chile for a cushy post in the Organization of American States in Washington—like Caus, he returned to Chile in 1974. A former dean of the School of Economy of Catholic University, he turned now to private business, rising to become the number two man—and largest shareholder—in the Vial Group. Luders left the group in March 1982 because of disagreements with Vial. Fontaine, op. cit., pp. 166–169.

48. Luders from a conversation with the author in Baltimore, June 4, 1988. On Monday, Pinochet put on his hat as military commander-in-chief and worked out of the Defense Ministry. The night of the bank intervention, Luders gave a nationally televised talk in which he sharply criticized economic consortia. Fontaine observes that Luders thereby put both the Cruzat and Vial groups in a pincers. Foreign creditors, listening to what he said, obviously would not now bail them out; the intervention of institutions in which they had such heavy interests (*Banco Hipotecario* and *Banco de Chile*, both in the Vial group, and *Banco de Santiago*, Cruzat group, headed then by Jorge Cauas, as well as the group's *Colocadora Nacional de Valores*), meant that their internal lines of credit were also cut. Other, more conservative groups, Fontaine adds, were able to "emerge vigorous from the crisis ... able to build on solid bases the advances begun by the Cruzat and Vial groups." Fontaine, op. cit., pp. 170–171. Luders was dismissed from his job on February 14, 1983—a "scapegoat," as *1984 Book of the Year*, op. cit., p. 233 (among others) would note. The economy minister's job, long a stepchild under Pinochet, became a revolving door thereafter—five would follow Luders between 1983 and 1988; two followed in the finance minister's job (Carlos Cáceres and Luis Escobar), before Hernán Büchi Buc would settle in on February 12, 1985.

49. Statement of Finance Minister Hernän Büchi, June 28, 1985, to the international finance community, in *Chile: An Appraisal of Investment Opportunities in the Equity Market*, op. cit., p. 21 (bank intervention; 42 percent reflects the 1980 share of those banks); Foxley & Piñera in *Perspectivas Económicas Para la Democracia*, op. cit., pp. 87 (emergency credits) and one hundred (crowing); Zahler, ibid., p. 31 (failure of model). Zahler wrote off the 1977–1980 boom as "a transitory bonanza" (p. 45); "The Chilean economic experience for the period 1974–1982," he asserted, "has been a failure ... the Chilean economy puffed up like a huge bubble in these years, people thought they were rich and increased their spending as a result" (pp. 39 and 41). Although it may be obvious, the authors in this book write from a Christian Democrat/statist economic bias.

50. "Las Fuerzas Armadas en el Acontecer Político," *El Mercurio*, September 22, 1985, p. 1 (Pinochet); "Warming to Popular Capitalism," in a special paid supplement in *Euromoney* magazine, September 1987, pp. 11–15 (banking).

51. *Poverty in Latin America*, op. cit., pp. 11–12 and 16 (indexing, "worst," and unemployment statistics, including 27 percent); *Indicadores Económicos y Sociales 1960–1985*, op. cit., pp. 282–284. The number covered by PEM declined steadily to 105,646 in December 1985, the last month covered by this report; POJH—*Programa Ocupacional para Jefes de Familia*, or Occupational Program for Heads of Family—remained at high levels through 1984–1985; at year's end, it still stood at 171,360.

52. Fontaine, for example, attributes the moves to Pinochet's affinity for "balances and counter-weights"—a variation of "rolling with the punches," op. cit., p. 174. From the beginning, the new Finance Minister, Carlos Cáceres Contreras, found himself checkmated. Among those who accompanied him to Washington for his 1983 conversations with the International Monetary Fund was a man who had come to enjoy Pinochet's confidence: Hernán Felipe Errázuriz, then president of the Central Bank, but who had previously (1982–1983) served as the first civilian secretary-general of the government. Pinochet later named Errázuriz to another delicate job: ambassador to Washington, still later (1988), Foreign Minister.

53. Frederick N. Nunn, "One Year in the Life of Augusto Pinochet: Gulag of the Mind," *The Americas*, October 1985, pp. 204–205. Nunn, on the faculty of Portland (Oregon) State University, said he interviewed Pinochet on September 5, 1983.

54. The 1982 Food for Peace total was $2.3 million; in 1983, the last year, $1 million.

55. *Indicadores Económicos y Sociales 1960–1985*, op. cit., pp. 164 (exchange rates) and 148 (CPI for 1981 and 1982); 1985 figure from *Economic and Social Progress in Latin America: 1987 Report*, p. 20. In 1985, Mexico's CPI index was 57.7, Peru's 163.4, Nicaragua's 219.5, Brazil's 227, Argentina 672.2 and Bolivia a preposterous 11,749.6. Chile's dropped to 17 percent in 1986—second only to the 1981 figure as the lowest in 20 years. (Source: *Chilean Review*, op. cit., Vol. 1, #5, June 1987, p. 5; that same source shows a lower figure for 1985: 26.4 percent.)

56. *Country Reports on Human Rights Practices for 1984* (Washington: U.S. Government Printing Office, 1985), report by the State Department to the House and Senate foreign affairs and relations committees, respectively (U.S. aid); Patricia Brenner, of the IMF Western Hemisphere department, "The IMF View," in *IMF Survey*, September 23, 1985, as reproduced in *Chile: An Appraisal of Investment Opportunities in the Equity Market*, op. cit., pp. 17–20 and 28–35 (details of the recovery plan and IMF/World Bank support); Gallagher, ibid., p. 25.

57. Brenner, op. cit., p. 28, projected and comparative prices; *Indicadores Económicos y Sociales 1960–1985*, op. cit., p. 172, for 1984–1985 prices; (both the forecast and prices given were in 1984 dollars); *1986 Book of the Year*, op. cit., p. 574, for earthquake. As if that were not enough, international interest rates rose by about 1 percent in 1984, a heavy blow to a big debtor nation.

58. Brenner, op. cit., p. 18 (GDP) and Büchi, op. cit., pp. 22–23 (duties and imports); *Indicadores Económicos y Sociales 1960–1985*, pp. 243 and 246–247. Büchi noted that import surges such as those in 1984 "are commonly observed in adjustment processes," and reflected not only the upturn in the economy "but efforts to replenish the greatly diminished stocks of intermediate products and imported capital goods." Although Chile's economy in 1986 was bigger than it was in boom year 1981, oil imports were $322 million in 1986, $983 million in 1981. Only one other net-importer country on the South American continent—Brazil—managed a similar feat through aggressive development of its own oil resources. Source: *Economic and Social Progress in Latin America: 1987 Report*, op. cit., p. 482.

59. The appointment of Büchi, former superintendent of banks, banished any doubts about whether Pinochet intended to abandon free market strategies. In the phrase of the *1985 Book of the Year*, "the new minister's appointment was a cause of alarm among the domestic business community because Büchi was seen as chief promoter of the Chicago-style monetarism that [Luis] Escobar had been specifically appointed to change," op. cit., p. 574. Those changes, however, did not represent a "change," but a pragmatic interim measure. As to "nervousness," it was confined to those traditional businessmen accustomed to having the government rush to their rescue in times of crisis. Büchi's program, called "Structural Adjustment," assumed rapid export growth, and rapid it was. Son of an air force officer (with Swiss blood on his father's side, Yugoslav on his mother's), Büchi won fame in Chile for his austere habits. Writes Fontaine: "Instead of long lunches, he

meditates while jogging the streets of Santiago, or, in the eastern section of the city, uses a bicycle as his ministerial means of transport . . . he is the kind of high official not often seen in Chile . . . he knows the problems of bus-riders from the inside, for example, and not just of the passengers, but of the drivers, as well. He knows, for example, what lack of change means, and warns the Central Bank of the possible lack of 50-peso coins 'for the mini-buses.' " Fontaine, op. cit., pp. 181–182.

60. The article entitled "Trade Liberalization in Chile," was reprinted in its entirety in *Chilean Economic Report*, a publication of the New York office of CORFO, #193, August 1987, pp. 4–5.

61. Allen A. Boraiko, "Acts of Faith in Chile," *National Geographic*, July 1988, pp. 54, ff. Although the *Geographic* admittedly does not specialize in socio-economic or political reporting, it is carefully researched, and so it is somewhat astounding to discover not only careless repetition of the hollow clichés but also downright error. Examples of the first: "longest tradition of political stability and civil liberty"; "habitual division of Chileans into right, center and left voting blocs"; "Pinochet quelled the disorder—sown in part by CIA aid to Allende's opponents." Of the second: in discussing soup-kitchens, for example, there is no mention whatever of the government's extensive and highly effective food distribution program. Another publication which does specialize in such reporting—*The Economist*—regularly sermonizes about the efficacy of economic policies which are precisely the ones Chile has developed so successfully. Yet that publication, when it does take note of progress in Chile, almost invariably manages to lace praise with arsenic. One example among many: "Chile: Something to smile about," June 20, 1987, p. 74, wedged into the opening paragraph that GDP per capita remains below its 1981 level, and that "even the dictatorship itself admits that 'at least 14 percent of the population lives in extreme poverty.' " Chile's GDP in 1981 was at the highest level in the country's entire history; and a more honest poverty statement would have been that "the dictatorship might claim credit for reducing extreme poverty by fully one-third, from 21 percent of the population in 1973 to 14 percent in 1986."

62. *Economic and Social Progress in Latin America: 1987 Report*, op. cit., p. 68; *Poverty in Latin America: The Impact of Depression*, op. cit., pp. 20–21. The *Forbes* quote is in *Chilean Review*, op. cit., Vol. 1, #12, February 1988, p. 2. Later data showed even greater improvements in every area, including education. The *Poverty* study echoes the IADB finding on food distribution: "The examples of Chile and Costa Rica demonstrate that it is possible to protect the poor from the adverse effects of reduced national income on health. This was achieved by targeting the most vulnerable groups in society, which was possible because reasonably efficient bureaucracies existed in the social areas. Linking food distribution and primary health care has shown great benefits. For instance, in Chile the National Food Program administered by the Ministry of Health has been one of the main factors behind the rapid decline in infant mortality rates. Food distribution, in addition to improving the nutrition of both mothers and children, has attracted poor families to the health centers. . . ." Ibid., p. 23. As to education, the aforementioned 1987 *Economic and Social Progress* report notes (Tables IV-7 and 8, p. 65) that Chile and Argentina were the only two countries in all of Latin America and the Caribbean to reach 100 percent enrollment rates for children between ages 6 and 11, and recorded the highest enrollment rate for

children between ages 12 and 17. For the former, the figures were: 1965, 84.6
percent; 1975, 100 percent; 1985, 100 percent. For the latter: in 1965, 69.5
percent (slightly behind both Guyana and Jamaica that year); 1975, 85.2
percent (already the highest in the region); 1985, 92.8 percent.

63. Until 1988, when it was still true (though every day less so), such comparisons were frequently made. In 1988, it became a political issue in the course
of the previously discussed April television appearance of Ricardo Lagos,
president of the very leftist Party for Democracy. Lagos, however, went
beyond those who took 1981 as the baseline for "proving" their anti-market
claims, asserting that per capita income was down from 1970. According to
what are probably the most commonly used statistics in hemisphere
affairs—those contained in the annual *Economic and Social Progress*
reports—that was not even true for 1986, much less 1987, when the Chilean
economy grew again by 5.8 percent. The 1987 report (Table 3, p. 426), using
1986 dollars as the common denominator, gives Chilean per capita income
in 1970 as $2,275; for 1986, the provisional figure in that report was $2,306
(the actual figure was probably higher because GDP rose higher than was
shown provisionally in that report). Interestingly, per capita income did
decline during the 1970–1986 time frame in such relatively rich countries
as Argentina, Jamaica, and Venezuela. The 1988 projection is from *El Mercurio* international editions, June 2–8, "5.2% Creció el PGB En Primer
Trimestre; Informe Del Banco Central," p. 4, and June 9–15, 1988, "Economía en Crecimiento," p. 3. The newspaper noted that this was the 19th
consecutive quarter of growth, and that put GNP at nearly ten percent
above the 1981 level. A final observation: the gloomy World Bank prediction
that Latin countries would be lucky to match in 1990 per capita incomes
they enjoyed in 1970 because of the trauma of the severe recession early in
the decade was proving true. Chile was one of only four countries in the
region to show higher incomes for its people in 1986 than in 1970. The
others were Brazil, Colombia, (which had become an important oil
exporter), and the altogether artificial economy of Panama.

64. *Poverty in Latin America*, op. cit., p. 3; "External Public Debt Outstanding
by Country, 1970, 1975, 1977–1985," in *1987 Economic and Social Progress*
report, op. cit., Table 60, p. 466.

65. "Is anybody paying?" *The Economist*, March 14, 1987, p. 76. It was November before Brazil reached agreement with creditor banks: Brazil agreed to
pay $500 million of the amount due in the fourth quarter of the year, the
banks themselves lending the remaining $1 billion—a bizarre arrangement
in which, in effect, the banks "loaned" money to themselves. The next day it
was learned that the banks had agreed to lend an additional $2 billion, and
Brazil to put up $1 billion to pay the $3 billion Brazil had skipped paying—
but not until agreement was reached on the $10.4 billion in new loans Brazil
wanted over three years. The *Washington Post:* "Brazil Agrees to Resume
Debt Payments to Banks," November 6, 1987, p. F–3, and "Brazil's Lenders
Gained Hard-Fought Concessions," November 7, 1987, p. A–17. Eight
months later, the talks were still floundering. A news analysis zeroed in on
the dilemma: "It isn't difficult to understand why bankers would resist the
idea of lending more billions of dollars to Brazil. This is a country, after all,
where the inflation rate has been running at nearly 20 percent a *month*
[emphasis in original], where economic policies change in an afternoon,
where the national assembly recently voted to set interest rate ceilings by

the constitution. But about 600 banks around the world . . . are being asked to throw good money after bad in the hopes that the injection of fresh capital will help invigorate the Brazilian economy and increase the likelihood that Brazil will be able to pay interest on its borrowings. . . ." Paul Blustein, "Brazil's High-Stakes Debt Talks: Throwing Good Money After Bad?" the *Washington Post*, May 24, 1988, p. C–1. Socialist President Alan García of Peru—implanting policies in many ways resembling those which Allende used to create the artificial boom of 1971—developed a new strategy which made his country the pariah of international banking: He announced in 1986 that Peru would limit its debt payments to 10 percent of exports—period. The presidents of Mexico, Brazil, Argentina, Colombia, Venezuela, Panama, Uruguay, and Peru met in Acapulco in November and warned creditors to ease their debt burdens or face "unilateral measures"—which, in fact, Brazil and Peru, of that group, had already taken, "8 Latin Leaders urge New North-South Economic Talks," Acapulco-datelined dispatch in the *Washington Post*, November 30, 1987, p. A–27. Although neither Argentina nor Mexico had resorted to "unilateral measures," both were troubled economies: Argentina's GDP in 1986 was still well below 1980 levels, and Mexico in 1986 experienced one of its not infrequent deep year-to-year declines. On October 14, 1987, its much-hailed "Austral Plan" of 1985 a shambles, Argentina announced a new austerity program designed partly "to curb the country's raging inflation and ensure economic stability." Martin Edwin Anderson, "Austerity Plan Unveiled in Argentina," the *Washington Post*, October 15, 1987, p. F–3. It is, of course, too soon to evaluate the results of that program.

66. These debt extrapolations were done by Chilean economist Antonio Recabarren in response to Lagos' televised claims: "Abrumadora Cantidad de Inexactitudes," *El Mercurio* international edition, April 28–May 4, 1988, p. 7; the $40 billion figure, and 1970–1987 per capita comparison, from the same edition, p. 7, statement made by Economy Minister Brigadier General Manuel Concha, "Sus Propuestas nos Recordaron el Caos de la UP." Of the South American countries, only Ecuador experienced poorer terms of trade for the years 1982–1986; see individual country profiles in the 1987 *Economic and Social Progress* report. Chile's net international reserves in 1987 stood at $1.6 billion.

67. "Have Debt Will Travel," in *Euromoney*, op. cit., pp. 10–11. "Re-programming" debt appears in the "Socio-Economic Platform [*Compromiso*] of the Campaign for the 'No,' " unveiled by the Christian Democrats and a cluster of smaller parties early in May 1988. That plank speaks of "the need to solve the problem of the 'overdue debt [*cartera*] of the poor,' in the same way that the State took charge the debts of the big banks and corporations." "Cambios de Fondo Propone Programa Económico Opositor," *El Mercurio* international edition, May 5–11, 1988, p. 6.

68. Steve H. Hanke, "The Anatomy of Successful Debt Swaps," typescript version of a chapter from the book *Privatization and Development*, Steve H. Hanke, ed. (San Francisco: Institute for Contemporary Studies Press, 1987); "New Zealand Investors Buy $165 Million of Chile's Debt," *Chilean Review*, Vol. 1, #1, February 1987, p. 4. (It was the investment firm of Carter, Holt, Harvey International, Ltd., which had already invested $50 million in a fuel distribution and cellulose and fishmeal exports firm.) "Their exits and their entrances," *The Economist*, September 12, 1987, p. 86. The article said, "Argentina's attempt to turn some of its foreign debt into securities has

also flopped. . . ." *Friedberg's LDC Debt Commentary,* a publication of Friedberg Commodity Management, Inc., Toronto, March 10, 1988, p.. 1; "US $178 Millones Bajó la Deuda Externa en Marzo," *El Mercurio* international edition, May 26–June 1, 1988, p. 4 (1988 figures); "Chilean Peso," in *International Currency Review,* Vol. 18, #3, May 1987, p. 113. The Baker plan contained three essential elements: (1) comprehensive macroeconomic and structural policies by debtor nations to improve growth and reduce inflation; (2) a continued central role for the IMF, in conjunction with increased and more effective structural adjustment (policy-based) lending by the multilateral development banks; (3) increased lending by the commercial banks in support of debtors' reform efforts. (Summary from Morris B. Goldman, "Confronting Third World Debt: The Baker and Bradley Plans," A Heritage Foundation "Backgrounder," #559, January 22, 1987, pp. 5–6.) Hanke described Chile's debt-swap design thusly: "Suppose a Chilean note has a $100,000 face value, and is sold at a discount in the secondary Latin debt market for $67,000. The purchaser of the Chilean debt then 'takes' the dollar-denominated note to Chile. By utilizing Chapter XIX of the Chilean International Exchange Norms, the note is redenominated in Chilean pesos and sold in the Chilean money market for $100,000 in pesos. Through this process, what was an external debt denominated in dollars becomes an internal debt denominated in pesos. No new pesos are printed by the Central Bank. This feature distinguishes Chile from other Latin swap operations, where dollar-denominated notes are exchanged at the central banks for local currency that is created by turning the central banks' printing presses a bit faster." The investors, he adds, "have made a handsome profit by turning a $67,000 investment in dollars into $100,000 in pesos . . . to purchase equities in Chile." Hanke, "Forcing Banks to Mark Down Loans," the *New York Times,* October 5, 1986.

69. Steve H. Hanke, "Chilean Flight Capital Takes Return Trip," the *Wall Street Journal,* November 7, 1986, p. 33. Chapter XVIII, specifically aimed at Chilean investors as part of the 1985 debt swap program, allows Chileans to use their assets abroad to purchase external debt and convert it into domestic debt. The scheme allows for an arbitrage profit on repatriated flight capital, adding to the yields on investments made with those funds. Other sources have estimated Chilean overseas deposits/investments as high as $7 billion.

70. From an analysis done in November 1987 by Friedberg Commodity Management, Inc., (FCMI) of Toronto. The firm operates a mutual fund in Santiago, Toronto Trust. Income yields from *Chilean Review,* op. cit., Vol. 1, #6, July/August 1987, p. 5. As of May 24, 1988, Australia was, year-to-year, down 18.5 percent; Hong Kong, down 14.3 percent; Italy, down 32.1 percent; Singapore, down 20.7 percent. "World Bourses," *The Economist,* May 28, 1988, p. 102. By contrast, from November 30, 1987, to June 24, 1988, net asset value of shares on the Santiago market leaped from 1,293.36 pesos ($5.50) to 1,977.36 ($7.87)—a 43 percent appreciation (source: FCMI).

71. Shirley Christian, "Chile's Privatization Pleases Investors," a Santiago-datelined dispatch in the *New York Times,* July 20, 1987, p. D-6. She quoted Manual Mayca, "normalization manager" of CORFO, as saying all those enterprises were profitable. The 1973 loss figure was given by Economy Minister Brigadier General Manuel Concha, "Sus Propuestas nos Recordaron el Caos de la UP," *El Mercurio* international edition, April 28-May 4, 1988, p. 7. He was responding to the Ricardo Lagos' controversial television

remarks. Had those companies remained in state hands, he said, subsidizing them would be equivalent to 130,000 pesos coming out of the pockets of each and every family in Chile—the equivalent of nearly six months of minimum wages. More than just a steel company, CAP is a holding company which includes mining, forest, lumber, and service industries.

72. "Chilean Privatisation Grows Apace," *Euromoney*, op. cit., p. 6; "Chile: A Leader Country in Latin America," *Chile Now*, op. cit., p. 8; "Administrators of Pension Funds," *Chile Today*, #56, August 1987, pp. 20–21 (this was the forerunner publication of *Chile Now*); José Piñera, "Chileans Unravel Social Security Tangle," the *Wall Street Journal*, January 3, 1986, reproduced in *Chile: An Appraisal of Investment Opportunities in the Equity Market*, op. cit., pp. 53-54 (including direct quotes).

73. Christian, op. cit., (Briones); Tyler Bridges, "Pinochet's Reforms Boost Chilean Economy," a Santiago-datelined story in the *Washington Post*, September 6, 1987 (p. H-6) (Banker Geert Geisterfer quote); "Cambios de Fondo Propone Programa Económico Opositor," *El Mercurio* international, May 5-11, 1988, p. 6. Among those "profound changes," the program calls for constructing "a unitary" social security system, labor law reform, and promotion of small companies, cooperatives, and worker-owned companies. The latter two are sloganeering buzz-words for a return to politicized labor movements tied to a tutelary state. Of the fourteen "parties" which make up that coalition, as of late May 1988, only the Christian Democrats and the Humanists had managed to round up enough signatures to qualify as national parties. It should be remembered that nine of those fourteen were active members of the Popular Unity government, and that only one of the fourteen is on the Right, and it is a miniscule token member. Not surprisingly, the government employee union—stripped of most of its former powers and greatly reduced in size—urged a return to the old-style pension system ("ANEF Solicitó Volver al Antiguo Sistema Previsional," *El Mercurio* international edition, March 31-April 5, 1988, p. 4). Despite the headline—astonishingly positive for the *Post*—Bridges' story contained the usual digs: "millions of poor people are worse off," an assertion not only incorrect but bereft of evidence beyond an allusion to "critics of the government"; Bridges also included an astonishing canard: "Reagan officials . . . enthusiastically back the Pinochet government's market-based policies. . . ." That must have been read in Santiago as well as in Washington with something between disbelief and guffaws.

74. "Inquietudes Acerca Del Futuro de la Propiedad Privada en Chile," in *Puntos de Referencia*, #10, December 1986, p. 1 (Bitar) and 4 (Boeninger); "Plan populista sería un disparate solemne," *La Época*, June 9, 1987, p. 14. The former is a publication of the Centro de Estudios Públicos of Santiago. For yet another example of vintage Christian Democrat thinking, this time from one of the party's newer *wunderkind*, Alejandro Foxley: "The model is taking us into a society in which opportunities for making money, for access to education, health, housing and personal dignity, are distributed ever more unequally. In abdicating its functions, the State guarantees inequality as a norm of our existence. . . ." "La era de los 'Chicago boys,' " special edition of *Hoy*, May 1987, p. 39. A month later, he was quoted in the *New York Times* as saying that if his party took office, they would have "eclectic policies," but maintain a market orientation. Shirley Christian, Santiago-datelined story, "An Unlikely Lab for Free Markets," June 21, 1988.

75. Andrés Allamand Z., "Chile: The End of the Authoritarian Regime," a

speech delivered before a meeting of the Pacific Democratic Union and International Democratic Union in Honolulu in May 1988, p. 6 of typescript copy (job creation); "Unemployment at 15-year low," *Chilean Review,* op. cit., Vol. 1, #12, February 1988, p. 3; *Chile Economic Report,* op. cit., # 197, December 1987, pp. 4–5 and 8 (manufacturing & savings data; in 1982, manufacturing provided jobs for 356,000. The 1987 level was 8 percent above the previous all-time high); *El Mercurio* international edition, May 12–18, 1988: "Superavit Pasó los US $1,000 Millones," and "24% Aumentaron las Exportaciones de Fruta," p. 4. Allamand is vice-president of the National Renovation Party in Chile.

76. "Chile Breaks With Tradition," *Euromoney,* op. cit., p. 4, quoting Alfonso Serrano, vice-president of the Central Bank, as saying a "mini-adjustment" was needed when it appeared the economy could be over-heating. "The economy was growing 7 to 8% on an annual basis earlier this year," he said. "So we are slowing down a bit to avoid a future problem." Büchi was quoted in a *Reuters* dispatch by Richard Waddington, datelined Santiago, November 12, 1987. Buchi was right; after hitting a high of $1.45 at the end of 1987, it continued to slide afterwards, pricing at $1.12 late in May. The government assumed in its macroeconomic plan a price of 75 cents a pound. Just how radically those price swings could affect the country's fortunes was played out in *Friedberg's LDC Debt Comments,* March 10, 1988, op. cit.: at 75 cents, foreign debt would fall between 1988 and 1989 by $2 billion; $5.5 billion if copper were to average $1.30 per pound.

77. *El Mercurio* international editions: "Chile Ofrece Estabilidad Política," May 26-June 1, 1988, p. 1 (Kissinger); "EE.UU. Elogia Perspectivas de Economía Chilena," May 12–18, 1988, p. 1. Kissinger made those remarks at a benefit he addressed in St. Louis on May 26. *The International Economy,* January/ February 1988, reproduced in *Chilean Review,* op. cit., Vol. 1, #13, February 1988, p. 3. Other countries on the index were Argentina, Bolivia, Brazil, Columbia, Ecuador, Mexico, Peru, the Philippines, Uruguay, Venezuela, and Yugoslavia.

78. "Chile Breaks With Tradition," *Euromoney,* op. cit., p. 4 (Segal & Reed; the "best" part of the Reed quote is from *Carta Confidencial,* op. cit., #9, August 27, 1987, p. 21); *The Economist:* "Thump," and "Citicorp comes clean on third-world debt," May 23, 1987, pp. 12 and 77, respectively; the *Washington Post:* "Citibank Eases Objections, Giving Boost to Chile Loan Talks," February 20, 1987, p. F-1, and "Citicorp Move Brings New Era," May 21, 1987, p. F-4. Other major banks quickly followed Citicorp's lead in writing up reserve levels against losses. Citicorp's exposure with Latin America's big four debtors alone (Brazil, Argentina, Mexico, and Venezuela) was nearly $10 billion; Bank America, Manufacturers Hanover and Chase Manhattan were all in the $6–7 billion range. Chile owed Citicorp $600 million, but $800 million to Manufacturers Hanover. Finance Minister Büchi, reporting on the negotiations, said the agreements covered restructuring of $12 billion in maturities falling due between 1988 and 1999 for a period of fifteen years, with a six-year grace period; "retiming" the interest payments to annual instead of semi-annual footing, worth $447 million in savings in 1987–1988; and reduction in interest rates themselves, yielding savings of an estimated $606 million over the terms of the loans. Source: *Chilean Review,* op. cit., Vol. 1, #5, June 1987, p. 1.

79. Jose Piñera, "A New Chile," *Economía y Sociedad,* April 1988, based on a lecture he had given November 25, 1987, before the National Enterprise

Meeting; "US $273 Millones en Inversion Extranjera Ingresaron al País," *El Mercurio* international edition, May 19–25, 1988, p. 4.

80. Chavkin, op. cit., p. 246.

81. "Chile Bucks the Foreign Investment Trend," *Euromoney,* op. cit., pp. 22–23 (U.S. investments); *El Mercurio* international editions: May 19–25, 1988, op. cit., investment inflows; "Descubren Grandes Reservas de Cobre," and "US $180 Millones Invertirán en Mina de Oro y Plata La Coipa," March 31-April 6, 1988, p. 4; *Chile Economic Report,* op. cit., December 1987, pp. 2–4 (mining investments, statistics); "New Zealand Investors Buy $165 Million of Chile's Debt," *Chilean Review,* op. cit., Vol. 1, #1, February 1987, p. 4; "Gold Production," *Chilean Review,* Vol. 1, #15, May 1988, p. 3. Batista was already Brazil's second largest gold producer. Chilean gold production was expected to reach 6,500 kilograms by the end of the decade. In 1981, Exxon officials did inform Pinochet that they intended to discontinue their investment in *La Disputada,* giving as their reason their belief that the new constitution made such investments impossible. One interpretation was that they were reacting to the spate of criticisms of the constitution in the U.S. Fontaine, op. cit., p. 145, gives another: "We don't know whether they already perceived the adverse world market conditions for copper. The likelihood is that they already had in hand the figures for 1981 and mid-term projections." At all odds, they came back.

82. Piñera, "A New Chile," op. cit., p. 5. Piñera served from 1978 through 1980 as Labor and Welfare Minister, for nearly a year thereafter as Health Minister.

83. *The Economist,* "Poor man's Fund," and "Gain without pain?" pp. 14, 17, and 86, February 13, 1988. The study is entitled *Adjustment With A Human Face,* Giovanni Andrea Cornia, Richard Jolly, and Frances Stewart, eds., Oxford University Press.

84. "Evolución del Sector Exportador," *El Mercurio* international edition, April 21–27, 1988, p. 3.

85. Lavín, pp. 30–31. Lavín, who earned a master's degree in economics from the University of Chicago, and later served as Dean of the Faculty of Economics and Administrative Sciences of the University of Concepción, was then a senior editor of *El Mercurio.*

86. "Where Progress Makes Its Way," in *Chile Now,* #62, March/April 1988, pp. 3–6.

87. Lavín, op. cit., pp. 122–123; Pinera, op. cit., pp. 3 and 5.

88. Piñera, op. cit., p. 4; "Raising the Standard of Living," *Chile Today,* op. cit., August 1987, p. 7 (water/sewage); "Another Country," translated from *Economía y Sociedad,* February 1986, in *An Appraisal of Investment Opportunities in the Equity Market,* op. cit., pp. 57–58 (household construction details). Lavín, op. cit., p. 37 (cars). Lavín points out that the reason there are more of these things is that they cost less; citing a study done by Pablo Gómez of the Catholic University, he points out that the price of a black and white TV set decreased by 61 percent over the past ten years, while that of watches did so by 55 percent. So, too, did the value of cars, refrigerators, washing machines, and the like. For example, in 1976, a black and white TV set cost the equivalent of only 358 kilos. In 1976, the money needed to buy a refrigerator was the equivalent of the cost of 315 haircuts; in 1985, 136 haircuts (ibid., p. 37).

89. *Chilean Review,* op. cit., Vol. 1, #14, April 1988, p. 3.

90. *Chilean Review,* op. cit., April 1988, pp. 3 and 6.

Reflections

In one of his cogent essays, Jeffrey Hart, professor of English at Dartmouth College, wrote: "When history and experience are not consulted, fad is king and mindless utopias are culled out of the air."[1]

Perhaps in no country since Franco's Spain have history and experience been so little consulted as in Chile. Perhaps no revolution since the Spanish Civil War has been more maimed and mauled in the retelling than has the Chilean revolution of 1973, its causes as well as its effects.

In both cases, the Right defeated the Left, although it ought be noted that while the heavy hand of Moscow was visible in both dramas, there was no Nazi counterforce in 1973, nor, it is quite clear, would the Chilean revolutionaries have accepted one. What they did, they did alone. That would, however, not be sufficient to spare them the "fascist" label the Left applies so readily to those who truly oppose them, to those who smash their ikons. And, as MIT Professor Paul N. Rosenstein-Rodan observed a number of years ago, none among those ikons is greater than socialism itself: "Socialism," he wrote, "is a great, perhaps the greatest ideal of this century." For true believers, it is an ideal that dies hard. No matter that outside of college campuses and newsrooms hardly anyone seriously believes any more that socialism can actually work—certainly not in Beijing, nor Budapest, nor, it would appear, even in Moscow itself.[2] Those who raise their sword against the great ideal socialism have nevertheless defiled a treasured ikon and must themselves perish.

The foregoing would be mere fevered rhetoric were it not true of Chile, as it was of Spain. George Orwell, a Socialist at the time, fought on the Socialist (Republican) side in Spain. He would write later ("Looking Back on the Spanish War"): "At an early age, I became aware that newspapers report no event correctly, but in Spain, I read for the first time articles which bore no relation whatever to the facts, not even the relation implicit in an ordinary lie." It is difficult to come away from a conscientious examination of the scholarship and reportage on Chile of the years since 1973 without experiencing a similar sensation.

Fad is, indeed, king. It is a fad born of the mindless utopias so fashionable in the sixties. In no country of Latin America, and few in the entire developing world, were those confident prescriptions for a scientifically engineered Brave New World invoked with greater mystic fanaticism than in the Chile of the Christian Democrats of that era, to the enthralled huzzahs of "progressives" everywhere. What is truly astonishing is how many of those selfsame Christian Democrats, how many of their foreign apostles and disciples and heralds, have emerged now, two decades later, as though from long-lost time capsules, proclaiming that the road to Chile's future leads directly into that discredited past.

I have here, in these pages, attempted to confront and consult history and experience, painstakingly and—I suspect—not infrequently pungently. The purpose has been to create a record free of fad and mindless utopias, as meticulously and as scrupulously as the frailties of the human mind and emotions permit. It is a record that speaks not only of what the Chileans themselves did as they grappled with the intimidating task of governing themselves, but also of what outsiders have done, continue to do—because few countries in the modern world have been so pawed over by outsiders as has Chile.

Mao Zedong wrote some years ago that "a revolution is not the same as inviting people over to dinner or writing an essay or painting a picture . . . A revolution is an insurrection, an act of violence by which one class overthrows another."

A revolution took place in Chile in 1973. Although it was not originally intended that way, it became the profoundest revolution in the history of the country, and very likely, one of the most significant in the history of the Western Hemisphere. That will surprise most, because it is almost never described as a revolution outside of Chile itself. And yet it was a revolution, one which ended a half-century of an almost uninterrupted march into socialism and installed in its place the most self-consciously free market ("capitalist") system perhaps in the entire hemisphere, the United States of 1988 included. That march, at the end, in 1973, was close to culminating in the creation of a Marxist-Leninist totalitarian state from which—if the record of the modern world means anything—there would have been no escape. That is, in fact, the way the country's three living ex-presidents saw it, the way most of the country's responsible leaders saw it at the time. That is what they said then—however disenchanted many may have become with the subsequent course of events, and particularly when they discovered that it was not a revolution which would restore power to them and/or to their socialist nostrums.

But, as the arch-revolutionary Mao Zedong wrote, revolutions are not tea parties—a proposition well noted, and usually respected, by most of the world's "progressives." One need only look at the degree of tolerant understanding extended these days to Mikhail Gorbachev's efforts to salvage what has been one of the bloodiest, most murderous and conquest-minded tyrannies in the annals of man to understand the moral elasticity which surrounds "progressive" judgments about revolutions. (Die-hards who doubt the foregoing are invited to review the endless apologia proferred through the years by many among the world's intelligentsia that attempt to explain away the "excesses" or "shortcomings" of such sloganeering nation-wreckers as Fidel Castro, Mao Zedong, the Sandinista mob in Nicaragua; these and others of their Communist ilk, since 1917, have sacrificed more than 150 million human lives on the altars of their grotesquely failed revolutions. Incompetence and butchery need only call themselves "revolutionary" and occur on the "romantic" Left to bring out legions of predictable political scientists, herd reporters, "popular church" religious, demagogic [or worse: disingenuous] senators, deputies and orthodoxy-entombed diplomats ready and eager to counsel patience with "the revolution." The foregoing list omits, of course, the conscious or unconscious cats' paws of the Kremlin's $3 billion annual "agit/prop" propaganda-and-disinformation machine.) Chile's revolution has enjoyed no such dispensation, because Chile's revolution has been on the Right, and therefore does not qualify as a revolution.

Which is the first moral of the Chilean drama: beware the Hypocrites and the sermons they preach.

During the May 1988 Moscow Summit, Ronald Reagan raised the human rights issue again with the Soviet leaders (though he by no means pressed the issue). The *Washington Post*, the rule more than the exception among the world's major news media, explained to its readers on page one: "The bitter U.S.-Soviet dispute on human rights is based in great part on differences of definition." Since simply to say this could, understandably, appear to be a typographical error, or worse, a malicious invention, I hasten to add that the quotation appeared on page one of the Tuesday, May 31, 1988, editions. It referred the reader to an entire story on page A–10 "explaining" why the systematic extermination of as many as 25 million Soviet citizens and the subsequent and continuing subjugation of 277 million more amounted to "differences of definition." The twenty-four-inch story (" 'Rights' Definition at Core of Dispute") made no reference to the Soviet regime's long record of murder and mayhem, at home and abroad, nor did it include among the definitional "differences" the proposition that on the one side of the "misunderstanding" there stood an authentic democracy, on the other an authentic totalitarian despotism. It was enough to argue for patience, it would appear, that the Soviets had, in recent months, allowed a few hundred Jews to emigrate, released a few dissidents from their jails; besides, as the sub-headline noted, "Soviets Focus on Physical Needs, Not Personal Liberty."[3]

As the pages of this volume make plain, there have been serious human rights violations in Chile, particularly in the first years of revolution when the security services were rogue elephants. There have been far fewer in recent years than generally claimed. Chile has also opened up its political, civil, and human rights far more dramatically and effectively than one might dare dream the Soviets would ever do; Chile has also created an economy which, by contrast with the Soviet one, actually works, and thus has done a far better job of providing for "the physical needs" of its people in deeds as well as in words.

Which is, of course, the second moral of the story: the double-standard applied to regimes of the Right and of the Left. The Soviet Union is merely one such example; one might cite one after another of the leftist regimes of that dismal swamp of human rights—and dreams—which the African continent has become; or, for that matter, the contrast between the tolerance shown the leftist regimes of Latin America itself (Peru, Nicaragua, Cuba, among current examples) with the severity of the indictments returned against right-wing Chile.

It must also be said: Chile has been locked in a deadly war, one which has diminished sharply in recent years, but one which will burst anew in flames if outsiders continue to fan and feed the embers. On one side have been perhaps 10 percent of the country's population, who make up the hard core of the Communist party and far-left wings of the even more radical Socialist party, together with the guerrilla/terrorism appendages of both. On the other, a government determined to build a new kind of economic and social order combining the dynamics of market capitalism with the morality of a traditional religious and family based ethos. It is an order that leaves no room for the revolutionaries of the hard Left, nor for their ideas or values, so long as they persist in trying to implant those ideas. If that appears harsh from the outside, it clearly has not appeared that way to Chileans on the inside, because opinion survey after survey, since 1973, has shown that concern for human rights abuses has ranked well behind job security, terrorism and violence, the drug menace, and wage/price matters. This is not to say that Chileans are callous or bestial; it is to say that the human rights problem has not affected the overwhelming majority of Chileans directly, in their daily lives, but has involved almost entirely the armed or radical Left, and to a lesser extent, political activists on the Left.

Inevitably, there have been innocent victims, and one might well argue whether there can be *any* defense for hounding people for their political activities. To say these things, then, is not to justify human rights abuses, but to suggest that even within a *truly* moral framework, reasonable men may disagree on definitions.

It is also an attempt to put the issue in a Chilean context, rather than the one manufactured for consumption abroad. That context would include this: those political activists banished to external or internal exile—and occasionally even imprisoned—were not persecuted solely for their views, their ideas, which is the way the proposition is usually constructed. They were condemned because they not only opposed the creation of the new order, but fought to raise up anew the old one. To take one example among many: in a 1987 interview with the author, Gabriel Valdés Subercaseaux, then rounding out his fourth year as president of the Christian Democrat party, said: "We are convinced that when Pinochet goes, his legislation comes tumbling down, too. Just like Franco's, just as happened in Argentina." That is not simply an idea, a point of view. That is defiantly antirevolutionary. Revolutions which are indifferent to counter-revolution are not likely to endure. And, as the political scientist Michael Fleet has observed, "beyond a commitment to democratic rule . . . forces of the Left and Right [in Chile] have little in common. Their basic outlooks, social bases, and policy views differ radically. They are certain to turn on one another once military authorities have retired to their barracks." Wisely and well—or otherwise—it was precisely that sort of old-style politicization of the entire fabric of Chilean society that the revolutionaries of 1973 set out to expunge, once and for all. (Most recent public opinion polls, continuing earlier trends, would seem to indicate that, contrary to the international sound and fury, they have succeeded; a May 1988 Gallup showed only 10 percent of Chileans as indicating they believed they were represented by political parties, a figure that dropped to 7 percent outside of the political hot-house of Santiago.)[4]

As to the revolutionary Left: Does anyone remember, does anyone care, that (an example, again) the Allied occupation forces wrote into the constitution of postwar Germany provisions outlawing "anti-democratic parties"? This was done on the practical grounds that democracy, to grow, must also be able to defend itself against forces that are, by definition, antidemocratic. The Chilean Constitution of 1980, in one of the clauses most attacked by politicians at home and pundits abroad, did just exactly that in outlawing Marxist-Leninist and other totalitarian parties. Although the Chilean Left, in common with leftists everywhere, finds it excruciatingly difficult to acknowledge, Naziism is not the only mortal enemy of democracy; nor, in the modern world, even a relevant one. Communism is a far more dangerous enemy. (The usual sophistry invoked here is that the Communists grow and thrive when forced underground. There is no empirical basis for this claim. There is plenty of evidence that in Chile, inter alia, they reached the very peak of their power after twenty years of *legal* existence. Furthermore, even when legal, the party never abandoned its clandestine activities. Finally, the example of France, where the party has largely withered away, may become relevant when Chile achieves the socioeconomic and political maturity of France, and/or when the embarrassing example of the undiminished fortunes of the legal Communists in neighboring Italy no longer exists.)

Further, in the view of the leaders of the Chilean Revolution—in the view of many Chileans—what the country needed now was to build a new and different kind of democracy, not return to the formal but disintegrating democracy that gave the country the anarchy, chaos, and class warfare of pre-1973 Chile (nor, for that matter, to pre-1970 Chile) so that the country could again commit national suicide in the name of a "democracy" far more rotten and ruinous than real.

Is that the essence of the issue—who has a right to make a revolution, and what are the acceptable ground rules for revolution? Is any democracy preferable to all other political systems, at all times, and in all places? Questions to be examined in a moment, after a further word about human rights.

Indignation over human rights abuses is a clearly selective process. In neighboring Peru, for example, the security forces recently bragged that they had achieved "100 percent success" in an operation against three hundred partly unarmed *Sendero Luminoso* (Shining Path) prison rioters. That euphemism, as the *Economist* pointed out, meant simply that the security forces had wiped out—exterminated—all three hundred of them. At no time in the entire fifteen years of Chilean revolution, not even in the early days of secret executions (including a long hushed-up one in the Atacama Desert) has there ever been a serious insinuation of a three hundred-person massacre. Indeed, the world press treats death in democracies (Peru, in a truly tortured definition of the word, is a "democracy") in such an off-handed way that the *International Herald Tribune* of Paris relegated to "news brief" status a report that the guerrilla war in Peru had, so far, cost ten thousand lives.[5] None but the most delirious claim the death toll in Chile, 1973–1988, including the early days of bloody battles, reaches even half that number. (Nor, for that matter, are there cries of outrage in the U.S. Congress that 90 percent of all coca plants in the world are grown in two countries—Bolivia, which has actively cooperated with the U.S., and Peru, where police and military links to the drug barons are notorious and which actively opposes the United States on every conceivable front as its "populist" government continues to receive massive injections of Soviet arms and military advisers. "Populist" is the new media shorthand for Marxist.)

Or, to take another case: Cuba. As former UN Ambassador Jeane Kirkpatrick has pointed out, Cuba's record—a record of human rights violations with no equal in the modern history of the hemisphere—"has never come to the attention of UN human rights bodies because those institutions are 'wired.' " Among the nations that maneuvered to shield Cuba during the 1987 debate were Mexico, a one-party "democracy" for the past sixty years; newly democratic Argentina, which (for reasons of political expediency) later passed a law absolving lower military officers of complicity in the "disappearances" of ten thousand to twenty thousand persons during that country's "dirty war" of the 1970s and early 1980s; and such formal Latin democracies as Colombia and Venezuela. Yet that same UN Human Rights Commission that voted 19–18 (again) against examining human rights violations in Cuba, has for fourteen straight years voted to condemn Chile (over the objections even of its own special human rights *rapporteur* on Chile). It is also the same body which is routinely cited by such Torquemadas of Chile in the U.S. Senate as Edward M. Kennedy (D-Mass.) to justify their legal vendettas.

Nor were there cries to end U.S. aid to Israel—long the largest per-capita recipient of U.S. largess in the world—when, following the 1988 wave of demonstrations and counter-measures that claimed two hundred lives, it was reported that Israel was holding 4,800 "alleged activists and instigators" in prison, nine hundred of them "in administrative detention, where they can be held indefinitely without charge or trial." (Israel's population is one-third that of Chile's; in remarking on this, I am not either fixing blame for the events in Israel, nor dismissing Israel's right to defend itself against implacable enemies. The point concerns the reaction of the United States and other Western nations when rule of law is suspended in one country, as opposed to the reaction of those selfsame nations when Chile suspends rule of law for reasons its government deems vital.)

A final example: much attention has (properly) been focused on the plight of the starving refugees of Ethiopia. Virtually none has been centered on the country's monstrous leader, Mengistu Haile Mariam. His policies of Stalin-like collectivization of agriculture and enforced resettlement of 1.5 million peasants have claimed between 750,000 and 1 million lives in the past few years. The European Parliament, meeting in Strasbourg in July 1988, voted unanimously to call upon all Chilean political parties to express their "rejection" of President Pinochet in the

forthcoming plebiscite. It has never managed to vote a similar repudiation of Mengistu, but then, Mengistu has shown no signs of liberalizing
anything in his regime, backed by $3.5 billion in Soviet arms, much less
submitting his rule to a popular vote.[6]

> *Is it "Yankee imperialism" when the United States brings pressure*
> *against the government?*
> *No.*
>
> > Miguel Salazar, vice president of the far leftist
> > Christian Democratic Youth

Chile's Christian Democrats have always been in the vanguard of those
fighting "Yankee imperialism" in Latin America. The Christian Democrat government of Eduardo Frei, for example, was one of those most
vociferously denouncing U.S. intervention in the Dominican Republic
in 1965, even though that "intervention" was followed by a democracy
that has survived down to the present day. They have also, down to the
present day, been those in Chile most warmly embraced by the State
Department; as recently as May 1988, Secretary of State George Shultz
carved out time from his hectic, pre-Moscow summit schedule to
receive Patricio Aylwin Azócar, president of the Christian Democrats.
The Washington-PDC romance is nurtured by party leaders through a
nonstop "shuttle diplomacy" to Washington and other key capitals as
they seek to "internationalize" their country's domestic situation; one
source logged 652 trips abroad between 1986 and early 1988 by key PDC
leaders, including forty-two by the party's number two man, Andrés
Zaldívar Larraín. And the romance flourishes despite the undisguised
disdain of their dominant *chascón* ("long-hair," slang for leftist) wing for
the United States: in his farewell address in 1987, party President Gabriel Valdés described the United States as "an imperial republic" and
rebuked Washington's ideas on transition to democracy in Chile within
the framework of the neoliberal economic model as "completely
unworkable and ethically unjustified"; the preferable option, he said,
was to "perfect democratic solidarity" with the "Christian Democrat
and Socialist governments of Europe," as well as with like-minded
leftist governments of Latin America.[7]

Chile's Christian Democrats, however, have always applied a double-
standard when it came to U.S. intervention to help them—or to oppose
those they opposed. And well they might. CIA money helped to create
the Christian Democrats in 1962. In the 1964 election, the CIA dumped
$3 million into Chile to defeat Salvador Allende and elect Christian
Democrat Eduardo Frei. That worked out to roughly $1 per Chilean
voter. In the 1964 presidential elections in the United States, Barry

Goldwater and Lyndon Johnson together spent only 50 cents per voter. U.S. open and clandestine intervention in Chile, as amply documented in this book, continued unabated, despite the studied and systematic hostility of the Frei regime toward the United States, prompting later U.S. Ambassador Edward Korry to describe the clandestine support as "obscene." It was part and parcel of what the experienced diplomat Harry W. Shlaudeman told Congress in 1973 was the U.S.'s "highly paternalistic" policy then in vogue.

No one in the United States noticed, and when they did, several years later, there was scarcely a murmur of protest. By contrast, the entire world reverberated—and continued to reverberate for years later—to revelations (usually exaggerated) of CIA efforts to help the democratic opposition remain alive during the Allende years. The total actually expended was a piddling $6.5 million over three years. During that same period, Communist-bloc nations extended credits to Allende amounting to nearly $1 billion, not to mention immense injections of clandestine monies to radical groups such as the Movement of the Revolutionary Left and the Communist and Socialist parties themselves. Most of the U.S. money went to the Christian Democrats and opposition media (mainly the *El Mercurio* group, although the editors of the paper had no knowledge of it until afterwards, just as Frei himself denied knowledge of the 1964 CIA support). A total of $25,000 went to truckers locked in a series of turbulent (and important, but by no means decisive) 1972 and 1973 strike actions against Allende. Seven thousand dollars (!) went to the right-wing Patria y Libertad organization during the Allende presidency. Yet this insignificant and altogether ineffectual meddling would inspire countless frenzied lamentations in a seemingly endless series of newspaper and television reports, books, articles in "learned" journals, and the like—down to the present day.

A small digression is in order. In 1966, Sen. J. William Fulbright (D-Ark.) published a small volume entitled *Arrogance of Power* (New York: Random House). That book became immensely influential then, and again years later during the Carter administration. Its success was impelled at the outset by Fulbright's role as chairman of the Senate Foreign Relations Committee, but also because of his standing among intellectuals through his paternity of the Fulbright academic exchange program. But it succeeded also because it reinforced the conventional wisdom among intelligentsia. In it, Fulbright argued that it was wrong ("arrogant") for the United States to intervene to oppose revolutionary movements. He made it plain he had in mind leftist ("progressive") revolutions. The corollary of that—Fulbright must have known about the massive American meddling in Chile—was that it was our duty to intervene on behalf of leftist regimes. (Others would see that equation differently, but their voices tended to be drowned out, when not guffawed away; Henry Kissinger remarked ruefully that the United States seemed to excel at fomenting its own anti-American revolutions.)

Thus it was "wrong" for the United States to intervene in the 1970 elections: the United States spent the princely sum of $135,000 in a minicampaign of "scare" stories that mainly involved painting slogans on walls. No monies were expended in support of any party, of any candidate. It was even more wrong for the United States to intervene during the Allende years, even if only to help embattled democratic groups survive.

But it is "right" for the United States to intervene—blatantly and brazenly—against the Pinochet government in 1988. It is "right" notwithstanding that this government, in accord with a constitution overwhelmingly approved by the people of that country, is moving purposefully and openly toward a return to elections and democracy.

Why is it "right"? The United States, which lost 47,000 men and women and hundreds of billions of dollars trying to stop communism in Vietnam, contributes not one single cent of support to Chile as it fights to root out communism in its country. Nor has the United States given Chile little more than abuse and harassment in over a decade. (There was a brief respite during the first years of the Reagan administration; that withered away—as did so much of the rest of the conservative agenda—with the departure from the administration of one after another of the influential foreign policy conservatives; principally, Richard Allen as National Security adviser, in 1981; Jeane Kirkpatrick, as UN ambassador (and cabinet member) in 1985.)

Nor, of course, is it "principle." Pragmatism again and again finds reasons to overrule "principle"; witness again the willingness to overlook the abominations of the Soviet Union, the People's Republic of China, the Panama of Noriega (until he was no longer useful), the egregious human rights offenders of the Middle East and Africa; direct military as well as economic support for the Communist regime of Mozambique. Or, to take a more recent and seemingly "harmless" policy: the Reagan administration at mid-1988 announced plans to sell F18 fighter-bombers—"the navy's newest and hottest aircraft"—to Kuwait. Heretofore, the U.S. had sold them only to Canada, Australia, and Spain. What makes it notable is that Freedom House, in its 1987 survey of human rights around the world, ranked Kuwait dead-even in political rights and civil rights with Chile, a country cut off from *all* U.S. military aid since 1976. The administration justified the Kuwait deal on the grounds of enhancing security in the Persian Gulf. Indeed, each and every one of these lapses is excused on grounds of *realpolitik*; there is no room for *realpolitik* in the case of Chile, despite the country's immense strategic resources and geographic situation, a reality Moscow acutely recognizes and Washington will only belatedly recognize. Nor can U.S. policy toward Chile even be said to be rational: no country in all of Latin America more nearly embodies what the Reagan "Revolution" ostensibly is (was) all about than does Chile: a free market economy, decentralization of government together with a reduced role for government, sturdy opposition to communism, emphasis on traditional moral and ethical values.

Frank Ortiz, a former U.S. ambassador whose independence from State's "progressives" cost him repeatedly in his career, once told a group of editors: "We could turn Iowa into a wasteland with what we advocate for many foreign countries." He was speaking of so-called "agrarian reform." He might have easily been discussing political reform. If the United States were to do unto itself what it has foisted upon others in recent years, then we and not Iran might today be ruled by an Ayatollah—or by a Sandinista mob. With rare exceptions, the United States neither now nor in the past has created havoc or poverty abroad, domestic and foreign "blame-America" cliché-peddlers notwithstanding. But official Washington's "reformist" policies, particularly in recent years— and frequently behind the backs of the American people, or in defiance of their wishes—often aggravate and worsen already excruciatingly difficult situations. A smattering of examples: the U.S. forced Marcos out in the Philippines in 1986; despite over $1 billion in U.S. aid already to the autocratic but palpably incompetent government of Cory Aquino, that country is flying apart, and to make matters worse, turning increasingly hostile to the United States.[8] Washington pushed once stable and stunningly prosperous South Korea into an accelerated timetable for democratization in 1987, and when democracy returned, to further "liberalization"; that country is now increasingly benumbed by the riots and raucousness of a minuscule group of pro-Pyonyang fanatics who command only a single weapon: the sympathetic ear of the awesomely powerful international media. Haiti, long a socio-economic nightmare despite its standing as the second oldest independent nation in the Western Hemisphere, has been kneaded by Washington in recent years into a series of garish political shapes to the point where it has lost the one building-block quality it did possess, stability. It has been reduced to a condition so hopeless that the *Economist* would conclude that it may be the first "truly ungovernable" nation-state of modern times, dwelling in that "last circle of political hell . . . the collapse of all ordered society." Omitted from this brief recital are states such as South Vietnam or Cambodia (Kampuchea) the United States would first "save" and then abandon so that they are today just plain crushed and agonizing beyond rescue.[9]

* * *

This is approximately what the United States has been doing in Chile, although happily for the Chileans, thus far with less "success" than in the aforementioned countries. Further, Washington has been doing so under cover of what amounts to a conspiracy of silence of a conniving media. Under the sponsorship of Sen. Tom Harkin (D-Iowa), Congress late in 1987 enacted legislation requiring the National Endowment for Democracy (NED) to spend $1 million in Chile in 1988 to further the democratic process in a country already far along in furthering its own democratic processes. Only once before since its creation in 1983 had Congress ordered the Endowment to spend such a sum on a specific purpose: in 1987, on behalf of Solidarity, in Moscow-ruled Poland, which neither before nor since showed any signs of holding elections. But, then, NED did not need to be pushed: since 1985, it had earmarked a substantial slice of its budget to Chile. NED President Carl Gershman, himself a former Social Democrat activist, claimed he didn't have "exact" figures in an interview with *El Mercurio* early in 1988. But he did estimate that roughly 45 percent of the Endowment's fiscal 1987 ($15 million) and fiscal 1988 ($16 million) budget went to Latin America, and of that 15 percent to Chile. NED's spending paled, however, in comparison to that of yet another U.S. agency: the Agency for International Development (AID), which channeled a reported $3 million to Chile in 1987, virtually all of it for church or political groups clearly in opposition to the government. Still another U.S. taxpayer-funded agency, the Inter-American Foundation, has provided funds for a number of projects in Chile, including one headed by the Socialist Humberto Vega, as well as the Catholic church's Vicariate of Solidarity organization.

Among the principal beneficiaries of U.S. taxpayer funding has been Chile's Roman Catholic Jesuit order, an organization on the radical Left in Chile for more than two decades. According to *Carta Confidencial*— an insider publication in Santiago with reputed close ties to army intelligence—when the Jesuits learned the source of a $1.2 million grant in support of their supposedly nonpartisan electoral consciousness-raising program, they declined to take the money. The funds were then "laundered" (rerouted) through a Costa Rica-based organization (*Centro de Asesoría y Promoción Electoral,* affiliated to the Inter-American Institute for Human Rights), which then transferred the money to Chile.

Nor has Congress acted in isolation. An administration spokesman testified in May 1988 that the Reagan White House "enthusiastically backed" the special NED appropriation. The Chilean desk officer in the State Department, Peter Deshazo, told the Spanish news agency EFE in June 1988 that the administration was "concerned" about the lack of sufficient guarantees for an effective plebiscite. Johns Hopkins University specialist Riordan Roett translated that in an interview with EFE: Washington had let Pinochet know "indirectly" that "it would prefer" that he stand aside and put forward another candidate in the election. Arturo Valenzuela, a Chilean Christian Democrat long resident in the United States, said the White House had decided to abandon its policy of "quiet diplomacy" toward Chile in 1985 and switch to one of more active support for non-Marxist democratic opposition. That move was signaled when State Department insiders, who had long waged an internal guerrilla warfare against him, managed finally to ease out the relatively moderate U.S. ambassador James D. Theberge, replacing him with the "progressive" careerist, Harry G. Barnes, Jr. Barnes was posted to Santiago despite a State Department cover-up of a three-year liaison in Bucharest between his wife and the embassy chauffeur, a KGB agent, during Barnes' service as ambassador to Romania. Barnes' open courting of opposition leaders, including many on the ultra Left, won him such government enmity that Pinochet has refused even to see him since his arrival. By contrast to the experience of anti-Communist Ambassador Edward M. Korry in Santiago during the first Allende years, there was no press campaign to remove Barnes because he could not communicate effectively with the government he was supposed to be accredited to. But, then, there was no press outcry, either, about blatant and continuing American intervention in Chile now, as there was then.[10]

Altogether, an estimated $15 million was pumped into Chile from abroad in 1988 in support of opposition groups—roughly $6 million from U.S. public and private groups. The rest came from Austria, Belgium, Denmark, France, Holland, West Germany, Italy, Spain, Sweden, Canada, Panama, and Venezuela. (This does not include, of course, the unknown millions funneled in by the Soviet bloc, mainly via Castro's Cuba.) Among major private organizations active in Chile are the World Council of Churches, the Ford, Konrad Adenauer, and Volkswagen foundations, the U.S. Catholic Conference of Bishops, AFL-CIO, and the Brussels-based World Federation of Labor.[11]

As noted: by contrast with the banshee howls of the world media about outside intervention in Chile during the Allende years, there has been stony silence about the intervention of 1988. In the United States, the only major article I have been able to find in recent months appeared in the *New York Times* in June—and, with the exception of the headline, it was more misleading than revealing.

A footnote: On March 10, 1987, ignoring the massive evidence of political and human rights normalization in Chile, Sens. Edward M. Kennedy and Tom Harkin introduced a bill "to impose additional sanctions against Chile unless certain conditions are met." Quite apart from the arrogance of the language employed, the presumptuousness implicit in imposing "conditions" on a sovereign nation in disregard of that country's own laws, constitution and customs, the bill repeated the familiar demand in congressional resolutions and administration pontifications: that Chile, in effect, hand over the top officials of its long-disbanded state security agency for trial in the United States in the Orlando Letelier assassination case.[12] As far as can be ascertained, no nation has ever agreed to hand over the heads of its intelligence service to another nation for trial, for any reason. In this connection, it bears noting that when Spain's Socialist government, early in 1988, declined to respond to Chile's petition for extradition of César Bunster Ariztía—principal suspect in the assassination attempt on Pinochet's life which left five dead—there were no howls of "foul" in the world press nor from the European Parliament nor the halls of Congress.

An individual may on numerous occasions meritoriously indulge the emotions of generosity and benevolence, not only without an eye to, or even at the expense of his own interest. But a government can rarely, if at all, be justifiable in pursuing a similar course. . . .
                                        Alexander Hamilton, in *The Federalist*

Ever since Woodrow Wilson set out "to make the world safe for democracy," creating instead the conditions that would erupt in World War II, a number of influential American policymakers have ignored Hamilton's sage advice, with varying degrees of disastrous consequences. The most recent conspicuous example was Jimmy Carter, whose human rights fevers contributed importantly to such colossal human wrongs as the present mess in Central America (a thesis the author, together with Patricia B. Bozell, has, we believe, amply documented in *Catastrophe in the Caribbean: The Failure of America's Human Rights Policy in Central America*).*

Not infrequently, the charge has been led by those whose humanitarian pedigree and motives are themselves suspect, at the least. Such was the case of Chile, where before the smoke of battle had even cleared from the streets of Santiago, Sen. Edward M. Kennedy (D-Mass.), on October 2, 1973, proposed an amendment to cut off all U.S. aid to Chile. He continued to propose such amendments until, in 1976, he succeeded in cutting off all military aid, in 1981, all economic aid.[13]

That a Teddy Kennedy—aided, abetted, by such ultraliberals as The-

---

* Ottawa, IL: Jameson Books, 1984

odore Weiss (D-N.Y.); still later by Michael Barnes (D-MD), the former congressman who headed the House Subcommittee on Inter-American Affairs; and, in the Senate, most conspicuously, by Sen. Tom Harkin (D-Iowa)—should have chosen to direct such unremitting fire at an anti-Communist regime is not surprising. Nor, either, was there anything surprising about the hostility, from the outset, of the Carter administration.

What is notable is the hostility, since 1985, of an ostensibly conservative Reagan administration, a hostility which, in terms of practical measures, has surpassed anything achieved by its two postrevolution predecessors (Ford & Carter). Among the negative measures has been an end to the Food for Peace program, after decades of operation; withdrawal of U.S. support for Chilean loans from international institutions (despite the country's record as the *only* major Latin debtor nation yet to renege on them); cancellation of Overseas Private Investment Corporation insurance in Chile, although Salvador Allende had very nearly driven OPIC to bankruptcy through his brazen seizure of U.S. companies while the military, despite economic hardship, set about immediately to honor Chile's OPIC obligations; and ending of specialized trade preferences. But, as hurtful as these and other measures have been for the once staunchly pro-American Chilean leadership, none can rival as a source of fierce resentment Washington's arrogant and persistent intervention in the country's internal affairs. Continuing the policy of Carter, the Reagan administration has implicitly declined to recognize the legitimacy of Chile's 1980 constitution, approved in a plebiscite in which an unprecedented 6 million Chileans voted, and the process for political normalization which it created. Instead, the administration has thrown its weight openly and publicly behind opposition political figures. One searches one's memory and map of the world to find an example of such blatant U.S. intervention in the internal political processes of any leftist regime in modern times. Outright military intervention to oust or neutralize a dictatorship, yes; but bald intervention in the electoral process of a country with which Washington maintains diplomatic relations, no.

Ronald Reagan displayed prominently in the Oval Office the Harry Truman sign: "The Buck Stops Here." In the matter of Chile, it is doubtful that it did. It is doubtful, in fact, that either he or his secretary of state, George Shultz—who, since the 1987 death of CIA Director William Casey, expanded his already formidable power to exercise "vicar-general" control over American foreign policy beyond Alexander Haig's wildest dreams—have ever given more than cursory attention to that country. That is, of course, the continuation of a long history of official U.S. disinterest in Latin America, except in times of crisis.

Instead, control of foreign policy has devolved on a young (forty) and ambitious political appointee named Elliot Abrams. Abrams, whose first significant role in the administration was as assistant secretary of state for Human Rights, was moved into the revolving-door assistant secretaryship for Inter-American Affairs in 1984. A lawyer with no experience in Latin America, Abrams did, however, have an acute sense of opportunity. The Central American crisis was then at the top of the administration's foreign policy agenda—the covert as well as the overt one, as would be learned later. Abrams plunged enthusiastically into both, to the point where State Department insiders took to referring to him as the "assistant secretary for Nicaragua." For Abrams, from the first, Chile was a "throw-away" country—a sop, many claimed, which could be given to congressional and media liberals in exchange for tolerance of his hard-line views on the Sandinistas and support for the contras. Privately, through the still somewhat-recalcitrant ambassador James Theberge in Santiago, and publicly, through press statements and congressional testimony, Abrams maintained steady pressure on the Chileans. Explaining the unprecedented U.S. decision to abstain on the November 1986 $250 million World Bank balance-of-payments loan to Chile, Abrams said it was "a tactic, and we believe it was the right one." Then he added: "I hope that this abstentionist bloc grows. There were some European countries which did not join us and a number of Latin countries which did not. We hope that in the future they will." (One of the European countries that did: the Socialist government of France's François Mitterand.)[14]

By mid-1985, Abrams had a willing ally in Santiago in the person of Ambassador Harry Barnes. Barnes had not even presented his diplomatic credentials when he created an uproar by attending an antigovernment symposium conducted by Mónica Madariaga Gutiérrez, former justice minister in the Pinochet administration who returned from diplomatic duty in Washington in 1985 as one of the president's most caustic critics. A year later, he again made headlines: he and only one other ambassador—the other representing the Socialist government of France—attended funeral services for a Chilean youth doused with kerosene, set aflame and then left to die by soldiers after they had apprehended the youth and a young woman companion with Molotov cocktails during violent street demonstrations. The victim, Rodrigo Rojas Denegri, eighteen, was visiting Chile at the time from his home in the United States where he had obtained legal residence. (His companion, Carmen Gloria Quintana, nineteen, suffered hideous burns, but lived; their case became a worldwide *cause célèbre*.)

So actively and ostentatiously did Barnes court and cultivate ties with opposition leaders, from Christian Democrats to Socialists, that, as noted, the president of Chile refused even to receive the ambassador of the United States. (Negotiations on the delicate and volatile U.S. efforts to extradite two retired intelligence service chieftains and/or interrogate another were, perforce, handled by embassy subordinates.) The embassy itself, meantime, became both a forum for and a catalyst of antigovernment fervor; a U.S. delegation visiting Chile early in 1988 complained bitterly that the embassy's official briefing consisted of twenty-five minutes on human rights, barely five minutes on the country's spectacular economic success. The delegation was particularly indignant when their own meetings with independent human rights figures in Santiago revealed a far more benign picture of the human rights situation than the one portrayed by the embassy. An embassy spokesman, defending the briefing, said they were conducted that way "because that's what our visitors expect, that's what they want."[15]

An Arab proverb observes that the height of stupidity is the inability to distinguish between friend and foe. U.S. policies in Latin America over the past dozen years have been characterized by that inability, with the result that few friends remain, foes have multiplied. A *Miami Herald* year-end survey of the region at the close of 1987 concluded with this: "Seven years after the Reagan Administration swept into office with a promise to restore U.S. leadership in Latin America, Washington's relations with the region are at their lowest ebb since World War II, according to Latin American diplomats and U.S. officials and specialists. They say that the erosion of U.S. influence in the past few years has been so severe that it might take the remainder of the 20th century to rebuild even a measure of its former sway."[16]

As U.S. influence declines, Moscow has moved aggressively to increase its influence in the region. In 1987, Soviet Foreign Minister Eduard Shevardnadze visited Brazil, Argentina, and Uruguay—the first Soviet official of such high rank ever to visit South America. In 1988, Mikhail Gorbachev is to visit South America, part of what one dismayed U.S. diplomat called a policy of "smoothly calculated activism." A *Wall Street Journal* article noted: "Ironically, the Soviet efforts have been aided by the new wave of democracy . . . New civilian governments in Argentina, Brazil and Uruguay show their independence from the right-wing military regimes they replaced—as well as from the U.S.— by encouraging relations with the Soviet bloc." In 1986, Argentine President Raúl Alfonsín became the first chief executive of his country ever to visit Moscow, and Uruguay's president plans a visit for late 1988. Said Ilya Prizel, a University of Maryland professor specializing in Soviet activity in the Third World, "there's almost a competition among Latin American leaders over who will be invited to Moscow."

While U.S. economic aid to all of South America in 1987 amounted to only $173 million—3 percent of the worldwide total—the Soviets are buying Latin exports in increasing volume and offering low-cost loans and deals to build such projects as dams and hydroelectric plants. The 2,900 Soviet scholarships to Latins in 1978 were increased to ten thousand last year (while the U.S. offered about seven thousand). Even more significantly, the Soviets offered long-term scholarships in fields such as medicine—which the U.S. did not—creating a new wave of Soviet-trained elitists in the region.

Brazil and Mexico have long been the top targets of Soviet ambition in Latin America, and the Brazilians have shown themselves especially responsive to Soviet overtures. The closeness worries Chileans because of the long-standing Brazilian goal of exercising hegemony over its neighbors, particularly Bolivia and Paraguay. Bolivia—with Brazilian support, and tacit Soviet backing, as well—has recently revived its century-old campaign to recover the Pacific Coast territory it lost in the War of the Pacific, which left it landlocked. (Since its founding, Bolivia has lost more than 40 percent of its original territory, to Argentina, Brazil, Paraguay, and Peru, but has zeroed in only on the 9 percent it lost to Chile.) The principal prize is Chile's northern port of Arica—a prize the Soviets might well covet as an eastern naval anchor for their expanding Pacific fleet operations.[17]

So far, the U.S. response to Soviet initiatives in the region has been negligible to nonexistent.

In pursuing its policies, the administration has been driven, in no small measure, by simplistic notions about democracy, about its place in Latin America. Ronald Reagan was not alone in using the word as though it were a magic wand which, once waved over a country, would transform it into a promised land of felicity and prosperity. The problem is far more complex, more complex even than suggested by Winston Churchill's much-misunderstood aphorism to the effect that democracy is the worst political system, except when compared to all others. The problem begins with definitions; as *The Encyclopaedia of Philosophy* notes, "democracy is difficult to define, not only because it is vague, like so many political terms, but more importantly, because what one person would regard as a paradigm case another would deny was a democracy at all." But, as the *Encyclopaedia* adds, "the word has acquired a high emotive charge in the last hundred years; it has become good tactics to apply it to one's own favored type of regime and to deny it to rivals." Tocqueville warned of precisely such an outcome when he observed that unless the words "democracy" and "democratic government" were clearly defined and their definition agreed upon, "people will live in an inextricable confusion of ideas, much to the advantage of demagogues and despots." [18]

The "emotive" factor hinders dispassionate discussion of even the most basic proposition: obviously, democracy cannot and will not take root in all political soils, at all political seasons, and indeed, as Sartori observes in his important work, *The Theory of Democracy Revisited,* "democracies have always been, and still are, failure prone." The late political scientist Hans J. Morgenthau wrote of the "propensity [among self-proclaimed moralists in public affairs] for such moral and philosophical abstractions which has impeded the objective investigation of what other people want." He added a rebuke for those who imagine that "democracy is a kind of gadget which is capable of being installed in any political household, regardless of the qualifications and preferences of the inhabitants." The eminent theologian and liberal thinker Reinhold Nieubuhr sounded a similar warning, decades ago, about the tendency of liberals to live in an idealized world of make-believe:

> The democratic idealists of practically all schools of thought have managed to remain remarkably oblivious to the obvious facts. Democratic theory therefore has not squared with the facts of history. This grave defect in democratic theory was comparatively innocuous in the heyday of the bourgeois period, when the youth and the power of democratic civilization surmounted all errors of judgment and confusion of mind. But in this latter day, when it has become important to save what is valuable in democratic life from the destruction of what is false in bourgeois civilization, it has also become necessary to distinguish what is false in democratic theory from what is true in democratic life.

A more recent man of sweeping vision—Alexander Solzhenitsyn—has expanded powerfully on that construct. The West, he has written, trivializes what is important because the society itself, in its very essence, lacks a moral purpose. Its vaunted freedom is, in his terms, merely a formal freedom, directed to nothing beyond itself.

Taking note of Singapore Prime Minister Lee Kuan Yew's complaints of American meddling in the internal affairs of his highly successful country, Jim Hoagland, a *Washington Post* analyst of unusual thoughtfulness, referred to what he called "the American disease." It is a disease that causes the United States—and most particularly, its powerful press—to want to impose American (or, even worse, the liberal/left agenda of the press itself) on other countries. Few countries have suffered the consequences of that disease more than has Chile as it has gone about attempting to rise from the political and economic wreckage of its past. Although ignored by the world's press, few countries have, in fact, suffered such massive outside meddling in their internal affairs, leading one Social Democrat leader to remark: "It is my very considered opinion that Chile could become yet another link in the chain which is Angola, El Salvador, Nicaragua, or perhaps even a new Lebanon, because of the infusion into the country of arms and money from a wide range of sources."[19]

In Latin America, democracy has fallen on remarkably fallow soil. Between 1930 and 1966, there were fifty-eight military coups in Latin America. Between 1940 and 1980, expressed differently, democracy fell forty-six times; only ten survived more than ten years. Putting aside Mexico—an obvious caricature of democracy—only one democracy in all of Latin America (Costa Rica) has lasted as long, in fact, as the Stroessner dictatorship in Paraguay; only two (Costa Rica and Colombia, the latter by one year) have lasted as long as the Castro dictatorship in Cuba.

Nor, it should be quickly added, does democracy in Latin America mean what it does in the United States or Western Europe. For example, in Colombia and Venezuela—two of the longer-surviving democracies (since 1958 and 1961, respectively)—a handful of political parties selects candidates in private caucuses. In Venezuela, citizens then get to vote only for president, who in turn appoints governors. Congressmen are picked by the parties; voters get to vote only for the parties. A *Washington Post* writer wrote as the 1988 electioneering heated up: Venezuela's democracy "exhibits the kind of state management and party control more often associated with Soviet bloc nations . . . The influence of the major parties reaches into virtually every aspect of life here." (This is, of course, precisely the kind of party control Chile has sought to end, over the fierce resistance of old-time party leaders and their powerful allies in the U.S., Latin American, and West European governments.) As the *Economist* commented recently: "Both democracies are flawed. In Colombia, power is largely confined to the middle class and rich. In Venezuela, the bosses of the two main parties are overbearing . . . Voter turnout is normally low in both places, from 30 to 50 percent—perhaps because, as practiced in Venezuela and Colombia, democracy has been described as an artificial consensus that stifles the clear and public expression of different ideologies and economic interest." Nor, in long-violent Colombia, has democracy been able to secure two of government's fundamental responsibilities: personal safety and law and order. The lawlessness of the Medellín drug Mafia is now international legend—and scandal. Guerrilla forces and other freebooters of violence in 1987 took nearly two thousand lives in Colombia, including politicians, judges, newspaper editors.[20] Two years before, U.S. Ambassador Lewis Tambs had to be extricated from the country because of serious death threats against him and his family, threats the government was powerless to counter.

In Mexico, the July 6 elections focused serious widespread attention for the first time on the fraudulence of democratic pretensions in that country. Since 1917, a revolutionary dynasty has ruled the country uninterruptedly, power consolidated in a single party in 1928. That party—renamed the Revolutionary Institutional Party (PRI) in 1946—had, until this year, never lost a single election for president, governor, or senator, and had conceded the loss of only a handful of seats in the Chamber of Deputies in the 1985 elections, only rarely conceding defeat even in municipal elections. Under heavy pressure from the Left—the only kind the PRI can respond to—the electoral process was grudgingly opened up in 1988. The vote tallies revealed what specialists had long known: past vote totals were next to meaningless. When, after a week of stalling, official results were finally revealed, they showed Carlos Salinas de Gortari winning the presidency with only 50.36 percent of the vote, the closest win in fifty years. But the total vote itself was significant: 19 million of the country's 38 million voters went to the polls. In 1982, 23.6 million votes were "counted," giving Miguel de la Madrid his 74.4 percent "landslide" victory, although most observers agreed the 1988 turnout was greater than in 1982. There were, however, no National Endowment for Democracy grants to promote free and genuine elections in Mexico. Yet, as Harvard historian John Womack observed, "constitutionally republican since 1824, Mexican national politics has always happened mostly in private, in well-negotiated deals among a few politicians. Elections have had the status of public rituals—held not to decide national questions, but to ratify the already sealed decision."[21]

In Argentina, President Raúl Alfonsín appears assured of being the first civilian president to have completed a full term (in 1989) since 1929. It has been a far from perfect experiment in democracy; in the face of a fractious and obstructionist Congress, Alfonsín "has tended to rule by presidential decree whenever the law allows—and, critics claim, sometimes when it may not." Despite that, he has presided over an economic downturn which has revived the political fortunes of *Peronistas*, whose "reputation for political gangsterism" is well deserved; it was the demagoguery of Juan Domingo Perón and his followers that turned that once-rich and progressive country into the political and economic wasteland that it is today.

In Peru, which continues to welcome large contingents of Soviet military advisers and matching arms shipments, President Alan García came to power on a pledge of international irresponsibility—and kept that pledge: he said he would pay Peru's international debts only on his own terms, and he has. As a result, international credit has, of course, all but evaporated. Since the military in that country long ago marched to the Left, there has been no viable counterweight as Garcia embarked on a demagogic program of "populist" measures (price but not wage freezes, fueling an Allende-style artificial consumption binge; bank nationalizations). "The spectacle," commented the *Economist*, "makes Peru look ridiculous, and the nationalization is expected to make the economy get worse even faster."

Brazil, the seemingly unsinkable giant, is sinking into the worst economic morass in its history. Inability (and/or unwillingness) to service its debt obligations—largest in the Third World—has spawned a new and menacing xenophobia, including a parliamentary attack on foreign investment. It was foreign investment, during the long reign of the generals (1964–1982), that played a catalytic role in fueling and sustaining Brazil's "economic miracle."

From one end of the hemisphere to the other, incompetence and corruption run rampant. Corruption has long been described as the glue which held Mexico's political system together, but to that has been added economic mismanagement which has seen real wages fall by half over the past six years. In Peru, the founding of a small business, reports the *Economist*, is said to require up to three years of hunting for licenses, most of which are bought with bribes. Brazil, the report continues, "offers the most horrifying Latin example of a society run by charters, stamps, licenses and regulations . . ." "Latin democrats," the report said in another passage, "must stop the spiral whereby government in their continent is considered a device for awarding privileges and sharing spoils. Too often the easy way of becoming rich is not to produce something that people want to buy, but to obtain the right permits and pay the right bribes . . ."

Even worse, democracies have not, either, succeeded in making their countries havens of respect for human rights. The vice chairman of the very left-wing *Americas Watch* recently penned an article for the *New York Times* in which he said: "It has been an article of faith to the Reagan administration that elections and democracy guarantee respect for human rights. That faith is being betrayed in many newly emerging democracies, as I could not help but discover on a recent visit to Brazil . . ." While applauding Reagan initiatives in the human rights field, the writer, Aryeh Neier, after reciting examples of abuses, added: "Brazil demonstrates with painful clarity, however, that Washington has overstated the case for curative powers of democracy. It may even have done considerable harm in presuming that democracy automatically guarantees respect for human rights . . ." Nor, he made clear, was Brazil the only democracy where human rights abuses continued even after elections, citing Colombia, Peru, El Salvador, and Guatemala as additional cases. "Such is the case outside Latin America as well. In the Philippines, for example, violent human rights abuses have certainly not declined since Corazon Aquino replaced Ferdinand Marcos—far from it. They appear to have increased."[22]

Even the liberal press has taken note of the phenomenon in a spate of news stories, analyses and editorials. Wrote a *Washington Post* foreign correspondent: "Hopes persist that the current democratic era will yet prove a historical turning point in a region long afflicted by swings between dictatorship and democracy. Yet the failure of the free systems to deliver the economic gains, social advances and structural changes initially expected of them has soured national moods from Ecuador to Argentina and eroded the standing of all elected governments on the continent . . . Amid such gloominess, scattered voices in letters to editors and elsewhere have started calling for a return to military rule . . ." Chimed in the newspaper's editorial page: "Because Argentina and Brazil were the crucial cases [for democratic revival], it is troubling that a deep sense of disorder and decline has seized both countries. This disillusion is not yet irreversible, but the direction in which events are moving is not reassuring . . ." Commented the *Economist:* "Latin America's democratic moment is in danger . . ."[23]

Sprinkled amid these stories are a growing number of sullen references to the contrast between the economic cannibalism of the continent's formal democracies and the success of Chile's free market economy. To be sure, almost all such references are perverse, as is the political "reporting" on the country. Typically, such stories use outdated statistics to "show" that Chile may be succeeding, but per capita income is still below 1980 levels. By 1988, that (tendentious) comparison with an all-time peak year not only was untrue, but the assertion also omits the larger picture of Latin America (an overall drop of 6 percent in the level of real wages since 1980). It also omits the more agonizing experiences of some of the democracies—Mexico, for example, or Argentina where Alfonsín has driven real incomes down by 20 percent. (For that matter, one set of U.S. government statistics "proves" that "the real income of the typical American family after accounting for inflation was slightly lower in 1986 than in 1973.")

"News" stories from Santiago almost routinely assert that, well, the rich may be better off, but progress has been bought on the backs of the poor. Quite apart from the fact that the rich are better off everywhere, from the United States and Japan to the OECD countries, than they were fifteen years ago, in the case of Chile the assertion omits two key elements: the extreme "barbaric" poverty of Chile has been cut by one-third under the revolution, and the social safety net created by the government was the result of consistently higher levels of spending on health, education and welfare of *any* of the hemisphere's five largest democracies in recent years (see chapter 12). Earlier stories routinely "proved" the failure of the system by pointing to unemployment which reached 20 percent following the 1982–1983 regionwide depression; in Socialist Spain, unemployment last year reached a similar level without "benefit" of worldwide press fulminations about the failure of the system. Claims are routinely made that there may be progress, but then it never could have been done if the country had not been ruled by a dictatorship—overlooking the sorry records of dictatorships long entrenched in other Latin countries before they became models of democracy, overlooking the reality of draconian measures which those democracies have, in desperation, in fact imposed on their impoverished peoples (deliberately driving wages down in Mexico and Argentina, triggering runaway inflation in Peru and Brazil, etc.).[24]

October 5, 1988 broke bright, sunny and balmy in Santiago and most of Chile. Before the day was done, 7,236,241 Chileans cast their ballots in an election many—to the very end—said would never be held, and if it were, would never be held fairly. The outcome:

TABLE 56
VOTE IN 1988 PLEBISCITE

"Sí":	3,111,875 (43%)
"No":	3,959,495 (54%)
Blank:	70,356 (0.9%)
Void:	94,515 (1.3%)
Total:	7,236,241

Source: Electoral Service, as reported in *El Mercurio* international edition, Oct. 20–26, 1988, p. 5. Those figures represented 99.8% of the total vote, but were described as the third and final tally to be released by the Service.

The turnout represented 97.3 percent of the 7,435,913 persons who had registered to vote, and they, in turn, represented fully 92 percent of all those eligible to vote. [By contrast, just one month later in the United States—one of the countries whose State Department was loudest in carping that conditions were not simon pure perfect for "democracy" in Chile—fewer than half those eligible to vote bothered to do so in chosing George Bush as the country's 41st president.]

Furthermore, the vote was orderly, free of violence, and conducted under electoral rules which could be a model for nations everywhere. A veritable foreign legion of 3,000 "observers" from more than 50 countries, as well as close to 1,000 foreign journalists, were on hand to monitor the vote; only a handful of the countries they came from could themselves boast of a "democracy" superior in theory to the one being erected in Chile, and fewer yet among them of a democracy built on a sounder foundation of reality.

A "sí" vote would have meant eight more years of Pinochet; "no" meant that, under the 1980 constitution, elections for president and congress will be held on Dec. 14, 1989, the new authorities taking office on March 11, 1990.[25]

Although Pinochet himself clearly expected he would win right up to the time that, smiling and exuding confidence, he cast his own ballot at the downtown National High School, there was never even a serious intimation that the government—a supposed brutal "dictatorship"— would fail to do what dictatorships never do: honor the freely-expressed decision of the people and surrender power.

How and when to surrender power became the next line of attack for those who, from the U.S. Congress to the Kremlin, from the European Parliament to countless university lecture halls and editorial rooms, persisted in prescribing for Chile what the world has never been able to effect anywhere else: define and agree on what democracy really means, how, where and when it will even work. In the weeks following the plebiscite, with support from abroad (though in constantly-waning measure) the internal opposition demanded a speeded-up timetable for elections, as well as radical constitutional reforms. Pinochet was equally adamant: the Constitution of 1980 will apply in all of its dimensions, including timetable—until/unless a new elected government changes it. (It was rarely mentioned, but Pinochet lacked the power to amend the constitution; it would have taken another plebiscite to do that). In standing fast, he was bolstered by the reality, grudgingly recognized, that he without doubt remained the most popular single political figure in Chile: his 43 percent vote was, after all, against a united opposition made up of 16 political groups, including nine which actually managed to scare up sufficient signatures to qualify as "parties" in at least three of the country's 13 political regions. Popularity and an ambiguous constitutional situation notwithstanding, Pinochet indicated shortly after the plebiscite that he would not stand for election in 1989. [Interestingly, but not interestingly enough to still the heckling that he abandon office, Pinochet's 43 percent vote placed him far ahead of the 36 percent (of an electorate only half as large) which put Salvador Allende in the presidency in 1970. Inasmuch as his vote also represented around 38 percent of the total eligible vote, it also located Pinochet in terms of popular support well ahead of such U.S. presidents as Jimmy Carter and George Bush, both of whom reached the White House with around 27 percent of the total electorate; or even of Helmut Kohl, returned to power in West Germany in 1987 with roughly one-third of an electorate which votes in much higher proportions than that of the U.S.]

Such a recital too rapidly becomes defensive, churlish even, however powerful the provocation of international hectoring which reeks of intellectual colonialism. Chile is not, ought not be, anyone's colony. Democracy as practiced pre-1970 failed in that country; except for professional politicians, whose own base of popular support is acutely suspect, commentators on all sides of the Chilean political spectrum agree on that.[26] The country is well along the road to a new-style "guided" democracy, no less authentic than those in place in virtually all of the relative handful of Third World nations that live under anything resembling democracy. Whether that system is well-suited to Chile's political soil—whether Chileans even want to experiment with it—these now are questions Chileans ought to be allowed to resolve for themselves. In view of this observer, the Chilean model is, in fact, built on far sturdier economic and institutional frameworks than those in place in most of the world's crisis-ridden countries, and thus bids far better to serve well the needs of present and future generations of Chileans. It is a new-style democracy based on a sharply-diminished role for the state in the lives of the citizenry, a sharply expanded role for individuals—an end, in short, of what has been called "a society obsessed with the state." Furthermore, it is taking shape in the only country in Latin America that has created a truly modern economy: diversified, export-based, bringing hope and opportunity to a rapidly multiplying number of Chileans. In other words, a country which offers its people a better institutional and economic life than they had ever known before.

Prudence, a proper respect for the sovereignty of other nations and peoples, would thus demand that the Chilean revolution at least be given a chance. Even if the United States and other outsiders had shining records of success in intervening in the affairs of other nations in recent years, the vast majority of Chileans neither wants nor needs such foreign interference. Or does the world really need another Iran, another Nicaragua?

Chile asks not alms from others—only the right to be left alone, to work out its own destiny, in its own way. The rest of the world might even discover in the process that there really was a *vía chilena*, after all—a Chilean path to a better tomorrow, for themselves, for tens of millions of others.

Arlington, Virginia
November 1988

Notes

REFLECTIONS

1. Jeffrey Hart, "Does the University Have a Future?" *Dartmouth Review,* April 20, 1988, p. 10.
2. Paul N. Rosenstein-Rodan, "Why Allende Failed," *Challenge,* May-June 1974. The liberal columnist Robert J. Samuelson more recently quoted William Chandler of Washington's Worldwatch Institute as saying: "From the end of World War II until recently, centralized state planning served as a model for almost half the world. Newly independent Third World countries faced with a choice between centralized control and market orientation usually chose the former." Now, added Samuelson, "they are beginning to do the opposite. Central planning's false appeal rested on a naive theory of economic growth . . ." Samuelson, "Mikhail Gorbachev Rediscovers Adam Smith," *Washington Post,* February 4, 1987, p. G 2.
3. At the risk of inviting comparisons between the totalitarian Soviet Union and the loose authoritarian regime of the Chile of 1988—a regime on the verge of a restoration of democracy—it is interesting to cite recent remarks of Sergio Fernández, Chile's interior minister: Traditional Chilean democracy, he said, gave scant attention to "the more ordinary human rights, the freedom to work, to consume, to choose an education for one's children, to save and to choose a social security system, the right to undertake any economic activity, property rights and others formerly linked to the power of the State, which is today limited by legal provisions which protect individual rights, as well as by the principle of non-discrimination by the central government with respect to various activities and persons . . ." Quoted in *Chilean Review,* #13, March 1988, p. 4. Although each of the freedoms indicated above is real and close to full attainment in Chile, while the Soviet Union's promises of a better and freer life for its citizens remain mainly in the realm of slogans and promises, there were no backpedaling gestures of encouragement from the White House, nor anywhere else in the Western world.
4. Michael Fleet, *The Rise and Fall of Chilean Christian Democracy* (Princeton: Princeton University Press, 1985), p. 208. Poll data from "Fisonomía Política de la Sociedad Chilena," *Carta Confidencial,* #25, June 30, 1988, pp. 49–58. The Gallup Survey is derived from a sample taken: 10 percent from upper socio-income persons; 45 percent middle class; 45 percent lower classes. In 1987, as the political campaign was just getting started, 20 percent said they felt represented by one or another of the more than two dozen political parties then operating. It should be noted that similar laws banning totalitarian parties had been enacted in Chile back in the 1930s; one, promoted by the leftist Popular Front government then in power, sought to outlaw the home-grown Nazi party. On April 23, 1937, Chile's Supreme Court overturned the law, arguing that the National Socialist (Nazi) party was not contrary to democratic rule of law. The Communists, outlawed early

in the 1930s, were, of course, outlawed again by González Videla's "Accursed Law" of 1948.

5. "Lesson from Peru," *Economist*, May 29, 1987, p. 13. "31 Killed in Guerrilla Clashes in Peru," AP story datelined Lima in the "World Briefs" column of *International Herald Tribune*, July 6, 1988, p. 2.

6. Jeane Kirkpatrick, "U.N. Again Ignores Cuban Human Rights Atrocities," *Human Events*, April 11, 1987, p. 9; "Israel Deports Palestinians in Aftermath of Girl's Slaying," *Washington Post*, April 12, 1988, p. A–18; Cynthia Gorney, "Argentina Atrocities Described," San Francisco-datelined story in *Washington Post*, March 29, 1988, p. A–14; William Pascoe, "In Ethiopia, Mengistu's Final Solution," *Heritage Foundation* Executive Memorandum #200, May 12, 1988; "Rechazo a Decisión de Organismo Europeo," *El Mercurio* international edition, June 30–July 6, 1988, p. 1. In addition to Kremlin arms aid since 1977, Mengistu is supported by two thousand Soviet military advisers—and ten thousand Cuban combat troops. Mengistu's forced relocation was finally halted under international pressure after 600,000 peasants had been uprooted, but only after 100,000 of them had died of starvation on a gruesome death march. For further insights into human rights abuses in Africa—few, if any of which ever manage to inspire the indignation of parliaments from Washington to Strasbourg to Bonn and back—see Adam Wolfson, "Heart of Darkness: What Governments Do to Blacks in the Rest of Africa," in *Policy Review*, #34, Fall 1985, pp. 42–46.

7. "Periplos Opositores: Misión a Moscú," *Carta Confidencial*, #17, February 11, 1988, p. 22 (foreign trips) and "A la altura de los liderazgos," *El Mercurio* international edition, May 5–11, 1988, p. 6 (Zaldívar); "Las Líneas Estratégicas de Nuestra Acción Política," *Política y Espíritu*, #368, September 1987, pp. 12–14 (Valdés). Presumably because of Shultz' meeting with Aylwin, junta member Gen. Fernando Matthei excused himself from a luncheon appointment scheduled with Shultz for forty-eight hours after Aylwin's May 3 meeting on the grounds his Washington visit was "personal."

8. Nor is the Aquino government simon-pure democratic; not only did she ramrod through a combination constitution/presidential election using tactics that make Chile's 1980 constitution/presidential election look Boy Scoutish by comparison, but she signed 302 sweeping decree laws before Congress inaugurated its sessons in July 1987. Forty–two of those were banged out in the last twenty-four hours, including a sweeping agrarian reform law. Despite those autocratic measures, the U.S. and other nations continued to flood the country with aid. And, despite the aid, as the *Economist* observed, "under [her] inexpert captaincy" three-fifths of the 55 million Filipinos still lived below the official poverty line ("Gale-blown Aquino," October 17, 1987, p. 17). The new "democracy" she heads has, however, been resolute about one matter: imperiling the precarious franchise the U.S. holds on its vital naval and air bases in the Philippines.

9. "Nueve rostros para un perfil," *Qué Pasa*, March 20–26, 1986, p. 11 (Miguel Salazar); "Los Aportes del Tío Sam," *El Mercurio*, January 24, 1988, p. D–4 (for 1962 and 1964 CIA funding, and comparisons with U.S. electoral expenditures); *United States and Chile During the Allende Years, 1970–1973* (Washington: Government Printing Office, 1975), p. 168, Hearings of the Subcommittee on Inter-American Affairs of the Committee on Foreign Affairs, U.S. House of Representatives (Shlaudeman); Jon Basil Utley, "Why Land Reform Produces Poverty," *Conservative Digest*, February 1987, p. 99 (Ortiz); "The spiral down to chaos; The countries that could be following

Haiti down into the pit," *Economist,* August 22, 1987. Chile is not the only American friend to suffer State Department abuse; indeed, a paper summarizing recent U.S. hostility to Singapore's long-time leader Lee Kuan Yew summed it up: "State Department Reflex: Beating Up On America's Friends," *Heritage Foundation* Executive Memorandum #201, May 19, 1988. Instructive of how the media aids and abets State's self-flaggelation policies was reportage on the riots in South Korea in June 1988 following Washington-pressured "liberalization" on the part of the regime. One, preposterous even for the *Washington Post,* ought to be required reading for aspiring revisionist/propagandist journalists: Peter Maas, "Anti-Americanism Grows in South Korea; Revisionists Blame Washington for 1945 Partition of Peninsula." The "justification" for this journalistic hallucination was student protests that "have thus far failed to win widespread support." Except, that is, in the *Washington Post,* which then devoted thirty-five inches of newsprint to reportage so bizarre it is worth writing away for. For those who have not taken leave of their senses, it might be remembered that Pyonyang presides over one of the most thoroughly brutal and medieval totalitarian regimes in the modern world—an embrace scarcely to be desired.

10. "Triangulación Financiera," *Carta Confidencial,* #25 June 30, 1988, p. 30 (Jesuits); "Reagan Reconoce Su Poca Influencia Sobre A. Pinochet," a Washington-datelined EFE story in *El Mercurio* international, June 9–15, 1988, p. 5. As the headline indicates, the lead of the story referred to Reagan's "little influence" over events in Chile, though there was no further substantiation of that in the story. The Barnes cover-up scandal was first reported in the *Washington Post,* April 29, 1987, in a commentary by John M. Goshko, "Fraternization Abroad." The events took place during Barnes' service in Bucharest, 1976 through 1978. The State Department, responding then to press inquiries, acknowledged that it had known about the affair for years, but did nothing about it, by contrast to the vigorous prosecution in 1987 of Marine guards accused of fraternizing with Soviet agents. Indeed, the episode only came to light because of furious State Department behind-the-scenes moves to block a defector from revealing it during a CBS-TV "60 Minutes" appearance. Interestingly, the defector—Lt. General Ion Mihai Pacepa—omitted any mention of those events in his book: *Red Horizons: Chronicles of a Communist Spy Chief* (Washington: Regnery-Gateway, 1987). Those references reportedly were expunged from the original manuscript because of similar pressures. With the exception of Theberge, an early Reagan appointee, all American ambassadors to Chile since the 1973 revolution have radiated greater or lesser degrees of hostility to the regime. David Propper was succeeded early in 1977 by George W. Landau. Though not aggressively antagonistic, Landau was, after all, the man who testified at the Letelier trial in the United States in 1979 that Pinochet had personally asked Paraguayan authorities to issue false passports to two of the principals in the case: Michael Townley and Capt. Armando Fernández Larios (both of whom would later plea-bargain in turning state's evidence in the case). Pinochet repeatedly denied that claim.

11. Germany's Adenauer Foundation, closely tied to the ruling Christian Democratic Union (CDU), long considered the late President Eduardo Frei an "adopted son," and has generously provided not only scholarships for Chilean Christian Democrats, but funding for a cabbage patch of PDC think tanks, political action groups, institutes and the like. For years, Bonn made

the extradition of a minor Nazi war criminal named Walter Rauff the centerpiece of its pressure on Santiago. Rauff's death in 1984 removed that flashpoint; later, extraordinary attention was lavished on the sensational charges made to the extreme left German magazine *Stern* by persons who claimed they had been taken captive by Chilean security agents sometime prior to 1984 and spirited away to a small and isolated commune in the south of Chile operated by postwar German refugees. Once there, they claimed, they were tortured. Inevitably, the charges reinforced far left caricatures of the "fascist" regime in Santiago in sinister league with "Nazis." Those charges were seized upon both by the Bonn government and Amnesty International; as of this writing (mid-July 1988), after exhaustive on-site investigation with Amnesty and German government representatives present, no evidence has been produced to support the charges. The commune is called Colonia Dignidad, and is headed by a Dr. Harmut Hopp. In many ways, it resembles another self-contained (and long-isolated) German colony called Colonia Tovar, nestled in the mountains not far from Caracas, Venezuela. In a larger sense, it resembles many such efforts of small groups of persons who band together and create self-sufficient communities in isolation so as to preserve traditions or values which matter to them; one thinks of the Amish or Mennonites in the United States, the American Southerners who emigrated to Brazil after the Civil War and created Americus, a town in Sao Paulo state. To outsiders, such communities appear "strange"; to survive, all enforce strong rules to keep out intruding influences as well as intruders. (Quite obviously, not all such groups are harmless; witness Jonestown.) More recently, German indignation has centered on the cases of fourteen terrorists, some of whom face the death penalty, for a series of crimes including the cold-blooded murder on August 31, 1983 of retired Gen. Carol Urzúa Ibáñez; his driver, José Domingo Aguayo, and bodyguard, Carlos Riveros—cut down in a hail of sixty-two bullets fired in ambush. Most German sympathy centered on Beatriz Gudrun Brinkman Scheihing, a self-professed Communist who faced lesser charges. In August 1987, German Labor Minister Norbert Blum visited Chile and demanded that the fourteen be allowed to seek asylum in West Germany on the grounds (neither proved nor seriously supported) that they had been tortured while in detention in Chile. Of multiple other examples of foreign "concern," one bears special mention: the 49 million pesos (just under 2 million French francs) donated by the French Catholic Committee Against Hunger and For Development between 1982 and 1986 to twenty-three projects in Chile. Most of those funds (nearly two-thirds) were raised through special Lenten season collections in French churches. All twenty-three projects in Chile ranged from the far Left to the radical Left, and a 1986 investigation carried out by a French judge and two journalists failed even to identify seven of them. Among beneficiaries is the hard left magazine *Apsi* (12 million pesos), distinguished by such cover stories as "The erotic national press," "The loves of Marx," "Erotic Dictionary," "The psychotic [*psíquicos*] features of Pinochet." Another: the magazine *La Bicicleta* (3.5 million pesos in 1985), which the French investigators found was run by "youths" with "an ideological content of Marxist inspiration" and devoid of a Christian message. It should be noted that sermonizing apart, neither the Christian Democrat government in Bonn nor the Socialist one in Paris allowed its scruples to get in the way of business: the two have emerged as the principal source of arms sales to Chile, France most recently

(March 1988) selling Chile eight military helicopters. Socialist Spain took hypocrisy a step further: it was reported in May 1988 that the Spanish firm CASA eluded direct dealing with Chile by selling sixteen BO-105 military helicopters first to a West German firm which then sold them to the Chileans. Of passing interest is the half-million dollars provided between 1982 and 1985 by the Dutch Foundation for International Cooperation for Development (NOVIB) to the Communist-linked National Labor Coordinator (CNS); funding was suspended until early 1987 after it was discovered that $85,000 could not be accounted for. Sometime later, long-time labor leader Rodolfo Seguel decided to pull up stakes and move to Australia. It was then that Manuel Bustos assumed the mantle as top Chilean labor leader. Sources for the foregoing include: "Alemanes y la DC," El Mercurio, January 24, 1988, p. D-5; "Jueza Finalizó Inspección En la Colonia Dignidad"; El Mercurio international edition, May 5–11, 1988, back page; "Vino, intervino y se fué," and "Respuestas desde la cárcel," Qué Pasa, August 6–12, 1987, pp. 6–8, and Hoy, #524, August 3–9, 1987, pp. 17–18; "Ayuda Fraterna?" Que Pasa, #783, April 10–16, 1986, pp. 14–15; "Confirman Compra De 8 Helicópteros A Francia," El Mercurio international edition, March 31–April 6, 1988, p. 5; "16 Helicópteros Españoles Habría Adquirido Chile," an ANSA dispatch datelined Madrid, based on a report in the Madrid newspaper El País, published in El Mercurio international edition, May 26–June 1, 1988, p. 5. The same report said CASA had earlier sold twenty-four of those helicopters to Iraq and "scores" of military transport planes to Chile; "La 'Solidaridad' Internacional," Carta Confidencial, #9, August 27, 1987, p. 2.

12. "Los Aportes del Tío Sam," op. cit., pp. D–4, 5; "Who's Afraid of NED?" English-translation of El Mercurio January 1988 interview with Carl Gershman, in Freedom at Issue, May-June 1988, pp. 30–33; Shirley Christian, "U.S. Funds Are Aiding Pinochet's Foes in Chile," New York Times, June 15, 1988, p. A 1; "S. 709: A bill to impose additional sanctions against Chile unless certain conditions are met," U.S. Senate, March 10, 1987. Proposed sanctions included suspension of all commercial airline flights into the U.S. by Chile's state-run airline, a ban on Chilean copper imports that would have pushed U.S. prices up by 25 percent, and a cut-off of Overseas Private Investment Corporation loan guarantees in Chile, perhaps the only country in the world, that had discharged fully its obligations to OPIC (not all were finally imposed). The bill also included an outright falsehood: that Maj. Armando Fernández Larios, in his plea-bargained testimony in the U.S. in the Letelier case, "implicates General Pinochet directly in the 1976 assassination..." To the contrary: as Fernández Larios told El Mercurio in a February 13, 1987, interview (" 'Pinochet Ignoraba Plan Para Asesinar a Letelíer,' ") Pinochet "did not know about the murder... I believe that he only knew the cover story which was invented later." Christian's story, limited entirely to Endowment spending, makes the claim that $400,000 of the $1 million "was awarded to nonpartisan groups." That is preposterous. The biggest of those "nonpartisan group" grants was the so-called Coordinating Committee for Free Elections—whose principal leaders were Andrés Zaldívar, former president of the Christian Democrat party; Sergio Molina, a long-time Christian Democrat who served as finance minister in the Frei government; and Ricardo Lagos, a Socialist who had been Allende's choice to serve as ambassador to Moscow, and who exploded into prominence in a flamboyant national television appearance in April 1988 by defiantly claiming to represent the resurrection of the Allende socialist

tradition, a position he later soft-pedaled in appearances in the U.S. and elsewhere. The reality of the matter is that $950,000 of the NED award went to groups openly fighting against the government in the elections. The Christian article also included a gratuitous swipe at *El Mercurio*, which she described as "the pro-Pinochet newspaper." It would be tantamount to calling her newspaper the "pro-Sandinista newspaper" because, in the exercise of its free and independent judgment, it has found more to support in the Sandinista cause in recent years than it has in Washington's. She added that *El Mercurio*, a conservative but stoutly independent newspaper, "was identified in a congressional report as having accepted money from the Central Intelligence Agency to continue publishing during the Allende era." If she had read that much of the "congressional report," she might also have discovered from myriad sources, including the U.S. ambassador at the time, that *El Mercurio*'s editors did not know of the subventions, and thus their opinions were not "bought" by the CIA, as the reference would imply. It is also worth noting that although NED's Gershman claimed the awards were secret, a full nine days before the March 11 announcement, stories appeared in the Chilean press describing exactly how the monies would be allocated. Among beneficiaries of U.S. aid to Molina's Committee for Free Elections—a $10 million operation—is Ricardo Núñez, an ultra-left Socialist who spent part of his exile years in East Germany; one of his key men, Akin Soto, serves as executive secretary of the committee (source: "1988: Otro Dilema Para El Socialismo," *Carta Confidencial*, #17, February 11, 1988, p. 27).

13. In a vivid example of the law of unintended consequences—or the stupidity of sanctions—the U.S. arms embargo forced Chile to develop, for the first time, its own arms industry. By 1987, it was exporting $400 million worth of arms to other countries. The country's leading arms manufacturer, Carlos Cardoen, who earned a doctorate in metallurgical engineering from the University of Utah, founded his company in 1977. "I always say in a humorous way that I'm thankful for Senator Kennedy," Cardoen told an interviewer. Interestingly, observers of every ideological stripe recognize the ineffectiveness of embargoes—when it comes to applying them to states they want to do business with, anyway. For example, Sen. Bill Bradley (D-N.J.), in a 1987 *New York Times* article, argued that efforts to encourage Mikhail Gorbachev in his reforms "should not include embargoes or boy-cotts . . . the West . . . should treat its capital as a strategic asset and develop a plan for its flow eastward." The *Washington Post*, in an editorial criticizing congressional action in blocking arms sales to friendly Arab governments, noted that those states then took steps to buy arms elsewhere. "They often prefer to buy American, since with the hardware comes a valuable measure of political closeness and protection. There also comes at least an opportunity for the United States to shape the package and somehow moderate the recipients' policy toward Israel. This opportunity is lost when the Gulf States turn to Britain or other European suppliers, which are driven almost entirely by commercial considerations and are not in a position to attach political strings." Tyler Bridges, "U.S. Ban Set Chilean Arms Maker on Path to Success," a Santiago-datelined dispatch October 18, 1987, p. H–5, and "Triple Loss," July 12, 1988, p. A–22, both *Washington Post*.

14. Abrams served briefly as assistant secretary for International Organizations before being named to the human rights post. The late ambassador Theberge had told me of numerous instances of Abrams' back-stairs moves to apply muscle to Chile—and Theberge. The quote is from "Garrote y

zanahorias," *Qué Pasa,* January 22–26, 1987, p. 4. Chile got the loan. Following the October plebiscite, U.S. policy did change: the U.S. voted for a $35 IADB loan to Chile on Oct. 26; West European countries also backed the loan.

15. Barnes finished his tour of duty in Santiago—and diplomatic career—in November 1988, but not without a last hurrah. A few days before the plebiscite, he told a U.S. congressional delegation in an official briefing that best embassy information was that there was no way Pinochet could hope to pick up more than twenty percent of the vote. Though labelling it as a rumor, he also repeated an opposition-planted story that Pinochet was planning to create an incident which would give him a pretext for cancelling the plebisicte—a preposterous proposition denounced, among others, by the author, in the course of an Oct. 4, 1988 press conference in Santiago. State department officials later tried to defend the report on the grounds that it had strong intelligence source underpinning, and even to insinuate that part of the credit for the holding of the plebiscite actually belonged to Barnes. Indeed, the small cabal of anti-Chile leftists in Congress rammed through a resolution in October praising Barnes for his performance in Chile. Madariaga, an austere, severe spinster (the description is from *Los Presidenciables,* a publication of the pro-PDC magazine *Hoy*) claimed that during the eight years she served the Pinochet government in senior posts, she was like a sleepwalker. Then, she said, she was roused from her intellectual sleep by exposure to the stimulating personages of Washington while serving as her country's ambassador to the Organization of American States. [*Los Presidenciables: Diccionario Político,* in *Hoy,* vol. 2, June 1987, pp. 59–60.] The embassy briefing episode was reported to me by a member of a Heritage Foundation fact-finding team that visited Santiago in February 1988.

16. Alfonso Chardy, "U.S. clout falters in Latin America," a 200–inch comprehensive survey datelined Washington and published in *The Miami Herald,* December 27, 1987, p. 1A & 14A. I would disagree with many of Chardy's causes, but not his main conclusions.

17. Robert S. Greenberger, "Moscow Is Increasing Visibility and Influence in Latin Democracies," the *Wall Street Journal,* April 5, 1988, p. 1, and "Por la Errada Vía de la Multilateralidad," *Carta Confidencial,* #12 October 15, 1987, pp. 24, ff. There have been a number of articles in recent months similar to the one in the *Wall Street Journal.* In the face of mounting hostility from the Chileans, the Reagan administration did throw the Chileans a small bone: arranging in 1987 for the visit of four senior army officers to the U.S. as part of the U.S. Information Agency's International Visitors program. But training programs for Chileans, which continued even during the Marxist-Leninist government of Salvador Allende, remain suspended.

18. *The Encyclopaedia of Philosophy* (New York: MacMillan, 1972 reprint edition), vol. 1, p. 338. The Tocqueville quote is in Giovanni Sartori, *The Theory of Democracy Revisited* (Chatham, N.J.: Chatham House Publishers, 1987), p. 3.

19. Sartori, op. cit., p. xiii. Sartori reinforces the view of definitional confusion: "As we muddle through the 1980s the question is: Does a mainstream theory of democracy still exist? I think not." (p. x). Morgenthau: *Control or Fate in Economic Affairs,* ed., Robert H. Connery and Eldon L. Jones (New York: Academy of Political Science, Columbia University, 1971), pp. 199–200; Niebuhr: *The Children of Light and the Children of Darkness* (New York: Scribner's, 1960), p. 40. Solzhenitsyn, as paraphrased by James Finn,

"Taking Things Seriously (or, I'll Take L'Amour)," in *Freedom at Issue*, May/ June 1988, p. 3; Jim Hoagland, "The American Disease," the *Washington Post*, April 16, 1988, p. A-2. Hoagland quoted Lee as saying: "I am Asia. I am not America. I cannot allow American correspondents to decide my national agenda for me. An American journalist writes with the assumption that all governments are weak, that all politicians are venal. They would transpose their values to my society, and it is a set of values that we do not adhere to." Commented Hoagland: "His countercriticisms of the U.S. press and its frequently jaded assumptions about politicians and politics should not be brushed off. He has heard something disturbing in our current mood, something that is worth pondering as American voter turnout continues to sink toward a level that is considerably less than that of most industrial democracies"; "new Lebanon" in Carlos Neely, "Informe Político #4," September 1987, p. 3 of typescript version.

20. Francisco Cumplido Cereceda, "Los Límites del Pluralismo Político," in *Seminarios* S/4/86, the proceedings of an August 29, 1985, seminar in Santiago sponsored by the Instituto Chileno de Estudios Humanísticos, p. 1 (coups); Bradley Graham, "Calls for Change Rife As Venezuela Awaits Vote," Caracas-datelined story in the *Washington Post*, May 30, 1988, p. 23; "Colombia and Venezuela: Freedom to conform is not enough," The *Economist*, January 23, 1988, pp. 35–38.

21. Feuding continued among revolutionary factions following the promulgation of the new constitution in 1917—but from that point forward, the quarrels were internecine, with the party finally assuming the tutelary role. William Branigin, "Strengthened Opposition Charges Fraud in Mexico," Mexico City-datelined story in the *Washington Post*, July 15, 1988, p. A 1; Harvard historian John Womack, "Will Mexico's Political *Piñata* Break," in the *Washington Post* Outlook section, July 17, 1988, p. C–1; Larry Rohter, "Mexican Víctor Urges Party To Adapt to New Challenge," Mexico City-datelined story in the *New York Times*, July 14, 1988, p. A3.

22. From the *Economist:* "Argentina: Forward to the past," August 29, 1987, p. 35; "Argentina: The best since 1929, alas," March 12, 1988, p. 40; "Lesson from Peru," May 23, 1987, p. 12; "Peru: The man who broke the banks," October 24, 1987 (the episode referred to was the barricading of the president of the Association of Banks in his own small bank to protest bank nationalization); "To a different Latin beat," June 11, 1988, pp. 13–14 (licenses, bribes). Eugene Robinson, "Peronists Elect Populist in Primary," Buenos Aires-datelined story in the *Washington Post*, July 10, 1988, p. A 26; Womack, op. cit. (Mexican wages); Aryeh Neier, "A Dose of Democracy Isn't a Cure-all," a commentary originally in the *New York Times*, in the *International Herald Tribune*, Paris edition, July 6, 1988, p. 4.

23. Bradley Graham, "S. American Democracy Put to Test," a Buenos Aires-datelined story in the *Washington Post*, October 19, 1987, p. A 15; "South American Dilemmas," editorial in that newspaper December 15, 1987, p. A 22; "To a different Latin beat," in the *Economist*, op. cit.

24. "Spanish Unemployment Rises in October," Reuter dispatch from the news-wire itself dated November 12, 1987 (unemployment in October reached 20.69 percent, the second consecutive month of increase; it is worth observing that the Chilean generals inherited an economy in ruins; the Spanish Socialists inherited one already vigorous and growing, and would have the later advantage of affiliation with the European Economic Community); Spencer Rich, "Are Americans Better Off Than 15 Years Ago?" the *Washing-*

ton Post, July 14, 1988, p. A17 (the story cites one "widely-used Census Bureau measure" in arriving at the "worse-off," but points out that other indices contradict that—a reality reflected by the story's subheadline: "Government Statistics Say Yes, No and Maybe"—a proposition true of most economic statistics); "barbaric" is from the Chilean historian and educator Gonzalo Vial Correa, who pointed out that unlike the poor in the close-knit Indian societies of Peru and Bolivia, Chile's poor tended to be the displaced persons of urban shantytowns, cut off from interpersonal support systems; Rolf J. Luders and Steve H. Hanke, "How the Media Slight Pinochet," the *New York Times,* July 15, 1988, p. A31. The writers refer to a recent university poll showing almost 38 percent of the voters favoring any candidate presented by the junta, 29 percent opposed, and 27 percent undecided.

25. The new president will serve an eight-year term and not be eligible for re-election. The 120 deputies will serve four-year terms; the Senate will be made up of 26 elected senators serving eight years, and up to a maximum of 10 appointed senators, also serving eight years—with the exception of ex-presidents who would have life terms in the Senate. Among the international observers sent at taxpayer (or member) expense to the plebiscite were some 65 members of the Spanish parliament—a country then contending with 20-percent-plus unemployment and a resurgence of political violence—and around 90 officials of the AFL-CIO. That organization has worked feverishly to implant a union hegemony in Chile which it has failed to achieve in the U.S., efforts in part bankrolled by U.S. taxpayers through generous Agency for International Development and National Endowment for Democracy grants.

26. Citations abound in the text; to add two more recent ones from the far Left (it is, of course, assumed that the Right agrees with the collapse theorem): Luis Maira, of the radical breakaway splinter from Christian Democracy, the Christian Left (IZ), writing in the ultraleftist magazine *Análisis:* "What led to the collapse of the political system in Chile was the absence of any limit on the behavior of the leadership [*directivas*] of the parties and the over-ideologized character of their decisions. In such a context, whatever the correlation of forces, the tragedy could be repeated . . ." (June 15–21, 1987, p. 6; that is, of course, almost precisely what the military have been arguing for the past fifteen years); Clodomiro Almeyda, Allende's last foreign minister and leader of the most radical of the major Socialist parties: "The fracture which slowly insinuated itself into Chilean society and which evidenced its first acute symptoms during the presidency of Frei, which deepened during the government of Popular Unity, and which manifested itself in all of its crudeness, radicalism and violence with the military coup and the counter-revolutionary dictatorship, is very deep and difficult to repair . . ." (*Reencuentro Con Mi Vida* [Santiago: Ediciones Ornitorrinco, 1987], p. 32). Further apropos the generalized economic slump in Latin America, a framework persistently absent in "yes—but" stories about Chile, Gert Rosenthal, executive director of the UN Ecomomic Commission for Latin America, remarked recently: "We've been calling the 1980s a lost decade. The region hasn't grown. It has moved backward. Unless a number of factors change, the 1990s may not prove much better" (Bradley Graham, "No Quick End in Sight For Latin Debt Malaise," Buenos Aires-datelined story in the *Washington Post,* April 12, 1988, pp. C 1, 3).

Appendix I

Much ado has been made over a flurry of meetings and memos in Washington immediately before and after Chile's presidential election of September 4, 1970. The plans and schemes, a belated reaction to a largely unforeseen and clearly threatening occurrence—the election of Salvador Allende Gossens as Chilean president—addressed the question of how to protect U.S. interests under an anti-American Communist regime. But the protagonists in this titillating sideshow—the International Telephone and Telegraph Corporation (ITT) and the U.S. Central Intelligence Agency (CIA)—never were really more than bit players in what always was an all-Chilean drama.

Years later, in a peevish commentary on the bureaucratic infighting that virtually emasculated U.S. policymakers' ability to influence the outcomes of the popular election and the congressional balloting, President Nixon's national security adviser, Henry Kissinger, noted, "Our refusal to face the reality that what was going on was a deadly political struggle and not a debate between economics professors transformed us by 1970 from the dominant element of 1964 into a sort of mother hen clucking nervous irrelevancies from the sidelines."[1]

In contrast, Chile was uppermost on the mind of ITT's chief executive officer, Harold S. Geneen, as he called to order a board meeting in New York on September 9 of that fateful year. Besides other investments, ITT owned a 70 percent interest in the Chilean Telephone Company (CHILTELCO), which it valued at more than $150 million. Allende's Unidad Popular coalition had already targeted Chiltelco for expropriation once their man was in office. Geneen recounted:

> Mr. [John A.] McCone [former CIA director and then still a consultant to the agency] expressed to me disappointment with the results [of the election] since it represented reversal for U.S. policy of many years standing. Chile was apparently turning to a Marxist philosophy of government on a mandate of only one-third of the voting electorate. He [McCone] felt that the Chilean people might still arrive at a

democratic coalition solution, which would be more representative of the majority of the electorate. He felt the timing was already late but there was still a chance that our government might develop a plan that might provide the chance for a democratic coalition. Even if this should not develop, it seemed to me that the narrowness of Dr. Allende's victory gave room to hope that Allende's nationalization program could be moderated. Thus, it seemed to me that some sort of plan might be developed by our Government that might induce Dr. Allende to proceed with nationalization in a way that would permit orderly recovery of the vast U.S. investments, including ITT's, that were at stake. . . .

Of course, our thinking was very preliminary and we had no specific plans, but we did think that some socially constructive joint private industry and Government projects could be part of the overall plan. Such a plan might well envision the willingness on our part and others risking reasonable additional funds in order to safeguard the very large amounts which were at risk.

Through Mr. [ITT's senior vice president Edward J.] Gerrity, I directed that an approach be made to both the State Department and Dr. Kissinger's office, to tell them we had grave concern over the outlook for ITT's investment and we were desirous of discussing our thoughts in Washington and willing to assist financially in any Government plan to help protect private American investment in Chile. The amount mentioned of up to seven figures was intended to show a serious intent and to gain serious attention from the Government.[2]

A few days later, one of Gerrity's key Washington operatives made the first moves. On September 11, Jack D. Neal, a veteran of thirty-five years with the Department of State and then ITT's director of international relations, telephoned Viron P. Vaky, assistant to Kissinger on the National Security Staff for Latin America, and repeated Geneen's seven-figure offer. Though he assured Neal he would pass the information on to his boss, Henry Kissinger, Vaky failed to do so.

"I did not for two reasons," Vaky said. "I did not think the substance was worth further consideration, and I didn't think it worth bringing to his [Kissinger's] attention. I also had the impression, and I must explain that the call came out of the blue, so to speak, as far as I was concerned. I had known Jack Neal previously and I had the general impression that this was Jack Neal talking in terms of what I suppose one might call a normal lobbying effort to establish a position, to establish a view of things." He added that the purpose of the seven-figure offer was never clarified during the call.[3]

Neal did not have much better success with the next person he called: Assistant Secretary of State Charles A. Meyer. Meyer later could remember nothing more substantial about the conversation than Neal telling him: "Mr. Geneen just wants you to know if there is anything he can do, he would be delighted to help." Meyer added that he was "sure" he would have remembered mention of a seven-figure offer had it been made.[4]

At approximately the same time, McCone himself was moving to an even higher level.

"I came to Washington," he said, "and I met with Mr. [CIA Director Richard M.] Helms and I told him of this availability of these funds and I also met with Mr. Kissinger and I told him, if he had a plan—now, Mr. Kissinger thanked me very much and said that I would hear from him. I did not hear from him again and, therefore, I assumed that no such plan was adopted as a matter of national policy and that was the end of it so far as I was concerned." Both McCone and Geneen emphasized that the one and only offer of an unspecified amount of money to the CIA was the one turned down on July 16 by William C. Broe, chief of the agency's Western Hemisphere Division, in a meeting with Geneen, and that the seven-figure offer was not made to the CIA.[5]

In his memoirs, Kissinger wrote, "I learned later that some representatives of the CIA had informally advised some American business interests in late July and August where to channel funds during the election. This was not known at the White House or in the State Department; at any rate, it also was too late. My own attitude was that any covert action in Chile should be carried out exclusively by our government; this was not a field for private enterprise. Accordingly, I turned down ITT's offer of $1 million to help influence the election. I have agreed with the object, but certainly not the vehicle."[6]

Following Geneen's meeting with Broe, ITT did contribute $350,000 to the Alessandri campaign and another $100,000 in support of *El Mercurio*, one of the oldest and most highly respected newspapers in Latin America.[7]

As of mid– or late September, only one concrete "plan" had emerged from official Washington—apparently with the blessing of the Forty Committee, the interagency panel responsible for authorizing all covert activities. That "plan" was as short-lived as it was reckless: to "bribe" the Chilean Congress with $350,000 to vote against Allende. Quite apart from the fact that the amount involved would have allowed a paltry $5,000 and change for each of the sixty-three votes the Nationals needed, besides their own, to block Allende, the "plan" ignored the reality that the Christian Democrats who held the key votes were diehard leftists who never ceased to regard the Right as their mortal enemy. Such men and women, members of Latin America's most durable legislature, were not susceptible to "bribing."

"There was no attempt at any time to bribe any member of the

Chilean Congress," was ex-Ambassador Korry's reply to later reports. Korry added that he was "dead set against Dr. Allende as a candidate and everything he stood for. Dr. Allende knew my position . . . I would have gladly welcomed the Chilean Congress voting to keep him out of office, or the Chilean people doing whatever they would. I was against the United States doing it."

Korry had his reasons for opposing Allende: "The American public was unaware, because it often tends to give others the benefit of a doubt and look at it from a superficial point of view—that is, look at the mask rather than the reality behind it—the American public did not realize that we [the U.S. intelligence apparatus in Chile] were privy, chapter and verse, because we had penetrated the Chilean Communist party at the highest levels, were privy to everything they did, long before Allende's election, knew exactly what they were planning and how; I knew the Socialists as well—how they were going to gradually wipe out democracy as we understood it . . . wipe out and convert a democracy into a people's democracy. . . ." Korry pointed out that shortly after the election, Luis Corvalán Lepe, secretary general of the Chilean Communist party, told an interviewer from *L'Unita*, the official organ of the Italian Communist party, that the changes in Chile's political structure would be "irreversible." "Nobody that I knew in Chile," Korry commented, "took that to mean anything other than what it literally signified, that there would be no way you could reverse it for many years to come. There might be *pro forma* elections but no way to change the situation."

Korry gave Senate investigators a similar reading of the Chilean situation: "I want to make clear what I am saying. This is not a play of words. What I am saying is that when one employer has control of a country, that when the state controls everything of any significance, there cannot be a free press, there cannot be free trade unions, and there cannot be what I would consider a free election. That is what I was saying, and I said the Communist party of Chile and the Socialist party of Chile had spelled out these goals clearly over a long period of time, that all you had to do was sit in Chile and listen to the radio blaring out the propaganda every day from these people on the radio, in the press, in their theoretical journals and it was difficult to escape that conclusion."[8]

Richard Milhous Nixon had come to a similar conclusion about the fate of Chile under Communist rule, in part, no doubt, because of prodding from ITT. On September 14, Nixon also got a first-hand report from Agustín Edwards, publisher of *El Mercurio*, in a White House meeting arranged by a mutual friend, Pepsi-Cola president Don Kendall. Unlike Korry, however, Nixon felt the United States should do something to stop the Communist candidate from becoming president of Chile.

On September 15, the president held a secret White House meeting on Chile attended by Kissinger, Helms, and Attorney General John Mitchell, then the president's closest political confidante. According to Kissinger, Nixon told Helms he "wanted a major effort to see what could be done to prevent Allende's accession to power. If there were one chance in 10 of getting rid of Allende, we should try it. If Helms needed $10 million, he would approve it. AID programs to Chile should be cut, its economy should be squeezed until it 'screamed.'

". . . Nixon did not in fact put forward a concrete scheme, only a passionate desire, unfocused and born of frustration, to do 'something.' "9

Thus was born what Senate investigators later would dub "Track II." On September 21, the CIA station chief in Santiago was told to discard "parliamentary legerdemain" and concentrate instead on a "military solution." He was explicitly told that the Forty Committee, the State Department, Ambassador Korry, and the embassy were not to be told about his activities or be involved in any manner.10

Years later, Kissinger wrote that there was always less to Track II than met the eye. "Nixon was given to grandiloquent statements on which he did not insist once their implications became clear to him. . . . In the case of Track II, for example, not only was there no expenditure of $10 million, no specific sum was ever set aside. The expenditures, if any, could not have amounted to more than a few thousand dollars. It was never more than a probe and an exploration of possibilities, even in Helms's perception."11

Two days after the White House meeting, ITT's top Latin American reporting team—Bob Berrellez and Hal Hendrix, a Pulitzer Prize winner who, like Berrellez, had long experience in the region—dispatched a cable from Santiago with a phrase that would continue to loom larger than life long after it had been denied to death.

"Last Tuesday night," the fifth paragraph of the long "situationer" began, "Ambassador Edward Korry finally received a message from the State Department giving him the green light to move in the name of President Nixon. The message gave him maximum authority to do all possible—short of a Dominican Republic-type action—to keep Allende from taking power."12 "Last Tuesday" was, of course, the day of the White House meeting. But Hendrix, who later claimed authorship of that passage, also admitted that he had embellished it with third-hand information.

The source, Hendrix said, was "highly placed in the Christian Democratic movement, and very, very close to Mr. Frei." He said the two met in a coffee bar in downtown Santiago, a block or so from the presidential palace, on the morning of September 16.

"We were discussing the so-called Alessandri formula," Hendrix said, ". . . so, during the course of my questioning and discussion of this, this gentleman said, and I can only paraphrase from best recollection, that 'I had heard this morning . . . that a very important, a very strong, very hard message had been received at the embassy last night.' " The informant, whom Hendrix had known since 1963, several times said his source was "muy alto, muy alto"—very high, very high. From this, Hendrix said, he himself "inferred" that the source was President Nixon. Hendrix conceded that his source had not mentioned Nixon. "I had been led to believe from listening to newspaper friends that I had seen on this quick trip [Hendrix had arrived only a day or two before] that Korry was not getting much response to any message he was sending to Washington. So I presumed that he had gotten something from high. And [when] he had emphasized that it was a high, very high place, I interpreted this to mean State and I guessed on Mr. Nixon. . . ."

As to the phrase, "short of a Dominican Republic-type action," Hendrix admitted that he "stuck in that language" himself "to emphasize to Mr. Gerrity that nobody down there is talking about sending troops . . . I may have exaggerated the import of what this man had heard. I do not know to this day whether it is factual or exaggeration . . ."[13]

Korry, however, said he—the man who supposedly received the "green light"—did know. "There was no green light or anything approximating it," Korry testified under oath. ". . . my recollection of all my instructions is that I did not receive that kind of message" ("that kind" being to "do all that you could to stop Allende from being elected president by the Chilean Congress").[14]

If such a message, to "unseat the Marxist," had been sent to Korry, one of the three men who should have been aware of it managed to conceal his secret the very day after meeting with Nixon. At a background briefing for Midwestern editors in Chicago on September 16, Henry Kissinger fielded a question about Chile.

"In Chilean history," Kissinger said, "there is nothing to prevent it, and it would not be at all illogical for the Congress to say, 'Sixty-four percent of the people did not want a Communist government. A Communist government tends to be irreversible. Therefore, we are going to vote for the No. 2 man.' This is perfectly within their constitutional prerogatives. However, the constitutional habit has developed that Congress votes for the man that gets the highest number of votes. . . . so both the internal structure of the Congress, plus constitutional habits, would argue that Allende is likely to win the congressional election, barring something extraordinary. . . ." Since the information provided at the briefing was not attributable to him by name, Kissinger spoke with greater candor than would have been the case if he had been speaking for attribution, particularly when he speculated on what an Allende win would mean.

"So, I don't think we should delude ourselves that an Allende takeover in Chile would not present massive problems for us," Kissinger said, "and for democratic forces and for pro-U.S. forces in Latin America, and indeed to the whole Western Hemisphere. What would happen to the Western Hemisphere (Inter-American) Defense Board, or to the Organization of American States, and so forth, is extremely problematical. So we are taking a close look at the situation. It is not one in which our capacity for influence is very great at this particular moment now that matters have reached this particular point."[15]

In remarking that an Allende victory would "present massive problems for us," Kissinger was seconded by the Soviet Union, except that where he saw cause for woe, the Soviets saw reason for jubilation. A Soviet analyst described Allende's victory as "second only to the victory of the Cuban revolution in the magnitude of its significance as a revolutionary blow to the imperialist system in Latin America."[16]

On September 22, ITT's Washington chief William R. Merriam entered the picture, hosting a quickie (forty-five minute) luncheon for the CIA's Broe at the posh Metropolitan Club in downtown Washington. Broe remarked that since "Merriam knew very little about Chile," they did not have a "full discussion" of the situation in that country. Most of the conversation, Broe said, centered on a series of five recommendations made by Berrellez and Hendrix in their September 17 report to their home office. Four of the five were public relations/propaganda measures, two of them involving support for the *El Mercurio* newspaper group. The fifth was to assist in setting up a "family relocation center" in Mendoza or Buenos Aires, Argentina, for wives and children of about fifty "key persons" in the fight against Allende. Hendrix clarified that the fifty were newsmen who wanted to "stay and keep on writing in the same manner they had, but they were sincerely fearful, scared, frightened, for their wives and children. . . . There had been a threat to burn down the Mercurio building, physically burn it down. . . . [Their fight] was to keep the paper, keep writing the way they wanted to write, keep the paper [*El Mercurio* and its sister papers] going. There was no physical fight."[17]

Broe said Merriam asked him for his opinion—not approval—of the recommendations, and he replied that he said he thought "they are all right. There was no discussion." Broe also said Merriam made no mention at that luncheon of ITT's seven-figure offer.

One week later, at Helms' bidding, Broe went to New York to see Gerrity for what would be the final—and decisive—contact of any consequence between ITT and the CIA. Broe described it, in fact, as the "only operational discussion" he had with ITT.

"At that time," Broe said, "September 29, the Christian Democratic members of Congress were showing indications of swinging their full support to Allende in the belief that they could make a political bargain with him. It was felt that if a large number of congressmen, Christian Democratic congressmen, swung their support to him, he would take office with a mandate from the majority and he would be in a very strong position. At the same time, the economic situation had worsened because of the reaction to the Allende election, and there were indications that this was worrying the Christian Democratic congressmen. There was a thesis that additional deterioration in the economic situation could influence a number of Christian Democratic congressmen who were planning to vote for Allende. This is what was the thesis. . . .

"I explored with Mr. Gerrity," Broe concluded, "the feasibility of possible actions to apply some economic pressure on Chile; yes, sir."

Broe also explained to Gerrity that ITT was the only company he had had any contact with on the Chilean situation. He then discovered Gerrity was not buying.

"I must say," Broe recalled, "Mr. Gerrity was very negative about it [the economic pressure idea]. He in no way indicated that it made any sense or it was exactly what he wanted out of it. . . .

"We talked about 25 minutes and I came away from there feeling that if he talked to anybody about it, Mr. Geneen or anybody else like that, he gave me every indication that he did not think it would work."[18]

That very afternoon, Gerrity fired off a coded telex to Geneen, then on one of his frequent trips to ITT's European headquarters in Brussels.

"Subsequent to your call yesterday, I heard from Washington and a representative called on me this morning. He was the same man you met with Merriam some weeks ago. We discussed the situation in detail, and he made suggestions based on recommendations from our representatives on the scene [Berrellez and Hendrix], and analyses in Washington. The idea he presented, and with which I do not necessarily agree, is to apply economic pressure. . . . I discussed the suggestions with [John W.] Guilfoyle [ITT's vice president for Latin America]. He contacted a couple of companies who said they had been given advice which is directly contrary to the suggestions I received. Realistically, I do not see how we can induce others involved to follow the plan suggested. . . ."[19]

The next day Gerrity followed up with a memo to Merriam, Neal, and John Ryan of the Washington office:

> Yesterday, subsequent to my visit from Mr. Broe, Jack Guilfoyle was advised of the following by Enno Hobbing of the CLA [Council for

Latin America, a private organization of American businessmen active in Latin America].

Hobbing was visited yesterday by Gregorio Amunátegui, who is an Alessandri representative. Gregorio had come from Santiago and his message to Hobbing from Alessandri was—keep cool, don't rock the boat, we're making progress.

This is in direct contrast to what Broe recommended.

I will call you later to discuss HSG's [Geneen's] reaction to my telex in some detail. He agrees with me that Broe's suggestions are not workable. However, he suggests that we be very discreet in handling Broe.[20]

A week later, on October 6, Broe dumped bad news on ITT: the Christian Democrats were going to back Allende. He added that it was his "personal estimate that the military would not act against Allende, so there would not be anything happening." Three days later, his "personal estimate" became an Agency estimate. "Our coverage of the military," Broe told Merriam, "gave no indication they would take action." It was a measure of just how far the CIA was really out of it that at the precise time Broe and the CIA were concluding that "the military would not act against Allende," two separate military plots to block Allende's taking office were being hatched in Santiago.

Broe's telephone call to ITT on October 6 was his last significant contact with the company—or ITT's with the CIA. Three lunches later—one after the congressional election and none of them "substantive"—he would fade back into the shadows of espionage.[21]

The day after Broe unloaded his bad news on Merriam, Merriam had more gloom for Gerrity: "Repeated calls to firms such as GM, Ford, and banks in California and New York have drawn no offers to help. All have some sort of excuse."[22] The American company with the biggest stake of all in Chile—Anaconda Copper—approached the brink with seeming fatalistic resignation. On October 9, J. E. Byrne, head of the company's Chilean operations, wrote a matter-of-fact report to his New York headquarters reporting on a Korry briefing. Apart from the laconic, resigned tone of the memo, it was significant in reinforcing the belief that official Washington had come to the conclusion that there was no stopping Allende.

"Allende will be ratified as President on the 24th," Byrne wrote, "with the approval of the Unidad Popular and the Christian Democrats. Accommodation to this position is becoming so widespread that it is not unlikely that the Alessandri supporters will also vote in favor of Allende. . . .

"There is no evident support for the rumors that a military takeover is possible here. There is very little activity in this area and it is only being talked about by a few retired military people. . . ."

Byrne's letter contained another revealing passage: Korry, Washington's man in Santiago, not only believed Allende to be "an honest man, a man who will support his promises and live up to his convictions," but that U.S. companies nationalized by Allende "will receive adequate, just and timely compensation."[23]

By early October, both corporate and government staffs seemed to have run out of contingency plans acceptable to the decision-makers above them—a distinction both McCone and Assistant Secretary of State Meyer would insist on making.

"... Mr. Broe had a shopping list, and the staff of the CIA had a shopping list," McCone said. "Sometime in October, I discussed this with Mr. Geneen, and told him, and in telling him I think I was just concurring in his judgment, that I thought that the plans were totally impractical. . . .

"I think we must differentiate very precisely," McCone said, "between the policies of the corporation or the policies of an agency of the government as finally decided by the final authority and the staff thinking. That is what you have staffs for, to think up the alternatives, and then that is why you have bosses, to make the decisions as to what you do."[24]

"One of the problems facing this distinguished committee and to that degree the American public," Meyer told a Senate subcommittee headed by Senator Frank Church (D-Id.), in March 1973, "is the distinction between policy and examinations of feasibilities. . . . I find personally that there is nothing that is sinister or that indicates a change in policy to have learned that Mr. Broe, on the 29th of September, had discussed or had explored, brainstormed, if you will, a policy option, if you will, in terms of economic pressures on Chile as stipulated, because it was not policy. The policy had not changed. . . .

"The policy of the government was that there would be no intervention in the political affairs of Chile. We were consistent in that, in that we financed no candidates, no political parties, before or after September 8, or September 4. . . ."[25]

Meyer, who according to Kissinger had been a strong advocate in the Forty Committee's deliberations for staying out of internal Chilean politics, had purposely not been made aware of the Track II activities.

A precedent for U.S. covert activities in Chile had been well established during two previous Democratic administrations.

In a January 9, 1977, interview with CBS's "60 Minutes," Korry revealed that both the Kennedy and Johnson administrations, through the CIA and the Agency for International Development, funneled "tens of millions of dollars" to Chilean political parties, beginning with the 1963-64 presidential election campaigns. Korry said he was told by the CIA station chief in 1967 when he took over as U.S. ambassador that he could not cut back on these payments because "this lifetime annuity had been promised and I couldn't do anything about it."[26]

"Two of the leading Christian Democrats sent their closest representatives to me," Korry continued. "The right-wing candidate, Alessandri. All of them. I mean, just incessantly, and through the multinationals and through the CIA, just leaning on me for . . . from the day I got there."

(CBS reporter Mike) Wallace: "For money?"

Korry: "For money, for money . . . even Allende, in 1970, his campaign manager asked me in my house for a million bucks."

Korry said he turned them all down.

But, according to Kissinger, the CIA did not.

Referring to the millions of dollars in covert funds and assistance funneled to Allende by Cuba and other Communist sources (the CIA estimated that Allende received $350,000 from Cuba and an undetermined amount from the Soviet Union during the 1970 campaign,[27] Kissinger felt the U.S. expenditures—contributions to prodemocratic political parties and media organizations—were "neither morally nor politically unjustified. There was nothing sinister about the desire of the United States to make it possible for democratic parties to maintain competing radio or television outlets or newspapers."[28]

But the pace of covert activities in Chile had slowed considerably under the relatively new Republican administration. Kissinger says the Forty Committee considered Chile only four times in the twenty-one months before Allende won a plurality in the September elections: in April 1969, it deferred taking a decision on any Chilean actions; in March 1970, it allocated $135,000 for propaganda (posters, leaflets, newspaper advertisements); in late June, it allocated "a somewhat larger sum" for the same purpose—but in total still only 15 percent of what the U.S. spent covertly in 1964, and the funds reached Chile barely four weeks before the election, too late to be of any use. In August 1970, the Forty Committee decided that nothing further could be done before the election.[29]

The heavy-handed way the CIA went about spending even these relatively small amounts during this critical period ironically might have produced an effect on the Chilean electorate opposite to the one intended. Less than five weeks before the election, a Chilean Chamber of Deputies investigating committee, probing outside financing of presidential campaigns, received a sheaf of confidential documents stolen from an ad agency handling the Alessandri campaign. The records showed campaign donations from *El Mercurio*, two U.S. banks, the Anaconda Copper Co. and a total of $600,000 from a mysterious "Charlie," whom leftists promptly labeled as being a (CIA) conduit for money from ITT and other U.S. businesses.[30]

The Church Committee found that the Forty Committee approved nearly $2.6 million for covert activities in Chile during Allende's first year (November 1970 to November 1971). Between November 1971 and Allende's ouster on September 11, 1973, additional disbursements of about $4.7 million were approved, although the last $1 million authorized on August 20, 1973, had not been spent when the coup intervened. This makes a total of $6 million for covert actions in three years—about $2 million a year. Most of the money went to the Christian Democratic Party, lesser sums to the National party and to splinter factions of the Radical party.

El Mercurio, which survived, in Kissinger's words, "a relentless campaign of harassment, intimidation and economic pressures," received $965,000 between November 1971 and September 1973 and $700,000 in September 1971 from the U.S. government for a total of $1.7 million for the three years.[31]

These latter CIA funds were to enable opposition media—and freedom of expression—to survive the communization of Chile. Allende was barely in power when he contrived to seize the country's biggest publishing house. He used every device at his command, from cajoling to threats of economic strangulation, in his attempts to seize control of the country's biggest newsprint supplier—the only independent one, inasmuch as the other one was owned by the government—and it was only the determined resistance of the opposition in what came to be a nationwide crusade that blocked Allende from gaining a stranglehold on newsprint. Since the government controlled 70 percent of the country's productive capacity, government advertising was crucial for the media, and government advertising all but disappeared from opposition pages and airwaves. The government also used its formidable power to coerce independent firms from advertising with opposition media.[32] Individual radio stations were harassed constantly and ordered off the air repeatedly for minor infractions, and in October 1972, the government began compelling all stations to join national networks broadcasting government propaganda, a practice the government continued even after the courts ruled the measure unconstitutional and ordered the jailing of a Cabinet minister for refusing to heed a court order. Small newspapers and radio stations suffered repeated attacks by goon squads. The University of Chile television plant was invaded and held for nine months by leftist extremists protected by the government, which refused to honor repeated court orders to oust them, giving the government control of two of the three national television networks. In August of 1973, a mob cordoned off the area around the big tabloid, *La Tercera de la Hora,* and refused to allow a "reactionary newspaper" to publish in "a worker neighborhood."

Funds that the CIA provided *El Mercurio* and other beleaguered Chilean news organizations was virtually all that saved many of them from financial ruin.

As a result of the September 15 White House meeting, Thomas Karamessines, the CIA's chief of covert activities, was dispatched to Chile for an on-the-scene assessment of the stop-Allende efforts. On his return to Washington he reported to Kissinger that retired Gen. Roberto Viaux had formed a group that was plotting to kidnap army commander Gen. René Schneider, a strict constitutionalist who had rebuffed feelers from his colleagues about joining in a military coup. Unbeknownst to the White House at that time, the CIA also had made contact with a group of active military officers, headed by Santiago District Commander Gen. Camilo Valenzuela, through the well-connected U.S. army attaché in Santiago, Col. Paul M. Wimert, Jr. Beginning on October 5, 1970, Wimert contacted these two groups of conspirators a total of twenty-one times.

Kissinger, swayed by Karamessines' pessimistic report on the chances for success by Viaux's group, ordered the retired general's coup plot "turned off" on October 15 and later wrote, "Nixon, [Gen. Alexander] Haig and I considered it the end of both Track I [the Forty Committee] and Track II [CIA answering directly to the White House]. The CIA personnel in Chile apparently thought that the order applied only to Viaux; they felt they were free to continue with the second group of plotters, of whom the White House was unaware."[33]

On October 16, the day Kissinger says the thought Track II ended, the CIA cabled Santiago: "It is firm and continuing policy that Allende be overthrown by a coup. Viaux is to be encouraged to join forces with other planners. . . . There is great and continuing interest in the activities of Valenzuela et al."[34] Confusion, born in Washington, quickly spread to Santiago.

On the next day, two officers from the Chilean army and navy met with Wimert and requested eight to ten teargas grenades, three 45-caliber machineguns and five hundred rounds of ammunition. On October 18, six gas grenades originally intended for Viaux were delivered to the Valenzuela group and a day later the machineguns and ammunition were sent by diplomatic pouch from Washington.[35]

For Kissinger, "military plotters that needed foreign weapons should not have been regarded as serious. For they were not. In a comedy of errors worthy of the Keystone Kops, the plotters were set to kidnap Schneider in his car after a dinner party on October 19; they missed him because he left in a different car. The next day they tried again but lost sight of Schneider's car in Santiago traffic."[36]

On October 22, Wimert delivered the sub-machineguns and ammunition to his Valenzuela contact, but they were never used because now the Viaux group resurfaced unexpectedly.

On October 17, the CIA station chief in Santiago had transmitted to Viaux's group Kissinger's October 15th order to call off the plot and had advised them "that their scheme would fail, would thus backfire and should not be carried out." But on October 22, according to Kissinger, the Viaux group proceeded on its own "in defiance of CIA instructions and without our knowledge."[37] The kidnapping attempt was bungled and Schneider, who resisted his would-be captors, was shot and died three days later. That suspended further coup talk by the Chilean military until 1973 when U.S. involvement was studiously avoided.

The U.S. Senate Select Committee that investigated Schneider's death and the extent of CIA involvement found that, "Although the CIA continued to support coup plotters up to Schneider's shooting, the record indicates that the CIA had withdrawn active support of the group that carried out the actual kidnap attempt on October 22, which resulted in Schneider's death." The committee also concluded that arms and ammunition supplied by the CIA to coup plotters in Santiago were not used in the attempted kidnapping, nor did the CIA plans ever anticipate the assassination of Schneider.[38]

A subsequent Chilean judicial investigation revealed that the Valenzuela group's initial plan called for the kidnapping of the nation's four top army generals so Valenzuela could succeed, under military rules, as army chief. Then a junta headed by Adm. Hugo Tirado, navy commander, was to take over and President Frei would go into exile. Six months later, Frei would be allowed to return and run again in new elections as the candidate of the democratic forces.[39]

Back in Washington, Nixon administration spokesmen were putting out the word that no effective obstacle remained to Allende's taking power. Meyer told an overseas writers' luncheon in early October that the best thing to do would be "just let Chile make a mistake." As to military intervention, Meyer said he could give an "ironclad pledge": there would be none—by the U.S. or anyone else. "The Latin governments I have talked to are all concerned about Allende," he said, "but nobody has any Carthaginian ideas of crossing the Andes on elephants."

As to the future, Meyer said the United States would deal with Chile the way Chile wanted to be dealt with. "In other words," he said, "the ball is in their court."[40]

According to David Atlee Phillips, the chief of the CIA's Western Hemisphere division in the early 1970s, agents in Santiago returned to the more mundane work of collecting intelligence and maintaining their Chilean contacts following the Schneider debacle. Phillips, who was on an overseas assignment in 1970, consulted his deputy, identified only as "Abe," who gave the following account of what happened to Track II (and its swashbuckling schemes):

> It just faded into oblivion as new crises demanded Kissinger's attention. We did not think Track II was workable in the first place, and were quite content, as the White House chiefs turned to other matters and relaxed the pressure on Karamessines, and he on us, to put it on the back burner. This is not to say that we forgot Track II. Chile was still a concern in 1971 and something could happen that would set off a spasm of renewed interest and requirements for status reports on our Track II progress.
>
> In fact, Track II really expired in November 1971 or shortly thereafter. Abe was in charge between two chiefs of the division. He sent a written dispatch—not a telegram—to Santiago, gently suggesting, almost, that it was time to forget about a coup and concentrate on intelligence reporting. It was not an order (Abe did not have that authority), but rather a philosophical exposition....[41]

By the end of September, Korry had become convinced that Frei would not back the Alessandri formula (having Congress elect Alessandri and Alessandri immediately call elections in which Frei would run against Allende). He arrived in Washington on October 11 and stayed until October 20, drafting a position paper for the State Department that would become the basis of U.S. post-Allende policy.

He also agreed at this time to a request from ITT's Neal for a meeting. Neal later would report to his superiors: "The Ambassador said there are several alternatives of action, the main ones being to provoke Allende and cause a rupture in our relations with Chile, thus, lose all without a try.

"The second would be to try to live with Allende—not appease him— take a firm line, but attempt to negotiate at every turn.

"The second alternative seems to be the one the U.S. will take."[42]

The same day Neal met with Korry, ITT was taking the wraps off its newest investment in Chile, the San Cristóbal Sheraton Hotel. General Manager Fernando Hoffman said his first guests were a group of about seventy-five people on an American Express tour and he had several more such tour groups booked for the coming months, enough "to keep it afloat." (The San Cristóbal, and her older sister, the Sheraton Carrera downtown, were the only major ITT investments in Chile that would, in fact, remain afloat.)

A week later, Schneider was shot and two days after that Allende was ratified by Congress.

* * *

On October 9, ITT's Merriam complained to the CIA's Broe about the "softness" of U.S. policies in Latin America. Merriam mentioned, for instance, the failure of the U.S. to take tough reprisals the year before against the leftist military junta in Peru when it seized International Petroleum Company's installations. Broe—who was not a policy man even with the CIA, and who was not privy to policy-planning anywhere—said he gave Merriam his "opinion that if Allende was elected, the U.S. government approach would be severe. That is what I told him. I thought it would take a stronger position."[43]

Broe's speculation surfaced a few hours later in a memo Merriam dashed off to McCone, in which he said that he was "rather surprised to learn that in this man's opinion, the Nixon Administration will take a very, very hard line when and if Allende is elected."[44]

This would later become the basis for an ITT mindset about what it could expect by way of support from the White House. On October 23, Merriam wrote Kissinger a six-page position paper on Chile, outlining ITT's views and recommendations, couching them in what he no doubt believed was suitable "hard-line" language. Merriam said ITT did not "visualize retaliation or vengeance as part of our policy," but one of the four specific recommendations called for putting a hold on all AID monies to Chile, "with a view to a permanent cutoff, if necessary."

The memo brought an immediate retort—from within ITT's own ranks. A senior staffer in ITT's law department, R.R. Dillenbeck, protested sharply that the letter was not cleared with other members of the company's Chilean "team" in their legal and treasury departments. Besides, said Dillenbeck, it wouldn't work: "Identifying ourselves as being opposed to well-defined State Department policy at a time when it is imperative that we have the full confidence of our opposite numbers in State and at AID's successor, OPIC (Overseas Private Investment Corporation), seems to be possibly to jeopardize efforts which will be made to collect on the AID guarantee insurance." Dillenbeck, in language which had all of the grace of legalese and the pungency of diplomatic indirection, was making the point that such tactics could cost ITT support on their insurance claims if and when Allende should grab their property. ITT's policy on its telephone company was for $108 million, the biggest single OPIC exposure in Chile, and one of the largest the government agency had anywhere. To support his arguments, Dillenbeck attached a position paper which was authored by an authentic Latin scholar on the legal staff, Robert D. Crassweller.[45]

Kissinger waited better than two weeks to react, and when he did it was with a seventy-four word brushoff: "Thank you very much for your letter of October 23 and the enclosed paper on United States policy toward Latin America. I have read it carefully and I have passed it to those members of my staff who deal with Latin American matters. It is very helpful to have your thoughts and recommendations, and we shall certainly take them into account. I am grateful for your taking the time to give them to me."[46]

It was the last "satisfaction" an increasingly embattled International Telephone and Telegraph Company would receive from its government.

Just one year to the day after Neal's meeting with Korry, Neal was beseeching the State Department to tell him just what *was* U.S. policy toward Chile. For ITT, it was no longer an academic question: Allende had already seized their telephone company. And a week after that, on October 21, 1971, ITT complained that Secretary of State William Rogers was "going along with Meyer and Company's soft-line, low-profile policy for Latin America."[47]

"The United States had three policy choices that it laid out at the time we considered this seriously just before Allende was confirmed by the Chilean Congress in October 1970. These three choices were to seek to have a modus vivendi with them. Get along with them as best we could and try to accommodate them. Two, to have what was called a correct, but minimal relationship with them. And third was to seek to isolate, and hamper."

The speaker was Ambassador Edward Korry. He continued: "Now the President of the United States and the entire foreign policy-making process in the United States came down on number two, correct but minimal. But in point of fact, we carried out role three and to the surprise of Mr. Nixon and others we began with number one: that is, to seek an accommodation. . . .

"Immediately after the inauguration in early November of Mr. Allende," Korry continued, "I decided that even if our analysis is airtight, even if everything we said that Allende was going to do would in fact be carried out, that we had an obligation to the American public and to history to demonstrate that we did not operate to fulfill our own prophecies, that we had to test our assumptions. . . .

"I walked over to their foreign minister who described himself in that period as an all-out Maoist (and this is in the period of Beijing's ruthless Red Guard), Clodomiro Almeyda—and not only had described himself to me that way but to interviewers later and before—and I said, 'You know my view of what I think Dr. Allende and you represent in the way of political forces, in this country, in the hemisphere and in this world. You know that I was opposed to you, but you are now the representative of a sovereign power, and I am the representative of a sovereign power. And we are both mature individuals.

" 'Our job, therefore, is to seek to avoid problems if we possibly can and that I would suggest that I brief you on where our relationship was as of the day that Dr. Allende was inaugurated and that what I view as the unavoidable problems that will arise between our two countries and a process by which we may seek to avoid conflict and confrontation.'

"And I explained the rationale as to why I thought this would be in their interest and ours. I said that Marx had never said that you had to go to socialism by tying your legs and your hands and crawl on your belly to it, that it could be done in a comfortable way, that the United States was not opposed to socialism. We were opposed to somebody exercising irrationality or hostility to everything we stood for."

Korry added that the process of "accommodation" began tentatively, but by April and early May of 1971 it was "really taking off" when "suddenly, it was stopped."

"Now we learned," Korry went on to explain, "and it was confirmed to us by Dr. Allende's closest advisers, that the reason he stopped was that a veto was interposed by the then-head of the Socialist Party, Senator [Carlos] Altamirano. The Socialist Party, incidentally, it should be emphasized, is in Chile far to the left of the communists and there was an unending roar between these two parties before and during and I'm sure after Dr. Allende's election, with the communists accusing Altamirano of reckless leftism. That was the term they used.

"And Altamirano wanted to have a violent class war. He wanted no agreements with the United States. He wanted to have these dramatic encounters."

Phase one—seeking a modus vivendi—lasted for five or six months, according to Korry. He said the United States was still behaving according to phase two—"correct but minimal relationship"—when he ended his four-year tour as ambassador in October 1971.[48]

Long after the swirl of events of the autumn of 1970 had been replaced by a domestic tempest created by the piecemeal publication of a part of the so-called "ITT Papers" by columnist Jack Anderson, ITT Board Chairman Geneen gave his own summary of what had—and had not—happened. For all the publicity it got, he might as well have offered it in Sanskrit.[49]

Said Geneen—under oath:

"ITT did not take any steps to block the election of Salvador Allende as president of Chile. . . .

"ITT did not encourage or participate in any alleged plot for a military coup in Chile to block the election of Dr. Allende. . . .

"Nor did ITT contribute money to any person or to any agency of any government to block the election of Dr. Allende. . . .

"ITT did not take any action to cause economic chaos in Chile in an attempt to block the election of Dr. Allende, nor did it advocate that any others take such steps. On the contrary, it continued to operate its telephone subsidiary in Chile as efficiently as possible and continued its expansion problem of Chiltelco as best it could until it was seized by the Allende government on September 29, 1971. . . .[50]

". . . I firmly believe that fair-minded persons would agree that ITT should have tried to protect its investment in Chile in the face of a Marxist takeover and all it implied, and that we should have sought the help of our own Government. That is what we did and that is all we did. The U.S. Government, for its own reasons, took no action, and we accepted that decision and operated within the framework of U.S. government policy. There may have been better ways for us to have proceeded, but certainly American companies should have the right to seek and depend upon support from their own Government in protecting their legitimate interests abroad. . . ."[51]

Senator Church, who headed the subcommittee that investigated ITT's activities in Chile, was a man of decidedly antibusiness views. The chief counsel for the committee was Jerome Levinson, a man who hewed to the thinking that American foreign policy in Latin America had too often identified with the interests of American business, when preferably the two—foreign policy and American business interests—should often be at cross-purposes.[52] The committee was anything but "sympathetic" to ITT before, during, or after the hearings. Inasmuch as three of the five senators were Democrats, they could not be expected to deal too kindly, either, with a Republican administration.

The committee's investigative work began in September 1972, and the hearings were held from March 20 through April 2, 1973. On June 21, 1973, the committee issued its report. It contained nine specific conclusions taken directly from the testimony, followed by several thousand words of text which included a number of judgments not directly supported by the testimony.[53]

The main conclusions were: "On July 16, 1970, Geneen offered "a substantial fund to the CIA to be used to support the conservative candidate Alessandri in the Chilean election of September 4, 1970. This offer was turned down. . . .

". . . Geneen, Gerrity and McCone, considered a plan proposed to them by the CIA on September 29, 1970, to create economic chaos in Chile but rejected it because they thought it 'unworkable.' "

No truly neutral observer of events in Chile in the early 1970s has ever seriously intimated that the CIA had any direct involvement in the military coup that finally toppled Salvador Allende on September 11, 1973. The most that has been alleged is that the CIA worked behind the scenes to create the chaotic conditions that led up to the coup. But the testimony of those who made U.S. policy, since made available in their published memoirs, portrays a U.S. government standing very scrupulously on the sidelines as the Chilean tragedy unfolded.

William Colby, who succeeded Helms as CIA director, repeatedly denied that the agency had any role in the coup or the truckers' strike or that he had ever used the word "destabilization" to characterize U.S. policy toward Allende. This was a word attributed to Colby in a letter written by ultra-liberal Congressman Michael Harrington (D-Mass.), summarizing Colby's secret testimony to the House Armed Services CIA Subcommittee. The description of Colby's testimony by Harrington, who opposed U.S. policy in Chile, was based on the congressman's recollection of his reading of the secret testimony, since he was not a member of the CIA subcommittee and, therefore, was not present when it was given. The letter was subsequently leaked to the *Washington Post* and the *New York Times*, and "destabilization" became the catchy new word to describe U.S. policy toward Chile. Colby never used it, an examination of his testimony revealed, but his assertion, in a 1974 letter to the *New York Times*, that U.S. policy had been one of "encouraging the continued existence of democratic forces looking toward future elections," was little noted or, when noted, believed.[54]

As resistance to Allende within Chile grew and even the Christian Democrats began to lose hope of a constitutional resolution of the crisis, Ambassador Nathaniel Davis, who succeeded Korry, said, "The U.S. government could have done little to prevent or slow this trend and, seeing this, we tried to avoid bankrolling the plotters and to keep away from the plotting. As pro-coup sentiment spread, the effort became more and more difficult, but it was honestly sustained.

"The U.S. government wished success to opposition forces, a position intrinsically counter to the governing coalition's interest. Is that 'destabilization'?"[55]

According to Davis, Chile's congressional elections of March 1973 was the last time U.S. covert financial aid to the country's political parties was relevant. "By mid 1973, it was becoming clear to responsible U.S. officials in Washington as well as in Santiago that the U.S. record of abstention from coup plotting was going to be more important than any resort to increasingly superfluous covert intervention," he said.[56]

Davis went out of his way to make sure neither the embassy nor the CIA was associated in any way with the leading anti-Allende opposition groups.

"... I am confident that no element of the U.S. mission in Chile extended financial support to the strike movements of October 1972 and August-September 1973," Davis wrote a dozen years later. The ambassador even avoided opportunities to meet the leaders of the shop-keepers, the professionals, the land transport confederation, and the truckers.

Kissinger added, "The mythology that the U.S. relentlessly assaulted Allende after he was installed is the opposite of the truth. We had not changed our original judgment but we were prepared to make an effort at coexistence. So many other problems were clamoring for our atten-tion that Chile kept sliding on our list of priorities, except when some provocation by Allende forced us to react. . . ."[57]

Two persons who would know to what extent the United States was involved in the events that led to Allende's fall were the CIA's Western Hemisphere division chief, Phillips, and his deputy, Abe.

"Abe described two cables sent to our Santiago station during the month of May 1973," recounted Phillips, now retired. "In a rather abrupt departure from CIA custom, these instructions pointed out the proba-bility of an opposition move against Allende and the inevitability that the CIA would be blamed as the instigator of any coup. The station response to the first message reminded headquarters that the CIA con-tinued to have the responsibility of predicting a coup—ringing the gong—and the station could hardly be expected to do that unless its agents penetrated all conspiracies.

"The second headquarters cable countered this valid argument saying that this time keeping CIA's record clean was more important than predicting a coup."[58]

Kissinger would acknowledge that the U.S. intelligence agency was aware "of what was well known to every Chilean, including Allende: that the military who already controlled key positions in the govern-ment were seriously considering the takeover that had been virtually invited by the Chamber of Deputies and the president of the Christian Democratic Party. But we were unaware of any specific plan or date. And we were party to none."

Kissinger quotes from memoranda on Chile from the summer of 1973 prepared for him and the Forty Committee by his deputy in charge of Latin America, William Jorden. These corroborate the hands-off policy described by Kissinger and the CIA officials.

In one such memo, dated July 10, 1973, Jorden counsels, "The U.S. lacks powerful or reliable levers for influencing the final outcome. Continued encouragement of constraining forces within Chile and con-tinuing economic pressures could have some limited impact. But a policy of open all-out economic pressure would help Allende more politically than it could hurt him economically." Jorden recommended that the Forty Committee take no action in Chile. In every case, Kis-singer said, the Forty Committee followed his deputy's good advice.[59]

The U.S. policy of supporting the Christian Democrats in 1964 was considered by Kissinger to have been a success because Frei defeated Allende. But the Christian Democrats went on to become one of the most snarling, U.S.-baiting regimes in the hemisphere. In 1970, the U.S. was backing a third-place finisher and the effectiveness of its subsequent support for the PDC was questionable given the party's propensity to play ball with Allende until it, like other democratic parties, was forced to join the growing opposition to his chaotic rule.

The U.S. government's first contact with the military junta leaders came on September 12, 1973, the day after the coup when army General Augusto Pinochet initiated a secret meeting with the head of the U.S. Military Assistance Advisory Group. In his report to Nixon on this contact, Kissinger noted that Pinochet stressed that "he and his colleagues had not even hinted to us beforehand of their planned action and said he thought it had been better that way."[60]

In 1970-1973, the money spent on politicians may have been useful in keeping democratic forces alive, but it was a waste of money in terms of getting rid of Allende. In the end, the coup was made by the Chilean military and only the military, in response to their own consciences, in response to the clamor of their own people.

Notes

APPENDIX I

1. Henry Kissinger, *The White House Years* (Boston: Little Brown and Company), p. 664. Kissinger blames the State Department's refusal to do anything that would aid right-wing candidate Jorge Alessandri for Allende's victory. "Had I believed in the spring and summer of 1970 that there was a significant likelihood of an Allende victory, I would have had an obligation to the President to give him an opportunity to consider a covert program of 1964 proportions, including the backing of a single candidate. I was resentful that this option had been foreclosed without even being discussed, first with the argument that a substantial program was unnecessary (Alessandri led in the pre-election polls) and later because it was then too late" (ibid. p. 669).
2. *Multinational Corporations and United States Foreign Policy*, Hearings of Subcommittee on Multinational Corporations, Committee on Foreign Relations of U.S. Senate ("Church Committee"), Parts 1 and 2, March 20–22, 27–29, April 2, 1973 (hereafter *Multinational Corporations*). Geneen's testimony April 2, 1973, pp. 459–560.
3. Ibid., pp. 435–436.
4. Ibid., p. 423. Neal's September 14 memo to his boss, Merriam (text on pp. 599–600 of vol. 2) gave the distinct impression of a dynamic and well-connected man of action—which, after all, is what lobbyists are supposed to be—moving easily and forcefully through these invisible corridors of power. But then, Neal also called Meyer "Chuck" in that memo, and Meyer's nickname is "Charlie."
5. Ibid., pp. 102, 460. McCone's testimony clearly indicates that the former CIA director's knowledge of Chile—and events in that country—was imperfect, at best.
6. Kissinger, op. cit., note p. 667.
7. Anthony Sampson, *The Sovereign State of ITT* (Stein & Day, New York, 1973), pp. 264–265, 276–277; also, U.S. Congress, Senate, *Covert Action in Chile, 1963–1973*, Staff Report of Select Committee to Study Governmental Operations with Respect to Intelligence Activities, Washington, D.C., 1975, pp. 11–13, 21.
8. Transcript of "Firing Line" program, September 29, 1974, pp. 2, 14, and *Multinational Corporations*, March 27, 1973, p. 300. Whatever his other qualities, there are three which need to be noted here. (1) Korry is, by no stretch of the imagination, a man who would take the rap for someone else, perjuring himself, for example. At the time of his testimony, he was out of government service. And yet, when he felt that loyalty, or decorum, or the limits of his own information impinged, he would not testify on a topic, lending further credence to what he did say. (2) Korry had long experience in international affairs—communist affairs, particularly—before arriving in

Chile in October 1967. In 1943, he began a career as a United Press foreign correspondent in Europe that spanned eleven years and included two years (1949–1951) as chief correspondent for Eastern Europe, based in Belgrade. (3) The third quality, complementing his skill—and zeal—as a reporter, was the breadth of his international experience. Besides UP, he served 1955–1960 as European editor for *Look* magazine. From 1963–1967, he served as American ambassador to Ethiopia, and from 1967 to October 1971 in the same capacity in Chile. It is highly unusual for a noncareer appointee to be given two consecutive ambassadorial appointments; rarer yet to be retained by three presidents; and unheard of when those presidents happen to be of opposing parties. Korry was neither a conspicuous contributor nor a political activist, which says even more.

9. Kissinger, op. cit., p. 673.
10. Paul E. Sigmund, *The Overthrow of Allende and the Politics of Chile, 1964–1976* (University of Pittsburgh Press, Pittsburgh, Pa., 1977), p. 115. Sigmund quotes the CIA station chief apparently from testimony he gave to Senate investigators.
11. Kissinger, op. cit., p. 674.
12. *Multinational Corporations*, Part 2, p. 608. The same memo contained another oft-quoted point (#9, p. 610). Reporting—again—on the Berrellez September 6 meeting with Dr. Matte, Alessandri's campaign manager, Hendrix and Berrellez said: "The anti-Allende effort more than likely will require some outside financial support. The degree of this assistance will be known better around October 1. We have pledged our support if needed." Berrellez later denied (p. 165) that he had pledged financial support on behalf of ITT. Gerrity testified Berrellez was "not authorized" to make such an offer (p. 177) and Matte later said that Berrellez "offered assistance but money was not mentioned" (p. 504). The reference to a "Dominican-type action" was, of course, an echo of Lyndon Johnson's decision to send 23,000 U.S. marines and soldiers ashore during the 1965 civil war to prevent a feared Communist takeover.
13. Ibid., pp. 130–132, 146–147, Hendrix testimony March 21, 1973. Hendrix admitted that the reference to the Dominican Republic was his, and that he "guessed" the instructions came from Nixon, and that his source was a Chilean who supposedly got the information from an even higher-ranking Chilean who, in turn, supposedly got it from the U.S. Embassy (p. 1490). None of those qualifications appeared in Hendrix report to ITT headquarters in New York. Timing would seem to favor the belief in the authenticity of the Hendrix report: Nixon met with Helms and Kissinger on September 15, and that night the "green light" allegedly was flashed to Korry. Yet Helms notes of the September 15 meeting contain the notation, "No involvement of [U.S.] Embassy." ("Nixon Ordered Chile Coup," a Chicago Daily News Service story datelined Washington in the *Miami News*, November 21, 1975, reported—with a badly misleading headline—on that phase of the Senate Intelligence Committee's final report.) Despite the questionable ancestry of the "green light" theory, it went on to become an uncritically accepted element in the Allende mythology, routinely repeated in press accounts as if it were an established fact.
14. *Multinational Corporations*, pp. 286, 288, Korry testimony on March 27, 1973.
15. Ibid., Part 2, pp. 542–543.

16. Gouré and Rothenberg, *Soviet Penetration of Latin America* (Miami: Center for Advanced International Studies, University of Miami, 1975), p. 97.

17. *Multinational Corporations,* Broe's testimony March 27, pp. 248–249; Hendrix' testimony March 21, p. 143. ITT's top man in Latin America, John W. Guilfoyle, would later testify (p. 222) that ITT did not, in fact, increase its advertising in the *El Mercurio* group as Berrellez and Hendrix had urged.

18. Ibid., pp. 250–251, 255–256. Neither Hendrix nor Berrellez—busily tuning in for news of conspiracies in Santiago—knew about these ITT-CIA contacts in the U.S. (see pp. 148–149 and 167, respectively, of their testimony).

19. Ibid., Part 2, pp. 626–627. The only Hendrix-Berrellez "recommendations" were the four for shoring up the opposition press and view from abroad, and to assist in the "relocation project." It would appear, then, that Gerrity was imputing to his men a role they had not played. Interestingly, too, not only were Hendrix and Berrellez unaware of the CIA-ITT contacts, they did not even know that their Washington office was reading their output.

20. Ibid., Part 2, p. 636. Presumably, Amunátegui was "encouraged" by the report, around September 21, that Frei was ready to acquiesce in a plan for a military coup.

21. Ibid., pp. 252–253 (Broe and CIA estimates of the military). Broe would lunch with Merriam on October 9, again on October 18 or 19, and finally in December. He said that at his luncheon meetings with Merriam, he "did not have what I would call operation discussions" but that he merely gave Merriam general assessments of the situation (p. 254)—fodder for a number of important sounding Merriam memos.

22. Ibid., Part 2, p. 643.

23. Ibid., Part 2, pp. 1050–1051. Before too much virtue be written into Anaconda's behavior, it must be remembered that Anaconda's confidential files were not ransacked and later scattered to the media winds. The record does, however, contain no indication whatever of maneuvering—by Anaconda or any other American company—to influence events in Chile during this delicate period. Then, too, Anaconda had been badly burned only six years before because its management believed the company's best chance for survival in an increasingly hostile nationalistic environment was in "manipulating the politics of Chile behind the scenes." The other American copper giant, Kennecott, opted for disengagement (i.e., a phased sell-out). The policy bought Kennecott short-run popularity and handsome financial rewards—handsome, that is, until Allende buried both companies alive. For a thorough account of copper in Chile, see Moran, Theodore H., *Multinational Corporations and the Politics of Dependence: Copper in Chile* (Princeton University Press, Princeton, New Jersey, 1974). For a discussion of the differing 1964 strategies, see, particularly, pp. 132–138; the "manipulation" quote is taken from note 20, p. 132. As for Korry, he was not wavering in his belief that Allende's convictions were "all . . . contrary to the free enterprise and capitalistic system" (p. 105), or that Allende was inimical to the U.S. But Korry seemed to have underestimated Allende's freedom of action within the coalition and overestimated Allende's altruism.

24. *Multinational Corporations,* pp. 103, 106.

25. Ibid., pp. 398–399, 420, from his March 29, 1973, testimony. Meyer was, by then, out of government. Senator Church attempted to dispute Meyer's interpretation by saying that "we are talking about a CIA agent meeting with a high official of ITT and laying before that official a plan of action

which, as it happened, was rejected" (p. 402). Church seems to have forgotten that Broe himself had described the "plan" as a proposal. "These were ideas staffed, they were passed up to me, by people who work for me. I went upstairs. I talked to the people upstairs and I was sent out to check out if they made any sense at all" (p. 256). Gerrity—and ITT—told him they did not. There is no evidence they were ever executed, and certainly not during the crucial period in question. And so, it would appear, it was ITT that dashed Nixon's ambitions to "make the [Chilean] economy scream"—in the phrase from Helms' notes of the September 15 meeting (as reported in the November 21, 1975, news story—see note 76). McCone made the same point about staff proposals vs. plans: "Mr. Geneen summarily rejected any such ideas [for creating 'economic chaos'] that came up from his staff. Now I understand that various ideas were generated at the staff levels of the Central Intelligence Agency. They were never approved by Mr. Helms, never were submitted to this inter-departmental group, and therefore, were not policy. This must be clearly understood, that this is the differentiation between staff thinking and policy determination" (p. 103). Though he was no longer with the CIA, McCone at that time was a consultant to the Agency and a close friend of Helms, and presumably was in a position to make such a statement as part of his sworn testimony.

26. "The Korry File," segment of "60 Minutes," vol. IX, no. 16, as broadcast over CBS Television Network, January 9, 1977. Korry's reference to "tens of millions" was probably the kind of hyperbole meant to gain the attention of a vast television audience. Kissinger (*White House Years*, p. 661) estimates that the Kennedy and Johnson administrations had pumped about $3 million into the campaign of Allende's chief opponent, Frei, between 1962 and 1964 (though apparently without Frei's knowledge).

27. U.S. Congress, Senate, *Covert Action in Chile, 1963–1973*, staff report of Select Senate Committee on Intelligence Activities, 1975, pp. 20–21.

28. Kissinger, op. cit., p. 659.

29. Ibid., pp. 665–666. Kissinger states that the State Department representative on the Forty Committee went along with the expenditures only after warning that if any of the funds tended to endorse Alessandri, its support would be withdrawn forthwith. He noted his frustration over this years later: "The concept of defeating one candidate without helping his principal opponent was rather original; it was not obvious how Allende could be defeated without benefitting Alessandri. The appropriation and the caveat canceled each other out."

30. Sigmund, op. cit., pp. 103–104. On July 21, five young men entered the agency in downtown Santiago and forced the manager at gunpoint to turn over all records, including financial accounts. Five days later, two journalists who said they had received the documents from "anonymous sources," turned them over to the committee. Sigmund cites examples of the anti-Communist newspaper ads sponsored by Chile Joven (Young Chile) and Acción Mujeres de Chile (Women's Action of Chile). They featured pictures of firing squads, an Iron Curtain, political prisoners, and the caption: "This is communism. Do you want this for Chile?"

31. Nathaniel Davis, *The Last Two Years of Salvador Allende* (Cornell University Press, Ithaca and London, 1985), p. 308. Davis said he personally vetoed attempts to channel U.S. financial assistance to groups such as many private sector groups and unions "because of their possible involvement in

anti-government strikes," although the Society for Manufacturing Development (or, National Manufacturing Association, as it is sometimes loosely translated), known by its Spanish acronym SOFOFA, did receive $24,000 on September 21, 1972, to help pay the salaries of economists transferred to an affiliated economic "think tank."

32. The largest mineral water firm, for example, found its supply of bottles from the state glass company cut off for a full year because it persisted in advertising on Radio Agriculture.

33. Kissinger, op. cit., p. 676.

34. *Alleged Assassination Plots Involving Foreign Leaders*, U.S. Senate Select Committee to Study Governmental Operations, Washington, D.C., 1975, p. 242–245.

35. Sigmund, op. cit., p. 122.

36. Kissinger, op. cit., p. 676.

37. Ibid.

38. *Alleged Assassination Plots Involving Foreign Leaders*, op. cit., p. 5.

39. Sigmund, op. cit., p. 122.

40. Notes on the briefing were provided me by Juan J. Walte, of United Press International, who attended.

41. Davis, op. cit., p. 314. Davis (and the Senate Select Committee's report) says Abe's message was provoked by one sent to Washington by the Santiago station chief in which it was suggested that the U.S. objective was a coup. Davis, whose information came from Phillips, writes: "Abe responded by rejecting that formulation of the objective and cautioning that the CIA did not have Forty Committee approval to become involved in a coup. He also admonished the station to report history, not make it" (p. 315).

42. *Multinational Corporations*, Part 1, pp. 295, 314, Part 2, p. 658.

43. *Multinational Corporations*, Part 1, p. 254. It is probable that Broe was reacting to the earlier instructions to the CIA from the White House to explore all possibilities of blocking Allende. Again, Helms' notes of the September 15, 1970, meeting with Nixon—as reported in the previously cited Chicago Daily News Service story—convey the image of Nixon at his imperial worst: "*One in 10 chance, perhaps, but save Chile! *Worst spending *Not concerned risks involved . . . *$10,000,000 available, more if necessary *Full-time job—best men we have . . . *48 hours for plan of action." But Nixon would shortly discover that he was as powerless to manipulate Chilean events, in the final crunch, as he was the American system.

44. Ibid., Part 2, p. 645.

45. Ibid., Part 2, p. 723. Crassweller's observations are on pp. 726–728. As so often is the case with scholarly analysis, Crassweller erred on the side of caution—as events in Chile would later demonstrate. Crassweller is primarily known for his work on the Caribbean, including his excellent book, *Trujillo* (New York, The MacMillan Co., 1966).

46. *Multinational Corporations*, Part 2, p. 730.

47. On March 10, 1971, top ITT officers met with Allende to begin what they thought would be "negotiations" on the future of Chiltelco. What they got were six months of stalling, a cost-price squeeze, a ludicrous offer ($19 million for a property they valued in excess of $150 million and which was insured for $108.5 million), contrived labor troubles, double-talk, and growing abuse in the government-controlled press, accompanied by increasing pressure on their other Chilean subsidiaries (one of them was seized on May

15). Finally, on September 2, Chiltelco's bank accounts were frozen; on September 13, the company was formally "intervened," as Allende's press and ministers had been "predicting" would happen for months. On September 25, four ITT executives (all Chileans) were jailed, including the seventy-one-year-old head of Chiltelco, and one—a man who had been locked out of his office since May 15—held incommunicado. *El Mercurio* editorialized that if the government had reason to believe the company should be nationalized and could not reach agreement with the owners, it should have sent legislation to Congress, as it did in the copper takeover. Instead, "following the customary illegal procedures, it [the government] again ignored Congress and through administrative measures, went after the *de facto* seizure of the Chilean Telephone Company. This is an act of force that adds another shadow to the political experiment initiated by President Allende under the reiterated promise to act within the constitutional framework existing when [he] was elected. . . . each expropriation carried out behind the back of Congress gives the so-called 'Chilean model' the appearance of the 'international model' used so often by communists around the world. . . ." On October 15, 1971, in response to Neal's appeal to define State Department policy, Meyer told him: "The whole matter of Chilean relationships and expropriations of American investments [is] under review" (vol. 2, p. 964). On October 21, ITT concluded, after its representatives joined those of Ford Motor Co., Anaconda, Bank of America, First National City Bank and Ralston Purina for a meeting with Secretary of State William Rogers: "In summary, the entire meeting indicates that the Secretary is pretty much going along with Meyers & Company's soft-line, low-profile policy for Latin America" (p. 79). So much for ITT "clout" and the "very, very hard line."

In 1975, ITT and OPIC arbitrated their differences, including a dispute over a clause in ITT's insurance contract that invalidated OPIC coverage if it could be shown that expropriation was the result of provocation by the investor. An arbitral panel of three judges ruled in favor of ITT, and the OPIC insurance was not invalidated. ITT received $34,706,917 in cash and a guarantee of $59,384,614. It was one of twenty-six settlements by OPIC involving U.S. companies operating in Chile during the Allende years (Davis, op. cit., p. 71; also, *Insurance Claims Experience to Date: OPIC and Its Predecessor Agency,*" OPIC news release, June 30, 1987).

48. "Firing Line" transcript, op. cit., pp. 8–9, 12. That the U.S. was still very much stuck on phase two—"correct but minimal"—is amply reflected in the record of public statements and actions, including the aforementioned "soft-line" response of Secretary Rogers to U.S. businessmen. It was further demonstrated by the U.S.'s accession to renegotiating Chile's huge and unmanageable foreign debt during the "Paris Club" negotiations of April 1972. It was further demonstrated by the quiet and unobtrusive *increase* in U.S. Food for Peace shipments to Chile during the Allende years.

49. The *Washington Post*, the *Wall Street Journal*, and the *Associated Press* all gave over the vast bulk of their reports to questioning about ITT's two money offers. The *Post* buried deep in its story a single paragraph of Geneen's defense of ITT's actions; the AP version (as published in the *Miami Herald*, April 3, 1973), a very lengthy story, did not even mention it. Not even the *Wall Street Journal* gave Geneen's defense more than a single paragraph—the next to last in its story.

50. This was six months before Anderson published the purloined "ITT Papers,"

which Allende's government would seize upon as the pretext for formalizing what it had, in fact, done the previous September: namely, grab the telephone company, without compensation. In fact, it was exactly what they said they intended to do even before Allende was elected. (Allende referred to the need to nationalize Chiltelco in a campaign speech on September 1, 1970, echoing what the platform-drafters had decided months before.)

51. *Multinational Corporations*, pp. 458–459, 461. McCone also alluded to the wisdom of the tactics used, while staunchly defending what was behind them and the decisions actually taken. He said there were "a great many unfortunate things that happened in connection with ITT's activity in Washington—and, when the whole thing surfaced, very radical changes were made in the organization . . ." (p. 106). Among those "radical changes": Merriam was transferred to Rome, the office was demoted from vice-presidential level to that of a firmly subordinated adjunct of New York headquarters, and the public relations professional staff reduced from sixteen (in 1970) to five (by 1975).

52. This view permeates, for instance, the book Jerome Levinson co-authored with Juan de Onis, the *New York Times, The Alliance That Lost Its Way* (Chicago: The Twentieth Century Fund, 1971). Levinson is remembered by colleagues I know at the Inter-American Development Bank as a man as deeply congenial to leftist economic theory as he is hostile to capitalistic ideology.

53. *Multinational Corporations, op. cit.* June 21, 1973, pp. 16–17. The harshest finding in the report says (p. 18): ". . . but what is not to be condoned is that the highest officials [sic] of the ITT sought to engage the CIA in a plan covertly to manipulate the outcome of the Chilean presidential elections." It should be remembered that the one and only such "covert" approach to the CIA in that sense was the one made by Geneen on July 16, 1971—and that one died as quickly as it surfaced. The uses and purposes of the later million-dollar fund remained blurred in the testimony, but did *not* include the CIA. Even the nine specific conclusions contain questionable language, such as the statement (#8, p. 16) that "early in 1971, negotiations undertaken with a view to convincing Allende that if he made a deal with ITT, he could confiscate, with impunity, other U.S. companies in Chile." Nowhere in the ITT Papers does the "impunity" suggestion appear. What does appear (vol. 2, pp. 799–800) is a suggestion from Gerrity to Geneen, on February 11, 1971, that since ITT's days in Chile appeared numbered, "we might suggest to Allende that he make an agreement with us on the best possible terms we can arrange so that when he has to come to grips with problems, which will flow from his treatment of other American investments in Chile, he will be able to point to a satisfactory agreement with us. In short, when the critics descend on him, assuming he has made a reasonable agreement with us, he can point to us as an example of how a fair deal can be completed if both sides approach the matter sensibly." Gerrity then added a phrase to demonstrate what he meant by "sensibly"—in other words, a genuine *quid pro quo* in bargaining: "I think we have a couple things going for us. One, we own two major hotels in Santiago and we can point out that if he treats us fairly we would do everything possible to promote tourism both in Chile's interest and in our own . . . I am suggesting for your consideration that we try to evolve a plan which would provide a mixture of good international relations

for Allende and which would also provide an agreement that would be good business both for Chile and for the United States with us as the vehicle."

54. Davis, op. cit., p. 320. Davis also notes that Harry Shlaudeman, then deputy assistant secretary of state, remembered hearing the term for the first time in his life when Harrington himself used it repeatedly in badgering questioning of Shlaudeman on June 12, 1974, three months before the leaks.

55. Davis, op. cit., p. 328.

56. Ibid., p. 329.

57. Kissinger, *Years of Upheaval* (Little Brown and Company, Boston and Toronto, 1982), p. 378.

58. David Atlee Phillips, *The Night Watch: 25 Years Inside the CIA* (Robert Hale Limited, London, 1977), p. 238. Davis, op. cit., p. 349, quotes Phillips in a letter to him, as saying: "Of one thing I am morally certain. We did not promote or assist that coup and we did everything we could possibly do to avoid any inference of involvement, short of closing down the station and leaving Chile."

59. Kissinger, *Years of Upheaval*, pp. 401–404.

60. Ibid., pp. 407–408.

Appendix II

In September 1970, a handful of the vanquished, military men and civilians, began to take the first tentative steps in a desperate effort to stop Salvador Allende from becoming president.

In an instant of panic, however, these men, moved by a deep sense of patriotism, immolated themselves, as well as the last faint hopes of their compatriots, to save their beloved Chile from what many considered an impending disaster.

Two years later, three of the principals reconstructed those tormented days of September and October in a series of conversations with the Chilean journalist Florencia Varas.[1]

"On the night of September 4, I opened a few bottles of red wine and a few of white wine, and I got drunk." So said Luis Gallardo Gallardo, forty-one, industrial chemist, a leader in the campaign of Jorge Alessandri, a mustachioed man with thick black hair and the facial features and mien of the prototype middle-class Chilean man.

No doubt, it would have been much better for Luis Gallardo—and, perhaps, for Chile—if, in the company of a few Second District campaign coworkers, he had gotten as drunk that night as he had hoped.

But as it happened, the telephone rang; it was a special caller who said he had to see him, right away. Some time later—Gallardo doesn't remember when—the caller arrived, and seeing there were others in the house, said he preferred to stay outside. The two men chatted on the front lawn.

The visitor was a high official in "Investigaciones," the national police detective force. He came to tell Gallardo, among other leaders of the Alessandri campaign, that many high officers of Investigaciones shared his feelings: it would be dangerous for Chile to fall into Communist hands and he, together with the others, was ready to cooperate in any effort to prevent it.

"It was," Gallardo said, "a small beacon of hope."

Gallardo went back inside and, "even before I knew what I felt," he began calling his colleagues. One call hit paydirt: retired army Gen.

1057

Héctor Martínez Amaro, also a leader of the Alessandri campaign and president of the embryonic National Popular party, made up mostly of retired military men. The two agreed to meet the following day.

"We went over the situation," Gallardo said, "and we arrived at the conclusion that so long as the electoral process was not over, we should continue fighting to keep the Communists from taking power." The fight was designed to persuade Congress to choose Alessandri, and to carry it out, they organized a "Republican Independent Front," headed by General Martínez.

While organizing the front, Gallardo discovered that another group was forming around still another retired military man: Gen. Roberto Viaux Marambio.

On October 21, 1969, Viaux, a blunt and scrappy artillery officer who had been promoted to general only ten months earlier, became a hero to most of Chile's dispirited officer corps, chafing under five years of systematic neglect: he led a pocket revolt that more nearly resembled the first "strike" in the military's history (see chapter 4, pp. 179–192).

Discontent had been boiling up for some time. Two years earlier, the army was unable to hold maneuvers because it lacked enough shoes for the men. Pay had fallen so far behind other levels that a lieutenant colonel with twenty-five years service earned no more than the starting pay for the lowest-rated laborer at the Chuquicamata copper mine. At Viaux's army First Division in Antofagasta, fifty officers had to crowd into BOQs (Bachelor Officer Quarters) designed for half that number. Housing for noncommissioned officers was so bad that many lived in shanties with no roofs. In 1968, four hundred of the army's officers resigned en masse—an act that forced Frei to reshuffle the high command. The new defense minister, retired Gen. Tulio Marambio Marchant, and the new army commandant, Gen. Sergio Castillo Aránguiz (a man with family ties to top Christian Democrats), promised relief within nine months. They failed to deliver.

Into the breach marched Viaux, agitating through channels for action. Late in September 1969, he got it: a summons to Santiago, ostensibly to sit on an army promotion board. He began demanding immediately—as was his right—a meeting with Frei, but was persistently brushed off. Instead, he was told he was to be retired, and should make ready to hand over his command. Shortly after, back in Santiago, officers turned up at his house late on the night of October 20 asking him to head an insurrection. At 2:30 A.M., he agreed to take over the Tacna armored regiment in Santiago and declared himself in "professional rebellion" against the government. Numerous other units quickly pledged support, while Frei massed a "defensive force" of garbage trucks around the presidential palace in downtown Santiago.

Late that afternoon, after daylong negotiations, Viaux agreed to end the "revolt" in return for a five-point agreement, under which Frei pledged to cashier his defense minister and army commander and to "resolve in urgent form the economic problem of the armed forces."

Inasmuch as it was clear that Viaux probably could have seized the government that day—other army units refused to obey orders to act against him—his punishment was limited to retirement and a suspended sentence.

In the months that followed, he toured Chile from one end to another, while refusing to become involved in politics. (He did, however, poll twenty thousand votes to win a popularity contest in the small town of Calama, near his last post.) Viaux claimed envoys from both Alessandri and Allende approached him as the elections drew near, asking for his support, and that after the elections, Carlos Lazo Frías and others attempted to enlist his support for Allende in the congressional runoff.[2] Lazo, named by Allende as head of the Bank of the State, emerged as the brains of a conspiracy to organize secret cells within the armed forces so as to neutralize their power to oppose Allende.

But the voices of the Left were not the ones Viaux was listening to on those charged September days.

Through his father-in-law, retired Col. Raúl Igualt Ramírez, Viaux was put in touch with an old friend, Gen. Camilo Valenzuela Godoy, commander of the Santiago army garrison. At the first session, they felt each other out. Later, they became more specific; the circle of like-minded men expanded to include Gen. Joaquín García, number two man in the air force; Adm. Hugo Tirado Barros, number two in the navy; and Gen. Vicente Huerta Celis, commander of Carabineros, the quasi-military, 26,000-man national police force. Others would later join, some would drop out (Valenzuela, Tirado, and Igualt were the only high military officers later convicted of various degrees of complicity in the plot).

"From the first meetings," Viaux said, "the unknown was the commander-in-chief of the army: General René Schneider Chereau." That man was, in an ironic sense, a creature of Viaux's own invention. Following Viaux's one-day "war," he was asked who he believed ought to be the new army commander. Viaux replied that it should be the general with the most seniority, General Mahn. Instead, Frei decided to name Schneider, whose sympathies in favor of the Christian Democrats were well known.

Early in the campaign, on May 7, Schneider issued a statement in which he said the army would accede to the decision of Congress if, as expected, the election were thrown into the Congress—no matter who the winner might be. The statement was designed to reassure Allende's forces that the rules of democracy would not be suspended should their man win.

Viaux said he later learned that Valenzuela had informed Schneider of his meetings with Viaux and the other military commanders still groping for legal means to block Allende. (He said Huerta also kept his superior, Frei's civilian interior minister Patricio Rojas, informed.)

"Around that time," Viaux said, "it became known that President Frei had had a long meeting with General Schneider behind closed doors. It was said that the purpose had been to sound him [Schneider] out on a possible move outside the Constitution. We did not learn the outcome. . . ."

Parallel with his talks with military commanders, Viaux met with the civilian group headed by Gallardo and retired General Martínez. "He gave us a tremendous lift," Gallardo said, "because we discovered that, like us, the great majority of Chileans felt the same anxiety, and that many political personages and people from other walks of life had visited him starting on September 5th, seeking in him a leader with sufficient resolve to block the Communist aims."

Later, to still the growing anxiety of those around him, Gallardo agreed to serve as a bridge to Viaux, bringing to his house every day, starting September 14th, a different group representing mainly working-class neighborhoods.

"I do not exaggerate," Gallardo said, "when I tell you of the veritable transformation which came over visitors who came to listen to him and recover their faith. But I also observed that this constant dialogue with common people who brought their fears to him caused the general to become more and more thoughtful, perhaps realizing that without wishing it, he had become the repository for the hope of an entire people. . . ."

Such a man was José Jaime Melgoza Garay, a powerfully built man of five feet, ten inches, one of three children of a Spanish immigrant who worked as a skilled laborer in the coal mines of Lota, and a woman past forty when he was born. At twelve, Jaime was already driving buses. He would later work as a used car salesman and on the railroads. Until the fall of 1970, he had never taken part in politics. In March or April of that year, he found himself spending more and more time with a cousin, who treated him like a younger brother, and her husband, a law student named Juan Enrique Prieto Urzúa.

Prieto was a middle-level leader of an organization called the Alessandri Legion, made up of far right remnants of the defunct Conservative party who felt that the National party—mainstay of the candidacy of Alessandri, himself an Independent—was too bland. Prieto gradually interested Melgoza in the legion. Melgoza was then twenty-nine and his political outlook had been heavily shaped by the European immigrants he knew in the southern coal mines around Lota, men and women with a deep-seated hatred of the Marxist regimes many had fled. (That area was also, paradoxically, the region of Allende's greatest strength.)

When the Republican Independent Front was formed after the election, Prieto went along as representative of the legion. Melgoza tagged along to the meetings, held at a house on 1900 Catedral in downtown Santiago, the former command post of worker organizations backing Alessandri. There, the first talk of a coup d'état surfaced. And there it was decided that the only man able to lead such a movement was Roberto Viaux. There, too, it was agreed that because of the rumors flying around Santiago about such talk, and the threats that had already been made on his life, Viaux needed special protection.

A ten-man flying squad was formed to protect him. One member: Jaime Melgoza, chosen because of his command of karate and his obvious strength. Melgoza would become one of the general's true disciples.

Hope of a nonviolent solution had not yet disappeared, however. Viaux recalled:

> Around the third week of September, I learned through my contacts that Frei was at last ready to act. My source also told me that Mr. Zaldívar, the finance minister, would make a speech on the state of the economy in which he would depict the situation as unfavorable as a result of the outcome of the election. This he did do on September 23. After the speech, four ministers would resign, I was told, and this in turn would trigger the resignation of the entire Cabinet.
>
> Next, Frei would name a transition Cabinet, made up of personal friends and officers on active duty, among them General Schneider. That would solve the problem of the command of the army and our hands would be freed to act. In that way, the president and commander-in-chief of the army would also keep up constitutional and legal appearances.
>
> Time passed, and the finance minister's speech was made.
>
> It must have been around the first week of October—remember, I'm telling you this off the top of my head—when Guillermo Caray[3] told me that the president was just then anxious for a coup. Afterwards, a military junta would take over the government, exiling the president and, in that way, nothing would be known about Frei's participation in all this. . . .
>
> Beyond this, I received from the lips of Nicolás Díaz Pacheco[4] a message that President Frei sent me through his cousin, Father Ruiz Tagle, telling me that I had a green light to act, but that I should do it cleanly, with complete assurance of succeeding because if I did not,

then he would be forced to take action against me. Caray later confirmed this message, in the same words. . . .

With the assurance that the president's own decision to act gave me, I took this message to the meetings we held in different places with the generals I have mentioned. But we still had the problem of the commander-in-chief of the army, and another, which General Valenzuela raised. He preferred to act under the orders of a senior general, since he, as a member of the corps of engineers, could not, under the rules, take command of the army.

So he thought of General Prats [General Carlos Prats González], who followed Schneider in seniority . . . After several false starts, the meeting was arranged for mid-October, at 10:00 P.M., in the home of Guillermo Carey. We waited for Prats until 11:00 P.M. As I was about to leave, [Carlos] Arriagada (who had arranged the meeting) arrived to say that Prats sent his apologies but at the last minute several officers had showed up at his house unexpectedly, and he had to see them. . . .

Prats, in his memoirs, gives a sharply different version of meeting with his old Military School classmate. Prats says that Arriagada, who had called earlier that evening to request the meeting, arrived about 10:00 P.M. The two went into his study where Arriagada came quickly to the point: he had been asked to invite Prats to meet with Viaux that very night. Prats says he reacted angrily, telling Arriagada he not only had nothing to discuss with Viaux but that he (Arriagada) had showed disrespect toward him by even suggesting such a thing. He then said that if Arriagada truly believed he was a friend, he would tell Viaux that if Viaux had it in mind to plot with him, he (Prats) would report it to the authorities. According to Prats, the next day Arriagada returned to say that Viaux believed it was Prats who wanted to talk to him, and there the matter rested. That same day, Prats did report the entire incident to General Schneider. Prats said nothing about other visitors arriving that night, but he did say that he had to excuse himself from family members in the house when Arriagada arrived: his wife, an unmarried daughter, a married daughter and her husband.[5]

If Viaux actually was told of Prats' rebuff, he did not show it by his actions; he continued to believe that this man who would succeed Schneider as army chief was favorably disposed to the plotters. That, at least, is the version of the plotters themselves. The other possibility, of course, is that Prats had not told Arriagada what he claimed to have said in his memoirs.

Again according to Viaux:

The following Monday, Arriagada told my cousin Julio Fontecilla that General Prats had commissioned him to relay word that the

following day there would be good news, and that Prats had to travel
to the north on official business.

The good news did, in fact, come when the government retired the
commander-in-chief of the navy, Admiral Fernando Porta Angulo,
and replaced him with Admiral Hugo Tirado Barros. It was said that
with his retirement, several admirals, with his permission, had gone
to pay their respects to Allende, in defiance of the defense minister's
orders that military chiefs stay clear of all candidates. . . .

The news from Prats not only appeared to demonstrate his own
favorable position and that of Frei, but also solved the problem insofar
as the navy was concerned since Admiral Tirado was in contact and in
agreement with us.

There was no further chance to meet with General Prats. Besides, in
one of the later meetings with the generals, it was concluded that his
[Prats'] vacillation or absence was not important because, once we
moved, he would join in. We had the same feeling about the commander-in-chief of the air force. . . .

While the military conspirators plotted in terms of a link with the
government, the civilians abandoned hope, first that the "Alessandri
formula" would be accepted, and then that Frei would act. Their first
response was to arm themselves to repulse the kind of violence Allende
and his cohorts had threatened in the event the Congress should veto
him. It was a short step from defensive to offensive thinking.

Arms, however, were not to be found. Carlos Labarca Metzger, one of
the conspirators who was familiar with weapons, turned down offers of
"poor quality" arms. Later, they were able to make a deal with an arms
collector for a big lot—"enough to arm our group in good style."[6]

Viaux's men, with time running out before the Congress was due to
meet and give Allende the presidency, still lacked the pretext they
believed Frei wanted for them to act. And they still did not know the
mind of Schneider (Schneider's widow would later be quoted as saying
that a few days before the plot exploded, she heard her husband say that
if he were to turn on the radio and hear a news flash that he had been
kidnapped, it wouldn't faze him in the slightest).[7]

Still, they did not know, and so it was decided to kidnap Schneider and
hold him for forty-eight hours. "This idea," Viaux said, "was approved
unanimously, that is to say by the five of us [Admiral Tirado, Army
General Valenzuela, Air Force General García, Carabinero General
Huerta, and himself].

"When we got to the question of who would take charge of the actual
kidnapping, it seemed logical," Viaux continued, "that it should be done
by personnel of the army itself. But General Valenzuela was opposed to
having subordinates confront their superiors, for obvious and fundamental reasons of discipline.[8]

"For that reason, I decided to give the job to a group of Nationalists, but admonishing them that they must, in every way, give deferential treatment to General Schneider. . . ."

As his envoy to the "Nationalists," Viaux chose Juan Diego Dávila Bastorrica and insisted that Dávila have complete command of the operation. Dávila was enthusiastic to discover that Gallardo's group was already armed and resolved to do whatever necessary to stop Allende. The next day, Dávila introduced Gallardo to other like-minded civilians who had contacted Viaux, including Juan Luis Bulnes.

Together, they went to work on Plan Alpha: the kidnapping of General Schneider. They also put together three supplemental plans: Beta, Gamma, and Delta, for the kidnapping of three other high-ranking generals.

Gallardo arranged through a friend for a downtown apartment hide-out for those who would take part in the caper. They nicknamed the place "the aquarium," because it was located across the street from a nightclub called La Sirena. There were beds there for four persons. Labarca obtained another nearby with beds for two more.

While part of the group put together a complete dossier on the habits, security arrangements and other details of each of the kidnap targets, Gallardo took his group to remote places on the outskirts of the city for shooting practice.

On Saturday, October 17, Viaux ended the tension of the long wait: they would strike the following Monday, October 19. That Monday, the corps of generals was giving a banquet in Schneider's honor at the official residence of the commander-in-chief (which Schneider had never bothered to move into). It was expected the banquet would end around 1:00 A.M. As Schneider made ready to leave, Valenzuela was to invent some pretext for detaining him for fifteen or twenty minutes. When he finally did leave, the streets would be quiet—no Carabineros patrolled until 2:00 A.M.

Schneider then would be taken to a secret place known only to Dávila and Gallardo. The next day, a note would be sent to Frei, on behalf of a fictitious commando group, demanding that Frei name a military Cabinet in return for Schneider's release. Gallardo was assured that "Frei would accede immediately." Frei would resign, Admiral Tirado, as interior minister, would become acting president, and new elections would be called.

The plot collapsed on a single detail. The person charged with shadowing Schneider when he left his house to report on which car he was using, how he was dressed, and so forth, failed to do so. The lookout decided to "wing" it and told Gallardo and Dávila that Schneider had used the Mercedes he usually favored, and had gone first for a cocktail at the Argentine Embassy. The kidnappers waited tensely until 3:00 A.M.

on darkened Inca Street for Schneider to pass. They would discover later that he had glided past them nearly two hours earlier—alone, at the wheel of the family Opel.

The plotters decided to seize the initiative themselves and began actively tailing Schneider to discover his exact habits, resolved to kidnap him at the first opportunity. They finally decided on a place: Martín de Zamora Street, where it meets the more heavily traveled Américo Vespucio. Martín de Zamora was narrow, it took a sharp bend about 125 feet before meeting Américo Vespucio, and there was a stop sign at the corner. The plotters used model cars to rehearse the details and went about assembling their tools: a spray can with teargas, chloroform, rope, milled pepper, a hammer—and an arsenal of hand guns, sub-machine-guns and grenades.

The plan: a lookout would signal with a handkerchief as General Schneider emerged from his house and climbed into the car. An "alert" car would then speed down Zamora toward Vespucio to alert the others—parked along the way, or on small tributary streets—that Schneider was coming. Another would then divert traffic on Zamora above the general's house. As he cruised along Zamora, three cars with plotters would fall in in front of him, and a jeep would follow. Around fifteen other cars—manned by persons not totally aware of what was happening—would form a "screen" to congest traffic.

The jeep (driven by Labarca) would bump into Schneider's car from behind at the Vespucio stop sign. As the general's driver alighted, the men in the three forward cars would jump out, weapons in hand. Two would flank the car on the left, while one of them smashed the windows with a hammer. Two others would do the same on the right, while one—Andrés Widow—would open the door and cover Schneider.

Melgoza's mission: knock the general's driver senseless with a karate chop.

On Wednesday, October 21, Gallardo ordered his men "to the mattresses," at the two downtown hideouts, for final briefings. Dávila, General Viaux's emissary who was supposed to command the operation, failed to show for two scheduled meetings and was, in fact, nowhere to be found. Gallardo decided to go ahead himself, and he, Widow, and Labarca worked on the final details without letting the others in on the plan. When Labarca opened a map in the presence of the others and pointed out the place where they would strike, Gallardo fumed and ordered everyone confined to quarters.

He said he was especially worried about Melgoza, because Melgoza had protested the plan. He ordered Melgoza watched carefully, an order he would later claim was disobeyed.

At ten o'clock that night, he and Widow went to Viaux's house to bring him up to date on the final plans. Dávila was there, and Viaux repeated his order that Dávila run the operation and take personal charge of Schneider.

He then repeated still another order:

"Under no circumstances is there to be any shooting."

From Viaux's house, Gallardo went directly to Cousiño Park, a sprawling parade ground and park just off the downtown area, where his men were to hold their one and only dress rehearsal. Even that, however, was aborted; Gallardo claims it was because Melgoza began to "shout hysterically." Dávila, who was supposed to follow him to the park to supervise the dry run, failed to show for that rendezvous also.

It was their last chance. D-Hour had been set for the following morning, Thursday, October 22. Only two days remained before the Congress was to meet.

It was 4:00 A.M. before the plotters slept. At 6:30 A.M., they were on their way: two in a borrowed Peugeot; two others with Gallardo in his own Borgward (it was later pointed out that the plot was so amateurish and hastily improvised that the would-be kidnappers hadn't even thought to use stolen cars); Dávila and two others in another car. Widow was waiting for them at the rendezvous point, the end of Américo Vespucio North, together with the occupants of the "screen" cars, most of them strangers to Gallardo.

Gallardo repeated the orders: there was to be no shooting. The submachineguns and grenades were to be kept in the cars, taken later to the place where Schneider was to be held and used if the Left should discover the hideout and decide to attack.[9]

At 7:45 A.M., Gallardo began a slow swing around the perimeter of the operation to make sure all was in readiness.

At 8:15 A.M., Schneider left his house. One minute later, his car, driven by Cpl. Leopoldo Maura, eased onto Martín de Zamora. One minute later, about sixty-five feet before reaching the corner of Américo Vespucio, a yellow Ford Falcon moving in the opposite direction swerved in front of the Mercedes, colliding with it. A khaki-colored jeep pulled in front, blocking the street at Américo Vespucio. A white Peugeot pulled up behind the Mercedes. A blue Dodge Dart pulled alongside the Mercedes on the right.

The occupants of the four cars scrambled out, guns in hand. Gallardo was still on his rounds, a block away, when he heard shots. If he had counted, he would have heard ten, but he was too nervous to count.

The mission had been bungled.

General Schneider was mortally wounded with eight bullet wounds. Three days later he was dead. President Frei and President-elect Allende were pallbearers at his funeral.[10]

Two days after the shooting, a stunned Congress voted to confirm

Salvador Allende Gossens as president of Chile, without even waiting for approval of the Statute of Guarantees.[11]

Dreams or delusions of armed resistance to the Marxist president died with General Schneider. It would take Salvador Allende himself to resurrect them, but not before the country he was called to lead was torn asunder.

Notes

APPENDIX II

1. Details of Gallardo's experiences are from a statement written by him, reproduced in Florencia Varas, *Conversaciones con Viaux*, (Santiago: Impresiones Eire, 1972), pp. 149–170.
2. Ibid., pp. 118–119. Viaux notes that Frías and others named by him later denied those contacts. Details of Viaux's activities from Varas, op. cit., pp. 126–127, and Alain Labrousse, *El Experimento Chileno: ¿Reformismo o Revolución?* (Barcelona: Ediciones Grijalbo, 1973), p. 252.
3. Guillermo Carey Tagle, Viaux's main pipeline to the Christian Democrats. Carey was associated in a business venture with Finance Minister Zaldívar.
4. Díaz Pacheco was not otherwise identified.
5. Carlos Prats González, *Memorias: Testimonio de un Soldado* (Santiago: Pehuen Editora, 1985), 2nd ed., pp. 181–182. Prats describes Arriagada as one of those drawn into the right-wing plot against the Popular Front government in 1939, then being expelled from the army and exiled for a time to Argentina. As for Viaux, he said Arriagada should inform him that whereas he had nothing personal against him, he never shared Viaux's ideas, which he considered nefarious for the army. Arriagada said he had been asked to make the overture to Prats in a telephone call from a person he did not know, so he could not be sure that it was Viaux who had initiated the move. Given Prats' very visible condemnation of Viaux following the 1969 uprising, it does seem improbable that those with knowledge of senior commanders in the army should have imagined that Prats would have cooperated with them.
6. This occurred in late September—nearly one month before the CIA, "for a few hours," toyed with the idea of providing three sub-machineguns—not to civilians, but an army general!
7. Viaux said the report was published in *Puro Chile*, the Communist party tabloid; it was never denied by Mrs. Schneider.
8. Such behavior—conspirators fretting about protocol—may appear bizarre to civilians, but it is entirely consistent with the mentality and attitudes of the Chilean military, as I have observed them.
9. The Left did, in fact, penetrate the group. *Punto Final* was on the streets the very day of the attack on Schneider with a detailed account of the plot to kidnap Schneider and force Frei to resign.
10. The men, untrained civilians, only a few of them experienced in handling firearms, simply panicked. Before Schneider's driver even had a chance to alight from the car, one of the attackers was already smashing the windows with a red hammer, causing the driver to dive for his gun, believed to be in the glove compartment. Schneider also pulled his gun. Within seconds, the attackers fired ten shots, eight of which hit the general, two others going wild. Death was caused by two 38-caliber bullets. Within three days, 250

people had been picked up for questioning, thirty of them held. On October 29, Viaux, Igualt, and Gallardo gave themselves up. Labarca and others were apprehended two days later. Widow managed to escape. In the eight-month investigation that followed—perhaps the biggest ever in Chile and conducted with the full weight of the Allende government behind it—there was no serious intimation that the CIA or any other foreign agency had been involved. In Florencia Varas's book, *Conversaciones con Viaux*, the CIA is not even mentioned, although Viaux, Gallardo, and Melgoza's lawyers all talk freely—very freely—about the plot, each other, and outsiders, and make countless accusations and allegations. On June 16, 1971, the military court martial handed down its sentences: Melgoza, life in prison for homicide; Viaux, twenty years in prison and five years in exile for planning a kidnapping; Igualt, ten years in prison, three years in exile, same charges; Gallardo, fifteen years in prison, same charges; Dávila, ten years, same charges; sentences ranging from three to ten years also were handed down to fifteen others convicted of participating in the plot. Valenzuela, Tirado, and three others were sentenced to three years in exile; lesser penalties were handed down to eleven others. Seventeen actually served time—from sixty to 305 days—before all but Melgoza, Viaux, and Dávila—were paroled. Melgoza's lawyer—Juan Prieto, himself among the convicted—said Melgoza was "framed" by his coconspirators as the one who fired the first shot because he was an unknown, whereas some of the others were from first-rank families (as many others were ordinary workers). Prieto points out that a single shot "escaped" from Melgoza's gun, and it was an unusual hammer-action 45-caliber revolver, whereas Schneider was killed by two .38 slugs. As to Gallardo's claim that Melgoza had "disappeared" into his house for fifty minutes the night before the shooting, Prieto said it was a lie, and attributes Gallardo's animosity to rivalry over a girl. There were widespread reports later that the MIR had infiltrated the ranks of the conspirators, and Melgoza was frequently "fingered" as the MIR man who deliberately fired so as to provoke the panic which occurred. Prieto heatedly denies that. Of the ten bullets, eight were from Argentine 38-caliber Ruby revolvers, one from a 35-caliber pistol, and one from Melgoza's pistol.

11. They were voted on December 21 and signed into law January 21, 1971.

BIBLIOGRAPHY

Reference Works; Special Studies/Reports/Documents; Speeches

Algunas Características del Proceso de Toma de Decisiones en la Gran Empresa y la Dinámica de Concentración, Oscar Guillermo Garretón and Jaime Cisternas Pinto (Santiago: ODEPLAN, mimeographed study, March 1970)

Algunos Fundamentos de la Intervención Militar en Chile, Septiembre de 1973 (Santiago: Editora Nacional Gabriela Mistral, no date)

Allamand, Andrés Z., "Chile: The End of the Authoritarian Regime," print-out copy of a speech delivered before a meeting of the Pacific Democratic Union and International Democratic Union in Honolulu, May 1988

Alleged Assassination Plots Involving Foreign Leaders (Washington: U.S. Senate Select Committee to Study Government Operations, 1975)

Allende Gossens, President Salvador, booklet distributed by the Embassy of Chile in Washington containing the text of his speech before the United Nations General Assembly, Dec. 4, 1972

The Almanac of American Politics, Michael Barone and Grant Ujifusa, eds. (Washington: National Journal, 1986)

Almanaque Mundial, 1973 (Virginia Gardens, FL: Editorial América, S.A., 1974)

Analysis of the Economic and Social Evolution of Latin America Since the Inception of the Alliance for Progress (Washington: Inter-American Economic and Social Council of the Organization of American States, August 1971)

The Annals of the American Academy of Political and Social Science, "Interest Groups in International Perspective," Robert Presthus, ed. (Philadelphia: American Academy of Political and Social Science, May 1974)

Annual of the Institute of Strategic Studies (London: Institute of Strategic Studies, 1973–1974 edition)

Atlas de la República de Chile (Santiago: Instituto Geográfico Militar, 1972)

Atlas Regionalizado de Chile (Santiago: Instituto Geográfico Militar, 2nd ed., 1981)

Boletín Estadístico de la OEA; Statistical Bulletin of the OAS, Vol. 9, No. 1–2 (Washington: Organization of American States, Jan.–June 1987)

Braden, Amb. Spruille, "Soviet Threat to the Panama Canal," printed copy of a speech delivered before the Belair Council of the Navy League of the U.S.A., Feb. 28, 1977

Brenner, Patricia, "The IMF View," in *IMF Survey,* Sept. 23, 1985

Canal Beagle: Laudo Award 1977 (bi-lingual edition covering the hearings and arbitration award in the Beagel Channel dispute, published by the Government of Chile)

Carter, President James, private message to President Augusto Pinochet dated Dec. 15, 1978 (copy obtained by the author)

Chile (Washington: American Nation Series of the OAS, 1969)

Chile: An Appraisal of Investment Opportunities in the Equity Market (Toronto: Friedberg Commodity Management, Inc., 1986)

Chile: An Economy in Transition (Washington: The World Bank, 1980)

Chile: Caos o Democracia; Crónicas de la Guerra Irregular, 48-page booklet produced by the government following the assassination attempt on President Pinochet's life in September 1986 (no pub. data)

Chilean Economic Report, a publication of the New York Office of CORFO (Corporación de Fomento de la Producción) "Trade Liberalization in Chile," #193, Aug. 1987; #197, Dec. 1987

Chile: 11 de Septiembre de 1974 (Santiago: Dirección Nacional de Communicación Social de Gobierno, 1974)

Chile 1980 Economic Profile (New York: CORFO, 1980)

Chile: Guía turística '71 (Santiago: Seccion Publicaciones, Ferrocarriles del Estado, 1971)

Chile: Under Military Rule. Gary MacEoin, guest ed. (New York: IDOC/North America, 1974)

Chile's Defense Needs (New York: American-Chilean Council, 1975)

¿Cómo Llegaron las Fuerzas Armadas a la Acción del 11 de Septiembre de 1973?, Arturo Fontaine Aldunate and Cristián Zegers Ariztía, eds., special supplement published by *El Mercurio*, Santiago, on the first anniversary of the revolution, Sept. 11, 1974

Compañía Manufacturera de Papeles y Cartones, S.A., annual report for 1971–1972 (22-page booklet published in Santiago, Oct. 1972)

Compendio Estadístico 1986 (Santiago: Instituto Nacional de Estadísticas, Ministerio de Economía, Fomento y Reconstrucción, 1986)

Country Reports on Human Rights Practices (Washington: U.S. State Department), 1979, 1984 and 1986 editions of the annual reports to the House Foreign Affairs and Senate Foreign Relations Committees

Covert Action in Chile 1963–1973: Staff Report of the Select Committee to Study Governmental Operations with Respect to Intelligence Activities, United States Senate (Washington: U.S. Government Printing Office, 1975) (see also "Select Committee to Study Governmental Operations With Respect to Intelligence Activities")

Current Biography (New York: H.W. Wilson, Sept. 1971)

Declaración de Principios del Gobierno de Chile, booklet issued by the government's Division of Communications containing statements of principles announced March 11, 1974

The Development Data Book; Social and Economic Statistics on 125 Countries (Washington: The World Bank, 1984)

Diccionario de la Lengua Española (Madrid: Real Academia Española, 1970)

Diccionario Político de Chile 1810–1965, Lía Cortes and Jordi Fuentes, eds. (Santiago: Editorial Orbe, 1967)

Documentos del Episcopado: Chile 1970–1973 (Santiago: Ediciones Mundo, 1974)

Documentos Secretos de la ITT (Santiago: Empresa Editora Nacional Quimantu, 1972), a publication of the Government of Chile

Dow Latina, Vol. 1, January 1974, company publication published by Dow's Latin American headquarters, Coral Gables, Florida

Economic and Social Progress in Latin America (Washington: Inter-American Development Bank), annual reports 1973 through 1987

El Desarrollo Económico y Social de Chile en la Década 1970–1980 (Santiago: ODEPLAN, Aug. 1970)

Elección de Parlamentarios 1973, Boletín de Información General # 67, Oficina de Informaciones, Senado de Chile, June 30, 1973

Elección Ordinaria de Presidente de la República, Viernes 4 de Septiembre de 1970 (Santiago: Dirección del Registro Electoral, 1970)

El Once, Hora por Hora, special edition of *Qué Pasa* magazine, # 177, Sept. 10, 1974

El Papel de las Fuerzas Armadas en la Redemocratización de Chile, Francisco Orrego Vicuña, 33-page paper prepared for a conference on the involvement of the Armed Forces in the Chilean political system, organized by the Centro de Estudios de Desarrollo of Santiago. My typewritten version bears no date, but it was approximately 1986

Encyclopaedia Britannica (Chicago: Encyclopaedia Britannica) 1967 and 1975 editions

Encyclopaedia Britannica Year Books (Chicago: Encyclopaedia Britannica), 1968 through 1988 editions

The Encyclopaedia of Philosophy (New York: MacMillan, 1972 reprint edition)

Estadísticas de Comercio Exterior al 30 de Abril de 1974 (Santiago: mimeographed study issued by the Government of Chile, July 5, 1974)

Estudio Económico de América Latina (Santiago: U.N. Economic Commission for Latin America, 1978)

Expropriation of El Teniente (New York: Kennecott Copper Corp., 1971) (Supplements were published by the company in 1972 and 1973)

Facts on File, 1979 Yearbook, Vol. 39 (New York: Facts on File, 1980)

Fodor's South America (New York: David McKay Company, 1974)

Foreign Assistance and Related Programs: Appropriations Bill, 1971 (Washington: Committee on Appropriations, U.S. House of Representatives, June 1, 1970), Report # 91–1134

Freedom at Issue: Freedom Around the World (New York: Freedom House, 1982)

Freedom in the World: Political Rights and Civil Liberties 1979, Raymond D. Gastil, ed. and principal author (Boston: G. K. Hall & Co. and New York, Freedom House, 1979)

Friedberg's LDC Debt Commentary (Toronto: Friedberg Commodity Corp., March 10, 1988)

Fuentes, Jordi, and Cortes, Lía, eds., *Diccionario Político de Chile, 1810–1965*

Garretón, Oscar Guillermo and Cisternas Pinto, Jaime, "Algunas Características del Proceso de Toma de Decisiones en la Gran Empresa y la Dinámica de Concentración" (Santiago: ODEPLAN, mimeographed study, March 1970)

Heritage Foundation, Washington, D.C., internal memorandum dated April 12, 1988 reporting on the findings of a Heritage study mission to Chile in March of 1988

Heritage Foundation

Morris B. Goldman, "Confronting Third World Debt: The Baker and Bradley Plans," *Backgrounder* # 559, Jan. 22, 1987

William Pascoe, "In Ethiopia, Mengistu's Final Solution," *Executive Memorandum* # 200, May 12, 1988

"State Department Reflex: Beating Up on America's Friends," *Executive Memorandum* # 201, May 19, 1988

"A Strategy for Keeping the U.S. Bases in the Philippines," Asian Studies Center *Backgrounder* # 8, May 20, 1988

Huneeus, Carlos, *Los Chilenos y la Política; Cambio y Continuidad en el Autoritarismo*, book-length (241-pages) report on an ambitious public opinion survey carried out in the Greater Santiago area in June 1986 by the Centro de Estudios de la Realidad Contemporánea of the Academia de Humanismo Cristiano

Indicadores Económicos y Sociales 1960–1985 (Santiago: Dirección de Estudios, Banco Central de Chile, 1986)

Infancia y juventud de la junta, Sunday magazine supplement of *El Mercurio,* Feb. 3, 1974

Informe de la Comisión Chilena de Derechos Humanos Sobre la Situación de los Derechos Humanos en Chile (Santiago: 1986 and Feb. 1987 reports)

"Insurance Claims Experience to Date: OPIC and Its Predecessor Agency," Overseas Private Insurance Corporation news release RJ/771, June 30, 1987

Inter-American Press Association (Miami), "The Chilean Presidenta," an article by IAPA scholarship winner John Adam Moreau and distributed to North American and Latin American newspapers, Dec. 8, 1971

International Currency Review, Vol. 18, # 3, May 1987

International Financial Statistics, Vol. XXXV, # 1 (Washington: International Monetary Fund, Jan. 1982)

La Acción del Ejército en la Liberación de Chile (Historia Inédita), a 50-page pamphlet printed on plain newsprint, circulating in Chile in 1974 and widely ascribed to President Pinochet

La Cultura Política Chilena Según las Encuestas de Opinión Pública (Santiago: Instituto Chileno de Estudios Humanísticos, 1986)

La Economía de Chile durante el Período de la Unidad Popular: La Vía Chilena al Marxismo (Valparaíso: Escuela de Negocios de Valparaíso, Fundación Adolfo Ibáñez, March 1974)

La Iglesia y la Experiencia Chilena Hacia el Socialismo (Santiago: 1974, no further pub. data)

Lasky, Victor, "Turning Defeat into Victory," booklet published by the American-Chilean Council, New York, Sept. 1975

Latin America, Vol. 3, # 17 (Washington: Organization of American States, April 27, 1973)

Latin American Economic Study, Rep. Thomas M. Rees (D.-CA) (Washington: Committee on Banking and Currency, U.S. House of Representatives, 1969)

The Latin American Scene of the Seventies, a Basic Fact Book, Irving B. Reed, Jaime Suchlicki and Dodd L. Harvey, eds. (Miami: Center for Advanced International Studies, University of Miami, 1972)

Libro Blanco de la Ingeniería Chilena (Santiago: College of Engineers, 1973)

Libro Blanco del Cambio de Gobierno en Chile (Santiago: Editorial Lord Cochrane, S.A., 1973)

Lo Que Usted Nunca Supo del Día 11 . . . , a special supplement published by the Santiago newspaper *La Segunda,* Sept. 10, 1974

Los Chilenos y la Política; Cambio y Continuidad en el Autoritarismo, Carlos Huneeus

Los Presidenciables, three booklets published by the magazine *Hoy* in June 1987, containing biographical sketches of some 140 presidential hopefuls or possible candidates

MacHale, Tomas P., *Poder Político y Comunicación en Chile: Marzo a Septiembre de 1973* (Santiago: Cuadernos del Instituto de Ciencia Política, Universidad Católica de Chile, March-April 1977)

McDonald, Rep. Larry (D-GA), extension of remarks, in the *Congressional Record,* June 24, 1977 (on U.S.-Chilean relations)

The Multinational Corporation; Studies on U.S. Foreign Investment, Vol. 1 (Washington: U.S. Department of Commerce, 1972)

Multinational Corporations and United States Foreign Policy, report on hearings in March and April 1973 before the Subcommittee on Multinational Corporations, U.S. Senate, published in two volumes (Washington: U.S. Government Printing Office, 1973) Testimony extracted from that report herein includes that of the following [date(s) of testimony follows names]:

    Berrellez, Robert, March 21, 1973 (ITT official)
    Broe, William C., March 27 (CIA officer)
    Geneen, Harold S., April 2 (ITT President)
    Gerrity, Edward J., March 22 and April 2 (ITT official)
    Guilfoyle, John W., March 22 (ITT official)
    Hendrix, Hal, March 21 (ITT official)
    Korry, Amb. Edward M., March 27
    McCone, John A., March 21 (ITT Board member)
    Meyer, Charles A., March 29, (Ass't. Sec. of State)
    Neal, Jack D., March 20 and April 2 (ITT official)

Multinational Investment in the Economic Development and Integration of Latin America (Washington: Inter-American Development Bank, 1968) (based on an IADB round-table held in Bogota, April 1968)

Neely I., Carlos
    "Informe Político # 2," May 1987
    "Informe Político # 4," Sept. 1987
    (from a series of typewritten reports prepared for the leadership of the Social Democrat party in Chile)

New Deal in Chile: Will Revolution in Liberty Succeed? Great Decisions, # 6 (New York: Foreign Policy Association, 1967)

The New York Times Encyclopaedia Almanac, 1971 edition (New York: *New York Times* Book and Educational Division, 1971)

Nueva Enciclopedia de Chile, Francisco Javier Díaz Salazar, ed. (Buenos Aires: Ediciones Copihue, Fotomecánica Futura, S.R.L., Ediciones Libra, 1974), in four volumes

Nunn, Frederick N., "One Year in the Life of Augusto Pinochet: Gulag of the Mind," in *The Americas* magazine, Oct. 1985

OAS 1974 Human Rights Report (Washington: Organization of American States, 1974), CP/Doc. 381.74

Observations by The Government of Chile on the 'Report of the Status of Human Rights in Chile' (Washington: Organization of American States, 1974), mimeograph document CP 385/74

The Oligarchy Muddle, James L. Payne, monograph prepared for delivery at the 1967 annual meeting of the American Political Science Association in Chicago, Sept. 5–9, 1967, c 1967, American Political Science Association

Orden Económico y Democracia (Santiago: Centro de Estudios del Desarrollo, 1985)

Origen, Contenido y Práctica de la Constitución Política de 1980: Su Significado desde la Perspectiva de los Derechos Humanos (Santiago: Commission on Human Rights, no date)

Orrego Vicuña, Francisco, *El Papel de las Fuerzas Armadas en la Redemocratización de Chile*

Overseas Private Investment Corporation, 1986 Annual Report (Washington)

Payne, James L., *The Oligarchy Muddle*

Pike, Frederick, and Bray, Donald, "A Vista of Catastrophe: The Future of U.S.-Chilean Relations"

Pinochet Ugarte, President Augusto

"Palabras del Jefe Supremo de la Nación, Augusto Pinochet Ugarte al Conmemorarse el Primer Aniversario de Gobierno, mimeograph text distributed by the presidential press office of his address, Sept. 11, 1974

"Mensaje al País de S.E., del Presidente de la República, General de Ejercito, D. Augusto Pinochet Ugarte, al Conmemorarse el 6° Aniversario del Gobierno," mimeograph text distributed by the presidential press office of his address Sept. 11, 1979

Pocket Data Book, U.S.A., 1971 (Washington: U.S. Commerce Department, May 1971)

Políticas de Desarrollo, mimeographed report combining analysis and prescription for Chile's economy developed during 1972 and 1973 by a group of young free-market economists who, because so many had studied at the University of Chicago, came to be known as "the Chicago Boys." That secret plan—which they nick-named "The Brick"—came to form the basic economic strategy of the Junta following Allende's overthrow. The author's copy is numbered # 188.

Poverty in Latin America; The Impact of Depression (Washington: The World Bank, 1986)

Prewett, Virginia, "The Mysterious Letelier Affair: Another Rush to Judgment?," a special report published by the Council for Inter-American Security, Washington, Sept. 1978

Programa de Desarrollo de Chile a Corto y Mediano Plazo (Santiago: Editora Gabriela Mistral, 1974)

Recent Developments in Chile, October 1971, report of the Subcommittee on Inter-American Affairs of the Committee on Foreign Affairs, U.S. House of Representatives (Washington: U.S. Government Printing Office, Oct. 15, 1971)

Report of the Federal Trade Commission on the Copper Industry (Washington: U.S. Government Printing Office, 1947)

Report on the Status of Human Rights in Chile (Washington: Organization of American States, 1985)

Seminarios, Francisco Cumplido Cereceda, ed., "Los Límites del Pluralismo Político," proceedings of an Aug. 29, 1985 seminar sponsored by the Instituto Chileno de Estudios Humanísticos (Santiago: May 4, 1986)

Select Committee to Study Governmental Operations With Respect to Intelligence Activities, U.S. Senate, (Washington: U.S. Government Printing Office, 1976), covering hearings and amassing of documents, September–December 1975, published in seven volumes with six volumes of supplements. Material relating to Chile is contained primarily in Volume 7 ("Covert Action") and a supplemental volume ("Alleged Assassination Plots Involving Foreign Leaders," Interim Report dated Nov. 20, 1975), p. 5, pp. 225–253, 262 & 273.

Síntesis Estadística (Santiago: Instituto Nacional de Estadísticas, Dec. 1974)

Situation, Principal Problems and Prospects of the Chilean Economy, study done by the ad-hoc review group of the Inter-American Economic and Social Council (Washington: Organization of American States, March 6, 1975)

Social Indicators of Development 1987 (Washington: The World Bank, 1987)

Social Progress Trust Fund, Annual Reports (Washington: Inter-American Development Bank), 1963 and 1969

Socio-Economic Progress in Latin America, Annual Reports (Washington: Inter-American Development Bank), 1970 and 1971 (Beginning with 1972, these annual reports were renamed: *Economic and Social Progress in Latin America*)

South America '78, booklet published by the *Chicago Tribune*, containing a series of articles produced by a team of the newspaper's reporters and photographers criss-crossing the continent and whose work appeared in the newspaper from Jan. 22 to Feb. 1, 1978 and Feb. 28 to March 1, 1978.

The 1987 South American Handbook (Bath, England: Trade & Travel Publications, Sept. 1986)

1971 Statement of Loans; Appendix to the Annual Report (Washington: Inter-American Development Bank, 1972)

Statement made by Fernando Leniz, Jorge del Canto, Walter Sedwitz and Paul Rosenstein-Rodan to CIAP Subcommittee meeting in Santiago (Santiago: Editora Nacional Gabriela Mistral, 1974) (booklet)

Statistical Synthesis of Chile, 1981–1985 (Santiago: Dirección de Estudios, Banco Central de Chile, 1986)

The Theory and Practice of Communism, Part 5: (Marxism Imposed by Chile-Allende Regime), report on hearings Nov. 15, 1973 and March 7 and 13, 1974, before the Committee on Internal Security, U.S. House of Representatives (Washington: U.S. Government Printing Office, 1974)

Three Years of Destruction, booklet published by the Chilean Printers' Association (ASIMPRES), apparently in 1974

Tomic, Amb. Radomiro, "Chile Faces Human Development," mimeograph text of speech delivered at Notre Dame University colloquium, March 8, 1967, distributed by the Chilean Embassy in Washington

Topics, Vol. 3, # 2, April 1974, "Chile Makes First Payment to OPIC," newsletter publication of the Overseas Private Investment Corporation, Washington

Turistel 87; Guía Turística de Chile (Santiago: Compañía de Teléfonos de Chile, 1987)

United States and Chile During the Allende Years, 1970–1973, report of the Subcommittee on Inter-American Affairs of the Committee on Foreign Affairs, U.S. House of Representatives, based on hearings in 1971, 1972, 1973, and 1974 (Washington: U.S. Government Printing Office, 1974)

Following is a listing of major works from that volume cited in this book:

Birns, Laurence,
    "Chile: The Frying Pan Awaits the Fire," *American Report*, Vol. III, No. 22, July 30, 1973;
    "Chile: The Path Ahead," ibid., Vol. III, No. 23, Aug. 13, 1973;
    "Chile: A Bloody Fall," *Worldview*, Nov. 1973
Chile: A Chronology, report prepared by the staff of the Congressional Research Service, Library of Congress
Cline, Ray S., "The Value of the CIA," *New York Times*, Nov. 1, 1974
Colby, William E., Director, CIA, testimony, Oct. 11, 1973
Crimmins, John H., Testimony, March 6, 1973 (he was then acting Assistant Secretary of State for Inter-American Affairs)
Fagen, Richard R.,
    "The United States and Chile: Roots and Branches," *Foreign Policy*, Jan. 1975;
    Letter, *Foreign Affairs*, Jan. 1975

Farnsworth, Elizabeth. "Chile: What Was U.S. Role? More Than Admitted," *Foreign Policy*, Fall 1974

García Márquez, Gabriel, "The Death of Salvador Allende," *Harper's*, March 1974 (translated by Gregory Rabassa)

Gil, Federico "Socialist Chile and the United States," *Inter-American Economic Affairs*, Autumn 1973

Hagen, Virginia M., analyst in Latin American Affairs, Foreign Affairs Division, Congressional Research Service, report entitled "U.S. Relations With Chile Under the Government of Salvador Allende (November 1970–September 1973); Background and Current Developments"

Ibáñez, Sen. Pedro, "The Chilean Crisis and Its Outcome"

Korry, Amb. Edward M.,
Testimony, July 1, 1971;
"Ambassador Korry on a 1971 Proposal to Allende," *Washington Post*, Sept. 29, 1974

Lefever, Dr. Ernest, testimony, Aug. 5, 1974

Landsberger, Henry A.,
"Answers to Some Questions About the Military Coup in Chile," Sept. 30, 1973;
"Major Characteristics of Chile's Political Life: Developments Up to 1970," Feb. 1974

Landsberger and McDaniel, Tim, "Mobilization as a Double-Edged Sword, 1970–1973: The Allende Government's Uneasy Relationship with Labor, 1970–1973," July 1974

Martin, Everett G., "Did the Chilean Press Need CIA Help?," *Wall Street Journal*, Sept. 18, 1974

Mays, Marshall T.,
testimony, Oct. 15, 1971;
letter transmitting "Decline of OPIC business in Latin America and OPIC Insurance Trends," and "Expropriated U.S. Interests in Chilean Copper Mines: Comparison of Chilean Controller General's Evaluation and OPIC Expropriation Coverage"

Meyer, Assistant Sec. of State Charles A., testimony, Oct. 15, 1971

O'Leary, Jeremiah, "Peru Watched for Move Against Chile," *Washington Star-News*, Aug. 4, 1974

Petras, James F., and LaPorte, Robert Jr., "Can We Do Business With Radical Nationalists? Chile: No," *Foreign Policy*, Summer 1972

Petras, James F., testimony, Sept. 18, 1974

Sanford, Jonathan E., analyst in International Relations, Foreign Affairs Division, Congressional Research Service, Library of Congress, report entitled "The Multilateral Development Banks and the Suspension of Lending to Allende's Chile," August 6, 1974

Schlaudeman, Harry W., Deputy Assistant Sec. of State, testimony, Dec. 7, 1973

Sigmund, Paul E.,
"The 'Invisible Blockade' and the Overthrow of Allende," *Foreign Affairs*, Jan. 1974;
"Allende in retrospect," *Problems of Communism*, May-June 1974;
"Chile: What Was U.S. Role? Less Than Charged," *Foreign Policy*, Fall 1974;
Letter, *Foreign Affairs*, Jan. 1975

Stern, Laurence,
   "CIA $ 400,000 Chile Fund Reported," *Washington Post*, March 28, 1973;
   "Aid Used as a Choke on Allende," ibid., Sept. 16, 1973;
   "Chile: The Lesson," ibid., Nov. 1973
Theberge, Amb. James A.,
   "Kremlin's Hand in Allende's Chile," from *The Soviet Analyst*,
   Aug. 15, 1974;
   Testimony, Sept. 18, 1974;
   Conference Report, "Understanding the Allende Revolution and the Fall of
   Chilean Democracy," Center for Strategic and International Studies,
   Georgetown University, Aug. 1974
*U.S. Overseas Loans and Grants and Assistance from International Organiza-
   tions; Obligations and Loan Authorizations, July 1, 1945–Sept. 30, 1978*
   (Washington: U.S. Agency for International Development, 1979)
Vial Correa, Gonzalo,
   "Historic Factors and Their Influence in Chile," mimeograph copy of an
   address to the Chamber of Commerce of the United States in Chile, in
   Santiago, Aug. 1986
Ware, Richard A., *The Pentagon's Office of International Security Affairs, 1969–
   1973*, brochure published by American Enterprise Institute, Washington,
   1986
Weill, Kurt and Brecht, Bertolt, *The Threepenny Opera (Die Dreigroschenoper)*,
   original cast recording by MGM Records (E3121) of the musical, adapted to
   English by Marc Blitzstein
World Almanac (New York: Pharos Books), 1987 edition
World Armies, John Keegan (New York: Facts on File, 1979)
The World Bank Atlas (Washington: The World Bank), 1986 and 1987 editions
World Bank, Discussion Papers, # 5, Guy P. Pfefferman, "Public Expenditures in
   Latin America; Effects on Poverty" (Washington: The World Bank, 1987)
World Bank Operations: Sectoral Programs and Policies (Baltimore and London:
   Johns Hopkins University Press, 1972)
World Development Indicators (New York-Oxford-London: Oxford University
   Press, for the World Bank, 1987)
*World Development Report; National and International Adjustment; World
   Development Indicators* (Washington: The World Bank, Aug. 1981)
*World Development Report 1987; Barriers to Adjustment and Growth in the
   World Economy; Industrialization and Foreign Trade*
World Tables, Third Edition, vol. 1 ("Economic Tables") (Baltimore and London:
   Johns Hopkins University Press, 1984)
Zaldívar Larraín, Andrés, "Una Solución Para Chile Por la Razón y No Por la
   Fuerza," booklet published by the CIPIE Foundation, Madrid, July 1986

Articles/Broadcasts (Periodicals, selected major magazine articles/ issues; transcripts of broadcasts)

American-Chilean Council Report (published by the New York-based public
   interest and lobbying group of the same name, 1975–1977)
   "Chile's Defense Needs," undated, early 1975;
   "Turning Defeat into Victory," by Victor Lasky, Sept. 1975;
   (Additionally: numerous excerpt citations)

Análisis (Santiago magazine)

"Carmen Gloria Quintana: yo era como toda joven chilena . . .", Jan. 27–Feb. 2, 1987;

"Los laberintos del corredor," June 8–14, 1987;

"La historia secreta del GAP," ibid;

"Crónica de una oposición descontrada," June 15–21, 1987

APSI (Santiago magazine)

"Discurso del ex-Presidente de la República, Eduardo Frei, el miércoles 27 de agosto en el Teatro Caupolicán," # 84, Sept. 21-Nov. 3, 1980

Bolsa Review (monthly publication of the Bank of London and South America, London; numerous citations from vols. 7–10, Oct. 1973 through Nov. 1976

Business Week

"A Future for Business in Chile," Sept. 29, 1973

Carta Confidencial (magazine-style newsletter published in Santiago beginning in 1987)

"El Pacto de Reconciliación Nacional," # 3, May 2, 1987

"Khadafy y el Terrorismo Continental," # 4, May 18, 1987

"La 'Solidaridad' Internacional," # 9, Aug. 27, 1987

"Los Planes de Mr. Reed," ibid.

"Predominio de la Corriente Liberacionista," ibid.

"Socialismo II," ibid.

"El País," # 10, Sept. 15, 1987

"Los Micropartidos," # 11, Sept. 30, 1987

"Una Simpatía de Antigua Data," # 12, Oct. 15, 1987

"De Simpatizante a Candidato," ibid.

"Las Confesiones de Dieter," ibid.

"Por la Errada Vía de la Multilateralidad," ibid.

"U.F. y Alza del Cobre," # 15, Dec. 11, 1987

"Plan Piloto Revolucionario," ibid.

"Un Documento con Nombres y Sin Firmas," ibid.

"Humanistas: ¿Partido Verde, Naranja o Rojo?," ibid.

"La Habana Da Instrucciones Para el Plebiscito," # 16, Jan. 15, 1988

"Radicalización de la Iglesia," ibid.

"Periplos Opositores: Mision a Moscú, # 17, Feb. 11, 1988

"1988: Otro Dilema Para el Socialismo," ibid.

"Fundamentos del Retiro de una Candidatura de 'Marca Registrada,' " # 18, March 2, 1988

"La Inscripción Táctica," ibid.

"US$ 4.612.949 Pide Oposición a Comunidad Economica Europea," # 19, March 18, 1988

"Una Posible Escisión," # 20, April 5, 1988

"Dos Discursos," ibid.

"Plebiscito para Octubre," ibid.

"Lo Que Ocultan Los Segundos Planos," # 21, April 20, 1988

"El País," ibid.

"El Movimiento, Los Humanistas y Los Verdes," # 22, May 9, 1988

"Estallido de Masas. Nueva Ilusión del P.C.Ch.," ibid.

"Atacando Los Centros Conservadores," ibid.

"Filipinización y Fechas," # 23, May 25, 1988

"Medios y Planes," ibid.

"Los 'Manques' en Acción," ibid.

"El País," ibid.

"Candidatos y Candidaturas," ibid.

"Intensa Pugna Aplaza Junta Ordinaria del P.D.C.," ibid.

"Fisonomía Política de la Sociedad Chilena," # 25, June 30, 1988

"Triangulación Financiera," ibid.

Challenge

Rosenstein-Rodan, Paul N. "Why Allende Failed," May-June 1974

Chile Now (publication of the Chilean Foreign Ministry, Santiago)

"Carretera Longitudinal Austral; Where Progress Makes Its Way," March/April 1988

Chilean Review (publication of the Chilean Embassy in Washington)

"New Zealand Investors Buy $ 165 Million of Chile Debt," vol. 1, # 1, Feb. 1987

"Ex-Agent Confesses Role in Letelier Murder," ibid.

"Fund To Get Terrorism Victims Back On Their Feet," vol. 1, # 4, May 1987

"Chilean Terrorists Belong to Transnational Terror Rings," vol. 1, # 5, June 1987

"Chilean Quotes," ibid.

"Bishops Urge Chileans To Register to Vote," ibid.

"Chilean Economic Indicators," ibid.

"President Makes Cabinet Changes," vol. 1, # 6, July/Aug. 1987

"Unemployment at 15-Year Low," vol. 1, # 12, Feb. 1988

"The Foreign Press on Chilean Economic Policy," ibid.

"Opposition Invites Foreign Observers," vol. 1, # 13, March 1988

"Opposition Leaders to Respect Will of Majority," ibid.

"President Pinochet's Address to Nation," ibid.

"Human Rights," vol. 1, # 14, April 1988

"Cuban Official Admits Training Guerrillas," vol. 1, # 15, May 1988

"Gold Production," ibid.

Chile Today (publication of Chilean Embassy, Washington)

"Administration of Pension Funds," # 56, Aug. 1987

Conservative Digest

Cline, Ray S., "The Ballad of Cory and Johnny," Feb. 1987

Utley, Jon, "Why Land Reform Produces Poverty," ibid.

Dartmouth Review

Hart, Jeffrey, "Does The University Have A Future?," April 20, 1988

Dissent (Magazine)

Galt, Norman, "Chile: The Struggle in the Copper Mines," Winter 1973

Economía y Sociedad (Santiago)

Piñera, José "A New Chile," April 1988

The Economist

"Is Anybody Paying?," March 14, 1987

"Chile: As the general said to the pope," April 4, 1987

"Prising out Pinochet," April 11, 1987

"Thump," May 23, 1987

"Citicorp comes clean on Third World debt," ibid.

"Lessons from Peru," May 29, 1987

"Chile: Something to smile about," June 20, 1987

"Friends like these," Aug. 8, 1987

"The spiral down to chaos: The countries that could be following Haiti down into the pit," Aug. 22, 1987

"Argentina: forward to the past," Aug. 29, 1987
"Sea seek again, señor?," Sept. 5, 1987
"Their exits and their entrances," Sept. 12, 1987
"Peru: the man who broke the banks," Oct. 24, 1987
"Poor man's fund," Feb. 13, 1988
  "Gain without pain?," ibid.
"World Bourses," May 28, 1988
"To a different Latin beat," June 11, 1988
Encounter (Magazine)
  Holden, David, "Allende and the Myth Makers: Political Realism and Rev-
  olutionary Romance," Jan. 1974
  Moss, Robert, "Chile's Coup and After," March 1974
Epoca (Magazine, Rome)
  Salvatore, Gaston, "Unidad Popular: Los sueños, las victorias, las luchas
  intestinas, la misión a Cuba. El amor a Salvador. Y después, el golpe. El
  asedio a La Moneda. El suicidio con la metralleta de Fidel . . . Catorce
  años después, por primera vez, habla la mujer del presidente chileno."
  Contreras yo, la amante de Allende," an interview in Paris by Gaston
  Salvatore with Miria Contreras Bell de Ropert, published in the Italian
  magazine January 10, 1988, translated and re-published in *El Mercurio*,
  Jan. 14, 1988, on p. 1, under the headline "Revelaciones de la secretaria
  de S. Allende"
Ercilla (Santiago)
  "Prats: El Hombre, el general, el vicepresidente," Nov. 29–Dec. 5, 1972
  "General Pinochet, el hombre del 'Día D,' " March 13–19, 1974
  "Almirante Merino: análisis de doce meses," Sept. 11–17, 1974
    "El difícil cambio de rumbo," ibid.
Euromoney (magazine)
  "Warming up to popular capitalism," Sept. 1987
Firing Line (television program)
  Transcript of Sept. 29, 1974 interview with Amb. Edward Korry
Foreign Affairs
  Fagen, Richard R., "The United States and Chile: Roots and Branches," vol.
  53, # 2, January 1975
  Foland, Frances M., "Agrarian Reform in Latin America," vol. 48, # 1,
  October 1969
  Frei Montalva, Eduardo, "The Second Latin American Revolution," vol. 50,
  # 1, October 1971
  Lowenthal, Abraham F., "Alliance Rhetoric Versus Latin American Reality,"
  vol. 48, # 3, April 1970
  Oliver, Covey T., "Foreign and Human Relations with Latin America," vol.
  47, # 3, April 1969
  Sanders, Thomas G., "The Church in Latin America," vol. 48, #2,
  January 1970
  Véliz, Claudio, "Centralism and Nationalism," vol. 47, # 1, October
  1968
Foreign Policy
  Moran, Theodore H., "New Deal or Raw Deal in Raw Materials," Winter
  1971–1972
Fortune
  Meyer, Herbert C., "Down Picks Up The Piece in Chile," April 1974

Freedom At Issue (publication of Freedom House, New York)
  Finn, James, "Taking Things Seriously, (or, I'll Take L'Amour)," May–June 1988
Harpers
  García Márquez, Gabriel, "The Death of Salvador Allende," March 1974
Healine Series (New York: Foreign Policy Association)
  Stephansky, Ben S., "Latin America: Toward A New Nationalism," # 211, June 1972
Hoy (Santiago)
  "Las dudas del plebiscito," Aug. 20–26, 1980
  "Cuestión de medios," Sept. 2–9, 1980
  "Cuando las aguas se calman," Sept. 17–23, 1980
  "La Década de Hoy," special edition, May 1987
  "Con la mirada en la historia," June 8–14, 1987
  "A tres bandas," June 15–21, 1987
    "El dilema de un candidato civil," ibid.
  "Respuestas desde la cárcel," Aug. 3–9, 1987
    "Ahora en el re-exilio," ibid.
    "Definiciones en Punta de Tralca," ibid.
    "Chicago 'Boys' Miran al 2000," ibid.
  "El Derrotero del PDC," Aug. 10–16, 1987
  "Luces para el debate, Plebiscito III," Sept. 10–16, 1987
Human Events
  "Kirkpatrick, Jeane, "U.N. again ignores Cuba human rights atrocities," April 11, 1987
  Brownfeld, Allan C., "Constitution was a spectacular success of Founding Fathers," July 18, 1987
International Currency Review
  "Chilean Peso," vol. 18, # 3, May 1987
The Mindszenty Report, vol. XVII, # 11, Nov. 1976 (Washington, D.C.)
National Geographic
  Boraiko, Allen C., "Acts of Faith in Chile," July 1988
National Review
  Moss, Robert, "The Tribulation of Chile," Oct. 10, 1975
New Republic
  "President Frei and the Copper Goose," Dec. 18, 1965
Newsweek
  Barnes, John, "Slaughterhouse in Santiago," Oct. 8, 1973
  Pringle, James, "Chile: Stability of a Sort," March 11, 1974
  "Private Lives," Oct. 20, 1975
New York Times Magazine
  Collier, Bernard, "A Revolution Without the Execution Wall," January 17, 1967
New Yorker
  Kraft, Joseph, "Letter from Santiago," Jan. 30, 1971
Noticias (weekly digest of hemisphere news, published by the National Foreign Trade Council, Inc., New York), numerous items, 1970–1974
Policy Review (Heritage Foundation quarterly)
  Falcoff, Mark, "The Coming Crisis in Chile," # 34, Fall 1985
  Wolfson, Adam, "Heart of Darkness: What Governments Do To Blacks In The Rest of Africa," ibid.
Política (Instituto de Ciencias Políticas, University of Chile)

Vial Correa, Gonzalo, "Perfil Histórico de la Democracia," vol. II, Jan. 1977
Political Science Quarterly (New York: Academy of Political Science, Columbia University)
    Hyman, Elizabeth H., "Soldiers in Politics: New Insights on Latin American Armed Forces," Vol. LXXXVII, # 3, Sept. 1972
Política y Espíritu (Centro de Estudios Públicos, Santiago)
    "Las Líneas Estratégicas de Nuestra Acción Política," Sept. 1987
Política y Geostrategia (Academia Nacional de Estudios Políticos y Estratégicos, Santiago)
    Vial Correa, Gonzalo, "Decadencia, Consensos y Unidad Nacional en 1973," # 36, 1985
Puntos de Referencia (Santiago)
    "Inquietudes Acerca Del Futuro de la Propiedad Privada en Chile," Dec. 1986
Qué Pasa (Santiago)
    "El Who is Who de Carabineros," Sept. 6, 1973
    "Carabineros: ¿Siempre los mismos?," ibid.
    " 'Estado Mayor' tecnico para la junta," March 22, 1974
    "Habla el Almirante Merino," ibid.
    "En un año, otro país," Sept. 17, 1974
    "Las forjas de vulcano," Sept. 27, 1974
    "Los que vinieron a vernos," June 10, 1976
    "Frei: ¿es alternativa?," Sept. 4–10, 1980
    "Nueve rostros para un perfil," March 20–26, 1986
    "¿Ayuda fraterna?," April 10–16, 1986
    "Chile y su futuro," April 24–30, 1986
    "Al calor de la contienda electoral," April 23–29, 1987
    "Vino, intervino y se fue," Aug. 6–12, 1987
    "La definición de la PDC," ibid.
Radio Agricultura (Santiago)
    Tape recordings of junta communiques and final Allende speeches, Sept. 11, 1973 (copied by the author)
60 Minutes (television program)
    Transcript of "The Korry File," a segment of the program aired Jan. 9, 1977 (Vol. IX, # 16), on CBS-TV
Soviet World Outlook (published in Washington by the Advanced International Studies Institute, in association with the University of Miami)
    Vol. 5, # 4, April 15, 1980
Time (magazine)
    Eisendrath, Charles, "The Coup: The view from the Carrera," Sept. 24, 1973
    "The Price of Order," Dec. 31, 1973
    "In a Shadow Country," April 22, 1974 (unsigned)
Visao (Rio de Janeiro)
    Prado, Antonio Alberto, "O limbo gelado de Dawson," Feb. 25, 1974
World Marxist Review
    Teitelboim, Volodia, "For a victorious revolution," # 11, Nov. 1973
    Sobolev, A.I., "Prelude to Victory," # 3, March 1974
    "Latin America: A continent in struggle," June 1981

Books

Agee, Philip, *Inside The Company: CIA Diary* (New York: Stonehill Publishing Co., 1975)

Agor, Weston H., *The Chilean Senate* (Austin & London: University of Texas Press, 1971)

Agrarian Problems and Peasant Movements in Latin America, Rodolfo Stavenhagen, ed. (New York: Doubleday, Anchor Books, 1970)

Alexander, Robert J., *Communism in Latin America* (New Brunswick, NJ, Rutgers University Press, 1957)

Allende Gossens, Salvador, *Allende: Su Pensamiento Político* (Buenos Aires: Granica Editor, 1973)

Almeyda Medina, Clodomiro, *Reencuentro Con Mi Vida* (Santiago: Ediciones Ornitorrinco, 1987)

Antología de la Filosofía Americana Contemporánea, Leopoldo Zea, ed. (Mexico: B. Costa-Amic, 1968)

Arellano Iturriaga, Sergio, *Mas Allá del Abismo* (Santiago: Editorial Proyección, 1985)

Arriagada Herrera, Genaro,
   De La Vía Chilena a la Vía Insurreccional (Santiago: Editorial del Pacífico, S.A., 1974)
   La Política Militar de Pinochet (Santiago: Impresor Salesianos, 1985)
   Chile: Sistema Político Futuro (Santiago: Editorial Aconcagua, 1985)
   Pinochet: The Politics of Power (Boston: Unwin Hyman, 1988) (translated by Nancy Morris, with Vicent Ercolano and Kristen A. Whitney)

Baltra Cortés, Alberto, *Gestión Económica de la Unidad Popular* (Santiago: Editorial Orbe, no date)

Bethel, Paul D. *The Losers* (New Rochelle, NY, Arlington, House, 1970)

Birns, Laurence, ed., *The End of Chilean Democracy* (New York: Seabury, 1978)

Bitar, Sergio, *Chile: Experiment in Democracy* (Philadelphia: Institute for the Study of Human Issues, 1986)

Blasier, Cole, ed., *Constructive Change in Latin America* (Pittsburgh: University of Pittsburgh Press, 1968)

Boizard, Ricardo,
   El Ultimo Día de Allende (Santiago: Editorial del Pacífico, S.A., 1973)
   Proceso a Una Traición (Santiago: Ediciones Encina, 1974)

Bravo Lira, Bernardino,
   De Portales a Pinochet: Gobierno y Regimen de Gobierno en Chile (Santiago: Editorial Jurídica de Chile, Editorial Andrés Bello, 1985)
   Regimen de gobierno y Partidos Políticos en Chile, 1924–1973 (Santiago: Editorial Jurídica de Chile, 1986)

Breve Historia de la Unidad Popular, Teresa Donoso Loero, ed. (Santiago: Editorial Lord Cochrane, S.A., 1974), a chronology of key dates and events during the Allende years, 1970–1973, taken from the pages of *El Mercurio*, and published by that newspaper

Brownfeld, Allan C., and Waller, J. Michael, *The Revolution Lobby* (Washington: Council for Inter-American Security, 1985)

Bulnes Aldunate, Luz, *Constitución Política de la República de Chile: Concordancias, Anotaciones y Fuentes* (Santiago: Editorial Jurídica de Chile, 1981)

Calvo, César Hidalgo, *Teoría y Práctica de la Propaganda Contemporánea* (Santiago: Editorial Andrés Bello, 1986)

Carrasco Delgado, Sergio, *Alessandri: Su Pensamiento Constitucional; Reseña de su Vida Pública* (Santiago: Editorial Jurídica de Chile, Editorial Andrés Bello, 1987)

Central America: Anatomy of Conflict, Robert S. Leiken, ed. (New York: Pergamon Press, 1984)

Chalmers, Douglas A., ed., *Changing Latin America: New Interpretations of its Policies and Society* (New York: The Academy of Political Sciences, Columbia University, 1972)

Chamudes, Marcos, *Chile: Una Advertencia Americana* (Santiago: Ediciones P.E.C., 1972)

Changing Latin America: New Interpretations of its Policies and Society, Douglas A. Chalmers, ed. (New York: The Academy of Political Sciences, Columbia University, 1972)

Chavkin, Samuel, *Storm Over Chile* (Westport, CT: Lawrence Hill & Co., 1982 and 1985) (published originally as *The Murder of Chile*)

Chile: A Critical Survey, Tomás P. MacHale, ed. (Santiago: Institute of General Studies, 1972)

Following are the principal articles from that work cited in this book:

Baraona Urzúa, Pablo, "The reality of Chilean agriculture"
Cox, Ricardo, "The Collapse of Democracy"
Fontaine A., Arturo, "Revolution on official stamped paper"
Garrido Rojas, José, "The increasing social participation in Chile"
Guzmán E., Jaime, "The Church in Chile and the political debate"
MacHale, Tomás, "Ideologies in the reform of the Universities"
Martínez Williams, Jaime, "Education under the government of the Popular Unity"
Orrego Vicuña, Francisco, "The system of Chilean foreign policy: rise or fall?"
Pérez de Arce, Hermógenes, "Between socialism and freedom"
Sanfuentes Vergara, Emilio, "The economic policy of the Popular Unity"
Silva Carvallo, Alfredo, "The battle for freedom of expression"
Zegers Ariztía, Cristián, "The Armed Forces: support of a democratic institutionality"

Chile: An Economy in Transition (Washington: World Bank Country Study, 1980)

Chile: The Balanced View, Francisco Orrego Vicuña, ed. (Santiago: Institute of International Studies, University of Chile, 1975)

Following are the principal articles from that work cited in this book:

Blakemore, Harold, "Chile: Current realities and historical perspectives"
Del Canto, Jorge; Leniz, Fernando; Rosenstein-Rodan, Paul; and Sedwitz, Walter, "An Overview of the Chilean Economic Policies"
MacHale, Tomás P., "The Chilean Approach to International Relations under the Government of the Popular Unity"
Mamalakis, Markos J., "The Allende Experiment"
Moss, Robert, "Chile's Coup and After"
Orrego Vicuña, Francisco, "Some International Law Problems Posed by the Nationalization of the Copper Industry by Chile"
Ratliff, William E., "Chile"
Sáez, Raúl, "Chilean Short and Medium-term Development Program"
Trucco, Amb. Manuel, "Foreign Armed Intervention in Chile"

The Chilean Road to Socialism, Dale L. Johnson, ed. (Garden City, NY: Anchor Doubleday, 1973)

The Chilean Road to Socialism, J. Ann Zammit, ed. (Austin: University of Texas Press, 1973)

Connery, Robert H., and Jones, Eldon L., *Control or Fate in Economic Affairs* (New York: Academy of Political Science, Columbia University, 1971)

Constructive Change in Latin America, Cole Blasier, ed. (Pittsburgh: University of Pittsburgh Press, 1968)

Corbett, Charles D., *The Latin American Military As A Socio-Political Force* (Miami: Center for Advanced International Studies, University of Miami, 1972)

Correa, Enrique, and Viera-Gallo, José Antonio, *Iglesia y Dictadura* (Santiago: Centro de Estudios Sociales, approximately late 1986)

Correa Morandé, María, *La Guerra de las Mujeres* (Santiago: Editorial Universidad Tecnica del Estado, 1974)

Corvalán Lepe, Luis,
>   *Camino de Victoria* (Santiago: Impresora Horizonte, 1971)
>   *Nuestra Vía Revolucionaria* (booklet published in 1971, presumably in Santiago)

Crassweller, Robert D., *Trujillo* (New York: The MacMillan Co., 1966)

Cuadernos de Información, # 3/1986, Tomás P. MacHale, ed. (Santiago: Centro de Estudios de la Prensa, Pontificia Universidad Católica de Chile, 1986)

Cumplido Cereceda, Francisco, *Una Salida Político-Constitucional Para Chile* (Santiago: Instituto Chileno de Estudios Humanísticos, 1985)

Custine, Marquis de, *Journey for Our Time: The Russian Journals of the Marquis de Custine* (Washington: Gateway Editions, Regnery Gateway, 1987)

Cutler, Julio, and Fagen, Richard, *Latin America and the United States: The Changing Political Realities* (Palo Alto: Stanford University Press, 1974)

Davis, Nathaniel, *The Last Two Years of Salvador Allende* (Ithaca: Cornell University Press, 1985)

Debray, Regis, *The Chilean Revolution: Conversations With Allende* (New York: Vintage Books, Random House, 1971)

de Castro, A. Pineda, *Pinochet: Verdad y Ficción* (Madrid: Vasallo de Mumbert, 1981)

Democracia Cristiana y Partido Comunista (Santiago: Editorial Aconcagua, 1986)

de Onis, Juan, and Levinson, Jerome, *The Alliance That Lost Its Way* (Chicago: The Twentieth Century Fund, 1971)

de Tocqueville, Alexis, *Democracy in America,* 1833 and 1840 editions, Henry Steele Commager, ed. (New York: Harper & Row, 1947)

Deutscher, Isaac, *The Prophet Unarmed: Trotsky, 1921–1929* (New York: Random House, Vintage Books, 1965)

Domic K., Juray, *Destrucción de las Fuerzas Armadas por el Partido Comunista* (Santiago: Editorial Vaitea, 1975), 4th edition

Donoso Loero, Teresa,
>   *La Epopeya de las Ollas Vacías* (Santiago: Editora Nacional Gabriela Mistral, Ltda., 1974)
>   *Breve Historia de la Unidad Popular,* ed. (Santiago: Editorial Lord Cochrane, S.A., 1974)

Dooner, Patricio, *Periodismo y Política: La Prensa de Derecha en Chile, 1970–1973* (Santiago: Instituto Chileno de Estudios Humanísticos, no pub. date)

Echeverría B. Andrés, and Frei B., Luis, eds. *La Lucha Por La Juridicidad en Chile* (Santiago: Instituto Chileno de Estudios Humanísticos, 1985)

Edmund Burke (New York: P. F. Collier & son, Harvard Classics, 1968)

Edwards, Jorge, *Persona Non Grata* (Barcelona, Buenos Aires, Mexico: Ediciones Grijalbo, 1976)

89/90: Opciones Políticas en Chile, Patricio Tupper, ed. (Santiago: Ediciones Colchagua, 1987)

The End of Chilean Democracy, Laurence Birns, ed. (New York: Seabury, 1978)

Feliú, Manuel, *La Empresa de la Libertad* (Santiago: Editorial Zig-Zag, 1988)

Fermandois, Joaquín, *Chile y El Mundo 1970–1973; La Política Exterior del Gobierno de la Unidad Popular y el Sistema Internacional* (Santiago: Ediciones Universidad Católica de Chile, 1985)

Filippi, Emilio, and Millas, Hernán, *Anatomía de Un Fracaso: La Experiencia Socialista Chilena* (Santiago: Empresa Editora Zig-Zag, S.A., 1973)

Fleet, Michael, *The Rise and Fall of Christian Democracy* (Princeton: Princeton University Press, 1985)

Fontaine Aldunate, Arturo, *Los Economistas y el Presidente Pinochet* (Santiago: Editorial Zig-Zag, 1988)

Frei Montalva, Eduardo, *Un Mundo Nuevo* (Santiago: Ediciones Nueva Universidad, Universidad Católica de Chile, 1973)

Fuentes Wendling, Manuel, *Terrorismo Comunista; Su Accionar en Chile* (Santiago: Ediciones E.C.O.S., 1981)

Fuerzas Armadas y Seguridad Nacional (Santiago: Ediciones Portada, 1973) (anthology)

Fulbright, Sen. J. William, *Arrogance of Power* (New York: Random House, 1966)

Furci, Carmelo, *The Chilean Communist Party and the Road to Socialism* (London: Zed Books, Ltd., 1984)

Galdames, Luis, *Historia de Chile: Prehistoria a 1970,* 14th edition (Santiago: Productos Raval, 1974)

Garrido, José R., ed., *Historia de la Reforma Agraria en Chile* (Santiago: Editorial Universitaria, 1988)

Gil, Federico G., *El Sistema Político de Chile* (Santiago: Editorial Andrés Bello, 1969)

Goure, Leon, and Rothenberg, Morris, *Soviet Penetraton of Latin America* (Miami: Center for Advanced International Studies, University of Miami, 1975)

Gunther, John, *Inside South America* (New York: Harper & Row, 1966)

Hanke, Steve H., ed., *Privatization and Development* (San Francisco: Institute for Contemporary Studies Press, 1987)

Harrington, Edwin and González, Mónica, *Bomba en una Calle de Palermo* (Santiago: Editorial Emision, 1987)

Horne, Alistair, *Small Earthquake in Chile* (New York: The Viking Press, 1972)

Huneeus, Carlos, *Los Chilenos y La Política: Cambio y Continuidad en el Autoritarismo* (Santiago: Salesianos Printers, 1987)

Huneeus, Pablo, *Los Burócratas; un nuevo análisis del estado* (Santiago: Editora Nueva Generación, 1973)

Jerez Ramírez, Luis, *Chile: La Vecindad Difícil* (Holland, no pub. data)

Johnson, Dale L., ed. *The Chilean Road to Socialism* (Garden City, NY: Anchor Doubleday, 1973)

Johnson, Paul, *Modern Times: The World From the Twenties to the Eighties* (New York: Harper & Row, 1983)

Kantor, Harry, *Patterns of Politics and Political Systems in Latin America* (Chicago: Rand McNally, 1969)

Kautsky, John H., *Political Change in Underdeveloped Countries: Nationalism and Communism* (New York: John Wiley & Sons, n.d.)

Keegan, John, *World Armies* (New York: Facts on File, 1979)

Kissinger, Henry,
> *The White House Years* (Boston: Little Brown Co., 1979)
> *Years of Upheaval* (Boston: Little Brown Co., 1982)

Labin, Suzanne, *Chile: The Crime of Resistance* (Richmond, Surrey, England: Foreign Affairs Publishing Co., Ltd., 1982)

Labrousse, Alain, *El Experimento Chileno; ¿ Reformismo o Revolución?* (Barcelona, Mexico: Ediciones Grijalbo, S.A., 1973) (published originally as *L'Experience Chilienne*)

Lafourcade, Enrique, *Salvador Allende* (Barcelona, Mexico: Ediciones Grijalbo, 1973)

La Lucha por la Juridicidad en Chile, Andrés Echeverría B., and Luis Frei B., eds. (Santiago: Instituto Chileno de Estudios Humanísticos, 1985)

Latin American Politics, Robert D. Tomasek, ed. (Garden City, NY, Doubleday, Anchor books, 1966)

Lavín Infante, Joaquín, *Chile: A Quiet Revolution* (Santiago: Empresa Editora Zig-Zag, 1988)

Leiken, Robert S., ed., *Central America: Anatomy of Conflict* (New York: Pergamon Press, 1984)

Levinson, Jerome, and de Onis, Juan, *The Alliance That Lost Its Way* (Chicago: The Twentieth Century Fund, 1971)

Libertad de Expresión; Etica Periodística y Desinformación, Tomás P. MacHale, ed. (Santiago: Pontificia Universidad Católica de Chile, 1988)

MacHale, Tomás P.,
> *La Libertad de Expresión en Chile* (Santiago: Ediciones Portada, 1973)
> *Chile: A Critical Survey*, ed. (Santiago: Institute of General Studies, 1972)
> *Libertad de Expresión, Etica Periodística y Desinformación*, ed. (Santiago: Pontifica Universidad Católica de Chile, 1988)

Magnet, Alejandro, *Operación Primavera* (Santiago: Editorial del Pacífico, 1973)

Marchetti, Victor, and Marks, John D., *The CIA and the Cult of Intelligence* (New York: Dell, 1974)

Martínez Ocamica, Gutenberg, ed., *Una Salida Político-Constitucional Para Chile* (Santiago: Instituto Chileno de Estudios Humanísticos, 1985)

Marx, Karl, *The Eighteenth Brumaire of Louis Napoleon; Selected Works* (New York: International Publishers, n.d.)

Millar, Walterio, *Historia de Chile* (Santiago: Editorial Zig-Zag, Dec. 1973), 29th edition

Miranda Carington, Sergio, *Las Fuerzas Armadas En El Ordenamiento Jurídico de Chile; Fuerzas Armadas y Seguridad Nacional* (Santiago: Ediciones Portada, 1973)

Moran, Theodore H., *Multinational Corporations and the Politics of Dependence; Copper in Chile* (Princeton, NJ: Princeton University Press, 1974)

Moreno Beauchemin, Ernesto, *Historia del Movimiento Sindical Chileno: Una Visión Cristiana* (Santiago: Instituto Chileno de Estudios Humanísticos, 1986)

Moss, Robert, *Chile's Marxist Experiment* (New York-Toronto: John Wiley & Sons., 1973)

Muñoz, Heraldo, *Las Relaciones Exteriores del Gobierno Militar Chileno* (Santiago: Las Ediciones del Ornitorrinco, 1986)

Neruda, Pablo, *Pablo Neruda: Selected Poems*, Nathaniel Torn, ed. (New York: Delacorte Press, 1972)

Niebuhr, Reinhold, *The Children of Light and the Children of Darkness* (New York: Scribner's, 1963)

Orrego Vicuña, Francisco, ed., *Chile: The Balanced View*, (Santiago: Institute of International Studies, University of Chile, 1975)

Pacepa, Lt. Gen. Ion Mihai, *Red Horizons: Chronicle of a Communist Spy Chief* (Washington: Regnery Gateway, 1987)

Papi Beyer, Mario and Urzúa, Germán, *Historia y Proyección Socialdemócrata en Chile* (Santiago: Editorial Andante, 1986)

Pensamiento de Portales (Santiago: Colección Ideario, 1974)

Perlmutter, Amos, *The Military and Politics in Modern Times* (New Haven: Yale University Press, 1977)

Perspectivas Económicas Para la Democracia: Balance y Lecciones Para la Experiencia Chilena, Jorge Rodríguez Grossi, ed. (Santiago: Instituto Chileno de Estudios Humanísticos, 1984)

Petrei, A. Humberto, *El Gasto Público Social y sus Efectos Distributivos; Un examen comparativo de cinco países de América Latina* (Petropolis, Brazil: Editora Vozes Ltda., 1987), project of the Programa de Estudios Conjuntos Sobre Integración Económica Latinoamericana

Phillips, David Atlee, *The Nightwatch: 25 Years Inside The CIA* (London: Robert Hale, 1978)

Pike, Frederick, *Chile and the United States, 1880–1962* (South Bend, IN, University of Notre Dame Press, 1963)

Pinochet Ugarte, President Augusto,
> *La Acción del Ejército en la Liberación de Chile, Historia Inédita* (a 50-page booklet printed on newsprint quality stock, believed to have been written by Pinochet. Devoid of any identifying marks or dates, it appeared in Santiago at about the first anniversary of the revolution, or September 1974. It was not released to bookstores and copies were extremely hard to come by. The booklet describes Pinochet's own role in the revolution—no other military commander is named in it—and that of the army.)
>
> *El Día Decisivo: 11 de Septiembre de 1973* (Santiago: Editora Andrés Bello, 1980)

Pinto, Silvia, *Los Días del Arco Iris* (Santiago: Editorial del Pacífico, S.A., 1972)

Pocock, H.R.S., *The Conquest of Chile* (New York: Stein & Day, 1967)

Powers, Thomas, *The Man Who Kept Secrets: Richard Helms and the CIA* (New York: Alfred A. Knopf, 1979)

Prats González, Gen. Carlos,
> *Una Vida por La Legalidad* (Mexico: Fondo de Cultura Económica, 1976) (Five years after its appearance, his three daughters disavowed the legitimacy of the book)
>
> *Memorias: Testimonio de un Soldado* (Santiago: Editorial Antártica, 1985), 2nd edition, edited by his three daughters, Sofía, María Angélica and Cecilia

Puga, Alvaro, *Diario de Vida de Usted . . .* (Santiago: Ediciones Encina Ltda., 1973) (The book appeared under his pen name, "Alexis")

Quantitative Latin American Studies, James Wilkie and Kenneth Rudle, eds., (Los Angeles: University of California at Los Angeles, 1977)

Rama, Carlos M., *Chile: Mil Días Entre la Revolución y el Fascismo* (Barcelona: Editorial Planeta, S.A., 1974)

Ravines, Eudocio, *El Rescate de Chile* (Santiago: Empresa Editora e Impresora Edimpres Ltda., 1974)

Reforma Constitucional 1970 (Santiago: Editorial Jurídica de Chile, 1970)

Robb, Edmund W., and Robb, Julia, *The Betrayal of the Church: Apostasy and Renewal in the Mainline Denominations* (Westchester, IL: Crossway Books, 1986)

Rodríguez Gross, Jorge., ed., *Perspectivas Económicas Para La Democracia: Balance y Lecciones Para La Experiencia Chilena* (Santiago: Instituto Chileno de Estudios Humanísticos, 1984)

Rojas Sanford, Robinson, *The Murder of Allende* (New York: Harper & Row, 1976)

Sampson, Anthony, *The Sovereign State of ITT* (New York: Stein & Day, 1973)

Sartori, Giovanni, *The Theory of Democracy Revisited* (Chatham, NJ: Chatham House Publishing, 1987)

Septiembre de 1973: Los Cien Combates de Una Batalla (Santiago: Editorial Gabriela Mistral, apparently late 1973), book published by the Chilean Armed Forces highlighting events of the revolution

Shakespeare, William, *Romeo and Juliet*, The Yale Shakespeare series, Richard Hesley, ed. (New Haven: Yale University Press, 5th printing, 1965)

Shultz, Richard H., and Godson, Roy, *Dezinformatsia: Active Measures in Soviet Strategy* (Washington: Pergamon, Brassey's, 1984)

Sigmund, Paul E., *The Overthrow of Allende and the Politics of Chile, 1964–1976* (Pittsburgh: University of Pittsburgh Press, 1977)

Silva Henríquez, Cardinal Raúl, *La Misión Social del Cristiano: ¿ Conflicto de Clases o Solidaridad Cristiana?* (Santiago: Ediciones Paulina, 1973)

Silva, Lautaro, *Allende: El Fin de Una Aventura* (Santiago: Ediciones Patria Nueva, 1974)

Smith, Brian H., *The Church and the Politics of Chile: Challenges to Modern Catholicism* (Princeton: Princeton University Press, 1982)

Solaun, Mauricio, and Quinn, Michael A., *The Politics of Military Intervention in Latin America* (Urbana, IL: University of Illinois Press, 1973)

Stavenhagen, Rodolfo, ed., *Agrarian Problems and Peasant Movements in Latin America* (New York: Doubleday, Anchor Books, 1970)

Szulc, Tad, *Twilight of the Tyrants* (New York: Henry Holt, 1959)

Theberge, Amb. James D., *The Soviet Presence in Latin America* (New York: Crane, Russak & Co., 1974)

Thomas, Hugh, *The Spanish Civil War* (Harmondsworth, Middlesex, England: Penguin Books Ltd., 1965), revised edition

Tomasek, Robert D., ed., *Latin American Politics* (Garden City, NY, Doubleday, Anchor books, 1966)

Transición a la Democracia. América Latina y Chile, Augusto Varas, ed. (Santiago: Asociacion Chilena de Investigaciones para la Paz, 1984)

Tupper, Patricio, ed., *89/90: Opciones Políticas en Chile* (Santiago: Ediciones Colchagua, 1987)

Ulam, Adam B., *The Bolsheviks* (New York: The MacMillan Co., 1965)

Una Salida Político-Constitucional Para Chile, Gutenberg Martínez Ocamica, ed. (Santiago: Instituto Chileno de Estudios Humanísticos, 1985)

Uribe, Armando, *The Black Book of American Intervention in Chile* (Boston: Beacon Press, 1975) first published in French by Editions du Seuil in 1974 as *Le Livre Noir de L'Intervention Americaine au Chili*

Valdés Subsercaseaux, Gabriel, *Por La Libertad; Discursos y Entrevistas, 1982–1986* (Santiago: Ediciones Chile y América, approx. 1987)

Varas, Augusto, ed., *Transición a la Democracia. América Latina y Chile* (Santiago: Associacion Chilena de Investigacione para la Paz, 1984)

Varas, Florencia,
  Conversaciones con Viaux (Santiago: Impresiones Eire, 1972)
  Gustavo Leigh: El General Disidente (Santiago: Editorial Aconcagua, 1979)

Varas, Florencia, and Vergara, José Manuel, *Operación Chile* (Santiago-Buenos Aires: Editorial Pomaire, 1973)

Vergara, Pilar, *Auge y Caída del Neoliberalismo en Chile* (Santiago: Facultad Latinoamericana de Ciencias Sociales, 1985)

Whelan, James R., *Allende: Death of a Marxist Dream* (Westport, CT: Arlington House, 1981)

Whelan, James R., and Bozell, Patricia, *Catastrophe in the Caribbean: The Failure of America's Human Rights Policy in Central America* (Ottawa, IL: Jameson Books, 1984)

Wilkie, James, and Rudle, Kenneth, eds., *Quantitative Latin American Studies* (Los Angeles: University of California at Los Angeles, 1977)

Wolfe, Bertram D., *Three Who Made A Revolution* (New York: Dell Publishing, Delta Books, 1948)

Zaldívar Larraín, Andrés, *Eduardo Frei: Pensamientos* (Santiago: Ciceros, 1987) (booklet)

Zammit, J. Ann, ed., *The Chilean Road to Socialism* (Austin: University of Texas Press, 1973)

Zea, Leopoldo, ed. *Antología de la Filosofía Americana Contemporánea* (Mexico: B. Costa-Amic, 1980)

Personal Interviews

All interviews were conducted in Santiago unless otherwise noted; although I returned to Chile several times between researching my first book on that country and this one, the meetings/conversations I conducted were not in the form of "interviews;" nor does this list include scores of persons interviewed in the course of reporting trips to Chile in the 14 years before beginning work on these books. The list, in a word, is by no means all-inclusive:

"Aide-de-camp," Oct. 23, 1974. The former Allende aide requested anonymity, but consented to have the interview tape-recorded.
Alarcón, Ricardo, April 4, 1974
Allamand, Andrés, June 15, 1987
Allende Gossens, President Salvador, September 1972
Arnello, Mario, Jan. 28, 1987
Arriagada Herrera, Genaro, April 23, 1974
Arriagada Moreno, Eduardo, April 15, 1974
Baeza, Gen. Ernesto, Oct. 16, 1974
Barnes, Amb. Harry, June 16 and 18, 1987
Barros, Tobías, April 11, 1974
Bernath, Dr. Zoltan, April 24, 1974
Brady Roche, Gen. Herman, in April and October 1974
Boeninger Kausel, Edgardo, Jan. 30, 1987
Brana, Jorge, April 1974

Briones Olivos, Carlos, May 13 and Oct. 10, 1974; June 15, 1987
Caamano, Juan (Juanito), May 1, 1975
Canessa Roberts, Col. Julio, April 30 and May 1, 1974
Carmona Peralta, Sen. Juan de Dios, April 7, 1974
Carneyro, Mario, March 25, 1974
Castillo, Jaime, June 19, 1987
"César," key civilian in planning and operation of the secret radio network that linked military commanders on Sept. 11, 1973 fearing later reprisals, he asked for anonymity. Interview in Santiago, Oct. 17, 1974.
"CIA agent," in Washington, June 2, 1974. A retired officer, he requested anonymity.
Committee for Peace, various persons, April 30, May 1, 3, and 6, 1974
Correa, Pedro, Jan. 28, 1987
Cox de Valdivieso, Mrs. Alejandrina, October 1974
Cuadra, Francisco, Feb. 2, 1987
Cubillos Sallato, Hernán, Aug. 13, 1988
Cuevas Farren, Gustavo, January 29, 1987
Cumsille Zapata, Rafael, Oct. 11, 1974
Díaz, Mrs. Silvia Galarze de, May 9, 1974
Domic K., Juray, June 16, 1987
Donoso Loero, Teresa, May 7, 1974
Durán Caceres, Héctor, in Miami, over several months, in 1975
Errázuriz, Hernán Felipe Amb., numerous, in Washington and Santiago, 1987–1988
Ewing Hodar, Col. (later Gen.) Pedro, Feb. through May and October 1974 and June 10, 1987
Ferrari S., Roberto di., May 1, 1974
Figueroa, Jorge, April 1, 1973
Figueroa Toro, Pelayo, May 8, 1974
Filippi, Emilio, June 15, 1987
Fontaine Aldunate, Arturo, several 1972–1984
Frei Montalva, President Eduardo, May 7, 1974
Gallegos Dubost, Miguel (Mike), March 14, 1974
Garrido Gonzalez, Vicente Adrian, in Miami, April 9, 1974
Gordon, Gen. Humberto, June 10, 1987
Grez, Commander Jorge, Oct. 24, 1974
Grove Kimber, Jaime, Oct. 23, 1974
Guijon Klein, Dr. Patricio, a series of interviews beginning on April 4, 1974, and continuing over the next five weeks, carried on subsequently by mail, and resuming personally over a three-week period in October 1974; and again, June 17, 1987
Guijon, Mrs. Silvia, several conversations in April and May, 1974
Guzmán Errázuriz, Jaime, April and Oct. 13, 1974
Halsema, James J., March 29 and May 2, 1974
Hernández, Francisco (Gabito), April 3, 1974
Hidalgo, Cesar, June 12, 1987
Hinojosa, Mrs. Esther, April 3, 1974
Huerta Celis, Gen. Vicente, Oct. 9, 1974
Huidobro, Rear Adm. Sergio, Oct. 24, 1974
Humeres, Héctor, April 1974
Huneeus, Pablo, April 9, 1974

Ibáñez, Pedro, Jan. 30, 1987
Kelly, Roberto, en route to Miami, June 21–22, 1987
Leigh Guzmán, Gen. Gustavo, Oct. 14, 1974 and June 16, 1987
Leiva Lillo, Sgt. Alfredo, May 12, 1974
Leniz Cerda, Fernando, May 8, 1974
Letelier, Mrs. Isabel, May 8 and May 12, 1974
Letelier, Orlando, in Miami, May 1973
Lira, Juan Enrique, March 28 and April 8, 1974
MacHale, Tomás P., numerous, 1972–1987
"Mario," key civilian in organizing and operating the secret radio network which linked military commanders on the day of the revolution. Fearing later reprisals, he asked for anonymity, but did permit the author to transcribe textually and directly from the tape recordings those command network exchanges. Based on a series of interviews with him in Santiago, beginning on May 4, 1974 and extending over the next ten days, and again on Oct. 17, 1974
Martínez Ocamica, Gutenberg, Jan. 29, 1987
Mason, Roberto, April 17, 1974
Massa Armijo, Jorge, Oct. 10, 1974
Matthei Aubel, Gen. Fernando, June 15, 1987
Medina, Mrs. María, May 11, 1974
Mendoza Durán, Gen. César, Oct. 14, 1974
Merino Castro, Adm. José Toribio, Oct. 18, 1974 and June 9, 1987
Morandé Errázuriz, Francisca, Jan. 29, 1987
"Navy steward," Oct. 24, 1974 (assigned to the presidential household at Tomás Moro on Sept. 11, 1973, he requested anonymity but consented to the tape-recording of our interview)
Navasal, José, May 7, 1974
Neely, Carlos, June 11, 1987
Ossa, Mrs. Nena, numerous, in Miami, July 1975, and Santiago, June 1987
Pati Beyer, Mario, Feb. 2, 1987
Pinochet Ugarte, President Augusto, Oct. 22, 1974 and June 11, 1987
Phillips, David Atlee, May 1975
Pizarro Mora, Cpl. 2nd Class, Pedro, Oct. 14, 1974
Polloni Pérez, Col. Julio, Oct. 23, 1974
Puga, Alvaro, a series of interviews in October 1974
Ramírez, Luis, Feb. 2, 1987
Ramírez Jald, Lt. Hernán, May 13, 1974
Ravera, Hugo, Oct. 21, 1974
Sáez Ayala, Col. Iván, May 9, 1974
Sepúlveda, Col. Eduardo, in Miami, beginning in August 1974 and continuing into early 1975
Sepúlveda, Mrs. Marisa, late 1974, early 1975, in Miami
Terreros Fernández, Vicente, Mrs. Terreros, and their daughter, María, numerous in March, April and May 1974
Theberge, Amb. James, numerous, in Washington and Santiago, 1984–1987
Tonini, Frank, March 29, 1974
Toro, Pedro A., May 7, 1974
Urrutia, U.S. Army Col. Carlos, April 24, 1974
Urrutia Manzano, Chief Justice Enrique, May 9, 1974
Valdés Subercaseaux, Gabriel, June 30, 1987
Valentín Ferrada, Luis, numerous, in Washington and Santiago, 1986–1988

Valenzuela Valderrama, Héctor, April 25, 1974
Véliz, Claudio, several, 1972–1973
Vial Correa, Gonzalo, Jan. 28, 1987
Vicariate of Solidarity, various persons, June 17 and 18, 1987
Videla Cifuentes, Gen. Ernesto, June 19, 1987
Vilarín, Leon, Oct. 15, 1974
Willoughby MacDonald M., Federico, June 16, 1987
Zaldívar Larraín, Andres, Jan. 29, 1987

Newspapers

The Baltimore Sun
Buffalo (N.Y.) News
The Chicago Tribune
Christian Science Monitor
El Caribe (Santo Domingo)
El Centroamericano (Leon, Nicaragua)
El Mercurio (Santiago)
International Herald Tribune (Paris)
Journal of Commerce (New York)
La Epoca (Santiago)
La Gaceta (Tampa, Florida)
La Nación (Santiago)
La Prensa (Lima)
La Prensa (Managua)
La Segunda (Santiago)
La Tercera (Santiago)
Las Ultimas Noticias (Santiago)
The Los Angeles Times
Manchester Guardian
Manchester Guardian-Le Monde Weekly
The Miami Herald
The Miami News
The New York Times
Novedades (Managua)
The Rocky Mountain News (Denver)
San Francisco Examiner
Tribuna (Santiago)
The Wall Street Journal
The Washington Post

INDEX